Sociology
in
perspective

Mark Kirby

Warren Kidd

Francine Koubel

John Barter

Tanya Hope

Alison Kirton

Nick Madry

Paul Manning

Karen Triggs

Heinemann Educational Publishers
Halley Court, Jordan Hill, Oxford OX2 8EJ
a division of Reed Educational & Professional Publishing Ltd

OXFORD   BLANTYRE
MELBOURNE   AUCKLAND
IBADAN   JOHANNESBURG   GABORONE
PORTSMOUTH NH (USA)   CHICAGO

Text © Mark Kirby, Warren Kidd, Francine Koubel, John Barter,
Tanya Hope, Alison Kirton, Nick Madry, Paul Manning, Karen Triggs, 1997

First published 1997

99 00 01 10 9 8 7 6 5 4 3

British Library Cataloguing in Publication Data
A catalogue record for this book is available from the British Library

ISBN 0 435 33156 6

Designed by Jackie Hill
Cover design by Balvir Koura
Typeset by Wyvern 21 Ltd
Printed in Great Britain at The Bath Press

Acknowledgements

The authors' acknowledgements appear on page 8.

The publishers would like to thank the following for permission to use photographs:
P. G. Brunellei/Repfoto p. 228; Camera Press p. 742 bottom; Camera Press/Glenn Harvey p. 743 top;
Thalia Campbell p. 179 top; J. Allan Cash Ltd. p. 761; the Cooperative International College p. 179 bottom;
Frank Spooner Pictures/Gamma pp. 742 top, 743 bottom; Topham/Picturepoint p. 206; Wendy Wallace p. 637.

Copyright acknowledgements appear on page 765.

The publishers have made every effort to trace copyright holders. However, if any material has been incorrectly
acknowledged, we would be pleased to correct this at the earliest opportunity.

Contents

1

Introduction

1.1 **What is sociology?**

What is sociology and is there a need for it?

On one level the answer to this question is that sociology is a subject you have chosen to study with the aim of obtaining a qualification. You might need such a qualification to obtain a job or to go to a university. But this does not differentiate sociology from a multitude of other subjects that can be studied, nor is it particularly inspirational.

The literal meaning of the word 'sociology' is the 'science of society', and it is one of the most popular social sciences concerned with understanding human behaviour. This tells us it is an '-ology' – a science, but again this can be said about many other subjects dealing with human beings, such as biology and psychology. To justify the need for sociology it must be possible to show that its knowledge provides something more than, and arguably superior in some respects to, these other worthwhile disciplines.

The obvious difference is the 'socio-' bit of the word, meaning the study of society. However, this leads us no further than to ask the obvious question: 'What is society?', and here we begin to get a feel for a real debate. There are those who would deny that such a thing as society exists.

Margaret Thatcher, when prime minister, once declared that 'there is no such thing as society, merely individuals and their families' (Kingdom, 1992, p. 1). But if this is true then there is clearly no need for a science to study society, no need for sociology.

Does society exist?

A number of points can be raised to question the validity of this notion. First, Margaret Thatcher was able to make her statement and to communicate it to others because of the existence of language which prescribes certain rules for communication. Which individual invented this language? It is impossible to answer, for the simple reason that the existence of language is proof that we do not exist merely as individuals but as social animals interacting with others. If we lived as individuals why would there be any need for language, or indeed any other form of communication? If an individual wanted to invent their own language, what language would they use to think it up?

Secondly, it can be asked, who invented the family? Why should individuals suddenly all decide (as individuals) to invent a particular way of living found in 250 societies of widely differing types (Murdock, 1949) and call it a family? (For an outline of Murdock's argument and the critical debate that followed, see Section 7.1.) Furthermore, even if one individual did decide, by what method did he or she get the rest of humanity to adopt this way of acting?

Thirdly, who invented the concept of the 'individual'? While they are biological and psychological entities, individuals have not in all societies and at all times been seen as the key basis of society. Arguably the 'individual' was only really invented by the rise of ideas in the seventeenth and eighteenth centuries, which in many ways reversed older ways of thinking and set in train major changes in society, including the invention of sociology (see Sections 2.2 and 16.1).

This celebration of the individual arises out of monumental changes in the way people lived and thought. These events involved individuals of course, but individuals acting in social groups and affected by forces that went beyond the control of any one individual to control. We can therefore say that the individual and the celebration of the individual is not some natural truth, right for all times and places, but was the result of a number of social forces (going beyond any one existing individual) and the consequences of the way they interacted. This invention and the idea that people should have some say in events and society led eventually to democracy (see Section 17.1), to the election of Margaret Thatcher to the position of prime minister and the power that goes with that post, including the power to invent a National Curriculum (see Section 8.10) for secondary schools that excluded sociology, and to make statements attempting to deny even the existence of its subject matter. If any one of these events had turned out differently, the world might have become a very different place; and while individuals might have played a role in all this, they did so only on the basis of being part of social forces and organizations whose influence cannot be grasped solely on the basis of the individuals prominent within them.

It is this idea that there are forces beyond the overall control of any one individual that allows us to reject Margaret Thatcher's pronouncement, since it is this which we see at the heart of notions of society and sociology.

The social patterning and determination of individual action

How, for instance, can we understand the fact that whether one is born a man or a woman (something an individual can have absolutely no control over) can have an effect on one's life experiences? For instance, why in 1996 – according to government statistics (Osbourne and Nichol, 1996) – is the average weekly pay of women working full-time only 72.3 per cent of the average weekly pay of men working full-time? And why does this sort of disparity of payments occur at all levels of job? (See Chapters 4, 5 and 6, and Sections 9.3 and 14.8.) This is evidence of a force which goes beyond the ability of any one individual woman or man to control, yet it affects their lives regardless of the individual talent they each possess.

To take another example, why is it likely that a sociology class will be composed predominantly of females, something it is likely to have in common with a class of biology students. In contrast, if one visits a physics or computing classroom there is likely to be a predominance of male students (see

Section 8.7). No one (presumably) forced them to choose these subjects, and as individuals they did make a choice – yet year after year, and in institution after institution, these patterns are evident.

Discussion point
To what extent does the regular occurrence of such patterns undermine notions that we are all individuals able to exercise free choices?

It is this regularity which suggests that there is something beyond the individual (and therefore beyond psychological aspects of humanity) which cause these patterns (see Section 10.1). It is of course possible to argue that it is biology that causes men and women to behave differently, but this would require that all men behaved in a certain way and all women behaved in a certain different way, and this can be shown to be false (see Sections 5.1 and 6.4). Although a majority of candidates for A level Sociology are female, it is far from being exclusively a subject studied by females.

The conclusion seems to be that there are certain forces which go beyond the individual and which are not biologically programmed into us – forces that tend to make us act in certain non-random ways, even if we think we are all acting as individuals. It is this non-random social patterning of behaviour that is the basis of the idea of society, and therefore the subject matter of sociology. (See also Sections 2.6 and 5.2.)

Human creativity and action

It would be wrong to suppose that people are all puppets controlled by unknown forces, since the authors of those forces are none other than ourselves. Individuals and social groups find themselves subjected to forces beyond their control, but also help in the construction of these forces and the maintenance and reproduction of society. Sociology does not treat us all as robots (although some approaches may run close to this), because if society exists then people must have built it – and people can, if they wish, try to change it. In order to decide whether some aspect of society should be changed, it is first necessary to understand how it operates – and this is precisely the purpose of sociology. (See also Chapters 2 and 3.) One of the most eminent contemporary British sociologists has explained the purpose of sociology as follows:

Sociological thinking is a vital help to self-understanding, which in turn can be focused back upon an improved understanding of the social world. Studying sociology should be a liberating

experience: sociology enlarges our sympathies and imagination, opens up new perspectives on the sources of our own behaviour, and deepens a sense of cultural settings different from our own. In so far as sociological work challenges dogma, teaches appreciation of cultural variety and allows us an insight into the workings of social institutions, the practice of sociology enhances the possibilities of human freedom.

(Giddens, 1989, p. 2)

So not only does studying sociology give one a chance to gain vital points towards university entrance, the subject also offers the chance to develop self-understanding, to enlarge one's imagination and enhance human freedom. Not many subjects can offer this intoxicating combination of benefits. Since sociology does, you should grasp it and dive into it with great enthusiasm. Okay, it may not always seem like that on a wet morning in February when you haven't quite got to grips with a particularly stubborn concept and an essay is two days overdue, but like anything else that is new it takes time to develop your understanding, and explanations sometimes become complex. However everything is understandable if one takes the time and effort. Your tutor or teacher will positively encourage discussion about anything that is unclear, and in sociology there are lots of opportunities to debate issues and the society we all live in. Everyone can contribute since they are part of society and therefore part of the subject matter of the topic.

One example of such a debate concerns the place of sociology itself. It is certainly the case that some right-wing political and social thinkers have shown great hostility to the subject. Roger Scruton, professor of philosophy at the University of London, declared:

I suspect a lot of people feel this about sociology, that there are certain matters which should not be pried into, least of all by half-baked lefties from universities. . . . I would say also because of this relentless questioning of human institutions and human realities it may be inappropriate for young people to study it.

(Scruton, 1991)

Discussion point

To what extent do you agree that there are certain things which it may be inappropriate for young people to study? What sort of things might they be?

The usefulness of sociology

Reading all this one is in danger of being left with the thought that sociology either studies a non-exis-

tent subject and is therefore pointless or alternatively is positively dangerous to impressionable young minds! The charges outlined above are serious. However, they do introduce you to the notion that sociology is a controversial subject in some respects. Before you are put off studying sociology, we would want to argue that the charges are wrong, for the following reasons.

Human societies are fantastic things because they result from the interaction of countless numbers of highly creative and active beings, which raises questions about how societies should be and how humans should treat each other. While some might find this threatening, sociologists do not. We are all part of society and we all want to live meaningful and fulfilled lives, and consider the best way this can be achieved. Studying society is therefore partly about studying oneself and one's experiences, and you should have some views on that. This questioning leads to new insights and ways of looking at the world. As a leading professor of sociology, Zygmunt Bauman, puts it:

As long as we go through the routine and habitualized motions which fill most of our daily business, we do not need much scrutiny and analysis. When repeated often enough, things tend to become familiar, and familiar things are self-explanatory; they present no problems and arouse no curiosity. In a way, they remain invisible. . . . In an encounter with that familiar world ruled by habits . . . sociology acts as a meddlesome and often irritating stranger. It disturbs the comfortingly quiet way of life by asking questions no one among the 'locals' remembers being asked, let alone answered. Such questions make evident things into puzzles: they defamiliarize the familiar. Suddenly, the daily way of life must come under scrutiny. It now appears to be just one of the possible ways, not the one and only, not the 'natural' way of life.

(Bauman, 1990, p. 15)

In this respect you should question everything, considering what you once saw as natural as now problematic, and asking questions such as why, how and for whose benefit did the things you took for granted come about. We would argue that this is not a threatening or destructive act, but allows one to develop insights and understanding. This is of course a continuing process, a point also made by Zygmunt Bauman:

Sociology is an extended commentary on the experiences of daily life; an interpretation which feeds on other interpretations and is in turn fed into them. Sociological thinking does not stem, but facilitates the flow and exchange of experiences. . . . The great service sociology is well prepared to render to

human life and human cohabitation is the promotion of mutual understanding and tolerance as a paramount condition of shared freedom.
(Bauman, 1990, pp. 231–2)

While studying sociology, you are also part of that flow and exchange, and are helping to construct, challenge and think about how the society that you are living in will develop. So get stuck in!

1.2 The changing nature of sociology

Towards the twenty-first century

For a long time, A level sociology has been seen to consist of a framework constructed by sets of ideas which were developed and elaborated in the period roughly covering the 1930s to the 1950s. It is these ideas around which exam questions still sometimes tend to be framed.

As we approach the twenty-first century, this framework is increasingly beginning to show its age and arguably can no longer be adapted to either the reality of the world around us or even the reality of sociology around us. Some have suggested that we quickly electrify the tracks to allow for the speedy transmission of post-modernism and other currently fashionable notions. It is inappropriate to jump directly from the 'old' sociology to the question of the validity and usefulness of the post-modernist world viewpoint, since this merely creates a dialogue of the deaf. Equally, we sometimes wonder whether it is still useful to continue to present, as contemporary explanations, ideas from the 1930s and 40s. What is the point of teaching students, in detail, ideas which no longer inspire or relate to the world around them? The time for the 'Talcott Parsons, boo! hiss!' (to use a notable phrase of Aidan Foster-Carter) version of A level sociology is over. The world (and sociology) has moved on.

Building bridges

However, the world did not simply move on by rejecting functionalism and jumping into the warm embrace of post-modernism. Things happened in between which we feel need to be included. These are the bridges which link the 'old' to the 'new'. These bridges have not yet been built in sufficient detail to enable a critical appraisal of the value or otherwise of the new ideas. Our aim is therefore to build such bridges, and to illuminate them in the hope that this will help you to see with greater clarity how today's debates have come about. We hope it offers a richer, deeper version of what sociology is.

We have tried to give what we see as a good coverage of the main elements which constitute sociology today. In order to do this, we have consulted a wide variety of sources and have undoubtedly been influenced by them. As far as possible the sources are mentioned so that you can be aware of where the views originate. We hope we have done this fairly and have interpreted what others say accurately. The aim is to throw light on what these others say, and to encourage you to follow these up by seeking out some of the references quoted.

Sociology should, if it is to have any meaning, shed light on the real world. In this book, contemporary case studies are used to illustrate certain ideas and themes. The skill of application in A level exams requires the presentation of relevant examples, so you should be inspired to seek out your own.

Sociology is inherently a discursive subject – best approached through discussion and active learning. In this book, activities are designed to enable you to reflect, interpret, apply, analyse and evaluate the theories, ideas and evidence presented. These activities are labelled in terms of the skills you are required to demonstrate in the final exam, in the hope that this will increase your awareness of exactly what the Chief Examiners require. In our teaching, we have found these very useful instruments, but with one potential weak spot. Given activities to complete, it is sometimes the case that students become individuals or very small groups and silence fills the room. We strongly believe in the importance of discussion, so 'discussion points' appear throughout the book to encourage people to discuss ideas. In a supportive environment, this is what learning is all about: talking and discussing with others, where all contribute and all gain. These discussion points are purposely intended to encourage maximum discussion, and it is of course entirely up to you and your colleagues where such discussions lead.

We have endeavoured to ensure the information in *Sociology in Perspective* is up-to-date, empirically and theoretically. We hope this is recognizable to you.

1.3 How to use this book

The chapters

The chapter headings in *Sociology in Perspective* reflect the format adopted by the A level syllabuses produced by the Associated Examining Board (AEB), the Interboard Consortium (IBS) and the Northern Examinations and Assessment Board (NEAB). The content of each chapter is designed to cover the issues contained in those syllabuses. We have, however, included separate chapters on Theory and Methods, although they are often examined together. There are two simple reasons for this:

- Theory and Methods is the compulsory element on the AEB syllabus.
- These topics contain a vast amount of material and have a major impact on framing the construction of sociological knowledge in all other areas of the subject.

We have placed these chapters at the front of the book, because we believe the topics are important. Cross-references to these chapters appear in the rest of the book.

We have also included three separate chapters on Stratification. Again there are two reasons for this.

- Stratification is the compulsory element on the IBS syllabus.
- This topic equally contains a vast amount of material and is also very much a foundational basis for the material in other chapters.

Since virtually all the other chapters make reference to stratification by including sections on class, gender and ethnicity within them, in the Stratification chapters we have focused on the theoretical debates surrounding stratification itself. As a result the material in these chapters follows on from the Theory and Methods chapters and is also cross-referenced to other chapters. Since in reality people are not merely identified as being of a particular gender, ethnicity or age, or as a member of a particular class, but can be identified on all these dimensions of stratification, the last section of each of these chapters considers the issue of the links between the three chapters and also between the particular aspect of inequality covered in that chapter and age. We felt this was the best way to try to show the links between them.

The remainder of the chapters reflect the headings developed by the examination boards in their most recent syllabuses.

Reading the chapters

Since there are increasingly moves towards varying degrees of modularity in assessment procedures, it is unlikely that you will study all the topics in this book. Instead you are more likely to study between five and eight topics. We cannot know which elements of the book you will use, so we have tried to ensure that each chapter is self-contained while at the same time providing cross-references to other sections in the book to allow you to consider the links between topics that exist. One of the key elements of the skill of application is the ability to select and use relevant material, and this can mean looking at parallels which cross the boundaries of the syllabus areas. We would therefore encourage you to follow up these cross-references to deepen your sociological knowledge and understanding and allow you to

apply material where you think it is relevant.

Each chapter is numbered, as are the sections within it. So, for example, a cross-reference to Section 12.5 refers to the fifth section of Chapter 12.

The content of the chapters

Each chapter begins with a chapter outline detailing the main debates covered to assist in locating the section most relevant to your needs. The cross-references that are included are mostly to sections rather than chapters.

Within each chapter we have tried to cover both classical theoretical and empirical material and recent developments, including the most recent material available to us, while also drawing out the links between the 'old' and the 'new'.

We have included a considerable number of quotations so that you can learn about the work of sociologists in their own words. Full page references are given to facilitate ease of access to the material quoted. A date in brackets appears after each author – for example McRobbie (1994) or Eldridge (1993). The date refers to the year of publication of the piece of work referred to, and the details of it can be located in the bibliography at the back of the book.

Active skills-based learning

Although the idea that it is best to learn by doing has been around for a long time, it is only relatively recently that textbooks have begun including activities which encourage this. In *Sociology in Perspective*, each chapter includes a number of activities. These are highlighted with the following symbol:

 Activity

We have tried to make these intrinsically interesting things to do, and we have also tried to use them to help you to develop the skills approach which is now a standard requirement of all sociology syllabuses.

The syllabus published by the relevant exam board should of course be consulted. Your tutor or teacher will be able to provide other relevant material produced by exam boards. You will also no doubt get plenty of opportunities to read about, or hear the views of, the Chief Examiner and Senior Examiners. Their thoughts should of course be taken into account in planning your overall study approach.

The skills laid down in the various sociology syllabuses are extremely similar. They can be summarized as follows:

- Knowledge, Understanding (K, U)
- Interpretation, Application or Analysis (I, A)
- Evaluation (E).

Activity

a Obtain a copy of the syllabus you are intending to follow.

b Make a note of those elements of the course which are compulsory and those which are not. Confirm with your tutor or teacher that your interpretation of what is compulsory on your syllabus is correct.

c Make a note of any choices you have to make about the exact nature of your A level in Sociology (for example, whether you will be doing coursework or not).

d Discuss with your tutor or teacher how decisions will be made in relation to these choices.

e Read the section of the syllabus concerned with the topic you are going to be studying first, and make a note of any terms you do not understand. Repeat this exercise for all the other elements of your course when you start them.

f Using a dictionary of sociology (available in your local reference library if not in the school or college library) look up the meanings of these words and write these out in your own words.

g Read the section of the syllabus concerned with the skills you are required to demonstrate in the assessment procedures of your course. Ask your tutor or teacher to identify material where you can read more about the meaning of each of these skills. Locate this material, read and make notes on it. Apply these points throughout all your work.

h Discuss your findings with your class colleagues.

U, I, A

Following the Dearing Review of Qualifications for 16–19 year olds, all exam boards' syllabuses were revised and restructured to take account of the introduction of a new Advanced Subsidiary (AS) level. This will be examined for the first time in 2000 and is designed to assess the skills, knowledge and understanding of a candidate who has completed the first half of a full A level course. The standard of this new qualification represents work of a quality intermediate between GCSE and A level.

As a result, the skills weightings applied by the syllabuses will change, as will the actual title of the skills assessed. The new sociology core laid down two Assessment Objectives for Sociology (AO1 and AO2) which will therefore apply from 2000. These are:

AO1 Knowledge and Understanding (K, U)

AO2 Identification, Analysis, Interpretation and Evaluation (I, A, E).

While the assessment pattern and the relative balance of these skills will change from 2000 onwards (and you should consult your teacher for more information on this), the techniques you are required to use in order to demonstrate that you have developed the skills necessary for an award to be made are very similar to the present skills. The activities in this book will help you to develop the new skills and we have therefore identified the skills each activity relates to.

Each activity has capital letters which relate to these skills at the end of the activity. These letters indicate which skill or skills we feel the activity tests. This makes the activities closely tied into the development of skills required by the syllabuses, and should also make the skills basis of A level Sociology more transparent. Your tutor or teacher can offer more guidance on the skills basis of the exams and on which particular skills you might need to develop. Most of these activities are based around the development of skills by requiring you to engage in some form of written work.

However since sociology is at its most enjoyable when it involves discussing the state of society today, discussion points are included to form the basis for class discussions and discussions among students away from class. These are each highlighted using the following symbol:

Discussion point

As far as possible they are related to contemporary events. There is no right answer to these discussion points (it follows logically that there is no wrong answer), and you should therefore not feel too intimidated to become involved. Recognize that your experiences and views are as valid as anyone else's. Discussion in a friendly and supportive atmosphere is one of the best ways to learn. So get involved and enjoy your sociology: make it meaningful to you.

Exam questions and coursework suggestions

Recent past exam questions are included at the end of each chapter to illustrate the kind of questions you might be expected to confront in the exam, and to enable you to consider the style and format of these. Your tutor or teacher will be able to provide you with more past exam questions and probably the comments of Chief Examiners and the mark schemes for these exam questions. You should also regularly consult the Examinations Matters section of *Sociology Review* for advice on tackling exam questions.

A number of coursework *suggestions* appear at

the end of each chapter. You might consider these, or even adapt them to your own needs. We must stress that the choice of coursework topic is a matter you must discuss with your tutor or teacher, who should of course be kept fully informed of what you propose to do before you embark on any coursework.

Further reading

It is important that you actively engage with the material in your sociology course, and we hope that *Sociology in Perspective* offers a sound foundation to enable you to do this. However, we must stress that you will need to read widely so that discussions and written work are informed by a high level of sociological knowledge and a detailed understanding of it. For this reason, we have included some suggestions for further reading at the end of each chapter. Most of these should be readily available, while others might form the basis of detailed reading if you find yourself drawn to a particular topic, perhaps for your coursework. They are not intended to be exhaustive and you should of course consult your tutor or teacher and the various suggested reading lists provided by the exam boards for other sources of material on particular topics. *Sociology Review* is particularly useful here and the back copies of this (and its predecessor, *Social Studies Review*) provide a wealth of useful information both on substantive sociological debates and articles aimed more specifically at developing your skills in sociology.

Using the bibliography

The bibliography is there to help you to locate the exact source of the material referred to. For instance, in the bibliography you will find that the references quoted in the section on the content of chapters above (see page 5) relate to:

McRobbie, A. (1994) *Postmodernism and Popular Culture*, London, Routledge.
Eldridge, J. (1993) 'News, truth and power', in Eldridge, J. (ed.), *Getting the Message: News Truth and Power*, London, Routledge.

If there is more than one publication by an author in any one year – or two or more publications in the same year by authors with the same surname – this is indicated by the use of letters to differentiate between the two. For example, Fiske (1989a) and Fiske (1989b) refer to:

Fiske, J. (1989a) *Understanding Popular Culture*, London, Unwin Hyman.
Fiske, J. (1989b) *Reading the Popular*, London, Unwin Hyman.

The use of dates in the text will allow you to be aware of the broad period when work was produced, and therefore to contextualize the ideas being discussed. You would expect ideas about popular culture to be different in the 1950s and 60s to those in the 1990s, and this can help you make that connection.

This approach also provides a format or template which you can use yourself, for example in the presentation of your coursework. It is similar to the format adopted by many books.

Where the date of publication is misleading – for example where books by long-dead sociologists have been reprinted in recent years – the original date of publication is given as well to avoid confusion.

Using the indexes

To find out where the writers referred to above are discussed in this book, you should refer to the Index at the very back of the book. There are two indexes, one based on subject topics and one based on authors. The authors mentioned above can be located in the author index and you will find that the page numbers referred to fall largely in Chapters 10 and 15. Equally if you are considering the changes in the way we look at the world – for example the move from religion to science as the key basis of knowledge – index entries will take you to Chapters 18 and 13; and if you then go on to look at the statistics produced by this new scientific method you will find important debates in Chapters 13 and 11, as well as Chapter 3. Indexes can therefore help you draw out the links between topics.

They can provide a quick way of finding cross-references, since all other references to a particular author or a particular subject area will also be listed in the index. You should therefore use this as a way of finding other references to the particular author or subject you are discussing or working on.

Conclusion

This introduction has given a brief flavour of what sociology is about and what you will be looking at while you study the subject. We would underline one final piece of advice, which is that you should use the book in conjunction with advice from your tutor or teacher. This will ensure that you follow a course of study designed to achieve your maximum potential.

Good luck, we hope you enjoy sociology.

Further **reading**

Books aimed at helping to develop skills needed for A level Sociology are:

- Kirby, M., Madry, N., Koubel, F. (1993) *Sociology: Developing Skills Through Structured Questions*, London, Collins Educational.
- Lawson, T. (1993) *Sociology for 'A' Level: A Skills-Based Approach*, London, Collins Educational.

Books designed to help with coursework are:

- Barrat, D. and Cole, T. (1991) *Sociology Projects: A Student's Guide*, London, Routledge.
- Harvey, L. and MacDonald, M. (1993) *Doing Sociology: A Practical Introduction*, London, Macmillan.
- Howe, N. (1994) *Advanced Practical Sociology*, Walton-on-Thames, Nelson.
- Langley, P. and Corrigan, P. (1993) *Managing Sociology Coursework*, Lewes, Connect.
- Williams, L. and Dunsmuir, A. (1991) *How To Do Social Research*, London, Collins Educational.

The following are summary and revision guides:

- Harris, S. (1994) *Sociology Revise Guide*, London, Longman.
- Selfe, P. (1995) *Work Out Sociology*, London, Macmillan.

The following are dictionaries of sociology:

- Jary, D. and Jary, J. (1991) *Collins Dictionary of Sociology*, London, HarperCollins.
- Marshall, G. (ed.) (1994) *Concise Oxford Dictionary of Sociology*, Oxford, Oxford University Press.

Authors' **Acknowledgements**

A book like this involves the work of a whole army of people of whom the nine mentioned on the cover are really only the tip of the iceberg. While those nine are the ones who take full responsibility for the book, they would not be in that position without the help, support, advice and encouragement of a lot of others.

First the team would like to thank Sue Walton at Heinemann for her total and unswerving support for the project and her expertise and assistance in seeing it through. We would also like to thank Alistair Christie at Heinemann for keeping the whole thing going and remaining calm even under provocation. Roger Parker, Heather Serjeant, Fiona Barr, Sandra Stafford, Trish Stableford, Victoria Ramsay, Helen Maxey, Rachel Caldin and Jane Tyler also contributed with their particular forms of expertise.

Our first attempts were kindly read by a group of academic sociologists and their extremely helpful comments and advice were much appreciated. We would therefore like to thank Bob Blanchard, David Booth, Phil Brown, Stephen Edgell, Helen Fawcett, David Gillborn, Lesley Hoggart, Kate Nash, Alan Scott, John Solomos, Merl Storr, Bill Sugrue, Steve Taylor, Kenneth Thompson, Frank Webster and John Westergaard. It is important to stress that none of these bears any responsibility at all for the final book, but we would like to thank them and let them know their comments were both incisive and helpful, an extremely useful combination.

Writing a book like this requires reference to an enormous amount of material and it is therefore appropriate to thank the various libraries and library staff who always proved invaluable in assisting us in locating such material.

We would also like to thank all those who contributed to this book by designing it, typesetting it and printing it. Your skills mean the book looks good despite the material we provided you to work with.

Finally we would like to thank our families and friends for putting up with our obsession, and our students for humouring our early attempts and for re-creating the correct atmosphere of humility in the team members.

Mark Kirby
Warren Kidd
Francine Koubel
John Barter
Tanya Hope
Alison Kirton
Nick Madry
Paul Manning
Karen Triggs

May 1997

Sociological theory

2.1 **Do we need theory?**

Let the facts speak for themselves?

It might be argued that if our task is to understand the world, we should simply set about gathering together as many facts as possible and use them to develop a picture of society. Then perhaps we should compare that information to our idea of the type of society we want to live in, measure the extent to which the two diverge and set about devising a programme of changes to bring the two into line. Surely this would be a purposeful activity and would allow sociology and sociologists to contribute to the creation of a better society. What is more we would not need to delve into all this dreadful theory.

While this idea might at first seem popular, it is not a route we can really take. You might have gathered that this was the case already, since this book includes a chapter on theory. It is there because we really do need theory. Why?

We might assume that facts are unproblematic entities, waiting around for us to scoop up through questionnaires, interviews or observations but they are not.

Take the facts in Table 2.1 about income inequalities in the UK taken from a government publication, the *New Earnings Survey*, 1995:

Table 2.1 Average gross weekly pay for full-time workers on adult rates whose pay was not affected by absence

Region	Male manual	Male non-manual	Female manual	Female non-manual
South East	£310.70	£506.30	£208.50	£326.10
East Anglia	£283.30	£402.70	£175.30	£264.00
South West	£276.50	£410.00	£178.00	£267.30
West Midlands	£285.20	£410.20	£186.40	£264.20
East Midlands	£282.40	£395.80	£177.20	£262.80
Yorks & H'side	£285.50	£390.60	£176.20	£259.30
North West	£290.40	£414.40	£182.00	£270.60
North	£286.40	£385.40	£180.30	£258.70
Wales	£284.40	£386.80	£185.40	£264.90
Scotland	£284.50	£413.20	£186.00	£272.70

Source: *New Earnings Survey*, 1995

On the surface these appear to be facts and they are, in one sense. If we assume that the statisticians have done their job properly (see also Section 3.11) the figures do tell us that the average gross weekly pay for female manual workers in the East Midlands in 1995 was £177.20. It follows that if we were asked whether this group earned more than £200 per week, we could confidently answer no, and quote the survey findings as the basis of this statement. (See also Section 14.8.)

The social construction of facts

However, if we delve deeper and consider how these facts came to be collected and presented, the role of human action in the construction of these statistics becomes clearer. There are a whole range of questions that might be asked (as indeed all good sociology students should ask) about the accuracy of these figures, but another issue which we will consider here, is why the categories outlined above were chosen. Why do they decide that it was important to divide the figures between male and female, or between manual and non-manual workers, or into regions? Why, for example, did they not provide figures divided up by shoe size, or inside leg measurement? Surely such a table would also yield facts. The answer (unless you consider shoe size or leg length an important social variable) is that some ways of categorizing things are more important than others. But how do we decide which are more important than others, and so which facts are more important than others? We do so by thinking, by developing models, or to put it another way, by theorizing. So, you cannot have facts without theories because in order to decide which questions to ask and which way to present your findings:

- You have to decide on some way to classify all the possible facts floating around in the world.
- You have to decide on the relative importance of facts.

If this seems very obvious, consider the following system of classification devised for animals:

Animals are divided into: (a) belonging to the Emperor (b) embalmed (c) tame (d) sucking pigs (e) sirens (f) fabulous (g) stray dogs (h) included in the present classification (i) frenzied (j) innumerable (k) drawn with a fine camelhair brush (l) et cetera (m) having just broken the water pitcher (n) that from a long way off look like flies.
(Foucault, 1970, p. xv)

This classification was fictional, and might be the subject of argument if it was proposed as the basis of a census for animals in the UK in the 1990s; but on what basis would we argue? In his commentary on this classification, French post-structuralist social thinker Foucault (see also Section 2.10) points out that one of the reasons it appears absurd is because we judge it on the basis of our own pre-existing ideas. When it was suggested that the earth was round and revolved around the sun, this undoubtedly seemed absurd to those who believed the earth was flat. So when we decide how to classify facts, we decide on the basis of theory. The whole of the knowledge of society, which constitutes sociology, requires the existence of theories.

So although it might be nice to think that we could dispense with all these nasty, difficult and sometimes seemingly impenetrable theories, and simply go about the business of collecting facts, we can't, because without theories there are no facts.

On a more profound level, even if we assume we can devise what we see as sensible categories, we could still not dispense with theory.

Facts do not explain themselves

What are we to do with such a collection of facts? Leaving aside for the moment the important question of the accuracy of government statistics (see Section 3.11), we can say that arguably the presentation of the statistics on income distribution in the UK in 1995 has been based on sensible and meaningful categories and that, therefore, the table is useful. However, where do we go from there? We would want to know why such a distribution occurred (see also Section 14.9) and what mechanisms existing in our society cause such an outcome, and possibly what we can do to change this outcome. The table itself does not give us the answers to these questions, so yet again we need to think (theorize) to try to answer these questions.

So we need theory to get facts and then we also need theory to try to make sense of these facts. As you can see, theory is indispensable.

Although the writing of some theorists may seem initially to be impenetrable, they are all seeking to do the same as you: to understand the nature of the society in which we live. The notion of theory can be seen as quite simple, a point made very eloquently by contemporary social theorist Kilminster:

What is a theory? Contrary to expectations, the answer to this question is fairly simple. A theory is an organising framework of concepts, established by empirical evidence, which explains why society or some aspect of society works as it does. It also makes connections between aspects of society which would otherwise seem to be unconnected, thereby enabling us to organise a good deal of disparate empirical knowledge.
(Kilminster, 1992, p. 139)

A sociology book without any theory would simply be an arbitrary, jumbled set of facts with no discussion of any possible connections between them and no reasons given why those facts are placed where they are. So think of theories as ways of understanding and you will see they are there to help you make sense of the world you live in. Of course, you yourself have to decide whether the theories are any

good, but this is a matter of choosing between theories rather than choosing between theory and no theory.

Discussion point

What might a sociology without sociological theory be like? Could it exist? Would you prefer it?

An invitation to theorize

The centrality of sociological theory can be obscured if we treat it merely as an exercise in listing the historical development of sociological theory. Rather we should see theory as a way of considering the contemporary usefulness of what sociological theorists of the past have developed. Merely knowing what Talcott Parsons, Max Weber, Karl Marx and Emile Durkheim said is a necessary but not sufficient exercise. The important point is to consider whether and how their concepts help us to explain the contemporary world, and how these concepts are used by contemporary theorists. The key point is whether their ideas can be applied to the analysis of contemporary society and it is your job to evaluate their usefulness in this respect. As Ian Craib puts it in his book, *Modern Social Theory*:

The problems which lead people to theory are problems we all face in our everyday lives. I think the truth is that we all think theoretically, but in a way of which we are not often aware.
(Craib, 1992, p. 7)

If this is true, and we think it is, then surely we must try to apply our natural inclination to theorize to the questions sociologists have asked. To be a sociologist is surely to approach a problem in the way sociologists do, rather than simply knowing what some people called sociologists have said in the past. This opens up the study of sociological theory and suggests the limits of seeing it only as historical knowledge. This is explained by Craib in a way far better than we can:

Because we start with the result, it is too easy for students and teachers to imagine that the whole process is a matter of learning what various theorists have said – of learning theories. It is that, of course, but in one sense that is the least important aspect. . . . Another way of putting this is that it is less a matter of learning theory than of learning to think theoretically. . . . Perhaps the best way to learn 'theoretical thinking' is not just by reading and understanding theory but by asking the theory

questions and speculating on the answers.... The first step is always to speculate, to try to invent an answer.
(Craib, 1992, pp. 5–10)

This book is designed to help you pass your A level so it does include descriptions of what sociologists have had to say. This should provide you with knowledge and understanding. However, in an attempt to incorporate some elements of the approach identified by Craib above, and also to encourage you to think about sociological theory as a way of thinking about the society you live in, we will start by encouraging you to speculate as Craib suggests. We think this is also the way you should approach the information and problems considered by the theorists discussed in the rest of this chapter.

You live in society and experience it, so draw on that experience for the following activity aimed at getting you into the swing of thinking about theories of society. The activity contains a (not exhaustive) list of questions we think sociological theories consider.

Activity

Organize yourselves into groups of about four and then discuss each of the following questions. Add other questions of your own. Do this before your read any other sections.

a What exactly is society and in what ways does it affect the lives of individuals?
b How are societies possible, and do we need them?
c In our lives how much individual choice do we really have?
d How are/should decisions be made in society?
e Do societies change; if so how and why?
f What are the most important relationships and institutions in society and how do they work?

Provide your own versions of answers to these questions. These should be as detailed as possible. Speculate, try to invent an answer, as Craib puts it.

Write summaries of your answers on large sheets of paper and stick these up on the wall. You should then continuously modify your own answers and compare them to the answers provided by the thinkers referred to in this chapter as you read your way through it. In what ways are the answers they give better than yours and in what ways worse?

I, A, E

For example, you might argue that the answer to the question on how society is possible is the fact that we all need each other and we all need to live in some degree of agreement. However you should then consider what exactly we need to agree on, what things we don't need to agree on, whether that means we are individuals or not and what mechanism we can use to make a decision, that is, to reach an agreement.

On the other hand you might argue that society is possible because some people have access to guns, planes and bombs while some others don't and that therefore fear and power underlies our adherence to laws and routines which is the reason society exists in the form it does. However, you then need to ask where these people get these weapons from, whether in fact they would use them, why everyone doesn't have such things and why the people who fear the use of these weapons agree to the existence of them and indeed pay for them through taxes.

In other words, once you have thought about the big issues, follow your process through and consider any weaknesses of your answers or any areas where further explanation is necessary. We hope you will find you are now theorizing and providing answers you can use for comparison purposes when looking at the thoughts of some other sociologists contained in the remainder of this chapter.

2.2 Modernity and the emergence of sociology

The rise of modernity

Although thinkers have commented on the nature of society since the beginning of humanity, sociology as a distinct subject only emerges in the nineteenth century. Why?

It can be seen to follow from two broad sets of changes occurring in the eighteenth century:

- changes in the way people lived, most notably seen in the Industrial Revolution and the French Revolution
- changes in the way people thought about the world, particularly in the rise of the set of ideas known as the Enlightenment.

The first important material change was the Industrial Revolution, a process begun in England and spreading out across Europe (see Section 9.2). This brought a total change in the way people lived their lives. Work was concentrated in specific places built for that purpose, namely factories. This led to a split between the place of residence and the place of work. People were no longer spread out across the land growing crops, but became concentrated in cities. (See Section 16.1.)

At the same time, traditional notions of how society should operate were being undermined by changing ideas, notably through the process known as the Enlightenment. This phrase covers a whole development of thinking culminating in the mid-eighteenth century, with the rise of science as a method of explanation and as a result the declining importance of religion. (See Section 18.1.)

The idea that people were not merely the passive subjects of God's will but were in some way able to comprehend and master their own world also had political repercussions. The French Revolution of 1789 and the American Revolution of 1776 were the most important early results of this new way of thinking and the impact of these events shook the whole world.

In short, the world was turned upside down. Science replaced religion as the main basis of knowledge, notions of the people and democracy replaced religion and monarchy as the main form of government (see also Section 17.1), and industrial production and urbanization transformed previously agricultural, rural societies. These developments collectively have been seen as the emergence of modern society and modernity. For anyone interested in human affairs, this was a period of intense change and inevitably led many to ask about the implications of these changes for society and the way people lived. In relation both to political authority and to more general knowledge about the world, the idea that people could understand the world and could therefore participate in the construction and administration of that world was the central theme. From being objects of the world, people saw themselves as able to shape their own destiny. What was required was the knowledge to do so. Sociology was to be that knowledge.

The entrance of sociology

What knowledge was needed to understand the changes society had been through? Some argued that there was a need for sociology to restore a degree of stability to society, while others argued it was needed to ensure that future changes to society were made on the basis of informed scientific statements. In either case, sociology would play a central role. We can consider two contrasting reactions to this situation by early sociologists.

Comte: sociology as a reforming ideology for the state

Auguste Comte (1798–1857) is most famous for actually inventing the term sociology and for promoting it as the main element in his positive philosophy (Comte, 1877, orig. pub. 1830–2). He believed that society progressed through a number of stages reflecting the development of human ideas. The first two of these, the theological and the metaphysical, represented eras when the clergy and philosophers respectively were the ultimate arbiters of knowledge and clearly represented Comte's view of the development of human society up to that point. His third stage, positivism, represented the triumph of science (see Section 3.1). He argued that an understanding of human society could and should be developed on a scientific basis. This knowledge was to be used to effect changes beneficial to society. Comte believed that with the growth of economic specialization and the division of labour whereby people specialized in different tasks, the notion of community, of having something in common with others, which had been the main basis of social integration in pre-industrial society, might break down (see Section 16.1). He therefore set out to produce an outline of changes needed to avoid this situation. Central to this was the state, which he saw as the only real potential unifying force in this new period of individualism. The problem was to get people to recognize the validity of the state's right to regulate their lives. It is here that sociology comes in, since Comte argued that the authority of the state would be greater if it was backed up with a specific intellectual doctrine. Sociology was therefore assigned a central role in the reconstitution of a notion of community in society, through providing authority for state regulation over society. It might be argued that this presents a very authoritarian vision of society, with directions given by sociologists and enforced by the state.

Spencer: society as a marketplace

In contrast, Herbert Spencer (1820–1903) argued that the state was not needed and insofar as it did intervene, it had the effect of stifling the individual initiative which was now the key basis of economic and societal development. Drawing on the ideas of Adam Smith, Spencer (1874, 1896) argued that society was now regulated merely by the mutual self-interest of individuals and all that was needed was exchange and trade between individuals. He argued that the move from military societies of the past to the industrial society had led to a decline in the need for state regulation. Societies would therefore almost automatically stabilize as long as individual self-interest was not stifled.

We all like our own individual freedom when it is threatened, but perhaps we are not so enamoured of individual freedom when it involves our neighbours' freedom to play loud music until four in the morning. Every day we face the problem of how we can retain individual freedom while at the same time living in some relationship with others in society.

It is in respect of this dilemma that Comte and Spencer offered contrasting views. Comte worried that in the face of the new ideas of individualism society might break down. He argued for a strong state to limit this individualism. Spencer saw individualism not as a threat but as the hope for the future, and argued that trade and exchange (in short, the market) provided all the cement that was needed to keep people together in some sort of civilized relationship.

The relationship between society and the individuals within it forms the key continuing focus of sociological theory. Should we view society as the construction of individuals and therefore understand it by looking at how those individuals interact together to make and remake society, or should we instead see individuals as the product of society and therefore start our analysis at the level of society?

Activity

Suggest ways in which the themes and arguments presented by both Comte and Spencer are present in contemporary debates about society. Make a list of the advantages and drawbacks of each of these two schemes. Which of these two contrasting visions of society do you think offers the best blueprint for contemporary society?

I, A, E

The answers to these questions form the starting point for sociological analysis and the contrasting answers given by Comte and Spencer form the backdrop to the ideas developed by the three generally acknowledged founders of modern sociology. These in turn form the basis for all subsequent theory.

If you are wondering why we are spending time looking at how some dead sociologists reacted to events over 100 years ago, the answer is quite simple. The problems they considered, the questions they asked and the answers they provided, are still relevant today, as Kilminster put it:

One reason we return to Marx is that there is still a class struggle, even though its form has changed. One reason we return to Durkheim is that the problem of solidarity in an individualistic society is still an issue for us. One reason we return to Weber is that power relations continue to proliferate on many other dimensions than the economic.
(Kilminster, 1992, p. 153)

Discussion point

To what extent do you agree that these phenomena are present in contemporary society? Are there other issues which are more important today? Discuss the relative importance of all these issues in contemporary UK society.

2.3 The development of classical sociological theories

This section considers in some detail the key ideas of the three thinkers commonly identified as the founders of classical sociology: Karl Marx, Emile Durkheim and Max Weber. It also looks at some of the diverse ways their ideas have been later interpreted.

Karl Marx

Marx (1818–1883) grew up in the Rhineland area of what is now part of Germany; a society obsessed with the implications of the French Revolution, and how to stop such a thing happening in Germany. Marx himself gravitated towards a group of thinkers who developed rather more radical ideas out of Hegelian philosophy. The central insight which Marx took from Hegel was the idea that things develop through the clash of contradictions. For Hegel, this meant a clash of ideas, but Marx argued that real material existence was more important and therefore argued that the clashes were real material clashes between human beings.

Historical materialism

Marx argued that the fundamental element of human society is the need to produce the basic needs of humanity: food, shelter and clothing. All this needs to be done before people can reflect and develop ideas. Marx therefore argued that production combined with the social relationships which people entered into to meet these needs, was the fundamental element of society. By around 1845 Marx and his close collaborator, Friedrich Engels, were closely involved in the growing communist movement and also wrote a number of works, such as *The German Ideology* (1974, originally written 1845) where they arrive at an outline of their own thinking, which came to be known as historical materialism. Their work considers topics which today would clearly be called sociology as we can see from the following quote from the *Communist Manifesto*:

the essence of man is no abstraction inherent in each single individual. In its reality it is the ensemble of the social relations.
(Marx and Engels, 1968, p. 29, orig. pub. 1848)

Class struggle and social change

Production and the social relations they entail are therefore central to Marx's analysis. However what makes it distinctive is the way in which he does two things:

- He argues that the relations created in the process of production have always entailed conflicts of interest which lead to social conflicts between classes and social change. Class conflict is therefore the central motor of history.
- He argues that the relations created in the production sphere have an effect on all other social relations in society.

In relation to the first of these, the description contained in the *Communist Manifesto* (Marx and Engels, 1968, orig. pub. 1848) provides a summary of this notion of human society developing through successive conflicts centred on production:

The history of all hitherto existing societies is the history of class struggles.

Freeman and slave, patrician and plebeian, lord and servant, guildmaster and journeyman, in a word, oppressor and oppressed, stood in constant opposition to one another, carried on an uninterrupted, now hidden, now open fight, a fight that each time ended, either in the revolutionary reconstitution of society at large, or in the common ruin of the contending classes.

(Marx and Engels, 1968, p. 36, orig. pub. 1848)

The theory of exploitation

The important question to ask here is why these relations were antagonistic, that is, between oppressor and oppressed. To answer this question, we need to examine the labour theory of value, which Marx supported. This is an abstract concept which tries to describe the fundamental relations within production. Marx uses it (1954, orig. pub. 1867; 1956, orig. pub. 1885; 1959, orig. pub. 1894; 1973, orig. pub. 1857) to develop an analysis of actually existing society. It focuses on the fact that the important thing about production is not technological change, but change in the way it is socially organized.

The theory argues that the inherent value of anything is based on the number of socially necessary hours needed to produce it since that is what things have in common. The term 'socially necessary' is used because otherwise a table made by an incompetent carpenter who takes a very long time would be extremely valuable, and this would be a nonsense. On the basis of this theory, it is only by being directly involved in production that people produce value. But Marx noted that in all social relations of production up to that time some of the people involved in production actually did no direct work at all. Marx argued, however, that since they produced no value themselves, their money must arise from the work of others. In simple terms, part of the value created by workers was taken not by them but by the capitalists. This is what Marx meant by exploitation, the expropriation of money from workers by capitalists. It is also the basis of Marx's notion of alienation since by this, Marx meant the way in which things which we made come to have a power over us. Money is a prime example of this, since it is not a natural thing, but a human invention which now occupies much of our thoughts and often worries. The lack of it restricts our ability to engage in certain activities. Production, which Marx saw as potentially liberating, both in terms of the goods it could provide and the satisfaction to be gained from making things, in fact became a drudge, a necessity and an arena in which one group lived by exploiting another.

Marx therefore argued that the direct producers, meaning the workers who produced things, would rise up and overthrow their oppressors and would create a society where the surplus was shared by all, a communist society. Production and the producers (the working class) were therefore central to his analysis.

The economy and society

To return to the second point above: how does this affect the rest of society? In *Capital* Marx provides the following summary of this argument:

The specific economic form, in which unpaid surplus-labour is pumped out of direct producers, determines the relationship of rulers and ruled, as it grows directly out of production itself and, in turn, reacts upon it as a determining element. Upon this, however is founded the entire formation of the economic community which grows out of the production relations themselves, thereby simultaneously its specific political form. It is always the direct relationship of the owners of the conditions of production to the direct producers – a relation always naturally corresponding to a definite stage in the development of the methods of labour and thereby its social productivity – which reveals its innermost secret, the hidden basis of the entire social structure, and with it the political form of the the relation of sovereignty and dependence, in short, the corresponding form of the state. This does not prevent the same economic basis – the same from the standpoint of its main conditions – due to innumerable different empirical circumstances, natural environment, racial relations, external historical influences, etc., from showing infinite variations and gradations in appearance, which can be ascertained only by analysis of the empirically given circumstances.

(Marx, 1959, p. 791, orig. pub. 1894)

This has come to be known as the base-superstructure model of society, since it suggests that the way production (the economic base) is organized will have a determining effect on all other relations in society. However, the point about the possible varieties of society that are compatible with the same economic base leads to the conclusion that Marx meant that the way production was organized put definite limits on the way the rest of society could be organized.

Ideology and class consciousness

The implication of this is that workers engaging in struggles over production, will, if they are successful, cause changes not only in the sphere of production but in all other areas of society as well. This is the meaning of social revolution. Put together these elements provide both a view of historical changes and a vision of the future, a communist society. Marx was centrally involved in the setting up of the First Communist International, an entity dedicated to organizing to develop the struggles taking place in society to the point where a social revolution would occur. This suggests that Marx believed such a process was not automatic.

One of the major reasons for this was his belief that the ideas in people's heads reflected the ideas of the people in charge of society. Ideologies kept existing society going and they were an important part of the circumstances within which people struggled to change society. This idea is encapsulated in the following extract from the *Communist Manifesto*:

Men make their own history, but they do not make it just as they please; they do not make it under circumstances chosen by themselves, but under circumstances directly encountered, given and transmitted from the past. The tradition of all the dead generations weighs like a nightmare on the brain of the living.
(Marx, 1968, p. 96, orig. pub. 1872)

The idea is expressed more specifically in what has come to be known as the Dominant Ideology Thesis which states that:

The ideas of the ruling class are in every epoch the ruling ideas: i.e. that class which is the ruling material force in society is at the same time its ruling intellectual force.
(Marx and Engels, *The German Ideology*, 1977, orig. written 1845; quoted in Callinicos, 1987, p. 140)

This suggests that the struggle to change society is not merely an economic one but must also engage in ideas and ideological struggle, in order first to persuade workers that the ideas in society are not correct and merely justify their treatment.

Criticisms of Marx

The centrality of production in Marx's work has also been the basis of one of the most oft-repeated criticisms, namely that Marx's work is an example of economic determinism. This has led to criticism that such an approach ignores those social relations not directly involved in production and those people not involved in production. Feminists (see Section 2.6) have argued that Marxism downplays conflicts in the domestic sphere, and post-modernists (see Section 2.10) have argued that in contemporary society, processes of consumption are more important in the formation of identity and social relations than production. Despite this criticism, it seems clear that the level of economic production does at the very least place clear limits on other aspects of society. Whether it is so utterly determining as some interpretations of Marx would suggest is open to question.

A related criticism is that class conflict as a theory of social change cannot explain other aspects of inequality which exist and which can operate to achieve social change. The women's movement (see Chapter 5) and black nationalism (see Chapter 6) are the most obvious, but included here would also be the more recent New Social Movements which often consciously organize themselves around identities which have nothing to do with the sphere of production.

Finally, the link between Marxism and the working class has led to criticisms along the lines that since the working class has not as yet led a revolution in western Europe, Marx's analysis of the process of social change is flawed. It is arguably this last point which has been the spur to the various interpretations of Marx that have developed in recent years.

Interpretations of Marx

Some followers of Marx, notably those leading the Second Communist International, tended towards an evolutionary view which relied on developments in technology to produce a communist society. This led to divisions when revolutionary Marxists split from the Second International to create the Third Communist International. The leaders of this included Lenin, Trotsky and Stalin, who themselves were later to diverge in their analysis.

The revolutionary tradition continued in the period after the Russian Revolution of 1917, but the failure of the revolution to spread to western Europe led to the growth of what has been called Western Marxism of which there are many variants. It is undoubtedly versions of this which are most prominent in contemporary Marxist sociology. These developments have led to a multitude of Marxisms:

Structural Marxism: Marx's focus on how the structure of production relations has a determining effect on other aspects of society has led some to see Marxism as a version of economic determinism, in other words a belief that the economy determines everything else. In some versions of Marxism, this led to a belief that economic and technological developments will almost automatically lead to socialism. More recently, reacting against this, Althusser (1966, 1968) developed what came to be known as Structural Marxism, structural since it denied any place in the theory for human action despite Marx's statements about men making history. These interpretations of Marx are discussed in more detail in Section 2.5.

Humanist Marxism: In contrast to Structural Marxism, humanist interpretations of Marx stress his critique of capitalism as dehumanizing social relations, and further, they stress the potential for people to overcome this and create a fully free society. The various strands of this approach are examined in Section 2.5.

Marx and ideology: The comments Marx made about ideology have led to the rise of interpretations of his arguments which stress that economic struggle alone is not sufficient to cause social change, but that instead Marxists need to engage in ideological and cultural struggles to achieve social change. This relies on an interpretation of the work of Italian Marxist Antonio Gramsci (1971, orig. written 1929–35) but can also be seen in the work of the Frankfurt School and the development of Critical Theory. These approaches are examined in more detail in Section 2.5.

Emile Durkheim

Society as a reality, a 'social fact' and the need for sociology

Durkheim (1858–1917) argued that society was a reality *sui generis* (a unified whole). Society is not reducible to the sum of individuals within it, it is exterior to them, but it is nonetheless a social fact since it effects a constraint on their actions. The idea that we live a life determined for us is clear from the following extract from Durkheim's *The Rules of Sociological Method* (1938b, orig. pub. 1895):

When I fulfil my obligations as brother, husband, or citizen I perform duties which are defined, externally to myself and my acts, in law and custom. Even if they conform to my own sentiments, and I feel their reality subjectively, such reality is still objective, for I did not create them; I merely inherited them through my education . . . the church member finds the beliefs and practices of his religious life ready made at birth; their existence prior to him implies their existence outside himself (Durkheim, 1938, orig. pub. 1895; in Jones, 1993b, p. 25)

Activity

Looking at the three roles outlined by Durkheim above, suggest what the law and customs define as the obligations of these roles.

Provide two examples of roles of your own and explain how the law and custom constrains the people in these roles to act in certain ways.

A

Durkheim goes on to set out the implications of this for sociology. While he argued the new subject had to be scientific, he believed that economics, the social science which had most followed the methodology of the natural sciences, had erred by starting from the notion of the isolated individual. Given Durkheim's definition of society he could not accept this. Instead he argued that sociology should study 'social facts' which were exterior to individuals and were not directly observable by watching the actions of these individuals (see Sections 3.1 and 3.3).

Discussion point

Why is society distinct from the individuals who make it up? Could we not simply understand what happens in sociology as the result of the actions and motivations of the collections of individuals within in? Durkheim's answer to this would be a clear 'No'. How far do you agree with him?

Durkheim argued that sociology should concern itself with the causes of these 'social facts' but also the reason for their persistence over time. In order to study this latter aspect he argued that we needed to consider the functions these social facts served, reasoning that if they did not serve a function they would die out. The application of this methodology to produce a specifically Durkheimian approach can be seen in his other main works.

The division of labour in society, the moral basis of society and *anomie*

Durkheim's first book dealt with the problem of the relationship between the individual and society in the context of the transition from pre-industrial to industrial society. (See also Sections 9.2 and 16.1.) Durkheim argued that we could not understand society simply on the basis of agreements between individuals. *The Division of Labour in Society* (1938a, orig. pub. 1893) was dedicated to a critique of this position, and the allied theory that society resulted from a contract. Durkheim rejected this view of the origin of society and he did so by arguing that for people to make a contract they must have a prior basis on which to do so:

In Durkheim's celebrated phrase, there is 'a non-contractual element in contract': the existence of contractual exchanges presupposes moral authority, the authority which renders contracts binding. (Giddens, 1978, p.10)

Durkheim set out to show how the individualism of modern society, which was absent in traditional societies, could be explained in terms of changes to this moral order. Durkheim called this moral order the 'conscience collective' emphasizing that it was both a moral and a rational outlook. Durkheim argued that in traditional societies, the conscience collective formed a strongly-defined moral consensus. The usual method of transmission of this moral consensus was through the Church and religion. Subject to a powerful and all-embracing moral order, people were essentially very similar. He argued that this was what kept society together. He called this 'mechanical solidarity' emphasizing its similarity to a biological organism composed of cells very similar to each other.

However, modern society was very different since important changes had taken place due to industrialization and urbanization. Most notably, the implementation of a division of labour had occurred. This meant that the work done in society was divided out and people began to specialize. Durkheim was concerned to consider its social effects. He argued that society was now based not on people being similar but on people being seen as individuals. For this to come about there needs to have been some transformation of the nature of the conscience collective. This social force needed to alter to allow for the growth of the notion of individualism. Individualism was therefore not the product of individuals but of the changing moral order of society. Society created individuals and individualism. Society now survives, because individuals need each other. Since there is now specialization, no one individual can perform all the tasks they need to survive and are therefore mutually dependent on each other. This Durkheim calls 'organic solidarity'. This different type of society has a different moral basis, but it still does have a moral basis:

This is not to say, however, that the conscience collective is likely to disappear completely. Rather it increasingly comes to consist of very general and indeterminate ways of thought and sentiment, which leaves room open for a growing variety of individual differences. There is even a place where it is strengthened and made precise: that is, in the way in which it regards the individual. (Durkheim, 1938a, p.146, orig. pub. 1893)

Durkheim recognized that in the transition from mechanical to organic solidarity there might be some problems which might result in a 'forced division of labour' leading to some people failing to be properly integrated into the new society. He used the phrase '*anomie*' to indicate this state of being outside societal regulation and he argued that this might be seen to lie behind such phenomena as industrial conflict, unhappiness and rising levels of suicide. Nonetheless, he argued that this was an abnormal state of affairs and a result of the great transformations that had taken place. He looked forward to a return to social stability given time.

The normal state of affairs was therefore a society where there was a clear moral consensus and social stability. *Anomie* was therefore a problem but a temporary one. This concept also illustrates another strand of Durkheim, which distinguishes him from the earlier positivism of Comte. He argued that there are forces and processes in society which are not reducible to individuals and are not therefore directly observable from viewing individuals. This view is known as realism (see Section 3.3) and Durkheim's method is therefore arguably a combination of positivism and realism. This can perhaps best be seen in his study of suicide (1979, orig. pub. 1897).

Anomic suicide resulted when the individual was insufficiently regulated by society and this occurred when the value consensus holding society together began to break down, particularly during periods of social change resulting in uncertainty for individuals. While there are major debates about the validity of this piece of work as an explanation of suicide (this issue is covered in more depth in Section 3.3) it illustrates a number of key Durkheimian themes:

- the power of society over the individual
- the superiority of sociological analysis
- the use of science as a method via the collection and analysis of facts, in this case statistics on suicide rates
- the belief that the key variable in society is the moral order and the way this integrates individuals into society, and that the variability of this can explain variations in individual behaviour.

Society, religion and rituals

The final aspect of Durkheim to consider is his analysis of religion (1982, orig. pub. 1912). This is more fully examined in Section 18.3. However some comments are required here because of its importance in the overall Durkheimian schema. When Durkheim analysed religious rituals he came to the conclusion that their function was to facilitate people coming together and that through such rituals, people, and therefore society, were bonded together.

The importance of rituals based on Durkheim's ideas was studied by Shils and Young (1953) who viewed the coronation ceremony of Queen Elizabeth II as just such a ritual allowing the reaffirmation of certain values and support for such values. A similar analysis was provided of the rituals surrounding the investiture of the Prince of Wales:

The feelings about the Queen and Prince Charles which the Investiture invoked, managed to fuse personal with public concerns in a symbolic fashion that Durkheim would have understood.
(Blumler *et al.*, 1971, p. 170)

💬 Discussion point

How might such theorists view the divorces in the Royal Family? What might they view them as indicating and what vision of the future might they foretell?

For Durkheim, the analysis of religion served to underline the need for a moral order to exist in society and it is clear that he saw the need to develop a secular morality to replace the declining religious value system. This led him to be concerned with ways in which the moral basis of society could be reinvigorated.

Criticisms of Durkheim's approach

The first obvious criticism of Durkheim concerns his notion of a society. He argued that it had an existence which cannot be reduced to the experiences of individuals within it. This is a controversial point, since it appears to attribute life to something which is an abstraction, and this reification of society is a point of criticism made of him. Durkheim tended to see society as similar to the human body with interrelated elements each fulfilling a function. The danger of this is that it can lead you to see society as a living organism, which it isn't.

💬 Discussion point

How much individual free will is there in society according to Durkheim? How might his idea be applied to the choice of A level subjects by students?

Durkheim has also been criticized for overstating the degree of consensus in society. He held that in his mode of organic solidarity the normal state of affairs was for society to be an integrated whole. The problem here is that anything that diverges from these modes is then discounted as 'abnormal' or to use Durkheim's word 'pathological'. In the section of *The Division of Labour in Society* (1938a, orig. pub. 1893) where he discusses the reality of the situation in France at the time, he presents a picture of class conflict, rising dissatisfaction and rising levels of suicide, all described by his famous concept of *anomie*.

There is, however, a clear contradiction in his analysis. He saw sociology as the study of social facts which he defined as something present in the average of societies. In France at the time he was writing, social conflict and unrest was clearly a social fact on this basis, yet he himself chose to describe it as an abnormality:

As a result, he tended to idealise societies he thought of as integrated, ignoring the tensions and conflicts within them, while seeing the realities of his own society only as the pathological deviations from its future, normal, ideally integrated state.
(Lukes, 1973, p. 30)

💬 Discussion point

What is normal and what is abnormal and how do we decide?

Lukes further argues that Durkheim's notion of rituals uniting people is unacceptable since it can be shown that societies exist where there is no consensus (such as Northern Ireland) and that some rituals do not serve an integrating function. Rituals such as the Orange Order parades in Northern Ireland do not lead to greater social integration but instead intensify differences.

These potential contradictions in his thought are the basis of recent attempts to provide a radical interpretation of Durkheim, one of the ways in which Durkheim's ideas have been interpreted in sociological circles. There are arguably three differing interpretations:

- *Durkheim as a forerunner of functionalism:* Durkheim argued that everything that survived over time did so because it served some function. His view of society as a system of interrelated parts which form a whole also leads to a functional analysis. This stress on the interrelatedness of parts and the function each fulfils in maintaining the whole became a central part of functionalist analysis. While it is clear that the idea of function is central to Durkheim's sociology, whether the interpretation of Durkheim in functionalist sociology is totally justified is an area for debate. It is however certainly this interpretation of Durkheim which is most prevalent in sociology (this approach is explored further in Section 2.4), though it has recently been challenged by two other contrasting versions.

- *Durkheim as a forerunner of structuralism:* Structuralism might be defined as follows: The whole is more than the parts, and cannot be reduced to the parts. What is important is the relationship between the parts. This view of Durkheim as a structuralist is clearly held by Bottomore and Nisbet (1979) who argue that Durkheim must be regarded as: 'the prominent structuralist in French sociological thought' (1979, p. 565).

  Structuralism became an important component of French thought through the work of anthropologists, but became more widely used in sociology, primarily through the development of Structuralist Marxism and the work of Althusser. The way in which structuralism has developed and the way some of these ideas can be traced back to the legacy of Durkheim will be explored more fully in Sections 2.5 and 2.10.

- *Radical Durkheimianism:* Although as a theorist, Durkheim has often been portrayed as a rather conservative thinker overly concerned with order and social integration, Pearce (1989) and Gane (1992) have both argued that he should be seen as a radical thinker, concerned with the inequalities of industrial society. The notion of a radical Durkheim will be explored in Section 2.10.

Max Weber

Social action and *verstehen*

Max Weber (1864–1920) is seen quite rightly as one of the originators of the approach in sociology usually known as Social Action Theory. This means that we need to see society as the result of the actions of human individuals and in contrast to the extreme structural views, Weberian sociology always starts off with the notion of an active humanity. Weber's stance on this can be grasped from the following extract where he talks about the way we need to understand social phenomena:

these collectivities must be treated as solely the resultants and modes of organisation of the particular acts of individual persons, since these alone can be treated as agents in the course of subjectively understandable action.
(Weber, 1968, p. 13, orig. pub. 1921, in Lukes, 1973, p. 20)

The last phrase of this statement is also important since it brings us to his second point about the study of sociology. This is that we need to study the meanings people give to their actions, we need to understand the way they look at the world and how this influences their action. Weber gave the name 'verstehen' to this approach, meaning 'to understand'. This implies a very different theoretical and methodological approach from the positivist tradition (see Section 3.2).

The theory of rationalization

Weber's key concerns in sociological theory (1968, orig. pub. 1921) were the effects of the rise of rationalization in society and his fear that the growth of bureaucracy would become a threat to individual freedom, an 'iron cage' as he put it (see also Section 9.7). At the same time, Weber was clearly a German nationalist, proud of the cultural traditions of Germany. His work is therefore concerned with the development of rationalism and its potential effects on western and more specifically German civilisation. These concerns led to a number of recurring themes running throughout his work. These may be summarized as:

- a continuing debate with Marx rejecting his exclusive emphasis on material and economic factors and stressing instead the role that ideas, culture and non-economic factors can play in life
- the analysis of rationalization both as a set of ideas and a set of institutional processes leading to a discussion of power and the political sphere.

His first work was as an analyst of a study of peasants in eastern Germany. Following German unification in the 1870s landowners in eastern Germany began replacing German workers with foreign migratory workers. This led him to study the way in which farm workers who shared the same basic economic relationship nonetheless differed in their status, notably because of the precarious status of foreign workers as guest workers in Germany

Here we can see the basis of the later famous distinction Weber draws between class (a purely economic relationship) and status, relating to non-economic notions of prestige but also a basis for inequality. (This aspect of Weber's thinking is considered more fully in Section 4.2.)

What also emerges out of this early study was the argument that economic conduct could only be understood by also analysing the ideas that people held and which affected the way people pursued their economic aims. When later refined and developed into the analysis of the general process of the growth of rationality the study of ideas and their role in history can be seen to be the basis of perhaps Weber's most famous work, *The Protestant Ethic and the Spirit of Capitalism* (1930, orig. pub. 1905).

Religion, ideas and social change

Marx had argued that history was understandable in terms of the development of material factors but Weber disagreed and argued that ideas could also be an important basis for social change. These were seen as a crucial factor in the rise of capitalism in western Europe:

Weber had no regard for comprehensive accounts of history, seeing, instead, the contemporary developments as entirely distinctive to the history of Western Europe and the United States and unmatched elsewhere. . . . Acquisitiveness and avarice are common throughout all societies. In other societies, work and the pursuit of wealth are regarded as necessary evils, as means which provide the good life; they do not in themselves make up the good life. In modern capitalism, by contrast, work has a morally positive character.

(Hughes *et al.*, 1995, p. 95)

According to Weber, it is this 'spirit of capitalism', this positive idea of hard work as a duty which distinguishes western civilisation. Capitalism cannot be seen as pure individual acquisitiveness since this was often greater in pre-capitalist societies. It is the idea, the ethic, the spirit that makes it distinctive. (See also Section 18.6.)

He notes that there was a correlation between the rise in commercial activity and the adoption of Protestantism, particularly that of Calvinism:

business leaders and owners of capital, as well as the higher grades of skilled labour, and even more the higher technically and commercially trained personnel of modern enterprises, are overwhelmingly Protestant.

(Weber, 1930, p. 35, orig. pub. 1905)

He sought to explain this by examining the impact of belief on the lives of people in a specific Protestant doctrine, Calvinism. Calvinists argued that all people were predestined either to be saved or damned. This meant there was actually nothing they could do to change this. However, uncertainty about whether they were in fact chosen would lead people to look for a sign. This allied with the Puritan disdain for possessions would lead them to work hard and reinvest any surplus rather than spend it on material goods:

The spirit of modern capitalism is thus characterised by a unique combination of devotion to the earning of wealth through legitimate economic activity, together with the avoidance of the use of this income for personal enjoyment. . . . the performance of 'good works' became regarded as a 'sign' of election – not in any way a method of attaining salvation, but rather the elimination of doubts of salvation.

(Giddens, 1971, pp. 126–9)

In his study of Weber, Bendix (1963) does point out that Weber also made reference to material factors that were necessary for the rise of capitalism. In particular, Bendix points to Weber's analysis of the rise of the independent power of the city. Weber argued that trade in mediaeval cities was regulated by ethical ideas, which can therefore also be seen as precursors of the spirit of capitalism. He argues that what was different about the rise of cities in Europe was that all inhabitants were made citizens of the city, whereas elsewhere they were not. The importance of this is that the ethical regulation over trade in European cities covered all inhabitants and was therefore much more powerful. A second important fact was that one of the requirements of citizenship (see Section 17.5) in European cities was to participate in military service. This gave European cities a basis for independent power, and this local autonomy further reinforced their power to regulate commercial activity. Thus Bendix argues that material factors are arguably as important as ideas in Weber's explanation overall, though it is clear that it is an emphasis on the ideas of Calvinism that has dominated later commentary.

In his comparative studies of religion, Weber (1951, orig. pub. 1915; 1952, orig. pub. 1917; 1958, orig. pub. 1916) further fleshed out his idea that the belief in certain ideas may have an effect on the level of development of rationality in the economic sphere and in society in general. It is clear that Weber broadly argues that the differences in the religious ideas can be seen as one issue for investigation of the reasons why economic rationality first developed in Europe. Briefly Weber saw that most of the material prerequisites for capitalism were also present in China and suggests its non-emergence there may be due to differences between Calvinism and Confucianism, or more properly the social effect of these different theologies.

Discussion point

Bearing in mind the rise of countries such as Japan and South Korea to contemporary economic prominence, how might such developments question Weber's focus on religious differences as a key explanatory variable in explaining economic development?

Criticisms of Weber

Weber's theories about Calvinism has been subject to a number of criticisms. First it has been argued that there were some areas which were strongly Calvinist where capitalism did not develop early on, notably Switzerland, Scotland and the Netherlands. A second criticism is that capitalism predated Calvinism, which would of course eliminate all possible consideration of it having some potential causative relationship.

In a contribution to a recent debate about Weber's Protestant Ethic thesis, MacKinnon (1994) has argued that Weber misinterpreted Calvinism. He argues that Calvinism also allowed for 'good works' to be merely spiritual. If true, there would be no need for them to engage in economic activity to look for a sign of their salvation, which would undermine the central correlation of Weber.

His rather pessimistic analysis of the effects of rationalization have also been subsequently questioned, most notably by Habermas. (see Section 2.9). More generally, Weber's views about the importance of ideas and of analysing society in terms of the meanings developed by individuals clearly provide the basis for contrasts between his work and that of Durkheim and Marx.

Activity

Using material from the above section, suggest how Marx would respond to Weber's emphasis on the importance of ideas and how Durkheim would respond to Weber's conception of society. Write short summaries of the differences you have identified.

In each case, suggest which theorist you feel has the stronger argument and why. Remember that you should consider how useful these ideas are in explaining contemporary society.

I, A, E

Interpretations of Weber

Weber, rationalisation and critical theory

Weber's studies of religion were all concerned with an attempt to investigate the relationship between ideas and action and this can also be seen in his major overall theme: the rise of rationality for the basis of action and its effect on social life (see also Section 9.7). Bendix argues that:

Weber was preoccupied throughout his career with the development of rationalism in Western civilisation.
(Bendix, 1963, p. 9)

It is this strand in Weber's thinking that has influenced the development of critical theory (see Section 2.5) through the work of the Frankfurt School as well as more recent thinkers broadly in this tradition such as Habermas (1972, 1976, 1981a). They can be seen to be engaged in a reworking of the meaning and

significance of this process of rationalization (see Section 2.9). This idea has also had an influence in the Marxist tradition through the work of Lukács (1971, orig. pub. 1923).

Weber as an alternative to Marx

A common interpretation of Weber involves the idea of him engaging in a debate with the ghost of Marx which leads to the development of a very different analysis of power and inequality in society, through conflict theory (see Section 2.6). Crucially, this involved the development of his argument that not all conflicts or social developments can be explained with reference to economic factors.

Weber and social action theory

It is clear that Weber saw human meaning as central to the study of sociology and this insight is a key basis for the social action tradition in sociology. This can be contrasted to versions of Durkheim and Marx who, it can be argued, see individuals almost as puppets with their lives determined by structural forces in society. Weber can be seen as providing insights which develop into the contemporary approaches of symbolic interactionism (see Section 2.7), phenomenology and ethnomethodology (see Section 2.8).

Activity

Using a large sheet of paper, present the above information in diagram form. Start at the top with Marx, Weber and Durkheim. Using the sections on interpretations of these three writers try to draw further arrows suggesting the more contemporary ideas which show the continuing influence of these three classical sociologists.

U, I, A

2.4 Functionalism and neo-functionalism

Functionalism

Functionalism is an important part of sociology because it was principally through the interpretation placed on them by functionalism that the writings of Durkheim and Weber first really came to be discussed. It is also the earliest example of an attempt to provide a 'grand theory' of sociology and as such was extremely dominant in the 1950s and 1960s. Society is seen as resulting from agreement (consensus) about what is important (values), and how we should behave (norms) in particular situations (roles) (see Section 10.1).

Talcott Parsons and normative functionalism

Talcott Parsons (1902–79) set out to produce a theory of social action, of how humans act. Parsons (1937) considered human beings to be rational but he wanted to consider the way the choices rational humans made resulted in stable societies rather than anarchy. He argued that an analysis based simply on individual action could not explain the emergence of a society where those activities were regulated. This is explained by Coser (1977) in his history of sociological thought:

Human actors were seen as capable of making choices of courses of action, but these choices were constrained by biological and environmental conditions and, more importantly for Parsons, by the values and norms governing the social structures in which they were variously enmeshed.
(Coser, 1977, p. 564)

Activity

Which theorist do you think provides the basis for Parsons' emphasis on values and norms?

Over the course of Parsons' life, although he initially set out to provide a theory of social action, in the end he almost denied that such a thing existed (Parsons, 1951) and saw people almost as the puppets of society. In a critical comment, contemporary sociological theorist, Mouzelis states:

Parsons – especially when his analysis progressed from his early theory of social action to a theorisation of social systems, and their long-term evolution – over emphasised the systemic functionalist dimensions of social systems at the expense of agency. His theory either portrays agents as passive outcomes of a system of core values, or ignores them altogether.
(Mouzelis, 1995, p. 4)

This quote highlights the centrality of cultural values to functionalist theories. Parsons, like Durkheim (see Section 2.3), was interested in the question of how society could survive in the new age of individualism and his answer was also similar to Durkheim's. He argued that what keeps society together is agreement on central values. Values are broadly moral statements and underpin society. Since Parsons argues that there is broad agreement on what these are, he talks about a value consensus underlying society. These broad values are translated into more specific norms of behaviour relating to particular roles. These are passed on to new generations through the process of socialization (see Section

10.1). The picture this provides is of a harmonious society where everyone agrees with and is happy about the value consensus. The key problem with this vision is that if we are living in agreement why is there any need to change? Since we know social change does occur, this presents something of a problem for functionalism and Parsons in his later work dealt specifically with this issue.

Functionalism and social change

Parsons (1951) argued that societies exist in a state of equilibrium (meaning there is no pressure to change). He identified four subsystems in society which together provided all the functional prerequisites of society – the things it needs to survive.

These four subsystems meet the four key needs of society which are:

- *Goal attainment:* Societies need to set goals for their members to achieve. This requires some kind of political decision-making body and a legal system to enforce decisions.
- *Adaptation:* Every society needs to adapt to its environment, at the simplest level to provide food and shelter. This all requires social organization.
- *Integration:* There is a need to maintain society as a cohesive whole and this requires some form of authority, principally the legal system in contemporary societies.
- *Pattern maintenance (latency):* The value commitments which hold society together need to be maintained. This requires that the values be passed onto new members of society such as children. The process of socialization where parents teach children is therefore central to this need.

Parsons argues that all aspects of and institutions in societies meet at least one of these needs and are therefore functional, since they serve to keep society going.

Parsons further argues that the key subsystems of society which meet the needs specified above are all in some way interrelated. He argues that it is quite possible for one subsystem to change and will do so, since although society is in equilibrium it is never possible to achieve a perfect equilibrium. There will, therefore, be demands for change which arise in one of the societal subsystems from time to time and society therefore constitutes a 'moving equilibrium'. Since all the subsystems are related together, change in one will have an effect on the rest and therefore on society as a whole. This does constitute a theory of social change, though not one with which all would agree.

More fundamentally, Parsons adapts the evolutionary views of Herbert Spencer (see Section 2.2) and suggests that all societies evolve from the more simple to the more complex forms through a process of structural differentiation. This refers to the process whereby functions previously undertaken by the primary unit in society – the family (see also Section 7.4) – are now undertaken by specialized agencies:

What has recently been happening to the American family constitutes part of a process of differentiation. This process has involved a further step in the reduction of importance in our society of kinship units other than the nuclear family. It has also resulted in the transfer of a variety of functions from the nuclear family to other structures of the society.
(Parsons and Bales, 1955, p. 192)

The value system of society has also evolved. Parsons identifies two broad sets of values which he groups together into pattern variables and he argues that over time societies have evolved from one broad set of pattern variables to another set.

The pattern variables he identifies are shown in Table 2.2.

Table 2.2 Parsons' pattern variables

Pattern variable A	Pattern variable B
Ascription	Achievement
Diffuseness	Specificity
Particularism	Universalism
Affectivity	Affective Neutrality
Collective orientation	Self-orientation

Source: Parsons, 1951, p. 67

In some ways these lists of pattern variables are a much more detailed version of the classical dichotomies present in all the evolutionary schemas set up by various sociologists, such as Durkheim's contrast between mechanical and organic solidarity (see Section 2.3). However, since they are more detailed they allow for the possibility of societies making a number of choices and permutations. They therefore undermine notions of any one unilinear development. One problem that remains is that while trying to portray the complexities of society, Parsons is nonetheless trying to present one grand unified theory capable of explaining everything.

Merton's reformulation of functionalism

This approach was rejected by a second functionalist thinker, Robert Merton (1968) who argued instead that there was a need for 'middle-range' theories which merely aimed to explain one or other aspect of society. The basis of this modification was Merton's rejection of Parsons' argument that all parts of a social system work. Instead he argued that such links did not necessarily exist, and therefore the question of whether they did exist in any particular situation had to be left to research. The implication of his argument is that

there may be a great degree of functional autonomy between institutions in society.

He secondly argued that there is no necessary basis for Parsons' argument that all elements of society work together to benefit the whole. He argued that certain actions might actually be dysfunctional (harmful) in relation to the social system as a whole, and also that actions may be functional for some while being dysfunctional for others. He further argued that some actions might have no consequences for the system as a whole at all. These he called eufunctional.

The point of this development is that by moving away from a position that argues that everything is beneficial (functional) Merton is able to deal with the existence of strains and conflicts in society. This can be seen, for example, in his application of strain theory to an understanding of crime and deviance (see Section 11.4), or his argument that people in roles may come under conflicting pressures from people in surrounding roles (see Section 9.7) leading to role conflict. For example, teachers may face conflicting pressures to give less homework (from pupils) or more homework (from parents). In this situation people need to make a choice about their course of action. The importance of this is that it presents a vision where people can actively respond to the situations they find themselves in and have an impact on society. This moves functionalism away from the vision of humans as puppets determined by the socialization process to follow a preset route, which is an implication of Parsons' deterministic vision.

Activity

Summarize in your own words the differences between Parsons and Merton as functionalist thinkers.

Criticisms of functionalism

Functionalism has often been criticized for portraying societies as consensual entities, though the work of Merton is less open to this criticism than that of Parsons. One of the ways functionalists tried to deal with these sort of criticisms was by arguing that although conflicts do exist in society, they are in fact in some sense functional on the whole. For example, Coser (1956) argued that by allowing some degree of conflict, pressures which would otherwise have built up and threatened the whole stability of society are released. This did not, however, satisfy the critics from conflict theory, and some have even argued that there is no need for society to be consensual at all. However the criticism remains and was the inspiration for the rise of conflict theory examined in Section 2.6.

The work of Mann (1973) showed that this picture of a consensual society was in fact far from accurate. He argued that there is a much lower level of consensus than is assumed by functionalist theory. The implication of this is that we cannot explain social stability through some general adherence to a value consensus, which leads directly to arguments which see some form of power underlying social stability.

Steven Lukes (1973) points to Northern Ireland, where there is no shared value consensus, and yet society there retains some degree of stability. What this means is that not only is there little evidence of a value consensus, but that something else must be responsible for retaining social stability:

value consensus is not merely insufficient to ensure social integration; it is not even necessary. There are, to put it another way, functional alternatives to value consensus.
(Lukes, 1973, p. 64)

What he broadly seems to mean by alternative is coercion or ideological power.

While Merton's work did include reference to the importance of material inequalities and power inequalities (again his analysis of crime and deviance is an example) such views did not entirely satisfy the critics who still argued that this aspect of society was downplayed in functionalist analysis.

Discussion point

How far do you agree that there are functional alternatives to value consensus as a basis for stability in society? What might these be? To what extent might these be considered dysfunctional in some respects?

Finally functionalism has been said to operate with an oversocialized conception of humanity as Wrong (1969) famously argued. By this he meant that functionalism suggested that through socialization (see Section 10.1) people's lives were almost determined and this left very little room for notions of human agency. A very similar criticism has been made more recently by Walsh (1972), a phenomenologist who argues that human beings actively construct their world and that Parsons' theory presents people almost as automatons, with lives determined and programmed through the processes of socialization and social control.

Classical functionalism was largely discredited by the mid-1970s, owing to the criticisms mentioned above and also the fact that a theory of society as a harmonious entity found it difficult to explain the upsurge of popular protest that swept across the world in the late 1960s. Despite this, it is important to remember that Parsons was the first modern theorist to try to come up with an overall theory of society, and the profusion of perspectives which arose in sociology in the 1970s and 1980s reflects both the fact that such a project is hard and also the lack of success on the part of any one approach in replacing functionalism in the pivotal role it had held in sociology in the 1950s and early 1960s (Holmwood, 1996).

Neo-functionalism

Although the overall schema of normative Parsonian functionalism is no longer accepted there has nonetheless been a renewed interest in the work of Parsons generally, and more specifically in the rise of a neo-functionalist approach based in American and Germany sociology. The key thinkers in this approach are Alexander (1985, 1987, 1995), Münch (1987) and Luhmann (1982). Holmwood summarizes Alexander's intentions as follows:

In our current social and political circumstances, it is perhaps understandable that there are attempts to return to the 'old orthodoxies' which existed prior to the theoretical upheavals of the 1960s ... But even this theoretical recidivism is not new. A moment's reflection will be sufficient to recognise that the 'new' paradigms of the 1960s and after were, for the most part, themselves returns to even 'older' paradigms. Then we were offered neo-Marxism and neo-Weberianism (among others), to which Alexander now is proposing should be added, neo-Parsonianism.
(Holmwood, 1996, p. 19)

Alexander (1985) argues that there is a need to reconsider functionalism by considering the criticisms made of the original Parsonian version and his response to these is as Craib puts it: 'simply to accept them' (1992, p. 56).

Alexander argues that Parsons' later work which included the vision of people as almost totally determined by structures has to be rejected. The determinism of Parsonian functionalism is therefore totally dispensed with and instead we are presented with a vision of society as open-ended. In this Alexander uses Parsons' idea of society as a moving equilibrium, he merely emphasizes that this is a permanent state of affairs. Alexander retains from the original functionalist analysis the idea that we need to consider society as composed of a social system, a cultural system and a personality structure. He also argues that the view of social change occurring through structural differentiation is still valid.

In essence, Alexander argues that although conflict theory (see Section 2.6) led to the wholesale abandonment of functionalism, conflict theory itself cannot offer an adequate explanation of the importance of stability and consensus in society, although he recognizes that it is important to see that the appearance of consensus can sometimes be the result of the imposition of norms and values. What Alexander sees as most important in Parsons is the recognition that we need to understand that there are multiple layers and causes operative in society. Although this was later developed into an overly-deterministic model of society, if this is dispensed with the central insight remains valid.

Craib points out that the return to Parsons has also been conditioned by changes in the world. At the time he was originally writing, he was seen as a Cold War warrior and squarely on the right wing of sociology. However with the rise of the New Right and the fall of the eastern European regimes it is argued that Parsons:

now represents the 'moral high ground' of pluralistic liberalism, encouraging openness and tolerance; certainly in the USA the neofunctionalism of Alexander has become associated again with the progressive liberalism with which Parsons once associated himself.
(Craib, 1992, p. 62)

Münch (1987) sees neo-functionalism as a basis for attempting to integrate micro and macro sociological analysis. He argues we need to see action as directed towards goals (following Parsons) but also that these are shaped by social norms (also following Parsons). He develops a notion of society as divided up into four subsystems also resembling Parsons' original analysis. Arguably, however, this turns out to be more macro than micro, albeit without the notion of people as puppets in the original Parsonian analysis. Again as with Alexander, Münch argues that we need to note that there is a multiplicity of elements which have an effect on the way society develops. He has used the notion of the links between societal subsystems developed by Parsons to explain the evolution of modern law.

Luhmann (1982) has been mostly concerned to apply the idea of social change occurring through structural differentiation. He argues that the key problem with Parsons' original formulation was that it overemphasized functional differentiation, whereas in fact it is the process of structural differentiation which is more important. He applies this notion to develop the idea that this differentiation means that societies have developed to have three different levels of action: the interactional, the organizational and the societal levels. He argues that these have also become relatively autonomous of each other and yet they remain connected in that the higher levels set a framework within which the lower

levels of interaction can occur. He also offers an implicit theory of the basis of social conflict, namely that there are problems if any of the different levels get too much out of synch with the other levels.

Neo-functionalism is therefore a pluralistic functionalism which retains a desire to consider social norms and societal consensus as important real phenomena which need to be included in any overall theory of society. Despite starting out as an attempt to explain social action, functionalism was deterministic and tended to see social actors as puppets whose lives were wholly determined through the transmission belt of socialization. It is this particular aspect of functionalism that neo-functionalism rejects. The rise of neo-functionalism shows the enduring appeal of some elements of the original functionalist approach.

Activity
Make a list of the similarities and differences between functionalism and neo-functionalism

U, I

2.5 Marxism and neo-Marxism

This section will consider the ways in which the original ideas of Marx (examined in detail in Section 2.3) have been incorporated into sociological analysis, and the multitude of different versions of Marxism that this has led to.

Evolutionary Marxism
Marx argued that history progresses through changes in the forces and relations of production. He also argued that the development of capitalism would lead to increasing poverty and economic crises.

Followers of his in Germany in the late nineteenth century found themselves in a situation where there appeared to be increasing prosperity and a distinct lack of class conflict. This led a number of authors, including Dühring, to argue that there was a need to revise Marx's notions. His arguments were attacked by Engels in *Anti-Dühring* (1986, first written in 1878), and it was Dühring's arguments presented as Marxism that led Marx to state that 'All I know is that I am no Marxist'.

Despite this rejection by Marx of attempts to modify his ideas in a reformist manner, Bernstein (1961, orig. pub. 1899) decided Marx's ideas needed revising. He argued that capitalism was not producing conflict and disorder but instead growing order and stability. Since socialism in Marx's original schema required the breakdown of capitalism, Bernstein argued this was now unlikely. He sought instead to argue that socialism would arrive on the basis of rational debate and discussion, and there was no need to undertake major changes to the economy since this was already delivering increased prosperity.

Instead, socialists should campaign for an extension of voting rights to all, an increase in powers for Parliament and an end to restrictions on trades unions. The leaders of the Second Communist International therefore rejected revolution for reform, and this, allied to their failure to campaign against the First World War, led to a split with the formation of the Third Communist International by leading figures such as Lenin who rejected Bernstein's arguments.

The Third Communist International argued that Marx's writings were not a form of economic determinism. If Marx had believed that socialism would arise inevitably as the level of technology increased, then there would be no point at all in engaging in political activity. It would be more rational to sit back and wait for the arrival of socialism. There was therefore, according to these thinkers, still a need to organize to overthrow the capitalist system and that required the construction of a revolutionary party and a willingness to engage in revolution. It is this view which can be seen to underlie the Russian Revolutions of 1905 and 1917, events which probably had the most effect in bringing the ideas of Marxism to the attention of the world in general and social scientists in particular.

Precisely because this view of how social change and socialism would come about was not accepted by the evolutionary wing of Marxism, Marxist and socialist thought has until this day been characterized by an important schism which can be summarized as that between those who advocate social reform and those who advocate social revolution.

The enshrinement of Marxism almost into a religion by Stalin can also be seen to embody some element of evolutionary thinking in the centrality placed on raising the productive level of the Soviet economy. Certainly this brand of thinking embraced economic determinism, though whether it remained Marxist is very much open to doubt. The abhorrence of Stalinism was a key motivation in the development of other Marxist perspectives, notably those associated with Western Marxism.

Revolutionary Marxism

The term revolutionary Marxism can be reserved for those classical Marxist thinkers who continually adhered to the need for revolution. This tradition would include both Lenin and Trotsky but also Rosa Luxembourg and Antonio Gramsci (1971). A leading

contemporary advocate of this approach is social theorist and revolutionary socialist, Alex Callinicos (1982, 1987, 1989, 1995).

Callinicos has argued that there is a need to try to provide a Marxist account of society which encompasses both the structural and social action approaches and therefore his arguments deal with the most long-standing and arguably important dichotomy in sociological theory. He himself argues that to base Marxism either on one or the other is mistaken since:

structure and agency are so closely interwoven that to separate either and give it primacy over the other is a fundamental error.
(Callinicos, 1987, p. 7)

Callinicos is attempting to provide from a Marxist perspective the kind of unified theory which has also been sought out by others in competing approaches, notably the structuration theory of Giddens (cited favourably by Callinicos, and examined in more detail in Section 2.9).

Callinicos (1987) recognizes Marx's attempts to provide this, notably in his phrase:

Men make their own history, but they do not make it just as they please; they do not make it under circumstances chosen by themselves, but under circumstances directly encountered, given and transmitted from the past.
(Marx, 1968, p. 96, orig. pub. 1852)

In this single sentence, Marx presents his own view on the structure/agency debate. The first part of this sentence appears to presents a social action/agency view, while the latter half present a fairly traditional view of the way social structures constrain individual action.

However, Callinicos argues that it is a flawed view since here Marx views structures as purely negative entities, merely constraining the actions of individuals. He argues that we need to develop a more positive notion of social structures both constraining and enabling social action to take place.

Activity

Callinicos argues that Marx's formulation of the agency/structure debate (quoted above) is flawed.

a Explain in your own words Callinicos' criticisms of this statement.

b In what way might we note a similarity between Callinicos and Giddens in relation to this issue?

c Rewrite Marx's statement in the light of Callinicos' criticism to see if it can be reworded to take this criticism into account.

I, A

Western Marxism

Western Marxism is the name given to a group of approaches which grew up in western Europe reacting against events broadly spanning the period between the two world wars. Examples of these include:

- the collapse of the German revolution in 1919 which led to the isolation of the Bolsheviks and the distortion of Marxism into Stalinism
- the rise of Fascism and the repression of Marxist and radical ideas, notably the imprisonment of the Italian Marxist, Antonio Gramsci and the removal of the Frankfurt School from Germany to the USA
- the strength of post-Second World War capitalism and consequent pessimism about the prospects for revolutionary change in western Europe.

It was the attempt to react to and explain these developments while living through their consequences that characterizes Western Marxism. The continuing grip of Stalinism on what was seen as orthodox Marxism meant that this trend in Marxist thinking was notable for being largely divorced from any practical involvement and further contributed to the characteristic pessimism about the possibilities of the organized working-class effecting socialist transformations.

Nonetheless, these thinkers remained Marxist in the sense that they identified in different ways with the original project of Marxism, and all were concerned to try to explain the failure of revolutions to take place in western Europe. In order to explain this Western Marxists sought to go back to the philosophical underpinnings of Marxism, most notably involving reinterpretations of Hegel. It is possible to argue that this is what different Western Marxists have in common, as McInnes comments that:

the history of Marxist theory in this century can be told as the story of successive re-readings of Hegel. (McInnes, 1972, p. 131)

Of course the term Western Marxism covers a variety of approaches best examined in separate sections. The following divisions seem important:

- Lukács and Hegelian Marxism
- Critical theory and the Frankfurt School
- Althusser and Structural Marxism
- Gramsci and Cultural Marxism.

Lukács and Hegelian Marxism

Lukács in *History and Class Consciousness* (1971, orig. pub. 1923) was trying to reassert the importance of Hegel to re-create Marxism and distinguish it from the crude vulgar Marxism then dominant in Germany. The version of Marxism presented in the Second International (what we have here called evolutionary Marxism) presented history as proceeding through the development of technology with such changes automatically leading to other changes in society. This has been widely criticized as technological determinism and it certainly crudely portrays what Marx meant by the forces and relations of production.

Lukács sought to reassert classical Marxism in opposition to this crude representation. Central to this was the need to avoid focus on any one element (such as technology) and instead to see society as a totality. His initial opposition to capitalism was based on the idea that it had sullied life, cheapened it, and although the book was immediately denounced by the Stalinist-dominated Communist International, its fame stems from some similarities it has with the writings of the young Marx (at that time still unpublished and only becoming available up to 50 years after Marx's death).

Lukács took over the notion of a total theory of society from Hegel and argued that it is only possible to have knowledge of anything in particular if we have knowledge of the totality of any social formation. What he means by this is the need to understand things in their historical context. So the same item can have a very different significance in different periods of time. However, what allows us to develop this knowledge in any period is praxis, that is practical involvement as well as thinking. We need to be both the object and the subject of history. Knowledge comes from action in the world, which itself creates change, and therefore a different world and different forms of knowledge. Lukács argued that in capitalism it was such knowledge which made exploitation and domination seem natural.

Lukács most important contribution was the idea of reification. By this he meant that human relations and humans themselves came to be seen as objects (something controlled or dominated). The origin of this notion is Weber's (1968, orig. pub. 1921) theory of rationalization which Lukács applied to Marx's idea of commodity fetishism. This is simply the notion that in capitalism everything is seen as a commodity which can be bought and sold, even people.

He argued that practical involvement or praxis was necessary to undermine this, and he argued that through the application of Marxism, the working class could become the identical object/subject of history. In other words he argued that by virtue of their position in the objective social structure of capitalism, they would almost automatically come to revolutionary consciousness. The key problem with this formulation is that by and large it hasn't happened, and to view it as happening almost automatically massively understates the political problems involved in the development of such consciousness.

Critical theory and the Frankfurt School

The origins of this approach are in 1923 when an institute to promote Marxist studies was set up at Frankfurt University funded by a wealthy businessman. The leading thinkers of this group are undoubtedly Horkheimer (its director from 1930), Marcuse and Adorno. Its site in Germany at that time also shaped its later development. Fascism was clearly on the rise at the time. The Stalinist communist parties consistently underestimated this threat and also denounced socialists as social fascists. The absurd optimism of the Stalinists can be contrasted with the more realistic pessimism of the Frankfurt School about the prospects of socialist uprisings at the time. A further factor contributed to this pessimism and also further divorced the School from an active involvement in political practice. In 1934 with the rise of the Nazis the Institute was transferred to the USA which had no tradition of mass socialist parties. When it returned to Germany in 1950 it was at a time when the German Communist party was banned and capitalism was resurgent. These factors clearly had an influence on the ideas of the School, which have generally come to be described as 'critical theory'.

In the *Dialectic of Enlightenment* Adorno and Horkheimer (1979, orig. pub. 1944) argued that there can be no separation of knowledge of the world and actual social practice. This led them to criticize science and technology. They argued that the idea that these were neutral techniques was false, and that such knowledge is used merely as a way of dominating and controlling the world. A key example of this new 'instrumental reason' was positivism which was seen as non-critical and they sought to establish a critical theory to replace it. (See also Section 3.2.)

However their rejection of the scientific method led them to argue that the world was dominated by ideologies and that people themselves were unable to see through these. As such, the working class, the traditional agent of change in Marxist theory, was seen as impotent in the face of this instrumental reason – the name they gave to what they saw as the new form of knowledge which was characteristic of the times.

Further they argue that the rise of this instrumental reason far predates the rise of capitalism. The effect of this argument is to undermine the notion that the abolition of capitalism will lead to freedom, and insofar as Marxism remains rooted in the idea of science then it will merely lead to a different form of domination. This is their view of what had happened in eastern Europe. The solution lay with the development of a different kind of knowledge, critical theory, and the alliance of critical theorists with the working class; though owing to the concrete circumstances of the Frankfurt School

theorists this never became a reality. Critical theorists saw the working class successfully integrated into capitalism by the power of instrumental reason and they saw Stalinist Marxism as simply another variant of this. The result is a very pessimistic account of the potential for human change, closer to Weber than Marx. Adorno and Horkheimer therefore argued that there was a need to reject any idea of a total theory of society and instead argued that we should concentrate on localized small-scale struggles which would show up the contradictions in the system and undermine the instrumental reason which was its ideology. In that way, it was possible to further the struggle for human freedom.

Marcuse (1955, orig. pub. 1941, 1964) argued that the triumph of the Nazis showed that the unfolding of history would not inevitably lead to the victory of the workers' movement and that this notion of the unfolding of history (taken from Hegel) needed to be abandoned. He argued that the centrality accorded to economics, technology and science in earlier formulations of Marxism were thus mistaken since these could also be turned to repressive ends. Instead he argued that what was important in Hegel was the distinction he made between the real essence of things and the surface phenomena. He translated this into an argument about the way that real progress would only occur when the real essence of things was involved. In society, he argued that this distinction could be seen in the difference between authentic real needs and wants and the false manufactured wants that capitalists used to keep people happy. (See also Sections 10.3 and 15.10.) However if the issue was real wants and needs versus false ones, the link to production as a central element of Marxism is abandoned and there is no need to have the working class at the centre of such an analysis. In fact, Marcuse argued that the workers were unable to distinguish between false and real needs and desires and believed themselves free when they pursued false needs even though these represented no possibility of human progress.

Such ideas fed into the growth of the New Left, a term covering various movements which grew up in the 1960s such as the anti-Vietnam War protests, peace campaigners, hippies, students, the black and women's movements. It is these movements which have fed into contemporary concerns with New Social Movements, which are generally conceived as an alternative to the working class as agents of social transformation. (See also Section 17.5.)

The key problem with this is that while it might be argued that the working class in western Europe has not as yet successfully led a revolution, its centrality in Marxism rests more on the point that it is the only group with the potential power to effect such a transformation. In other words, the working class are central because of their place in the social and economic structure rather than because of any inherent progressiveness. In contrast, while the various New Social Movements might be composed of people with radical ideas, they have little or no power and often lapse simply into lifestyle politics where the only thing they try to change is themselves. This leads to individualism and mysticism and far away from any connection with Marxism and the transformation of society.

A key criticism of the overall approach of critical theory is that its pessimism resulted from its implicit belief that capitalism could now successfully manipulate people's needs and this was because of the prior belief that capitalism could now exist as a system without economic crisis. In the 1990s, with its period of economic recessions and booms and slumps, such a view seems unduly optimistic about the stability of capitalism.

Critical theory's overall interpretation of Marxism was no doubt aided by the publication of Marx's early writings, where he does talk of humanity, reason and progress rather than the working class. The question of whether this was the 'real' Marx was central to the ideas of another influential Marxist thinker, Althusser.

Louis Althusser and Structural Marxism

Althusser was a member of the French Communist party (PCF) although his sympathies lay more with China than with Moscow.

Althusser (1966, 1968) argued that Marxism was, and should be seen as, scientific. This clearly placed him in a position diametrically opposed to the anti-scienticism of most Western Marxism. He argued that the interpretation of Marx as a humanist concerned to struggle for a rational humane society was false. Instead he argued that these early works did not represent Marx's fully worked out views. He argued that there was a clear break (an epistemological break to use his terminology) between these early works and the later mature works of Marx such as *Capital*.

He also argued that all the existing versions of Marxism were reductionist in that they sought to explain social change as resulting from change in the economy. He argued that this reductionism resulted from the retention of the Hegelian notion of the totality and that instead all social formations needed to be seen as structured complex unities within which various elements in society actually had a degree of relative autonomy from the economic, which, however, remained determinant in the last instance. This allowed Althusser to argue that Stalinism was a political and ideological phenomenon which had grown up although the economy in the Soviet Union was socialist. In essence, Stalinism was bourgeois while the economy was socialist. This criticism of Stalinism fitted in with his preference for Maoism.

This view is structuralist since Althusser argued that people are not active subjects of history but only the bearers of objective structures. The important relations are the relations of production stressed by Marx in *Capital* and it is therefore at the level of these structures that change takes place. This retains a notion of the class struggle albeit without the idea of consciousness and political action. Althusser argued that 'history is a process without a subject' and therefore rejected any attempt to suggest that socialism was predetermined by the progress of history. He suggested that revolutionary change required people to break from the ideology created by capitalism and in order to do this Marxist leaders needed to engage in theoretical practice.

The most notable criticisms of Althusser came from humanist Marxists for whom notions of conscious activity were central. This view can be seen for example, in the work of French philosopher, Sartre (1960, 1974) whose work merged Marxism and existentialism, a brand of philosophy much influenced by phenomenological notions (see Section 2.8). This approach later brought Sartre into arguments with Michel Foucault. However probably the most direct attack on Althusser's ideas came in the work of Thompson. Thompson (1978) argued that what was crucial to Marxism was the notion that people are active and he pointed to his own research on the *Making of the English Working Class* to show that throughout history people have organized to fight oppression and domination. If anything, it can be argued that while Thompson was right to point to the centrality of active struggle involving real humans in Marxism, his own brand of Marxism tends to underplay the structural realities within which such lives are lived.

Problems in Althusser's (1971a) theory of ideology were to lead to the breakdown of Structural Marxism and the emergence of post-structuralist approaches. However his emphasis on ideology can also be seen in a different way in another Western Marxist, Gramsci, arguably the most influential of this group.

Antonio Gramsci and Cultural Marxism

The key contribution Gramsci (1971) made is his concept of hegemony. By this he meant that capitalist rule does not depend solely on force but also involves the active consent of the population through ideas in society. The implication of this was that Marxist struggle must also include cultural and ideological struggle so the proletariat can grasp this hegemony from the bourgeoisie. Since he argued that this hegemony of the bourgeoisie was more deeply entrenched in western Europe than it had been in Russia, he felt that revolutionary transformations in western Europe would not necessarily take the same route as the Russian Revolution. The implications for socialist strategy thus have to be rethought. For example, by promoting such things as democratic reforms people's ideas can be changed and the influence of dominant ideas over them (which in his concept of hegemony he never saw as total) can be overcome.

The importance he attached to ideological and cultural struggle has sometimes seemingly been interpreted as a requirement that these are the most important or fundamental types of struggle. This can best be seen in the type of analysis promoted by *Marxism Today* (see Hall and Jacques, 1983, 1989), influential for a time in the 1980s and explicitly devoted to cultural and ideological struggle, as well as in the work of the Centre for Contemporary Cultural Studies at Birmingham University (see Section 10.4).

Such interpretations of Gramsci have been criticized for an almost exclusive concern on cultural and ideological struggle rather than these being seen as part of an overall political struggle as envisaged by Gramsci. This over-emphasis on culture combined with influences from post-modernism, particularly the emphasis on diversity, have led a number of ex-Gramscians to move over to a position of post-Marxism rather than neo-Marxism.

Nonetheless, the utilization of Gramsci's ideas within Marxist traditions continues since his theory is seen as the most sophisticated attempt to come to terms with the ideological and cultural aspects of capitalist domination.

Analytical Marxism

The most recent variant of Marxism to emerge is known as Analytical Marxism. Its most notable advocate in sociology today is the American, Erik Olin Wright. (See also Section 4.3.)

The key basis of this approach is the belief that Marxists should share the same foundations regarding questions about the status of knowledge and truth, and the same approach to scientific methodology as other approaches. In essence, this is a rejection of Stalinist notions that there was a bourgeois science and a proletarian science, an idea now thoroughly discredited, although it is not suggested by Analytical Marxists that all other forms of Marxism lacked scientific approaches. From this start point, Analytical Marxism argues for the need to explain things using conventional scientific criteria, and more specifically through the systematic develop-

ment of concepts at the core of Marxist theory such as class, exploitation and capitalism, and logical analysis of the interrelationships between them. Finally the approach argues that the intentions of individuals are an essential part of explanations and theories.

An example of this approach can be seen in Wright's own work which has involved the systematic elaboration of concepts to explain the class structure, starting with his analysis of the term 'middle class' and its conceptualization in Marxism. The most controversial aspect of Analytical Marxism is undoubtedly the last, namely the concern with the intentional actions of individuals. This is controversial since it is seen by some as a belief that we can explain things on the basis of rational choices by individuals, a position more closely associated with Weberian and more right-wing thinking than Marxism. Wright denies that this is the case although admits the criticism exists. He says that such an approach does not argue that social processes can be reduced to individuals, but that we cannot ignore their conscious choices nonetheless. This does however lead to the question Wright acknowledges:

Analytical Marxists reject claims about the methodological distinctiveness of Marxism; they adopt the full repertoire of 'bourgeois' scientific practices; and they constantly question the core concepts and traditional theses of Marxism. What, then, is Marxist about this theoretical enterprise? I would emphasise three things in answer to this question.
(Wright, 1994a, p. 191)

Briefly, these are that Analytical Marxism works on Marxism as a tradition of thought, poses questions and considers topics rooted in the Marxist tradition and uses concepts and language deeply embedded in Marxism. It is clear that this approach remains controversial, largely because not all Marxists are convinced it is a form of Marxism, but it is nonetheless a growing trend.

2.6 Conflict theory

Conflict theory is a mixture of Weber and Marx (overwhelmingly the former) which arose in reaction to the emphasis on consensus in the then dominant functionalist approach (see Section 2.4). As its name suggests, it argued that society was characterized by a number of fundamental conflicts and not by consensus. The demise of classical functionalism can be seen as one of the results of this approach. Initially it reacted to modifications of functionalism made by Coser (1956) who had argued that in some respects conflict can be functional for society, most notably by the fact that tolerating a certain degree of conflict will stop such conflicts threatening the whole basis of a consensual social structure.

The critique of functionalism

Conflict theory proper developed among a number of writers influenced in particular by Weber, who felt that Coser's notion of functional conflict underplayed the importance of conflict in society. The appeal of Weber's writing lies in his rejection of the Marxist argument that there were only two fundamental classes in society, and furthermore that not all conflicts were economically based.

John Rex (1961) argued that if we look at society there are conflicts over values which are deeply embedded in society:

Instead of being organised around a consensus of values, social systems may be thought of as involving a conflict situation at central points. Such conflict situations may lie anywhere between the extremes of peaceful bargaining in the market place and open violence.
(Rex, 1961, p. 129)

In particular he referred to the work on 'race' relations in the USA, where clear lines of conflict were emerging with the rise of the Black Civil Rights Movement, whose arguments made it difficult to sustain the notion of a society in harmonious equilibrium. His argument was that in such a situation, groups in conflict over values will be likely to interact in a conflicting way:

For in the process of conflict the actors might be expected to look for allies who will add to the strength of the sanctions they can bring to bear against the other side. Allies will be found who have a similar situation and out of the alliances there will emerge groups structured for participation in conflict.
(Rex, 1961, p. 122)

Conflict theory versus Marxism

Rex argues that the most basic cause of the conflicts will be over access to material resources and he points to the way this can be seen in Marx's theory of class conflict. However he argues that this was one particular sub-type of the sort of conflict he was talking about, and one which could not explain all conflicts that emerged in society.

This argument emerges more clearly in his studies of 'race' relations in Birmingham (Rex and Moore, 1967; Rex and Tomlinson, 1979). These studies (considered in more detail in Section 6.4) highlighted the importance of ethnicity as a social division in relation to the distribution both of employment and housing. Their concept of housing classes is quite clearly more in line with Weber's notion of market situation as the basis of class than Marx's notion of class as based on relationship to the means of production. (Their differing notions of class are examined in more detail in Section 4.2.) Their finding that immigrant workers were systematically disadvantaged compared with white working-class people also emphasized the possibility of divisions other than between the bourgeoisie and the proletariat and these are key works in the development of the Weberian structural version of the underclass thesis (examined in more detail in Section 4.8).

The idea that Marx's theory of class conflict was not adequate to explain the totality of divisions and conflicts in Britain was also the basis of the work of Dahrendorf (1959). He argued that there have been important changes to the class structure since Marx's time which have rendered his concentration on conflict centred between the bourgeoisie and the proletariat outdated. He points to the growth of a middle class and the growth of social mobility as loosening the class bonds identified by Marx. He also argues that the growing divorce between the owners and managers of industry means that the wealthy are no longer necessarily those with power in society. It is this conflict over power which Dahrendorf sees as characteristic of more modern societies. He also argues that Marx's notion of class conflict is merely one possible example of this, rather than the primary or most fundamental form of conflict. Here we can see quite clearly, the legacy of Weber's original argument against Marx expressed in his argument that inequalities and conflicts can also arise between status groups and those with or without power as well as on the basis of class.

Social integration and system integration

In a further theoretical development of conflict theory, Lockwood (1964) criticized structural functionalism in the guise of Parsons (see Section 2.4) for concentrating on norms and values and therefore the cultural aspects of society. He argued that this ignored the material aspects of society, by which he meant access to economic resources and property. This, argued Lockwood, is a crucial element in determining people's life-chances and the fact that these are unequally distributed is an important basis for conflict because it leads people to have differing material interests. In a situation of scarcity where not everyone's needs can be met, there will be inherent conflicts of interest as one group tries to change the distribution of resources and power. In this sense, the notion of whether there was a real value consensus was questioned and the potential for conflicts over access to scarce material resources was highlighted. The Parsonian emphasis on value consensus was said to ignore the fact that the norms and values of society always rest on a structure of power which arises out of conflicts. These conflicts emerge because of the conflict of interests in the material substratum of society.

In order to explain the possibility of conflict and to deny that society was in equilibrium, Lockwood argued that it was necessary to distinguish between 'social integration' and 'system integration'. Social integration refers to relations between individuals and social groups in society, while system integration refers to the relations between institutions and spheres of society. He says that while it might be possible to argue that there is a degree of consensus at the level of social integration, this cannot be assumed just because we can outline the way the various structures of society are integrated together to form system integration. Conflict theorists pointed out that the appearance of consensus might reflect the operation of power in society and that at the level of social integration it was possible to conceive of either situations of order or of conflict.

Discussion point

To what extent is it possible to differentiate between the way people behave if they genuinely agree to something and if they are somehow coerced into agreeing to something?

What are the implications of this for the debate about whether society can be characterized as being consensual or conflictual?

Secondly, Lockwood argued that even if it is possible to identify genuine social integration, this cannot be taken as proof of system integration. Even if we find a degree of value consensus among individuals and social groups, because this ignores the material aspects of society, it ignores the possibility of strains and conflicts at the systemic level of society, shown for example in periodic economic crises. Thus, the functionalist's almost exclusive concentration on norms and values ignores the material realities of society. Although at any one point there may be no apparent conflict, this is not proof of equilibrium if there are potential strains and conflicts of interest in society.

In a later work, Lockwood (1992) argues that the origins of the problems he identifies in functionalism arise from Durkheim's 'ambiguous and contradictory explanation of disorder and anomie' (1992, p. 3), a point commented on by others, leading to the growth of interpretations of Durkheim other than

those contained in Parsonian functionalism. (See also Section 2.3.)

Criticisms of conflict theory

The critique of Marxism contained in conflict theory did lead to a response from Marxist theorists and the most notable outcome of this has been the continuing debate between neo-Marxist and neo-Weberian thinkers over how best to conceptualize class and other conflictual relations in society. This debate is examined in detail in Section 4.3. However it is also important to notice that there were criticisms of conflict theory from the functionalist camp and from those who argue that it has not really broken out of the mould of functionalism. Starting with the latter, Craib (1992) argues that particularly with reference to Dahrendorf, this is simply arguing that in some instances conflict is more likely than consensus, or as he puts it:

Conflict theory is just a way of looking at the world. On Friday afternoon, the world is bright and happy; on Monday morning, it is grey and miserable.
(Craib, 1992, p. 58)

In other words, all this does is say conflict is possible, and it develops no further than this since it does not provide a causal theoretical mechanism which would allow us to decide whether conflicts were endemic to the system or not. While Lockwood's work builds towards this, Craib argues his insights have never been built upon further.

In relation to the criticisms from the functionalist camp, Alexander (1987, 1995) argues that the key problem with conflict theory is that if it is taken as theory, it is unable to explain the degree of stability in society other than by recourse to some notion of power and domination, but this moves the analysis away from being based on action by groups which is seen as the basis of conflict. This does highlight a central problem which is that a situation where there is a genuine consensus might outwardly look exactly the same as where people are coerced somehow to behave in certain ways. This problem is at the root of sociological theories of power. (This debate is explored in detail in Section 17.4.) It is the feeling that social stability is an important element in society in need of explanation that is the central motivation behind the rise of neo-functionalism (see Section 2.4).

Neo-Weberian conflict theory

The contention of early conflict theory that class conflict was only one example of the possible conflicts that could occur is the central insight underlying more recent versions of Weberian-influenced conflict theory. These developments have included contributions to various versions of radical elite theory on the nature of the state (see Section 17.3) but also more general investigations into the nature of power in society. While it is clear that Giddens might arguably fit into this category, (being more Weberian than Marxist) his work is examined in Section 2.9 and so here we will focus on another writer in this tradition, Michael Mann.

In his ongoing study of the sources of social power in society covering the period from the beginning of human society to the present, Mann (1986, 1988, 1993) argues that it is not possible to explain all forms of power as flowing from economic activity since the key to power in modern societies is control of the state, and he points to the fact that the state élite are different from, and to some degree independent of, economic classes. He explains his theoretical outlook as follows:

Four sources of social power – ideological, economic, military, and political – fundamentally determine the structure of societies . . . What are the relations among these four power sources? Is one or more of them ultimately primary in structuring society?

The greatest social theorists gave contrary answers. Marx and Engels replied clearly and positively. In the last instance, they asserted, economic relations structure human activity. Max Weber replied more negatively, saying 'no significant generalizations' can be made about the relations between what he called 'the structures of social action.' I reject Marxian materialism, but can I improve on Weberian pessimism?
(Mann, 1993, p. 1)

His answer is to argue that in the eighteenth century, economic and military power were predominant, but in the nineteenth, military power came to be subsumed into states and therefore economic and political power took over in importance. What this means in terms of the overall conflict theory approach is that at no time can we rely on a theory based simply on economic (class) conflict. The development of nation-states has meant that political power, which is to an important extent autonomous from economic power, has risen in importance. In political sociology, this has led to the growth of theories of the state which reject older arguments seeing the state as operating at the behest of one or other economic class, and instead arguing that the state must be treated as an autonomous element in modern society. This has been called the state-centred approach (see Section 17.3) and it is clearly inspired by the fundamental notions of conflict theory derived from Weber's critique of Marx.

This would, of course, not be accepted by Marxists. Brenner (1986) argues that the growth of military expenditure cannot be explained by a desire to combat external foes (as Mann broadly argues) which points towards political reasons for this growth, but instead should be seen as a response to internal economic crises and the desire to shift more of the burden of taxation onto the poor. In other words he argues that the military did operate at the behest of the rising capitalist class. This illustrates the point about the degree of state autonomy from capitalism and dominant classes that is central to contemporary versions of the Marx versus Weber debate. Since this is centred around the extent to which all social relations in society can be explained ultimately on the basis of economic relations, this question has also surfaced in other forms. One such form is the argument by feminist writers that the position of women in society cannot be explained through class analysis, developing in this respect both critiques of Marxism and Weberianism.

Feminism

Feminism can be seen as a version of conflict theory in that it is clearly based on the idea that there are fundamental conflicts of interest in society in this case between men and women. Since these conflicts are not all related to economic factors, there was a debate within feminism over the extent to which Marxism could be used to explain the subordinate position of women in society. While a version of Marxist-feminism did emerge, it remains a matter of debate whether it was successful or not. (See Section 5.4 for more details.)

The critique of malestream sociology

As well as developing theories to explain the oppression of women in society, feminists were also concerned to secure consideration of these inequalities as an integral part of sociology and criticized what they saw as 'malestream' sociology for ignoring this and effectively becoming a sociology of men:

The feminist challenge to malestream sociology is one that requires a radical rethinking of the content and methodology of the whole enterprise, one that recognises the need to see society from the position of women as well as from the standpoint of men – to see the world as fundamentally gendered.
(Abbott and Wallace, 1997, p. 3)

One important element of the critique of malestream sociology by feminist thinkers has been the argument that by premising itself on a scientific approach, sociological knowledge marginalises women's concerns and views these as purely subjective. In this sense, science and rationality are seen as male approaches to social investigation, and the fact that these are viewed as superior to other possible bases for knowledge is seen as another reflection of male domination. Sociology as the science of society might therefore be seen as part of the problem, rather than part of the solution. This has led feminists influenced by phenomenology and ethnomethodology, such as Stanley and Wise (1983, 1993), to develop notions of a specifically feminist methodology (examined in further detail in Section 3.2).

Feminism and gender relations

Perhaps the most notable early exponent of a feminist approach in sociology is Oakley (1972, 1974a) who criticized earlier functionalist accounts of the gender division of labour and pointed out that there was nothing natural in this. Furthermore she highlighted the way women were ignored through her studies of housework which she analysed using categories developed to describe the work of males in car factories. (These studies are covered in more detail in Section 5.1.)

Since that time, feminism has been accepted as a perspective in its own right and the study of gender and gender inequalities has become an integral part of most substantive areas of sociology. The rise of feminism in sociology undoubtedly followed from the rise of feminism in society in general in the 1970s and 1980s, and these developments are explored in more detail in Section 5.4.

The term feminism covers a wide variety of approaches and these present often conflicting theories about the nature of gender relations in society and suggested changes to eliminate the inequalities surrounding them. The earliest form of feminist theory can be described as liberal feminism in that it was concerned principally with legal restrictions on women, and the effect of these on the construction of gender inequalities. Such views can be seen to underlie legal changes such as the 1970 Equal Pay Act and the 1975 Sex Discrimination Act. While these left women legally equal to men in many respects, they did not of themselves eliminate inequality. This led to the development of more structural perspectives linking the position of women in society to longer more deeply embedded structures in society.

Radical feminists such as Firestone (1970) and Millett (1970) argue that the oppression of women is a universal feature of all human societies. They developed the concept of patriarchy, broadly meaning the rule of men, to describe this situation. Most of their work has focused on the way that men oppress women through direct physical acts, such as rape and wife-battering, and also the way that child-bearing and child-raising roles which are seen as primarily a female responsibility affect the lives of women and maintain patriarchal inequalities. The key division in society is that between men and women since men benefit from the oppression of women.

Marxist feminism emerges from the attempt to argue that the crucial basis of the oppression of women is their exclusion from the sphere of paid employment, either literally or from the best-paid jobs, owing to the expectation that they will fit employment around domestic responsibilities (see also Section 9.3). The origins of this approach are in Engels' (1972, orig. pub. 1844) work *The origins of the Family, Private Property and the State*. This locates the development of monogamy as a way for men to ensure their property passes to their biological offspring. This only becomes important with the growth of private property under capitalism. In contemporary Marxist-feminist approaches, such as Rowbotham (1973), it is argued that the free labour women provide in the form of housework (see Section 7.5) is a benefit to capitalism since the costs of providing childcare commercially would bankrupt the capitalist system. Women also provide benefit in that their care provides capitalism with a new generation of workers. Marxist feminism rests on the proposition that working-class men and women have a common interest in overthrowing capitalism. Such a view is rejected by French materialist feminism, most notably in the work of Delphy (1977, 1984) who applies class analysis to the relations between men and women and argues that they exist as separate and conflicting classes. The key to this is the argument that marriage is a form of slavery since it is based on unpaid labour and that this constitutes a domestic mode of production where men exploit women.

The extent to which women's oppression can be explained by either capitalism (as Marxist-feminists argue) or patriarchy (as radical feminists argue) is the starting point for the development of the dual-systems perspective, most notably associated with Walby (1990). She argues that it is necessary to see the position of women as resulting from the operation of these two systems in parallel, meaning that both must be considered as the basis of women's oppression (explored in more detail in Section 5.4).

Black feminism arose owing to concerns by black women that the feminist approach as it developed did not take into account the effect of racism on black women and black men. Anthias and Yuval-Davies (1983) argued that the effects of racism meant black women faced a different situation from white women, meaning that a specifically black feminist approach was needed in order to explain the particular form their oppression took. (See also Section 6.6.)

The notion that there is not one universal form of the oppression of women has been taken further by post-modernist feminists (see also Section 5.5), who have emphasized that there is a need to consider the way that the terms 'woman' and 'man' cover a multiplicity of existences and identities. There is therefore a need for all of these to be taken into account through the production of multiple discourses of the way women are oppressed. They reject the idea that one overarching true theory of gender oppression can emerge. Butler (1990) has argued that we need to understand the way the category 'woman' is actually a construction which carries with it assumptions about relationships between men and women. The implication is that women can never achieve emancipation while they adhere to the universal category, 'woman' owing to the ideas surrounding the construction of this term (see also Section 5.1).

Activity

We have identified seven feminist perspectives: liberal/reformist, _____, radical, dual-systems, postmodernist/post-structuralist, _____ and Black feminist. All these perspectives address the question of what constitutes the oppression of women, and all suggest strategies for overcoming it. All argue that women are oppressed in Western industrial societies but they differ in their explanations of the 'cause' of oppression and their suggested strategies for overcoming it.

_____ is concerned to uncover the immediate forms of discrimination against women in Western societies and to fight for legal and other reforms to overcome them. Marxist feminists argue that the major reason for women's oppression is the exclusion of women from _____ production and that women's struggle for emancipation is an integral part of the fight of the _____ (working class) to overthrow capitalism. Radical feminists see male control of women (_____) as the main problem and argue that women must fight to free themselves from this control. Materialist feminists argue that women as a _____ are exploited and subordinated by men as a class. _____ feminists argue that women's oppression is both an aspect of _____ and patriarchal relations. An end to capitalism, they argue, will not lead automatically to the emancipation of woman – women also need

to fight to free themselves from control by men. Postmodernist/post-structuralist theories argue that the ideas which are the foundation of social divisions can be explored only through texts or _____. The challenge is to construct a discourse from a woman's point of view. They also argue that rationality, and therefore sociology, is a product of a masculine attempt to objectify and control the world. The solution is to reject _____ as a form of explanation. _____ feminists argue that a feminist perspective needs to take into account the differential situation for racialised women as well as racialised men, and therefore the solution is to fight for liberation for Black people as well as women.
(Abbott and Wallace, 1997, p. 31)

The phrases below have been taken from the extract above. Copy this out and fill in the gaps with the appropriate phrase. Each phrase is to be used only once.

liberal feminism	materialist
patriarchy	public
rationality	social class
Black	proletariat
language	Marxist
Capitalism	dual-systems

I, A

2.7 Symbolic interactionism

Georg Simmel (1858–1917): society as the sum of interactions

Although often omitted today, Simmel was in his time as important as Weber. Simmel (1968, orig. pub. 1908); 1978 (orig. pub. 1900) saw sociology as a kind of art form, and as such he stands squarely in the tradition of those opposed to the positivistic notion of sociology as a science. This can be seen from Simmel's argument against purely objective notions of a science of society:

There is no science whose content emerges out of mere objective facts, but rather always entails their interpretation and ordering according to categories and norms that exist a priori for the relevant science.
(Simmel, 1890, p. 3)

He argued that sociology should not be concerned with the attempt to eliminate subjective categorizations, but instead should seek to understand them and the implications they have for the way society develops. The task of sociology is therefore to describe and understand human communal existence. This requires an analysis of the interactions between individuals since society is:

only the name for the sum of these interactions
(Simmel, 1890, p. 15)

Simmel argued that a sociology was necessary since although we need to start from individuals, what is important is the idea of interactions that they engage in. He saw society as composed of these interactions and it was therefore in a state of permanent flux. The interactions which people enter into become social forces which have a real effect and are also determining factors in people's lives.

Simmel's idea that interaction and exchange were the fundamental elements of society led him to consider the role of money in society, since money is something that is involved in both interaction and exchange. It also enabled him to consider Marx's theories (see Section 2.3) about the effect of the rise of capitalism and the commodification of everything. He was centrally concerned with the impact of this on the culture of society, that is, the emotions and interests of individuals, institutions and society.

The importance of consumption

In contrast to Marx, who argued that the key basis of society was production, Simmel argued that it was consumption (see also Section 10.9) that was the prior basis. The reason we produced things was because we wanted to consume things. It is the world of consumption which determines the value of things.

It is the need to exchange which underlies both the formation of society through interactions and the development of social institutions such as money. In his study of Simmel's ideas, Frisby (1984) argues that although his views are critical of the idea that culture can be read off from economic phenomena, he was only really critical of the crude versions of Marxism prevalent at the time in Germany, rather than socialism as such.

Although he differed from Marx on whether production or exchange were the key basis of society, his theory of money also contained an idea very similar to Marx's notion of alienation. Simmel argued that although money was a human creation, it often confronts us as something alien. His point was that monetary relationships are always in reality relationships between people, which further underlies the emphasis on interaction.

In *Sociology* (1968, orig. pub. 1908) Simmel posed the question 'How is society possible?'. He argued that the creation of society was a choice and not inevitable. This means, according to Simmel, that individuals are never fully involved in society since they retain some individual elements within them. In contrast to Durkheim and the later functionalists (see Section 2.4) who essentially saw individuals through the process of socialization as totally integrated into society, Simmel saw a continuing area where people would retain individual identity. This idea provides the basis for refusing to see individuals as merely passive recipients of societal norms and instead for retaining a notion of human individuals as active and therefore interacting and through this creating and re-creating society. He further linked the growth of money to the increasing rationalization of society in ways very similar to the better-known theories of Weber (see Section 2.3), though Simmel is much more interested in the small-scale way that such changes are reflected in social interactions.

Simmel's work has become popular of late because of certain themes running through it which (see Section 2.10) mirror the central interests of sociologists influenced by post-modernism. Simmel was much more interested in sociology as an art form, as a study of aesthetics, and this idea can also be found in contemporary post-modernist statements. The influence of German philosopher Nietzsche is also a similarity with post-modernism.

Finally Simmel, along with Mead, can be seen as the originator of the theories of interaction which emphasize communication as the basis of interaction. This provides a commonality with present-day post-structuralist theories which are also based on analysis of language.

Perhaps the reason why Simmel is often forgotten is the fact that he often provided little evidence to back up his statements. Giddens says :

Simmel's use of empirical method is cavalier: he quotes examples without documentation as if truth were self-evident – although this is bound up with what he repeatedly stressed as the provisional and exploratory character of his work. Simmel's terminology often tends to be loose to the point of carelessness.
(Giddens, 1969, p. 172)

Despite this, his ideas were clearly influential in the rise of American symbolic interactionism and have belatedly become influential in European sociology through the rise of post-modernism.

Symbolic interactionism

Perhaps the most important origin of symbolic interactionism is the writing of George Herbert Mead (1863–1931). Mead was familiar with the work of Weber and Simmel and shared the emphasis on human beings as creative and active.

Mead and the Chicago School

Mead is clearly the founder of the most important form of symbolic interactionism, that associated with the Chicago School, so named because its leading advocates have all been associated with the University in Chicago and used the city of Chicago as the basis of their research.

Mead argued in *Mind, Self and Society* (1934) against the crude behaviourism dominant in psychological circles at that time. Briefly, behaviourism is the belief that a given stimulus elicits an automatic given response from a person. It has thus been represented as a stimulus–response model of society. The criticism of this is that in order to respond to any given stimulus, a person first has to understand it or construct a meaning from it. In short, before they respond, they think. It is this notion of humans as active thinking beings that underlay Mead's rejection of orthodox behaviourism. This insight led Mead to develop his ideas. These culminated in his argument that our behaviour is the result of constructing meanings, but also that these meanings are constructed bearing in mind our membership of social groups and they are therefore social meanings. Since it is this process which distinguishes us from animals, it also undermines attempts to understand humans on the basis of the natural sciences or behaviourism, both of which fail to make such a distinction.

Mead argues that the way we make sense of the world is through language which is inherently social in nature, and this underlines the need for a theory of humanity to embrace the notion of the social as a fundamental element. His most famous distinction on this basis is between the 'I' and the 'me'. What he meant by this was the distinction between the real inner self ('I') and the public front, the social image we present of ourselves ('me').

Both of these are creative and active but the 'me' is a reflection that our behaviour is affected by others, that we are social. We sometimes abstain from doing things we might wish to do because we fear the negative reaction of others. Mead recognized that we do not know everyone we meet, but they have a potential effect on us since, through our knowledge that others will react to what we do, we construct a generalized notion of the 'other' which is contrasted to our notion of 'me'. He also points out, however, that some others will have more of an effect on us and our notion of self and therefore our behaviour. He called these 'significant others'.

This highlights the way we think about our action before we respond, and our thinking is guided by attempting to work out what others will think of our particular responses as well as about what effect our actions will have on others. We are not there-fore the pure selfish 'I' celebrated in free market theories but we are self-regulating on the basis of our internal calculation of the likely consequences of given responses. Interaction thus needs to be considered on the basis of these internal thought processes that mediate between stimulus and response. This is ultimately social, since it occurs in symbolic form, notably language.

There are different symbols in different social groups, and therefore the meaning of any symbol is particular to a social group – which provides the possibility of a variety of different meanings in different social contexts. Even so there is a common structure underlying all of this, providing the basis for the integration of all of these sub-groups into wider society. That common structure is language.

Blumer (1969) further developed this idea to suggest that although we have to be active in constructing meanings, we draw upon accepted meanings and do not invent new meanings in every interaction we take part in. These meanings become part of the culture of society and provide a framework within which people can construct meanings in any particular interaction. However, since people encounter new situations or new meanings they are having to constantly monitor their responses. In other words although people act within a social framework this is never conceived as a fixed order and people are always having to check that the meanings they are using are still appropriate.

Craib (1992, p. 87) summarizes the views of Blumer as three insights:

- Human beings act towards things on the basis of the meanings these things have for them.
- These meanings are the product of social interaction in human society.
- These meanings are modified and handled through an interpretative process that is used by each individual in dealing with the signs each encounters.

Since interactionists see society as simply the meaning constructed through these interactions, this gives us a notion of society constructed and changing through interaction and therefore always in a state of flux.

This idea of symbolic interaction was used in a number of studies of Chicago undertaken by various members of the department. Most notably there was the study of the effect of large-scale immigration from Europe and of large-scale migration of black Americans from the South. Both of these led to a specifically Chicago School perspective on 'race' relations (see Section 6.4).

The idea of people having to construct meanings and therefore reality through interactions has led to the development of explanations of the social construction of deviance and the development of the notion of labelling through the work of Lemert and Becker (see Section 11.5).

The empirical studies of the Chicago School have therefore led more people to consider the usefulness or otherwise of the general symbolic interactionist approach.

Varieties of symbolic interactionism

The dominant school of symbolic interactionism has always been the Chicago School though its influence fell in the 1960s. It was revived by the work of Becker on deviance but it is again somewhat on the decline. Perhaps the most important development out of this school has been the notion of institutions as negotiated order. The original emphasis on face-to-face interaction rather limited the ability of symbolic interactionism to investigate anything other than purely interpersonal encounters, but this more recent emphasis has enabled symbolic interactionism to be applied to institutional settings.

Strauss and interaction as negotiated order

This is known as the 'negotiated-order' approach and can best be seen in the work of Strauss (1979). He argues that organizations cannot be understood as simply places where action is determined by rules, but instead as places where such rules are always in a state of negotiation. Joas provides a neat summary of this argument:

For their existence, organisations are dependent on their continuous reproduction in action; they reproduce themselves in and through the medium of action. Goals and strategies of organisations are a matter of controversy; agreement can assume many different forms . . . Every agreement is of a conditional and transitory character. The actors themselves have theories, drawn from their everyday experience, about the nature, scope and probable success of negotiation processes.
(Joas, 1987, p. 107)

The idea of structures as the result of previous and continuing actions is clearly in this tradition though it goes beyond a concern with the purely face-to-face interaction.

The Iowa School

A move closer to an integration of concern with social structures can also be seen in a second variety of symbolic interactionism, the Iowa School. Sociologists in this tradition have tried to integrate into their approach some notion of objective structures existing beyond the subjective notions of social actors. Further, it tends towards assuming a rela-

tively stable self which is then amenable to quantitative measurement, in contrast to the idea of a self in continuous flux as seen in the Chicago School variant. This leads them to take the notion of structures seriously. In his book *Symbolic Interactionism: A Social Structural Version*, Stryker (1981) argues that it is important to consider the way in which such structures exist and constrain the actions of social beings. The importance of this is that it becomes possible to argue that certain roles are in some cases imposed on people rather than being actively constructed by them, and the extent to which this happens depends upon the effect of larger structures within which interactions take place.

Goffman and dramaturgy

However, by far the most influential development of the symbolic interactionist tradition can be found in the work of Goffman, who has developed what has been called a 'dramaturgical' approach. Goffman starts from the premise that the expectations that others have of us are the basis of roles, and that these expectations form a kind of script which we then act out. Social life is really therefore all an act, it is a drama (hence dramaturgical) during which we play different roles and all the time strive to manage our performance.

Goffman did fieldwork in the Shetland Islands for his book *The Presentation of Self in Everyday Society* (1971) and discovered that the people there let the appearance of their cottages decay so that the landlord would not put up their rents. They were presenting themselves as poor to achieve this effect. This can be called impression management. Craib points out the implication of this:

That 'impression management' is going on all the time, as if we were all advertising agents. We use our physical surroundings as props and maintain areas of privacy 'backstage' where we can relax from our performances (the toilet, for example).
(Craib, 1992, p. 89)

As Craib and others point out, this distinction between the performance and the relaxed artist backstage is in effect a reworking of Mead's 'I' and 'me', pointing to the continuities in the symbolic interactionist tradition.

However, Goffman develops this insight to the point where it might be argued that everything we do is an act and it is not clear whether a real coherent self is ever present. If this is the case, this takes Goffman's ideas close to the post-structuralist notion that there is no real essence or truth.

Goffman conducted a number of famous studies in developing this dramaturgical approach. In *Asylums* (1968) he studied the way in which the routines employed in asylums for the mentally ill are actually manipulated to effect change in people's self-identity as a way of enforcing social control over them. In studying interactions within institutional settings Goffman argues that there is both an inter-action order and an institutional order and that the two are distinct but loosely coupled (see also Section 9.7). Although he is here trying to recognize that there is more to life than face-to-face interactions and that there are also institutional orders which cannot be fully explained on the basis of the inter-action orders he identifies, he nonetheless uses this distinction to underline the need for separate studies of micro and macro phenomena.

However, others are critical of such a distinction. Elias, for example, in his concept of figurations (see Section 2.9) explicitly denies what Goffman sets out to argue, namely that we need to distinguish between interactions and institutions. Elias argues that both are the result and also part of a wider set of figurations which include but extend beyond face-to-face interaction. However Elias has been criticized in turn for failing to make this very distinction.

Since Goffman is effectively concerned to maintain some distinction between the micro and the macro (action and structure) he is obviously criticized by those who wish to overcome this division. Giddens, for example, argues that by restricting his work to the analysis of small-scale face-to-face interactions, Goffman's work is limiting and does not allow him to consider the way in which interactions actually con-tribute to the reproduction of institutions.

However, it is also clear that Habermas' idea of communicative rationality (see Section 2.9), since it is based on the idea of interaction and communica-tion through language, does draw upon the interac-tionist insights, particularly the early work of Mead and Blumer on language. The common link here seems to be Simmel, since it can be argued that Habermas is trying to Simmelize Weber's notion of rationality.

Criticisms of symbolic interactionism

The most long-standing criticism of this approach is that in focusing almost entirely on small-scale face-to-face interactions, it ignores any notion of struc-ture and constraint. In extreme versions, society is simply the result of interactions and is therefore seen as a permanent flux. Such a view undermines any notion of structure since this implies some relatively enduring element in society. The key question is whether this is true, and it can be seen that there are differences within the symbolic interactionist approach on this question. The Iowa School seem much more willing to talk of some notion of struc-

Discussion point

Goffman's work on interaction orders does essentially define interactions as being face-to-face.

a How might phone conversations or communication by letter be considered on this basis?

b Goffman saw them as reduced forms of real interaction. What do you think is reduced in this form of interaction and what remains?

c Do you agree with Goffman or can the notion of interaction orders be applied to these forms of communication?

d What are the implications for the future of symbolic interactionism bearing in mind the growth of electronic forms of communication.

e How real is virtual reality on this basis?

ture, while the Chicago School and Goffman seem less inclined to integrate notions of structure into interactionist analysis.

Since it is argued that structural factors are important in shaping the way people interact, this is a key criticism. Craib argues that the refusal by some symbolic interactionists to acknowledge the existence of a society outside people's immediate interactions actually leads to a contradiction of the premises of symbolic interactionism because most people do interact on the basis that such a thing exists:

To suppose 'society' to be a fiction, to suppose that it is unorganised, and so on, is to ignore the expe-rience of its effects amongst those we study. In other words, it is to do precisely the opposite of what symbolic interactionism sets out to do.
(Craib, 1992, p. 92)

This leads on to the second criticism which is that symbolic interactionism cannot conceptualize power since this is linked to a notion of social structure. Mouzelis points to the failure of an exclusively micro-focus to even explain all individual interactions:

Where does an interaction fit in between a few indi-viduals (mega actions) who happen to be heads of state and whose decisions may have world-wide repercussions?
(Mouzelis, 1995, p. 18)

Interactions, therefore, appear to take place in a vacuum and society is essentially the result of these meaningful interactions. The implicit point here is that symbolic interactionism tends to imply that society (as they understand it) results from some sort of consensus achieved through interaction but also – since we do not come into an empty world – through learning how to interact and the rules for interaction through socialization. This criticism can certainly be levelled at some elements of symbolic interactionism. The early Chicago School influenced accounts of 'race' relations assumed that assimilation, meaning the integration of newcomers into the value system already existing, would occur unproblematically. When this proved not to be the case, they merely argued that the process would take longer than originally anticipated rather than making the alternative interpretation that such relations were characterized by conflicts of interest and inequalities of power. Feminists have pointed out that the focus on interactions might serve to obscure such inequalities since women might interact with men in a certain way because they have less power than them. This point would be obscured by a focus on the interaction alone.

More recent variants of symbolic interactionism do at least try to answer this criticism since they include some notion of structure in their ideas. Strauss's idea of negotiated order does allow for conflicts and debates to take place and therefore also for a calculation of power in negotiations. It might also be argued that power is actually a micro as well as a macro phenomenon and therefore we can study power in interpersonal interactions. It is suggested that when it does focus on conflict, symbolic interactionism only focuses on fleeting trivial issues and that these are peripheral to a real analysis of society. In response, symbolic interactionists would argue that this really rather depends on what you consider trivial and that this is not obvious.

A final criticism is that symbolic interactionism is too based on American society to be of use anywhere else. Critics such as Shaskolsky (1970) argue that its emphasis on individuals interacting reflects the individualistic ethos of the USA with its stress on individuality and freedom. However, it might be argued that the dominant notion of individualism and freedom in the USA is actually based much more on economic and financial factors and therefore takes the form of the contemporary New Right (see Section 2.10). It is precisely this idea that everything can be explained on the basis of self-seeking individuals that Mead set out to criticize by pointing out that the construction of individuals is inherently a social act. Nonetheless it is clear that symbolic interactionism is a form of liberalism and therefore the more radical critics of capitalism would find it wanting.

2.8 Phenomenology and ethnomethodology

The differences from symbolic interactionism

Symbolic interactionism, phenomenology and ethnomethodology are often considered together as varieties of social action approaches. While this is true it often leads to problems. As Cuff *et al.* put it:

Many people . . . profess that they are unable to tell the difference between symbolic interactionists and ethnomethodologists.
(Cuff *et al.*, 1990, p. 211)

However, it is important to be aware that they are different and we need to know what these differences are as well as the similarities. Rather fortuitously, Cuff *et al.*, having identified the problem, also provide the solution:

Interactionist studies typically are concerned to identify 'social meanings' that some group of actors share and to explain these meanings in terms of the relation the actors have with one another and with other groups. Thus the interactionist is concerned with actors, their beliefs, actions and relationships. The ethnomethodologist, in contrast is concerned with activities rather than actors. Ethnomethodological studies inquire not so much into meanings, as into the work which makes meanings possible.
(Cuff *et al.*, 1990, p. 191)

So interactionism is concerned with the actors (people) and ethnomethodologists are concerned with activities (process). In effect ethnomethodologists are concerned with the process whereby people construct meanings and they are therefore working on the stuff which becomes the basic material that interactionists work on. While these differences do mean that they are two distinct approaches, they are both clearly concerned with social action and the micro end of sociological analysis.

Having established that there is a difference we now need to investigate in more detail the meaning of ethnomethodology. This requires an explanation of the rise of phenomenological sociology.

Phenomenology and sociology

The whole basis of phenomenology in sociology is a total rejection of the idea of social structures. While these structures are almost an absent presence in symbolic interactionism, they do not exist for phenomenologists. The only reality for them is the way the social world is given meaning by the actions of individuals.

Phenomenology came into sociology via the work of Schutz (1972). He said that while Weber through his concept of *verstehen* (see Section 3.2) had argued that it was necessary to understand the actor's point of view, he nonetheless also asserted that such a study needed to take into account the social structural and historical circumstances within which such action took place. This, Schutz argued, actually leads to researchers constructing meaning themselves. What starts out as an attempt to understand the subjective world of the social actor in the end becomes a social scientific description of how the actor sees the world. Schutz argues that in creating meaning social actors create first-order typifications, but that sociologists have their own way of organizing material dictated by the convention of attempting to arrive at a rational explanation of the social world. Their constructions are therefore 'second-order typifications'. Schutz points out that the two are not the same thing and that we should therefore simply concentrate on how actors themselves create meanings and therefore construct society. This means a sole focus on daily experience and the way in which actors draw upon taken-for-granted knowledge to enable them to interact with others.

Schutz developed a number of concepts to explain this process, notably those of 'typification' and 'meaning contexts'. Craib explains the significance of these as follows:

He attempted to show how we build our knowledge of the social world from a basic stream of incoherent and meaningless experience. We do this through a process of 'typification', which involves building up classes of experience through similarity . . . Thus we build up what Schutz calls 'meaning contexts', sets of criteria by means of which we organise our sense experience into a meaningful world and stocks of knowledge, which are not stocks of knowledge about the world but, for all practical purposes, the world itself. Action and social action thus become things that happen in consciousness: we are concerned with acts of consciousness rather than action in the world, and the social world is something which we create together.
(Craib, 1992, p. 99)

This phenomenological approach has been used in a number of more recent sociological works. Berger and Luckmann (1967) presented a view of sociology strongly influenced by phenomenology but yet still wishing to retain some notion of a world which exists beyond the level of meaning central to phenomenology. In other words, while they start from the notion of individuals constructing meanings they go on to consider how these meanings become solidified into institutions. Craib argues that this in effect brings their end-product close to functionalism even though it is clearly inspired by phenomenology. In a later work, Berger and Kellner explore this idea further:

Every human institution is, as it were, a sedimentation of meanings, or, to vary the image, a crystallization of meanings in objective forms. As meanings become objectivated, institutionalised, in this manner, they become common reference points for the meaningful actions of countless individuals, even from one generation to the next. But these institutionalised meanings can also be interpreted – 'retrieved' or 'unwrapped', from their seemingly inert forms.
(Berger and Kellner, 1981, p. 37)

Activity

a What elements of the above formulation point towards a phenomenological approach?

b To what extent do you agree with Craib's argument that their formulation also has great similarities with functionalism?

I, A, E

The radical implication of phenomenology, that there is no world separate from the consciousness of individuals and the meanings they work to actively construct, has been drawn out much more consistently by the rise of ethnomethodology.

Ethnomethodology

The key work in the origins of ethnomethodology was written by Garfinkel (1967). It focuses on the way that meanings are constructed in the way suggested by phenomenological approaches, but suggests that these should be investigated as a kind of method that people develop in order to deal with everyday experiences. What is interesting is an analysis of the way this method works, how it is constructed and therefore how people use it to construct meanings and localized worlds. The world is therefore seen as a product of these constructions of meaning. Clearly this implies a total rejection of any notion of social structure separate from the meanings of individuals interacting in localized settings. To use Garfinkel's phrase, social order is 'participant produced'. The way in which people actively construct meanings and therefore make their everyday experience understandable is precisely the way social order is produced. This is the basis of social order. While the question of the basis of social order is most famously associated with Parsons and functionalism, Garfinkel was concerned to look at all the assumptions Parsons made about society and consider them instead as problematic areas in need of investigation:

Although sociologists take socially structured scenes of everyday life as a point of departure they rarely see, as a task of sociological enquiry in its

own right, the general question of how any such common sense world is possible. Instead the possibility of the everyday world is either settled by theoretical representation or merely assumed. . . . My purposes in this paper are to demonstrate the essential relevance, to sociological inquiries, of a concern for common sense activities as a topic of inquiry in its own right and by reporting a series of studies, to urge its 'rediscovery'.
(Garfinkel, 1967, p. 36)

The breaching experiments

This idea about the way everyday social order is actively created can be seen in the breaching experiments documented by Garfinkel in *Studies in Ethnomethodology* (1967). These were concerned with a central element of the ethnomethodological analysis, namely the existence of rules on which everyday behaviour is based. However the rules are not conceived of as fixed, but as starting points which may then be broken, bent, reinterpreted or not. Precisely because they exist, social life is possible, but because they exist in our consciousness we often forget they exist. Garfinkel set out to demonstrate their existence by getting researchers to consciously break certain rules, thus:

'making commonplace scenes visible'
(Garfinkel, 1967, p. 36).

A few examples of these studies will demonstrate the general approach.

Students were asked to involve themselves in conversations but to respond to every statement by asking 'What do you mean?' Since this breaches normal rules, it elicits often hostile responses as the following extract shows:

(S) Hi, Ray. How is your girl friend feeling?
(E) What do you mean, 'How is she feeling?' Do you mean physical or mental?
(S) I mean how is she feeling? What's the matter with you? (He looked peeved)
(E) Nothing. Just explain a little clearer what do you mean?
(S) Skip it. How are your Med School applications coming?
(E) What do you mean. 'How are they?'
(S) You know what I mean.
(E) I really don't.
(S) What's the matter with you? Are you sick?'
(Garfinkel, 1967, p. 42)

In other experiments, Garfinkel instructed students to spend 15–60 minutes in their parents' home acting as if they were paying lodgers. The point was to try to get students to look at familiar activities (family interaction) from a new viewpoint and also to breach the conventions of the rules concerning such a situation to see what happens. Parents interpreted the odd behaviour of their offspring in a variety of ways, from believing that they wanted something and were therefore being extra-nice through to concerns that they were sick. These reveal both that people react, often negatively when unspoken rules are broken, but also that they act to make sense of the situation, to construct some meaning which explains the unforeseen event. In this respect, Garfinkel argued that people actively construct meanings and that this showed the falsity of views which saw people as passive creations of society, as for example in functionalism.

This idea of the construction of meaning was also explored by Garfinkel (1984) through an experiment in counselling. If it can be shown that people make sense of a situation that has no sense then this notion that sense and meaning are constructed is underlined. He invited students to get involved in a new form of counselling. The two people involved would sit in separate rooms and communicate via an intercom. This allowed Garfinkel to set up a situation where the 'counsellor' was instructed to answer only 'yes' or 'no' to questions and the answer they gave would be determined by reference to a random number table. This creates a situation where all possible objective sense is removed. Nonetheless, he found that the people being counselled found it helpful and used their own experiences and meanings to make sense of this situation.

Indexicality

The advantages of this approach are that it clearly illustrates that people are active and knowledgeable. Garfinkel refers to the indexicality of everyday life, by which he means that the meanings of particular words can only be understood in the particular context in which they appear. He argues further that we have to actively engage with each word to try to construct some meaning to it, through a process he calls glossing. This points to the way human society is constructed through the active construction of meaning through interaction, and that people are reflexive, to use Garfinkel's term.

Criticisms of ethnomethodology

The question of whether this illustrates anything beyond the level of everyday experiences is open to question. While ethnomethodologists would argue that there is nothing beyond this level, the more structurally-inclined sociologists would point to a number of examples of things that happen which people do not need to make sense of. For example, the dropping of the atomic bomb on Hiroshima can be seen as an instance of something which had an effect on the people of that city without them ever having to consider its meaning or make sense of it. The bomb will still kill you even if there is no construction of meaning. Although the ethnomethodologists concentrate on the construction of meaning, they do not talk about the ways in which meaning can sometimes be imposed and they have no explanation of why people would adopt certain meanings. The implication of this criticism is that the way people construct meanings does not only depend on what is happening in a local context but on their placement and experiences in the wider world. This requires a notion of social structures which exist beyond localized meanings. Some notion of power and interests therefore needs to be integrated for ethnomethodology to be useful.

It is therefore argued that such studies simply concentrate on the trivial aspects of life and only tell us what we know already. In their account of ethnomethodology, Haralambos and Holborn (1995) quote the criticisms of ethnomethodology made by Gouldner who developed a parody of an ethnomethodological experiment:

An ethnomethodologist might release chickens in a town centre during the rush hour, and stand back and observe as traffic was held up and crowds began to gather and laugh at policemen chasing the chickens. Gouldner goes on to say that Garfinkel might say that the community has now learned the importance of one hitherto unnoticed rule at the basis of everyday life: chickens must not be dropped in the streets in the midst of the lunch rush hour.
(Haralambos and Holborn, 1995, p. 903)

The emphasis on the ever-changing nature of reality, and therefore the impossibility of ever arriving at a final truth, has in more recent times been taken up by post-structuralist and post-modernist influenced sociologists (see Section 2.10), though with the important difference that here social actors are back in the role of cultural dope ultimately powerless in the face of the mass media. In one sense, therefore the insights about the continual relativity of meaning remain a part of sociology.

Activity

Explain in your own words the difference between symbolic interactionist approaches and ethnomethodology with respect to:

a the construction of meanings
b the notion of social structures.

I, A

Conversation analysis

The most recent development of ethnomethodology is the growth of conversation analysis. This is developed directly out of the insights Garfinkel developed from his experiments, many of which involved the analysis of conversational settings. Sacks (1984, 1992) argues that it is through the analysis of conversations that an empirical account of the way people construct meanings through interaction can be arrived at. By this method they aim to uncover the social competencies which are revealed by the fact that the interaction takes place. He therefore set out to analyse and describe the rules and structure of conversations, including the idea that people take turns and that broadly only one person speaks at a time. He investigated conversation through research at a suicide prevention centre, studying how people started their telephone conversations. Further studies have focused on how endings of conversations are managed or how new topics are introduced. Conversation analysis has been taken up in the UK by researchers such as Atkinson (famous for his phenomenological interpretation of suicide) and Heritage (see Atkinson and Heritage (1984) and Heritage (1987)).

While conversation analysis remains faithful to the idea of an investigation of the way people construct meanings and operate on the basis of these shared rules in localized contexts, and is therefore still indexical, May (1996) in his study of social theory argues that it:

has moved ethnomethodology even further away from its phenomenological input.
(May, 1996, p. 94)

Basically this is because of the overt emphasis on observable empirical data as the basis of conversation analysis which moves it away from a consideration of the way people create interpretations (the basis of phenomenology).

2.9 Putting sociology back together again?

The preceding sections have outlined the diverse ways in which sociological theory has developed since the subject was invented by Auguste Comte. This has been characterized as 'the war of the perspectives'. However, in recent years a number of different sociologists have attempted to synthesize approaches and in particular to try to overcome the division between social structural approaches and social action approaches that has been evident for so long. The writers explored in this section all argue that this is something which should be considered, even though their proposed solutions differ.

Norbert Elias

The work of Elias has become more central to sociology in recent years. There are two main reasons for this. First Elias always denied that it was possible to sustain the structure/action split, and so he fits alongside others who have sought to go beyond this conceptual split. The second reason is the influence of his work on the sociology of sport and leisure (see Section 9.8), areas of growing interest within sociology in general and post-modernist circles more particularly.

He is concerned with the process whereby people and the ideas they hold are constituted through chains which stretch back through the generations. Society is seen as the result, often accidental, of all the interweavings between social actors. He used the term figurations to describe this:

From the interweaving of countless individual interests and interactions – whether tending in the same direction or in divergent and hostile directions – something comes into being that was planned and intended by none of those individuals, yet has emerged nevertheless from their intentions and actions. And really this is the whole secret of social figurations.

(Elias, 1982, p. 160, orig. pub. 1939)

Central to his sociology is an examination of the processes whereby such figurations work themselves out. This emphasis on dynamism and process is central to his rejection of the structure–action dichotomy. The individual and society are not two different things, merely two different perspectives on the same thing. This leads him to examine the nature of the structures which emerges from these interdependencies and the way this leads to the formation of later structures. His work is therefore an examination of the evolution of both structures and individual personalities within sets of interdependencies. Although he shares the idea of evolution with the functionalists (see Section 2.4), he saw their work as overly static. His work therefore emphasizes dynamism, albeit evolutionary dynamism. His attraction to post-modernist thinkers arises because of his emphasis on the way people exist as pluralities:

Since people are more or less dependent on each other first by nature and then through social learning, through education, socialisation and socially generated reciprocal needs, they exist, one might say, only as pluralities, only in figurations.

(Elias, 1978, p. 261, orig. pub. 1939)

The Weberian strand of his thinking comes across in his consideration of power which he sees as a characteristic of all social relationships, though he differs in the consideration of the extent and meaning of the idea of the growing rationality of power.

Elias's central work is *The Civilising Process* (1978, 1982) originally published in German in 1939. In it he presents an analysis of the evolution of human

manners and the way in which changes in the social structure change aspects of our personality structure, namely our feelings for others. Elias studied court society (primarily in France) between the thirteenth and the nineteenth centuries. He argues that if you look at certain forms of human behaviour such as handling food, farting, burping and spitting, these have undergone a long-term evolution described as the continuous civilizing of behaviour with an increase in social pressure on people to behave in certain ways. He argues that this process led to a change in psychological development so that the constraints on the way people behaved, which were originally external, now became internal and therefore self-restraint. He emphasizes that this is not to suggest that the past was totally uncivilized since he argues that the civilizing process is a process without a beginning. There is, nonetheless, a clear idea of the evolution of manners and embarrassment and shame thresholds over time. He argues that this cannot be explained on the basis of material changes or changes in knowledge about health, but instead is related to respect for others. The cause is changes in the social relations between people. These occurred first in the upper class and then filtered down.

Elias links this changing behaviour to the formation of states (thereby showing the way micro and macro issues can be linked) by arguing that it is possible to investigate the process through which states gained monopoly power in respect to taxation and the legitimate use of violence. As a result conflicts became more a matter of who ran the state rather than whether one should exist at all and Elias argues this has led to the progressive reduction in the use of violence. Centralization and integration are key processes here and Elias emphasizes the way competitors to state power were eliminated (thereby coming close to neo-Weberian accounts of the state which emphasize military conflicts) although he argues that the monopoly over taxation is also needed. He further argues against Marxism by saying that neither of these monopolies can be understood to arise from strictly economic processes:

Elias is emphatic that the monopolisation of the means of violence and of taxation is not reducible to an economic process.

(Mennell, 1989, p. 70)

Although his emphasis on people interacting has similarities with symbolic interactionism, the emphasis there is always on people interacting face-to-face. Elias's idea of figurations, or chains of interdependence stretching back over time, emphasizes that our actions are also affected by the fact that we are interdependent on people we have never met. While this is clearly true in one sense, it has been criticized.

Layder points out that he is wrong to suppose that there is no real difference between face-to-face interaction and the other type of connections encompassed within the term figurations:

dealing with someone on a face-to-face basis (say in a family, or a coffee bar) is very much influenced by the reality of the presence of other people. . . . As social relations stretch away into the impersonal realm of institutional phenomena, say our connection with some government agency, we find that our ties of interdependence are based primarily upon an absence rather than a presence. We do not experience the presence of the government as such; there is no face-to-face encounter with the institution. . . . We must be aware that the defining characteristics of institutions are not to be found in the connectedness of people as such. . . . It is the nature of the ties between people (rather than the fact of ties per se . . .) that is the crucial defining feature.
(Layder, 1994, p. 122)

Discussion point

Elias's notion of figurations implies that we are affected by chains of interdependencies stretching back through the ages. To what extent do you feel that these can be analysed in the same way as face-to-face interactions?

Elias's work has become much discussed in sociology, but it is not without its critics. His emphasis on evolution has led some to argue that he is merely reasserting the ideas of some of the earlier sociologists such as Spencer and Comte (see Section 2.2) and the whole idea of evolution has been criticized as tending towards presenting a hierarchy of societies with some seen as more advanced than others. Giddens for example argues that:

Elias does stress certain specific characteristics of the modern West, but these are largely submerged in a generalised evolutionism. In the 'less complex societies' there is lower individual self-control, greater spontaneous expression of emotion, etc. People in such societies are rather like children, spontaneous and volatile.
(Giddens, 1984, p. 241)

Giddens points out quite clearly that he believes this view to be wrong.

The idea of a progressive growth in civilization is also open to question. Mennell (1987), although a supporter of Elias's approach, points to two key criticisms of this argument. First, it is argued that there was civilized behaviour in stateless societies. This criticism undermines the idea of the progressive evolution of civilization, although Elias was careful to argue that

the process had no beginning, in other words, there were no societies which had no civilization. A second line of criticism points to the way levels of barbarism have increased in recent years and particularly towards the rise of the Nazis and the Holocaust as key examples. It is clear, however, that his work is an attempt to go beyond structure versus action and the phrase he used to describe the level of personality characteristics people share with others is *habitus*, a word since also used by Bourdieu. What they both point to, albeit in different ways, is the need to think about the process linking people and society or structure and action rather than just portraying it as an empty space between these two opposing views.

Pierre Bourdieu

Bourdieu's (1977, 1984, 1990, 1993a) argument centres around the need to see social practices as the central subject of sociological analysis. He argues that both structural and action-based theories have produced rather one-sided accounts of human life. By social practices he means the way that people create and recreate the objective structure of society in certain ways. In contrast to structuralist accounts this does take the notion of humans as agents seriously and in contrast to action-based sociology it retains a notion that there are objective structures beyond us which nonetheless constrain our actions. What provides the link is the social practices people engage in.

The central concept he develops to provide a link between the structural and action aspects of society is that of 'habitus'. This term refers to the actual means by which people produce and reproduce social circumstances. In particular, Bourdieu wishes the term to refer to the way certain forms of behaviour become so internalized that they appear almost, though not quite, automatically:

with the notion of habitus you can refer to something that is close to what is suggested by the idea of habit, while differing from it in one important respect. The habitus . . . is that which one has acquired, but which has become durably incorporated in the body in the form of permanent dispositions. . . .

But then why not say 'habit'? Habit is spontaneously regarded as repetitive, mechanical, automatic, reproductive rather than productive. I wanted to insist on the idea that the habitus is something powerfully generative. To put it briefly, the habitus is a product of conditionings which tends to reproduce the objective logic of those conditionings while transforming it. It's a kind of transforming machine that leads us to 'reproduce' the social conditions of our own production, but in a relatively unpredictable way.
(Bourdieu, 1993a, p. 86)

The knowledge gained from living in a particular culture or subculture in a sense predisposes the choices that we will make, although not entirely and we still have to actually make a choice. The *habitus* is therefore history embodied in human bodies as opposed to in objects such as books and buildings.

Activity

Suggest ways the *habitus* embodied in yourself has predisposed you to make choices in your life in a particular way.

A

While Bourdieu's theory does therefore include a strong theory of constraint, it might be said that Bourdieu is then open to the criticism that although he talks about choices, in effect he sees most of these as predetermined. This point is made by May when he says that:

The result is that the habitus may be read as a gun out of which the individual is shot, thereby determining their social trajectory.
(May, 1996, p. 127).

He goes on to say however that such an interpretation would be counter to Bourdieu's wish to view the *habitus* as open and flexible to some extent. He quotes Bourdieu as follows:

Habitus is not the fate that some people read into it. Being the product of history, it is an open set of dispositions that is constantly subjected to experiences . . . that either reinforces or modifies its structures. . . . Having said that . . . most people are statistically bound to encounter circumstances that tend to agree with those that originally fashioned their habitus.
(Bourdieu, in May 1996, p. 127)

It seems that Bourdieu believes that things are determined but not totally so and not passively so. They are only determined insofar as people so determine them. However he wishes to retain a clear notion of objective structures and rejects the attempt to argue (originating in phenomenological views but also present in some post-structuralist formulations) that ideas and subjectivity are the only real basis of things. Instead he argues that:

Only by constructing the objective structures (price curves, chances of access to higher education, laws of the matrimonial market, etc.) is one able to pose the question of the mechanisms through which the relationship is established between the structures and the practices or the representations which accompany them, instead of treating these 'thought objects' as 'reasons' or 'motives' and making them the determining cause of the practices.
(Bourdieu, 1977, p. 21)

Bourdieu insists, however, that his serious attention to the cultural sphere reveals that he is interested in subjectivity and is seriously trying to avoid the determinism evident in other versions of structuralism (see Section 2.10). Despite this insistence, the criticisms remain, and in this respect his weaknesses can be seen to be the opposite of those of Giddens' theory of structuration (see below). Alexander argues that this does mean that his work ultimately falls back on a form of determinism. In looking at Bourdieu's work on the 1968 revolts in France, Alexander argues that:

His theoretical interest is in denying the voluntaristic, self- or value-generated dimension of critical change. . . . Even in Bourdieu's efforts to make this crisis model more complex, the subjective element falls away.
(Alexander, 1995, p. 148)

The similarities and differences between Bourdieu and Giddens are examined by Layder who argues:

Habitus is the means through which people produce and reproduce the social circumstances in which they live. This makes it similar to Giddens' idea about structures being both the medium and the outcome of activity. Bourdieu is much more inclined to view social circumstances in the more conventional 'objective' sense of structures and institutions than is the case with Structuration Theory.
(Layder, 1994, p. 144)

It is this attempt to retain some notion of structure which arguably causes Bourdieu some problems. In some accounts, he argues that these structures are the result of human social practices but he also wishes to see them as embedded in power relationships.

His theory of distinction emphasizes the way in which social factors affect the choices we make about leisure (see Section 9.8) but also shows that these choices are affected by the degree of capital we have. He wished to move the notion of capital away from the purely economic connotation of that term evident in orthodox Marxism and also included the idea of cultural capital. This can be seen in his analysis of education (see Section 8.2) whereby some people can translate their economic capital into cultural capital (buy a good education) which then becomes the basis for the accumulation of further economic capital. He therefore emphasizes the cultural construction of inequality and the way in which social divisions are produced and reproduced through cultural tastes and actions.

The key problem this poses is that if he believes all our choices are essentially rooted in some form of inequalities of power, this places him very close to the notion of all knowledge being rooted in power, which underlies post-structuralist accounts.

Bourdieu does not want to encompass this idea, since he wishes to retain some notion that it is possible for sociologists to gain some objective knowledge of the world, and for this his theory must require some notion of objectivity. This points to a long-standing problem in social thinking. If the view of the sociologist is no more valid than any other, why should anyone listen to the sociologist? This relativism is clear in post-structuralism. If to avoid this, one suggests that there is a difference (usually seen as the more scientific nature of sociology compared to commonsense) then how can one retain some notion of humans as active agents, since they clearly do not possess all the necessary information to make real choices?

Discussion point

To what extent does the notion that sociology is superior to commonsense undermine the notion that humans are active knowledgeable agents? Are sociologists merely imposing their view on the world?

It is perhaps clear that in trying to overcome the structure/agency division Bourdieu tends towards the more structural type of analysis. Lash (1990) argues that Bourdieu only allows a minimal amount of autonomy for humans from the power embedded in structures, and May therefore argues that Bourdieu's work has:

the tendency, despite his wish to avoid this very problem, for an ahistorical structuralism to reassert itself.
(May, 1996, p. 133)

Anthony Giddens

Giddens' most notable contribution to sociological theory has been his development of structuration theory, which is most certainly an attempt to consider and go beyond the division between structural and social action approaches to sociology. Giddens (1977, 1979, 1987, 1990) has been developing some of the elements of structuration theory for some considerable time, but it is probably best developed in his book, *The Constitution of Society* (1984). At its heart is his own particular conception of structure. While conventionally the notion of social structure has been seen as placing limits on the extent of choice individuals have, and therefore constraining, Giddens argues that social structures should be viewed as having a dual character, what he refers to as 'the duality of structure'. The centrality of this notion to his theory can be grasped from his own exposition of the problem he sees at the heart of social theory:

Of prime importance in this respect is a dualism that is deeply entrenched in social theory, a division between objectivism and subjectivism ... In spite of Parson's terminology of 'the action frame of reference', there is no doubt that in his theoretical scheme the object (society) predominates over the subject (the knowledgeable human agent). ... By attacking objectivism – and structural sociology – those influenced by hermeneutics or by phenomenology were able to lay bare major shortcomings of those views, but they in turn veered sharply towards subjectivism. The conceptual divide between subject and social object yawned as widely as ever.

Structuration theory is based on the premise that this dualism has to be reconceptualised as a duality – the duality of structure.
(Giddens, 1984, p. xx)

We obviously need to know what Giddens means by this phrase. In essence, his argument is that neither social structures nor social actions can exist independently of each other, and therefore accounts which focus on one or the other are deficient. Social structures should not be seen as purely constraining our actions, but also as enabling them to take place. For example, the structure of a language, its rules of grammar and construction are clearly a structure in that they exist independently of any one individual. We can view them as constraining our action insofar as they limit the particular ways we communicate. This aspect of structure is familiar and conventional. It is the enabling aspect of structures that is novel. However, to use the example of language again, we can see that Giddens has a point. Without a structure of language shared between individuals, no communication would be possible. So the structure of language enables us to engage in the social activity of communication and of course all other possible social actions are based on this ability to communicate. To take the example further, new words emerge in languages and therefore not only does the structure of language enable social action to take place, but that structure is itself created, recreated and changed through social action. This is an example of what Giddens calls rules, by which he means the principles which regulate social action. Human agents can and do transform as well as reproduce structures. The duality of structure therefore emphasizes that structures both constrain and enable social action to take place.

Structural approaches to sociology usually make reference to inequalities of power in society, but Giddens also argues that we can see power as enabling action in certain circumstances, and further as something which does not exist unless it involves human action. He argues that the resources we use can be divided into allocative resources, by which he broadly means raw materials such as land and technology, and authoritative resources, by which he broadly means systems of power and authority. His point is that in both cases neither of these exist in a usable form unless human actions turn them into resources. So structures of production, power and authority can also be traced back to human action and as such power can be viewed as a resource. Here Giddens partially supports Parson's view of power as a capacity to achieve outcomes.

Structures consist of rules and resources:

In structuration theory 'structure' is regarded as rules and resources recursively implicated in social reproduction; institutionalised features of social systems have structural properties in the sense that relationships are stabilized across time and space. (Giddens, 1984, p. xxxi)

However, since both rules and resources are created by humans the clear link between structure (in Giddens' sense) and action is maintained. Structures do exist independently of individuals but only insofar as they are reproduced by human action. Humans are viewed by Giddens as 'knowledgeable agents' and in this respect his work draws on both Goffman and Garfinkel in emphasizing the way that humans are active and attempt to make sense of the particular situations they find themselves in. Giddens argues that humans desire a degree of predictability in their lives and as a result, create institutions and structures which exist beyond the control of any one individual. However, they are created by human action and for the purpose of facilitating and helping human life.

Since he views structures as the result of knowledgeable human agents, he is very critical of the conventional structural argument that our lives are determined in some way. He argues that there are very few situations where as individuals we have no choice. In particular he argues that constraints often only mean a limited course of action given aims set by ourselves. He refers to Marx's argument that propertyless labourers must sell their labour power but comments that:

there is only one feasible option, given that the worker has the motivation to wish to survive (Giddens, 1984, p. 177)

The implication here is that the worker did face a choice, that of choosing either to live or die and that although if they choose to live, they do have to work, this may itself involve choices between different jobs. Giddens argues further that this choice is also enabling since it does allow the worker to make a living and therefore enable existence. What appears

like a constraint is seen by Giddens to result from the motivations and choices of actors. However, whether the choice between living and dying is seen as sufficient degree of choice to enable us to talk of people having choice, is a matter of debate. Although it is clearly true that we do have an option in life or death situations, this might be seen as offering only pyrrhic choice. It is this perception that Giddens' attempt to merge structure and action operates only by redefining structure in such a way that notions of constraint almost disappear that has been the main source of criticism of his work.

Archer (1982, 1988, 1995) argues that Giddens underplays the importance of structures and constraint. She argues that his emphasis on agents recreating the world tends to imply that if different choices are made, the world can be changed almost at will. This she argues is incorrect. She points to the constraint involved in Cuba's literacy programme based on getting one literate person to teach one illiterate person. The key constraint here was the number of existing literate persons. She further points to physical constraints such as volcanoes and floods. Although these would appear as factors in Giddens' notion of allocative resources, she argues that their effect on humanity does not depend on humans exercising a choice, although it might be argued in response to this that it might be another example of life or death being seen as a choice. She therefore argues that structure and action have to be understood as linked but distinct levels of analysis.

Activity

a Suggest a number of possible situations where it might be said that human action is constrained.

b In each instance, try to think of a list of possible choices still open to knowledgeable actors in these situations.

c On the basis of these examples, summarize the relationship between freedom of choice and determinism in human society.

d Evaluate the notion of choice embodied in Giddens' structuration theory and consider whether you think it effectively provides for sufficient real choice among human actors.

I, A, E

From a different angle, New (1993) suggests that Giddens' theory does not provide much of a conception of human agency either. She argues that although it may be technically true that people always have a choice, some people have more choice than others and for some their options are severely limited. This means he does not address questions such as: 'Who can transform what aspects of social structure and how?'. Her point is that by emphasizing choice as present in all situations, the fact that some social structures are more impervious to change than others is obscured and so therefore is the issue of the extent to which human agency can have effects.

Jürgen Habermas

Habermas is the most recent thinker in the critical theory tradition which stretches back to the writings of the Frankfurt School (see Section 2.5). Their work was influenced by a number of key social thinkers, notably Marx, Weber and Freud. However Habermas (1972, 1976, 1981a) has added to this tradition by making his own distinctive contribution which also weaves in the influence of Durkheim, Mead and Parsons.

One controversial aspect of his work is his refusal (Habermas, 1989) to accept the arguments of post-modernism (see Section 2.10). Habermas refuses to accept the post-modernist notion that it is impossible to rationally understand the world. As such he stands (along with Anthony Giddens) as a key defender in contemporary times of the inspiration behind the rise of sociology, namely the enlightenment notion that it is possible to understand the world and to use that knowledge to construct a better world. He argues that post-structuralism and post-modernism are merely one variant of the re-emergence of conservative thinking, arguing that they are the 'young conservatives' who are merely recreating the nostalgic longing for a pre-capitalist order which has for so long been a trend in social thinking. This argument illustrates what has been his main aim, namely to reformulate the meaning of rationality to remove what he sees as distortions introduced by positivism and also by Weber's pessimism about the future. At the heart of his work is a reconsideration of the notion of rationalization.

Thinkers in the Frankfurt School have long been critical of positivistic conceptions of science (see Section 3.1), seeing in its attempt to remove all notion of subjectivity both a falsehood, but also almost an arrogance about the power of science. Habermas builds on this by arguing that any notion of understanding something must involve both an object and a subject and that therefore no science is able to be purely objective. In this respect and in the importance accorded to communication in his overall theory, he is building on the insights of the interpretive tradition in German thinking, but arguably also the way this was incorporated into symbolic interactionism. (see Section 2.7.)

His book, *Knowledge and Human Interests* (1972) is a critique of the positivist conception of science,

and argues for the need to rescue the notion of rationality from such interpretations. The process of rationalization is of course a central element in Weber's work (see Section 9.7) and this shows the influence of Weber on Habermas. However Habermas argues that Weber's analysis, ending in the idea of a world strangled by the 'iron cage' of bureaucracy, highlights the potential downside of the growth of rationality. He feels that Weber's conclusion is overly pessimistic and it is the attempt to rescue rationality as a positive force that underlies all his work. He argues that the central reason for Weber's pessimism was that he shifted emphasis in his study of the process of rationalization from an early concern with the development of rational thinking by humans to a later concern with the development of rationalization as the growth of bureaucratic institutions. As a result he lost sight of the cultural process involved in the process of rationalization. Weber's analysis led to the problem of how to develop a rational critical theory if rationalization was identified with domination.

Habermas argues that it is necessary to redefine the meaning of rationalization so that it is not conceived simply as an objective process concerned with the achievement of clearly-defined goals by precise calculation but also as an active process of the development of the subjectivity and knowledgeability of humans. At the heart of this is the idea of communication and understanding, a theory he fully developed in *The Theory of Communicative Action* (1981a). Rationality is redefined away from an exclusive focus on the development of instrumental rationality towards a notion of communicative rationality. In capitalist society this means a critique of seeing the pursuit of profit by clear means as the only rational course, instead talking of rationality as containing an ethical element involving the development of mutual self-understanding. In this sense rationality can be equated with freedom since it enables people to see through falsehoods and thereby enhance their power.

Habermas argues that we can distinguish two types of action, first instrumental action which is

Activity

Consider the following passages from Scott and answer the questions following them:

In order to build his theory of communicative action, Habermas turns to Mead's symbolic interactionism. ... He also turns to ethnomethodology for insight into communicative action. Unlike Giddens, however he sees the ethnomethodologists as providing merely a rather extreme formulation for Mead's ideas. Ethnomethodological ideas must be reined

> *back and consolidated into the mainstream of symbolic interactionism . . .*
>
> *The claims of ethnomethodology were largely ignored by orthodox sociology until they were taken up by Giddens. It is through Giddens' work that ethnomethodology has been brought into the mainstream of sociological analysis. . . .*
>
> *Social development has always been seen by Habermas as a process of evolution, a directional process of change . . . This teleological view of social development differs sharply from the strictly anti-evolutionist model outlined by Giddens, though his actual description of the course taken by social development has considerable similarity to that given by Giddens*
>
> (Scott, 1995, pp. 194, 239, 245)

a Summarize in your own words the differences between Habermas and Giddens as outlined in these passages.

b What similarities might be noted about the aim of both Giddens and Habermas.

c Using material in this chapter and elsewhere, explain exactly what it is in Mead that Habermas uses, and what it is in Garfinkel and ethnomethodology that Giddens uses.

I, A

basically action orientated towards the achievement of a specific goal and the key measure of this action is in terms of success and failure. Getting promoted, pursuing a career or trying to become a millionaire might fall into this category. The second type of action is what he calls communicative action where the aim is not a specific goal but simply understanding and the reaching of agreements.

Since communication is central to understanding and agreement, Habermas is also concerned with language, ideas and symbols and the role they can play in the struggle for emancipation. It is his notion of the importance of agreements which allows Habermas to quote Parsons approvingly, although he is arguing that the goal of such a society is desirable rather than that such a society exists, as Parsons argued. It might be argued that Habermas therefore seeks to construct the theory of action Parsons set out to achieve in his early work but quickly abandoned for the structural emphasis of his later work. In this sense, Habermas is clearly in tune with one of the most notable elements of modern social theory, namely the attempt to consider human as actors and to focus on the process of action rather than simply the identification of actors.

The notion of communicative rationality and communicative action is offered as a way we can retain reason as a liberating force and a standard against which we can measure existing societies. Culture, norms and values are seen as of prime importance and this leads Habermas to reject Marxist attempts to argue that they are in some way purely derived from economic phenomena. However he recognizes the power of the Marxist criticism of capitalism and he himself talks of the way labour relations are exploitative. In essence he sees all these phenomena as examples of the ways culture and structures of power both develop. His aim, of course, is to rescue rationality from the exploitative and dominating ways it has been applied in capitalist society.

He distinguishes between the lifeworld and system. The lifeworld comprises the set of taken-for-granted assumptions that underlay interactions. The lifeworld is the mediation between culture, ethics and social structures. Society evolves through the rationalization of the lifeworld. What this means is that the growth of critical and reflexive thinking allows us to reject traditional customs from the past. This process thereby promotes learning and the evolution of society. His concept of the lifeworld also includes institutions, norms and social practices that help to reproduce society. In contrast, by system he refers to things not linked through shared human communication, and this essentially means those areas where money and power rule, since here there is no need for agreement to be reached. He argues that areas of the lifeworld have become subject to control through money and power and this vision points towards the danger of the system overcoming the lifeworld. For example, information and education are now in some respects commodities sold for profit rather than promoted for mutual understanding. Habermas (1976) calls this the colonization of the lifeworld, but he also argues that this is not seen as legitimate by many people and leads to crisis of legitimacy in modern societies that are more important in many respects than economic crisis. People no longer see corporations and the state as acting in their interests, but instead see them as instruments of domination. Communicative action aims to rescue all aspects of the lifeworld from the stranglehold of the system, thus expanding the areas of social life governed by agreement and communication, rather than by money and power.

The important implication of this is his belief that the positive features of rationalization (that is the growth of rational standards of interpersonal behaviour and the way we reflect on our actions and communicate through arguments judged by their logic and truth) are still evident in society and can therefore be used to create a better world. In summary,

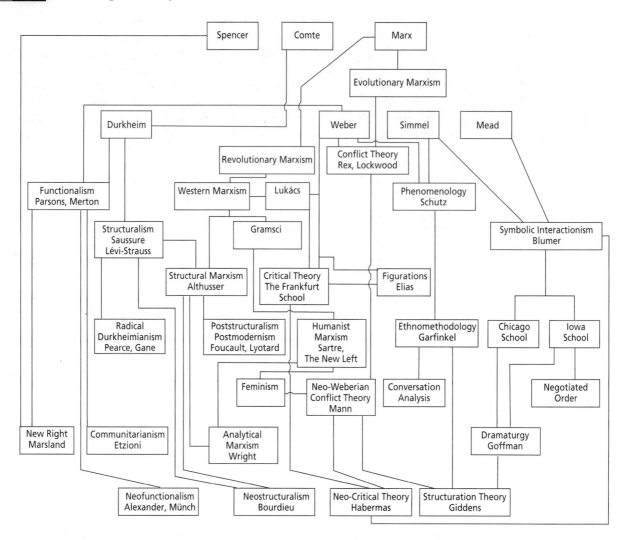

Figure 2.1 Sociology, the war of the perspectives and bringing it all back together again: an interpretation

he turns round Weber's pessimistic ending to provide the opportunity for a happy ending where rationality still has a role to play. This focuses on the way language and communication can be used to achieve agreement and sustain social relationships. In this, however, he faces a key problem explained by Giddens:

Truth is agreement reached through critical discussion. Here Habermas's standpoint seems to face a major difficulty. How are we actually to distinguish a 'rational consensus' – one based upon reasoned agreement – from a consensus based merely on custom, or power?
(Giddens, 1985, p. 130).

Habermas' answer is to argue that the difference is that a consensus arrives purely from the use of logical argument. He sets out a model of what would be required for such a condition to be met which he calls an 'ideal speech situation'. There are essentially two conditions required for such a situation:

- all relevant evidence is presented
- nothing apart from logical argument is involved.

Giddens provides a summary of what this would mean:

An ideal speech situation is one in which there are no external constraints preventing participants from assessing evidence and argument, and in which each participant has an equal and open chance of entering into discussion.
(Giddens, 1985, p. 131)

Habermas' idea is to provide a model of what would be required for society to allow for the full development of communicative rationality. Since this is based on language, it underlies all other possible forms of rationality, including instrumental rationality. Its neglect has not, therefore, meant its elimination and the one-sided nature of the rationalization process can therefore be rectified. The model of communicative rationality would serve as a standard against which we can measure existing societies to see how far they

Activity

Consider the UK today.

a How far do you think discussion and decision-making in the UK meets the criteria of an 'ideal speech situation'?

b Make a list of all the possible ways in which discussion and decision-making in the UK falls short of such a situation. One example might be that the UK possesses a very wide-ranging Official Secrets Act which means that all the evidence might not be presented in all cases, particularly relating to defence. As such this means discussion might fall short of the first criteria Habermas sets for an 'ideal speech situation'.

c On the basis of your answer to (b) discuss in groups reforms which might be made to move the UK closer to the ideal of an 'ideal speech situation'.   **I, A, E**

fall short of this standard. The gap also provides the key areas for campaigns for social change.

It is clear that Habermas' work involves integrating elements from many thinkers, but perhaps the most notable line of criticism is that his work, in contrast to the earlier Frankfurt School, is not critical enough. Marx is less of a presence and Weber and Parsons more of a presence, the latter particularly being the most likely basis for this criticism. In an ideal world we should rationally reach understanding as a way of running society, but the question of how we arrive at that situation and stop the colonization of the lifeworld by the system – to use Habermas' phrases – is a big question and the agent of that change is not entirely evident. Habermas focuses on the New Social Movements (see Section 17.5) but whether they can achieve this remains to be seen.

2.10 Contemporary influences on sociological theory

In this section we will examine some bodies of thought which have widely influenced contemporary sociological debate although they are not confined to or arising solely from sociology itself. These broadly fall into two categories. The first of these is the influence of post-structuralist philosophy and the rise of post-modernism as an approach in sociology.

The second is the influence of political doctrines on social debate. The New Right in particular have been important in affecting both social thinking and the actual social structure through their place in government. Arguably one of the effects has been the radical reshaping of social-democratic thinking and we will examine the rise of communitarian ideas. One of the key critics of the ideas now forming the basis of the New Right was Durkheim. As well as communitarianism we have recently seen the rise of attempts to portray Durkheim as a radical thinker. These ideas will be examined in this section.

Structuralism, post-structuralism and post-modernism

Theories of language have played an increasing role in social thinking in recent years. The reason for this is twofold. First language is inherently social. Even if you wanted to invent a private language you would have to think about the new language in an existing language. There would also be little point in a private language, since language exists to communicate.

The second reason is that when we look for answers to questions (as sociologists do) we think about them and write about them in the form of language. Language not only underlies our existence in society, it also underlies our attempts to analyse that existence through sociology.

'So what?' you might ask. And indeed that would probably have been the common response until 40 or so years ago because it was only then that theories of language changed. It is the implications of that change which have led to post-structuralism and post-modernism.

Conventional theories of language stressed that there was some intrinsic link between an object and the word used to describe it such that the word's meaning rested in some aspect of the object it described. So there is some link between the word 'cat' and the small furry creature with claws that miaows. The link between these two is human consciousness. The implication of this was that through rational thinking, humans could gain knowledge of the outside world.

Structuralism

Saussure (1974, orig. pub. 1915) rejected this approach, though his ideas took until the 1960s to filter to a more general audience. Saussure argued that words, or rather sound-images were not linked to objects in the real world but only to concepts of those objects. He divided language into two elements, the signifier (the sound-image) and the signified (the concept). The way a particular signifier comes to represent a particular signified is seen by Saussure to imply no correspondence between the sound and the object, thus there is no intrinsic link between the sound 'cat' and our concept of the object that word represents.

Instead, Saussure argues that meanings arise from differences between words. In simple terms, this means that the link between language and reality implied by the original correspondence theory of language has gone, language now floats free of the world. Meanings arise simply from the existence of differences. This approach is known as structuralism because it denies any basis for humans being active since human consciousness is no longer seen as the basis of meaning in language. Again underlining this, Lévi-Strauss (1963) argued that language arises from the unconscious.

Post-structuralism

The key shift to post-structuralism came when thinkers such as Lacan (1977) and Foucault (1970, 1972, 1979, 1980) started to argue that the signifier and the signified were not simply two parallel systems but that the signifiers had priority. They argued that there were more signifiers than signified in the world. Whereas with structuralism, the signifier (sound) was always linked to a signified (concept) now this link is broken. Even when talking about the unconscious in the case of Lévi-Strauss, or ideology in the case of Althusser, there is still some link between humans and language even though they are not conscious of it. With post-structuralism even this last link disappears. The importance of the notion of the overabundance of signifiers is that this potentially leads to confusion, in the sense that there are a multitude of ways a particular idea can be expressed. Since there is no link between the words, the ideas and the real world (the link finally destroyed by post-structuralism) we have no access to a measure in the real world by which to decide which of these possible meanings is correct. Humans cannot therefore arrive at anything they can confidently call the truth. Instead all we are left with is collections of statements or 'discourses' whose meaning can only be arrived at by considering their similarity or difference to other discourses, not by recourse to the outside world. The most important implication of this is that the original sociological mission to arrive at a scientific understanding of the world is totally undermined because this requires that our concepts have some relation to the real world, which post-structuralism denies.

Foucault (1980) links these insights with a notion of power to argue that the assignment of meanings is not arbitrary but is a reflection of power struggles (see also Section 17.4). Knowledge is therefore always linked to power and it is those who are powerful who are allowed to define their ideas as the truth. Finding the truth is no longer an objective scientific quest but a power struggle, and science is simply one among many other discourses engaging in this power struggle. The implication is that the nice friendly sociologist who is asking you questions to try to find truths to provide the basis for reforms to make a better world is in fact engaging in a power struggle and is part of the problem, not part of the solution. The applications of science for negative purposes such as the development of nuclear weapons and in the Holocaust fed into this pessimistic image of science. Weber's pessimistic conclusion to his analysis of the process of rationalization also contributed to this atmosphere.

The certainty about the possibility about gaining knowledge of the world is known as modernism. The destruction of this optimism by the arguments of the post-structuralists is therefore one of the main origins of post-modernism. Now it was argued that not only was it not possible to arrive at a final truth, but that such attempts were dangerous. Here Marxism (see Section 2.5) was cited as a doctrine which believes that you can arrive at a final truth and the reality of Stalinist Russia and the Gulag Archipelago was held up as the end result.

Post-modernism

Post-modernism also drew upon critiques of the increasingly bureaucratic and controlling nature of society. As a result it tended towards anarchic calls to celebrate chaos and to live for the moment because there was now no ultimate purpose in life, no overarching reason to human existence. Those who still maintained there was a purpose were denounced as dangerous and potentially authoritarian rulers.

The notion that there is a superabundance of signs was used by Baudrillard (1981, 1983b) who argued that with developments in the media and culture, we now actually consume not necessarily objects but signs or symbols (see Section 10.9). These proliferate as time goes on and this increases our confusion to the point where we are unable to tell the difference between reality and fiction. Commodity production moves from copying the real object to the point where production is a copy of a copy of a copy of a copy and the real object is left far behind. This is what he calls hyperreality where 'reality' is entirely a product of the media and its production of signs. The only form of resistance to this is to refuse to care, to be apathetic, because the ideologies of the mass media depend on us caring. Instead then we should simply treat life as a joke, a game and abandon any attempt to seriously resist or analyse it. Just enjoy the ride while it lasts.

The rather bizarre implications of this line of thinking came out in newspaper articles Baudrillard wrote about the Gulf War in 1991 (see Section 15.6). He argued that it could not happen and then afterwards that it had not happened. The point he was making was that this was a war broadcast directly over the media, but there was no way of telling whether the pictures we were seeing were 'real'. The denial of any access to the truth meant that this was a fruitless question.

The truth about post-modernism

One of the key critics of this approach, Norris, highlighted his belief in the possibility of arriving at truths by entitling one book *The Truth about Postmodernism* (1993). His critique of Baudrillard is brought home in a book written in response to his comments on the Gulf War. Norris argues this position is merely a reflection of intellectual cowardice in the face of US firepower:

one could justifiably argue that Baudrillard was waiting at the end of the road that structuralism and post-structuralism had been travelling for the past three decades and more. . . .

It has finished by promoting a postmodern-pragmatist worldview, which blithely deconstructs the 'notional' difference between 'war' as a simulated pseudo-event . . . and war as a real-world state of affairs in which countless thousands of Iraqi civilian men, women and children were daily being killed in an aerial bombardment of unprecedented scale and ferocity. Small wonder, as I say, that Baudrillards' ideas have achieved such a cult following at a time and in a context – that of the current US drive for renewed world hegemony – when few intellectuals seem able or willing to resist these pressures of ideological recruitment. . . . it brings home with particular force the depth of ideological complicity that exists between such forms of extreme anti-realist or irrationalist doctrine and the crisis of moral and political nerve among those whose voices should have been raised against the actions committed in their name. . . .

The apparent inability of much of what currently passes for critical theory to take any principled oppositional stance on issues of local or world politics must surely be a cause for concern.
(Norris, 1992, p. 27)

The idea that there was nothing we could do clearly outrages those who still desired to develop critical theories of society. Not that this stopped Baudrillard again courting controversy. Bourdieu and Haacke (1995) provide the following comments :

People in New York were not amused by his comparison of AIDS with a 'viral catharsis' which, in his terms, is 'a remedy against total sexual liberation which is often more dangerous than an epidemic' . . . What he and his disciples have lost since is a sense of history and social conflict, which, in spite of the fireworks of the latest intellectual fash-

ions, do not dissolve in the virtual. In short, they have lost a sense for the real.
(Bourdieu and Haacke, 1995, p. 37)

Not surprisingly, post-modernism, while fashionable in certain quarters, has also been incredibly unpopular in others where it is seen as a form of conservatism. This is the view of Habermas (1989), whose project to reformulate the notion of rationality is based on the premise that it is still possible, a view clearly at odds with post-modernism.

The suggestion that there might still be some basis for rational and critical discussion also appears to have surfaced in Foucault's later work. His work on sexuality (1986) led him to suggest that there were possibilities for resistance based on localized struggles and ultimately struggles over the modelling of the human body. Towards the end of his life in a lecture on Immanuel Kant, a philosopher linked to the idea of the existence of reason, Foucault presented Kant not as part of a power-driven process of discourse formation, but as standing at the head of a tradition of critical thinking stretching back through Western Marxism and the Frankfurt School, to which Foucault added his own name. Habermas gives the following account of this change of approach:

Foucault had previously traced this will to knowledge in modern power formations only to denounce it, he now displays it in a completely different light: as the critical impulse that links his own thought with the beginnings of modernity, an impulse worthy of preservation and in need of renewal.
(Habermas, 1989, p. 178)

There is therefore perhaps the hope that post-modernism can draw back from the rather nihilistic versions which have been fashionable for so long and return to the sphere of reason and rationality.

The New Right

The New Right is the name given to the set of ideas which have underlain the relative success of the political right in recent years, perhaps best exemplified in the Thatcher governments in the UK and the Reagan administration in the USA. (See also Sections 4.8, 6.5, 7.4, 8.9, 11.9, 13.6, 14.2, 15.3, 17.3.) These ideas comprise a combination of faith in neo-classical or free market economics emphasizing freedom of choice, but also more conservative notions emphasizing the need for authority and the preservation of traditional institutions in society, notably the family.

The free market

The key rallying theme of the New Right has been opposition to state intervention in people's lives and the extension of the free market to enhance freedom of choice. It is argued by economist Milton Friedman (1980) among others that the free market is an inherently superior way of distributing goods since it enforces efficiency and meets consumer demand. The free market had fallen into intellectual disrepute following the economic depression of the 1930s and instead governments had actively intervened in the economy to try to maintain full employment and economic growth.

Friedman argued that not only was state provision less efficient than private-sector free market provision, but further that state provision actually harmed the free market. This was because government borrowing to pay for public expenditure pushed up interest rates, thereby increased business costs and forced private sector companies out of business. It was therefore argued that there was a need to reduce government expenditure, a need further enhanced by the desire to cut taxes to reduce the burden of the state on people's lives. This aim was based on the ideas of Austrian philosopher von Hayek (1944, 1960) who argued that all forms of state intervention were merely a backdoor way of introducing socialism. He argued that socialism was a system based on the denial of individual freedom. The reasoning behind this was that states are coercive institutions with the power to force people to pay taxes and do certain things. Any increase in power of the state was therefore, in Hayek's phrase leading to 'the road to serfdom'.

Such ideas influenced the development of privatization policies where state-run industries were sold to private investors, with the hope of also encouraging a share-owning democracy, but also with an emphasis on cutting taxation and reducing state expenditure. A particular emphasis was placed on cutting back on welfare expenditure since it was held that this turned people into creatures dependent on the state. This notion underlay arguments about the creation of an underclass possessing separate cultural values from the rest of the population and thereby threatening the fabric of society.

Traditions and families

Despite their support for individual freedom, the New Right were clear on their support for traditional institutions in society, most notably the traditional family. Mount (1982) argues that this is the natural way to care for children and bases this argument on notions of a biological ethic. This approach led him to argue that the development of other forms of family life were subversive of the traditional family and ultimately of society. The growth of single-parent families was seen as leading to the rise of social problems such as juvenile crime and poor educational achievement.

The critique of the welfare state

The welfare state was implicated since it was argued that without the support of benefits provided by it, people would not be able to choose to live in these non-traditional and harmful ways. The New Right supports the notion of a return to traditional family values and this requires changes to the welfare state and the remoralizing of society (see Section 14.3). Perhaps the leading sociologist supporting New Right ideas in the UK is David Marsland. The following extract from his book, *Welfare or Welfare State?* (1996) ranges over some of these topics and provides an indication of the links drawn by the New Right between them:

In studies of youth unemployment, I have regularly found that many young men, unemployed since leaving school at the earliest opportunity, and supported in a life of futile idleness by state benefits, family support and a variegated repertoire of scrounging skills, simply do not want to work. . . . The attitudes they have learned in school and especially at home towards work and money equip them for little but idle moaning, and certainly include little trace of the work ethic. A successful modern society requires the maintenance of a system of economic incentives which reward initiative, enterprise and effort, and penalize laziness and failure. This in turn implies commitment by the population at large – including the less successful and less well-paid – to defending this reward system. . . .

Murrays' [Charles Murray, author of an influential report on the growth of an underclass in Britain, see Section 4.8] *plea for self-reliance, like mine, is precisely a condemnation of specific members of the governing élite for what they have done, and for what they are still doing, to hurt and damage ordinary capable, British people.*

It is socialist politicians, academics and journalists who invented and imposed the Welfare State. It is the fanatical ideologues of collectivist welfare who have undermined the good sense and sound moral values of ordinary people with their 'sophisticated' permissivism. It is the overprivileged intelligentsia who subverted the family, the neighbourhood and the police, and thus sabotaged the normal, natural and necessary process of social control which every community needs.
(Marsland, 1996, pp. 112–16)

The somewhat controversial nature of the Thatcher governments has led to criticisms of the New Right, most notably recently by Will Hutton (1996) who argues that the economic reforms introduced by the New Right have harmed economic prospects, and by increasing levels of inequality have been socially divisive. However the very success of the Conservative

Party while promoting these ideas has led to some reassessment on the political left. This can be seen in the shifts occurring inside the Labour party and we now turn to the emergence of some of the ideas underlying these shifts. (See also Section 17.2.)

> ### Activity
> a Make a list of the social ills identified by Marsland in the extract above.
> b Identify the ideas, individuals or social institutions which he feels are responsible for the growth of these problems.
> c Identify the more general New Right concepts which he is drawing upon in this analysis.
>
> **I, A**

New Labour and sociology

The classical social-democratic project can be seen as active involvement of the state in the economy with the aim of achieving some redistribution of income and wealth and also the liberalization of society to allow more personal freedom in the social sphere. It is clear that some recent trends in social-democratic thinking represent a radical departure from this approach. This shift has been enshrined in the emergence of New Labour whose leader Tony Blair became famous for his argument that there was a need to be tough on crime and tough on the causes of crime. The second part of this statement offers at least some difference from a New Right approach (see Section 11.9) but nonetheless seems to argue for a need to restore law and order. In early 1997, Gordon Brown stated that he would not alter the Conservative government's spending plans for the next two years if elected to government. For many this seemed to signal that there was little prospect of any great change as a result of this election and thus underlined the shift in thinking inside the Labour Party. These themes can be seen in the following extract from a statement by Tony Blair:

How do we construct a society which is cohesive and ordered whilst still allowing individual enterprise and initiative to flourish? . . . the problems posed by this question arise from a failure to understand what radical politics is about. It is not a rigid formula or policy. It is a set of values, an attitude to mind. It believes in progress through reason and justice. It is broadly social in outlook, not narrowly individualistic.
(Blair, 1996, p. 26)

While the last aspect of this clearly provides some degree of differentiation from the New Right, the emphasis on values is seen as an element of the reemergence of a Labour Party based on ethical or moral socialism. Some of the inspirations for this can be seen to come from certain sociological ideas.

Communitarianism

Perhaps the most important of these ideas is the growth of communitarianism (see also Section 16.1), most notably associated with the American sociologist, Etzioni. In his book *The Spirit of Community* (1995) he argues that there is a need to engage in a recommitment to moral values and this leads to a number of more specific arguments concerning the need to save the family, develop a moral aspect to education, restore law and order and for an increase in community through an emphasis on increased social responsibilities. If the old-style social democrats believed in economic collectivism and social liberalism, this rather points to a turn back from social liberalism.

At the same time, the Left appears to now believe in the power of the free-market seemingly on the basis that the process of globalization offers little choice and rules out large-scale state intervention. The emphasis on the need for a moral basis to society, if it has a sociological origin, can be located most obviously in Durkheim (see Section 2.3) though disillusioned ex-Marxists have also recently tried to present Durkheim as a much more radical figure.

A radical Durkheim?

It could be argued that Durkheim is more radical than the present Labour Party. If you read his comment on the condition of workers in France at the time he was writing (the 1890s) you might be excused for thinking the quote came from Marx. For example:

one social class is obliged, in order to live, to offer its services at any price, while the other can do without them, thanks to the resources at its disposal, which are not however necessarily due to any social superiority, the second unjustly dominates the first. In other words, there cannot be rich and poor at birth without there being unjust contracts.
(Durkheim, quoted in Lukes, 1973, p. 175)

Pearce (1989) argues that Durkheim's radicalism is often overlooked because Durkheim was critical of socialists in his time, but Pearce argues that such criticisms may have been caused by the adventurist nature of revolutionary socialist thinking in the nineteenth century. He suggests that a particular interpretation of Durkheim can be used to amend a Marxist understanding of society (see Section 2.5) in order to arrive at a revised version of socialism consisting of:

slimmed down versions of both traditions
(Pearce, 1989, p. xiv)

In essence, this is a reflection on the problems of Marxist analysis in the wake of the collapse of

Structural Marxism and the 'actually existing social-ism' of eastern Europe, but also an attempt to avoid the pessimism of the post-structuralists about social-ist transformations, as Gane makes absolutely clear:

It is now becoming increasingly evident that much of recent conventional commentary on Durkheim and Mauss in English seriously misread just how radical the Durkheimian project attempted to be. Often treated as simple-minded, introductions to sociology present a contrast between Marx and the revolutionary tradition and Durkheim in a conser-vative tradition (Weber representing something of a sophisticated agnosticism). After the historic events in Russia, Eastern Europe and China in the late 1980s, it is now timely to look once again at the writings of Durkheim and the warnings it provided against simplistic revolutionism.

(Gane, 1992, p. 1)

Pearce's evidence for the existence of a 'radical Durkheim' consists of the neglected analysis of the forced division of labour and fatalistic suicide.

It is in this section of the *Division of Labour in Society* (1938, orig. pub. 1893, see Sections 2.3 and 9.2) where Durkheim talked about the appearance of abnormal and pathological elements of modern life. While he foresaw these being eliminated in the full course of the development of organic solidarity, such an evolutionary optimism was very weakly explained and later in life Durkheim reiterated the importance of the need for secondary associations to get involved in social life. He also clearly called for reforms, such as the abolition of inherited wealth, which are most certainly radical. He also provides a clear justification for the involvement of the state in the provision of collective welfare:

If today we have a large number of social vagrants, people from all ranks of society, it is because there is something in our European societies promoting such a condition ... Such obviously social evils require social treatment ... The only effective rem-edy lies in the collective organisation of welfare.

(Durkheim, 1893, in Pearce, 1989, p. 43)

Having demonstrated that it is possible to draw out a version of Durkheim startlingly at odds with the Durkheim filtered through functionalism, Pearce argues that his analysis can provide the basis of a version of socialism.

The limitations of Durkheimian socialism

Now the major criticism of this might be twofold. In essence, it suggests a reformist rather than a revolutionary road to socialism and the previous experience of the Labour Party in government does not suggest this can be guaranteed to deliver. Nonetheless it is clear that the notion of morality has become an important influence on the contemporary Labour Party who could therefore in some sense be described as Durkheimian. Levitas (1996) has used the term Durkheimian to describe some of the key ideas informing contemporary Labour Party ideas, and she is very critical of the idea that these can be seen as radical. Again at the heart of this is the con-trast between normality and pathology emphasized in Durkheim's *Division of Labour in Society* (1938, orig. pub. 1893). She cites Will Hutton's book *The State We're In* (1996) as an example of this type of thinking:

Hutton's book ... presents an essentially Durk-heimian view of the world. Hutton explicitly pur-sues 'an efficient and socially cohesive capitalism' [1995]. Moreover his basic argument is that the ills of contemporary British society stem not from the nature of capitalism, but from the particular pathologies of British financial and governmental institutions. Despite the undoubted merits of Hutton's analysis of the workings of the British economy, this assertion that it is a pathological and abnormal form – and hence that the social divisions engendered are also essentially pathological and abnormal – is as implausible as Durkheim's origi-nal argument that the forced division of labour as expressed in actually existing capitalist society con-stituted a pathological and abnormal form of the division of labour.

(Levitas 1996, p. 17)

She goes on to argue that there are problems with the proposed Durkheimian solution based on social inclusion since this is invariably defined in terms of paid employment. It thus ignores inequalities among those in employment and also ignores the issue of unpaid work, a particular issue with great relevance for the position of women in society.

This leads to the second criticism. Although Pearce demonstrates convincingly that there are ambiguities in Durkheim, they remain this and ulti-mately it might be argued that his emphasis on the need for moral order and social integration enforced by the law and the state if necessary present a rather authoritarian picture of society. This can certainly be said to be true of the other main contemporary off-shoot of the Durkheimian tradition (albeit one not very radical and much influenced by functionalism), namely communitarianism.

Further **reading**

- Slattery, M. (1991) *Key Ideas in Sociology*, Basingstoke, Macmillan.

  This contains summaries of about 50 sociolo-gists outlining the key concepts they developed.

- Jones, P. (1993b) *Studying Society: Sociological Theories and Research Practices*, London, Collins Educational.

  This book gives very readable accounts of sociological theory and includes arguably the best explanation of the ideas of post-structuralism and post-modernism. It also shows the clear links between theories and methods.

- Cuff, E. C., Sharrock, W. W. and Francis, D. W. (1990) *Perspectives in Sociology*, 3rd edn, London, Routledge.

  An extremely useful book covering all the major sociological theories in a very user-friendly way. The third edition also includes a chapter on critical theory including reference to both the Frankfurt School and Habermas.

The following recent books consider contemporary developments in theory:

- Craib, I. (1992) *Modern Social Theory*, 2nd edn, Hemel Hempstead, Harvester-Wheatsheaf.

- Layder, D. (1994) *Understanding Social Theory*, London, Sage.

- Scott, J. (1995) *Sociological Theory: Contemporary Debates*, Aldershot, Edward Elgar.

- May, T. (1996) *Situating Social Theory*, Buckingham, Open University Press.

Back issues of the periodical *Sociology Review* (formerly known as *Social Studies Review*) also contain many articles on this field of sociology and many others.

Exam **questions**

1 Compare and contrast the contributions of structural theories and interactionist theories to an understanding of social life.   [25 marks]
(AEB, Paper 2, Summer 1995)

2 Compare and contrast Marxist and functionalist theories of social change.   [25 marks]
(AEB, Paper 2, Summer 1996)

3 Assess sociological explanations of the role of ideas in both promoting and preventing social change.   [25 marks]
(AEB, AS level, Paper 2, Summer 1996)

4 Assess the claim made by interactionists that the social world has to be explained in terms of the meanings that actors give to their actions.
[25 marks]
(AEB, Paper 2, Summer 1994)

Coursework **suggestions**

Your coursework needs to include both theoretical and empirical elements but one way in which to approach this is to apply concepts developed by sociologists to a particular situation. All of these require you to consider the meaning of these concepts in detail and then operationalize them in a way which allows you to gather empirical material. The following are suggested:

1 **Compare the analysis of power and institutions provided by Foucault and Goffman and apply them to old people's homes in your area.**

2 **Compare the Durkheimian concept of *anomie* and the Marxist concept of *alienation* and apply them to a study of the attitudes of young people to contemporary society.**

3 **Compare the functionalist concept of value consensus and the notions of conflict theory and apply them to an analysis of pupil–teacher relations in your school.**

4 **Adapt one of Garfinkel's breaching experiments for your own use.**
   The example of being a lodger in your own home offers some possibilities.

As always you should consult your tutor or teacher fully before engaging in any aspect of sociology coursework.

3

Research methods

3.1 Positivism as a methodological tradition

The basic starting point for positivists is a belief that sociology should be scientific – meaning that it should use, as far as possible, the procedures for considering evidence developed by the natural sciences. Positivists believe that the relationship between evidence and explanation is based on the notion that concepts which try to describe classes of phenomena are not real in the sense that individual

things are. This position is known as 'nominalism'. One important variant of this is the doctrine of 'empiricism' which stresses that science can proceed only by the collection of facts, by which is meant observable phenomena only. Not all positivists are empiricists in this sense, though the two terms have often been confused. Christopher Bryant particularly emphasizes this when he states:

Comte condemned theory without observation as 'mysticism', and observation without theory as 'empiricism' (1844, p. 25). The latter in particular

cannot be overstressed given that many contemporary social scientists simply equate positivism with a crude empiricism.
(Bryant, 1985, p. 14)

This point serves to underline the fact that sociologists disagree about the meaning of 'positivism'. This section considers the three major variants of positivism in sociology, based largely on distinctions elaborated by Bryant (1985), namely:

- classical positivism
- logical positivism
- instrumental positivism.

Classical positivism

Classical positivism derives from the work of Saint-Simon (1819, 1825) and Auguste Comte (1830, 1851) who saw sociology's role as providing information which would inform the new enlightened rulers of society. In order to do this, Comte (see also Section 2.2) argued that sociology should use the methods of the natural sciences. It is this belief which is the central defining aspect of positivism, as Bryant makes clear:

Positivism in sociology has come to be associated with the very idea of a social science and the quest to make sociology scientific.
(Bryant, 1985, p. 1)

The reason for this desire was the important role the natural sciences played in the Enlightenment, being seen as the epitome of the new form of knowledge which offered tremendous possibilities and benefits for humanity. If sociology could imitate the methodology of the natural sciences, Comte reasoned, then it would be able to provide information of a calibre required to fulfil the role he defined for it.

Comte's most famous notion is the idea that society – or more specifically the human mind – has evolved through three stages of development. This is his Law of the Three Stages:

- In the first stage, the 'theological', everything is assumed to be caused by some supernatural being and therefore humanity searches for the origin and purpose of everything in some wish of this supernatural being.
- In the second stage, the 'metaphysical', deities are replaced by abstract forces of some nature present in all things, and debate is about the nature and correct identification of these forces through speculation and philosophical reasoning.
- Abandonment of the search for absolute causes characterizes the emergence of the third, 'positive', stage:

In the final, positive stage, the mind has given over the vain search after Absolute notions, the origin and destination of the universe, and applies itself to the study of their laws – that is, their invariable relations of succession and resemblance. Reason and observation, duly combined are the means of this knowledge.
(Comte, 1853, vol. 1, p. 1)

There are two important points here. First, the quotation above demonstrates Comte's belief that there are laws which explain how society works. Secondly, through reasoning and observation, particular facts can be linked to these laws, allowing us to gain knowledge of them – which, however, exist whether we know about them or not. In other words, the world has an *objective existence*.

As science progressed, society could be fully explained by these laws. This would allow knowledge to be used for *positive* reasons – that is, for social reform. Comte believed that science in this sense implied abandoning any metaphysical or philosophical speculations about the origin of things, and instead confining oneself to theories about accessible (that is, observable) phenomena. In simple terms, the positivists believed that sociology should seek to adapt the methods of the natural sciences so that the scientific method becomes the basis of a positivist methodology. That which cannot be known scientifically cannot be known, as science becomes the only basis of knowledge. Positivism in sociology might therefore be summarized as:

. . . the assertion that the concepts and methods employed in the natural sciences can be applied to form a 'science of man', or a natural science of sociology.
(Giddens, 1974, p. 3)

This leads to the question of how sociology could, or should, imitate the natural sciences. The central method of the natural sciences, the experiment based in a laboratory, was mentioned by Comte as one possible method, but it is not something sociology could easily utilize. One cannot literally put society in a laboratory; and while it is possible to test human behaviour in a laboratory the unnatural environment would most likely lead to unnatural behaviour which would undermine the whole enterprise. However, the aim of making sociological findings scientific could still be approached even though the exact mechanisms of the techniques to be used needed to be worked out.

As well as experiments, Comte argued that the methods of observation, comparison and the historical method could be used. Comparison allows us to look at two different societies or different phenomena and, by observing similarities and differences, gain knowledge of how they operate. Comparison of societies at different periods in history allows us to look at the way things change.

It is perhaps with the implications and use of this knowledge that Comte's beliefs become more controversial. He argued that the adoption of the scientific method would ensure that the laws of the universe were uncovered, thus ending the need for choices to be made. Bryant spells out the implications of this:

Once such laws are presumed to obtain, there can be no more justification, as Comte pointed out, for freedom of opinion in social matters than there is in astronomy. Instead the laws of social statics and dynamics provide applied sociology with the means to determine all moral and political questions scientifically.
(Bryant, 1985, pp. 20 and 32)

As sociology was the highest science, sociologists would determine policy. It is this approach which led Comte later in his *System of Positive Polity* (1851) to see sociologists as the priests in his 'religion of humanity'. Saint-Simon had earlier emphasized the need for a 'new Christianity' (1825) – meaning a new set of ethics – because he believed that, while the educated would accept the findings of science and would comply, the ignorant might still need some form of religion. Similarly Comte argued that such a 'religion of humanity' was needed to instil correct behaviour in the working class, through festivals emphasizing adherence to Humanity rather than God and underlining their social duties.

Evaluating classical positivism

While these notions of 'religion' were dismissed by other social thinkers and later by Durkheim, they do offer an insight into the possible realization of the limitations of the development of science and positivism which undermines the earlier confidence of Comte and Saint-Simon. However, what both the earlier and later versions share is a view of sociologists telling people how to live their lives – a fairly authoritarian view. This aspect of positivism has led to later criticism, notably from the Frankfurt School.

Although notions of a 'religion of humanity' would not be taken particularly seriously today, the question of how sociology can use the scientific method is clearly still an important one. A number of questions flow out of this. Most importantly, how can sociology adapt the methods of the natural sciences?

Since the object of research is different, we cannot simply apply without modification the methods of the natural sciences, since this would entail the banal conclusion that society and people within it can be investigated by means of pouring acid on them, heating them up or putting them in a test-tube to see what would happen. Clearly this is not what is meant. However, it leads to the question of how far a modification creates not an adaptation but a new qualitatively different methodology.

So exactly how much adaptation is allowed before we are dealing with something else altogether? The basic point to be adapted seems to boil down to the notion that all knowledge derives from observation and reasoning, and that all such knowledge must be verified by reference to the real world, which operates according to laws or law-like generalizations which are discoverable by application of this method of observation and reasoning. This general view is applicable to any object (either natural or social) and this, then, is what is meant by the adoption of the methods of the natural sciences.

The emphasis on laws is perhaps the weakest aspect of positivism, since this leads to a contradiction. If society is governed by laws that operate independently of our awareness of them (it is not necessary for you to be aware of the law of gravity for the apple to fall), then why should we need a priesthood of sociologists or sociology at all, since whatever was going to happen according to the laws of society would happen anyway? If laws of society are held to operate in the same way as the laws of the natural world:

. . . it would make no difference whether positivist sociologists succeeded or not in the accumulation of positive knowledge.
(Bryant, 1985, p. 17)

Some theories do indeed present humans as being like puppets who are simply determined by the operation of laws. The presence of this notion of laws (not only of sociology but of society) is the most problematic aspect of positivism. Comte did believe in some way that such knowledge could help us to predict the future; but that implies that the laws are in some way not laws, or that we might know when something was going to happen but not be able to do anything about it. All the time this comes back to the fundamental question of sociological theory: are humans' experiences totally determined for them, or can they make real choices and so affect the course of human development?

Discussion point

To what extent do you think sociology can help humankind to predict the future? Would such knowledge be of any use?

Today, few would accept Comte's rather rigid belief in the laws of society (arguably few did even in Comte's time). This does not necessarily entail disavowal of the scientific method, though it does mean we cannot accept the full-blown version of Comtian positivism. Emile Durkheim (1938a; orig. pub. 1893), for example, does not seem to argue that society is based on the operation of inviolable laws, since his analysis of the 'division of labour' (see Sections 2.3 and 9.2) at least allows for the possibility of society developing in normal or abnormal ways – and therefore the need for action in the form of reforms to avoid abnormality. This is clearly not a totally determinist view, but Durkheim (1938b, orig. pub. 1895) shares with Comte the idea that society is a reality *sui generis* and therefore independent of the actions of the individuals within it; and there is still therefore a degree of determinism in his views which would certainly be unacceptable to sociologists in the social-action tradition influenced by phenomenological views (see Sections 2.7 and 2.8).

Thus, while positivists share the idea that the social sciences should seek to be scientific – and that this involves adapting in some way the methods of the natural sciences – the actual way in which that view is worked out differs. In other words there is more than one variety of positivism, and these variants developed by thinking about the problems in Comte's schema. In terms of the development of sociology in the UK, it is arguably *logical positivism* that has had the greatest influence, and which people are generally referring to when they talk of 'positivism'.

Logical positivism

The Vienna Circle and the 'verification principle'

This version of positivism grew out of attempts in the 1920s and 30s by analytical philosophers known as the Vienna Circle (1929) to define a universal method for science. This attempt was supported by three representatives of the scientific world, namely Albert Einstein, Bertrand Russell and Ludwig Wittgenstein.

They argued that there were really only two bases for science, namely (a) empirical statements and (b) analytical statements of logic. This meant that only empirical data could serve as a basis for knowledge, and in considering such data scientists must apply the rules of logic to their theories. As Bryant comments:

The logical positivists went much further than Comte in that they demanded something he opposed, the identification of positivism with empiricism.
(Bryant, 1985, p. 112)

The aim was to resolve age-old philosophical debates by rendering them into statements which could then be tested through empirical investigation, known as hypotheses. They allowed of no notion that there were things unamenable to such testing, since they were unknowable or unobservable. Such statements merely existed because methods to observe and test them had not yet been properly worked out.

Once the data have been collected, the question arises of whether the hypothesis is confirmed or not. In relation to this, the Vienna Circle argued that the issue was of *verification*. If the hypothesis is confirmed or verified by the data, then it counts as scientific knowledge. Otherwise, not only is the hypothesis not scientific knowledge, it is utterly meaningless.

The implication of this was that statements only had meaning in so far as they referred to observable experience in the world. Everything – even the meanings people construct – is a physical event located in a particular space and time. Thus the social sciences could use the same method and verification test as the natural sciences, and there was no justification for the argument (associated most famously with Max Weber, and the basis for the whole social-action tradition in sociology – see Sections 2.7 and 2.8) that there was a need for a separate notion of social research based on 'understanding', as opposed to the natural scientific notion of 'explanation'.

The key problem with this idea is that it set up a standard, the verification principle, which cannot itself be verified. Jary and Jary explain this as follows:

A further telling criticism – the so-called 'paradox of positivism' – is that the Verification Principle is itself unverifiable.
(Jary and Jary, 1991, p. 485)

Karl Popper and 'falsification'

Karl Popper (1959), philosopher of science, wrestled with the verification paradox by arguing that it was necessary to set a different standard. He argued that instead of seeking to verify their hypotheses, scientists should instead seek to falsify them. He argued that it was not true to say that statements that are not verifiable are meaningless, and he instead argued that they are simply statements that have not yet been falsified. If we wish to develop these into scientific knowledge, we must recast them in terms which would allow of the *possibility* that they could be falsified. The importance of this is the rejection of the idea implicit in the original positivist formulation that it is possible to approach universal knowledge.

Popper argued that just because something has been verified lots of times, this is no proof that it will always be true (thus identifying the central problem of inductive reasoning) and it is possible it might be falsified at some point. The true test of knowledge is whether it is formulated in ways which *allow* of this falsifiability, and the true test of science is that it should seek to falsify things. It is knowledge if it has resisted falsification so far, despite being framed in such a way as to allow falsification. This does not, however, imply that it will be knowledge for all time.

This means that science needs to start with statements that can be tested – 'hypotheses'. In order to ensure it can be tested, a statement should be as precise as possible. The inspiration for a hypothesis might come from observation, but equally it might come from thinking about something. Sense-experience is therefore not seen as the sole basis of scientific knowledge. This is the basis of the approach known as the 'hypothetico-deductive' methods, the stages of which are illustrated in Figure 3.1.

Because statements may be falsified at some point in the future, Popper's argument points towards the impossibility of ever arriving at absolute knowledge – since this depends on being able to count something as true for all time and gradually adding to such statements until everything is known. An important implication of this is that the kind of grand schemas for wholesale societal reform outlined by Comte (see Section 2.2) are undermined. According to Popper, science cannot predict the future, merely know something about what is true today. In practical policy terms this points towards the advocacy of piecemeal social reform and gradual evolution, a view which also led Popper to be critical of Marxism.

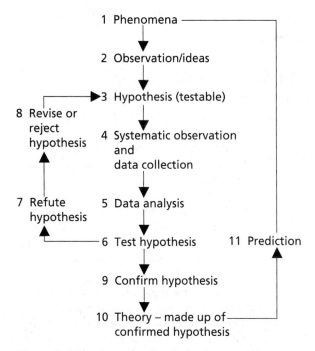

Figure 3.1 The hypothetico-deductive model.
Source: McNeill (1985, p. 42)

The distinction between verification and falsification means that, although Popper had some connections with the logical positivists, he is not really a positivist in this sense – and he himself rejected the label. Actually his ideas tend to point towards a realist view of science. This is because he rejected the idea of induction, and because he argued that as a consequence all scientific statements are intrinsically theory-bound. However, his argument that the facts (theory-bound though they are) could be tested empirically at least left him associated in many eyes with positivism, widely defined.

Evaluating logical positivism

Popper was attacked as a positivist by those in the 'critical theory' tradition (see Sections 2.6 and 3.2) who argued that, if facts were theory-bound, then so were the tests designed to falsify or verify those facts. Thus science was not a method capable of escaping the theories out of which its statements emerged. Positivism was therefore necessarily adopting concepts which promoted the interests of powerful groups, since these arose from the existence of a 'dominant ideology' in society (see Section 17.4). By disavowing criticism as value-laden, positivists did not arrive at a scientific truth, merely a form of ideology which justified the existing state of society.

This line of argument has also been taken up by another philospher of science, Thomas Kuhn, whose book *The Structure of Scientific Revolutions* (1970) emerged out of a series edited by two members of the Vienna Circle. Basically Kuhn argues that scientists work within sets of ideas or paradigms that do not derive from, and are not sustained by, their proximity to facts alone. Because their careers depended on it, they were unlikely to take risks most of the time. This idea undermined the notion of the scientist as a detached observer, concerned with the careful testing of hypotheses – and therefore ultimately undermined the notion of science the logical positivists had sought to build on. Kuhn's work is examined in more detail in Section 3.3.

Instrumental positivism

This version of positivism grew up in the USA in the late 1930s, and has dominated American sociology. The term 'instrumental positivism' to describe this school originates with Bryant (1985). It is positivist in the sense that it is based on the idea that we should generate knowledge through empirical research; but its key distinguishing characteristic is the belief that research should be confined to areas where research techniques which would provide such evidence already exist.

The implication is a clear limiting of the areas of social scientific investigation, and implicitly this pushes instrumental positivism much more towards empiricism than can be found in either logical or classical positivism. There is an almost complete reliance on quantitative data in the form of statistics (see Section 3.6), and the development of ever more elaborate statistical techniques to analyse data. This can be seen in the book *The People's Choice* by Lazersfeld *et al.* (1944) (see also Section 15.9), which was an empirical investigation into political decision-making through refinement of the opinion poll technique.

This overall approach meant that sociology was to be based on the gradual accumulation of knowledge, primarily through statistical analysis. It was to be scientific in the sense of not being concerned overtly with the question of the uses to which the data were to be put, or indeed with any attempt to argue that sociological knowledge could help create a better society. 'Taking a stand' was seen to undermine objectivity, leading to their promotion of value-freedom as a key element in the instrumental approach. Equally, theory was rejected as not being based on data and as such effectively excluded from what counts as sociology.

That said, it did appear that instrumental positivists acted on an implicit theory of society, since they believed that knowledge could be based on the findings generated by questionnaires administered to individuals, summarized as:

> ... the development of a total portrait of man derived from the combination of discrete question-naires, surveys and other 'atomic' facts.
> (Horowitz, 1968, p. 200)

This points to a view which believes that society is merely the sum of the individuals within it, fitting in with the individualistic ethos of the society in which this variant of positivism was born. An important implication is that any notion of social structures, which cannot be measured by such methods, disappears.

Such an approach in American sociology contrasts with the attempt by Talcott Parsons (1937, 1951) to arrive at a 'grand theory' of society (see Section 2.4). The rise of functionalism to prominence in sociology undermined the appeal of instrumental positivism's attack on theory, but did not necessarily undermine the use of the approach they identified. Statistical analysis remained dominant.

Evaluating instrumental positivism

The disdain for theory and social structures in this approach led to it being criticized in the 1960s and 70s. In his book *The Sociological Imagination*, C. Wright Mills (1959) described it as 'abstracted empiricism' whereby sociology became merely a matter of considering individuals abstracted from their place in wider social structures. Thus he argued that Lazersfeld and colleagues had tried to examine American politics merely by reference to the voters' choices and the media, without examining the wider structures of power within which they operated. Other radical sociologists also suggested that the notion of value-neutrality held by these researchers in effect meant that sociologists became merely empirical researchers up for hire to the highest bidder. This, it was argued, made them complicit with various questionable operations undertaken by the American government, notably in Latin America. The key example of this is the notorious Project Camelot. The nature of this project and the issues surrounding it have been summarized by Bilton *et al*:

> In its natural concern for social order in the lower half of the continent, the Pentagon wished to discover the causes of revolt and remove them. In order to achieve this, they planned to spend up to six million dollars and recruit a huge team of political scientists and sociologists to work in the countries concerned. Their employer made the aims clear in a recruiting letter: 'The US Army has an important mission in the positive and constructive aspects of nation-building in less-developed countries as well as a responsibility to assist friendly governments in dealing with active insurgency problems.' The aims were equally clear to the South American governments concerned, and they rapidly forced the abandonment of the project, with accusations of spying and covert intervention by the United States. All this came as a shock to those who agreed to take part, for they believed they were aiding those countries by advocating policies such as land reform which would remove the need for revolution. It is a sad comment on social scientists that they could be so naive about the intentions of the powerful.
> (Bilton *et al.*, 1987, p. 607)

Activity

Suggest elements of Project Camelot which identify it as being derived from the ideas of instrumental positivism.

I, A

3.2 Hermeneutics and phenomenology as a methodological tradition

While positivists stress that sociology can in some sense adapt the methods of the natural sciences to its own purposes, since the social world just like the natural world is an objective reality which exists independently of our awareness and knowledge of it, it is the denial of this point that marks out phenomenological and hermeneutic approaches. This leads to an approach which stresses the importance of *interpretation* and the way knowledge is socially constructed.

Hermeneutics arose originally as a way of interpreting texts and other static representations of human life. It is this approach which lies behind Max Weber's famous notion of *Verstehen* as the central aim of sociology, since this means 'to understand'.

Phenomenology equally seeks to understand, but in this case is concerned with understanding the way that order and regularity are actively created by humans through the construction of meanings. It is further concerned with explaining how these constructions come to be seen as natural. This brings it into clear conflict with positivism which believes the world is a reality external to individuals. These insights have had various implications for discussions about methodology which will be examined here.

The key point of phenomenology is that humans think about things: they are conscious beings and their actions are therefore not equivalent to those of atoms or rocks. The ideas that a person has in his or her head as part of this consciousness are a crucial part of being human. Any study of humanity cannot therefore rest on a notion of an objective world existing in isolation from our awareness of it. In fact our awareness of the world is an important part in its construction, since humans are active thinking beings and any notion of human society and the study of human society must start from this insight. It follows that we cannot utilize the methods of the natural sciences because one of the key differences between the natural and the social sciences relates to their subject matter. The social sciences are interested in the actions, motives and intentions of human beings: 'intentional explanation is the feature that distinguishes the social sciences from the natural sciences' (Elster, 1983, p. 69).

People make choices, and this makes the social world to some extent unpredictable and not therefore amenable to law-like statements, unlike the natural world. This has a further important implication for the question of whether we can simply observe a world which exists separately from our observations of it. Anthony Giddens (1976) wrote his book *The New Rules of the Sociological Method* partly as a conscious refutation of the positivistic elements to be found in Durkheim's earlier *Rules of the Sociological Method* (see also Section 2.3). Giddens explains this in his later book on positivism and sociology:

Durkheim proposed that social phenomena should be treated like things: we should regard ourselves as though we were objects in nature. Thereby he accentuated the similarities between sociology and natural science. . . . although this type of standpoint has been very pervasive in sociology, it is one I reject. . . . We cannot approach society, or 'social facts', as we do objects in the natural world, because societies exist in so far as they are created and re-created in our own actions as human beings. . . . It follows from this that the practical implications of sociology are not directly parallel to the technological uses of science, and cannot be. Atoms cannot get to know what scientists say about them, or change their behaviour in the light of that knowledge. Human beings can do so.
(Giddens, 1986, pp. 11–12)

Discussion point

What are the implications of Giddens' arguments for the actual methods of research adopted by sociologists and for whether sociology can be a science?

This view leads on to the phenomenological and hermeneutical approaches in sociology, centred on the idea that it *does* matter crucially that the object of analysis is qualitatively different from that of the natural sciences. This is not an excuse to reject rigour in methodology, but instead a belief that sociologists cannot simply adapt the methods of the natural sciences. So, reflections on the nature of humanity lead to the rejection of positivism.

The most notable classical contribution to his approach came in the work of Max Weber (see also Section 2.3). He argued that the starting point for any sociology was an understanding of the subjective meanings that people use in the process of interaction. Thus, social research cannot exclude consideration of the subjective feelings of people as positivists had suggested, since in reality the object of sociological research *is* a subjective being. The reality that we wish to investigate is in fact made by people through the active construction of meanings which people engage in when they interact. Weber argued that it was necessary to reject the notion that there could be any universal causal laws governing society, which was a key element of classical positivism. He argued instead that it was necessary to understand the *motives* behind any particular action in order to arrive at an understanding of a situation. He said this should be the task of sociology, starting from a recognition of the importance of seeing humans as engaging in subjectively meaningful actions, and therefore as different from the objects of research in the natural sciences. McNeill provides the following summary of Weber's approach:

If we are to explain some event in the social world, our explanation has to take into account what the people involved think and feel. We must not regard them simply as helpless puppets.
(McNeill, 1985, p. 111)

The reasons for human behaviour are therefore internal to people, not external as classical positivism claimed. Following this line of criticism of positivism, Georg Simmel – a contemporary of Weber – even went so far as to argue that sociology should be seen almost as an art form (see Section 2.7).

Discussion point

a To what extent does the fact that human beings are subjective conscious actors undermine the idea that sociology can be a science?

b Should it be seen as an art form?

c What do you think sociology as an art form would involve?

In contrast, Weber did wish to retain some notion of sociology as a science, by which he meant it must have methodological rigour. He rejected the particular version of sociology as a science embodied in positivism because of his views on the centrality of human subjective consciousness to an explanation of human action.

However, a second element of Weber's argument has been the subject of much later controversy. While rejecting positivism, he asserted that there needed to be a clear distinction between facts and values in social research. He argued that it was possible to arrive at an objective understanding of the subjective meanings people attribute to their actions in the world.

It is important at this point to distinguish Weber's position from the rather cruder versions of this idea present in instrumental positivism (see Section 3.1). That view of sociology – almost merely as a technique – meant that instrumental positivists saw it in principle as usable by anyone, and they further felt that to let values enter into decisions about who or what is studied was not objective. As we have seen, this led them to fail to avoid becoming the handservants of the US military in various pieces of 'social research'. This is not at all what Weber wanted to say, since he argued (a) that scientists should be responsible in their approach and have a concern for the consequences of their work: 'An attitude of moral indifference has no connection with scientific "objectivity"' (Weber, quoted in Giddens, 1971, p. 138); and (b) that values do enter into the choices of subject

matter to be researched. The reason for this rests on his rejection of the possibility of ever arriving at an overall universal theory of society. Instead he argued that the problems arise in particular historical circumstances. Since these particular circumstances will also affect the values individuals hold, and so dictate what will be of interest to them, the choice of topics for study is inherently value-relative, that is governed by people's values.

This did *not* mean that Weber was willing to reduce science merely to values, since he did believe it was possible ultimately to arrive at an objective understanding of society. He thought it was not possible to arrive at statements of policy from statements of fact; that is, one cannot derive *evaluative* statements about what should or should not be by starting from statements about *what is*. (This comes from the philosophical argument that one cannot derive an 'ought' statement from an 'is' statement.) Weber contended that while it was the duty of sociologists to outline to the best of their competence the facts, they should not – as the classical positivists had suggested was possible – argue that this negates the need for moral and political choices to be made. Indeed Weber was insistent that such responsibilities not only could not, but should not, be lifted from the citizens by sociologists. The contrast with classical positivism can be seen in the comparison of statements by Weber and Comte:

It can never be the task of an empirical science to provide binding norms and ideals from which directives for immediate practical activity can be derived.
(Weber, 1949a, p. 52; orig. pub. 1904)

The social sciences, which are strictly empirical sciences, are the least fitted to presume to save the individual the difficulty of making a choice, and they should therefore not create the impression that they can do so.
(Weber, 1949b, p. 18; orig. pub. 1917)

Science would ensure that correct policy was followed whatever the situation; indeed it would make moral and political 'choice' a misnomer insofar as man possessed of positive knowledge has only the choice between compliance with what the laws of succession and resemblance require or non-compliance, which has as its inevitable consequence eventual failure accompanied by the generation of unnecessary social costs.
(Bryant, 1985, p. 20 – describing the views of Comte)

His attempt to create some more general notion of society led him to construct 'ideal-types'. By these, Weber meant effectively simplified abstract notions of what exists in the ideal world of thought, rather

Activity

a Explain in your own words the difference between Comte and Weber over the issue of whether sociology can be used to determine policy choices.

b Suggest the key distinct problems associated with each of these two contrasting views.

c Evaluate the relative merits of each position in relation to contemporary social policy debates.

I, A, E

than actually representing something which concretely exists in the world. The ideal-types would not in all likelihood exist in their full-blown versions: they represent Weber's attempt to argue that, while it should be recognized that we are imposing order on a rather more complex reality through the methods of science, nonetheless this is a necessary stage in ensuring coherence and direction to sociological enquiries.

This highlights Weber's rather ambiguous position. While wishing to start from the basis of subjective experiences, he nonetheless wants to cling to some notion of objective understanding.

The phenomenological critique

The ambivalence of Weber's position presents a problem. Alfred Schutz (1972) argues that the attempt to scientifically understand human subjective behaviour was flawed because the interpretation of events and meanings given by the social scientist could differ from those of the person being studied. Schutz therefore argued that sociology should confine itself to the actual methods people used to construct meanings, rather than trying to impose meanings. It is this insight which led to the development of phenomenology and ethnomethodology (see also Section 2.8).

The methodological implications of this line of argument are, first, that sociologists should observe behaviour in its natural setting; and secondly, that the overall aim must be to achieve an understanding of the thought processes of humans which direct their actions.

The approach of the Chicago School which developed out of the insights of George Herbert Mead (1934) and 'symbolic interactionism' (see Section 2.7) can be seen as an important example, providing a clear contrast to the statistically driven view of sociology as a technique presented by instrumental positivism, but arising at broadly the same time.

The Chicago School argued that the key problem with the questionnaires and opinion polls used by instrumental positivists was that they were written by the researchers and were therefore based on assumptions about what was important. The Chicago School asserted that no assumptions should be made beforehand, and so they advocated the use of observation techniques (see Section 3.9) to allow researchers to get involved with people engaged in everyday activities. The belief that people should be studied in their natural environments also contained a critique of positivism, since it was argued all other forms of research, including questionnaires (see Section 3.7), were an unnatural form of communication. Thus there was no guarantee that such methods would arrive at a valid – that is to say, accurate – portrayal of human action and thought.

The whole tradition of 'social-action sociology' therefore rests on statements concerning human consciousness, and the implication that the methods of the natural sciences are not appropriate to the study of human interactions (or society).

However, while this approach stressed the need to study human subjectivity in a naturalistic setting, it did nonetheless assume that the facts generated by such observation were available to be collected and did represent reality. Against this it has been argued that what are considered 'facts' are mediated by our theories of the world, and so there is no such thing as a natural fact waiting to be gathered. This was the basis of realist criticisms of phenomenologically inspired methodologies, which are examined in Section 3.3.

The Frankfurt School and 'critical theory'

At this point it is necessary to return to a second aspect of Weber's thinking which led to later criticisms – namely his attempt to argue that sociology could be both value-relative and value-free. The context of this criticism was debate between the logical positivists and the 'critical theorists' of the Frankfurt School (see also Section 2.5).

In 1961 a debate was held at Tübingen in Germany between Karl Popper and Frankfurt School theorist Theodor Adorno concerning the status and methodology of the social sciences – themes also taken up in a later debate between Hans Albert and Jürgen Habermas. These debates summarized the differences between positivism represented by Popper and Albert (although Popper rejected that label himself) and the 'critical theory' of Adorno and Habermas (Adorno et al., 1976). 'Critical theorists' reject positivism for two main reasons.

The first rejection of positivism

Critical theorists reject the idea (most prominent in logical and instrumental positivism) that empirical data are the key element of science. Bearing in mind that the Frankfurt School had been located in America between 1934 and 1950, its leading lights had had the opportunity to witness American social science at first hand, and by and large they did not like what they saw. What was presented as social science was, in essence, large amounts of opinion polls. Social surveys, no doubt technically correct in relation to sampling and the wording of questions, simply elicited people's opinions on a wide range of subjects. Pollack rejected the idea that these findings could be seen as scientific:

The concept of opinion held by current opinion . . . operates with a subjective concept of truth, without even a glance at the problem of the objective. Objectivity, on which it prides itself so much, is nothing but a generality abstracted from subjectivities of this kind – the common denominator of opinions, as it were, unrelated to their objective validity.
(Pollack, 1955, p. 85; quoted in Bryant, 1985, p. 122)

To clarify what Pollack meant, consider a hypothetical finding of a social survey. If it asked people whether the earth was flat and found that 70 per cent did believe that the earth was flat (admittedly unlikely, but certainly not impossible), what could one conclude? Does this present objective proof that the earth is flat, or merely objective demonstration that the subjective beliefs of most people are wrong?

Discussion point

If 70 per cent of people in a survey thought the earth was *not* flat, would that make the findings more scientific or not?
What can this tell us about notions of objectivity and science?

In case you are thinking that this example is so far-fetched as to be unbelievable, let us look at a real example:

The age of the American hero is dead and most Americans can no longer tell right from wrong, according to a new study.

Based on 1800 question interviews with 2000 Americans held simultaneously at 50 locations, with privacy and anonymity guaranteed, 'The Day America Told the Truth' found that 91 per cent of Americans lie regularly both at work and at home.
(*The Guardian*, 2 May 1991)

The second rejection of positivism

Critical theorists also reject the fact/value distinction which leads to the idea that sociology should be value-free. The ideas they are attacking can best be found in American social research and the work

Activity

a What exactly did the *Guardian* survey reveal, if anything? (Think carefully before you answer.)
b How would Pollack respond to such research? Would he consider it objective?
c What do you think about this piece of research?

I, A, E

of Weber. The Frankfurt School argued that it is impossible to be value-neutral, since this implies that social scientists cannot really have any say in the way society develops. Weber argued that sociology could not arbitrate over questions of ethical, moral and political choices, and he makes a clear distinction between 'science' and 'politics'. However, the Frankfurt School argued that this meant that sociology would, for example, have nothing to say about the advent of Hitler to power – since that was a political rather than a scientific choice. Even worse, it can be argued as a development of this position (and certainly was in the USA) that sociologists can advise governments and societies of the means to a predetermined end, but not about which end to adopt.

In other words, Weber's distinction actually does not work in practice. Certainly the Frankfurt School saw this idea of a value-free sociology as a way of creating an uncritical science because it did not effectively ask questions of the uses to which its knowledge was put.

Furthermore, they argued that this was not simply a question of some errors by particular sociologists, but that such positions necessarily arose from the nature of positivism itself. What they meant by this is that the concentration on 'objective knowledge' in positivism was linked to a desire to control nature (see also Section 2.5). Herbert Marcuse in *Reason and Revolution* (1955) argues that positivism was a reaction to Hegelianism, seen as negative in the context of conservatives frightened by the French Revolution. Positivism thus set about restoring order:

The laws positivist science discovered and that distinguish it from empiricism, were positive in the sense that they affirmed the prevailing order as a basis for denying the need to construct a new one. . . . Observation instead of speculation means, in Comte's sociology, an emphasis on order in place of any rupture in the order; it means the authority of natural laws in place of free action, unification in place of disorder. The idea of order, so basic to Comte's positivism, has a totalitarian content in its social as well as its methodological meaning.
(Marcuse, 1955, orig. pub. 1941, p. 348)

Thus it is people's interests that will necessarily dictate what is to count as objective knowledge. In a society riven with conflict, ideas will inevitably be distorted. As Lee Harvey puts it:

At the heart of critical social research is the idea that knowledge is structured by existing sets of social relations. The aim of a critical methodology is to provide knowledge which engages the prevailing social structures. These social structures are seen by critical social researchers, in one way or another, as oppressive structures.
(Harvey, 1990, p. 2)

The focus on universal laws in positivism denied this possibility and denied people the possibility of making choices, an aim the critical theorists saw as central to their whole approach. This issue did, however, also bring them into conflict with Weber's value-relative stance on methodology.

Critical theorists say that it is not possible, as Weber arguably tried to do, to stand outside such conflicts and retain an objective stance. Weber's position was that while science could contribute to policy by informing debate it could not actually make choices for people. The problem with this is that it says nothing about how such choices are to be made, and his support for the need for strong leaders has been seen as leaving little defence against force as the ultimate decision-maker. This issue was of importance in Germany, owing to the rise of Hitler. Weber's position appeared to offer no defence against this sort of decision-making.

Habermas has focused on how decisions can be reached. He argues that what is needed is a reformulation of rationality to allow for the development of communicative action – by which he means a situation wherein we can all freely talk and arrive at agreement, thus reaching a consensus of truth (see Section 2.9).

Feminist criticisms of positivism and science

Comte argued that science would eventually make all other forms of knowledge redundant. In the positive age, science would become the only *acceptable* form of knowledge. He saw science as based on reasoning and observation, the use of humankind's rational faculties to understand the world. However, he also believed that men were superior to women in terms of their intellectual capacity while women were superior to men in terms of affectivity and emotionality. Put simply, this suggests that men are rational and women are emotional. A similar view of women can be seen in Durkheim's writings. It implies two things:

- women can never be as good as men at understanding science
- since science was to be the exclusive basis of knowledge, such knowledge would be exclusively defined by men.

Not surprisingly, this is a position feminists and other contemporary sociologists reject. However, the feminist rejection is complicated by the division among feminists over their views on the nature of women (discussed in detail in Chapter 5). Put simply, some feminists see women and men as *essentially similar* and explain inequalities between them on the basis of social constructions which can be changed to achieve equality. Other feminists say that women and men are *essentially different* and that women are more in touch with their emotions (see Section 5.5). While this latter position mirrors Comte in arguing that there is an essential difference between men and women, some feminists argue that the fact that women can be both rational and emotional while men cannot suggests that it is men who are inferior.

Feminists go on to suggest that a true knowledge of society needs to recognize both the rational and the emotional aspects of behaviour, and so science (as conceived by positivists) is not and cannot provide a complete picture of society. Furthermore, the general acceptance of science as the highest form of knowledge perpetuates the oppression of women since it is a form of knowledge based on a way of thinking in which men are perceived to be the strongest. Scientific thinking therefore leads to domination by men both as researchers and as subjects of research, since science concentrates on the study of measurable phenomena and ignores 'emotionality and values'. Science is therefore not only an inadequate model for sociology, it is also a model that furthers the oppression of women.

In this sense, feminist criticisms mirror the critique of positivism put forward by the Frankfurt School, though they apply the notion of science as oppressive to women in particular.

This approach can be seen in the work of Liz Stanley and Sue Wise (1990, 1993), who draw on elements of phenomenology and ethnomethodology to suggest that science is a social construction, just like everything else. The search for a 'feminist science' is therefore rejected, and instead it is argued that feminists should adopt a reflexive attitude to research uncovering the variety of forms of knowledge that women have. This can only be done by women because only they share the experience of oppression:

Thus there is no way of moving outside of experience to validate theories 'objectively' – nothing

exists other than social life, our place within it and our understanding of all this.
(Stanley and Wise, 1993, p. 193)

Ray Pawson (1992) is critical of claims that there is a need for a specific 'feminist methodology'. He argues that even though one can find views about women in Durkheim and others which are clearly wrong, this does not in itself mean that all Durkheim's insights can be set aside (although it does point to the fact that there did exist for a long time a blind spot about gender in sociological research). Further, the claim to base research solely on experience is invalid since it leads to a form of relativity where all experiences are true, but this leaves no way to judge between which of the different and contrasting accounts of experience are valid.

This problem of relativism has surfaced more generally in recent arguments about methodology with the rise of post-modernism and its influence on methodological debates.

Post-modernism and methodology

Post-modernists see the ideas of reason and of the free individual as the key legacies of modernist thinking (see also Sections 2.10 and 10.11). This led to the notion that rational thinking individuals could gain insight into the real nature of the world, an insight that clearly lies behind all theories of methodology. It is this which post-modernists reject.

Instead they argue that the notion of gaining control over the natural world and the attempt to arrive at a total theory of society leads to authoritarian ends. This is because of their belief that all forms of knowledge are merely forms of power (Foucault, 1980), which seek to arrive at a uniform truth only by denying the differences which are an important part of humanity. The search for truth is therefore something that can never be finally solved, for two reasons:

- there is no ultimate truth, and
- what are presented as truths are merely those ideas which are the most powerful at any one time, but not necessarily for ever.

Science is therefore the form of knowledge which is presently winning the power-struggle, but that is all it is.

Critics of this argue that it leads straight to a very strong form of relativism which ultimately leads to the proposition 'anything goes'. In terms of social theory it is criticized as being a cowardly response to contemporary society by giving up on any prospects of human emancipation and instead becoming a celebration of the expression of difference through consumption – again seen as an excuse for the

excesses offered to some in the era of late capitalism (Callinicos, 1989).

The argument that we can still rely on some form of rationality and seek out ways to establish the truth has, however, had to take account of the critiques of the positivistic approach outlined in this section. This has led to the emergence of a revised notion of a scientific approach, which is known as 'realism'.

3.3 Realism as a methodological tradition

Realism defined

The distinguishing characteristic of positivism and empiricism is that sociology is a science, and this has most often been interpreted as meaning it should confine itself to analysis of things that can be directly observed. Phenomenological views suggest that this is in fact all there is, since the idea is rejected that there is an objective truth behind the various subjective accounts research can generate.

Realism rejects both those positions. It holds that there *are* real structures which underlay surface phenomena. These may be unobservable directly, but that does not prove they do not exist; and realists argue that such entities do exist.

In contrast to the positivists, it is argued that it is essential that these real material bases of society be included in an overall analysis if we are to claim to give a full account of society.

Realism can therefore be summarized as the belief that there are real structures of society which exist, but which are not necessarily open to observation. The implication of this is that the pure empiricist position, which is to go out and collect facts and to consider only these as scientific, must be rejected as presenting an incomplete view of the world: it cannot account for the fundamental structures of society. Theory and method are therefore intrinsically linked together, since sociologists need a theory of society couched in theoretical terms which provides the basis for empirical research.

The appeal of realism arises partly from the failure of natural and social scientists to be able to prove that what they did in actuality matched up to the rules of science as defined by empiricism and positivism. This can be seen in the work of Kuhn (1970). In *The Structure of Scientific Revolutions*, Kuhn argued that there is a need to consider what it is that scientists actually do in the course of their work, and this led him to devise the term 'normal science'.

Kuhn argued that all such normal science operated within a paradigm, by which he meant a set of concepts, theories and methods which define both areas of research and methods to be adopted. As such, the paradigm effectively provides both the questions and the answers – and therefore frames and limits the reality of scientific investigation. Furthermore, since these paradigms are laid down by the scientific community, the acceptance or rejection of a paradigm is not a purely objective matter but involves social considerations and conflict. Scientists have a vested interest in maintaining their academic careers, and this leads them to argue for the retention of paradigms within which they work.

Kuhn asserted that it is only occasionally that discoveries occur which cause the replacement of one paradigm by another. When this happens 'scientific revolutions' occur:

Paradigm changes do cause scientists to see the world of their research-engagement differently. In so far as their only recourse to that world is through what they see and do, we may want to say that after a revolution scientists are responding to a different world.
(Kuhn, 1970, p. 110)

He outlines how one such revolution occurred with the rise of Copernicus' discovery in 1543 that the sun, not the earth, is at the centre of our universe. More recent examples of 'scientific revolutions' include the impact of Newton's theory of gravity in 1648 and the way this revolutionized physics – only to be overcome by the paradigm shift initiated by Einstein's 'general theory of relativity' in the 1920s and Heisenberg's 'uncertainty principle' in the 1930s. Once these scientific revolutions have taken place 'normal science' is resumed until the next paradigm shift occurs.

So natural scientists do not proceed solely by empirical testing which yields new knowledge, but instead new knowledge flows out of the theoretical breakthroughs which initiate paradigm shifts and therefore scientific revolutions. These occur because existing theories begin to break down under the weight of evidence, but it requires new theories to initiate the paradigm shift. This further underlines the theory-laden basis of scientific knowledge.

A second implication for the social sciences was that since natural scientists were not as 'scientific' (as conventionally defined) as was thought, then it was possible for social science to be similar to the natural sciences – as long as the reality of the natural sciences was recognized along the lines set out by Kuhn.

Clearly such a view undermines the basis of most variants of positivism (see Section 3.1), since science is considered no longer to rest purely on observation. However, in integrating the notions that scientists hold their views for non-scientific reasons,

Kuhn's approach created support for those who argued that science was a social construction (see Section 3.2). Ultimately this leads to a relativist position, since scientific theories constructed in different paradigms cannot be tested against each other, and the history of science could therefore be seen as a succession of paradigms none of which could ultimately be tested against another.

It is this relativist conclusion that realists seek to avoid. This is the importance of their idea that there is an independent reality to which our theories are answerable, even though this reality cannot be grasped by the empirical testing posed by positivism.

Imre Lakatos (1975), another philosopher of science, criticizes Kuhn's notion of scientific revolutions by arguing that it is not the case that a single paradigm is all-powerful at any one time, and in fact in reality many paradigms compete all the time. He goes on to say that the truth of these statements cannot be proved by reference to empirical testing alone, but he nonetheless argues that it is possible to arrive at an objective standard by which to judge the relative merits of different theories:

One cannot prove statements from experiences. . . . all propositions of science are theoretical and, incurably, fallible.
(Lakatos, 1975, vol. 1, p. 16)

This link to the theory-bound nature of science, and the idea that nonetheless we can and should seek to arrive at objective measures of the truth, builds towards the realist argument that rejects empirical testing as the sole criterion of truth:

The rejection of empiricism is the basic trend which marks the distinctiveness of modern realism from earlier variants.
(Outhwaite, 1987, p. 27)

Realism and classical sociology

The most obvious candidates for inclusion in the category of realist among the classical sociologists are Emile Durkheim and Karl Marx (see Section 2.3). Durkheim is often thought of as a positivist, though he himself rejected the term and was critical of Comte's claim to have found a way of explaining all societies on the basis of one universal law. While he can clearly be seen as a positivist in his belief that we can view society as being similar to the human organism, and his adoption therefore of the organic analogy, his writings reveal an interest in things which could not be directly observed. Bryant describes his work as follows:

The strength and penetration of the currents which impel us to marry, have children or commit suicide, for example, are reflected in the level and stability of

the marriage, fertility and suicide rates for different groups. The rates serve as indicators of phenomena whose dimensions are not immediately graspable.
(Bryant, 1985, p. 35)

This indicates that Durkheim in his choice of subject matter, notably in the case of suicide, was interested to discover more than simply the surface 'facts' about these phenomena as revealed in the statistics; instead he saw such 'facts' as indicators of more deep-lying 'social facts'. Positivism is involved since he looks for something observable and measurable (suicide statistics), but his analysis is also realist since these statistics are held to indicate something else – that is, the level of social integration or the lack of it. His explanation for the variations in the levels of suicide was squarely in terms of the power of society over individuals. In other words, he was using suicide as an example to demonstrate the power of the social.

Realism is the belief that there are certain processes which are real, but which nonetheless are not directly observable. Durkheim used suicide rates as an indicator of these forces. While his use of official statistics has therefore led to him being labelled and criticized as a positivist by phenomenological writers such as J. Douglas (1967) and J. M. Atkinson (1978), realist accounts point quite clearly to the idea that Durkheim saw these statistics as indicators of deeper structures in society. One cannot, for example, find any statistics or hope to directly measure something like *anomie*. This, however, does not mean it does not exist.

Steve Taylor (1982), in his study of suicides and deaths on the London Underground, argues that in order to understand suicide we cannot rely simply on empirical evidence, but instead need to outline the underlying unobservable structures and causal processes which contribute to suicide. He argues that this approach is realist – and points to his view that Durkheim's original study of suicide was as well – which undermines phenomenological criticisms of it based on the question of empirical data.

On the other hand, Bryant asserts that some accounts of the attempt to define Durkheim as a realist only succeed by presenting a caricatured version of positivism. He includes Taylor's work in this category. Bryant argues that this problem arises because the main view of positivism in some realist approaches is that of logical positivism. While this type of positivism is clearly incompatible with realism, since it insists that anything which is not observable is nonsense, Bryant argues that:

. . . although some positivisms are incompatible with realism, that of the French tradition is not.
(Bryant, 1985, p. 55)

This leaves open the view of whether we should see Durkheim as a positivist or a realist, or possibly as veering between one and the other.

Jane Clarke and Derek Layder (1994), like Taylor, see Durkheim's suicide analysis as a key example of a realist approach, as Figure 3.2 (taken from their work) indicates.

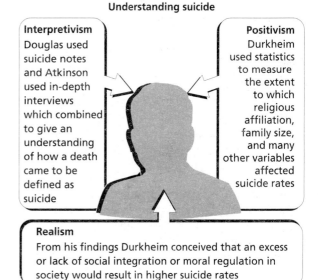

Understanding suicide

Interpretivism
Douglas used suicide notes and Atkinson used in-depth interviews which combined to give an understanding of how a death came to be defined as suicide

Positivism
Durkheim used statistics to measure the extent to which religious affiliation, family size, and many other variables affected suicide rates

Realism
From his findings Durkheim conceived that an excess or lack of social integration or moral regulation in society would result in higher suicide rates

Figure 3.2 Theorizing suicide.
Source: Clarke and Layder (1994, p. 8)

They summarize the main points of realism as follows:

1 *Firstly, realism concentrates on the nature of society as a whole rather than the smaller elements that make it up.*

2 *Realism tries to combine an interest in the analysis of human activity as it occurs in face-to-face encounters with an interest in the institutional elements of society, such as economic and political organization, or religious ideas.*

3 *Realism is interested in aspects of society which may not always be apparent to an observer or even a trained researcher.*

4 *Realism searches for explanations in terms of underlying causes.*
(Clarke and Layder, 1994, pp. 7–8)

Activity

a Write out Clarke and Layder's summary of realism in your own words.
b Suggest criticisms of this view which might be made by a positivist sociologist.
c Suggest criticisms of this view which might be made by a phenomenological sociologist.

I, A

As an example of something which exists and is important, but which is not directly observable, Clarke and Layder cite racism. They argue that racism and similar doctrines are:

... not easily observed since it is their 'low profile' which serves to maintain and enforce them in the first place. ... In this respect it is important to accept that underlying causes ... may not be readily observable in the way that other aspects of social life are.
(Clarke and Layder, 1994, p. 8, see also Section 6.1.)

Discussion point

a If something is not easily observed, how do we know it really exists?

b How might we set out to test the existence of things not easily observed?

With regard to Marx, the picture is also of someone who accepted the need for science to go beyond surface observations in order to understand the real nature of society. In fact Marx saw the existence of such entities as the key reason for the need for a scientific approach, since:

... all science would be superfluous if the outward appearance and the essence of things directly coincided.
(Marx, 1959, p. 817; orig. pub. 1894)

He labelled as 'the philistines' those who believe that things can be understood simply by looking at surface appearances (the empiricists of their day).

Discussion point

Marx here provides a particular view of how science can be distinguished from other forms of thinking, and of its uses. To what extent do you agree with this as a view of what science is?

Scientific realism

While the theories espoused by Durkheim and Marx provide the basis for the emergence of realism, only in recent times has it emerged as a distinct view of how social research should be conducted. Writers who have developed the notion of realism significantly are Roy Bhaskar (1978, 1979, 1986), Russell Keat and John Urry (1975) and Andrew Sayer (1979, 1984). There are differences between the approaches of these writers, but they have all contributed to the development of what is now known as 'scientific realism'.

Essentially, scientific realism arose out of a dissatisfaction with the positivist view that anything that could not be verified or falsified purely through empirical testing could not count as evidence or knowledge. Such a view is certainly associated with logical positivism and instrumental positivism, though arguably not with classical positivism (see Section 3.1).

The underlying structures of society

Realists claim that in order to examine phenomena in both the natural and the social world, it is necessary to take account of the underlying realities of society (hence 'realism'). Bhaskar argues that it is possible to use the methods of the natural sciences, but not in the way advocated by positivists. The important thing to remember, he says, is that although humans create their world, they do not enter into a vacuum so their actions need to be understood in relation to an already existing underlying structure of society. In order to fully understand things, therefore, sociologists need to concentrate not on static visions of either individuals in society or of structures impinging on individuals, but instead on the social relations that exist and which both constrain and enable action to take place.

Not everything is directly observable (*alienation* and *anomie* for example), but since realists argue that they exist they need to be incorporated into explanations. This requires the construction of models of society which account for and can explain those phenomena that are observable. These explanations should then be subjected to empirical research, and the results will provide further issues for debate and research. The important thing is to test the usefulness of different theories and explanations. Testing these theories allows us to identify how the underlying structures of society work, and thereby design effective research methods.

It is important to recognize that, while classical empiricist research sought simply to identify relationships between observable variables, realists seek to establish links between observable phenomena and the underlying generative mechanisms which are not necessarily directly observable. This requires that researchers engage in theory first in order to establish detailed explanations of these generative mechanisms which can then be tested. A second implication of this is that all variables need to be considered in a particular context, and cannot be viewed as true for all times.

Realism versus positivism

This leads to two key ways in which such an approach differs from positivism. First, in rejecting the belief that theory arises from empirical data and consists of statements made only about such observable data, realists can be distinguished from both logical positivists and instrumental positivists.

Secondly, in rejecting the idea that sociology can discover laws which are applicable for all times, realists reject elements of the Comtean version of positivism. Precisely because they view society as a dynamic set of relations, such iron laws do not exist. Things may generate effects, but whether those effects take place or not depends on a whole series of complex relations which also need to be taken into account. The picture of society offered is therefore much more complex than the original positivist view based on the notion of unchanging causal laws.

In essence, this means that all empirical statements are theory-dependent – that is, they can make sense only in the context of an overall theory. This does *not* mean that empirical research is rejected, as Outhwaite explains:

The realist emphasis on the legitimacy and the importance of theoretical argument should not be understood to imply the depreciation of empirical research. What it does suggest, I think, is that such research cannot achieve useful results in the absence of theoretical reflection on the structuration of empirical data and a rejection of empiricism, understood as an exclusive focus on social phenomena which are empirically observable and measurable.
(Outhwaite, 1987, p. 60)

We therefore need to underline the point that empirical research, meaning the collection of data should not be confused with empiricism. Empiricism is based on the notion that data exist independently of theories and therefore leads to the belief that theories can be empirically tested, and indeed that this is the only way theories can be tested.

The use of the word 'structuration' is not accidental since Bhaskar makes conscious use of Giddens' 'theory of structuration', in showing the need to go beyond positivism and phenomenology and their links to exclusively structural or action sociologies. However, although realists argue that it is necessary to study both structures and social actions, they are also critical of Giddens' approach as Margaret Archer (1995) makes clear in her argument that what is needed is:

a theoretical approach which is capable of linking structure and agency rather than sinking one into the other. The central argument is that structure and agency can only be linked by examining the interplay between them over time . . . When discussing 'structure' and 'agency', I am talking about a relationship between two aspects of social life

which, however intimately they are intertwined . . . are none the less analytically distinct.
(Archer, 1995, p. 65)

This debate further underlines the link between theoretical developments and methodological developments.

Realism versus phenomenology

The key claim of realism is that, while rejecting the positivist characteristics of empiricism and attempts to discover the laws of humanity, we should nonetheless seek to establish sociology on a scientific footing. This leads realists into clashes with phenomenologically inspired versions of sociological methodology. The key difference here is the realist's insistence that there are deeper structures in society than the merely surface phenomena, which is all that phenomenologists claim there ever is. However, realists take from the phenomenological tradition the idea that the active nature of humanity must be taken into account in any conception of social science. They hold that this does not mean that sociologists cannot learn from the natural sciences, and here they draw on reflections on the actuality of the way natural scientists work, as opposed to the textbook model of natural science.

Realism and science

Here it is possible to identify a number of elements, the first being the importance of *theory* in natural sciences. Natural scientists do not confine themselves to that which is observable. Keat and Urry (1975) cite biological and medical sciences, where the idea of viruses existed before they were empirically identified. The idea was used to explain diseases for which other bacterial agents could not be found. Later the idea was of course found to be empirically valid. However, the theory came before the empirical validation.

A second important point about natural sciences is that the classical laboratory experiment cannot be applied in many instances. Sayer (1984) points to the important distinction between closed and open systems as subjects of scientific enquiry. A laboratory is set up as a closed system where everything apart from one variable is controlled. Although this is seen as the epitome of natural scientific research, it has limited application. In particular, certain sciences – such as meteorology – have to operate with open systems where such controls are not available. Meteorologists have to work with the weather in the real world, rather than in a laboratory, so their findings are much less precise. It is no accident that the recent emergence of 'Chaos Theory' in natural sciences came originally from meteorology.

The impact of Chaos Theory is instructive. In attempts to arrive at certain scientific laws, small differences were ignored as insignificant. The neatness of the laboratory is, however, undermined by the real world, where meteorologists found that tiny differences do have an effect and so cannot be ignored. This is best summed up in the famous phrase:

A butterfly stirring the air today in Peking can transform storm systems next month in New York.
(Gleick, 1987, p. 8)

Recognition of this meant that laboratory approximations were simply no longer good enough and would in any case never be able to predict accurately. Since small differences matter, explanations have to be for particular circumstances and have to be put in the context of an overall theory. In this sense, natural sciences (as opposed to the traditional image of them) are similar to what social scientists do, in that both in reality are often faced with open systems where the laboratory experiment is inapplicable or useless.

Chaos theory has major implications for the natural sciences, since it posits that small changes cannot be ignored. However, it nonetheless argues that there is an underlying order to all this. Chaos theory is not, therefore, similar to post-modernism (see Section 2.10) but is in fact its opposite. The ideas of chaos theory might be applicable to sociology in that societies might be viewed as chaotic systems.

💬 Discussion point

a To what extent do you agree that societies might be chaotic systems?

b What implications does this have for sociology as a science of society?

A second point of similarity between the natural and the social sciences is that both suggest that things are affected by underlying structures. So realists suggest that the social sciences can be like the natural sciences as long as we have a realistic understanding of the way natural scientists operate. In this respect, the work of both Popper and Kuhn in explaining exactly how natural scientists operate is relevant.

Popper was in effect a scientific realist. He said that the Vienna Circle was wrong to reject as 'nonsense' everything except that which could be verified:

A metaphysical position, though not testable, might be rationally critisable or arguable. I had confessed to being a realist, but I had thought that this was no more than a confession of faith.
(Popper, 1976, p. 150; quoted by Outhwaite, 1987, p. 29)

It is also the case that Kuhn's work on scientific revolutions was instrumental in getting recognition of the reality of exactly what natural scientists did. Although he and Popper disagreed on some points, Kuhn himself pointed to the fact that he was largely in agreement with Popper:

On almost all the occasions when we turn explicitly to the same problems, Sir Karl's view of science and my own are very nearly identical.
(Kuhn, 1974; quoted in Derry, 1996, p. 18)

In conclusion it can be re-stated that a realist's account of natural sciences is very different from the model presented by positivists. Exactly what sociology has to do to be scientific is thus very different.

Case study – A realist investigation of CCTV

An example of realism is the work of Ray Pawson and Nicholas Tilly (1996) on closed-circuit television (CCTV) and crime detection. (CCTV is also discussed in Section 11.9.) They argue that quasi-experiments which aim to measure the effects of such initiatives as community policing fail, precisely because they try to keep everything constant except one variable and then measure the difference between an area where community policing has been applied and one where it has not:

Our point is that programmes are the products of skilled action by human agents, not reducible to the 'facticity' of a given event. It is not programmes that 'work' as such, but the practitioners' attempt to change the reasoning processes of their subjects. It is not contact patrols that 'work' as such, but something about the character of the contact. Quasi-experimentation gazes past these vital issues, since the experimental/control comparison, which is at the heart of the logic, demands that we see the programme as a kind of binary dosage which is simply 'present' or 'absent'.
(Pawson and Tilly, 1996, p. 38)

However, they say that this does not mean that we cannot come to scientific conclusions. They wish therefore to arrive at a scientifically valid study of crime detection, but one which avoids the problems of the experimental method – namely that it ignores the whole network of events and sequences, including human action, which needs to be considered if an adequate explanation is to be provided.

This requires a look at the overall context in which CCTV might be employed since it is never employed in a social vacuum (precisely why experimental methods fall down):

Just as there is nothing about police patrols which intrinsically reduces fear of crime, so too there is nothing about CCTV in car parks which intrinsically inhibits car crime. It certainly does not create a physical barrier making cars impenetrable. The scientific realist begins by pondering the rather different mechanisms through which CCTV may, nevertheless, lead to a reduction of car crimes and the contexts needed, if these potentials are to be realised.
(Pawson and Tilly, 1996, p. 45)

They suggest nine mechanisms by which CCTV might work. These include the idea that CCTV may deter potential offenders; it may reduce crime by making the apprehension of actual offenders more likely; or it may, by the use of notices, jog drivers' memories about the potential for car crime and lead them to be more careful in securing vehicles. They also say that the use of CCTV needs to be considered in specific contexts, and they identify five in which CCTV might be used. These include whether the car park is long-stay or short-stay; whether the CCTV in one place merely leads to increased car crime elsewhere; and the extent to which it is deployed in conjunction with other security measures.

They argue that a full study of the effect of CCTV needs to take into account these variations in both the context of its applications and the actual mechanism of its usage. Such an approach widens enquiry out from a simple consideration of the use of CCTV to a whole series of networks of connections with wider features of society – thus illustrating the classical realist themes that:

- things need to be considered as parts of networks of connections
- empirical research needs to be informed by the theoretical reasoning that allows one to come up with a number of potential contexts and mechanisms.

Although these researchers found that CCTV does tend to reduce car crime, they conclude that it does not do so by catching offenders. They go on to point to further lessons learned:

Most else remains unclear. It does so, so to speak, because the scientific realism entered too late. That which would need to be measured could not be reconstructed after the event with the data available. Consider, for example, the possibility that the 'appeal to the cautious' mechanism may play a part in certain contexts. In relation to this, a survey of cars parked before and after installation of CCTV, together with signs indicating its operation, could ascertain changes in the numbers left locked and in the extent to which attractive goods were left on

display. . . . It is by no means transparent at first sight that looking inside parked cars would comprise part of the evaluation process. This needs early thought and pre-planning.
(Pawson and Tilly, 1996, p. 49)

It is the need to consider, identify and theorize about all the possible contexts and mechanisms in which CCTV might contribute to a reduction in car crime that marks this out as a study conducted using a scientific realist approach. As the researchers admit, this entered late into their study, which meant the data were not necessarily collected to enable a full realist evaluation to take place. Here is an illustration of the pitfalls of a purely empiricist strategy of merely going out and collecting the facts: it is first necessary to theorize about exactly what data are needed, some of which may not be obvious (see also Section 2.1).

Sociology and science: the ongoing debate

The aim of Sections 3.1–3.3 has been to provide a detailed consideration of the question of whether sociology can, and whether it should, seek to be scientific. The answer ultimately rests on various notions of what being 'scientific' implies, and these have altered over time – from the view of natural sciences held by classical positivism, through to the criticisms of this position in the work of Kuhn.

The question rests also on whether objective knowledge is possible. Here the criticisms made by phenomenology and hermeneutics are relevant, and the later argument of the post-modernists (see Section 2.10) that all forms of knowledge are inevitably subjective and reflect power relations in society. Thus it is argued that it is not possible to distinguish between objectivity and subjectivity in a way that allows us to distinguish truth from opinion.

Some (including feminist sociologists) have argued that the use of science as a model for sociological methodology is problematic because science rests on a particular form of knowledge, which denies the importance of personal experience and emotions. In this view, if sociology tries to mimic science it risks becoming subject to the oppressive structures science itself is part of. It risks becoming part of the problem rather than part of the solution.

This denial of the possibility of objectivity is rejected by realists. The latter nevertheless argue that we cannot rely on purely empirical testing, since all empirical statements are theory-laden and not everything that is relevant is directly observable. Thus, while sociologists can still attain an objective – and therefore scientific – methodology, what is meant by science and scientific testing is very different from the notions developed by positivism.

Activity

Use the material in Sections 3.1 to 3.3 – and Lawson's (1986) article if you can locate it in your library – to answer the following questions:

a On what basis did positivists argue that sociology could be a science?

b What are the key strengths and weaknesses of this approach?

c What are the key points of phenomenological and hermeneutic criticisms of positivism?

d What are the implications of these criticisms for the methods sociologists should use?

e What are the criticisms of the phenomenological position made by realist sociologists?

f Which of these three positions do you think provides the best basis for a sociological methodology? Should sociology seek to be scientific?

U, A, E

It is important to realize that the questions of (a) how we know things and (b) how statements are tested are the basic starting point for the development of sociological methods and techniques. This has implications for the issues concerning methods considered in the rest of the chapter. As Tony Lawson has written:

Positivists believe that only by adopting a position of total objectivity towards the subject matter or phenomena can unbiased knowledge or theories be produced. ... adopting a positivist perspective towards the search for knowledge implies a certain type of methodology. But the social sciences will clearly have difficulty in putting such ideas into practice, if only because, unlike rocks, plants and animals of the natural sciences, the subject matter of the social sciences – human beings – think. This awareness, or consciousness, about what is happening to them makes the subject matter of the sociologist extremely difficult to control. ... These obvious difficulties have led some sociologists to question whether it is possible to adopt positivistic procedures or methods, and others to suggest that the subject matter of sociology is so different from the natural sciences that is it not desirable to follow them at all. ...

However, many natural scientists have themselves dismissed the idea that research into chemistry, physics, biology and the rest is carried out in the way that the positivists suggest. ...

If neither the social, nor the natural, sciences, measure up to positivistic standards in the search for 'truth', are they both equally non-scientific? ... Science, therefore, casts a shadow over sociological research, and it is in the context of the positivistic model that the relationship between theories and methods in sociology must be understood.
(Lawson, 1986, pp. 37 and 38)

The debate about whether sociology can or should be a science goes on today. All the research cited in this book was done by sociologists who at some stage had to address this issue.

3.4 Ethical issues in social research

Sociologists conduct research to try to understand the world, and possibly to try to influence policy decisions. This research can have real effects on the lives of people. Sociologists need, therefore, to think about the ethical issues, before, during and after their research.

The ethics of research relationships

At the heart of the way sociologists treat respondents in research is the notion of 'informed consent'. All people should be participants out of free choice, rather than face pressure of any sort to take part. It follows from this that they should be aware of the fact that the researcher is doing research, and something about the nature of that research.

Once the sociologist has collected data, there is still a responsibility towards the respondents. Information gained in the process of research should be treated as confidential, and people should be granted anonymity when the findings are published. This is not always easy. For example, if a researcher is doing research in a school, omitting someone's name while identifying them as a head of department might make it possible for that person to be identified. On the other hand, to leave this information out might not provide a full context in which to consider that person's statements or actions.

So, although it is relatively straightforward to think about these issues and to outline some general principles, the application of the principles in research is sometimes difficult and involves sociologists in ethical and professional dilemmas. This section looks at two actual sociological studies as a way of considering how ethical issues arose and how sociologists tried to deal with them.

Case study – Tearoom Trade

With regard to covert participant observation (see Section 3.9), one of the most famous cases is that of

Laud Humphreys study (1970), which he called *The Tearoom Trade*. In this research he observed gay sexual encounters in public restrooms. He wished (a) to explain how such encounters, and the social structure they required, worked; and (b) to investigate the rules and meanings attached to the encounters by the participants. In order to do' this he engaged in covert participant observation, but also later with follow-up interviews (see Section 3.8).

Humphreys became a part of the gay scene in Chicago by visiting gay bars and attending balls, and so became an accepted part of the scene. He adopted the role of 'watch-queen', meaning a lookout, but also someone who got satisfaction from watching others engage in sex. Publication of the study attracted some controversy.

Discussion point

To what extent do you think controversy over the methods used by Humphreys was related to the subject matter of his research?

He noted 134 car number-plates and, using contacts with the police force, obtained the addresses of the owners. He later got 100 of these addresses included in a survey on health he was involved with a year later. In that year, having changed his appearance, he called on the 100 people in the guise of the health survey to conduct further research. May (1993) recounts the details of the response to this research:

The reactions to the publication of his study were variable. As Humphreys notes in a postscript to the book: 'several have suggested to me that I should have avoided this research subject altogether' (1970:168). He was accused of deceit, the invasion of privacy and increasing the likelihood of the sample's detection by the police force. One account suggests that some faculty members at Washington University were so outraged 'that they demanded (unsuccessfully) that Humphreys' doctoral degree be revoked' (Kimmel 1988:23). On the other hand: 'The research was applauded by members of the gay community and some social scientists for shedding light on a little-known segment of our society, and for dispelling stereotypes and myths' (Kimmel 1988:23). . . . In this sense, the means justified the end. He brought into the public domain an understanding of an issue which American society had done so much to repress. To his critics, however, the means can never justify the ends: 'Social research involving deception and manipulation ultimately helps produce a society of cynics, liars and manipulators, and undermines the trust which is essential to a just social order' (Warwick 1982:58).
(May, 1993, p. 46)

Activity

In your own words, explain (i) the case for supporting Humphreys' research methods, and (ii) the case for opposing his methods.

Case study – The Moonies

Another example of the issue of ethics in social research can be found in Eileen Barker's study in 1984 of the 'Moonies', members of the Unification Church. (The findings of this study are discussed in Section 18.5.) She argues that conducting the study seemed difficult or impossible without gaining access and becoming a member of the church, but she was unwilling to do this, partly because of ethical questions:

It seemed unlikely that I would be able to obtain much information unless I was to pretend to become a member myself. This was out of the question for a number of reasons. First, I would have been unhappy about the deception on purely ethical grounds; secondly, I had no desire to give up my job; and thirdly, even if I were to have joined, I would not have been able to go around asking questions on any sort of systematic basis without arousing suspicion.
(Barker, 1984; quoted by Dunsmuir and Williams, 1991, p. 60)

She eventually became an *overt* participant observer (see Section 3.9), following an invitation from the Unification Church itself. Although this clearly did not involve the deception she had worried about, which had led her to abandon covert observation, this method was itself not without problems, as she recounts:

The people I was studying could be influenced by my presence because I was studying them. . . . There were several occasions on which I mediated between a Moonie and his parents. . . . These interventions . . . I undertook with an awareness that what I was doing could affect the situation. There were also numerous occasions on which my influence was unintended. . . . One occurred while I was on a 21-day lecture course at which the participants were expected to deliver a lecture. The subject I was allocated was 'The Purpose of the Coming of the Messiah'. I did not exactly enjoy this aspect of my research, but participant observation does involve participation, so I gave the talk, carefully punctuating its delivery with phrases such as 'The Divine Principle teaches that . . .' or 'According to the Principle . . .'. When I had finished, a member of the audience declared that she had been extremely worried about this particular part of the doctrine, but now she understood it, and she fully accepted that the Reverend Moon was indeed the Messiah. I was horrified. 'But I don't believe it,' I insisted, 'I don't think it's true.' 'Perhaps not,' interrupted the Moonie in charge, 'but God has used Eileen to show Rosemary the truth.'

(Barker, 1984; quoted by Dunsmuir and Williams, 1991, p. 62)

Activity

With reference to both the studies by Humphreys and by Barker, consider the following questions:

a To what extent do you support the notion that social researchers should never lie in their research?

b To what extent do you support the notion that social researchers should never invade people's privacy in research?

I, A, E

3.5 Obtaining a research sample

The one instance in which an individuals's participation in social research is not optional is the national Census (see Section 3.11) of the whole population. People are legally required to fill in a questionnaire and can be fined if they fail or refuse to do this. The Census costs so much to conduct that it is done only every 10 years. The resources needed to conduct research on this scale are unavailable to other sociologists, who are therefore required to fall back on the use of *samples* of the population for their studies. However, this is problematic since most pieces of research will want to draw conclusions about the UK as a whole.

How are sociologists to select people to be studied, and how are they to get them to agree to participate?

Sampling

The first thing to be clear about is the population to be studied. Population in this context does not refer to the population of the whole country, but all those people in the group to be studied. Thus a study of the effects of unemployment might have as its population all those who lived in households where at least one member was unemployed.

While this may suggest that deciding on a population is relatively straightforward, this is deceptive. While the suggested population does not limit itself to individuals who are unemployed, it does limit itself to households and it can be argued that the effects of unemployment spread much wider than that. For instance, shopkeepers in an area with a large number of unemployed people might be affected, while not being unemployed themselves. Equally, given the known links between unemployment and ill-health (see Section 13.2), it is possible to argue that levels of unemployment would have an impact on demand for health services, and thereby affect the length of time non-unemployed people have to wait to see their doctor. It is also the case that since the level of unemployment affects the costs of social security (see Section 14.2), and has an impact on the level of economic output of the economy, it could be said that unemployment affects every person in the UK even if they as an individual are not unemployed or have an unemployed person as a member of their household. So, identifying a population to be studied requires much reflection on the nature of the problem at issue, and the possible aspects of it that might need to be considered.

Despite the fact that a population in this sense contains a much smaller number than the whole of the population of the UK, it still may involve impracticably large numbers. So sociologists seek to select a sample to represent, or stand-in for, the population they wish to study. In order to be able to make general statements about the whole of the population they are studying, they need to ensure that the sample selected is representative of that population. This introduces the important concept of representativeness:

This refers to the question of whether the group of people or the situation that we are studying are typical of others. If they are, then we can safely conclude that what is true of this group is also true of others. We can generalize from the example that we have studied. If we do not know whether they are representative, then we cannot claim that our conclusions have any relevance to anybody else at all.

(McNeill, 1985, p. 13)

The procedures used to ensure that any sample is representative are known as 'sampling techniques'. They involve several stages, issues and choices which are examined in this section.

Discussion point

What problems might arise in trying to define a population to study the effects of a school opting-out of local education authority control and becoming grant-maintained?

The sampling frame

The first problem (and an extremely important practical one) is how to obtain a complete list of the names of the population to be studied. This is known as a 'sampling frame' because it provides the list from which the sample will be selected. Sometimes people seem to assume these just exist, but this is a misconception.

Lists that are openly available are those making up the electoral registers, compiled for the purposes of checking eligibility to vote. These are by polling district and are available at local reference libraries. They contain the names and addresses of all people eligible to vote in that particular district. Since a roll is updated every year, it will provide an up-to-date list.

The Post Office General Address File lists all the addresses in the UK, and if one were trying to select a sample based on households rather than individuals this would provide a possible starting point.

Various professionals, such as doctors, have lists of people in their area and it might be possible to try to utilize these. However, the issue of confidentiality may lead to access to these lists being denied. Howard Newby (1977) points to some problems he faced in his study of agricultural workers in Suffolk (see also Section 16.5):

I sampled farms rather than farm workers, since I believed I could obtain a reliable sampling frame of farms (mistakenly, since the Ministry of Agriculture refused to co-operate and I was forced back on to Yellow Pages*) and then contact the workers via an employer. This was not only an administrative convenience, but probably also an administrative necessity. However, the result was that, in common with so many other sociological studies, I was taking the easy option of homing in on a captive set of respondents.*
(Newby, 1977, p. 114–15)

Activity

a What problems did Newby encounter in the construction of a sampling frame?

b Explain why he described his sample as a 'captive set of respondents'.

c Suggest reasons why he did not sample farm workers.

I, A

This example illustrates the point that it should not be assumed that existing data will automatically be made available to sociological researchers.

A further problem might be that no potential sampling frame exists covering exactly the population one wishes to study. If, for example, one wished to study relations between parents and young children, school lists would not include those under school age, and an electoral roll does not include children under seventeen or eighteen.

All this serves to emphasize that populations do not simply exist nicely lined up in alphabetical order on sampling frames waiting for a sociological researcher to turn up. Constructing a usable sampling frame might in itself involve a considerable amount of work.

Sampling procedures

Once a researcher has managed to obtain or construct a sampling frame, he or she is in a position to select a sample from it. There are a variety of ways of doing this.

Random sampling

The idea behind truly random sampling is that everyone in the population has an equal chance of appearing in the sample, so ensuring that the sample is not biased. This 'equal chance' is based on probability theory, and random sampling is sometimes known as probability sampling for that reason. The technique is therefore not haphazard, as its name might suggest, but based on clear scientific principles.

The most basic form of random sampling involves selecting people through the use of a random-number generator on a computer. This selects numbers randomly and adds the names and addresses which correspond to those numbers onto the researcher's population list, up to the required amount to form a sample. Alternatively one can scan the population list and select every tenth, twentieth etc. name, depending on the sample size required. Lee Harvey and Morag MacDonald call this 'systematic random sampling' and they explain its potential pitfall:

There is a possibility that this process might give an unrepresentative sample if the lists are ordered in a particular way. For example, if the list was an address list in house number order then every tenth house might generate only even numbers that would (in Britain) lead to the houses selected all being on one side of a street. It is possible that this might generate a sample with an unrepresentative housing class.
(Harvey and MacDonald, 1993, p. 118)

Stratified random sampling

This method divides the research population into a number of strata based on what are seen as significant variables – for example, gender, ethnicity, class, age. Samples are then randomly drawn from each of the strata and combined together to form the final sample. Decisions about the precise way the final sample is to be made up can be made on the basis of the respective importance of the substrata in the population as a whole.

Stratified sampling allows the researcher to ensure that all potential target groups within a population are represented in the final sample, and that all variables considered potentially important (or in which they have a special interest) are covered.

Cluster sampling

This method can be used when no sampling frame is easily available. It is based on identifying a number of clusters in the population, such as schools or classes within schools, and then selecting individuals from within these clusters. While this allows the construction of a sample in a much quicker way than would be possible if it were necessary to construct a sampling frame and construct a simple random sample, it is also problematic in that it can be biased. In selecting clusters before individuals are selected, not every individual has an equal chance of being selected, and the overall sample might therefore not be representative of the population under study.

Multi-stage random sampling

Here the selection of a sample goes through various stages. Each stage involves the selection of a sample from the previous sample chosen, until the researcher arrives at a list of individuals. This method was employed, for example, by Marshall *et al.* (1988) in their study *Social Class in Modern Britain* (the findings of the study are discussed in Section 4.9):

A three stage design was employed. This involved the selection of parliamentary constituencies, polling districts, and finally individuals. . . . One hundred parliamentary constituencies, then two polling districts from each sampled constituency, were selected with probability at both stages proportionate to size of electorate. . . . Nineteen addresses from each sampled polling district were then selected by taking a systematic sample through the list of elector names and noting the address of the elector on which the sampling interval landed.
(Marshall *et al.*, 1988, p. 288)

The main potential drawback with this method is that, if parliamentary constituencies have differing total numbers of electors, then the chances of individuals being selected at the final stage become unequal. This issue explains the concern in the extract above with ensuring that probability was proportionate to size of electorate, but this entails careful attention to the detail of the sampling.

Panel studies

While all the above methods relate to one-off samples, the idea of a panel study is to conduct research on the same sample over a period. Such an approach is important when one wishes to consider changes over time. The original sample can be constructed using any of the above methods. Key problems are, first, convincing people to agree to be questioned on more than one occasion; and secondly, keeping in contact with the original sample if, for example, they change residence. Because of these problems such studies tend to have relatively high drop-out rates which may make the sample progressively less representative.

For example, Himmelweit *et al.* (1985) selected a sample of 450 men who were 21 years old in 1959 and considered their voting behaviour (see Section 17.2) through to the October 1974 General Election. By 1974 the sample numbered only 178 and all were now middle aged. Since their sample was also overwhelmingly non-manual workers, their findings were criticized as not being representative.

Spatial sampling

If it is required to study the participants at a particular event, then one can choose respondents randomly from within a group of people gathered together in a certain space (hence 'spatial'). This is random in so far as it selects people randomly from within a *given* population. The method might be employed to study people on a demonstration, or at a concert, since they will be gathered together for only a short time and this means more conventional methods are inapplicable.

Non-random sampling

While it is often thought that a sample should always be representative of the population, this is not in fact the case. There are instances when one might purposely wish to select a sample that is not representative. It is not therefore a criticism of these approaches to say that they are not representative since they do not aim to be, neither do they claim to be. As with random sampling there are a number of forms this type of sampling can take.

Accidental sampling

Here the researcher studies all individuals he or she comes into contact with over a given period – for example from 3 pm until 4 pm on a Tuesday in a shopping centre. Such an approach tends to be associated with qualitative research, or for the pilot stage of quantitative research where the main aim is to test the usefulness of a questionnaire.

Such an approach does not yield a representative sample. For example, a researcher in the high street on Tuesday afternoons is unlikely to obtain responses from those with full-time employment working conventional hours.

Purposive sampling

Here the researcher selects people on the basis that they are likely to be relevant to the subject being studied. This of course means that the sample reflects judgements made by the researcher which may be open to question. However, it does allow researchers to include significant individuals within their research.

Volunteer sampling

In this method, people volunteer to be studied. It has its limitations:

Ien Ang's (1985) study of viewers' attitudes to Dallas *was based on a volunteer sample of people who responded to her advertisement in a Dutch magazine. Volunteer samples are thus self-selecting and usually biased as they are a subgroup of a population who are prepared to be involved in the research. Sometimes researchers have to resort to volunteer samples as there is no other way of reaching sufficient numbers of people to build up a sample.*
(Harvey and MacDonald, 1993, p. 120. This research is discussed in Section 15.9.)

Activity

Suggest two potential research topics where researchers might have to 'resort to volunteer samples'.

A

Quota sampling

Quota sampling is similar in some respects to stratified sampling. Instead of choosing randomly from strata within the population, the researcher sets a quota precisely outlining the number of individuals meeting certain criteria that are to be included in the sample.

An interviewer might therefore be told to ensure that the sample comprises 10 men over 40 years, 10 men under 40, 10 women over 40 and 10 women under 40. The interviewer would be left to select individuals who fit these criteria.

The first stage is to decide on the important variables, and then investigate how they are located in the population as a whole, probably by consulting the national Census. For example, according to the 1991 Census 56 per cent of the economically active population were in non-manual employment and 44 per cent in manual employment, so these proportions could be used as the basis of a quota instruction. The final sample would then fit the population as a whole on this criterion. There is,

however, the problem that the interviewer is left to decide which individuals are to be questioned, out of all the possible ones who fit the criteria. This can lead to problems:

Problems of abuse and bias caused by the interviewer, who may turn to the first available, convenient or least resistant person, are hard to avoid. However, quota sampling normally is not meant to be a random procedure, and should not be expected to provide random data.
(Sarantakos, 1993, p. 139)

Snowball sampling

Here researchers start with very few people and ask them for recommendations of further people to interview who fit the criteria of the study. When interviewing these people the same procedure is applied and gradually a sample is built up.

A sample can be constructed when no sampling frame is available, and when studying a close-knit group of people who, however, do not necessarily appear on any lists. Roseneil (1995) used this method to construct a sample for the interview stage of her study of feminist activists at Greenham Common (see also Sections 3.9 and 5.4).

This is a method often associated with participant observation. The links between individuals that such approaches reveal can unveil important insights, as well as providing one with a sample.

From sampling to research

This section has considered the various methods available to sociologists to select a research sample from a population. Arriving at a sample is itself a task which requires skill, time and effort. When reading a report it is sometimes easy to concentrate solely on the findings, and to forget that before a single question was asked a lot of hard work had to go into the construction of a sample, and possibly into persuading the sample to participate.

There is nothing to prevent a significant proportion of a carefully selected sample declining to help, and thus undermining the representativeness of the sample. The standard way to deal with this is to construct a bigger sample on the assumption that there will not be a 100 per cent response rate. This of course requires an estimate of the likely response rate, and consideration of other potential reasons why individuals in the sample may end up not answering one's questions.

Each stage in the construction of a sample and contacting the sample members engages researchers in much time-consuming and probably costly effort. This is, however, an indispensable part of any research project which cannot be ignored.

3.6 Deciding on a research technique

Methodological theories and choice of method

The techniques sociologists use to obtain research data are just that – techniques. There are, of course, points concerning the correct application of these techniques (examined in Sections 3.7–3.11), but nonetheless they remain techniques. So why do researchers choose to use a particular technique rather than another? It is here that the relevance of theoretical and methodological debates becomes clear:

In a sense, methods are a-theoretical and a-methodological (meaning, independent from methodology). Interviews, for instance, like observation, experiments, content analysis etc., can be used in any methodology type, and serve any chosen research purpose. The same methods can be used in the context of different methodologies, and the same methodology can employ different methods. ... Nevertheless, although methods are in general a-methodological, their content structure and process are dictated by an underlying methodology. Although interviews, for instance, can be used in a qualitative and a quantitative methodology, the former employs an unstructured, open or in-depth interview, while the latter normally opts for a standardised interview. In a similar vein, participant observation is used in qualitative studies while structured observation is employed in quantitative studies.
(Sarantakos, 1993, p. 33)

So theoretical and methodological approaches play a large role in decisions about which particular research technique or method to use. It is for this reason that Sections 3.1–3.3 considered methodological debates, and why they come before the discussion of actual methods in this chapter. We need to look now at how such debates frame choices of method. Bilton et al. (1987) point to how these theoretical outlooks impact on the choice of a suitable method to be employed (see Figure 3.3).

So, positivists have traditionally been inclined to methods which will produce *quantitative* data (i.e. in the form of numbers or statistics), while anti-positivists have been more inclined to those methods which will produce *qualitative* data (i.e. in the form of words).

Today we would wish to add the approach known as realism. Because realists argue that we need to take into account both that humans are conscious, active agents and that there are underlying structures of society, their approach cannot so easily be placed on a qualitative–quantitative continuum. The

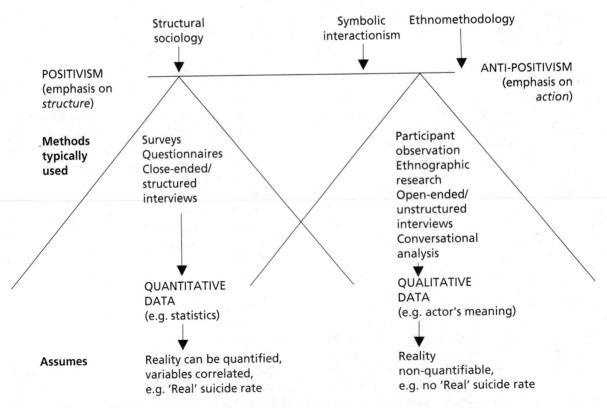

Figure 3.3 A summary of the relationship between theory and methods. Source: Bilton *et al.*, 1987, p. 550

implication of their approach is that these choices would provide one-sided accounts of reality. This issue is explored further later in this section.

Owing to its association with radical and critical approaches, the realist approach is sometimes also described as the 'critical approach'. The differences between the three are contained within Table 3.1.

The differing ways in which these methodological approaches seek out knowledge impacts on – though does not totally determine – the specific method adopted.

As the discussion above shows, theoretical and methodological outlooks will play a large part in deciding which particular technique to use in the research process. This is as it should be; otherwise all the arguments which rage in sociological theory about the nature of society, and all those which rage in relation to methodology about how or whether we can know the reality of a situation, and whether sociology should or can be a science, would be utterly pointless. People spend time on these arguments because they matter. This point further underlines the fact that there can be no separation between theorizing and empirical research, since in either case this would lead to pointless and useless activity.

Positivism and quantitative methods

The positivists' desire for quantitative data arises from their belief that humans are in essence subject to the laws of society. Their view of humanity means it does not really matter what people think since this can have no real influence on the direction society will take, and this leads to a concern with delineating the structures of society. Their belief in the superiority and precision of the scientific method is a further factor influencing them to move in the direction of quantitative research, since this will lead to the production of data in the form of numbers – essentially statistics which can then easily be manipulated to consider trends over time or differences between various social groups according to certain criteria. This leads them to seek connections – and ultimately causal connections – between variables. One could, for example, look at church attendance by age group, or average GCSE scores by father's occupation, to discover whether these showed consistent trends and correlations which would point to a likelihood that the two factors were linked in some way.

The problem of correlation and causation

Demonstrating a link (correlation) between two variables is merely evidence there might be a relationship between them. It is important to remember that it is *not* evidence that one *causes* the other. Unfortunately this is often the basis for dubious interpretations of statistical findings. For example, in looking at the statistics relating to number of marriages and number of wedding rings purchased one would expect to find that they were linked – when one rises, so does the other. However, it would be foolish to argue that the reason people get married is because they have bought a wedding ring. Clearly some *other* factor is here causing a change in people's behaviour such that they (a) buy a wedding ring and (b) get married. It might be said that the causal factor was 'falling in love', or 'a baby due to be born'. Here a third factor – which can be debated – causes changes in the first two factors.

Another important example of this is the doctrine of monetarism. On the basis of studies of the American economy, monetarist economists noted that there was a link between the rise in the level of money in circulation and the rate of inflation. They demonstrated that the two variables were correlated. However, monetarists then went on to argue that this was a causal link whereby increases in the supply of money in circulation were the cause of inflation. This argument is hotly disputed by other economists, but it is this economic doctrine which underlies much of the economic policy of the New Right in the 1980s and 90s (see Section 2.10).

In summary, never confuse *correlation* with *causation*. One does not prove the other, and one should always be careful to check that this slippage

Table 3.1 Summary of the three epistemological approaches

	Positivism	Phenomenology	Critical
Knowledge via	Explanation	Interpretation	Understanding
Seeking out	Causes	Meanings	Structural relationships
Type of 'data'	Social facts	Social interactions	Historical, structural, ideological
Analytic approach	Scientific method	Direct involvement	Dialectical

Source: Harvey and MacDonald (1993, p. 9)

is not occurring when reading accounts of sociological research.

Strengths of quantitative methodology

Statistics play an important role in sociology because they do allow us to consider trends over time. Since numbers provide a common currency with which to compare social groups in relation to certain issues, quantitative research remains very popular.

Quantitative data can easily be analysed using statistical techniques, and this attractive feature has been enhanced in recent years by the availability of computers that can process data very quickly. This allows sociologists to obtain findings from social surveys with large samples with relative ease. Computers also permit one to re-analyse data easily, so later sociologists can go back and re-use primary data that have been collected earlier.

Problems with quantitative methodology

Those influenced by phenomenology and hermeneutics would suggest that at the heart of all problems is the nature of humanity espoused by positivism, namely the way humans are viewed as puppets subject to forces and laws external to themselves.

The construction of questionnaires and interview schedules often reveals this problem, with a limited number of options being offered and no space being given to allow people to explain in detail the reasons behind their choices. This reflects the positivists' belief, but it is of course rejected by phenomenological sociologists who argue that it is precisely in the process of interaction and the construction of meaning that humans not only have choices, but make the choices which make the world the way it is. This is central to sociology, they argue, and it is largely missed out in quantitative methodology, which instead imposes its own framework of meaning on those being researched.

It is therefore argued by phenomenologists that, although quantitative methods can be shown to be reliable (in the sense that if repeated they will produce the same result), this reliability is of no use because the findings, although constant, are not valid. Rather, they represent the 'reality' imposed on people by the researcher. Furthermore, it is this which also accounts for the the data's reliability, since the findings are a reflection of the methodology used rather than the superiority and accuracy of the method.

Those who criticize quantitative methods therefore say they lack validity, in that the findings do not really represent the reality of those being studied.

The belief that facts are value-free and theory-free is at the heart of the empiricist approach which underlies positivist methodology, and this is of course rejected by those who argue that facts only make sense in the context of theories. The danger is of generating reams of 'facts' without any coherent theoretical framework with which to make sense of it all.

Phenomenological and hermeneutic approaches

For research sociologists, the central defining aspect of these methodological approaches is that reality is the result of human interactions, and the way people interpret their world and try to construct meanings out of it.

So the key concern is a wish to describe and analyse how people interact; and although it is possible to do this using quantitative methods, these are largely rejected because they impose a frame of meaning on the subject being researched.

For example, a questionnaire framed to elicit quantitative data will allow only responses picked from a preselected number of alternative answers. People might be forced to place themselves within a category which does not really represent their true situation, and it is also possible that two people with widely differing views might end up in the same statistical mass. For instance, in a survey asking people whether they are (a) impressed or (b) unimpressed with the current leader of the Labour Party, the group of responses in the second category might include Conservatives, Liberal Democrats and left-wing socialists. This category would thus include a very diverse range of people who made their choice for divergent reasons. Conservative Party supporters might be unimpressed because they see the Labour leader as a socialist, while left-wing socialists might be unimpressed because they see the same person as not enough of a socialist.

To explore more deeply the meanings and attitudes behind responses like these requires the asking of further questions, and this leads towards a qualitative methodology. Those adopting a qualitative methodology argue that research should be approached without any preconceptions or structures, and treat people as conscious, active subjects in order to capture the full depth and detail of how people interact meaningfully to create the world. This reality, they say, is far too complex to be captured by pigeon-holing people into the categories associated with quantitative methodology.

Strengths of qualitative methodology

The key advantage claimed for qualitative methods is that they allow a deeper – and therefore more valid – picture to emerge of the particular set of social relationships under investigation. By focusing on interactions, they allow sociologists to look at the dynamic and fluid nature of society, and by focusing on the meanings people construct they concentrate on the active nature of humanity.

In so far as social researchers wish to view people in this way and to focus on the cultural and social processes by which they live their lives, then this approach has clear advantages over the more static fixed pictures which emerge from quantitative methods.

This is seen as much more important than defining so-called objective variables which are merely seen as the imposition of researchers on a somewhat more fluid, subjective reality. Ultimately the advantages of qualitative methods are related to the methodological theories out of which they flow, and if one disagrees with the theories then the approach will seem subjective and unreliable. Justification of such criticism relies on a more positivistic view of the world than those undertaking qualitative research will accept.

Problems with qualitative methodology

The key criticism, resting implicitly on positivistic notions, is that qualitative approaches are subjective. The implied charge in this is that data produced using such approaches should not ultimately be taken too seriously. Sometimes this criticism is extended to say that qualitative methods tend to be applied towards the more trivial aspects of life, but this obviously depends very much on your point of view.

A potentially more serious criticism made of qualitative methods is that they are unreliable. By this is meant that a second researcher repeating the research using the same techniques – or even the same researcher repeating the research at a later date – will not be guaranteed to achieve the same results. While it is clearly the case that techniques such as participant observation do rely very heavily on the personal characteristics and skills of the researcher – and therefore another researcher is unlikely to be able to repeat the research precisely – this may be missing the point:

It might be that the positivist's research tool consistently and reliably measures the variables but if what is being researched is invalid then the whole process is rather pointless. . . . For example, intelligence tests are reliable measures of intelligence quotients but whether this has anything to do with intelligence is debateable.
(Harvey and MacDonald, 1993, p. 188)

In other words, a method that consistently measures things inaccurately or wrongly in some sense can still be considered reliable, but ought to be considered rather pointless and arguably dangerous in certain contexts.

Positivistic research uses preset categories of answers, whereas proponents of qualitative research claim that it overcomes this imposition problem. Ray Pawson, however, argues that there is nonetheless an imposition problem involved in qualitative methods. As an example he cites the large amount of material generated by Ann Oakley in her study of the experiences of motherhood (see also Sections 5.2 and 7.5), which involved 233 interviews and produced 545 hours of tape-recorded data. It is clear that not all of this material appears in the final report of her research project. (This is a general problem with all research that produces qualitative data.) In the final report, the data are represented by quotations from the material, but not by production of the whole data set. The problem with this is outlined by Pawson:

The phenomenological schools as a whole have traditionally been very tough on quantitative methods for imposing meaning. . . . This very familiar anti-positivistic missile has now been trained inwards and applied to participant observation. 'Field research' in general and by its very nature, tends to produce findings which are anecdotal and massively selective in terms of the ratio of events reported to those witnessed. In this process of the selection and packaging of evidence, the possibility of imposition of meaning again looms large.
(Pawson, 1989, p. 161)

Discussion point

To what extent do you agree with the argument that both positivist and phenomenological approaches suffer from the imposition problem? Do they suffer from it in exactly the same way, or differently?

A final criticism of qualitative methods is that, since they build on theories which tend to deny the existence of any social structures beyond those constructed at the level of interpersonal interactions, their approach is deficient in considering the whole ensemble of relations which make up society.

Realism and methodological approaches

In terms of methodology, the distinction between qualitative and quantitative as a broad dividing line is inapplicable to realism. This is because the latter argues that, while it is indeed necessary to take the proposition that people are conscious human agents seriously, there is also the need to uncover objective truths about the underlying causal mechanisms of society.

Thus realism seeks to understand the meanings that people arrive at, but within the context of the existence of real underlying structures which help to generate those meanings. This leads to a desire to place studies of society in an overall historical context and, using theories and concepts abstracted from the reality of everyday society, to try to illustrate the underlying mechanisms.

'Cultural reproduction' theory (which, depending on the variety, draws on both Durkheim and Marx – see Sections 8.2 and 10.2) is an example of this type of study, as is the more recent work by Paul Willis (1977). He was concerned to show how what takes place in school leads to working-class children getting working-class jobs. His study adopted primarily an ethnographic method. Harvey and MacDonald explain the methodological implications of this in the context of Willis' study:

Critical Ethnography usually starts by examining the social structure rather than taking it for granted. The ethnographic enquiry provides detailed data that helps to assess the structural analysis. However this is not done by testing a hypothesis with a view to falsifying a theory (as a falsificationist might). There is a two-way development of understanding. The ethnographic material is used to re-examine the structural relationship and, at the same time, the structural analysis will help to make sense of the ethnographic data.
(Harvey and MacDonald, 1993, p. 185)

> ### Activity
> Select the correct words from the list below to fill the gaps in the extract that follows (each word is used only once):
>
> *reliability, ethnographer, representative, survey, bias, sample, validity.*
>
> *Where the _____ researcher may claim _____ and representativeness, the ethnographer will claim _____. The survey enthusiast will point out the dangers of _____ and unreliability in ethnography, and stress how the representativeness of a _____ can be calculated precisely. The _____ may concede all this, but would point out that it is not much use being able to produce the same results over and over again, and to say how _____ they are, if they are invalid in the first place.*
> (McNeill, 1985, p. 114)

In contrast, in the studies conducted by the Glasgow University Media Group, which were concerned with analysing the content of the media as a form of ideology, it can be seen that they primarily used the quantitative method of content analysis. (Content analysis and semiology, as methods associated with the study of the media, are covered in detail in Section 15.2.) The GUMG's aim was, nonetheless, still to reveal the underlying structures of ideology which permeated the media.

Realism, therefore, does not fit very easily into a quantitative–qualitative dichotomy, precisely because it denies the validity of the methodological theories behind this distinction and which tend to pose it as an either/or choice.

Using more than one method: triangulation

Triangulation refers to the use of more than one method in order to try to counter the weaknesses of one particular method by combining it with another which is strong in that area. So, for example, structured interviews might be combined with participant observation. It is also possible to use both structured and unstructured interviews, the logic behind doing so being to try to gain the highest levels of both validity and reliability.

The classical exposition of this approach is in Barkers' (1984) study of the Unification Church, better known as the Moonies. Details of the study can be found in Section 18.5, but here we wish to concentrate on the methodological implications. In her study, Barker used participant observation, questionnaires and interviews. Information from the participant observation (which lasted six years) and from the interviews (which consisted of 30 interviews lasting between six and eight hours) was used to gain a detailed picture of the Unification Church, and this information was then used to enable the researcher to draw up more detailed hypotheses for later investigation using questionnaires.

Barker argued that by combining these methods her study of the Moonies gained greater validity and reliability than would have been the case if she had conducted the study using only qualitative or only quantitative methods. Since research methodology allows us to be fairly sure about the relative strengths and weaknesses of the various techniques, and since this information is now widely available, more and more sociologists are seeking to use triangulation, or 'methodological pluralism' as it is sometimes called.

As another example we can look at the points made by Pierre Bourdieu when being interviewed about his book *Distinction* (Bourdieu, 1984) (this is discussed in more detail in Sections 9.8 and 10.4):

Q: I'd now like to turn to the question of the relationship between sociology and the neighbouring sciences. Your book Distinction *opens with the sentence: 'Sociology is rarely more akin to a social psychoanalysis than when it confronts an object like taste.' Then come statistical tables, and accounts of surveys – but also analyses of a 'literary' type, such as one finds in Balzac, Zola or Proust. How do these two aspects fit together?*

A: The book results from an effort to integrate two modes of knowledge – ethnographic observation, which can only be based on a small number of cases, and statistical analysis, which makes it possible to establish regularities and to situate the observed cases in the universe of existing cases. So you have, for example, the contrasting description of a working-class meal and a bourgeois meal, each reduced to their pertinent features. On the working-class side, there is a declared primacy of function, which appears in all the food that is served: the food has to be 'filling, body-building' as sports are expected to be (weight-training etc.), to give strength (conspicuous muscles). On the bourgeois side, there is the primacy of form, or formality, which implies a kind of censorship and repression of function, an aestheticization, which is found in every area, as much in eroticism, functioning as sublimated or denied pornography, as in pure art which is defined precisely by the fact that it privileges form at the expense of function. In fact, the

analyses that are described as 'qualitative' or more pejoratively, 'literary', are essential for understanding, that's to say fully explaining, what the statistics merely record, rather like rainfall statistics. They lead to the principle of all the practices observed, in the most varied areas.
(Bourdieu, 1993a, p. 14)

While it might be seen that this approach can allow research strategies to be developed that avoid the problems associated with using only one method, it should be noted that it does not eliminate these problems – it merely covers them over by utilizing other methods with strengths in the areas of weakness in the first method. Rather than a unified overall methodology, it is a form of using complementary methods. As Tim May has pointed out:

While triangulation might appear attractive, it is not a panacea for methodological ills.
(May, 1993, p. 90)

Nonetheless it is clear that triangulation can offer real benefits and is leading to more and more sociologists adopting the principles that lie behind it. Case studies focusing on specific issues but using more than one methodological technique, or even methodology, have risen in popularity in sociology recently. While this might put a spotlight on the issues of validity and reliability, it could also impact on the issue of representativeness. For instance, the famous study by Goldthorpe and colleagues, *The*

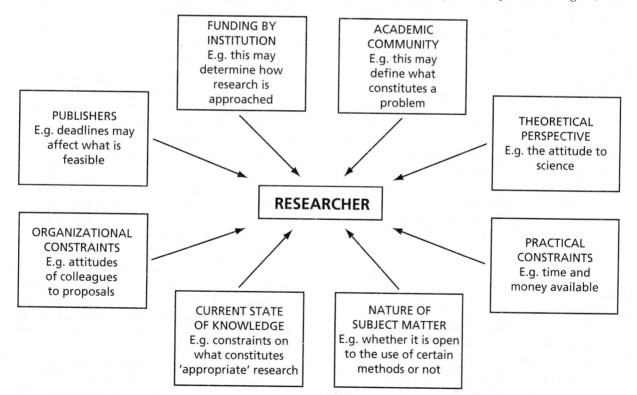

Figure 3.4 Influences on the researcher's choice of method. Source: Lawson (1986, p. 40)

Affluent Worker (1968), chose to study workers in Luton, not because they were representative, but because this seemed the most likely place to find 'affluent workers'. In this sense an extreme case was picked rather than a representative sample.

Each of the sections in the third part of this chapter (3.7–3.11) contains extracts from sociologists talking about their research, and more than one method was used in many instances.

Whether a unified methodological toolkit can be devised which would go beyond triangulation remains to be seen.

Non-theoretical factors impacting on the research selection process

This sub-section of the chapter would be redundant if we lived in a world where sociologists were allowed to propound their theoretical arguments (positivism *versus* phenomenology *versus* realism) and then choose research methods solely on that basis. Of course, we do not live in such a world. Structures of power exist (see Section 17.4), and these impinge upon – and are created by – sociologists in the world of sociology just as in every other sphere of society. These structures therefore have an impact upon how research is done.

Obvious constraints are *money* and *time*. Funding is not always easy to come by, and awarding bodies may require the sociologist to undertake research using specific methods as a condition of their funding. Equally, if a research report is required in four months one is unlikely to have the luxury of choosing in-depth participant observation. Lawson (1986) has provided a useful summary of possible constraints on researchers (see Figure 3.4).

Lawson points to how the subject matter itself can constrain choices:

Interactionists are likely to be highly disposed towards observational techniques. But if you are a fifty-year-old female sociologist interested in football hooliganism, it is going to be difficult to perform a participant observation study of that topic! Similarly, if you are a positivist wishing to investigate illiteracy, a written questionnaire is not an option you can easily take.
(Lawson, 1986, p. 41)

Activity

Suggest two examples of your own of how (i) the nature of the subject matter, and (ii) practical constraints such as time and money, may serve to affect choices over research methods to be employed.

A

The points made above about resources serve as a reminder that sociological research (as opposed to reading about it) operates in a world where the people with power might not care much for your ethnomethodological predilictions. They might want just the bare statistics, and they could withdraw funding if they do not get their way. Of course, it is likely that such a project would be entrusted to a sociologist already quantitatively inclined, but this would leave our ethnomethodologist without a grant and therefore possibly unable to do research. The nature of what is researched, and how it is researched, would therefore still be influenced.

The remaining sections consider each of the main methods employed by sociologists, and some of the points made here are underlined. Those sections should be read while bearing in mind always the frameworks in which research operates, discussed in this section.

3.7 Questionnaires and social surveys

The term 'social survey' refers to a study which aims to gain data from large numbers of people, generally through the use of various types of questionnaire and interview methods. A questionnaire, which is a list of organized questions, is the primary research tool in much sociological research.

The basic questionnaire method involves providing respondents with a printed list of questions to be answered. If, on the other hand, the questions are asked verbally by the researcher, then this situation becomes an interview. Many interviews involve some kind of questionnaire and must take into account the methodological rules devised for drawing up, administering and analysing questionnaires. There are further issues relating to interviews which are dealt with in Section 3.8.

Questionnaires are most usually used when there is a desire to gain information from a large sample of people. There is a minimum number which must be reached if the sample is to stand a chance of being representative – though this is a necessary but not sufficient basis for representativeness.

By ensuring that each respondent is faced with an identical stimulus – that is, an identical questionnaire – the method aims to be reliable. Variations in answers will not be the result of any variations in the questions, or the order in which they were asked, or the manner in which they were asked. As May comments:

The theory is that if all respondents are asked the same questions in the same manner, and if they express a difference of opinion in reply to those ques-

tions, these variations result from a 'true' difference of opinion, rather than as a result of how the question was asked or the context of the interview.
(May, 1993, p. 67)

The validity of findings from a social survey using a questionnaire is related to the actual wording of the questions, so extreme care must be taken at the stage of designing and wording the questionnaire. If questions are ambiguous, or if the instructions on how to complete the questionnaire are unclear, it might be that the answers given do not reflect the true situation. The design of a questionnaire and its testing through a pilot study are therefore very important.

Piloting a questionnaire

A pilot study is a small initial study conducted with the first draft of a questionnaire, with the sole aim of testing whether it is clearly worded and contains questions that are both understandable and answerable. At this stage it is hoped that any sociological jargon will show up, and any questions that remain unclear can be rectified. In a pilot study, therefore, respondents are asked an additional question: to comment on the questionnaire. On the basis of this study, careful consideration must be given to any possible need to rewrite or reorder the questions.

This stage is important since once questionnaires have been issued it is unlikely that they can be reissued if any problems emerge. The final questionnaire must be clear of any technical blemishes.

Administering a questionnaire

There are a number of ways of asking people questions, and consideration must be given to the choice of method of administration of a questionnaire. There are four main methods:

- respondents' self-completion
- delivery by mail
- delivery by telephone
- administration by an interviewer.

In the first two cases the questionnaire will be completed by the respondents, so there is a particular need for the wording of the questions to be as clear as possible. Instructions on how to complete the questionnaire have to be drawn up and attached to the front.

Respondents' self-completion

This occurs when questionnaires are handed to respondents who are then asked to complete them themselves. Such delivery requires that the sample be concentrated in one area and accessible to the researcher. This is most likely to occur when the

questionnaire is being administered to people in an institutional setting, such as workers in a factory or students in college.

Delivery by mail

Mailed questionnaires are sent via the postal system to the sample selected, with a reply-paid envelope for return of the document. Since there is no obvious reason why the sample should complete the questionnaire, such surveys require the researcher to draw up a covering letter explaining the purpose of the research and asking for the co-operation of the respondent. Since the researcher and the respondent will in this case be geographically distant, it is impossible for the researcher to clarify any questions or instructions that are unclear. It is therefore vitally important that careful attention be paid to the design and piloting of the questionnaire.

Mailed questionnaires are popular for surveys because they allow researchers to select a sample from a geographically disparate population, and they are cheaper to administer than questionnaires delivered by an interviewer. Catherine Hakim (1987) estimates that their cost is about half that of interview-administered questionnaires.

However, a major problem with postal questionnaires is the often low response rates. May (1993) suggests that a figure of 40 per cent is not uncommon. This creates a difficulty because the people who do respond to the questionnaire cannot be said to be representative of the sample as a whole (they are clearly unusual in one sense, in that they chose to respond). May provides the following example of the problems that can result:

It is possible that only some groups will reply and not others. The replies might then by systematically biased towards one part of the population. For instance, in one health survey, people appeared more healthy than was generally thought the case. An examination of replies found that those in more deprived areas had a low response rate. As there is a relationship between health and income, this biased the results showing a more healthy population than was actually the case.
(May, 1993, p. 72)

Clearly such problems need to be considered and possible solutions suggested. It is likely that it will be necessary to issue reminders, probably enclosing a second copy of the questionnaire to non-respondents to try to ensure that a high response rate is achieved.

However, there are also a number of problems with this. First, if the questionnaire is anonymous, the researcher will not be able to tell which members of the sample have responded and which have not. Secondly, the cost of the survey is increased if two letters have to be sent to some respondents.

The other two forms of administration involve the researcher, or interviewers working on his or her behalf, filling in the answers. Here, careful training is needed to ensure that the interviewers apply the questionnaire in a standardized way and record the answers accurately. There is a degree of personal interaction, and so issues relating to interview technique are involved.

Delivery by telephone

Although the researcher in this case is not involved in face-to-face interaction, it is necessary to consider issues relating to the manner and tone of the conversation.

The key problem with the use of the telephone to administer a questionnaire is the potential for the sample being unrepresentative. May (1993) points out that in many households it is a male in whose name the telephone is registered, and whose name will therefore appear in the telephone directory. It is also the case that some people choose to be ex-directory.

Discussion point

What other problems might arise from the use of a telephone directory to obtain a research sample, and the telephone to administer a questionnaire?

As a result of these problems, telephone administration is considered the most likely to be problematic with regard to representativeness – although, as May points out, if one is studying a *particular* population with virtually 100 per cent ownership of a phone, this problem is likely to be less. Although telephone surveys are often used by private research organizations, and tele-sales are now common, they are rare in sociological research.

Administration by an interviewer

In this case, all the points about the need for questions and instructions to be clear still apply, and in addition there is the need to train interviewers. Interviews are dealt with in greater detail in Section 3.8.

Closed and open-ended questions

Closed questions allow only a limited number of possible responses. Often these responses are written on the questionnaire, where a space or box is allocated for a tick or a cross. Another variety of closed questions is those which attempt to elicit the attitudes of people by providing them with a set of scales, ranging from, say, 'strongly agree' to 'strongly disagree'. Other scales are possible.

Alternatively questions may be 'open-ended'. Here the respondents are provided with spaces in which they can construct their own answers.

Some questionnaires contain a mixture of closed and open-ended questions, with closed questions used to identify the person on a set of social variables such as gender, occupation (and thereby class), age, and locality. If statistical information is needed then it is likely that the vast majority of the rest of the questions will also be closed.

There is a link between the choice of type of question and a sociologist's theoretical and methodological beliefs, since closed questions will result in quantitative data and open-ended questions will result in qualitative data. Whether or not statistics are required will therefore be a consideration in the design and construction of the questionnaire, and methodological beliefs are likely to play a part in this decision (although they are unlikely to be the only factor).

A comparison of the two types of question

By limiting the number of possible responses, closed questions allow the data to be produced in quantitative form, which is ideal for statistical analysis. The advent of computers has meant that large amounts of data can be compiled into statistical tables and graphs relatively easily and quickly, and this has to some extent led to a resurgence in interest in quantitative social surveys.

The main criticism of this type of question is that, since the researcher constructs the possible answers, this forces people to pigeon-hole themselves, and the possible responses may not in fact cover all possibilities. Further, the meanings of the possible responses may vary between respondents, and so what looks like a homogeneous block of people who all respond in the same way might in reality not be such. Sociologists influenced by the phenomenological approach therefore argue that closed questions do not reveal in-depth insights into the people being studied, and the results can be an artifact of the way the survey was constructed. McNeill summarizes this view as follows:

The questionnaire may produce the same statistics whenever it is used, but this may be just a matter of repeating the same distortions. The survey style of research imposes a structure on that which is being researched, rather than allowing the structure to emerge from the data as it is collected.
(McNeill, 1985, p. 114)

The choice of categories can attempt to minimize this problem, by ensuring that all possible alternatives are included and by adding an 'other' category. These are issues to address at the pilot stage. However, this will not eliminate the fact that the researcher is imposing a structure, albeit possibly a looser one than a poorly designed questionnaire would impose. In essence, at the heart of this is a philosophical and theoretical debate about whether sociologists can use categories at all. Some would argue that, for example, social classes do not exist in any real sense and are merely constructions of researchers.

There are definite practical advantages in the use of closed questions. Generally they are very quick to administer, and are therefore correspondingly cheaper than other methods. If proper attention is paid to issues of questionnaire design they will produce a reliable research instrument. However, their key weaknesses remains a question-mark over their validity and the imposition of the researcher's framework through the pre-set selection of possible answers.

Open-ended (or simply 'open') questions are designed to avoid this problem. By allowing respondents to speak for themselves, they are not limited in their possible responses. However the great problem with this is, of course, that it becomes extremely difficult to make comparisons between the answers because there is no way of ensuring that all respondents interpret the questions in exactly the same way. There is no guarantee that there will be any overlap in their answers which would allow comparisons. In effect, results can be reported only by quoting the comments of the people who have responded. Can it be claimed that the conclusions are valid if in reality only a sample of all the answers is quoted in the final report or book, and the decision over which bits to include lies with the researcher? Questionnaires conducted using open-ended questions can therefore be criticized over their validity and representativeness, unless all the answers are included in the final research report (which is unlikely).

So, while in the use of closed questions a researcher imposes a meaning on the situation *prior to* the answers being given, a similar process happens with open-ended questions *after* the questions have been answered.

Case study – Age barriers at work

In one of the contributions to Arber and Ginn's study of the connections between gender and ageing, Miriam Bernard *et al.* (1995) looked at how processes in the workplace impact on women in later life. As part of this they commented on the findings of a piece of research (known as the METRA study) conducted by two of their number, Catherine Itzin

and Chris Phillipson (1993). This sought to look at how age barriers might operate in the context of local government employment. The following draws on their comments on the methodology employed in this research:

The ... Metropolitan Authorities Recruitment Agency study ... was a large-scale national survey examining the position of mature and older male and female workers in the context of local government. ... The METRA study had three major phases. The first phase involved a postal questionnaire to all local authorities in England and Wales and was carried out in the spring of 1992. Of 449 authorities, 221 completed the questionnaire, a response rate of 49 per cent. The second phase involved case-study fieldwork in a representative sample of 11 local authorities. Each case study looked at the corporate policies and practices of the authority and then focused on the particular situations within different service departments. Tape-recorded in-depth interviews were held with managers, and group interviews were held with older employees in senior management, in administrative and clerical work, and in manual work. Group interviews were also carried out with women aged 35–50 in middle management. Overall, around 350 people were interviewed in one form or another in the case studies. The third phase involved a self-completion questionnaire sent to 476 senior managers in 8 of the 11 service departments selected for the case-study research. Three hundred and three questionnaires were completed, giving a response rate of 64 per cent.
(Bernard *et al.*, 1995, pp. 59–60)

Activity
a What were the response rates achieved in the two questionnaires mentioned in the extract?
b Explain why the researchers feel it is important to mention this.
c Apart from questionnaires, what other methods were used in this research?
d Identify the distinct sample used in each phase and suggest how these samples were arrived at.

I, A

3.8 Interviews

While all research involves asking questions in some way, if a questionnaire is administered by a person face to face then this becomes an interview. Here not only do the issues surrounding the design of the questionnaire remain important, but a whole list of issues which arise from the fact that an interview involves interpersonal interaction also need to be considered. The relative importance of these varies according to the actual type of interview conducted.

Types of interview

All interviews involve communication between people, but the way in which this occurs can vary.

The degree of structure

Structured interviews occur when a questionnaire is administered face to face and the interviewer is not allowed to deviate from the wording of the questions nor the order in which they are asked. The aim is to standardize the experience so that the only variations should reflect real variations in the answers given. Since this type of interview is used mainly by those interested in obtaining quantitative data, the questions will usually be of a closed type. Structured interviews were used by Marshall *et al.* (1988) in their study of social class in modern Britain (see also Section 4.9). The methodological issues surrounding this piece of research are considered in detail later in this section.

Unstructured interviews occur when there is no rigid format imposed on the interviewer. The latter may decide the order in which questions are asked, and indeed the questions themselves. In this type of interview, it is unlikely that a detailed list of questions would be drawn up beforehand. Instead the researcher is likely to draw up a list of potential *areas for discussion* and use interviewing skills to frame questions to cover these areas. Questions are likely to be much more open than those used in structured interviews. The aim is to try to make the interview feel as natural as possible, almost like a conversation. The lack of structure permits the interviewer to react to the actual answers given by the respondent, by modifying the particular questions asked or their order.

As the name suggests, *semi-structured interviews* fall in between the above two extremes. The questions are not set down in detail beforehand, thus allowing the interview to proceed in a natural way. The interview will focus on certain predetermined topics, but without preset questions. Alternatively it could be that some questions *will* be preset, especially those relating to the social characteristics of the interviewee which the interviewer has deemed to be possible significant variables. This allows consideration of the way responses might vary according to these social characteristics, but also ensures that the overall sample is representative of the population to be studied in respect of the social variables identified.

The extent of the structure of the interview is likely to be affected by the general methodological beliefs of the researcher. The more structured interviews are likely to be part of social surveys aimed at producing quantitative data, while more unstructured interviews tend to be favoured by those seeking qualitative data and looking for a more natural – and therefore more valid – interview process.

Number of interviewees

Should people be interviewed individually or as a group? Group interviews allow the researcher to consider the views of a lot of people in a shorter time than it would take to interview them individually, and in certain circumstances this might also be seen to be more natural. Paul Willis (1977) adopted the group-interview method in his study of working-class male pupils because he interviewed some of the 'lads' together (see Section 8.2). He argued that since they acted together as a group, interviewing them as a group would create a more natural setting which would also allow him to observe interactions between them while conducting the interview.

A potential problem is that people are required to respond in the presence of others, and this may affect the accuracy of the answers they are prepared to give. If, for example, a group of workers were interviewed together with their boss, they might be reluctant to be openly critical of the management. The question of whether people should be interviewed individually or in a group is therefore an issue requiring careful thought.

Discussion point

What would be the advantages and disadvantages of interviewing students from the same group in a joint interview? To what extent might this depend on the topic being researched?

The depth of interview

Ethnographers have developed what are called 'in-depth interviews', which are now used more widely in sociology to uncover the cultural meanings perceived by individuals. Rather than talking to a large range of people, the aim here is to focus on one person or a few people (possibly seen as key individuals). Thus by talking to a few people over a long period of time, issues can be considered in detail and points which emerge followed up.

Such information may then be used as the basis of interview schedules for more standard samples, or the method may stand on its own as a distinctive approach concerned more with depth than with breadth.

Issues in the interview process

An interview is similar to (though not the same as) a conversation in that it involves interaction between at least two people. In order to make an interview work it is necessary to build up some form of relationship with the person being interviewed, if only to encourage them to participate. The role of the interviewer also involves making contact with potential interviewees and gaining their co-operation. The interview process clearly involves the use of interpersonal skills.

A problem may arise over objectivity if the personality of an interviewer intrudes into the research process. This is particularly true if more than one interviewer is used, since the intrusion of their different personalities will mean that the interview experience varies between the interviewees. The actual experience of the interviewees will therefore not be the only variable involved, so the research experience will not have been standardized. This would place a question-mark over the reliability of the research findings.

This issue has been investigated by looking at the outcome of interviews conducted with variations in the characteristics of the interviewers. May (1993) quotes a study of the levels of satisfaction of black Americans with their social, economic and political lives, showing that the answers given differed according to whether respondents were interviewed by white interviewers or black interviewers. Given that the interviews were conducted in the southern US state of Tennessee, it is likely that the overall context of racial relations there had an effect, but it was manifested in variations in response according to the social characteristics of the interviewer.

Labov (1973) also found that black children responded very differently when interviewed by white and black interviewers. In this case the findings from the interviews with white interviewers had been used to define the black children as linguistically deprived, and such a conclusion was the basis of programmes of education based on the assumption that black children were somehow deprived. Labov clearly showed this finding to be invalid, instead reflecting the extent to which black children in a country with high levels of racism would openly respond to white people.

That is a clear example of what is called the 'interviewer effect'. This stresses that the characteristics and behaviour of the interviewer can be an important factor in affecting the answers that respondents give. It is in order to minimize the problem that surveys using more than one interviewer often involve training (sometimes of many days duration), covering issues of how the interviewer is to behave in order to try to standardize as far as possible and minimize the interviewer effect. This issue is of extreme importance if the research findings are to be used for practical social reform.

It is also clear that when choosing both interviewers and the location of the interview, researchers must be aware of the potential for these to affect the research findings. This is known as the 'interview problem'. Oakley (1979) highlighted this by pointing out that an interview is an artificial situation. It is therefore likely that, however hard the interviewer tries to create a naturalistic environment, respondents may choose not to reveal certain things – this being particularly true of any questions relating to sensitive issues. Thus we can only be certain that an interview reveals that which respondents are willing to say, which may not be the same as what they actually think or do.

Conducting an interview

Precisely because an interview is an artificial situation, with the need to develop and continue a rapport with the respondent, there have been a number of debates relating to the actions and stance the interviewer should take within it. The early position on this stressed that the interviewer should adopt a neutral role and avoid any commentary on the answers respondents gave to avoid their response affecting further answers. This is known as a *non-directive interview*.

This view is rejected by Howard Becker (1971), who feels that in certain circumstances a more directive and aggressive style of interviewing is needed. The aim here is to arrive at the truth, rather than simply the information the respondent is apparently willing to provide. Becker most famously used this method when interviewing 60 Chicago teachers about their attitudes to pupils (see Section 8.3). He argued that a non-directive interview would have provided information only on what teachers thought they were *supposed* to think about pupils. Since he was aiming to discover the reality of how teachers actively labelled pupils, he adopted a sceptical stance to their answers. This approach, he says, allowed him to discover the reality of the views they held of pupils. Clearly, research into events which happen but which are not officially meant to happen could require such an approach to break through the bland responses that might result from a non-directive interview.

Another debate about interviews was sparked off by Oakley's (1979) work on the experience of motherhood, and her further reflections on issues arising out of the interview process (Oakley, 1990). She argues that textbook models of interviewing tend to stress the need for the interviewer to remain detached and neutral (the classic non-directive interview). The interview is totally controlled by the interviewer, but she argues that this tends to set up a hierarchical relationship where only the interviewer is allowed to ask questions, while remaining aloof from the respondent beyond the minimal need to establish rapport. Her argument is that this style of interviewing results from a desire to be seen as scientific and to remain the detached researcher. She rejects this model on the basis of her experiences of interviews in relation to her study of motherhood. She argues that there is a need to include values such as subjectivity and equality in the research process, and sees the objective detached model as infused with patriarchal values linked to science.

In her research Oakley conducted repeat interviews with women, and the relationship she built up with them involved her answering their questions as well as them answering hers. She sees this as a more equitable and therefore non-oppressive form of interviewing. A similar approach was taken by Kelly (1988) when interviewing women about domestic violence.

The centrality of personal experience to feminist views in sociology leads them to reject impersonal interviews. This is because the interviews tend to under-value the personal experiences of the interviewees. It is also sometimes argued that to operate on the principles of the detached researcher is to strengthen what is seen as a patriarchal structure in society.

This points towards the idea that there is a distinctly feminist approach to methodology. Exactly what this might involve is a matter of debate. For instance, another feminist-inspired sociologist Angela McRobbie (1991a) has been critical of Oakley by arguing that all research involves some degree of power relationship, and that Oakley's research methods did not in fact overcome this. She points out that pregnant women in hospital were to some extent in a position of powerlessness, particularly *vis-à-vis* the doctors, and it may have been this that contributed to their willingness to participate in the research:

Their extreme willingness to participate in the research could also be interpreted as yet another index of their powerlessness.
(McRobbie, 1991a, p. 79)

Oakley presumed that her stance would at least not add to this sense of powerlessness on the basis of her common identification with the respondents as a woman. However, McRobbie suggests that this assumes that all women have a shared sense of oppression, a view she rejects since it rests on a unified notion of women. Although they may share gender, there are still other bases for power inequalities.

Evaluating interviews as a research method

In essence, the advantages and disadvantages of interviews depend on the degree of structure imposed.

One advantage of a structured interview is that it is possible to make direct comparisons between the responses given by different interviewees, given the commonality of questions asked and the attempt to standardize the interview experience. In so far as this is successfully done, such interviews can be said to have a high degree of reliability. In this respect they are similar to self-administered closed-question questionnaires. However, an advantage they have over these is the fact that there is someone present to clarify the meaning of any confusing questions, and secondly the response rate from social surveys using the interview method tends to be much higher (around 65–80 per cent) than is the case with mailed questionnaires.

A disadvantage of this method is that the structure of the interview is preset, and it is argued – particularly by qualitative researchers – that this precludes the respondent providing full and detailed responses. This results in a lower degree of validity than would be achieved by, for example, an unstructured interview programme.

That point leads on to the first advantage of the unstructured interview. Since respondents can respond in their own words, it is argued that this provides a more in-depth valid picture of reality. The interviewer can follow up issues which arise in the course of the interview. The more naturalistic setting is also likely to make the respondent more relaxed and willing to continue participating.

The key disadvantage of unstructured interviews is that there is no guarantee that there will be any great level of comparability between interviews in a research project. It is possible for two interviews which start at the same point to go off in different directions, making comparison difficult if not impossible. This lack of similarity undermines the reliability of the approach.

Interviews as a whole tend to gain a greater response rate than mailed questionnaires, but they also tend to be roughly twice as expensive to conduct. This will affect the number of people it is possible to interview. Time constraints also limit the number of people it is possible to interview, and therefore the size of the sample in interview programmes tends to be smaller than in mailed questionnaires. In particular the sample size in unstructured interviews tends to be between only 30 and 150, which means that careful consideration needs to be given to the sampling procedure to try to ensure that something approximating a representative sample is achieved. The smaller the actual sample, the more difficult this is.

Finally, with all interviews the skill of the interviewer is paramount. The selection and training of interviewers must be carefully undertaken to minimize the 'interview effect'. All of this adds to the time and cost of the method. Nonetheless, overall the interview method remains a very popular method of social research, with the potential to provide both qualitative and quantitative data.

Case study – Social class in modern Britain

Marshall *et al.* (1988) used the social survey method in their investigation of social class in modern Britain. Thus the study obtained sizeable amounts of quantitative data from a large number of people in a relatively short space of time. This was done using a large questionnaire administered by interviewers. (For further details of this study, see Sections 4.7 and 4.9.)

The questionnaire contained some 136 questions, though not every respondent was to be asked all of them. Sampling and training of interviewers were both key questions. The following lengthy quotation is provided here to reveal the various methodological decisions that were taken in relation to this piece of research:

AGENCIES
The Project Directors . . . were Gordon Marshall, Howard Newby, and David Rose. Carolyn Vogler was Senior Research Officer from January 1983 until August 1985. The Survey Research Centre at Social and Community Planning Research assisted with the questionnaire design, carried out the fieldwork, edited and coded the data, under the Research Directorship of Patricia Prescott-Clarke.

THE SAMPLE
The sample was designed to achieve 2000 interviews with a random selection of men aged 16–64 and women aged 16–59 who were not in full-time education. The Electoral Register was used as a sampling frame. . . .

A three-stage design was employed. This involved the selection of parliamentary constituencies, polling districts, and finally individuals. . . .

One hundred parliamentary constituencies, then two polling districts from each sampled constituency, were selected with probability at both stages proportionate to size of electorate. . . .

Nineteen addresses from each sampled polling district were then selected by taking a systematic sample through the list of elector names and noting the address of the elector on which the sampling interval landed. . . . One person at each address was then selected from those eligible for the survey. This selection was made by interviewers who were given the set of rules laid out in the respondent selection sheet that forms the frontispiece of the questionnaire. . . .

When deciding on the size of the starting sample of addresses two forms of sample loss, in addition to non-response, had to be taken into account. The smaller of these losses is the 'deadwood' contained in a sample of addresses selected via electoral registers. This comprises addresses which are found to be no longer occupied as residential properties. The usual allowance of 4 per cent was made for this factor. The other form of loss was related to the population to be surveyed – persons of working age who were not in full-time education. It was known that a proportion of sampled addresses would contain no such persons and therefore no interviews could be conducted at these addresses. (Some addresses, for example, would contain only persons of pensionable age.) Data from the 1981 Census were used as a basis for estimating the number of such ineligible households. These suggested that around 20 per cent of sampled addresses would be outside the scope of the survey and this too was allowed for in the sample size selected. It was decided, on the basis of these estimates and an anticipated net response rate of 70 per cent, to issue 3800 addresses (19 in each of the 200 selected polling districts).

Of the addresses issued, 165 were found to be non-residential, vacant, or demolished. At 805 of the 3635 occupied residential addresses in the starting sample, interviewers established that none of the occupants was eligible for the survey. A successful interview was conducted at 1770 of the remaining addresses (a response rate of 62.5 per cent). . . .

FIELDWORK AND QUALITY CONTROL
Fieldwork was carried out during the period 1 March to 3 July 1984. One hundred and twenty-three interviewers were employed on the survey. Six full-day briefing sessions were held, all of which were attended by a member of the Essex team, and interviewers were also given a full set of written instructions. The first three interviews conducted by

each interviewer were subjected to an immediate thorough checking in order that critical comments, where appropriate, could be conveyed. During the course of fieldwork the work of interviewers was subject to personal recall. Ten per cent of issued addresses were re-issued for recall (13 per cent of productive interviews). In addition, 36 interviewers were accompanied in the field by supervisors, as part of SCPR's standard supervision process. The mean length of interviews was 77 minutes.
(Marshall *et al.*, 1988, pp. 288–291)

Activity

a Explain the meaning of the terms 'population', 'sampling frame' and 'response rate'.

b What was used as a sampling frame in this study?

c Suggest reasons why this sampling frame was used.

d Bearing in mind the target population of the research, what problems might be involved in using the electoral register as a sampling frame?

e Apart from the example mentioned in the quotation, suggest one other type of household which would have fallen into the category of having no occupants eligible for interview.

f How did the researchers try to ensure that interviews were standardized?

I, A, E

3.9 Observational methods

Participant and non-participant observation are two important methods in sociology which arise from the ethnographic methods developed by anthropologists. The term 'ethnography' refers to the study of small-scale communities. It derives in particular from researchers such as Bronislaw Malinowski who, in order to study the Trobriand Islanders, actually lived in their society as a member and a researcher. He observed while participating.

While the term 'ethnography' is strictly wider than participant observation and includes a number of other possible approaches, such as interviews and document analysis (see Section 3.10 on Hey's research), it is undoubtedly true that participant observation is the most important legacy of ethnography in sociology.

The central idea is to study life 'as it really is', and to observe the meaningful interactions people engage in. In order to do this, it is argued that the best way to obtain the most natural and most valid picture is to use a naturalistic setting, observing life in as undisturbed a way as possible. While this aim is shared among all ethnographers, this section focuses on participant observation and the various debates about the use of that method premised on the idea of naturalistic research. What differentiates it as a sociological research method from purely journalistic descriptive accounts of lifestyles is that it is used to develop and test theories in a systematic way.

The key aim behind observational methods is to avoid the construction of an artificial research environment, which would occur if one approached somebody with a clipboard or even sent them a questionnaire through the post. The latter methods only provide a static snapshot of social reality, and as a result miss out the most important fact about societies – namely that they consist of people interacting in a dynamic way.

There are a number of approaches which can be classed under the heading of observation.

Non-participant observation

Non-participant observation involves a sociologist observing without actually participating in the events being studied. This method of observation is used both to capture the reality of a dynamic situation without affecting it with intrusive research situations (such as conducting structured interviews), and because it is believed that any such intrusion would actually affect the situation being observed. It is therefore a non-obtrusive method.

The most obvious way to observe something without affecting what happens is to do it from a distance or from behind a barrier such as a two-way mirror. Then those being observed are not aware of their status. This is to avoid the infamous 'Hawthorne effect', which refers to a piece of research conducted by Elton Mayo *et al.* (1933) and Roethlisburger and Dickson (1939) to study the effect of various changes in the workplace environment on productivity, in the Hawthorne works of the Western Electricity Co. in Chicago (see Section 9.7).

This was an example of a 'field experiment' in that it was conducted in the factory and variables were systematically changed and the results observed. However, the most famous finding of the study was that changes in productivity could only really be explained on the basis that workers responded in that way precisely *because* they were being watched – they knew the experiment was taking place.

Unobtrusive measures seek to avoid this. This may mean researchers not being visible to the group being observed; or, though visible, they do not announce that they are conducting research.

The most famous examples of this type of research are the various interactionist-inspired studies of education. In David Hargreaves' (1967) study, for example, observation occurred by the researcher sitting in on classes, and there is some evidence that his presence affected what subsequently happened. Some teachers and pupils clearly modified their behaviour under observation.

However, although this method has been used, one of its key drawbacks is the virtual impossibility of totally eliminating any trace of the Hawthorne effect (particularly in highly structured environments). It is for this reason that participation is considered as a cover for the observation. Such research then becomes a form of participant observation.

Participant observation

There are a variety of possible approaches to participant observation, reflecting the level of participation involved and whether or not the group being observed is made aware of the research being undertaken. Any one study may involve a variety of these subtypes, though it is usual for one to predominate.

With regard to the degree of involvement, it is possible to envisage either complete participation in all the activities of a group, or only partial involvement. Ned Polsky (1971), for example, in his study of poolroom hustlers, was involved in their activity in the poolroom (where his prowess as a pool player helped him) but was not involved in other activities of the group. In contrast, William Foote Whyte (1943) lived as a lodger in an Italian house with the group he was studying, even becoming a member of their street gang.

One important consideration concerns the extent to which total participation is possible. Clearly in order to participate the researcher has to share some particular social characteristics of the group to be studied. It would not be possible, for example, for a male middle-aged sociologist to engage in complete participant observation research of the Girl Guides, nor would a white sociologist be able to join the Black Panthers as a participant.

This issue is important because the question of who gets to be a professional research sociologist is affected by the unequal structures of society, just like anything else.

It also tends to place a limit on the type of groups than can be studied by this method. One obvious thing that is characteristic of researchers is that they are adults, and this limits the extent to which they can become complete participants in the activities of youths and children. Since the method has been popular in the study of juvenile delinquents, this issue has frequently surfaced, and the general

response has been to try to achieve an accepted status which means that one can hang around and observe. Paul Willis' (1977) study of male subcultures in a school environment (see Section 8.2) might fit into this category since as an adult he clearly could not be a complete participant but was allowed to hang around with the youths. Similarly, Howard Parker (1974), in his study of juvenile delinquents in Liverpool, used his position as a community worker to hang around and therefore observe.

Even if it is possible to participate, it might be decided against on ethical or personal safety grounds. As mentioned, many studies have used this method to study juvenile delinquents who in their activities engage in illegal activities. Clearly to be a complete participant involves the danger of being called upon to participate in such acts. 'James Patrick' (1973) found this was the case with his study of a juvenile gang in Glasgow: he was eventually forced to flee and abandon his research when he refused to carry a weapon and turn up to a gang fight. Another member of the gang, at that time in prison, threatened him with retaliation and the researcher was forced to leave and change his name – with the result that the real name of the author of *A Glasgow Gang Observed* is not known and he is referred to as 'James Patrick'.

Laud Humphreys (1970) was on occasions arrested by the police during his study of gays, and Michael Haralambos (1974) recounts episodes of being threatened with a gun several times while researching music and culture in Chicago.

It is essentially because of these dangers that Polsky argued against covert participant observation when studying criminal groups, since he believed that such observers would invariably be found out and would then face violent retribution.

This leads on to the question of whether the researcher should inform the subjects of study of what is going on, and thereafter engage in overt participant observation, or whether covert observation is the better choice? It might be argued that unannounced (covert) observation is the only effective way to engage in research on certain activities because some groups are unwilling to be observed openly. This is, of course, particularly true of any activities of a sensitive or criminal nature, and why therefore the research by Humphreys and 'Patrick' illustrate this point so well.

As well as these practical issues, there is also an ethical question surrounding covert participant observation. Should sociologists *ever* engage in research on people without their knowledge, since this involves a breach of privacy? This method of research receives special mention in the British Sociological Association's (1991) ethical guidelines:

COVERT RESEARCH

There are serious ethical dangers in the use of covert (or secret) research but in some circumstances covert methods may avoid certain problems. Covert methods violate the principles of informed consent and may invade the privacy of those being studied. Participant or non-participant observation in non-public spaces or experimental manipulation of participants without their knowledge should be resorted to only where it is impossible to use other methods to obtain essential data. Inexperienced researchers are strongly advised to avoid covert research. . . . Covert researchers should:

1 safeguard the anonymity of research participants

2 ideally obtain consent to the research after it has been concluded (prior to publication).

(BSA, 1991, p. 2)

Activity

a Explain in your own words the principle of informed consent.

b Suggest some problems that covert methods might avoid in certain circumstances.

c To what extent do you agree with the view that this method should be resorted to only where it is impossible to use other methods?

I, A, E

Case study – The Greenham Common 'peace camp'

Sasha Roseneil (1995) presents a specifically feminist portrayal of the actions of the women at the Greenham Common 'peace camp'. (This piece of research is also discussed in Section 5.4.) She was first involved with the camp as a participant but later went back to study it using the methods of observation, interviews and documentary sources. These methods, and some of the issues which arise out of them, are discussed by her in the extract below:

Three main sources provide the data on which the book is based; my own 'retrospective auto-ethnography', interviews with Greenham women, and documentary sources.

RETROSPECTIVE AUTO-ETHNOGRAPHY

In effect, the research for this book began back in December 1982, when I first visited Greenham for the 'Embrace the Base' demonstration. But this was not a conventional research trip; I was sixteen, and went to Greenham wholly as a participant. A year later I had left school and moved to Greenham, where I lived for ten months. During this time, I had a whole range

of 'Greenham experiences' – actions, arrest, court appearances, prison, evictions, harassment from police, soldiers and vigilantes, and, above all, being part of the camp, contributing to its daily re-creation and transformation. I kept a diary only sporadically and untrained and uninterested in the niceties of sociological research methods, I did not systematically gather 'data' on Greenham whilst there. However, my memories and reconstruction of experiences at Greenham have been plundered continually in the course of the formal research process.

Whilst 'insider research' is rarely discussed in texts on research methods, I am certainly not the first sociologist to use her personal experiences and unique life history for research purposes. Long before feminists were advocating this, Mills argued that the sociological imagination thrives on inward reflection: '[You] must learn to use your life experience in your intellectual work, continually to examine and interpret it. In this sense craftsmanship is the centre of yourself and you are personally involved in every intellectual product upon which you work (Mills 1958:196). . . .

My own involvement with Greenham locates me as anything but the unbiased, objective researcher required by the positivist tradition in sociology, or even of mainstream interpretive qualitative research. . . . Rather than 'bracketing' (Schutz 1967) my pre-existing experiences and politics, I sought to engage with them reflexively, to interrogate them, and to locate myself on the same critical plane as the women I interviewed and the archives I trawled. Indeed, I claim a high level of validity for my findings because of, not despite, my own involvement in Greenham. I do not claim that this work is in any way definitive, but I do believe that it is better than that produced by an outsider could have been.

That said, insider research is not without problems. The most obvious of these is the danger of being too close to the subject matter, either to see the sociological significance of that which appears completely normal, or to be able to frame criticisms – the 'rose tinted spectacles' problem. Had I started researching Greenham very soon after living there, with little time for reflection, desensitization through familiarity may have been a more serious issue. As it was, beginning four years after Greenham had last been my home, I came back to the subject matter refreshed. Throughout the formal period of my research I made a conscious effort to 'make the familiar strange', to attempt to see things as if for the first time and then to compare these observations with my immediate 'gut feelings'. As far as criticising Greenham is concerned, the proof of the pudding is in the reading – I have attempted to tell 'the truth' about Greenham as I understand it, warts and all. Here again the length of time between my living at Greenham and formally beginning my research, and my subsequent engagement with individual feminists and a feminist literature hostile to Greenham have, I believe, afforded me a certain degree of critical distance.

INTERVIEWS WITH GREENHAM WOMEN

As a loosely structured network of individuals and groups, Greenham had no membership list and hence no ready-made sampling frame from which to draw a probability sample. I therefore had to rely on my own knowledge of the social organisation of Greenham by gate-based networks. In sampling, I started from a small number of women I knew, most of whom had lived at Greenham between 1982 and 1985, and I worked outwards, using a 'snowball sampling' technique (Coleman, 1958). I was able very quickly to move beyond women of my acquaintance by asking each woman I interviewed to suggest further possible interviewees. Of the 35 women interviewed, 25 were not known to me prior to the interview.

In order to maximise the heterogeneity of the sample, and to challenge the popular stereotypes of Greenham women (the Guardian stereotype of the middle-class, middle-aged, southern England mother of four, and the Sun stereotype of the teenage lesbian punk), I used a method of 'judgment' (Burgess 1984) or 'strategic' sampling (Thompson 1988). Based on my knowledge of hundreds of women I had met at Greenham, I formulated a list of characteristics which I hypothesised were important variables, and sampled with these in mind: age when first involved; class; gate of association; level of involvement – 'camper', 'stayer', or 'visitor'; motherhood status before involvement; and sexual identity before involvement. I was concerned particularly to focus on women who had not been in the public-eye as media-chosen 'spokespeople'. Whilst the final sample is not statistically representative of the population of Greenham, it covers a very broad cross-section of the sorts of women who were involved, in different ways, and at different periods in the camp's history. . . .

My insider status and knowledge had many advantages in the process of interviewing Greenham women. Already 'empirically literate', about Greenham, I could avoid the faux pas of the visitors and journalists who besieged the camp at its peak. . . .

Many of the women said that they would not have agreed to be interviewed by an 'outsider', with a few commenting that our shared histories of involvement allowed them to discuss issues, particularly internal conflicts, which they would not have otherwise done. My membership of Greenham friendship networks also made it possible for me to interview many women whom an outsider would not have 'found'. . . .

The interviews, which were all tape-recorded, were semi-structured, and lasted between two and fours hours. . . .

The interviews were conducted between 1989 and 1991, up to ten years after the events they describe, and my use of auto-ethnography draws on experiences of over eleven years ago. The problem usually highlighted in relation to retrospective data is the possibility of distortions in memory, due either to memory failure, or influenced by subsequent changes in values and norms, which may unconsciously alter perceptions. Thompson (1988) argues that the most significant loss of material from the memory occurs very shortly after the event (within minutes). The process of discarding continues over time, but for the first thirty-four years is insignificant compared with the immediate phase of loss. Thus there seems to be a 'curve of forgetfulness' which inevitably affects even contemporary reporting and participant observers. Thompson also suggests that the memory process depends, to a large extent, on the interest of the interviewee in that which is to be remembered.

Greenham had been a very significant part of the lives of all the women, and all were keen to talk about it. Their memories were therefore probably aided by this, together with their interest in the research. . . .

DOCUMENTARY SOURCES

Various types of documentary sources were used in the research. First, I made use of my own quite extensive archive of Greenham paraphernalia, gathered over the years; this includes leaflets about actions, the irregularly produced Greenham newsletter (to which I contributed extensively in 1984), pamphlets and my personal diary. Second, I was given access to the archives of several other Greenham women, which complemented my own. Third, I consulted publicly available archives and newspaper libraries.

(Roseneil, 1995, pp. 7–11)

Activity

a Explain what Roseneil means by 'auto-ethnography'. How convincing do you find her defence of this method against the criticisms she herself notes?

b What are the advantages and disadvantages of 'insider research'?

c To what extent do you agree with her assertion that her findings were more valid precisely because of her status as a participant in what she was researching?

I, A, E

3.10 **Life documents**

Sociology seeks to consider social relationships, so the ways in which those relationships are thought about and communicated can become an important source of information. This leads to a consideration of the use of life documents. The term refers to documents created by individuals which reflect their own personal experiences of various events or reflect their feelings about certain things.

This sort of approach can be particularly useful when considering historical events, since the authors themselves may no longer be around but it may be possible to gain access to their feelings through documents they have written. The letters and diaries of soldiers killed in war can, for example, still give some insight into what the experience was like, and how social relationships within the army worked.

There is no reason why such documents should not also inform research about the present. One famous example of the usage of life documents is W. I. Thomas and F. Znaniecki's (1919) study, *The Polish Peasant in Europe and America*. In order to try to understand the experience of migration (see Section 6.1) for Polish peasants to America, they made use of an extensive collection of documents including diaries, 764 letters and articles from newspapers.

Ken Plummer (1983) identifies a number of other studies that have made use of life documents, including Oscar Lewis's (1961, 1968) studies of poverty in Mexico and Puerto Rica (see Section 4.8), and Clifford Shaw's (1931) life histories of delinquents in Chicago in the 1920s. Plummer says of this approach:

All this research is characterised by a lack of pomposity and pretension about methods: the researcher is merely there in the first instance to give 'voice' to other people; in some circumstances the voices may then be interpreted. Such studies rarely get bogged down in the abstract methodological and theoretical debate which characterizes so much social science today.
(Plummer, 1983, p. 1)

Discussion point

To what extent do you think it is a good thing to get away from the 'abstract methodological and theoretical debate which characterizes so much social science today'?

The sheer variety of source materials identified by Plummer as falling under the category of 'documents of life' is quite staggering:

The world is crammed full of personal documents. People keep diaries, send letters, take photos, write memos, tell biographies, scrawl graffiti, publish their memoirs, write letters to the papers, leave suicide notes, inscribe memorials on tombstones, shoot films, paint pictures, make music and try to record their personal dreams. All of these expressions of personal life are hurled out into the world by the millions and can be of interest to anyone who cares to seek them out.
(Plummer, 1983, p. 13)

One of the key issues in considering the use of such data is a possible concern with the reliability and validity of the material. People may keep diaries, but does the content of these diaries reflect the reality of their lives? On the other hand, what they say in their diary is a reality in itself, and this recalls W. I. Thomas's dictum that if people believe something to be real then it is likely to be real in its consequences.

The use of life documents reflects this interactionist approach to the study of society, and therefore seeks to consider the interpretations people make of events as real valid data.

Plummer points to the Polish peasant study as perhaps the best example of this type of research, and its popularity as a method seems to have risen and fallen with the star of interactionism since he broadly sees its most influential period as being the 1920s to the 1950s. Since then the tradition of oral histories and life stories has seen something of a re-emergence as a popular research tool.

Plummer makes the further point that the lack of regard shown to this method reflects the desire to adopt a scientific method as a framework for research. He quotes this view of Nisbet who laments the fact that sociology did not choose the arts as a discipline on which to model itself as the basis of a 'humanistic' sociology:

How different things would be . . . if the social sciences at the time of their systematic formation in the nineteenth century had taken the arts in the same degree they took the physical sciences as models.
(Nisbet, 1976, p. 16. Quoted in Plummer, 1983, p. 5)

Discussion point

How different do you think sociology would now be if this had been the case? Should sociology be a science or an art?

Plummer argues that life documents offer a richer, more in-depth, picture of the way people feel and act than is generally possible with social surveys and quantitative research, and he therefore sees them as having great validity. He accepts that there may be a problem with reliability, but is quite clear that this is of less importance than validity:

Validity should come first, reliability second. There is no point in being very precise about nothing! If the subjective story is what the researcher is after, the life history approach becomes the most valid method.
(Plummer, 1983, p. 102)

Case study – The study of girls' notes

An interesting variation on the use of life documents has been used by Valerie Hey (1997) in her study of girls' friendships in two London schools. Although the principal method used was participant observation, she also gathered girls' notes and examined their diaries. The study therefore combined a number of methods which result in qualitative data. She explains the collection and importance of the notes as follows:

In the course of my time in the schools I got to know about 50 girls reasonably well, 20 of these girls very well and three sufficiently well to have been invited to their homes and to have invited them to mine. One girl even sent me a note during a lesson. Others kept up communication after I left the schools, updating me on their present situation. . . . Yet other girls sent me notes which they had stored away; others offered me diaries to read. I offered mine in return. . . .

In so far as teachers noticed girls' extracurricular activities they called girls' notes 'bits of poison' or 'garbage'. Girls referred to them as 'bits of silliness'. As far as I was concerned they were sociologically fascinating because they were important means of transmitting the cultural values of friendship.

It emerged that not only did these writings constitute visible evidence of the extensive emotional labour invested by girls in their friendships, they also comprised a 'pocket ethnography' of girlfriend work.
(Hey, 1997, p. 50)

Activity
a Explain in your own words why Hey feels the notes were important.
b Apart from notes, suggest two other life documents which might be used in a study of friendships.

I, A

3.11 Secondary sources and sociological research

Official statistics

The term 'official statistics' refers to numerical data produced by government departments. They are official because they are produced by the state apparatus. As Martin Slattery (1986) points out, the word 'statistics' derives from the German word meaning facts and figures for the use of the state.

All of this information exists primarily for the purposes of government administration. There are data produced in the course of administering government policy, such as figures on the number of people receiving various benefits. Surveys are conducted with the aim of allowing policy to be formed on the basis of clear information – an example being the ten-yearly national Census. Their production in a political context is therefore something which should always be borne in mind.

There are a vast quantity of such statistics, and for sociologists this represents a mine of potentially useful information, easily and cheaply available. Official statistics are kept in reference libraries and university and college libraries. Production of the figures is co-ordinated by the Office for National Statistics (ONS) formed in April 1996 by a merger of the Central Statistical Office (CSO) and the Office of Population Censuses and Surveys (OPCS). This section of the chapter concentrates only on the most important sources from a sociological point of view.

The Census

Undoubtedly the largest survey, in terms of the amount of data produced, is the ten-yearly national Census, produced at some considerable cost. Slattery (1986) points out that the 1981 Census cost £45 million and involved the employment of 129 000 people.

The Census involves questionnaires being delivered to every household in the UK, with assistance being available to help people fill it in if necessary. It has been a regular feature of UK statistics since the middle of the nineteenth century and is clearly the most representative survey in existence since it involves everyone. The Census Act 1920 made completion of the form compulsory, and although there are some who refuse to fill it in, the threat of a £400 fine is sufficient to ensure that almost everyone complies. Slattery says that, in 1981, out of 54 million people only 6000 refused to fill it in and 700 of these were prosecuted.

The cost of the 1991 Census was £135 million, and the increasing cost is leading to debates about whether the present format should be changed so that Census forms are sent out by mail rather than given out by door-to-door enumerators (see also Section 3.7).

Discussion point

Do you agree that a shift to a mailed census is a good idea?

For the first time in 1991 a question was included on 'ethnicity'. Such a question had been planned for the 1981 Census but was eventually dropped after protests and debate in Parliament. (The issue of 'race', ethnicity and statistics is covered in more detail in Chapter 6.) The questions in the 1991 Census cover the following categories:

- Type of accommodation
- Amenities in household
- Type of household tenure
- Sex and age of people in household
- Marital status
- Household relationships
- Country of birth
- Ethnic group
- Long-term illness
- Work status
- Hours worked
- Occupation
- Journey to work
- Educational and professional qualifications

Activity

a The Census's main aim is to provide reliable information for the government to facilitate policy planning and administration. Suggest ways in which information collected using the categories listed above might be useful to the government in this respect.

b What other areas if any which are not presently included do you think should be included

I, A

Although the Census is generally considered reliable and representative, and as such is often used by sociologists as the basis of checking whether their sample is representative, the 1991 Census cannot be said to have achieved this level of accuracy. The reason for this is the existence of the 'poll tax' at that time. This extremely unpopular tax led to people avoiding payment, and in order to avoid detection they did not fill in any official documents. Recognition of this problem led to after-the-fact adjustments being made to the population figures derived from the Census.

There were further complaints following the 1991 Census, both about the Census in general and the 1991 one in particular. Some complained that the forms were difficult to understand and fill in and demanded a very high level of literacy. Also there were complaints from those administering the survey about the difficulty of contacting some people. Although there were attempts for the first time to attain a census of the homeless, the extent to which this was successful is a matter of debate.

In relation to the specific questions to be included on the 1991 Census form, there were debates over the inclusion of a question on ethnic origins, and on the issue of work which was defined in such a way as to exclude the work done by women as unpaid housewives. Both these debates reflect the fact that definitions used in official statistics do not always reflect sociological ideas in the areas they cover.

Additional categories to include in the 2001 Census are under consideration (Garrett, 1996). These include religious affiliation, levels of voluntary care provided to relatives and friends, access to a garden, and the level of qualification gained after leaving school.

Undoubtedly the most important possible additional category, however, relates to income, which has never been included on the Census form.

While these additional categories would undoubtedly provide useful information for sociological research in the future, there is also the suggestion that the inclusion of the question on income reflects commercial pressure. Such information, when cross-referenced to the other information from the Census, would give companies free (but very valuable) market-research information. Debate has therefore centred on the inclusion of the income question:

The ONS says that in 2001 such a question would be used to help government departments target areas of low income. But others suspect its inclusion has more to do with the ONS ... becoming more commercial, possibly as a precursor to privatisation.
(Garrett, 1996, p. 2)

Other government surveys

For sociologists, probably the most important of the rest of the surveys are the *New Earnings Survey*, the *General Household Survey* and the *Family Expenditure Survey*. Many of the results of these surveys can be found in the annual publication *Social Trends*, which is an extremely useful source of information for sociologists.

New Earnings Survey

As its name suggests, the *NES* covers income and is compiled using a 1 per cent sample of employers operating within the PAYE tax system. It provides information on earnings, broken down into various categories, and allows comparison by class (manual/non-manual), gender and locality. It is therefore one of the most important secondary sources in relation to income.

However, this survey is not without its problems. First, since it is collected using the PAYE tax data, those who do not earn enough to be liable for National Insurance or income tax are excluded from the statistics. This has a particular impact on the gender distribution on earnings, since the vast majority who fall into this category are women, and mostly part-time workers. Faludi (1992) estimates that the earnings of roughly 3 million people, mainly women, are excluded on this basis.

Secondly, the survey excludes the self-employed, and those elements of people's earnings which accrue from self-employment, even if they are employed as well. This is likely to affect the higher-paid categories.

As a result of both of these factors, it is likely that the *New Earnings Survey* considerably under-estimates inequalities in the distribution of income.

The Inland Revenue also publishes statistics on wealth, but these too are likely to be less than accurate since the information derives from their estimate of the value of the estates left by those who die. This ignores the many ways in which estate duty can be avoided, thereby under-estimating wealth. It also ignores the fact that in some cases there are disputes over the actual estimates of the value of estates.

Since Inland Revenue statistics are collected from data whose primary purpose is the administration of taxation – and given that many people wish to minimize their liability – they must be treated with extreme caution. The survey is, however, easily available and allows sociologists to consider some trends in the distribution of income (see Section 14.8).

General Household Survey

The *GHS* was started in 1971 and is based on interviews with 10 000 households. It covers such issues as household composition, population trends, health and illness, employment and education, all of which are of immense potential interest to sociologists. The usefulness of this survey is further enhanced by the fact that it has a very high response rate, with the latest estimate being 82 per cent. Early in 1997 this survey was at the centre of controversy when the government announced plans to suspend it. In response Anthony Giddens wrote an article defending it:

> *. . . dumping of the* GHS *is a symbol of a much larger and disturbing trend. It is a symptom of a society which is turning away from self-knowledge towards an ostrich-like inability to face up to a new and rapidly changing world. . . . One wonders whether* Social Trends *will be the next to fall under the axe. The 1997 version of* Social Trends *is due to appear this week. As with previous editions, it will be full of material produced by the* GHS. *It's hard to see where this information will come from in the future.* (Giddens, 1997)

This points to the important way in which political decisions can affect what information is readily available and what is not.

Activity

If you have access to a quality newspaper on CD–ROM, look up newspaper reports from January 1997 to follow up this issue.

K, A

Family Expenditure Survey

The *FES* comprises a diary completed for a fortnight by a sample of 11 000 households. It covers income as well as expenditure and considers expenditure under headings such as food, clothing and entertainment. One problem with this is a relatively low response rate of 67 per cent.

This survey has also been at the centre of controversy over government changes in presenting statistics on the poor (see Section 14.6). The new measure 'Households below average income' is based on data from the *FES* and has been criticized because such figures are based on households, not individuals. Critics point out that it is perfectly possible for an individual to be poor in a household which is not, but the government response is that it assumes households share their assets. It is this assumption that has been most criticized, precisely because it is an assumption rather than a fact, and one which has been shown to be not always true according to studies of household budgeting.

Problems with government statistics

The political context

Given that the government funds the production of official statistics, it is open to the suspicion that they might be manipulated for political purposes. The government might decide not to collect certain statistics or not to publish others. For instance, the famous Black Report on 'Inequalities in health' was originally published as only 260 photocopied reports on an August Bank Holiday Monday (see Section 13.2). This, it was thought, was an attempt to avoid drawing attention to a document critical of the government's policies on the health service.

The availability and accessibility of official statistics has been the subject of much debate. In essence, they were started because the government wanted to be actively involved in the administration of many services (notably the welfare state), and there grew a feeling that the general public should be informed about the state of the nation as a key basis of an enlightened democracy where people make choices on the basis of facts and figures. Although the ideas of the New Right (see Sections 2.10 and 14.3) have led to it being questioned whether the government should be responsible for producing all the official statistics, critics fear that any move to commercialize the collection, publication and distribution of statistics might lead to a reduction in their availability. The Rayner Reviews on government expenditure in the early 1980s considered this possibility, and at one time threatened the existence even of *Social Trends*. Subsequently the introduction to that publication was changed to stress its usefulness to the government, without any reference to the general public.

Although there has been a trend to more openness in the 1990s, and *Social Trends* is now seen as being aimed at the general public as well as the state, nonetheless there are still concerns. A particular row erupted over the claim by Muriel Nissel, the first editor of *Social Trends* that her proposed introductory article to the 50th issue of *Social Trends* had been 'blatantly suppressed' (Phillips, 1995). The article was rejected by William McLennan, Director of the Central Statistical Office because it was seen as too political. The article was critical of the pressures put on statisticians by the Rayner reviews of Official Statistics. This incident led to a debate in which the second editor of *Social Trends*, Eric Thompson, also intervened:

Impartial statistical information is not only needed to help make, manage and monitor government policies: it is also essential for informed public debate about those policies. Integrity in government statistics is essential for democratic debate. . . . As I had succeeded Mrs Nissel as editor in 1975, she let me comment on drafts of her article. I thought it a balanced review of the history of Social Trends *. . . though I regretted that she had felt it necessary to pull her punches when commenting on government*

statisticians' self-censorship after the post-Rayner attacks on government statistics in the early 1980s. This incident reinforces Mr McLennan's call for a UK Statistics Act to place the independence of government statistics on a statutory footing. Government statisticians should serve Parliament and the public as well as ministers.
(Thompson, 1995, p. 9)

Definitions in official statistics

The definition of various entities is an issue in relation to official statistics. Clearly, the government can decide on the definitions to be used, and it is not always the case that the definitions actually adopted will correspond to general sociological views, or even those held by the general public. Since the data are not collected by sociologists, there is little they can do about this. There are a number of notable examples of this problem.

First, the most commonly used measure of social class, until recently, was the Registrar General's measure of occupations (see Chapter 4). This was based on the relative prestige attached to various occupations, and in many ways it is therefore a measure of status rather than social class (see Section 4.4). Certainly there is no *direct* link between the social class on the Registrar General's scale and level of earnings; and it is also the case that those without an occupation are not included, this most notably excluding the capitalist class.

Consider also unemployment. The official definition of unemployment (see Section 9.6) is in fact a measure of those eligible for certain benefits, and so changes in the administration of the benefits system will lead to changes in the total number recorded as unemployed – regardless of whether the employment status of those affected has indeed changed. The definition of unemployment in this context has in fact changed over 30 times since 1979, and all but one of these changes resulted in a fall in the number classified officially as unemployed.

Another example is the way in which expenditure on the health service (see Section 13.6) can appear differently if the definition of a nurse is changed:

The number of nurses and midwives has risen, but the size of the increase is a matter of hot dispute. This is because in 1980 nurses' and midwives' contract hours were reduced. Because so many work part-time, they are usually counted in terms of 'whole-time equivalents' – in other words according to the proportion of the full week worked. When the hours were reduced, a nurse working the same hours became a larger whole-time equivalent overnight, so, according to the Radical Statistics Group, the 63,000 extra nurses and midwives fea-

tured in the Conservatives' 1987 election advertising would have amounted to only 32,000 if the change in definition had been acknowledged.
(*The Guardian*, 15 March 1989)

The examples considered in this subsection serve to underline the need for sociologists to check the definitions in official statistics to see whether there have been any (perhaps subtle) changes.

Other sources of statistics

Bodies such as trade unions, charities and independent research organizations conduct research and publish statistical information. For example, the Rowntree Foundation produces a wealth of data on income distribution, poverty and the welfare state, (see Section 14.8) which is of course potentially useful to sociologists. Harvey and MacDonald suggest that the name 'unofficial statistics' should be given to this body of data:

This should not be taken to mean that 'unofficial' are any less correct than official statistics. The distinction is simply that official statistics are the ones that 'officially' the government agencies collect and use.
(Harvey and MacDonald, 1993, p. 62)

Conclusion

The Enlightenment out of which sociology was born was based on the idea that humankind could use knowledge to gain control for the purpose of creating a better world. Without accurate information this project will flounder. While there are a multititude of questions which sociologists need to consider in relation to statistics, it is clear they are also a very useful and important source of data on society and the ways in which it is changing. This is why, despite all the shortcomings, sociologists will always flock to the various outpourings of the Office for National Statistics. It is their very importance that leads to concerns over their accuracy and fairness.

Further reading

The following are two useful introductory texts:
- Chignall, H. (1996) *Theory and Methods*, Lewes, Connect.
- McNeill, P. (1990) *Research Methods*, 2nd edn, London, Routledge.

The following is currently the best *video* available on sociology. It covers the philosophical and theoretical issues surrounding research, focusing on positivism, phenomenology and realism:
- Taylor, S. (1996) *Theory and Methods*, London, Vine Video.

A clear and comprehensive overview of the social research process can be gleaned from:
- May, T. (1993) *Social Research*, Buckingham, Open University Press.

The following book is comprehensive and packed with original extracts. It is of immense use to those wishing to consider methodological debates:
- Harvey, L. and MacDonald, M. (1993) *Doing Sociology: A Practical Introduction*, London, Macmillan.

Back issues of *Sociology Review* (formerly known as *Social Studies Review*) also contain many articles on this field of sociology and many others.

Exam **questions**

1 Evaluate the ways in which scientific thinking and methods have influenced sociological research. [25 marks]
(AEB, Paper 2, Summer 1995)

2 'Whether researchers adopt participant observation and/or non-participant roles when observing, they cannot avoid having some influence on those they study.'
   Compare and contrast the role of the researcher in both participant and non-participant observation. Illustrate your answer with examples of sociological studies using these techniques. [25 marks]
(IBS, Paper 3, Summer 1996)

3 'Sociologists who use personal documents, letters, diaries, etc. have to ask themselves whether the evidence is authentic, whether it is complete, how representative it is and whether it is distorted by personal bias of the writer.'
(Adapted from McNeill, P., *Research Methods*, 1990.)
Assess the value of personal documents in sociological research. [25 marks]
(IBS, Paper 3, Summer 1996)

4 Evaluate the advantages and disadvantages of using interviews in different types of sociological research. [25 marks]
(AEB, Paper 2, Winter 1993)

Coursework **suggestions**

- Those doing coursework *must* discuss their intentions with their tutor or teacher at each stage, and keep them fully informed.
- Consult the assessment criteria for the particular syllabus you are following. That said, it will be found that considering and applying method-

ological issues forms a major part of the available exam marks. In coursework pay particular attention to choice of methodology and explain why a particular approach was taken. In applying the chosen methodology pay particular attention to issues of sampling, reliability, validity and representativeness.

- It may not be possible to do coursework simply on a methodological issue. However, you can seek to study topics that have been researched by others, but using a different methodological approach or a different method to compare the results. (This, after all, is what underlies much of the debate about the sociology of suicide.) Such an approach, in allowing you to consider different theories through empirical research, presents some possibilities. First find a topic that is intrinsically interesting, and you will find that each of the other chapters in this book contains coursework suggestions relevant to that topic area.

Stratification: class

Chapter outline

4.1 **An introduction to stratification and inequality**

According to sociologist John Scott, at its most simple social stratification of a society can be defined as:

. . . its internal division into a hierarchy of distinct social groups, each having specific life chances and a distinctive style of life.
(Scott, 1996, p. 1)

The dimensions of class, gender and ethnicity are not mutually exclusive: they coexist, each type of inequality overlapping and compounding another. However, sociologists writing in the different areas may disagree about the relative importance of each dimension of stratification. This chapter considers the case of social class, while the next two look at 'sex' and gender and 'race' and ethnicity. Each chapter concludes with a discussion of how class, gender and ethnic divisions, as well as other factors such as age, interact in social stratification. (See also Sections 4.11, 5.7 and 6.6.)

Social stratification and social inequality

Every society tends to develop a pattern of 'distributive justice' or social inequality according to which the distribution of reward, honour and power is organized and legitimised – though, of course, in practice the pattern of distribution may appear to be anything but just! However, according to Scott:

Social stratification . . . is more than just social inequality. Structured social inequalities can occur around a variety of social differences, and they may involve a wide range of resources, capacities and possessions. Such inequalities include those associated with age, gender, sexuality, ethnicity, religion, language, region, and so on. Social stratification occurs when structured social inequalities are systemmatically interrelated in the way that they shape people's life chances and are involved in the formation of large-scale collectivities that stand in hierarchical relations to one another. The social stratification of a population, then, involves the formation of its members into a system of social strata that are distinguished from one another by their life chances and their life styles and by the particular causal mechanisms that are responsible for these.
(Scott, 1996, p. 91)

Social differentiation

There are a multitude of differences between individual people which may allow us to differentiate between them. Many of these differences are not significant, in the sense that they do not form the basis of identifiable structures of inequality and are therefore not normally a form of social differentiation. The term 'social differentiation' is reserved for those differences which are held to be important in terms of being attributed to positions carrying greater or lesser benefits in society. It *does* matter whether one is male or female, old or young, rich or poor in the sense that membership of social groups based on these social differences will profoundly influence every area of life.

Power and inequality

In evaluations of difference it is important to note the influence of power. As far as conflict sociologists (see Section 2.6) are concerned, the significance of power in evaluations of social difference lies in the fact that it will not be the difference itself which is so important as the power to make it an inequality. In other words those at the top of the hierarchy have a vested interest in perpetuating the high evaluation placed on those characteristics with which they are already endowed, and the ability to achieve this will reflect their power to maintain their relative position of privilege and prestige. Whenever there is inequality there are likely to be competing accounts about the extent to which it can be seen as either inevitable or justifiable, or both. There may be a dominant view according to which the existing social order is legitimized, or seen as acceptable, and this may be challenged by other groups. The supremacy of the dominant group might be achieved by force in some contexts but in others by its power to persuade the population of its 'legitimacy'. The possibility can never be ruled out that majority 'acceptance' of such legitimacy reflects conformity merely to the routine necessities of everyday life – adaptation merely to things as they are for want of practical alternatives – without positive endorsement of the social order.

Approaches that adopt a 'class-based' view of social stratification, according to which inequality stems from command over economic resources, tend to take the view that such economic power signifies class divisions even if the power is invisible to its wielders or its 'victims', or both. For instance, Westergaard (1995) argues that, while subjective evaluations of inequality are important in determining how people in a particular class location might see their situation and may or may not react to it, the point is that objective inequalities exist regardless of peoples' perceptions and evaluations of them. Scott (1996) makes a similar point:

While people in their everyday lives may, indeed, now be less likely to identify themselves in class

terms, this does not mean that class relations, as objective realities, have disappeared.
(Scott, 1996, p. 2)

He argues that much popular and academic discussion of class ignores this distinction between 'structure' and 'consciousness' whereby structural inequality exists independently of people's consciousness of it. Such discussions are not concerned with 'class' at all, but with what Max Weber termed 'status'. (See also Sections 2.3 and 4.2.) They focus on issues of prestige and social honour rather than those of differences in economic power.

4.2 Classical approaches to class analysis

Karl Marx and social class

Virtually all discussions of social class can be traced back to the writings of Karl Marx (1818–83) (see also Section 2.3), in the sense that his analysis of class and class conflict retain their relevance in contemporary society.

Although Marx would not have described himself as a sociologist, much of the history of the discipline has consisted of attempts to support or refute his work – what has come to be known as 'the debate with the ghost of Marx' – particularly in reference to the writing of Max Weber (1864–1920). Social class was a fundamental part of Marx's theory about the dynamics of human history – the structure of societies at different stages of development and the mechanisms which caused societies to change from one stage to another.

Marx believed that all societies beyond the most primitive are characterized by class conflict. In his thoughts on long-term social developments, he argued that this was likely to result in clashes between two fundamental classes in each mode of production; though he recognized that in certain historical circumstances intermediate class 'fractions' may exist. The respective classes change as the dominant mode of production changes from one stage to another, but the important thing is that the two fundamental classes at any given time are defined in terms of their relationship to the means of production. In every era one class owns the means of production which places it in a super-ordinate position to the rest because, according to Marx, political control stems from economic inequality. Those who own the production process are able to appropriate any surplus produced.

The relationship between the two classes is based on conflict over the economic exploitation of the oppressed by the oppressor – whether it be master versus slave in the ancient epoch, noble versus peasant in the feudal, or the bourgeoisie versus the proletariat in capitalist society. This antagonism or class conflict was, for Marx, 'the motor of history' because it contained the contradictory forces that ultimately lead to the transformation of society from one stage to another.

At the time Marx was writing he believed that the most advanced societies in the world had already reached the penultimate stage in this process – capitalism. Much of his writing was devoted to an explanation of the economics of the capitalist system, its impending demise and its ultimate replacement by a communist order. In capitalist society the two great classes defined in terms of their relationship to the means of production are (a) the bourgeoisie, the owners of capital, and (b) the proletariat, those who have little choice but to sell their labour power. (But see Giddens on this in Section 2.10.) According to Marx's theory of surplus value, workers are not paid the true value of what they produce (see also Section 2.3). Increases in productivity mean that more is produced than is required to provide a basic subsistence living to all under capitalism. Part of this surplus production is appropriated by the bourgeoisie. Employers are in a position to exploit owing to their power to hire and fire workers. Workers have little choice but to sell their labour power in return for wages, and will only be employed for as long as their labour power produces profit for capital. Marx believed that the exploitation of the proletariat would lead to entrenched conflict between two increasingly polarized classes in a context of widening inequality between rich and poor. (See also Section 14.8.)

The role of the proletariat, or 'working class', in Marx's theory of social change was to become a revolutionary class. However, he realized that it would not occur automatically: it depended on the establishment of 'radical class consciousness' on the part of the working class. In Marx's terms the proletariat had to be transformed from being a 'class in itself' (a group of people who objectively share a common position in relation to the means of production), to a 'class for itself' (one with subjective awareness of its common interests and an intention to overthrow the oppressors – the bourgeoisie).

Much of the subsequent debate on the Marxist view of class has been concerned with:

- whether or not a discrete and homogeneous proletariat exists
- the extent of class consciousness
- to what extent the contemporary working class constitutes a potentially revolutionary class.

These issues are dealt with in more detail in Section 4.7.

The Marxist conception of class cannot be reduced simply to income level or even occupation, because it is fundamentally an expression of a social relationship between people *vis-à-vis* the production process in which differences in income and work performed are secondary to the basic relationship of ownership or non-ownership of the means of production. Furthermore, even occupation itself cannot simply be equated with social class in the full Marxist sense of the word. There are significant differences between two people doing essentially the same work if one of them is self-employed and the other is not. What is important is not so much the work done as the degree of autonomy and control that flows from ownership of the means of production.

Marx placed such an emphasis on the social relationships of production because he saw the production process, owing to its absolute necessity, as the most fundamental feature of human existence. In producing things people are involved in definite relationships – what may be referred to as the social organization of production – which Marx saw as the determinant of all other features of life. Class relationships based on different positions in this social organization of production were for him the fundamental division in society and formed the basis for differences in interests between them.

The Marxist view of capitalist society portrays a dichotomous class structure (arranged on two sides) in which two polarized, antagonistic classes coexist in a relationship until such time as the proletariat overthrow their counterparts, thereby bringing about the transformation of society and simultaneously abolishing themselves as a social class.

Criticisms of Marx

Criticisms of Marx's theory of social class centre on two main issues:

- the likelihood of a class ever becoming fully class-conscious
- the inapplicability of his analysis to concrete historical situations generally, and in particular to capitalist society in the twentieth century.

Class consciousness is for Marx's critics an improbability, though not an impossibility. Max Weber in particular took issue with the Marxist assumption that radical class consciousness would occur. He suggested that it might be possible to envisage social circumstances which would facilitate its development but was of the opinion that it does not readily occur. The significance of this criticism is that Marx's theory relied on the concept of class consciousness which may have no objective basis in fact but could be said to be merely an ideological device. As Joyce puts it:

the consciousness of a class need not be the consciousness of class
(Joyce, 1992, p. 202).

Activity
Explain the quotation from Joyce in your own words.
U, I

A frequent criticism is that Marx's dichotomous view of class is far too simplistic to be applicable to any real situation. Clearly any theory is an abstraction from the real world, and Marx in his primary concern to point out the fundamental class division in society was aware of the numerous anomalies in such a classification. Many groups or individuals are in an ambiguous position, unable to identify their interests with either bourgeoisie or proletariat. However, according to Marx, eventually polarization would occur whereby more and more people would come to identify their interests with one class or the other. The capitalist system, with its tendency towards the concentration of capital in the hands of a shrinking bourgeoisie, would lead the vast majority to fall into a proletariat characterized by its homogeneity and subject to increasing 'immizeration'.

While some of the intermediary classes which Marx saw as transitional have disappeared, there has been an increase in the number of so called 'middle classes' (see also Section 4.6). This development tends to undermine Marxist theory as an explanation of the class structure of advanced industrial society. Marxist theorists have responded by claiming that such 'new' classes can be incorporated into a Marxist analysis on the basis that they have been 'proletarianized', but the failure of a proletariat thus conceived to develop class consciousness remains problematic for Marxist theory.

A further criticism of Marx's original theory claims that as a result of the 'managerial revolution' control of capital has now become separated from, and more important than, its ownership. Thus the notion of class based around ownership/non-ownership is no longer relevant and does not take into account the rise of the so-called 'managerial élite'. Marxists debate whether or not such separation has occurred and the extent to which this managerial group should be included as part of the bourgeoisie (see Section 4.5).

Max Weber: class, status and power

Weber's views on class and stratification can be seen as a debate with Marx, and in a number of respects he adds to or modifies Marx's theory. It should be noted that while Marx was unequivocally opposed to industrial capitalism, Weber approved of its rationality and was opposed to socialism (Edgell, 1993, p. 11). He thought socialism would weaken the incentive to work and exacerbate the dehumanizing consequences of rational–legal bureaucratization, which he saw as a regrettable concomitant of what was otherwise the most efficient form of administration. (See also Section 9.7.)

Unlike Marx, Weber was less concerned to link the analysis of class to a general theory of history. (See also Section 2.3.) While agreeing that class conflicts frequently occur, Weber denied them the central place accorded by Marx. Weber's main criticism of Marx was that he confused what is sometimes the case with what is necessarily the case.

Though not using the same terminology, Weber implicitly agreed with Marx's distinction between class 'in itself' and class 'for itself'. Weber made much the same kind of distinction when he described class as a potential basis – and hence not an ever-effectively active basis – for the mobilization of conflicting (class) interests. Thus Weber's disagreement with Marx did not concern their implicitly shared distinction between potentiality for class action and its realization, but rather the likelihood that the 'working class' in capitalist economies would ever actually unite in common – even revolutionary – cause. Weber pointed to a variety of class actions that could result from a particular class situation, and he stressed that in capitalist society class consciousness resulting in class conflict was by no means inevitable.

Weber argued that stratification has three conceptually distinct dimensions which relate to different spheres of power. Power for Weber refers to the ability of an individual or group to get what they want even against the opposition of others. Weber was interested in explaining the operation of institutionalized power: that is, the effective control over others that can be exerted in a legitimate and regular manner.

Weber's three spheres of power are the economic, the social and the political. Within each of these, individuals can be grouped according to the amount of that particular form of power they command. Power in the economic system is stratified into classes, in the social sphere into status groups, while the political is based on parties and interest groups. Weber noted that, of the three, 'class situation is by far the predominant factor' (1961, p. 190).

Class

Weber agreed with Marx that class is an economic phenomenon: a person's class situation is a function of their position within the economic structure. It is position within the market that determines a person's 'life chances', so for Weber class exists to the extent that a number of persons share a common chance in the market for the possession of goods and other opportunities for income. Weber claimed that 'property' and 'lack of property' were the 'basic categories of all class situations' (1961, p. 182). Thus for Weber, as for Marx, class situation pivots on ownership or non-ownership of capital; but for Weber it will also vary within and between these categories according to 'market situation'. In turn a person's market situation will depend on the skills and services they can offer in the labour market. In return for what people bring to the labour market (skills, qualifications etc.) they are rewarded differently in terms of income, job security, benefits, and opportunities for social mobility. The effect of these factors, according to Weber, is to discourage the development of class consciousness.

Weber's theory of class specifically allows for a multiplicity of classes. He distinguishes between two types of positively privileged classes – property classes and acquisition classes. The former is determined by the kind of property they own (e.g. land and machinery), while the latter is differentiated by the opportunity its members have for exploiting their services on the market (e.g. entrepreneurs, merchants, professionals and those with a monopoly in valued skills).

Weber also described six negatively privileged classes: three in terms of their lack of property, the unfree, the declassed and the paupers; and three in terms of their potential for acquisition, namely skilled, semi-skilled and unskilled workers. Furthermore, between both types of positively and negatively privileged classes Weber identified various types of middle classes (e.g. propertyless white-collar workers).

In an attempt to establish a definition of the concept, Weber argued that a social class is comprised of a 'constellation' or grouping of class situations which share a number of commonalities. There were four such constellations:

- the dominant ownership and commercial class
- the propertyless white-collar workers and intelligentsia
- the petty bourgeoisie (owners of small businesses)
- the manual working class.

Status

As part of his overall theory of power, Weber's analysis of class went beyond the economic dimension by linking it to the facet of status. If class reflects differences in economic power, status marks differences in the social sphere of prestige or honour. If social classes are distinguished in terms of their different 'market situation', status groups are distinguished according to different styles of life. According to Weber, 'classes' are stratified according to their relations to the production and acquisition of goods; whereas 'status groups' are stratified according to the principles of their consumption of goods as represented by 'special styles of life'. Status groups, unlike classes, tend *de facto* to have a sense of identity and common purpose.

Though class and status are not synonymous they are clearly related – if only by dint of the economic resources needed to live a particular lifestyle. The possibility exists for anomalies to occur in the relationship between class and status, as in the case of the *nouveau riche* or the impoverished aristocrat; but for the most part status groups tend to be tied to occupational grades or professions. According to Hamilton (1990, p. 194), Weber's main concern in defining these concepts is to characterize the stratification systems of societies as either class-based or status-based. Industrial capitalist society is predominantly class-based. Earlier forms of society have often been status-based.

Evaluations of status depend on a subjective, consensual notion by which they can be measured. Status thus involves a personal element which contrasts with the impersonality of class and which has implications for the kind of collective action that can arise from status groups as distinct from class action. Action based on status is concerned with 'social inclusion' and 'exclusion', status groups are concerned with maintaining social distance and exclusivity. Status groups can enjoy their privileges only to the extent that they have power to enforce the rules of exclusion and maintain a monopoly of access. Those sharing a similar status position often form communities which display themselves in a specific style of life, and may become highly self-contained. As a result status affiliations can cut across class lines. Classes and status groups are potentially competing bases of mobilization and group formation in relation to the distribution of power. Weber saw this as another impediment to the development of radical class consciousness.

Activity

Suggest one example of a status group which demonstrates cross-class allegiance, and one example which illustrates internal class conflict.

I, A

Party

Parties are groups which pursue political power in the broadest sense. Thus it includes political parties, trade unions, pressure groups and professional associations. In Weber's view the holders of power may not be the most wealthy or have the highest status. Parties are related to, but distinct from, class and status groups and represent a further dimension of Weber's overall discussion of power, his primary concern. Edgell (1993) argues that there is an emerging convergence betweeen Marxist and Weberian approaches to class. He sums up Weber's contribution as follows:

This essentially hierarchical and highly pluralistic account of class (and status) recognised that economic interests were at the root of class action, but also recognised that the expression of class interests was problematic, not least because of the variable connections between class and status, especially in relation to parties.
(Edgell, 1993, p. 14)

Activity

a Try to think of (i) indicators of *status* that have universal significance, and (ii) those indicators that are of relevance only to the members of a particular subcultural group. Make two lists and note any similarities and differences.

b Which list is most significantly linked to the possession of *power*?

c Assess the extent to which status indicators in each list correlate with *social class*.

d Describe the relationship between *class* and *Status*, and assess their relative importance in sociological analysis.

e Describe the relationship between *status* and *power*.

U, I, A, E

Comparing Weber with Marx

Weber's view of class can be contrasted with that of Marx on a number of grounds.

- Weber's is a pluralistic classification rather than a dichotomous one.
- It suggests that industrialization complicates patterns of stratification rather than simplifying them in the direction of two great classes confronting each other. For Weber the complexity of market relations generated by the division of labour in capitalism creates a variety of different and overlapping interests often making for cross-class allegiances and internal conflicts within classes.
- Class is seen as an objective fact about a person's life chances but it does not follow that people in

common situations always see that situation in the same way. In line with Weber's general sociological position (see Section 2.3), he gives a much greater role to subjectivity and meaning in the relationship between economic interests and class consciousness, seeing the development of class action as a voluntaristic process and as a result far from inevitable.

- Class is seen primarily in terms of market situation (the means of consumption) rather than in terms of the relationship to the means of production. Marx placed much greater emphasis on the latter.
- Weber places much more emphasis on the advantages that stem from the possession of knowledge.
- Weber stresses the importance of status as a basis of group formation.
- Weber rejects what is seen as Marx's economic determinism, by questioning the primacy of economic factors in shaping social life over others, such as political ones.

Essentially, then, while Marx predicted class conflict and polarization, Weber highlighted the problematic nature of class action and predicted a fragmentation of the class structure. Marx saw socialism as the final solution to end social conflict, while Weber argued that socialism might intensify the problem of dehumanization that was already endemic to the rationality of capitalism. The debate between these classical approaches to class analysis continues in the guise of neo-Marxist and neo-Weberian accounts of the class structure in contemporary capitalist society – accounts which utilize the conceptual tools provided by these classical accounts.

💬 Discussion point

Discuss the proposition that there are as many similarities as differences between Marx's and Weber's theories of social stratification.

4.3 Contemporary approaches to class analysis

The inheritance from Marx and Weber has continued to inform virtually all subsequent accounts of class analysis. This section considers ways in which neo-Marxist and neo-Weberian theory has attempted to adapt to changes in the class structure during the twentieth century.

Neo-Marxist theories

In the face of criticisms of its dichotomous view of class, neo-Marxists have responded by defending the logic of the basic division between those who own and those who do not own the means of production. They acknowledge the expansion that has occurred in non-manual occupations which ostensibly appears to have little in common with a proletarian condition. However, they argue that some such groups are in an 'intermediate position': they enjoy greater privilege than manual workers but remain 'hired hands' and subject to their employers' control. For this reason they are described as being in a 'contradictory class location'. The other groups, they argue, such as lower-grade clerical workers, despite differences in working conditions, share a class location with the manual working class.

The latter argument was presented by Braverman (1974), an American Marxist, who claimed that the proletariat in the USA then consisted of 70 per cent of the population. Braverman claimed that during the course of the twentieth century a polarization of control and skill in the workplace has occurred, whereby the 'mass of workers' has undergone a process of deskilling and proletarianization ('degradation'). (See also Section 9.7.) According to this approach the proliferation of white-collar occupations can be accommodated in Marxist theory by stating that these occupations bear the hallmark of the proletarian condition.

Wright (1976, 1985, 1997), another American Marxist, has developed neo-Marxist class analysis further. Wright devised a classificatory scheme which included the higher non-manual occupations which he described as being in a 'contradictory class position'. They are said to be in a contradictory location within class relations because they are located immediately between two other classes in a hierarchy based on differential access to control, one of which has more control while the other has less. Wright adds the dimension of organizational control to the more conventional one of ownership/non-ownership. He divides possession of organizational control into three types:

- control over investment
- control over the means of production
- labour power.

While the bourgeoisie possess all three, the contradictory classes show a mixed pattern – controlling some elements but not others, and having control over some while being controlled by others. This is illustrated in Figure 4.1 on page 116.

Wright devised four degrees of control which generated a four-fold classification of contradictory classes between the bourgeoisie and the proletariat. He also distinguishes between two sections of the bourgeoisie, the traditional capitalists and the

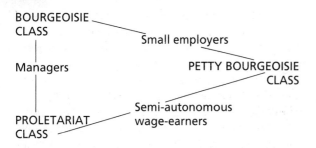

Figure 4.1 Wright's class map 1 (basic version): the relationship of contradictory class locations to the basic class forces in capitalist society. Source: Wright (1976)

corporate executives. When the proletariat, the semi-autonomous workers, the petty bourgeoisie and small employers are added to the picture, Wright's original class map contained ten classes. This was hailed as a significant development in dealing with the intermediate propertyless classes. But there were problems with trying to differentiate the proletariat from semi-autonomous workers.

Wright also went on to question the notion of contradictory classes on the basis that it placed too much emphasis on the concept of domination and took little account of exploitation. Wright revised his analysis with central emphasis on the concept of exploitation. He argues that it is not only the bourgeoisie who are able to exploit workers; some non-owners are able to exploit other non-owners owing to the fact that they possess capital in the form of educational credentials and strategic managerial

control, rendering them at one and the same time exploiters and exploited.

Wright thus constructs a class schema which is based around the Marxist notion of exploitation, while also making the distinction between owners and non-owners and accommodating the complexity of twentieth-century class relations (see Figure 4.2).

Wright's second map is to be read as follows. The distinction between owners and non-owners of the means of production is clear. Each class category is further differentiated; in the case of the owners the distinction is between those working for themselves and those who hire and fire others. Among employees the two key criteria are: firstly their location in the authority structure of the organisation i.e. the degree to which they possess managerial authority and secondly their possession of skills (including educational credentials). This generated six 'new' categories in the propertyless category. Wright is clear about the fact that the people in the property-less middle-class category have interests opposed to those of workers, so he describes them as being in contradictory locations within exploitative relations. Wright acknowledges, therefore, that his scheme implies that the process of class formation and class struggle is a far more complex process than Marx's original theory allowed.

Wright developed doubts about some aspects of his theory, notably the idea that managers are necessarily exploiters, that control is the basis of their exploitation, and that exploitation may be the basis for intra-class divisions rather than inter-class divi-

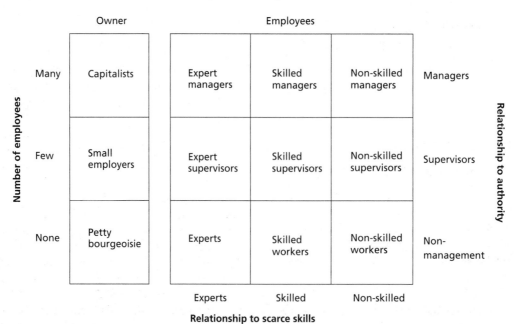

Figure 4.2 Wright's elaborated class typology. Source: Wright (1997)

sions. Others such as Savage *et al.* (1992) point out that it is unclear how a person with skill assets exploits the unskilled.

The most common criticism against Wright has been that his approach moves away from Marx towards Weber. This he denies, making the point that he has adhered to the Marxist notion that material interests in processes of exploitation are objective regardless of the subjective states of the actors.

Wright outlines the three defining chracteristics of a Marxist theory of class as follows:

- Class is defined in relational rather than gradational terms (i.e. the one significant class division that matters is between owners and non-owners of the means of production).
- Class relations are fundamentally shaped by the organization of production, not by the market.
- The analysis of class relations is rooted in the processes of exploitation rather than the technical division of labour.

Relational or gradational?

Wright has further defended his Marxist orthodoxy by arguing that his class map is 'relational' and not 'gradational'. In other words he claims that his map still contains the fundamental Marxist antagonistic dichotomy – capitalists and workers with different relationships to the means of production. However, once he starts to discuss the internal differentiation of the non-owning category he resorts to gradational measures. So, while his description of ownership exploitation is relational, differences in organizational and skill/credential assets are gradational. It is not clear, for instance, why the possession of organizational skills and/or credentials should lead to the exploitation of non-experts by experts. The possibility arises that the propertyless middle classes do not constitute a distinctive, relationally defined class.

Production or the market?

With regard to Wright's second defining characteristic of Marxist class theory – its production-centred nature – he accepts that both Marx and Weber used production-based definitions of class. The main difference between them was that, where Weber looked to the market exchange of assets, Marx looked at production in terms of the exploitation it generates.

Edgell (1993) has commented that on close inspection of Wright's scheme it is difficult to see how it differs from Weber's in practice: as well as using property, Wright suggests that other factors – such as skill – can create class differences among the propertyless.

Exploitation or division of labour?

Wright's final defining characteristic of Marxist class theory is the distinction between class and occupation, which is the source of the Marxist thesis of class relationships being inherently antagonistic. In his analysis of the contradictory 'middle class' locations he identifies them by reference to the occupational hierarchy. Therefore occupational considerations are not excluded from Wright's class analysis. It might be concluded that, even in terms of his own definition of Marxist class theory, neither of his two class maps are purely Marxist as they contain gradational as well as relational elements.

Neo-Weberian theorists

In the discussion of Weber's contribution to class analysis in Section 4.2, the distinctive elements of his view of class position were, on the one hand, the possession of property for exchange, and marketable knowledge/skills on the other. Goldthorpe (1987), following Lockwood's (1989, orig. pub. 1958) expression of Weber's two elements in terms of the distinction between work and market situation, attempted to combine both components into a single class scheme – which can thus be described as a neo-Weberian approach:

We combine occupational categories whose members would appear, in the light of available evidence, to be typically comparable, on the one hand, in terms of their sources and levels of income, their degree of economic security and chances of economic advancement [i.e. market situation]; *and on the other in their location within the systems of authority and control governing the process of production in which they are engaged* [i.e. work situation].
(Goldthorpe, 1987, p. 40)

Thus the Goldthorpe class map aggregates together those occupations that share broadly similar market and work situations and results in a seven-fold class scale. The logic of this is extended to the arrangement of these seven into three broad groupings – 'service', 'intermediate' and 'working' – according to the commonality of their market and work situation. Goldthorpe argues that his employment-based class scheme is 'relational' – that is as reflecting the actualities of class relations based around property ownership. However, to the extent that it is based on a distinction between manual and non-manual work it is also said to be gradational (hierarchical ranking by occupation). Thus in Goldthorpe's scheme a single class can include both the propertied and the propertyless (market situation) and manual as well as non-manual occupations (work situation). Those classes that include such a mixture are said to contain gradational as well as relational elements. These can be seen in Figure 4.3.

Activity

a Within Goldthorpe's three broad categories – service, intermediate and working – identify which ones contain a mixture of propertied and propertyless people.

b Which contain a mixture of both manual and non-manual workers?

c Describe briefly what is distinctive about the working class according to these criteria, and in what sense does this make them a 'pure' class?

d Which class would be described as the most heterogeneous (containing the most diverse elements)?

e Explain what you understand to be the distinction between relational and gradational class elements.

U, I, A

Criticisms of the Goldthorpe scheme

Criticisms have centred around the problem of trying to resolve the use of relational (ownership and non-ownership dimension) and gradational (occupational dimension) in one overall scheme and within class groupings. The relational definition implies the Marxist dichotomous model of two antagonistic groups, while a gradational definition tends at the very minimum to have three groups. Thus the merging of the two definitions is seen to be incompatible. Goldthorpe asserts that the scheme does primarily reflect the structure of class relations and is not consistently hierarchical.

Neo-Marxists such as Wright argue that, because it is based on occupational class rather than social class, the scheme obscures the fundamental social cleavage in a capitalist society – the conflict of interest between owners and non-owners of capital. Indeed, definitions which emphasize occupational groupings ultimately appear to exclude the capitalist (employer) class altogether.

A second and related point is that Goldthorpe's description of the 'service class' elevates their status by merging them with large proprietors, implying that they share similarities in income and power. However, this view is questioned on the basis that the impersonalization of control of capital has not reduced the privileged position of the capitalist class (Scott, 1991; see also Section 4.5).

Other criticisms relate to the problem of including disparate occupational groups within the same category. This is seen in the placement of routine white-collar employees in the same ('intermediate') class as small proprietors.

Finally, there have been feminist objections to the use of a male head of household as the unit of class analysis (see also Section 4.11), on the basis that this is no longer a salient measure of 'household class' owing to the increase in female employment and the growth in female-headed one-parent families. On the other hand it is also argued that, because women are concentrated in different segments of the workforce, especially routine non-manual work, then these classes need to be revised to make them more suited to the class allocation of women (Walby, 1986). Goldthorpe has responded to this by suggesting that in his scheme the routine white-collar jobs could be combined with the semi- and unskilled manual category.

Comparison of neo-Marxist and neo-Weberian positions

There has been a tendency to see an emerging convergence between the neo-Marxist and neo-Weberian versions of class analysis that have been

---

Occupational classes

Service Class

I   Higher-grade professionals; higher-grade administrators and officials; managers in large establishments; large proprietors

II Lower-grade professionals and higher grade technicians; lower-grade administrators; managers in small establishments; supervisors of non-manual workers

Intermediate Class

III Routine non-manual workers (largely clerical) in administration and commerce; sales personnel; other rank-and-file employees in services

IV Small proprietors, including farmers and small-holders, self-employed, artisans; other 'own account' workers (except professionals)

V   Lower-grade technicians; supervisors of manual workers

Working Class

VI Skilled manual wage-workers

VII All manual wage-workers in industry in semi-skilled and unskilled grades; agricultural workers

Figure 4.3 Goldthorpe's model of the British class structure (Nuffield Mobility Study). Source: Goldthorpe (1987)

Table 4.1 Comparison of neo-Marxist and neo-Weberian positions

Neo-Marxist class analysis	Neo-Weberian class analysis
Contains an occupational dimension to class which is essentially relational	Contains an occupational dimension to class which is essentially gradational
Incorporates the idea of a distinctive capitalist class	Obscures the existence of a small but powerful class
Sees the main 'fault line' in advanced societies as between employers and employees	Sees the main division as between non-manual and manual workers
Main advantage is ability to differentiate capitalists from non-capitalists	Main advantage is ability to differentiate between a variety of non-capitalist classes
Main disadvantage is that the proletariat is seen to include disparate groups such as routine white-collar workers and unskilled manual workers	Main disadvantage is that the service class is seen to include disparate groups such as employers and employees

Source: Adapted from Edgell, 1993

discussed in this section. However, Edgell identifies a number of important differences between them, as summarized in Table 4.1.

So, despite similarities between neo-Marxist and neo-Weberian theoretical approaches to class, they retain significant differences in their approaches to the problem of how to combine relational and gradational elements in a single classification.

Class formation and class action

In one major respect, neo-Marxist and neo-Weberian theories are united: they are both based around an 'employment-aggregate' model of class analysis. The main principle of this empirical approach is the statistical analysis of large national datasets which are then grouped into 'social classes'. They tend to concentrate on identifying the persisting effects of class inequality by providing a snapshot of the (employment) class structure at any given point.

Crompton (1993), in a review of debates between the various approaches to class, says that this employment-aggregate approach can be located within the broader sociology of class and stratification. She identifies three levels of class analysis as shown in Table 4.2.

The employment-aggregate approach (level 2) is thus only one strand of class analysis as a whole. Methodologically this approach has tended to be positivistic (see also Section 3.1) in its reliance on the social survey technique (see also Section 3.7) and secondary data (see also Section 3.11). During the 1970s the 'action' approach (level 3) which was emerging in sociology could be seen within class analysis as a range of studies that sought to focus on class processes; that is:

. . . the mechanisms through which the class structure changed and developed, and how different groups of class actors struggled for advantage within it.
(Crompton, 1996b, p. 20)

A further approach is known as 'class formation' (level 1). The way in which class formation differs from class structure is described as follows:

If class structure refers to the system of positions in the division of labour, class formation, on the other hand, tends to refer to the way in which these groups of people who occupy a common position in the division of labour may form as a social collectivity on the basis of these positions.
(Savage et al., 1992, p. 226)

Studies at level 1 have often been historical, charting the emergence and development of groups having

Table 4.2 Levels of class analysis

Level of analysis	Method of investigation
1 Class formation	Socio-historical analyses of change (e.g. Thompson, 1968)
2 Class placement in employment structures	Large datasets aggregating jobs (e.g. Goldthorpe, 1987; Wright, 1985)
3 Class consciousness and action	Contemporary case studies of specific groups (e.g. Newby, 1977; Savage et al., 1992)

Source: Crompton, 1996a

particular characteristics within the capitalist division of labour. Crompton (1996b) cites Braverman's (1974) approach as one such example of analysis of class formation. Braverman's argument was that 'de-skilling' was changing the class (occupational) structure through the proletarianization of white-collar work (see Section 4.6). Another example was that of Thompson (1968): working from a Marxist humanist perspective (see also Section 2.5), his historical account of the 'making' of the English working class stresses the importance of human agency (as opposed to the economic determinism of structure) and class consciousness. Lockwood's (1989, orig. pub. 1958) examination of the changing position of clerical workers can also be seen as part of this approach to class analysis.

According to Crompton, the other strand of the class-processes approach involves studies of class consciousness and action (level 3). These, she says, have often overlapped with level-1 type studies of particular occupational groups, but are often supplemented with contemporary empirical research. Her own joint research (Crompton and Jones, 1984) was one such example of empirical research into the 'proletarianization' of clerical, administrative and managerial workers.

Crompton (1996a) notes that by the 1970s and 80s within the area of empirical approaches to class analysis there had developed a divergence between case studies of class formation (the 'action' approach, i.e. levels 1 and 3), on the one hand, and the more quantitative employment-aggregate approach (level 2) on the other hand. She sets out the case for the class-processes approach as follows:

Both class formation, as well as class consciousness and action (i.e. levels 1 and 3), depend crucially upon organisations and processes which cannot be adequately investigated or grasped via macro level survey analyses alone. Households, communities and work-places – as well as trade unions, political parties, and other social movements – require analysis and investigation via quantitative and qualitative case studies and ethnographies, as well as sample surveys. In British sociology there is an important tradition of this kind of empirical work – the 'Affluent Worker' studies of Goldthorpe, Lockwood et al.; Newby's research on agricultural

workers; Hindess's work on local politics; Hill's study of dock workers; Crompton and Jones on clerical workers and so on. This kind of work has emphasised the significance of processes of class formation, as well as the links that may or may not occur between such formations and class consciousness and action.
(Crompton, 1996a, p. 120)

A recent example of the class-processes approach can be seen in the work of Savage *et al.* (1992). They argue that the 'middle classes' constitute classes in that they form cohesive social entities. Borrowing from Wright (discussed earlier), they look at how organizational assets can be seen as a source of power for those in middle-class positions. These can be used in conjunction with cultural assets – such as educational credentials – to secure and maintain their position (see Section 4.6 for more information on this). This study still relies on the use of quantitative class structure data, which is indicative of the difficulty of testing the findings of case studies on which class-formation analysis is based.

It seems that nowhere in sociology is the debate between structure and action more pertinent than in considerations of their relative merits for class analysis. Here perhaps Giddens' structuration thesis (see also Section 2.10) provides some hope, on the basis that structure and action are seen as 'two sides of the same coin' – which in terms of class analysis implies the need for study of the dynamic interrelationship between class structure and class processes. The findings based on the former tend to indicate the stability of the class structure and its enduring effects, while studies of class processes tend to portray changes, some of which seem to be undermining the very notion of class (see Section 4.10 for more information on this).

Crompton (1996b) argues that there is a place for both approaches in class analysis since each has methodological strengths (see also Section 3.6) lacking in the other. For instance it is difficult to study

Discussion point

The only sensible way forward for class analysis in sociology is to use a combination of quantitative and qualitative approaches. Is this likely to happen? To what extent do you agree with this statement?

Activity

a How would you go about carrying out a case study of 'the very rich', and what difficulties might arise?

b How would you select a sample of the 'under-privileged' in order to carry out a survey investigating their moral values?

c Using information from this section and elsewhere, evaluate the relative usefulness of the employment-aggregates and class-processes approaches to class analysis.

K, U, I, A, E

'the very rich' using the sample survey of the employment-aggregates approach because there are so few in this category they would not be represented in a sample; thus a case study would be more useful. However, she points out that claims of the supposed decline of moral values among under-privileged groups could only really be 'tested' in a large-scale survey.

4.4 Defining and operationalizing the concept of class

Alongside the protracted debates both within and between neo-Marxist and neo-Weberian schools of thought about the theoretical meaning of class and its empirical applications, there have been other, less theoretically informed attempts to operationalize the concept. These have tended to be based on the defining characteristics of occupations such as skill or prestige.

Objective definitions of class

The Registrar-General's definition of social class

The Registrar-General's classification was devised:

. . . so as to secure that as far as possible, each category is homogeneous in relation to the general standing in the community of the occupations concerned. This criterion is naturally correlated with . . . other factors such as education and economic environment, but it has no direct relationship to the average level of remuneration of particular occupations.
(HMSO, 1966; quoted in Crompton, 1993, p. 53)

This indicates that the Registrar-General's social class (RGSC) scale is based on the assumption of a hierarchy of occupational status, reflecting relative 'standing in the community' but closely related to educational credentials and skill requirements. Thus many have seen this as more accurately described as a status classification rather than a class one.

However, apart from a shift in emphasis from occupational prestige to skill as the basis of ranking in 1980, from 1911 until the 1991 Census (see also Section 3.11) this was the main way in which social class was measured in official statistics as well as in sociological research.

The RG model divides the population into six classes (since 1971) as in Table 4.3, which also shows their distribution.

Table 4.3 Social class distribution of the economically active population, by RG category (percentages)

		1971	1981	1991
I	Professional	4	4	5
II	Managerial and technical	18	22	28
IIINM	Skilled non-manual	21	22	23
IIIM	Skilled manual	28	26	21
IV	Semi-skilled manual	21	19	15
V	Unskilled manual	8	7	6

Source: Censuses 1971, 1981, 1991

Activity

a According to the Registrar-General's classifications in Table 4.3, which class has experienced the biggest percentage point increase in size since 1971?

b Identify the classes that have increased in size and those that have decreased.

The key division, as with most occupationally based schemes, is between the manual and non-manual categories. Thus classes I, II and IIINM are said to be non-manual and are also taken to represent the 'middle classes', while the remaining (IIIM, IV and V) consist of manual workers and are taken to represent the 'working classes'.

Since the scheme assumed that the hierarchy accurately reflected the regard in which each group was held, the belief that manual workers were inferior resulted in them being placed at the bottom of the class structure. The assumption of shared values is integral to this idea of a mutually agreed status hierarchy, and it places the RG scale within a functionalist perspective (see also Section 2.4) to stratification as does the notion of the naturalness and necessity of inequality.

A number of problems flow from the fact that the RG scale does not bear a direct relationship to the relative earning power of the various occupations. There are anomalies, such as the fact that priests (placed in class I) have an income which is considerably less than others placed lower down the scale. As it is based on 'general standing in the community' the RG scale owes more to ideas of inequality based on status than to social class. Since assessments of status are essentially subjective, this might be thought of as undermining the RG scale's claims of objectivity. Finally, the reliance on occupation as the determinant of class membership means that those without paid employment do not feature in it in their own right. This has proved particularly troublesome in terms of locating women in the class structure (see also Section 4.11), as the unit of class analysis is taken as 'male head of household'.

The Registrar-General's socio-economic groupings

This scheme, operative since 1961, seeks to provide a closer link between classification and command of economic resources by classifying people into socio-economic groups (SEGs) who share a similar social and economic status. It has been used in government surveys such as the *General Household Survey*. (See also Section 3.11.)

The 1991 Census provided data using SEGs and the RGSC measure, thereby allowing some comparisons to be made. In only ten of the seventeen socio-economic groups were all the members in a single RG social class category (mainly professional workers and all manual workers). In the case of employers and managers (SEGs 1 and 2), members of these groups were to be found across all six RG classes.

The difficulty with classifying managers, most of whom are in class II, and the problems noted earlier with placing clerical workers, suggest that of the six RGSCs it is II and IIINM that are the most problematic. This is all the more significant when it is considered that, according to the 1991 Census, these two groups make up 51 per cent of the economically active and 91 per cent of the middle class (i.e. classes I, II and IIINM). The growing preponderance of these occupational groups in the population suggests that the RG social class scale will become less useful.

How useful are these schemes?

Although it is still used widely for long-term comparisons in socio-medical data, the RGSC is now seldom used for most professional sociological purposes. Socio-economic grouping has a number of advantages. The SEG is a measure of employment status as opposed to skill or social standing. It also has seventeen categories, which makes it potentially more flexible.

However, apart from the lack of compatibility and the possibility of cross-mapping between the two schemes, the major weakness from which they both suffer is the fact that they ignore the 40 per cent (approx) of the population who do not have paid employment. Because of these problems, the Office of Population Censuses and Surveys (as it was then called – now the Office for National Statistics (ONS)) commissioned the Economic and Social Research Council (ESRC) to review the existing classifications (Rose, 1995).

Phase one of this exercise has been completed, the chief conclusion being that occupationally based classifications will continue to be important tools for policy analyses, despite the problems with the current classifications. On practical grounds, they are based on routinely and widely collected data; and on theoretical grounds they are useful in that a person's employment situation is a key determinant of life chances.

Gilbert sums up the conclusions of phase one as follows:

... it is not surprising if the RGSC is now considered inadequate by many academic researchers. ... the revision of government social classifications will have to be considered within the framework of current intellectual debates surrounding class analysis. Principal among these, of course, are the unit of analysis problem, the relationship between gender and class, the appropriate reference occupation for the retired, the unemployed and other significant economically inactive groups, and the even thornier problem of the very relevance of class analysis to contemporary society and social scientific explanation.
(Gilbert, 1995, p. 5)

In 1991 some changes were introduced by the government in response to the criticism that the classes in government scales are based solely on occupation, rather than any other factor relating to social class. They are now to be known as 'social class based on occupation' – not simply social class:

This was the result of a consultation exercise by the OPCS who found that while people had doubts about the title 'Social Class' they were reluctant to see it abandoned entirely in favour of names such as 'Occupational Skill Group' or 'Occupational Category'. In its defence, it was argued that the social status of occupations is related to other social class indicators such as income, security of employment, skill level and education. The compromise was to adopt the new name of Social Class Based on Occupation.
(Denscombe, 1993, p. 12)

The Standard Occupational Classification

This scheme (the SOC) was developed to replace the Registrar-General's scale. The argument was that social class was not adequately indicated by the single measure of occupation, and so the OPCS sought an alternative to social class on the pretext that the name:

... implies that the classification embraces many social characteristics whereas it is actually based on groups of occupations.
(Delamothe, 1989, quoted in McDonnell 1990, p. 30)

Thus the introduction of the SOC may be seen as intended to literally 'de-class' occupationally based schemes and its scope is stated as being simply to measure jobs. It classifies occupations according to the level of skill and qualifications involved. Some of the benefits of this new scheme are outlined here:

The designers of the SOC state that the concept to be classified is a 'job' which is seen as a set of skills or expertise. Assigning jobs to categories, they argue, does not require the ancillary information on status in employment, for example whether the person is self-employed or a supervisor . . . (McDonnell, 1990, p. 31).

This approach does appear to treat occupation as if it occurs in a vacuum. Critics of the introduction of SOC saw it as an attempt by a Conservative government via the OPCS (ONS since April 1996) (see also Section 3.11) to 'abolish social class' by defining it away. This argument is put specifically in relation to trends in differential mortality rates, which have shown a widening gap between rich and poor. (See also Section 13.2.) It is argued that changing the system of classification will disrupt comparisons over time and remove the social class component altogether. Health along with a number of other characteristics will thus be dissociated from social class.

The Surrey Occupational Class Scheme

This was an attempt to deal specifically with the problem of how to classify women in occupational class schemes, developed by Arber, Dale and Gilbert at Surrey University. It is based on 'individual classification' of women in their own right. It tends to highlight the differing proportions of men and women in different segments of the labour market. (See also Section 9.3.) Thus as well as showing women's disadvantage it also confirms male dominance of particular occupational groups and their preponderance in full-time employment. The compilers acknowledge a number of problems with using the part-time and unwaged classifications for women as these are often transitory occupations and without more information about their economic circumstances it is probably a fairly poor indicator of their socio-economic position. (Another similar scheme developed by Dex to accommodate women's class positions is described in Section 4.11).

Evaluation of occupationally based classifications of social class

Figure 4.4 shows some of the principal schemes based on occupation. Some of the advantages and disadvantages of these schemes are given below.

REGISTRAR-GENERAL'S SCALE (RGSC)	SOCIAL GRADING SCALE (SGS) – used in market research	HOPE-GOLDTHORPE SCALE (HGS) – excluded women for historical and comparability reasons	STANDARD OCCUPATIONAL CLASSIFICATION (SOC) – replacing the RGSC for official purposes	SURREY OCCUPATIONAL CLASS SCALE (SOCS) – (1986) including women and discriminating more finely in occupations where women are well represented
I	A	I	1	1
Higher professional/managerial		Higher professional/administrators/managers and large proprietors		
II	B	II	2	2
Lower professional/managerial		Lower-grade administrators; higher-grade technician and supervisory	Professional	Employers and managers
			3	3
			Associate professional and technical	Lower professional
IIIN	C1	III	4	4
Supervisory (over manual workers) and lower/routine non-manual		Routine non-manual	Clerical and secretarial	Secretarial and clerical
		IV	5	5
		Small proprietors and self-employed	Craft and related	Foremen and self-employed manual
		V	6	
		Foremen and lower-grade technicians	Personal and protective serivces	
IIIM	C2	VI	7	6*
Skilled manual		Skilled manual	Sales	Sales & personal services
				Skilled manual
IV	D	VII	8	7
Semi-skilled manual	Semi-skilled and unskilled manual, in industry, and agricultural workers		Plant and machine operatives	Semi-skilled
V			9	8
Unskilled manual			Other occupations	Unskilled
	E			
	Unemployed, pensioners, housewives, permanently sick and disabled			*Divided into two classes in some sources*

Figure 4.4 Some of the most widely used classifications based on occupation. Source: Swatridge (1995)

Advantages

- Such schemes are reasonably easy to understand.
- They are used regularly in research and are therefore familiar.
- They allow comparisons over time where a standard measure is repeated, and thus facilitate replication.
- For most people their occupation provides virtually all their income, and so this is a potent indicator of inequality.

Disadvantages

- Occupational dynamics make comparisons over time difficult or misleading.
- It is debatable whether a single criterion such as occupational status can capture the full significance of class, particularly in the Marxist sense of the word.
- Occupational scales are essentially descriptive, saying little about class processes or class relations. In particular they deny the existence of the capitalist class and are unable to explain the inequalities that arise from the ownership of capital.
- It is difficult to classify those who do not have a paid job. Classification on the basis of a previous job is unsatisfactory as it implies that an unemployed sales representative has the same command over resources as an employed teacher.
- Married women are not classified by social class according to their own occupation (except in the Surrey scheme).
- There are anomalies between occupational class and income. Someone who earns less than someone else may well be placed in a higher class.
- The class position of people is based on their current position in the occupational class hierarchy. This does not indicate either their class origins or their future aspirations.

Overall, then, while the use of 'occupation' as a proxy for 'social class' has some advantages these tend to be administrative rather than theoretical. Edgell (1993) describes how reviews of the history of official occupational classification schemes have concluded that they are an obsolete and simplistic, arbitrary and crude, but well used, measure of social inequality.

Discussion point

'It is difficult to conduct credible sociological research into class without using some sort of occupational-based scheme to categorize people, but the existing ones all seem to have their drawbacks.' Discuss this proposition. If it has any truth, should we still use these schemes?

Subjective definitions of class

In most of the objective class schemes noted above, people are assigned to a class according to the criterion of what job they do. But many people thus defined as middle class might well describe themselves as working class. The implication of this is that we can tell very little about levels of *class consciousness* from objective classifications alone. An example of the complexity of the relationship between objective and subjective data can be seen from Table 4.4.

Table 4.4 How a sample of people saw themselves, compared with their objective classification

Subjective social class	Objective social class (%)					
	I	II	IIINM	IIIM	IV	V
Middle class	74	71	48	37	21	29
Working class	11	23	42	56	66	62

Source: Roberts *et al.* (1977)

The anomalies produced by using objective and subjective classifications are dramatically illustrated also by the following example. In 1989 a MORI poll showed that 30 per cent of people described themselves as middle class and 67 per cent described themselves as working class. This contrasts with the objective data from the 1991 Census which showed that, of the economically active population, 56 per cent were middle class and 42 per cent were working class.

There have to be doubts about the wisdom of relying on objective measurements of class. This suggests the need for greater understanding of the perceptions of various groups of 'class actors', as favoured by the class-processes approach.

4.5 The dominant classes

Giddens (1980) has described the three main categories of rich people in the UK as (a) the 'jet-set' rich, who made their money out of the media, sport and entertainment, (b) the 'entrepreneurial' rich, whose money resides in stocks and shares, and (c) the land-owning rich. These three groups constitute less than 2 per cent of the total population, but they are extremely significant in terms of the concentration of wealth in their hands, the nature of that wealth and its disposal. (See also Section 14.8.) In 1992 the richest 1 per cent of the population owned 18 per cent of marketable wealth (*Social*

Trends, 1995). However the figure is much higher (29 per cent) if the value of housing is excluded from the calculation. Marketable wealth refers to anything that can be bought and sold.

Activity

a Suggest why the exclusion of the value of housing from assessments of personal wealth holdings seems to indicate an even greater concentration of wealth in the hands of the richest 1 per cent?

b How would you assess the significance of this disparity for the debate about the existence of a capitalist class?

I, A, E

While there are differences between these three rich groups regarding the type of capital they own, there are also many connections between the individuals and families that comprise them which have been documented since the 1970s (Stanworth and Giddens, 1974; Scott, 1985, 1991). Sociological interest in 'the rich', in terms of social stratification, concerns the extent to which they can be said to constitute an 'upper class' and whether or not their ownership and control of certain forms of capital means that this group constitutes a unified 'capitalist' or 'ruling' class.

As Edgell (1993) points out, the language of class is biased and this is well illustrated in relation to descriptors of the dominant classes. Neo-Marxist accounts, with their emphasis on economic exploitation, tend to employ the term 'capitalist class', while neo-Weberians, who stress political power as an alternative to economic power, distinguish between those who are positively privileged in economic terms and those with political power, the political élite. Those favouring an occupationally based definition tend to speak of the rich simply as 'the upper-class'. For this reason Edgell (1993) suggests that the term 'dominant class(es)' is a more neutral generic term for such groups.

Ownership and control

Marxist theory is the classical exposition of the concept of a ruling class. By virtue of its ownership and control of the means of production, the bourgeoisie is also a politically dominant class whereby it monopolizes power in the state as a tool of class dominance. (See also Section 17.3.) Furthermore the position of the bourgeoisie is consolidated by its power over the cultural sphere via the ideological control which both legitimates and obscures its dominance. It has therefore become important to investigate developments in the patterns of owner-

ship and control of capital, as changes in this area might undermine the Marxist concept of the ruling class.

In the third volume of *Capital*, Marx argued that a separation of ownership and the control of production would occur which would render capitalist owners superfluous to the production process – and hence conspicuously parasitic and expendable, precipitating their demise. Weber, on the other hand, recognized the tendency for managers to become key players yet, crucially, remain employed by the owners on the basis of their ability to 'turn a profit'. The question becomes one concerning the strategic position of such managers in relation to their employers and the workers they supervise.

Edgell (1993) identifies two main schools of thought about the significance of such a development, the managerialists and the non-managerialists. Both schools agree that a separation of ownership and control has occurred. However, the managerialists might argue that this has led to a major transformation of the upper end of the class structure, while the non-managerialists, who tend to be neo-Marxists, argue that it has not altered the underlying nature of capitalist class relations.

Aspects of what came to be called 'the managerial revolution' thesis were first proposed by Berle and Means (1968, orig. pub. 1932). It has been supplemented by numerous contributors since then, notably Burnham (1945) – who coined the term 'managerial revolution' – and Dahrendorf (1959). It was argued that the rise of the 'joint-stock company' or 'corporation', where managers had control over shareholders' capital, gave rise to the possibility that salaried managers could usurp the powers of the capitalists and become the dominant force in society. Berle and Means saw modern capitalism evolving towards management control of the largest enterprises, with a transfer of power from owners to managers, and Dahrendorf (see also Section 2.6) referred to this process as 'the decomposition of capital'. Further, as well as wresting control from the owners, the new managerial class would exercise their control in a more socially responsible, even benign, way, suggesting a regard for the needs of the wider community rather than simply the rational pursuit of profit.

Dahrendorf argued that there had occurred a significant shift in the values and motives of those in control of industry. He saw managers as more interested in bureaucratic efficiency than profit *per se*, because their authority was based on educational qualifications and their tenure of a position in the organization. Dahrendorf took this to signify the end of a capitalist system based on antagonistic class relations, and the dawn of 'post-capitalist' society in the sense that there was no longer a discrete and identifiable capitalist class of owners/controllers.

Scott (1985) asserts that the managerialist case cannot be sustained because it rests on inadequate evidence and faulty theory. The mere fact that the ownership of capital has taken on a more remote form (shareholding) does not alter the basic fact that capitalism is built on exploitative class relations. Edgell (1993) says that these criticisms can be characterized as follows:

- The fundamental necessity for capitalist enterprises to produce profit or risk collapse has not changed at all, regardless of who controls them. So the profit motive must be paramount to all other considerations in the decisions of the managers.
- There is evidence that managers are actively recruited and promoted on the strength of their profit-making ability.
- Despite the apparent separation, there is considerable social and economic unity between owners and managers.

Scott (1985, 1991) argues that management control was characteristic of only a short period of capitalist development. What has happened since then, he says, is that financial intermediaries (banks, insurance companies and pension fund-holders) have increased the proportion of company shares in their hands. Thus there has been a move away from personal and family ownership of businesses to more impersonal arrangements, which Scott refers to as a 'depersonalization' of property. This has led to the emergence of 'control through a constellation of interests', whereby the ownership and control of industry has taken on a 'corporate' form. Dominant groups of shareholders are often able to combine their holdings to form a large voting block; but since their interests are too diverse to have a consistently common policy, and although directors have to take account of the interests of such 'blocs', the latter retain some autonomy.

Because a board of directors are in such an important strategic position as mediators of the various interests that determine company policy, Scott argues that this is the focus of corporate control, so any study of the persistence of a capitalist class should look at the composition of company boards. It is here, he says, that the link between ownership and control is most visible. Pointing to the high degree of self-recruitment to an economically privileged upper class, he argues that here is considerable evidence to indicate the continuing existence of a distinctive upper class in British society.

Social unity between owners and managers

The pattern of social unity between owners and managers is based on the similarities in their social class origins and educational experience. One area which is highly instrumental in this respect is the role of the public school system in the self-perpetuation of recruitment to top positions in British society, a remarkable proportion of which are held by former pupils of public schools. Stanworth and Giddens, (1974) found that of those employed in each of the following occupational categories – bishops, senior ranks of the armed forces, principal judges, senior civil servants, Conservative MPs, and the directors of the largest industrial and financial corporations – more than half had been to a public school (in many cases the proportion was much higher). Some 73 per cent of the directors of industrial corporations and 80 per cent of the directors of financial firms had received a public-school education. The study drew the conclusion that the élite positions in the major institutional sectors in British society continued to be heavily dominated by individuals from a 'privileged social background'.

Scott's own later research (1991) demonstrates the continuing significance of the public schools in the process of class reproduction. In 1990, notes Scott, the heads of the top 200 wealthiest families included 35 Old Etonians – significant indeed when the public schools collectively took only 5 per cent of the male school population. Scott's main contention is that upper-class families have been successful in reproducing themselves not just through the transmission of economic capital but increasingly via cultural capital (see also Section 8.5), which is acquired by purchasing a privileged education. Scott summarizes the situation as follows:

The capitalist class no longer owes its privileges and advantages exclusively to inherited access to entrepreneurial locations. In the system of impersonal capital the recruitment of executive and finance capitalists depends upon the possession of educational credentials. Members of the capitalist class can use their wealth to purchase a privileged education for their children, so ensuring that they are well placed in the educational race and stand a much enhanced chance of attending the universities of Oxford and Cambridge. It is the degrees of these universities which are still regarded by those who recruit executives and directors as being most appropriate for a career in business. Wealthy families are able to convert their wealth into the 'cultural assets' of the educational system, which can

then be reconverted into enhanced economic opportunities and prospects for wealth accumulation.
(Scott, 1991, p. 115)

Scott goes on to point out that entry to capitalist locations depends not simply on educational credentials, but also on the social assets which are seen as desirable by those involved in the process of selection. The milieu for the development and reinforcement of these social attributes is the 'old boy network'. Scott concludes that there is a capitalist class with an inner circle of finance capitalists who are involved in a number of intersecting upper circles, and that it is through the informal social networks which connect these upper circles that class reproduction is ensured.

Activity

a Describe in your own words Scott's view of the part played by education in the process of class reproduction.

b Using information from the extract immediately above to illustrate your answer, suggest what effect the continuing existence of fee-paying education is likely to have on the degree of openness of élite positions in British society. **U, I, A**

Economic unity between owners and managers

Scott (1986) argues that, although most directors are salaried employees, they tend to benefit from two sources of privilege and power which distinguish them from the mass of salaried managers:

- To a certain extent they are able to determine their own pay and conditions of employment, so the way in which they are regulated at work gives them more in common with the owners.
- The majority of directors are substantial shareholders, which gives them an interest in the suc-

cess of the business system as a whole. In addition to this category of directors, it is also apparent that there are still many companies which bear a family name and are under the direct ownership and control of that family.

In opposing the managerialist argument, Scott states:

Top corporate decisions are taken by a group of directors with significant shareholding interests, often with controlling blocks of shares, and with interests which are closely allied with those of the financial intermediaries. . . . Top directors are tied together through 'the interlocking directorships' . . . which . . . casts the 'multiple directors' in a key role as coordinators of the business system as a whole.
(Scott, 1986, p. 6)

All this leads him to argue that top business controllers today are much the same as their pre-war counterparts. Despite the increasingly impersonal pattern of ownership, there has not been a disappearance of the upper class as an economic force; rather there exists in the UK a power bloc dominated by the capitalist class (see Figure 4.5).

Referring to Figure 4.5, Scott states that, while managerialists argue that the 20th century has witnessed a transition in the nature of capitalist economic locations from property ownership towards directorships, in reality there are numerous overlaps and interconnections between these four 'ideal-type' capitalist locations, among which mobility is both easy and frequent. Particular individuals may occupy a number of locations simultaneously. Scott rejects the managerialist claims and argues that

The capitalist business class of Britain today consists of those whose family wealth and life chances are generated by the involvement of their members in these capitalist economic locations . . . which . . . comprises about 0.1 per cent of the adult population, about 43,500 people and . . . there remain a

NATURE OF INVOLVEMENT

NO OF INVOLVEMENTS	PROPERTY-OWNERSHIP	DIRECTORSHIP
SINGLE	Entrepreneurial capitalist (Exercises direct and immediate control over all aspects of business operations)	Executive capitalist (Property-less salaried full-time manager of a joint-stock company)
MULTIPLE	Rentier capitalist (Passive recipient of share income from holdings in a wide range of industries)	Finance capitalist (Property-less but occupies directorships on boards of a number of companies)

Figure 4.5 Scott's four capitalist economic locations. Source: Adapted from Scott (1991, p. 66)

number of extremely wealthy families within the core of the capitalist business class.
(Scott, 1986, pp. 72 and 82–3).

Together with the service class and the entrepreneurial rich they constitute a 'power bloc' that is cemented together through interlocking directorships, family ties and the culture, lifestyle and status of 'high society'. Scott concludes that the capitalist class is the dominant, 'ruling' group in British society – a class which is dominant economically, integrated with other power groups and sustained by the operations of the state.

Westergaard, on restating the case that the managerialist thesis was always a mirage, expresses bemusement at the way in which:

. . . class-dissolution theorising of the 1980s has lowered the ceiling for its concerns. . . . It has had hardly anything to say about the concentration of power, influence and wealth at the very top.
(Westergaard, 1995, p. 123)

What he calls the new 'forget-about-class' wisdom of the 1980s has just not been much bothered with dominance and privilege at the top. He says it is tantamount to sociological blindness to forget about the upper class merely because it is so very small.

The main plank of Westergaard's argument is that the empirical evidence of the hardening of inequality in the 1980s and 90s can only be seen as undermining, among other things, the notion that a privileged upper class has disappeared. (See also Section 14.8.) He dismisses the notion of upper-class attrition by shrinkage of top income and ownership privilege. For him, this argument was hard enough to square with the facts before the 1980s, but since then income inequalities between richest and poorest have widened so dramatically – with a 'ferocious boom at the top' – that such a notion is 'quite out of the running'. In terms of wealth, too, there is an immense. concentration of measurable privilege vested in a tiny minority of hands.

Westergaard is equally dismissive of the claim that the upper class was waning through 'pluralism' in both economic and political decision-making. He argues that while organized labour may have had some influence as a participant in the corporatism characteristic of the British economy from 1945 to 1980, since then New Right-inspired legislation against trade unions, recession, and an insecure labour market have contrived to limit the influence of the general wage-earner. (See also Sections 9.4 and 9.5.) Like Scott he sees control in large corporations remaining at the top:

. . . as governance by dominant configurations of financial interests, at and around board level in companies linked into intricate webs through ties of leading capital ownership and credit deployment.
(Westergaard, 1995, p. 126)

When these facts are coupled with political reform that has resulted in the centralization of power into a strong if 'small' secretive state (see also Section 17.3), Westergaard argues that visions of a pluralistic dispersal of power from the top have not come out of the 1980s well. Furthermore, he emphasizes the fact that in practice wealth-privilege and power combine, and the rich command power directly and actively in terms of their purchasing power or their say in the deployment of multi-billion-pound assets. They also benefit passively from the tacit assumptions abroad in society about the rightness of the capitalist system and the notion that it would involve more trouble than it is worth trying to change it.

The following example can be used to illustrate Westergaard's position. In 1996, hundreds of individual British Gas shareholders wished to oust the unpopular managing director (the recent recipient of a huge pay increase) and tried to use their votes to bring this about. They were out-voted when the company chairman announced that the massive corporate shareholders' block votes were backing the MD.
In conclusion, Westergaard notes a paradox:

. . . there patently is an upper class and one indeed which, through dominance in a still more evidently capitalist economy, enjoys more power and privilege in Britain now than just a decade or two ago; yet . . . mode-setting opinion has blithely declared class a thing of the past nonetheless.
(Westergaard, 1995, p. 127)

He adds that the socio-structural weight of this group makes the society they top a class society, whatever may be the pattern of divisions below them.

Discussion point

To what extent do you agree that, far from disappearing in a Marxist revolution, the 'upper class' were the real winners of the 'class struggle' in the twentieth century.

4.6 The middle classes

Perceptions of the size and composition of the middle classes vary considerably. For some the term is used as a general description of those at the top end of the social structure, on the assumption that the upper class has disappeared; others as the broad middle band of a diamond-like structure; yet others as a narrow compressed stratum squeezed from above and below.

The boundary problem

Sociologists, too, have grappled with this 'boundary problem' – trying to decide where the middle class begins and ends.

Probably the most widely used (and simplistic) definition within sociology has been based on the distinction between manual or 'blue-collar' workers and non-manual or 'white-collar' workers, the former being designated as working class and the latter as middle. Section 4.4 showed that there are a number of weaknesses with measurements of class based simply on occupation. For example, defining the middle class as all those engaged in non-manual occupations is unsatisfactory because of the wide diversity of people included in this broad category. There is an enormous difference in income, status and lifestyle between the stockbroker at the upper end and the checkout assistant at the other. Also, in recent years there has been a tendency to see an incongruence between some routine non-manual occupations and the designation 'middle class'. Therefore it is perhaps more accurate to talk of the middle *classes* rather than one single homogeneous class.

The rise of the middle class

One thing is clear: changes in the occupational structure of society (see also Section 9.4), together with the expansion of higher education (see also Section 8.5), has seen the middle classes – if defined as all non-manual workers – make up an increasingly large proportion of the population. The 1991 Census, using the Registrar-General's classification, indicated that the 'middle-class' workforce was then made up as follows:

- class I: 6.84 per cent
- class II: 31.34 per cent
- class IIINM: 13.87 per cent.

In other words, just over a half were classed as 'non-manual' on the RGSC. According to Savage this under-estimates the real size of the middle classes:

In 1991, 29.4 per cent of those in the workforce worked in professions and management, a figure only marginally smaller than the 32.7 per cent who worked as manual workers. If one were to include the self-employed (10.7 per cent) and the routine white-collar workers (27.2 per cent) as part of the middle class, we would have to conclude that the middle classes now comprise a substantial majority of the employed population.
(Savage, 1995, p. 2)

Activity

a Draw up a list of the groups mentioned by Savage and write down the respective percentage of the workforce each group comprises.

b Work out what proportion (as a fraction) of the workforce is classified as middle class according to this scheme.

c What disadvantages might be involved in classifying the self-employed as middle class?

I, A, E

Savage argues that the growth of the middle classes has warranted new debate on the class structure and the way in which sociologists define class.

Edgell (1993) points out that it has been usual, after C. Wright Mills (1956), to distinguish between the 'old' propertied and the 'new' propertyless middle classes. Sometimes they are referred to as the 'petit bourgeoisie' and the white-collar non-manual classes respectively. The former comprises the self-employed and owners of small businesses, while the latter covers a multitude of non-manual employees ranging from routine clerks to highly qualified professionals.

The petit bourgeoisie

Marx predicted that the 'petit bourgeoisie', lying between workers and the large property owners, would find it impossible to compete with large capitalist organizations in the long run. Weber also believed their days were numbered and thought they would have to upgrade their technical expertise to survive.

Edgell identifies three lines of argument regarding the future of the petit bourgeiosie:

- terminal decline – or the demise thesis
- survival – or the marginalization thesis
- revitalization – or the demarginalization thesis.

The demise thesis

The number of people classified as self-employed was dwindling until about 1980 when it stood at 6.7 per cent of the workforce. During the 1980s their number increased by nearly a half, so by the 1990s they constituted over 10 per cent of the workforce – a change not unconnected with Conservative government policies which encouraged small business enterprises. However, one neo-Marxist response to this growth in petty capitalism is to see it as a more negative effect of the restructuring of the labour market, where self-employment has become a refuge from unemployment for the large numbers of people who have experienced redundancy. Gerry (1985) argues that in effect the self-employed have become a 'disguised proletariat' that is in the same class position as previously – still exploited and oppressed, though in the UK in the 1980s holding an individualist political orientation. (See also Section 17.2.) So despite the disguise, he says, this distorted version of the petit bourgeoisie still heralds its ultimate demise.

The marginalization thesis

This approach proposes that petit capitalism will not disappear altogether but will permanently occupy a marginal role between 'big capital' and organized labour. The reasons for its persistence are explained by the fact that business cycles and developments in technology frequently generate new entrepreneurial opportunities. The 'autonomy' of self-employment is then seen as an attractive feature. Furthermore, for the government in power it is both economically convenient to have a reserve capacity for (self-) employment (and its converse, a way of absorbing unemployment), and ideologically convenient as a bolster for the virtues of the capitalist endeavour. However, because of its precarious nature, it will only ever constitute a relatively small proportion of the workforce.

The demarginalization thesis

Edgell suggests five reasons why it may seem plausible to believe that, far from declining, the petit bourgeoisie are an expanding class:

- A service economy favours small businesses because it is more labour-intensive than capital-intensive. (See also Section 9.4.)
- Developments in information technology have facilitated the ability of small firms to compete with larger ones, as witnessed by the archetypal 'electronic cottage industry'.
- The concerns about rehumanizing work have led to a 'small is beautiful' philosophy in the organization of work.
- Enterprise culture became fashionable in the 1980s, linked as it was with notions of meritocratic social mobility. (See also Section 4.9.)
- There was a minor trend to co-operatives or collective self-employment as alternatives to unemployment or work in a large bureaucratic corporation.

Research by Fielding (1995) seems to support the demarginalization thesis. It was found that the self-employed constitute a relatively stable group in that, over a ten-year period 1981–91, around 67 per cent stayed in self-employment – a much higher figure than for the period 1971–81. This led him to con-

clude that the petit bourgeoisie was becoming a more secure, distinct and visible group. Butler and Savage (1995) suggest that self-employment, traditionally seen as being fairly humble, has generally received a boost in status as its ranks have been swelled by increasing numbers of 'consultancy' workers in, for example, financial services or 'high-tech' areas.

On a more negative note, Edgell cites comparative research by Bogenhold and Staber (1991) who argue that rising self-employment is symptomatic of labour market deficiencies rather than providing a cure for them.

Edgell concludes that, on balance, the marginalization thesis is the most promising since it 'rules out both terminal decline and unlimited growth'.

Weberian approaches to the new property-less middle classes

The fragmented middle classes

While the majority of non-manual workers readily ascribe themselves to 'the middle class' in surveys based on self-assignment, this is rather unsatisfactory because the term middle class means various things to different people. Roberts *et al.* (1977) examined the attitudes of 243 male white-collar workers and found a number of different 'images' of the middle class held by the respondents:

- 52 per cent held a 'middle-mass' image of society, seeing themselves as part of a massive group in between a small, powerful upper class and a small, poorer lower class
- 19 per cent saw themselves as part of a compressed middle class between increasingly powerful working and upper classes
- 15 per cent (typically professionals) expressed no class loyalty and often rejected the idea of class, preferring instead to see society in terms of a finely graded ladder of opportunity
- 14 per cent (typically lower-grade clerical workers) saw themselves as working class with more in common with the proletariat than with managers.

Roberts and his colleagues concluded that the days when it was possible to speak of 'the middle class' are gone, preferring to describe it as a number of increasingly fragmented strata based around different lifestyles and class images. The advantage of this approach is that it demonstrates the importance of subjective awareness of class for the process of class formation and class action, and the interpretative complexity involved in trying to understand the middle orders of society.

In contrast, Giddens (1980) argues the case for seeing the middle class as a discrete united stratum on the grounds that their possession of educational credentials distinguishes them from other social strata: from the upper class who also have property income, and from the working class who have neither. He argues against assuming the primacy of subjective factors at the expense of objective criteria such as income and market capacity. Giddens believes that a class can exist in an objective sense without necessarily having class consciousness.

The service-class thesis

This approach takes the view that it is possible to identify a distinctive middle class of professional, managerial and administrative workers known as 'the service class' or 'salariat'. The term 'service class' itself is thus slightly misleading and should not be confused with the generic term for work in the service sector of the economy. (See also Section 9.4.) It actually refers to professionals providing specialist services or knowledge and managers who exercise delegated authority. This group have tended to be highly rewarded in terms of salary, job security and prospective career opportunities. The term was used to describe the growing number of occupations – particularly those in the public sector but also those in profit-making organizations – which appeared not to be characterized by exploitation. By virtue of their knowledge and expertise, the 'new class' of employees were afforded a certain amount of autonomy in their work which was not possible for most other groups of workers.

The 'service-class thesis' is now primarily a Weberian approach and has come to be most closely associated with the work of Goldthorpe (1982). As a result of his work on social mobility (1987) he argues that, although the service class still contains a preponderance of those who were born into it, around 60 per cent of its members are drawn from other class backgrounds – it could therefore best be described as 'a class of low classness'. In other words, the widening of its recruiting base made the service class much less coherent and more heterogeneous.

A feature of Goldthorpe's description of the service class is his tendency to see professionals and managers within this group as interchangeable, in the sense that they share a similar experience in pay and conditions of employment. He portrays them as a fairly contented, and therefore conservative, group who are unlikely to form the basis of significant class action as a result of their lack of cohesion. He suggests that they are a conservative force in society because they enjoy the privileges associated with their occupations and are primarily concerned to maintain the status quo in order to preserve their relative position. However, Goldthorpe's more general assertion regarding the contented and politically apathetic nature of the middle class has been criticized by a number of Marxist theorists, particularly Savage et al. (1992). (See page 133.)

Neo-Marxist and post-Marxist approaches to the new propertyless middle classes

The 'new class' thesis

Gouldner (1979), working in a broadly Marxist framework, saw the rise of a potentially radical new class which stood outside traditional class divisions as a result of its ability to engage in new ways of living and new forms of dissent. He was referring to a group who might be called 'humanistic intellectuals', those with a political and social conscience. Their dominance was based on the possession of cultural capital (see text on Bourdieu in Section 2.10) as opposed to economic capital, which is why, according to Gouldner, 'the new class' is immersed in the 'culture of critical discourse'. Others (e.g. Ingleheart, 1971) have seen this group as the harbingers of 'post-materialist political values'. (See also Section 17.5.) The affluence of its members allows them the luxury of not having to worry about securing the material necessities of life, so they divert their energies to other, more 'expressive', issues such as those related to personal and psychological need, ecology and human rights.

The progressive nature of the politics of this class is usually illustrated by reference to its involvement in 'new social movements', especially the environmental movement. For Gouldner, the 'new class' is:

... the most progressive force in modern society and is a centre of whatever human emancipation is possible in the foreseeable future.
(Gouldner, 1979, p. 88)

A middle-class proletariat?

Marx noted a rise in the supply of white-collar workers. As part of his theory of class polarization he predicted the 'proletarianization' of such workers, in the sense that they would experience worsening pay and conditions and would eventually, literally, become proletarians as members of a 'universal working class' in society. Their proletarianization would be complete when they developed proletarian class conciousness. In short, Marx saw that proletarianization could take three forms: of work, of society and of consciousness. Weber later outlined a much more prosperous and privileged future for such workers.

In debating the place of the middle class in society it has therefore become a major concern to analyse the nature of non-manual employment. One 'solution' here might be to suggest that Marx and Weber were both correct in the sense that the middle class can be divided into two groups: routine non-manual workers and professional/managerial workers. So while Marx's prediction applies to the former, Weber's seems more appropriate for the latter.

Non-manual employees doing routine tasks still enjoy considerable advantages over their manual counterparts in terms of pay and conditions. Despite this one neo-Marxist response has been to see large swathes of non-manual employees as, to all intents and purposes, belonging to the proletariat. This is a development of Marx's original belief that capitalism would bring about the real subordination of labour through an erosion of skill differentials between different groups of workers, leading to their homogenization at a relatively low level of skill.

This 'deskilling' argument was adopted by Braverman (1974) and applied to developments in what he called the 'deepening degradation of work'

in the twentieth century. (See also Section 9.7.) He addresses two of Marx's forms of proletarianization – of work and of society.

Braverman is particularly concerned to describe the way in which manual workers lose autonomy and control over the work process as a result of the separation of the 'conception and execution' of work. But he extends the argument to encompass non-manual work and claims that the twentieth century witnessed the proletarianization of both manual and mental labour. He argues that many white-collar jobs that were once seen as being of high status have become marked by the 'proletarian condition'. Professional workers, too, he claims, have also been proletarianized, such that they have become merely the trained servants of capitalism, in many cases undertaking alienated labour in large corporations. Braverman argues that the massed ranks of draughtsmen, accountants and technicians are the new proletariat and the terms 'worker' and 'working class' refer to everyone who has to work for a living whether they be professional, middle class, routine white-collar or manual workers.

This does not necessarily mean that these people perceive themselves in this way, which presents the central problem for Marxist theory of the failure of class consciousness to materialize. In fact one of the main criticisms of Braverman is his failure to con-

Power, control and struggle

CLASSES ARE not stagnant categories. The working class changes over time.

The working class consists of anyone who is separated from ownership or control of the means of production and is therefore regularly compelled to sell their labour in order to live.

So it includes miners, steel workers and postal workers, but also secretaries, teachers and nurses.

Being working class cuts across the false divisions of manual/white collar and services/manufacturing. As a data processor or checkout operator you face the same discipline, the same low pay and the same pressure as a factory worker.

The working class includes people who work 60 hours a week for a boss and the unemployed and retired.

When Marx was writing about class in the 1860s the biggest single category of workers in Britain was female domestic servants. His analysis did not change because other groups, like min-

ers, and engineers, became larger.

Today, far from everyone becoming middle class, more people are forced to recognise themselves as workers.

At one time bank staff were seen as middle class. Today they join unions and go on strike.

Groups like further education lecturers face increasing attacks from their bosses and in response act more and more like "traditional" workers.

You do not have to recognise that you are a worker to be working class. But it is significant that in 1949 some 43 per cent of people regarded themselves as working class whereas in 1990 this had risen to 67 per cent.

So a large majority of the population is working class. In contrast the ruling class is very small.

One study estimates that the people who make crucial decisions about investment in Britain, with their families, number between 20,000 and 50,000 people.

Because this ruling class is so small,

and because it has to administer the whole of production, there is a genuine middle class of people who share some of the characteristics of both bosses and workers.

They sell their labour for a salary but at work they act to control the labour of other people.

This class of line managers, top education and health administrators and so on makes up between 10 and 15 per cent of the population.

We are not a one-third, two-thirds society. We are a four-fifths, one-fifth society with at least 80 per cent having a clear interest in overthrowing the system and replacing it with one where workers are in charge.

In the end Marx's analysis of class is so powerful because it points to the struggles which will one day enable the overwhelming majority to run society in the interest of the overwhelming majority.

Source: *Socialist Worker*, 3 September 1994

sider the third of Marx's forms of proletarianization – political consciousness – by confining himself to an analysis of the working class as a 'class in itself' rather than a 'class for itself'. The effect of this, it has been argued, is to portray the working class as powerless and docile.

Critics of the deskilling thesis in general argue that it has a romanticized image of craft production in the past which tends to overstate the degree of skill and autonomy of such work, thereby making comparisons with contemporary work unrealistic. Pahl (1984), for instance, believed Braverman was deluding himself about a past 'golden age' of work.

Activity

First read the article 'Power, control and struggle' on page 132.

a Explain how this article supports the ideas of Braverman.
b What do you think is meant when the article states that 80 per cent of the population 'have a clear interest in overthrowing the system'?
c To what extent do you think that they do?
d How valid do you find Braverman's classification of 'the professions' as proletarian?

I, A, E

Erikson and Goldthorpe (1992) are also not convinced by claims of proletarianization. They assert that the test must be to show that those engaged in 'degraded jobs' have been 'forced down' from more advanced positions and have little chance of escaping. Most research on routine clerical workers (e.g. Stewart et al., 1980; Marshall et al., 1987) show that this is not the case, at least in the case of males.

It does, however, appear that there may be grounds for arguing that female clerical workers have been affected by proletarianization. This idea of a 'white-bloused proletariat' (Crompton and Jones, 1984) is not new, but there is growing evidence that some workers in certain service-sector jobs – notably those often defined as 'women's work' – are being proletarianized. Gallie (1991) believes that the gap in the skill levels used by men and women in employment widened during the 1980s. This was partly due to the preponderance of women in part-time employment which tends to be inherently low in skill requirements and responsibility. (See also Section 9.3.)

The result is a broad agreement between neo-Marxists and neo-Weberians that:

. . . men in blue-collar jobs and women in routine white-collar jobs increasingly resemble each other in terms of their work and market situations.
(Edgell, 1993, p. 81)

Class formation and the middle classes: managers and professionals

With regard to the other segment of the new middle classes – entrepreneurs, professionals and managerial workers who comprise about a third of the workforce – an approach has been advanced by Savage et al. (1992) which draws on the neo-Marxist perspectives of Wright (1985) and Bourdieu (1984).

Savage and colleagues see major differences between professionals and managers based around the mode by which they achieved their position. They argue that there are long-standing divisions in the British middle class between those who have thrived on cultural assets and those whose position rests on other factors, primarily money. The conflict around this division, they say, is becoming more severe as they each try to improve their position in a hostile market. In their view professionals are currently faring better than managers in this respect because they have more flexible skills; managers on the other hand are becoming more marginalized.

Labour market restructuring and changing conditions of employment have tended to erode the security and the predictable pattern of remuneration that used to be a feature of middle-class career trajectories. (See also Section 9.4.) Even these groups of workers may now be subject to fixed-term contracts and individually negotiated performance-related pay deals, as opposed to the previous pattern of collective bargaining. Savage (1995) cites the case of banking, where pay and conditions used to be related to seniority, had guaranteed incremental rises and were negotiated between unions and management. But in the 1980s performance-related pay became the norm and many senior employees were 'shaken out' through early retirement or voluntary redundancy. This suggests to Savage that Goldthorpe's notion of a cushioned and contented 'service class' is outmoded. The struggle for economic survival has not been overcome, it has been intensified, and Savage's main point is that the recent experiences of managers and professionals, both male and female, have been very different (see Table 4.5 on p. 134).

Table 4.5 Social class transitions for men and women in England and Wales, 1981–91

Social class in 1981			Social class in 1991			
	PRO	MAN	PB	WC	BC	UE
Males						
Professionals	63.45	18.63	4.01	4.04	6.56	3.31
Managers	13.91	54.16	11.58	7.41	8.12	4.82
Petit bourgeoisie	3.58	6.70	70.67	2.27	11.15	5.63
White collar	12.09	23.67	7.96	38.12	12.39	5.76
Blue collar	4.39	6.17	11.23	3.73	65.23	9.26
Unemployed	5.52	5.52	14.43	5.16	35.91	33.72
Education	13.90	8.30	6.08	16.50	35.90	19.32
Other	12.13	10.99	11.11	14.34	33.33	18.10
Females						
Professionals	77.40	5.99	2.48	8.39	3.80	1.93
Managers	16.52	36.83	8.41	28.50	6.10	3.64
Petit bourgeoisie	7.03	7.51	48.41	24.38	10.33	2.34
White collar	7.24	9.65	4.32	62.30	12.54	3.95
Blue collar	4.55	3.18	3.35	22.66	60.00	6.26
Unemployed	11.78	5.68	4.70	35.78	24.98	17.07
Education	16.06	8.10	1.80	47.28	13.55	13.21
Other	11.39	5.31	7.21	44.81	25.60	5.69

Source: OPCS Longitudinal Study 1991

The careers of managers show much higher rates of instability, as seen in their more rapid turnover and some evidence of demotion on a fairly large scale. Professionals have not fared nearly so badly. Further evidence of fragmentation is found in the differences in political orientations of the two groups. Studies of voting patterns point to a cleavage between the university-educated public-sector intellectuals on the Left and the private-sector managers with no further or higher education who have tended to support the Conservative Party. (See Section 17.2 for more detail on social class and voting behaviour.)

Savage and colleagues conclude that Goldthorpe's notion of a unified service class ignores the divisions within it, and 'new class' theory may apply to just a small section of this class – the thinking radicals. So the expansion of the middle classes which appears to have gone against Marx's expectations of class

Activity

Study Table 4.5.

a Explain how this information indicates that managers experienced greater career instability than professionals in the 1980s.

b Was this instability greater for male or female managers?

U, I

polarization does not signify the end of the road for class analysis. There are new forms of conflict emerging as competition between middle-class occupational groups intensifies, which leads them to adopt positional strategies intended to maximize their market situation.

Discussion point

'The middle classes are now more fragmented than ever.' How far does the evidence support this assertion?

4.7 The working class

According to Marx the proletariat, having been created by capitalism, was destined to bring about its demise. However, thus far it has failed to fulfil Marx's expectations: the working class has not turned out to be 'the grave-digger of capitalism'. As Hamilton and Hirszowicz point out, if anything the opposite tendency seems more likely to occur:

Capitalism, having created the working class which it needed in its early development, is now rapidly dispensing with it. Rather than the working class abolishing capitalism, it is capitalism that appears to be abolishing the working class.

(Hamilton and Hirszowicz, 1993, p. 161)

Attention has therefore turned to identifying those factors which may account for the demise of the proletariat both as a 'class in itself' and as Marx's historic 'class for itself'.

Any claims about change in the characteristics of the working class are premised on a notion of what the traditional proletariat was like.

The changes to the class structure that are said to have led to the disappearance of this traditional working class, and reduced the significance of class divisions generally, include:

- the decline of traditional proletarian occupations and communities
- the expansion of working-class affluence
- the growth of white-collar employment
- the increasing participation of women in paid employment.

(See also Sections 9.3, 9.4 and 16.1.)

Changes in the occupational structure

It is clear that the proportion of the population employed in 'manual work' continues to decline, a trend that has been accelerating throughout the post-war period (see Table 4.6).

Table 4.6 Occupational classes: 1981 as percentage of 1951

Higher professions	227.6
Lower professions	258.4
Employers and proprietors	80.9
Managers and administrators	212.5
Clerical workers	156.4
Foremen, inspectors, supervisors	181.7
Skilled manual	79.6
Semi-skilled manual	86.2
Unskilled manual	91.8
All	112.8

Source: Routh (1987, p. 37)

According to Marshall (1987), these changes have typically been interpreted within one of two theoretical frameworks:

- what he calls a liberal perspective which can be traced back to the 'post-industrial society thesis' of Bell (1973)
- the Marxist response which argues that predictions of the end of class are premature and mistaken.

Bell's (1973) post-industrial society thesis emerged during the long economic boom of the 1950s and 60s. It was part of the post-war orthodoxy of social scientists whose main themes were:

- separation of ownership and control
- a consequent rise of a managerial technocracy
- fragmentation of social classes into clusters of overlapping interest groups
- the end of ideology and polarized class politics (see also Section 17.2) as the working class is incorporated into a post-industrial democracy.

The term 'post-industrial' implied the notion that work was becoming more pleasant for the majority as the basis of occupations shifted from industrial production to information processing. This 'deindustrialization' process was marked by the relative decline of manufacturing and an increase in service-sector jobs, creating a new 'knowledge society élite' workforce. The rise of a service economy and the central importance of the possession of knowledge were thought likely to produce a shift in the dominant values, norms and culture of this 'post-industrial' society. The traditional work ethic would be replaced by a greater emphasis on individual freedom and pleasure-seeking, market forces would be subdued by increased stress on social welfare and economic planning, and class-based conflict over the distribution of wealth would decline.

In common with this 'post-industrial thesis', the former Marxist Gorz (1982) argued that the term proletariat was obsolete, but for different reasons:

In place of the productive collective worker of old, a non-class of non-workers is coming into being. ... The majority of the population now belong to the post-industrial neo-proletariat which with no job security or definite class identity, fills the area of probationary, contracted, casual, temporary and part-time employment.
(Gorz, 1982, p. 67)

Gorz's argument was that technological developments were leading to a situation of 'jobless growth' whereby mass unemployment was the future scenario. He believed this to be potentially liberating for people, with exciting new possibilities for a better way of living if only people would seize the opportunities for greater autonomy outside the sphere of paid employment.

Activity
a Do you agree at all with Gorz's prediction of the future of the working class?
b In what sense, if any, would you describe him as optimistic? Give reasons for your answer.
c How might a Marxist approach be used to criticize Gorz's position?

I, A, E

The Marxist response to the post-industrial society theorists initially revolved around the work of Braverman (1974). For him, the labour process is increasingly subject to control from above and is thus becoming more, not less, proletarianized. Deskilling was becoming a more prevalent feature of manual jobs owing to their fragmentation into simple operations which also reduced the costs of easily replaceable workers. Further aspects of proletarianization could be seen in the intensification of the labour process (the requirement for increased productivity) and extensive use of techniques of surveillance to monitor the behaviour of the workforce (Thompson, 1993). As a result Braverman believed that manual workers, as well as many non-manual workers, were experiencing increased alienation and would resist the deskilling and close policing of their work. (See also Sections 9.2 and 9.7.)

For Marxists, then, the process of production is still seen as crucial to an understanding of these proletarianized workers' class-based images of society and the development of class consciousness, since the vast majority of the workforce is forced to submit to the control of capital, though they remain latently revolutionary.

Rising affluence and embourgeoisement

Although in many ways the 'embourgeoisement thesis' should have been consigned to sociological history, the significance of the debates around it remains because the social and political conditions of the late 1980s led to calls for its resurrection. The main points of the original debate will be briefly rehearsed before considering more recent contributions.

Zweig (1961) is thought to have coined the term, arguing that large numbers of the working class were on the move towards new middle-class values and middle-class existence. Embourgeoisement of the worker implied a number of related aspects of change within large sections of the working classes, which were described at the time as:

- economic advancement in terms of household income, family expenditure and possessions
- educational advancement
- greater family- and home-centredness
- shift of interest from job to consumerism
- contraction of class consciousness – the idea of class being relegated in the worker's mind to something unimportant.

These changes resulted, it was argued, in the individualization of workers in the sense that they were becoming less committed to the value of solidaristic collectivism – the traditional idea that their common purpose lay in 'sticking together' to advance their collective interests. It was also suggested that the worker became not only deproletarized but also disalienated.

One of the most influential sociological studies of the 1960s, *The Affluent Worker Study* (Goldthorpe *et al.*, 1969), deliberately sought to test the embourgeoisement thesis by investigating a group of 'affluent' (or relatively well-paid) workers in Luton who might have been expected to be showing signs of embourgeoisement. Their findings, which are presented here very briefly, indicated that while changes were occurring in this section of the working class they did not amount to embourgeoisement. The results may be considered under four headings.

- *Attitudes to work* – Since they were not interested in 'getting on', careers or intrinsic job satisfaction, they could not be said to have adopted the kind of orientation to work traditionally associated with white-collar workers. They had an instrumental attitude to work (primarily motivated by pay).
- *Friendships, lifestyle and norms* – The 'affluent workers' did not associate with white-collar workers outside work nor did they seek middle-class status and had not, therefore, developed middle-class patterns of sociability. However, they had developed a 'privatized' and home-centred lifestyle.
- *Outlook on life and image of society* – They had not adopted a middle-class outlook since they were not concerned with advancement in the 'prestige hierarchy', but were primarily focused on material benefits such as maintaining their relative position in terms of what they perceived to be a hierarchy of income differentials.
- *Political attitudes* – The majority (80 per cent) of the workers in the sample not only voted for the Labour Party but also saw it as 'the party of the working class'. However, they were less aligned to Labour out of a traditional sense of loyalty to their class, than by how they personally might benefit from voting for them. (See also Section 17.2.)

In conclusion, these 'affluent workers' held different views from traditional working-class groups but could not be described as having become middle class. The two respects in which they did differ from the traditional working class were (a) in the sense that they were more isolated from the community in their private family life, and (b) in how they saw trade unions as a way of promoting individual interests. Goldthorpe and colleagues agreed that there had been some convergence between the middle and working classes and that a 'new', possibly prototypical, working class may have been emerging as a result.

The Conservative Party's four General Election victories from 1979 onwards (see also Section 17.2.) gave a new lease of life to the idea of the transformation of the working class. The Conservatives owed their success in large part to the support from the C2 (skilled manual) segment of the electorate. Once again this was most prevalent in the prosperous regions, and the sobering statistic for the Labour Party in 1987 was that the Conservatives led it by 46 per cent to 26 per cent among the working class in the south of England. This general pattern continued into the 1990s when, according to a MORI poll of 22 727 voters during the General Election in 1992, Labour managed to improve its share of the C2 vote but still only gained two in five of the votes in this group. 'The fact remains that nearly as many skilled manual workers vote Conservative as they do Labour' (Denscombe, 1993, p. 44).

The restructuring of distributional conflict

While there was a consensus of opinion that the 'new' affluent workers were significant in terms of their shifting political allegiances, it was also felt that the term embourgeoisement – and for that matter its twin proletarianization – were unable to explain the complexity of changes that were happening in society. An alternative view was that class conflict had been restructured around new divisions brought about by the economic reorganization associated with global competition. (See also Sections 9.9, 10.10, 16.8 and 17.6 for details about globalisation.)

With more reliance on market forces, less government intervention, increased flexibility of labour, the adoption of microelectronic technology, the decline of the manufacturing sector, and the increasing participation of women in paid work, employment has become insecure and fragmented. These changes are said to have reduced the significance of the manual/non-manual divide. In addition, 'postmodern' culture (see also Section 10.11) has developed in which work is 'decentred' as a source of identity and consciousness, to be replaced by issues of individualist consumption, whether it be housing or state benefits. Work is no longer a way of identifying oneself, more a means of acquiring desirable goals – a tendency which leads to a decline in traditional class politics and the death of the possibility of working-class revolution.

Lukes (1984) identifies a number of divisions emerging in British society which, though related to class, could also be seen as independent of it:

- owner-occupiers *versus* tenants
- waged *versus* welfare claimants
- declining regions *versus* prosperous ones
- secure core workers *versus* peripheral casualized workers.

Activity

a Suggest other sources of division which might be added to Lukes' list.
b To what extent do you agree that these divisions are now more important than social class for the analysis of stratification in contemporary UK society?

U, I, A, E

The picture that emerged from this theory of restructured class conflict was one of sectionalism, instrumentalism, and privatism:

- sectional in the sense that the monolithic labour movement had been replaced by numerous sectoral interests each resigned, in an era of recession, to the pursuit of its own economic interests
- instrumental in that the workers had embraced the capitalist economic values of an acquisitive society and saw labour organizations as a way of maximizing their level of consumption
- private in view of the tendency of members of the working class to withdraw from class politics into the private world of the family.

Thus it was claimed that the restructuring of distributional conflict had seen a shift from issues of production and class to those of consumption and status.

Marshall (1987) notes the irony of the fact that this analysis of the effects of recession on the working class seems to confirm many of the findings of Goldthorpe's *Affluent Worker* study which, it should be remembered, were conducted against a backdrop of rising prosperity.

Abercrombie and Warde (1994) argue that the changes taking place in the working class need to be considered in relation to three areas:

- class position
- lifestyle and culture
- degree of class consciousness.

Class position

In terms of market situation it is probably true that, taken as a whole, the working class enjoys a better standard of living in absolute terms than previously. However, interpretations of this are complicated by a number of factors, primarily the difficulty of generalizing about all members of the working class.

For example, while the average wage of manual workers is higher than that of routine non-manual workers, it is below average for the non-manual sector as a whole. In other words the average conceals some very low wages in the manual sector, and during the 1990s the relative earnings of the lowest-paid 5 per cent fell further behind the average (see Section 14.8). It is also the case that manual workers tend to work longer hours than those in non-manual work, but earn this lower average income.

Internal divisions in the working class are potentially created by the large discrepancy in earnings from the top to the bottom of the working class, but the differentials between skilled and unskilled rates of pay have reduced. The most significant source of division is related to the increasing participation by women in paid employment (see Section 9.3). Abercrombie and Warde (1994) surmise that the inferior positions of women and ethnic minorities in the labour market could create deeper and highly visible intra-class divisions.

In terms of the work situation it is evident that manual work generally affords little control and discretion, so the primary orientation to work remains an instrumental one and the potential for solidarity among workers over pay and conditions remains. While a convergence between the conditions of lower non-manual and manual work has been suggested, it is still the case that the conditions of manual work are inferior. Within the working class, variations in the work process experienced by different workers are not thought sufficient in themselves to be capable of creating antagonistic relationships between different groups of workers.

Working-class lifestyle and culture

Two aspects of changing lifestyle are thought to have eroded working-class solidarity, namely consumption patterns and the tendency to privatism. (See also Section 10.9.)

Consumption patterns

Increasing affluence has seen the spread of consumer durables to the working class and a growth in home-ownership. However, despite an apparent convergence in this respect, consumption patterns remain significantly unequal between classes, reflecting the market positions of the classes (see Table 4.7).

Despite the fact that these relative class differences in standards of living are still evident, the trend to individualist consumption is thought to be leading to an acceptance of the values of

Table 4.7 Expenditure by households of employees, by occupation of head of household in 1988

	Average weekly household expenditure (£)	Average weekly expenditure per person (£)
Professional	318	113
Employers, managers	339	114
Intermediate non-manual	242	96
Junior non-manual	221	89
Skilled manual	230	71
Semi-skilled manual	195	67
Unskilled manual	164	61

Source: *Family Expenditure Survey*, 1988

Activity

a Compare the expenditure pattern of the junior non-manual category with that of the skilled manual.

b How would you account for the apparent difference between the amounts spent per household and the amount spent per person?

c To what extent does this type of evidence undermine the notion that class differences in consumption have become less significant?

I, A, E

capitalism – creating new divisions around participation in private ownership versus reliance on public services, notably in relation to housing. Abercrombie and Warde, however, argue that it is doubtful whether housing tenure (see also Section 16.7) in itself causes people to alter wholesale other aspects of their behaviour.

Privatism

Privatism refers to a pattern of social life that is restricted largely to the home and the conjugal family. This was held to be another tendency that was reducing traditional working-class solidarity. However, according to Abercrombie and Warde, the extent of conviviality outside of immediate kin relations said to be typical of traditional working-class communities may have been exaggerated, and the privatized pattern of sociability was not unknown in the past. It is true that urban redevelopment and the relocation of industry have led to a more geographically dispersed population, but working-class social contacts remain extensive, though less intense and less centred around masculine roles. (See also Section 7.2.) Furthermore it is probably the case that increased female participation in the labour market has led to a decline in home-centredness on their part.

Saunders (1987, 1990b) rejects the argument that increasing home-ownership has encouraged privatism. The intensity and frequency of neighbourhood relations were more a function of how long people had lived in an area. He also found little difference between home-owners and council tenants in participation rates in leisure activities outside the home. The conclusion that there is little difference between social classes in terms of privatism is supported by both Marshall *et al.* (1988) and Devine (1992). Abercrombie and Warde conclude that 'manual workers are neither obsessed by consumerism nor excessively privatised'. They go on to say that although a few more prosperous regions may exhibit privatism:

. . . no one has yet demonstrated that there is a systematic structural basis for variation in privatism, or that it has been responsible for undermining solidarism.
(Abercrombie and Warde, 1994, p. 167)

Class consciousness

Concern with what is happening to the working class ultimately relates to the degree to which it retains the potential for radical class consciousness.

Evidence strongly suggests that the traditional proletarian outlook with a view of the social structure based on conflict between 'the bosses' and 'the workers' is quite common and almost universal among the working class. Marshall *et al.* (1988) attempted to assess the extent to which social class remains a common and salient source of identity. They discovered that 63 per cent of their sample (see Section 3.8 for an account of their methodology) held this proletarian image. It was also the case that, while members of the lowest social classes were slightly more likely than others to describe the existing pattern of distributive justice as unfair, this was the view commonly held by members of all classes. According to Marshall:

Britain remains a class society rather than a post-industrial or post-class one. Class is still a common and salient source of collective identity. Naturally,

class identities do not constitute class consciousness, at least in the sense that most Marxists would intend. Britain is not a nation of class warriors resolutely involved in a power struggle to achieve specifically class objectives. Nevertheless, our research does confirm that class is still a crucial factor in the understanding of social change in contemporary Britain. It is not, as many accounts of the restructuring of distributional conflict would have it, an obsolete concept.
(Marshall, 1987, p. 40)

Further evidence on class imagery can be seen by looking forward to Table 4.11 on page 151, which shows an increase in the extent to which there is an awareness of class in the UK. In their 1993 survey, Gallup reported that 87 per cent of people agreed with the statement 'the rich get richer and the poor get poorer' and 71 per cent agreed that 'the people running the country don't really care what happens to me' (quoted in Allan *et al.* (1994, pp. 10–11)). Although these findings apply across the class structure, Abercrombie and Warde conclude that:

. . . working class people do still feel some sense of class and consider it affects their lives. . . . However, class identity only sustains a radical, alternative political value system among a minority of manual workers and is not often translated into class based political action.
(Abercrombie and Warde, 1994, p. 169)

To what extent this reflects the fact that the proletariat has dissolved into a competing crowd of individuals, or how much it is due to apathy, or a sense of powerlessness, remains debatable.

Devine's (1992) study of 'affluent workers' in Luton sheds some light on this. She found that interviewees' consumer aspirations were not entirely individualistic but were framed with reference to other ordinary people who worked for a living. Sharing similar standards of living and striving for more improvements was an important dimension of their class identity. They adopted a 'pecuniary model' of the class structure, seeing money and its associated lifestyle – and, crucially, how these were acquired – as a way of identifying different social classes. However, there was resentment at what was perceived as the inequitable distribution of resources in society, in particular the notion of inherited wealth. They aspired to a society which was more equal and in which people were rewarded more fairly, and this vision of an ideal society was not confined to the capitalist system. Devine concludes that the everyday economic realities of people's lives act as a powerful constraint on them doing anything other than accepting things as they are. But this constraint in itself may imply a lack of acceptance of the existing system. She suggests that lack of collective action on the part of the working class can be largely put down to the failure of the trade unions and the Labour Party to mobilize working-class support for change.

Abercrombie and Warde warn, however, that the incorporation of the working class is never likely to be complete because of its exploitation at work and it would be unwise to anticipate the end of working-class politics. Writing in 1994, they pointed to both the unfavourable economic climate (a recession) and the political climate (with a party balance still in favour of the Conservative Party) as explanations of the failure of the working class to mobilize its opposition.

They also conceded that the working class is fragmented. Fragmentation occurs in the sense, first, that gender and ethnic identities stemming from depressed market situations may inhibit class solidarity. Secondly, there has been a tendency for trade unions to become increasingly sectionalist as instrumentalism reaches new heights, with individual plant bargaining as opposed to national pay deals. A third area of potential division is between organized labour and those who are marginalized. The Trades Union Congress (TUC) has been effective in representing the most powerful groups among the working class, but the unorganized are ignored and in some respects form a sub-proletariat. Abercrombie and Warde do not believe that such divisions are new and therefore cannot be said to imply a new type of politics.

Discussion point

The term 'working class' has ceased to have much meaning for most people. How far do you agree that this is the case?

4.8 The 'underclass'

According to Saunders (1990a) there are four key features of the underclass:

- it suffers multiple deprivation
- it is socially marginalized
- it is almost entirely dependent on state welfare provisions
- its culture is one of resigned fatalism.

This section considers the extent to which such a marginalized underclass (see also Section 14.7) exists in an objective sense, and how far the differing interpretations of the concept are rooted in ideological and political debates about the extent and causes of poverty (see also Section 14.6).

The concept of an underclass located in a substratum can be traced back to the Poor Law and beyond (see also Section 14.1). Debates about the underlying causes are not new either. Perspectives on the existence of an underclass and explanations of it tend to be divided into those that stress the importance of subcultural values, and those – particularly on the Left – which look at the underlying social structure.

In short, the differences are expressed in the question as to whether members of an underclass are 'depraved or deprived', which raises the further question of whether it is possible to use the term 'underclass' in a neutral way.

Mann (1995) suggests that participants in the underclass debate fall into three categories:

- advocates of the concept who view the culture and behaviour of members of this supposed class as posing a danger
- advocates who are sympathetic to the plight of this class and who tend to point to structural explanations for its existence
- those who reject the analytical validity of the term and the policy implications.

Cultural explanations and dangerous behaviour

Attempts to explain the persistence of poverty (see also Section 14.7) among certain subcultural groups on the basis of their behaviour and values can be traced back to a study of the urban poor in Mexico. This 'culture of poverty' thesis (Lewis, 1968) argued that poverty could not be eradicated simply by giving more money to the poor because they had developed a way of life which would not allow them to improve their position simply by having more money. Their culture was said to be characterized by short-term horizons, indifference to work, apathy, inertia and feelings of resignation; in other words they had a fatalistic philosophy which in turn feeds back on itself and becomes self-fulfilling. Furthermore this culture was said to be transmitted from one generation to the next, setting up a cycle of deprivation and a culture of dependency.

The 'culture of poverty' thesis was largely discredited because it seemed to ignore structural causes of deprivation and failed to demonstrate that the cultural values developed in response to deprivation cannot be altered through effective structural change (Pilkington, 1992). However it did gain academic credibility in some circles in the US and was adopted by those of a New Right persuasion in order to attack the 'waste and futility' of state welfare programmes (see also Sections 2.10 and 14.3). The problem of poverty continued to grow despite the increasing amount spent on the social welfare budget – or, in the view of those on the Right, because of it.

The New Right had begun to espouse market liberal economic theory which emphasized the need for reduced state intervention in the economy to allow market forces to operate freely. One of the principal areas of state intervention was in social welfare expenditure, and this came under attack from the New Right thinkers such as Friedman (1980) and Hayek (1949) as they blamed the postwar expansion of welfare for, among other things, the growth in criminality, and the decline of community responsibility as functions of a culture of dependency (see also Section 14.3). In order to gain support for policies which justified reduced public spending, the Right linked the most deprived groups in society with the culture of poverty according to which an undeserving poor are blamed for their deplorable behaviour. Hence the New Right version of the underclass is said to be based on a cultural explanation.

This view was put forward by Murray, initially in the US (1984) and subsequently in relation to the British underclass (1990). He argued that welfare actually fostered dependency and supported a deviant, antisocial lifestyle. He went on to claim that public policy intervention was doomed to fail and so it was a bad investment. Murray sought to provide an intellectual and moral justification for policies of neglect in which the poor were seen as politically disposable. These themes have been developed in his most recent work (Herrnstein and Murray, 1994) which claims that members of the lowest stratum are limited in terms of their intelligence by genetic factors, and therefore do not warrant significant educational investment. (See also Sections 6.4 and 8.9.)

For Murray, the defining characteristic of the underclass is not so much the degree of poverty, it is the *type* of poverty. He characterizes the underclass as having high rates of birth outside marriage (see also Section 7.4), violent crime and dropout from the labour force. Of these he saw birth outside marriage as the most indicative of the existence of an underclass. He argues that the increase in birth outside marriage is strikingly concentrated among the lowest social class. This is taken as a symptom of social decay because it is seen to represent (in the lowest class) a pathological type of family based on moral turpitude, absent fathers, inadequate parenting, lawless children, idle young men and reliance on financial support from the state.

This analysis tends to be accepted (by and large) among the New Right. It fits into the 'Thatcherite' belief that the poor need to be weaned off dependency on 'the nanny state'. It is not dependency in itself which concerns them – indeed, private dependency within the family is considered acceptable and even desirable (Lister, 1991). As well as wanting to tighten restrictions on social benefits and encourage the value of self-reliance, the New Right attacks the lifestyle and values of the poor by stressing the need to return to 'family values'. Targets include never-married single mothers, social security 'scroungers', 'New Age' travellers and aggressive street beggars (see also Sections 7.4 and 7.6).

The language used to describe the underclass from this perspective portrays it as a threat. According to Lister it is the language of disease and contamination. Murray, for instance, described himself as a 'visitor from a plague area, come to see if the disease is spreading'. Lister argues that such language:

. . . encourages a pathological image of people in poverty as somehow different from other people and to be feared. The danger is that the concept of the 'underclass' is so imprecise that it gets stretched to describe the poor generally, and so value-laden and emotive that it stigmatizes them as a group apart. (Lister, 1991, p. 194)

Discussion point
To what extent is the term 'underclass' and the language associated with it insulting to those it is meant to describe?

The right-wing journalist Bruce Anderson has written of the new 'Dickensian underclass' in his attacks on the reborn 'dangerous classes'. According to Robert Reiner and David Downes of the London School of Economics, writing in *The Observer* on 11 August 1996, the new language is part of the reinvention of the moral economy of Victorian England with its vocabulary of exclusion (see also Section 17.5) whereby whole classes are regarded as outlaws.

The term 'underclass' was readily associated with disorder and crime (see also Section 11.10), and by the late 1980s even some of the journals of the Left began to include articles which described the underclass as a severe threat to social order. In 1991, a BBC1 *Panorama* broadcast on youth disturbances on the Meadow Well estate in Newcastle used the term freely.

Structural explanations and sympathy

Despite its current associations with the New Right, the term 'underclass' was first used by the liberal Left to describe those who were being marginalized from the labour market by structural changes in the economy (Myrdal, 1962). The term was used by Rex and Tomlinson (1979) to describe the relative deprivation of ethnic minorities in relation to employment, housing and education which was compounded by their experience of racism and discrimination. (See also Section 6.4.) Such approaches tended to have sympathy with the plight of those thought to constitute the underclass and predicted social conflict as a result of the exclusion of the 'have-nots' from the general rise in prosperity.

In the USA, liberals have tried to reassert their ownership of the concept in structural terms. Wilson's book *The Truly Disadvantaged* (1987) saw people in poverty as relatively powerless in the face of deep-seated economic and social structural forces. In the USA, structural changes primarily related to removing low-skill inner-city employment have created an underclass of poor black families isolated in ghettos. (See also Section 6.4.) The behaviour of such people, far from being the symptoms of depravity, are a rational response to their restricted opportunities. Thus generally the term 'underclass' in the USA has become equated with inner-city black populations.

Lister's criticism of the use of the term 'underclass' applies equally to structural theorists. Wilson was uneasy about using the term but argued that it is justified because there was a reality to the ghetto underclass that could not be just theorized away. Out of such debates has come a general agreement that the term means more than just 'poor' – it refers to the truly disadvantaged. While the Left and the Right might argue about the causes, there is some consensus on what the commonly shared experiences of members of the underclass are. In 1982 these were summarized by Cottingham (quoted in Robinson and Gregson, 1992) as:

- severe income deprivation, leading to poverty and dependency on welfare (see also Section 14.3)
- unstable employment, or unemployed/unemployable)
- low skills
- limited access to, or involvement with, education, social services etc. (see also Section 13.5)
- persistent poverty – not just temporarily poor, but enmeshed in intergenerational poverty
- spatial concentration – the underclass typically exists in ghettos (see also Section 16.7)
- high incidence of health problems, physical and mental (see also Section 13.2).

In the UK the structural approach has tended to find more favour among sociologists and politicians of the Left who have portrayed the poor and the unemployed as largely victims of circumstances. Frank Field MP, a long-time campaigner on poverty issues, in 1989 detected an underclass comprising the long-term unemployed, single-parent families and elderly pensioners. His use of the term is imprecise, but he claimed to have shown that such groups had missed out on the general rise in affluence during the 1980s. He believed that rising unemployment (see also Section 9.6), a relative reduction in the value of benefits (see also Section 14.2), and a hardening attitude towards the poor had created 'a subtle form of political, social and economic apartheid' (Field, 1989, p. 4).

Morris and Irwin (1992), while rebutting the idea that the long-term unemployed constitute an underclass of their own making, argues nevertheless that there are stuctural, economic and labour market obstacles which make the long-term unemployed more vulnerable than others. Morris (1994) also concludes that, despite the popular image of a class of unemployable and feckless people, labour market exclusion of certain groups was at the root of the problem rather than an underclass that was culturally inclined to unemployment.

Criticisms of the analytical use of the term 'underclass'

Pilkington (1992) identifies four main criticisms of the use of the term. First, he agrees with Lister's view that the very use of the term can be disturbing and can lead to pathological views of people in poverty. He also believes the term is used in a variety of different ways to describe a very heterogeneous range of people, from all those in the secondary labour market to just the long-term unemployed, itself a varied category.

Secondly, he notes the tendency to use the term to link numerous trends – such as growing crime rates (see also Section 11.1) and increasing racial disadvantage (see also Section 6.2), and single parenthood (see also Sections 7.3–4) – as if they are all necessarily associated with all those who characterize the underclass. This he argues is to see the underclass as a uniform group exhibiting identical behaviour patterns, but there is a world of difference between the young unemployed and elderly pensioners.

Thirdly, he argues, even the structural approach is in danger of tacitly accepting some of the assumptions of a culture of dependency and the idea of widespread participation by the underclass in the informal economy. There is no evidence that members of the underclass do not want 'conventional' lives.

Fourthly, Pilkington questions the extent to which the underclass possess a distinctive and coherent set of attitudes, or even has stability in its composition. While there is a residual group of long-term unemployed they are no more fatalistic than other groups and share similar aspirations.

Heisler (1991) argues that as the underclass lacks a meaningful market position it should be seen as a social category outside the class structure, rather than as a class. However, according to Edgell (1993) this tends to blur the distinction between social marginalization (in citizenship terms – see also Section 17.5) and minimal labour market power (class position), the former being a function of the latter. The rationale for seeing the underclass in class terms is confirmed by the role it performs for capital as the disposable labour force and the expression of its class interests through riots (collective bargaining by force). (See also Section 16.7.) Edgell concludes that the underclass should be seen as a regular feature of the class structures of advanced capitalist societies:

It is arguably more constructive to regard the underclass as the under-employed and the unemployed fraction of the working class, characterised, like all social classes, by shifting population of variable size, but distinctive in its poverty.
(Edgell, 1993, pp. 79–80)

Gallie (1994) specifically tried to test the usefulness of the concept of the underclass for understanding the situation of the long-term unemployed. He found little evidence in support of the cultural arguments, in that:

. . . the long term unemployed were clearly not, on the evidence of their past work histories, inherently unstable members of the workforce.
(Gallie, 1994, p. 755)

He found a strong commitment to employment among the unemployed. However, he also found little evidence that long-term unemployment led to a distinctive subculture of radical solidarity and resistance of the kind predicted by some structural accounts of the underclass. Rather, they were more likely to align themselves (see Section 17.2) with the Labour Party. Gallie concluded that the use of the term 'underclass' in analyses of the unemployed:

. . . would appear to obscure rather than clarify the major determinants and implications of unemployment.
(Gallie, 1994, p. 756)

While for some the term 'underclass' has been a useful way of asserting the interests of the poor at a time when it has been difficult to get these on to the political agenda, Mann (1995) argues that this does not justify the resurrection of such a pejorative term with its overtones of blame. In his view:

. . . what distinguishes the critics, both from advocates of the term 'underclass' and from each other, is not whether there are real social divisions or not but how we account for the obvious divisions that exist. Whereas advocates of the term underclass can debate the respective weighting they give to structural and behavioural factors, critics reject the term precisely because it focuses attention on aspects of the behaviour of the poor. Whereas 'good' behaviour and structural disadvantage means the advocates of the concept see sections of the poor as 'deserving' it is more likely that attention will shift and become obsessed with 'bad behaviour'.
(Mann, 1995, p. 55)

The effect of this is to increase public support for restricting eligibilty for welfare, to stigmatize claimants and encourage a moral panic of 'scrounger-phobia'. (See Section 15.5 for more information on 'moral panics'.)

Mann also suggests that the '1990s remix' of the underclass concept may perform a similar ideological function as it did in Victorian times. The portrayal of the poor as 'idle, thieving bastards' (Bagguley and Mann, 1992) may serve to alleviate the class consciousness of guilt among the middle classes.

According to Mann, some feminists have construed concern about the underclass concept as part of the backlash against feminism. (See Sections 5.4 and 5.6.) This can be observed in discourses about the underclass, lone mothers, welfare dependency and changing employment patterns.

Activity

a With reference to the discussion in this section and elsewhere, explain why the increasing willingness to use the term 'underclass' could be seen as 'just another moral panic'.

b To what extent would you agree with Mann's view that, however the term 'underclass' is intended, 'attention tends to shift and become obsessed with "bad behaviour"'?

c Justify your support for one of the three main positions on the underclass debate that have been outlined in this section.

K, U, I, A, E

Whatever definition one adopts to describe a 'new' subclass, the distinctiveness of its deepening poverty and the sheer scale of its effects tend to undermine the notions of classlessness, active citizenship and opportunity.

4.9 Social mobility

Social mobility is of central concern to sociologists for a number of reasons. It is important in the sense that the prospect of upward mobility may help to legitimize the existing social structure in the eyes of individuals, thereby reducing the potential for class conflict. But it is also important at a structural level, since according to Weberian sociologists, it is related to class formation, the sense of class cohesion and the possibility of class conflict. Where there is considerable social mobility there tends to be a blurring of the edges between classes.

Ascribed and achieved status

Sociologists have distinguished between different systems of stratification according to whether they can be described as relatively open or closed. An 'ideal type' closed system is one in which social positions are determined by birth and a person's status is said to be 'ascribed'. Each social stratum is closed in that there is no possibility of movement between the various strata either through marriage or merit. Each stratum is thus totally recruited from within its own ranks. At the other extreme a totally 'open' society would be one where there was 'perfect' social mobility according to which class origins are completely unrelated to eventual class destinations. This implies fluidity of movement between the classes to the extent that those in the top stratum should contain by origin roughly equal proportions of people from each of the other strata. In such a society social positions would be said to be achieved – the true meritocracy – in which people would be totally responsible for where they end up. This arrangement might result in dysfunctional (see also Section 2.4) consequences such as arrogance on the part of those at the top and demoralization of those at the bottom, with attendant possibilities for conflict (Young, 1961). However, it is still seen as a desirable direction in which to be moving.

In attempts to measure the extent of social mobility, a complicating factor is that the occupational structure is changing; therefore mobility is related to the changing nature of jobs (see also Section 9.3) as well as to the fluidity of the structure at any given time. Sociologists have distinguished between *absolute* mobility, on the one hand, which refers to the total amount of movement going on in the class structure and the net changes in the size of each class, and *relative* mobility on the other hand, which refers to the chance of an individual from each class going up or down by a certain distance. Both types of mobility need to be measured by comparing class status over successive generations – this is known as *intergenerational* mobility. The three main factors which affect social mobility are the number of positions to be filled, the methods of access and entry to positions, and the number of offspring to fill these positions.

Payne (1987) says that the occupational transition that has occurred in post-war Britain has helped to generate upward mobility, because there are more professional and managerial posts to fill. Most of these jobs require educational qualifications. It has also been the case that the fertility rates of those in the highest classes have been too low to fill all the new posts with their own offspring, so opportunities for upward mobility from below have arisen. Figure 4.6 shows the importance of educational credentials for achieved status (in this case measured by income). As a result of the growth of educational opportunities, a debate has arisen as to whether a meritocracy has been established in Britain.

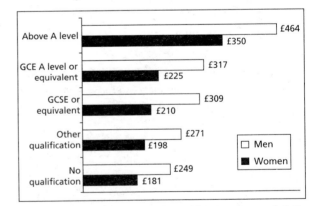

Figure 4.6 Average gross weekly earnings of full-time employees in Great Britain in 1994. Source: *Employment Gazette*, May 1995

Discussion point
If class conflict might occur even in a truly meritocratic society, is it still an ideal worth striving for?

Evidence on social mobility

Studies of social mobility are expensive and cumbersome to conduct because they depend on large sample surveys. (See also Section 3.7.) Glass (1954) and his LSE colleagues carried out the first major twentieth-century British survey of social mobility in 1949. The main finding was that the class structure was fairly static, with the number who rose roughly equaling the number who fell.

More recent studies have been undertaken: those carried out by Nuffield College, Oxford, in 1972, and the follow-up re-analysis of data collected in 1983 as part of the British General Election Study (Goldthorpe, 1987); and the Essex University Class Project in 1984 (Marshall et al., 1988). The first two of these concentrated entirely on males for reasons of cost, while the latter included both male and female mobility.

Absolute social mobility

The Nuffield study was based on a survey of 10 000 men aged between 20 and 64 and was based on the Hope–Goldthorpe classification (see Figure 4.4 on page 123). The picture that emerged was significantly different from that found by Glass in 1949. In terms of absolute mobility, the proportion of people in the top two classes (Goldthorpe's service class – S) had increased. Of those men born in the period 1908–17, only 22 per cent were in the service class in 1972 while the figure for those born in 1938–47 was nearer 30 per cent. The less well-off classes (intermediate and working – I and W) had declined, and the historic working class appeared to be diminishing towards less than two-fifths of the British population.

When they compared the jobs of the 10 000 men with those of their fathers, they discovered that there had been substantial net upward mobility over the 60 years to 1972.

What had happened was that the service class had almost doubled, and inevitably it had to recruit new members from the intermediate and working classes. One important consequence of this was the fact that the sons of the service class are more likely to stay where they are – which has an impact on relative mobility – and this is discussed on page 146. In terms of the degree of openness of the top classes, while the service class still contained a majority who were born into it, there had also been an influx from other classes. Thus there has been a widening of its recruiting base

and a consequent decline in the extent to which it is self-recruited.

Also in contrast to Glass, the Nuffield team found evidence of 'long-range' upward mobility. This contrast is illustrated by the fact that in the 1949 survey the percentage of people of class 7 origins who had reached a class 1 destination in 1949 was 0 per cent, while the equivalent figure in 1972 was 7.1 per cent. There was clearly 'more room at the top' and the survey found about 750 who had moved from the bottom to the top.

The 1983 study confirmed the strong upward trend of absolute social mobility. In 1972, just under half the respondents said they had manual jobs; by 1983 the figure was nearer one in three. And one in three had service class jobs, compared with about one in four eleven years previously. The one note of change was that long-term unemployment (see also Section 9.6) had increasingly come into the picture, but as might be expected its effects were felt most by the manual working class. So, while in 1972 sixteen per cent of the men from working-class backgrounds aged between 20 and 34 had moved up the ladder into the service class, and 60 per cent had stayed in the working class, by 1983 22 per cent had moved up and only 40 per cent had stayed there. But 11 per cent of these were unemployed.

Goldthorpe also noted that it was becoming increasingly difficult to escape from the working class later in life, and as a result those who stayed in the working class were becoming more homogeneous. This point is salient to debates about developments in the working class and the 'underclass'. So the overall picture continued to be one of a growing heterogeneous middle class underpinned by an increasingly tight self-recruited working class. Rose (1988) has argued that the growth of middle-class jobs has ended, and points out that even if more were created – which is unlikely – they would most probably go to the children of this new expanded middle class.

The 1984 survey produced quite similar results, as can be seen from Table 4.8 which has been simplified by omitting the data on the intermediate class.

Table 4.8 Absolute male social mobility in three British studies (percentage of origin)

Origin	Destination	1972	1983	1984
Service	Service	58	62	60
Manual	Service	16	24	20
Service	Manual	19	16	20
Manual	Manual	61	53	51

Source: Payne (1991)

Payne summarizes the 1980's findings thus:

Moves up from manual to service class tend to be higher by the 1980s. . . . people born in the service class are able to retain their position . . . and fewer of those born in the working class remain there. (Payne, 1991, p. 13)

Occupational transition as the basis of increased absolute social mobility

Such findings on the increase in absolute social mobility might be seen by some as evidence that the UK has become a more open society and even a 'classless' one. However, Goldthorpe (1987) and Marshall *et al.* (1988) have argued that the increased levels of social mobility are not necessarily indicators of equal opportunity or a classless society, but are instead to be explained by changes in the occupational structure.

More recent evidence on changes in the occupational structure from 1971 to 1991 based on Census data is illustrated in Figure 4.7. This shows clearly the changes in the relative numbers of people in each

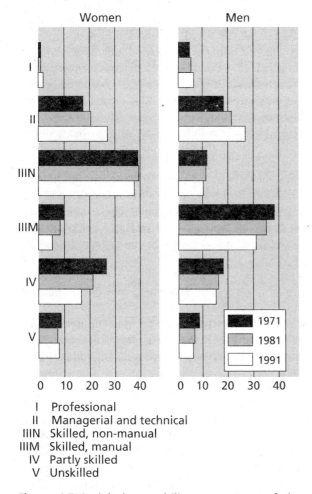

I Professional
II Managerial and technical
IIIN Skilled, non-manual
IIIM Skilled, manual
IV Partly skilled
V Unskilled

Figure 4.7 Social class mobility: percentage of the UK population by social class and sex.
Source: Census/*The Guardian*, 25 February 1995

class and the net result of social mobility.

Goldthorpe (1987) and Halsey (1980) conclude that the upward mobility was wholly explained by the UK's general post-war economic expansion, social reforms such as the 1944 Education Act having contributed nothing. Goldthorpe says:

Even in the presumably very favourable context of a period of sustained economic growth . . . the general underlying processes of inter-generational class mobility – or immobility – have apparently been little altered.

(Goldthorpe 1987, p. 86)

Halsey shows that the main effect of educational reform was in fact to increase the proportion of middle-class children going on to university. (See also Section 8.5.) The message is that policies of social democracy had not brought about greater equality of opportunity. The middle classes managed to be the prime beneficiaries of welfare services provision (see also Sections 13.2 and 14.4), and this is evidenced by continued differences in relative opportunities for upward mobility.

Relative social mobility

While it is clear that absolute levels of mobility have increased, this does not necessarily mean that inequalities of access based on social class background have been eliminated. What really matters are the chances that, say, two children from very different class backgrounds have of reaching the top. This is what is measured by relative social mobility, and it emerged that despite the general opening-up of chances, the odds were still stacked against the sons of working-class fathers. The 1972 study found that the service-class children were three-and-a-half times as successful (in ending up in the service class) as children of manual workers. By 1984 this had fallen to a still significant 3 to 1 advantage. If the effects of occupational transition are controlled for (using statistical techniques), then according to Goldthorpe (1987, p. 252) 'no significant reduction in class inequalities has in fact been achieved'. Marshall *et al.* concluded that 'there have been no changes in social "fluidity" – that is, in the direction of greater equality of opportunity' (1988, p. 137).

The Essex mobility findings on relative mobility have been presented in the form of 'odds-ratios'. Marshall explains the principle of this technique by reference to the example of betting odds. A very good horse and jockey may be expected to win a race and be given odds of 2 to 1, whereas an outsider might be given odds of 200 to 1. Then the odds ratio – that is the difference in their relative chances – is 200/2, or 100. The Essex team worked out such ratios for mobility chances and these are shown in Table 4.9.

Table 4.9 Transition from class of origin to present class position

Pairs of origin classes 'in competition'	Pairs of destination classes 'competed for'					
	Men			Women		
	S vs I	S vs W	I vs W	S vs I	S vs W	I vs W
S vs I	2.75	3.09	1.12	1.67	3.75	2.23
S vs W	4.00	7.35	1.82	3.77	12.95	3.43
I vs W	1.47	2.37	1.62	2.23	3.45	1.54

Note: S = service class; I = intermediate class; W = working class.
Source: Marshall *et al.* (1988, p. 105).

In order to understand this table examine the transition for men from service and working class backgrounds competing to end up in a service class rather than a working class destination. The odds ratio here is 7.35 to 1, which is the measure of the advantage held by the former over the latter in this particular competition. In other words the chances of someone starting in the service class being found in the service class rather than the working class are over 7 times greater than the same chances for someone starting in the working class in the case of men, and almost 13 times greater in the case of women. If there were no class inequality in this respect then the odds ratio in any given comparison would be simply 1. All the figures in the table are over 1. What is more, these relative mobility chances do not vary much over time, so the odds ratios have remained remarkably constant.

Activity

Identify those 'competitions' where the odds ratio is greatest and smallest in the case of men. Repeat the exercise for women.

Saunders (1990a) has accused Goldthorpe, Marshall *et al.* of being unrealistic, on the grounds that it is inappropriate to expect the odds ratios to be identical and it is wrong to ignore the occupational transition effect. He says that they will not accept that there is equality of opportunity until destination is completely unrelated to origin. He argues that greater affluence has been significant in causing large numbers of people to experience upward mobility and this cannot simply be ignored on the grounds that we are not yet totally equal in access to opportunity. Marshall and Rose argue that Saunders is wrong to simply assume that because considerable numbers of people have experienced upward mobility it follows that they have done so meritocratically. Payne sheds light on this debate with the following example:

Suppose that 70 per cent of today's service class are recruited from origins in other classes; is this high or low, good or bad? If 85 per cent of the population started in the other classes, then 70 per cent is not too bad, but it means that the other classes are not achieving their share (i.e. 85 per cent) of the best occupations. Saunders is stressing that the 70 per cent is quite good, while Marshall and Rose are saying the missing 15 per cent is what really matters.
(Payne, 1991, p. 13)

Saunders (1996) has also been associated with the argument that the odds ratios are not necessarily the result of class inequality but can be explained by other factors, such as genetic superiority or better parenting on the part of the middle classes. Such views have been rejected by Marshall and colleagues. Table 4.10 shows that class origins *do* make a difference to social mobility chances, even when educational level is taken into account. Saunders believes that IQ (ability) has an effect over and above the effect of educational qualifications and has replaced social privilege as the major factor determining where a child is likely to end up in the class structure. (For further details of the debate about IQ and educational achievement, see Section 8.9.)

Most of the material discussed in this section has related to male mobility. As can be seen, the Essex Class Project also included an investigation of female mobility. In order to overcome the automatic sexism in most social mobility studies, they used the term 'chief childhood supporter'. Most of the findings confirmed the view that women experience sex segregation in employment which disadvantages them. This probably explains the most striking fact about women's class trajectories: regardless of starting point, anything from a third to a half end up in class III (by their own occupation). Table 4.10 indicates the different trajectories of men and women when controlling for level of educational attainment. The social fluidity among men and women is virtually the same; that is, taken as separate entities the internal characteristics of their mobility patterns are similar.

Table 4.10 Mobility trajectories (%)

Educational attainment		Male destinations			Female destinations			All destinations		
		S	I	W	S	I	W	S	I	W
HIGH	origins S	92	3	5	78	22	0	86	11	3
	origins I	90	5	5	63	35	2	75	21	3
	origins W	91	9	0	57	39	4	76	22	2
MEDIUM	origins S	43	32	26	30	61	9	39	41	20
	origins I	31	41	29	22	63	16	27	49	24
	origins W	15	37	43	21	60	19	17	47	36
LOW	origins S	33	27	40	0	57	43	23	36	41
	origins I	13	33	54	13	37	50	13	34	53
	origins W	II	25	64	2	43	56	7	33	60

Source: Marshall and Swift (1993)

But equality of opportunity for women appears to be limited because their destinations (jobs) have in the past tended to be less advantageous than those of men (see Section 4.11 for a discussion of class and gender).

Activity

a State in your own words how the information in Table 4.10 demonstrates that differences in social mobility chances cannot be explained by superior educational attainment alone.

b To what extent does the evidence in the table support the claim that male and female patterns of mobility are different?

I, A, E

In conclusion, if a classless society is one where there are only weak links between peoples' origins and where they end up, then even on this definition the UK cannot be said to be classless. It has a far from perfectly mobile society, and studies of social mobility demonstrate the continuing effects of class origins on eventual class destination. (See Section 4.5 for details on élite self-recruitment). In the words of Heath, 'silver spoons continue to be distributed' (1981, p. 77). Marshall and colleagues sum up the situation thus:

Such upward mobility as has existed is the result of changes in the shape (rather than the openness) of the class structure.
(Marshall *et al.*, 1988, p. 137)

Activity

Explain the last statement from Marshall *et al.* (1988), and evaluate its validity using information from this section.

I, A, E

4.10 Classlessness and the end of class analysis?

A 1996 Gallup poll result, that 76 per cent of the population 'thought there was a class struggle in Britain today', seems to fly in the face of the media which has either ignored class struggle or proclaimed that it is over. Class struggle is not the same as class, but here too the media has tended to propagate the view that the nature of the new class structure is such that people can become upwardly mobile simply by changing their tastes and cultural habits. In the journalese of Hadfield and Skipworth (1994), class is about lifestyle and self-conscious conspicuous consumption. It has become quite common for sociologists to argue that class is an outmoded concern. Pahl, for instance, has suggested that:

. . . if the concept does not do any useful work for us we should cease behaving as if it did.
(Pahl, 1989, p. 710)

People, particularly non-sociologists, now talk about class and classlessness in different ways, but within sociology the notion that class is redundant takes on two main forms: 'the myths of classlessness' and the 'death of class' (Lee and Turner, 1996, p. 3):

- *The myths of classlessness* are theories that assume the obsolescence of class, in the sense that classlessness has been achieved through changes in the actual distribution of class power and privilege in modern industrial nations.
- *The death of class* refers to the obsolescence of class analysis, on the basis that class is no longer a useful tool with which to understand society.

These two views are, of course, closely related because the rationale for those holding the latter position is in part based on assumptions of the former.

The myths of classlessness

Edgell (1993) identifies three possible interpretations of the notion of classlessness: total classlessness, one-class classlessness, and multi-class classlessness.

Total classlessness

In Marxist theory, total classlessness would be achieved only following a proletarian revolution with the dismantling of capitalist class relations and the establishment of a communist order. (See also Section 2.3.) Clearly this is not the version of classlessness which is heralded by media pundits and politicians. It is the notion of classlessness that survives among neo-Marxists who urge that it is necessary to abolish private property as the basis of economic inequality. This would involve a radical overhaul of existing society or its complete transformation.

One-class classlessness

This variant is part of the long-standing debate about alleged embourgeoisement which was discussed in Section 4.7. According to Lee and Turner (1996), the oldest such myth of classlessness originated in Germany at the end of the nineteenth century. Then, Eduard Bernstein argued that the conditions of the working class had improved such that revision of the Marxist doctrine of revolution was required as capitalism could be reformed through parliamentary politics. (See also Section 2.5.) Lee and Turner suggest that the second myth of classlessness was the 'separation of ownership and control' thesis (discussed in Section 4.5), according to which capitalist ownership was said to have been democratized, and the capitalist class had disappeared. These myths were implying that the Marxist model of class formation was outmoded, and by the 1950s it was felt that capitalist society was safe from the threat of revolution. On the contrary, it was argued, communist societies were more

likely to change in the direction of capitalism. This was known as the 'convergence thesis' (Kerr *et al.*, 1973, orig. pub. 1960).

One-class classlessness theories contain the suggestion that class differences no longer exist since all people belong to a single (middle) class. This view tends to focus on the distribution of income and wealth in the middle ranges of the class structure, where class inequalities are said to have disappeared, or at least to have declined considerably – though, as the later part of this section will demonstrate, income inequalities are wider than ever before. (See also Section 14.8.) As for embourgeoisement, the view that rising affluence automatically translated into class transition was soundly rejected (Goldthorpe *et al.*, 1969), and more recently the evidence suggests that there remains a distinctive working class which retains the potential for class action. Middle-class classlessness according to Edgell is therefore a myth. There are similarities between the embourgeoisement thesis and later versions of a similar idea which are associated with the 'new' myths of classlessness such as citizenship, post-industrialism, post-Fordism, post-Marxism and post-modernism – which are discussed below.

Multi-class classlessness

According to Edgell, this multi-class type of classlessness which emanated from the work of Weber finds its most extreme form in the functionalist model which 'involves the equal opportunity to be unequal and has been called non-egalitarian classlessness' (1993, p. 120). The implicit assumption of this whole approach is that, just as success is related to individual ability and effort, failure is due to lack of one or the other, or both. This has been seen by many as a major force in the legitimization of the capitalist order – a point not lost on right-wing political administrations on either side of the Atlantic.

The main objection to this view of classlessness is the continued existence of obvious material inequalities which appear to have hardened (Westergaard, 1995; see page 150). Sennett and Cobb (1977) write of 'the hidden injuries of class', by which they mean the guilt and social humiliation that accompanies failure to be successful.

Edgell concludes that none of the foregoing versions of classlessness stands up to criticism:

Hence, what needs to be explained is not the presumed demise of class, but the tenacity of class-based patterns of inequality and politics, and much else besides.
(Edgell, 1993, p. 122)

New myths

In recent decades, changes in ownership, employment and labour markets have given rise to 'new' myths of classlessness. (See also Section 9.3) The suggestion here is that class analysis is obsolete because class differences are being replaced by other inequalities and influences such as those based on gender, ethnicity, age, region, housing tenure (owner-occupiers/tenants), employment sector (public/private), employment (waged/welfare recipients) (Saunders, 1987). These forms of social cleavage are often associated with reduced alignment between class and voting patterns (Crewe, 1987). (See also Section 17.2.) The changes include:

- the shift from individual to corporate wealth (contested by Westergaard, 1995)
- the restructuring of work (including the increasing participation of women)
- the decline in manufacturing and the rise of services
- the decline of class-related organizations such as trade unions.

We are said to be experiencing 'the end of work', as witnessed by increasing long-term unemployment, early retirement, longer periods in education, and fewer lifetimes spent in work. Allied with such changes is the growth of individualism and consumption as an expression of personal identity in conditions of cultural flux divorced from the structural determinacy associated with class. Thus, if work as employment is declining in its significance, it is argued that consumption is becoming more relevant in the sense that people's identities are increasingly expressed and manifest through consumption, rather than production. (See also Section 10.9.) Class as a concept based on productivism should, it is argued, therefore be abandoned. Crompton sums up these views as follows:

Thus, it is argued, 'class' (i.e. employment) is becoming relatively less significant in terms of both 'life chances' and as a source of identity.
(Crompton, 1996b, p. 19)

Another type of argument for 'the end of class' is the apparent failure of organized class action to materialize. This view has been massively reinforced in popular opinion by the fall of state socialism in a 'post-Marxist' eastern Europe. In the West, changes in employment have undermined the numerical dominance of manual work, which has led to the increasing fragmentation of the workforce. This mirrors the fragmentation effected by the post-Fordist organization of work based around the principles of flexible specialization. (See also Section 9.4.) It has prompted Clark and Lipset

(1991) to argue that this has led to an increasing fragmentation of political orientation and behaviour. Class (i.e. economic position) no longer determines political preferences, it is argued, particularly among the young. Pahl (1989) also argues that consumption-related sources of identity have led to a decline in class-related political attitudes and behaviour. A further strand of thinking is that notions of citizenship and welfare intervention (See also Sections 14.3 and 14.4.) have reduced the salience of class divisions.

Lash and Urry (1987) suggest that the characteristics of post-Fordism signalled the end of 'organized capitalism' and the start of 'disorganized capitalism'. With more reliance on market forces, less government intervention, increased flexibility of labour, the adoption of microelectronic technology and the decline of the manufacturing sector, employment becomes less secure and fragmented. The result is the emergence of a 'post-modernist' culture based on fragmentation and pluralism in which class is 'decentred' as a source of identity, being replaced by individualist consumption. (See also Sections 10.9 and 10.11.) Work is no longer a way of identifying oneself, more a means to acquiring desirable goals, a tendency which leads to a decline in traditional class politics and the death of the possibility of working-class revolution.

These theories have questioned the significance of classes as significant forces in late twentieth-century capitalism. However, they do not suggest that capitalist societies are not highly unequal. As Crompton points out:

. . . although 'work' may have declined as a significant source of social identity, work is still the most significant determinant of the material well being of the majority of the population. Thus descriptive class indexes continue to show the structure of inequality in contemporary societies.
(Crompton, 1993, p. 18)

In defence of traditional forms of class analysis, sociologists such as Westergaard (1995), Goldthorpe and Marshall (1992) and Hout *et al.* (1993) have argued that liberal and post-modernist myths of classlessness have ignored the findings of rigorously conducted research.

Westergaard (1995) criticizes the fashionable argument of classlessness, claiming that it is very much at odds with the facts. He argues that such a view has misunderstood the fundamental nature of social class and has ignored hardening class inequalities. Westergaard, adopting a Marxist position, reasserts the salience of class predicated on social divisions arising from a society's economic organization. From this flows differential command over resources, and consequently (drawing on elements of Weberian analysis) he notes the existence of differential access to rewards which are to be seen in fundamental aspects of people's life experiences or 'life chances' in the form of various inequalities. Westergaard is aware of the need for class consciousness if a 'class in itself' is ever to become a 'class for itself', but he also points to the importance of the objective features of class 'in itself' in shaping the character of society and people's experiences. Westergaard's main argument is that the 1980s and 90s saw the effects of class increase in their potency.

Economic and political command

Westergaard (1995) argues that within the UK there has been a trend towards the increasing concentration of capital and a consolidation of upper-class power and privilege (see Section 4.5), which is strengthened by the increasing globalization of its scope. He thus argues that the notion of mass consumer empowerment seems rather hollow in the face of this increasing concentration of productive property. This is reinforced by the increasing inequality of incomes (see also Section 14.8) which has brought consumer empowerment far more to the few than to the many. Westergaard accuses the class-denying theorists of ignoring the question of an upper class, as the mere existence of this upper circle means there is a class structure. This is where students of stratification should look, he argues, for it is here that power is concentrated: power to consume, in that the richest 5 per cent of the population command as much post-tax income as the entire poorest third. It is also the case, he argues, that there has been increasing concentration of economic command in terms of top decision makers' power in the financial markets. He also notes the increasingly tight links between business and political élites.

Westergaard's overall contention is that there exists a business hegemony which is underscored by its increasing power and privilege at the top of society, and its very existence makes a mockery of the idea of classlessness.

Class inequalities of life experience

Westergaard acknowledges the widening of systematic inequalities of income that have occurred since 1979 (see Figure 4.8). However, he says that their full significance has not been appreciated. The argument that average income has risen is used by some to defend the redistribution that has occurred. Others argue that the significant feature is the exclusion of a minority underclass fallen behind the

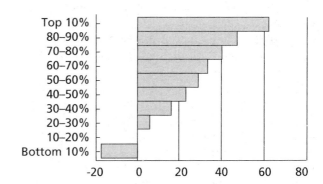

Figure 4.8 Percentage changes in real income (after housing costs), 1979–92. Source: *Households Below Average Income*, London, HMSO, 1994

average. But Westergaard argues that the average is an artefact which is skewed upwards because of the massive incomes of a few. Most increases in income have been below this 'artefactual average', so our attention should be focused on the majority experience of lagging steadily more behind upper-level incomes.

Westergaard describes the class-eclipse theorists as engaging in sociological fantasy rather than fact.

Table 4.11 Gallup's long-running poll result

'There used to be a lot of talk in politics about a "class struggle". Do you think there is a class struggle in this country or not?'			
	'Is'	**'Is not'**	**'Don't know'**
1961 (Dec)	56	22	22
1964 (Aug)	48	39	13
1972 (Jun)	58	29	13
1973 (Feb)	53	33	14
1973 (Apr)	60	29	11
1973 (Dec)	57	29	14
1974 (Jan)	58	31	11
1974 (Feb)	62	27	11
1974 (Apr)	60	29	12
1975 (May)	60	29	11
1981 (Mar)	66	25	9
1984 (Mar)	74	20	6
1986 (Feb)	70	24	6
1991 (Jul)	79	16	4
1993 (Sep)	77	17	6
1994 (Mar)	78	16	7
1995 (Nov)	81	12	7
1996 (Aug)	76	15	9

1996 percentage agreement by voting intention:
Labour 81, Conservative 66, Liberal Democrat 77

Source: Gallup Organization

The facts of income inequality signify a widening of consumer inequalities of choice. He concludes that all this has made for more class-divided life experiences in all respects, including illness and the risks of death. (See also Section 13.2.)

Westergaard also notes that class-denial theorists have been too quick to announce the eclipse of class politics. He contends that voters still vote as much along class lines as they did in relative terms in the 1960s and 70s. (See also Section 17.2) Importantly they continue to show unease about inequality generally and concentration of power at the top.

Gallup's long-running poll results on the British public's awareness of 'a class struggle' would seem to be further indication of growing awareness of 'the hardening of class inequalities' in modern times (see Table 4.11).

Lee and Turner concur, with the conclusion that:

. . . the existence of class divisions and their profound effects on people's lives is an objective finding which sociology can claim to have established. (Lee and Turner, 1996, p. 9)

Activity

a Describe in your own words the overall trend suggested by the information in Table 4.11.

b Suggest at least one methodological limitation of such research.

c How might a 'class-denial' theorist interpret the findings of these polls?

d Using information from this section and elsewhere, to what extent do you either agree or disagree with the claim that the UK has become a classless society?

U, I, A, E

The death of class?

The debate about the conceptual issues surrounding the sociology of class broadly revolves around a distinction between what Crompton (1996b) has called the 'employment aggregates model' and the class-processes model.

There are also methodological differences between them. The employment class-aggregates view tends to be seen as more positivistic and derives from large-scale survey data (see also Section 3.7), while the class-processes view derives from the 'action' approach with its stress on the socially constructed nature of class formation – concentrating therefore on how the class structure changes and individuals and groups compete in it (see Table 4.12). The division between these two approaches was centred on the contradiction: 'How could a constantly changing structure be studied using fixed occupational categories?' (Crompton, 1996b, p. 21).

The dominant 'employment-aggregate' school has argued that, although changes have been taking place in employment, they have not resulted in a transformation of the link between (employment) classes and other phenomena such as voting behaviour, chances of social mobility etc. So in defending the rationale for their class schema they point to the persistence of class-related differences. Thus although the class structure is changing it is relatively easy to show its persistent effects.

Crompton argues that the debate over the death of class is a 'pseudo debate' which has arisen as a result of the misinterpretation by the protagonists on each side of each others' work. It is really a question of different emphasis – whether the changes are more significant than the constants. She proposes that both of the approaches can play a useful role in class analysis and concludes that, since access to property and employ-

Table 4.12 The employment class-aggregates model and the class-processes schools compared

Employment aggregates	Class processes
Positivistic	Action
Based on statistical analysis of national data sets grouped into 'social classes'	Based on socio-historical analyses of change or case studies of specific groups
Emphasizes stability rather than change, such as the persistence of relative social mobility	Reveals the extent of changes in employment patterns, workplace organization and the class structure, such as net upward mobility
Concentrates on the persistence of class effects	Concentrates on instability and change and new bases of social cleavage

Source: Adapted from text in Crompton (1996b)

ment resources are the most significant source of life chances in capitalist societies, they are still class societies and:

> . . . *at the present time it makes little sense for sociologists to be arguing that 'class' is no longer a useful concept in sociology.*
> (Crompton, 1996b, p. 22)

Discussion point

To what extent do you agree that class is still an important sociological concept?

Bradley (1996, p. 79) strongly defends 'modernist' theories derived from traditional class analysis. She also recognizes the need for an awareness of the insights provided by 'post-modernist' writings. She argues that neither class (as a set of lived economic relationships) nor class analysis (as a set of social categories) is dead. But there must be recognition of how class relations are shaped by other forms of inequality.

4.11 The interacting dynamics of inequality

It is necessary to consider the debates over the salience of class analysis for explanations of other forms of inequality and the links between them. According to Bradley (1996), class must be viewed as an interaction with other dynamics of inequality.

Gender

Bradley argues that gender has historically served to divide the working class: men and women have been in competition over employment, resulting in the economic and political marginalization of women in secondary roles. (See also Section 9.3.) Classes are also 'gendered' in the sense that gender is integral to processes of class formation, action and identification. This is witnessed by womens' contributions to the reproduction of working-class culture, both in their position in the family (see also Section 7.5) and the community, often bearing the brunt of poverty, and increasingly through proletarianized paid employment of their own.

At various levels of the class structure the effects of gender are seen. At the highest levels women are conspicuously absent from senior positions, but they play a key role in the economic and social reproduction of capital through their role in maintaining 'élite cohesion' and the transmission of dominant values. In the middle classes the effects

of gender are most evident in the feminized nature of lower-grade non-manual work, a trend which is likely to continue according to Esping-Andersen's (1993) account of the feminized nature of the emerging post-industrial service classes. At the lower end women are an important element in the 'underclass' as a result of the 'feminization of poverty', whereby women are particularly vulnerable to dependency on benefits as single parents, as pensioners, as low-paid workers and as wives of unemployed men. (See also Section 14.6.) Bradley thus concludes that:

> . . . *gender is significantly involved in processes of class recomposition.*
> (Bradley, 1996, p. 75)

Women and class theory

Feminists have criticized traditional approaches to stratification as 'malestream' sociology (see also Sections 2.6 and 5.3). Women have traditionally been excluded on the grounds that:

- the family household is the unit of analysis
- the head of the household is male
- women are not continuously in the labour market, and their class is determined by their husbands' jobs.

Acker (1973) argues against deciding the social position of a family by the occupation of the male head of household. She claimed that it was inappropriate to subsume women's class position with that of her spouse or partner. She believes that women should be classified in their own right because they can be seen as constituting a 'caste-like' status group within social classes as a result of sharing certain social characteristics within occupational categories that distinguish them from men at a similar level of the class hierarchy.

Delphy (1977b) argues that married women constitute a distinct social class, because they are involved in distinct (patriarchal) relations of production based on exploitative domestic labour. Allen (1982) claims that, just as on marriage a wife does not acquire her husband's education, nor should it be assumed that the wife assumes his position in society. This focuses on the importance of power in class and other relationships, rather than merely viewing class as being based on income.

In the face of such feminist criticisms, Goldthorpe (1983) attempts to defend the conventional view. He claims that it is not based on 'intellectual sexism' but on a realistic understanding of the position of women:

- According to Goldthorpe, women do not have equal opportunities for participation in the labour market because conventional norms associated with familial ideology (see also Sections 5.3 and 7.1) force them into a situation of dependency. Thus the notion of the male as chief breadwinner for the purposes of class analysis is justified, he argues, because women's participation in paid employment is intermittent, limited and conditional owing to the constraints of family and domestic responsibilities.
- Furthermore his main reason for defending the conventional view is that the employment opportunities of married women vary directly with the occupations of their husbands.
- Finally, he contends that contemporary marriages are largely homogeneous with respect to class (i.e. they share similar class origins and/or occupational level).

In a revised formula, Goldthorpe now argues that the head of the household is the person whose occupation is highest on the basis of status of employment and hours employed – and accordingly the whole 'family' is best classified according to the highest level of labour market participation.

According to Wright (1997), three main criticisms have been levelled against Goldthorpe:

- Although families may pool income, husbands and wives do not necessarily always share the consumption of that income equally.
- Since class is more than simply about income, merely showing that married couples share the same consumption class does not prove they share the same class (as defined by Marxism).
- It is not the case that families rather than individuals are the units of class mobilization.

While generally agreeing with these points, Wright is more interested in providing a specific critique of Goldthorpe's stance on the classification of married women:

Goldthorpe argues that because the economic fate of the family is more dependent upon income from the husband's job than the wife's, the class location of the family should be exclusively identified within his job. . . . Family strategy, then, is not some kind of negotiated weighted average of the class-based imperatives linked to each spouse's job, but uniquely determined by the class imperatives of the male breadwinner. This claim is simply asserted on Goldthorpe's part, unbacked by either theoretical argument or empirical evidence. Of course, there are many cases where a story of this sort has considerable face validity. . . . But there is no reason to assume that this particular situation is universal.
(Wright, 1997, pp. 255–6)

Wright believes that family-income maximization strategies are affected by the class character of both spouses' jobs:

Even where the wife contributes less than the husband, therefore, the class character of her paid work could systematically shape family strategies, and thus the class character of the family unit.
(Wright, 1997, p. 257)

While it is unjustified to equate the class location of married working women with the job class of their husbands, it also seems unsatisfactory to treat their class as simply based on their own immediate work.

Direct and mediated class locations

Wright offers a conceptual solution by distinguishing between direct and mediated class locations. Direct class locations exist through the link between individuals and productive resources constituted by their immediate job and their direct personal control or ownership of such resources. It is also the case that peoples' material interests are shaped by a variety of other relations which link them to the system of production – typically kinship relationships and those to the state. These indirect links between individuals and productive resources are mediated relations resulting in mediated class locations. According to Wright, an adequate picture of the class interests of, for instance, children, housewives, the unemployed, pensioners and students cannot be gained simply by examining their direct participation in the relations of production. Wright thus conceives of a class structure in which mediated relations loom very large for some people and not for others in shaping their material interests, and thus their overall position in the class structure (see Figure 4.9).

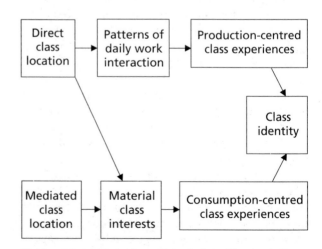

Figure 4.9 A general model of the effects of direct and mediated class locations on class identity

Wright has sought to test the relative salience of direct and mediated aspects of the class location of married women for the probability of having a working-class identity – subjectively considering oneself in the working class – using comparative data from the USA and Sweden. In other words, to what extent are individuals' (both husbands' and wives') class identities influenced by the effects of their own paid employment, and to what extent by those of their partner?

Wright's main conclusion is that direct class location has a much bigger effect on class identity in Sweden than in the USA for both men and women. This is due in part to the lower degree of economic dependence of wives on husbands in Sweden. It is also a function of the greater salience of class experiences within work on the lives of Swedish workers in general, in contrast to the United States where classes are constituted primarily in the realm of consumption. Thus Wright accepts that Goldthorpe's conceptualization of class – that classes consist of families as units of common material interests/consumption – is much more appropriate for the class structure of the United States than for Sweden:

In the former no predictive power is lost by defining the class location of women in the labour force by the class of their husbands, whereas in the latter this is not the case.
(Wright, 1997, p. 269)

However, he believes that the couplet of direct/ mediated class relations offers a way of linking a Marxist class analysis to an analysis of gender relations without simply subsuming the latter into the former. The addition of the concept of mediated class relations:

. . . makes it possible to move away from a view of class and gender in which these two kinds of relations are treated as entirely distinct, separate structures. And it does not move all the way toward the view that class and gender constitute a unitary undifferentiated system. Mediated class relations therefore provides a basis for conceptualising one form of interaction of class and gender without collapsing the distinction itself.
(Wright, 1997, p. 277)

According to Abbott and Wallace (1997), taking the family as the only relevant unit of analysis obscures the inequalities between women and men within it, and the different market and work situations which they face outside it. Women are concentrated in low-paid low-status jobs, many of which have become 'sex-typed' as 'female jobs' historically and are now seen as the very justification for their low pay and status. (See also Section 9.3.) Thus, they argue, it is important to consider the ways in which female wage labour and domestic wage labour are combined and interact with each other and with the capitalist system, with complex consequences for class structure and class consciousness.

A number of attempts have been made to create a separate classification for women, such as the following by Dex (1987):

1 professional occupations
2 teachers
3 nursing, medical and social occupations
4 other intermediate and non-manual occupations
5 clerical occupations
6 shop assistants and related sales occupations
7 skilled occupations
8 childcare occupations
9 semi-skilled factory work
10 semi-skilled domestic work
11 other semi-skilled occupations
12 unskilled occupations.

However, the new difficulty such separate classifications create is that of comparability between men's and women's occupational schemas.

Another alternative approach – 'individual classification' – refers to the notion of couples being allocated individually to a social class, and where the partners are in different classes then they are said to constitute a 'dual-class household'. This is favoured by Abbott and Wallace as the only meaningful way to analyse social mobility of women. Goldthorpe rejects joint classification because he does not believe that women make that much difference to the class position of families. In terms of individual classification, he claims to show that married women's life chances are in fact most fully explained by their husbands' occupations.

Abbott and Wallace conclude, first, that the study of women's class demonstrates the need to look at family members in their own right rather than assuming a common experience for all members of the same family. Secondly, in reviewing the evidence on female social mobility, they note the disadvantages faced by women in mobility opportunities compared with men, and the significance of this for understanding the enhanced social mobility of men. However, they do acknowledge that while women have such disadvantages in common they are also divided by class.

Gender inequalities do not abolish the need to look at class inequalities; they exist, and are demonstrably important.
(Abbott and Wallace, 1997, p. 66)

They are prepared to contemplate the idea that class may be a more important principle of stratification than gender, but argue that this must be demonstrated and not taken for granted as has been the case in some traditional malestream sociology.

Discussion point

Discuss the statement: 'Women are in a class of their own'.

Ethnicity

According to Bradley (1996), 'race' and ethnicity act as a source of division within classes in the form of competition between black and white workers for employment. Like gender, 'race' contributes to processes of class formation in an integral way. The emergence of capitalist production, its continued development, and more recently its globalizing tendency, have in large part been made possible by the exploitation of both colonial slave populations and internationally migrant labour. (See also Sections 6.1 and 6.2.) Migrant labour characteristically fills the worst, low-status, 'dirty' jobs rejected by the indigenous population. To use Bradley's words:

Labour, therefore, is not an ethnically neutral category. The working class is composed of ethnically distinct layers, shaped by the particular pattern of migration in each country.
(Bradley, 1996, p. 76)

According to Abbott and Wallace (1997), two major theories of ethnicity and 'race' have emerged in sociology. The Marxist view explains racial disadvantage in terms of the class structure under capitalism, according to which racialized groups are part of the proletariat, exploited to suit the requirements of international capitalism. However, because of the history of colonialism they encounter prejudice from white working-class people and are scapegoated as being to blame for lack of jobs etc. This deflects attention away from the 'real' causes of the problems, which is exploitation of the working class as a whole.

Weberian sociologists see racial disadvantage as the result of competition over scarce resources such as housing. White native groups have practised social closure against racialized competing groups.

Marxists underplay the distinctiveness of 'race', while Weberians do not explain how some racial characteristics come to be chosen rather than others

as the basis of social closure. Both theories have been criticized by Bryan (1985), a black feminist, for not realizing that the experiences of racialized women and how they are exploited are different from those of racialized men. (See also Sections 5.3 and 6.6.)

Abbott and Wallace were particularly interested in examining the situation of 'black women' who had come to the UK as migrants, and their daughters. They use the term 'black' to refer to those who experience the racism directed at non-white people – at racialized groups. They argue that black women face exploitation and subordination as women, as members of the working class and on the basis of their colour. Thus they conclude:

Black women are oppressed not only by their gender but by the intersection of class, 'race' and gender. On the whole they suffer the worst of all groups in terms of disadvantage.
(Abbott and Wallace, 1997, p. 76)

Age

Bradley (1996) calls age 'the neglected dimension of stratification'. Research has been focused on the experience of specific age-groups, such as childhood and old-age. While these provide insights into inequalities associated with age, they are not usually located within a general theory of age and inequality. Bradley argues that age should be seen as a dimension of inequality because, like class, gender and ethnicity, it involves the construction of social differences which result in differential access to wealth status and power. Ageism refers to discrimination against people on the basis of characteristics imputed to them solely because of their age and, for Bradley, all age-groups are adversely affected by ageism.

Discussion point

To what extent do you think it will ever be possible to overcome stereotyped thinking about age?

Bradley believes that young people have been particularly susceptible to the worst forms of capitalist exploitation, whether it be in the nineteenth century or at the end of the twentieth. Globalizing capital continues to make use of child labour in both first-world and third-world settings. (See also Sections 12.5 and 12.8.) Traditionally the most lucrative and secure jobs at all levels in the class structure have been, and still are, held by middle-aged people. According to Bradley, young people are 'at the sharp end of the changing class dynamic' (p. 77). She argues that young people's awareness of class is less developed than in the past, owing to two factors:

- periodic increases in relative affluence, and the spread of a consumer culture, and
- the growth of youth unemployment which has eroded the experience of workplace socialization and its attendant emphasis on collective class action.

However, despite appearing to be at the forefront of post-modern cultural change, young people are actually feeling the effects of class polarization more than most – effects which vary greatly according to the social class of the individuals concerned. (See also Sections 10.4 and 10.5.)

The elderly tend to suffer from the effects of 'role loss', the most significant of which is withdrawal from the full-time labour market, and they experience increasing dependence on others. For many people, old age is a period of diminishing power and fewer resources, together with the debilitating effects of ill-health, negative social stigmatization and social exclusion (Field, 1992). Once again the experience of individuals in these respects varies according to their lifetime earning power and accumulated resources. Class inequality is often most marked among the elderly.

Class and other inequalities: contemporary debates

Bradley (1996) accepts that societies are becoming fragmented, and that social identities are more fluid. But she rejects the idea that materially based class inequalities have lost their significance. She also believes that it is inappropriate to attach primary importance to class, arguing the case for an increasing emphasis on non-class forms of oppression. Her main point is that class and other forms of inequality – such as gender, ethnicity and age – 'merge together to form the complex hierarchies which are characteristic of contemporary societies' (p. 203).

Westergaard (1995) has challenged attempts to relegate the importance of class inequality relative to gender and ethnic inequality to the point where, in some accounts, they are seen as essentially parallel. While recognizing that class, gender and 'race' are distinct dimensions of inequality, and that gender and racial subordination cannot be primarily explained by the workings of capitalism, Westergaard nonetheless contends that in the public sphere, gender and ethnic inequality operate and are mediated largely through class inequality. That is to say, the results of gender and racial inequalities are primarily seen in terms of their economic consequences.

According to Wright (1997), there is still a general expectation by Marxists that class and non-class forms of oppression will tend to reinforce each other. There are two broad theses about the interconnection of class and other forms of oppression that flow from this:

- *Non-class oppression translates into class oppression.* Those oppressed through non-class mechanisms will be especially exploited within class relations because they are denied access to resources which matter for class. Thus women and racialized groups will be over-represented in the working class.
- *Class oppression translates into non-class oppression.* While all capitalist societies are exploitative, the degree of inequality varies, as does the extent of non-class oppression. The extent of non-class oppression depends on the power of the exploiting class to take advantage of them and perpetuate them. A class analysis of non-class oppression would, therefore, predict that 'the more oppressive and exploitative are class relations within capitalism, the more oppressive these other forms of oppression will tend to be as well'.

Wright's results on class and gender distribution tend to provide support for the first thesis. In international comparisons, women are much more proletarianized than are men. The picture is similar in terms of the relative authority in the workplace of men and women. The case of 'race' and class indicates that black people are significantly more proletarianized than white people, and black women are the most proletarianized of all 'race' and gender categories.

However, some surprise results ran counter to the expectation in the second thesis that gender

Activity

a Describe in your own words Bradley's view of the relationship between class and other forms of inequality.

b Identify any similarities and differences between the views of Bradley and those of Westergaard and Wright.

c Using information from this chapter and elsewhere, describe the extent to which you believe that class deserves to retain its central position in the sociological analysis of inequality.

K, U, I, A, E

inequalities will be greatest where class inequalities are greatest, thereby supporting the feminist thesis that gender relations are autonomous from class relations and can vary independently of each other. For Wright this is not to deny the oppressive features of class inequality that impinge on women's lives.

Further **reading**

- Abercrombie, N. and Warde, A. (eds) (1994) *Stratification and Social Inequality: Studies in British Society*, Lancaster, Framework Press.
- Bradley, H. (1996), *Fractured Identities*, Cambridge, Polity Press.
- Crompton, R. (1993) *Class and Stratification: An Introduction to Current Debates*, Cambridge, Polity Press.
- Edgell, S. (1993) *Class*, London, Routledge.
- Hamilton, M. and Hirszowicz, M. (1993) *Class and Inequality*, Hemel Hempstead, Harvester Wheatsheaf.
- Lee, D. and Turner, B. (eds) (1996) *Conflicts About Class*, Harlow, Longman.
- Scase, R. (1992) *Class*, Milton Keynes, Open University Press.
- Scott, J. (1996), *Stratification and Power*, Cambridge, Polity Press.
- Westergaard, J. (1995) *Who Gets What?*, Cambridge, Polity Press.
- Wright, E.O. (1997) *Class Counts,* Cambridge, Cambridge University Press.

Back issues of *Sociology Review* (formly known as *Social Studies Review*) also contain many articles on this field of sociology and many others.

Exam **questions**

1 **Item A** Giddens argues that class relations are shaped by such factors as the division of labour in production, authority relations in employing organisations, and patterns of consumption. These all help to determine the 'structuration' of classes – the degree of consciousness, solidarity and cohesion which they can achieve. The development of the division of labour, for example, has tended to sharpen the distinction between manual and non-manual workers – between working class and middle class. This sharpening has been reinforced by the involvement of non-manual workers in the exercise of

authority over manual workers on behalf of the owners and controllers of businesses. Consumption patterns, similarly, reinforce class relations by creating for example a residential neighbourhood segregation of middle class and working class 'communities', each with their particular and distinct styles of life and pattern of living.

Source: Adapted from Scott, J. *Social Stratification, Developments in Sociology Vol. 7*, Causeway Press

Item B Marx sees a particularly strong connection between class and culture. Marxists often use the term 'class culture' to refer to a way of life – physical and mental – and behavour typical of a given class . . . Weber did not think that culture was quite so closely connected with class as do Marxists. Indeed, he often used the term 'life-style' rather than culture, which has a deliberately more individualistic sound to it. For him, the working class person with middle class values, friends and leisure pursuits is a relatively common exception requiring no special explanation. People develop their own cultural habits which can easily cut across class lines. Functionalists, including Durkheim, tend to regard it as the major role of culture to unite rather than to divide society. In particular, Durkheim was concerned to bridge the rift between capitalist and worker.

Source: O'Donnell, M. (1992) *A New Introduction to Sociology*, Nelson

Item C Mrs Thatcher was on record as saying there was no such thing as society – only individuals. Her successor as Prime Minister, Mr John Major, had a different opinion. On taking office he spoke of Britain as moving towards a 'classless' society – a society of opportunity based on merit and effort. He said 'what people fulfil will depend upon their talent, their application and their good fortune'. This vision is well known to sociologists as the 'meritocracy' concept. Mr Major came from a grammar school background and left school at 16. His rise to the top job in the land illustrates the possibilities.

Source: Denscombe, M., *Sociology Update 1991*, Olympus Books

a What does Giddens mean by 'the structuration' of social classes (**Item A**) [1 mark]

b To what extend do sociologists agree that manual workers and non-manual workers are still sharply distinct (**Item A**)? [7 marks]

c Using material from the **Items** and else-where, assess the evidence for the existence of class cultures in modern Britain. [8 marks]

d How far does sociological evidence support the idea that Britain is a 'meritocratic' society (**Item C**)?   [9 marks]

(AEB, Paper 1, Summer, 1993)

2 **Item A The Decline of Class?**

Gordon Marshall *et al.* have conveniently sum-marised the alleged 'decline of class' in Britain in the following way. The first factor is the restruc-turing of capital and labour. The decline of manufacturing industry and the rise of service industries have led to the numerical decline of the manual or traditional working class. Capitalists are considered to have used the changing economic situation to reassert control over labour. Secondly, a greater variety of social, cultural and political differences and identities are considered to occur within the major class groups than in the past. Thirdly, instrumental collec-tivism means that workers in a particular industry are members of a union to pursue their own sectional interests rather than the interests of the working class as a whole. Fourthly, individuals and families are seen as becoming home-centred and privatized, enjoying relatively affluent consumer lifestyles. Finally, due to these developments, issues of inequality are either obscured or seen as less important.

Source: Adapted from O'Donnell, M. (1992) *A New Introduction to Sociology*, 3rd Ed., Nelson

Item B Social Class of all Persons in Employment (percentages): 1971–1991

	1971	1981	1991
Professional and managerial	22%	26%	33%
Clerical	21%	23%	23%
Foremen and skilled manual	28%	25%	22%
Semi and unskilled manual	29%	26%	22%

Source: Calculated from *Censuses of Population* 1971, 1981 and 1991

a Briefly outline in your own words what is meant by 'instrumental collectivism' in **Item A**.   [3 marks]

b In your own words briefly describe how **Item A** suggests 'the restructuring of capital and labour' has affected the working class.   [5 marks]

c Summarise the changes in the social class structure shown in **Item B**.   [6 marks]

d Outline and critically assess the view that class remains the most significant aspect of social inequality in the UK.   [16 marks]

(IBS, Paper 2, Summer 1996)

See also exam question 4 in Chapter 5, p. 196.

Coursework **suggestions**

1 **Investigate public attitudes on social class, images of society and political perspectives**

You could carry out an investigation of public views on such matters as class structure and class consciousness, in order to try to ascer-tain whether or not class is still central as a source of identification for people, and to what extent people are concerned with class solidar-ity and issues of social justice. You could get an idea of how to go about this by reading *Social Class in Modern Britain* (1988) by Gordon Marshall *et al.*, a book which contains copies of the type of questions that were used in their study. Fiona Devine's 'Affluent workers revisited' (*Sociology Review*, February 1994) indicates the type of questions that might be included. An article by Jane Clarke and Carol Saunders entitled 'Who are you and so what?' (*Sociology Review*, September 1991) provides some discussion of alternative notions of identity. They suggest some questions that would be relevant for use in this topic.

2 **Try to answer the question: 'How unequal is British society?'**

Using secondary data, you could investigate the nature and extent of inequality in British society, to build an up-to-date picture of the extent to which the nation is divided in terms of various criteria, such as income and other aspects of 'life chances'. It would be advisable to concentrate on one basis of inequality – choosing from class, gender, ethnicity, age or disability – though an adventurous project would be to demonstrate any links between these areas.

Stratification: sex and gender

5.1 Sex and gender: 'What is a woman?'

Are men and women different? There are anatomical differences, of course. But does this fact mean that men and women can be expected to think and behave differently in everyday life? And even if they can at times be observed to think and behave differently, how can this phenomenon be explained? Are men and women biologically programmed to act in certain 'masculine' and 'feminine' ways? Or are their respective behaviours socially constructed, arising from, for example, gender-role socialization?

Biologically determined or socially constructed?
Debates about gender hinge on sociologists' answers to the question 'What is a woman?' While this may at first seem like a silly question – a woman is a physical being with certain distinguishing biological characteristics – it is difficult to make any further assertions which are not open to question. Does the

fact that some women can give birth indicate that all women have a 'natural' inclination to care for children and carry out associated domestic tasks? (See also Section 7.5.) Does a woman have particular mental processes which lead her to favour certain modes of behaviour?

French feminist philosopher Simone de Beauvoir asked some of these questions in her book *The Second Sex* (1953), arguing 'One is not born, but rather becomes a woman'. It was not the case, said de Beauvoir, that women were naturally inclined to housework or to childcare, as had been previously supposed, but rather that social and economic circumstances had tended to channel women into occupying such roles. De Beauvoir's work flew in the face of a received wisdom which referred to 'masculine' and 'feminine' traits as innate characteristics, paving the way for other social scientists to question what had been perceived to be the natural social places of women and men.

Sex and gender

Many sociologists, subsequently questioning the social relationships between women and men, have made use of a distinction between 'sex' and 'gender' coined in the 1960s by American psychoanalyst Robert Stoller (1968). Stoller suggested that the anatomical features which mark out men and women might be labelled 'sex', while the behaviour – or the cultural practices – of men and women should be referred to as 'gender'. In other words, 'sex' is a biological characteristic, while 'gender' is culturally constructed. If this was the case, argued Stoller, there was no necessary correlation between 'sex' and 'gender'. It did not always follow, for example, that a boy must behave in a 'masculine' way, or a girl in a 'feminine' way. Thus, it became possible to suggest that women generally shouldered the bulk of domestic responsibilities in any given household because that was seen as culturally appropriate feminine behaviour, and not because they were biologically inclined to do so.

This distinction had important implications for the life-choices of men and women. Once women and men were freed from the biologically based assumptions that governed their social behaviour, they could begin to justify any attempts that they made to behave differently. If, for example, it is no longer 'natural' that women should take on the bulk of domestic responsibilities, then there are grounds for arguing that such tasks should be shared (see Section 7.5).

Sociologist Ann Oakley (1972) has similarly contended that 'sex' and 'gender' are separate, and in her groundbreaking studies on women and housework (1974a) she argued that the numerous social

scientists who claimed it was 'natural' for women to take a caring role in the family – and thus to look after children and perform household tasks – had been tricked by their own prejudices into assuming what it meant to be a woman.

In particular, Oakley took issue with anthropologist George Peter Murdock (1965; orig. pub. 1949), who argued that the biological differences between men and women underpinned the sexual division of labour – the allocation of social and economic tasks by gender – in society. Murdock claimed that as men were in the main stronger, and as women in the main bore children, it made sense for a society to organize tasks in a manner which recognized this. Murdock found, in a survey of 224 societies from around the world, that women and men tended to undertake different social and economic duties – women gathering vegetables, cooking and caring for children, and men hunting and mining. Murdock argued that where so many societies were organized around the same sexual division of labour it must be the case that gender was a product of biology, in the sense that such divisions reflected the most logical form of organization given the different biological characteristics of males and females. (See also Section 7.1 for discussion of Murdock.) But Oakley argued that Murdock's conclusions were flawed. She pointed to 38 societies included in his sample in which cooking was an activity shared equally between women and men. She also examined a number of other societies, not part of Murdock's sample, in which women's roles could not be said to be determined in the manner proposed by Murdock. For example, the Mbuti Pygmies, who inhabit the rainforests of the Congo, did not divide tasks by sex, so that men and women hunted together, and shared the care of children. It was also the case, argued Oakley, that in some Asian and Latin American countries, for example, approximately a quarter of miners were female, while women undertook combat roles in the armed forces of nations like Israel, Cuba and China. Thus biological sex did not determine gender in the way that Murdock imagined.

Oakley also took issue with the work of functionalist sociologist Talcott Parsons (1959) and with psychologist John Bowlby (1965), influential thinkers who had suggested that women were primarily fitted for the role of giving emotional support and socialization to children. While their work respectively spoke of the 'expressive female' who provided her family with emotional security and nurturance, and the genetically determined psychological need that is the basis of a deep attachment between mother and child, Oakley appeared to show that it was perfectly possible for a woman to give care of her child to others for significant periods with no ill-effects for

Sexism that starts in the nursery

Children are able to distinguish between male and female, daddy and mummy, from the age of about six months, through a combination of hair length and voice modulation. Toddlers tolerate members of the opposite sex, although they are happier playing with same-sex children. By about five or six years, a period of separation begins which ends in puberty when the two sides come together out of sexual interest.

Dr Charlie Lewis of Lancaster University conducted an experiment with young babies where different-sex children were dressed in white clothes so that only their name tags distinguished their sex. Some of the name tags had been swapped around, so adults who were asked to play with the children were sometimes playing with a Joe, when in reality the baby was a Joanna. Dr Lewis comments:

'We did find differences in the adults' reaction to the children, depending on whether they thought the child was male or female. Babies thought to be female were treated more gently. However what we did find was that all
the biological females stayed within three feet of the adults, whereas the biological males were far more adventurous, crawling off to discover new horizons.'

At such an early age, it is difficult to argue that these different characteristics are anything more than biologically driven. But external factors also come into forceful play. Parents, especially fathers, are better disposed to male offspring. Dr Lewis discovered that fathers held their newborn sons for longer periods than their daughters, and even stayed longer in the delivery room to make sure their partners were well if they had given birth to a son.

Women are more likely to breast-feed their sons than their daughters. In an examination of Italian mothers' breast-feeding habits, 66 per cent of mothers of girls breast-fed their babies, compared with 99 per cent of mothers of boys. The mothers' view seemed to be that boys needed to develop to be stronger, and that it was a basic maternal duty to give the son the start in life he needed.

Children also learn about their gen-
ders by the response they get from their parents: if little boys are frowned upon for playing with dolls, then they soon stop playing with dolls and play with trucks and blocks instead. Parents are far more concerned when their boys play with ironing boards than when their daughters play with trucks.

The view that boys are more valued by society is backed up by the attention boys receive in schools. An experiment was carried out by the Department for Education at the University of Surrey on a group of teachers who were given a pupil's report. The pupil was unruly, inattentive, but managed to gain good marks in some, not all, subjects. The name 'John Smith' was attached to the report for one half of the group and 'Joan Smith' for the other half. The teachers who read John Smith's report decided he was 'possibly very bright', with 'good career prospects' if he received more attention. Many of his problems were seen as his teachers' fault. Joan Smith was dismissed as a potential dropout with no intellectual potential.

Source: *The Observer*, 18 June 1995

---

the child. She pointed to the Indonesian Alor islanders, whose economy is horticulturally based. In this society women, who grew and harvested vegetables, generally gave over the care of their children to a member of their extended family, about two weeks after giving birth. Oakley also refers to the many UK studies which demonstrated that no emotional harm seemed to come to children whose mothers left them in the care of others for long periods while they were at work.

Oakley's studies found that the social role that has been ascribed to women – that of wife and mother – existed for the convenience of men. Male theorists like Murdock, Parsons and Bowlby, she argued, conducted research which reflected their own claim to dominance over women. As these theorists carried out their studies they assumed the inevitability of women's traditionally ordained social roles. Thus it is not surprising that their work simply reinforced traditional ideas about the social relationships between men and women.

Having claimed to have exploded the myth that the social behaviour of women and men was a product of biology, or 'sex', Oakley went on to attempt to demonstrate that there is no necessary correlation between 'sex' and 'gender', and that

'gender' is in fact culturally produced. Having understood that men and women learn the particular behaviours which correspond to the norm for their 'sex', it became apparent to her that 'gender' was simply a product of socialization – the ways in which a society inscribes socially acceptable behaviour into its members (see also Section 10.1). Girls and boys, women and men, are produced by gender-role

Activity

On the basis of the foregoing discussion, and your reading of the articles on this page and page 163, answer the following questions.

a List the arguments which support the biological origins of gender differences and those which support the idea that these are socially constructed.

b To what extent does the existence of women who have XY chromosomes undermine the argument that one's sex is determined by purely objective scientific definitions of male and female?

I, A, E,

A case of mistaken identity

Helen Mather did not suspect she was any different from other women her age. But two factors worried her. At 19, she'd never had a period. And penetrative sex had always been impossible.

Mather went for tests at the Elizabeth Garrett Anderson Hospital for women. Here it was discovered that she did not have a vagina, or uterus, fallopian tubes or ovaries. She was told she had a rare genetic condition called Androgen Insensitivity Syndrome (AIS). She would have been born a boy, but an insensitivity to androgens, or male hormones, caused the foetus to develop along female lines. Tests showed that she was biologically male and had XY chromosomes, but in every outward way, she appeared female.

"It would be grotesque to suggest I'm anything other than female," says Mather, now 46. "I wouldn't know how to be a man."

There are around 500 women in Britain with AIS. The condition shows physically in the reproductive organs and ranges from complete AIS (completely female genitalia in appearance, although the vagina is usually short or absent) to partial AIS (almost completely male).

Her mother considered her condition so embarrassing that she swore Mather to secrecy – presumably unaware that AIS is mostly inherited via the maternal line. Her father was simply never told. "At times I felt fearful and lonely. If you have chickenpox, you can tell people about it. You can't with AIS. The hospital didn't offer me counselling to cope with the psychological effects. It just wasn't considered then."

Philippa Blackman was diagnosed as having AIS at 16. Her doctor told her nothing of her condition, only that she'd need surgery to remove her "ovaries". This was a medical euphemism for a gonadectomy, or the removal of the testes, which occur in all women with AIS and which were undescended and not visible in Blackman's case. However, her condition and the surgery were not mentioned again beyond that day.

Blackman, like Mather, was registered female at birth and reared as a girl. Unlike Mather, however, her vagina developed to a normal length and penetrative sex was possible, although in fact she remained celibate for 10 years.

At 28, she produced a documentary on women with AIS and, listening to them talking, realised that she couldn't have children either. Then, when being examined by an osteopath following an accident, she admitted she'd never had a period and didn't know why. Going to a GP for the first time in 12 years, she was diagnosed as having AIS. "I remember the female doctor saying: 'You can consider yourself female, if you like.' I'd never thought of myself as anything else."

Reassurance came from Howard Jacobs, professor of reproductive endocrinology at Middlesex Hospital. "He told me I am completely female, but my genes are male. That was the first time my condition had been explained to me. I had always felt like an outsider; the one who didn't have periods. I'd spent years wondering: will anyone want me?" They did: Blackman plans to marry her long-term boyfriend next year.

Naomi Walters certainly wishes there had been more honesty in her case. When she was a child, strangers would stop her mother in the street and say: "What an adorable little girl." She looked female, but Walters had been registered male at birth, as she was born with male genitalia (albeit smaller than average).

From three years old, she underwent many surgical operations to augment her "maleness".

She was never comfortable as a boy, she recalls. "My best friends were girls. I leaned naturally towards female behaviour." Her confusion about her gender was exacerbated in her teens by the non-appearance of male sexual characteristics, such as facial and body hair, a deep voice and muscles. Then she discovered painful "lumps" in her chest. "I was terrified. I thought, boys don't develop breasts, do they?"

It wasn't until her mid-twenties that Walters found the courage to live as a woman. After consulting a psychiatrist, she began surgery, including a vaginal reconstruction using a section of her bowel, and hormone replacement therapy. Switching gender roles was no problem for her – she'd always been mistaken for a female anyway – and her mother, she says, coped with it well.

She is currently taking time out from her career in agriculture to have her first counselling sessions and "to discover who I really am. I've never had a relationship. I know I could have a sex life now, but I don't feel any sexual attraction to anyone, male or female. I have the stigma of having male on my birth certificate and as I have XY chromosomes, I can't get that changed. I envy someone born with AIS now. People are so much more realistic and open today."

Source: *The Guardian*, 29 August 1996

---

socialization. For Oakley it is therefore human nurturing, rather than biological nature, that is the key determinant of gender identities. Furthermore, she argues – attempting to put paid to the claims of biological determinists once and for all – gender-role socialization is a more important factor in creating 'masculine' men and 'feminine' women than any genetic traits which men and women might be discovered to have, which might predispose them to certain behaviours. As evidence for these claims Oakley cited studies, like those of Hartley (1966), which showed that parents treated their male and female children differently from birth.

Feminist anthropology

The notion that 'sex' and 'gender' exist separately was taken up by feminist social scientists wishing to comprehend the nature of men's dominance over women. As feminists sought proof that women's social, political and economic roles were culturally constructed rather than biologically determined, they turned for help to anthropology – the study of human cultures. Anthropological studies provided numerous examples of the variability of gender roles in different societies.

But while anthropological evidence showed that gender roles could be – and were – variable, it also appeared to demonstrate that women were subordinate to men in all societies. So no matter that women and men undertook the same tasks in some societies, men were still more powerful than women, taking decisions on important matters.

How could feminists account for this? Feminist anthropologists Sherry Ortner (1974) and Michelle Rosaldo (1974) each devised a theoretical model in an attempt to explain women's universally subordinate position. Ortner argued that women tended to be associated with 'nature', in part at least because they could bear children, while men were associated with 'culture'. Individual societies ascribed 'nature' a lower status than 'culture' and thus male dominance over women was assured.

Rosaldo also referred to reproduction and child-bearing, linking women to the home and domesticity – the private sphere – and pointing out that men tended to play public socio-economic and political roles – in the public sphere. Having created a distinction between 'public' and 'private', individual societies then proceeded to view 'private' as inferior to 'public'. This meant, of course, that women, associated with the private sphere, came to be constructed as inferior to men who operated in the public domain.

Gayle Rubin (1975), a feminist anthropologist, discusses the idea that women are invariably associated with 'nature' and thus devalued in relation to the male 'culture'. In her essay 'The Traffic in Women', she suggests that the distinction between 'nature' and 'culture' made in many societies underpins what she calls a 'sex/gender system':

A sex/gender system is the set of arrangements by which a society transforms biological sexuality into products of human activity, and in which those transformed sexual needs are satisfied.
(Rubin, 1975, p. 159)

In other words, biological 'sex' turns into 'gender' – particular versions of masculinity and femininity – when it is overlaid by culture. It is the sex/gender system that Rubin describes which is responsible for constructing constraining models of subordinate femininity.

What would solve the problem? Rubin argues that if the kinship system – norms associated with the way in which people relate to each other by 'blood' – were to be transformed, then individual psyches – masculine or feminine – would also

change, along with the meanings ascribed to 'nature' and 'culture'. Finally the sex/gender system itself would inevitably be reshaped and men's and women's places in the social structure of any given society would change.

The insights of feminist anthropologists were important to the (new) definition of 'woman' that feminist social scientists tried to establish, as they sought some justification for their claims that men were more powerful than women, and that this was not a 'natural' state of affairs. The theoretical models produced by Rosaldo, Ortner and Rubin proposed a

'socially-based account of women's position in society, and the origins of gender difference'
(Moore, 1994, p. 80).

Their answer to the question 'What is a woman?' could have been: 'a person showing female biological characteristics whose behaviour is culturally determined by gendered expectations, relating to the socially constructed distinctions'.

By extension, it might then be possible for feminists to argue that women were not 'closer to nature', or especially given to housework by choice, but rather that men had forced them to take up those positions. It might then be the case that some women who had been compelled to adopt a certain set of behaviours, to be played out as their relationships to 'nature' and the 'private sphere' (the family and domesticity), would wish to operate elsewhere, in the realm of culture, or in public spaces. (See also Sections 7.5 and 17.4.)

However, as feminist anthropologist Henrietta Moore (1994) has pointed out, the categories 'nature', 'culture', 'public' and 'private' were soon found to be historically and culturally variable, not universal:

Feminists of colour, feminists from the developing world, and lesbian feminists ... challenged the notion of the universal category 'woman' and the assumption of underlying commonalities of existence for all women.
(Moore, 1994, p. 80)

In other words, women's (and men's) ideas about their places in society depended on their own particular social and economic circumstances. Thus, a woman who is also black occupies a social position that differs from that of a white woman – the way in which the categories 'nature', 'culture', 'public' and 'private' impact on the former, frame the life of the latter differently.

More recent feminist thinking has called into question the biological definitions on which the sex/gender distinction was based. Moore comments:

Discussion point

To what extent does the often-rehearsed argument that there have been relatively few 'great' women artists demonstrate that men are culturally superior to women?

Gender was seen as socially constructed, but underlying that idea was that although gender was not determined by biology, it was the social elaboration in specific contexts of the obvious facts of biological sex difference.
(Moore, 1994, p. 81)

The suggestion was that even the notion of 'biology' was historically specific. Consequently, feminists concerned to answer the question 'What is a woman?' were forced to think again about the relationship between 'biology' and 'culture'. If 'biology' does not exist as a fixed conceptual point which acts as a marker of difference, then it becomes necessary to reassess ideas about the way in which gender is culturally produced.

Judith Butler (1990), a post-modern feminist theorist, has recently argued that the very idea of 'femininity' is problematic – thus further unpicking the supposed relationships between the notions 'sex' and 'gender'. She questions the assumption that an individual with a particular set of genital or biological characteristics must also, inevitably, have a gendered identity. She points out that much of feminists' work on gender assumes that a female human individual – a woman – has a coherent set of interests relating either to her sex or her gender or both. A 'woman' may assume that her interests are at least to an extent defined by her capacity (or not) to give birth. Alternatively, she may assume that she is subject to male oppression because she is a 'woman', and thus that some of her interests address themselves to challenging that oppression.

Butler questions assumptions like these, arguing instead that even to ask the question 'What is a woman?' is to present a ready-made answer that necessarily refers to oppression and subordination. The very construction 'woman' carries with it ideas about a fixed set of relationships between women and men, and amongst women. Butler's arguments rest on the suggestion that feminists and other thinkers have been asking the wrong questions about the links between the ideas and concepts that have attached themselves to the visible differences between men and women, and amongst women. But while her arguments are very abstract, they have important practical implications for feminists wishing to act on women's unequal social status.

Butler suggests that 'woman' is a concept which carries with it a particular view about women's social places. But this must mean that women as a group can never achieve emancipation because their unequal status is a vital component of social and political life as it stands. In fact, as soon as women begin to ask 'who they are' in an attempt to define their status, and speak of 'femininity' as a way of answering their questions about themselves, they necessarily conspire in their own oppression. Butler contends that if women insist on defining themselves through their 'femininity' it is no wonder that they have not become wholly equal with men: the task of attaining equality is impossible by its very nature.

Butler's contentions beg an important question about how women, and by extension other oppressed groups, can ever shake off their subordinate status, if the very ways in which they understand the world around them favour the powerful. Feminist theorist Alison Assister (1996) has responded to Butler's work, pointing out that her arguments make it difficult to give any credence, for example, to feminists' activism in the early 1970s (see Section 5.5). It would be nonsense, says Assister, to dismiss as self-deluded those feminists who ran campaigns on issues like abortion, sexism in education, and domestic violence. Neither could it be correct to claim that those campaigns had no influence and did not facilitate or effect any changes.

It is difficult to quantify the influence of the feminist movement on contemporary society. But it is possible to gain a broader understanding of its objectives, and thus to ask whether they have been achieved. The sociology of gender exists as an aid to this task. As Abbott and Wallace (1997) point out in their survey of feminist approaches in sociology, within and simultaneously framing the sociology of gender there exists a feminist sociology:

. . . one that is for women, not just or necessarily about women, and one that challenges and confronts the male supremacy which institutionalises women's inequality.
(Abbott and Wallace, 1997, p. 17)

5.2 Gender and stratification: differences and inequalities

Sociobiology: the natural order

Those sociologists and scientists who favour the long-standing idea that women and men fill 'naturally' ordained social places base their views on biological evidence. They point out that the biological make-up of men and women is intrinsically different, citing evidence gleaned from genetics, and research into hormonal differences to support their cases. This evidence leads them to suggest explanations for the apparently different behaviour and preferences of men and women. These explanations are summarized below.

Hormonal influences

The bodies of men and women produce differing amounts of certain hormones – bodily chemicals which control the development of reproductive capacities. Women's bodies secrete higher levels of progesterone and oestrogen, while men produce more testosterone, and other similar hormones called androgens. Testosterone has been linked, in animal experiments, to aggressive behaviour. This has led researchers to claim that observably aggressive behaviour in men is linked to testosterone levels. More broadly, it is easy to see how this evidence could be used to support the claim that women are naturally peaceable, while men are naturally violent.

The practice of using animal behaviour to explain human activity has been subject to much criticism. Suggesting that the effects of hormonal differences on behaviour in animals can also explain human behaviour involves a leap of faith that is scientifically questionable. It is difficult to see how valid and reliable conclusions about human behaviour can be drawn from observing animal behaviour.

Further research has claimed that the differing amounts of hormones secreted by men's and women's bodies affect the development of the brain. What has been called the process of 'brain lateralization' refers to evidence that the brain's left hemisphere – held to be responsible for language and analytical skills – is more dominant in girls as they mature, while the right hemisphere – held to be responsible for skills relating to mathematics, engineering and artistic creativity – is dominant in boys (see also Section 8.7). However, brain lateralization studies are not conclusive. The measurable differences in women's and men's thinking skills are very small, and could result from environmental differences – that is, differences in socialization – rather than from biological differences.

Genes and evolutionary theory

Some sociologists and anthropologists have used genetic theory and evolutionary theory in order to explain the observable differences in men's and women's behaviour. Anthropologists Tiger and Fox (1972) claim that humans are to an extent 'programmed' by their genetics, and thus their behaviour is to an extent determined. They call this genetic programming the 'human biogrammar'.

Tiger and Fox suggest that humans have evolved their current behaviours based on their comparatively recent existence as primitive hunter-gatherers. Genetic change occurs slowly, so that even in a modern industrial society – which has generated some cultural belief in 'equality' – women and men are bound by their genetic 'natures'. These 'natures' are adapted to a sexual division of labour in a hunting society, where men are hunters and protectors and women bear and nurture children. According to this scheme, it is small wonder that equality between women and men has not been wholly achieved – any attempt to abolish gender roles is doomed to failure in the short term, as men and women are simply 'wired' for their particular behaviours.

Tiger and Fox's conclusions are not incontestable. It has been argued that the primary emphasis they place on hunting is simply a reflection of their own prejudices. In fact, gathering vegetables and hunting small animals has been the main means of human subsistence over the centuries, and these activities have in the main been carried out by women. At the same time, if genetic change is as slow as has been claimed, it is difficult to see how male dominance can have evolved, bearing in mind that the earliest conclusive evidence shows that the systematic hunting, by males, of large animals began only 500 000 years ago.

Natural selection

A further attempt to link gender differences to genetics and evolution has been made by sociobiologists. Sociobiology has its genesis in a particular interpretation of Charles Darwin's evolutionary theories, although it develops these extensively. Sociobiologists believe that all species, including humans, evolve and change over time via a process of natural selection. (See also Section 6.4 for discussion of sociobiological theories of racial and ethnic inequalities.)

Sociobiologists argue that human behaviour is ultimately governed by genetic instructions which urge men and women to maximize the chance of passing on their genes through reproduction. Thus, men and women behave differently in order to maximize their chances of becoming parents to children who are likely to survive and prosper.

Sociobiology thus provides a context for observable male promiscuity and culturally deviant activities such as rape. It suggests that males have evolved with the need to spread their genetic material as widely as possible. Therefore they are likely to attempt to impregnate the maximum number of females. Females, on the other hand, who gestate and then raise children, are likely to be selective about their male sexual partners, needing quality of genes rather than quantity. Sociobiologists might argue that the root causes of war and territorialism are found in men's attempts to secure and retain access to their own females. At the same time they deny that any of their claims are sexist, suggesting that men and women are different, and simply pursuing their own ends in the most productive fashion.

Sociobiologists have been heavily criticized by feminists, many of whom regard sociobiology as a spurious attempt to provide scientific justification for male power.

> ### Discussion point
> To what extent can a sociobiological perspective explain the high incidence of rape in the UK?

Gender and the relations of production

The work of Marx and his successors has offered a challenge to biological theories which attempt to account for inequalities between women and men by calling them 'natural'. Rather than being 'natural', argue Marxists, all inequalities – class, 'race', gender, and so on – are products of particular historical conditions (see Sections 2.3 and 2.5). Marxists suggest that human beings have no 'natural' tendency to behave in particular kinds of ways. While similar sets of inequalities appear to exist across the world, this is because the course of history – rather than the course of 'nature' – determines their existence. Crucially, the course of history can change, and quickly, where tensions over inequalities between classes, in particular, become too much for a society to bear. This is in contrast to biological and evolutionary theories which give scope to conceive only gradual social change, in tune with biological evolution.

Marxists have argued that women's oppression is generated, like other sets of exploitative relations, through the workings of capital. Friedrich Engels (1972; orig. pub. 1884) identified the cause of inequalities between women and men in his 1884 pamphlet *The Origins of the Family, Private Property and the State*. (See also Section 17.3.) Engels wrote of an historical phase, early in the development of all societies, in which men and women carried out work-tasks according to a division of labour by sex. But while men were hunters and women were responsible for domestic work, men did not dominate women, and women were not subordinate to men. Furthermore, no restrictions were placed on sexual activity – monogamous marriage as contemporary western societies would understand it, did not exist – and men and women could have sexual intercourse with many partners if they so wished. This meant that the male parentage of children was uncertain, and so private property, of which there was very little – tools, cooking pots and so on – was handed on through the maternal line.

But as humankind began to herd animals, rather than simply to stalk them in the wild, the concept of private property took on greater importance. This was because a trade in meat and skins emerged. As this trade developed, so did men's power relative to women: men controlled the animal herds, and thus the key to early economic success. Not wishing to relinquish control of their own animal herds to a child of uncertain parentage, men found ways to restrict women's sexual choices. As they did so they created the patriarchal family, in which men dominate and control women and children (see Section 7.5). In this way, women suffered what Engels called a 'world-historic' defeat. Furthermore, the subsequent development of the capitalist economic system has meant that they have been unable to correct the imbalance in power.

All Marxist theorists share Engels' assumption that inequalities between men and women have arisen historically – that is, that inequalities have emerged during a period in which societies have, one way or another, changed their day-to-day practices. Marxist theorists also argue, as did Engels, that women's subordination is basically a product of economic circumstances.

Contemporary Marxist theorists have attempted to correct Engels' anthropological assumptions, focusing on more recent data in order to underscore the complexity of class and gender relationships (Coontz and Henderson, 1986). However, many of the most compelling modern accounts of women's subordination do not predicate themselves on Marxist theory alone. Rather they draw on feminist theory too. In this way it has been possible for theorists to separate class exploitation and women's subordination, allowing questions about whether economic conditions and historical circumstances are solely to blame for gender-related inequalities, and allowing theorists to look closely at inequalities between women.

While Marxist theorists have offered explanations for women's subordination and racial subjugation, both black writers and feminist writers have argued that Marxism cannot satisfactorily explain the complex entirety of inequalities. They suggest that Marxism is effectively gender-blind and 'race'-blind. (See also Sections 6.4 and 6.6.)

Case study – Gender and ideology

Marxist concepts have infused contemporary sociology with a historically based understanding of inequalities. In particular, the notion of an 'ideology' has proved useful for those wishing to consider the way in which inequalities are culturally justified and legitimated. Abbott and Wallace define ideology as:

[a] *pattern of ideas (commonsense knowledge) – both factual and evaluative – which purports to explain and legitimate the social structure and culture of a social group or society and which serves to justify social actions which are in accordance with that pattern of ideas.*

(Abbott and Wallace, 1997, p. 9)

Thus, ideology 'works' to shape beliefs about appropriate social behaviour for all socio-economic groups, by acting to present a dominant socio-economic group's views as 'natural'. Ideologies are phenomena which impact historically, emerging at particular times, in response to particular sets of social and economic circumstances, as a means for a dominant group to preserve and retain power over other groups. (See also Sections 15.6 and 15.7.)

Feminists have used the Marxist concept 'ideology' to explain how dominance by men over women is culturally constructed and maintained. They refer to 'patriarchal ideologies'. These are ideas which suggest that some forms of behaviour and some social roles are more appropriate for men than women, and vice versa. Patriarchal ideologies reinforce men's dominance over women by suggesting, for example, that 'a woman's place is in the home'. As Abbott and Wallace have put it:

Patriarchal ideologies have the effect of disguising the actuality of male power. Men defined themselves as powerful because of their ability to master nature – to be dominant. Women, because of their biological role in reproduction, are defined as being closer to nature than men, thus justifying their domination by men. Male ideology confirms and reinforces men's dominant status by devaluing women's work and reproductive functions while at the same time presenting male work as of cultural importance, and as necessary.

(Abbott and Wallace, 1997, p. 10)

Activity

Mrs Sarah Stickney Ellis was an early-nineteenth-century writer of books for women. Her books advised on 'correct' feminine behaviour.

a   With reference to the following extract, suggest how women are constructed as being of the private, domestic realm via the injunctions of Mrs Ellis.
b   To what extent do you feel Mrs Ellis' attitudes have a familiar ring to them?
c   Suggest examples of how the views she espouses are reflected in contemporary popular culture.

I, A, E

MRS SARAH STICKNEY ELLIS

Mrs Sarah Stickney Ellis was probably the best-known ideologue of domesticity, one of a number of women writers in the genre in the second quarter of the nineteenth century. Indeed conservative thinkers were sometimes worried at the extent to which advice books were written by women. 'We doubt much', complained one critic, 'whether women are the best direct preceptors of women'. . . .

Her best-known books were the series on the wives, mothers, daughters and women of England. Mrs Ellis will soon, commented one unsympathetic reviewer, 'have circumnavigated the female world; every variety of female condition will have had its separate book . . .'.

She was particularly concerned with those families of traders, manufacturers and professionals where there were one to four servants, where there had been some kind of liberal education, and where there was no family rank. 'False notions of refinement' were rendering their women 'less influential, less useful, and less happy than they were'. This was a moral crisis for the nation and her concern was to find ways of improving 'the minor morals of domestic life'. Once again the family was to provide a secure basis for national stability. Men did not have the time; they were occupied in the world of business and politics. Women had both the time, the moral capacity and the influence to exercise real power in the domestic world. It was their responsibility to re-create society from below. . . .

Mrs Ellis's belief in the separate spheres of men and women went together with a conviction that women's influence could be felt far beyond her own limited circle. *Influence* was the secret of women's power and that influence, as wives and mothers, meant that they did not need to seek other kinds of legitimation. Having been criticized for placing women on too low a scale Mrs Ellis responded by arguing: 'I still think that as a wife, woman should place herself, instead of running the risk of *being placed*, in a secondary position; as a mother, I do not see how it is possible for her to be too dignified, or to be treated with too much respect.' . . .

Women could find the true meaning of their lives in the family which was a woman's profession, the love that she would find there would answer her needs. For women, wrote Mrs Ellis, love was her very being 'In that *she* lives, or else *she* has no life', unlike a man who has his public character. To love was woman's duty; to be beloved her reward. Women's aim should be to become better wives and mothers.

Source: Davidoff and Hall, 1987, pp. 182–3)

The Marxist concept of an 'ideology' has helped feminists to uncover and challenge male dominance. It has enabled them to reveal the cultural and historical means by which patriarchy maintains itself.

Feminist historians Leonore Davidoff and Catherine Hall's study *Family Fortunes* (1987) documents the emergence of modern gendered inequalities alongside the emergence of the modern capitalist economy. The abridged extract reproduced here, 'Mrs Sarah Stickney Ellis', shows how patriarchal ideologies constructed the concept of a private sphere – a separate space for women at home. This occurred as production moved from domestic workshops and into factories during the industrial revolution.

5.3 Feminist sociology and patriarchy

Feminist sociologists – and other feminist writers – have argued that the social and economic odds are always stacked against women. Contemporary British society, many have argued, is a patriarchal one in which men have tended to determine the broad patterns of women's lives and choices. The term 'patriarchy' is used by some feminists to describe and analyse the unequal distribution of power between women and men. This power differential has been variously called subordination, oppression, or exploitation. Each of these terms suggests women's relative lack of power and status, but the emphases on each differ slightly.

- Subordination refers to the manner in which patriarchal social structures inevitably produce unequal interpersonal relations between men and women.
- Oppression refers to the manner in which women experience sexism, a process of unfounded social discrimination whereby men claim authority over women.
- Exploitation, a term borrowed from Marxists (see Section 2.3), refers to the manner in which men appropriate women's skills and labour without rewarding them.

Activity

Study Table 5.1 and suggest ways in which its information supports the idea of the existence of patriarchy in the practices of everyday life.

I, A

Feminist research argues that the unequal practices referred to above add up to a systematic form of oppression. Their concept 'patriarchy' forms a lens through which they can view that system. Maggie Humm, a professor of women's studies, has suggested that the concept 'patriarchy' is:

. . . crucial to contemporary feminism, because feminism needed a term by which the totality of oppressive and exploitative relations which affect women could be expressed.
(Humm, 1995, p. 200)

At the same time the concept is intended to be flexible enough to allow feminists to make multiple assessments of the causes of inequality.

Varieties of feminism

In the 1970s and 80s several schools of feminist thought emerged, each developing their own theory of patriarchy. Radical feminists, like Shulamith Firestone (1979) and Kate Millett (1970), argued that the primary oppression women suffered was based around an entrenched gendered social divide. Men, they said, benefited both individually and collectively from women's unremunerated labours in the home. A male-dominated society, they added, would tend to deny women access to positions of power, in order

Table 5.1 How people spent their time (in hours) in May 1995

	In full-time employment		In part-time employment		Retired		All
	M	F	M	F	M	F	Adults
Weekly hours spent on:							
Sleep	57	58	62	60	67	66	61
Free time	34	31	48	32	59	52	40
Work, study and travel	53	48	28	26	3	4	32
Housework, cooking and shopping	7	15	12	26	15	26	16
Eating, personal hygiene and caring	13	13	13	21	15	17	15
Household maintenance and pet care	4	2	6	3	9	3	4
Free time per weekday	4	4	6	4	8	7	5
Free time per weekend day	8	6	8	6	10	8	8

Source: ESRC Research Centre on Micro-social Change, from *Omnibus Survey/Social Trends* 1996, p. 216

to maintain and consolidate their own standing. Early Marxist feminists like Sheila Rowbotham (1973) contested radical feminists' views, instead laying emphasis on the exploitative nature of the capitalist economic system. Like radical feminists, Marxist feminists focused on women's unpaid work in the home, but suggested that the owners of the means of production were the primary beneficiaries of this free labour: benefits accrued to men as a by-product of capitalism.

Radical feminism

Shulamith Firestone asserts that the difference between men and women structures every aspect of human social life. In *The Dialectic of Sex* she suggests that men are able to oppress women because their physical strength is often superior and because women are disadvantaged by their childbearing and childrearing roles. Based in biology, men's power is inevitably reflected in culture and patterns of socialization. What would be her solution? She would want to see social institutions, like the nuclear family (see Section 7.1), restructured so that women would no longer be dependent and subordinate, and – with a utopian vision presaging the advanced reproductive technology 25 years away – to 'end the tyranny of reproduction' (p. 221) so that women were freed from the biological process of giving birth (see also Section 13.3). This, Firestone argues, would mean an end to patriarchy, as women became men's biological equals, and were also able to control their participation in childrearing.

While many radical feminists did not share Firestone's views on childbearing, and have subsequently disagreed over the extent and nature of necessary social transformation, their assessment of the causes of women's oppression has remained broadly similar: women are categorized 'as an inferior class to the class "men" on the basis of . . . gender' (Humm, 1995, p. 231). Patriarchy, for radical feminists, is society's defining principle and the primary explanation for gender stratification.

Marxist feminism

In contrast, early Marxist feminists like Rowbotham (1973) argued that patriarchy operated within the capitalist economic system. Rowbotham's evidence for this claim was drawn from her analysis of men's and women's work. She showed how the taken-for-granted division between work, which takes place outside the home, and leisure, which takes place inside the home, was a division which exists only for men. Far from being a place of rest for women, argued Rowbotham, the home was a place of work. In fact, women's unpaid work in the home – child-care, domestic labour, giving of emotional care – enabled capitalist and patriarchal social relations to reproduce themselves. Men exploited women within the environment of home and family, from whence a new generation of workers would come, fully socialized into the ways of capitalism and patriarchy. (See Section 7.5.)

Socialist feminism

Many feminists argued, however, that Marxism – a theory which purported to explain all social, political and economic relationships in the terms of its materialist analysis – viewed the exploitation of women as ultimately less important than the class struggle it aimed to resolve. For this reason, feminists wishing to make use of Marxist insights, but certain that Marxism could not explain the totality of women's oppression, developed a dual-systems theory. In order to distinguish their perspective from Marxist feminism they often referred to themselves as 'socialist feminists'.

Socialist feminist dual-systems analyses were intended to show how capitalism and patriarchy acted together, infusing and moulding a social structure which created women as subordinate to men, both at work and at home. Feminists found it difficult to construct a coherent dual-systems perspective, however. They argued that this was because Marxist theory could not easily accommodate feminist ideas.

Feminist social theorist Michèle Barrett undertook to explore the troubled relationship between Marxism and feminism in *Women's Oppression Today* (Barret, 1989, orig. pub. 1980), as did Marxist feminist theorist Heidi Hartmann (1981) in an article 'The unhappy marriage of Marxism and feminism'. While Hartmann argues that the relationship between Marxism and feminism is tense but necessary, and only a combination of both sets of ideas can unpick the role women play in reproducing capitalist relations, Barrett's tone is less certain that the two theories could co-exist. Reflecting almost ten years later in a revised edition, she writes that her book was part of an attempt:

. . . to bring together two world-views that have continued to go their separate ways in spite of our efforts at marriage guidance.
(Barrett, 1989, p. v)

Activity

Read the extract 'The unhappy marriage of marxism and feminism: towards a more progressive union'.

a Explain in your own words the limitations Hartmann identifies with respect to marxist analyses of relations between men and women.

b Why does Hartmann feel that a feminist analysis alone cannot account for inequalities between men and women?

The unhappy marriage of marxism and feminism: towards a more progressive union

The 'marriage' of marxism and feminism has been like the marriage of husband and wife depicted in English common law: marxism and feminism are one, and that one is marxism. Recent attempts to integrate marxism and feminism are unsatisfactory to us as feminists because they subsume the feminist struggle into the 'larger' struggle against capital. To continue our simile further, either we need a healthier marriage or we need a divorce.

The inequalities in this marriage, like most social phenomena, are no accident. Many marxists typically argue that feminism is at best less important than class conflict and at worse divisive of the working class. This political stance produces an analysis that absorbs feminism into the class struggle. Moreover, the analytic power of marxism with respect to capital has obscured its limitations with respect to sexism.

While marxist analysis provides essential insight into the laws of historical development, and those of capital in particular, the categories of marxism are sex-blind. Only a specifically feminist analysis reveals the systemic character of relations between men and women. Yet feminist analysis by itself is inadequate because it has been blind to history and insufficiently materialist. Both marxist analysis, particularly its historical and materialist method, and feminist analysis, especially the identification of patriarchy as a social and historical structure, must be drawn upon if we are to understand the development of western capitalist societies and the predicament of women within them. We suggest a new direction for marxist feminist analysis.

Source: Adapted from Hartmann, 1981 p. xxx

Black feminism

Feminists writing from black perspectives have criticized both radical feminist and Marxist/socialist feminist theories of patriarchy. Black women theorizing about gender have never constituted a self-perceived, unified grouping like radical feminists and Marxist feminists; nonetheless they have tended to agree that, while the concept of patriarchy refers to gender subordination and class exploitation, it does not address 'race'-related oppression. (See also Section 6.6.) Black feminists like Floya Anthias and Nira Yuval-Davies (1983) have pointed out that radical feminists and Marxist feminists – in the main white women – have tended to 'forget' ethnicity in their analyses. Black feminists have termed this forgetfulness 'ethnocentrism' – citing generalizations made by white feminist theorists who have claimed to speak on behalf of all women, but who have failed to notice the dissimilarity between some aspects of the experiences of white women and black women. Amina Mama (1989) points out, for example, that social policy impacts differently on black women and white women. She comments:

The 'deserving' and 'reputable' groups earmarked for good welfare services and provisions exclude women who are not in traditional nuclear families and Black people.
(Mama, 1989, p. 35)

She supports her case by stating, for example, that:

Black women with British-born children are threatened with deportation when they leave violent husbands. Or Black women rehoused under the domestic violence policies fought for by feminists in some Local Authorities can find themselves housed in accommodation which had to be abandoned by the previous Black family because of racial harassment.
(Mama, 1989, p. 35)

Valerie Amos and Pratibha Parmar (1984) make a similar point, referring in particular to the assumptions of sociologists and anthropologists as they have attempted to define the role of black women in the family. (See also Section 7.3.) Amos and Parmar argue that feminist theories of the family have tended to trade in stereotypes about black women, so that in white feminists' accounts of family life we hear of passive, oppressed Asian women, and resilient African–Caribbean women badly treated by their sexist male partners. They comment that:

White feminists have fallen into the trap of measuring the Black female experience against their own, labelling it as in some way lacking, then looking for ways in which it might be possible to harness the Black women's experience to their own.
(Amos and Parmar, 1984, p. 11)

Mama, for one, argues that white feminists are likely to find it difficult to take 'race' issues fully on board. Even when feminist theorists have attempted to add 'race' to their analyses, as some later Marxist feminist work has, they tend to 'miss the point' by failing to readjust their concepts 'gender' and 'class'. Amos and Parmar are particularly critical of those

Marxist and socialist feminists who they feel have simply added 'race' as a third factor in their analyses of women's oppression.

Many black feminists have argued that the concept 'patriarchy' is unlikely to be able to include 'race'. They suggest that 'patriarchy' is a fully formed concept already and that in these circumstances 'race' can only stand as a further oppression suffered by women, rather than operating as a form of oppression in its own right. Such an understanding does not speak to the experiences of black women, say black feminists, who point out that a black woman is both 'black' and 'female' at the same time, not primarily 'female' and then 'black' (or vice versa). Stanlie James and Abena Busia (1993) have spoken of the principle of the 'simultaneity of oppression' as a way of understanding how 'race', 'gender' and 'class' operate together to construct women's lives. They suggest that 'race', 'class' and 'gender' are relational categories – that is, they do not operate separately on the lives of individual women, and they should not be conceived of as separate analytical categories or abstract concepts. (See also Sections 4.11, 5.7 and 6.6.)

Walby: triple-systems theory

Sylvia Walby (1989, 1990), a feminist sociologist, has attempted to synthesize feminists' competing explanations of subordination, oppression and exploitation. She says that 'patriarchy' is too useful a concept to be abandoned: rather, it needs reworking so that it can incorporate the experiences and analyses of black women. Hence she has developed what Sasha Roseneil (1994, p. 92) has called a 'triple-systems theory' of patriarchy.

Walby proposes that patriarchy should be understood as a system of abstract relationships between women and men – but a system that intersects with capitalism and racism. This means that there are three likely sets of inequality-inducing factors working to produce any empirically observable social or economic phenomenon. Thus, sociologists making use of triple-systems theory might undertake a study of black women's employment. (See also Section 9.3.) Having found that the majority of working black women occupy low-paying jobs that are relatively worse-paid than the low-paying jobs occupied by the majority of white working women, triple-systems theorists would then refer to Walby's system of abstract relations, explaining black women's position of relative disadvantage according to the manner in which patriarchy, capitalism and racism act on women as a group, and on individual women.

Walby's triple-systems theory does not understand patriarchy itself in terms of a single ultimate cause-and-effect mechanism. Instead Walby argues that patriarchy consists of six social structures which are at once relatively autonomous and relatively interdependent. Roseneil (1994, p. 92) has summarized these six social structures as follows (see Figure 5.1):

1 *The patriarchal mode of production*, which refers to the exploitation of women's labour by husbands/cohabitees within the household. (See also Section 7.5.)
2 *Patriarchal relations in paid work*, which serve both to exclude women from high-status well-paid jobs, and to segregate women in particular low-status low-paid jobs. (See also Section 9.3.)
3 *Patriarchal relations in the state*, which means that the state tends to operate in the interests of men rather than in those of women. Examples of this include the recent policy of community care, which has returned, largely to women, the responsibility for caring for sick and elderly relatives; and the weakness of equal-pay legislation and the lack of investment in the machinery to implement the legislation, which means that women still earn about £0.75 for every £1.00 earned by men. (See also Sections 13.3, 14.2 and 17.3.)
4 *Male violence against women*, which takes the form of rape, sexual assault, wife-beating and sexual harassment. (See also Section 7.7.)
5 *Patriarchal relations in sexuality*, exemplified by the almost compulsory nature of heterosexuality and the stigmatization of lesbianism, and the sexual double standard, which values multiple partners and sexual encounters for men, yet labels women who behave similarly as 'slags' (Lees, 1986). (See also Sections 10.7 and 13.3.)
6 *Patriarchal relations within cultural institutions*, such as the media, the education system and religion, which serve to create masculine and feminine subjectivities and identities. (See also Sections 8.7, 15.7 and 18.3.)

Activity
a Suggest an example of patriarchy 'in practice' for each of the six structures identified in the list and Figure 5.1. 'Sexuality' has been done for you.
b Consider whether you would add any further structures to Walby's six. What would they be? Explain your choices. **A E**

Where Walby refers to the form and degree of patriarchal oppression, she indicates her attempts to address the shortcomings of earlier, more limited theories of patriarchy. She acknowledges that inequalities between men and women vary over time and in intensity, pointing, for example, to changes such as the fact that young women are on average attaining

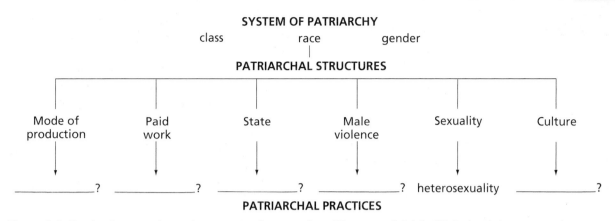

Figure 5.1 Patriarchy as a three-tier system of oppression. Diagram of Sylvia Walby's triple-systems theory.

better educational qualifications than young men (Walby, 1990, p. 23). (See also Section 8.7.)

At the same time, she argues that the prevailing characteristics of patriarchy are subject to transformation, pointing to a shift from private patriarchy to public patriarchy in the last 100 years. Prior to the twentieth century the household was the main site of women's oppression. During the nineteenth century middle-class women in Britain were increasingly restricted to the home; and even while most unmarried working-class women were engaged in paid work, an ideology of domesticity (see Section 7.5) restricted their access to a variety of jobs, education and other forms of public life. No woman could hold a legitimate place in the public sphere, and she had no voting rights and few property rights, while her husband had the legal right to beat her. Women tended to exist under the control of their fathers and then their husbands, residing within the home, with few opportunities for economic or social independence.

In late twentieth-century Britain this picture of patriarchy is much less recognizable. Walby claims that this is because patriarchy has adjusted itself to fit women's relatively recently acquired civil and political rights. Women have won the right to vote and participate as citizens in public life, while enjoying a greater degree of freedom and independence than ever before. (See also Section 17.5.) At the same time, they are poorly represented at higher levels within the state and private-sector businesses, tending to be concentrated in lower-paying, lower-status occupations (see Section 9.3).

Furthermore, women are culturally represented in what is arguably an increasingly sexist manner: television, film and advertising in the main portray women as sexual objects (see Sections 10.7 and 15.7). Evidence like this points to the existence of a public patriarchy which controls women's lives, even as they have become more independent of individual men.

Although Walby's theory of patriarchy represents an attempt to address some of the problems of earlier theories, and thus to answer feminists' questions about male dominance over women more effectively, some critics have suggested that her modern reworking of patriarchy is still inadequate. Feminist sociologist Joan Acker, for example, has pointed out that the search to 'theorize male dominance as a systemic process at the societal level' (Acker, 1989, p. 236) was stilled in the late 1970s and early 80s as feminist theorists realized that they had perhaps bitten off more than they could chew at that time.

- First, says Acker, feminist theorists had not compiled a full-enough record of women's histories and experiences to be able to formulate a theory that spoke to all women.
- Secondly, 'the territory to be encompassed was enormous and complex' (p. 236).
- Thirdly, the more general theories of society on which feminists had drawn to create their own large-scale understanding of male dominance claimed to be gender-neutral, but '[feminist] theorists understood that standing behind [concepts like] the gender-neutral human-being and gender-neutral societal processes were assumptions based on men's experiences' (p. 237).

As Acker unequivocally reminds us:

Building a one-system theory meant confronting these difficulties inherent in the most fundamental concepts of sociological theory and method.
(Acker, 1989, p. 237)

Walby's theory of patriarchy does not attempt to construct a one-system theory, but rather presents itself as a two- or three-system theory. Nonetheless, Acker argues that early problems with the theoretical understanding of male dominance have buried themselves within later ideas, and ultimately this must mean that Walby's theory is inadequate. A closer look at Walby's ideas about patriarchy shows, for example, that when she addresses women's subordination in the workplace she does so using Marxist concepts like 'the relations of production'. Marxist theory, contends Acker, is

relatively untouched by the feminist critique, with the old patriarchal images still embedded in an apparently gender-neutral framework'
(Acker, 1989, p. 258)

It cannot, therefore, provide a satisfactory explanation of women's subordination. (See also Section 2.6.)

Acker contends that in order to produce a more adequate theory of male domination a shift in analytic approach is necessary. Suggesting that Walby is making incorrect assumptions about the way in which social life is structured by gender, class and race relations, she proposes that the concept 'patriarchy' be abandoned. A more useful way of theorizing male domination, she says, might be to speak of the manner in which 'gender' is interactive, and inseparable from other social sets of social relations like 'class' and 'race', rather than to imagine, as Walby does, that 'gender', 'class' and 'race' as analytical concepts, and as sets of social relations, exist separately. By way of illustration, Acker points out that:

. . . gender and class relations may be produced within the same ongoing practices. Looking at them from one angle we see class, from another we see gender, neither is complete without the other.
(Acker, 1989, p. 239)

Rather than a theory of patriarchy like Walby's – that begins life in the realm of the abstract and conceives of male domination as filtering down to the level of the everyday – what is needed, claims Acker, is a theory that starts in the realm of the particular, at the level of everyday experience. In this way the complex links between 'gender', 'race' and 'class' subordination (see Sections 4.11, 5.7 and 6.6) will be understood differently, and perhaps more clearly. Acker cites Cynthia Cockburn's (1983) study of the working relationships between men and women in the printing industry as an example of such an understanding. The study *Brothers* demonstrates the way in which:

. . . male workers dealt with technological threats to their class status and in the process defined and redefined both their masculinity and an opposing, subordinated femininity.
(Acker, 1989, p. 239)

Acker admits that a move away from the unambiguity of a theory of patriarchy to the more fuzzily defined 'gender' means that what she calls 'critical-political sharpness' is lost. A theory of patriarchy like Walby's is a way of stating male domination and women's subordination unequivocally – and only later working out the precise details. Conversely, Acker's suggestion that 'gender' is linked to 'class' is linked to 'race', and that those linkages are best

investigated through the medium of women's everyday experiences, represents an uncertainty about the nature of male domination and women's subordination. But it may be that an adequate analysis of women's social, political and economic roles will in this way be lost. Those researching the links may be induced, by their very uncertainty, into placing 'gender' second to 'class', for example. In this example any conclusions drawn will look similar to the early conclusions of Marxist-feminists – conclusions that those using 'gender' as an analytical concept have already rejected as wrong.

Case study – Rational-choice theory: a riposte to feminists

Feminist theories have influenced contemporary sociology to a degree that has led some critics to suggest feminism constitutes a new and unwelcome orthodoxy in sociological thinking. One such critic, Catherine Hakim, suggests that feminists have over-emphasized their research findings in order to corroborate their strongly held beliefs. While she does not deny that in the past women have been subject to discrimination, she argues that feminists' theories of patriarchy are misleading, in the face of evidence which shows women making rational choices about their day-to-day lives, and about the longer term.

In a controversial article *Five feminist myths about women's employment*, Hakim demonstrates that far from being victims of unfair employment practices, women actively choose part-time work in order to manage the domestic responsibilities with which they actively wish to be engaged. (See also Section 9.3.) While she takes issue with feminist claims about women's participation in the labour market, her argument, by extension, is critical of a spectrum of feminist assumptions in other areas of sociological study. Hakim's claims are listed below:

1 There has been no substantial increase in women's labour market participation, contrary to feminists' perceptions and claims. Whilst the economic activity rates for women of working age have increased in the last 50 years, this increase can be explained mainly in terms of the substitution of part-time for full-time jobs and the substitution of married women for single women workers.

2 Women part-time workers are less 'committed' to their jobs than their male full-time counterparts. Hakim writes:

The commitment of a part-time worker to a part-time job is not equal to the commitment of a full-time worker to a full-time job. At the minimum the two levels of commitment differ in degree, and arguably they differ qualitatively as well.'
(Hakim, 1995, p. 434)

This is because many more women working part-time have traditional attitudes towards women's role in the home and at work, than do their full-time women counterparts. Hakim suggests that while some women give priority to careers and training, others choose to give priority to what she calls the 'marriage career'.

3 A lack of available and affordable childcare is not a major barrier to women's employment. This is because women with access to birth control can choose whether or not to have a child. If a woman chooses to have a child, rather than simply having a child by default, it is likely that she will prioritize childrearing over employment.

4 Female part-time workers are not 'exploited'. Hakim responds to writers who have argued that part-time jobs should accrue the same benefits as full-time jobs, pointing to evidence which shows that part-time workers make a qualitatively different compromise between market and non-market activities. She argues that part-time workers are adequately protected by law and have adequate rights at work.

5 Women and part-time workers have higher absentee rates and higher instability rates than do their male and full-time counterparts, owing to differing 'work orientations' (Hakim, 1995, p. 448).

It can be seen that Hakim thinks that feminist sociologists have skewed the evidence on women's employment and women's labour market participation to suit their own ends. She writes:

In each of the five cases examined, feminist orthodoxy has replaced dispassionate social scientific assessment of the evidence on women's position in the labour market, effectively dictating a narrow range of acceptable conclusions (broadly, that women are victims who have little or no responsibility for their situation) and even eliminating certain topics from the research agenda.
(Hakim, 1995, p. 448)

Hakim argues that, while feminists have contributed much to knowledge about women's position in society, they have also:

. . . created a new set of feminist myths to replace the old patriarchal myths about women's attitudes and behaviour.
(Hakim, 1995, p. 430)

Her point that women are capable of making intelligent choices emphasizes the discomfort many feel on learning from feminist theory that they are the victims of a patriarchal society.

Responses to Hakim

Hakim's work has been labelled provocative by those feminist sociologists and economists seeking to

---

Whose myths are they?

Hakim's attempt to re-establish the myth of women as unstable, unreliable workers is the most disturbing part of her paper. It is, of course, true that, taken as a whole, women have higher turnover rates and shorter job tenure durations than men.

The results of a regression analysis of job duration for all those employed and living in South East England in 1993, suggests that the effects of gender are relatively small once occupation, age and type of job are controlled for. Though job duration rose by about 4 months for every extra year of age, women without dependent children had on average been in their jobs just 1 year less than men without children. The average duration of current jobs for mothers was *ceteris paribus* 2 years and 8 months less than fathers, which is hardly surprising given the norm that it is women not men who leave their jobs when starting a family. In some occupations – catering and routine assembly, for example – women tend to have been in jobs longer than men, in each age group.

Of course there is considerable room for discussion about what is and what isn't an appropriate control. It is possible to follow human capital theorists in arguing that women choose occupations in which high turnover is not penalized; equally the same data can be used to argue that employers select women for occupations where high turnover is not costly. Either way, higher turnover amongst women workers is not inherent, but the result of an interaction between occupation and gender.

Source: Breugel (1996, p. 176)

---

defend themselves against her accusations.

In one article, feminist social scientist Irene Breugel (1996) suggests that Hakim caricatures feminist ideas in order to shore up her argument, deliberately understating the complexity of much feminist work. At the same time, says Breugel, Hakim uses statistics to suit her own purposes, reading from a set of figures that best match her own thesis, rather than surveying all the available evidence, including that pointing in another direction. An extract from

Activity

a Referring to 'Whose myths are they?', summarize Breugel's argument in no more than 50 words.

b From 'Feminist fallacies: a reply', match Ginn *et al.'s* refutations of Hakim's five claims to the appropriate myths in the earlier list.

c To what extent do you think that taking issue with the statistical evidence cited by Hakim, as Ginn *et al.* and Breugel do, refutes Hakim's argument?

I, A, E

Feminist fallacies: a reply

Extract A The reasons for women's shorter job tenure (whether they leave for job-related reasons, for childbirth or for other domestic reasons including their partner's job moves) and the extent to which job quits reflect job changes or interrupted employment are important.

Recent work confirms that the gender difference in turnover rates is attributable to the occupation rather than the person and that, once factors such as occupation, sector, firm size and age are controlled, women employed part-time are *less* likely to leave their jobs than those working full time (Elias, 1994).

Hakim's rejection of childcare as a major explanation of women's shorter job tenure is unconvincing. First, her data shows that women with dependent children have shorter job tenure than those without. Second, although women without dependent children also have shorter job tenure than men, they need to be disaggregated into women who are childless and those whose children are no longer dependent (p. 171).

Extract B It is well known that part-time jobs are not only worse than full time, in terms of hourly pay, training opportunities, fringe benefits and statutory rights, but are also at a lower level in Britain than in other Western countries (Dale and Joshi, 1992).

Expressed 'satisfaction' by part-timers with their job is likely to reflect their lack of alternatives and weak bargaining position with employers because of having to accommodate domestic responsibilities. Rubery *et al.* (1994) show that women part-timers are overqualified for their jobs and that their initial 'satisfied' response in surveys is not confirmed on examination. For example, they were less likely than women full-timers to say their current job was the one they liked best: over half women part-timers, compared with a third of full-timers (women and men), said that given their qualifications and experience they could expect a better job.

A key issue is whether women prefer part-time *jobs* or jobs with *short hours*. If women were able to stay in the same job, with the same employment conditions, status and level of responsibility, but reduce their hours to accommodate family commitments, would they choose to switch to jobs in the part-time sector of the labour market, with all the disadvantages characteristic of such jobs? Evidence from Sweden and Denmark, where working hours can be reduced in this way, suggests that they would not (p. 170).

Extract C Hakim points out that the total hours of female employment, in terms of full-time equivalents (FTEs), have increased little in the postwar period up to 1987 in spite of the dramatic rise in the number of women employed. We are unaware that recent feminist writing has claimed otherwise. But FTEs are not necessarily the most relevant measure of women's employment and oversimplify a complex set of changes.

For many research purposes, the proportions of women employed, either full time or part-time, are more useful than FTEs.

Even if two part-time jobs are comparable with one full-time job for statisticians, this is not so for those who hold the jobs nor for their employers (p. 167).

Extract D Hakim reports evidence of gender equality since the late 1980s in non-financial commitment to work, which is confirmed by her own data. However, in spite of this evidence, and the equal proportions of women in full- and part-time employment who show non-financial work commitment, Hakim remains unconvinced that women and men are equally committed to work and dismisses what is surely a most impressive change in employed women's attitudes.

Curiously, Hakim states that commitment to a part-time job 'is not equal to the commitment of a full-time worker', without explaining how equating commitment with hours can be justified. She suggests that the women working part-time may well express greater commitment to their families than full-timers, but this is likely to reflect differences in their family situation. It is possible to be highly conscious of the needs of one's family and at the same time to care deeply about maintaining employment. As Dex observes, 'Most women . . . want to enjoy both work and home life to the full' (Dex *et al.*, 1994 p. 168).

Extract E Hakim cites studies 'showing that part-time work is chosen voluntarily by women' (e.g. Hakim, 1991), claiming this refutes the view that childcare problems are a major barrier to women's full-time employment.

Where women state a preference for part-time work, this must be understood in the context of demands on their time and childcare costs, which limit their employment options more than men's.

Clearly other factors besides current childcare responsibilities influence women's employment. Breaks in employment and part-time work while children are young tend to confine women to a narrow segment of the labour market, reducing their chance of returning to their previous full-time occupation. In addition, having adult children in the household increases the likelihood that mid-life women work part time, suggesting that the domestic workload associated with non-dependent children restricts women's capacity to take full-time employment (Ginn and Arber, 1994).

The evidence that childcare is a major factor in restricting British women's full-time employment seems undeniable (p. 169).

Source: Ginn *et al.* (1996)

Breugel's response is reproduced here as 'Whose myths are they?'

In another response, ten writers (Ginn *et al.*, 1996) respond to her claims, closely examining the evidence that she cited, and finding it possible to make further, contradictory interpretations. Extracts from their article are reproduced here as 'Feminist fallacies: a reply'.

5.4 Feminism in action

Sociologists have adopted a number of theoretical approaches in order to explain gendered inequalities. It is feminists' theories which have proved the most influential, however, in reshaping sociology's traditional concerns, and delineating new areas for sociological investigation. (See also Section 2.6.)

Feminist sociologist Mary Maynard (1990) has argued that feminists' theories of gender have changed the overall shape of empirical sociology in two main ways. The first she calls the 'additive approach'. This, says Maynard, is:

. . . designed to bring women's lives into view, take seriously the female experience and compensate for their previous neglect.
(Maynard, 1990, p. 270)

Feminist sociologists have added women to already-existing areas of sociological research – education, employment, crime and deviance, and so on. (See Sections 8.7, 9.3 and 11.7.)

Secondly, argues Maynard, feminism has introduced new areas of study to the discipline of sociology, focusing, for example, on housework and resource allocation in households, motherhood, childbirth and pregnancy, and issues regarding sexuality, none of which had previously been thought to be central sociological concerns (see Sections 7.5 and 10.7). She writes:

These areas of concern were previously ignored, either because they were regarded as inconsequential or because it was not recognised how significant they were in the structuring of women's lives.
(Maynard, 1990, p. 270)

Just as feminists have suggested new avenues for sociological research, they have also developed a set of research methods which, they claim, are better able to take account of women's experiences and ideas than more traditional ways of asking sociological questions (see also Section 3.2). They point to much sociological research conducted prior to 1970 to support their case. Until this time, they suggest, the bulk of sociological research was firmly 'malestream'. Using this pun on the word 'mainstream', feminists have been able to show how sociology had privileged men and male concerns as it sought research subjects, and how it subsequently generalized the findings of such research to account for the actions of both men and women. This sort of practice, say feminists, has produced sociological knowledge which is misleading and inaccurate. Thus, feminist research has conceived of itself as a corrective to sociological inaccuracy, as much as it has sought to establish a new sociological paradigm.

Currently feminist work in sociology includes empirical research and fieldwork as well as what Maynard (1990) has called the 'middle-range' theory generated by such work. At the same time feminists are producing theory based on their assumptions about 'capitalism', say, or 'patriarchy' – theory which is derived from material observation and which expects to generate feminist political activity. Lastly, feminists are constructing other types of theories about gender which are not necessarily concerned

with women's lived experiences – rather these theories refer to the way in which feminists have conceived what a woman is. These theories also question the assumed relationships between feminist theory and feminist activity made by feminist sociologists working in the first two areas.

The remainder of this section concentrates explicitly on feminists' theories and feminist activism in an attempt to explain the relationships between the two as feminists have conceived them. Understanding these relationships entails addressing the genesis of feminist thought. It is through considering feminism as a body of ideas with a history and a particular terrain that we are able to assess critically the extent of its impact on sociology.

What is 'a feminist'?

Journalist Rebecca West said in 1913:

'I myself have never been able to find out precisely what feminism is. I only know that people call me a feminist whenever I express sentiments that differentiate me from a doormat or a prostitute.'
(West, 1982, p. 219)

Maggie Humm affirms the difficulty of defining feminism, pointing out that feminists have widely different concerns and analyses. She has, however, suggested that all feminists share a 'woman-centred perspective' (1995, p. 95).

But while feminism means paying attention to the particular experiences of women where they have previously been rendered invisible, or differently understood, feminists do not agree on the precise nature of the political, social and economic changes that will be required to improve women's lives. In fact, change is an imprecise term which speaks differently to feminists depending on the way they view women's subordination. So while Marxist feminists might envisage change as an end to capitalism's exploitation of women and men (see Sections 2.6 and 5.3), radical feminists are likely to imagine a change in the nature of sexual and family relations as patriarchal domination is eroded (see Sections 5.3 and 7.5).

Certainly men are implicated in any proposed changes to the established order, given that they have been deemed to be responsible, intentionally or unconsciously, individually or collectively, for the subordination of women. Thus, feminists have been critical of individual men when they think and behave in a sexist manner. Feminists have also been critical when male-dominated institutions have excluded or marginalized women. But many men and male-dominated institutions have been slow to change their ways in response to feminists' demands. This has meant that feminists have used, and continue to use, a variety of tactics to persuade them that change is necessary (see Section 5.7).

Feminist activists have often used very familiar mechanisms of protest to state their demands for change, organizing meetings and marches, petitions and letter-writing campaigns in order to express their views. For example, feminists concerned with women's safety issues periodically organize 'Take Back the Night' marches. Such a march is intended to reflect women's (and men's) collective strength in precipitating a change to established norms and material circumstances. Activists may request, say, that their local authority installs more effective street-lighting in a particular area, which will in turn allow women to feel safer if they are walking alone after dark. If better lighting is subsequently installed then feminist activists have enjoyed a measure of success because change has occurred.

'Liberal feminism'

Those feminists who have been wedded to the use of 'official' political mechanisms – like meetings and letter-writing campaigns to voice their concerns about women's status – are often referred to as liberal feminists. This is because liberal feminists' concerns are focused on fitting women into existing social and political structures – the structures of liberal democracy. Liberal feminists wish to bring women into the decision-making processes of all public institutions on an equal basis with men, so that those bodies will take account of women's issues.

Liberal feminists are closely associated with the rhetoric and practice of equal opportunities. While they seek to improve women's access to work and education, and to codify their legal rights, subsequently an individual woman can choose to take advantage of the opportunities that have been created for her – or not. Thus, any changes in women's status and conditions tend to occur on an individual basis rather than for women *en masse*.

Most importantly, liberal feminists do not seek to reshape liberal democracy fundamentally. For this reason they have been criticized by other feminists who argue that their position cannot lead to the attainment of equality for most women.

Feminist forms of action

Although marching, petitioning and letter-writing have served feminists well, they are very traditional forms of protest. Increasingly feminists have used their imaginations to think up newer ways of drawing attention to sexism, oppression, exploitation and inequality. Often these forms of protest have served other causes simultaneously. When feminist peace activists camping outside the nuclear weapons base at Greenham Common in the 1980s adorned miles of the fence surrounding the base with ribbons, children's toys and photographs, they had established as much a peace movement-derived protest as a feminist protest.

Protests that do not fit the familiar letter-writing and marching mould, but involve a non-violent presence that disrupts the usual activities of the institution that is the target of the protest, are often referred to as 'direct action' (see also Section 17.5). Thus, feminists living at the women's 'peace camp' at Greenham Common nuclear base often climbed the fence to enter the base, forcing military workers to eject them. The act of entering the base was a constant reminder for the military of the women's feminist, anti-nuclear stance.

Alongside their direct actions or more familiar forms of protest, feminists have also pressed into service what have been seen as women's traditional skills – sewing and knitting, for example – to create decorative banners for display. Banners are historically associated with movement-based protests. They symbolize the strength and solidarity of the group they represent. The banners pictured in Figure 5.2 demonstrate feminist strength and solidarity using emblems of women's traditionally ascribed concerns.

Activity

Suggest reasons why feminists have used symbols of 'traditional' womanhood to represent their cause, as in the banners in Figure 5.2.

I, A

Thinking about activism

Just as feminists have worked to expand their repertoire of methods of activist-style protest, many have suggested that thinking and writing are forms of action too. When feminists write books or articles in which they try to explain their ideas about the need for change, they are in a very real sense 'speaking out'. The term 'feminist activity' refers to *all* feminists' efforts to precipitate change – grassroots activism as well as thinking and writing.

Gabriele Griffin, a professor of women's studies, has suggested that feminist activity is currently characterized by:

. . . a discontent with the present, and possibly the past; a desire for improvement in the future; and a (self-)questioning in the face of struggle.
(Griffin, 1995, p. 1)

While this section has already dealt with Griffin's first

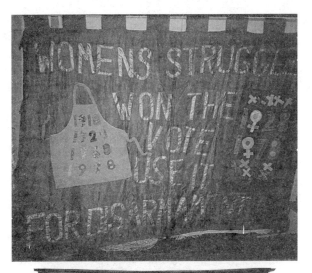

Figure 5.2 Banners in support of a cause, using 'traditional' images of womanhood

ment have been critical of the assumptions of their middle-class counterparts. Thus differences between women are emphasized as part of a process in which feminists take issue with each other's answers to the questions 'What is a woman?' and 'What is a feminist?'

Feminists' agendas for change are invariably redrawn when lesbian feminists point out that those agendas are heterosexist, or working-class women point out that middle-class values are inscribed into statements about what women and feminists want.

'I'm not a feminist, but . . .'

Thus far it has been intimated that all feminists are activists or thinkers/writers who share a woman-centred perspective that encourages them to push for changes to an established order. There are, however, many women who are broadly in agreement with feminists' objectives but are not prepared to call themselves a feminist. Some women live in circumstances which make it difficult for them to speak out, finding themselves ostracized by family and friends if they openly criticize, say, the unequal distribution of household duties between their male partners and themselves.

Furthermore, popular culture has constructed a negative stereotype of 'the feminist'. While caricatures of crop-haired, man-hating feminists are only the most recent incarnation of a centuries-old attempt to 'keep women in their place', those who have no sources of information about feminism bar, say, the tabloid press are likely to be wary.

Discussion point

To what extent do you think describing herself as a feminist is an important part of a woman's personal identity?

two claims, her third statement speaks to the ambivalence with which feminists have always determined their allegiances. For example, many feminists have necessarily 'blamed' men as a group for the subordination of women. At the same time, those feminists each have male friends who may be consciously acting to frame their personal behaviour in a non-patriarchal way. In this way a feminist analysis which apportions 'blame' to men is problematized: men are not as similar as some feminists' theories would suggest (see Section 5.6).

Neither are all women as similar as might be supposed. Lesbian feminists, for example, have criticized the heterosexist nature of some feminists' assumptions about women's lives. In the same way, working-class women active in the feminist move-

The Enlightenment: dreaming of equality

If women have been protesting about their unequal condition for hundreds of years, why have changes taken so long to occur? One important reason is that until at least the mid-eighteenth century the notion of equality itself was not firmly established.

It is hard to imagine a time when people did not perceive each other as equal citizens, but certainly prior to the eighteenth-century's Enlightenment (see also Section 2.2) the social and economic status accorded by circumstances of birth would designate a person's place in the world. In other words, a child born to a peasant family was imagined to be a person of lesser character, lesser intelligence and lesser capability than a child born to an aristocratic family. Similarly females were thought to have less all-round ability than males, while ideas about the superiority of white Europeans acted to justify imperialism and slavery (see Section 6.2).

What does the term 'Enlightenment' mean? It refers to a then-radical body of work emerging from eighteenth-century writers and philosophers across western Europe. This challenged existing views about the proper organization of society. More than anything, the thinkers of the Enlightenment hoped to challenge the control exerted by a powerful clergy over the way most people saw the world (see Section 18.4). In particular they asked questions about the authority of kings, suggesting that more power should be vested in the people through democratic bodies like parliaments (see Section 17.1).

Ideas such as these proved the catalyst for revolutions in France, the USA and elsewhere, as large groups of dissenters rejected absolute rule.

What was so persuasive about Enlightenment ideas? The concepts 'equality' and 'freedom' provoked a sense of excitement among many who sought emancipation from their immutably fixed social, economic and political statuses, and the accompanying material conditions of their lives.

Although Enlightenment thinkers spoke of 'equality' and 'freedom' as rights which were desirable for members of a modern society, these were rights that did not really extend beyond a relatively small circle of middle-class white men. It seems, in fact, that the Enlightenment imagination was strangely limited. 'Equality' and 'freedom' were not conceived to apply in the case of the enslaved Africans on whose forced labour the relative economic prosperity of the period rested.

Neither did 'equality' and 'freedom' extend to women. Enlightenment thinkers did not perceive women as individuals in the same way as men: they assumed that men's powers of reasoning were superior to those of women (this was certainly true of Auguste Comte, the founder of sociology – see Sections 3.1 and 3.2). This was an assumption that pre-dated the Enlightenment and one which justified the barring of women from sustained formal education.

Women's lack of education bred a vicious circle. Men could point to women's lack of intellectual distinction to explain their second-class status, even though it was men – as fathers and then as husbands – who prevented their daughters and wives from acquiring learning.

Vindication of the rights of women

Some girls and women – mainly middle-class – slipped through the educational net. One such, Mary Wollstonecraft (1759–97) was one of the earliest writers to espouse principles similar to those of modern feminists. Wollstonecraft was part of a group of radical, forward-thinking intellectuals who supported the principles of the Enlightenment and the French Revolution. She saw no reason why the principles of 'equality' and 'freedom' should not be extended to women.

In a book, *A Vindication of the Rights of Woman* (1792), she claimed that women should be educated properly as part of the acquisition process. Educating women, she argued, had indisputable social benefits. Wollstonecraft focused her concern around the social role of mothers.

Wollstonecraft's work – which at the time amounted to little less than a revolutionary statement – attracted ferocious criticism from the British conservative establishment. But her ideas were welcomed by supporters of the revolution in France, even though most did little to practically advance her cause.

A Vindication of the Rights of Woman emphasized that a woman's primary social roles were as a wife and mother. These roles tended to be carried out privately, in the home, just as men were a family's representative, or public face, outside. But while women and men occupied different spheres, because their inherent differences suited them for particular roles, they could still be *equal*.

Carole Pateman (1992), a feminist theorist, has pointed out that it is difficult for feminists to argue they are different from and yet equal to men. This is because such an argument supposes that the principle of equality can be applied in the large to connect dissimilar sets of circumstances. Where women possess a set of particular qualities – nurturing, caring and so on – and are thus necessarily attached to the private sphere, and where men possess a different set of publicly-applied qualities, no mechanism exists to ensure that power is evenly spread between the two groups. (See also Section 17.3.) The principle of 'equality' cannot in fact perform the task of distributing power equally because it assumes the same point of departure for each individual or group to whom it is applied. Thus it is easy to posit 'equality' between white male citizens operating in the public sphere, but the notion simply was not designed to fit the case of women or, of course, the colonized and enslaved peoples of the British Empire.

One way to avoid this problem might involve thinking of women as potentially similar to men in every respect. Such an argument would mean that women could conceive themselves competing with men on their own terms. But using the notion of 'equality' like this would necessarily mean that feminists played down differences between men and women (in this case), suggesting that women were essentially 'like men'. What Wollstonecraft – whose argument was predicated on essential sexual differences – did not want, however, was that women should have to become 'like men' in their quest for equality. She wanted women to be able to retain what she supposed were their feminine virtues, which were expressed in carrying out domestic duties and looking after children. (See also Section 5.5.)

Pateman has called the attempt to rationalize the argument that women are different from men, and yet the same as men, 'Wollstonecraft's dilemma'. She argues that this 'dilemma' is still very relevant for feminists. In fact, some contemporary feminist writers have suggested that what they call the 'equality/difference' debate underpins much recent feminist thinking (see Section 5.5). This is because when feminists suggest ways in which inequalities between men and women could be ironed out, they are in effect telling us what their version of an 'ideal world' would look like. In that ideal world it is likely to be the case that women are as powerful as men – after all, empowering women is a central feminist objective. But will that mean that women must become 'like men' in order to escape oppression? Or could it be that women can find a way to express their differences while managing to avoid subordination?

Feminist activity from the mid-nineteenth century

Assumptions about 'equality' and 'difference' have generated currents of thought which are clearly traceable in the feminist activity of the last 150 years, but particularly in the twentieth century. Feminist activity in the twentieth century is often characterized as occurring in two waves, 'the first sweeping over Europe and America in the mid- to late-nineteenth century, the second crashing against the post-war consensus a hundred years later' (Phillips, 1991, p. 121).

- First-wave feminists, campaigning for change around the turn of the century, were very much concerned with attaining legal and political rights – the vote, access to higher education, and so on – in an effort to become socially and financially independent of men.
- Feminists in the second wave began to emphasize what they identified as women's ways of thinking and living and the curtailment of these in a male-dominated society.

Without wishing to suggest that feminist activity occurs in isolated bouts as women formulate a series of demands which are then granted, the rest of this section focuses on first- and second-wave activity in an attempt to explain the relationship between feminist theory and feminist activism, and the relationship of these to the recent reshaping of sociology.

The first wave

From the 1850s onwards, feminists were broadly agreed that women's views ought to be more adequately represented in Parliament, preferably by women MPs. It stood to reason, they argued, that women should be able to choose who their representatives were. This would necessitate giving the vote to women: their enfranchisement. But enfranchisement would mean more than choosing parliamentary representatives. It would also give women an 'official voice' with which to speak on other diverse matters of concern such as sexual morality, or the acquisition of property rights.

Although support for the suffrage campaign was fairly widespread, women campaigners did not necessarily agree on the appropriate tactics for persuading the government of their case. Some campaigners thought that women should focus their activities on attaining the vote: if the government granted women a vote, this was tantamount to an admission that women were capable, rational human beings.

Some women saw enfranchisement as just the tip of the feminist iceberg, arguing that the granting of the franchise was appropriate and useful only as part of a package of reforms designed to improve women's social and political condition. Working women in particular wanted the vote as part of a package which was focused on improving the poor conditions endured by all working people – women, men, and the colonized peoples working in the British Empire.

Suffragettes and suffragists

Women campaigning for the suffrage and other reforms quickly established allegiances with particular organizations. Those who were prepared to take direct action through civil disobedience, and who were concerned with enfranchisement above all else, joined the Women's Social and Political Union (WSPU). Calling themselves suffragettes, these women were prepared to use unorthodox means to get attention. Thus, some women famously chained themselves to the railings outside Downing Street and others smashed windows and stormed public meetings. Some were prepared to go to prison for the cause, having been caught perpetrating acts of violence against property, for example.

The WSPU were not alone in campaigning for the vote and attendant reforms. Feminist historians Jill

Liddington and Jill Norris (1978) point out that conventional histories of the suffrage movement almost invariably portray a middle-class, London-based campaign. But in fact, campaigns led by working-class women, particularly in the Lancashire area, had a tremendous impact on the popular consciousness, and played an important part in the suffrage movement as a whole. Women involved in such campaigns were known as 'radical suffragists'.

Radical suffragists called for the vote for all adults over the age of 21. This would mean enfranchisement for women and for the small number of white working-class men who were still disenfranchised. Their demands existed in contrast to the position adopted at one stage by the WSPU leadership, who had suggested that giving the vote only to those women who owned property would be acceptable as a prelude to total enfranchisement. Clearly, such a partial enfranchisement would mitigate against poorer women – the very women that most needed a legitimate political voice in the eyes of the radical suffragists.

Working women, trade unionism and Empire

Women began to organize against poor working conditions towards the end of the nineteenth century – particularly in the textile industry where many were employed. A major focus of their concern was an exploitative outworking system known as sweating. Factory owners had found that they could produce goods more cheaply if they employed women and children working from home or in cramped workshops that were not restricted under existing governmental guidelines on employment. They often paid piecework rates, remunerating workers per item and not per hour, forcing them to keep up production or lose income.

Women workers made up a large part of the sweated labour force. Women trade unionists like Emma Paterson (1848–86) – founder of the first women worker's organization, the Women's Trade Union League (WTUL) in 1874 – argued that the Factories Acts, which legislated to 'clean up' factories by requiring higher safety standards and better cleanliness, had pushed women out of factory-based employment and into the unregulated labour market because employers hired men in preference to women. Thus, said Paterson and her supporters, the Factories Acts benefited men, but not women, and they lobbied against the introduction of further legislation. In 1875 Paterson was one of two women delegates to the Trades Union Congress (TUC). At this and at subsequent congresses she opposed the Factories Acts, calling them 'man-made' restrictive legislation on women's employment.

But having initially believed that effective trade union-style organization of women workers would bring about improved working conditions, the WTUL later came to favour further governmental regulation. While allowing the state to determine women's choices about the hours they worked and the trades they worked in was an unsatisfactory state of affairs for some trade unionists, they argued that governmental legislation could act to improve working conditions across the Empire (women trade unionists were very concerned at the unfettered exploitation of colonized women and their families).

Taken together the nineteenth-century evidence demonstrates that even while women attempted to improve their circumstances by campaigning for the suffrage, access to higher education and better working conditions, these actions were framed by inequalities of class, 'race' and gender.

The second wave

After all women aged over 21 had been given the franchise in 1928, some suffrage groups disbanded. This did not mean that women stopped writing, thinking and campaigning for change, however. Feminist campaigns continued across the world through the mid-century period. But what has been called a 'second wave' of concentrated feminist activity gathered momentum in the UK in the late 1960s, taking some of its inspiration from an earlier burst of similar activity in the USA.

Second-wave feminism flourished in a time of political ferment, from the late 1950s and mid-60s onwards, in the USA and Europe, respectively. The relative success of the 'civil rights' movement in securing new freedoms for black US citizens fuelled other groups' desire to express their widespread disillusionment with political systems as they stood. An explosion of political activity across the USA and western Europe emerged from opposition to US involvement in the Vietnam War, while 1968 saw a Europe-wide wave of student-led protests and demonstrations. In the UK a politics of anti-racism was developing, as was a fledgling lesbian and gay-liberation movement. (See also Section 17.5.)

The concerns of each of these movements influenced the growth of second-wave feminist activity, which then achieved its own momentum. Audrey Battersby, a feminist activist involved with early second-wave campaigns, writes of that momentum:

I think everybody was being carried forward on a kind of tidal wave, and it wasn't just to do with the women's movement, it was also to do with the late 1960s and early 1970s and what was going on at the time worldwide. There was a surge of optimism towards radical change.

(Quoted in Wandor, 1990, p. 115)

Simultaneously, economic and technological changes had acted to make women feel a little more sure of themselves. Innovations in reproductive technology, and in particular the introduction of the contraceptive pill, meant that for the first time women were able to control their own fertility (see Section 13.3), while more women than ever before were entering the labour market (see Section 9.3). However, employment opportunities for women were still very restricted, and they were paid less than men. The following pages show how these issues and others were of primary concern to particular groups of women as they participated in second-wave feminist campaigns.

The Women's Liberation Movement

During the late 1960s and early 70s, small women's liberation groups appeared in many large towns. These groups often met in members' homes to discuss issues of women's rights. The groups arguably had a dual function – consciousness-raising and campaigning.

The extract reproduced here from a Women's Liberation Workshop promotional leaflet shows the idea.

Activity

a Explain in your own words why Women's Liberation Workshops are closed to men.

b What criticisms of the 'leaderless' structure of meetings might be made by activists and sociologists from other perspectives, such as Marxism?

What was consciousness-raising? Women felt that they needed to be able to discuss the difficulties that they faced on a day-to-day basis, with other women. That way, they argued, they would be able to find a collective strength to solve their problems. At the same time, they argued, the minutiae of women's lives should no longer be seen as trivial and unimportant. Instead women's feelings were worth exploring and addressing. Kathie Amatniek, a member of a US consciousness-raising group, suggested that: 'Our feelings will lead us to ideas and then to action' (quoted in Rowbotham, 1989, p. 246).

Women were able to share their knowledge with other women outside the group, via newsletters and magazines, as well as larger meetings and conferences. This often led to the mounting of protest marches and demonstrations as well as smaller, well-orchestrated direct actions. In November 1969, for example, women entered the BBC studios where the Miss World beauty contest was being transmitted live and disrupted the broadcast. In 1970, during a

WOMEN'S LIBERATION WORKSHOP

Women's Liberation Workshop believes that women in our society are oppressed. We are economically oppressed: in jobs we do full work for half pay, in the home we do unpaid work full time. We are commercially exploited by advertisements, television and press; legally we often have only the status of children. We are brought up to feel inadequate, educated to narrower horizons than men. This is our specific oppression as women. It is as women that we are, therefore, organizing.

The Women's Liberation Workshop questions women's role and redefines the possibilities. It seeks to bring women to a full awareness of the meaning of their inferior status and to devise methods to change it. In society women and girls relate primarily to men: any organization duplicates this pattern: the men lead and dominate, the women follow and submit.

We close our meetings to men to break through this pattern, to establish our own leaderless groups and to meet each other over our common experience as women. If we admitted men, there would be a tendency for them, by virtue of their experience, vested interests, and status in society, to dominate the organization. We want eventually to be, and to help other women to be, in charge of our own lives; therefore, we must be in charge of our own movement, directly, not by remote control. This means that not only those with experience in politics, but all, must learn to take their own decisions, both political and personal.

For this reason, groups small enough for all to take part in discussions and decisions are the basic unit of our movement. We feel that the small group makes personal commitment a possibility and a necessity and that it provides understanding and solidarity. Each small group is autonomous, holding different positions and emerging in different types of activity. As a federation of a number of different groups, Women's Liberation Workshop is essentially heterogeneous, incorporating within it a wide range of opinions and plans for action.

The magazine, Shrew, is produced by a different group each month. Thus, to a certain extent, it reflects the preoccupations of the group producing it. WLW meets monthly, the small groups weekly. We come together as groups and individuals to further our part in the struggle for social change and the transformation of society.

Source: Peckham Rye Women's Liberation Workshop Collective (1971)

similar demonstration a bomb exploded under a BBC outside-broadcast van. Five women were subsequently arrested (Rowbotham, 1989, p. 248).

Women's liberation groups worked with the belief, above all, that 'the personal is political'. They argued that daily life tended to be thought of as taking place either in the public sphere or the private sphere. Feminists argued that any distinction made between public and private was artificial and acted to prevent women from speaking out. As Rowbotham has put it:

The separation of personal and public spheres was seen as a way of restricting women's articulation of grievances.
(Rowbotham, 1989, p. 246)

Women in the early second wave were adamant that their concerns should be heard in the public arena, and furthermore that they should have some input into public decision-making processes. Their voices had been absent for too long.

The National Women's Conference, Oxford, 1970

Some of the women attending liberation groups, and a number of other women working in universities, decided that they would hold a general conference on women's liberation in order to develop their ideas about the freedoms women wanted. Rowbotham describes what happened:

The Four Demands

At the first national women's conference at Ruskin College, Oxford, in February/March 1970, the following four demands were formulated.

EQUAL PAY
We have to understand *why* we don't have equal pay. It's always been said that a woman's place is in the home. We don't want to do equal work and housework as well. We don't want to do equal work when it's shit-work. Equal pay means not just the same money for the same work, but also recognising how many women work not because they want to, but because they *have* to, either for money or for friends. Equal pay is the first step not just to more money, but to control over how, why, and for whom we work.

EQUAL EDUCATION AND OPPORTUNITY
We don't want to demand an education equally as bad as that of men – we want equal resources, not equal repression. We want to fight for real education, to make our own jobs and opportunities.

24-HOUR NURSERIES
We need somewhere for the kids, but we have to choose as to whether the kids will be kept out of the way or given their own space, and whether, freed from children, we just manage to survive through working or make the time to discover who stops us from living.

FREE CONTRACEPTION AND ABORTION ON DEMAND
We want to be free to choose when and how many kids to have, if any. We have to fight for control over our own bodies, for even the magic pill or (in the case of mistakes) abortion on demand only gives us the freedom to get into a real mess without any visible consequences. We still can't talk of sex as anything but a joke or a battle-ground.

Source: *Women's Newspaper*, 6 March 1971.
Reprinted in Wandor, 1990, p. 242–3

We thought perhaps a hundred women would come. In fact more than 500 people turned up, 400 women, 60 children and 40 men. . . . I'd never seen so many women looking so confident in my life before.
(Quoted in Wandor, 1990, p. 22)

The conference lasted a weekend and formulated four demands (see the box). These represented some of the early aims and objectives of the women's movement. At subsequent similar women's conferences, further demands were added, including legal and financial independence for women, an end to discrimination against lesbians, and freedom from intimidation by emotional abuse or sexual violence.

Activity

a Identify any links between the areas of women's lives referred to in 'The Four Demands'.

b Suggest how you would modify or add to the original demands if you were writing them today. Provide reasons for any changes you would make.

I, A

The strike at Ford, 1968

The Women's Liberation Movement was not exclusively the preserve of middle-class women. But it did not always focus on issues that were at the forefront of working-class women's feminist agenda. Women trade unionists and factory workers were very much occupied with the question of equal pay for work of equal value. Working women had been lobbying business and government on this issue for years with no success.

In 1968, women workers at the Ford car plant in Dagenham, East London, went on strike. As sewing machinists who stitched car upholstery, they were angry that the company refused to acknowledge their skills and reward them with a higher level of pay. Audrey Wise, a trade-union activist involved with the women's campaign, remembers the strike's effects:

'What is really central in my mind is the fact that they stopped the whole factory. Everybody thought of cars as being about the track, about engines and metal, and here you had women working with soft materials, sewing, and they could stop a huge car factory. So it was an indication to those women and lots of other people of the power in their hands. Women are not used to feeling powerful, so it had a very great effect on them.'
(Quoted in Wandor, 1990, p. 202)

The Ford women formed an action committee along with other trade unionists from across the country – both men and women – to help them decide how to run the strike and to plan further campaigns of action. In May 1969 the committee organized an 'equal pay and equal rights' rally in Trafalgar Square. This was one of the very first large protests organized by women in the early second wave of feminist activity. Wise further comments:

'The first women's liberation demonstration in 1971 is usually referred to as being the first big demonstration after the suffragettes, and it just isn't true, because it's got to do with this idea that only middle-class women are interested in feminism.'
(Quoted in Wandor, 1990, p. 204)

Black women organizing

Many black women involved with the Women's Liberation Movement noted that its agenda did not seem to reflect their concerns, and that some of its ideas – about the nature of family life, for example, and about reproductive rights – explicitly excluded their experiences. In response to these omissions, and alongside their developing politics of anti-racism, black women began organizing independently.

Black women in Brixton, London, formed one of the earliest second-wave African–Caribbean women's organizations in 1974. Initially a study group, members met in a back room at the bookshop or at each other's houses, although by 1980 they had their own black women's centre. At the same time Asian women were active in campaigning from the late 1970s. One of the earliest Asian women's groups, Awaz, drew attention to immigration issues, highlighting the so-called 'virginity testing' occurring at airports as Asian women affianced to British Asian men attempted to gain entry to the UK.

Asian and African–Caribbean women worked together through the Organization of Women of Asian and African Descent (OWAAD). (See also Section 6.6.) This was formed from a 1978 conference of 250 black women, at which topics for discussion included immigration rights and the law as it appeared to discriminate against black people. OWAAD spawned a number of other black women's organizations, and attempted to maintain links between them. But as feminist political scientists Joni Lovenduski and Vicky Randall (1993) have pointed out, OWAAD's very attempt to bring black women together was bound to draw attention to the differences between them. Successive conferences in the early 1980s ended in bitter divisions (mirroring arguments similarly occurring at WLM conferences at this time).

Sisterhood: women working together for change

Women working for change in the second wave have often had an uneasy relationship with each other. While some feminists have wanted to emphasize the togetherness of women – their sisterhood – in the face of male oppression, others have argued that it is not easy for women from different backgrounds to metaphorically link hands. Women, it is said, have such varied and different life experiences that attempts by some feminists to present the movement as a united front must be doomed to failure.

Sisterhood is ...

Sisterhood becomes possible when, at last, we become aware of ourselves as women in common plight with other women. It is, for the individual, a consciousness of her situation *vis-à-vis* men and society.

However it seems to us that Sisterhood really only exists when the individual goes out and relates to and acts with other women in the light of this consciousness. We identify with other women in terms of our common oppression and servitude and we have a solidarity between us born from this.

In our discussions, in our minute examination of how we see ourselves and how we really feel towards our sisters, and towards men, is formed a bond of communication and understanding. This is the confidence of Sisterhood, which is constantly confirmed through our action in the workshops.

Source: *Shrew*, **3**, no. 5 (July 1971)

The early Women's Liberation Movement operated on the assumption that women had a set of common demands that could be identified and then realized. The 'four demands' statement of 1970, reproduced above, might seem to suggest that all women in the UK in 1970 shared a common bond by virtue of their oppression and could be read as a demonstration of feminists' agreement about what needed to be done to end the oppression of women.

It is easy to see why some feminists might have wanted to suggest that all women have a common bond. It could be argued that their sisterhood claim gave legitimacy to all feminist activity. The notion of sisterhood suggests that feminist campaigns operate for the good of all women, and furthermore that all women will benefit in a similar way from any changes that are made in legislation, in attitudes, in employment practices, and so on. However, is this really the case?

Discussion point

To what extent might the concept of 'sisterhood' mitigate against the recognition of differences between women? Does this matter?

Case study – The Equal Pay Act

Do all women benefit in the same way from changes in legislation? An examination of the impact of the Equal Pay Act 1970 might suggest that this is not so. The Act legitimized the principle of equal pay for work of equal value. Introduced to Parliament by Labour MP Barbara Castle, it was intended to end wage discrimination on the grounds of sex. In 1984, following a European court ruling, its scope was extended to allow claims for equal pay on the basis of equivalence of skill, effort and decision-making.

Critics of the Act argued that it would do little, in practice, to alter the imbalance between men's and women's pay. If employers could not discriminate against women overtly, then they would do it covertly, by regrading work tasks within a firm, so that they could suggest women were undertaking less-skilled work than men. Thus they could evade the Act.

Other critics of the Act argued that, while it might be effective where women were doing jobs that could be directly compared to the type of jobs that men did, it could do nothing to change the low pay received by women in largely gender-segregated occupations like cleaning and catering. Cleaning and catering work was – and continues to be – performed almost exclusively by women. (See also Section 9.3.)

Feminists monitoring the immediate effects of the Equal Pay Act noted that it had seemed to have little impact in the large. Mandy Snell commented:

Although most women received some increase in pay as a result of the Equal Pay Act, many are still underpaid in relation to the men they work with, and in relation to their level of skill and effort. . . . Most women are still concentrated in low-grade, low-paid women's jobs with little prospect of better-paid jobs or promotion.
(Snell, 1986, p. 34)

Although feminists welcomed the Equal Pay Act, many considered that it had a very limited scope. As Snell has commented:

The women's movement has always been ambivalent about the value of legislation in bringing about real change. On the one hand women have campaigned vigorously for legislation to improve women's domestic, economic and political positions. On the other hand, women inevitably find that laws, once passed, are unsatisfactory and that the inequalities they were intended to remove still remain.
(Snell, 1986, p. 12)

Case study – Feminisms

In order to better address the inequalities noted above, feminists changed tack. Where previously they had attempted to present a united front, now feminism became 'feminisms', as women joined together in smaller, identity-based groups in which they could discuss issues and plan campaigns.

Black women formed groups in which they could consider feminism and racism at the same time – something that the mainly white Women's Liberation Movement was not doing. Some lesbian women met together to consider feminism alongside the homophobia and heterosexism of the WLM and wider society.

'Feminisms' have thus emerged as a series of often-conflicting ideas and arguments, based around the differences between women, rather than as a unified and universally agreed-upon set of principles and demands.

Roseneil's (1995) research (see also Section 3.9) on the women's 'peace camp' at Greenham Common focuses on the differences and resultant productive tensions between women activists at the camp. Women peace activists maintained a constant presence outside the nuclear air base at Greenham Common, near Newbury in Berkshire, from 1981 to 1994. Ostensibly, they were protesting at the deployment of US Cruise missiles to the UK. But importantly the protest was organized and carried out by women, many of whom were informed by feminist ideas.

Initially women had camped at 'Yellow Gate' or 'Main Gate' near the main entrance to the base. But as more women arrived and differences of outlook began to assert themselves, those who shared common interests or attitudes set up camp at other gates. This affected the nature of the camp as a whole, as Roseneil comments:

[There was] *a discourse at Greenham which constructed the gates as different from each other in important respects. In the case of Blue Gate, for example, this meant that working class women living there felt an enhanced sense of identity and community with the women around them, and were able to distance themselves from some of the aspects of Greenham which they found oppressively middle class. Similarly, many women, aware that Greenham was often thought of as 'spiritual' and 'earth-motherly', and rejecting that aspect of Greenham, were able to construct the 'cosmic' as other, by locating it at Green Gate. There were two women, both visitors, who in the course of their interviews expressed disapproval of the behaviour and high visibility of lesbians at Greenham, and sought to disassociate themselves from the 'militant feminism' (which is frequently a euphemism for lesbianism) of some of the women. They were, in part, able to do this by pinpointing gates which they did not visit . . . and thus separating themselves from those features of Greenham which they disliked.*
(Roseneil, 1995, p. 79)

Compulsory heterosexuality and lesbian existence

But whatever its origins, when we look hard and clearly at the extent and elaboration of measures designed to keep women within a male sexual purlieu, it becomes an inescapable question whether the issue feminists have to address is not simple 'gender inequality', nor the domination of culture by males, nor mere 'taboos against homosexuality,' but the enforcement of heterosexuality for women as a means of assuring male right of physical, economical, and emotional access.

One of many means of enforcement is, of course, the rendering invisible of the lesbian possibility, an engulfed continent which rises fragmentedly into view from time to time only to become submerged again. Feminist research and theory that contribute to lesbian invisibility or marginality are actually working against the liberation and empowerment of women as a group.

The assumption that 'most women are innately heterosexual' stands as a theoretical and political stumbling block for feminism. It remains a tenable assumption partly because lesbian existence has been written out of history or catalogued under disease, partly because it has been treated as exceptional rather than intrinsic, partly because to acknowledge that for women heterosexuality may not be a 'preference' at all but something that has had to be imposed, managed, organized, propagandized, and maintained by force, is an immense step to take if you consider yourself freely and 'innately' heterosexual.

Yet the failure to examine heterosexuality as an institution is like failing to admit that the economic system called capitalism or the caste system of racism is maintained by a variety of forces, including both physical violence and false consciousness. To take the step of questioning heterosexuality as a 'preference' or 'choice' for women – and to do the intellectual and emotional work that follows – will call for a special quality of courage in heterosexually identified feminists, but I think the rewards will be great: a freeing-up of thinking, the exploring of new paths, the shattering of another great silence, new clarity in personal relationships.

Source: Rich, in *Blood, Bread and Poetry* (1994).

Activity

Read the extract 'Compulsory heterosexuality and lesbian existence'.

a To what extent do you agree that heterosexuality is 'imposed, managed, organized, propagandized and maintained by force'?

b Suggest examples which might illustrate each of these points.

I, A, E

5.5 Equality and difference

Invoking 'equality' while recognizing differences has been shown to be a key aspect of feminist thought and a basis around which feminists have attempted to organize.

Many feminists have suggested that it is possible for women to be equal to men, without becoming *like* men. These feminists want a share in what are currently men's exclusive privileges. At the same time, they want to retain the way in which women and men are seen to be different from one another, each possessing a distinct set of qualities. Carol Gilligan (1982) suggests, for example, that women and men have different cognitive processes and that this affects their respective moral viewpoints. Women's moral viewpoints are based on an 'ethic of care' which is produced through their concern with the nurturance and moral development of children. Hence women tend to conceive morality as an understanding of relationships and responsibilities towards others. Men, on the other hand, tend to conceive morality in terms of 'fairness' and 'justice', focusing on the construction and maintenance of a system of 'rights' for individuals.

Gilligan's influential arguments have been taken up, for example, by feminist peace activists or ecofeminists, who have used them to support their claims that women are essentially more peaceable than men, say, or more conscious of the relationships between human beings and their natural environments. If attaining 'equality' involves becoming 'like men', contend these feminists, women would be forced to emulate men's war-mongering and environmental destruction. Instead it is better for women to concentrate on preventing war and devastation. Thus 'difference' is emphasized, although it is assumed that 'equality' between men and women can emerge when men disarm and turn away from war, or consider 'green' claims about pollution.

Gilligan and her supporters seem to suggest that an 'ethic of care' or an inclination for peace are somehow 'built in' to women. Other feminist theorists using psychoanalytic concepts to address women's ideas about mothering have made assumptions in a similar vein. Nancy Chodorow (1978), for one, has argued that there are systematic biological and behavioural differences between men and women. But while women's behaviour does not necessarily relate to their biological status, neither can it be explained with reference to the process of socialization they have undergone. In Chodorow's account women's behaviour is produced by a feminine sense of self. Instructions from a peculiarly female psyche are an important factor in the

construction of that self. That all human beings possess a gendered psyche – a naturally existing psychological imaginary – is assumed in her argument.

Discussion point

Do you think that women are naturally
more peaceable than men?

Feminists who argue that the differences between
men and women are socially constructed and historically produced have taken issue with claims
like these, calling them 'essentialist'. In her book
*Inessential Woman: Problems of Exclusion in
Feminist Thought*, Elizabeth Spelman (1990) has
suggested that, not only is it incorrect to imbue
women and men with 'natural' qualities, when those
qualities are assumed but never explained; but
furthermore that it is impossible to speak of 'gender'
– of differences between women and men – without
also speaking of other differences such as 'race' and
class. Those who, like Chodorow, suggest that gender
is linked to 'race' and class, but can be analysed
separately, speak of 'men' and 'women' as if these
categories are not mediated by other differences.
Thus, in focusing on the differences between men
and women, Chodorow has omitted to address the
differences between women (and, by implication,
between men).

Spelman's insistence on recognizing differences
between women puts another spin on the equality/
difference debate. It is much more difficult to speak
of equality with assurance when a plethora of differences enter the theoretical arena. If experiences
of mothering, say, are different for black women and
white women, working-class women and middle-
class women, then gender identity itself is problematized. As Spelman has put it:

[Do] *we have gender identity in common? In one
sense, of course, yes: all women are women. But in
another sense, no: not if gender is a social construction and females become not simply women,
but particular kinds of women.*
(Spelman, 1990, p. 113)

In this argument the differences between women
are made manifest by observable inequalities. Put
another way, the existence of inequalities between
women presumes differences. Thus, by addressing
differences between women, feminists can simultaneously address 'equality' as it is implicated in the
notion 'inequality'. Spelman argues:

[If] *the meaning of what we apparently have in common (being women) depends in some ways on the
meanings of what we don't have in common (for
example, our different racial or class identities),*

*then . . . attention to race and class . . . helps us to
understand gender. In this sense it is only if we pay
attention to how we differ that we come to an understanding of what we have in common.*
(Spelman, 1990, p. 113)

What Spelman suggests is that 'equality' can never
be achieved without considering the full gamut of
culturally constructed human differences that appear
as inequalities. But conceiving of differences as
culturally constructed begs a further question. Will
gender, 'race' and class disappear as equality is
attained, leaving a world of 'sameness'?

For many this is equality's sticking point. While
differences currently produce inequalities they also
produce cultural richness and diversity. So even as
black people experience racism, they may want to
hang on to their sense of themselves as 'black', as
this sense of self mediates and constructs, say,
particular family relationships or forms of artistic
expression. In the same vein many women derive a
great deal of satisfaction from performing their
traditionally ascribed roles, particularly caring for
children, and might suggest that their rich experiences of mothering are not something they feel can
be shared beyond the level of giving responsibility
for particular tasks to a partner at particular times
(see Section 7.5).

While it seems that 'equality' between men and
women and between women is desirable, 'difference'
currently acts as an apparently insurmountable
stumbling block to its attainment. Alternatively, one
might argue in this case that the existence of 'difference' undermines the notion of 'equality'. If men
and women become equal in the sense that the
notion 'equality' describes, then women may lose
what is precious to many – a particular sense of their
relationships to others. But if they emphasize their
differences from men, suggesting that these are in
some way 'natural', they fall prey to traditional ideas
about women's cultural roles. So, if women's and
men's differences rest on women's capacities for
mothering, for example, then women who choose
heterosexual nuclear family-style personal relationships are effectively arguing themselves back into the
home. But if differences between women and men
are culturally constructed then women have no insu-
perable claim to staying at home caring for children,
which many of them in fact wish to do.

At the 'equality' end of this debate there is, in
effect, no way for those women who are mothers to
describe and understand their often powerful feelings about motherhood. If men can have those same
powerful feelings too – because looking after children must be seen in terms of gender-neutral parenting, rather than gender-specific mothering or

Source: Women's Community Press

fathering – then a feminist vision of womanhood that involves mothering is negated. No problem? But many women who are mothers have described the 'realness' of their powerful feelings.

Pateman (1992), a feminist theorist, has suggested that 'equality' can accommodate 'difference'. She argues that it is the inequalities attendant on 'difference' that present problems, rather than differences themselves (see also Section 17.5). She writes:

[The] *meaning of sexual difference has to cease to be the difference between freedom and subordination. The issue in the problem of 'difference' is women's freedom.*
(Pateman, 1992, p. 28)

Pateman speaks of 'equal worth', arguing that 'equality' can flexibly accommodate both a predisposition in women towards motherhood, and a desire for equal status that relates only to the potential similarities between women and men, and between women. She invokes the notion of 'citizenship' – social, political and economic participation – to frame her argument, suggesting that women must be free to make life-choices for themselves. She argues:

If . . . women's citizenship is to be worth the same as men, patriarchal social and sexual relations have to be transformed into free relations. This does not mean that all citizens must become (like) men or that all women must be treated in the same way. On the contrary, for citizenship to be of equal worth, the substance of equality must differ according to the diverse circumstances and capacities of citizens, men and women.
(Pateman, 1992, p. 29)

Men and women, while making a claim to the right of self-determination of each, might thus conceive of themselves as having the potential to be 'differently equal' and 'equally different'.

5.6 What about men? Studies of masculinity

Feminist critics of 'malestream' sociology have argued that much sociological research ignores and excludes women. Consequently, much current sociological knowledge is biased, rather than gender-neutral as it purports to be. The remedy, argue feminist sociologists, is to write women back in. But it is not enough simply to begin including women in empirical studies: theorists must address women's exclusion too.

Perhaps unsurprisingly, feminist sociologists and theorists have tended to concentrate their efforts on putting across women's points of view. Thus, until very recently, relatively little attention was paid to the manner in which social constructions of masculinity operated to make men powerful. Of late, however, feminists and male theorists taking their cue from feminism have begun to develop perspectives on male attitudes and behaviour. At the same time, male theorists who are 'opposed' to feminist arguments have also made an entrance into the field of study.

The first group considers that without knowledge about masculinity, studies of gender may tend to construct men as 'gender-neutral' while regarding women as inherently gendered beings. The second group – those 'opposed' to feminist arguments – take a different view. This latter group includes men's rights activists, as well as the followers of US men's movement leaders like Robert Bly, who lay emphasis on the supposed spiritual qualities that constitute the basis of masculinity. They consider that feminists are wrong when they call men 'oppressors'. In reality, they say, men are as oppressed as women have claimed to be. For example, it has been traditionally expected that men will work long hours to maintain a family. After separation or divorce, custody of children is usually awarded to women, and men are granted only restricted rights of access. The theoretical basis for the claims of both groups is considered below.

Male theorists working alongside feminisms

Feminists have argued that inequalities between women and men are perpetuated both by the sexist behaviour and assumptions of individual men in public and private spheres, and by 'institutionalized' discrimination – in the labour market, in the family and so on. The two operate in conjunction to produce 'patriarchy'. Feminists have always understood the necessity for wholesale changes in male behaviour and attitudes and have argued, like Lynne Segal (1989), that:

We want to see an end to the self-centredness, arrogance and insensitivity which accustomed privilege and authority bring to so many men when simply functioning within the day-to-day rituals which simply confirm their relative superiority to women. We want, most urgently, an end to the fear of men's violence towards women (and other men) in which their affirmations of a perhaps precarious sense of masculinity become one and the same as their expressions of fear and contempt for 'femininity'.
(Segal, 1989, p. 16)

Some men, broadly in agreement with these views, have subsequently been involved in a rethinking of aspects of male behaviour – taking the position that men must listen to women and take note of their prescriptions for change, as well as proposing their own vision of a reworked masculinity. These men have sometimes been involved with men's groups, akin to feminist consciousness-raising groups. One such group has intermittently produced a men's magazine *Achilles Heel*, which has carried articles on men and parenting, on domestic violence, and on men's use of pornography, for example. (See also Sections 7.5 and 7.7.)

In this vein, theorist of masculinity Geoff Hearn (1987) has identified men as the oppressors of women and of other men. Questions as to the genesis of male domination of women and other men, and the social and emotional costs of men's dominant behaviours – to men and to women – emerge from a perspective such as this. Theorist of masculinity Victor Seidler (1989) has argued that, while the traditional, dominant western model of masculinity is often perceived to be 'natural' to men, it has only developed comparatively recently.

Seidler explains that in western cultures the male mind and masculine ways of thinking are characterized by logic, rationality and objectivity, while masculine identities are strongly linked to the public rather than the private sphere. Men's restricted association with the private sphere means that they may have less of a chance than women to develop emotional skills that would allow them to address the needs of others. At the same time men are discouraged from expressing their emotional needs by a socially constructed dominant masculinity which emphasizes aggression and competition, and are forced to 'prove' their masculinity by competing with other men. This need to prove one's 'manhood' spills over into male sexuality and sexual behaviour. Marsh *et al.* (1996) summarize Seidler's argument in this respect, outlining his view that:

... as part of this competitive struggle men approach sex as something closely connected to individual achievement and something which signifies their position in the pecking order of masculinity. Male sexuality is part of the development of a masculine identity in which sexuality is seen in terms of power and conquest. Sex becomes a way of proving manhood.
(Marsh *et al.*, 1996, p. 284)

Johnathan Rutherford (1988) also links 'dominant' conceptions of masculinity to ideas about sexuality. He argues that masculine identity is tied to particular dominant forms of heterosexuality. These forms are 'white' constructs. They are also constructed within a patriarchal tradition. But recently, as these dominant forms of heterosexual masculine identity have been challenged by gay men, by women and by black men, individual white heterosexual men have, of necessity, begun to reassess their masculinity. Those who have done this, and as a consequence have begun to change their behaviour – attempting, for example, to more freely express an emotional side of themselves – have been dubbed 'new men' by the media. But does the 'new man' really exist? Rutherford draws on sociological evi-

Discussion point

Does the 'new man' exist, or is he simply a media construct? Are younger men more likely to be 'new men'?

dence to suggest that, while some appearances may have changed, men are still taking a great deal less responsibility than women at home, for example.

An anti-feminist backlash

Some men have responded with relative hostility to the criticisms of conventional masculinity raised by feminists. Taken as a whole their responses might be characterized as an anti-feminist 'backlash'. US journalist Susan Faludi (1992) has catalogued the evidence for such a 'backlash' in her book of the same name. She writes:

> [The] *last decade has seen a powerful counter-assault on women's rights, a backlash, an attempt to retract the handful of small and hard-won victories that the feminist movement did manage to win for women.*
> (Faludi, 1992, p. 12)

Faludi argues that the anti-feminist backlash is occurring on a number of fronts as men attempt to regain the power and status that they perceive themselves to have lost to women. The 'backlash' deploys the claims of some 'research', alongside the moralizing of the popular media that attempts, via popular culture, to deride and undermine women's claims to equality. (See also Sections 10.7 and 15.7.) In the USA it is also manifested, for example, in the angry condemnations of women's independence by New Right politicians, or the fire-bombing of women's clinics by anti-abortion protestors.

It has to be asked, if there is a 'backlash', why is it occurring when inequalities between women and men and between women all too clearly do still exist? Faludi suggests that, as women have not yet achieved equality with men, the 'backlash' acts like a pre-emptive strike:

> *The anti-feminist backlash has been set off not by women's achievement of full equality but by the increased possibility that they might win it.*
> (Faludi, 1992, p. 14)

However, she concludes that rectifying inequalities is a just cause, and hence that it will be difficult to prevent the eventual attainment of equality between men and women.

Not all feminists would agree with Faludi's prognosis. Theorists like Judith Butler (1990) who take an explicitly post-modern approach might argue that 'equality' as it is currently conceived mitigates against its own attainment. It is a concept which masquerades as 'gender-neutral', but in fact sets terms for women's emancipation. Thus, in order to become equal with men, women must construct themselves in men's image – an impossible and perhaps undesirable task as far as many feminists are concerned. However, post-modern feminists are unlikely to suggest that women should stop trying to change their conditions in both public and private spheres.

Men's rights and the men's movement

Some men have attempted to imitate what they understand to be feminist 'successes' and have explicitly characterized themselves as part of a men's movement – stating the need to 'reclaim' what it means to be a man. US poet and writer Robert Bly has been seen at the forefront of this initiative. In his book *Iron John* (1991), Bly argues that the behaviour which is now understood to constitute masculinity – the dominant western model of masculinity – is in fact a condition out of touch with 'true' masculinity, a spiritual state connected to the purported existence of male 'instincts'. In order that men can get in touch with their 'real' masculinity – a wild, primitive and deeply hidden part of themselves – Bly and others like him organize workshops and country weekends where men participate in what is essentially group therapy, exploring their emotions through the enactment of rituals.

Clearly, Bly and his supporters believe that masculinity and femininity are to some extent 'natural' and given – although men also naturally have a feminine side, and women a masculine one. But at the same time Bly claims a relationship to the feminist movement, arguing that his position is not anti-feminist, but rather pro-men. Women and men may have more chance of achieving equality across their differences, he claims, if men can undo the ravages of contemporary culture and inhabit their true masculinity, just as women have begun to challenge patriarchy and claim new social, economic and political roles for themselves.

Bly himself is keen to keep his distance from men's rights activists who contend that feminism has 'gone too far', affecting the self-concepts of men and devaluing masculinity. These men claim the necessity for 'men's rights' to be addressed in the law and social policy – citing in particular the Child Support Agency as an institution which constructs them as absent fathers, while Family courts are simultaneously restricting their access to the children they are supporting. One example of such a men's rights organization is the group Families Need Fathers.

Discussion point

Do you agree that men are suffering oppression at the hands of traditional social and economic expectations? Are they suffering oppression at the hands of the feminist movement? To what extent are 'men's rights' already enshrined in the law?

Masculinities

Is it correct to characterize men as conforming to one masculine stereotype or another? Or could it be argued that there are many different forms of masculinity? While the behaviour of some men is undoubtedly in keeping with images of dominant masculinity, most men's behaviour is like this only sometimes, while some individual men do not behave 'like men' at all. This may seem encouraging news for feminists and others who seek to undermine dominant masculine forms, but at the same time it underlines the complexities of the operation of patriarchy.

Just as some women are more powerful than others, so masculinity too is modified and reframed by 'race', class and sexuality, making some men more powerful than others. Given that dominant forms of masculinity are predicated on male power, less-powerful men may express their masculinity differently. Is it more appropriate, then, to refer to 'masculinities' rather than the singular 'masculinity'?

Jeffrey Weeks (1986), a theorist of gay masculinity and sexuality, has argued that what it means to be a man or a woman in contemporary society is, in fact, always contradictory:

[We] *learn early on in our particular society that to be a man is not to be a homosexual. Male homosexuality has been stigmatised through several centuries as effeminate, an inversion of gender, precisely unmanly. Yet we also know that many 'real men' do see themselves as homosexual and that the 1970s saw a general 'machoisation' of the gay world. Here conventional views about what it is to be a man conflict with sexual desires and (probably) sexual activities: yet for many gay men the two are held in tension.*
(Weeks, 1986, pp. 58–9)

Weeks argues that, while masculinity and femininity are not unified concepts, nonetheless gender acts as a critical social divide. Thus he is able to conclude that, although there have been and continue to be constant battles over forms of masculinity and femininity at both individual and collective levels, 'the battles are against, and within the limits set, by the dominant terms' (p. 59). Hence it may be correct to refer to 'masculinities' rather than 'masculinity', but 'masculinities' too act to affirm dominant forms, and to oppress women.

5.7 Injustices? Gender, class, ethnicity and age

Differences and inequalities between men and women and between women have framed social relationships between groups and individuals in the twentieth cen-

tury. Sociologists and other theorists asking 'how' and 'why' such differences and inequalities exist have generated a series of explanations of men's and women's contemporary social, political and economic roles. These explanations and analyses coexist and intersect with theorizations of class and 'race' stratification. (See also Sections 4.11 and 6.6.)

Feminist theorists have highlighted the complex links between gender, 'race' and class as stratifying agents. In this vein, Abbott and Wallace have argued that:

. . . *racialised women in Britain suffer discrimination, exploitation and subordination because they are Black as well as because they are women.*
(Abbott and Wallace, 1997, p. 80)

They also contend that inequalities can become lesser or greater during the course of a lifetime:

While middle-class women are more advantaged than their working-class sisters, this does not prevent them becoming poor if they become a head of a lone-parent family or from suffering relative poverty in old age.
(Abbott and Wallace, 1997, p. 80)

Hence the inequalities of gender, 'race', class and age which sociologists have identified and theorized can act in a compound fashion on particular groups of women, or on individual women.

Gender and 'race'

Feminists writing from a 'black' perspective have attempted to theorize the link between gender and 'race'-related oppressions. This has, however, revealed a number of tensions and contradictions within the 'black feminist' perspective. Gemma Tang Nain (1991) points out that many black women are ambivalent about feminism:

- On the one hand, black women may be critical of the sexist attitudes of some black men.
- On the other hand, they may feel protective of those same black men, given that those men are seen as already the subjects of racism.

It is temptingly easy for white people and institutions to view black women's criticisms of black men as supporting their claims about the inferiority of black people in general. Tang Nain argues (1991, p. 2) that black women's ambivalence about feminism stems from:

- an assessment of feminism as a white ideology and practice which is anti-men
- a sense that it is incompatible with the black struggle against racism and that attention to it will detract from and divide that struggle
- a belief that it does not address issues of relevance to black women

- disenchantment over the experience of racism (and/or indifference to it) by black women who were involved in the movement
- the 'race'-blindness of some of the concepts of 'mainstream' feminism
- the insensitivity of some of the practices of mainstream feminism to the experiences of black women and the whole black population.

Controversy has arisen, in particular, over 'white' feminist analyses concerning reproduction, patriarchy, the family, abortion, and male violence towards women. These analyses, it is argued, have not taken the experiences of black women into account.

Tang Nain concludes that, while feminism is necessary for black women in order to understand those aspects of their experiences which are gendered, black feminists could occupy a central role in generating a new feminism – giving equal space to inequalities of gender, 'race' and class. Such a feminism might be called 'anti-racist/socialist feminism'.

How would such a feminism differ from the socialist feminism discussed in Section 5.3? Most importantly, it would not simply add 'race' to its already existing analyses, as 'socialist feminism' did. Rather, it would generate its analysis directly from black women's experiences and ideas.

Gender and class

The early days of second-wave feminism saw the construction of Marxist and feminist analyses that attempted to understand women's oppression as it was mediated by class. Feminists observed inequalities in the labour market that could not be explained with reference to class alone, as had been previously argued by Marxists (see Section 9.4). They also constructed an analysis of inequalities between men and women in the domestic sphere, pointing to women's unpaid domestic labour as evidence of oppression and exploitation (see Section 7.5). One group of Marxist feminists argued that there should be a formally constituted, state-run system of 'wages for housework' (Dalla Costa and James, 1972).

Many years later the British government stated its intention to include an estimate of the economic value of domestic labour alongside its calculations of gross national product, although this figure will not be formally included in the total GNP. In a small way, this represents a recognition, at least, that domestic labour constitutes 'work' or productive labour of some kind (see Section 9.1).

Discussion point

Do you think women (or men) should be paid wages for housework?

Michèle Barrett (1989) writes:

. . . socialist feminism's influence within feminism as a whole has been steadily declining. . . . [The] negotiations of socialist feminism with the issues of men and class have been relatively displaced. . . . [The] voices now most effectively addressing questions of class, inequality, poverty and exploitation to a wider public are those of black women, not white socialist feminists.
(Barrett, 1989, pp. xxiii and xxiv)

This does not mean that 'white' feminists have nothing further of use to say about class, or do not continue to act around inequalities of class and gender. In the 1984/85 miners' strike (see Section 9.5) women in mining communities formed Women Against Pit Closures (WAPC), an organization that supported the striking miners but also campaigned on its own behalf. Some male strikers initially reacted adversely to the relatively autonomous activities of WAPC, precisely because the organization gave women a voice of their own. Some women found a new confidence as a result of their involvement with WAPC, and have subsequently been actively involved with reconstructing their economically devastated communities, setting up women's centres and education and retraining programmes. Castleford Women's Centre, in West Yorkshire, is an example of one such centre which offers education to women.

Injustices

Where sociologists have identified inequalities of gender, 'race' or class, they have also necessarily identified injustices. Why uncover and analyse them otherwise? An exhortation to justice is clearly visible in the sociology of gender, particularly as feminist sociologists have been instrumental in developing and shaping this field.

Feminist sociologists and other feminist theorists have prescribed remedies for the gender-related inequalities they argue are caused by women's oppression. These may relate to the behaviour of individuals, or to the rethinking of institutional policies and practices. Nancy Chodorow (1978), a feminist theorist, proposes that men and women ought to share parenting activities more equally. Alternatively, some black feminist theorists have prescribed anti-racist and anti-sexist education, incorporating 'black' history as determined by 'black' theorists, and Women's Studies – a mixture of history, sociology, politics, literature and feminist theory – as a means by which to combat gender and 'race'-related inequalities in tandem.

A range of feminist ideas have been taken up by institutions in recent years. There has been a strong current of feminist sensibility in Labour-run local authorities, for example. The former Greater London Council (GLC) was the first to set up a Women's Committee, in 1982. The task of this was to promote women's needs and interests within local-authority decision-making and service provision, and to administer a budget for the resourcing of women's groups and activities in London. It has been much imitated by other authorities seeking a way to incorporate women's needs into their provision. Additionally, some major employers have introduced 'equal opportunities' codes of practice and monitoring systems, and flexible working hours so that those with care responsibilities – often women – can start work early, say, and then leave early to meet children from school.

Many feminists have argued that recent changes (particularly in institutional practices) – which have been spawned by analyses of gender, 'race' and class-related inequalities – have been 'token' and have failed to address the 'real' issue of the gendered division of labour within families. Even when some men and women have transformed their personal behaviour, or have practised feminist parenting, this has not meant, it is argued, that others have chosen to follow suit.

It can also be argued that oppressions related to gender, 'race' and class are structural phenomena, held in place by the British economic and political systems, and so the changed behaviour of a few individuals is likely to have little effect in alleviating society-wide inequalities. Feminist political theorist Anne Phillips (1996) argues that there is still a persistent association between women and care work:

As long as boys and girls continue to grow up with such different expectations of the way they will balance out work and family, this will inevitably affect the choices they make in developing their 'endowments'. As long as women continue to find themselves with the primary responsibility for the young, the sick or the elderly, this will inevitably translate into systematic disadvantage in the labour market. If the post-war expansion of women's employment tells us anything, it is that the sexes cannot be equal in their job opportunities when they are so profoundly different in their domestic lives. Unless the responsibilities of care work are equalised between women and men (which depends not only on the level of social provision, but also on major restructuring of the hours and conditions of paid employment), women's income, position, and conditions will continue to reflect the bad luck of being born female.

(Phillips, 1996, p. 38)

Phillips' argument cuts across the 'public/private' division that structures the British socio-political imagination. In short, she points out that unless things change at home, they cannot change at work. Conversely, in order for men and women to be able to equalize their domestic roles, the expectations of employers and social policymakers must change. What is required is the wholesale adoption of new working practices, which do not demand, for example, that men or women who seek promotion must work long hours over a five-day week to 'prove' themselves, or that men and women who choose to work a four-day week in order to take on caring responsibilities on the fifth day, are seen as 'uncommitted' to the firm (see Section 9.3).

Gender and age

Is it realistic to make proposals for wholesale, large-scale change? Is this kind of change possible? One recent piece of research suggests that it may be. Having studied the attitudes and behaviour of young people between the ages of 18 and 34, Demos – an independent 'think tank' – has argued that amongst this age group there has been a profound shift in ideas about gender. In *Freedom's Children*, Helen Wilkinson and Geoff Mulgan (1995) argue that as young women achieve success in the education system (see Section 8.7), and 'male' jobs in the army, manufacturing and construction dry up (see Section 9.3), there has also been what they call 'a swing away from traditional masculinity' (p. 31). They describe a '"feminization" of men's values' (p. 31) where younger men are professing to want intimacy and emotional honesty, previously seen as the domain of women, as well as wanting more involvement with parenting, and being more prepared to work in 'caring' jobs. At the same time young women are becoming 'masculinized'. This means that they are more prepared to take risks, but also that they are becoming more attached to violence. This evidence speaks to the documented rise of 'girl gangs', for example. Demos expects these broad trends to continue, and successive generations to take these changes further. (See also Sections 10.5 and 10.7.)

These findings are important because young people's current values, aspirations and experiences contrast sharply with those of previous generations. While this may be an effect of economic trends – the feminization of the labour market, say, or job insecurity – the evidence cited by Wilkinson and Mulgan shows, for example, that while young women still do more housework than young men:

. . . the ratio of time spent by working women relative to men in cooking, cleaning and doing the

laundry has fallen from 3 amongst 35–55 year olds to 2.3 for 25–34 year olds, and just 1.75 for 16–24 year olds. . . . Perhaps even more striking is the fact that the amount of time spent by the youngest working woman is barely a third of the time spent by the oldest working woman. At this rate of change we might expect the gender gap to have disappeared within a decade or so. Perhaps too, despite hi-tech washing machines and hoovers, the young are becoming the dirty generation as masculinised new women accept male standards of cleanliness rather than the other way around.

(Wilkinson and Mulgan, 1995, p. 76)

The broad implication of Demos' argument is that if enough people – a critical mass – change their attitudes and behaviour, then gender-related inequalities will begin to disappear. At the same time, policymakers in particular will need to address changing social attitudes amongst British people. The UK is a democracy, and so the policy decisions of government and its agencies must generally reflect the will of the people (though see Section 17.1). Thus, institutions like these will be forced to rethink their practices. This extends to employers too. If employees are generally less prepared to work long hours, then employers – given that they need to employ workers – will be forced to allow for this by building in further flexible working patterns or by changing their 'office culture'.

Demos' trend-spotting points to new prospects for feminists and others interested in promoting equality. If young people are leading a 'genderquake', as Demos have suggested, then those who wish to actively address today's social inequalities must ensure they make room for them to thrive.

Further **reading**

The following are two short books on gender written specifically for A level study:

- Garrett, S. (1987) *Gender*, London, Tavistock.
- Mayes, P. (1986) *Gender*, London, Longman.

A wide-ranging and inclusive compendium of work on the sociology of gender is:

- Abbott, P. and Wallace, C. (1997) *An Introduction to Sociology: Feminist Perspectives*, 2nd edn, London, Routledge.

For more detailed information on feminist thinking and feminist actions, consult:

- Lovell, T. (ed.) (1990) *British Feminist Thought: A Reader*, Oxford, Blackwell.
- Tong, R. (1989) *Feminist Thought*, London, Unwin Hyman.

Exam **questions**

1 Assess the influence of feminist perspectives on sociological research. [25 marks]
(AEB, Paper 2, Summer 1996)

2 'Despite increasing evidence to suggest equality in educational performance, women still remain occupationally disadvantaged in earnings, job-security and promotional opportunities. Their primary roles are still seen as domestic.'
What explanations have sociologists offered for the continuing subordination of women in society? [25 marks]
(NEAB, Summer 1996)

3 'Our contention is that mainstream sociology is inadequate because it ignores, or distorts, or marginalises women'. (Abbott and Wallace, *An introduction to Sociology: Feminist Perspectives*, 1990).
Using examples, outline and assess the contribution feminist research has made to mainstream sociology. [25 marks]
(IBS, Paper 3, Summer 1996)

4. Read the following data carefully and then answer the questions that follow.

Item A Sociologists such as Goldthorpe have traditionally argued that gender inequality is not particularly important for understanding the unequal distribution of resources in society, or the causes of political change. They assert that this is because women's social and economic position is determined by the position of the family in which they live, and this in turn is determined by that of the male breadwinner. This view, that gender inequality is almost irrelevant for mainstream sociological theorizing, has met with an onslaught of criticism by writers who have argued that it is inappropriate to take the family as the unit of analysis in such a way. These criticisms include the points that: firstly, there is inequality between men and women within the family; secondly, women's earnings are important in the standard of living and position of the household; and thirdly, not all people live in households where there is a male wage earner, let alone one in which such a man brings in all the family income. That is, the critics assert that there is a significant inequality between men and women, and for a woman to be married to a man does not mean that she gains all the privileges he has access to.

In complete contrast to the view that gender inequality is not important, radical feminists have argued that it is one of the most, if not the most, significant forms of social inequality. radical feminist theorists argue that the oppression of women by men is the most important aspect of inequality in society, and that men's exploitation of women is not a by-product of other forms of inequality. Such forms, for example those based on ethnicity and class, are important, but do not alter the fundamental nature of patriarchal power.

Dual system theorists have attempted to incorporate both class and gender inequality into their analysis. Here, the analysis of gender inequality as a system of patriarchy is combined with an analysis of capitalism. For instance, Hartmann argues that male workers are able to keep women out of the better jobs because they are organized, and that, as a consequence, women are obliged to marry on unfavourable terms, such that they have to do most of the housework. Hartmann argues that there is a vicious circle in which patriarchy and capitalism tend to maintain each other.

Source: Adapted from Abercrombie, Warde *et al.*, (1994) *Contemporary British Society*, 2nd edn, Cambridge, Polity Press

Item B Social class by sex, Great Britain, 1991 (percentages)

Registrar-General's social class	Men	Women	Total
I: Professionals	7	2	5
II: Managers	28	28	28
III N: Skilled non-manual	11	39	23
III M: Skilled manual	33	7	22
IV: Partly skilled	16	17	16
V: Unskilled	5	7	6
Total	100	100	100

Source: *Census of Population*, 1991, 10% sample

a Draw two conclusions from the data in the table in **item B**. [4 marks]
b Briefly outline what is meant by 'dual systems theory' (line 39 in **item A**). [4 marks]
c Using the information in **item A**, outline the problems faced by sociologists in identifying the class position of women. [6 marks]
d Evaluate how sociologists have explained the class differences between men and women.
[16 marks]

(IBS, Paper 2, Summer 1995)

5 Read the following data carefully and then answer the questions that follow.

Item A The Boys are Back in Town

A white male backlash apparently got under way this week in the United States. After 30 years of affirmative action in favour of women and minorities, men signalled their dissatisfaction. A campaign began in California to outlaw positive discrimination.

If Britain follows where America leads, what will this trend mean for men here? This country does not have the banks of laws and regulations that the US has. Yet some indicators demonstrate that, relatively speaking, men are not doing as well here as they once did. Men still earn more than women, but the gap has narrowed. Meanwhile the number of women in work has increased by 18 per cent since the late seventies while male employment has fallen 7 per cent. Girls are overtaking boys at school. Research suggests that men still enjoy more leisure than women but the difference has diminished significantly. Could this provoke a British male counter-offensive?

The intellectual thought that might justify such a backlash is available. Thinkers such as Charles Murray argue that the best way to rescue the self-esteem of young men in the 'underclass', caught in crime and unemployment, would be to restore them as the bread-winners responsible for supporting wife and family.

But this is an absurd dream. Propping up the old male stereotype would require changes right through society. It would mean diminishing the role of women in education and the labour market. Wage rates for women would have to be cut to render them incapable of supporting themselves and their children. Equality laws would have to be rolled back.

Men must reconcile themselves to the changed world they live in. Today men are expected to be totally committed to work, yet they are also told they should be full-time fathers. It is an impossible task. Women know that from the bitter experience of trying to fulfil twin roles. Only if men campaign for shorter hours, more flexible working and paternity leave will they be able to resolve such contradictions.

Source: adapted from the Opinion Column of *The Independent*, 14 January 1995

a Explain briefly and give two examples of what is meant by 'positive discrimination' (line 6). [4 marks]

b What do sociologists mean by an 'underclass' (line 25)? [6 marks]

c Using the data in the passage, and any other evidence about the UK with which you are familiar, examine the view that, compared to women 'men are not doing as well here as they once did' (line 12) [8 marks]

d Outline and critically assess two sociological explanations of economic differences between men and women. [12 marks]

(IBS, Paper 1, Summer 1996)

Coursework **suggestions**

1 Carry out a survey on a particular aspect of gender relations

In the final chapter of her book *Sex, Gender and Society*, Ann Oakley (1972) makes a number of observations about the status of women in British society, relating to paid employment, domestic labour and politics. Pick one of the topic areas she discusses and carry out a survey on this particular aspect of gender relations, in order to consider the extent to which there have been changes since the time when the book was written.

2 Investigate women's and men's experiences in employment

Using material from the most recent national Census, and your own observations, consider the extent to which men and women inhabit different 'spaces' in relation to paid employment. If you have a job, paid or otherwise, use it – and the jobs of your friends – as an opportunity to obtain information.

3 Investigate the 'genderquake'

Obtain a copy of Demos' report on the 'genderquake' (Wilkinson and Mulgan, 1995) and design a questionnaire to test whether the findings reflected in that research are also found in a representative group of pupils at your school/college.

Stratification: 'race' and ethnicity

Chapter outline

6.1 **Introducing 'race' and ethnicity**
page 198
A critical examination is undertaken of the terms 'race', 'ethnicity', 'ethnocentrism', 'ethnic minority', 'racism', 'racialism', 'nationalism' and 'black'.

6.2 **The history of 'race relations' in the UK**   *page 203*
This section explores black people's presence in the UK before, during and after colonialism, concentrating on migration after the Second World War. Irish migration is examined in order to compare state attitudes to black and white migrants. A chronological account of legislation on 'race' is given.

6.3 **Theories and research on 'race' and ethnicity – an overview**   *page 209*
The 1970s, 1980s and 1990s each had specific developments in academic investigations into 'race' and ethnicity, and these are put into perspective in an overview.

6.4 **Classical approaches to 'race' and ethnicity**   *page 213*
This section examines five classical approaches to the study of 'race' and ethnicity:

* *Biological approaches* – So-called scientific approaches to 'race' are considered. The contribution of contemporary sociologists' applications of this classical approach are evaluated, as is the move into sociobiology.
* *Marxism* – The use of Marxism in the field of 'race relations' is investigated, with a focus on Cox and Miles' contributions.
* *Weberian approaches* – Connections between Weberian and Marxist perspectives are critically evaluated before a detailed appreciation of Rex's

contributions is made. Recent developments using a classical Weberian approach are briefly examined.
* *Functionalism* – Two models based on functionalist principles are investigated: functional segmental theory and functional/cultural pluralism.
* *Symbolic interactionism* – This approach to the study of 'race' and ethnicity is considered through a review of the work of the Chicago School, in particular Park and Blumer.

6.5 **Contemporary approaches to 'race' and ethnicity**   *page 221*
This section presents an investigation into the more recent sociological perspectives:

* *Neo-Marxism* – A critical examination is made of neo-Marxism in relation to 'race' and ethnicity, concentrating on the relative autonomy model versus autonomy model debate.
* *The New Right and 'new racism'* – The development of the New Right and 'new racism' in the UK is critically evaluated, focusing on the use of nationalism and the notions of 'race', ethnicity and culture.
* *Postmodernism* – This section looks at the application of postmodernist ideas to the study of 'race' and ethnicity, with particular reference to notions of identity. A critical evaluation of these ideas is also given.

6.6 **Conclusion: 'race' and ethnicity, class, gender and age**   *page 228*
This final section examines 'race' and ethnicity in relation to other factors that are also part of the stratification system in contemporary British society – class, age and gender. An examination is made of feminist contributions towards the study of 'race' and ethnicity, focusing on the 'black feminist' developments in this field.

6.1 **Introducing 'race' and ethnicity**

All human beings are born free and equal in dignity and right. They are endowed with reason and

conscience and should act towards one another in a spirit of brotherhood.
(United Nations Declaration of Human Rights, Article 1)

It is widely recognized that although individuals enter this world on an equal basis, society constructs labels, based on physical differences, which are used to differentiate unequally between people. There is no scientific basis for 'race' as a classification, yet 'race' and the related concept of ethnicity exist as frames of reference in contemporary society. Individuals, groups, institutions and the government perpetuate meanings associated with an ideology of 'race' and ethnicity. The consequences of this in the UK are far-reaching, resulting in continued and widespread prejudice and discrimination. Despite legislation outlawing racial discrimination, people have failed to act towards each other in a 'spirit of brotherhood'. Racial and ethnic disadvantage is prevalent in the 1990s; for example, 60 per cent of Bangladeshis and 47 per cent of Pakistanis are reported to be living in overcrowded conditions, as opposed to 3 per cent of whites (Anthias and Yuval-Davis, 1993).

Defining key terms

Before we begin it is necessary to examine the key terms used in any discussion of 'race' and ethnicity. Generally sociologists have tried to use terms in their studies of 'race relations' which are preferred by members of the various groups themselves. For example, in the UK 'black' was adopted as a political identity by people of African–Caribbean and Asian descent (Bradley, 1996) and sociologists used this as a term to describe those groups.

However, Modood (1992) claims that all-encompassing terms such as black conceal the differences of distinct groups. As an alternative frame of reference it has been proposed that each group should be referred to by its cultural identity, be it Pakistani, Bangladeshi or whatever. Yet it must be remembered that differences of experience exist even within these identities. (The issue of identity is also discussed in Chapter 10.) Sociologists remain divided on this issue, but for the purposes of this book it is important to account for existing definitions within the sociology of 'race' and ethnicity.

'Race'

'Race' has been used to refer to real or perceived biological differences which have been given a social meaning, such as skin colour (phenotype). As Mason explained:

. . . race is a social relationship in which structural positions and social actions are ordered, justified and explained by reference to systems of symbols and beliefs which emphasize the social and cultural relevance of biologically rooted characteristics.
(Mason, 1995, p. 9)

'Race' as a biological characteristic is seen as a delusion based on unsubstantiated scientific research (see Section 6.4). As Donald and Rattansi noted:

. . . the physical or biological differences between groups defined as 'races' have been shown to be trivial. No persuasive empirical case has been made for ascribing common psychological, intellectual or moral capacities or characteristics to individuals on the basis of skin colour or physiognomy.
(Donald and Rattansi, 1992, p. 1)

Despite this, discrimination based on 'racial' assumptions is widespread in the UK. Whether 'race' exists or not, the racial frames of reference do and these have social consequences. People act as if 'race' is an objective category, and this is reflected in political discourse. As O'Donnell acknowledged:

'Race', understood in biological terms, has proved remarkably unsuccessful as a basis for categorising people and of explaining differences in their behaviour. However, this has not stopped people seeking explanations of others' behaviour in terms of their supposed race.
(O'Donnell, 1991, p. 3)

'Race' as a social construct to which meanings are attached is very real, as are its effects. Consequently it has been argued that 'race' could be seen as the construction of differences based upon non-existent biological differences which are expressed, or believed to be expressed, in cultural activities (Anthias and Yuval-Davis, 1993). 'Race' is therefore grounded, as Anthias and Yuval-Davis noted 'on the separation of human populations by some notion of stock or collective heredity of traits' (p. 2).

Ethnicity

'Ethnicity' as a concept is more social and rooted in self-definition than 'race'. There is no single definition of ethnicity, but it has been suggested that the most important factor that creates an ethnic group is culture. (The issue of culture is also discussed in Chapter 10, and Section 10.6 looks at culture, identity and ethnicity.)

Ethnic groups may be defined (or define themselves) on the basis of language, religion or nationality, but the idea of shared culture is perhaps the crucial issue.
(Bradley, 1996, p. 121)

Therefore, ethnicity becomes a characteristic of social groups based upon a shared identity (real or perceived) rooted in common cultural, historical, religious or traditional factors, and who are regarded so by others.

'Ethnicity' as a term used to be treated cautiously, because it was suspected that its links with culture would carry connotations of failure: for example, the under-achievement of 'black' pupils being linked to cultural deprivation through ethnicity. (This issue is

RACE – THE FACTS

VIOLENCE
Racist attacks are on the increase in many parts of the world.
• Indigenous Canadians are six times more likely to be murdered than other Canadians.[1]
• In the UK Asians are 50 times and West Indians 36 times more likely than Whites to be victims of racial violence.[14]
• In the US, 6 out of every 10 hate crimes had a racial motivation and a further 1 in 10 an ethnic motivation. 36% were anti-black, 21% anti-white and 13% anti-Jewish.[15]

IMPRISONMENT & EXILE
Belonging to the 'wrong' group increases the chances of imprisonment and asylum rejection.

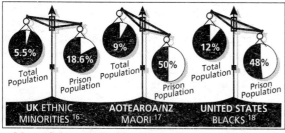

5.5% Total Population 18.6% Prison Population 9% Total Population 50% Prison Population 12% Total Population 48% Prison Population

UK ETHNIC MINORITIES [16]   AOTEAROA/NZ MAORI [17]   UNITED STATES BLACKS [18]

• Most of the world's 15 million refugees come from the South and seek refuge in neighbouring countries. One person in 10 was a refugee in Malawi in July 1993, compared to one in 5000 in the UK. The rate of asylum refusal on appeal in the UK has risen from 14% to 72%.[19]

WORK
Racial prejudice affects access to jobs.
CANADA – indigenous people are twice as likely to be jobless as the rest of the population.
US – blacks are twice as likely to be jobless as whites.[1]
UK – ethnic minorities are twice as likely to be jobless. Ethnic minority women are three times as likely to be jobless as other women.
AUSTRALIA – Aboriginal people are more than three times as likely to be jobless as the general population.[3]
• But in **INDIA** 10% of higher level jobs in the public sector now go to people from the Scheduled Castes (more than 16% of the total population) compared with only 3.5% in 1972.[4]

STRIFE & GENOCIDE
Half of the world's states have recently experienced inter-ethnic strife.
The result has been:
• In Afghanistan 1 in 6 people have been disabled by a landmine.
• In Zaire more than 800,000 people have been displaced.
• In Sri Lanka more than 14,000 have died in clashes between Tamils and the Sinhalese.
• In former Yugoslavia more than 130,000 people have been killed since 1991.[1]
• Up to 50,000 people were killed in Burundi in 1993.[20]
• In Rwanda the attempted genocide of Tutsis has resulted in an estimated 200,000–50,000 deaths.
• In Brazil an average of one tribe a year has been wiped out since 1990.[10]

HEALTH, WEALTH & HOUSING
How we live, where we live and how long we may live may often be determined by race.
In the **US**
• Nearly 50% of the black population live in polluted areas, compared to 30% of the white population.[1]
• 40% of Native Americans live below the poverty line. 37% die before the age of 45.[10] They are 10 times as likely to die of alcohol abuse.[11]

In **AUSTRALIA**
• Aboriginal people's life expectancy is 15 years lower than the rest of the population. Infant mortality is three times higher.[3]
• The suicide rate is six times higher.[10]
• Aboriginal family income is about half the Australian average.[12]

In **SOUTH AFRICA**
• The white 14% of the population owns almost 90% of the land.
• Life expectancy for whites is 73 years, for blacks 57. Infant mortality among whites is 13 per 1,000; among blacks, 57 per 1,000.[9]

In the **UK**
• People from ethnic minorities are four times more likely to be homeless in London than whites.[15]

EDUCATION
Discrimination affects the languages we speak and the education we get.
Fewer than 5% of the world's languages are given official recognition by governments.[5] No more than 100 people can speak Japan's indigenous Ainu language fluently.[6]

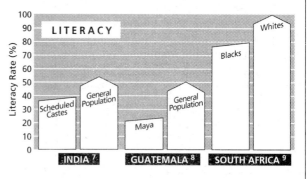

LITERACY — Literacy Rate (%)

Scheduled Castes / General Population — **INDIA** [7]
Maya / General Population — **GUATEMALA** [8]
Blacks / Whites — **SOUTH AFRICA** [9]

1 UNDP *Human Development Report*, 1994. **2** 1991 Census; Crown copyright. Through NEMDA. **3** NSW Task Force on Aboriginal Health, 1987. **4** *India Today*, 30 April, 1994. **5** Minority Rights Group. **6** *COLORS* 4, 1993. **7** Indian Census 1991. **8** Phillip Wearne, *The Maya of Guatemala*, MRG, London, forthcoming. **9** *Choices*, UNDP, June 1994. **10** Survival International. **11** *Talking Stick* 1, 1993. **12** 1986 Census, Australian Bureau of Statistics. **13** *Race through the 90's*, Council for Racial Equality and BBC, 1993. **14** Institute of Race Relations. **15** *Uniform Crime Report*, March 1994, FBI, reported by Center for Democratic Renewal. **16** Home Office Statistical Bulletin 9/91. Through NEMDA. **17** Julian Berger *The Gaia Atlas of First Peoples*, 1990. **18** Bureau of Justice Statistics, in *New Statesman and Society*, 1 April 1994. **19** *WUS Update*, June 1994. **20** *UNHCR Information Bulletin*, 10 December 1993.

Source: *New Internationalist*, October 1994

discussed in the chapter on education and training, in Section 8.5.) However, ethnicity can be a useful concept in many ways, such as allowing for conflicts within groups not distinguishable on racial grounds (e.g. Indian Sikhs and Hindus), or to refer to a sense of belonging within a community. It must be remembered that, as with 'race', the notion of ethnicity is still a differentiating force within society:

'Race' and ethnicity are social categories used in reference to divisions within a particular society.
(Bradley, 1996, p. 122)

In contemporary society the term 'ethnic' is quite often used as a synonym for someone seen as culturally different. This may possibly result in 'ethnocentrism' which has been defined as:

. . . the practice of evaluating other groups, and their cultures and practices, from the perspective of one's own.
(Mason, 1995, p. 10)

Judgements (good or bad) are made of another group based on our own subjective experiences, and Mason argues that these usually entail misunderstanding and possibly result in racism. The term 'ethnic minority' has also been seen to have potential problems, because it is used in reference to a group of people in a population whose cultural origins lie in another country and are therefore 'different'. However, not all 'ethnic' or 'minority' groups are perceived as 'ethnic minorities' – consider Polish (white European) immigrants.

'Ethnicity' as a concept has gained credibility because it recognizes the shortcomings of assimilationist assumptions (that all ethnic minorities should absorb themselves into the culture of the country in which they live) and accepts the permanence of these communities. It also avoids the biological determinism of 'race' by concentrating on culture and diversity.

Racism and racialism

'Race' and ethnicity as terms and concepts have the potential to clarify, yet also foster, racism and racialism. The concept of racism was first used as the title of a German book by Magnus Hirschfield in 1933 (Miles, 1993). However, it was not defined until the 1940s when Ruth Benedict (1943) used the term in reference to Nazi Germany:

. . . the dogma that one ethnic group is condemned by nature to congenital inferiority and another group is destined to congenital superiority.
(Solomos, 1993, p. 97)

Racism therefore involves racial prejudice, which is the holding of preconceived attitudes and beliefs about others and prejudging them on that basis, usu-

ally in a negative way. Racism is an ideology based on non-existent biological divisions (Miles, 1990). Mason saw it as:

. . . situations in which groups of people are hierarchically distinguished from one another on the basis of some notion of stock difference and where symbolic representations are mobilised which emphasise the social and cultural relevance of biologically rooted characteristics.
(Mason, 1995, p. 11)

This definition of racism brings in a notion of action, a concept involved more usually in racial discrimination or racialism, which is the behavioural manifestation of racial prejudice. Cashmore defined racialism as:

. . . the action of discriminating against particular others by using the belief that they are racially different, and usually inferior. It is the practical element of the race concept.
(Cashmore, 1983, p. 37)

Activity

Consider these two reported cases, cited by Jacobs (1988, pp. 116–17):

Five Asians were arrested following clashes between Asians and white youths in Spitalfields in London's East End. The fighting started after a white man was reported to have sprayed Bengali children with beer and called them 'Pakis'. Following disturbances, a number of shops in the area were damaged.

Two white youths were reported to have thrown a petrol bomb into an Asian family's home in Bradford. The youths, aged 16 and 15, told police that they had thrown the missile 'for fun' and admitted arson.

To what extent could the actions in these cases be perceived as racist?   I, E

Mason, however, has used the term 'racism' to encompass both racial prejudice and discrimination. In this sense racism becomes a relative concept, changing according to time, place and situation. As Cohen noted:

Racism has always been multi-dimensional and specific to different contexts.
(Cohen, 1988, p. 136)

It has been argued that a distinction between 'racism' and 'racialism' should be retained, because if 'racism' incorporates theory and ideology, while 'racialism' involves practice and behaviour, then each requires combating in different ways – possibly through socialization to change racism, or legislation to prevent racialism. 'Institutional racism' as a concept utilizes a general idea of racism, involving belief and behaviour, when it is seen as racial inequality within the structure of society. It involves treating ethnic minorities differently in social situations, such as employment, just because they are members of that minority group.

Activity

. . . there are aspects of national and international processes that have an indirect but fundamental impact on black people's housing situation, notably government immigration and housing policies, the structure and workings of the labour market, and the interactions between 'race' and other major lines of stratification, particularly class and gender. These processes may be described as structural racism, because they are not tangibly institutionalized in the local housing scene; they are institutionalized in the socioeconomic structure beyond immediate housing institutions.

(Ginsberg, 1992, p. 109)

a Explain 'structural racism' in your own words.
b Investigate how Marxists and Weberians would explain the disadvantaged position of black people in relation to housing. (You will find information on this in Sections 6.4 and 6.5.)

U, I, A

Nationalism

The term 'nationalism' also implies thoughts and actions when it suggests that national boundaries should coincide with ethnicity; that is, all those, and only those, who belong to an ethnic group should share a common territory. This incorporates racial prejudice and racial discrimination, because it relies on beliefs about national identity and ultimately on behaviour which reinforces boundaries.

In the UK nationalism has been intensified by the rise of 'new racism' (see Section 6.5), which has focused on the cultural incompatibility of ethnic minorities and indigenous populations. It stems from the idea of 'nation', which implies a distinct political territory linking people together, even though most of the population of a community do not know each other. This sense of 'nation' has been employed by Bradley (1996) as an explanation of 'race' and ethnicity in general:

'Race' and ethnicity are two of the social categories which have evolved to explain lived relationships which emanate from territorially based groups around the world.
(Bradley, 1996, p. 114)

It is argued that migration (by coercion and/or exploration) has mixed up groups of people from different territorial groupings and resulted in 'social pluralism', where a multitude of ethnic groups coexist. However, the term 'immigrant' (any person who has recently arrived from another society in which they have habitually lived) still carries the negative associations developed when the UK was a colonial power (see Section 6.2), quite often resulting in unequal treatment for the immigrant. (You will also find discussion of the sociological implications of nationalism in Sections 10.10, 16.8 and 17.6.)

'Black'

Racial and ethnic disadvantage has common themes, and it is argued that it is appropriate to use the term black for those who are victims of white racism/racialism. This idea has been challenged. Brah (1992) has argued that black people may have a similar structural position in post-war Britain (e.g. the lowest stratum in the socio-economic system), and experience similar racism, but the ideologies which racialized them were different. In other words the experiences of African–Caribbeans was very different from those of Asians. Brah concluded that the term black falsely homogenizes diverse groups. Modood (1988) and Hazareesingh (1986) both stated that black should only be used in reference to people of sub-Saharan African descent, because it has no cultural meaning to southern Asians. However, it might be proved that on this basis the term black would also ignore differences within African groups. (This issue is also discussed in Section 10.6.)

Black has varying meanings both historically and in a contemporary context. In the nineteenth century the colour black was a representation of evil; in the 1960s it represented political pride; and in a contemporary context being 'black' provides homogeneity as a political force or represents a basis for dividing ethnic minority groups. Consequently the notion of being black has been interpreted differently by sociologists, either as a tool for unifying oppressed ethnic minorities, or conversely as a way of concealing their differences. Brah realized that changing the term black would have few structural ramifications:

It is unlikely that replacing black by some other politically neutral description will secure more equitable distribution of resources.
(Brah, 1992, pp. 129–30)

Activity

In Britain there were no legal definitions of a black person, or legal restrictions on mixed marriages. This may have been in part because until the mid-1950s the number of black people in Britain was very small – never more than 15,000, often less. The few 'half-castes' were generally recognised by both black and white people as different from black. But they were stigmatised as much in Britain as elsewhere, perhaps more so, since they were usually born into the poorest sector of society, whilst in other countries they tended to be part of the intermediate class. ... Since the 1960s there have been major changes in both Britain and the USA that seem likely to have led to both black and mixed-parentage people developing more positive identities. The scientific discrediting of theories about the superiority of the white race, and the increasing liberalisation of white attitudes, have tended to reduce the stigma attached to being black or of mixed parentage.
(Tizard, 1994, p. 3)

Explain, in your own words, why Tizard thinks that black or 'half-caste' people are more likely to be stigmatized in the UK than elsewhere. In what ways does Tizard think this situation has changed since the 1960s?

Sociologists are therefore faced with the problem of occasions that necessitate a generic term to describe general processes of exclusion for certain sections of society.

In this chapter the term 'black' will be used to refer to all ethnic minorities who are not white when reference to historic countries of origin are not possible. The term black will not, however, appear in inverted commas because it is argued that it has been adopted by some ethnic minorities as a political identity (see Section 6.5) and should not be viewed in the same sense as 'race'. The term 'racism' will be used to refer to both racial prejudice and racial discrimination, unless otherwise stated.

6.2 The history of 'race relations' in the UK

Only by analysing the way in which history overlaps the present is it possible to understand the continuities and discontinuities between contemporary racial ideologies and previous forms.
(Solomos, 1993, p. 39)

An historical context of racial and ethnic divisions is necessary to understand the processes that produce and reproduce these social distinctions. It also enables us to understand contemporary social relationships.

However, many studies of 'race relations' in the UK after 1945 have a curious lack of historical and comparative analysis. This is strange because the UK's 'race relations' situation has been shaped by the complex migration and settlement structures of the past.

Black people in the UK

Black people have been in Britain since Roman times (Small, 1994). By 1596, Queen Elizabeth I was demanding the extradition of 'black infidels', partly as a response to economic pressures (see the box 'History of Black people in Britain: some important dates').

In the eighteenth century Asian immigrants found work in the UK in domestic service, as soldiers and as sailors. By the nineteenth century significant numbers of 'black professionals' were in the UK, such as the Lascars (Indian seamen employed by the East India Company). It should be noted, however, that

---

HISTORY OF BLACK PEOPLE IN BRITAIN: SOME IMPORTANT DATES

1596 Elizabeth I issues proclamation to send 'Blackmoores' out of England.

1772 Judge Mansfield rules black people cannot be forcibly removed from England.

1807 The Slave Trade is abolished in the British Empire.

1823 The 1823 Navigation Act denies Lascars the right to work on British ships, except in times of war.

1834–8 Slavery is abolished in the British Empire, with a five-year 'apprenticeship' system for the former slaves.

1892 Dadabhai Naoroji is the first Asian elected to House of Commons.

1919 Anti-Black riots in Liverpool in which Charles Wootton is murdered.

1925 The Special Restrictions (Coloured Alien Seamen) Order, prohibits Black British sailors from working on British ships, and forces some Black sailors born in Britain out of the country.

Source: *Small, S. Sociology Review*, April 1994

most black people ended up in England as slaves to become domestic servants. Solomos concluded that:

The historical presence of black communities within Britain can be traced back over several centuries. Black communities and individuals were a feature of British society and culture for centuries before the arrival of Asian and African–Caribbean immigrants after 1945.
(Solomos, 1993, p. 47)

Colonialism and migration

Historically, migration for conquest and warfare have established great empires, including Greece and Rome. European colonialism succeeded this and promoted intercontinental migration, which laid the basis for the racial and ethnic hierarchies which still characterize the post-colonial world. Pilkington (1988) and Bradley (1996) claim that the roots of contemporary racial divisions lie in the expansion of European empires, particularly during the eighteenth and nineteenth centuries when those empires straddled the world. The British empire extended to the Far East, but more significant was the occupation of India, Pakistan, large parts of Africa and several islands of the West Indies.

A key factor in laying the foundations for later racial conflict was the exploitation of Africans, especially West Africans, mainly through the slave trade. Slave traders, mainly from the UK, the United States, Spain and Portugal, bought and kidnapped Africans and transported them to the southern United States and the West Indies, where they were sold to work on plantations. It was believed by the imperialists that black people were somehow inferior savages who would benefit by being brought into the *civilized* world. This perception was used to justify imperialist behaviour and became the basis for the biological theories of 'race' being developed at that time (see Section 6.4). Therefore Bradley (1996) shows that colonialism and slavery can be seen as central to the formation of racist ideologies.

The UK's colonization policies had the long-term effect of promoting migration to 'the home country'. For example, the Jamaican economy had been geared to the needs of Britain, with profits from sugar being transferred to Britain, resulting in the under-development of that country. Migration to the UK was seen as a way in which Jamaicans could improve their situation. In India a similar process of under-development occurred. After the East India Company established trading posts in the seventeenth century, the British gradually took power. As in Jamaica, the economy was made to serve the needs of Britain. In fact, Britain used India as a 'crutch' when other countries were catching up economically. The conse-

quence was that India could not generate enough jobs for a rapidly growing population. Migration to the UK was again seen as a solution. (The impact of colonialism on social and economic development is also discussed in Section 12.3.)

The entry of Commonwealth subjects into the UK, who were considered of a 'different race', was restricted by legislation not only after 1945, but also before. An Act in 1813 made the East India Company responsible for providing subsistence to Indian sailors in Britain until they returned to India, while section 5(2) of the Alien Restriction (Amendment) Act 1919 legalized different rates of pay for British subjects employed as seamen according to their 'race'. Solomos (1993) argued that the state was responding to local racist agitation caused by unemployment and the fear that the seamen would reproduce with the indigenous women.

Irish migration

Similar restrictions were *not* placed on immigrants whose skin colour was 'white'. Take for, example, Irish migration to the UK in the late eighteenth and early nineteenth centuries. This was a period of rapid economic change, with the emergence of industrial capitalism so that European societies were transformed from rural agriculture to industrial bases. Mason (1995) realizes the importance of this time on migration patterns, arguing that it altered both 'the scale and character of international migration' (p. 21).

Less developed countries, such as Ireland, filled labour shortages in countries that were expanding rapidly. In the UK, urbanization and class formation resulted in a demand for new sources of labour. At the same time in Ireland people were being ejected from their land. Early Irish migration to the UK took on a seasonal pattern, with Irish peasant farmers planting their crops before seeking work in the UK to meet rising rent demands. It also supported the development of the infrastructure in building and road construction. The potato famine in Ireland in 1845 consolidated this migration and led to the formation of Irish communities in the UK with identifiable cultural differences.

Over the past two centuries the number of Irish migrants to the UK has been in excess of any other migrants, yet there has been little state response to this (especially relative to black migration). This can be partly explained by the 1800 Act of Union, which incorporated Ireland into the UK and gave the Irish common citizenship. This 'union' has been maintained through the formation of the Republic of Ireland in 1922, the exit of the Irish republic from the Commonwealth in 1947, and the British Nationality Act of 1948 (which gave citizens of the Republic of Ireland freedom to enter, settle, work and vote in the UK).

Emigration 'poses huge danger to Irish health'

Cal McCrystal

IRISH immigrants die earlier and suffer from alarmingly high rates of disease in their adopted countries, studies in Britain, the United States, Canada and Australia have revealed. North American surveys show they experience increases in mortality rate for every disease – including cancers and diseases of the respiratory system.

The report, 'Migration and Health in the Nineties' by the International Organisation for Migration, says: 'For those diseases where an increase in mortality rates was expected, there was a substantial overshoot past the mortality level of US whites. For those diseases where a decrease was expected, the Irish exhibited patterns of divergence; that is, there were large increases in mortality.'

So alarming are the statistics that a flurry of studies are under way, among them one in Liverpool funded by the Economic and Social Research Council (ESRC), another in Glasgow backed by the Medical Research Council and a third by London's Guildhall University. The results of a fourth were published a week ago in the *British Medical Journal*. It revealed that first-generation Irish immigrants in England and Wales had a death rate higher than the average for the host countries by about 30 per cent for men and 20 per cent for women.

Most puzzling of all was the discovery that second-generation Irish in these countries were also unhealthier than the general population – 'a cause for concern', the *BMJ* said.

Professor Maggie Pearson, of the University of Liverpool's Institute of Celtic Studies, who has just completed the ESRC report, said last week: 'We can define the problem, but we are still unable to explain it.'

She and others, including psychiatrists, have considered the possibility that an unusually high cancer rate among migrant Irish – far higher than the Irish in Ireland – might be brought on by racist attitudes in the host country.

Sociologist Seamus Taylor, chairman of the London-based Action Group for Irish Youth, says that anti-Irish feeling is exacerbated 'every time an IRA bomb goes off'.

Such a view appeared to be supported by the *BMJ* report. It suggested that the Troubles in Northern Ireland and a 'negative perception of Irishness might have created cultural pressures on the Irish to become English'.

This was the case with Mr Taylor's aunts, both nurses in England. 'It got to the point where they wouldn't read an Irish newspaper on the Tube,' he said. 'So they tried to recreate themselves as lower middle-class English women.'

Yet the *BMJ* report acknowledges studies of second-generation Irish children also showed a resistance to the process of assimilation. The studies were of second-generation Irish aged 15 or over in England and Wales in 1971 who died in the subsequent 18 years.

Socio-economic disadvantage, which may have predisposed first-generation Irish towards higher levels of mortality, was 'not the full explanation. There seem to be other important elements of being Irish that influence their patterns of morbidity and mortality, although what these are ... remains unclear.'

The British study found excess mortality for most causes of death, but it was particularly high for tuberculosis, diseases of the respiratory and digestive systems, certain malignant tumours and for external causes of injuries and poisonings (including accidents and violence).

Source: *The Observer*, 9 June 1996

It would appear, then, that the British government has maintained a policy of control against those migrants who are noticeably different, such as by skin colour. However, it should be remembered that although legislation has allowed free access to Irish immigrants, hostile responses and inequalities have been experienced by the Irish in Britain (as the article from *The Observer* shows). This racism is based upon anti-Irish images in popular culture which represent the Irish Celts as biologically inferior (Curtis, 1968), as well as on the self-definition of the 'English'. However, 'white' images of 'English' uniqueness and purity have shaped political debates about migration in general, and they have had particular effects on black migration and settlement (Solomos, 1993).

Black migration after 1945

Black migration and settlement in the early twentieth century resulted in the formation of domestic ideologies and policies towards 'coloured workers' and their communities. Racial difference played a central role in the politics of immigration, despite the relatively small size of the black population and the fact of their right to citizenship:

By the Second World War there was already a long historical experience of political debate and mobilisation around issues of ethnicity, 'race' and religion. (Solomos, 1993, p. 51)

Black workers helped in the war effort, and soldiers from the colonies fought in the British army.

After World War II, migration by ex-colonized citizens, 'black' and 'white', was a response to labour

Activity

The article 'Emigration "poses huge danger to Irish health"' suggests that Irish migrants experience worse health and premature mortality when living in another country. Make a list of the reasons given in the article for this phenomenon. Can you suggest other possible causes for Irish migrant ill-heath and early death?

Figure 6.1 Indian soldiers fighting as part of the British army in Burma in World War II.

shortages in the UK and their hope for a better life. In fact, most migrants arriving in the UK between 1945 and 1954 were from other European countries (e.g. Polish exiles totalled 157 300 by 1954). However, the British society responded predictably to the situation and placed tight controls on the arrival of black migrants, making calls for repatriation based on images of black communities as sources of social problems. White migrants, however, were treated in a *laissez-faire* manner. Therefore it becomes quite clear that the government perceived black migration in a different way from white European migration, hoping to stop the former. As Solomos notes:

Privately the government was considering the most desirable method of discouraging or preventing the arrival of 'coloured' British citizens from the colonies.
(Solomos, 1993, p. 56)

Immigration legislation

In 1948, the Labour government introduced the British Nationality Act, which established the right of all citizens of Commonwealth countries to enter the UK to work and to settle. The government encouraged white immigrants from Europe, who received very little media coverage. However, the arrival of 417 Jamaicans on *The Empire Windrush*

in May 1948 was splashed over the tabloids and portrayed as a problem.

It may have been legal for all Commonwealth citizens to enter the UK between 1948 and 1962, but both Labour and Conservative governments took a number of measures to discourage black immigration. The 1958 Notting Hill and Nottingham riots helped to publicize and politicize the image of black immigrants as 'undesirables' whose numbers should be controlled. This resulted in state intervention under the Conservative government's Commonwealth Immigration Act of 1962, which limited British entry to those either born in Britain, holding a British passport, people included on a British passport, people with work permits and/or close relatives. In reference to this legislation, William Deedes, then minister in a Conservative cabinet, stated:

The Bill's real purpose was to restrict the influx of coloured immigrants. We were reluctant to say as much openly. So the restrictions were applied to coloured and white citizens in all Commonwealth countries – though everybody recognised that immigration from Canada, Australia and New Zealand formed no part of the problem.
(Deedes, 1968, p. 10)

The Labour Party supported immigration controls. From 1964 to 1970, when a Labour government was in power, they became forced on to the defensive about immigration policies. Enoch Powell's 'Rivers of Blood' speech in Birmingham in 1968 (see box below) called for strict control on immigration and for repatriation. He popularized the argument that the UK would have the same racial tensions as the USA if something was not done by the British government.

Activity

As I look ahead, I am filled with foreboding. Like the Roman, I seem to see 'the River Tiber foaming with much blood'. The tragic and intractable phenomenon which we watch with horror on the other side of the Atlantic, but which there is interwoven with the history and existence of the States itself, is coming upon us here by our own violation and our neglect.
(Enoch Powell in *The Observer*, 21 April 1968)

a Explain Powell's speech in your own words.
b Investigate the extent to which views like Powell's are present in state legislation on 'race relations'.

I, A, E

In 1969, Labour introduced the Immigration Appeals Act, which gave the right of appeal to special tribunals, but placed further restrictions on entry by limiting the number of dependants who could enter. On one level this seemed positive, but in reality it meant that the government could now practise deportation when conditions of entry were broken.

The Conservative's Immigration Act in 1971 qualified the notion of citizenship. Patrials (anyone with at least one British grandparent, or who had been naturalized, or had lived five years in Britain) could enter freely. Anyone closely related to them, or who had been resident in Britain before 1973, or who was an Irish or EEC citizen, had right of entry. All other immigrants needed permits, which were usually short-term work permits. The 1971 Immigration Act has been seen as a founding stone in institutionalizing racist immigration controls:

The 1971 Act eventually took away the right of black commonwealth immigrants to settle, and this represented an important step in the institutionalisation of racist immigration controls.
(Solomos, 1993, p. 70)

From 1979 onwards the Conservatives based their 'race relations' legislation on the philosophy that black communities threatened British social and cultural values (see Section 6.5). Controls on immigration were heightened even further with the 1981 Nationality Act. This Act constructed nationality along racial lines, in that citizenship was only given to those who were either settled in the UK already, or those with one British parent who were registered abroad at birth. Those with British passports who had lived abroad and had no recent connection or residence in the UK would not be allowed to enter and settle. The Immigration Act of 1988 imposed the 'independent of public fund' test on those dependants of people who had settled before 1973. Public funds are defined as income support, housing benefit, family credit, council tax benefit and housing under the homeless persons provisions of housing legislation. Any immigrant must satisfy the authorities that they can live without recourse to public funds – they must be able to maintain and accommodate themselves and any dependants adequately in accommodation they own or occupy exclusively. (This issue is also discussed in Section 14.4.)

In 1993 the UK government enacted the Asylum and Immigration Appeals Act. This established a narrow interpretation of the British government's obligation towards refugees and asylum seekers. The Act did provide a right of appeal to all asylum seekers, but also introduced curtailed appeal procedures for many categories of asylum seekers. It also placed major restrictions on the housing rights of asylum

Activity

The following extract is from the Citizens Advice Bureau publication *A Right to Family Life* (March 1996):

A British man had married a Pakistani woman in Pakistan. The man was now working in the UK and earning £90 per week. He lived in a three bedroomed house which he owned himself, and on which there was no mortgage. The entry clearance officer refused the application on the grounds that there was no adequate support available without recourse to public funds. The case went to appeal, where more evidence was produced regarding the man's job and savings – which were looked after by the man's mother, who lived next door. The adjudicator dismissed the appeal because he was not satisfied that the man's savings would be used to support him and his wife, as he would also be supporting his mother.

a Which test in which immigration Act is being applied to the case above?
b To what extent does this example support the idea that there has been a divorce between being British and being entitled to the rights of British citizens?

I, E

seekers. It had an immediate effect on those detained while seeking asylum.

In March 1994, more than 9000 asylum seekers and other immigrants were incarcerated in British prisons and detention centres. In the month following the Act, the number of detentions doubled (Skellington, 1996). In July 1994 the Runnymede Trust revealed that refusals of entry rose from 14 per cent of decisions to 74 per cent after the Act. It is ironic that in the summer of 1994 the government announced new immigration rules designed to target migrant millionaires from Hong Kong and South Africa. It was hoped that they could be encouraged to buy their way into Britain, fast-tracking them through the system in order to attract investment (*The Independent*, 25 May 1994). The state once again reaffirmed its stance that some migrants are more welcome than others.

The 1995 Asylum and Immigration Bill proposed a further series of restrictions to the rights of asylum seekers, including additional restrictions on appeal rights, further cuts in housing and social security entitlement, and the creation of a 'safe list' of countries from which asylum is not deemed necessary.

Table 6.1 Entry clearance applications for temporary purposes

Country	USA	Jamaica	Africa	Indian sub-continent
Successful applications	56 280	2650	114 840	152 070
Refusals	130	910	20 450	23 510
Refusals as a percentage of successful applications	0.23	34.34	17.81	15.46

Source: *A Right to Family Life* (Citizens' Advice Bureau, 1996)

Activity

Study Table 6.1 before answering the following questions:

a Identify in the table the country with the highest and lowest refusal rates for temporary entry into the UK.

b Make a list of the possible reasons for the wide divergence in refusal rates between Africa/the Indian subcontinent/Jamaica and the USA.

c Assess the following statement: 'This table can be seen as an example of "race relations" legislation having racist consequences'.

I, A, E

Alan Travis (1996c) wrote in *The Guardian* that the government has had a 'crackdown on illegal immigrants and asylum seekers', figures for deportation notices being 20 per cent higher than the previous year. According to Mason:

It is no accident that the clearly consistent theme of immigration and citizenship legislation since 1962 has been a distinction between those who were thought of as 'white' and those who were not. Each successive measure sought to close the door to dark skinned potential migrants, while keeping it open to 'whites' from the countries of the Old Commonwealth and South Africa.

(Mason, 1995, p. 31)

Protective 'race relations' legislation

'Race relations' legislation which attempts to avoid racial discrimination in the UK has been relatively toothless in removing or abating racial discrimination. Massive inequalities still exist for Britain's ethnic minorities.

The 1965 Race Relations Act (enacted by a Labour government) made it a crime to discriminate on the grounds of colour, race or ethnic origin, in provid-

ing goods, facilities or services. It also established the Race Relations Board to monitor the Act and advise complainants. The 1968 Race Relations Act (also Labour) gave more power to the Board and established the Community Relations Committee (CRC), whose job it was to advise the government and foster better 'race relations' in the community. The 1976 Race Relations Act (also Labour) broadened the scope of legislation further and included the restriction of practices which, irrespective of intention, had the effect of discriminating against ethnic minorities – such as rigorous language qualifications for manual jobs. It also merged the Race Relations Board with the CRC to become the Commission for Racial Equality (CRE), which had powers to formally investigate and prosecute offenders under the Act. In addition, it banned positive discrimination in favour of ethnic minorities.

In 1981 the Scarman Report called for more anti-discrimination legislation in the UK, but not much has been done in the intervening years.

The history of government measures outlawing discrimination and promoting racial harmony is hardly an unqualified success. It is difficult to prove racial discrimination, expensive to pursue and the penalties for offenders are very small (which in itself is not much of a deterrent). The British government has never endorsed a notion of a truly multi-cultural society; it has instead responded, historically and contemporarily, to racist demands. A series of immigration laws have been passed which enshrine racist assumptions. For example, black immigrants are seen as a problem whose numbers must be limited. Harsh enforcement of immigration laws convinces 'confused' white people that they were correct to listen to racist discourse. It would seem appropriate to conclude that throughout Britain's history the state has reinforced racialism, by the maintenance and perpetuation of practices that support racist ideology, with only half-hearted attempts to cover their beliefs (Richardson and Lambert, 1985; Dummett and Dummett, 1982).

6.3 Theories and research on 'race' and ethnicity – an overview

Theories and research in the USA

Academic enquiry into 'race' and ethnicity began by focusing on scientific differences (see Section 6.4), but when these were discredited social scientific investigations started to take place. Bradley concluded that:

There has been a growing interest in the study of 'race' and ethnicity in Britain over the course of the twentieth century.
(Bradley, 1996, p. 143)

In the USA in the 1920s, Robert Park established the study of 'race relations'. He focused on the social and economic inequalities experienced by black people, their cultural and psychological backgrounds, their family relationships and political isolation. In 1944 Gunnar Myrdal foresaw, through documenting the history of inequality in the United States, the assimilation of the American black population into mainstream society. Assimilation is defined by Lawson and Garrod as:

. . . a view of 'race relations' which sees the host community as culturally homogeneous and the task of the immigrant community is to be absorbed into the host community as quickly as possible, by adopting host features. Sensitivity to cultural differences is minimal so that ethnic minority culture is disparaged.
(Lawson and Garrod, 1996, p. 14)

This work developed ideas on racial conflict and their origins and became known as the assimilation model. It enabled social scientists to see that 'race' became important only after cultural and social meanings were attached to the physical traits of a particular group.

Theories and research in the UK

Theorising and research into 'race' and ethnicity in the UK began in the 1940s. It then concentrated on immigration and the role of colonialization in creating popular conceptions on colour and 'race' (Glass, 1960). Marxist and Weberian perspectives were developed to examine these areas, focusing largely on concepts of class.

In the 1950s and 1960s, Glass (1960), Rex and Moore (1967) and Patterson (1963) carried out studies into 'race relations', concentrating on interactions between minority and majority communities in employment, housing and other social contexts. However, it has been noted that there was a lack of clear theoretical perspective about the object of analysis (Solomos, 1993). Consequently, in the 1960s problematic 'race relations' became the dominant area of research.

The 1970s

As all good students of sociology know, a theoretical perspective can dictate how research is carried out. Therefore, the absence of a clear theoretical approach can make research confusing or ambiguous. In the 1970s the work of John Rex provided a theory of 'race relations' in the UK, defining it in a structural sense based on conflict over scarce resources and conditions of exploitation and occupational segregation.

Later, Rex and Tomlinson's (1979) study of Handsworth discovered that immigrants held a place outside that of the working class in employment; they were seen as an 'underclass' who occupied the lowest stratum in society, resulting in discrimination in education and housing. Their examination of blacks as an 'underclass' established a model of political action, raising the issue of politics and racism. (The 'underclass' debate is also examined in Section 4.8.)

The 1980s

The 1970s saw class and social differentiation on racial/ethnic grounds as the major theoretical theme. However, in the 1980s criticism of Marxist ideology began to emerge based on three factors:

- Marxism's reliance on class obscures any analysis of racial/ethnic phenomena in their own right. This issue became the focus of important debates.
- It provided little historical or theoretical reflection on the role of slavery/colonialism etc. in the capitalist mode of production.
- Marxist's work showed use of dormant racial stereotypes and uncritical use of racist imagery.

Miles (1984) offered a debate on the Marxist framework, initiating a more theoretical investigation into 'race' and ethnicity. He viewed the analysis of racism as integral to capitalism and examined it via its political, class and ideological relationships. He concluded that 'race' is a human construct which hides real economic relationships. Therefore racism is a consequence of:

. . . on the one hand the need of the capitalist world economy for the mobility of human beings, and on the other the drawing of territorial boundaries and the construction of citizenship as a legal category which sets boundaries for human mobility.
(Miles, 1988, p. 438)

For Miles, 'racial identities' are ideologically constructed by the state in order to fragment the working class racially and reduce class conflict.

Concern with the ideological and cultural dimensions of 'racism' opened the way for the Centre for Contemporary Cultural Studies (CCCS) in Birmingham, which offered a contemporary analysis of 'race' and ethnicity. The CCCS was concerned with the changing nature of politics and 'race', and *The Empire Strikes Back* (1982) analysed the social and political construction of 'race'. This type of investigation into 'racism' did not occur in the United States for another decade, when Omi and Winant (1994) examined the processes of 'race formation' and the influence of political and legal relations on these.

The 1980s also saw the development of national quantitative data on ethnic minorities in the UK, which has not been freely available before, as Gordon acknowledged:

Until the mid 1980s relatively little statistical information about minority ethnic group people in Britain was collated at a national level or, indeed, in any systematic way.
(Gordon, 1996, p. 22)

Before the 1980s virtually no relevant national data was collected regularly on education, health, housing, welfare, social services, the criminal justice system, policing or racial violence. Therefore it was virtually impossible to know the extent of racial disadvantage or discrimination. The available sources were:

- the national Census, carried out every ten years but only providing direct data on ethnicity since 1991
- immigration data
- the Labour Force Survey, carried out every two years.

Organizations within the fields of 'race relations' wanted statistical data to back up their arguments on racial inequalities in the UK.

However, it must be remembered that 'racial groups' which are used in statistics are social constructions, rather than objective scientific categories, and that this can affect the collection of 'racialized data'. For example, the 1991 Census gave respondents nine 'race' categories to choose from, resulting in very different information based on changed perceptions of 'race groupings'

This problem of creating suitable categories has been impossible to overcome, with some institutions appearing to produce racial identifications in a racist manner. For example, Anthias and Yuval-Davis (1993) argued that the police have carried out ethnic monitoring using a visual assessment of 'racial' physical characteristics, such as colour of skin, type of hair and nose shape. Therefore their 'monitoring' is neither objective (country of origin), nor a classi-

Activity

In March 1982, the Metropolitan Police issued its statistics on crimes recorded in London in 1981. The figures highlighted two things. First, an 8 per cent rise in serious crime over the previous year and, second, an increase in 'mugging' and the alleged disproportionate involvement of black people in this crime. The figures stated that the 'appearance of the assailant' had been described as white by just under 5000 victims, but as 'coloured' by more than 10,000. This was the first occasion on which police statistics had been racialized in this way.
(Gordon, 1996, p. 29)

Prepare the arguments for *both* sides of the following debate:

- 'We believe that the police perpetuate racist beliefs by issuing statistics on crime and "race".'

This activity will involve your sociological understanding of 'race' and ethnicity in relation to crime, deviance and research methods.

K, U, I, A, E

fication based on the people's own perception of their ethnic identity.

However, researchers have generally attempted to improve categories by including a mixture of 'racial', national and ethnic classifications. The 1991 Census referred to 'race' (skin colour), nationality (Indian/Pakistani etc.) and ethnicity.

It has been argued that data on ethnicity, despite the usual methodological problems (some of which are discussed in Section 3.11), is useful on three levels:

1 *Fact-finding* – General observations can be made about 'race' and ethnicity.

Activity

First read the article 'Will ethnic data promote equality?' and then respond to the following:

a Draw up a table of the main arguments put forward in this article, (a) for and (b) against ethnic monitoring in education.

b Add points of your own to the table based on other sources.

c Evaluate the arguments surrounding the inclusion of questions on ethnic minorities in official statistics.

K, U, I, A, E

Will ethnic data promote equality?

PETER FOSTER

In an edited letter (*TES*, May 3) Herman Ouseley argues strongly in favour of ethnic monitoring in schools. This proposal is not new. It was recommended 11 years ago in the Swann Report. Indeed, in the late 1980s the Government appeared to support the idea, and Department of Education and Science's Circular 16/89 required local education authorities and grant-maintained schools to collect information on pupils' ethnic backgrounds on entry.

This commitment was abandoned last year. The Department for Education and Employment has been extremely reticent about the reasons for the change, but it seems the data has been difficult to collect and returns from LEAs have been inconsistent and unreliable. I also suspect that certain ministers have been reluctant to become associated with a racial equality policy reminiscent of certain left-wing councils of the 1980s. However, continued evidence from sample surveys and LEAs of differentials in attainment between ethnic groups has raised again the question of whether data on ethnic origin should be routinely collected. It might be hopeful, therefore, to review the arguments.

First, what benefits might such a policy bring? There is no doubt it would allow much more valid comparisons of the educational achievement levels of pupils from different ethnic groups. Currently it is difficult to judge the representativeness of information from sample surveys and individual LEAs, and therefore to form a broader national picture.

Large-scale data collection would also permit more differentiated comparisons, looking for example, at ethnic groups which are numerically small, or at sub-groups within ethnic groups, such as gender or social class.

Data on a national scale would also facilitate more sophisticated comparisons, not only of average levels of achievement, but also of the distribution of individual achievements within groups. Such within-group differences are frequently neglected in the analysis of current data. If data were collected when pupils enter school it would also allows schools, LEAs and the DFEE to compare not only educational achievements, but also the educational progress of students from different ethnic groups.

Finally, ethnic data would enable administrators to identify the location of pupils from different ethnic groups more accurately, and to target resources should this be desired.

But there are also significant limitations in what can be done with ethnic data, and problems in its collection. Sometimes it is argued that the collection of ethnic data will enable the identification of racial discrimination in education. Unfortunately, this is not the case. Inequalities in educational outcomes (achievement or progress) between ethnic groups at school, LEA or national level may be the result of discrimination, but equally they may be the result of factors external to the school or system. We cannot assume racial discrimination from unequal outcomes.

Ethnic data tells us little about the causes of any inequality between groups, and thus little about what might be done to rectify it. To argue, as Herman Ouseley does, that where an inequality is discovered "resources can be directed and strategies for improvement implemented", is simplistic. This suggests that inequality is necessarily iniquitous, and that remedial resources or strategies can easily be identified and uncontroversially put in place by policy-makers and teachers. If the continued presence, despite educational reform, of social class inequalities in education has taught us anything, it is that things are not so simple.

Another limitation in the use of ethnic data is that it tends to encourage the view that the education system is working as it should as long as the average achievement levels of pupils from different ethnic groups are the same. But this, too, may not be the case. Students from one ethnic group may achieve on a par with those in another even though they have been treated less favourably, because they have been able to overcome such treatment by commitment and hard work or as a result of a better ability profile.

Moreover, equal ethnic group outcomes may occur even though individuals and sub-groups within the broader group do badly. In short, broad ethnic group comparisons may mask significant inequities and we would be foolish therefore to rely on them.

Another problem relates to people's perceptions of the collection of ethnic data. Despite the efforts of the Commission for Racial Equality and some LEAs to convince parents and teachers that such data will be used benignly, some remain suspicious. Ethnic minority parents sometimes feel that the information may be used to stereotype and discriminate against their children.

Some white parents are also sceptical because they think that information may be used to favour ethnic minority children. Some teachers are wary because they feel that placing children into broad ethnic groups yields little additional information to enable them to cater more effectively for individual pupils' needs. These worries mean that the collection of ethnic data at school level is by no means straightforward or uncontroversial.

It also has costs. Reliable and consistent systems must be developed; they must be explained to schools and parents; the data must be requested from parents; if forthcoming it must be compiled by schools and supplied to LEAs, the DFEE and perhaps examination boards; these bodies in turn will have to conduct analyses, and supply composite information to policy-makers and practitioners.

Whilst these costs are not enormous we must decide whether they are justified given the benefits which ethnic data could bring.

Peter Foster is senior lecturer in education at Manchester Metropolitan University.

Source: *Times Educational Supplement*, 17 May 1996

2 *Informing government policy* – Data collected can assist in creating legislation.

3 *Social reform* – Using the data, areas can be identified where ethnic minorities may be subject to discrimination. Then policies can be implemented to promote equal opportunities.

However, it must be remembered that *all* statistics are open to misuse by way of an alternative interpretation. A government, for example, could use secondary data for purposes other than for which it was intended – information on client problems during migration could be used to tighten immigration controls. Gordon is clear to point out both the advantages and the disadvantages of collecting racialised data, but concludes that it is justifiable as a route to removing racial disadvantage:

The collection of ethnic data is not an end to itself but a means to an end: that of implementing equal opportunities and racial equality.
(Gordon, 1996, p. 41)

The 1990s

A key concern of studies in the UK on 'race' and ethnicity has been the need to develop ideas of racialization and its effects on politics and ideology. New theories are emerging, such as post-Marxism and post-modernism (see Section 2.10), which avoid a homogenous conceptualization of 'race' and ethnicity, with the differences within ethnic minority groups being emphasized. These contemporary theories have broadened studies on ethnicity, focusing on identities, the inter-connections between 'race' and nationhood, nationalism, cultural practices and racial discourses in post-colonial society (Gilroy, 1987; Phizacklea, 1983; Anthias and Yuval-Davis, 1993; see also Section 6.5 and Chapter 10)

The study of 'race relations' is politically charged and results in different theories, 'making imperialist demands to command the whole field to the exclusion of all other theories' (Rex, 1988, p. 64). However, as Solomos notes:

Not one theoretical perspective is dominant at the present time.
(Solomos, 1993, p. 36)

This could be attributed to the way in which the separate theories complement each other, rather than discredit each other. Rex (1988) highlighted three areas where potentially contradictory theories could support general investigation into 'race' and ethnicity:

• different theories deal with different kind of issues
• different perspectives may see the same issue in a different way

• different approaches may operate on different levels of abstraction, such as macro and micro levels.

Sociological approaches to 'race' and ethnicity are complex and variable. Contemporary perspectives may have arisen from previous theories, but they have progressed a great deal from the classical approaches which concentrated mainly on biology, industrial development and cultural assimilation – although a recent resurgence in biological examinations of 'race' and ethnicity has stunned the social scientific world (Herrnstein and Murray, 1994).

6.4 Classical approaches to 'race' and ethnicity

Biological approaches

Rapid social changes from the 1600s onwards ultimately resulted in industrialization, and with this came scientific explanations for natural and social phenomena (see also Section 2.2). Europeans began to have greater contact with other human societies and were aware of the physical differences in appearance, especially skin colour. 'White' skin and 'black' skin became associated with the qualities that colour suggested in the Christian Bible: 'white' for good and pure, 'black' for bad and corrupt (Jordan, 1974). The expansion of science sparked off quests to explain human differences.

The concept of 'race' emerged amidst European domination of the 'unknown world' in the eighteenth and nineteenth centuries. As Mason points out:

Race and ethnicity are modern concepts. They have their origins in the global expansion of European societies which gathered pace from the late 15th century onwards.
(Mason, 1995, p. 5)

The term 'race' was first used, however, in the English language in 1508 in a poem by William Dunbar (Banton, 1987). Science began to characterize human diversity, and by the mid-nineteenth century divisions had been drawn between separate 'races' based on biological and heritage differences. This displaced biblical teachings, which implied that all humans were basically equal, being descendants of Adam and Eve (Banton, 1987).

Phenotypes

In 1839 an American doctor, Samuel James Morton, developed a 'new' approach to 'race' which attempted to distinguish racial groups based on physiological characteristics (phenotypes). He measured the sizes of skulls of potentially different groups and concluded that five 'races' were evident through noticeable and relevant size differences. For example the average cubic capacity of an English skull was 96 cubic inches, compared with 82 for a Chinese skull. His five racial groups were:

- Caucasian (Europeans, Indians, some North Africans and people in the Middle East)
- Mongolian (Chinese and Eskimos)
- Malay (Malaysians and Polynesians)
- American (native Americans from the North and South)
- Ethiopian (sub-Saharan Africans).

Morton, however, related skull size and cranial capacity to intelligence, resulting in the claim that Europeans were more intellectually advanced than other 'races'. His 'scientific' approach has been criticized on many levels, such as the use of averages and the fact that skull size could be a response to diet (Gould, 1981). Linking brain size to intelligence remains totally unsubstantiated. Darwin's ideas of natural selection were incorrectly utilized by Social Darwinism in the nineteenth century, which claimed that all human groups struggle for survival, so the dominant groups must be the fittest or superior. Herbert Spencer wrote at this time that social evolution could define 'races' and consequently societies could consist of one 'race', but often consisted of a mixture of 'races'. The degree to which a society developed was influenced, according to Spencer, by 'race', some being superior to others.

Activity

The typical African of his 'race'-type is a happy, thriftless, excitable person lacking in self-control, discipline and foresight, naturally courageous, and naturally courteous and polite, full of personal vanity, with little sense of veracity, fond of music, and 'loving weapons as an oriental loves jewelry'.
(Lugard, 1929; quoted in Miles, 1989, p 103)

Make a list of the ways in which biological theories of 'race' and ethnicity may, judging from the one above, have caused or exacerbated the view that there are natural and innate differences between 'races'. Consider the extent to which the sentiments of this article are still evident today.

I, A, E,

Genotypes

As notions of 'race' based on phenotype were undermined, another biological criterion emerged. Genotypical differences (those based on different genetic structures) were used as an explanation for categorizing 'races'. It was argued that different 'races' had different genetic make-up which predisposed them to being superior or inferior.

Steven Jones (1991), a geneticist, found some differences between human groups – Europeans, for example, were able to hold their drink better than the Japanese, because of the different enzymes produced by their livers. However, he does not see this as a scientific basis for grouping people by 'race'. He concludes that people are divided by many things – culture, language, skin colour – and that 'race' is just another social construction for differentiating groups. This rationale has not stopped contemporary sociologists and sociobiologists from attempting to explain 'race' and ethnicity from a genotypical basis.

Contemporary applications of biological approaches

Kohn (1995) has argued that 'race' is a biologically meaningful concept, because humans come in different types which constitute a 'race gallery'. He states that this is not a racist claim, merely a scientific appreciation of 'real' human biological diversity. However, he is critical of sociologists who associate biological characteristics with social and cultural abilities, such as Herrnstein and Murray.

Herrnstein and Murray (1994) brought back into the 'race' and ethnicity debate the idea of social inequalities between ethnic groups being biologically based. Their 'New Right' publication, *The Bell Curve: Intelligence and Class Structure in American Life*, attempts to explain the inferior position held by some individuals and groups in America in terms of lower intelligence caused largely by genetic make-up. They claim that black people are concentrated at the lower end of the intelligence curve – scoring, on average, 15 IQ points behind whites – and that this is the main cause of growing poverty and unemployment. They emphasize biological inheritance as the main factor of IQ differences, arguing that environmental differences have been mostly solved, making social causes practically irrelevant. Despite Herrnstein and Murray's claims that 'a person should not be judged as a member of a group, but as an individual' (p. 550) and the fact that they insist on separating themselves from their unspoken conclusion – that black people's genes are the cause of social problems – their book still evoked an avalanche of criticism because of its racist connotations, as Richardson astutely recognized:

. . . some reviewers felt that publication of the book was likely to contribute to racism by giving bogus 'scientific' support to notions of racial superiority and inferiority.
(Richardson, 1996, pp. 68–9)

Steven Gould (1995), a biologist, has put forward a critique of Herrnstein and Murray's work. He argues that all the key biological assumptions in *The Bell Curve* were incorrect. Intelligence cannot be predicted by an IQ score alone (as Herrnstein and Murray tried to do), it is multi-dimensional. Therefore it is impossible to use IQ to rank people. Also, their idea that 60 per cent of differences in intelligence can be linked to genetics is considered wrong, because academics largely agree that only a small percentage of intelligence rests on hereditary factors (Rose, 1984). Social factors are agreed upon as making the largest contribution to intelligence (Gardner, 1995). (The debate about IQ tests and intelligence is covered in more detail in Section 8.9.)

Sociobiology

These arguments have not deterred sociobiologists, who believe that social behaviour does have a biological cause. Van den Berghe realized that this perspective was not widely accepted:

> . . . *I knew my book was touching on practically every raw nerve in the Social Sciences, since I had the audacity not only to espouse the label of Sociobiology but also to apply it to the most burning ideological issues of our time: race ethnicity and, in another book, sex.*
> (Van den Berghe, 1988, p. 246)

Van den Berghe had argued that it is the ideological connotations of sociobiology which make it distasteful (i.e. that black people are inferior), but he claims to have disassociated himself from any ideology in order to explore the issues scientifically and objectively. However, as shown in Chapter 3 of this book, scientific approaches do not necessarily equate with objectivity, all people (including sociobiologists) being products of their environment.

Van den Berghe described his approach as a mixture of biology interacting with culture to govern behaviour:

> *It is an interaction model in which genes, biotic and physical environments and, in the human case, culture always interacts to produce behaviour.*
> (Van den Berghe, 1988, p. 257)

Van den Berghe (1982) argued that ethnicity is linked to kinship, both of which are based on genetic predispositions to ensure survival of our own genes. He explains domination of 'racially inferior' groups in biological terms – the dominant group is merely that which emerges with the 'fittest' genes. Evolutionary success is therefore based on reproductive success, and this, he argues, is based on human behaviour and culture. He accepts that culture is not genetically transmitted, but that if humans did not reproduce, then culture would not carry on. Culture, therefore, is allowed to continue and develop initially because of humans' genetic ability for mental capacity and hence being able to generate and perpetuate it.

Sociobiology offers a gloomy forecast for reducing disadvantages based on ethnicity, since it argues that 'selfish genes' (Dawkins, 1976) will always exist and that this behaviour is rational. Sociologists, as sociobiologists are aware, largely reject the idea that 'ethnic' behaviour is determined by genetic make-up, but the New Right have adopted some of these notions into 'new racism' (Taylor *et al.*, 1995) (see Section 6.5). The 1990s has seen a worrying reemergence of biological explanations for 'racial' and ethnic differences, but sociologists and natural scientists alike give them little, if any, credibility.

Conclusion

'Race', as a scientific phenomenon, was examined by the United Nations after the Second World War, because of the racist nature of Nazism. Biologists and social scientists analysed the meaning of 'race' and concluded that humans had a single origin and were distinguishable only on the basis of physical characteristics such as skin colour, but that even these overlapped. Psychological and behavioural differences were found not to correlate with physical ones (O'Donnell, 1991). Therefore the notion of 'race' has been scientifically discredited for at least 50 years.

Sociologists, on the whole, now accept that 'racial groups' are socially rather than biologically created. Most reject concepts which perceive real differences (especially intelligence) between 'races'. 'Race' is recognized as a social construction, a term used in popular language based on ideology and myth to differentiate – usually in a disparaging way – between people who appear different.

Marxism

Marxism is characterized by three central beliefs (Pilkington, 1984):

- the economy is of primary importance
- class conflict is central to any social analysis
- ultimately this conflict will result in an egalitarian society.

However, the history of Marxism has carried a major tension between those who stress structural constraints (Althusser, 1971a) and those who stress the possibility of 'action' (Thompson, 1978). (The general sociological approach of Marxism and differences within it are discussed in Section 2.5.)

Marxists who adopt a structural approach argue that the needs of the system determine human behaviour. The economy is seen to ultimately determine capitalist production, but politics and ideology can have effects on the economy too – for example by maintaining fundamental economic relations. The action approach, however, argues that objectives are achieved by the meanings assigned to them by people.

This tension has been evident in the different approaches to the study of 'race' and ethnicity. Marxists who have taken a structuralist approach see the state reproducing the relations of production, resulting in the domination of other countries in the quest for profit. The consequence of this is the reproduction of racism caused by contributions to underdevelopment and the necessity of members of that population to migrate and play a disadvantaged role in the host country (Sivanandan, 1982). 'Action'-based Marxists argue that state action is not determined by capital, but is a result of choices (Ben-Tovim and Gabriel, 1982). Prejudice is used by the bourgeoisie to justify exploitation and to fragment the proletariat. Therefore racialism and racism are seen to be fully intended.

Marxists do agree that conflict is inevitable between the dominant and subject social groups and therefore believe that 'race relations' can be explained through incorporation into their analysis of the capitalist mode of production. Two main concepts have arisen from this belief (Bradley, 1996):

• 'race' is a special case of labour/capital relations
• 'racial' division has served to further the interests of capitalism.

Oliver Cox (1970), in classical Marxist terms, argued that class is the primary division in society and that capitalists exploit racial divisions to divide the working class. He went further to define prejudice in terms of the propagation of negative attitudes of a social group by the ruling class, in order to maintain the exploitation of that group. Therefore racism is viewed as an ideological construction and a by-product of class oppression. It exists because capitalism uses it to exploit groups within the subject class. Cox's work has been criticized along the following lines:

• It is argued that racism can exist outside a capitalist and colonialist context, but his theory does not account for this.
• His views are too simplistic. Neo-Marxists, for example, suggest that capitalism does not determine all social phenomena (see Section 6.5).

Robert Miles (1982) concentrated on specific racial disadvantage using a Marxist framework. He argued that African–Caribbean and Asian workers in the UK are a 'racialized fraction' of the working class. Ethnic groups are stereotypes which cast them as 'racially different', and this ideology results in discrimination

and the accepting of certain jobs that have been rejected by the majority of whites. Black workers remain as part of the proletariat, but are more disadvantaged than their white peers.

Miles therefore stressed ideology and racial formation. He argued that 'race' does not exist as a biological category, but the idea of 'race' suggests that certain social relationships are natural and therefore inevitable. 'Race' is presumed to be a biological reality which determines historical processes. Hence Miles argued that the idea of 'race':

. . . amounts to a process of reification, as a result of which that which should be explained becomes an explanation of social relations.
(Miles, 1993, pp. 44–5)

For Miles, 'race' is a socially constructed ideology based on erroneous assumptions, but with real social effects. It is an idea created by human beings and used to represent and structure the world in which they live for certain political reasons. Therefore he claims that 'race', as an idea, is essentially ideological. Racism is multi-dimensional and can be seen as the use of any physical characteristics of an individual or group to differentiate them negatively from others. In order to understand racism fully, Miles claimed that it has to be located within capitalist class relations. It is an ideology used to explain class position, hiding real economic relations and thereby promoting false class consciousness. No direct link is seen between ideas and action and social inequality is constructed by many factors; hence racism has to be perceived as ideological.

Miles has supported the claim of Castles and Kosack (1973) that migrants can be seen as a reserve army of labour. They can be utilized or 'let go' at the will of the employer, because they form a good supply of cheap workers to supplement the indigenous proletariat. Asian workers settled in the UK, for example, have 'former migrant' status, with different experiences of working conditions in their country of origin that have made them vulnerable to exploitation. For Miles, racism creates real divisions within the working class, and so the term 'race' should not be used in social science because it supports and solidifies these constructed differences. He believes, however, that these 'fractures' can be overcome. (The links between class and ethnicity are also explored in Sections 4.11 and 6.6.)

Summary

The Marxist approach to 'race' and ethnicity is useful because it examines the capitalist exploitation of the labour of racialized groups, and how racist policies are promoted by the state. Its main assumptions can be summarized as follows:

- Racism is a result of the capitalist economic structure, thereby linking racial inequality to social inequality.
- Racism is a form of dominant group control, promoting class division and false class consciousness.
- Ethnic minorities form a reserve army of labour and suffer all the disadvantages associated with this, such as poor living conditions.
- Ideology perpetuates negative images of ethnic minorities, via the media and other parts of the superstructure, which 'justifies' their disadvantaged position.

Criticisms of Marxist approaches

Marxist analyses of 'race' and ethnicity have been criticized generally on five counts:

1 By viewing class as the most important division in society, determining all others, 'race' and ethnicity as concepts become marginalized (Anthias, 1990).
2 All racialized groups are seen as part of the proletariat, but ethnic minorities do not all constitute part of the working class (witness the growing Asian petit bourgeoisie and black middle class). Post-modernism challenges the idea of racial minorities forming a homogeneous whole.
3 Weberian approaches (see later) argue that the notion of power has been ignored, in that not all members of ethnic groups in the UK are in disadvantaged positions.
4 The importance of racist attitudes and practices among the white population is generally underplayed.
5 It is implied that racial disadvantage will only be overcome by a unified proletarian revolution, which offers a bleak future for 'race relations'. This determinism has been challenged by racial formation approaches which argue that societal structures are formed by the actions of human actors (Omi and Winant, 1994).

Weberian approaches

It has been argued that there is a considerable overlap between Weberian and Marxist thinking on 'race' (Anthias and Yuval-Davis, 1993). Both approaches see racial disadvantage in primarily economic terms and in its relationship to class. As O'Donnell (1991) noted, John Rex (Weberian) and Robert Miles (Marxist) agree on two important aspects of racism:

- It is a form of ideology based on biological assumptions of 'race'. In South Africa, for example, apartheid was justified with reference to the Bible and its portrayal of white superiority.

- It reflects structural realities in a specific historical and contemporary context. For example, the colonial past has resulted in the disadvantaged position of black people in the UK.

However, despite these apparent similarities many differences do exist between the two approaches. (The general theoretical approach of Weber and conflict theory is discussed in Section 2.6.)

Weber saw stratification as deriving from the distribution of power, which provided a more flexible approach to the study of 'race' and ethnicity. It was realized that there was no need to reduce everything to class. Parkin (1979) used the concept of status (the amount of social esteem given to an individual or group by others) to examine 'race relations'. He argued that ethnic groups were negatively privileged status groups. By this he meant that social boundaries exist between groups which maintain existing hierarchies. (See also Section 4.2.)

John Rex has provided the major Weberian analysis of 'race', linking racial disadvantage to class position and market situation. His analysis was formed in South Africa where the situation did not conform to a classical Marxist model. He noticed that 'real' privileges existed for whites, rather than a Marxist notion of 'false class consciousness' making them appear so to disadvantaged blacks. Rex realized that Weber used the concept of capitalism in both a 'wide' sense (i.e. that it allowed market opportunity to develop peacefully or in the spirit of adventure, as in imperialism), and in a 'narrow' sense (i.e. just peacefully). The relatively unfree labour of black workers could only be understood, argued Rex, in terms of a Weberian approach, which allowed for classes being generated by differential control of, or access to, property:

. . . the best way to approach the study of a multiracial, multi-cultural society is to look at its mode of production and at the conflicting interests and relationships which this generates.
(Rex, 1988, p. 70)

In 1967, Rex published research carried out with Moore on the Sparkbrook area of Birmingham. They discovered that black immigrant groups were confined to certain types of housing, mainly decayed inner-city properties. Also, in attempting to acquire accommodation, different ethnic groups were thrown into conflict. With Tomlinson (1979), Rex suggested that black minorities may form a distinct 'underclass' (a class below the working class) because of their disadvantaged position in employment, education and housing. He went on to argue that members of ethnic minorities in employment were subject to a 'dual labour market', where black and white workers were segregated into jobs with different characteristics. The primary labour market provided mainly whites with well-paid work, good conditions and promotion prospects. The secondary labour market offered part-time, low-paid work in poor conditions, usually to black employees.

It has been noted (Bradley, 1996) that contradictions appear to exist in Rex's Weberian analysis. He defined race relations as different unequal groups in conflict, with membership of those groups being fixed or ascribed on the basis of deterministic belief systems – such as the biological view of 'race'. Consequently his approach viewed 'race' as an aspect of the stratification system distinct from class. However, it is argued that his research drew on class theory to explain the specific position of black minority groups. This potential paradox could be explained by the belief that 'race', unlike class, is not a 'real' category and therefore needs to be connected with something that is (Bradley, 1996). However, some sociologists claim that Rex's notion of class is clearly Weberian, rather than Marxist, because it focuses on the distribution of economic rewards by the state or the marketplace and therefore Rex's work does not contradict its Weberian roots. (This issue is also discussed in Sections 4.2 and 4.3.)

In his later work Rex has noted that the class position of ethnic minorities has fundamentally altered owing to rising unemployment, the undermining of the working class, and the decline of the welfare state. The white working class have moved into a similar position of ethnic minorities in the 1960s. This has meant that many Britons have been forced into an 'underclass' position. Rex argues that this may result in two possible outcomes:

- All deprived members of the working class and the unemployed are forced into class struggle, unifying black and white together.
- Some whites may challenge the minority groups with whom they are in competition, in pursuit of their own economic interests (rather than as part of a racist ideology).

Discussion point

To what extent does this suggest that the term 'underclass' is not appropriate today? (See also Section 4.8.)

Using a Weberian framework, Rex has put forward an analysis of 'race relations' which moves beyond economic determinism, incorporating a 'methodological individualism' that allows for actors to have 'interests' in the way the world is organized. These 'interests' become evident depending on the level of material constraint; that is, racism is related to people's perceptions which are constructed by daily interactions and historical conditions.

Criticisms of the Weberian approach

Criticisms of the Weberian approach to 'race' and ethnicity have been put forward by Marxists, who challenge:

- the emphasis on status rather than class
- the privileging of social action over structural considerations
- the focus on black workers as objects of discrimination, obscuring their position as members of the working class.

More generally, this approach has been argued to separate 'race' from inequality in general, which is regarded as imprecise (Bradley, 1996). It may also be seen to present a picture of society that is more fluid than it actually is: competition for scarce resources, for example, can restrict the *mobility* of ethnic minorities.

Recent developments in Weberian perspectives

Despite the foregoing criticisms, contemporary sociologists have noticed a swing towards the Weberian perspective. Jenkins (1994a) used the notion of 'history constraining actions' to develop his argument that ethnicity is a relational process by which one group defines itself by another, coupled with external categorization. He linked this idea to Foucault's classification of populations, claiming that power and authority are used in classifying ethnicity. (The work of Michel Foucault is discussed in more detail in Sections 2.8, and 10.2 and 17.4.) Jenkins was able to incorporate notions of power at both micro and macro levels, fusing a number of perspectives together to produce a notion of ethnicity as variable and dynamic, but allowing for power. Only by encompassing Weberian ideas was he able to achieve this. The Weberian approach allows for an optimistic overview of 'race relations', believing racism can change with the 'interests' of individuals and groups in that society. It is a multi-dimensional theory of stratification based on interaction between different groups competing for power and resources.

Functionalism

Functionalism is a theoretical perspective developed around the notion of 'value consensus': that is, agreement on what is good and worthwhile in society. (The general sociological approach of functionalism is considered in more detail in Section 2.4.) When applied to the study of 'race' and ethnicity, racial disadvantage is explained as a consequence of the cultural characteristics of the minority group; so ethnic minority groups do not 'fit in' with society's traditional norms and values, but will do so in the future and this will allow society to function (by assimilation).

In the 1960s, functionalists argued that all societies consist of various 'segments', each with their own subculture. Conflict was seen to be based upon cultural differences, with the host society being concerned about immigrants' differences such as skin colour and traditions. It was expected that immigrants would integrate and assimilate into society. In 1968 the Home Secretary, Roy Jenkins, argued that integration promoted equal opportunities and cultural diversity. As we can see in the article 'CS gas squirted at handcuffed man', this was a highly optimistic forecast.

The functionalist perspective also advocated the idea of assimilation. By this is meant that the host society, with agreement on basic values, expects immigrants and ethnic minorities to adapt and change their norms, values and beliefs to 'fit in' smoothly with their adopted society. It is argued that conflict is a consequence of ethnic minorities failing to adopt mainstream values. It is a consequence of the cultural characteristics of the minority group.

However, Horace Kallen argues that, in the USA, acceptance of the cultures of different immigrant groups (i.e. integration rather than assimilation) is more typical. He agrees that cultural value consensus has to occur in order to maintain societal equilibrium, but denies the need for assimilation (see the later discussion in this section on the Chicago School). Therefore, functionalist analysis of 'race' and ethnicity can be interpreted in two ways:

- as a call for assimilation to stop any potential 'racial' conflict
- as a call for multi-culturalism and the acceptance of a plurality of cultures to stop any potential 'racial' conflict.

In the UK, an acceptance of multi-culturalism is evident in, for example, educational policies in inner-city areas. It is argued that this approach will result in harmonious relations between ethnic groups, based on acceptance and tolerance. However, this theory still expects immigrant groups to change *their* culture, even if not to the same extent as an assimilation model would.

Functionalist theory on 'race relations' is all about a cultural consensus resulting in a balanced and functional society. This aim is based on the premise of equal access to societal goals, within the constraints of individual talent and ability. The rational-choice model put forward by Banton (1983) can in part be linked to this assumption. This model argues that an individual's course of action is rational in attempting to realize preferred goals. However, immigrant groups are perceived by the whole society as a potential threat, both to scarce resources and cultural resources, and this may result in conflict.

CS gas squirted at handcuffed man

JASON BENNETTO
Crime Correspondent

A man who died in police custody after CS spray was squirted into his face had his arms handcuffed behind his back at the time, the *Independent* has learned.

It is also understood that at least five officers were attempting to restrain Ibrahima Sey, 29, at a police station in east London in March, when he was sprayed with the incapacitant.

Initial findings of the police inquiry into the death at Ilford police station, in east London, are understood to have found that Mr Sey was handcuffed at the time he was sprayed, and was struggling, but contrary to some reports he was not headbutting officers. Sources suggest that shortly before the struggle he attempted to kiss a woman police officer.

A friend of Mr Sey, Paebou Ndimbalan, who had travelled with him to the station in a police van, has claimed that up to 12 officers were involved in his arrest and restraining him at the police station.

CS spray, which causes breathing difficulties, streaming eyes and nose, is designed to be used defensively to restrain violent people.

A post-mortem examination showed that Mr Sey, who was 6ft 3in and weighed 18st, collapsed after a period of exertion and was suffering from hypertensive heart disease. Death was not a result of being sprayed. However, further toxicology tests are being carried out on his brain to see whether it was a contributing factor.

Police from Forest Gate station in east London were called to Mr Sey's home in Forest Gate at 4.24am on 16 March, where they found his wife standing in the road. She had jumped from their first-floor flat. Mr Sey was allegedly holding his six-month-old baby and shouting through an open window.

Mr Ndimbalan eventually persuaded Mr Sey to get into the back of a police van with him. When they arrived at the police yard of Ilford station the two men were separated.

A scuffle took place in which Mr Sey was handcuffed. Shortly afterwards he was sprayed in the face, during which several people suffered from the effects of the incapacitant and were replaced by other officers.

Mr Sey was placed in a cell and subsequently complained of feeling unwell. He was taken to hospital where he later died.

An inquiry is being led by Frank Wilkinson, Assistant Chief Constable of Hertfordshire police, and the case is being overseen by the independent Police Complaints Authority.

Source: *The Independent*, 24 April 1994

A functionalist analysis of 'race' and ethnicity has not been developed in contemporary approaches. The potential racist outcomes of functionalism, such as blaming cultural differences for social problems, has consequently made it problematic/outdated as an explanation for 'racial'/ethnic relations.

Symbolic interactionism: the Chicago School

In the 1920s and 1930s, a group of sociologists at the University of Chicago investigated the poor communication between dissimilar groups in the cities. In Chicago in 1930, 35 per cent of the city's population were foreign born, with 6.9 per cent of the population being African–American. These black people had come to the city to escape racism in southern USA and to find work (Lal, 1988). However, the stigma associated with their colour resulted in them attaining a worse position than the white immigrants. Therefore it was concluded that social organization works on two levels, biotic and cultural. The biotic level referred to the idea that human ecology (where someone originates from) could help to explain the cultural level of African–American's physical and cultural isolation.

These discoveries resulted in further studies into relationships between ethnic groups, based on interactionist principles. The Chicago School believes that meaning emerges from interaction. 'Gestures', involving interpretation and modification, are flexible and influenced by history/socialization. Consequently meaning is related and constantly changed and updated through socialization, enabling us to take on new roles. Symbolic interactionism (Blumer, 1969) argues that interactions are always in a state of flux, because they are a condition of, as well as an outcome of, interpretation. This theoretical perspective influenced their research methodology and resulted in huge monographs into 'race

---

Black rap puts teacher on trial

TONY ALLEN-MILLS
New York

EIGHTEEN months ago a middle-aged St Louis schoolteacher named Cissy Lacks set up a video camera in her classroom and taped her black students reading out their homework. It was a routine creative writing assignment, one of many Lacks had set in her 25 years as an English teacher.

It was also to cost her her job, as a local row about students using bad language snowballed into a national controversy about freedom of speech, racism in schools and the extraordinary difficulties of teaching students whose home lives are frequently ravaged by drugs, guns or gangs.

At a prize-giving dinner in New York last week, Paul Newman, the actor, presented Lacks with a $25,000 cheque for her outspoken defence of her students' right to express themselves in the language they know best: the profanity-laden street slang of what has become known as the "hood" – the neighbourhoods where rapping gangstars have, thanks largely to MTV and Hollywood, become the most dynamic linguistic force currently reshaping the English language.

Lacks, 50, was sacked for allowing her students to swear. In most English schools, any teacher who allowed students to sprinkle their essays with four-letter words and references to "niggers" and "motherf******" might meet the same fate. But most English schools are not like Berkeley High in St Louis's hard-boiled Ferguson-Florissant school district.

A painful example of America's failure to desegregate its school system, Berkeley is 99% black. "There are kids from varying backgrounds," Lacks said last week, "but they've all had a life a lot tougher than mine. Some have been involved in gang violence. They have seen people killed. They have suffered the deaths of their friends."

As a white Jewish teacher assigned to the school five years ago, Lacks was immediately presented with the kind of challenge beloved of Hollywood scriptwriters in recent films such as Mr Holland's Opus, starring Richard Dreyfus as a teacher struggling to inspire his students, and Dangerous Minds, starring Michelle Pfeiffer in a similar role.

"I've always liked my students and they've always liked me," said Lacks. "But the first year at Berkeley was really hard. They really didn't like me. I had to fight that mistrust."

By the second year she had started a student newspaper and was helping run a literary magazine. Despite an enormous cultural and racial divide, Lacks felt she was making progress. Her mistake was to videotape the assignment in which she had encouraged her students to write "natural dialogue".

"These students were mumbling a lot and there was just no point in trying to get them to write something pompous and ineffective. They needed to write something important to them, from their own lives. To write as the people they know speak," Lacks said.

They eventually produced a script about gang members. "Yes, there was a lot of street language," Lacks said. She had videotaped the proceedings so the students could judge for themselves how effective or natural their dialogue appeared. But the tapes went missing from her locker, and ended up in the hands of Berkeley's black principal, Vernon Mitchell, who promptly fired her for failing to enforce the school's rules that forbid student profanity.

Lacks, who is suing the school for reinstatement, accuses Mitchell of bowing to political correctness and failing to live up to his responsibilities as an educator. She also suspects a racial motivation. According to court records, Mitchell told some of Lacks' students: "You made black fools of yourselves and you let white folk tape it."

The case has divided St Louis, with some parents taking the view that cursing should be kept out of the classroom, and many others insisting that Lacks was right to encourage her students to explore their creative instincts and express them in the language they best understood.

Source: *Sunday Times*, 28 April 1996

relations'. (Symbolic interactionism is considered in more detail in Section 2.7.) According to Blumer:

No theorising, however ingenious, no observation of scientific protocol, however meticulous, are substitutes for developing a familiarity with what is actually going on in the sphere of life under study. (Blumer, 1969, pp. 38–9)

Activity

First read the article 'Black rap puts teacher on trial'. Then draw up a list of the elements within it that support the interactionist perspective.

I, A

Park (1950) argued that 'race' prejudice was part of a changing relationship between racial groups, and that it emerged when a real or imagined threat occurred to an existing pattern of 'social accommodation' (consensus about social life). He believed that 'racial problems' emerged in cities where racial groups were either (a) previously isolated, or (b) had a 'fixed' place in 'social accommodation', but were now competing for jobs and housing, challenging their position to preserve or change their group status. He saw this as part of a four-stage cycle – where immigrants or different racial groups would:

- have 'contact' with the host population
- get into a 'conflict' situation with them
- this would result in 'accommodation'
- concluding with 'assimilation'.

This is interactionist, because it views conflict arising from lack of communication about different self-perceptions.

Park termed conflict groups 'publics' and argued that they were differentiated in terms of membership and goals, but may negotiate the division of scarce resources. However, to fully understand 'race relations', Park pointed out that a knowledge of history was essential to enable social attitudes and opinions to be related to experiences and meanings. Ultimately, however, 'racial' tension would disappear as different ethnic groups became assimilated.

Blumer (1969) agrees with Park's idea that racism is an aspect of groups rather than of individuals. He extends Park's work further in the following three ways.

First, he argues that social change is initiated by political leaders, rather than by personal experience. Leaders alter objective conditions in which racial groups co-exist, or by changing the imagery (ideology) surrounding these groups. This can result in variable 'race relations'.

Secondly, he developed the notion of 'collective definition', which is the way in which racial groups see each other and themselves and how this guides their interactions. Relations are seen to be aligned and realigned as others evaluate interpretations and their views influence the definition. Therefore 'racial groups' interact in a variety of situations.

Thirdly, he argues that 'dualisms' exist where the subordinate groups reiterate their 'specialness' and thereby either reinforce the solidarity of the group, or comply with dominant group expectations to improve the rank of the group. The dualism is therefore 'separatism' or 'assimilation'. Blumer argues that group members may do both at the same time: they may, for example, emulate the dominant group in times of economic prosperity with the hope of an improved lifestyle, while adopting the 'specialness' label when economic movement is unlikely, resorting to political action to improve their social position. Lal (1988) suggests that dualism was not a response to economic conditions but a strategic device to facilitate improvement in the collective status of the group, securing a larger share of scarce resources.

Criticisms of the Chicago School

Criticisms of the Chicago School have been put forward by sociologists, as follows:

- It is too relativistic, concentrating on individual situations and thereby revealing little about 'race relations' as a whole.
- It attempts to analyse complexity/diversity and makes generalizations that are contradictory, because individual cases cannot be used to make universal statements. Duster and Blumer (1980) account for this by saying that 'race relations' operate within a common framework, but this claim does not justify the methodological anomaly.
- Marxists claim that it overlooks the significance of class.
- It is confused over whether the social actor or social variable should be the centre of analysis (Lal, 1988). That is, should an individual within an ethnic minority group be studied, as opposed to the racism that they experience?

Lal (1988) believes that a new approach to 'race relations' was emerging based on symbolic interactionism, which focuses on:

- 'race'/ethnic relations and the 'transformation of traditional culture'
- 'race' and ethnicity as variables, rather than constants in on-going group life, which are constantly negotiated and renegotiated
- meanings, subjective and symbolic aspects of 'race' and ethnic relations
- concern for historical events, such as migration, and human experiences arising from them.

Lal concluded by summing up the value of a symbolic interactionist approach:

The logic of symbolic interactionism is to argue that the meanings of objects, including categories of people such as racial groups, are influenced by the nature of the specific situation in which the interaction occurs.
(Lal, 1988, p. 297)

(The work of the Chicago School is also considered in Sections 11.4 and 16.1.)

6.5 Contemporary approaches to 'race' and ethnicity

Neo-Marxism

Classical interpretations of Marxism have tended to reduce 'race' to a facet of class exploitation. However, since the 1960s Marxist sociologists have relied less on economic reductionism, focusing instead on areas such as the extent of autonomy in the field of 'race relations'. As with early Marxism, neo-Marxism consists of competing schools of thought. Two of the main approaches are the 'relative autonomy model' and the 'autonomy model'. (The general sociological approach of neo-Marxism is considered in Section 2.5.)

The relative autonomy model

This approach was developed by the Centre for Contemporary Cultural Studies (CCCS, 1982). The CCCS aimed to establish an analysis of racism which:

- accepted the relative autonomy of 'race' from class-based social relations
- acknowledged its specific historical position in relation to capitalism.

Their approach has also been termed 'cultural Marxism' (Bradley, 1996), because of its emphasis on imperialism and the use of racism in strengthening cultural hegemony in the UK.

The CCCS began examining racism in the early 1970s (Hall *et al.*, 1978) when attempting to explain 'moral panics' on mugging (see Section 11.8). The construction of 'race' as a social problem and political issue was investigated and paved the way for the influential CCCS publication *The Empire Strikes Back* (1982). This book suggested the following:

- Previous sociological/Marxist accounts of 'race relations' have not furthered our knowledge of racism and may even have reproduced ethnocentrism.
- A greater emphasis should be placed on 'state racism'.

- The relationship between 'class' and 'race' should be reconceptualized as relatively autonomous. This was initiated by Gilroy, who more recently has presented a post-Marxist, post-modernist approach.

The CCCS's approach is based on a theory of racism which deals with the economic and structural features, but also with its historical and social distinctiveness. Hall (1980) suggested three main areas which critical Marxist analysis of 'race' should involve:

- an attempt to understand what causes racism in a particular society, because it is an historical phenomenon
- an understanding of racism being relatively autonomous from other social relations – working separately from, but at the same time affecting, social relations
- an understanding that 'race' and class have to be analysed together.

The work of Hall and the CCCS has influenced later sociological developments in the study of 'race' and ethnicity. The idea that 'racisms' rather than 'racism' should be considered results in an understanding of racism as a multi-faceted phenomenon that develops in specific situations. The CCCS has been criticized for neglecting the economic context when emphasizing relative autonomy. This criticism, however, appears trivial in the wake of post-modernist reactions to studies of 'race relations', which remove 'racial' and eth-

Activity

Another major influence in recent debates about the politics of race can be traced to the work of authors who have at one time or other been associated with the Birmingham Centre for Contemporary Cultural Studies (CCCS). This research was stimulated in many ways by the publication of Hall's programmatic essay on 'Race, articulation and societies structured in dominance' (1980). Hall's most important argument was that while racism cannot be reduced to other social relations, neither can it be explained autonomously from them. Thus, racism commands a relative autonomy from economic, political and other social relations.
(Solomos and Back, 1995, p. 25–6)

What do you understand by Solomos and Back's conclusion that, in Hall's approach, 'racism commands a relative autonomy from economic, political and other social relations'?

U, I

nic relations from part of the class structure, replacing them in an analysis based on cultural diversity (see post-modernism later in this section).

The autonomy model

The autonomy model criticizes relative autonomy as still being ultimately 'reductionist', because it reduces 'race' to one aspect of class. This does not allow racial inequality or discontent to form a separate issue in political struggles, as it is seen as part of class conflict in general. Gabriel and Ben-Tovim (1979) analysed 'race' not separately from its social and class relations, but as a product of contemporary and historical struggles, which could not be reduced to wider economic and social relations. Therefore they perceived 'race' and racism to be autonomous from other social relations.

Gabriel and Ben-Tovim started by examining various struggles – local, national, political and ideological conflicts – in which 'race' was socially constructed. They were aware that wider structural constraints could affect these struggles, but they argued that it was not known to what extent. Gabriel and Ben-Tovim therefore concluded that 'race' could not be reduced to class on any level, and that all Marxist analysis of racism should start by examining the ideological and political practices which work autonomously to produce this phenomenon.

An overview of neo-Marxism

The autonomy model was a breakthrough theoretically from normal Marxist concerns, but it has

Activity

First read the article 'Black student killed "out of racist hatred"'. Just over a week after this article appeared, *The Observer* (28 April 1996) reported that the Crown Prosecution Service (CPS) official, Howard Youngerwood, who withdrew murder charges against the alleged killers of Stephen Lawrence, was later accused of 'covering up racism where the CPS paid damages to a black manager'.

Taking into account the article and the later revelations about Youngerwood, evaluate the neo-Marxist belief that racism can only be examined autonomously. **U, I, A, E**

resulted in the following irreconcilable rift within neo-Marxism on 'race' and ethnicity (Solomos, 1988):

1 It cannot be agreed whether 'racial' and ethnic categorizations are 'relatively autonomous' or 'autonomous' of economic and class determination.
2 The role of political institutions and the state in reproducing racism in capitalist society cannot be agreed upon.

Marxism has moved on from the days when it was seen as just a deterministic theory of social development. Many neo-Marxists challenge determinism (Wright, 1980) and analyse specific areas of industrial society. This has complicated neo-Marxist

---

Black student killed 'out of racist hatred'

MICHAEL STREETER

A black student was murdered by a gang of white youths simply because of the colour of his skin, a court heard yesterday. Stephen Lawrence, 18, died from two stab wounds inflicted by racist attackers, motivated by a "deep-felt hatred" of blacks, the Old Bailey was told.

Michael Mansfield QC, prosecuting, told the all-white jury: "There can be no mistaking that it was an unprovoked, unwarranted attack by those who hold not just racist views but racist views which involve the desecration of those who are black by injury and possibly death. Whoever did this was someone who had a deep-felt hatred of black people existing."

Later, Mr Lawrence's friend, Dwayne Brooks, described seeing the A-level student stabbed and then collapsing on the ground "with blood running on the floor".

Three men are the subject of a private prosecution brought by the Lawrence family. All deny murder.

Mr Mansfield outlined the events leading up to the killing on 22 April 1993, almost exactly three years ago. Mr Lawrence, who attended Bluecoat School in south-east London, was an "ordinary" young man who started that day not knowing it was to be his last. He and Mr Brooks were on their way home from an evening with Mr Lawrence's uncle when they stopped at a bus stop in Wellhall Road, Eltham after 10pm, said Mr Mansfield. Soon afterwards, they were approached by a group of four to six white youths – whom the prosecution says included the defendants – one of whom shouted "What, what, nigger" to them. When

approached, the black men tried to run but Mr Lawrence was not as quick to escape as his friend, Mr Mansfield said.

Mr Lawrence was surrounded and struck by an overarm blow with a weapon such as a "rather large, kitchen knife". Two wounds, on either side of his chest severed vital arteries and he was pronounced dead on arrival at hospital.

Mr Mansfield said the jury might think that the white youths, who fled into the night, had only one object on their minds that evening, which was to cause serious injury to one or other of the black youths. "This attack was swift, merciless and vicious. They approached together, attacked together and disappeared together."

The case continues.

Source: *The Independent*,
19 April 1996

analysis, making it impossible to construct an acceptable framework of 'racism' for all to follow. Solomos (1988), however, has proposed a Marxist approach that shows how racism is interconnected with wider social relations, but also has autonomy:

1 'Race relations' form part of the structural features of capitalist society.
2 Each historical situation needs to be examined in its own specific context, and therefore no general Marxist theory can be applied.
3 Structural contradictions cannot totally explain 'race' and ethnic divisions.

Solomos believes that economic and social conditions do play a role in structuring racism as an ideology and as a specific set of practices. He concludes that Marxism may involve diverse perspectives, but in relation to the analysis of 'race' it has homogeneity on two levels:

Marxist theories of 'race' are heterogeneous in approach, though it can be argued that they are unified through a common concern with (a) the material and ideological basis of racism and racial oppression, however it may be defined, and (b) the role that racism plays in structuring the entire social, political and economic structures of societies.
(Solomos, 1988, p. 107)

Neo-Marxism has made the debate over 'race' more challenging, touching areas of concern to non-Marxists (e.g. the origins of racist ideologies) and thereby stimulating further investigations. As Solomos wrote:

... a sizeable and growing body of theory and research in the area of 'race' and ethnic relations is based on or draws inspiration from Marxism.
(Solomos, 1988, p. 86)

The New Right and 'new racism'

Unlikely as it may seem, the theoretical work of Italian Marxist Antonio Gramsci, particularly his concept of hegemony, has been appropriated by the New Right.
(Seidel, 1986, p. 107)

The New Right in the UK is associated with the right-wing politics of Conservative administrations since 1979. As a sociological perspective (see also Section 2.10) it utilizes conservative traditions, and:

... insists on the freedom of the individual and the primacy of the free market in all social and economic arrangements.
(Lawson and Garrod, 1996, p. 178)

This emphasis on capitalist free enterprise is where Seidel (1986) has made the connection to Gramsci. Hegemony (class domination) has two aspects,

coercion and consensus. Thus the state has the apparatus to force procedures or produce and diffuse its chosen ideology. It is argued that the New Right is attempting to construct their own dominant ideology – in market relationships as the basis of social life – replacing post-war liberal democracy:

(The New Right) is engaged in a cultural battle to unsettle and displace the dominant ideology which constructed the post-war liberal and social democratic consensus.
(Seidel, 1986, p. 107)

In order to do this, language has to be manipulated and cultural and political history redefined. Seidel argues that Roger Scruton and the New Right publication *The Salisbury Review* have been vehicles for the construction of a new political language, the focus of which has been 'nation' and the construction of racist ideologies.

Casey (1982), in *The Salisbury Review*, based the idea of 'nation' in authority and an assumed common culture. He argued that West Indians are a 'problem' because they are different, not accepting authority and therefore prone to criminality. This led Seidel to observe:

... the New Right's racism does not require the hypothesis of innate superiority, only that of cultural difference.
(Seidel, 1986, p. 114)

'New racism'

The New Right is seen to support some elements of the 'new racism' (a term first coined by Barker, 1981). This is based on supposedly fixed cultural differences between ethnic groups, in contrast to 'old racism' which was based on the supposed biological superiority of whites. However, the Conservative party deny that they support racism, as did Enoch Powell in 1969 after his 'Rivers of Blood' speech. Yet in 1979, Prime Minister Margaret Thatcher claimed that 'people are really rather afraid that this country might be swamped by people of a different culture'.

Mason outlined what he perceived to be the basis of 'new racism':

Proponents of the idea that there is a 'new racism' draw attention to the increasing frequency with which political arguments in favour of the exclusion of migrants, or the segregation of members of different population groups, appeal to notions of cultural incompatibility and to the allegedly mutually disruptive and negative consequences.
(Mason, 1995, p. 10)

It is argued that language and discourse create values and ways of thinking, which channel our political behaviour and action in certain directions. Discourse which involves racism rests on institutional support; for example, immigration legislation and nationalism is both ideological and institutional. Gilroy (1992) states that this is incorporated into 'new racism' via three main concepts:

1 'Race' is central to political discourse, but is never used as a term. Seidel (1986) explains this as part of a larger New Right strategy – if 'race' has no meaning then agendas such as repatriation cannot be seen as racist.

2 It identifies 'race' with culture and identity, rather than biology.

3 It links 'race' with notions of nationalism, presenting an imaginary definition of the nation as a unified cultural community.

However, Mason (1995) is clear to point out that while 'new racisms' focus on cultural rather than biological differences, this has not altered popular conceptions on 'race'. In fact on 30 August 1992 *The Independent on Sunday* included an article by a sports commentator who explained that Pakistani fast-bowler success in a Test Match against England was based on the distinctiveness of their sweat in polishing the ball! Also, the recent work of Herrnstein and Murray (1994) has argued that cultural incompatibility is part of the biological view of 'race' (this is considered in more detail in Section 8.9).

Activity

Twenty years ago attitudes were overtly racist, with the assumption that immigrants should 'fit in' with British cultural expectations. The British media today is on the whole less racist, although nationalism bordering on racism can occasionally be found in the tabloids. The article discusses the changing attitude of the media towards the UK's ethnic minority population. Using your sociological understanding, take words from the list below and place them in the most appropriate gaps.

racialist	immigration
racists	fierce
increase	media
host community	black
demands	

Some 20 years ago the BBC ran a series called The Editors. *One day, July 13 it was, they invited a group of _____ editors on. Gurdip Singh Chaggar, a young Sikh from Southall, had been murdered by a group of _____ whites. And Southall had exploded.*

We, a group of black and Asian editors of London papers, were called to the BBC's studios to discuss the issues.

We laid heavy blame at the doors of the national _____ for helping to create a climate in which racial murders were taking place. We identified the major perpetrator as a programme in the BBC's Open Door *series which had been made by the 'Campaign against _____'. Then, as now, we had no illusions about attitudes and personnel which that campaign conceals. Our criticisms were _____. But the specific _____ that we made – for black programmes, black reporters, black feature writers, black columnists – ended up on the cutting room floor . . .*

Today I doubt very much whether any access series on the BBC would allow _____ disguised as decent Britons to putrefy our screens with the garbage of 20 years ago. And there has certainly been an _____ in the numbers of black programmes broadcast . . . [however] *It is difficult to avoid the conclusion that there is a tendency among the _____ to balk at a concentration of blacks. The readiness to disperse us has, in fact, been a constant feature of our presence in this country, something that no one should feel particularly proud of.*

(Darcus Howe, *Black, white and yellow journalism. New Statesman*, 6 September 1996)

I, A

'New racism' and nationalism

Nationalism in the UK today is tied up in its history of colonial conquest, jingoism and the construction of the national identity built on racist definitions about who is British. (Nationalism is also discussed in Sections 16.8 and 17.6.) In Europe, essentialism, which involved each individual being assigned a specific ethnicity or situational ethnicity (Barker, 1981), was linked to fascism in Nazi Germany and has been associated with the increase in neo-fascist movements in recent years.

Essentialist ideas have been attractive to fascism because ethnic difference is assumed by this concept to make a difference. These differences are used as the basis for, and justification of, racial prejudice and discrimination against ethnic minority groups. As Solomos (1993) notes, the 1990s have shown rapid change in the politics of 'race', which includes the rise of racist social and political movements in western and eastern Europe. Neo-fascists and right-wing political parties use popular issues, such as immigration, to attract support and perpetuate the myth of 'us' and 'them'. Education has been a recent tool of the New Right for attracting anti-anti-racist support (Gilroy, 1992). It is argued by the New Right that:

- schools are repositories of the authentic national culture
- multi-culturalism in the curriculum is a 'bastardization of genuine British culture'.

Therefore education is seen as an area where anti-racist policies should be abolished and a clear 'British identity' established. (This issue is also discussed in Sections 8.9 and 8.10.)

Discussion point

What do you think has caused the recent resurgence of neo-fascism in Europe?

Activity

Ray Honeyford, former head teacher of Drummond Middle School, Bradford, is well known for his outspoken views on 'race relations' issues and education. Using the following statement by Mr Honeyford, and knowledge you have attained elsewhere, outline and evaluate his views on multi-cultural education.

A 'racist' is to the race relations lobby what 'Protestant' was to the inquisitors of the Counter-Reformation, or witches to the seventeenth-century burghers of Salem. It is a totem of the new doctrine of anti-racism. Its definition varies according to the purpose it is meant to achieve. It is a gift to the zealot, since he can apply it to anyone who disagrees with him – and he often ejaculates the word as though it were a synonym for 'rapist' or 'fascist'. It takes force not from its power to describe but from its power to coerce and intimidate. It is attached to anyone who challenges the arguments or rhetoric of the race relations lobby. It is more a weapon than a word.
(Honeyford quoted in Lewis, 1988, p. 1)

I, A, E

The New Right has put 'new racism' on the political and academic agenda. It has linked national identity with culture, with black people being perceived as having a different culture and therefore constituting a threat. However, as Gilroy points out, no culture is completely segregated from others, so:

There is no neat or tidy pluralistic separation of racial groups in this country.
(Gilroy, 1992, p. 57)

Activity

The *Daily Mirror* newspaper printed a controversial front page with the headline 'Achtung! . . . Surrender' (below) the day before England were due to play Germany in a football match during the Euro 96 championship. It was accompanied by a note from the Editor issuing a 'declaration of war' against the Germans on the football pitch. The language was reminiscent of Neville Chamberlain's announcement of the outbreak of the Second World War and was intended to evoke feelings of patriotism, using lines such as 'Wherever there is a television set, loyal English hearts shall beat with pride and the Cross of St George shall wave in all its glory'.

Suggest ways in which newspaper articles might support the idea that there is a link between nationalism and racism.

I, A

Figure 6.2 The front page of the *Daily Mirror* on the eve of the England–Germany football match in the Euro 96 championship.

It is useful to note the responses to the *Daily Mirror*'s actions the following day by the quality newspapers. *The Times* wrote that:

The Editor of the Daily Mirror *has apologised after hundreds of people protested about yesterday's front page.*

The jingoism was not confined to the *Daily Mirror*. *The Sun*, which in common with *The Times* is owned by News International, ran the headline 'Let's Blitz Fritz' on an inside page. *The Independent* noted on its front page that:

The British still seem obsessed by Nazism and the War – more so than the occupied countries of Europe still are – and resentful of post-war German prosperity.

The next day, 26 June 1996, *The Independent* published the following poem by Martin Newell on its front page.

1966/1996

*Oasis aren't the Beatles
And Blur are not the Kinks
As Double D. and Watney's Pale
Were not designer drinks
And aerials weren't dishes
And football songs weren't hip
As monocles and spiky hats
Weren't German football strip
And Mitchell wasn't Garnett
As Heath was not a fool*

*And Hamburg found the Mersey Sound
As much as Liverpool
And Klinsmann isn't Haller
As Shearer isn't Hurst
And Ramsey was as much revered
As Venables is cursed*

*But mad old Tommy Tabloid
Still hammers at the hun
A powdered egg-bound xenophobe
Marooned in '41
He hears the grainy wireless
Across the sun-parched lawn*

*"4–2, 4–2." He must be true
To lion and unicorn
And younger generations
For whom his cant is meant
Will dress alike and dance alike
With or without consent
As sons of Thames or Tyneside
The Elbe, Rhine and Spree
Will only speak in footballese
Upon the field of play.*

Activity
Newell's poem is about Euro 96, but what is it saying in relation to nationalism and 'race relations'?

I, A

Post-moderism

The notion of 'post-modern' evokes images of something that comes after the modern age. Modernity, according to Lyon (1994), was a social order that developed after the decline of medieval European society. As it progressed it became industrial, capitalist, bureaucratic with a central state apparatus and adopted, on a cultural level, the values of enlightenment (secularism, materialism, rationalism, individualism and progression). Sociologists and cultural theorists have claimed, however, that the modern age is being replaced by a new social order – post-modernity. (This debate is also covered in Sections 2.10 and 10.11.) The post-modern society contains, as Richardson notes:

. . . more flexible (post-Fordist) forms of technology, new communication systems (e.g. global networks) and new social and political institutions (e.g. grouping of nation states in to larger units such as the European Union.
(Richardson, 1996, p. 72)

As part of the post-modern society a new set of values, lifestyles and art forms have emerged (post-modernism), creating a whole new cultural ethos. Post-modernism challenges former doctrines of objectivity, great art and seriousness, finding value in relativity, popular culture and superficiality (see also Chapter 10).

Where the modern age bred uniformity, post-modernism revels in diversity, fragmentation and rapid social change.
(Richardson, 1996, p. 70)

In relation to the study of 'race' and ethnicity, post-modern perspectives offer a critique of one-dimensional modernist theories such as Marxism, which claims that 'race' and ethnicity are secondary aspects of stratification determined by capitalist relations:

. . . a post-modern approach allows for the development of a multi-dimensional account of inequality, in which each dimension can be accorded equal weight. 'Race' and ethnicity are considered crucial aspects of social differentiation in their own right.
(Bradley, 1996, p. 130)

Post-modernism and post-structuralism

Post-modern and post-structural theories have, according to Bradley (1996), the following elements in common:

1 *The stress on difference and diversity.* Brah (1992) and Madood (1992) argue that each ethnic group experiences different patterns of disadvantage and develops distinctive responses within their own culture and community. For example, Gujaratis and Punjabis are both Asian groups, but have vastly different experiences, histories etc. Therefore, ethnicity and culture are emphasized rather than 'race'. The UK is seen as a patchwork of heterogeneous groups (Anthias and Yuval-Davis, 1993).

2 *The attack on essentialism.* Donald and Rattansi (1992) argue that various groups and individuals have divergent experiences. 'Race' is a social construction which reveals very little about the group it is trying to investigate. Post-modernists see ethnicity as fluid and complex, thereby guarding against 'ethnic absolutism' (Gilroy, 1987, 1993) which implies that all ethnic groups share the same experiences. It is argued that we are all 'mongrels' because ethnic purity does not exist:

There is no such thing as a 'pure' culture, since all have been inevitably affected by processes of migration, travel and tourism, cultural exchange and communication.
(Bradley, 1996, p. 134)

3 *Rejection of the presentation of racialized minorities as victims.* Gilroy (1987) argues that even during slavery African exiles developed their culture and that oppressed and racialized minorities do the same in contemporary society. Black groups are not passive recipients of racism and discrimination, they are active in opposing their own subordination through political and counter cultural forms (e.g. pop music).

4 *The analysis of discourse.* Hall (1992a) believes that ideas are perpetuated by various forms of discourse such as the portrayal of white superiority in literary texts. Post-structuralists argue that this helps to embed differences between nations and ethnic groups. Gilroy (1987) traced a discourse of black criminality which had developed since post-war Britain. Black was represented in the media as 'criminal'.

Sleeve notes

Controversy? Paris has it oozing from his every creative action. Even the inner sleeve artwork for the new album has got temperatures raised. On one side there is a picture of Paris behind a tree, gat in hand, ready to shoot the president in front of the White House. On the other a collage inscribed with the words "Land of the weak, home of the slave". What's it all about?

"The entire collage is the way that black America destroys itself. You see police violence, domestic violence, a little boy with a gun, a man with Uzis, a drug deal, Colin Powell and Clarence Thomas – those are basically people in allegiance with the oppressor by destroying ourselves. That's what 'Sleeping With The Enemy' is about.

"Originally on that statue it says 'Land of the free, home of the brave' but it's not applicable to us because we're not free and we're not brave. This country is weak and black people are still slaves here, but it's much more subtle now. It's more mind slavery because we don't think freely, we don't do for ourselves. That collage, that shows how a lot of us act as a result of this slave mentality."

Source: *Hip-Hop Connection* (HHC) Feb 1993.

Activity

Study the accompanying 'sleeve notes' of one of hip-hop artist Paris' records. What images are used? How could these images be seen to support a post-modernist perspective?

I, A

Identity

All four of the points discussed above have become evident in one area of post-modernist investigation into 'race' and ethnicity – that of identity. Post-modern theorists argue that identity was once a concept which people believed to be firm and fixed, but that social change has undermined this. New identities have been created via globalization, which has brought different cultural groups into closer contact, that are both fragile and complex. People adopt different identities to match the diversity in their everyday lives. Individuals no longer identify only with their class position, but with gender, age, disability, race, religion, ethnicity, nationality, civil status, music styles, dress codes etc. (Cohen, 1992). An individual will pick and choose, mix and match, the identity/identities with which they feel most comfortable (e.g. a 'Pakistani, black, male, youth, British rapper').

However, identities are fragile or precarious, because in a post-modern world where everything is changing, people are no longer sure who they are. This can also be used to explain the recent 'revival' of racism, or 'new racism', in terms of worries over identity. Individuals may feel threatened by losing their previously stable sense of identity and search for a more secure identity, which often takes an ethnic form (Hall, 1992b).

Criticisms of the post-modern approach

Criticisms have been levied at post-modern theory which not only challenge its fundamental basis, but also its application to 'race' and ethnicity (Richardson, 1996):

1 'The idea of post-modernity may yet turn out to be a figment of overheated disappointed radical hopes' (Lyon, 1994, p. 4). It has been argued by some sociologists that today's society is not a radical post-modern departure from the modern world, but a 'reconstituted modernity' (Smart, 1994) or 'late modernity' (Giddens, 1990).

2 'Racial' and ethnic post-modern theories remain under-developed and ambiguous (Hall, 1992a).

3 Post-modernism places too much emphasis on 'new ethnicities' and new identities, which is not an accurate reflection of everyday life for the

UK's ethnic minorities who value traditional culture (Modood, 1994). A balance is needed between traditional ethnicity and post-modern identities.

4 Post-modernism ignores socio-economic differentiations between racial and ethnic groups (Sivanandan, 1995). Materially disadvantaged groups cannot participate in post-modern consumer culture in the same way as affluent ones.

5 Post-modernism has been accused of underestimating racism and even reducing it to just another passing 'fad' of a pluralist society (Harris, 1993).

Whether it does or does not progress, postmodernism is a challenging new perspective in the examination of 'race' and ethnic issues in contemporary society. (This debate also effects theories of divisions based on class and gender. See Sections 4.10, 5.5 and Chapter 10.)

6.6 Conclusion: 'race' and ethnicity, class, gender and age

Our world is currently characterised by increasing ethnic and Nationalist tension on a global scale, and by polarization of racial inequalities often exacerbated by the whipping up of race hatred within nations.
(Bradley, 1996, p. 144)

Racial disadvantage and racial conflict are obvious aspects of contemporary British society. It has been argued that it is another stratum in our society's stratification system, along with class, gender and age. In other words, it is a way of dividing society up unequally. 'Race' as a basis for differentiation may, as we have seen, have no scientific justification, but it pervades everyday ideology to be taken as something real. The consequences of this have been noted by O'Donnell:

... members of Britain's black minorities disproportionately experience negative differentiation, with the result that their members are more likely than most others to occupy lower positions in stratification hierarchies (including those based on race, class or gender).
(O'Donnell, 1991, p. 39)

Therefore ethnic minorities not only suffer discrimination based on racism, but may have to face class, gender and age inequalities as well. In real life, all these are combined in specific individuals. This section will therefore consider the way in which these

Figure 6.3 The group Kula Shaker have combined Asian and western sounds to create a commercially successful post-modern blend of 'Britpop'

other aspects of stratification interact with 'race' and ethnicity to create specific inequalities. (See also Sections 4.11 and 5.7.)

Class

The relationship between 'race', ethnicity and class has been discussed in relation to the Marxist and Weberian perspectives. It was noted that racialized minorities occupied mainly the bottom of the socio-economic system, because of the nature of capitalism's class-based colonial roots and post-colonial attitude towards migrant labour. The Rowntree Foundation in 1995 claimed that ethnic minorities are more likely than whites to be part of the poorest fifth of the population, and less likely than whites to be in the richest fifth. However, attention has focused recently on the growing number of black middle-class professionals: self-employment in 1994, for example, was more common among Indian men (23 per cent) than white men (17 per cent), according to the Labour Force Survey.

According to Cross (1992), a change in class position for some of the UK's ethnic minorities has raised three issues:

- *Ethnic difference*. It has been argued by some sociologists that some ethnic groups are 'culturally predisposed' for enterprise.
- *Ethnic markets*. Do the markets that ethnic minorities sell to provide for ethnic groups only, or all consumer needs?
- *Reasons for enterprise*. Has discrimination *forced* ethnic minorities to start their own businesses because of limited chances in the open labour market? (See also Sections 9.3.)

Cross focused attention mainly on Asian businessmen. However, as demonstrated by the article 'The African–Caribbean network for science and technology', African–Caribbean communities are in the embryonic stages of filtering into the middle class, taking jobs in commerce and other professions.

Two distinct attitudes have emerged towards 'buppies' (black yuppies). The first is that they provide inspiration for other black people, as Richardson nicely summed up:

It could be argued that the success of middle class blacks helps the black community: they create jobs for other black people, they contradict racist stereotypes held by non-blacks, and they provide role models for young black people.
(Richardson, 1996, p. 67)

The second belief is that the black middle class has 'sold out' to the black community and the black working class, being more interested in their own careers than securing improved conditions for black people as a whole (Sivanandan, 1990).

THE AFRICAN–CARIBBEAN NETWORK FOR SCIENCE AND TECHNOLOGY

This group of 60 scientists, mathematicians, medical professionals and engineers was set up last year in response to growing concerns about the under-achievement of black Caribbean pupils. Based in Manchester but with a national membership, it works with schools; colleges and education authorities by:

- aiming to motivate children's interest by highlighting the achievements of black people in the professions
- providing a mentoring scheme with black scientists and other positive role models
- using a schools outreach service in which black professionals spend time in classrooms assisting multicultural maths and science modules
- making tutorial support available for children and young people from the age of nine through to undergraduates, every day after school, Saturday mornings and during school holidays
- running regular short courses to explain the education system to parents and an information service to help pupils and students who are interested in entering careers in science and technology.

To find out more about the African–Caribbean Network for Science and Technology, contact Liz Rasekoala at 19 Dorchester Road, Swinton, Manchester M27 5PX.

Source: *Times Educational Supplement*, 26 April 1996

Whichever position is adopted, the stability of this new stratum is presumed. In contrast, Daye (1994) argues that black middle-class workers are highly marginalized and therefore 'it is debatable whether in fact they will form a permanent grouping in the British class structure' (p. 280). Whether this small upwardly mobile group is here to stay remains to be seen.

Gender

Feminism

Structures of class, racism, gender and sexuality cannot be treated as 'independent variables' because the oppression of each is inscribed within the other – is constituted by and is constitutive of the other.
(Brah, 1992, p. 137)

The main objective of feminism has been to change the social relations of power based on gender. Knowles and Mercer wrote that:

. . . a feminist perspective is one which prioritizes the identification of, and opposition to, actions, practices and procedures which have the effect of excluding women or disadvantaging them relative to men.
(Knowles and Mercer, 1992, p. 105)

Black feminism

Feminists therefore have a common identity and a common goal, despite political and theoretical diversity in the feminism movement. (This issue is examined in more detail in Chapter 5.) Part of this diversity emerged in the 1970s when black feminists vocalized their discontent with the western feminist perspective's lack of attention to the racialization of gender (Brah, 1992; Knowles and Mercer, 1992; Mama, 1992). Black feminists, such as the Organization of Women of Asian and African Descent (OWAAD), identified little theoretical support for disadvantaged black women, on issues such as immigration and deportations, in white feminist analysis. They therefore sought to challenge specific forms of oppression faced by different black women and the specificity of black women and their relationship to the family, patriarchy and reproduction (Carby, 1982). Mama wrote that:

Black feminism has emerged as a collective political perspective that demands a coherent and co-ordinated rebellion against the varied manifestations of class, race and gender oppression.
(Mama, 1992, p. 97)

Knowles and Mercer (1992) identify a paradox in black feminism, which could account for the collapse of organizations such as OWAAD in the 1980s. They claim that the term 'black women' is used by 'black feminists' to account for both the diversity of lifestyles and similarity of experience which unite women from ethnic minority groups.

It would appear, therefore, that black feminism wants it both ways: to expose the plurality of experience for black women, but when necessary show that they are a unified category too. Knowles and Mercer (1992) also point out that black feminism has distanced itself from feminism as a whole on three issues:

1 *The family.* White feminism argues that both black and white women are oppressed and exploited within the family. However, black feminists argue that black women are not oppressed by the family because they are less dependent on men (Carby, 1982). The family is actually perceived as a factor in the fight against racist oppression. (See also Section 7.4.) Knowles and Mercer support this challenge that the family is a site of female oppression, but argue that it cannot be divided into black and white, the term 'black family' being a political construction, because no single type of family structure exists:

The position of black women in their families, once we reject the stereotypes of the African–Caribbean one-parent family and the Asian woman without rights of disposal over her own body and labour power, is infinitely varied.
(Knowles and Mercer, 1992, p. 107)

2 *Reproduction.* Black feminists claim that black women experience different reproductive issues than white women. For example, black women have to protect their fertility, while white women protect their right to 'infertility' by means of the contraceptive pill or abortion. In developing countries, birth control drugs such as Depo Provera have been given to women before they have met safety standards in the UK. This indicates how black women are perceived in a certain social context, but it reveals little about black women's position in the UK. (See also Sections 12.8 and 13.3.)

3 *Patriarchy.* It is argued that because of racism black men do not benefit from patriarchy in the same way that white men do (Carby, 1982). Therefore, patriarchy is not a central issue to black feminists, although white feminists retain it as the main social division. (The concept of patriarchy is discussed in more detail in Section 5.3.)

Black feminism claims that black women experience more oppression than white women in the form of 'race' and gender, 'race' taking primacy. Mama supports this argument, stating that black women are exploited in employment:

Black women enter the labour market facing the dual constraints of race and gender.
(Mama, 1992, p. 82)

She claims that black women have the lowest pay and the longest hours (see also Section 9.3), which reflects their general position in the British stratification system. Unfortunately, she believes that the situation is getting worse:

The sexist and racist devaluation of black female labour in Britain is not only historical but also a contemporary fact, and the situation, far from improving, appears to be deteriorating.
(Mama, 1992, p. 85)

She bases her claim on the fact that many black women find employment in healthcare (catering, cleaning, 'caring'). Here, privatization has made jobs more scarce and black women workers have been 'let go' in order for white workers to retain theirs.

Knowles and Mercer (1992) argue, from a pluralist perspective, that racism and sexism are not an *inevitable* part of capitalism and colonialism: they are, rather, a series of effects without a single cause. Therefore it is pointless to develop strategies to strike out capitalism and patriarchy, another politics of action is required (e.g. the identification of practices and procedures in social institutions which produce 'race' and gender inequalities and the challenging of these). Racism and sexism are seen as political constructs, ways of interpreting behaviour and events. Therefore black women in the UK will experience racism and sexism in different ways, not in a unitary fashion, as Carby (1982) and Parmar (1982) argued.

Conflict in feminism

Black and white feminism appear to have very different focuses. This has resulted in claims that the women's movement in general is racist (Knowles and Mercer, 1992), because it:

- excludes black women's political concerns, and when they are included it interprets their social lives incorrectly
- historically and currently acts as an agent of oppression of black women.

Activity

The feminist group Women in Nigeria started in 1982 at the University of Zaire. It developed the notion of black women's oppression in Nigeria, but viewed the family and marriage as acceptable organizations and by no means oppressive. Its focus was on land reform, rural development and the position of co-wives in polygamous marriages. This is very different from the focus of black women's movements in the UK, which concentrate on racism within institutions and organizations.

Explain why the Women in Nigeria group had different concerns from British black women's movements.

I, A

Barrett and McIntosh (1985), both white feminists, admit that their work is ethnocentric, but not racist. However, black women's issues are 'tacked on' to their analysis of female oppression, with gender retaining the primary role. Their theoretical approach has obviously not been responsible for contributing to the material disadvantage of black women, but it has done little to challenge the inequalities that they experience. What all this shows is the conflict existing between black and white feminist theories:

... what is strongly evident is black feminist anger and white feminist angst around the whole issue of feminism and anti-racism. Missing are any systematic discussions of what might be initiatives that could incorporate and develop feminist anti-racist strategies.
(Knowles and Mercer, 1992, p. 115)

In other words, feminism needs to get itself sorted out if it is to challenge female and racial disadvan-

tage. It is therefore difficult to support Brah's conclusion that:

... black and white feminism should not be seen as essentially fixed oppositional categories but rather as historically contingent fields of contestation within discursive and material practices in a post-colonial society.
(Brah, 1992, p. 126)

Women in an ethnic minority are confined to the least privileged sections of the employment sector, suffering the effects of 'race', class and gender stereotypes. This, therefore, challenges any perspective which claims that the position of black women is essentially similar to that of white women. Feminism has consequently been divided into white and black feminist theory.

Age

Ethnic minority groups in the UK are relatively young compared with whites, because it was mainly young adults who migrated in the 1940s and 1950s. This has resulted in young black people being prominent in certain social areas, such as education (for discussion of this see Section 8.6). Their age structure makes them highly 'visible'.

Unemployment is another example: it has been high among young black people since the late 1970s and has been used as a tool for sustaining prejudice and discrimination by the state and the media. Unemployment has not been blamed on the large-scale economic circumstances which caused it, but rather on the black unemployed themselves. The urban 'riots' of the 1980s, too, were seen as a reaction to their resentment of the situation (see also Section 16.8).

On a cultural level, the children of further generations of immigrants have had different cultural experiences, e.g. a British education (see also Sections 8.6 and 10.6). Bradley (1996) has argued that this has resulted in young ethnic minorities conforming, on the whole, to British values. It is feared, however, that continued discrimination could make racial conflict a serious problem in the future:

... the situation may deteriorate and the problems experienced in some cities in the United States, such as New York, Los Angeles and Chicago, could be replicated in Britain.
(Bradley, 1996, p. 143)

Most sociological studies of 'race' and age have concentrated, for obvious reasons, on the young. However, the UK's ethnic minorities are steadily 'ageing'. Proportionately there are a lot fewer 'old' black people than white, but the numbers are significant and 'race' can be seen to affect ageing:

Ethnicity makes a substantial difference to the experience of ageing. For example, minority elder's experience of ageing is effected by the expectations and status of old age in their former country. (Richardson, 1996, p. 64)

Blackmore and Boneham (1994) built up a profile of 'minority elders', describing them as more likely to be female, few over 75 years old, predominantly working class, but also with diversity between groups, gender, cohort and individuals. They concluded that they all, however, suffered a 'triple jeopardy' of racism, ageism and material disadvantages associated with being working class. They also noted that old white people are disadvantaged in inner cities, therefore age may actually act as a 'leveller' to reduce inequalities between white and black people.

Class, gender and age are all important factors in the process of stratification, and in terms of people's lives they interact with 'race' and ethnicity. It is extremely important to recognize the different ways in which individuals and social groups are shaped by all these structures of stratification.

Further **reading**

A useful book concentrating on the UK is:

- Jones, T. (1993) *Britain's Ethnic Minorities*, London, Policy Studies Institute.

The following is a very good introductory text:

- Mason, D. (1995) *Race and Ethnicity in Modern Britain*, Oxford, Oxford University Press.

A clearly written and easily available introductory text is:

- O'Donnell, M. (1991) *Race and Ethnicity*, London, Longman.

The following is an interesting collection of essays for students who want a more detailed approach to specific areas of 'race' and ethnicity:

- Donald, J. and Rattansi, A., eds. (1992) *'Race', Culture and Difference*, London, Sage.

The following provides information on a wide range of social areas relating to 'race' and ethnicity:

- Skellington, R. (1996) *'Race' in Britain Today*, London, Sage/Open University Press.

A very useful text for those wanting more detailed information on 'race' and ethnicity is:

- Solomos, J. (1993) *Race and Racism in Britain*, London, Macmillan.

Exam **questions**

1 Assess the view that the mass media are the major source of stereotypes of ethnic minorities. Illustrate your answer with reference to sociological evidence.   [25 marks]
(AEB, Paper 2, June 1996)

2 Read the following data carefully and then answer the questions that follow.

Item A: Male and Female Earnings
'In 1983, women's average full-time earnings were only two-thirds those of men's. One reason for this is that men tend to work longer basic hours than women, even when women are engaged in full-time work. A second reason lies in the effects of overtime, since men work substantially more overtime than women. A third reason why women's weekly earnings are on average lower than men's is that women tend to be concentrated in low-paying industries and in sexually segregated occupations.'

Source: adapted from Veronica Beechey, *Women's Employment in Contemporary Britain* (in Beechey V. and Whitelegg E., *Women in Britain Today*)

Item B: White and Black Workers' Earnings
'White men on average earn a good deal more than black men, although the differences between the groups of women is much less. A study conducted in the early 1970s found that non-manual ethnic minority workers earned 77% of the earnings of their white colleagues; skilled manual earned 89%; while for semi-skilled and unskilled manual workers the earnings were the same. However, in this last case, in order to achieve this equality of earnings, ethnic minority workers have to do more shift work because their jobs are intrinsically worse paid. These differences derive from a number of factors. For example, black workers are concentrated in certain industries which traditionally pay low wages. Again, it is the case that in certain occupations, older people are paid more than younger ones. The black population is younger than the white, and this will in itself depress wages. Further, within any broad socio-economic category, white workers tend to occupy more promoted positions. But lastly, having eliminated all these factors, black workers seem to be paid less than white ones simply because they are black.'

Source: adapted from Abercrombie, Warde *et al.*, *Contemporary British Society* (1994)

a Using **Item A**, describe in your own words **two** reasons why full-time women workers earn less on average than full-time male workers. [4 marks]

b Using the information in **Item B**, outline the reasons for differences in earnings between white and black workers. [4 marks]

c Identify and explain **two** other areas of social life where black people suffer disadvantage. [6 marks]

d Critically assess sociological explanations of racism which seek to show why 'black workers seem to be paid less than white ones simply because they are black' (**Item B** lines 24–6)
(IBS, Paper 1, Summer 1995) [16 marks]

Back issues of *Sociology Review* (formerly known as *Social Studies Review*) also contain many articles on this field of sociology and many others.

Coursework **suggestions**

1 Test the hypothesis that black people's success in British sport is used to perpetuate racist ideologies in the UK

Black people in the UK are subject to racist stereotypes in all areas of their social lives. Positive achievements by black people may be interpreted negatively by individuals and social groups, resulting in the continuation of stereotypical images. One area where this seems to occur in the UK is within sport. When black athletes such as Linford Christie, Daley Thompson and Fatima Whitbread are successful, it is often assigned to prejudiced biological assumptions associated with their colour. In this piece of coursework you could investigate people's perceptions of black athletes by using a questionnaire and/or interviews. You may decide to carry out content analysis of newspaper reports on successful black athletes (perhaps comparing tabloid with broadsheet representations). Your context could involve a critical examination of relevant theories and studies: for example, biological explanations of 'race', labelling theory in education (black children may not be perceived as academics by their teachers or themselves, but rather as sports people and therefore they take up this area).

2 Test the hypothesis that Asian rap musicians can be used as evidence for the existence of post-modern identities

Asian rap music, such as that of Apache Indian, appears to represent the mixing of different cultural identities in a unique blend of music e.g. African-American rap with British-Asian experience. In this piece of coursework you could investigate whether Asian rappers are seen as new and individual musicians, or whether they are perceived as a mixture of different 'identities' that have been adopted from other cultures. This could be carried out using social surveys of a relevant population. It may also be useful to carry out content analysis of Asian rappers performing to assess the 'outward' expression of their identity. The context could involve a critical examination of the relevant theories and studies, such as post-modernism, Cohen (1992), or even youth culture.

The family

Chapter outline

7.1. What is the family?

Morgan (1996) argues that, despite its centrality to much earlier sociological study by key writers such as Parsons (1959), Murdock (1949) and Young and Willmott (1957, 1975), studies in the sociology of the family virtually disappeared in the 1970s. However, concepts of family have changed quite profoundly since the 1960s, as have sociological conceptions of family life.

The family is often considered by non-sociologists to be one of the few 'natural' institutions in society.

People often express concern about its 'health', regarding healthy families as good for society and being fairly sure that they know what a 'healthy family' is. It is considered 'ideal' that the family should consist of two parents of different sexes and one or more children – preferably their own. This model of the ideal family is shared by some sociologists. Others tend to denigrate it as the 'cereal packet' family – a dream promoted by advertisers to sell other products or an ideology designed to produce a stable concept of society which ignores the variety of family life both throughout the world and within our own society today (see Figure 7.1).

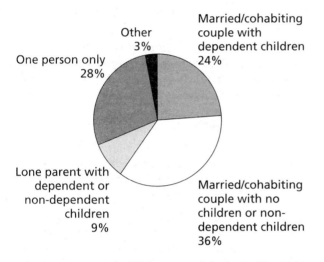

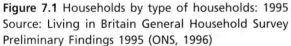

Figure 7.1 Households by type of households: 1995 Source: Living in Britain General Household Survey Preliminary Findings 1995 (ONS, 1996)

Clearly, some form of social network is required to introduce children to their own culture. Human beings take a long time to develop and they need to learn the culture of their own society if they are to exist within it in any acceptable way. Evidence of feral children and those unsocialized by their parents (see Section 10.1) shows that human beings need to learn such skills as speaking, affection, toilet control, tolerance and patience. What people eat, wear, believe in, aspire to and reward, as well as how they behave, has to be learned from someone. This process is often called socialization by sociologists. It is the way that the culture of a society is passed from one generation to the next. It teaches us the norms and values attached to particular roles or positions in society, such as how to be a student, a shopworker, a teacher, a friend or a parent.

Families are sometimes described as 'the agency of primary socialization'. They are usually the first group in which we learn aspects of our culture, although we continue to learn new roles, norms and values throughout our lives. We also learn

through many other socializing agencies such as school, friends, work, partnerships, the mass media.

Some writers who promote the traditional model of the family suggest that children who are not brought up in this sort of environment are more likely to become deviant and that changes to this structure are therefore a sign of social decay. Often moral pronouncements are made which attribute many of our social ills to the 'decline of family life'. The family (or family-style structures) can be seen as one of the most controversial institutions in society today.

Activity

Which of the examples below would you consider to be families and which not? Give reasons for each answer. Suggest other forms of living arrangements that might be defined as a family.

a Man and woman married for ten years without children

b Man and woman married for six years, two children at boarding school

c Man and woman cohabiting for three months with his daughter aged four

d 16-year-old girl living with her mother and her mother's boyfriend

e 16-year-old girl living with her boyfriend, his mother and his sister

f Man and woman, married and living with their four children, under age 10

g Woman cohabiting with her male partner and their baby, and a child from each of their previous marriages

h Woman cohabiting with her male partner and three young children from his marriage

i Woman cohabiting with her female partner and three young children from her marriage

j Two males cohabiting with an adopted son

k Man and woman cohabiting with an adopted son

l Woman living with her sister and her sister's husband

m Man living with his two children, his wife died last year

n Man and woman with a child, but living separately due to work

o Man and woman married for 25 years, both children away at university

I, A, E

Virtually every sociologist defines the family in a different way. Traditional functionalists (see Section 2.4), who see a traditional family structure as essential for the maintenance of society and the transmission of any social group's culture to the next generation, offer quite a narrow definition.

Murdock (1949) defined the family in the following way:

The family is a social group characterised by common residence, economic co-operation and reproduction. It includes adults of both sexes, at least two of whom maintain a socially approved sexual relationship, and one or more children, own or adopted, of the sexually co-habiting adults.
(Quoted in Haralambos and Holborn, 1995, p. 317)

However, a more inclusive view is taken by Giddens (1993a), who suggests this definition:

A family is a group of persons directly linked by kin connections, the adult members of which assume responsibility for caring for children.
(Giddens, 1993a, p. 370)

Discussion point

What criteria would you use for defining 'a family'?

Perhaps the term family is no longer really appropriate for describing the way we live our lives today. It may be more accurate to incorporate more inclusive terms such as households or household units as suggested by Nik Jorgensen (1996). Despite these problems of definition, we shall continue to use the term 'family', as it remains such an important social institution, even if its exact structure is increasingly varied, flexible and diverse.

The family as a universal institution

Much of the evidence of a universal family structure comes from the work of Murdock (1949). As a functionalist, he sought to show that some form of family structure was the basis of all societies – that is that the family was universal. He argued that the family performs three key functions without which society could not survive:

- it stabilizes sexual and reproductive functions
- it provides basic economic requirements such as food and shelter
- it provides the function of socialization of the next generation into the norms, values and other aspects of culture in that society (see Section 10.1).

Most sociologists who support a traditional family

structure (such as that outlined by Murdock) argue that the family is universal because it serves particular functions for society and for all its members. Not all functionalists agree totally on which functions are essential. Parsons (1959) argued that in modern societies there are only two 'basic and irreducible' functions:

- stabilization of the adult personality
- primary socialization of children.

Most of these writers agree that evidence and arguments can convince us that a family structure is essential for the maintenance of society and this will always be the case. The family is universal because its functions cannot be performed by any other institution.

The basic functions of reproduction, satisfying sexuality and the rearing and caring of children are necessary to ensure (society's) survival. The most efficient way of achieving these ends is the nuclear family.
(Muncie *et al.*, 1995, pp. 11–12)

From a social anthropological point of view, examining families from a number of different societies, O'Connell (1994) suggests that the family is definable only by its functions. She claims that:

While there is no universally applicable definition of the family, there is a broad consensus about the role of the family in society and the functions it should perform, namely, procreation, socialisation, providing affection and emotional support. In particular the family has a central role in the education, socialisation and care of children.
(O'Connell, 1994, p. 1)

Activity

Identify the key functions of the family suggested by the above authors. To what extent are these functions served by your parents or other kin members? Can you think of any other institutions which serve these functions?

I, A, E

The debates about whether the functions of the family have changed or not continue (see Fletcher (1966) and Shorter (1977)), but the basic insistence on the family as essential for the maintenance of society (and therefore natural and inevitable) remains. An interesting evaluation of this viewpoint which sees the family as functional for capitalist society, and therefore universal only under capitalism, comes from Marxists (see Section 2.5) and, in a moderated form, from Marxist feminists. (See also Section 5.2.)

In a book first published in 1884, Marx's colleague Frederick Engels (1972, orig. pub. 1884) demonstrated how the family arose in response to the development of private property and the need for men to pass on their property to their own offspring. Thus he saw the main function of the family as the reproduction of the capitalist system. Beechey (1977) argued that housewives perform major functions for capitalism by providing free care for current and future (male) workers and also as a cheap 'reserve army of labour', easily returned to the home in times of recession. Furthermore, Zaretsky (1976) claimed that as an area of personal freedom and release, the family helps to support capitalism, although often at the expense of greater oppression of women. However, from an interactionist viewpoint, Duncombe and Marsden (1995) argue that women in fact do a 'triple shift' – as workers in paid employment and in the domestic sphere, while also providing most of the 'emotional' work required in marriages.

From a Marxist-feminist perspective, Barrett and McIntosh (1991) suggest that the nuclear family is an ideological instrument whereby the nuclear family is presented as an ideal for us all to aspire to. This makes the concept of the family 'anti-social', as it presents other forms of family life as inferior. Thus, single or homosexual and lesbian parents can be presented as deficient, while single people are often to be pitied (see Section 5.4). This ideological view of the family allows the state to stereotype and scapegoat alternative family structures.

Most of these arguments suggest that the family – as a concept, anyway – serves the interests of capitalism. However, many feminists argue that men benefit most from familial arrangements. Evidence to support this 'radical feminist' approach comes from the fact that far more women than men sue for divorce (about 72 per cent of divorce petitions are initiated by women), while men are more likely than women to re-marry – although this may reflect their greater opportunity to do so. Gittins (1993) suggests that because men generally marry women younger than themselves, they tend to have a wider choice of potential partners after divorce than do women.

Radical feminists suggest that patriarchal ideology (the concept of male domination, derived from the superior role of the male in the family) leads to the tyrannization of women and children both within the family and within the wider society. Rape and sexual assault are seen as evidence of male power and the family is the key site of its maintenance. (See also Sections 5.3 and 7.7.)

Liberal feminists blame neither men nor capitalism for the unequal treatment of women and children in the family. They have argued for legal changes in order to ensure equality of opportunity. The most important pieces of legislation related to equal opportunities for women are the Equal Pay Act (1970) and the Sex Discrimination Act (1975), although they mostly affect women in the public arena rather than in the home. Of more consequence for women in the family have been the legal changes that outlaw rape within marriage and a greater awareness of the nature of domestic violence.

Activity

a Using material which can be found in your local library, outline the main ways in which these two Acts of Parliament have sought to equalize opportunities for women and men.

b From Marxist feminist and radical feminist perspectives, suggest reasons why legal changes alone might be unlikely to equalize the position of women and children – especially in the family.

K, U, I, A

Sociobiological views of the family

The zoologist Desmond Morris in *The Naked Ape* (1968) argued that it is essential for both animal and human societies to pass on the culture of the group. With 'naked apes' (i.e. human beings) this is particularly essential owing to the long period of dependency of the young on their mother. This also tied the mother to the home base and meant that hunting parties were all-male groups. To limit the threat to his family unit while the male was away hunting, the 'pair-bond' evolved in order to reduce sexual rivalries between males, maintain female commitment and co-operation and ensure maximum care for the offspring. These fundamental patterns have laid down the foundations of love and pairing that we find today in nuclear family structures.

Such views are shared by a number of sociologists such as Tiger and Fox (1972) who argue that men and women possess a different biogrammer – or biological programmer – which means that each sex 'naturally' adopts different roles, especially in regard to family life. Therefore men are seen as 'naturally' more aggressive and promiscuous while women are considered 'naturally' more faithful and caring – especially to their children. (See also Sections 5.2 and 6.4.)

Alternative family structures

One of the main problems with these functionalist and sociobiological analyses of the family is the evidence of diversity that exists in family structures all over the world. To suggest that the family as defined by them is universal means that there cannot be an example of an effective system of socialization which contradicts the parameters which Murdock and other writers regarded as essential. The ideological argument is that any system which tries to radically change their family structure will not survive. Murdock and Parsons were Americans writing at the time of the Cold War between the USA and the Soviet Union. Some Marxists argued that the family was a bourgeois institution, i.e. one which served the interests of the ruling class and which must therefore be abolished. Therefore, the functionalist argument that families were both universal and functional was at least partly intended to challenge communist ideology in the 1940s and 1950s.

The evidence of alternative family structures is certainly very convincing, although many might argue that they are variations on a theme.

The Nayar

An anthropologist, Gough (1972) studied the Nayar tribe in Southern India to show a picture of their family life. Girls were married before puberty, but men did not live with their wives and the only obligation the woman owed was to mourn at her husband's funeral. After puberty women could receive visiting 'husbands', as the men spent most of their time away as fighters. They would visit other 'wives', although the husband took priority when he was home. Either party could end the marriage or relationship at any time. The care of children was shared by women and the paternity of the child was not relevant. In a matrilineal society like the Nayar what little property there was descended through the female line. Males also made little economic contribution to their children's upbringing and this role was mainly played by brothers and sisters who tended to form an economic unit based on shared maternity.

The Oneida community

Founded by a Christian preacher John Humphrey Noyes in 1848, the aim of this community was to establish complete spiritual, economic and sexual equality. They set up a system of economic communism and group marriage where everyone contributed equally to the group. As well as the system of group marriage, the community introduced a programme of eugenic breeding, where only those considered suitable were allowed to reproduce, while other, controlled forms of sexual activity were allowed among other members where both parties agreed. After early care by the mother, children were raised communally and treated equally by community members.

The Kibbutz

In Israel in the 1940s, collective settlements were set up based on a system of collective ownership and childrearing. While marriage was monogamous (one spouse), children lived in collective dormitories and were raised by a number of child caretakers or educators. Children would spend an hour or so daily with their parents, but their sibling group was effectively made up of all the children of a similar age. Parents and children did not comprise an economic unit as all worked for the good of the kibbutz and needs were provided for collectively. Spiro (1968) argued that this system of childrearing cannot fit into Murdock's definition of the family, although the kibbutz could be seen as a form of extended family. Communes established in the 1960s also adopted a similar form of collective childrearing, although they tended to be short-lived.

The New World black family

In many parts of the Caribbean and among black families in the United States, matrifocal families, based on mother, children and grandmother make up a larger than average percentage of the population. Melville Herskovits (1958) suggested that this reflected traditional family structures in West Africa, from which many black Americans and African–Caribbeans had originated before being captured and enslaved. M. G. Smith (1962) claimed that mother and child formed the basic family unit under slavery, as the father was often sold separately, partly to ensure sexual access for white slaveowners to black female slaves. (See also Sections 6.2 and 6.3.) Other writers such as Liebow (1967) argued that most black men were so poorly paid that they were unable to maintain a family, so it made economic sense for the woman to receive sexual favours and economic contributions from a number of different fathers. Lewis (1959) saw the matrifocal family as part of the culture of poverty which poor people use to make sense of their situation. (See also Sections 4.8 and 14.7.)

Activity

Explain at least three alternative models to the traditional nuclear family. Suggest reasons why each of them may experience problems in modern industrialized societies and how they may make it easier for some people to raise children in society today. **I, A**

Defining the family

As Leonard and Hood-Williams (1988) point out, a lot of the problems involved in this debate relate to the way the family is defined. To merely define it as mother and offspring is clearly too inclusive, but as soon as we try to incorporate the idea of two adults, then the definition does not allow for diversity between social groups or even within them.

However, there is a political dimension to the debate which is probably unavoidable in such an emotional issue. The promotion of the ideal family does have important implications, suggesting the inferiority of other family types. There is a further important question to be asked here – who does the defining? One problem is that sociologists search for a definition which is both meaningful and valid, but one which they can operationalize in order to test hypotheses.

Activity

Draw up your own family tree. Decide who to include and who to leave out. Think about the criteria you use to define who is a member of your family and who is not. What sort of family do you come from (nuclear/extended/reconstituted etc.)?

Compare your family tree with other people you know to identify similarities and differences.

I, A

The ideology of the family

Gittins (1993) argues that the ideology (see Section 17.4) of the universal nuclear family is more important than the reality, as this ideology has major consequences for our view of society. (See also Section 5.3.) She demonstrates how a number of aspects that we tend to take for granted as 'natural' are in fact very different in different social conditions and are therefore socially constructed. Our concept of marriage as a binding contract between one male and one female is challenged by the existence of polygamy in many societies and serial monogamy in western societies today. The idea that marriage has always been (and is) based on love and mutual attraction was not only uncommon in many societies, but remains questionable in many cases in our own.

However, she concludes that some sort of definition of the family is important if we are to debate issues within it. She believes that relationships between people can be extremely varied, but that the ideological view of the 'good' family is based on long-term heterosexual relationships which always incorporate childbearing. Although such a formation may be an ideal in our society, this does not make it either universal or natural.

Furthermore, as Barrett and McIntosh (1991) point out:

The way in which family life is privileged makes it harder for people to live outside families. . . those who choose to challenge the hegemonic power of familialism have (also) been beleaguered in a climate of market individualism allied to moral conservatism.

(Barrett and McIntosh, 1991, pp. 163–4)

It appears that the ideology of the family is becoming stronger than ever as diverse forms of family life may well be on the increase. Despite larger numbers of people choosing to cohabit or live alone, the ideal of the family, best epitomized by the 'Back to Basics' campaign of the government in the early 1990s, is promoted ever more strongly. Choosing not to marry (although for many it was not really a choice) was seen as a valid way of life in pre-industrial society. Now, single men are regarded with suspicion and single women still often looked on as unfortunate. (See Figure 7.2 on page 240.)

Discussion point

Identify the negative and positive views about living alone presented in the article in Figure 7.2. What do you think is the writer's view of single people? Do you agree with her or not? How does this article reinforce the ideology of familialism?

Like Gittins, Barrett and McIntosh do acknowledge the popularity of 'familialism' (the promotion of family life) and admit that most alternatives are often perceived as unsatisfactory. They propose three ways in which familialist ideology (see also Section 5.3) could be undermined so that people would be free to choose their lifestyles more freely:

- encouraging variety – e.g. communes, single households, same-sex pairings
- avoiding oppressive relationships – giving support to those who find family life oppressive and may wish to escape from it
- avoiding domesticity – basic domestic chores to be carried out equally by all members of the household, so that the living arrangements of each person serves their own needs rather than those of society. (See also Section 7.5.)

Discussion point

How do you think these aims might be achieved within your own or your ideal familial arrangement? Are there any other ways you can suggest to avoid familialism?

Will you be lonesome tonight?

They're stylish, ambitious and rich. There are more of them than ever. But, argues **Angela Lambert**, the lives of the young and single often hide an aching loneliness

Takeaway meals, lonely-hearts columns, men's "lifestyle" (not "girlie") magazines, late-night shops, video hire, supermarket wines, cookery classes for men, body-building classes for women, dating agencies, singles holidays, cheap air-travel, sexual tourism, surfing the Internet . . . all these benefit from a vast market.

They value all these objects as an opportunity for self-indulgence ("presents for the house"); self-advertisement ("look how discriminating my taste is: clock how much money I've got"); and self-definition ("I am the sort of person who can afford these sort of tricks"). But this display hides the absence of any deep emotional commitment.

For in all this consuming, what they are unconsciously doing is buying parenting, in the form of food and treats, to make up for the absence of the reassurance that parents – or a spouse – would otherwise supply. For despite being in work and earning good money, loneliness is prevalent among them. They disguise it all too well by joining sports clubs and gyms, roller-blading, eating out at weekends or going clubbing in shiny clothes.

Naturally they don't call it loneliness, which they regard as a stigma – the lonely always do. They define living alone as the pursuit of individuality. Yet loneliness is the most obvious and predictable consequence of late marriage and even later child-bearing.

It is not just that they find it difficult to establish relationships based on real intimacy. They even find meeting people difficult. Relationships with colleagues of the opposite sex – potential partners, cohabiters or spouses – are complicated by political correctness. Except in a few die-hard, macho City office environments, it is more prudent not to flirt.

The number of people using introduction agencies, as marriage bureaux prefer to be known, has doubled in the last 15 years, from around 50,000 in 1980 to 100,000 this year. There are an estimated 200 in the UK, of which some 25 per cent close every year, usually having taken the money and run, trusting to the embarrassment of clients not to pursue publicity. Many use accommodation addresses and are untraceable once they have folded.

Given these risks, many single people prefer to place an advertisement in one of the lonely hearts columns that have grown tenfold in recent years. Those in the upmarket national newspapers have proliferated, catering as they do for an audience of young ABC1s.

There is no doubt that these single high-pressured lives come with an enormous downside: the aching loneliness that comes from lack of commitment. Asked by Mori in 1993 to list what they most disliked about being single, 37 per cent of single young people cited loneliness; 16 per cent sleeping alone; 15 per cent the lack of emotional security; 9 per cent felt unprotected; 8 per cent feared they would never have children; 7 per cent hated cooking and eating alone. It forms a bleak catalogue of the terrors of the single life, in which it is hard to recognise the joys of bachelordom so ardently recommended by *Cosmo* and *GQ*.

It is my theory, based on dozens of conversations, that the single greatest reason why this generation avoids commitment is the failure of marriages in their parents' generation. They have become suspicious of commitment, worried that it will cramp their style and ambition.

When I married in the early Sixties, we were both 22, and no one, least of all us, thought twice about it. Most of my contemporaries were walking up the aisle at about the same age. That was just before things really began to swing. Since then we've had the Pill, flower power, women's liberation, feminism, equal opportunities legislation and political correctness, all of which have done their bit to alter the way the sexes meet, mate and relate.

Today's young are marrying later than their parents, if at all; later than a generation unencumbered by war has ever done. When my stepson married at 20, the general reaction was one of astonishment. "He's how old? And his girlfriend is 21? But they're so young!" In that year, 1992, the average age of first marriage for women was 26, and for men, 28.

One-third of this age-group cohabit, most of them claiming that their pair-bond or family unit is at least as secure as their parents' marriages. They need no formalities to undo the relationship. They decide between them who gets the flat, the furniture, the cat, and the CDs, and go their separate ways.

By the early Nineties, the UK had the highest divorce rate in the European Union. The word "family" has taken on a new connotation. It does not necessarily imply a blood link; instead, the family network has become a living reminder of past relationships and love affairs.

Permanence and good example, let alone religion, has played little part in their lives. It is no exaggeration to call these 25- to 35-year-olds spiritually lost and dislocated. Those too sceptical or too intelligent to join one of the clubs that spring up like dragons' teeth are resolute atheists. Most are driven by work, ambition and money. They have pleasures and desires, hobbies and pastimes, but little by way of what someone older would recognise for spiritual ballast. They fight alone in a competitive world.

Figure 7.2 Article on the single life. Source: adapted from *The Independent*, 19 October 1995

It is clear that neither Barrett and McIntosh nor Gittins believe that the family is natural or universal, regarding such claims as part of the ideology designed to control people in society and, in particular, to limit the range of opportunities for women. The view of the family adopted by most feminist approaches are summarized by Edholm (1991), who concludes that:

The family, particularly the nuclear family, can be seen through comparative analysis, as just one very specific means of organising the relationships between parents and children, males and females. It is not, as so often has been claimed, some kind of 'natural', instinctive and 'sacred' unit. . . . Universal definitions of human relations must be constantly questioned and the whole notion of the

'natural' must, in terms of human relations, be challenged, and the 'unnatural' – in these terms the social construction of relationships – must be fully recognised.
(Edholm, in Loney *et al.* (eds), 1991, p. 152)

However, it is important to remember that the idea of the family as a natural institution with a specific and desirable nuclear, heterosexual, two-parent structure still dominates most political, media and 'commonsense' discourse about family life.

7.2 The relationship between the family and social change

The family and industrialization

Many sociologists have argued that the coming of the industrial revolution (see also Sections 2.2 and 9.2) brought about huge changes in society, including changes to the structure of family and kinship networks. Pre-industrial families tended to be mostly involved in production for use, selling some of their surplus in the market place. All members of the family were involved in the production process and they usually lived near each other. There were some relatively wealthy families who owned larger amounts of land. Often there was a system of rights and obligations between landowner and the peasants who worked on his land, known as feudalism (see Section 16.5). So land was, for most people, the only form of wealth, and production was mostly for personal consumption. The family was the main unit of production.

Historians such as Lane (1979) argue that the key change brought about by industrialization was the move to production for exchange. Wealth was held in the form of capital (money, factories and machinery) and the aim of production for the capitalists was to make a profit, often for further investment. Workers worked for wages when they were needed but the whole family was usually no longer involved in the production process. One result was that men mainly sold their labour power while women – although many did work for wages – tended to stay in the home and care for children, often dependent on the earnings of the husband. Although the process of industrialization varied in terms of class, region and throughout different periods of time, the industrial revolution brought important changes to the way families were structured and how their members related to one another.

Functionalist views of families and industrialization

Pre-industrial societies

Functionalists (see Section 2.4) stress the relationships between institutions in society and how changes in one aspect of society, for example, the economy, will bring changes in other institutions, including the family. They, therefore, see the family as changing and responding to the needs of society before, during and after industrialization. Drawing on the example of Irish families in rural areas in the 1940s (see Arensburg and Kimball (1968)), they argue that most pre-industrial families existed in a patriarchal extended family structure. This usually meant that the landholder dominated his wives and children, while even his adult sons and their wives lived with and deferred to him. Functionalists therefore argue that the nuclear family mainly developed as a result of industrialization.

However, this view has been challenged by social historians such as Laslett (Laslett and Wall, 1972), who showed convincingly, from the evidence provided by a study of parish registers in the seventeenth century, that families in much of pre-industrial northern Europe were most likely to consist of a more nuclear family structure of adults and their dependent children and siblings. He suggested that this was mainly due to the late marriage and relatively short life expectancy of most people at that time.

> ### Discussion point
> What problems do you think might arise when trying to study family structures of hundreds of years ago?

Industrialization

Fletcher (1962) argued that the long hours of work required by early industrialists meant that family members rarely saw each other, apart from a few hours for eating and sleeping. Low wages and poverty meant that the home was often poorly furnished and uncomfortable. Arguably this led to high levels of deprivation and all forms of vice including drunkenness and incest. With the development of industrialization, and especially improved systems of transport, people were more able to move away from their family of origin. This often allowed them to live in more pleasant, suburban surroundings. As a consequence the isolated nuclear family developed owing mainly to increased geographical mobility.

Increased prosperity also gave people greater economic independence from their family of origin.

Activity

Draw up a map to show the distribution of your immediate family members. Does it show that your family is geographically isolated from the rest of your relatives? Speak to parents and grandparents to identify if any changes have taken place over the past 50 years or so.

I, A

Fletcher therefore concluded that industrialization led to a move from extended to nuclear families. He also believed that this indicated that family members were consequently closer to each other and more supportive than they were before industrialization or during the period of early industrial production. Therefore, the nuclear family today is not evidence of decline, but of a growth in family ties.

However, evidence once again has been used to challenge functionalist views of family structure. Michael Anderson (1971) studied the 1851 census records in Preston, which was then at the centre of the cotton industry. Here, he found evidence of extended family networks among nearly a quarter of all households. If Laslett was right, these had developed largely since industrialization. Anderson suggested this was mainly due to the hardship and uncertainty experienced by workers at the time. The only way families could survive was as a system of reciprocal support which benefited all parties. Those who could work did so, while others cared for the children, and in many cases, the orphans, of the workers.

However, functionalists still tend to argue that changes in the process of production will lead to changes in other institutions. Therefore Fletcher is arguing that the structure of the family has changed to 'fit' better into the productive process and that this is beneficial to family members. Similarly Parsons (1959) argued that there is a functional relationship between the family and the economy, as the isolated nuclear family facilitates both geographical and social mobility.

Discussion point

What are the advantages and disadvantages of living in extended and nuclear families?

The conjugal family

Goode (1964) argued that the nuclear or conjugal family developed in a variety of ways, but to some extent these did have to suit the 'needs' of an industrialized system. This was particularly related to the need for social mobility (see Section 4.9) which meant that status was largely achieved through the particular demands of the job rather than being ascribed at birth by the family of origin.

The conjugal family establishes its own household, largely ignoring ties of wider kinship. Most importantly, often the family of origin no longer assists its younger members in gaining jobs or finding partners and unless this is the case, contact with wider kin is reduced. The close ties between conjugal family members also provides a form of emotional satisfaction not found in most areas of industrial employment.

Young and Willmott (1975) have also argued that industrialization led to a change in relationships between family members. They showed how the family moved from the pre-industrial unit working largely as a team to far more segregated conjugal roles during industrialization, where husband and wife tended to work and socialize in largely separate social spheres. They contend that conjugal roles are now far more symmetrical with the family operating as a unit of consumption, sharing social and leisure time and contributing similarly to the running of the family unit.

Their 1957 study of East London showed extensive evidence of close-knit, kinship-based communities in Bethnal Green among working-class families in the 1950s. Such groups were mainly mobilized by women, incorporating grandmother, her daughter and the daughter's children. Like Anderson, they concluded that these networks developed during industrialization as a result of poverty and as insurance against disaster. Young and Willmott also found, in a follow up study in 1973, that slum clearance of the East End (see also Section 16.8) had largely diminished these communities (and changed relationships between spouses), although some older parents would follow their children into the suburbs when possible.

Research (Bott, 1971; Rosser and Harris, 1965) shows that there have always been complex patterns of family interaction and structure. According to Morgan (1975), Litwak argued that we should talk about the 'modified extended family' to demonstrate the close links between family members of apparently nuclear families and their wider kin. Allan (1985) prefers the term 'modified elementary family' because people tend only to keep in touch with closer family members. Willmott (1988) favours the term 'dispersed extended family' (see Figure 7.3) to show close kinship links between wider family groups, even though they may live quite a distance away. None of these models can really account for all the different patterns that seem to exist today.

Activity

This model suggests that families maintain limited but important bonds with their wider kin. Draw a diagram to identify which members of your family you see, how often and how near (or far away) they live to you. You may wish to incorporate other forms of contact, such as telephone calls.

I, A

The traditional extended family

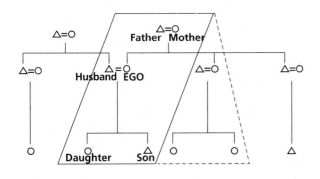

Social networks

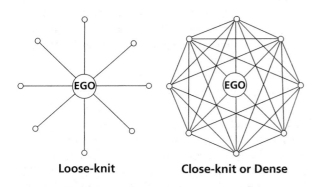

Loose-knit   Close-knit or Dense

Figure 7.3 Modes of kinship. Source: developed from Willmott (1988)

The working-class family in the 1990s

O'Brien and Jones (1996) returned to the parts of East London studied by Young and Willmott in the 1950s and 1960s to see what, if anything, had changed. The main pattern they observed was one of diversity in family and household composition. There were far more one-parent households, divorce, re-marriage and cohabitation compared to the 1950s. In fact these family structures appeared to be more common in their study than in the population as a whole. There were also higher levels of dual income households and ethnic diversity than

found either in the 1950s or in many other parts of the UK.

Such changes clearly reflect the increase in divorce rates, as well as changes in the roles of women – the majority of whom are now in paid employment (see also Section 9.3) – and in the ethnic composition of the UK (see Section 6.2). Although they found considerable structural differences between family composition in the 1990s compared with those in the 1950s, they also identified a number of patterns which had shown little change. One striking example was the persistence of 'matrilocality', that is, married women whose own mother (and father) still lived in the area. The maternal grandmother remained a particularly popular and important figure in the family household.

Social and geographical mobility were comparatively low in the area, suggesting a link between close family ties and low educational achievement, although there was also evidence of higher aspirations among younger people, who also generally expressed a greater desire for equality in the home between men and women. Overall, though, O'Brien and Jones found surprisingly little change in kinship patterns in East London, despite a pluralization of household structures and lifestyles and higher educational and occupational aspirations among large numbers of people in the area – especially women.

Industrialization and the role of women in the family

Feminists have particularly noted that industrialization affected men and women differently. Oakley (1974a,b) showed how women moved from being equal partners when the family was a pre-industrial unit of production to being increasing constricted and confined to the home by industrialization and factory legislation. She suggests that these changes, accompanied by Victorian ideology about the role and nature of women (see Section 5.2), resulted in the 'mother-housewife role' becoming the dominant role for women in industrialized societies.

Hall (1982) extends this analysis to show how as men became increasingly identified by their work, the separation of work and home became more important. Men and women increasingly operated within separate spheres, men with business and politics (the public domain) and women with the home and children (the private domain). Men whose wives went out to work were considered inadequate providers, while waged females such as mill girls were notorious for their independence and cheekiness.

However, O'Day (1983) argues that the roles of males and females were often quite separate before industrialization. Davidoff (1979) suggests that many women earned money from within the household. Both these writers suggest that the separation of home and work was neither so dramatic nor so complete as writers such as Oakley and Hall contend.

Whatever the reasons, it can be seen that the idea of the male breadwinner and the female domestic carer was well established by the end of the nineteenth century. Hartmann (1981) argued that this was largely due to an alliance between capitalist employers and working men (see also Section 5.3 and 9.3) to ensure high profits for the former and reasonable wages for the latter, although this view has been challenged by Humpheries (1977) who regards the fight for a family wage as a form of resistance by working-class people against capitalist exploitation.

Activity

Hartmann can be described as a dual-systems feminist, while Humpheries argues from a Marxist feminist position. Explain in your own words, taking material from this and other units in this chapter, their different views of the influence of industrialization on the working-class family.

U, A

Comparative approaches to the family

O'Connell (1994) argues that:

Despite massive research, historians have failed to locate 'a golden age of the family'. Rather, the evidence indicates that flux and inequalities characterize the family throughout its history.
(O'Connell, 1994, p. 6)

Thus, family patterns may be the result of economic changes in society, but there are a wide variety of factors which influence the structure equally profoundly. These include slavery, colonization and political factors, such as the rise of communism or Nazism.

O'Connell accepts that the introduction of capitalist industrial production has affected family structure by separating work and home in a way unimaginable in most former economic systems. However, the extent of such changes varies widely between countries. She suggests a number of common factors including:

the weakening of some traditional family ties and the emergence of new forms of family solidarity; changing relations between women and men within the family, and rising divorce rates; fewer children per family, and increasing longevity.
(O'Connell, 1994, p. 7)

Her evidence for such changes is taken from a wide variety of societies, but they demonstrate differences as well as similarities. In most industrializing societies there is considerable migration to the towns, most often among men. In Latin America and the Philippines, however, the majority of migrants, both to the cities and to work abroad, have been women. This clearly affects family life in a number of ways. Young people are less easily controlled by their parents when they move away, and while they may benefit from greater freedom, the authority of older family members is consequently weakened and less well established. Urban living also seems to reduce marital stability. For example, she suggests that some men living and working in the cities in many parts of Africa are often reluctant to support their wives, children or other family members who remain in rural areas.

Geographical mobility is a feature of most industrial societies but, for a number of reasons, moving the family for work is not considered advisable by many Japanese people. They fear the detrimental effects on family life, especially the disrupted schooling of their children. If moving is necessary, husbands will most likely live near their work place in the week and return home at weekends. This means that many mothers are single parents in all but name, while alcoholism and depression is a not uncommon result of such a disrupted lifestyle for a number of Japanese men. O'Connell suggests that as many as 60 per cent of Japanese men no longer eat breakfast with their children owing to work commitments.

The Indian family has long been traditionally patriarchal, with property passing down from father to son and the male head of household having unquestioned dominance over his wife and children. Urbanization and industrialization, accompanied by considerable increases in educational opportunity, might have been expected to change the gender roles and relationships within the family. However, the greater earning power of males has, if anything, increased the prestige of males in the family.

The above material suggests that industrialization has a very variable effect on family structure and relationships and that the symmetrical family (see Section 7.5) is certainly not commonly found throughout industrialized societies. It seems to be part of the diversity of family structures to be found in modern and modernizing societies.

Two more commonly identifiable trends are those of smaller family size and greater longevity, similar to the structures found in British society today. While these changes raise points in particular about care of the elderly, this is a far more serious problem in the United States of America, Japan and Northern Europe, with their rapidly ageing populations,

---

Household size

During the '70s and '80s and the first half of the '90s, there has been a gradual reduction in the average (mean) size of households from 2.91 in 1971 to 2.51 in 1989 and to 2.40 in 1995. This has reflected a combination of:

- the gradual ageing of the population;
- a decrease in the number of live births;
- an increase in the proportion of one-person households;
- a reduction in the proportion of large households (5 or more persons);
- an increase in the proportion of lone-parent families.

Family groups

In 1995, the most frequent family types in private households were:

- couples (married or cohabiting) with no dependent children (36%);
- persons living alone (28%);
- couples (married or cohabiting) with dependent children (24%).

Figure 7.4 Household composition and family groups. Source: *Living in Britain* General Household Survey Preliminary Findings 1995 (ONS, 1996)

Activity

From the material in Figure 7.4, identify five key trends each in household composition and family groups in recent years.

than in most areas throughout Africa and Latin America.

However, as O'Connell (1994) points out, while fewer children and increased longevity seems to raise a problem of caring for the elderly, not all families follow the apparent trend in the West for smaller, more isolated, family units. She found that:

Urbanisation has not led inevitably to nuclear family units; rather there seems to be an increase in the average size of households. In Kenya, households are generally larger in urban than in rural areas. Various reasons are suggested for this. The rising age of first marriage means that young adults remain in their parental families for longer, and economic difficulties hamper couples establishing separate residential units. In addition, individuals who migrate to the cities usually live with other family members and frequently depend on them for employment.

(O'Connell, 1994, p. 10)

The key finding throughout our study of the impact of industrialization on family structure is that of diversity and change. It is essential to study such processes in more detail if we are to really understand how family structure and family life is organized in contemporary societies. One argument is that we now live in a post-modern, post-industrial society (see Sections 9.4 and 10.11), and that this, too, is having a profound influence on family structure.

Post-modern views of the family

In trying to explain how post-modern thought affects our view of family life, Cheal (1991) argues that:

Postmodernist theorists have begun to grapple with the possibility that many of the features of social life that were taken for granted for a long time will have to be rethought.

(Cheal, 1991, p. 145)

He suggests that the key aspects of post-modernism are pluralism, disorder and fragmentation, and these concepts can be seen to be particularly relevant for a description of family life in many societies today. The post-modern view of family life is very different to seeing the family as the entity which more or less defined our gender roles – female as mother and carer and male as breadwinner – throughout the past 200 years at least. At one time, some parents called each other 'mother' or 'father' within the family.

Morgan (1996) suggests that from a post-modern approach:

'family' and 'gender' can be seen as increasingly problematic and theoretical entities with relatively little direct connection between them. This may roughly be identified with the analysis of postmodern society.

(Morgan, 1996, p. 73)

From this view, lone parents, surrogate mothers, lesbian households or gay couples, for example, are not seen as problematic, although many people in our society still consider them to be so. Most feminists argue that the basis of gender differences in the labour market are seen as being largely constructed through the domestic division of labour (see Section 7.5) and the different expectations about working mothers and working fathers. Women who work outside the home (as the majority now do) are expected to combine this with taking on most of the responsibility for childcare and domestic work. As a result of this, most children still grow up expecting their mothers to do more in the house than their fathers and women see domestic responsibilities as their own.

While this arrangement is not fixed, and cannot always be seen as disempowering women, it does reinforce the claim of some feminists, post-modernists and post-structural feminists that gender identity is largely constructed by familial expectations, rather than male and female roles being a social expression of their biological differences. This debate about the domestic division of labour is explored more fully in Section 7.5, but from this point of view, traditional two parent families can be seen as reinforcing the gendered division of labour in our society.

Morgan (1996) also argues that in some cases the family can obscure gender relationships. Marriage is still seen as the central domestic relationship for most people. We may accept some reduction of gender differences in marriage, but expectations about the sexual role (and sexual orientation) of married couples remain important. There are expectations now that most women will seek to combine a job or career with marriage (and often with children), while men are generally expected to contribute far more to the parenting of their children than was previously the case.

It appears that a more varied and complex set of domestic arrangements is becoming acceptable to many people. However, certain commonsense assumptions about marriage remain, including an assumption that both partners are exclusively heterosexual and that they marry with the intention of staying together.

There still seems to be a general rejection of the idea in our society that people should marry for money, or to help someone stay in the country or to suit the wishes of their parents and other family members. Clearly, post-modern views consider diversity in family life to be largely acceptable and desirable. As we shall see, not all sociologists or politicians share this view. Indeed it has become very much part of the current debate about the decline of morality and the lack of societal stability that many people perceive as characteristic of post-modern (or at least changing) society. For sociologists, it is important to examine the evidence about family structures more fully before we explore debates about their implications.

7.3 **Contemporary family structures**

Patterns of family life

In the UK in the late twentieth century, we seem to have more varieties of family types that ever before. There are dual-parent families where both partners work, one partner works or neither partner works – all with or without children. There are more single-headed families (usually headed by women) than previously, although it is far from a new phenomenon. We see more people living alone, co-habiting, divorcing, re-marrying, as well as different types of extended families and a whole range of 'nuclear' families, some more 'isolated' than others.

Statistical patterns in family life

Table 7.1 on page 247 shows that the nuclear family (married couple with dependent children) now only constitutes about 25 per cent of households in the UK today. Approximately 28 per cent are single households and about half are made up of adults only. However, this approach ignores the effect of the lifecycle on family life. Many people living alone, or adults without children, may have lived in nuclear type families in the past and/or may do so in the future. To see the nuclear family as the only acceptable form of family life for all ignores the extremely wide diversity of family and household arrangements found in modern societies.

Changing patterns of family life?

The 1995 OPCS report on marriage statistics in England and Wales highlights the trends. Table 7.2 compares 1993 statistics with those from 1983.

Types of diversity

The apparent diversity of family structures in modern industrial societies has been the subject of much sociological debate. Functionalists argue that the nuclear family still predominates or has been replaced by a similar type of 'reconstituted' family structure (incorporating step-parents and step-children). Others accept that family life is certainly changing, but regard this as a sign of moral decay – this can be seen for example in the New Right's call for a return to traditional family values or the 'ethical socialist' concern with the effects of absent fathers (see Section 2.10). Others, especially some feminist writers such as Gittins (1993) and Barrett and McIntosh (1991), welcome and celebrate the diversity of family structures in modern societies. Such diversity can be divided into groups, although

Table 7.1 Types of household: 1979 to 1994

	1979	1981	1983	1985	1987	1989	1991	1993	1994
				Percentage of households of each type					
(a) Households									
1 person only	23	22	23	24	25	25	26	27	28
2 or more unrelated adults	3	3	3	4	3	3	3	3	3
Married couple									
with dependent children	31	32	30	28	28	26	25	24	25
non-dependent children	7	8	8	8	9	9	8	7	6
no children	27	26	27	27	27	27	28	28	27
Lone parent									
with dependent children	4	4	5	4	4	5	6	7	7
non-dependent children	4	4	4	4	4	4	4	3	3
Two or more families	1	1	1	1	1	1	1	1	1
Base = 100%	*11454*	*11982*	*10031*	*9993*	*10367*	*10085*	*9955*	*9852*	*9663*
				Percentage of persons in each type of household					
(b) Persons									
1 person only	9	8	9	10	10	10	11	11	11
2 or more unrelated adults	2	3	3	3	3	3	2	3	3
Married couple									
with dependent children	49	49	47	45	44	42	41	41	41
non-dependent children	9	10	11	11	12	12	11	9	8
no children	20	19	21	21	21	22	23	23	23
Lone parent									
with dependent children	5	5	5	5	5	6	7	8	8
non-dependent children	3	3	3	4	4	3	3	3	3
Two or more families	2	2	2	1	2	2	2	2	2
Base = 100%	*30546*	*32310*	*26425*	*25454*	*26314*	*25269*	*24657*	*24079*	*23475*

Source: Living in Britain General Household Survey 1994 (ONS 1995)

Table 7.2 1993 and 1983 marriage statistics

	1993	1983
Average age of divorce	men 37 yrs women 35 yrs	men 36 yrs women 34 yrs
Average length of marriage before divorce	9.8 yrs	10.1 yrs
Divorcing couples with children under 16	95,000	87,000

these, too, are only models. These can be classified as organizational diversity, cultural diversity, class diversity, regional diversity, lifecycle differences and cohort differences.

Activity

Identify the main trends in the statistics in Tables 7.1 and 7.2..

Organizational diversity

It appears that the traditional 'cereal packet family' no longer makes up the majority of households in the UK today. Oakley (1974a) defined this as the advertisers' ideal family with the mother at home with a child of each sex and the father obviously leaving the happy home (and breakfast) to go off to work. Table 7.1 clearly shows that in 1992 only about 25 per cent of households consisted of two married people with dependent children – and few of these now contain only the one male breadwinner.

Organizational diversity is the term used to describe the variety of family structures that can be found in the UK, e.g. dual income families, non-employed families, same-sex parents, single-parent families, reconstituted families (formed after divorce and re-marriage) etc. These last two appear to be increasingly numerous in British society and there is also an increasing number of families with vertical extension as elderly parents move in with their children and children-in-law. This is due mainly to the ageing population found in most western societies and the government's policy of 'Care in the Community' (see Section 14.2), which encourages

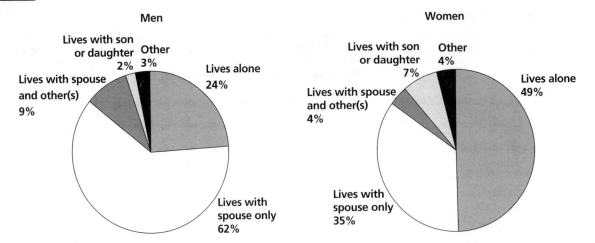

Figure 7.5 Elderly household type by sex: Great Britain, 1994. Source: Living in Britain 1994 General Household Survey Preliminary Results 1996 (ONS, 1996)

people to care for the elderly or infirm in their own homes rather than them being cared for in larger state-run institutions. However, as Figure 7.5 illustrates, most elders still live alone or with their spouse.

Activity

Identify the percentage of elderly households of each type in the UK in 1994 for both women and men. Suggest reasons for any differences between them.

I, A

Same-sex families

We tend to assume that people who have relationships with others of the same sex are unable or unlikely to have children. While some may choose not to do so, as do an increasing number of heterosexual couples, there is a small but growing number of same-sex parents. Some women leave a heterosexual relationship to live with another woman, taking their children with them.

This is often not an easy task, as there have been instances when charges of lesbianism have been used to suggest that a woman is unfit to be a mother, although there is no evidence to support this. It appears that the only disadvantage suffered by children brought up in lesbian households was the response of others to their situation.

Plummer (1976) argued that homosexuals are less likely to establish long-term relationships because of societal disapproval of homosexuality which makes it more difficult to meet potential partners. Furthermore, existing norms among gay men at least, tend to stress transient rather than long-term relationships. Nor can homosexuals marry or have children in the conventional ways that heterosexual

couples tend to. However, Plummer also argues that many homosexuals seek the ideal of a life-long partnership despite these discouragements, although many homosexual and heterosexual people do not seek such a relationship. The idea that two homosexual men can bring up a 'normal' child is often considered unacceptable and lesbian mothers are often seen as deficient in some way. Such prejudices do not appear to be supported by any evidence of greater levels of dysfunction among homosexual-headed families.

Re-constituted and neo-conventional families

An increasing number of people are getting divorced, and although many become single-headed families for a while, large numbers of divorced people remarry, forming 're-constituted families'. This means that many children are growing up with step-parents and, in some cases, step-siblings as well. Chester (1985) argues that despite these changes, most people are now brought up in what he terms a 'neo-conventional family', where there are two parents, a small number of children and long-term commitment. The main difference between this and the conventional 'isolated nuclear family' is the number of married women who are now economically active outside the home, although often working part time while their children are very young. Table 7.3 on page 249 shows the percentages of different types of these families.

Although it appears that the family is becoming more diverse in modern industrial societies, we need to remember that there have always been a range of family structures, with class differences still evident. For example, there are still some families – mainly upper and middle class – for whom state education is not considered acceptable and where

Table 7.3 Step-families with dependent children in 1995[1, 2]

(Family head aged 16–59) GB

	%
Couple with child(ren) from the woman's previous marriage	86
Couple with child(ren) from the man's previous marriage	10
Couple with child(ren) from both partners' previous marriages	4
Base = 100%	*193*
All families with dependent children whose family head is aged 16–59	*2305*

[1]Dependent children are persons under 16, or aged 16–18, and in full-time education, in the family unit, and living in the household.
[2]Includes previous cohabitations

Source: Living in Britain General Household Survey Preliminary Results 1995 (ONS, 1996)

boarding schools, nannies and au-pairs are the norm. (See Section 8.11.)

There have also always been many single parents and second marriages, although this may have been more likely to be due to death of a spouse than to divorce or choice. The assumption that there is an ideal family type and that structures which differ from that norm are somehow 'deviant' or deficient is probably more problematic than diversity in itself. Feminist writers such as Gittins (1993) argue strongly that the ideology of the nuclear family (see p. 239) is actually far more important than the way families are actually constituted in society.

Cultural diversity

One of the major advantages of living in a multi-ethnic society (see Section 6.1) like the UK is the con-tributions different ethnic groups make to diversity in society. There are a number of culturally specific family structures, but you need to be aware that these are generalizations and that many people from the ethnic groups outlined here do not live in the family structures identified (see Table 7.4). One of the problems for sociologists looking at cultural differences is the tendency to produce stereotypes, and all students of sociology need to be aware of this pitfall. The three groups explored here are South Asians, Cypriots and African–Caribbeans.

South Asian families

Ballard (1982) draws some generalized findings from his studies of migrant families from the Punjab, Gujarat and Bengal. Such families are usually patriarchal and ideally all the family co-reside in an extended pattern where all contribute to the domestic and wage-earning tasks. Although the work of women and men is usually highly differentiated, Ballard found increasing numbers of women needing to work outside the home. Often extended families were split into smaller, more nuclear family units. Some British-born Asians have rejected the traditional family authority structures. He found that many children co-existed in two cultures, conforming largely to peer expectations outside the home and parental demands within the home.

Cypriot families

Oakley (1982) also found extended family patterns among Cypriot families, most of whom migrated to the UK after the Second World War, although some came earlier. He found strong connections between married children and their parents, with considerable emphasis on family support rather than external agencies. Children, as in many South Asian families, were expected to contribute to the family businesses. Similar patterns can also be seen in

Table 7.4 Ethnic group of head of household, by household size, Spring 1995 (GB, percentages)

	One person	Two people	Three people	Four people	Five people	Six or more people	All (=100%) (thousands)
White	28	34	16	15	5	2	22 548
Black[1]	31	29	20	12	4	4	379
Indian	9	17	20	26	16	12	265
Pakistani/Bangladeshi	8	11	14	21	15	31	163
Other[2]	28	23	20	19	6	5	239
All ethnic groups	28	34	16	15	5	2	23 597

[1]Includes Caribbean, African and other black people of non-mixed origin.
[2]Includes Chinese, other ethnic minority groups of non-mixed origin and people of mixed origin.
Source: Labour Force Survey, Central Statistical Office in *Social Trends 1996*

closely-knit Italian migrant communities, for example in Clerkenwell in London.

African–Caribbean families

Barrow (1982) identified three types of family structures found in the Caribbean:

* conventional nuclear families found among religious and/or economically successful groups
* common-law families where less well-off unmarried couples cohabit and raise children who may or may not be their own biologically
* the 'mother household' where the mother (or sometimes grandmother) is head of household, adult males are absent or transient and most support comes from the wider female kinship group.

There is evidence of all these sorts of structures among African–Caribbeans in the UK, although women are more likely to be the main breadwinner in many households. There is less opportunity for input from other female family members, but many African–Caribbean women have extensive female support networks in areas of high black population. According to Barrow, this form of mother-headed family commonly found in Jamaica offers alternative family arrangements both in the Caribbean and for some women in the UK. Women in Jamaica have always been strong, both in the home and in public life such as teaching and politics. Single women have problems of unemployment or, if employed, finding childcare. Formal nurseries are one solution, but in more rural areas this role usually comes from within the extended family.

Working mothers will often find that their mothers and sisters can offer informal childcare, either within Jamaica if they have to migrate to find work, or within the UK. This suggests that many white British people often have little understanding of the importance of the role of the grandmother in African–Caribbean society, which is to provide support and strength for her daughters and nurture for grandchildren. This also provides a useful role for older women in society, something which is too rarely found among many British families. She attributes the cause of this family structure to slavery, as nuclear families were not encouraged by slave-owners (see Section 6.2). One positive outcome of this has been the tradition of mutual support found between women in a largely matriarchal society.

One of the problems with seeing the nuclear family as the norm is that other family structures are judged to be inferior. Dallos and Sapsford (1995) warn strongly against this form of ethnocentrism (seeing your own culture's social arrangements as superior to those of other social groups):

In thinking about ... other cultures it is important not to be trapped into a Eurocentrist perspective. Afro-Caribbean families, for example, may be different in many ways to white, British nuclear families, but it would be a mistake to regard these differences as an attack on family life. In fact the reverse could be argued: there is often a strong sense of family life and respect for it, and moreover the family can represent or offer a 'haven' for black people from the racial prejudice they may experience in white society.
(Muncie *et al.*, 1995, p. 146)

Discussion point

Why might families among some South Asian, Cypriot and Italian migrants in the UK wish to maintain a traditional family structure or mother-centred families be more often found among African–Caribbean households? What are the problems that might arise if these stereotypes are seen as the norm for people from non-white ethnic groups in society?

Regional diversity

According to Eversley and Bannerjea (1982) different patterns of family life can be found in certain parts of the country. Many southern coastal regions have large numbers of retired couples and single households. Two-parent families are more commonly found in the south east, while inner-city areas tend to have higher levels of single-parent families and ethnic minorities. Strong kinship networks are maintained in most highly rural areas. Particularly in areas of high unemployment, adult children may remain living with their parents to the age of 30 and beyond.

Evidence of family diversity appears quite convincing, but it is equally true that these are only snapshots of a society at a particular time. Over the last twenty years, trends related to increased cohabitation and, probably more importantly, never-married single parenting, have been at the heart of the debate not only about the family but about the morality and structure of society itself.

7.4 Family change – diversity or decline?

Having identified many of the varied family structures to be found in modern Britain, it is important to go on to look at the implications of such diversity. 'Traditional' nuclear family structures are far from universal although many people live part of their lives in them. The main debates about non-nuclear families seem to relate to single parents (particularly to mothers who have never been married) and, to a lesser degree, the implications of step-parenting and cohabitation. We shall focus mainly on the lone parent issue here, as it illustrates many of the salient points and has been the focus of much sociological and media attention and debate. First, some comments about cohabitation and step-families.

Cohabitation

Evidence from Table 7.5 suggests that many people are marrying later and that this often involves a period of cohabitation first. In the 1960s, cohabitation was often called 'trial marriage', perhaps to give the term respectability. Now, a considerable number of people, although the statistics are not always reliable, seem to marry after the birth of a child or children, while, as McRae (1993) shows, many choose

not to marry at all. A considerable proportion of people cohabiting will include at least one partner who is separated or divorced from someone else.

Activity

Summarize the key trends to be found in Figure 7.6 and Tables 7.6 and 7.7. What are the arguments for and against the idea of changes in levels of cohabitation? **U, I, A**

Table 7.5 Percentage of men and women aged 16–59 cohabiting, by sex and age: GB 1995[1]

| Age | Percentage cohabiting | | Base = 100% | |
	All	Non-married[2]	All	Non-married[3]
Men				
16–19	1	1	415	415
20–24	13	14	527	484
25–29	22	36	663	417
30–34	13	35	724	271
35–39	9	30	776	238
40–44	5	20	649	171
45–49	6	27	696	162
50–54	4	18	643	135
55–59	2	12	572	114
Totals	*9*	*21*	*5665*	*2407*
Women				
16–19	4	4	386	382
20–24	21	25	573	477
25–29	17	34	785	402
30–34	10	28	1027	374
35–39	8	24	838	275
40–44	5	19	707	193
45–49	5	19	856	205
50–54	3	11	695	171
55–59	3	12	599	143
Totals	*9*	*21*	*6466*	*2622*

[1]Same-sex cohabitees excluded.
[2]Men and women describing themselves as 'separated' were, strictly speaking, legally married. However, because the separated can cohabit, they have been treated as if they were not married.

Source: Living in Britain General Household Survey Preliminary Findings 1995 (ONS, 1996).

Women outside marriage

Despite the pluralism of living arrangements, marriage remains a normal and expected part of female biography in Britain. Mansfield and Collard's study of newly-weds (1988) provides an account of the continuing attractiveness of traditional marriage to many young couples. However, although the vast majority of women still expect to marry at some time, and at least once, in recent years there has been some decline in the popularity of marriage. In 1971 only 4% of women remained unmarried by 50, but by 1987 the proportion had grown to 17%. Women today are marrying older and marrying less.

However, much of this debate hinges on the differences drawn between cohabitation and formal marriage. In historical and cross-cultural studies (Gillis 1985; Smith 1988) the differences more obviously blur. But they are also not that clear in contemporary analyses. Here it is useful to note that the Census uses self-identification to place people in the combined category of married or living as married, while the Registrar records only formal marriages, counting only those entering and leaving marriage as a legal estate. Consequently, it is important not to assume that marital status is synonymous with living arrangements. Not only do the non-married cohabit, but the married may live apart, separated, for example, by the demands of employment or because their husbands/partners are in prison.

Whatever the complexities of these trends one thing is sure – the changing patterns of marriage and the relative longevity of women are increasing the numbers of women without husbands and blurring the boundaries between marriage and non-marriage (Chandler 1991). In discussion of marriage and 'the family' there is often a clear delineation: women are either married or they are not. In reality women not only have a variety of marital statuses, they also have a range of domestic and sexual relationships with men.

Figure 7.6 Women outside marriage. Source: adapted from Chandler (1993)

Table 7.6 Percentage of people who feel cohabitation[1] is wrong, by gender, 1994

	Males	Females
Year of birth		
1960–1978	7	6
1950–1959	10	8
1940–1949	16	14
1930–1939	23	22
Before 1930	40	34
All	17	16

[1]Percentages who agreed with the statement that living together outside marriage is always wrong.

Sources: British Household Panel Survey, ESRC Research Centre on Micro-social Change, *Social Trends* 1996.

Table 7.7 Attitudes to unmarried cohabitation in selected western countries

	Britain	USA	Nether-lands	West Germany
Advice respondents would give a young woman[1]:	%	%	%	%
Live with steady partner and then marry	43	26	45	50
Marry without living together first	37	46	24	19
Live alone without a steady partner	4	9	2	5
Live with steady partner without marrying	4	3	8	11
Can't choose	11	14	20	15

[1]The advice that would be given to a young man was substantially the same.

Sources: Scott (1990), Elliot (1996)

It is assumed that many cohabiting couples eventually marry or (in many cases) re-marry. This also means that there are a number of step-families. Therefore cohabitation and re-marriage are not usually seen as evidence of family decline in the way that lone parenting is sometimes presented.

McRae (1993) carried out a postal survey (see Section 3.7) of new mothers in 1988. From the replies received, she found that about 7 per cent were living in consensual or cohabiting units and her follow-up study on this group found a number of interesting differences between them and married mothers. She found that it was possible to identify those women who had cohabited with their partners before the birth of their child or children and continued to choose to do so afterwards.

As most women marry before or after the birth of their children, this group offered an example to investigate why some people reject marriage despite quite strong societal expectations that parents should marry. Her research identified a number of interesting trends. Cohabiting mothers tended to be younger than married mothers. They tended on average to have more children (some from previous relationships for themselves or their partners). Their family income tended to be markedly lower than for married couples, partly due to their lower involvement in paid employment. However, cohabiting mothers are usually considered as less of a 'problem' for themselves or society as a whole, than single mothers who have divorced or have never married and who are living without a partner.

Discussion point

What are the advantages and disadvantages for men, women and any children in a cohabiting household?

Divorce, re-marriage and step-families

About 5 per cent of women in the population are divorced and slightly fewer men, who tend to re-marry more quickly (Gittins, 1993). Despite this, about 70 per cent of divorce petitions are initiated by women. One notable trend is that those who re-marry are slightly more likely to divorce than those marriages where both partners have never married before. There are also more widows that widowers, primarily due to the longer life expectancy of women. More people are choosing not to marry at all, and certainly the average age of marriage has risen for both females and males. This means there is greater diversity in marital roles adopted throughout society and within many people's individual lifetimes.

People are now divorcing in greater numbers and earlier in the relationship than previously. As Gittins (1993) points out, large-scale divorce is a relatively recent phenomenon, being an expensive luxury until 1857. Even then, the Matrimonial Causes Act required greater culpability on the part of the husband than the wife in order for the latter to secure a divorce. Divorce became easier to obtain for poorer people throughout the twentieth century, culminating in the 1971 Divorce Reform Act. This allowed two people who had lived separately to claim that the marriage had irretrievably broken down, thus there was no need for blame to be allocated. However, the continuing popularity of divorce since

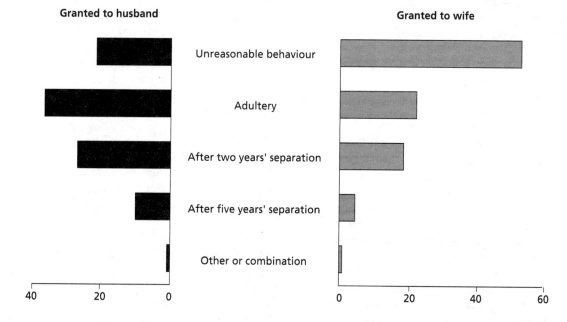

England, Wales & Northern Ireland
Percentages

Figure 7.7 Divorces granted, by ground, 1993. Sources: OPCS/General Register Office (Northern Ireland)/ *Social Trends* 1996

Table 7.8 Divorce: by duration of marriage (UK, percentages)

	1961	1971	1981	1991	1993
0–2 years	1	1	2	9	8
3–4 years	10	12	19	14	14
5–9 years	31	31	29	27	28
10–14 years	23	19	20	18	18
15–19 years	14	13	13	13	12
20–24 years		10	9	10	10
25–29 years	21	6	5	5	5
30 years and over		9	5	4	4
All durations (=100%) (thousands)	27.0	79.2	155.6	171.1	180.0

Sources: Office of Population Censuses and Surveys: General Register Office (Scotland); General Register Office (Northern Ireland), *Social Trends* 1996

Activity

a Identify the trends in divorce shown in Table 7.8.

b With reference to Figure 7.7, to what extent are the grounds for divorce given by men and women different?

I, E

this time, in most western industrialized societies at least, has been a subject of much sociological debate. Statistics for separation and cohabitation are a lot less reliable than divorce statistics, but not all couples can or do choose to divorce even if they are unhappy and many maintain what are known as 'empty-shell marriages', with limited joint social interaction.

Causes and consequences of marital breakdown

The rise in divorce statistics is often seen as problematic. Some sociologists, especially functionalists (see Section 2.4) such as Fletcher and Parsons and other promoters of family life, argue that it reflects higher expectations of marriage (especially) by women. The evidence for this is the high rate of re-marriage, although Gittins (1993) argues that most people tend to re-marry for economic and ideological reasons rather than any other.

Writers such as Dennis (1975) claim that the family now has fewer functions and, consequently, fewer things which tie people together. The modern isolated nuclear family is rarely a unit of production (although it may still often share an economic function as a unit of consumption). The lack of other functions leads to the centrality of the affective relationship. In other words, if people are no longer in love, they have nothing else to keep them together and so they decide to divorce. This reflects the sort of family structure required by industrialized society and high divorce rates are therefore seen as a consequence of industrialization. As O'Connell (1994) shows, this trend in divorce is found throughout the industrializing world and not just in the western societies identified in Table 7.9.

Many writers feel that divorce is now too easily obtained. Not only is it reasonably easy to divorce legally, secularization – the decline in religious practice and belief – means that divorce is no longer taboo. (See Section 18.4.) However, divorce may have a different impact on different family members and is still rarely an easy option for most women. Both Gittins and Chandler point out that divorce for men and women is a different experience.

Gittins (1993) also suggests that many men benefit financially from divorce and often find it easy to attract other (often younger) women as new partners. Women, especially if they have custody of children (which most of them desire), may be unable to find appropriate work or be limited to low-paid casual or part-time employment (see Section 9.3). As women still tend to earn only about 72 per cent of male earnings, even full-time employment reduces their standard of living. They are also more likely to be considered a sexual threat to friends' husbands and may become socially isolated. Thus more divorced men re-marry, despite the higher economic and social necessity for many divorced women to do so.

Table 7.9 Marriage and divorce rates: EC comparison, 1981 and 1993

| | Rates per 1000 population | | | |
| | Marriages | | Divorces | |
	1981	1993	1981	1993
United Kingdom	7.1	5.9	2.8	3.1
Denmark	5.0	6.1	2.8	2.5
Finland	6.3	4.9	2.0	2.5
Sweden	4.5	3.9	2.4	2.5
Belgium	6.5	5.4	1.6	2.1
Austria	6.3	5.6	1.8	2.0
Netherlands	6.0	5.8	2.0	2.0
France	5.8	4.4	1.6	1.9
Germany	6.2	5.5	2.0	1.9
Luxembourg	5.5	6.0	1.4	1.9
Portugal	7.8	6.9	0.7	1.2
Greece	6.9	6.0	0.7	0.7
Spain	5.4	5.0	0.3	0.7
Italy	5.6	5.1	0.2	0.4
Irish Republic	6.0	4.4	–	–
EC average	6.1	5.3	1.5	1.7

Source: Eurostat, *Social Trends 1996*

Hart (1976) argues that the increasing divorce rate reflects the conflict generated by contradictory demands on women to be both economic and domestic workers. Women, when they can, work to provide the increasing material demands of most families, but they are not fully supported in the domestic or emotional field by their husbands. She believes that the major cause of conflict leading to marital breakdown is the result of the increasing demands on women without enough male support.

Discussion point
What do you think are the main reasons that people get divorced? How are different members of the family likely to be affected?

Re-marriage and step-parenting
Although it is difficult to generalize about those who re-marry, it is argued by many writers that the popularity of re-marriage demonstrates the strength of family values (or, at least family ideology) for most people. Although Gittins argues that, for women with children at least, re-marriage is an important financial prerogative, writers such as Fletcher and Murdock point to re-marriage as evidence of the high value we place on traditional family life.

This trend towards a cycle of marriage, divorce and re-marriage is sometimes described as serial monogamy and this is the pattern identified by writers such as Fletcher (1965) as evidence of our commitment to the nuclear family. This view suggests that although more marriages are likely to end in divorce, due to greater longevity and (until recently) earlier marriage, it remains a popular institution.

Re-marriage is usually considered to be the best option for the children of divorced parents. It is argued that step-parents may offer a 'new' (possibly extended) family for these children and that they will therefore be less prone to the emotional and personal disruption associated with lone parenting. However, a report produced in 1995 by the National Child Development Study suggests that girls in particular tend not to benefit from step-parenting. More children in a step-family leave school at 16, leave home at 18 after family arguments, get poorer educational qualifications and marry younger than do those from lone parent households. There is also evidence that girls are more vulnerable to sexual abuse from step-fathers than from any other family member, although this problem is clearly not found in all step-families. (See Section 7.7 for a fuller discussion of this issue.)

Discussion point

What are the main advantages and disadvantages for the children, mother and father if their parents remain together, divorce, re-marry etc.? Consider factors such as the age and gender of the children, the number of siblings and the economic situation.

Lone parents

As noted earlier, the increase in the number of single-headed families is usually seen as one of the most important – and problematic – changes in the structure of family life. As we have seen throughout much of this chapter, the nuclear family is actually quite rare in many cultures and at different points in time.

Lone-parent families

Since 1971 there has been a marked increase in the proportion of families with dependent children headed by lone parents, in particular those headed by single mothers. The latter rose from 1% of all families with dependent children in 1971 to 8% in 1993. Since then there has been no increase in the proportion of families headed by single mothers.

The proportion of lone-father families has remained at 1% or 2% since 1971.

Figure 7.8 Lone-parent families. Source: Living in Britain General Household Survey Preliminary Findings 1995 (ONS, 1996)

Gittins argues that there are three main differences between families in modern industrialized society and others:

- More families are single-headed due to divorce rather than death, implying some notion of choice. One key result of this is that single-headed families tend to be found among the poorest members of society where divorce rates are higher, whereas death is more evenly distributed among the classes (although it is worth remembering that poverty is linked to lower life expectancy).
- The modern nuclear family is less likely to have close kinship ties or family support of the kind found in less industrialized societies and is therefore more likely to require help from the state (although close kinship ties were and are found among groups of Jamaican women both in Jamaica and the UK).
- The ideology of the traditional nuclear family is so strongly promoted by politicians, advertisers and a host of others with vested interests that alternative family structures may be seen as deficient.

Discussion point

Why might
a politicians
b advertisers
be keen to promote the nuclear family?
Discuss the benefits for each group.

Land (1995) shows how, in the mid 1980s, the government of the day was beginning to get concerned about the cost of lone parents. Not only were their numbers growing (see Figure 7.8), but they were disproportionately dependent on benefits, as single mothers in particular found it difficult to get a job which paid well enough to cover childcare as well as other expenses. Single parents tend to be the largest recipients of income support and housing benefit compared with other family status groups – see Table 7.10. (See also Section 14.4.)

Particularly noticeable is the increase in the number of mothers who have never married (Table 7.11). Although most of these women are involved in a stable relationship with both parents' names on the birth certificate and often a shared place of residence, this group are seen as the most problematic for the government. Many of them are teenagers and they are least likely to have a well-paid job and so be reliant on state benefits. Often young-never-married mothers are portrayed as welfare scroungers. Sometimes single motherhood is linked to aspects of ethnicity, especially in America, where about a half of all never-married mothers are defined as African–American or Hispanic. The Conservative MP John Redwood has suggested that single parents should put their babies up for adoption if their own parents are unwilling to provide for them, an idea borrowed from the New Right in America.

In an extensive article in *Community Care* magazine, Burghes and Roberts (1995) suggest that the rise in the number of lone parents has been generated into a 'moral panic' by politicians and the media. They argue that in the 1990s single parents have been presented as a major social problem. Since the 1980s, the increasing level of state support for lone parents has led to a number of research projects designed to develop policies to reduce the cost of such families to the state. Policies such as the introduction of the Child Support Agency were designed to stress the individual responsibility of parents (both fathers and mothers) towards their children.

Table 7.10 Benefit units by family status and combinations of benefits received (percentages)

Family status	On no benefits	Only Child Benefit	Only non-income related benefits	Only income related benefits	Income related and non-income related benefits
Pensioner couple	1	0	75	–	24
Single pensioner	–	0	51	1	48
Couple with children	1	71	12	–	15
Couple without children	72	0	18	4	5
Single with children	1	5	14	1	79
Single without children	70	0	7	16	7
Total benefit units	*34*	*15*	*25*	*6*	*21*

Source: *Living in Britain 1994*

One attempt to gain public support for this move was a concerted media attack on lone parents by (among others) Virginia Bottomley, Peter Lilley, John Redwood and Michael Howard, all Conservative cabinet members in the 1980s and 1990s. Other groups such as the Institute of Economic Affairs produced studies such as *Families without Fatherhood* (Dennis and Erdos 1992; see p. 257). Although not associated with the right wing of the Conservative party, the journalist Melanie Phillips, who is sometimes seen as part of the 'ethical socialist' tradition, has also produced articles about the rights and responsibilities of parenting. (See Section 2.10.)

Burghes and Roberts (1995) point out, however, that the reality does not support the idea that lone parenting is a major social problem, although their numbers have increased. They claim that the main reason for the development of such a moral panic (see Section 15.5) was to reduce state spending on lone-parent families, who are certainly disproportionately reliant on benefits. This is especially the case for less well educated women who find it difficult to gain paid employment that covers both living expenses and childcare costs, so that single mothers face particular problems in escaping dependency on welfare and state support. (See Section 14.3.)

However, the implicit argument was that the breakdown of the family was leading to a decline in morality and this could therefore also explain rising levels of crime, delinquency and drug-taking, particularly among young people. In response to this many people would argue that there is a problem with the growth of lone parenting, whether it is one for the state, the mothers or the children themselves. If this is the case, were the politicians not right to panic? Burghes and Roberts conclude that:

Table 7.11 Family type, and marital status of lone mothers: 1971 to 1995 (GB, percentages)

Families with dependent children[1]	1971	1974	1981	1984	1991	1993	1994	1995
Married/cohabiting couple[2]	92	90	87	87	81	78	77	78
Lone mother	7	9	11	12	18	20	21	20
single	1	1	2	3	6	8	8	8
widowed	2	2	2	1	1	1	1	1
divorced	2	2	4	6	6	7	7	7
separated	2	2	2	2	4	4	5	5
Lone father	1	1	2	1	1	2	2	2
All lone parents	8	10	13	13	19	22	23	22
Base=100%	*4864*	*4309*	*4445*	*3365*	*3143*	*3145*	*3168*	*3022*

[1]Dependent children are persons aged under 16, or aged 16–18 and in full time education, in the family unit and living in the household.
[2]Including married women whose husbands were not defined as resident in the household.

Source: Living in Britain General Household Survey Preliminary Findings 1995 (ONS, 1996)

. . . they were absolutely right to be concerned but seriously wrong in how they went about it, the way they initially attributed causes and effects, and therefore, their analysis of the policy options. Most of all, they were wrong to play to the media gallery, to go for the quick social security fix and so encourage a panic.

(Burghes and Roberts, 1995, p. viii)

Activity

Use the above material and the statistical information presented in Figure 7.8 and Tables 7.10 and 7.11 to summarize arguments for and against the view that lone mothers are a problem to society.　**I, A, E**

There has also apparently been an increase in the number of fathers who do not support their children. The Child Support Agency (CSA) was established in 1991 to ensure that absent fathers paid maintenance for their offspring. This initiative is an interesting example of the kind of policies that are being applied to reduce the 'burden' of single parenting, and the dependence of lone parents, on the state.

Dallos and Sapsford (1995) point out that being a lone parent can take a variety of forms, although in most cases lone-parent families are headed by the mother who takes prime emotional (and often financial) responsibility for the offspring. They also found from talking to lone mothers that a period of initial doubt and anxiety was often followed by feelings of increased self-confidence and the enjoyment of independence and autonomy. They conclude that in many cases lone parenthood reflects the choice of at least some women. This is supported by evidence such as the decline in the popularity of marriage and rising rates of births outside marriage (see Figure 7.9).

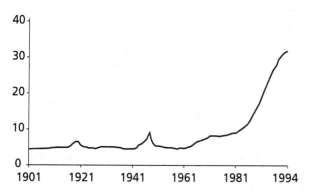

Figure 7.9 Live births outside marriage (in the UK) as a percentage of all births. Sources: Office of Population Censuses and Surveys/*Social Trends 1996*

Issues of family diversity – in particular families that end up in need of state support – are an important aspect of the debates explored more fully in the unit of this chapter on the relationship between the family and the state. Other sociologists criticize the development of single parenting from the view-point that the decline in traditional parenting has led to a decline in the stability of society itself.

Fathers and families

In *Families without Fatherhood*, Dennis and Erdos (1992) argue that the riots which terrorized both Chicago in the USA and North Tyneside in the UK in the early 1990s could not be attributed to poverty alone. In fact, despite the problems of poverty and inequality which persist in those areas, the standard of living has improved for all but a tiny minority of working-class people.

Far more hardship was endured by working people in the 1930s and 1950s, with far less social upheaval or unrest. They further found that riotous behaviour was condemned by many working-class people in the areas they studied, and blame was focused on a relatively small sub-group within the wider social network.

This suggests that economic deprivation alone cannot explain social unrest. One proposal was that lone parenting – found commonly in areas of social disintegration – might be at least a contributory factor to the distribution of social upheaval within working-class groups. Dennis and Erdos set out to investigate whether the correlation between changes in family life – including rising divorce and increasing lone parenting – and declining civil life and commitment to community were, in fact, causally related. As all social scientists know, it is important not to assume that two variables which change in the same direction are necessarily causing each other, although they may be interrelated. For example, over the past five years, girls have, overall, achieved higher GCSE grades than boys. Over the same time period the frequency of soap operas on TV has risen (correlation). Does this mean that watching soap operas on TV makes girls more intelligent (causation)? The answer is obviously no.

Writing from a perspective defined as 'ethical socialism' (see Section 2.10), Dennis and Erdos (1992) argue that a number of factors can be identified as contributing towards the decline of moral standards which they found among some groups in society. First, they suggest that most professional welfare workers no longer believe that they have any right to comment on the behaviour of others. While accepting that there needs to be a fine line between intervention and interference, Dennis and Erdos argue that such moral apathy may not always prove beneficial to the wider society. From this morally neutral viewpoint, the Victorian distinction between the 'deserving' and the 'undeserving' poor becomes meaningless.

The 'undeserving' poor were seen as feckless, work-shy and self-indulgent who spent their ill-gotten gains on drink, gambling and indulgence. On the other hand, there were sober and hard-working people who, through no fault of their own, found it difficult to make ends meet. The argument that we should help the latter and not the former is eroded under a system of morality which denies all blame or culpability among the poor. However, as they argue, the judgementalism of the Victorian era remained strong among those most negatively affected by the indolence of the idle and unclean, the respectable working class. (See Section 14.1.)

According to Dennis and Erdos, social theorists, who they call 'the reforming intelligentsia of non-working-class origin' (1992, p. 11) – reserved their sympathy for those who rejected the values of hard work and thrift which were the mainstay of working-class values. They saw the respectable working class as indoctrinated by 'bourgeois' values which really only served the interests of their employers. In relation to the family, therefore, sociologists have traditionally sympathized more with the single mother on benefit than with the woman who struggles at home on a limited income, either alone due to widowhood or trying to keep her husband in work and her children clean, well-fed and out of trouble.

Until the 1960s, a distinction had prevailed between the widowed mother and the never-married single mother in terms of both moral views and welfare entitlements. However, by the 1970s, the marital status of the mother and the legal status of the child had become irrelevant. If a women could not or did not work she was entitled to benefit for herself and her child. No one – not even the Church – was entitled to make moral judgements about the sexual behaviour of anyone. As a result, many children were being raised largely without a father for much of their lives.

Discussion point

To what extent do you think that young, unmarried mothers – and fathers – have done something immoral?

Dennis and Erdos attack the view (which they see as a commonly-held one) that single parents are just as successful as those where both parents bring up the children. They argue that boys in fatherless families in particular grow up without the restraints on their behaviour that a father might impose and without any expectations that they should take any responsibility for their own children when they become fathers themselves. Boys (especially) brought up without a father do less well at school and are more likely to gain a criminal record than those with two parents, even when class and income are held constant. Their evidence comes from a study of 1000 children born in Newcastle in 1947, who exhibited a greater statistical chance of having poor physical health, low IQ scores and a criminal record if they were in an 'unfathered' or 'poorly fathered' group.

So far, many of their views seem similar to those expressed by the New Right, but while their ideas about the cause of social problems seem similar, they suggest different solutions to the problem. They reject the idea that the free market and the rolling back of state support available to single parents will immediately wean them from their dependence on welfare. In fact, they suggest that the 'free-market' has become part of the thinking of many young males, who deny any social responsibility for the children they produce. This debate remains the focus of considerable current political concern and the assumed link between crime and lone parenting remains central to the debate.

Crime 'due to lax morality'

SEXUAL freedom and the lax moral attitudes of single mothers and the unemployed are responsible for the rising tide of crime, according to a report published yesterday by the rightwing thinktank, the Institute of Economic Affairs. The report also challenges the belief that crime and poverty can be linked, describing that concept as "fundamentally flawed".

The report's author, the social scientist Norman Dennis, claims the freedom of men "to engage in sexual intercourse without being powerfully constrained" by the pressure to become monogamous husbands or fathers can be linked to crime. Mr Dennis, a guest fellow at Newcastle-upon-Tyne University's religious department, also argues that the unemployed and single mothers should partly take the blame for their own low incomes.

Claire Rayner, the agony aunt, said his views were "utter bollocks". "Sexual probity is a luxury. You have got to have a roof over your head and a job to afford a wife and children," she said. – *Alison Daniels*

Figure 7.10 Article on crime and morality. Source: *The Guardian*, 2 January 1997

Back to the 1950s
LARRY ELLIOTT

Now it looks as if the 1950s are coming back: or rather, one bit of the 1950s. What we are not getting is the full employment, the progressive taxation and the determination of an interventionist state to use active welfare policies to reduce the gap between rich and poor.

What we are being offered instead is social authoritarianism; a crackdown on law and order and discipline in schools; a willingness to tell people how they should conduct their relationships and bring up their children.

This combination of the free-market economics of the 1980s and the social policy of the 1950s is being sold as a cure-all solution to society's ills. But this is not a social policy, nor even a moral policy. It is a policy of cut-price containment – a cheap way of coping with the middle-class fear that a burgeoning "underclass" is out of control.

The underlying analysis has some merit. Crime has doubled since the 1970s, almost half of new marriages end in divorce, there is a hardcore of disruptive pupils who do not want to learn. Once, politicians would have looked for an economic answer to these problems.

Some of the signs of a 1950s revival were implicit in the abortive Back-to-Basics campaign of three years ago, when the Government attempted to reassert its authority after the economic débâcle of Black Wednesday. But what is different this time is that Labour's adoption of a more authoritarian social policy stance has legitimised the drift to the right.

Women should be aware that the emphasis on family values and the need for parents to teach their children the difference between right and wrong is by no means the whole agenda. There will be pressure for tougher laws on abortion, and before long almost certainly calls for the ideal family unit to be made up of one male breadwinner and a wife who stays at home to care for the children. Just like the 1950s.

Stand back a second from the sense of moral panic that the politicians have stirred up, and what we see is not the inheritance of the permissive society but the inevitable consequence of an economic system built around exclusion, alienation and greed. As the American writer EJ Dionne puts it in his new book: "It's [the moral crisis's] roots lie deeper, in a society built on individualistic and market values that steadily cut away the bonds of solidarity, morality and trust."

The particularly harsh variant of free-market capitalism championed over the past two decades has led to the widest income distribution since records began. More than that, workers have found that the consumer society cuts both ways: they themselves are now commodities to be bought and sold in the flexible labour market.

This is in stark contrast to 40 years ago. Then, it was taken as read that the government should use demand management to create jobs, and that progressive taxation should redistribute income. The result – not just in Britain but in the whole of the West – was rising real incomes, a narrowing of income differentials and a stable society.

Ironically, it would be much simpler to re-create the economic conditions of the 1950s than to turn the clock back to 40 years ago, when homosexuality was a criminal offence, the Lord Chamberlain acted as the censor for the theatre and the death penalty was still in operation.

Of course, this won't be tried. Higher taxation for the rich is not on the agenda, because as we have been told countless times over the past two decades, it is bad for the economy and bad, ultimately, for the poor themselves. There is absolutely no evidence, even in the United States, that cutting taxes, either on rich individuals or on wealthy corporations, leads to higher investment or stronger growth. On the contrary, American growth rates were strongest when the top rate of tax was above 80 per cent.

It's a nice idea that cutting taxes for the rich makes everybody better off by unleashing a new wave of entrepreneurial activity. But in reality, all it has done is make a lot of rich people a whole lot richer and left a hole in the finances that has had to be filled either by raising taxes on the less well-off or by borrowing at damagingly-high rates of interest.

Ultimately, the question is whether compulsory parenting classes, minimum sentences and bans on guns and knives can fill the gap where economic policy used to be. Some of these reforms might be desirable; some may have a limited impact. But the experience of the US, where the crackdown on the poor is already well advanced, suggests otherwise.

Figure 7.11 Article on attempts to recreate the past. Source: adapted from *The Guardian*, 31 October 1996

• Labour is to support proposals by a group of right-wing Tories to teach all schoolchildren the importance of heterosexual marriage. In a late change to the Education Bill now going through Parliament, the Conservative family values campaigner, Edward Leigh, has tabled a clause to promote marriage and parenthood in maintained schools. The proposal would mean rewriting the national curriculum to include lessons about the positive aspects of marriage and heterosexual parenthood.

Activity

Using the material in Figures 7.10–7.12, the material above and any other sociological arguments with which you are familiar, discuss and evaluate the view that our society is suffering from moral decline as a result of family disintegration.

K, U, I, A, E

Figure 7.12 Article on promoting marriage. Source: *The Observer*, 26 January 1997

7.5 **Power relationships in the family**

We are used to considering the family as a very positive institution in society, based on ties of kinship or emotional and sexual attachment. It is certainly the case that everyday visions of the family project this image. Such a positive image also underlay early sociological visions of the family, seeing in it the ultimate basis for the consensus and harmony that exists in the rest of society. As an example of this we can quote the work of Shorter (1977):

The nuclear family was a nest. Warm and sheltering, it kept the children secure from the pressures of the outside adult world, and gave the men an evening refuge from the icy blast of competition. And as the nuclear family rose in the nineteenth century, women liked it too, because it let them pull back from the grinding exactions of farm work, or the place at the mill, and devote themselves to child care.

(Shorter, 1977, p. 279)

Activity

What assumptions does Shorter make about the roles of men and women, both in society and in the family?

I, A

We are presented with a vision of the nuclear family as a structure that benefits all members. However, it is also important to note the implicit assumptions about the roles of family members contained within this passage. It suggests that a division of labour exists whereby men go out to work and expect emotional and material comfort from the family, while the women stay at home looking after the children.

The feminist critique of 'happy families'

The rise of feminist thinking in sociology (see Section 5.4) has led to a questioning of the idea of the family as a harmonious unit. The view that family structures can lead to the oppression of women by either men and/or capitalism, depending on the variety of feminism, has led to analysis of family units in terms of relationships which involve unequal power struggles. The feminist slogan that 'the personal is political' encapsulates this notion precisely, if by political we mean the question of the distribution and use of power in society (see Section 17.4). As a result, the vision of the family produced by feminist writers is very different from the one quoted above. For example:

The family-household system of contemporary capitalism constitutes not only the central site of the oppression of women but an important organising principle of the relations of production and the social formation as a whole.
(Barrett, 1980, p. 211)

The reasoning behind feminist analysis was the experience of women in family life. This ranged from emerging evidence relating to domestic violence, marital rape and other very negative parts of family life, which only really began to emerge with the rise of the women's movement and feminist analysis; see Section 7.7.

The second part to the idea of the oppression of women within the family centred on the existence of the gendered division of labour and the notion that this was somehow a natural outgrowth of biological differences. Feminists rejected this and saw the growth of such forms of societal organization as a key example of patriarchal relations whereby men gain at the expense of women. The whole debate about the 'domestic division of labour' and its implications in wider society has therefore become central to discussions of the family. It is argued that this division is not one which everyone is happy with, but is instead something embodying differential power within personal and societal relationships.

The domestic division of labour debate

It is clear that the rather cosy views of family life presented by the early functionalists would not be endorsed today. However the question of whether the family is evolving towards structures which do at least allow a degree of equality and freedom to all parties or whether they still represent patriarchal oppressive structures is central to the domestic division of labour debate. The start of this debate can be traced to the mid-1970s with the publication of two books with radically different conclusions on family life and relationships within it.

In 1975, Young and Willmott published a book entitled *The Symmetrical Family*. It was based on both historical evidence plus work from their earlier studies of family life (Willmott and Young, 1971) and outlined their views on the way in which family life was changing. Central to this was the notion of changing roles for men and women in society in general and the family in particular. They argued that families have gone through a pattern of change leading to the emergence of the 'symmetrical family' in late industrial society. The most important indicator of symmetricality is the move towards a balance or symmetry between the roles of males and females inside families.

The evidence for this was twofold. First, there

was the increased tendency for women to engage in paid employment outside the home (see also Section 9.3), and secondly, the increase in the amount of work males do around the house (domestic labour). In line with their more general views on evolution and the principle of 'stratified diffusion', Young and Willmott argue that these developments occurred first in middle-class households and were later being adopted in working-class households. Their view of the 'symmetrical family' was therefore something of a prediction about the future at the time it was written as well as a description of how some middle-class couples lived.

This view came under sustained criticism in Ann Oakley's book on housework (1974a). She argued that the idea of symmetry presented in this work is a myth since Young and Willmott's own statistics show that only 72 per cent of husbands 'help' their wife in some way. She points out that this is a very loose notion and, more importantly, the idea that husbands 'help' their wives shows that the prime responsibility for domestic labour is still seen to lie with women.

One key spur to Oakley's work was the series of studies of the frustrations faced by male assembly-line workers such as Blauner's (1964) study on alienation (see Section 9.7) and work, and Goldthorpe and Lockwood's affluent worker study (1968) (see Section 4.7). She wished to analyse housework using similar categories to underline her argument that it should be treated as work. Some of her findings in this regard are presented in Table 7.12

Table 7.12 The experience of monotony, fragmentation and speed in work: housewives and factory workers compared (percentages)

Workers	Monotony	Fragmentation	Speed
Housewives	75	90	50
Factory workers	41	70	31
Assembly-line workers[1]	67	86	36

[1]The assembly-line workers are a sub-sample of the factory workers
Source: Oakley (1974a), p. 87

Activity
Which group experienced the highest levels of monotony, fragmentation and speed? To what extent does this information contradict Shorter's view of family life?

I, E

Secondly, her research indicated that far from males becoming more involved in domestic tasks –

although middle-class males helped slightly more than working-class males – most support related to childcare rather than to general housework duties. Overall she rejects the notion of progress implied by the idea of the development of the symmetrical family, since:

only a minority of husbands gave the kind of help that modern assertions of equality in marriage imply (Oakley, 1974a, p. 138)

She argued that the construction of the housewife role must be analysed on the same basis as the construction of predominantly male employment (see Section 9.1). Despite the fact that women spend up to 77 hours per week on this work, this has not in fact been the case. As a result, the domestic arena and its contribution to society are consistently downplayed, so that the link between the social construction of the housewife role and women's systematic structural oppression in society is obscured.

According to Oakley, the oppression of women occurs through this role since:

The characteristic features of the housewife role in modern industrialised society are (1) its exclusive allocation to women, rather than to adults of both sexes; (2) its association with economic dependence i.e. with the dependent role of the woman in modern marriage; (3) its status as non-work – or its opposition to 'real' i.e. economically productive work; and (4) its primacy to women, that is, its priority over other roles.
(Oakley, 1974a, p. 138)

Discussion point
In the above passage Oakley makes a number of statements about the situation of housewives. Discuss whether each of these is still valid today.

Decision-making and power inequalities in the family

Further criticism of the notion of increasing domestic equality came from Stephen Edgell's (1980) study of middle-class couples. Given that the theory of 'stratified diffusion' suggested that this was where most equality would be found, his conclusion was that in fact no such equality was present and that:

In contrast to certain optimistic theorists who claim that the nineteenth-century patriarchal family has been superseded by a more democratic type . . . the present study provides abundant evidence of the survival of patriarchalism.
(Edgell, 1980, p. 105)

Recent developments in the domestic division of labour debate

Research on this issue has mushroomed since the 1970s. Pahl (1989) studied the issue of who controls finances in the family and found that while there were some instances where women controlled the finances, in these cases women used their budgeting skills to provide goods for their husbands or children, often themselves going without in the process. Therefore even when women gain some control, ultimately it is men who benefit from this.

She suggests that there are a number of factors that contribute to decisions over the control of money within marriages. She found that there were four main ways in which family finances could be organized: control by wife, control by husband, or pooling arrangements controlled either by the wife or the husband. The factors which affect this are summarized in Figure 7.13.

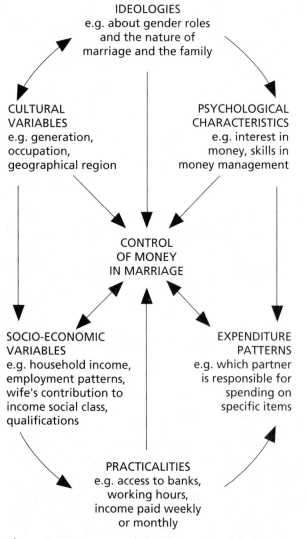

Figure 7.13 Money and marriage: a model. Source: Abercrombie and Warde (1994a)

Discussion point
How do you think each of these factors may have an effect on the management of money in households?

Pahl (1993) also found that the way finances were organized seemed to make a significant difference to the level of marital happiness expressed in the families she studied (see Table 7.13 and Figure 7.14).

Table 7.13 Marital happiness by control of finances: wives' answers (husbands' in brackets)

	Wife control	Wife-controlled pooling	Husband-controlled pooling	Husband control
Marriage described as:				
Happy/very happy	13 (13)	23 (25)	37 (35)	13 (16)
Average/unhappy	1 (1)	4 (2)	2 (4)	9 (6)
Total number of couples	14	27	39	22

Source: Pahl (1993)

We cannot be certain whether husband control leads to unhappiness or whether marital discord provokes the husband into taking control of finances. However, there was a very significant association between male control of money and marital unhappiness, which applied both to men and to women.

So the way in which a couple organise their finances reflects the resources which each brings to the relationship and affects the quality of the relationship. Ideology has the power to mitigate or to exacerbate structural inequality. An ideology which stresses the sharing of resources helps to conceal the structurally weak position of those who do not earn. An ideology of separateness in financial matters strengthens the position of those who earn compared with those who do not.

The control and allocation of money in marriage has proved to be an exciting new area of sociological enquiry, and one which provides many opportunities for small-scale, qualitative studies. In the past, the 'sociology of work' was largely separate from the 'sociology of the family'. Now we can see that the broader socio-economic context shapes the control of money within the household, which itself shapes the experience of individual members of households. Asking about money offers a revealing way of exploring the differences between 'his' marriage and 'her' marriage – and it is a topic which no couple beginning a serious relationship can afford to ignore.

Figure 7.14 Happiness and financial control. Source: adapted from Pahl (1993)

Activity

Summarize Pahl's main findings about the relationship between financial control in families and marital happiness. Can you suggest any other variables which she may have considered?

I, A

Also considering power over financial resources within the household, Lydia Morris (1987, 1993) conducted a case study of family relationships in Hartlepool. One of the reasons for this was her desire to investigate the effects of the recession and unemployment (see Section 9.6) on family structure and decision-making. She concluded that while changes in the economic structure of society have led to the demise of the idea of the male as an exclusive bread-winner for the whole family (owing to the rise of unemployment, which had reached 27 per cent in Hartlepool by the time of her fieldwork in 1986) and the idea of the 'family wage' has been undermined (see also Section 9.3), nonetheless, in relation to gender roles this has not led to a great deal of change.

She points out that most employment opportunities for women are part time and when women took such jobs their household roles were not largely taken over by husbands but predominantly by female relatives and friends. Therefore, even when men were unemployed, gender roles remained 'traditional' and women still undertook most household tasks, even if that meant a network of women rather than one individual woman. In relation to finance, however, she argues that the effect of the recession with the growth of male unemployment and consequential low household incomes has meant some greater influence for women in budgetary matters.

Generally, the wives of unemployed men are more likely to be unemployed (see also Section 9.6) than the wives of employed men (largely due to the disincentive effect of the operation of the social security system) so women gain greater control but over smaller amounts of money; merely giving them a greater say in poverty. You can find a more detailed summary of this piece of research in an excellent article in *Sociology Review* by David Abbott (1994).

A similar study by Wheelock (1990) looked at what happens when the husband is unemployed and the wife still has paid employment. For a number of reasons this is an unusual scenario, since most studies show that when the husband becomes unemployed the wife is very likely to become unemployed as well. However, it does provide a situation where it is possible to test out whether men would adopt domestic duties if their wife was working.

She studied 30 such families in the north east of England, and found that although women still retained primary responsibility for core household tasks, the men did become more involved in various activities. However, their involvement remained limited. The amount of help in domestic work given by husbands did seem to vary in line with the number of hours paid employment the wives were doing.

Negotiations around family responsibilities

Finch and Mason (1993) looked at the ways in which families tended to negotiate family responsibilities. This involved various expectations about obligations to family and wider kin, and they found that there was no general agreement about the level of help and obligation one should feel towards family members. They therefore argue that we should talk about guidelines rather than rules in this respect, as what is expected within families seems to be so varied.

It is here that the importance of negotiation becomes apparent as the lack of clear rules leaves room for discussion which takes the form of negotiations about the type and amount of help to be given or expected. In particular this is the case in relation to the issue of looking after elderly relatives, often provoking discussion and negotiation between the children of the elderly person and also between their children and their spouses.

A number of studies (Elliot, 1996; Hicks, 1988) have examined the gendered aspects of caring for the elderly, especially the way that the majority of care for the elderly seems to be delegated to daughters and daughters-in-law. However, men and women equally provide care for a spouse and both male and female carers experience similar problems in acquiring the levels of support they need. Figure 7.15 shows the average hours per week that men and women spend as carers.

Foucault, power, the family and the body – the control of populations

The work of the French philosopher, Michel Foucault, is now filtering down into sociological analysis. At the heart of Foucault's thinking is the idea that people are constituted by ways of thinking which he calls discourses. Such discourses, which effectively constrain the way we think, therefore gain power over us. This notion of power/knowledge is eminently applicable to the way in which discourses have developed about family structure in societies. (See also Sections 9.7 and 17.4.)

Foucault argues that the most important discourses in contemporary societies are those concerned with

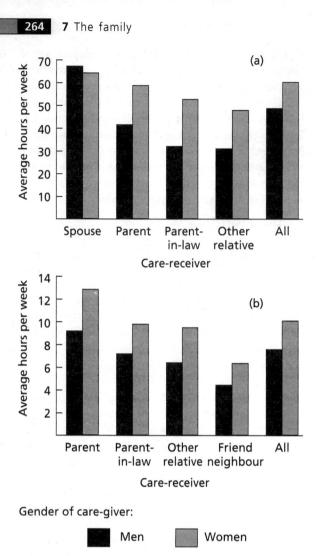

Gender of care-giver:

■ Men   ▨ Women

Figure 7.15 Average hours of informal care provided by (a) co-resident carers and (b) carers in a separate household, by relationship between carer and cared for and by gender of carer. Source: Arber and Ginn (1991) in Elliot (1996, p. 134)

regulation of populations and particularly with regulation of bodies. This explains Foucault's interest in the growth of medical discourses that he sees replacing religion as the most important discourse. Central to this control of populations are the structures of the family:

The reproduction of human populations and the restraint of single bodies require at the institutional level a system of patriarchal households for the control of fertility and at the level of the human individual a culture of asceticism for the regulation or delaying of sexual gratification in the interests of familial control.
(Foucault, 1977, p. 142)

The growth of medical discourse is the new means by which surveillance of the population can be carried out and such new discourses applied to control

their behaviour. (See Section 13.9.) The growth of medicine and other allied disciplines such as social policy and social work are therefore, for Foucault, new discourses that allow new forms of social control to be put into place. The history of the regulation of the family is simply a power struggle between different discourses with the Church losing out to medicine.

Modernist thinkers view the triumph of medicine over religion as the triumph of the rational over the irrational and therefore as progress. However, Foucault's adherence to post-structuralist (see Section 2.10) notions of relativism does not allow him to view this as the emergence of the truth or as progress. It is simply the emergence of a new discourse that controls people's behaviour just as surely as the old discourse did, albeit in slightly different ways.

Also examining the family from a post-modern perspective, Morgan (1996) suggests that:

Family practices are, to a very large extent, bodily practices. Family themes and family concerns revolve around issues of birth, death and sexuality.
(Morgan, 1996, p. 113)

There is a focus on the control and regulation of the body over both the self and others. Men and women have both used violence and the promise (or threatened withdrawal) of sexual favours in order to control each other (see also Section 7.7). While adultery, for example, is no longer ascribed the taboo once associated with it, it remains a powerful weapon within family situations. Children, too, are controlled in terms of their bodily processes especially through toilet training and restraints on sexual expression. There is still considerable debate about whether parents should smack their children or not, and, as Morgan points out, the threatened withdrawal of love may be as powerful a form of bodily control as any physical methods of chastisement. Few young people pass through adolescence without some debates over the limits and boundaries to their freedom.

💬 **Discussion point**

How might the behaviour of members of a family be controlled? To what extent does gender or age affect what people are allowed to do and the sorts of sanctions imposed?

Food and power in the family

Beardsworth and Keil (1993) point out that food is central to the cultural identity of most ethnic groups. While it is fairly easy to design a basic nutritional diet, few people would relish having to eat it every day. This is because it offers little in the way of physical or psychological pleasure and ignores any cultural or social differences between groups in what they choose to eat. For many households, the sharing of meals is part of what defines family and non-family relationships. Sharing meals is often particularly important in rituals and festivals such as Christmas, Divali and Passover.

The allocation of food in many households still delineates adults from children and, in many societies, men from women. In most families the preparation of food largely remains the responsibility of women, although men may 'help' clear up. Christine Delphy (1979) found that the male head of household tended to be better fed than other members of the family, while O'Connell (1994) suggests that Indian girls generally learn their inferiority to boys from birth, not least through their reduced access to good food within the family. Such a pattern was repeated in many poorer countries including Mexico and South Korea, and was commonly found among English working-class families in the 1950s (Dennis *et al.*, 1956).

Nowadays, in western societies, children are sometimes criticized for not eating enough and many families worry about children (especially daughters) becoming anorexic. This is an interesting contrast to the struggle for food in other families and cultures (see Section 12.9), although obesity remains, literally, a growing problem in many western countries, especially in the USA and, more recently, in the UK.

Discussion point

How is food allocated in your home? Do some people have more say than others over what is eaten and when? Do some members eat more or less than others? Are there any disputes over the amount you eat or what you eat in the family? To what extent is gender or age an aspect of differences in food choice, preparation or consumption patterns in your family?

There are a vast number of cookery books and magazines largely aimed at women, and traditionally, women have passed their knowledge about food and cooking skills informally to their daughters and daughters-in-law. However, men often have considerable input into what is eaten in the home (and when it is eaten) and are more frequently defined as the 'top' chefs in many countries.

A study of family eating habits by Charles and Kerr (1988) found that:

there was a very strong emphasis on the importance of the 'proper meal' (centred on a hot, freshly-cooked main course consisting of meat, potatoes and vegetables) and on the role of women as providers and servers of food. However, although women bore the main responsibility for purchasing, preparing and serving food, in practice the husband's taste tended to dictate which foods were bought and which recipes were selected. Thus, in a sense, women were in a position where they bore responsibility for feeding the family, but could not exercise very much power over the choice of food.
(Quoted in Beardsworth and Keil, 1993, p. 13)

Other studies support this view. They suggested that the 'cooked dinner' in particular reinforced a number of notions about familial expectations and, especially, the expectations about the role of women in the family. Meat remains important in our society as a symbol of social importance. Although vegetarianism and non-meat eating is increasingly popular (and possibly itself a cause of family friction), meat still remains important in a 'proper dinner', despite scares about BSE and battery chickens.

The study of the use of food in families is therefore an extremely useful way of examining differences and similarities in family life. While it is often assumed that cultural variations in eating habits have largely disappeared as we adopt an increasingly undifferentiated eating pattern owing to globalization (see Section 10.10), large differences remain. This not only reflects class, cultural and ethnic diversity but also differences of power and access to resources within the family. Table 7.14 shows the amounts of food eaten by men, women and children.

Gender seems to be a common variable as women tend to be more involved in feeding the family while often having less access to the food itself. Children (and sometimes older people) may have more or less power within the family set-up to decide how much or even what they eat. While economic power or earning potential may be at the root of such dominance or subordination, access to food also reflects and reinforces power relationships in family life.

Morgan (1996) concludes that:

Food and food preparation, therefore, do not simply create or reinforce unities within family groups; they may also provide the resources about which differences and divisions may be expressed.
(Morgan, 1996, p. 158)

He also suggests that differences between households, especially in terms of ethnicity, are frequently expressed in terms of food. Multi-culturalism at a popular level has entered not just the eating but the cooking habits of many British families – although some migrant groups and their offspring still remain

Table 7.14 Average incidence of consumption of main food items over a two week period (women's standardized food consumption = 100)

	Men (N=151)	Women (N=157)	Children (N=289)
High status meat	109	100	69
Medium status meat	132	100	78
Low status meat	133	100	102
Whole fish	112	100	53
Low status fish	94	100	106
Eggs	116	100	80
Cheese	104	100	68
Green leafy vegetables (cooked)	97	100	72
Other vegetables (cooked)	104	100	86
Raw vegetables	106	100	46
Fruit	88	100	124
Potatoes (boiled/roast)	103	100	98
Chips	100	100	57
Bread	114	100	92
Breakfast cereal	102	100	200
Cake	109	100	73
Biscuits	80	100	141
Puddings	100	100	133
Sweets	74	100	231
Crisps	133	100	222
Baked beans, etc.	105	100	153
Milk	105	100	358
Soft drinks	74	100	833
Tea/coffee	94	100	23
Alcohol	163	100	7

Source: Charles and Kerr (1994, p. 38)

sceptical about the attempts of native Britons to reproduce the cuisine of their culture of origin. Poverty and class differences can be seen not only in what families eat and how they organize their food consumption throughout the day, but also in their choice of food (white bread or wholemeal) and even where they go shopping. Each supermarket has a clear class profile of their 'typical' customer. Morgan (1996) concludes that food is so bound up with our personal, cultural and familial identity that we can see it as a defining aspect of our cultural selves, and therefore worthy of considerable sociological investigation when we examine power relationships in the family.

7.6 The family and social policies

The family is generally represented as a private institution in society where individuals have a great deal of autonomy from state regulation. However this is something of a myth as the state has always intervened in family life and certainly it is possible to trace a consistent approach in terms of social policy in this century to the production of particular types of familial arrangements.

This point is underlined by Muncie and Sapsford (1995):

social policy not only has a caring welfare objective but also carries with it notions of 'normality' to which families are directed to conform (Muncie and Sapsford, 1995, p. 29)

The family and the state

While the state provides a number of support mechanisms for families such as child benefit, the education system and income support, it does not do so without families meeting certain criteria and without certain assumptions underlying the systems that are developed. Public policy therefore shapes the way we live our supposedly private lives. At the same time this notion of privacy can be used to hold back from intervention in certain circumstances. The key question to ask is whether this notion of normality is one which is a true reflection of the way people live their lives or whether it is an ideological construction reflecting the beliefs of certain groups of people or interest groups about how we should live our lives.

Given that states generally do have the power to enforce their will, the normality which is presented to us might affect our individual autonomy and supposed privacy. Certainly the enforcement of such normality might lead to certain individuals losing out to others. An important point made by feminist sociologists such as Gittins and Abbott and Wallace is that the imposition of a particular family structure through the operation of social policy can contribute to the continued oppression of women and their dependence on men within family structures.

Functionalist sociologists (see Section 2.4) in the 1940s and 1950s saw the family becoming a much more specialized institution with many of its previous functions being taken over by the state. The growth of the welfare state in the post-war period (see Section 14.1) has indeed meant that many services previously provided in a private family context were now provided through public funding, especially education and health services (see Sections

8.5 and 13.5). Also, public support was given to the family in the form of child benefit and other welfare payments.

An important question over the relationship of the family to the state therefore arises. Does the state provide support for a natural family structure or does it shape the structure of the family in ways which are detrimental to family members, in particular, women? Gittins (1993) summarizes this debate as follows:

Essentially the controversy amounts to disagreement as to whether the growth of the state, and the Welfare State in particular, has actually enhanced the position of families and family 'solidarity', or whether it has exacerbated a decline and erosion of what is seen as a previously greater family solidarity and support.

(Gittins, 1993, p. 133)

Pateman (1988) has talked of the way in which the development of modern liberal-democratic societies included this division between the public sphere and the private sphere (see also Sections 5.4 and 17.3). She argues that democracy was only ever identified with the public sphere of society and this left the family (seen as part of the private sphere of society) as undemocratic with male patriarchal authority over women undiminished by the democratic reforms occurring in the public sphere of society.

Her work therefore points to the importance of the state defining what was to be private, meaning that even the notion of where the state was not going to intervene was a decision taken by the state. The 'privatization' of family life is therefore an inherently political decision. However it does point to an important assumption about family life which has not entirely been eliminated today, namely that the family is an arena where male authority over females should not be questioned by the state. This view is shared by some but not all MPs who are seen as on the 'right-wing' of the Conservative party.

The state and the reinforcement of inequalities

The extent to which the state, through legislation and intervention, served to problematize only certain families, and certain people within those families, can be seen in the example of the Poor Law Act of 1899. This Act gave Poor Law Guardians the power to remove children from unsuitable parents. This allowed a class-based definition of good parenting, and good mothering in particular to be enforced by middle-class guardians on working-class parents.

Gittins (1993) argues that this legislation was:

both class-specific (middle-class women never had their children removed from the family; whatever

horrors of incest or brutality might occur, middle-class families and mothers were by definition good families and mothers) and sex-specific – although it was considered irresponsible if working-class men failed to provide adequately for their children financially, they were seldom penalised in the ways mothers were if they were deemed to be bad mothers.

(Gittins, 1993, pp. 145–6)

One of the important elements of the notion of a 'good mother' was that she should not work in paid employment outside the home (see also Sections 5.3 and 5.4). This effectively made working-class women financially dependent on men to avoid being classified as a 'bad mother' and face the threat of having their children removed. However, as Gittins also points out, the wages for semi-skilled and unskilled male workers were often too low to provide enough money for a family. The definition of 'good mothering' did nothing to increase the wages paid, leaving working-class women the choice between being a good mother in poverty or working to supplement the family wage under constant threat of the removal of children:

State legislation was effectively trying to undermine many of the ways in which the poorer sectors had coped, while at the same time reinforcing the middle-class ideology of a patriarchal household with a dependent wife and children supported by a male breadwinner. 'Deviant' (i.e. poor) families were more and more subject to surveillance and interference by State agencies.

(Gittins, 1993, p. 146)

The assumptions underlying social policy

The most important developments in social policy in relation to the family were arguably the series of pieces of legislation passed in the late 1940s which created the welfare state (see Section 14.1). These changes were identified in the *Beveridge Report* of 1942 which set out a blueprint for such a state and laid the foundations for this legislation.

While it is undoubtedly true that the aims of this document were ones which broadly set out to produce a more equitable society with its emphasis on the elimination of the five social evils (squalor, disease, ignorance, idleness and want), it is nonetheless also true that this intervention contained within it a set of assumptions which have important implications even for contemporary welfare policy. These centre on Beveridge's notions of what family life involved and in particular on his ideas of the very different roles of men and women within families.

Beveridge and the family

The main form of provision enshrined in the *Beveridge Report* was for a system of national insurance which would provide financial assistance to those who were unemployed or sick, and would also provide pensions for those in old age. This was to be paid for through contributions collected from both employers and employees. It is here that the main problem is encountered since it does not consider how those without paid employment could make a contribution and therefore whether they would be entitled to the benefits available through this scheme.

In fact this became the basis on which married women were largely excluded from many of the benefits available since it was assumed that they would be looked after by their husband. In effect, this meant that married women were made economically dependent on their husbands. This was not accidental since it reflected Beveridge's ideas about what normal family life constituted, and in particular his view that on marriage women would cease to be employed outside the home. Married women were seen as mainly being provided for by men and generally not employed in paid work, therefore having a restricted entitlement to benefits.

Muncie and Wetherall (1995) point out that even at the time this was conceived it was a somewhat less than accurate reflection of reality since in 1943 40 per cent of married women were in employment, and after the Second World War the number of women in employment increased rather than decreased as Beveridge expected. Today, most married women work in paid employment (see Section 9.3) for a considerable portion of their lives. The assumption about how people live their lives was therefore never a reflection of reality, simply a particular view about how people should live their lives. Nonetheless, despite its lack of link with reality, the assumptions held by Beveridge continue in some respects to underlie the benefits system, often leaving women worse off than men.

The New Right and the family

[The] *New Right in both Britain and the USA has long seen itself as developing a 'new' morality through its approach to sexual and family matters. Its particular emphasis has been on redefining women's place within the family, especially as mothers. This focus on the family is central to New Right ideology.*
(David, 1986, p. 136)

The New Right have had most influence in the UK on the Conservative Party, which had a continous period in government in the UK in the 1980s and 1990s. (See also Sections 2.10 and 17.2.) The notion that a new ideologically inspired radical right agenda was needed developed in the 1970s following the defeat of the Conservative government by the miners in 1974. Central to the ideas of the New Right was the notion that the state is a negative, almost parasitic, entity in society. This view had clear implications for the idea of a welfare state. This set of institutions which grew up after the Second World War were seen by New Right thinkers as creating a culture of dependency (see Section 14.3) which encouraged laziness, leading to economic decline. The structure of the family was also central to this theory of economic decline. The New Right believe in the notion of the stable nuclear family as the bedrock of society (see Figure 7.16). Paul Johnson provides an example of this:

The ideal society must rest upon the tripod of a strong family, a voluntary church and a liberal minimal state. Of these, the family is the most important.
(Paul Johnson, *The Observer*, 10 October 1982)

A further development of this line of argument (which meets the neo-liberal desire for cuts in government expenditure) is that welfare state payments which encourage people to engage in family structures other than the perceived norm of the stereotypical nuclear family, lead to moral decline and a lack of personal responsibility (see also Sections 2.10 and 4.8). Such is the intellectual basis of the attack on lone parent families. They cause concern also since they are mainly supported by welfare benefits, leading to a rise in welfare expenditure in most cases.

This view has particular implications for women. The attempt to rein back the welfare state has not in fact led to the disappearance of the social problems that the welfare state sought to deal with. Instead, the New Right has attempted to privatize these problems by seeking to push responsibility back to the family unit. Within this family unit it is clear that it will be largely women who are expected to assume the traditional role of unpaid carer. Abbott and Wallace (1992) make this point clearly, as well as exposing the mythical nature of the New Right vision of the family:

The appeal of the New Right is one of nostalgia for a lost past when children respected parents, the crime rate was low, marriage was for life and the streets were safe for everyone to walk in. What is concealed when this image of the past is invoked is that it was never a reality but an ideal, a middle-class dream . . . the lost society is not a 'golden age' but one that secured the interests of capitalism and patriarchy at the expense of the working class, of

Family values and relationships

A critical aspect of the appeal of 'family values' to the political right is that they unite two very different groups of supporters. On the one hand, 'family values' appeal to conservatives; that is, to those who see the world as suffering from a long-term decline or decay from an earlier 'golden age' of order and stability. Typically, conservative thought stands for an intuitive nostalgia for a world we have lost. This world is conceived as based on small-scale and intimate collective units, such as family, village or tribe, believed to have been suffused with an unquestioned reverence for rank and authority. Where larger-scale social units are recognised, such as the nation, they are cloned in mystical sentiments generated around supposedly cohesive and tightly knit blood-ties of kith and kin. Thus, the British nation is headed by a royal family that incorporates the virtues of family solidarity and respect whilst providing a symbol of unity and belonging that all can comprehend.

Conservatives typically adopt an embattled outlook. Decency, respect for authority and order are breaking down everywhere. The failure of family bonds to restrain and constrain behaviour results in the original sin (which is believed to lie at the heart of human nature) to burst out in the form of greed, selfishness, decadence, destructiveness and anarchy. Conservative supporters of 'family values', then, see themselves as stalwart defenders of the ancient truths on which civilised life is based.

During the 1980s a second strand of right-wing thought came to prominence, based on a very different philosophy but no less committed to family values. Neo-liberalism rests on the principle of the primacy of individuals over all collective or social entities (Arblaster 1984). Individual initiative, liberty and creativity are regarded as of supreme value; the search for individual rewards is seen as the motor of all social life. Individuals are not seen as social products but rather as biological entities that are part of the natural order that precedes social institutions. Markets are regarded as the expression of this pre-social human nature. In this sense, markets are not social phenomena but the natural expression of unfettered human freedom.

In this view, then, there is nothing to fear from unrestrained human nature. Indeed, it is collective and social restraints that are seen as inherently dangerous to individual freedom. Such restraints might include the tribal loyalties of the past or the totalitarian bureaucracies of the present (Butler 1983). Neo-liberalism is, therefore, an inherently radical ideology that is willing to sacrifice all manner of traditional and long lasting institutions in the name of market dynamics.

It might well be thought that this philosophy would have little time for family ties. However, in recent years the mainstream of neo-liberal thought has portrayed family relations as part of the biological and pre-social expression of innate human needs and desires. Thus, when Margaret Thatcher enunciated her famous dictum that 'there is no such thing as society' she followed it up with the remark that there are only individuals and families. Maintenance of 'family values', therefore, became part of the neo-liberal agenda in the 1980s. Policy objectives were presented as returning choice, independence and responsibility to families. This was the flip side of rolling back the state, deregulation and privatisation. Thus, the two strands of contemporary right-wing thought, conservatism and neo-liberalism, are bound together as political allies in part by the appeal of 'family values'.

Figure 7.16 The appeal of 'family values' to the political right. Source: adapted from Jewson (1994)

women and of children. Indeed, this is what many in the New Right would appear to want to recreate. (Abbott and Wallace, 1992, p. 6)

Discussion point
To what extent do you think that most people have a nostalgic view of society in the past?

Public policy and the family

It appears that the family remains central not just to debates about family life, but also to policies concerning familial arrangements. Smart (1991) points out that although aspects of family structure have dominated state policy for years, the recent focus on the family has been unprecedented. Much of this, she suggests, was due to the New Right's desire to cut support for lone mothers. She argues that a number of policies can be seen to be combined into a singular attack on lone mothers.

These include the Social Security Act (1986) which stressed the need to support the 'responsible family' as part of its agenda. There have also been tax changes to encourage marriage and discourage cohabitation (for example in the allocation of mortgage tax allowance), although there are still few tax incentives for people to marry. One area, that of divorce and the pension entitlements of a divorced wife, still remains problematic. Changes in unemployment allowances and benefits have also made it increasingly difficult for lone parents to take paid employment.

Smart points out that the taxation and benefits system is so complex that the implication of such changes for the family are difficult to assess. However, it is clear that the more benefits are likely to require means testing – such as the repayable and means-tested loans which replaced the Social Fund special payments in 1991 – the more that people on benefit will be disadvantaged. Undoubtedly, this will not work in the interests of single parents who find it more difficult than most to find work that makes childcare a financial option. Whether this will stop women choosing lone parenting, as is sometimes argued from a New Right perspective, remains to be seen.

Child Support Agency

One problem identified by both the New Right and 'ethical socialists' such as Dennis and Erdos is the need for fathers to take more responsibility for their children. Set up by the government in 1991, the Child Support Agency was intended to bring errant fathers to heel and make them pay for the maintenance of their children. While few apparently disagreed with such an aim – at least publicly – there were a number of problems with such a policy (see Figure 7.17).

The Child Support Agency (CSA), established in April 1993, has been charged with the task of assessing and collecting maintenance payments from absent parents. The CSA uses a standard formula to assess levels of child maintenance based on the ability of both parents to contribute. This approach assumes that parents have just as much responsibility for children conceived through a previous relationship as they do for children of any current relationship. It differs from that used by the courts who used discretion in individual cases when determining the level of child maintenance. When the parent with care is on welfare benefits, successful enforcement by the CSA will result in considerable savings for the state. The reported concentration of the Agency's efforts on relatively well-off absent parents, whose former partners are currently on welfare benefits, has attracted the strongest criticism.

The survey shows strong support for the principle that maintenance should be paid by absent parents according to what they can afford. Ninety-four per cent agree that a divorced father should pay maintenance to support a primary school-aged child of his who remains with the mother. Ninety-one per cent agree that the amount of that maintenance should depend on the father's income. However, there is some disagreement over where paternal responsibility should come to an end. A substantial majority (about two-thirds) think that the amount of maintenance should depend on the mother's income also – in other words, that questions of need as well as biological responsibility are relevant. When asked to consider what should happen if the mother re-marries, only about two in five say maintenance should definitely continue, while a similar number say it should depend on the new husband's income.

The absent parent is of course most commonly a man. This subject thus raises important questions about relations between men and women as well as between the family and the state. Unsurprisingly, while nearly half of women take the view that a remarried mother should definitely continue to receive payments from a previous partner irrespective of her new husband's income, less than one in three men do so.

Figure 7.17 The family and welfare. Source: Jewell *et al.* (1995)

First, the father had to be identified and found and then he had to be made to pay the correct amount. The benefit would come from him paying for the children so that the state would no longer be doing so, although often getting the money would prove to be very expensive. However, the stated aim was as much ideological as it was financial, inasmuch as it was designed to make men more aware of their familial responsibilities.

Overall, policies which apparently promote responsible parenting have attracted a number of criticisms. Elliot (1996) argues that policies such as the Child Support Agency:

have won support from lone parent pressure groups but are opposed by the Left because the deduction of maintenance from income support means that lone parent family poverty is not alleviated; by many lone mothers because it keeps alive links with former partners which they may wish to sever; by feminists because women are not compensated for the costs they bear as a consequence of inequalities in marriage and childrearing; and by men on the grounds that the way in which their obligations are calculated sweeps aside clean break settlements, jeopardises the financial viability of their second families and takes no account of the 'blame', of their possible entrapment into fatherhood and of their limited access rights.
(Elliot, 1996, p. 27)

Activity
Identify the aims of the Child Support Agency.
Outline the advantages and disadvantages for:
a children
b fathers
c mothers
d the state.

U, I, E

Homosexuality, childlessness and the family

While social policy seems to stress the importance of traditional family structures, other options have always been adopted, although there appears to be something of a backlash against certain forms of households, especially same-sex arrangements. Weeks (1977) pointed out that although the legislation relating to homosexuality was liberalized in 1967, the number of convictions for homosexual offences had actually increased. Attitudes towards same-sex families have similarly come under considerable attack. Lesbian couples are increasingly being refused opportunities for artificial insemination and mothers are now more often refused custody of their children if it can be shown that they have entered a lesbian relationship.

Van Every (1995) further suggests that increasing numbers of people are choosing to remain voluntarily childless. While policies have yet to be introduced to reward mothers who produce large families – as was the case in France after the Second World War – tolerance of alternative arrangements appears to be more common in 'everyday' experience than in political rhetoric. As Gittins (1993) shows, the expansion of the state in modern industrial society has resulted in an ever-growing body of legislation which, in different ways, affects families and the individuals who live in them. How such legislation affects individuals depends very much on both their sex and their social class. One law may act to the detriment of one member of the family while another law may benefit another member of the same family. Legislation on sexuality, marriage, divorce, childcare, abortion, birth control, mothering all have crucial effects on families in different ways.

Protective legislation

This name has been given to a series of Acts which restricted the employment of women and children in certain areas, notably the mines. It is clear that these Acts might be seen as protective in that they stopped women and children being exposed to dangerous working conditions. However, in doing so they also acted to restrict job opportunities available to women. Certain feminists argue that this is a reflection of patriarchy on behalf of both the state and male-dominated unions who wished to restrict access to work to retain high wages. (See Sections 5.4 and 9.3.) The question of who protective legislation actually protected is therefore very much a matter of debate.

In fact, very little legislation is particularly protective towards women, but acts rather to ensure that they fulfil their appointed roles as wives and mothers 'properly'.
(Gittins, 1993, p. 153)

Formal and informal caring

The push towards more privatized family care and the move away from large-scale institutionalized care has indeed led to more pressure on women to care for elderly relatives (see Section 14.2). Claire Ungerson (1995) has argued that the traditional distinction between formal (paid) and informal (unpaid) care tended to assume that unpaid care was done for love. However she points out that changes to the care system mean that now both formal and informal caring contain elements of labour and love. This

is due to the development of 'waged care' in the form of 'paid volunteering':

the payments that they make look very much like wages, in the sense that the payments are conditional on evidence that specific work has been undertaken and successfully carried through.
(Ungerson, 1995, pp. 33–4)

While it can be argued that this is a partial recognition of the work done predominantly by females in the family setting, it has sparked off a debate since it can also be argued that this money constitutes an extra pressure on women by pushing them into traditional stereotyped roles. As Ungerson (1995) also comments:

part of the underlying reason for the development of these systems in the first place is to reinforce and ensure an adequate supply of informal caring labour in the face of rapidly growing demand for care . . . . [They might] constitute an extra pressure particularly on women to give up more conventionally paid work. Thus there is a powerful argument that such payments are entrapping rather than liberating.
(Ungerson, 1995, pp. 47–8)

Activity

Using material from this chapter and other sections in this book (Sections 13.6, 14.2 and 14.3), summarize the debates about the roles of informal care in the family. How do members of the family operate as informal carers? Who does most of the caring?

I, A

Decommodification and the family

The most influential account of welfare-state regimes at the moment is that devised by Gøsta Esping-Andersen (1990) (see also Sections 14.3 and 14.4). He argues that we can look at welfare states in terms of the extent of 'decommodification', by which he means the extent to which transactions are removed from a market context (where money changes hands). The main idea is that the more services are offered without market transactions the greater the extent of welfare services.

This is clearly one of the ways in which welfare states were designed to redistribute wealth. Since there was no need for you to contribute directly to the entire cost of any services you may require, they were instead funded on the basis of ability to pay. The assumption therefore is that transactions outside the market place are inherently beneficial.

However a problem has arisen with this notion relating to how the domestic labour of housewives can be accommodated within this scheme. Since housework is unpaid (see also Section 9.1), it is by definition already decommodified. This is not something which is generally seen as being a great step forward for women. This therefore brings into question the usefulness of the concept of decommodification in relation to the position of women in society:

while the concept of decommodification makes sense for those women fully engaged in the labour market, it applies significantly less well for those who are not.

(Shaver and Bradshaw, 1995, p. 13)

Back to basics?

One of the key Conservative policies of the 1990s was that of 'Back to Basics' which sought to reintroduce traditional family and moral values into soci-

ety. This remains a focus of considerable political and media debate. One aspect of this is that politicians are themselves being expected to adopt a more moral aspect to their behaviour, although the launch of the 'Back to Basics' campaign was undermined by evidence of sexual misbehaviour among a number of Tory MPs (see Figure 7.18). There are also debates about personal morality concerning the views of politicians on all moral issues, especially that of abortion. This suggests that the family, and its relationship to private and public morality, will remain at the centre of both political and sociological discourse.

7.7 The dark side of family life

Despite numerous criticisms, the family is still usually considered one of the most significant social institutions in society, linked closely with notions of love and caring. It can therefore be something of a shock to find out that there is a dark side to family life. Sociologists need to consider the reality of the way people live their lives in contemporary society. They therefore seek to understand some of the activities within the family which constitute a threat to some or all of its members. It is important to discover whether darker aspects of family life such as domestic violence and child abuse are exceptional acts committed by deviant people (see Chapter 11) or whether they are at least partly the result of the privatized nature of family life itself.

Violence against women

The extent to which women face domestic violence came to prominence as one of the key campaigning issues of the women's liberation movement and the rise of feminism as a perspective within sociology has led to continuing sociological concern (see Sections 5.3 and 5.4). The largest study of domestic violence is that by Dobash and Dobash (1980). They studied crime statistics in Scotland and came to the rather frightening conclusion that 25 per cent of all serious assaults were committed by husbands on their wives, although their methods and statistics have been questioned. When one takes into account their view that this study, if anything, underestimates the extent of 'wife-battering' due to the fact that this type of offence is not always recorded in crime statistics, it shows the rather dangerous prospects women face in conventional heterosexual partnerships. However, instances of domestic violence have also been recorded between same-sex couples and by women on men. While such occurrences often receive a lot of publicity, male violence on women is

Sex scandals that have shaken the Tory party

A long line of Tory sex scandals stretches back to the last election in April 1992.
• September 1992: Heritage Secretary David Mellor resigned after an affair with actress Antonia de Sancha and a free holiday with a PLO official's daughter.
• October 1993: Transport Minister Steve Norris admitted having five mistresses but avoided the sack.
• December 1993: Environment Minister Tim Yeo quit after fathering a love child by a Tory councillor.
• January 1994: Back-bencher David Ashby admitted to sleeping in the same bed as a young male friend. He later lost a libel action against a newspaper which claimed he was gay.
• January 1994: The wife of Transport Minister Lord Caithness killed herself after discovering his affair with another woman.
• February 1994: Eastleigh MP Stephen Milligan was found dead dressed in stockings and suspenders following an "auto-erotic" experiment which went wrong.
• February 1994: Hartley Booth, a Methodist lay-preacher, resigned as a ministerial aide after a relationship with Commons researcher Emily Barr, now a Labour Parliamentary candidate.
• May 1994: Government whip Michael Brown, a bachelor, resigned after allegations of gay sex with an under-age student.
• March 1995: Citizens' Charter Minister Robert Hughes resigned after an affair with a constituent who had asked for his help.
• April 1995: Richard Spring stepped down as a ministerial aide after a three-in-a-bed romp was exposed.
• June 1996: Welsh Office Minister Rod Richards quit over a fling with a PR girl.

Figure 7.18 Sex scandals. Source: *The Express on Sunday*, 5 January 1997

by far the most frequently recorded aspect of domestic violence.

The extent to which our society's notions of conventional family structure serve to reinforce this situation can be seen from their findings that one of the major factors precipitating assaults was the husband's perception that the wife was not performing her domestic duties to his satisfaction. Insofar as our society still accepts a domestic division of labour which allocates the majority of domestic duties to the female, this leaves women vulnerable to this sort of criticism, and possible subsequent assault.

However, the problems go further than this. Since domestic labour is unpaid and most women are in poorly rewarded jobs when they do work outside the home (see Section 9.3), it leaves many females economically dependent on male wages. Dobash and Dobash also found that although most women who were assaulted left home, many were forced to return. This was largely due to their economic dependency, but also because of the stigma surrounding the break-up of marriage. Many radical feminists argue that this stigma is based on the idea of heterosexual coupling as the normal form for family life.

A document produced for the Fourth UN Women's Conference held in 1995 implies that this problem has not disappeared. It points out that a quarter of the world's women suffer domestic violence, five women are burned to death in dowry disputes in India every day (see also Section 12.5), more than a million newborn girls are murdered or left to die every year and 90 million girls have endured genital mutilation. (See also Section 12.8.)

The report also makes a number of points about the economic situation of women worldwide. Women do two-thirds of the world's work, earn one-tenth of the world's income and own less than one hundredth of the world's property. There are twice as many illiterate women in the world as men, while their wages are between 30 and 40 per cent lower than those of men.

Activity

Write a short report of about 250 words on how the economic inequalities outlined above might contribute to the violence against women also outlined above. Are there any examples of domestic violence that cannot be accounted for by economic inequalities?

I, A, E

Cheal (1991) argues that feminist and Marxist theories have allowed sociologists to understand more about the problems that occur within families. They examine the structural causes of problems rather than accepting individual explanations for behaviour within what had always been conceived of as a private institution. Psychologists use what is known as 'family systems theory' to explain abusive patterns in family life, but they tend not to identify the relationship between the private and public aspects of family life.

This has resulted in the 'invisibility' of battered women whose unseen (and often unacknowledged) abuse is compounded by low self-esteem where women often blame themselves for their suffering. Cheal argues that such isolation:

is not a purely individual phenomenon. It has its roots in the social isolation experienced by many women living in private families. Separations of family life from public life and the role that women are expected to play as 'binding agents' in maintaining family integrity (Liljestrom, 1982), both reinforce cultural beliefs that family problems are private troubles and that women have the primary duty of resolving them.
(Cheal, 1991, p. 83)

Discussion point

To what extent do you agree that problems between domestic partners are largely a private matter?

Problems such as 'wife-battering' (now more commonly included under the phrase domestic abuse) have largely been ignored by police and courts, who have traditionally been reluctant to intervene in family disputes. Such views are linked to the idea that families are private institutions.

Cheal points out that the idea that external groups should not intervene in domestic matters highlights three key concepts that we have about the family. One is the idea that the family is a private institution where public groups have limited access. Another is the idea that individuals act as free agents; so that women can just leave the abusive relationship rather than being accountable to various notions of expected behaviour by women, especially those with children.

Finally, there is the concept of interest, where the interests of the individual (private interests) are seen in opposition to their position in the family where they act in the interest of the whole family group as publicly defined by politicians and welfare agencies; for example, the idea that parents should stay together (or part) for the sake of the children. This again assumes that all family members are completely free agents. According to this viewpoint Cheal suggests that:

These three ideas – access; agency/accountability; and interest – together define the cultural ideal of the private family in liberal western democracies. Family members define their projects with reference to personal desires, rather than public goals, and they are free to implement them to the limit of their resources
(Cheal, 1991, pp. 83–4)

Discussion point

How free do you think men, women and children are to act as individuals within their own families?

Domestic violence throughout the world

Domestic violence against both women and children is not just a problem in western democracies. O'Connell (1994) argues that:

Men have always used violence against women to perpetuate the gender hierarchy: to keep a woman 'in her place', to stifle her right to speak, to come and go, to make decisions and to control her sexuality.
(O'Connell, 1994, p. 79)

She suggests that in many cultures a man is seen as having the right to beat his wife, his children and other female members of his family. As many other writers have also conceded, she accepts that violence is not solely a male phenomenon, but argues that females are the most common victims of domestic violence. Her point is that violence against women in the home is rarely seen as any violation of human rights, and often, not even as a criminal action. She sees a link between the level of familial violence considered acceptable and the amount of violence used by the state to ensure its own survival, for example in Colombia.

However, other factors need to be considered in an explanation of why men are permitted (or take) so much physical power over women. For many societies, it seems to be a result of the belief that men are inherently superior to women, and many women accept the situation for economic and cultural reasons. Many women are, apparently, almost literally beaten into submission and share their husband's view that they deserve to be punished. While arguments for the criminalization of domestic violence as

a specific offence seem convincing, the results are often less than helpful, resulting in judicial and prison overcrowding and doing little to address the underlying problem.

Activity

Summarize the advantages and disadvantages of prosecuting men for violence in the family. Suggest other ways in which this problem could be approached.

I, A, E

Rape within marriage

Until legal changes in 1991, a women in England who was forced to have sex against her will by her husband had no recourse in law. This reflected the idea of the wife as the property of her husband. Although this has been amended, it is still rare for a woman to bring a dispute of this kind to court, especially if she still lives in the same household as her husband.

In a survey of practices in a number of countries, Connors (1992) found that few penalized rape in marriage while some countries still excuse a man who kills his wife if he suspects her of adultery. For most feminists, rape in marriage is an extreme example of violence found – and accepted, or at least tolerated – in many patriarchal families. Connors also found that women throughout the countries she studied experienced considerable mental and psychological oppression alongside their physical abuse. However, things are beginning to change.

Responses to domestic violence

Connors suggests that for a legal system to control domestic violence adequately all legal limits to female equality must be redressed and women must be assured that legal advice is available. Changing attitudes among the police and the judiciary are also required if anything is to change. In many cases, the most effective action has been taken by groups of women themselves. The Women's Aid movement set up refuges in America, the UK and a number of other countries. This sort of action appears to be more effective when combined with educational programmes, such as those in Papua New Guinea and Australia. Many sociological explanations of violence in the family tend to combine the abuse of women and children as problems with a similar cause. For this reason it is important to look at the way child abuse within the family has been examined over the past twenty years or so.

Child abuse

In the 1960s, radical psychologists such as Laing and Cooper argued that the family might literally drive children mad (see also Section 13.8). From their studies of family interaction, they argued that the conflict between spouses could lead to attacks of schizophrenia among adolescent offspring as they struggled to deal with the competing demands on them from their parents and other family members.

While their views on both family life and schizophrenia have been strongly challenged, they did highlight the psychological dangers of families to children, although they did not look at sexual or physical abuse as many theorists do today. One of the most emotive debates of recent years has been that surrounding the issue of child sexual abuse.

Table 7.15 Parent-to-child violence in 1975 and 1985 in the USA

	Rate per 1000 children[1] 1975	1985
A. Minor acts of violence		
1. Threw something	54	27
2. Pushed, grabbed, shoved	318	307
3. Slapped or spanked	582	549
B. Severe acts of violence		
4. Kicked, bit, hit with fist	32	13
5. Hit, tried to hit with something	134	97
6. Beat up	13	6
7. Threatened with gun or knife	1	2
8. Used gun or knife	1	2
C. Violence indices		
Overall violence (1–8)	630	620
Severe violence (4–8)	140	107
Very severe (abusive) violence (4, 6, 8)	36	19

[1]Aged 3 to 17.
Source: Straus and Gelles (1986) in Elliot (1996)

This issue came to prominence in the 1980s with a number of media stories concerning the actions of social workers in Cleveland who had removed children from their parents because of suspicions about abuse. The incident provoked numerous debates about the power of social workers and a disbelief that parents could really abuse their children, culminating in a number of stories in which the picture of child abuse became mixed up by the media with images of satanic rites, such as

the events reported (and subsequently disproved) in the Shetland Islands.

Gittins (1993) argues that the topic of child abuse – or more precisely, child sexual abuse – has become increasingly important to debates about the family. She claims that it is predominantly males who sexually abuse children and in this sense she adopts a standard radical feminist argument which suggests that children are endangered by males in the home, which implies that it may be better to bring children up in a male-free environment.

Marxist-feminist critics of this position, such as Elliot (1996), point to the way in which the issue of child abuse is an example of how middle-class social workers seek to stigmatize and control the lives of working-class parents in order to enforce a dominant code about parenting. They also argue that the feminist concentration on child sexual abuse is not actually giving the full picture since, if all forms of abuse are included, women are also abusers of children. Although it may be argued that sexual abuse is in some way worse than other forms of abuse, it is also difficult to maintain that a male-free environment leads inevitably to a completely safe domestic environment for all children.

Explanations of abuse in the family

Elliot (1996) suggests that there are three main explanations of domestic violence: psychopathological, sociological and feminist. Psychopathological debates come mainly from psychologists and mental health therapists, who focus on individual pathology where domestic violence is viewed as both rare and deviant.

Men who beat their wives or children apparently often hold very fixed views about roles within families and are often found to have been victims (and/or witnesses) of abuse in their own childhood. They are often seen to be weak and frustrated men, while women who punish their children severely are presented as even more deviant, not just in terms of their own psychological damage but also in terms of the expected role of a mother. Women are also seen as provoking violence from men and condoning or accepting their husband's abuse of the children. Often a child's sexual abuse is deliberately blamed on the inadequacy of their mother.

According to Elliot (1996), such women are:

portrayed as denying their husbands sex, as unable to maintain a nurturing, affectionate relationship with their husbands and daughters, and as physically absent from the household. Whatever the cause of these circumstances – pregnancy, illness, exhaustion, imputed personality defect, the necessity of taking on a breadwinning role or the sexual boorishness, impotence or drunkenness of the husband – men's sexual desires tend to be privileged and mothers are seen as forsaking their wifely and maternal roles and so producing an incestuous relationship.
(Elliot, 1996, pp. 168–9)

Children, too, may be pathologized, with some little girls in particular being presented as either compliant and accepting or, in extreme cases, as infant seductresses who the father is somehow helpless to resist. These sorts of explanations tended at one time to be shared by most child professionals and still appear regularly today in, for example, incest cases. However, the idea of male abuse of children as a rare but almost 'normal' response to pathological female behaviour has been criticized by sociologists and feminists, although they differ in their explanations.

Sociological explanations of domestic abuse

Non-feminist sociological approaches to child abuse often link it to economic deprivation and the development of a particular set of sub-cultural beliefs. Poverty, overcrowding and poor educational and occupational opportunities lead to frustration and repression which may result in abusive behaviour where men seek to establish power over at least some aspect of their lives. Abuse of children is apparently accepted in such families and this belief is transmitted to the next generation. Such behaviour is enhanced through the number of lone mothers and their tendency to have numerous sexual relationships with men other than the father(s) of their children. Structural explanations, too, tend to regard deprivation as the key to understanding child abuse, as violence and inappropriate sexual behaviour can be seen as 'normal' responses to blocked opportunities. Violence, stress and conflict are constant aspects of working-class life, so that structured age and gender inequalities can be seen as explanations of domestic violence – even if sexual abuse is harder to understand.

While these explanations move beyond simplistic notions of individual pathology, Elliot shows that they, too, can be widely criticized. First, there is an assumption that child – and other forms of violent and sexual – abuse only takes place in deprived families, whereas increasingly this has been shown not to be the case.

It also ignores gender differences in patterns of abuse and there is also a tendency to treat statistics relating to child abuse as unproblematic.

The validity of child abuse statistics

Debates about the cause of abuse in the family often focus on the problems of definition and, especially, measurement, of such a phenomenon. By its very nature, domestic abuse – and especially the sexual abuse of children – is a secret and usually deliberately hidden phenomenon. While the number of recorded cases of child abuse has increased in recent years, there is a debate about how much this reflects changes in patterns of behaviour and how much it reflects changes in awareness and reporting.

Defining parental abuse is problematic. When does a smack turn into abuse? Even the definition of sexual abuse is complex, as one of the key aspects of the parent–child relationship is cuddling and showing affection. The level of child abuse, therefore, depends to a great extent on the definitions used which include or incorporate certain actions. The widest definitions suggest that a large proportion of children experience some form of sexual abuse, mainly in the home with someone they know, quite often a relative or friend of the family.

Table 7.16 Experiences of sexually abused children, British data[1]

	%
Abuse by a stranger	51
Abuse by a known person	49
Abuse by a family member	14
Non-contact abuse	51
Contact abuse not involving intercourse	44
Abuse involving intercourse	5
One incident involving one person	63
Repeated abuse	23
Multiple abuse	14

[1]This survey was based on a random national survey of 2019 women and men and used an omnibus definition of abuse that included contact and non-contact experiences.

Source: Baker and Duncan (1985) in Elliot (1996)

While Table 7.16 shows a wide variety of abusive behaviour experienced by children, it cannot show the range of experiences nor how these have changed. Elliot quotes a study by Russell which shows that recorded child abuse quadrupled between 1900 and 1970. Girls are more likely to be abused than boys, especially within the home and incestuously, while the great majority of abusers are men.

While child abuse is clearly a growing problem, not just for sociologists but for social workers, family therapists and psychologists as well, we need to be cautious about seeing it as a 'new' phenomenon. There are no statistics to illustrate its occurrence, but it is possible that there is less child abuse than, for example, in Victorian times when child prostitution was common and children were considered the possessions of their fathers. One of the key benefits of the greater equality of power between parents and children – partly resulting from feminist challenges to patriarchy – is to empower children to challenge abuse by adults in ways that they could not do in the past.

Feminist explanations of domestic abuse

Although they differ widely in their approaches, feminist writers tend to focus on male domination of society as the key cause of abuse of both women and children – and even of the elderly – within the family. Elliot argues that this is based on two linked arguments. First, there is the assumption that all male domination is, in the last resort, supported by physical force. Secondly, there is an equally persuasive assumption that male sexuality is both powerful and irresistible, i.e. that men cannot help themselves. She therefore suggests that:

Feminist discourse suggests that aggression and abuse are inherent in this construction of masculinity and seeks to show that wife-battering and killing, date-rape and marital rape and child sexual abuse are extreme forms of the sexual aggression which women and children routinely experience.
(Elliot, 1996, p. 178)

Feminists also suggest that such a construction of masculinity puts women at constant risk of sexual harassment, that male sexual fidelity is all but impossible, and that children are at risk of sexual abuse unless men are regularly 'serviced'. Some feminists also claim that male sexual violence receives institutional support from the law, judges and the media. This means that the dark side of the family is, in fact, the most common picture of family life.

This highly negative picture of family life has also received considerable criticism. Not surprisingly, on an individual level, most men reject the image of themselves as inherently violent, potential (or actual) abusers of women and children with no control over their sexual feelings and desires. (See also Section 5.6.) Many men regard the sexual or physical abuse of women and children as deviant, and convicted child abusers usually have to be kept apart from other prisoners for their own protection. Some women, too, agree that it removes all blame from those men who, they argue, in most cases, choose to attack or abuse.

Such an approach also fails to explain abuse of children and men or other women by women, which, although apparently less common than that by males, appears to be a growing phenomenon. Nor does it really explain violence in homosexual and lesbian relationships or abuse of people by others of the same sex both within and outside of the family, often discussed as a form of 'bullying'. It also ignores age-related abuse by both men and women of elderly parents within the household.

It is important to remember that while many families do have their darker aspects, most people gain considerably from family relationships. While critics of the family tend to stress its dark side, and supporters its caring and supportive role, the diversity of family structures tells us that the concept of one family type, structure, relationship or household is probably less useful for explaining family life than it has ever been.

Activity
Using the material above, summarize and assess different explanations of child abuse.
I, A, E

Black feminism and the family

Elliot (1996) points out that black feminist perspectives from writers such as b. hooks (1982) offer some interesting insights into our understanding of both ethnicity and family structure. They argue that feminist ideas of universal male oppression and violence tend to ignore racial oppression in society. (See also Sections 5.7 and 6.6.) Arguments about abortion and contraception are very different for black women in poor countries, where contraception is often imposed upon them rather than their being offered much option about their fertility. Their arguments do not deny instances of male oppression of women within the black families, but they do highlight the fact that inequalities exist in more than the one dimension that some radical feminists seem to suggest. This shows the varied nature and perceptions of the family, which, for all its faults, seems to offer many of us some escape from the perceived stresses and problems of the world outside.

Abuse outside the family

While we are shocked at examples of violence or sexual abuse within families, it is important to remember that, as far as can be seen, most children have limited experience of such activity personally. Other forms of child-rearing (usually considered second-best in our society) such as children's homes, have also often been at the centre of scandals of child abuse.

Conclusion

However we define or understand the family or household unit, it seems that sociologists have an important job to do. We need to uncover the evidence about the family to show how it operates, rather than following either a falsely cosy or blindly antagonistic view of family life. The debates about how the family should or should not operate are largely political ones, but it is important that, as a sociologist, you have a clear idea of how you view the diversity, ugliness, strength and beauty of family life. It is the one institution that undoubtedly affects us all, both as children and when we form our own families – however structured – or households.

Further **reading**

- Abbott, P. and Wallace, C. (1992) *The Family and the New Right*, London, Pluto Press.
- Abercrombie, N. and Warde, A (eds) (1994) *Family, Household and the Life-Course*, Lancaster, Framework.
- Barrett, M. and McIntosh, M. (1991) *The Anti-Social Family*, 2nd edn, London, Verso.
- Gittins, D. (1993) *The Family in Question*, 2nd edn, London, Macmillan.
- Jorgensen, N. (1995) *Investigating Families and Households*, London, Collins Educational.
- Leonard, D. and Hood-Williams, J. (eds) (1988) *Families*, Walton-on-Thames, Nelson.
- Muncie, J., Wetherell, M., Dallos, R. and Cochrane, A. (eds) (1995) *Understanding the Family*, London, Sage.

Back issues of the periodical *Sociology Review* (formerly known as *Social Studies Review*) also contain many articles on this field of sociology and many others.

Exam **questions**

1 What has been the contribution of feminist sociology to our understanding of relationships in the family? [25 marks]
(IBS, Paper 1, Summer 1995)

2 To what extent have recent debates on single parents ignored sociological research?
[25 marks]
(IBS, Paper 1, Summer 1995)

3 Read the following extract and answer the questions which follow.

Women have been on the receiving end of male violence for centuries. But now, increasing numbers of men are reporting being battered by their female partners. Consider the figures collected by police Domestic Violence Units.

Number of men hurt by their spouses (reported)

	London	West Midlands
1987	441	249
1992	887	506

Men now account for 12% of victims in domestic incidents. This increase in domestic violence by women coincides with a rise in the overall number of women convicted of violent crimes. Home Office records shows that 1300 women were committed for trial at Crown Courts for offences of violence against the person in 1993. 100 more than in the previous year.

What sociologists need to consider is how far the statistical trends described in this report are socially constructed and to what extent they represent a new set of social facts.

a Define and illustrate the following terms:
(i) social facts [3 marks]
(ii) socially constructed. [3 marks]

b What factors might lead to increasing numbers of men reporting being battered by their female partners? [6 marks]

c With reference to another area of social life (e.g. unemployment, poverty, suicide, family breakdown, white-collar crime) outline why official statistics should be interpreted with caution. [8 marks]

(NEAB, Paper 2, Summer 1996)

4 Read the following passage and answer the questions which follow.

Many areas of social life come under scrutiny by the press, by the government and by society in general. In recent years for example the alleged decline of so-called 'shared family values' seems to have produced widespread political and press comment. 5

The structure of family life has clearly changed dramatically over the last twenty years. However, areas like housing policy and social security provision in society have contin- 10 ued to treat women as dependent on their wage-earning husbands and have failed to respond to the changing situation of increasing numbers of female earners, single parents and elderly women. Much policy and provision has 15 been based on the assumed predominance of

the nuclear family form. This served to stigmatize those not living in such a household like
single people, single parents and partners of the
20 same sex. It also led to the view that the steady
departure from this norm constituted a social
problem in itself. This had been particularly the
case with single parents. The increase in the
numbers of single parents has been viewed as a
25 social problem, indeed as a social issue!
Government commentators have noted that:–
'one of the biggest social problems of our day is
the surge of single parent families'. The media
have also helped to create this image and in
30 many ways have created a moral panic.

Various media claims have been made which
directly link lone-parent families and criminality, and studies have been cited as evidence that
the presence of a father is critical to the well-
35 being of the child. However, a report which
reviewed all the main studies of family disruption stated that:– 'no child growing up in a one
parent household is inevitably destined to do
less well than one raised in a stable marriage'.

40 Nevertheless, such media claims are used to
inform Government policy decisions. Various
policy recommendations were made, from
reducing benefit to single parents in order to
discourage them, to setting up a Child Support
45 Agency to track down missing fathers. There
has always been a relationship between the
academic discipline of sociology and social
policy. Policy makers in this case however, seem
to have made selective use of sociological
research in developing social policy recommen-
50 dations. However, sociologists do attempt to
provide explanations and identify causes of
'social problems' although these will depend
upon the perspective which they use to examine
social life.

a Explain what is meant by 'shared family
values'. (line 4)   [2 marks]

b Using the functionalist perspective, explain
how a departure from the nuclear family
norm comes to be seen as a social problem.
[5 marks]

c i Explain what is meant by a 'moral panic'.
(line 30)   [3 marks]

  ii With reference to the example of 'single
  parents' discussed in the above passage,
  examine the role of the media in creating
  a 'moral panic'.   [3 marks]

d Outline the contribution which sociologists
have made to the understanding of a different 'social problem' from the one discussed
in the passage.   [6 marks]

e What contribution could sociology make to
influencing Government policy?   [5 marks]

(NEAB, Paper 2, Summer 1995)

5 Item A Rapoport identifies five types of
contemporary diversity in the family:
organizational, cultural, class, life-course and
cohort.

Families today organize their respective individual
domestic duties and their links with the wider
social environment in a variety of ways. The
contrasts between 'orthodox' families – the woman
as 'housewife', the husband as 'breadwinner' –
with dual-career or one-parent families, illustrate
this diversity. Culturally, there is greater diversity
of family beliefs and values than used to be the
case. The presence of ethnic minorities (such as
West Indian, Asian, Greek or Italian communities),
and the influence of movements such as feminism,
have produced considerable cultural variety in
family forms. Persistent class divisions, between
the poor, skilled working class, and the various
groupings within the middle and upper classes,
sustain major variations in family structure.
Variations in family experience during the life
course are fairly obvious.

Source: Adapted from Giddens, A. *Sociology,*
Polity, 1993.

Item B The idea of 'the family' or 'the nuclear
family' is an idea with remarkable strength
and power – it is something which just about
any member of our society can define and
which many powerful lobbies (political, moral,
religious) claim to support and revere. The
image of 'the family' is quite clear.

Our traditional family model remains central
to all family ideology. This is a model of a
married heterosexual couple with children,
and a sexual division of labour where the
husband as a breadwinner provides economic
support for his dependent wife and children.
While the wife cares for both husband and
children.

I propose that there is no such thing as 'the
family' and in reality, no such things as
'normal families'. The simplest approach is at
the statistical level of counting how many
families do correspond to the clear image of
'the family'. Work on the 1981 Census suggested that few households corresponded to the
image.

Source: Adapted from Bernades, J. *The Family
in Question, Social Studies Review,* 1990.

Item C Preliminary results of the 1989 General Household Survey by the Office of Population Censuses and Surveys show continued growth in the number of single-parent families. The proportion of such families rose from 8 per cent in 1971 to 17 per cent in 1989, of which lone mothers were 15 per cent and lone fathers were 2 per cent.

At the same time, the proportion of households containing only one person rose from 17 per cent in 1971 to 25 per cent in 1989, with only 26 per cent of households in 1989 comprising a married or cohabiting couple and children.

Source: Adapted from Brindle, D. *The Guardian,* October 1990.

a State the increase in the percentage of lone-parent families between 1971 and 1989 (Item C). [1 mark]

b Identify one way in which the presence of ethnic minorities has contributed to the 'contemporary diversity' in the family (Item A). [1 mark]

c How far do you agree with the idea expressed in Item B that the 'traditional family model remains central to all family ideology'?

Support your argument with appropriate examples. [6 marks]

d Using information from the Items and elsewhere, to what extent does sociological evidence support the idea that there is a 'contemporary diversity' in the structure of the family? [8 marks]

e With reference to any of the issues raised in the Items, assess the contribution of feminist perspectives to an understanding of contemporary family life. [9 marks]

(AEB, Paper 1, Summer 1993)

Coursework **suggestions**

1 **Carry out extensive secondary research into contemporary family structures**
You could combine this with an in-depth study of a small group of families with which you have some personal contact.

2 **Use an attitude survey to investigate whether there are any structural differences (e.g. age, class, gender) in views about less traditional family arrangements; e.g. mothers working full-time, lone parenting, same-sex couples, voluntary childlessness etc.**

3 **Carry out an extensive investigation of media and political views of different family structures in contemporary society**
The findings could be compared to secondary data about family structure.

4 **Compare the allocation of housework, food provision and consumption and decision-making in terms of age, gender and financial input in a number of different households.**

8

Education and training

Chapter outline

The first part of this chapter focuses on the main perspectives in the sociology of education, using up-to-date examples of research. The second considers how ethnicity, gender, social class and learning difficulties and disabilities affect educational achievement. The third covers recent debates in the sociology of education and training. 'Education' is used as a broad term for skills and knowledge acquired both inside and outside formal educational institutions; 'schooling' is a term used mainly by Marxist theorists to describe preparation through school for the labour market; and 'training' is the teaching of skills required for a particular occupation.

PERSPECTIVES IN THE SOCIOLOGY OF EDUCATION

SOCIAL INEQUALITIES AND EDUCATIONAL ACHIEVEMENT

KEY ISSUES IN THE SOCIOLOGY OF EDUCATION AND TRAINING

8.1 Functionalism

French functionalism

Emile Durkheim (1858–1917) has been very influential in the sociology of education, especially in the work of Basil Bernstein. Bernstein constantly acknowledges the influence, particularly as he feels Durkheim rather than any other social theorist is a source of what the term 'social' means. Bernstein explained the importance of Durkheim to him:

[I read] *Durkheim and although I did not understand him it all seemed to happen. I did not care that he was a naughty functionalist with an oversocialised concept of man, that he neglected the institutional structure and the sub-strata of conflicting interests, that his model of man contained only two terms, beliefs and sentiments. In a curious way I did not care too much about the success of his various analyses. It was about the social bond and the structuring of experience.*
(Quoted in Atkinson, 1985, p. 21)

These concerns about the 'social' became central to Bernstein's sociology. What did Durkheim have to say about education? Durkheim emphasized the moral force of education, the way in which children internalize the values and beliefs of society to become 'social' beings. The main function of education was the development of social solidarity through the transmission of a collective culture. The main problem was to resolve the divisions of modern industrial society, especially reconciling individualism and social solidarity.

Bernstein was particularly drawn to Durkheim's work on the division of labour, the distinction between mechanical and organic solidarity – mechanical solidarity characterizing pre-industrial societies with a simple division of labour, and organic solidarity characterizing industrial society with a complex and interdependent division of labour. Durkheim used them to characterize whole societies, but Bernstein uses them to look at principles of differentiation within societies. Specifically he looks at the nature and consequence of the change from mechanical to organic solidarity on education systems. This is clearly seen in his work on the organization and transmission of school knowledge. Durkheim's work and his influence on functionalism generally are also discussed in Sections 2.3, 2.4 and 10.2.

The notion of boundaries between subjects is a key theme in Bernstein's work, and this brings us on to another influence. Traditional forms of knowledge are regarded as sacred and have strong boundaries. Newer forms of knowledge have weaker boundaries. This work on boundary maintenance between subjects is partly the result of the influence of Mary Douglas, a structural anthropologist. Her work (1966) focuses on why some things – particularly food – are considered polluting and dangerous. This is because they break systems of classification.

Discussion point

For Douglas, matter out of place breaks classification systems and is considered dangerous. What other areas of social life could this be applied to?

Bernstein applied this notion to the classification of school subjects. Classification is the organization of knowledge into curricula – what is thinkable and what is not. Strong classification means that the curriculum is highly differentiated and separated into traditional subjects, and weak classification means that the boundaries are fragile. 'Framing' refers to the degree of control teachers and pupils have over the selection, organization, pacing and timing of the knowledge taught and learnt. The curriculum, the teaching methods and evaluation are three message systems. Underlying these message systems are codes, rather like Bourdieu's *habitus*, a regulating grammar. (This is like the grammar in a language which tells you which words you can or cannot put together, and how to do so.) These codes were developed into two **ideal types** which do not exist in pure forms – integrated code and collection code (see Table 8.1).

Table 8.1 Collection code and integrated code

Collection code	Integrated code
Strong classification and framing	Weak classification and framing
Highly specialized pure forms of selection and combination	Flexibility of control of knowledge
Hierarchical relationships	Horizontal relationships
Authoritarian control	Self-regulatory control
Visible pedagogy	Invisible pedagogy
Traditional academic Examples: Physics, Maths, English, Latin, History	Progressive Examples: Integrated Humanities, Media Studies, Women's Studies
Sacred	Profane
Pure	Polluting

Bernstein looked at the way in which the change from collection code to integrated code represents the change from mechanical to organic solidarity. The curriculum is the message system of the school which privileges middle-class pupils because they come to school with access to the codes. Working-class pupils, on the other hand, are not able to meet their requirements. In this way the message system reproduces within schools the social class inequalities of the society. There is a link between the codes of the school and the families that they serve.

Conflicts between the 'old' and 'new' middle class were reflected in the debate over progressive education in the 1970s: the integration code was favoured by the new middle class and the collection code by the old middle class. More recently there have been conflicts over the curriculum: vocational education emphasizing skills is favoured by neo-liberals, and traditional subjects are favoured by neo-conservatives. (See Section 8.12.)

Bernstein's work is difficult to understand and largely theoretical. It does provide a useful theory of the 'how' and 'what' of the curriculum and the relationship between power and knowledge. The curriculum is seen as a codified reflection of societal and ideological interests. In this way Bernstein's work sits firmly in the French structuralist tradition. (See Section 8.4 for an explanation of structuralism.)

Activity

a Why might certain subjects in the curriculum be considered dangerous or polluting? Use Table 8.1 to help you answer this question. Has this affected the subjects' status or popularity?

b What is the relationship between production, the needs of employers and the curriculum in schools and colleges?

c Where pupils have some control over the selection, organization, pacing and timing of the knowledge taught and learnt, is this to their advantage?

I, A, E

American functionalism

Functionalism was developed by American sociologists like Talcott Parsons and Davis and Moore between the 1930s and 1960s. (See also Sections 2.4 and 10.2.) Central to this work was an analysis of the ways in which the educational system functions in society. If talent is unequally distributed then the education system plays a central role in the allocation of the most talented to the occupations that are functionally most important for society. This implies

a meritocratic model in which everyone has an equal chance to be unequal. (See also Section 4.9.) *P144*

Discussion point

Are a meritocracy and an equal society the same thing?

Functional importance is decided by the length and specialist training required for particular occupations. It is claimed that to be a brain surgeon, for example, takes much more talent, education and training than to be a nurse. Therefore in order to ensure that people are prepared to undertake long and expensive training the rewards offered must be substantially greater for surgeons than for nurses:

A medical education is so burdensome and expensive that virtually none would undertake it if the MD did not carry a reward commensurate with the sacrifice.
(Davis and Moore, 1945, p. 244)

Inequality is therefore functionally necessary. If everyone had the same levels of pay and status no one would be prepared to take on the more difficult and responsible jobs, it is argued.

There are many criticisms of this position on the role of education. It assumes firstly that all pupils start from the same point – a level playing-field – whereas in fact some children start with large amounts of cultural capital in the form of language, attitudes, confidence and manners that privilege them in schools. Parents pass on such advantages to their children. Looked at closely it may not take a lot more training, education and skills to become a surgeon rather than a nurse. This difference may be a mechanism to protect the privileged position held by the minority in the top jobs. It also assumes a value consensus where everyone agrees about the most important jobs and shares the same values to be transmitted through society by schools.

Activity

'The best people get the best jobs because they have received the best education.' Evaluate this statement by drawing up three arguments *for* the statement and three *against*, using a functionalist perspective on education.

A, E

Functionalism is not a dominant perspective in sociology at the moment, but some of the ideas in crude form seem similar to New Right ideas. (See Section 8.9 for a discussion of this.)

P313

8.2 Marxism

In the sociology of education there are a variety of 'Marxisms', all drawing on different interpretations and developments of the work of Marx. It can be useful to divide them into structuralist and humanist Marxisms. (See also Section 2.5.)

Marxists like Bowles and Gintis, Bourdieu and Althusser come from the structuralist perspective within sociology. The term 'structuralist' has two meanings. Firstly it means theories that put emphasis on the structure of society as a system of functioning institutions as their starting point. The second meaning is quite difficult to understand but important to do so in order to understand post-structuralism. Structuralism has been influenced by anthropology, mainly the work of Lévi-Strauss: it means that language defines social reality for us. The structures of society are internalized in us through language, a social system of signs and symbols which we use when we think and speak. We only know the meanings of things because we can name them. This theory signals the death of the 'subject'. We are determined, our stories are written for us. (See also Sections 2.10 and 10.11.) This is the opposite of social action theory where social actors create their social worlds:

Althusser rejects completely the idea that humans can be 'subjects' – creative agents . . . in charge of their lives and worlds. For him, human life is always entirely structured. . . . Althusserian Marxism thus sees itself as heir to the late Marx – to writings produced towards the end of Marx's life, when he tried to build a scientific analysis of the structure of capitalism – as opposed to the work of the 'young' or early Marx whose heirs are humanist Marxists like Gramsci.

(Jones, 1993b, p. 63)

Humanist Marxists give much more power to human agency as a means of change.

Althusser: the role of education in society

Althusser (1971b) identified three levels in class society, the economic, the political and the ideological. Although the economic determines the other levels in the last instance, the ideological and political have 'relative autonomy' and are not directly or crudely determined.

Althusser looked at the way in which the state exercises power through repressive state apparatuses like the courts, army, police and law. The state also rules through ideology, using ideological state apparatuses, like the media, culture, religion and education.

Education has now replaced religion as the main ideological state apparatus. In schools children receive the ideology that prepares them for their role in capitalist society. This includes the rules of good behaviour, skills and knowledge needed by capitalism. Althusser has been criticized for the similarities between his analysis and functionalism. His theory leaves little room for struggle or contradiction.

Discussion point

How is education ideological?

Bowles and Gintis: schooling in capitalist America

Bowles and Gintis (1976) were influenced by Althusser in their study of the relationship between the education system and the economy. They state that the roots of inequality in the USA are in the class structure, and the school system is one of the institutions that perpetuates this inequality. Despite educational reforms and claims that the USA is a meritocracy, educational achievement is just as dependent on parents' socio-economic background as it was 30 years before. The association between the length of schooling, ability and how much you earn is dependent on factors other than ability. Parents' social class and the fact that ability improves the longer you stay in school are crucial factors. IQ is evenly distributed in society, but power and income are not. The use of IQ to justify inequalities of outcome places the blame for educational failure on the students themselves:

The predatory, competitive and personally destructive way in which intellectual achievement is rewarded in US schools and colleges is a monument not to creative rationality, but to the need of a privileged class to justify an irrational, exploitative and undemocratic system.

(Bowles and Gintis, 1976, p. 107)

They claim that schools reflect the hierarchical division of labour in the economy through a correspondence between the social relations of production, school and family. This is transmitted through the values and organization of the school, in grades, fragmentation, alienation because of a lack of control over the curriculum, and discipline. Working-class schools are authoritarian whereas middle-class schools are more open and democratic, in the same way as workplaces. This correspondence allows the education system to produce an amenable and fragmented labour force.

📰 **Discussion point**

To what extent does daily life in your school or college correspond to that in the workplace?

Bowles and Gintis conclude that the creation of an equal and liberating school system requires a revolutionary transformation of economic life. They encourage teachers to become effective subversives by teaching the truth about society, encouraging a sense of collective power and fighting ideologies of privilege like racism and sexism.

Bowles and Gintis have been criticized for ignoring the role of the state and its mediation between education and the economy. They are seen as being over-deterministic in that they see students as somewhat passive receivers of ideology (this is a criticism also made of Althusser). They also ignore what is transmitted by schools – the content of the curriculum.

Bourdieu: cultural reproduction

Bourdieu (1977), another structuralist Marxist, looked at the way schools in France reproduce social and economic inequalities. (The work of Bourdieu is also considered in Section 2.9.) He looked at the relationship between the culture acquired in the family, the school and that of the ruling class. Central to this are three concepts: cultural capital, *habitus* and relative autonomy.

Through their families children of the dominant class acquire cultural capital. Their culture is similar to that which permeates education. They have the right manners, accent, confidence and know-how. This is the same culture as the teachers who teach them. They have the right language (linguistic capital) to unlock the categories used in formal education. Possession of cultural capital means the ability to engage with the high culture so prized in traditional academic education. Education is a message system. Possession of cultural capital privileges middle-class children who arrive at school equipped with the code to decipher the message of the dominant culture. These underlying rules, like grammar in a language, are what Bourdieu calls *habitus*, the rules of the game to succeed. Bourdieu also uses the concept of relative autonomy. This means that schools have the appearance of being independent of the economy. This makes them appear neutral and fair.

The sum of these processes, according to Bourdieu, is the social reproduction of the dominant class. The main function of the education system is not to transmit knowledge but to select, to differentiate, to categorize. This is achieved by making socially acquired linguistic and cultural competencies appear natural in those students who succeed. Bourdieu recognizes that some working-class children do break the code and succeed against the odds.

Bourdieu has been criticized for the same reasons as Bowles and Gintis and Althusser. He sees only one culture, that of the dominant class, and students are cultural dupes who passively accept their failure. Such theories are also very abstract and not rooted in the complexities and contradictions of real classrooms and schools. However, they have been very influential in the development of further research by sociologists. Their real importance lies in exposing the power relations at work in educational systems that appear neutral and fair. They also help to account for the persistence of working-class underachievement.

Cultural reproduction, resistance, accommodation and transformation

Since the early work on reproduction theory, subsequent research has given a much more guarded and complex account of the reproduction of social class inequalities. The theory has also been applied to the reproduction of gender and 'race' inequalities.

Taking a humanist Marxist position, and to counter the over-determinism of structuralist Marxist accounts, Willis' classic study (1977) specifically sought to study the resistance of the 'lads', a group of working-class boys in a secondary school in the Midlands. He asked the question 'How do working-class kids get working-class jobs?' (what he meant in fact was boys!).

Willis showed that the resistance these lads displayed to schooling came from their working-class culture which prized manual over mental labour. Despite the fact that the lads enjoyed bunking off and making teachers' lives difficult, their resistance was ultimately reproductive as they ended up in manual jobs as a result of the absence of qualifications.

McRobbie (1978) carried out a similar study of working-class girls in a youth club. She found that these girls also regarded school as a place to celebrate their culture of femininity by smoking, gossiping about the boys they fancied, playing up teachers (sometimes using their sexuality). They dismissed successful middle-class girls as 'swots' or 'snobs' with whom they could compete academically but chose not to. Their response to schooling both liberated and trapped them by reproducing gender and class relations. Their future roles as wives, mothers and low-paid workers loomed large in their lives.

McRobbie did report that feminist teachers could have a role in challenging the inevitability of such futures.

Both the foregoing studies were very important in identifying the complex and contradictory nature of social and cultural reproduction. Willis has been criticized for ignoring girls, and for celebrating the lads' culture of masculinity despite its sexism and racism. He also ignored the conformist lads in the study – the 'earoles'. It would have been interesting to compare their destinations with those of the lads to see whether conformity and qualifications made a difference.

Using ethnography (a method derived from symbolic interactionism – see Sections 2.7 and 3.9) within a Marxist framework was also very productive, allowing both macro and micro analysis. The ethnographic data produced a richly detailed picture of working-class children's experiences of schooling, giving them a voice. This work has inspired further study and the development of social and cultural reproduction theory: in Australia the work of Connell, Ashenden, Kessler and Dowsett (1982), and in the USA that of Anyon (1983).

Anyon added the useful concept of 'accommodation'. Her study of girls in five elementary schools found that the girls' responses were complex when faced with two ideologies of femininity, one passive and nurturing, the other confident and competitive. The way they responded was complex and depended on their social class and home background. She considers that neither acceptance nor rejection accurately describe what occurs; it is much more a process of simultaneous accommodation and resistance. These concepts were later used by Mac an Ghaill (1988) to describe the responses of a group of black A level students, the 'black sisters', who practised resistance with accommodation. They adopted subtle forms of resisting the institutional demands of the school, such as by being late for lessons, but they were in favour of education. Qualifications were highly prized as they provided the opportunity to escape traditional black working-class 'female' work.

Discussion point

Do you ever resist following the rules in school or college? If so, how far do you go, and in what ways do you do it?

Modes of challenge and resistance

Peter Aggleton (1987) was interested to discover whether the potential to transform society lies with the traditional working class, or whether disaffected middle-class groups had revolutionary potential. (This issue is also discussed in Sections 4.6 and 4.7.) Building on the studies outlined above, he developed social reproduction theory by refining the concept of resistance and introducing a much more finely tuned account of modes of student challenge. He undertook an ethnographic study of 27 students taking A levels in a college of further education. His central concern was to discover the reasons for their educational under-achievement despite their privileged middle-class backgrounds. Related to this was the question of whether this under-achievement was resistance to schooling and had the potential to transform society. He studied these students at home, at school and college, and in their sub-cultural world.

The parents of the students in Aggleton's sample tended to be members of the 'new middle class', whom Bernstein (1977) termed the agents of symbolic control. In these homes there was a weak distinction between adults and children, a high degree of autonomy, parents and children discussing all sorts of issues openly, an implicit system of rules, and a blurring of distinctions between work and leisure. Such progressive values led students into conflict with the values of their schools. They objected to the way in which their schools attempted to regulate their personal dress and appearance, the boring routines, the lack of creativity, and teachers whom some of them regarded as illiterate. College, they felt, would allow greater degrees of personal autonomy:

[Tom] *'I went to college because I thought that I wouldn't have to come across authority. I hated having to do things like go to assembly, being there to register, having to be in school at lunch hours, that sort of thing.'*
(Aggleton, 1987, p. 68)

At college these students regarded themselves as a cultural élite. They tried to negotiate their educational experiences with teachers and chose subjects like fine art, communication and theatre studies in order to display their creativity, originality and culture. Other students who pursued courses considered unfashionable, such as industrial training, building or engineering, and those who worked hard, were looked down on:

[Ric] *'They're all so macho those engineering "lads" (sneer). All they ever do is go around getting pissed and trying to pick up secretaries ... They're sort of really thick and brutish and boring.'*
(Aggleton, 1987, p. 71)

Similarly, female students who worked hard and conformed to dominant images of femininity, usually following vocational courses, were looked down on by female respondents:

[Norma] *'And it (the common room at college) was taken over by other sections, people from the other side, secretaries, they rather took it over.'*

[P. A.] *'What was wrong with that?'*

[Norma] *'We didn't want to be associated with them.'*

[P. A.] *'Why not?'*

[Norma] *'Well, we looked down on the secretaries and catering students. They were only doing it to get jobs which were really boring. They're going to go and get some shitty job which pays £30 a week and that's it. I think we felt that we were more liberated than them, and that our horizons were wider. And they were all so feminine.'*
(Aggleton, 1987, p. 75)

Outside college the rebels spent a lot of time in a public house called the Roundhouse. As was the case in college, their major concern was to gain control for themselves over space, time and systems of meaning. These places were central to their subculture and were valued because exciting people in exotic clothes met there, political discussions took place and gossip was exchanged. The rebels also engaged in what Aggleton calls 'displays to be observed', such as arriving at the benefits office in a taxi and dressed in a cocktail dress with your boyfriend dressed like something out of Somerset Maugham, or causing a disturbance at midnight Mass on Christmas Eve. (See also Section 10.5.)

Discussion point

Are there students in your school or college who regard themselves as a cultural élite? If so, what are their 'displays to be observed'? Do these relate in any way to their educational achievement?

The academic under-achievement at college of Aggleton's Spatown rebels did not have such dire consequences for them in terms of employment as would be the case for, say, the 'lads' of Willis' study:

Fifteen out of twenty-seven students in the present study left Spatown college with no qualifications other than those they had possessed when they enrolled. Six years later, however, at a time of high national youth unemployment, such under-achievement was found to have relatively insignificant consequences for students' employment. Every student was in paid employment at this time – working as theatre staff, video and film technicians, servers in cocktail bars and chic restaurants, or as personal assistants to those in the worlds of fine and media arts.
(Aggleton, 1987, p. 135)

This indicates that something other than educational qualifications was instrumental in their employment. Possibly the network of contacts through their parents and their possession of cultural capital helped. Aggleton concludes that the children of the new middle class are not interested in transforming society, and thereby losing the privilege which their class position provides.

He provides a useful if rather complex grammar of modes of challenge, developing and refining the concept of resistance. He distinguishes between resistance and contestation. Resistance is the mode of challenge to structural relations of power, and contestation refers to struggles against control in a particular social practice or site, as in the case of the rebels, to win personal autonomy and reject the dominant ethos of schooling, within existing class relations.

Aggleton's study has been praised as an excellent ethnographic study that includes young men *and* women, which adds to our understanding of middle-class students' under-achievement. But it can also be criticized. The strongest of these would be to ask the question why he thought such privileged young people might be resistant to wider power structures or interested in the transformation of society. He also neglects to address the transition of these young people from school to work – which the title of his book suggests – or to compare them with any other groups, either achievers or under-achievers, who come from similar backgrounds.

Transformation

The foregoing studies of social and cultural reproduction have led to interesting debates by Marxists about the role of education in society, and particularly how teachers as organic intellectuals can change society. Organic intellectuals are those workers who attempt to develop a socialist political consciousness in those with whom they work.

The American sociologists Apple (1986) and Giroux (1989) have focused on the possibilities for counter-hegemonic struggles in schools and the development of radical pedagogy. (This issue is also discussed in Section 12.9.) Radical pedagogy means developing in students the ability to act and think critically so that the true nature of class society is uncovered and possibly transformed. The terms hegemonic and organic intellectuals come from Gramsci, a humanist Marxist. (See Section 2.5.) Hegemony helps to explain how the ruling class hold on to power over subordinated groups in society. They do this by winning the consent of subordinated groups to the existing social order in a way that this order is taken for granted, seen as natural and normal. This has to be constantly fought for and is done by taking seriously some of the interests of subordinate groups. Schools are possible sites for counter-hegemonic struggle, rather than merely passing on dominant meanings and values according to Giroux.

These ideas have recently come under attack from feminist post-structuralists like Ellsworth (1989) and Lather (1991). They are particularly critical of the notion of radical pedagogy which they feel speaks in an abstract and disempowering way about all classrooms, all teachers, all students. They find it arrogant and prescriptive – 'what we can do for you! – which disempowers the very people it seeks to empower. They say it hides such educators' own positions as wielders of power in education. Education itself is regarded by feminist post-structuralists as fundamentally a paternalistic project.

Activity

Working in small groups, discuss the following statements and sort them into 'agree', 'disagree' and 'don't know'. Report back to the whole group.

- 'Teachers working as organic intellectuals is the same as indoctrination.'
- 'Teachers are relatively powerless to change society.'
- 'Any attempts at radical pedagogy are now impossible because of the National Curriculum.'
- 'The idea of schools as sites for counter-hegemonic struggles is totally unrealistic in the 1990s.'
- 'Students are interested only in good grades, not in transforming society.'
- 'New Right ideas are dominant in education because of the failure of socialist educational reforms.'
- 'Some small gains can be made by the collective action of teachers, parents and students.'

U, I, A, E

8.3 Interactionism

Symbolic interactionism covers a range of different approaches (see Section 2.7) and traditions but is mainly associated with the Chicago School. It has its roots in the work of John Dewey, George Herbert Mead, and Herbert Blumer. In relation to education, some of the most interesting work in this perspective has been produced by Howard Becker. His work on labelling and the self-fulfilling prophecy, sub-

cultures, educational careers and the ideal client has been very influential in the work of sociologists studying education. Ethnographic studies of schools which originated from within this perspective also have an established place in sociology.

Labelling theory and the self-fulfilling prophecy

Labelling theory was developed by Becker (1951, 1963) in relation to the study of deviance and was later applied to the study of teachers' interactions with pupils. Two classic studies illustrate this work well.

In Rist's (1977) ethnographic study of an elementary school in a black community of St Louis, USA, a teacher made children sit at tables according to her evaluations of their academic ability. These were based on social class. The poor children whose parents were on welfare became known as the 'clowns', by second grade, and sat at one table; the working-class children, the 'cardinals', sat at another; and the 'tigers', the middle class, sat at a third. Rist followed these children through first and second grades and found that the initial labels had stuck. What had begun as subjective evaluations became objective ones as the school continued to process the children on the basis of the initial labels.

Becker (1963) measured how the teacher operationalized her expectations of these groups of children by the amount of time she spent with them, and her use of praise. He then applied the concept of a self-fulfilling prophecy. He reminds us of the central premise of this:

If men (sic) *define situations as real, they are real in their consequences.*
(W. I. Thomas, 1909)

So if the 'clowns' accepted the false initial definition of their ability and performed on the basis of it over a period of time, then it has become a self-fulfilling prophecy.

A second study, the controversial *Pygmalion in the Classroom* by Rosenthal and Jacobson (1968), also illustrates early work in this area. They found that when teachers were told that some pupils whom they had randomly chosen were 'intellectual bloomers' (i.e. bright) this caused the teachers to treat them differently, and they performed better at the end of the year. This study received a great deal of criticism, mainly about the methods used as they had not actually observed changes in expectations and behaviour. They analysed pre- and post-test data (IQ scores) but not what happened in between. This led Rist to reiterate that teachers' expectations are *sometimes* self-fulfilling.

Discussion point

To what extent do you agree that students disregard the labels teachers attach to them because 'teachers are not significant'.

Labelling theory has been used to investigate deviance in schools through the social typing of pupils. Amongst others, Hargreaves (1967) looked at sub-cultural development in a secondary school through the labelling of pupils. Ball (1981) studied the banding of pupils in a comprehensive school moving to mixed-ability teaching. He analysed the ways in which teacher expectations affected the academic performance and behaviour of pupils in different bands. (Labelling theory is also discussed in Section 11.5.)

Case study – The ideal client

A study by Gillborn (1990) aimed to understand the experiences of African–Caribbean and South Asian pupils in a comprehensive school in the English Midlands. It was strongly influenced by Howard Becker (1951). Gillborn drew especially on Becker's work on teachers' notions of the 'ideal client', a construction drawn from their own lifestyle and culture:

Professionals depend on their environing society to provide them with clients who meet the standards of their image of the ideal client. Social class cultures, among other factors, may operate to produce many clients who, in one way or another, fail to meet these specifications and therefore aggravate one or another of the basic problems of the worker–client relation.

(Becker, 1952; quoted in Gillborn, 1990, p. 149)

The focus of Gillborn's study was the ways in which ethnic differences influence how teachers perceive their pupils. He found that African–Caribbean pupils, both male and female, received a disproportionate amount of punishment and criticism from teachers. Even where pupils from different ethnic groups were engaged in the same behaviour, it was the African–Caribbean pupils who were singled out for criticism. Gillborn gives an example of this from his classroom observations:

Paul Dixon (Afro-Caribbean) and Arif Aslam (Asian) arrived seven minutes late for a mixed ability lesson that I observed. ... almost half an hour into the lesson most of the group were working steadily and, like the majority of their peers, Paul and Arif were holding a conversation while they worked. The teacher looked up from the pupil he was dealing with and shouted across the room: 'Paul. Look, you
come in late, now you have the audacity to waste not only your own time but his (Arif's) as well.'
(Gillborn, 1990, p. 31)

Paul is blamed whereas Arif is regarded as a blameless victim. But was this just an isolated incident? Gillborn asked pupils in his two case study classes to answer some sentence completion items, such as '____ is picked on by some teachers'. Half the pupils nominated African–Caribbean pupils, yet they constituted only 10 per cent of the age group. This was supported by data from interviews with pupils:

[D. G.] *'Do you think the teachers particularly like or dislike some people?'*

[James (a white pupil)] *'I think some are racialist.'*

[D G.] *'In what ways would you see that?'*

[James] *'Sometimes they pick on the blacks. Sometimes the whites are let off. When there's a black and a white person, probably just pick on the black person.'*
(Gillborn, 1990, p. 31)

Many teachers were unconscious of their behaviour. The source of this conflict was often in the teachers' responses to the pupils' sense and display of their ethnicity, such as styles of speech, dress and manner of walking. This was considered by some teachers as a challenge to their authority, which Gillborn calls 'the myth of the black challenge'. He is careful to point out that this process is complex. Often work in the symbolic interactionist field is accused of claiming that once a person is 'labelled' he or she will automatically internalize that judgement and act accordingly by committing further deviant acts. Instead Becker identified several factors which may lead to the development of a 'deviant career'. Among the most important is when those in authority, in this case teachers, go on to constantly reinforce the initial negative judgement in subsequent interactions. By analysing official disciplinary procedures, such as report cards, detentions and exclusions, Gillborn found that this was the case: report cards were a possible source of the reinforcement of 'deviant' labels. With such cards the total number given was small, but a much greater proportion of African–Caribbean pupils received at least one report card: 37 per cent compared with 6 per cent of pupils of all other ethnic origins. Similarly with detentions: 68 per cent received at least one senior management detention during the research period. This was true for both sexes and unique to pupils of African–Caribbean origin. A majority of these went on to have a total of four or more such detentions. In this way their 'deviant careers' begun in classroom interaction were developed and continued through the school's disciplinary procedures.

How did these pupils respond to such conflictual relationships with their teachers? Gillborn outlines two forms of response at each end of a range of different adaptational styles and sub-cultures. He focuses on three lads, Wayne, Barry and Roger, who formed a sub-culture but who were not anti-school: theirs was not a counter-school culture. Nevertheless, increasing conflict with the school led to their educational failure – one expulsion and no exam passes. This sub-cultural group's responses were compared with those of another African–Caribbean pupil, Paul, who avoided conflict by playing down his ethnicity in order to succeed academically against all odds. He carefully distanced himself from other pupils who were regarded as trouble and from teachers with whom he was likely to come into conflict.

Gillborn does emphasize the complexity of interactions: he says it is not an either/or question of 'resist' or 'accommodate', but rather a spectrum of possible responses. He also studied the experience of South Asian male pupils in the school and found it different from both their African–Caribbean and white peers. He found that teachers' stereotypes of Asian culture and traditions did not mean that all of their assumptions operated against the pupils' interests, as it did with African–Caribbean boys. Asian pupils were much more likely to have positive relationships with teachers, who tended to regard them as hard-working and from homes where education was highly valued.

Gillborn focuses on male experience and ethnicity. The influence of gender, though mentioned in his book in relation to other ethnographic research, is not fully explored. This is a pity, especially as he found that black male and female pupils experienced the same level of conflict with teachers but he studied only the male response. This raises an interesting issue about whether it is possible for male researchers to develop the rapport and interaction with female pupils necessary in this kind of research.

Discussion point

What problems do you think may be encountered, by either male or female researchers, in schools or colleges when carrying out research on students of the opposite sex?

8.4 Post-structuralism

It has been argued that there has been something of a crisis in sociology generally with the development of new perspectives, namely post-structuralism and post-modernism.

Post-structuralism is a sociological perspective which developed out of structuralism, whereas post-modernism is a much broader term. Sometimes the two terms are used interchangeably.

Post-modernism describes a movement which encompasses architecture, the arts and sciences as well as sociology. Post-modernists are critical of the Enlightenment period, which began in the seventeenth and eighteenth centuries, when science replaced religion to explain social phenomena, capitalism replaced feudalism, and rationality replaced superstition. Events in the twentieth century such as the use of science for war and destruction, the demise of the Soviet Union and the continuation of sexism and racism have led post-modernists to question grand theories like Marxism, as well as the products of rationality and science. (See also Sections 2.10 and 10.11.)

What is post-structuralism?

The central concept in this perspective is *discourse*: specific ways of thinking and talking about aspects of the world. Discourses are forms of knowledge which work like languages. Such languages or discourses have power over us because they define what we can think and say about the world. They are the thinkable and the unthinkable and the yet-to-be-thought. These discourses create us, our identity and subjectivity, they constitute us.

Discursive practices provide a link between thought, knowledge, language and action and are at the root of social life. These ideas come mainly from the French philosopher and historian Foucault. His ideas are difficult because of the language used and because they changed and developed over time. Foucault's work is, nonetheless, becoming very influential in the sociology of education. (His work is also examined in Sections 2.10, 10.2 and 17.4.)

Feminist post-structuralism

There are several examples of feminist research in the sociology of education using a post-structuralist framework. (This general approach is discussed in more detail in Sections 5.5 and 10.7.) It is valued because it allows a move away from former macro-theories of education (grand theories that explain everything) which reduce everything to a single cause, usually either patriarchy or social class, towards much more complex and fluid notions of power:

When girls are seen as multiply located, and not unambiguously powerless, a feminist approach to classroom research must shift away from the 'disadvantage' focus. An interest in the unevenness of power means that ... studies might focus on the ways in which girls are variously positioned in the classroom. (Jones, 1993a; quoted in Weiner, 1994, p. 69)

As early as 1981, Walkerdine's research in two nursery schools showed that both female teachers and small girls have identities which in terms of power are constantly changing; at one moment they are powerful at another powerless. She describes a teacher aged about 30, sitting at a table with a group of children aged 3 and 4:

The children are playing with Lego; there are three children: a 3-year-old girl, Annie, and two 4-year-old boys, Sean and Terry. The teacher's name is Miss Baxter. The sequence begins when Annie takes a piece of Lego to add on to a construction she is building. Terry tries to take it away from her to use himself, and she resists. He says: 'You're a stupid cunt, Annie!' The teacher tells him to stop, and then Sean tries to mess up another child's construction. The teacher tells him to stop. Then . . .:
Sean: 'Get out of it Miss Baxter paxter.'
Terry: 'Get out of it knickers Miss Baxter.'
Sean: 'Get out of it Miss Baxter paxter.'
Terry: 'Get out of it Miss Baxter the knickers paxter knickers, bum.'
Sean: 'Knickers, shit, bum.'
Miss B.: 'Sean, that's enough, you're being silly.'
Sean: 'Miss Baxter, knickers, show your knickers.'
Terry: 'Miss Baxter, show your bum off.' (they giggle)
Miss B.: 'I think you're being very silly.'
Terry: 'Shit Miss Baxter, shit Miss Baxter.'
Sean: 'Miss Baxter, show your knickers your bum off.'
Sean: 'Take all your clothes off, your bra off.'
Terry: 'Yeah, and take your bum off, take your wee wee off. Take your clothes, your mouth off.'
Sean: 'Take your teeth out, take your head off, take your bum off. Miss Baxter the paxter knickers taxter.'
Miss B.: 'Sean, go and find something else to do please.'
(Walkerdine, 1981, pp. 14–15)

This transcript illustrates how small boys can take away the adult power of a woman teacher. Their power comes from their refusal to be powerless objects in *her* discourse, and in the way that they recast her as the powerless object of *their* own discourse. She hasn't stopped being a teacher, but she has stopped *signifying* as one. In this discourse both the adult teacher and the small girl Annie are reduced to sex objects, owners of the same qualities – in this case possessors of tits, bums and cunts.

Case study – Frogs and snails and feminist tales

More recently, but drawing on Walkerdine's work described above, Davies (1989) carried out research in Australia using a post-structuralist framework. She values this perspective because:

If we see society as being constantly created through discursive practices then it is possible to see the power of those practices not only to create and sustain the social world but also to see how we can change that world through a refusal of certain discourses and the generation of new ones.
(Davies, 1989, p. xi)

Her research was inspired by two events. Firstly her reading *The Paper Bag Princess*, a feminist fairy tale, to a 5-year-old girl. In the story Prince Ronald is rescued by Princess Elizabeth, but instead of being pleased he is appalled by her appearance. The story ends with the princess skipping off into the sunset and the words 'They didn't get married after all.' Davies realized that the ending was not appreciated by the 5-year-old, and that the story she was hearing was not the same story that the child was hearing.

The second event involved the same child's response to another girl called Penny, who looked and behaved like a boy. The first child was outraged that other children were calling a 'boy' by a girl's name.

These experiences raised the following questions: Why had the child not appreciated the feminist story? Why is it so important to get people's gender right? Why was Penny regarded as a problem by parents and other children?

Davies decided to investigate this in a two-year systematic exploration of children's understanding of feminist stories. She chose eight children aged four and five from varied social class backgrounds and spent hundreds of hours reading feminist stories to them. She also observed pre-school children playing and read them stories so that she could fit children's understanding of the stories to their actions in the everyday world.

Using post-structuralist theory, she found that when children insist on sticking to traditional forms of femininity and masculinity it is because the male–female dualism is so central to the way their human identity is constructed. Children had difficulty with feminist stories because their ideas had already been shaped by the discourses of traditional children's stories in which all the characters are positioned as either male or female. That was what they had come to expect and how they made sense of the world.

Davies hopes that through this kind of action, the reading of feminist stories, children will be able to see masculine and feminine qualities as a range of options rather than two types of behaviour – these types being related to biological reproduction and relatively minor bits of anatomy. She hopes we will come to question how the social world could have been seen in terms of two types of people.

Davies' research can be criticized for not considering sufficiently how her presence may have affected the children's behaviour. She perhaps should also have considered how a child's experience of the world differs from that of an adult, as a framework to discuss their responses.

A critique of post-structuralism and post-modernism in education

Beverley Skeggs (1991) provides an interesting and amusing critique in which she states that her aim is to stop educationalists wasting their time over ideas that are of very little use or have been said before. Here is a summary of her criticisms:

1 Post-modernism is an attempt by disillusioned male academics to win back power and influence in a world where there is a decline in the demand for their services.

2 Theorists like Lyotard claim that one of the purposes of post-modernism is to destroy meta-narratives (grand theories), yet he simply constructs another called post-modernism.

3 The ideas have an exclusive status because only the highly articulate can play confidently with the language.

4 Foucault's ideas are useful for understanding the role of education in the reproduction of techniques of discipline and surveillance, but they cannot explain the effect of the central power of the state. For post-structuralists the state is seen as simply a multitude of local sites of micro power. For example, how can the imposition of the Education Reform Act 1988 be explained in post-modern terms, of a multitude of local sites of micro power alone?

5 Adopting a post-modernist position could lead to political inactivity and conservatism. If subjectivities (identities) are multiple and changeable and power is diffuse, then political struggle is difficult.

Activity

This is an activity to test your understanding of the various perspectives in the sociology of education. It is adapted from 'As if . . . an introduction to perspectives', in *A Handbook for Sociology Teachers* by Gomm and McNeill (London, Heinemann Educational, 1982). The class should be divided into small groups and each group allocated a 'statement' from the seven choices that follow. Your group should first identify the perspective and then discuss the questions *as if you are sociologists*

from that perspective using material from the whole of this chapter, finally report back to the whole group.

1 'We would like you to think of the educational system as a means of producing a highly motivated, achievement-oriented workforce. Both the winners (high achievers) and the losers (low achievers) will see the system as just and fair because status is achieved in a situation where all have an equal chance.'
   a Identify the perspective.
   b How would you explain working-class under-achievement?
   c How would you explain the existence of independent (private) schools?

2 'We would like you to think of the educational system as a site of a series of complex interactions between teachers and pupils. Through these interactions teachers label pupils as bright or dull or troublemakers, and these labels become self-fulfilling prophecies with pupils behaving accordingly. These labels are not fixed or unchangeable but are socially constructed.'
   a Identify the perspective.
   b How would you explain working-class under-achievement?
   c Suggest how teachers might improve pupils' educational achievement.

3 'We would like you to think that the main role of the educational system is not to reduce inequalities but to reproduce them. Pupils are prepared for their work roles through a close correspondence between the social relations of the workplace and the social relations of the school. Subordinacy and discipline are rewarded while creativity, aggressiveness and independence are penalized.'
   a Identify the perspective.
   b How would you explain how the educational system appears to be fair?
   c How would you explain teachers who encourage pupils to be critical of society?

4 'We would like you to think of the educational system as a marketplace.

Parents and pupils are consumers, education is the product and teachers are deliverers of the curriculum. Through competition and choice the best use is made of educational resources and the wasteful role of local education authorities is minimized.'

a   Identify the perspective.

b   How would you explain a centrally imposed, statutory, National Curriculum?

c   How would the market work for parents with statemented children with special educational needs?

5   'We would like you to think of the educational system as a male-dominated hierarchy with men in most of the powerful positions. In the curriculum, history and literature reflect the interests and activities of white, middle-class males. The main aim of the education system is to prepare young women for a domestic role in the family and that of a flexible worker in the economy.'

a   Identify the perspective.

b   How would you explain girls' success at GCSE relative to boys?

c   How would you explain the improved take-up of places in higher education by mature women returners?

6   'We would like you to think of the educational system as the micro-politics of power relations in different localities. Schools, like prisons and hospitals, have their own histories and techniques of discipline and surveillance. Localized complexity describes such sites rather than any notion of centralized power.'

a   Identify the perspective.

b   How would you explain educational inequality?

c   Explain how discipline is exercised by teachers.

7   'We would like you to see the educational system as a means by which some working-class lads celebrate their culture of masculinity by playing up teachers and being anti-academic. Pupils who conform to school rules by wearing uniform, carrying a briefcase, respecting teachers and working hard are ridiculed by these 'lads'. They think university is

for middle-class hippies.'

a   Identify the perspective?

b   How would you explain working-class boys who achieve academically?

c   How would you explain the behaviour of girls who behave in the same way as the 'lads'?

U, I, A

8.5 Social class and educational attainment

It is interesting that there has been very little sociological research on social class and educational attainment in the 1990s, given that this has been the major preoccupation of sociologists of education since the 1960s. (See also Section 4.10.) In what has come to be known as the 'old' sociology of education, working-class under-achievement was explained largely by cultural factors outside the school. These were investigated by empirical studies of educational inequality. They were influenced by American functionalism but this was implicit. Karabel and Halsey describe the approach:

British researchers in education were as preoccupied with 'wastage' and 'dysfunctions' as their American colleagues but perhaps more animated by the egalitarian concerns of a country with a long established and politically organised Labour Movement. The attack by British sociologists on inequality of educational opportunity was not only that it was unfair, but also that it was inefficient. (Karabel and Halsey, 1977, p. 10)

Their approach has been called 'political arithmetic', derived from mobility studies (examined in detail in Section 4.9) and aimed at calculating the chances of reaching different levels in the educational system for pupils of different social class origins. The 1944 Education Act opened up educational opportunities to working-class pupils by making education free and compulsory for all pupils to age 15. Thus financial barriers which may have denied them access to education were removed. Despite this, class differences in educational attainment persisted.

The home and the school

Sociologists such as Douglas (1964) focused on home background to explain the relative failure of working-class children compared with their middle-class counterparts. He conducted a longitudinal study of 5362 children born in 1946, tracking them through primary and secondary schools. Douglas found that children of similar measured ability at age 7 varied a great deal in their educational attainment, and by 11 the gap had widened and these differences related to social-class background. Pupils were also much more likely to stay on at school if they were middle class.

Douglas claimed that the greatest influence on attainment was parental attitudes. He measured this by the number of times parents visited the school. He also outlined other factors such as family size, early child-rearing practices, health and the quality of the school.

Discussion point

What are the factors that might affect the number of times parents visit a school? Is this necessarily a good indicator of their interest in their child's education?

Compensatory education

The old sociology of education has been criticized for focusing on the form rather than the content of education. This was evident in the support for the comprehensivization of secondary education as a reform that would improve educational opportunities. There was also a rather naive belief in educational reform and the power of education to bring about social change or to reduce inequalities.

Studies like Douglas' also gave rise to the idea that working-class culture was to blame for under-achievement. This resulted in compensatory education schemes like educational priority areas established as a result of the Plowden Report (1967) and Operation Headstart in the USA. These schemes attempted to compensate for the perceived cultural deficit of black and working-class pupils. (See also Section 6.3.)

The old to the new

Challenges to the political arithmetic approach occurred within the sociology of education in the late 1960s. De-schoolers like Ivan Illich began to challenge the content and form of education and the idea that education was a good thing *per se*. Studies began to focus on schools and what happened in them, rather than on the effects of the environment and home background.

Case study approaches were used by Hargreaves (1967), Lacey (1970) and later Ball (1981) to investigate the ways in which school organization worked against working-class pupils, particularly the effects of selection by the 11-plus examination and streaming. Hargreaves (1967) used some qualitative methods such as participant observation (see Section 3.9) to investigate social relations in a secondary modern

school. He found that working-class boys in lower streams developed an anti-school subculture as a response to their lack of educational success. Not only had they failed to get a place in grammar school, they were also negatively labelled by teachers and placed in the bottom stream. By inverting the culture of the school they produced an alternative value system from which they could derive status.

These studies began a change of focus in the sociology of education, away from explanations of failure in terms of home background towards a focus on school organization, teacher–pupil interaction and the content of the curriculum and school knowledge. This shift was influenced by 'interactionist' perspectives, with sociologists undertaking ethnographic research into classrooms. (This is also discussed in Section 10.5.)

The new sociology of education

The 'new' sociology of education had several strands, the two most important being phenomenology and cultural Marxism. These strands did, however, share certain concerns, which were to challenge taken-for-granted assumptions about what counts as legitimate school knowledge, educational success and failure.

They were critical of functionalist explanations of working-class failure. Pupils and teachers were viewed as creators of meaning rather than passive receivers of 'education'. The content of the curriculum and what counts as legitimate knowledge came under scrutiny from sociologists like Young and Whitty (1971). The assertion that all knowledge is equally valid led to interesting debates about cultural relativism.

The social construction of reality in schools and classrooms was the approach taken by the phenomenologists. The emphasis here was on subjective meanings of how pupils and teachers make sense of their experiences of the culture and knowledge of schools.

Who has benefited from educational expansion?

The political arithmetic tradition in the sociology of education did, however, survive the challenges of the new sociology of education. In 1980, Halsey, Heath and Ridge produced *Origins and Destinations*. Using data from the Nuffield mobility study (1972) of 8529 men born at different times in the twentieth century (see Section 4.9), they investigated two issues:

1 to determine to what extent the educational system had achieved its professed goal of meritocracy

2 to test Bourdieu's theory of cultural capital – that while schools appear fair and meritocratic, in

reality they privilege pupils with the requisite cultural attributes. (Bourdieu's work is also considered in Sections 2.9 and 10.4.)

They found that despite the expansion of the educational system, relative chances remained the same or in some periods worsened. Before the 1944 Education Act service-class men were eight times more likely than men from the working class to go to university; after 1944 this increased to 8.5 times:

The 1944 Education Act brought England and Wales no nearer to the ideal of a meritocratic society. . . . Secondary education was made free in order to enable the poor to take advantage of it, but the paradoxical consequence was to increase subsidies to the affluent.
(Halsey *et al.*, 1980, p. 210)

They found that the existence of private schools structured class chances and built bias into the meritocratic development of the state system of education. The two systems, private and state, remained divided along class lines. (The impact of private education is also considered in Section 4.5.) They did find a large volume of intergenerational educational mobility, so cultural capital is not an exclusive means of cultural reproduction of social classes. Those from privileged social class backgrounds were more likely to stay on at school (70 per cent of Social Class 1 pupils went on to university). They concluded

that qualification inflation could lead to social class inequalities becoming a permanent aspect of education.

Since Halsey *et al.*'s study there has been very little large-scale research. Two studies, by Drew and Gray (1990) and Jesson *et al.* (1992), indicate that while the proportion of pupils entered for examinations at 16 has expanded massively, social class differences in educational performance remain.

A multi-dimensional approach – ethnicity, gender and social class

What *has* increased in recent years is research that considers together the various factors that may affect the educational achievements of pupils, including gender, ethnicity and social class. Such a multidimensional approach, though often complex, is extremely important. Pupils do not experience the effects of gender, 'race' and class separately; these work *together* to influence performance at school.

A report from the Office for Standards in Education (Ofsted), prepared by Gillborn and Gipps (1996), focuses on the achievements of ethnic minority pupils. It reviews research on the effects of social class, race and gender, and its findings are interesting and revealing. Some of their findings are reported in Figure 8.1.

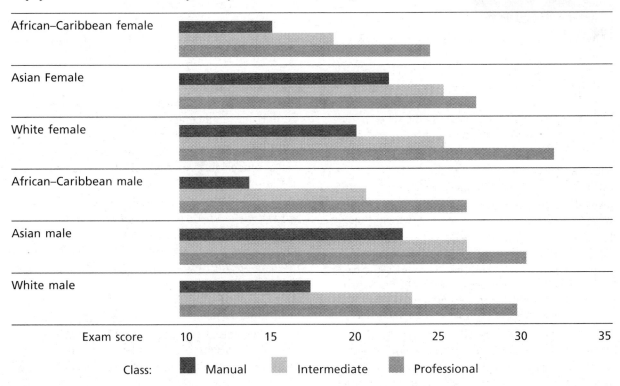

Figure 8.1 Average exam scores by ethnic origin, gender and social class (England and Wales, 1985).
Source: adapted from Drew and Gray (1990) 'The fifth year examination achievements of black young people in England and Wales', *Educational Research* 32(3), pp. 107–17

Activity

a Study Figure 8.1. What does it tell us about the primacy of social class?

b What does it *not* explain?

c How satisfactory are the categories used for ethnicity?

I, A, E

Social mobility: assisted places

Following a promise in the 1979 Conservative election manifesto to provide a ladder of opportunity for academically able working-class pupils, the 'assisted places' scheme was introduced as part of the provisions of the 1980 Education Act.

The scheme was intended to enable academically able pupils whose parents could not afford the fees to benefit from education at an independent school. Between 5000 and 6000 means-tested places were to be made available. This was justified as a way of improving parental choice, rescuing pupils from the 'wreckage' of local comprehensives, necessary as their opportunities had been restricted by the demise of so many maintained grammar schools.

Edwards, Fitz and Whitty (1989) carried out an evaluation of the scheme. Their aim was to look at the political and ideological context and sources for the scheme and to test empirically some of the competing claims being made for and against it. They collected evidence on three levels:

- national statistics on the allocation and take-up of places
- the scheme's implementation in selected geographical areas with high concentrations of assisted places
- how individuals were affected by the scheme (they interviewed 600 pupils in independent and maintained schools and over 300 of their parents).

What is especially interesting here is the social origins of pupils with assisted places. These researchers used the Hope–Goldthorpe classification of eight groups within three broad classes: 'service' (higher and lower grade professionals), 'intermediate' (white-collar workers, small business people, technical foremen), and 'working-class' (skilled, semi-skilled, unskilled). (This is discussed in more detail in Sections 4.3 and 4.4.) They found very few children of working-class parents among their sample of pupils with assisted places:

In the assisted places scheme, it is noticeable that while children from single-parent families constitute the largest category of beneficiaries identified in relation to social 'need', as successive ISIS surveys have emphasised, children from other kinds of family also thought to be widely disadvantaged are either much less prominent (like the unemployed) or conspicuously under-represented (parents in semi-skilled and unskilled manual work, black and Asian families.)
(Edwards *et al.*, 1989, p. 166)

They found a high proportion of service-class occupations and a conspicuous absence of 'unambiguously working-class occupations' amongst the parents participating in the assisted places scheme in their sample. This supported earlier research by Salter and Tapper (1986) who found that a large proportion of the beneficiaries were relatively impoverished but educationally aware members of the petite bourgeoisie.

Yet head teachers, when asked how they allocated the places, were very keen to emphasize the working-class pupils they recruited:

[Head of Milltown Grammar] *'I'm trying to decide who will get the last five assisted places this year, and it's awful trying to weigh one up against the other . . . but the occupations we are talking about are . . . we've got a lorry driver, a British Rail guard, window cleaner, school meals assistant, . . . that's a single parent family . . . van driver, textile worker, unemployed, and two of these boys are actually . . . both sons of first generation Pakistani immigrants who work in textile firms as operatives. So overwhelmingly our application this time is bringing in poor children from inner cities.'*
(Edwards *et al.*, 1989, p. 115)

Heads when interviewed cited various reasons for entering the scheme, including helping individual children and serving the local community. Some claimed the school benefited from the improved social mix and that attracting high-fliers helped their exam results and competitive edge. There was some evidence of bright children being talent-spotted in primary school. A matron at one of the prestigious public schools described the effect on the social mix of the school:

[Cathedral College] *'It's good for them to realise that not everyone has three cars and two houses . . . It's the old thing of the nobility freshening their blood by marrying pretty shop girls. I think it's the same principle really. Introducing fresh blood into the school.'*
(Edwards *et al.*, 1989, p. 102)

In another school a teacher viewed the assisted places scheme as rescuing the school from *nouveau riche* parents with 'thick' and uncultured children, by providing bright working-class pupils who were preferable.

There was a stereotyped assumption amongst many of the parents interviewed that independent schools were better. However, out of the 470 schools who initially offered places, 200 were discarded as unsuitable for explicitly academic purposes.

The research seems to show that the assisted places scheme, despite its rhetoric of justification, is not drawing in pupils from inner-city neighbourhoods, and is 'saving' middle-class rather than working-class children from comprehensive schools. With potentially their best students creamed off, comprehensives are placed by the scheme in a position of increased competition, and of having to mimic independent schools in order to attract able pupils.

This research has been strongly criticized by John Marks (1991) who carried out an appraisal of the scheme for the Independent Schools Information Service. He used data from a Mori survey of 3475 pupils which found that roughly four in ten assisted places are from working-class backgrounds. This is higher than the findings of the Edwards *et al.* research, which found only one in seven from working-class households.

Discussion point

What type of questions would you ask of both pieces of research in order to evaluate their findings and account for the discrepancies?

By 1995 there were 33 000 assisted places being taken up and plans to double the number – seen as an attempt to put 'clear blue water' between the Conservative government and the opposition parties. It was considered better value than investing in state schools. The Independent Schools Information Service considered the scheme a great success, claiming that 80 per cent of people receiving assisted places had parents earning below the national average wage. Their wish was to extend it to non-academic pupils.

Discussion point

Could the assisted places scheme provide equality of opportunity? Is it meritocratic?

Access to higher education

Eighteen year olds today have a nearly 60 per cent chance of going to university, either straight from school or later in life, full or part time. In 1900 it was 1.2 per cent, in 1938 it was 2.4 per cent and in 1962 it was 6.5 per cent (including teacher training).

(Smithers and Robinson, 1995, p. 2)

As we move from an élite to a mass system of higher education it is interesting to explore whether this

Discussion point

Will a mass system of higher education necessarily improve the relative chances of working-class students?

has improved relative chances for working-class students.

Egerton and Halsey (1993) identify three features in the history of access to higher education since 1900:

- a considerable expansion of tertiary provision
- no reduction of relative social class inequality
- a significant reduction in gender inequality.

They used a sample of 25 000 men and women between the ages of 20 and 50, drawn from the General Household Survey for 1985, 1986 and 1987. (This particular source of official statistics is discussed in Section 3.11.) They included the prestige of the institution and the age of attaining the qualification. Most studies use only academic qualifications as measures of tertiary educational attainment, but type of institution is also important in maintaining or reducing inequalities because the most prestigious institutions may be accessible only to the most privileged groups. The age of attaining qualifications was also considered as there is some evidence that qualifications gained later in life may lead to upward mobility. A three-point version of Goldthorpe's social class schema was used. (See Sections 4.3 and 4.4.)

Egerton and Halsey found social-class inequalities in access to all educational institutions (universities, polytechnics and colleges): the service class had an advantage over both the intermediate and the manual working class. Absolute access had increased for all, but the service class had maintained its relative advantage in both universities and polytechnics.

They found that students from service-class backgrounds were more likely to take degree courses in universities than working-class and intermediate-class students, who were more likely to take them in a polytechnic or college of further education. This supports the thesis that more advantaged groups tend to dominate more prestigious institutions. They sum up:

The overall picture for social class is of unchanging service class advantage. The children of managerial or professional families are more likely to gain access to university, more likely to have obtained the most prestigious qualification, a degree, at a university and more likely to have qualified earlier in life than people from an intermediate or manual class background.

(Egerton and Halsey, 1993, p. 189)

They did find, however, that the expansion in tertiary education has benefited women and it seems likely that women's educational achievement will soon be on a par with that of men.

The answer to the question 'Is social class still the most important determinant of educational attainment?' would appear to be yes. Despite the expansion of the educational system, relative chances have apparently remained the same. There is also some evidence that the assisted places scheme benefits service-class children even more than the bright working-class pupils it was set up to assist.

8.6 **Racism and education**

It is difficult to understand the position of the ethnic minorities, particularly African–Caribbean, African and South Asian pupils, in the educational system without reference to Britain's colonial past. After World War II, immigrants from the ex-colonies – now the Commonwealth – were recruited to meet Britain's post-war labour shortages. (This issue is discussed in more detail in Section 6.2.)

By the 1950s there was growing resistance to this immigration amongst the white population. In 1958 a series of attacks by youths led to riots, first in Nottingham and then in Notting Hill in London. This led to a call for action and it was to schools that the policy-makers turned. Before this, black children's needs had been relatively neglected. If black children would take on British traditions, values and mastery of the English language then the process of assimilation (see Section 6.4) would be smooth, it was assumed.

In 1966 a speech by Roy Jenkins, the Labour Home Secretary, was taken as the turning point in the movement away from an assimilationist position towards a more liberal integrationist phase. He advocated:

... *not a flattening process of assimilation but equal opportunities, accompanied by cultural diversity, in an atmosphere of mutual tolerance.*
(Quoted in Mullard, 1982, p. 125)

Whereas an assimilationist position meant total absorption, integration made allowances for cultural diversity. This approach resulted in multi-cultural education being developed by teachers, encouraged by some Local Education Authorities in the 1970s and 1980s.

There was also growing concern about under-achievement amongst black pupils. This it was felt was partly explained by the Eurocentric nature of the curriculum. It was felt that the curriculum should draw on the experiences and cultures of all ethnic minorities, and that this should permeate the whole curriculum. Multi-cultural education was interpreted very differently in different locations.

It was heavily criticized by some educationalists. Stone (1981) blamed multi-cultural education for the under-achievement of black pupils. She claimed that black pupils needed more formal methods rather than the child-centred approach implicit in multi-cultural education. Tailoring the curriculum to the needs of black pupils, she felt, was interpreted by teachers as encouraging them in sports and music. They should be encouraged to take academic subjects which would lead to educational success and upward mobility. Multi-cultural education was also parodied unkindly as 'saris, samosas, and steel bands' because of its focus on lifestyles rather than life chances. It was also regarded as ignoring structural racism in the wider society.

By the 1980s many teachers had adopted a much more political, anti-racist approach. This represented a move away from the pluralist model of multi-cultural education where all cultures were regarded as equal. It used a socialist or Marxist model of dominant and subordinate cultures, and neutrality for teachers was considered impossible where racism was concerned. Teachers tried to create an atmosphere of trust in classrooms so that 'race' and racism could be openly and honestly discussed.

This position also had its critics. Some multi-culturalists saw it as indoctrination by teachers who should remain neutral. In one school – Burnage in Manchester – it was claimed that a badly implemented policy contributed to the murder of an Asian pupil. The white working-class pupils of the school felt that the way in which the school's anti-racist policy was used ignored their needs and blamed them for racism. Such poorly implemented one-dimensional policies were condemned by an enquiry into the death, the Macdonald Report (1989).

Many schools developed much more comprehensive equal-opportunities policies to address the different and interconnected oppressions faced by pupils. They included 'race', gender, class, disability and learning difficulties and sexual orientation.

In the late 1980s there were attacks in the media on schools and LEAs with strong equal-opportunities policies. A more sophisticated version of the old assimilationist position was beginning to reappear. It emphasized the notion of difference rather than superiority or inferiority. The right-wing Hillgate group and academics like Roger Scruton claimed that multi-cultural education was a threat to the British way of life – that ethnic minority pupils should be encouraged to discard their culture and blend in. The Hillgate group were influential in planning the content of the National Curriculum, especially the teaching of British history, English literature and standard English. (See also Section 6.5.)

It is not just the right who are now attacking multi-cultural and anti-racist education. Recently sociologists like Gilroy (1990) and Modood (1989), influenced by post-modernist thinking, have criticized some anti-racist policies for their emphasis on 'colour racism', which focuses on the dualism of black and white and ignores other minority groups. (This issue is also discussed in Section 10.6.) Modood claims that religion as part of identity is more important to Muslims and possibly Sikhs and Hindus. Gilroy calls for the end of anti-racism as presently conceived, to be replaced by the new cultural politics of difference. He accuses modernist accounts of 'race' of being essentialist and reductionist:

- *Essentialism* means deciding who is racist and who isn't on the basis of a set of essential defining properties or dispositions.
- *Reductionism* means reducing everything back to a single cause, such as capitalism or patriarchy.

Celebrating difference, and understanding the complexity of identities, is important for teachers and pupils committed to anti-racism. (These issues are also discussed in Sections 4.11, 5.5 and 6.5.) These 'New Left criticisms' could have a demoralizing effect on teachers and contribute to political inactivity. As Epstein comments:

Essentializing slogans have played a necessary part in the construction of positive identities by people in subordinate groups, and the development of oppositional strategies has often rested on these identities.
(Epstein, 1993, p. 17)

Discussion point

What are the 'essentializing' slogans referred to by Epstein, and how might they be dangerous?

African–Caribbean boys at school

For a long time sociologists have focused on the educational achievement of groups from different ethnic groups. According to Gillborn and Gipps (1996) in an Ofsted report, African–Caribbean boys are over-represented amongst those failing in the educational system (see article on page 300).

African–Caribbean girls at school

There is some evidence that African–Caribbean girls perform better in examinations than their peers, but the data are from small-scale ethnographic studies and therefore not generalizable (see Section 3.9). Yet recent figures from the London Borough of Brent and from Birmingham show that, while there was an increase in what pupils of each ethnic group achieved, the gap grew between the highest and the lowest achieving groups (Gillborn and Gipps, 1996). This is between Asian and African–Caribbean pupils of both sexes (see also the evidence in Figure 8.1).

However, ethnographic work shows a very different response to schooling by black girls compared with their peers. Fuller (1980) studied a small group of girls of West Indian parentage who formed a discernible subculture (see Sections 10.6 and 10.7), by virtue of the girls' positive acceptance of the fact of being black and female. These girls, unlike their black male peers, directed their frustrations and anger towards achievement in school through the acquisition of educational qualifications. Their response to racism was to work hard and prove their worth. They were not, however, conforming, 'good' pupils. They were pro-education but not pro-school and had clever and subtle ways of showing their defiance. Teachers' expectations of them were unimportant:

In an ethnographic study of two south London comprehensives, Mirza (1992) found young black girls did better in exams than their peers and that the black girls aspired to careers in social classes 1 and 2. In the sample, 74 per cent of black females expected to find work in social class 1 or 2, compared with only 27 per cent of black boys and 35 per cent of white females. Mirza accounts for the difference by a comparison of second-generation African–Caribbean and Irish pupils. The black girls in her sample rejected the economic dependency desired by the young Irish women. They looked forward to relationships which 'have joint responsibility towards the household' within the context of *relative autonomy* between the sexes which are a common feature of West Indian family life.

Mirza also found that positive attitudes to education and lack of restrictions on the female labour market participation within West Indian families account for high aspirations amongst young black women. This presents an important alternative to pathological accounts of West Indian family life with an emphasis on strong mothers as role models which therefore marginalize black men. This issue is also discussed in Section 7.4.

Mirza's study is also a real indictment of careers advice available to young black girls. Such advice does nothing to challenge the gendered choices they make by widening their horizons and offering alternatives to those safe, traditionally female, occupations like teaching and social work. She shows, as do other studies like the Eggleston Report (1986), that the careers service plays a significant role in the reproduction of sexual and racial divisions in the

Caribbean boys fall far behind

NICHOLAS PYKE

Afro-Caribbean boys are marking up disastrously low scores in the crucial subjects of mathematics and science, according to worrying new studies.

A project by Birmingham education authority, one of the first of its kind, shows Caribbean boys scoring only a third of the male average in technical GCSEs.

The Birmingham analysis, based on 1995 GCSE results, shows only 8.6 per cent of black Caribbean boys getting grades A to C in maths, and 12.4 in science. The comparable figures for other groups of boys are: black African – 14.3 and 28.6; Indian – 34.2 and 44.1; and white – 32.2 and 36.9. Black Caribbean girls did considerably better, scoring 33.3 per cent A to C in maths and 37.5 per cent in science.

Another authority, which did not wish to be named, surveyed 1,508 pupils at 15 secondary schools and found that only 10 per cent of black Caribbean children got five grades A to C at GCSE (national average 43 per cent) and that only 7 per cent got any sort of GCSE pass in maths.

Birmingham produced its figures after working with the African-Caribbean Network for Science and Technology, a group of black scientists concerned about the failure of Britain's Caribbean pupils, boys in particular.

"What future will black Caribbean young people have in this Western, numerate, industrialised society?" asked the network's spokeswoman, chemical engineer, Liz Rasekoala. "They're not even qualified for an apprenticeship."

The network condemns the lack of detailed information. "Everybody was telling us there's a general problem. There was a lot of wringing of hands, moaning and groaning. But no one in the mainstream was willing to come out and say exactly what was going on.

"What we want from the Government is to have ethnic monitoring made statutory. As a result of gender monitoring there have been major improvements and support for girls. No one, apart from Birmingham, has had the moral courage to come forward with the figures."

Ms Rasekoala, who trained in Nigeria, said that black scientists are so rare they often feel isolated and may be tempted to seek other professions. She has spent her entire career as the only black individual at work and blamed low expectations at school for the failure of many black pupils in science.

Dr David Gillborn, a lecturer in policy studies at London University's Institute of Education, said that Birmingham's detailed figures are the first he has seen from a named local authority.

"Good quality ethnic monitoring is a crucial element in addressing existing inequality. But it must be with categories that are sufficiently detailed and meaningful." So far the Government is only proposing to collect very basic information.

Source: *Times Educational Supplement*, 24 April 1996

Activity

Read through the extract 'Caribbean boys fall far behind' and answer the questions. You will need to draw on Section 8.3 on interactionism and the information in Figure 8.1 to help you to answer the questions.

a Summarize the evidence that African–Caribbean boys under-achieve at school.

b Is racism to blame? What are the arguments for and against this?

c Is ethnic monitoring of exam results important? Why might there be opposition to this?

I, A, E

labour market. Such divisions are explored in more detail in Section 9.3.

Mirza found that black girls developed strategies to avoid teachers' negative assessments that were often detrimental to their own interests, and had little power to counteract negative outcomes.

These findings are very similar to those of Máirtín Mac an Ghaill's (1988) study of the 'Black sisters', a group of A level students who responded positively to education. They were pro-education but anti-school. They practised *resistance* with *accommodation*, finding subtle ways of resisting the institutional demands of the school and the racist curriculum, but at the same time succeeding academically. This accommodation came from wanting highly prized academic qualifications and the opportunity to escape from traditional black working-class occupations.

More recently Mirza (1997) has studied black supplementary schools in London which she regards as part of the transformative social movement developed by black women. Such women give up their Saturdays to teach black children what mainstream education fails to provide. Ethnographic research carried out by Mac an Ghaill (1991), in Marcus Garvey, a black voluntary school in the Midlands, suggests how maintained schools might incorporate more positive responses to the black communities they serve. The school was held in a community centre and was based on the values of collective self-help. Most of the black pupils attended local state schools with a majority of black pupils, but they felt them to be white institutions. The teachers lived out of the area. At Marcus Garvey the curriculum did not marginalize black people's culture, literature and history. The teachers were from the same area and were committed to promoting academic achievement through high expectations of their pupils. A positive use of creole was promoted, though there was a strong recognition that good English was also necessary. High priority was given to numeracy and literacy so that pupils could follow high-status academic courses.

South Asian pupils

South Asian pupils would appear to face a different

Activity

The following is a summary of the findings of an Ofsted report (Gillborn and Gipps, 1996) in relation to South Asian pupils:

- Indian pupils appear to achieve more highly, on average, than pupils from other South Asian backgrounds.
- Indian pupils achieve higher average rates of success than their white counterparts in some – but not all – urban areas.
- There is no single pattern of achievement for Pakistani pupils, although they achieve less well than whites pupils in many areas.
- Bangladeshi pupils are known on average to have less fluency in English, and to experience greater levels of poverty, than other South Asian groups. Their relative achievements are often less than those of other ethnic groups. In one London borough, however, dramatic improvements in performance have been made – here Bangladeshis are now the highest achieving of all major ethnic groups.

a Which ethnic groups are included in the term 'South Asian'? Why is the qualification 'South' added?

b Offer explanations for the differential achievements of pupils of South Asian origin, drawing on Brah's work described above.

I, A, E

---

set of barriers and prejudices from their African–Caribbean peers. The work of Avtar Brah (1992) focuses particularly on the position of South Asian girls. Firstly she rejects the fact that South Asian women are regarded as a homogeneous group when their country of origin, class, religion, language and gender systems are often different. (This issue is also discussed in Sections 6.5 and 10.6.) She rejects 'culturalist' explanations of South Asian girls' underachievement at school because they pathologize South Asian family life, blaming inter-generational conflict for educational failure. Attention is then diverted from teacher racism and a Eurocentric curriculum. In earlier research she found no evidence that the level of inter-generational conflict was higher amongst South Asian families.

Brah challenges orientalist ideologies that construct South Asian girls as passive. She points to the long tradition of resistance and struggle among South Asian women.

8.7 Is the future female? Gender and examination success

In the media recently there has been a moral panic about boys' under-achievement at school relative to girls'. The idea of a moral panic came from the study of deviance. Folk devils like the mods and rockers were considered a moral threat to society and this threat was sensationalized in the media (see Sections 11.2 and 15.5).

Discussion point

Consider the newspaper headlines. Are they sensationalizing this problem?

It is white working-class boys who are now the folk devils of the education world. Programmes on television have focused on girls' achievement and boys' relative academic decline at all levels of the educa-

---

Why flash boys shine at A-level
The Independent, 10 July 1996

They're falling rapidly behind girls at school. Are boys in terminal decline?
The Independent, 18 October 1994

Girls excel despite the male culture
TES, 26 April 1996

Male brain rattled by curriculum 'oestrogen'
TES, 15 March 1996

Go-ahead girls leave experts with a mystery
Sunday Times, 22 May 1994

Anti-school bias 'blights boys for life'
The Times, 6 March 1996

tional system. Interestingly, girls' success is not celebrated; instead there is a strong concern about boys losing out to 'girls with attitude'. The BBC's *Panorama* programme ('The future is female', 24 October 1994, and 'Men aren't working', 16 October 1995) compared boys' and girls' attitudes to education and doing well at school. Some of the boys described how being good at school conflicted with their 'culture of masculinity': they claimed 'it just isn't macho to work' and 'boys who work hard aren't boys'.

The popular stereotype of the female underachiever is now being challenged. This trend of girls doing as well as or better than their male counterparts is also part of a global trend in both the developed and developing worlds. Research conducted in the Caribbean islands of Jamaica, Barbados, St Vincent and the Grenadines found that, while subject choice followed traditional patterns, Caribbean females were out-performing their male peers (Parry, 1996). This has led to similar moral panics about the marginalization of men and men at risk (Miller, 1992).

Is this a new phenomenon?

In the UK, boys' under-achievement is not a new phenomenon, but it has been and still may be confined to working-class boys. It could be that the fact that schools are now having to publish their examination results has highlighted a problem hitherto hidden.

In his ethnographic study of working-class lads' responses to schooling, Willis (1977) found that they rejected the mental labour of school and the conformist culture – the 'earoles' – in favour of a counter-school culture. This involved bunking off to have fun, and playing up teachers. Manual labour was what 'real' men like their fathers did, and when it came to getting employment it was unofficial networks rather than paper qualifications that were useful.

McRobbie's (1978) study of working-class girls found a similar celebration of the culture of femininity, both trapping and liberating girls as the lack of academic success reinforced their futures as wives, mothers and unskilled workers.

Since these classic and important studies of the 1970s life has changed considerably for school leavers, especially for young men in working-class areas. In the Midlands and North East of England, traditional employment in manufacturing and mining has drastically diminished, resulting in high rates of youth unemployment. Often it is easier for young women to get jobs, but those that are available are part-time or insecure, low-paid and unskilled. (See also Section 9.3.) It is interesting that the two

Panorama programmes mentioned above were both filmed in the North.

The idea that girls do better than boys at school needs to be looked at very carefully. Which boys and which girls? Girls have always done better academically at primary level than boys. They were marked down in the 11-plus examination, otherwise there would have been a larger proportion of girls in grammar schools. When grammar schools were replaced in most LEAs with comprehensives and the 11-plus examination abolished and replaced with banding, some LEAs marked girls down and boys up to achieve an equal balance of sexes in schools. There is also some evidence from ILEA statistics (Mortimore, 1981) that the problem was more of under-representation than the under-achievement of girls. Where they were entered for mathematics and physical science they achieved better than boys. The fact was that they did not opt for these subjects.

Some educationalists have suggested that the moral panic about boys' under-achievement is part of a backlash against feminist teachers: that girls' success is at the expense of boys'. It is felt that such teachers may have focused attention on girls, especially in maths and science, because they were traditionally under-represented and under-achieved in this area. In some schools and LEAs, special projects were established to encourage girls into maths, technology and engineering. Equal Opportunities policies and practice also often stress the need for teaching methods and content to be structured to the needs of girls, and for there to be single-sex groupings in some subjects.

There needs to be a lot more research before it is established that Equal Opportunities policies and the efforts of teachers have significantly contributed to girls' improved exam performance.

Exam statistics

Over the last ten years girls have been out-performing boys at GCSE, as Table 8.2 shows. It has been suggested that the coursework methods of GCSE suit girls and account for the differences.

Research was undertaken in 1992 by the University of London Examinations and Assessment Council, in collaboration with NFER, to investigate the causes of differential performance between boys and girls in GCSE English and Mathematics. Data was collected by questionnaire from 200 heads of departments in schools and from 3000 examination scripts. This suggested that coursework played only a minimal role in explaining such differences, which were more likely to be a result of experiences that candidates brought with them to the exam and a complex interaction of all the elements within GCSE,

Table 8.2 Percentages of male/female entry and grade A–C results (all GCSE groups) in 1993

Subject	Male entry	Male A–C grades	Female entry	Female A–C grades	Mean difference % A–C (M–F)
Art /Design	48.7	45.7	51.3	62.6	–16.9
Biology	43.1	66.0	56.9	56.3	9.7
Chemistry	58.5	69.8	41.5	68.4	1.4
Combined Science	50.2	42.4	49.8	43.1	–0.7
Economics	65.5	55.9	34.5	56.3	–0.4
English Language	50.0	49.7	50.0	64.6	–14.9
English Literature	47.4	54.1	52.6	67.4	–13.3
French	45.6	42.3	54.4	53.7	–11.4
Geography	57.2	48.1	42.8	53.8	–5.7
History	48.1	51.4	51.9	58.2	–6.8
Maths	48.7	45.8	51.3	44.9	0.9
Physics	68.9	66.4	31.1	72.1	–5.7

Source: Inter-group Statistics (1993) Associated Examining Board; quoted in Elwood (1995b)

including teachers' expectations, entry policies, how coursework is regarded and different emphases in the syllabus (Elwood, 1995b).

Boys catch up at A level

It is interesting that the early pattern of success is reversed at A level, as demonstrated by Table 8.3. Despite its importance as the 'Gold Standard' of education, A level has been left out of the gender and equity debate.

One of the main changes in A level examinations over the last 20 years is female entry patterns. More females now enter for A levels: in 1990 they made up 48 per cent of the total entry, having been only 38 per cent in 1970 (Table 8.4; Elwood, 1995a). By 1993 the figure had grown to 51 per cent.

However, females do not leave post-compulsory education better qualified, in terms of the percentage of higher grades obtained, than their male counterparts. What, then, do the statistics tell us?

Table 8.3 Percentages with A–C grades at A level (all GCSE groups), 1990–93

Subject	Male (M) % A–C				Female (F) % A–C				Difference (M – F) % A–C				Mean difference 1990–93
	1990	1991	1992	1993	1990	1991	1992	1993	1990	1991	1992	1993	
Biology	43.7	40.6	45.5	44.4	41.4	38.8	43.1	43.9	2.3	1.8	2.4	0.5	1.8
Chemistry	49.6	49.3	51.5	51.8	47.6	48.0	49.5	50.3	2.0	1.3	2.0	1.5	1.7
Physics	44.6	44.7	46.2	48.7	44.2	43.7	47.3	49.6	0.4	1.0	–1.1	–0.9	–0.1
Mathematics	46.8	47.9	49.3	57.1	45.0	46.7	48.4	57.5	1.8	1.2	0.9	–0.4	0.9
French	54.5	54.9	57.7	58.7	50.5	51.4	52.5	54.1	4.0	3.5	5.2	4.6	4.3
English Lit.	53.3	51.9	54.1	55.4	50.4	48.4	51.8	53.5	2.9	3.5	2.3	1.9	2.7
Geography	42.6	42.2	44.9	44.8	42.7	45.8	48.4	47.7	–0.1	–3.6	–3.5	–2.9	–2.5
History	49.1	48.2	49.9	50.5	43.7	43.2	46.3	47.3	5.4	5.0	3.6	3.2	4.3
Total all subjects	45.5	45.4	47.2	48.6	42.7	43.1	45.7	47.8	2.8	2.3	1.5	0.8	1.9

Source: Inter-Board Statistics 1990–93, Associated Examining Board; quoted in Elwood (1995a)

Table 8.4 Entry figures for eight major A level subjects by gender, 1970–90

Subject	Sex	1970	1980	1990	Percentage differences 1970–80	Percentage differences 1980–90
Biology	Male	10 235	17 232	17 938	68.4	4.09
	Female	9 463	20 662	28 517	118.3	38.0
	Total	19 698	37 894	46 455	92.4	22.6
Chemistry	Male	23 385	24 836	27 427	6.2	10.4
	Female	7 385	12 408	18 769	68.0	51.3
	Total	30 770	37 244	46 196	21.0	32.1
Physics	Male	35 045	35 752	35 300	2.0	−1.3
	Female	6 501	9 406	10 029	44.7	6.6
	Total	41 546	45 158	45 329	8.7	0.4
Maths	Male	52 364	50 238	47 096	−4.1	−6.3
	Female	12 017	15 775	23 867	31.3	51.3
	Total	64 381	66 013	70 963	2.5	7.5
French	Male	9 822	7 456	7 445	−24.0	−0.1
	Female	16 103	18 640	19 799	15.8	6.2
	Total	25 925	26 096	27 244	0.7	4.4
English Lit.	Male	21 257	20 229	14 621	−4.8	−27.7
	Female	34 736	45 371	32 345	30.6	−28.7
	Total	55 993	65 600	46 966	17.2	−28.4
Geography	Male	19 421	20 714	23 524	6.7	13.6
	Female	12 347	14 360	18 146	16.3	26.4
	Total	31 768	35 074	41 670	10.4	18.8
History	Male	18 145	18 898	19 845	4.1	5.0
	Female	16 811	21 196	23 962	26.1	13.0
	Total	34 956	40 094	43 807	14.7	9.3
All Subjects	Male	189 674	195 355	193 196	3.0	−1.1
	Female	115 363	157 818	175 434	36.8	11.2
	Total	305 037	353 173	368 630	15.8	4.4

Source: Elwood (1995b)

Activity

Read the two extracts 'Under-achievement among boys' and 'They're falling rapidly behind girls at school . . .'. Then, using Tables 8.2–8.4 and information from this section and the rest of this chapter answer the following questions:

a From Table 8.2, in which subjects were boys ahead of girls in A–C grades at GCSE?

b From Table 8.2, in which subjects were girls ahead of boys?

c From Table 8.2, how do the percentages of male and female entry rates at GCSE differ? Offer possible reasons for this.

d Since 1988, GCSE has replaced CSE and O level, the National Curriculum has been implemented and league tables of exam results are now published. How might this affect teachers' expectations, entry policies, how coursework is regarded and how different syllabuses are viewed?

e From Table 8.4, analyse the change in entry pattern from 1970 to 1990 for A levels. Suggest reasons for these changes.

f From Table 8.3, in which subjects were males out-performing females at A level A–C?

g Using the sources here and elsewhere, make a list of the explanations for differential male and female success in GCSE and A level exams, and evaluate them.

h Offer possible reasons for the pattern of achievement being reversed at A level.

U, I, A, E

UNDER-ACHIEVEMENT AMONG BOYS

Boys, particularly from working class backgrounds, may be experiencing low self-esteem and poor motivation which is having an adverse effect on their educational performance. Research by Harris *et al.* (1993) into the attitudes of 16-year-olds from predominantly working class backgrounds towards schoolwork, homework and careers, confirms that many boys are achieving below their potential. It was found that girls tended to be more hard-working and better motivated than boys, whilst boys were more easily distracted in the classroom and less determined to overcome academic difficulties. Overall, girls were prepared to work consistently to meet coursework deadlines, whereas boys had difficulties organising their time.

There was a greater readiness among girls to do school work at home and they spent more hours on homework than boys. When thinking about the future, the young women recognised the need to gain qualifications for lives which would involve paid employment as well as domestic responsibilities. Generally, the males had not given much thought to their futures and seemed fairly unconcerned about poor school performance.

The authors relate their findings to the gender 'regimes' which the young people encounter in their homes and communities. Some of the girls, exposed to the image of woman as organiser, responsible for home and family and wage-earning, displayed similar characteristics themselves, i.e. being highly organised with school work and homework. Harris *et al.* argue that the dominant stereotype of the male in the working class communities they examined was highly 'macho'. Typically, this was characterised by a disregard for the authority of organisational structures and an enjoyment of the active company of other males. Some boys were already fulfilling such a stereotype in their approach to school, showing little regard for working steadily and dissociating themselves from formal requirements.

Source: Clark (1996) *Sociology Review* Vol 5. No. 4.

They're falling rapidly behind girls at school.
Are boys in terminal decline?

JUDITH JUDD

PAUL CAVANAGH, 17, is honest about why he did less well than he expected in his GCSE exams. "Complacency and arrogance," he says. "After our mock exams, the teacher predicted I would get six As. No trouble, I thought. I don't need to work. So I didn't and I got three As."

He is now in the sixth form at King Alfred's School, Wantage, Oxfordshire, preparing for four A-levels. He says he is working harder to get to a decent university but still not as hard as the girls in his physics group. "The group is mainly boys and they do almost no work at all, especially homework," he says.

Paul, according to national studies, is a typical male student. Girls work harder and are less confident of their ability. Working hard is not "cool" for either sex, but girls are less swayed by their peers' attitude to school work. Alison Francis, 15, another King Alfred's pupil, puts it this way: "Girls do more work at home even if they want to keep up an image of doing no work at school."

Girls' industry has been rewarded. In the days of the 11-plus 30 years ago, they did better than boys in primary schools. Recently they have beaten the boys at 16: more than four in 10 get top grades at GCSE compared with only a third of boys. Even in science and maths, traditionally male strongholds, girls have edged ahead. Last year, for the first time, they had more top grades in science.

A-Level has remained the bastion of male achievement but the gap is narrowing. More boys still get the top two grades but girls are cutting their lead. Already a higher proportion of 18-year-old girls than boys gets three A-levels. Male undergraduates do both better and worse – more firsts and more thirds – than their female counterparts, but the difference varies from university to university.

The inexorable march of girls towards better examination performance is not explained just by hard work. It is the result, too, of the equal opportunities revolution of the past 20 years. Girls have been encouraged by a generation of determined female teachers to tackle maths and science, to stay on at school, to go to university and to have careers.

Recently, however, concern has shifted. Experts have begun to suggest that schools, in their eagerness to encourage girls, have neglected boys. They say that, in precisely the same way as teachers in the past failed to interest girls in maths, they are now failing to make boys enthusiastic about English. Recently, Demos, the independent think-tank, suggested that the revolution in girls' education had a price: demoralisation of boys. As girls have become more optimistic, the report said, boys have become so pessimistic that their depression is affecting their academic performance.

If this is so, the pessimism has not yet reached King Alfred's boys. They are neither worried about job prospects nor dismal about the future. Complacency remains. Figures from the Equal Opportunities Commission show that there will be a fall in male employment of 300,000 by the year 2000 and 500,000 new jobs for women, but Paul says: "It's definitely easier for men to get jobs. There are still employers who don't want women because they may go off and have children or because they think they lack a hard-nosed attitude." Jonathan Spinage, another 17-year-old, agrees: "Men think, I'm bound to get a job. I'm a bloke'."

Far from being cowed, Paul and his contemporaries are ambitious. They want to be rich – but they are not sure that better qualifications mean a better job. Matthew Ryland, 17, explains: "Boys are more ambitious. The basic boy dream is to be rich, to have a big car and a nice house. It was always said that to get high up you need lots of qualifications. Now there are other ways of doing it."

Girls, says Kate Douglas, 17, take a different view: "With girls it's about succeeding in whatever they're doing. We're not just interested in the money."

Even when girls and boys dislike subjects, girls still do well. Both boys and girls challenge the view that boys perform less well than girls in English because teachers do not stimulate boys' interest. Girls, too, have difficulty seeing the point of English, one of the subjects in which boys trail farthest behind girls.

Are the boys of King Alfred's, a successful comprehensive with exam results well above the national average, unusually cheerful about their future? Research last year among 30,000 teenagers by John Balding, of Exeter University, suggests not. It shows boys have not sunk into gloom at the sight of girls' educational advance. Although fewer of them expect to continue in education, they are more confident than girls that they will have a worthwhile career and find a job. They also expect to meet less sex discrimination than girls when they are job-hunting.

Michael Barber, professor of education at Keele University, comments: "Ten or 15 years of equal opportunities have worked," he says. "That should be celebrated. But it is possible that we have taken away something from one group and given it to another. It is time to reconsider our equal opportunities strategy." In particular, he believes we need to tackle boys' literacy, which is already behind that of girls by the age of seven.

Yet any plan to redress the balance in favour of boys must be treated with caution. There is no evidence that girls' success has been at the expense of boys, nor that teachers are discriminating against boys. According to research by Peter Mortimore, director of London University's Institute of Education, the latter still dominate the classroom and grab most of the teachers' attention.

Source: *The Independent*,
18 October 1994

Single-sex schools
Primary schools

In the 1970s and 1980s, feminist researchers found that boys dominated co-educational classrooms to the detriment of girls. Researching primary school classrooms, Clarricoates (1978) looked at the operation of the hidden curriculum:

. . . in particular how teachers tailor the subject content to boys through the ostensibly non-sexist curricula, through the use of linguistic sexism, through preferences of teachers for pupils by sex, and through the link between the criteria for according status and sex appropriate behaviour.
(Clarricoates, 1978, p. 353)

She showed that control and discipline were the central concerns of most teachers. Because of this they spent more time listening to, talking to, and helping boys who were considered more undisciplined than girls.

Her research corroborates evidence from previous studies that girls are more academically successful at primary level in most subjects (Douglas, 1964; Sharpe, 1976). Teachers however, instead of awarding girls status as a result of this success, tended to see them as boring and conforming. Boys were considered more interesting and challenging to teach. Similar findings resulted from research by Walkerdine and Walden (1982), who found that teachers in primary schools 'explained away' girls' success in mathematics as not really 'success' but rather an ability to be neat, tidy and follow rules; whereas the boys' 'success' was defined as having 'real understanding'. This led them to develop a theory, using the work of Foucault, to find the way different 'truths' relating to girls' failure are constructed.

Discussion point
To what extent is the notion of the conforming, passive, girl a myth?

Secondary schools

In secondary schools, Spender (1980) found that sexism permeated the entire curriculum. Women's contributions to history and science were ignored and more male writers were included in English Literature examination syllabuses.

Spender also looked at the reasons for female non-participation in verbal activities in the classroom. She reviewed the research which showed that both sexes regarded talking in class, particularly questioning or challenging teachers, as specifically masculine behaviour. Therefore encouraging girls to take part verbally in class was requiring them to play what was considered an unfeminine role. Spender regarded talk as a powerful tool that teachers should encourage girls to use. She notes, though, that much of the language used then in textbooks and worksheets was sexist, using 'man' and 'he' to cover both male and female activities. This, she felt, was no linguistic accident but a rule intended to promote the primacy of man.

Discussion point
To what extent has the linguistic sexism described by Spender disappeared in schools and colleges?

Spender and Scott (1980) put forward a strong case for single-sex education for girls. There was some evidence at the time that girls did better in single-sex schools, but this was not supported at the time by findings in the ILEA (Mortimore, 1981). However, Spender and Scott based their evidence on research in mixed schools where boys received more attention from teachers, the curriculum was directed towards boys' interests, where 'success' in high-status subjects is defined as 'male success'. In such circumstances girls are at a disadvantage and single-sex education would be desirable:

When girls are educated in a context in which boys are absent, in which they are encouraged to grow and develop their human potential, then they will be in a much stronger position to resist oppression in the wider society.
(Spender and Scott, 1980, p. 65)

Stanworth (1983) found, in her study of A level Humanities classrooms in a further education college, that teachers paid more attention to the boys, asking them questions and giving them more help with their work. She also found that teachers held stereotyped views of female students' future careers, for whom marriage rather than a profession was considered appropriate. Teachers also found it difficult to remember their female students, especially the quiet ones. Quiet male students *were* remembered.

Throughout the 1980s, feminist teachers made a good case for single-sex groupings for girls, especially in Maths and Science. Some girls' schools were valued as havens where feminist teachers could develop anti-sexist strategies and courses, girls' groups and women's groups relevant to the needs of girl pupils and women teachers. Female teachers had better career prospects in girls' schools. However, there were some criticisms of those who defended single-sex schools for girls: that this promoted an image of girls as the problem, of 'passive' girls who couldn't stand up to the boys, of not challenging mainstream practice.

As a result of the kind of research and activities mentioned above, there was an assumption that single-sex education was better for girls. But was the case proved? As early as 1978 Byrne outlined what she called the 'aggregation of inequality' suffered by less able, lower social class girls in rural areas, whom she considered to be 'quadruply disadvantaged' in the education system. She claimed that unequal facilities and resources especially in single sex girls' schools went some way to explain this disadvantage. At this time many girls' schools did not have good science laboratories or equipment or workshops for practical subjects like metalwork and woodwork. Some girls' schools were chosen by parents for religious reasons and they sometimes had the effect of reinforcing traditional notions of femininity and restricting girls' choices.

Much of this research conducted was small-scale, focusing on classroom interaction, making generalizations about the benefits of single-sex schools difficult. The only large-scale study was undertaken by Dale (1969, 1971, 1974) who interviewed pupils and teachers and came down in favour of mixed schools on the basis that they promoted 'optimal adjustment to life for all students'. The problem in claiming definitively that girls' schools are better for girls is that there are so many other variables to take into account, such as type of school, location and social class. This was summed up by Bone (1983):

. . . the subject mixes taken by girls, their academic results and the responses of their schools to their more personal needs have been conditioned far more by the type of school they attend (comprehensive, grammar, modern or independent) and by the style of school (traditional or not) than by whether their school was single sex or mixed. The repeated absence of a strong indication in favour of either a girls-only environment or a mixed environment through the great variety of research reviewed, supports the conclusion that this aspect of schooling on its own has not been crucial.
(Bone, 1983, pp. 1–2)

Making a case for single-sex schooling also means that boys have to be educated in single-sex schools. In areas where girls' schools are popular then there may be a gender imbalance in the co-educational schools. This could possibly put girls in such co-educational schools at a disadvantage. Some educationalists also feel that working with boys, changing their attitudes and assumptions, is vital if the bad effects of sexism which affect both boys and girls differently are to be countered.

Some recent research has focused on the need to provide single-sex groupings and spaces for both boys and girls *within* co-educational settings. This is not a new idea and single-sex groupings for maths, science and sex education have been established practice in some schools since the 1980s. Epstein (1995) describes how in her primary classroom complaints from three girls about boys dominating the use of bricks led to a discussion of this with the whole class and a solution in the form of specific times for each group to have access to the bricks:

. . . gradually other girls also began to take the opportunities offered them to play with the bricks. . . . Within their domestic play, girls could adopt 'feminine' roles which had reference to future heterosexual expectations of marriage and motherhood. At the same time they could and did build complex structures with the bricks. Girls could, then, at one and the same time position themselves firmly as feminine and do the 'masculine' activity of building – thus giving lie to the notion that 'girls don't do bricks' and to the idea that they must be 'boys' if they wanted to play in this 'inappropriately' gendered way.
(Epstein, 1995, p. 64)

In interesting research in Denmark, Kruse (1992) describes how she divided pupils into single-sex groupings for the benefit of withdrawn and shy girls. She found that boys needed support in different ways and that more and more teachers are employing sex segregation because of repeated incidences of conflict between boys and girls. She states that the reason for employing sex segregation is that co-education renders power relations invisible. Sex segregation, she claims, helps to expose this power because of the absence of the other group. This helps pupils to relate and act differently, to become owners of their own learning. She says this power becomes clear to pupils when embedded, hidden knowledge is uncovered.

Discussion point

Discuss the proposition that if boys and girls are separated into single-sex teaching groups they will never learn to confront unacceptable behaviour from the opposite sex.

Does the market favour some girls' schools

Recent research on choice of school by parents and pupils in this new age of consumer choice in the education market has also thrown up interesting findings about single-sex and co-educational schools. As part of a larger study of education markets in practice, Ball and Gerwitz (1997) looked at two related questions:

- how girls' schools position themselves in competition with their co-educational rivals (and how they respond)
- how parents and their daughters perceive, evaluate and choose between single-sex and co-educational schools.

This analysis draws on interviews with parents choosing secondary schooling for their daughters and who particularly expressed views about single-sex schooling. Two over-subscribed state girls' schools, Pankhurst and Martineau, are used as case studies. They are positioned differently in the school market because of their intake, with Pankhurst being decidedly middle-class. They found that girls are one group who are advantaged in certain respects by the current structuring of educational markets. Single-sexness is now a unique selling point for schools in the marketplace. This is due to their favourable characteristics in the context of school competition, for example in performance in public exams and the positive impression they give about ethos and discipline. Both schools gave considerable attention to their corporate image. Part of this was school colour used as a symbol and identifier in both schools, but Martineau also had a logo, flag, flower and motto:

[Union representative, Martineau] *'Well . . . you see a lot more things like our new sign and that sort of stuff and the colours . . . so it's very much more emphasis on presentation and our prospectus is very glossy. I mean it's what you would imagine a public school or university, the style of it, and that sort of thing has become very important, and there's quite a lot of emphasis on style and dress for teachers as well.'*
(Ball and Gerwitz, 1997, p. 209)

School uniform was part of the complex semiotics of girls' schools: the cloistered, traditional ethos. This was based on the absence of and escape from boys. This traditionalism is often mixed with feminism posing as an equal curriculum, enabling girls to get access to computers, to not be afraid to be clever, to have a career and a commitment to modernism and academicism. Such conflicting messages are summed up:

In all this then, feminism and femininity, traditionalism and progressivism are wrapped up together in a sophisticated and sometimes confusing set of signs and meanings. At Martineau something of both is signalled in the school prospectus which announces the school as a 'Grant Maintained School for Girls', and is emblazoned with the school motto: *'The best education today for the woman of tomorrow'.*
(Ball and Gerwitz, 1997, p. 212)

Discussion point

How do some girls subvert school uniform to convey a very different image from that of the traditional and respectable?

Part of the image or 'presentation of self' was the promotion of dance and drama productions, and especially music. Schools in competition for middle-class parents have to promote the playing of an instrument as an option.

Local co-educational schools in the sample responded by placing emphasis on the recruitment of girls in their marketing, and some also emphasized girl-friendly strategies such as separate play areas and separate teaching. However, it was made clear that co-educational schools were interested in a particular kind of girl: not all girls, but swots.

Activity

a From the evidence offered above, list the advantages and disadvantages, first to girls and then to boys, of single-sex schools. What are your conclusions? Is the case for single-sex education proved?

b Discuss the effects of the marketization of education on single-sex girls' schools and co-educational schools. Who are the losers and who are the winners? **I, A, E**

8.8 Special educational needs: separation, integration or inclusive education?

Tomlinson (1982) makes a strong plea for a sociology of special educational needs which she says has been marginalized in the sociology of education for too long:

Over the last thirty years, sociologists have devoted much time and energy to demonstrating the inequities of selection by 'brightness' in education while ignoring the progressive removal of more and more children from normal education on the grounds of defect, dullness, handicap or special need.
(Tomlinson, 1982, p. 9)

She makes a case specifically for a sociology of special education rather than its dominance by psychology, which tends to consider individuals as divorced from wider social contexts. Sociology, she claims, would view it as a public issue, a social process with the categories used as socially constructed and ripe for some demystification. Drawing on C. W. Mills' concept of a sociological imagination, she says:

The promise of the sociological imagination is to help people understand the interrelationship between history and individual lives, between the so called private and the public. This imagination is urgently needed in special education to examine the way in which the private trouble of having produced, or being, a child with special needs, and the resultant referral, assessment, labelling and diagnosing, is related to the wider social structure, to processes of social and cultural reproduction, and to the ideologies and rationalisations which are produced to mystify the participants, and often to perplex the practitioners.

(Tomlinson, 1982, p. 25)

Since those words were written in 1982 the position of pupils with 'special educational needs' (SEN) and the language used to categorize them has changed considerably, in part due to legislation. This will be considered in detail, but first some historical context is necessary.

A brief history of special education

Tomlinson (1982) provides a sociological analysis of the social origins of special education. She points out that there are two main interpretations of the history of special educational needs provision. One regards it as fuelled by the motives of benevolent humanitarianism and the other by social, economic and political interests. The former has been disputed as the motive by sociologists like Barton (1986):

... the view that concern for the handicapped has developed as a result of progress, enlightenment and humanitarian interests, is totally unacceptable. The experience of this particular disadvantaged group has generally been one of exploitation, exclusion, dehumanisation and regulation.

(Barton, 1988, p. 276)

Let us look briefly at the historical evidence. Full state provision for all children began in 1870 with Forster's Education Act. State provision for special education in England and Wales dates from 1874 when separate classes for deaf pupils were established by the London School Board. In 1893 the Elementary Education (Blind and Deaf Children) Act required local authorities to provide separate

education for deaf and blind children. In the early 1890s the first classes and schools were set up for Special Instruction for 'Defective' Children in London and Leicester, and so the term 'special' entered educational discourse. Before the 1870s education was dominated by churches, especially the Anglican church, who showed no interest in the education of the handicapped. It was individual businessmen with the profit motive in mind who saw an opportunity to exploit them. In early schools for the deaf and blind, commercial interests dominated. This was justified as an attempt to save pupils from 'idleness'. In these schools trade and vocational training took place. This emphasis became more pronounced after the introduction of state education:

... the blind, deaf, dumb and the educable class of imbecile ... if left uneducated become not only a burden to themselves but a weighty burden to the state. It is in the interests of the state to educate them, so as to dry up, as far as possible, the minor streams which must ultimately swell to a great torrent of pauperism.

(Egerton Commission, 1889; quoted in Tomlinson, 1982, p. 38)

There was also a political motive in the social control of groups who may prove troublesome. Links had been assumed between defect, moral depravity, crime and unemployment. This was also true for the mentally handicapped for whom separate provision developed in the late nineteenth century. Contemporary echoes of this debate are examined in Sections 4.8, 14.7 and 16.8.

At this time the medical profession, struggling for professional recognition, also had a vested interest in the education of people with mental handicap. They claimed the right to oversee their education. Moves to segregate pupils with mental handicap stemmed from fears about possible dangers to society, especially the hereditary nature of such 'defects'. Also it was to allow normal schools to operate smoothly. Throughout the twentieth century the stigmatization and separation of children with special needs continued. In the 1920s another group of professionals entered the arena, psychologists. Cyril Burt, then considered a progressive, initiated the use of intelligence tests to decide whether pupils had learning difficulties.

The 1944 Education Act stated that LEAs were required to meet the needs of pupils suffering from any disability of mind or body. This transferred responsibility from the medical domain to the educational one. For most children this meant education in special schools because, despite the stated intention of the Act to teach the less seriously handicapped in ordinary schools, this did not happen.

A change of approach in the 1980s

In the Warnock Report and the 1981 Education Act it was stated that, in planning appropriate services, it should be assumed that about one in six children at any time and one in five at some time in their educational career will need some form of special educational provision. Such children will need one or more of the following (Warnock, 1978, 3.19):

- provision of special means of access to the curriculum through special equipment, facilities or resources, modifications of the physical environment or specialist teaching techniques
- provision of a special or modified curriculum
- particular attention to the social structure and emotional climate in which education takes place.

In the 1981 Education Act that followed the report, special educational needs (SEN) are defined in terms of:

- significantly greater learning difficulties than the majority of children of the age group
- having a disability which either prevents or hinders a child from making use of the educational facilities generally available in schools.

The Warnock Report and the legislation that followed contained some important and radical changes in the approach to special education. The first of these was that special educational needs were to be seen as a continuum from those with severe and enduring needs to those with milder and more temporary needs. Such children were not to be seen as discrete and separate from the rest of the school population, and of the approximate 20 per cent with SEN, 18 per cent would be taught in mainstream schools and 2 per cent would continue to be taught in special schools. Secondly, learning difficulties were to be seen as interactive, a result of complex interactions of the social and cultural and learning environment rather than a deficit in the pupils themselves. The social construction of special needs was recognized. As a result of this the system of categorizing children was to be abolished:

We believe that the basis for decisions about the type of educational provision which is required should not be a single label 'handicapped' but rather a detailed description of special educational need. We therefore recommend that the statutory categorisation of handicapped pupils should be abolished.
(Warnock, 1978, 3.25)

The decision about who was to qualify for this special provision was to be decided within a partnership between members of the various educational services and parents. There would be an assessment procedure in which the needs of the pupil and how the local authority would meet these needs would be stated. This became known as 'statementing'.

Discussion point

Are special educational needs socially constructed?

The 1981 Act was met with a mixed response. For some it was a welcome extension of the rights of parents and children, a move towards the flexible integration of pupils with special educational needs and away from the stigmatizing labels attached to them. Some critics of the changes pointed to the composition of the Warnock committee: the fact that no 'handicapped' person was a member, and that there was no ethnic minority member, despite the fact that a disproportionate number of black children were referred to schools for what were called then the 'educationally sub-normal' or 'maladjusted'. Another criticism was that the funding implications were not addressed, and without considerably more money the 18 per cent of children might be neglected. Yet another was that the concept of educational needs and integration also hides institutionalized discrimination. A study by Croll and Moses (1985) of the incidence of special needs in ordinary schools found, in terms of behavioural problems, boys outnumbered girls by almost four to one and that it appears that more children from ethnic minority backgrounds are seen to have special educational needs than white children.

Tomlinson (1985) asked why it was that if all children have special educational needs the system caters mainly for the children of the manual working-class. Whether the implementation of the Act has led to a real improvement in integration appeared to be influenced by a combination of the traditional practices of the Local Education Authority, politics and luck (Riddell and Brown, 1994).

After 1981, further Conservative educational reforms restructured education in fundamental ways that affected provision for pupils with special educational needs. The Education Reform Act 1988 set up the National Curriculum and Local Management of Schools (LMS). Since then there has been a debate about whether the effects of these changes have worked against or in favour of the progress made by the 1981 Act. Assessing the possible effects is a complex matter. There is a sense in which a national curriculum for *all* pupils including those with special educational needs can be regarded as real progress, an entitlement curriculum. It could mean that discriminatory practices that excluded many pupils with special educational needs from mainstream schools and their curriculum disappear. However, the effects of the market and LMS may work against progress made by a common curriculum. Bowe *et al.* (1992) looked at the effects of this on SEN policies in the schools in their study of the effects of the 1988 Act on schools. Figure 8.2 maps out the various constraints and possibilities affecting the working of the Act in relation to a school's SEN policy.

Formula funding by Local Educational Authorities means that statemented students have quite high 'price tags', but the other 18 per cent of non-statemented pupils do not (Warnock, 1978). Some schools responded like the one below:

'The deputy Head in charge of finances asked me whether I could get more children statemented so that we could get more money for the school.'
[Head of Department for SEN, 13 July 1990 p. 133]

This means that pupils with special educational needs are seen not in terms of their needs but in terms of their worth in formula funding. Under the pressures that the legislative changes have brought, schools are then faced with hard choices. Should they attract statemented pupils and risk their school having an image of catering for the 'less able'? Or should they try to attract more able pupils without special needs who are more likely to stay on in the sixth form and therefore attract extra funding?

Research carried out into the effects of LMS on special educational needs provision between 1989 and 1992 involved three questionnaire surveys to all LEAs in England (Lunt and Evans, 1994). The findings indicate that, despite the fact that LMS could have led to more openness, accountability, value for money and quality, it has in fact had a negative effect on the provision for special educational needs. These negative effects can be summarized as follows:

1   There has been a reduction in centrally provided special needs support services.
2   There has been an increase in the number of pupils seeking statements. This is a result of funding following the individual pupil rather than schools being allocated a budget that allows them to cater for a wide range of both statemented and non-statemented pupils (thus threatening the Warnock notion of a continuum of needs).
3   There has been a trend towards more placements in special schools. The move towards the integration of pupils with special educational needs into mainstream schools initiated by the 1981 Act should have resulted in the closure of special schools and the transfer of those resources to mainstream schools. Only 100 special schools have closed since 1982, and 100 000 children are still segregated (Swann, 1991; quoted in Lunt and Evans, 1994).
4   There has been a rise in the numbers of pupils excluded from schools.

A positive effect reported was that some LEAs have made substantial moves to monitor the effectiveness of SEN provision. However, LMS does seem to have impacted negatively on the integration of pupils with special educational needs into mainstream schooling.

The 1993 Education Act

The introduction of Parents' Charters in the 1990s included one for the parents of children with special educational needs. This stated that their children had the right to be educated in an ordinary school wherever possible and to follow all the subjects in the National Curriculum to the best of their ability. The right of such parents were then strengthened by the 1993 Education Act's code of practice which imposed on schools a clear procedure for the identification of special needs provision and a programme and timetable for each child as to how these needs were to be met. The responsibility for meeting these needs now lies with the ordinary classroom teacher supported by a team and SEN coordinator.

Case study – Inclusive education

The term 'integration' has recently come under attack. It can mean that pupils with special educational needs are educated in mainstream schools *geographically*, while in terms of their experiences they may still be excluded from the mainstream

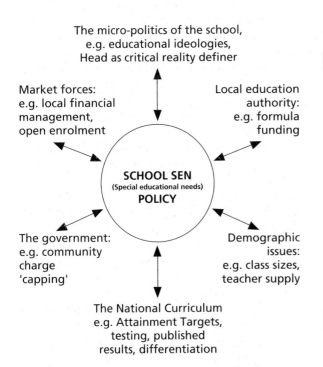

Figure 8.2 The constraints and possibilities which could affect a school's SEN provision. Source: Bowe, Ball and Gold (1992)

curriculum. More progressive boroughs and schools now prefer to use the term 'inclusive'.

Corbett (1994) explains inclusive education using a definition from Toronto in Canada:

'Inclusion means inclusion! It means affiliation, combination . . . Inclusion does not mean that we are all the same. Inclusion does not mean that we all agree. Rather inclusion celebrates our diversity and difference with respect and gratitude . . . Inclusion is an antidote to racism and sexism because it welcomes these differences, and celebrates them as capacities rather than deficiencies . . . Inclusion means all together supporting one another.'

(CIEC, 1992, pp. 1–4; quoted in Corbett, 1994)

Such a position seems to recognize other oppressions and to celebrate difference and diversity. What does it mean in practice? The London Borough of Newham provides us with a case study.

For Newham, firstly it meant closing all the special schools in the borough and all the pupils attending mainstream schools. Teachers in special schools were then employed in mainstream schools. The experience of Newham shows that some parents were happy for their children to attend mainstream schools. They wanted them to share the same educational experiences as other children and to avoid the stigma and the often unchallenging curriculum of special schools. Others feared for their children in what they saw as inhospitable mainstream schools and preferred the sanctuary of special schools where specialist staff and small classes ensured a safe environment.

Secondly it was part of an equal opportunities policy developed by Newham teachers and the LEA. Not all teachers supported the move unless there was careful planning, proper funding, resourcing and training. Some were suspicious that it was just a cost-cutting exercise.

Thirdly it meant that the aims of education were the same for all children and they were all to be taught the same National Curriculum.

This policy of inclusive education was a brave move by Newham, a borough that has high levels of poverty, homelessness and racial prejudice. This begs the question of whether progressive educational policies like this one can survive at a time when the introduction of market forces makes competition for scarce resources undermine the notion of working together for social justice.

Researching special educational needs

It is clear that the voice that is missing from all the debates on special educational needs is that of the pupils themselves. Some recent research has given a voice to those previously marginalized. Armstrong's (1995a) study is part of research undertaken in three local education authorities between 1989 and 1991, into the assessment of children having emotional and behavioural difficulties (Galloway, Armstrong and Tomlinson 1994). Armstrong interviewed 47 children forming three sub-samples: seven in an off-site unit, eleven in two residential schools, and 29 who were at the time of the study being assessed. He found that children felt they had not been allowed to tell their side of the story in their assessment, and that they had been disempowered by the process. An example of this is George's meeting with an educational psychologist:

[George] *'I've been visited by someone in school called a socialist* (sic) *I didn't like seeing her because I thought they were going to take me away. I couldn't talk to them and tell them about what I felt. They kept talking and I couldn't get a chance to speak. If I had the chance to speak I would have said I didn't want to go away. I wanted to stay with my parents and family.'*

(Armstrong, 1995b, p. 91)

Recently sociologists have suggested using a Foucauldian framework for researching special needs education:

Foucault (1967) argues that confinement, segregation, stigmatization and exclusion are all ways in which societies at different stages in their history have reacted to those construed as 'other', different and abnormal. Who is categorized in this way, on what grounds, and what happens to them is dependent upon the cultural and economic influences manifest in particular spatial and historical moments. Just as the ways in which society treats its 'deviants' gives us an insight into that society, we suggest that special education can be a particularly informative 'lens' through which to examine the changes occurring in the education system as a whole.

(Evans and Vincent, 1996, p. 102)

This offers insightful possibilities. As Allen (1994) states, Foucault is useful in two respects. His work on medicine, madness, discipline and punishment is relevant to the study of experiences of children with special educational needs. He provides us with a methodology of analysing the discourses of special education. (The work of Michel Foucault is examined in more detail in Sections 2.8, 10.2, 10.11 and 17.4.) Allen suggests that this analysis can operate on three levels:

- *macro* – what is said in official reports
- *micro* – informal accounts from SEN pupils, their classmates and teachers

- *meso* – what is said about pupils with SEN in statements and reports.

She used this approach to analyse how mainstreaming policies in Scottish schools affected a sample of 16 pupils with a range of special educational needs. Pupils were shadowed and they, their peers, teachers and parents were interviewed. The emphasis was on their conversations with others, rather than attempting to construct their reality of mainstreaming. School documents relating to these pupils were also examined. The results of this study are not yet available, but the methods themselves indicate possibilities for research projects. Handled with sensitivity such research can give a voice to those so absent from much research on pupils with special educational needs – the pupils themselves. As Allen concludes:

It also offers to explore the relationship between the 'prettifying euphemisms', adopted in our current climate of political correctness (Shapiro, 1993), and the ways in which children with special educational needs are spoken about in mainstream schools.
(Allen, 1994, p. 9)

Activity

a Analyse the times in your life when you may have had real difficulties with learning something. Compare this to times when your learning curve has hit the roof. How do these reflections relate to the idea that special educational needs are interactive and socially constructed?

b Analyse the terms used in this section to describe learning difficulties and disabilities from the nineteenth century onwards. How and why has it changed? What are the 'prettifying euphemisms' used? Is this language satisfactory? If not, how could it be improved?

c What does the position of students with special educational needs tell us about the effects of the marketization of education? Use the Evans and Vincent (1996) idea that: 'Special education can be a particularly informative "lens" through which to examine the changes occurring in the education system as a whole.'

I, A, E

8.9 The New Right and education

There has been a rise in the influence of New Right ideas in education (see also Section 8.11 and, for an outline of their general impact, Section 2.10). Some of these ideas have a resemblance to functionalist ideas, though in a rather crude form. An example of this is a book called *The Bell Curve: Intelligence and Class Structure in American Life* by Herrnstein and Murray published in 1994, which became a bestseller. Before the ideas in the book can be understood it is necessary to understand some of the debates about intelligence, intelligence testing and 'race'.

Intelligence, intelligence testing and 'race'

It was Binet, a French psychologist, who produced the first intelligence test in 1905 to identify children with special educational needs. Binet tried to separate out innate ability by using a variety of tasks that did not require reading or writing. This was because he believed that intelligence was too complex to reduce to a single number or score. The aim of his scale was to help children to develop and improve, not to label them as in deficit. Binet would not have approved of the subsequent use of IQ to label, limit and stream pupils.

It was then a German psychologist, Stern, who developed a measure known as an Intelligence Quotient (IQ), which is the ratio of a pupil's mental age to their actual age. This measure was welcomed by some as it allowed the abilities of pupils to be described through a simple number. This was potentially very dangerous. American psychologists then highjacked Binet's measures and called them intelligence *tests*. They assumed that intelligence was inherited and confused environmental and cultural differences with innate abilities.

In England it was psychologist Cyril Burt who promoted the idea that intelligence is innate, inherited and measurable. He claimed that intelligence, as opposed to knowledge, remains unaffected by teaching or training and can be measured with accuracy and ease. Burt thought that once the intelligence of a pupil was measured this should form the basis of selection to an appropriate type of education to meet the needs of the individual. There was a limited and biologically determined pool of talent and only these talented pupils were capable of academic success in higher education.

📢 **Discussion point**
How similar are Burt's ideas on intelligence to functionalist ideas on education?

After the 1944 Education Act, intelligence tests formed the basis of the 11-plus examination, used to decide whether a child should proceed to a grammar, secondary modern or technical school. Within these schools, and in larger primary schools, pupils were also streamed according to ability.

The result of this selection was that most working-class children ended up in secondary moderns and most middle-class children in grammar schools. To some educationalists this reinforced the idea that IQ is genetic, but to others it indicated that the whole basis of selection was unfair. The nature/nurture debate – of whether it is environmental or hereditary factors (or both) that determine educational and occupational success – continued to be waged.

The system of selection at age 11 was challenged by the movement towards comprehensive schools and the abolition of the 11-plus by most LEAs in the 1960s. In many schools, mixed-ability teaching replaced streaming. This was an attempt to break what was regarded as a socially divisive and unfair system of selection which labelled so many working-class children as failures.

In 1969, arguments about IQ and 'race' were sparked off when Jensen published a paper in the USA which claimed that Operation Headstart, a compensatory education scheme, had failed to improve the educational achievement of ghetto, mainly black, children – because of the belief that intelligence is genetically determined and cannot be changed by educational reforms. Jensen went on to argue that this justified a different basic education for black children and others with low IQs. For his evidence Jensen drew on statistics drawn up by Burt. This issue is also discussed in Section 6.4.

Why the use of IQ was discredited

Discrediting of the use of the IQ measure for determining a child's education was based partly on the discrediting of Burt's classic study of intelligence. He was found to have increased his sample of twins from less than 20 to more than 50 and to have produced correlations that were statistically impossible. His data on the IQs of close relatives were also found to be fraudulent. Was this carelessness or deliberate fakery? Two of Burt's 'researchers' were discovered not to have been involved in the research. Defenders of Burt claim that the attack on his work was part of a left-wing plot by those supporting an environ-

mental rather than an hereditary position on IQ. Others say that Burt was a sick man.

A second reason for discrediting IQ tests was that they were usually drawn up by white middle-class educationalists. So, despite claiming to test innate ability and often using non-verbal reasoning, the tests were seen to be still culturally biased.

📢 **Discussion point**
How would you test the IQ of a Martian?

A third reason for discrediting IQ tests was that the scores were unreliable because performance in the tests depends on many variables: where the test takes place, who does it, how confident the pupil feels. This also relates to the ethnicity of those involved in the testing. In 1968, a white psychologist carried out some testing with a black assistant in a south London comprehensive. African–Caribbean pupils were found to score much worse when tested by the white psychologist rather than by his black assistant.

Finally, some sociologists would claim that intelligence and intelligence testing are social constructs or discourses which change over time and in different locations, rather than being genetic or biological. They are, however, very political. Kamin (1974) states:

There exists no data which should lead a prudent man to accept the hypothesis that IQ test scores are in any degree heritable. That conclusion is so much at odds with prevailing wisdom that it is necessary to ask, how can so many psychologists believe the opposite?
(Kamin, 1974, p. 1)

He anwers his own question:

The IQ test in America, and the way in which we think about it, has been fostered by men committed to a particular social view. That view includes the belief that those on the bottom are genetically inferior victims of their own immutable defects. The consequence has been that the IQ test has served as an instrument of oppression against the poor . . . dressed up in the trappings of science rather than politics.
(Kamin, 1974, pp. 1–2)

Why the issue of IQ has re-emerged

Herrnstein and Murray's (1994) book mentioned at the start of this section argues that socio-economic differences between blacks and whites can be explained by differences in intelligence. Put crudely, what they are saying is that whites are cleverer than blacks, that low intelligence is largely the result of genetic inheritance. This they claim explains most of the problems faced by the USA, namely crime, poverty, dependency on welfare and unemployment. They state that new social policies are necessary which accept that social class and racial inequalities are inevitable. In relation to education they suggest scrapping affirmative action in higher education and shifting educational resources to more gifted students. Spending money on less intelligent pupils is a waste of money, they claim.

Affirmative action is rather like positive discrimination, and covers a range of measures to redress the balance in favour of under-represented groups. Some higher education institutions, for example, require different levels of qualifications for members of ethnic minority groups. One of Herrnstein and Murray's prominent themes is that such egalitarian policies victimize whites and privilege minority groups. Another theme is that IQ tests give a fair and accurate measure of people's abilities for selection to higher education and occupations.

The work of Herrnstein and Murray has been heavily criticized by educationalists and sociologists on both sides of the Atlantic. Drew *et al.* (1995) present an excellent critique. This can be summarized in the following points:

- Herrnstein and Murray do not present an objective case. Those criticizing IQ testing are presented as ideologically motivated charlatans whereas its supporters are seen as fair-minded and rigorous.
- They present only one side of the case, quoting only sources that support their position. They use racist sources from academics with poor records of research.
- They use simplistic and unspecified definitions of intelligence, intelligence testing and IQ testing. They substitute cognitive ability for intelligence and assert for general purposes that intelligence is the same as what Americans mean by being 'smart'.
- They claim that IQ tests are not demonstrably biased against social, economic, ethnic or racial groups.
- They ignore the contemporary consensus of those working in the field of intelligence that IQ is not fixed, that many IQ tests are not generally useful, and that there is no basis for the assertion that racial differences in IQ are due to genetics (Sternberg, 1995).
- They almost completely ignore the research on racism and educational and occupational inequalities, apart from a few grudging references to the work of W. J. Wilson, author of *The Truly Disadvantaged* (see Section 4.8).

Activity

1 James Tooley (1995) took up the arguments from Herrnstein and Murray in relation to education in an article in *Economic Affairs* entitled 'Can IQ tests liberate education?' Below are some quotes from the article in which Tooley espouses a New Right position on intelligence. Making use of the information in Table 8.5, evaluate each of the quotes.
a 'IQ is a better predictor of work productivity than any other single measure.'
b 'IQ stabilizes at about ten years of age.'
c 'IQ tests are more efficient than sorting pupils by GCSE or A levels.'
d 'Low scoring children will need to be warned that certain employment is likely to be out of reach.'
e 'Low scoring pupils can be provided with education that does not involve humiliating public examinations; the child can approach education for whatever intrinsic delights it holds.'
f 'Telling pupils that they can do well is rather like telling a boy who is short that, if only he will exercise enough, he can play in the top basket ball team.'
g 'If students do not want to partake of the riches of the curriculum offered to them, then they should be allowed to refuse . . . and take with them educational credits to be used when they want to avail themselves of learning opportunities.'

2 Draw up a chart of the similarities and differences between New Right, functionalist and Marxist ideas on education and intelligence. You will need to draw on the appropriate sections of this chapter.

U, I, A, E

- There is very little discussion of gender differences or of the interactions of ethnic, gender and social class interactions in their work.

Drew and colleagues thus conclude:

Despite its user friendly presentation, therefore, The Bell Curve *is bad science. It trades on the hard, factual image of statistical data and peddles conclusions which threaten to exacerbate, not lessen, the social divisions and conflicts which lie at the heart of the 'race' and IQ debate.*
(Drew *et al.*, 1995, p. 25)

Table 8.5 Myths, mythical counter-myths, and truths about intelligence

Myth	Mythical counter-myth	Truth
1 Intelligence is one thing, *g* (or IQ)	Intelligence is so many things you can hardly count them	Intelligence is multidimensional but scientifically tractable
2 The social order is a natural outcome of the IQ pecking order	Tests wholly create a social order	The social order is partially but not exclusively created by tests
3 Intelligence cannot be taught to any meaningful degree	We can perform incredible feats in teaching individuals to be more intelligent	We can teach intelligence in at least some degree, but cannot effect radical changes at this point
4 IQ tests measure virtually all that's important for school and job success	IQ tests measure virtually nothing that's important for school and job success	IQ tests measure skills that are of moderate importance in school success and of modest importance in job success
5 We are using tests too little, losing valuable information	We're overusing tests and should abolish them	Tests, when properly interpreted, can serve a useful but limited function, but often they are not properly interpreted
6 We as a society are getting stupider because of the dysgenic effects of stupid superbreeders	We have no reason at all to fear any decline in intellectual abilities among successive generations	We have some reason to fear loss of intellectual abilities in future generations, but the problem is not stupid superbreeders
7 Intelligence is essentially all inherited except for trivial and unexplainable variance	Intelligence is essentially all environmental except for trivial and unexplainable variance	Intelligence involves substantial heritable and environmental components in interaction
8 Racial differences in IQ clearly lead to differential outcomes	Racial differences in IQ have nothing to do with differential environmental outcomes	We don't really understand the relationships among race, IQ, and environmental outcomes
9 We should write off stupid people	There's no such thing as a stupid person – everyone is smart	We need to rethink what we mean by 'stupid' and 'smart'

Source: Sternberg (1996)

Sternberg (1996), concerned about the media attention to debates about IQ, attempts to outline the current state of knowledge and to avoid extreme positions. Table 8.5 lists the myths, counter-myths and what he believes to be truths about human intelligence.

8.10 **The National Curriculum and cross-curricular themes**

Is the National Curriculum new?

To a historian of education like Aldrich (1988), one of the striking things about the National Curriculum is that it is at least 83 years old. He makes a comparison of the subjects included in the syllabus prescribed by the Board of Education in 1904, following the 1902 Act which established state secondary schools and those of the 1987 National Curriculum:

1904	*1987*
English	English
mathematics	mathematics
science	science
history	history
geography	geography
a foreign language	a modern foreign language
drawing	art
physical training (PT)	physical education (PE)
manual work/	technology
housewifery	music

Thus the only subject not included in 1904 was music. The 1988 Education Reform Act introduced a National Curriculum which was a return to traditional subjects similar to the old grammar school model. It provided three core subjects, maths, English and science, and seven foundation subjects, art, music, technology, history, geography, a modern foreign language and physical education. In addition, locally determined agreed syllabuses for religious education were to be taught.

The curriculum for each subject was laid down in statutory orders, with attainment targets, programmes of study and ten levels of attainment defining what a pupil must know, understand and be able to do at each level. Pupil achievement was to be assessed through standard national tests at the ends of four Key Stages: at age 7 (KS1), 11 (KS2), 14 (KS3) and 16 (KS4).

The dismantling of the National Curriculum

No sooner had the National Curriculum been established than it became obvious that it would need to be amended. Key Stage 4 (KS4) was the first to be changed.

In 1991 the then Secretary of State for Education, John MacGregor, announced that curriculum overload could be solved by the introduction of short or combined courses at GCSE. Pupils could study either history or geography or a combination of both.

In 1992–3 there was strong opposition to the National Curriculum from parents, employers, the training lobby and teachers. It came to a head with a boycott of Standard Assessment Tests by all the teaching unions. This led the Secretary of State for Education, John Patten, to appoint Sir Ron Dearing as chairman of the School Curriculum and Assessment Authority (SCAA), to make recommendations to slim down the National Curriculum. Evidence collected during a three-month consultation period from teachers, industry and examination boards, amongst others, indicated that there was widespread support for the *principle* of a National Curriculum, but severe reservations about the way in which it had developed.

The most serious reservations were that it was over-prescriptive and administratively complex – especially regarding the mass of statements of attainment. There was strong feeling that it had been introduced too quickly and that teachers had not been properly consulted. This evidence informed Dearing's final report which recommended that the National Curriculum be slimmed down for 5–14-year-olds to make it less prescriptive, and to free 20 per cent of the teaching time for use at the discretion of the school. At KS4 only English, mathematics, single science, physical education, short courses in a modern foreign language and technology, religious education and sex education are now mandatory. To allow scope for vocational options at KS4, a General National Vocational Qualification (GNVQ)

was to be developed for 14–16-year-olds with the lead body for vocational qualifications (NCVQ). Their brief was also to investigate whether work undertaken as part of GCSE courses could count towards GNVQ accreditation. (For further information on vocational qualifications see Section 8.12.)

That the ten-level scale should be retained, but reformed, was also recommended. This was to be done by significantly reducing the statements of attainment and levels of attainment. Also recommended was that no further major changes should be made to the National Curriculum Orders for five years following the review. To satisfy the anti-SATs lobby, Dearing recommended that national tests were only to be held in core subjects. His recommendations were accepted and he moved on to a review of the post-16 curriculum.

Cross-curricular themes

In recognition that a broad and balanced curriculum requires that attention be given to a variety of issues not easily encapsulated within traditional school subjects, the National Curriculum Council added cross-curricular themes, dimensions and skills. These were added almost as an afterthought when it became increasingly obvious that the traditional subject model adopted was not well suited to the promotion of 'the spiritual, moral, cultural, mental and physical development of pupils at school and of society' and to the preparation of pupils 'for the opportunities, responsibility and experiences of adult life', as required by the Education Reform Act 1988. These cross-curricular themes were education for economic and industrial understanding, careers education, health education, environmental education and citizenship. Interesting research (Whitty *et al.*, 1994), using Bernstein's theories of the framing and classification of knowledge, analyses the relationship between cross-curricular themes and the core and foundation subjects. This research sought to discover how these themes would be organized and taught in schools. Schools were asked whether their delivery of the cross-curricular themes had changed as a result of the ERA 1988 and to identify how the themes were delivered. Various models of delivery emerged, including permeation through the core and foundation subjects, through personal and social education, through the pastoral system, and through integrated humanities.

Whitty *et al.* (1994) found that economic and industrial understanding was the most fully permeated theme. Health education and careers were the least permeated, having instead the status of quasi-subjects. Interviews were conducted with head teachers, teachers and pupils and classroom observations on cross-curricular work were conducted.

They found that some subject teachers in virtually all the schools visited intimated that they did not believe they should be asked to teach the themes. During an interview in one school a science teacher rejected his role in health education; he was quite happy to teach about tooth decay but not the necessity to clean one's teeth:

[Science teacher] *'It's not our job at all. We do do it, but we shouldn't have to. Parents should do it. Our main aim is to get them through the exam. . . . we're not nappy changers . . . nannies.'*
(Whitty *et al.*, 1994)

It was felt that cross-curricular themes 'polluted' the subject and were potentially threatening to the integrity of science as a subject. Thus the strongly framed and classified collection code of the core and foundation subjects sat uneasily with the weakly framed and classified integrated code of the cross-curricular themes.

One way of making sense of the difficulties of linking subjects and themes is Bernstein's work on different contexts being identified by different recognition and realization rules:

- Recognition rules are the clues that pupils use to determine what is a proper school subject. Does specialist equipment such as books, aprons, and PE kit have to be brought to lessons? Is there written work and homework?
- Realization rules tell pupils how or how not to demonstrate knowledge. What form does written work take, what is acceptable oral communica-

tion, activity in PE and what sort of things can be made in technology and art?

One of the key problems of using subjects to teach themes lies in the rules that relate to the use of *talk* in different contexts. The researchers found that pupils drew a strong distinction between subject discourses and talk, which they saw as not directly related to subjects. Chat in lessons had an illicit feel to it, associated with being off-task or something to get away with. It belonged to the world outside and was different from subject discourse. This ambiguity about the status of talk across different subjects and the importance of the talk of everyday life in teaching the themes also accounted for difficulties in a permeation model. If subject discourses are differentiated by their distinct recognition and realization rules, it will always be difficult to switch between subjects and themes.

8.11 The marketization of education

Hargreaves (1989) uses the term 'Kentucky Fried Schooling' to describe the education market as a system of franchises. What does the marketization of education mean in reality? Take, for example, the experience of the school cited in the following newspaper extract:

Commiserate, please, with Barclay School, a 980-seater mixed comp in Stevenage which won't be getting a £100 000 makeover courtesy of Glaxo Wellcome. Headteacher Russell Ball's imaginative scheme to rent the school's Henry Moore bronze (worth £2 million at the last count) to the multinational apothecary's Stevenage depot for four years in return for super new science labs has collapsed at the eleventh hour. Glaxo withdrew from the deal after union protests that it would be spending cash on a school at the same time as it was laying off its own scientists.
(*Guardian Education*, 9 January 1996)

School management teams spend a considerable amount of their time on budgets and raising money by sponsorship from local firms, or loaning out their Henry Moore sculptures. They have to ensure quality control and keep an eye on the opposition – the other schools in the area. Schools now have to compete for clients or consumers. They 'package' themselves using marketing strategies and by developing a corporate 'image': knowledge is now a 'product'. Parents have the power – 'parentocracy' (David, 1993) – to choose their school. Freedom from central government and local education authorities allows schools to determine how they spend their budget allocation.

Activity

a Develop the description of realization and recognition rules by comparing two subjects, one that is strongly framed and classified and one that is weakly framed and classified. How useful are the concepts?

b Carry out a small investigation into the importance of 'talk' or 'chat' in lessons. Interview students about how they view talk in different lessons. What are the rules that determine the use of talk and its status.

c National Curriculum history, English and geography are criticized by some teachers and educationalists for being Eurocentric and racist. Find copies of the most recent curriculum Orders for one of these subjects in your school or college library. Use content analysis to test the above claim.
(See also Section 6.5.)

K, U, I, A, E

Making sense of the marketization of education

It is useful to see the history of English education as a series of compromises between the old humanists, the industrial trainers and the public educators.
(Williams, 1961; quoted in Whitty, 1992)

The old humanists, or the neo-conservatives, represent the interests of the élite: they defend traditional academic education. The industrial trainers, or neo-liberals, defend narrow vocational or instrumental education. The public educators have struggled to develop an education relevant to all pupils in a democratic society. This provides a useful framework for analysing educational reform.

Until recently most battles were over the *form* of education rather than the *content*. ERA 1988 and the National Curriculum changed this. It was a victory for the old humanists defending the traditional grammar school curriculum. This was until the Dearing Report intervened and allowed pupils to choose a vocational path at 14 which marked the regaining of ground by the industrial trainers.

The 1988 legislation contains within it a powerful contradiction. The National Curriculum that it established prescribed, in law, what subjects and content teachers were to teach and how these were to be assessed. In this sense it was a centrally controlled prescriptive curriculum with very little choice for teachers, parents or pupils in the state system. This prescription sits uneasily with another part of the legislation which introduced 'the market' into education with the concept of LMS. This makes it a quasi-market. The 1988 Act also introduced other aspects of the market: formula funding, open enrolment, City Technology Colleges (CTCs), opting out, and grant-maintained schools. The introduction of the market was a victory for the New Right or neo-liberals.

What is 'new' about the New Right?

It is using the market in services like health and education that is 'new':

In the UK, the neo-Liberal, Hayekian vision of the market, to which Margaret Thatcher was converted in the mid-1970s, underpinned both the small-business, self-employment revolution in the UK economy in the 1980s and the market reforms being implemented in the education system and National Health Service.
(Ball, 1994, p. 106)

Hayek was an Austrian economist, not an educationalist. His ideas are favoured by the New Right (see Section 2.10) because they wanted to move away from monopolistic state provision to make schools more entrepreneurial and efficient, and to provide freedom of choice for the consumers – parents and their children. This was to be achieved by schools operating open enrolment, in which parents could choose which school to send their children, causing competition between schools. This, it was claimed, would improve educational standards generally. Schools would be forced to consider the wishes of parents rather than the needs of teachers and the social justice concerns of local education authorities. Schools were to manage their own budgets, free from the bureaucray of LEAs, with each pupil attracting a fixed sum. Successful schools would then become like successful businesses: cost-effective, with a positive image, responsive to consumer demand. They would produce a product (educated pupils) in line with National Curriculum specifications, though these subject specifications cannot be chosen. The philosophy behind this is a rational choice model in which the self-interested individual's choice will lead to what is in the interests of the whole community.

Discussion point
Discuss the proposition that if schools are more entrepreneurial, everyone will benefit.

The marketization of education is also an international phenomenon, with the New Right colonizing political agendas not only in the UK but also in the USA, Canada, New Zealand and Australia. The aim here is to make national economies internationally competitive as part of the global economy. (For more detail on this see Section 9.9.) Countries must make their economies more productive, efficient and innovative. Education and training are central to this.

Criticisms of education markets

Critics draw attention to the fact that markets in theory and markets in practice are very different. In practice, schools' selective and economic purposes become more important than their academic, pastoral and citizenship purposes. Markets put schools' educative purposes at risk because 'image' becomes more important than substance, the head teacher becomes a business-person, and resources for teaching get diverted into marketing.

The idea that all children have the right to equal access to good education is lost. Consumers get power but those with the greatest market capacity get the most. The market is only accountable to itself and therefore disregards policies and practices in education designed to redress inequalities. Also, the whole game is not taking place on a level playing field. Schools in middle-class areas which inherited good buildings and resources are in a much better position than schools in inner-city areas with run-down buildings and poor resources. League tables on which choices are to be made use raw data, making it impossible to compare like with like:

Activity

First read the extract 'Selling out on ideals to attract a better class'. Then role-play the choices facing Northwark Park school. Imagine you are at a governors' meeting where a decision must be made about employing a firm of educational consultants to implement plans to improve the image of the school. Students take on the roles of head teacher, parent-governor(s), teacher-governor(s), SEN coordinator and local employer representative. Debate the above decision and get the rest of the class to vote on the decision in the light of the debate.

I, A, E,

The implementation of market reforms in education is essentially a class strategy which has as one of its major effects the reproduction of relative social class (and ethnic) advantages and disadvantages. (Ball, 1994, p. 103)

8.12 **The academic/ vocational divide**

Why do England and Wales have such a divided system in post-16 education? Vocational education and training have always been the poor relation of the educational system. Skills training has traditionally been the apprenticeship system, developed outside the state system and privately organized by employers and craftsmen. This was 'on the job training' rather than theoretical study.

The theoretical study of science and technology was very under-valued in the UK in the nineteenth century compared with its European competitors.

Selling out on ideals to attract a better class

JUDITH JUDD

Northwark Park in London is a working-class school struggling for survival. It cannot attract enough pupils, and the majority of those it has are from ethnic minorities.

The school's governors and teachers know the answer: it must learn to compete for pupils in a marketplace set up by a government that funds schools according to the number of pupils they recruit, and fosters competition by the publication of exam league tables.

Northwark (not its real name) is committed to the comprehensive ideal, to opening its doors to all pupils whatever their needs, to co-operating with other schools and to teaching mixed-ability classes. Under sentence of death, however, it is rethinking its philosophy.

The story of Northwark is told in a study for the Economic Research Council by Sharon Gerwitz, Stephen Ball and Richard Bowe, researchers at King's College, London. They say the school is typical of those at the bottom of the league tables. Professor Ball suggests that their response is not, as the Government hopes, to start a programme of educational improvement, but to try to increase the intake of middle-class children and to reduce the proportion of problem pupils.

The decision to enter the market divides teachers and governors. At Northwark, the governing body, whose chair is an active socialist politician and which has a majority of left-wing members, is strongly opposed to abandoning the comprehensive ideal. The head and her deputy, however, appear to be toying with the idea of a grammar-school ethos and hinting at the attractions of selection.

The head comments: "I'm not saying we're looking for middle-class parents, but we're looking for motivated parents. Ideally, every school wants to be oversubscribed, so it does have some control over who comes in." Her deputy speaks admiringly of a nearby school: "I'm not saying it has lost its comprehensive ideals, but the head has set it up, as near as dammit, to a traditional girls' grammar school ... it's obviously attracted a lot of people."

In the drive for more pupils, the school's tradition of welcoming children with learning difficulties and teaching them in ordinary classes is thrown into doubt. The deputy head thinks special needs should be questioned: "That sort of provision is expensive, and if you're being asked to produce a good set of examination results, then you want as much of your resourcing as possible to be directed in that way."

The head of special needs feels educational considerations are already being subordinated to commercial ones. Staff, she suggests, are worried by the school's reputation for teaching special-needs children because of its effect on parents of more able children.

Much the same is happening over the exclusion of difficult children. The head and deputies are not discussing the educational merits of exclusions but the financial implications and whether or not they bring good publicity. Meanwhile, the school is attracting a large number of excluded 15-year-olds who depress its exam results.

The decision to review the policy of teaching children in mixed-ability classes has divided staff. The science department has begun to "set" children, and modern languages and maths may follow. The head of special needs is resisting the decision.

Researchers believe changes brought about by the marketplace in Northwark Park have implications for all British schools. They reflect a shift to a system that "rewards shrewdness rather than principles, and encourages commercial rather than educational decision-making. Concern for social justice is replaced by concern for institutional survival, collectivism with individualism, co-operation with suspicion and need with expediency."

Source: *The Independent*, 27 January 1994

Green (1990) explains this as part of the liberal tradition of *laissez faire* in education:

In part it resulted from the deep penetration within traditional education institutions of those conservative and anti-industrial values of the ruling elite. (Green, 1990, p. 293)

Liberal educational values stressed the importance of education for its own sake and its importance in relation to individual development. Élitist academic education should remain unsullied by being linked to usefulness in a future career, aiming rather to produce the 'educated' person. Vocational training, on the other hand, prepares people in a narrow way for a specific occupation. Recently this term has been replaced by 'new vocationalism', which seeks to produce trainees with flexible, transferable skills that can be used in a variety of low-skilled occupations. This is required because of a change in industrial production methods. (This issue is discussed in Section 9.4.)

The needs of industry: from Fordism to post-Fordism

There has been a move away from Fordism – line production of standardized mass-produced goods – to the requirement of flexible specialization and computerized control of production. (For more detail on this see Section 9.7.) This new emphasis on style, design and difference goes with what is called post-Fordism. Old proletarian-type industries, manufacturing and mining, have declined and are being replaced with service sector work. This requires a different type of labour force and training must meet these needs.

The fact that industrialists felt that education was not meeting these needs was expressed very strongly in what has been called the Great Debate. This arose from a lecture delivered in 1976 by prime minister James Callaghan, in which he called upon schools to respond more to the needs of industry. Several initiatives followed. For example, the Manpower Services Commission was set up in 1973. Then, in 1980, the Technical and Vocational Education Initiative (TVEI) was introduced to allow schools to bid for money to develop the work-related curriculum for 14–19-year-olds. The Youth Opportunities Programme (YOP) of 1978 was followed by the Youth Training scheme (YTS) in 1983, to be replaced by Youth Training (YT) in 1990 organized by Training and Enterprise Councils (TECs).

Sociological studies of such training schemes have been critical of their aims and their role in social reproduction. They have been seen as a means of covering up unemployment figures and providing a source of cheap labour. If young people went through a training scheme and still failed to find employment, then the responsibility for this was transferred to them. Such schemes were regarded as having a 'hidden agenda' of keeping young people off the streets and 'cooling out' young people who might otherwise turn to crime. Young people have complained about these schemes being a 'con' – not involving good training at all, but rather about them being used as skivvies (Lee, 1990).

Improvements to vocational training

Since the initiatives cited above, others have followed as attempts to improve the UK's training and industrial performance. The proliferation of vocational courses eventually led to the National Council for Vocational Qualifications (NCVQ) being set up to rationalize them. NCVQ devised five levels of National Vocational Qualifications in which sets of competencies were drawn up to be assessed by observation on the job. These have since been criticized for being expensive to administer, too narrowly defined, and related to the short-term needs of the employer rather than the long-term needs of the learner. They have resulted in an increasing number of certificates in circulation, rather than improving skills.

In May 1991 the Department for Education and Employment issued its White Paper *Education and Training for the 21st Century.* It set out the need for a range of general qualifications within the NVQ framework, and this was the beginnings of GNVQs. These are much broader taught courses, relating to wide vocational areas like health and social care or leisure and tourism. They include key skills of communication, numeracy and information technology. Assessment is by coursework and externally set and marked tests. They were designed so that students could combine them with A levels.

A national survey of school-leavers conducted by researchers at Southampton University (1996) indicates that government efforts to improve the status and value of vocational qualifications have failed. Students still regard such qualifications as work-related rather than leading on to higher education: only a quarter of those taking vocational qualifications were hoping to go on to such education. Students regarded them as second-rate qualifications, citing A levels as the gold standard and the natural route to a degree.

A levels: still the gold standard?

Despite repeated messages from successive education reports, the government has so far refused to change A levels. There has been some 'tinkering at the edges' in attempts to bring parity of esteem to the academic and vocational, but A levels – regarded as the gold standard of our élite system – remain unchanged. Only 30 per cent of each age cohort follow this academic track. Taking three or perhaps four A levels is widely regarded as too narrowly specialist. It compares unfavourably with all our major competitors, as do our staying-on rates and achievement post-16.

Defenders of A levels regard them as rigorous, even if they sometimes lack relevance. There are fears that this rigour and depth of knowledge will be lost if A levels are abolished.

The Higginson Report (1988) recommended that five subjects should be studied and that syllabuses be streamlined to allow for greater breadth. This is similar to Scottish highers and the International Baccalaureate. The government at the time endorsed the general aim of widening A levels but introduced

Activity

a First read the newspaper articles 'Aiming higher than Dearing?' and 'Compare France'. Draw up a list of the similarities and differences between the Dearing Report recommendations and those of the Labour Party in *Aiming Higher*.

b To what extent have the proposals for the British Baccalaureate and the French experience been adopted?

c Outline the problems and criticism of both approaches.

I, A, E

AS levels as a means of doing this. (A new AS Level will be introduced from 1998 following the Dearing Review.) These have not been a success and have

---

Aiming higher than Dearing?
KEN SPOURS AND MICHAEL YOUNG

The Dearing report has brought 14–19 qualifications to another watershed. The last was the 1991 White Paper *Education and Training for the 21st Century* which established a national triple-track qualifications system.

Now, for the first time we have overarching certification at different levels to broaden student programmes.

A week prior to the publication of Sir Ron's report, the Labour party launched its proposals for reforming the 14–19 curriculum, *Aiming Higher*.

In important respects the two documents occupy the same terrain – a framework approach to qualifications, emphasis on rigour, encouraging breadth, the merger of School Curriculum and Assessment Authority and the National Council for Vocational Qualifications.

However, a closer look reveals that they are pointing in significantly different directions. The main focus of the Dearing report is the development of a coherent national framework covering all present qualifications but keeping the three distinct tracks (A-levels, general national vocational qualifications and national vocational qualifications), and, in some ways, creating greater distinctions between them.

Dearing's dilemma is the tension between two objectives – providing distinctively different curricula for students with different abilities and trying to ensure that they are equally valued.

His answer is to introduce an overarching framework of certificates and diplomas to establish parity of esteem between academic and vocational learning and to increase the amount of external assessment in GNVQs.

His framework approach is essentially a way of increasing choices within the system as a whole while preserving A-levels.

Aiming Higher also starts with the idea of an overarching framework. However, it is presented as a first step towards a unified system in which diversity would be expressed in the range of modules (along the lines being developed in Scotland) and the separate tracks would eventually disappear. Implicit in *Aiming Higher* is a recognition that parity of esteem will only be achieved when students have a larger common component in their curricula and when the pathways operate within the same assessment and grading systems.

The proposal for a national framework in *Aiming Higher* has more in common with *Higher Still*, the Scottish model for post-16 reforms, than the three qualification tracks in England which Dearing seeks to retain.

On a number of key points the Labour party document takes a quite different view from Dearing. Notably on modularisation, review of NVQ/GNVQ design, establishing a credit framework and modular bank, extended study time, grade alignment and coursework assessment.

If these proposals were implemented by a Labour government it would mean a broader education for all and an improved vocational route and therefore it would have the basis for a substantially better system.

The key weakness in the Dearing report is its voluntarism. Post-16 schools and colleges will be able to choose to continue with A-levels and GNVQs and whether to offer the proposed new certificates and diplomas.

Here lies the possibility of proliferation of certification and increased confusion. In *Aiming Higher* there is also some ambiguity as to whether all students will be required to broaden their A level study and extend study time.

In government Labour is likely to have to face up to the policy alternatives: whether to find incentives to encourage greater breadth of study or to make greater breadth a requirement for all students.

As it stands, the comparative analyses suggest that there is sufficient common ground between Dearing and *Aiming Higher* for Labour to build on the framework proposals and to take "stakeholders" along towards a more unified system.

Ken Spours and Michael Young are based at the Post-16 Education Centre at the Institute of Education

Source: *Times Educational Supplement*, 19 April 1996

Compare France

... The French ... have created a more integrated system of general, technical and vocational *baccalauréats* offered within the *lycée* system. The qualifications all share the same prestigious title which confers right of entry to higher education; each track has a considerable component of general education, much of which is common to all; and modes of assessment and curriculum design have more consistency across the different tracks. The system has not yet achieved equal status for academic and vocational tracks but it has considerably more potential for doing so than our new system. It has also achieved a level of participation and qualification at 16–19 around 100% higher than our own (48% attain the *bac*).

Post-compulsory education in France and Britain in the 1970s faced many of the same problems which still face us now. It was highly elitist, not designed for mass participation and vocational routes had very low status. In France it has been improved through decisive and co-ordinated government action and by the adoption of a comprehensive approach to the planning of the whole post-16 sector. To achieve similar results in this country, our own government would need to adopt a similarly resolute and co-ordinated approach. Education and training would need to be brought together under a single department and planned as a whole; SEAC and NCVQ would need to be amalgamated with the new joint qualifications board responsible for creating a single national framework of qualifications. There would be an end to the absurd free-market approach to the setting and awarding of qualifications where over 300 independent bodies currently offer thousands of different certificates, each seeking its particular niche in the market, and in competition with the others.

If the government is serious about giving more choice to students, raising participation and achieving higher and more consistent standards, we need to see a little more rational planning and a lot less free-market dogma. In the meantime teachers will continue to struggle at the local level to make some sense out of the muddle created by myopic ministers and blind markets.

Source: Green (1993)

not been used to do what they were designed to do. The government also supported the notion of 'core skills' (now key skills) which all young people should acquire throughout the curriculum.

In 1990, the Institute for Public Policy Research published interesting proposals for a British Baccalaureate. These suggested a modular, unified system post-16 with three levels. They proposed that the whole of post-16 education should be modularized and include work-based or community-based learning. There would be a system of credit accumulation and transfer so that all students, including part-timers and adult-returners, could undertake a range of modules to build towards an Advanced Diploma. Such modules would be organized within three broad domains of study: social and human sciences; natural sciences and technology; and arts, languages and literature. Students would have to choose from three modules: core; specialist; or work- or community-based. This structure aimed to provide flexibility, choice, and a balance of intellectual and practical.

Further **reading**

The following is up-to-date and includes skills necessary for the A level examination:

- Heaton, T. and Lawson, T. (1996) *Education and Training*, Basingstoke, Macmillan.

A good introduction, with very up-to-date information, is:

- Trowler, P. (1995) *Investigating Education and Training*, London, Collins Educational.

The following, although a teachers' text, is recommended for its coverage of marketization of education, SEN and a post-structuralist approach to educational policy:

- Bowe, R., Ball, S. with Gold, A. (1992) *Reforming Education and Changing Schools: Case Studies in Policy Sociology*, London, Routledge.

The following is very useful and accessible, with good coverage of issues relating to equal opportunities:

- Gillborn, D. (1990) *'Race', Ethnicity and Education: Teaching and Learning in Multi-Ethnic Schools*, London, Unwin Hyman.

A very accessible introduction to all varieties of feminism and their approach to education is:

- Weiner, G. (1994) *Feminisms in Education: An Introduction*, Milton Keynes, Open University Press.

The following is useful for vocational training:

- Lee, D. (1990) *Scheming for Youth*, Milton Keynes, Open University Press.

Back issues of *Sociology Review* (formerly known as *Social Studies Review*) also contain many articles on this field of sociology and many others.

Exam **questions**

1 Evaluate the success of sociologists in explaining class-based inequalities in educational attainment.
   [25 marks]
   (IBS, Paper 2, Summer 1996)

2 Assess the contribution of studies of classroom interaction to sociological accounts of gender differences in education.   [25 marks]
   (IBS, Paper 2, Summer 1996)

3 To what extent might recent changes in the educational performance of boys and girls challenge established sociological explanations of gender inequalities in education? [25 marks] (IBS, Paper 2, Summer 1995)

4 a Briefly outline how social class might explain *one* aspect of ethnic inequality in education. [4 marks]

b Identify and illustrate *two* problems with using IQ tests to examine educational differences between ethnic groups. [4 marks]

c Outline the view that the family life of ethnic groups influences their educational attainment in the UK. [7 marks]

d Examine the significance of racism in the UK educational system in explaining ethnic inequalities in education. [10 marks] (IBS, Paper 2, Summer 1996)

Coursework **suggestions**

1 Investigate boys' under-achievement
Look at the exam results for your school or college. Do they conform to the national picture? Interview a sample of relatively successful and unsuccessful pupils about their GCSE results (be tactful). What factors affected their success or failure? How do these relate to different sociological explanations of under-achievement?

2 Investigate the place of sociology in the Curriculum
Why was sociology left out as a core or foundation subject in the National Curriculum? What is the status of sociology in the curricula of other countries? How is sociology regarded by the New Right?

3 Investigate the equal opportunities policy in your school or college
Does it include the needs of students with learning difficulties and disabilities? Is separation or integration or inclusion (or a combination) practised? Design and conduct a research project to investigate how well it meets the needs of students with learning difficulties and disabilities.

4 Investigate attitudes towards gender roles or the career aspirations of primary children
You could do this by getting them to draw pictures. Ask them to draw what toys boys or girls play with, or to depict what types of jobs boys and girls do when they grow up. Analyse these pictures and relate what you find to sociological theories of gender roles. Do children hold stereotyped views?

Work, organizations and leisure

9.1 Defining work and non-work

In order to discuss sociological theories of work, it is first of all necessary to discuss exactly what we mean by work, since without clearly differentiating it from other activities the sociology of work is in danger of becoming the sociology of everything.

Defining work: money or effort

Although the term work has a commonsense meaning as in the phrase 'I'm off to work', when we delve a little deeper it becomes clear that the meaning of the word can be contested.

Susan Himmelweit and Neil Costello (1995) provide the following examples and discussion of the problem of defining work:

One could say, for example, that it depends who the children are as to whether looking after them is to count as work or not. When you look after your own children that is not seen as work, but if you employ a child minder to look after them that is her job and it is her work . . . a market gardener who grows flowers to sell is more likely to see it as work than an amateur pursuing gardening as a hobby for its own sake. Similarly, some onerous tasks may count as work in some contexts but not in others. Writing lists and filling in forms is part of a clerical worker's job but it is also a chore most of us have to do at various times without considering it as work. . . . it is not what you are doing but the social context in which it is done which determines whether we see a particular activity as work or not.
(Himmelweit and Costello, 1995, p.10)

The construction of work as paid effort

The most important socially constructed distinction we use is that work is associated with paid labour, but we need to note that there is nothing natural or eternal about this (see also Section 2.3). Therefore, at some point, for some reason, the exchange of money must have achieved its present degree of prominence. While the exchange of money is a key feauture of capitalist societies, in order for capitalism to exist it is possible to identify a whole range of activities that are essential but which nonetheless are not based on the exchange of money.

Housework: work in reproducing society

The most obvious and important example is the work performed largely by women in the domestic sphere, i.e. housework – without which the whole social and economic system we live under would very quickly grind to a halt. (See also Sections 5.3 and 7.5.)

Why, if this is essential, is it differentiated from other activities by not leading to the exchange of money? This is a very good question and one which feminist sociologists have raised increasingly in the last 20 years. It is also a question which leads to the consideration of a very different way of conceptualizing work. Again Himmelweit and Costello (1995) summarize the differences between the two possible meanings of work that may arise out of this:

We have two meanings of the term 'work': one of them refers just to work done for money whereas the other usage of the term encompasses all activities necessary for the reproduction of society whether paid or not. Both correspond to ways in which the term 'work' can be used in everyday speech.

By the first definition, the content of the activity is irrelevant; it is the social context in which it is

done that defines it as 'work'. This is underlined by the tendency in our society for clear distinctions of time, place and attitude to be drawn between 'work' and 'non-work' in this first sense.

In the second sense, 'work' includes a number of activities that bring in no money to the person doing it, but are nevertheless important or necessary to society. Here it is the content of the work done that is significant and it may be done in different social contexts, for example be paid or unpaid, and still count as work.
(Himmelweit and Costello, 1995, p. 13)

Sociologists have been concerned to study the relationships between the two possible definitions of work to uncover the mechanisms by which one or the other is actually applied in concrete circumstances.

The three economies in society

Sociologists Jonathan Gershuny and Ray Pahl (1985) used the phrase the 'three economies' to try to capture all the possible different social relationships covering the expending of human effort. First they talk about the formal economy, by which is meant effort that leads to monetary reward and which is officially recognized as contributing to the economy. Secondly there is an informal economy which also involves effort but does not always lead to monetary reward or official recognition as work. This informal economy can be further sub-divided into two aspects:

- the household/communal economy
- the underground or hidden economy – 'the black economy'

They further argue that it is possible to identify ways in which specific tasks have moved from one economy to another over time; for example, they point to the way washing clothes started out in the home, then moved to the laundry, but now with the development of washing machines has moved back to the home (arrows 1 and 2 on Figure 9.1). Equally:

'the current prevalence of household construction work paid for in cash may indicate a shift from formal to underground, or 'black' production (arrow 3 on Figure 9.1), and if unemployment levels rise, the cost of black work will drop and some jobs, now DIY, will move across (arrow 6 on Figure 9.1)'.
(Gershuny and Pahl, 1985, p. 250)

Activity
Suggest an example of a change in economy location for each of the arrows numbered 4 and 5 in Figure 9.1.

A

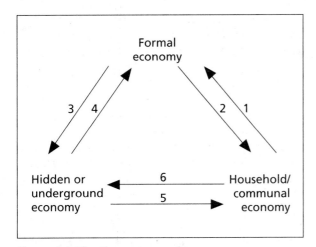

Figure 9.1 The three economies.
Source: Gershuny and Pahl (1985, p. 250)

One aspect of the household/communal economy is housework. The amount of effort expended here can be gauged from the figures in Table 9.1 which appeared in the *Daily Telegraph* in 1993.

Table 9.1 Average housewife's weekly timetable

	Hours	Cost if paid for(£)
Nanny	17.9	105.61
Cook	12.2	65.27
Cleaner	12.2	65.27
Laundress	9.3	35.34
Shopper	6.4	24.32
Dishwasher	5.7	21.66
Driver	2.6	11.70
Gardener	1.4	8.26
Seamstress	1.7	6.12
Other	1.3	5.20
Total	**70.7**	**348.75**

Source: *Daily Telegraph*, 3 February 1993

As the figures above show, the total number of hours is considerably higher than the number worked by those in full-time work and since the cost of providing these services through paid labour is considerably higher than average earnings (£316.90 in 1993) we can begin to understand why some feminists campaigned for wages for housework (see also Section 5.4).

It is of course important to say that cost should not necessarily be the criterion on which these things are decided, and that since housework is not paid, it is just as easy to point to the cost in terms of paid employment income lost to all the women who do, and have, engaged in housework. (See also Section 9.3.)

By communal economy, Gershuny and Pahl (1985) mean work done outside the household but without money exchanging hands. This covers the whole of what is normally called voluntary work (see also Section 14.2). It also covers kinship and neighbourhood-based networks providing services reciprocally.

By the hidden/underground economy, Gershuny and Pahl (1985) mean what is often called the black economy. This is where work is done in exchange for money but is not officially declared, particularly to the tax authorities. This is of course illegal and therefore poses the question of whether this should be considered as work or deviance. Interactionists might argue that it depends on whether you get caught. (See Section 11.5.)

Work and non-work

A consideration of some of the issues surrounding the definition of work therefore leads to the identification of a number of different ways in which it is possible to define work, and by extension, non-work. Non-work could be defined as those areas or aspects of society which are not included in the notion of work. Of course altering the definition of work will alter the definition of non-work too.

One important component of non-work is leisure activities (see Section 9.8), comprising those things we do for enjoyment; but depending on the definition of work adopted there are a number of other activities that, while not really leisure activities, might fit into the category of non-work, notably housework, crime and voluntary activities. Why these have in certain respects come to be defined as non-work is an interesting sociological question in itself, and one which exists as a backdrop to the rise and changing nature of the sociological study of work, most evidently in the case of arguments about the activities of women. While much of the rest of the chapter is concerned with the arena of paid employment, it must be remembered that exactly what this is cannot be taken for granted and that paid employment must itself be seen as a social construction and therefore open to debate concerning the possibility of change.

9.2 The sociology of work: classical approaches

The transformation of western European societies from being agriculturally-based to being industrially-based, along with the associated changes of the move from rural to urban societies (see also Sections 2.2 and 16.1), lay at the heart of the transformations which led to the rise of sociology. It is not surprising therefore that the world of work features heavily in the accounts of the founders of sociology. We will therefore examine these ideas with a particular emphasis on the concepts they developed.

Alienation and exploitation

Karl Marx is most famous for founding the approach to the study of society known as historical materialism (see also Sections 2.3 and 2.5). Marx believed that it was the material existence of people and their material needs (for example the need for food, clothing and shelter to survive) which were the most fundamental bases of society, and that it was the way the production of these goods and the social relationships entered into to produce them changed over time that created the process of social change and therefore history.

Marx starts from the premise that human beings are differentiated from other animals primarily in the way that they consistently act on nature to transform it to meet their needs. Labour is therefore a fundamental and central part of what it is to be human. In his writings Marx points to the vast accomplishments that human labour has achieved and the intrinsic satisfaction to be gained from the development of human skills in this respect.

However, he argues that under capitalism this great resource is utilized not for human need but for individual profit. Thus, for Marx, it is not the rise of industrial society but the system of capitalism that is the important motor. It is the fact that industrial production is organized along capitalist lines that is important.

Marx argues that in contracting to work for capitalists in return for wages, workers are actually entering an exploitative relationship. Marx follows the economists of the period in arguing that the only source of value in a good is the amount of socially necessary labour-time invested in its production. Only those who actually do work therefore create value. However not all of the profits from production flow to these workers, since the capitalists retain some for themselves in the form of profits and dividend payments on shares. The source of this money is the work undertaken by workers and Marx calls this an exploitative situation.

This is also the basis of his description of labour under capitalism as alienated labour. Marx argued that since workers were not paid the full value of their work, the goods that they produced would be too expensive for workers to afford. Workers could not therefore have the very products they created and in this sense the goods begin to have power over them. Additionally, since workers did not have any real control over the work process any more, the intrinsic satisfaction to be gained from labour had disappeared. Work is no longer a source of pride and offers no real potential for the full realization of the

self, and the fact that a person's work is valued simply in monetary terms divorces it from the potentially positive human relationships and cooperation that could characterize production. The continual division of tasks to increase profitability leads to dehumanizing, soul-destroying jobs and destroys the creative potential of human beings (see also Section 9.7).

Both alienation and exploitation as concepts imply that the social relationships surrounding work under capitalism are based on inherently conflictual relationships, even if no actual conflict occurs. Marx's view was quite clearly that such conflict would break out and it is on this basis that he describes capitalism as containing its own gravedigger since the workers employed by capitalism are the potential basis for Marx's revolutionary proletariat. The question of whether workers will fulfil this role is a central and continuing debate within sociology (see also Sections 4.7 and 9.5), but there were two key reasons contained within Marx's writings which at the very least provide the basis for such a hope. First, if workers are unable to afford the goods they produce, this will lead to unsold goods and a crisis of overproduction.

Secondly, earlier theorists had talked of labour as a commodity. Marx however pointed out that it is not labour that capitalists buy (since this would entail buying a person) but instead labour power. Because of the alienating nature of work under capitalism, and because labour is provided by people, in order to gain the maximum labour power from them capitalists would need to establish mechanisms of managerial control. This leads to the potential for disputes over production and the control of work.

The division of labour and *anomie*

Emile Durkheim (see also Section 2.3) was highly critical of the theories of those who in his time held similar ideas to those of the contemporary New Right (see also Section 2.10). Thinkers such as Jeremy Bentham and Herbert Spencer (see also Section 2.2) argued that the market was a fundamentally sound way of organizing production and society generally. Contracts, freely entered into, were seen as the basis of society. Durkheim was critical of this since he argued that there needed to be more than this, if only to ensure that people honoured their contracts. Without some potential for the enforcement of contracts, there would be little alternative but personal retribution if someone failed to deliver what they had promised to do.

He therefore argued that contracts and the market could only exist on the basis of a prior existing non-contractual element, that is a framework of commonly understood assumptions and agreement to run society on certain lines.

Having thus established that economic theories of society were inadequate since they failed to recognize the moral and social basis of economic behaviour, Durkheim set out to consider the implications of the industrial revolution and the wider social implications of this change. It is this which is the basis of his first book, *The Division of Labour in Society* (1938a, orig. pub. 1893).

Durkheim argued that since no one can be totally self-sufficient, production has always involved some division of labour whereby some people specialize in certain tasks. In traditional society, the division of labour is not particularly highly developed and people by and large engage in the same tasks (agricultural labour). As a result, their lives are very similar and it is this similarity which is what keeps society together. He calls this situation one of 'mechanical solidarity'. Common lifestyles and common ways of thinking create a common value system which Durkheim called the 'conscience collective'. This affects people similarly and, since it is strongly enforced, keeps people in line and therefore keeps society from descending into individualism, anarchy and chaos. However in contrast to other commentators on pre-industrial society, notably Tönnies (see Section 16.1), Durkheim viewed this all-encompassing conscience collective as rather suffocating and he was concerned to show how individual freedom could be reconciled with social stability.

However Durkheim was concerned with the social implications of this, namely that the individualism this implied could lead people to forget the need for societal integration.

The commonality of lifestyle which had been the glue which kept society together in pre-industrial times was clearly undermined by the specialization implied by the increased division of labour and Durkheim was worried that society might begin to fall apart. He argued that the solidarity which kept people together needed to be organized on a fundamentally different basis in industrial society, but nevertheless it was necessary for there to be some form of solidarity to avoid society falling apart.

Durkheim argued that it was possible for solidarity to develop in this situation on the basis that our dependence on others was increased by the development of specialization. It was this mutual dependence which brought forward a new form of solidarity, which Durkheim characterized as 'organic solidarity'.

He was, however, concerned that this might not develop automatically. He therefore argued for reforms and the development of associations of producers to develop the ethical and moral guidelines on which economic activity must be based if societal solidarity was to be upheld. This fact is highlighted by his discussion of the forced division of labour which he argued represented a pathological form of the development of the division of labour (see also Section 2.10). To admit that such a thing was possible was to underline his fear that society might not automatically develop along desirable lines.

The forced division of labour is the origin of Durkheim's most famous concept, 'anomie'. Durkheim argued that in the period of transition between mechanical and organic solidarity, an anomic division of labour might develop which is characterized precisely by the lack of normative regulation of action. People would not feel constrained by the collective conscience and would exist in a state of normlessness. People would therefore be unregulated. In essence, Durkheim is here describing life under a free-market based on extreme individualism and this point again underlines his opposition to such a way of organizing society. Durkheim outlined a number of possible indicators of the level of *anomie* in society, most famously the level of suicides (see Sections 3.3 and 11.11), but also the level of industrial conflicts and crime. It is because of these applications of the concept that it is most famous today. However it is also clear that the key implications of the concept, the need for some degree of moral regulation of society and the danger of theories based on pure individualism (such as the contemporary New Right), have more recently been discussed with the rise of communitarianism and the moralism evident in Tony Blair's New Labour, indicating a Durkheimian strand in contemporary thinking. (See also Section 2.10.)

The fact that Durkheim considered all the social ills he identified with *anomie* as being only temporary phenomena which would disappear when organic solidarity was properly established has led to a debate between Durkheimians and Marxists, since in this respect the argument that *anomie* is a temporary phenomenon leads to the conclusion that social ills can be solved under capitalism (albeit regulated capitalism) – a position Marxists would reject.

Bureaucracy and rationalization

The key contribution of Max Weber to an understanding of work and work organization is his theory of bureaucracy and rationalization. (See also Sections 2.3, 9.7 and 18.6.) These contributions are linked to his work on power and authority in society (see also Section 17.4). Basically Weber argued that the pre-eminent form of authority in pre-industrial times was that of traditional authority which was often religious-based and generally entailed the argument that the people in authority in society were somehow imbued with the authority of God. However the process of disenchantment that Weber saw, entailed a fall in the importance of religion and the divine right of kings had been fatally undermined by the French Revolution and calls for democracy.

Weber argued that we were therefore in modern industrial society much more likely to see authority based on legal and rational arguments. In short, this is a version of the argument that the rise of science was replacing religion as the key belief system. While many sociologists (notably the positivists, see Section 3.1) saw this as a very positive development, Weber's main contribution is to explore its potentially dark side.

While rationalization and the construction of bureaucracies staffed by technically competent, impartial officials getting on with specific tasks was seen as providing a potentially more efficient method of making decisions, and one less open to favouratism owing to the impersonality of the rules, Weber was very concerned that the power concentrated in the hands of the new bureaucracies would mean they might elude societal control and become an 'iron cage' threatening individual freedom. He therefore wrestled with the problem of how to benefit from the positive strengths of bureaucratic organization while avoiding the potential pitfalls. His debate led him to focus on democracy as a potential way to achieve such a balance. The extent to which this argument was accepted by later analyses of bureaucracy and organizations is the central theme of Section 9.7.

Keith Grint (1991) in his account of *The Sociology of Work* provides the following comparison of the approaches of these three classical thinkers:

while Durkheim focused on, and sought to extend, social solidarity, integration and control, Marx concerned himself with social fragmentation, disintegration and conflict and Weber developed his theory of rationality and bureaucracy. Durkheim was of a social democratic orientation though he was seldom directly involved in politics. . . . Marx, of course, was a revolutionary who railed against capitalism and actively promoted its overthrow. Weber, on the other hand, was a conservative liberal, anxious to preserve both the freedom of the individual and the sanctity of the German state. . . . Both Marx and Durkheim adopted structural arguments that delimited the influence and impact of individuals upon society and social change. The structural approach of Durkheim was, in fact, far more rigid and consistent than that of Marx. . . . Weber's individualistic sociology was clearly demarcated from the approaches of Marx and Durkheim.
(Grint, 1991, pp. 90–1)

The notions of alienation and exploitation have more recently been the subject of debates in industrial sociology (see Sections 9.5, 9.7), and Durkheim's notion of social solidarity was a key spur to the development of the Human Relations School of organizational analysis, again here criticizing views which

saw money as the sole determinant of behaviour. The theory of rationalization has an importance which spread far outside the sociology of work, but it does impact clearly on debates about organizational behaviour. These concepts are therefore still utilized in the sociology of work and organizations today.

Activity

Write a short explanation of the following concepts in your own words.

Alienation
Exploitation
The division of labour
Anomie
Rationalization
Bureaucracy

U, I

9.3 Patterns of employment in contemporary UK society

This section considers recent evidence about the experience of work as the basis for considering how patterns of employment are structured in contemporary Britain and how important work remains for diverse groups of people today. It will focus largely on gender and ethnic inequalities.

Measuring work participation in contemporary Britain

There are two official measures of employment used in the UK today (see Section 3.11). First the *Labour Force Survey* (LFS) which is based on interviews of people in households and is produced quarterly. The Summer 1995 *Labour Force Survey* showed that there were a total of 25.5 million persons in employment in the UK, of whom 19.3 million were in full-time employment and 6.2 million were in part-time employment.

Secondly there are the Workforce in Employment (WiE) statistics, derived from surveys of employers, also available quarterly. This measures employment that contributes to economic output as measured by gross domestic product (GDP), and is therefore a measure of jobs rather than people. One important implication of this is that people who have two jobs (800 000 people in 1995) would only be counted once on the LFS but twice on the WiE (this explains the greater number of part-time jobs shown in the WiE). In the summer of 1995, according to this measure, there were a total of 25 million persons in employment, comprising 18.1 million in full-time employment and 7.0 million in part-time employ-

Table 9.2 Comparison of published estimates by full-time and part-time status (GB, millions, seasonally adjusted)

LFS quarter / WiE quarter	1992				1993				1994				1995	
	Spr Mar	Sum June	Aut Sept	Wint Dec	Spr Mar	Sum June	Aut Sept	Wint Dec	Spr Mar	Sum June	Aut Sept	Wint Dec	Spr Mar	Sum June
Full-time														
LFS	19.3	19.3	19.1	19.0	19.0	19.0	18.9	19.0	19.0	19.1	19.2	19.2	19.3	19.3
WiE	18.7	18.5	18.2	18.1	18.1	18.1	18.1	18.1	18.1	18.0	18.1	18.1	18.1	18.1
Difference	0.7	0.7	0.9	0.9	0.9	0.9	0.9	0.9	0.9	1.0	1.1	1.1	1.1	1.2
Technical factors	-0.1	-0.1	-0.1	-0.1	-0.2	-0.1	-0.2	-0.2	-0.1	-0.1	-0.3	-0.3	-0.2	-0.3
Remaining difference	0.6	0.6	0.8	0.8	0.7	0.8	0.7	0.7	0.8	0.9	0.8	0.8	0.9	0.9
Part-time														
LFS	5.9	5.9	5.9	5.9	6.0	6.0	6.1	6.1	6.1	6.1	6.1	6.2	6.1	6.2
WiE	6.6	6.6	6.6	6.7	6.7	6.7	6.8	6.8	6.8	6.8	6.9	6.9	7.0	7.0
Difference	-0.7	-0.7	-0.6	-0.7	-0.6	-0.6	-0.6	-0.7	-0.6	-0.7	-0.7	-0.7	-0.8	-0.7
Technical factors	0.1	0.0	0.0	0.0	0.0	0.0	0.1	0.2	0.2	0.3	0.2	0.2	0.4	0.3
Remaining difference	-0.6	-0.7	-0.6	-0.7	-0.6	-0.6	-0.5	-0.5	-0.4	-0.4	-0.5	-0.5	-0.4	-0.4

Source: *Labour Market Trends*, (January 1996, p. 26)

ment. As can be seen, there is a significant discrepancy between the two figures (see Table 9.2).

The Times' labour correspondent Philip Bassett (1996) argued that this showed that:

Not only does the Government not know how many people are out of work in the UK, it doesn't even know how many people are in work . . . Does this matter? Well, yes. In terms of knowing about what is going on in both the labour market and the economy more generally, the number of people in productive work is clearly a key factor. Politically, job growth is a key goal: ministers proclaim the growth of jobs as a key indicator of the claimed success of Government policy.

(Bassett, 1996, p. 27)

Keith Perry (1996) of the Central Statistical Office (now the Office for National Statistics) argues that in the 1980s the two series of measures showed similar trends, but that since 1992 they have diverged:

Although the WiE was thought by some to more accurately reflect the 1992 fall in economic activity, the LFS seemed to be the more consistent measure during the early stages of the economic upturn.

(Perry, 1996, p. 20)

Perry argues that the technical differences between the two measures might explain some of the discrepancy (for example, the LFS includes unpaid family workers – i.e. people who work in a family

business – while these are excluded from the WiE). However, Bassett analysed figures from both the LFS and the WiE and argued that while the technical differences would mean that the actual numbers would differ, if they are both to be regarded as valid, the trends they reveal should be the same. However:

analysis of the figures over a year to last summer shows that in many cases they are not. The LFS, for instance shows employment up by 1.2 per cent. WiE figures show a fall of 0.4 per cent. Male employment is rising twice as fast in the LFS than in the WiE, while part-time work is increasing twice as rapidly in the WiE measure compared with the LFS.

(Bassett, 1996, p. 27)

He concludes that there is no evidence to show that one series is more reliable than the other, and this leaves us with a still unexplained gap of 500 000 in the figures for the number of people in work.

Gender and work

The pattern of women's involvement in paid employment has been an area of growing interest because women are increasingly involved in paid employment, and it is likely that at some point in the near future women will constitute a majority of the workforce. In certain areas of the UK, for example the north, the south-west and Scotland, this is already the case (Roberts *et al.*, 1996). In the UK overall in 1995, women formed 49.3 per cent of employees according to the Department of Employment's 1995 *Annual Employment Survey*. Frances Sly (1996) points out that in 1995 67 per cent of single women and 73 per cent of married and cohabiting women were economically active.

Perhaps the most important factor in determining whether women are economically active or not is the presence of children, and more specifically the age of the youngest child. Sly (1996) reports the following rates for women being economically active:

Table 9.3 Economic activity of women and age of children

Age of youngest child	Percentage economically active
0–4	52
5–10	71
11–15	78
Without children under 16	71

Source: Adapted from Sly, (1996, p. 93)

Childcare obligations also seems to explain why so many women work part time, allied to the very low level of publicly funded childcare support in the UK. Sociologists Rosemary Crompton and Nicky Le Feuvre (1996) argue that the differences in the level of such support are the key reason for the fact that while in France only 20 per cent of women work part time, the equivalent figure for the UK is 40 per cent:

Before the Second World War, British social policy in respect of child welfare worked so as to keep women out of the labour market in the interests of both the health of their infants and the national economy. In general, British women have been treated for social policy purposes as mothers, rather than as workers and, moreover, as mothers who will be provided for by a man.
(Crompton and Le Feuvre, 1996, p. 430)

They argue that there is still the expectation that women will primarily concern themselves with the household in support of their male partner's career (see also Sections 5.3 and 7.5). They also point out that if women wish to get on they are almost required to adopt 'masculine' patterns of work, meaning full-time continuous work. Obviously given the lack of childcare this in effect means women choosing between career and children.

Women and the workplace: segregated experiences

While it is clear that women's involvement in paid employment is increasing, we need to ask what types of job women are filling in order to consider the extent to which such involvement provides a degree of economic autonomy for women.

The first point is the much greater level of part-time working among women. In 1995 about 43 per cent of women in employment worked part time and women comprised 84 per cent of all part-time workers. In comparison 6 per cent of men in employment work part time (Sly, 1996). However since 1985 both full-time employment and part-time employment for women have risen by 10 per cent, so the rise in employment of women cannot be accounted for solely by changes in the structure of the labour market with the growth of part-time jobs. Indeed there is evidence that the changes in the labour market with the growth of temporary jobs have affected men more than women. Between 1985 and 1995 the number of women in permanent jobs rose by 12 per cent, while the equivalent figure for men fell 5 per cent. Both groups experienced a large rise in the number of temporary (fixed term or casual work) employment, with a 21 per cent rise for women and a 71 per cent rise for men. It is also the case that the gender differential in pay levels is much lower in part-time work than in full-time work and perhaps surprisingly, the average earnings of part-time workers are lower for men than for women (see Table 9.4) (although this might be affected by the fact that most male part-time workers tend to be young).

Table 9.4 Average gross hourly earnings of full and part-time employees of working age

Spring 1995 (UK)

	Women 16-59	Men 16-64	Female as % male
All employees	£6.19	£8.22	75.3
Full-time	£6.60	£8.40	78.6
Part-time	£5.63	£5.41	104.0

Source: Adapted from *Labour Force Survey,* (Spring 1995)

While these statistics indicate something of the nature of the changes described as the development of the flexible labour market (see also Section 9.4), and while they indicate that some men may be suffering the effects of this, this does not necessarily mean that women are gaining at the expense of men. In order to look at this we need to look at the type of jobs that women are involved in. Two concepts developed by feminist sociologists to explain the gender divisions in paid employment are useful here: horizontal segregation and vertical segregation.

Horizontal segregation refers to the way in which men and women are separated into different occupations and vertical segregation refers to the way that men and women tend to hold jobs at different levels in hierarchical structures.

Horizontal segregation

Evidence on horizontal segregation is a standard feature of *Labour Force Surveys*. In their survey of women and employment using statistics for 1980 from the Department of Employment, Jean Martin and Ceridwen Roberts (1984) reported that 63 per cent of women worked only with other women. In relation to the husbands of these women, 81 per cent worked only with other men. This clearly underlines the extent to which workplaces are horizontally segregated. More recent information on this can be found in the figures for Spring 1995 which are shown in Figure 9.2.

Activity

a From the information in Figure 9.2, identify the two industries with the highest proportion of women workers and the two with the highest proportion of male workers.

b Identify the two industries with the highest proportion of women part-time workers and the two with the lowest proportion of women part-time workers.

c Write a short summary of the patterns in the table.

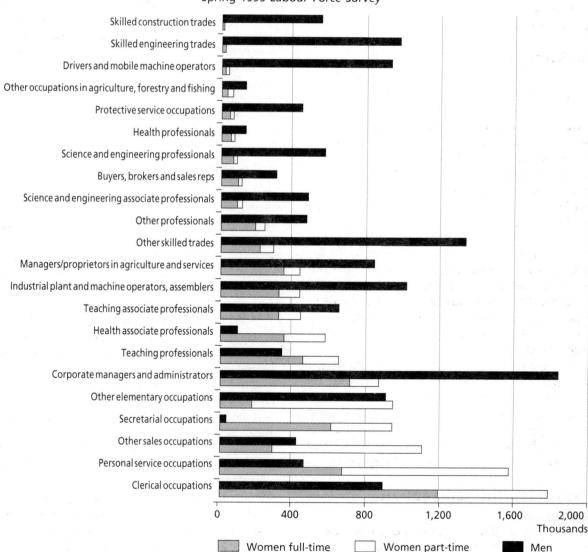

Figure 9.2 Numbers of women and men of working age in employment by occupation, Great Britain; Spring 1995 (not seasonally adjusted). Source: *Labour Market Trends*, (March 1996, p. 97 data from *Labour Force Survey*)

The survey that Table 9.4 is derived from found that the employment of men was roughly equally divided between manual and non-manual work, but that 70 per cent of women employees worked in non-manual jobs. Furthermore it found that 51 per cent of all women in employment worked in four occupation groups: clerical, secretarial, sales and personal service occupations. By looking in even more detail at horizontal segregation, that is at the level of individual occupations, we find that 92 per cent of receptionists are female, as are 87 per cent of nurses, 75 per cent of clerks and secretaries and 63 per cent of teachers. In contrast the occupations which are most male-dominated are in engineering, mechanics and agriculture.

The fact that there are no occupations where the gender division is equal (teaching is perhaps the nearest, although issues of vertical segregation matter here as we shall see) means that horizontal segregation continues to be relevant.

Vertical segregation

Vertical segregation is the grade at which people are located within occupations. While teaching is the occupational category closest to being equally divided between men and women, male and female teachers can be clearly differentiated in terms of the grade they work at. A National Union of Teachers (NUT) (1988) survey in 1988 found that while 50 per cent of male primary school teachers were head teachers, only 15 per cent of female primary school teachers were.

In relation to the effect of labour market segregation on pay, Michael Webb (1982) points to the following factors as explaining pay differences between males and females: 7 per cent could be accounted for by the differential distribution of men and women among occupations, 13 per cent by differences in hours worked and almost 80 per cent by differences within occupations.

In their research into the issue of work in five localities, Paul Bagguley and Sylvia Walby (1988) found that between 1971 and 1981 there had been a decline in the degree of vertical segregation between men and women as women gained access to the higher level jobs, but there had also been an increase in the extent of horizontal segregation.

Explaining the segregation by gender

Crompton and Le Feuvre (1996) provide the following summary of feminist arguments on this issue:

feminists have seen the restrictions on women's participation in paid employment . . . as reflecting the patriarchal control of women by denying them access to the kinds of employment which would generate a sufficient income to live independently (Crompton and Le Feuvre, 1996, p.427)

This still leaves open to debate the actual mechanisms by which such patriarchy operates.

Dual-systems theories

Heidi Hartmann

Dual-systems theorists focus on how patriarchy and capitalism together oppress women (see also Section 5.4). Heidi Hartmann points to the way this operates in relation to employment:

Job segregation by sex. . . is the primary mechanism in capitalist society that maintains the superiority of men over women, because it enforces lower wages for women in the labour market. Low wages keep women dependent on men because they encourage women to marry. Married women must perform domestic chores for their husbands. Men benefit then, from both higher wages and the domestic division of labour. This domestic division of labour, in turn, acts to weaken women's position in the labour market. Thus, the hierarchical domestic division of labour is perpetuated by the labour market, and vice versa.
(Hartmann, 1982, p.448)

Sylvia Walby

Perhaps the most substantial attempt to provide a dual-systems theory lies in the work of Sylvia Walby (1986, 1990). In relation to the sphere of paid employment, she argues that there are three key features of gender relations. First women earn less than men. Secondly they participate in paid employment less than men, and thirdly they do different jobs from men. (See also Section 5.3.)

Although she agrees with Hartmann that we need to consider the interplay between capitalism and patriarchy, Walby argues that Hartmann does not pay enough attention to the way in which there is a degree of tension between these two structures and she sets out to consider this.

First she argues that the emphasis on the family wage (meaning the idea that men on their own should earn enough to keep themselves and their family) is overplayed since many households do not operate on this basis. She points to the way in which the two demands on women's time, namely as workers for capitalists and as providing domestic work for husbands (see Section 7.5), potentially come into conflict, since time spent on one leads to less time for the other.

From exclusion to segregation

She points to the arguments which developed after

women first entered factories in large numbers in the mid-nineteenth century and the reaction which led to their exclusion from certain forms of employment under the Factory Acts legislation. This provides an example of her argument that in the past the key strategy for the subordination of women in relation to paid employment was exclusion.

This strategy is, however, no longer seen as the crucial one owing to developments such as the greater involvement of women in the workforce during the World Wars and the political campaigns which were waged to gain citizenship rights for women (see also Section 5.4). These had an effect on the way state policy reacted to the issue of women's employment. They undermined the basis of exclusionary strategies and led to a shift towards job segregation as the key contemporary basis of the oppression of women. Walby provides the following summary of what she means by segregation approaches:

The most important new form of labour market segregation in Britain since the 1940s is that of the division between part-time and full-time work, the former being performed almost exclusively by married women. The conditions of work are different between part-time and full-time in two main respects: part-time jobs pay less than full-time ones on average; part-timers have less secure contracts of employment, making them vulnerable to dismissal.
(Walby, 1990, p. 54)

She also points to the concepts of horizontal and vertical segregation, and argues that recent experience in the UK has been for a decline in vertical segregation to be matched with a rise in horizontal segregation.

So in the context of her overall argument about the changing nature of patriarchy, Walby argues that in relation to the sphere of paid employment this has taken the form of a shift from exclusionary strategies to segregation strategies as ways of enforcing gender inequalities in the paid employment sphere. These obviously have an effect on other areas of life. She concludes her arguments on paid employment with the following three points:

1 The Labour market is more important and the family less important as the determinant of women's labour force participation than is conventionally assumed.
2 Women's lesser participation in paid work is a result of material constraints rather than a matter of 'choice' or of cultural values, as is frequently argued.
3 Politics and the state are much more important in the structuring of the sexual division of labour than is often recognised; we need an analysis not merely of economy, but of political economy.
(Walby, 1990, p. 56)

Women, work and choice: Catherine Hakim

The idea that the reasons for the unequal position of women in the paid employment sphere are material and structural constraints rather than personal choice has recently surfaced as the basis of an argument raised in various publications by Catherine Hakim (1991, 1995, 1996b). She argues that it is primarily a question of choice that women have a different and unequal position in the paid employment sphere. Such an approach is clearly contrary to the approach of Walby and other feminist approaches. (See also Section 5.3.)

Hakim argues that the idea that inequalities in the workplace are the result of structural determination (whether capitalism or patriarchy) is wrong, and suggests instead that gender inequalities result from the differential behaviour and attitudes of men and women to work. To put it in simple terms, she argues that women have less commitment to work and it is this which is the basis of their inferior pay rewards. First she argues that, looked at in terms of the hours of paid employment:

there was absolutely no increase in the volume of female employment, measured in full-time equivalent numbers, from World War Two up to 1987 in Britain. Rather than underlining the increase in women's employment, we should be seeking to explain the long-term stability of female employment despite dramatic social and economic change over the past century.
(Hakim, 1995, p. 431)

Her own explanation for the pattern of stability she has outlined is basically that men and women do hold differential attitudes towards paid employment and that men have higher levels of commitment to work. She argues that when asked if they would continue to work, even if they did not need to financially, men outscore women, with two-thirds of women still preferring to have a job, compared with three-quarters of men. She argues that there is little difference among men and women working full time and that the overall difference emerges when looking at part-time working. She further argues that the level of commitment difference between full-time and part-time workers is not merely quantitative but qualitative as well (see also Section 3.6). This leads her to argue that we can identify two groups of women: first career women and secondly those women who:

give priority to the marriage career, do not invest in what economists term 'human capital', transfer quickly and permanently to part-time work as soon as a breadwinner husband permits it, choose unde-

manding jobs 'with no worries or responsibilities' when they do work, and are hence found concentrated in lower grade and lower paid jobs which offer convenient working hours with which they are perfectly happy.
(Hakim, 1995, p. 434)

She further argues that childcare problems cannot be the main reason affecting women's work since part-time working and not working at all extends well beyond those with childcare responsibilities.

Overall, her argument suggests that the lower commitment to paid employment by women is the key reason why part-timers and therefore women are treated differently in the labour market. In essence, it is women's choices about orientation to work which lead to gender inequalities in relation to paid employment.

Criticisms of Hakim

Rosemary Crompton (1997) argues that there are flaws in Hakim's argument. First she disputes the division between committed and uncommitted women workers developed by Hakim, pointing out that Hakim herself says that women will switch between these groups, which rather questions their existence as separate clear groups. Her evidence points to the fact that women want to be able to combine both domestic and market commitments and do therefore make choices. However she argues that Hakim consistently underplays the structures within which such choices have to be made. In particular she cites the development

of the 'male breadwinner' model and the way this has been enshrined in welfare state and other social policy developments (see Section 14.3), meaning that explanations based purely on notions of choice cannot explain all inequalities:

To be sure, women can and do make choices – although in aggregate, their relative lack of power and resources relative to men means that both today and in the past, they have been less able to do so than the opposite sex. Women – and men – can choose but are also constrained, a fact which lies at the root of sociological explanations of human behaviour. The tension between 'structural' and 'action' explanations is a long-standing one in sociological theory and research, and has not yet been satisfactorily resolved . . . However I am concerned that Hakim's oversimplified rendering of the complexities of the structuring of the gender division of labour, with its emphasis on one 'side' (choice) to the exclusion of the other, might focus the argument on the sterile dichotomies of choice or constraint, structure or action
(Crompton, 1997, p. 4–5)

(The debate surrounding Hakim's arguments is also considered in detail in Section 5.3)

Ethnic minorities and employment

There are clear differences by ethnic group (see also Chapter 6) in the economic status of people, and these differences are reinforced by gender differences as can be seen from Table 9.5.

Table 9.5 Economic status of people of working age: by gender and ethnic group, (GB, percentages, Spring 1995)

	White	Black[1]	Indian	Pakistani/ Bangladeshi	Other[2]	All ethnic groups[3]
Males						
Working full time	72	49	65	41	51	71
Working part time	5	8	7	8	8	5
Unemployed	8	21	10	18	12	9
Inactive	15	22	18	33	29	15
All (=100%)(thousands)	16,993	273	306	216	224	18,017
Females						
Working full time	38	37	36	12	30	38
Working part time	29	15	19	6	16	28
Unemployed	5	14	7	7	8	5
Inactive	28	34	38	75	46	29
All (=100%)(thousands)	15,420	296	279	191	238	16,428

[1]Includes Caribbean, African and other black people of non-mixed origin.
[2]Includes Chinese, other ethnic minority groups of non-mixed origin and people of mixed origin.
[3]Includes ethnic group not stated

Source: *Labour Force Survey*, quoted in *Social Trends*, (1996, p. 83)

Church and Summerfield (1996) in their *Social Focus on Ethnic Minorities* point out that in spring 1995, while 82 per cent of black Caribbean men and 70 per cent of black Caribbean women were economically active, only 66 per cent of Bangladeshi men and 20 per cent of Bangladeshi women were. While white males had an unemployment rate of 8 per cent, the rate for Pakistani/Bangadeshi men was 18 per cent and that for black men was 21 per cent. These differences will have an important effect on inequality given the importance of paid employment as a source of income.

The employment of ethnic minorities also appears to show the characteristics of segregation explored earlier in the section on gender. Employment in distribution, hotel and catering, are higher among South Asian groups than among whites, but both groups are likely to be employed in manufacturing industry, whereas for blacks the most likely sectors of employment are public administration, health and education. Nursing is one occupation with a large proportion of ethnic minority workers, but while 34 per cent of whites and 35 per cent of Asian nurses were charge nurses or senior nurses, only 29 per cent of black nurses were in these grades.

The employment of ethnic minorities in the Civil Service also shows that they are clearly under-represented among all but the lowest clerical grades.

Table 9.6 and other statistics show that ethnicity is a clear factor in determining the type and level of job occupied, generally meaning that ethnic minorities suffer worse working conditions and worse standards of remuneration.

Table 9.6 Percentages of UK civil service staff belonging to ethnic minorities: by grade level, 1989 and 1995

	1989	1995
AA	6.5	7.6
AO	5.6	6.7
EO	2.9	4.3
HEO	1.7	2.4
SEO	1.2	2.1
Grade 7	1.2	2.6
Grade 6	2.2	2.8
Grade 5	1.8	2.5
Grade 4	0.6	0.4
Grade 3	0.0	0.2
Grade 2	0.0	0.0
Grade 1	0.0	0.0
All grade levels (thousands)	18	23

Source: Cabinet Office, Church and Summerfield (1996, p. 43)

Statistics show that people from ethnic minority groups are much more likely to be temporary workers. In spring 1995, 7 per cent of white workers were temporary, compared with 8 per cent of Indian workers, 9 per cent of black workers and 13 per cent of Pakistani/Bangladeshi workers. Three-quarters of workers from Pakistani/Bangladeshi groups said this was because no permanent work was available, compared with less than half giving this reason among white workers. This ethnic difference is important in the context of the debates about the spread of flexible working practices. (See Section 9.4.)

These points contribute to differences in hourly pay rates as shown in Table 9.7.

Table 9.7 Average hourly pay of full-time employees: by gender, Winter 1994 to August 1995 (GB, £ per hour)

	Males	Females	All
Black	7.01	6.71	6.88
Indian	8.01	5.75	7.12
Pakistani/ Bangladeshi	6.87	4.78	6.43
Other ethnic minorities	7.70	6.66	7.32
White	8.34	6.59	7.73

Source: *Labour Force Survey*, Church and Summerfield, (1996, p. 47)

Explaining labour market inequalities by ethnic group

These inequalities have sometimes been explained by the idea that ethnic minorities along with women occupy a secondary labour market. This idea is explained by Webb as follows:

It is often argued that the 'secondary workforce' is composed of a number of groups which when needed can be channelled into jobs of low status and pay, and that ethnic minorities as well as the majority of women are such groups. Ethnic-minority women in the labour market may have a double handicap and form a very distinct segment in terms of levels of participation and types of occupation.
(Webb, 1982, p. 166)

Dual labour market theory

The notion that secondary labour markets exist is a development of the broadly Weberian notions of John Rex and Sally Tomlinson (1979), who argued that there are dual labour markets with a primary labour market consisting of well-paid secure jobs, and a secondary labour market with low wages and poor working conditions. They argued that this, along with discrimination in housing, meant that ethnic minorities did not identify with the white working class and this analysis has latterly been developed into the structural version of the underclass thesis. (See Sections 4.8 and 6.4.)

Reserve army of labour thesis

Marxist theorists have argued that ethnic minorities constitute a reserve army of labour who form a distinctive strata within the working class because of the discrimination they face from racism. They argue that their position derives from the fact that capitalism faced labour shortages, having exhausted the supply of indigenous women, and therefore turned to immigration as a source of a reserve pool of cheap labour which could be exploited. The issue of whether this means that they constitute a part of the working class distinctly separate from white workers or merely a disadvantaged part of the working class, is a source of debate among Marxists, with Stephen Castles and Godula Kosack (1973) taking the former position and Annie Phizacklea and Robert Miles (1980) taking the latter. (See Section 6.4.)

David Mason (1995) in his book *Race and Ethnicity in Modern Britain* points out that the position of ethnic minorities has been affected by the fact that large-scale migration in the 1950s (see Section 6.2) occurred because there were labour shortages which meant white workers could move up into higher level jobs, leaving the worst jobs for the new immigrants. This, and continuing racism, affects their position today. One contemporary example of the argument that racism contributes to the ethnic composition of the workforce arose in relation to a dispute at Ford UK where racism was alleged. *Guardian* journalist Seamus Milne (1997) reported that while 45 per cent of Ford shop floor workers are from ethnic minorities, only 2 per cent of prized jobs as drivers in Ford's truck fleet are.

9.4 Contemporary theories of work and society

This section considers debates surrounding the notion of a growth of flexibility and the suggested transition to post-industrial and post-Fordist societies. Theories of the post-industrial society suggest that we are moving from a period dominated by manufacturing industry and manual workers to one where the service sector and non-manual workers dominate. This has implications for debates about the class composition of the workforce. The more recent theories of a transition to post-Fordism also have implications for class analysis, since they

invariably also suggest either a decline in manual work, or the creation of important divisions within the working class. In effect, therefore, both these theories by implication consider the changing class composition of the workforce. (See also Section 4.7.)

The second industrial revolution?

The reason such a notion has arisen is the observation that the way we organize work has undergone a number of dramatic changes in recent years. The first element of this concerns the changing distribution of employment in terms of the three sectors of the economy, namely the primary, secondary and tertiary sectors. By primary sector is meant employment in agriculture and extraction, mainly mining. By secondary is meant employment in manufacturing – making things. It is the shift from predominance of the first of these to predominance of the second which is the central process underlying the industrial revolution. (See also Section 2.2.)

The tertiary sector means employment in service industries such as banking, hotel work or cleaning. One of the important trends noticed in recent years has been the rise of jobs in the service sector and the decline (both absolute and relative) in manufacturing industry, both in the UK and in other western advanced industrial economies.

The move to a service economy?

Ian Marsh *et al.* (1996) point to the change taking place in the distribution of the workforce in the UK as follows:

In the UK in 1946 the manufacturing, construction and mining industries employed about 45 per cent of the labour force. By 1990 this had dwindled to around 20 per cent. The teaching profession now employs more people than mining, the steel industry and shipbuilding combined.
(Marsh *et al.*, 1996, p. 160).

Looking at even more recent figures, Roberts *et al.* (1996) point out that the 1995 *Annual Employment Survey* in Great Britain showed that 75 per cent of employees worked in the services sector and 18 per cent in manufacturing. We can also look at the distribution of employees divided into men and women (see also Section 9.3) and whether they have full-time paid employment or part-time paid employment (see Table 9.8 and the associated Activity box on page 339).

The post-industrial economy thesis

This notion that advanced economies were moving from an industrial to a post-industrial stage first arose in sociology in the 1960s and 1970s. Daniel Bell (1973) argued that we were witnessing such a change characterized as he saw it by the change

Table 9.8 Employees in industry in Great Britain: September 1995 (thousands)

	Full-time	Part-time	All
Men			
All industries and services	9,735.3	1,135.3	10,870.6
Agriculture, forestry and fishing	176.7	41.8	218.5
Index of production and construction ind.	3,599.8	62.6	3,662.5
Manufacturing industries	2,750.2	50.0	2,800.2
Service industries	5,958.7	1030.9	6,989.6
Women			
All industries and services	5,801.2	4,766.5	10,567.7
Agriculture, forestry and fishing	33.9	27.6	61.4
Index of production and construction ind.	1,050.2	269.6	1,319.8
Manufacturing industries	925.9	218.5	1,144.5
Service industries	4,717.2	4,469.3	9,186.4

Source: Roberts *et al.* (1996, p. 491)

Activity

a Calculate the percentage of male employees working in service industries, and the percentage of female employees working in service industries according to the figures in Table 9.8.
b Summarize the differences between full-time and part-time workers in terms of their distribution between manufacturing and service industries.
c How might sociologists explain these patterns of employment?

I, A

from jobs based on physical strength to mental agility. He argued that this would lead to the growth of a knowledge-based society and as a result the arena of work would become much more pleasant since the dirty, dangerous jobs associated with industry would be replaced with safer, more pleasant and satisfying jobs which gave scope for the use of one's brain. (See also Section 4.7.)

Discussion point

Would such a change necessarily make people happier?

This analysis went beyond the scope of work with talk of how this would lead to a decline in the cohesiveness of social classes and the end of polarized conflict in both industry and politics, as the worst excesses of capitalism disappeared and benevolent employers concerned with their workers no longer acted solely for profit. The implications of this line of thinking were spelled out by Michael Burawoy (1979, 1985) in his Marxist analysis of the labour process:

The rise of 'end of ideology' through the 1950s led Daniel Bell, Clark Kerr, Seymour Martin Lipset, Talcott Parsons, Edward Shils and others to claim that the major problems of capitalism had been overcome. All that remained was to perfect modern society.
(Burawoy, 1979, p. 3)

These ideas were also present in 'convergence theory' (Kerr *et al.*, 1973, orig. pub. 1960) which argued that the needs of industrial society meant that similar levels of inequality and social structure were produced in both capitalist and self-proclaimed communist societies. The functional imperatives of industrial society would out, according to this theory, meaning communist societies would converge with capitalist societies. This would show that it was not capitalism but industrialism that was the key determinant of social structures. It is clear that these theories were influenced by a Cold War desire to discredit Marxism, in this case by arguing that it would end up like capitalism, and in Bell's case by arguing that capitalism had now changed its spots and would in the future act as a benevolent mechanism in society, one that would produce a more caring, democratically controlled form of capitalism. This rather optimistic picture of the emergence of post-industrial society has not held up very well in historical perspective. (See also Section 4.10.)

Criticisms of the post-industrial economy thesis

In *Prophecy and Progress*, Krishan Kumar (1978) argues that the notion of a 'great transformation' is not backed up by the facts. He points out that as long ago as 1900 the majority of workers in Scotland were in the service sector and that for the UK as a whole manufacturing employees were never in a majority, reaching a peak of 48 per cent in 1955. Frank Webster (1995) has also argued that no capitalist economy has ever had a majority of its workforce employed in manufacturing industry. The obvious point is that the image of industrial society against which the theories of post-industrial society were counter-posed were a severe exaggeration. We should also consider the nature of those service sector jobs that have emerged and see if they measure up to Bell's notion of a knowledge-based society.

Deindustrialization

In fact what appears to have happened is not the emergence of nice well-paid technologically-based jobs, but instead the emergence of service sector jobs that in many respects are similar to or even worse than the manufacturing jobs they have to some extent replaced.

Marxist social theorist Alex Callinicos (1989) provides the following description of the process in California:

Deindustrialization has been a painful process, with socially regressive results. Nowhere is this better illustrated than in California, the paradigmatic 'postindustrial society', strategically located on the Eastern edge of the dynamic Pacific economy, with 70 per cent of its workforce employed in services in 1985, ideally suited, thanks to Hollywood and Silicon Valley, to supply the world market with entertainments and information. The 1979-82 recession virtually wiped out the state's car, steel, tyre and other basic industries. High unemployment combined with an influx of (often illegal) immigrants to push down wages. Labour-intensive low-wage industries consequently expanded, in manufacturing as well as services. Employment in textiles, where California can now compete with Hong Kong and Taiwan, grew. As Mike Davis commented, 'LA industry has been turned back from 'Fordism' to 'Bloody Taylorism' of an almost East Asian standard.' A similar pattern can be observed in service industries, whose wages are on average 40 to 50 per cent lower than in basic manufacturing. Consequently, despite California's fabled wealth and dynamic growth rates, the state's per capita income fell from 123 per cent of the US average in 1960 to 116 per cent in 1980 and 113 per cent in 1984.

(Callinicos, 1989, p. 125)

The idea of high-quality lifestyles emerging from the shift to a service economy does not therefore seem to have occurred. However, it is important to point out that while it is clear that service sector jobs have grown and manufacturing jobs have declined in some countries, this is far from being true on a global level. There is evidence of some manufacturing industry shifting to parts of the newly industrializing countries (see Sections 12.5 and 12.6); and furthermore, in the advanced economy showing the most economic success in the 1980s and 1990s, Japan, the proportion of service sector workers actually fell between 1960 and 1982. The idea that shift-ing to a post-industrial service economy will provide economic success and growing prosperity does not seem to have universal support and the service sector jobs that have been created do not appear to adhere to the vision outlined by Daniel Bell.

This means that we have to seek alternative explanations for the shifts that are occurring and this leads on to a consideration of arguments that focus on the growth of flexibility in the period after the 1970s as a key explanation for the transitions.

Flexible production methods: post-Fordism or neo-Fordism

It is against the backdrop of problems in the system of mass production characterized as Fordism, that these theories have developed. First, therefore, we need to know what is meant by this term.

Fordism

The term was coined by Antonio Gramsci (1971) (see also Section 2.5) writing in his prison notebooks on *Americanism and Fordism* in the early 1930s. Gramsci highlighted the way that the adoption of mass production techniques utilizing some of the ideas of Scientific Management (see Section 9.7) by Henry Ford in 1913 changed the face of work. Such production forms required economic stability, and mass consumption changed other aspects of society, notably government economic policy and the advent of advertising and marketing on a mass level. He also argued that there was a clear element of social control involved in Fordism:

In America rationalization of work and prohibition are undoubtedly connected. The enquiries conducted by the industrialists into the workers' private lives and the inspection services created by some firms to control the 'morality' of their workers are necessities of the new methods of work. (Gramsci, 1971, p. 302)

It is this Fordist system that fell into crisis in the 1970s, and the possible consequences of this led to talk of a transition from Fordism to post-Fordism. The proponents of post-Fordism argue that the economic changes in the 1970s signalled the end of Fordism, first because the economic stability it required was undermined, but secondly because consumers were no longer happy to put up with the mass-produced range of goods Fordism offered and were looking for more choice. The system therefore lost legitimacy and was no longer able to operate either as a mode of production or a mode of regulation. This led to the emergence of firms operating on 'post-Fordist principles' described by Tony Watson (1995) as follows:

The post-Fordist regime of accumulation replaces the Fordist one with an emphasis on quality-competitive production for shifting and differentiated markets using qualified and highly skilled flexible labour and is supported by a post-Fordist mode of regulation in which there is reduction in state intervention in labour markets, a shift of responsibility for welfare provision from the state to the employers or private individuals and a more flexible and varied approach to employment relations.

(Watson, 1995, p. 343)

Within this argument about the end of Fordism, a number of propositions have emerged with slightly differing conclusions. We will therefore look at each in turn before going on to evaluate the whole debate about flexibility in the workplace.

Flexible specialization

The key work here is that of Michael Piore and Charles Sabel (1984). They argue that when technological choices are at issue we are in a period of industrial divides and these choices affect the social development of society for decades afterwards. The first industrial divide occurred with the development of mass production techniques at the end of the nineteenth century and the central argument of their book is that we are now at the threshold of a second industrial divide. They outline the choice this involves:

The reactions of firms and nations to the economic dislocations of the 1970s point to two contrasting ways out of the crisis. The world-car strategy suggests that one way is multinational Keynesianism: the extension of the principles of institutional organization that gave rise to the corporation and to macroregulation. . . . By contrast, the spread of flexible specialization suggests that the way out of the crisis requires a shift of technological paradigm and a new system of regulation. If recovery proceeds by this path, then the 1970s and 1980s will be seen in retrospect as a turning point in the history of mechanization: a time when industrial society returned to craft methods of production regarded since the nineteenth century as marginal – and proved them to be essential to prosperity.

(Piore and Sabel, 1984, pp. 251–2)

Although they argue that either outcome is possible, they themselves seem to prefer the move to flexible specialization, largely because they feel this offers the prospect of jobs which are satisfying. The advent of computers is a key component of this:

The computer is . . . a machine that meets Marx's definition of an artisan's tool: it is an instrument that responds to and extends the productive capacities of the user. . . . The advent of the computer restores human control over the production process; machinery again is subordinated to the operator.

(Piore and Sabel, 1984, p. 261)

In studies of how this operates, commentators point to what has been called the Third Italy – third since it is not the mass production industrial north, nor the still agriculturally dominated south. It broadly encompasses the areas of Tuscany and Emilia-Romagna, where production is dominated by small firms and workshops. The small workshops and factories in these areas produce high-quality sophisticated design-conscious products. Co-operation with other firms was also part of the set-up, based on sub-contracting which built relationships between these small firms, as did their tendency to group together to obtain specialist services such as accountancy and marketing. These local traditions were underpinned by the role of socialist and communist councils in the area.

As a result of this flexible specialization the area experiences high economic growth and high standards of living, all combined with stable permanent employment and social provision. Piore and Sabel consider it possible to identify certain areas in the USA which might also become areas of flexible specialization, notably Boston and Palo Alto in California. However this requires the setting up of the social infrastructures which are a part of the Italian examples. In summary, the notion of flexible specialization offers an optimistic view emphasizing the possibilities of an end to alienating work on mass production assembly lines and the return of craft work.

However, the example most often quoted of this type of operation, Benetton, might also be seen as a negation of this form of organization. Benetton is a company employing only about 1500 people directly but working with a number of sub-contractors. Their outlets are franchised but with an on-line link allowing them to make immediate note of trends in consumption, which it is claimed, allows them to respond to market trends in 10 days. However, while Benetton might have started out as a small firm, it is now a multi-national giant and therefore might be seen as coming:

ever closer to the 'world car model' that is the very antithesis of the post-Fordist concept.

(Kumar, 1995, p. 62)

Disorganized capitalism

Scott Lash and John Urry (1987, 1994) argue that we have moved from an era of organized capitalism characterized by high levels of state intervention and regulation of the economy, the domination of production by a professional, managerial and technical service class (see Section 4.6) and the cultural domination of modernism, rationalism and nationalism; into the era of disorganized capitalism characterized by the growth of multi-national capital, the further growth of a service class, the shift of manufacturing industry to the Third World and the fragmentation of cultural life with the decline of modernism and the rise of post-modernism. What differentiates Lash and Urry's analysis from other views is their argument that there are a number of causes of this change, notably the various processes identified by the phrase 'globalization' (on this see Sections 9.7, 10.10, 12.5, 15.11, 16.8 and 17.6). The implication for Lash and Urry is that the working-class movement is weakened:

The power of a mass industrial working class to shape society in its own image are for the foreseeable future profoundly weakened.
(Lash and Urry, 1987, p. 311)

The term 'disorganized capitalism' is also used by Claus Offe (1985a) He means by it that the mechanisms which supposedly organize sociopolitical systems in welfare state capitalism no longer seem able to fulfil this task (see also Section 14.2). Principally this applies to the trade union movement, which he argues is no longer able to act as the representative of unified working-class interests, owing to the growth of economic and cultural divisions within the working class, and because a number of groups such as the young appear to be turning their backs on the trade union movement. He argues that the trade unions can only restore their claim to act as a universal voice by extending their concerns beyond a consideration of people as employees. Again the implication of this is to argue that the working class and its representatives can no longer be seen as the key component of groups arguing for social change.

Post-Fordism as 'new times'

This term has been most notably associated with various commentators writing in the journal *Marxism Today*. Hall and Jacques (1989), for example, argue that changes in the 1960s and 1970s led to a crisis in the then-dominant Fordist system. This is being replaced by post-Fordism which is based on production being targeted much more specifically at segmented markets. Flexible specialization and the division of the workforce into core and periphery elements are seen as key consequences of this.

However, just as Gramsci's analysis of Fordism linked changes in production to changes elsewhere in society, so too does the 'new times' analysis. In essence, the analysis argues that the changes in production also produce changes in the role of education, the place of the state, and the nature of political -

struggle. This can no longer be seen as being embodied in a monolithic trade union movement; but instead, because of the divisions within the working class, requires the consideration of alliances and also a broadening out of political concerns to focus on issues of consumption. All of this is an attempt to engage in a battle for hegemony and this involves cultural struggle as well as economic struggle. (See also Section 10.2.)

Neo-Fordism

The notion of 'Fordism' was most fully developed by the French neo-Marxist 'regulation school' whose notable members were Michel Aglietta (1979) and Alain Lipietz (1987). It is this idea which forms the start point for post-Fordist theories. However, they themselves are sceptical of such approaches, arguing instead that what we are witnessing is really a form of 'neo-Fordism' which is merely the development of new strategies on the part of capitalism to try to survive. Fordism, in its classical form, no longer brings in the profits and therefore new ways have been developed. Crucially, they argue this has involved the development of 'global Fordism'. This means that labour-intensive parts of work have been shifted to parts of the developing world (see also Section 12.5), where the conditions resemble classical Fordism or worse, while the adoption of flexible strategies in the developed world have been aimed at breaking trade unions and labour organizations. Overall then, on a global level enough remains of the old Fordist methods to talk of neo-Fordism, and therefore, although the crisis of profitability may be staved off by the use of cheap labour in the developing world, the problems which led it into crisis in the 1970s have not been overcome.

Activity

Draw up a table summarizing the main views on a post-Fordist economy summarized above. This should contain a short summary, names associated with this view and an outline of differences with other versions of the post-Fordist thesis.

A final column can be used to make notes of criticisms of these theories.

I, A

Are we really living in post-Fordist times?

All of these approaches (with the partial exception of the neo-Fordist argument) share the broad belief that fundamental transformations are taking place, and this is captured in shorthand by the phrase 'from Fordism to post-Fordism'. This idea is however not without its critics.

One criticism of the 'post-Fordist' argument is that it is a version of economic reductionism, that is, it tries to explain social changes on the basis of changes in economic production. This is most clear in the emphasis on the effect of computer technology on production and society.

A second criticism of these arguments is that they overstate the dominance of Fordism in the twentieth century. Anna Pollert (1988, 1991) argues that Fordism was never as widespread as the proponents of post-Fordism claim, and it never became the universal form of capitalist production. She also argues that the attempt to point to 'flexibility' as a key characteristic of post-Fordism ignores the degree of flexibility which underlay Fordist production methods and was central to Taylor's Scientific Management (see Section 9.7). Taylorism was never meant only for mass production, so the emergence of smaller units of production does not mean Taylorism is no longer applicable.

Thirdly, it is argued that the developments in the Third Italy, focused on by Piore and Sabel as a key example of flexible specialization, are historically and culturally specific, meaning that they offer no lessons which can be applied more generally.

Fourthly, critics point to the non-universality of flexible working arrangements, assumed to be widespread in post-Fordist analyses. *Labour Market and Skill Trends 1995/6* (Department of Employment, 1996) reports that:

- the proportion of part-time employees in the UK rose from 21 per cent in 1981 to 28 per cent in 1993
- the number of temporary workers remained constant at about 5 per cent between 1985 and 1995
- 70 per cent of firms were sub-contracting 'non-core' operations in 1995.

While these trends do clearly indicate that flexibility is on the increase, it is questionable whether this is now the dominant form of employment relations as notions of post-Fordism would suggest: 56 per cent of people are employed by firms with more than 50 employees (33 per cent in firms with more than 500 employees), compared with 44 per cent of people employed in firms with fewer than 50 employees. This would tend to suggest that large units still predominate in terms of employment.

In other words the suggestion that we have moved from Fordism which was only mass production to post-Fordism which is only small-scale flexible specialization is not backed up by evidence. The contrast is too overdrawn. Kumar (1995) puts it as follows:

Mass production, whatever its strategic importance in the economy, was never, nor could it be, the dominant form of industrial production. Small firms and 'craft production' – not of course necessarily the same thing – always persisted alongside mass production, as had been the case since the Industrial Revolution; they performed then as now not vestigial but indispensable functions. There is no revival of these forms, merely their continuation. The opposition, 'mass production versus flexible specialization', is false.
(Kumar, 1995, p. 60)

Case study – Japan as an example of post-Fordism?

The organization of production in Japanese firms has long been a matter of interest to sociologists, an interest heightened by the relative economic success of that country. At the end of the Second World War Japan produced 1 per cent of the world's gross national product, and by 1992 this figure had reached 13 per cent. Its companies dominate the consumer electronics industries and it is also the leading world producer of steel and ships (Woronoff, 1992). Interest has also been spurred by the movement of Japanese and latterly South Korean firms into Europe and North America (see also Section 12.6). The Japanese method of production is often seen as post-Fordist since it involves flexible production techniques such as developing close relations with sub-contractors, reducing the level of stocks through the Just-In-Time (JIT) system, employing team working and quality circles and emphasizing Total Quality Management (TQM), job rotation and multi-functional operatives.

However, Ronald Dore (1987) used the phrase 'flexible rigidities' to describe Japanese operations owing to the highly centralized control evident in their corporations.

Some have argued that the movement of Japanese firms overseas has often led to them adopting western-style organizational forms. Mair (1994) identifies this in the case of Honda and argues that this points to the development of the global local corporation. Although Richard Florida and Martin Kenney (1996), in their study of Japanese car companies in North America, noted that the Japanese model was transplanted to North America, and saw it as a new form of production, they went on to say that:

We find little evidence to support the claim made by Sabel (1989) that the Japanese firm, as manifested by the transplants, is converging towards flexible specialization.
(Florida and Kenney, 1996, p. 77)

It is in the area of the actual organization of work that much talk of flexibility has emerged, but here again the evidence for great differences is not entirely convincing. What emerges from Kamata's (1984) participant study of life on the Toyota assembly line is the great similarity with accounts of life on UK mass production lines, such as that of Beynon (1973). As Andrew Sayer commented:

Whatever the conditions of mass production in the West it is alive and well in Japan.
(Sayer, 1989, p. 666)

As a result, many commentators have argued that Japan does not provide evidence of any shift to post-Fordism, but instead of a different form of Fordism. For example, Kumar comments:

Japan's pattern of 'flexible rigidities' (Dore 1987) shows a thriving system of mass production co-existing with a high degree of the 'vertical dis-integration' usually associated with flexible specialisation. By comparison with western economies, it is also a very organized form of capitalism. . . By any measure of significance, Japan is more central to the world economy than the Third Italy, the model type of post-Fordist practice. Its presence, even allowing for certain peculiarities of its economy, suggests not only that Fordism and post-Fordism are inextricably mixed up but that the future may lie more with a modified Fordism than with anything that looks like post-Fordism.
(Kumar, 1995, p. 166)

Farewell to flexibility?

What then is left of the calls for flexibility as a way out of economic crisis? In reality, flexibility has more often been seen as a way for capitalists to restore profitability by increasing the rate of exploitation. (See also Sections 2.2 and 9.2.)

This can only be achieved by inflating the alleged inflexibilities of the Fordist system, which provides the basis for talk of the need for flexibility and the division between core and periphery workforces – although the notion that the core workforce have any long-term job security is also open to question since *Labour Market and Skill Trends 1995/6* reported that in relation to restructuring to achieve flexibility:

Four in five restructurings had led to job loss at all levels, and seven in ten to the loss of at least one management layer.
(*Labour Market and Skills Trends*, 1996, p. 22)

Flexibility could therefore be seen as the latest development of techniques which remain within the Fordist system of mass production, aimed at restoring profitability, in a climate where the economic stability of the original Fordist project has gone. The continuities with the original form of Fordism are however more important that the supposed changes to a post-Fordist scenario, and the emphasis on the computer as a source of liberation can also be countered with analyses of the way that technology can be used to heighten the degree of surveillance of workers and others, albeit with their consent, as seen for example in the accounts of David Lyon (1993). (See also Section 17.4.)

> ### Discussion point
> Are computers the basis of a return to craft production or a way of achieving greater control and surveillance over our lives?

The debate is important precisely because if the post-Fordists are right the idea of a unified working class is part of history and any prospect of socialist change would have to rely on other actors; whereas if the notion of post-Fordism is overplayed, the working class may still be able to provide the basis of such a transition.

Doonesbury   BY GARRY TRUDEAU

Figure 9.3 A comment on flexibility

9.5 Recent trends in industrial relations

Considering the effect of the changes to industrial relations in the UK affected by the Conservative administrations of the 1980s, Will Hutton (1996) in his book, *The State We're In* comments that:

Fifteen years after the Conservatives' election the scope of labour reform exceeded even the wildest dreams of the New Right in the 1970s. There was no regulation of working time; no legally-protected conditions for labour hired under fixed term contracts; no minimum wage legislation; minimal employment protection; and employees had no legal right to representation at the workplace. The OECD, compiling a composite index of these measures, could by the summer of 1994, rank Britain at zero – the lowest, apart from the US, in the industrialised world. With the lack of legislation there was no obligation on employers to treat their workers other than as disposable commodities, or even to pay them fairly.
(Hutton, 1996, p. 95)

It is therefore clear that there have been major changes in this area and this reflects both the ideology of the New Right (see Section 2.10) concerning trade unions and the policies with which that ideology has been implemented.

The New Right believe that the free market works and that without any imperfections the wage rate will settle at a level which will lead to full employment. Their explanation for unemployment therefore centres on those institutions which attempt to limit the operation of the free market, notably the welfare state (see also Section 14.3) and trade unions.

Discussion point

To what extent do you agree that trade unions are the chief cause of unemployment?

As a result, trade unions came under critical fire from the very first Conservative administration in 1979 and that pattern continued, leading to the situation described by Hutton above, where to be a worker in the UK is to be totally bereft of rights.

The New Right in government and the assault on the unions

The implementation of legislative changes impacting on employment and trade unions shows the way in which this ideology was actually enacted.

In 1980 an Employment Act was passed which placed restrictions on picketing by making it illegal to picket anywhere other than at your own place of work, and by outlawing secondary action (i.e. action against other companies). A further Employment Act in 1982 made it possible for employers to sue trade unions for damages and also to take out injunctions stopping trade unions taking certain actions.

These pieces of legislation were first tested by the outbreak of conflict at a printworks in Warrington. Eddy Shah (later famous for printing *Today* newspaper, the first national colour daily) had set up a non-union printshop to produce one of his newspapers. This created problems since the rules of the relevant union, the National Graphical Association (NGA) forbade its members to handle work from non-union outfits. Fears that this plant would lead to job losses were heightened when the company had advertised some jobs.

Eventually this was to lead to a strike at one of the group's companies and striking printers picketing the works of another of the group's companies at Warrington. This led to the NGA being taken to court for secondary picketing since although the two companies were part of the same group and clearly had links, it was argued they were legally separate. This event rather showed how the law would be bound to conflict with trade union principles and effective action to protect them.

This issue was to rise again in perhaps the most important dispute of recent years, the miners' strike of 1984–5. In March 1984, miners at Cortonwood pit came out on strike when their mine was threatened with closure. This escalated into a national dispute, as other areas joined in to support the protest as allowed under the union rules. It quickly became clear that the government had put in place plans to defeat the miners and part of the reason for this appeared to be a desire to get even for the defeat the miners had inflicted on the previous Conservative government in 1974.

The miners received tremendous levels of support from around the country and inspired the setting up of a number of support groups, most notably Women Against Pit Closures which helped to break down the level of sexism evident in certain parts of the mining community.

The police were quickly called upon and the events of the following year witnessed a major escalation of the restriction of free movement, which were described by James Anderton, then Chief Constable of Greater Manchester, as being in some respects like those operative in totalitarian states. The level of violence inflicted by police in riot gear on protesting miners was broadcast to the whole nation in news reports from Orgreave in South Yorkshire in June 1984.

The miners bravely stayed out on strike for a year but their dispute was lost and as a result, the level of pit closures increased.

Although it would be possible to say that at this stage the organized trade union movement was somewhat on the defensive, the legal barrage against it continued. The 1984 Trade Union Act introduced a requirement that there be secret ballots before any industrial action and also for the election of union leaders. The 1988 Employment Act provided the right to ignore union ballot results and not to be disciplined by your union. The 1989 Employment Act placed restrictions on paid time off for trade union representatives. The 1990 Employment Act made unions liable for the actions of their members and effectively outlawed the closed shop. The 1993 Trade Union Reform and Employment Rights Act made it possible for ordinary members of the public to sue unions for losses arising from disputes and made unions provide notice of any industrial action, while also requiring that all strike ballots be postal.

The particular forms of democracy (see Section 17.1) and representation which workers had fought for ever since the first union members protested (The Tolpuddle Martyrs in 1834 who were transported to Australia because of their attempt to form a trade union) were systematically undermined in pursuit of the idea that workers should behave as individuals. The initial impetus for the formation of trade unions was the acknowledgement by workers that as individuals they would always be less powerful than employers and that their only way to seek to improve their conditions would be to join together in collective representation. This clearly went against the individualistic philosophy of the New Right and the legislation described above is the result.

Activity

a Construct a table summarizing all the pieces of legislation mentioned in the preceding pages. Place them in date order.

b Note the year and title and then summarize its effect in your own words.

c Use this information to evaluate the effect of legislative change on the trade unions in the 1980s and 1990s.

I, E

In a survey of the contemporary position of trade unions, sociologist John Williams (1997) points out that only 31 per cent of UK workers are now unionized, and for workers under 25, the figure is just 7 per cent. It is on the basis of figures like these that there has been talk of the end of trade unionism. However while it is the case that this situation has put trade unions on the defensive, it should not be assumed that this has stopped all protest. Indeed it is often the case that trade union activity has been instigated by the changes introduced by New Right reforms to the economy, with managers trying to reassert the right to manage and annoying workers to such an extent that they take action to defend themselves. The next two subsections will therefore consider in more detail recent examples where, despite the unfavourable legal context, workers have continued to act to defend their interests.

Discussion point

Why do you think young people seem relatively uninterested in trade unions?

Case study – Lecturers in further education colleges

Strikes and industrial action are often considered to be the preserve of manual workers. However the dispute which led to the largest number of strike-days in both 1994 (63 000; 22 per cent of total) and 1995 (39 000; 9 per cent of total) was centred on a group of non-manual workers, namely lecturers in further education (FE) colleges.

The 1992 Further and Higher Education Act removed further education colleges from the control of local authorities and turned them into corporations, a form of quasi-privatization. At the same time, the funding mechanism was changed and they were subject to requirements to make efficiency gains.

The key way in which this was to be achieved was through the introduction of a new 'professional' contract for lecturers. The model for this was produced by the College Employers Forum (CEF) a grouping which brought together managers from colleges who in all other respects argued that they were individual entities. The contract (compared to the existing nationally negotiated contract for college lecturers) increased the teaching load for lecturers by 26 per cent, increased their overall working hours by 23 per cent and also reduced their holiday entitlement. It was argued that this was needed to allow colleges to provide a flexible service in a new business-orientated environment.

Discussion point

Should business principles operate in an educational environment?

Lecturers and their union, the National Association of Teachers in Further and Higher Education (NATFHE), argued that such a change would not only worsen lecturers' conditions but would also have a negative impact on the level of quality of the education provided. The new contract therefore became the central issue in a rolling conflict.

Lecturers were balloted on industrial action over the proposed introduction of the contract and a positive result was then challenged in the courts by arguing that a national strike would be illegal since it involved employees from a number of different legal entities. The court ruled that such a strike would therefore be illegal. Despite the fact that the proposed new contract to be introduced into the colleges was based on a unitary model contract produced by the CEF to which most colleges were affiliated, a similar unified response from the union was deemed to be illegal because the colleges were legally individual entities.

While this means that the defence of existing conditions has been made harder, it does not mean the end of the dispute. For three and a half years lecturers have held out against increasing levels of pressure on them to sign the new contract. At the same time, there has been an increase in the use of part-time hourly paid lecturers and a decline in the employment of full-time lecturers as well as an increase in the number of redundancies in the colleges.

As well as the dispute over contracts, relations inside the colleges has been affected by changes in management style following their removal from local authority control. This led to fears that there now appears to be little public control over the activities of the managers of the colleges despite the fact that they are still largely publicly funded. This issue was highlighted at the end of 1996 by activities at Stoke-on-Trent College, one of the biggest colleges in the UK, where it was revealed that the college was having to cut £8 million from its budget. *Times* journalist, David Charter (1996) argued that:

a clearer picture has emerged of Stoke's descent into financial crisis. At the heart seems to lie a lack of accountability at the most senior level of the kind that further education colleges last year pledged to Lord Nolan's inquiry into standards in public life that they would strive to overcome.
(Charter, 1996, p. 37)

NATFHE members at the college had complained in a survey of the 'dictatorial and bullying style' of the Principal. The article in Figure 9.4 presents a view on some of the issues that arose out of the activities at Stoke-on-Trent College.

While it may be argued that this is an isolated case, the fact that it happened at all must mean that there are serious question marks placed over the level of public accountability (see also Section 17.1)

A lack of principal

NO ONE better understands the following ground rules for success in the newly-privatised further education colleges than Neil Preston, the principal of Stoke-on-Trent College.

1) Get a reputation at a smallish college for a nasty and dictatorial management style without the slightest concern for accountability to anyone. Preston achieved this triumphantly at Amersham College, Bucks, where, as principal in 1992 and 1993, he caused widespread anger and chaos. At one stage he proposed that he, not the students, should appoint the president of the students' union; and on another he provoked a group of parents to declare a vote of no confidence (see *Bucks Examiner, passim,* March 1992 to September 1993).

2) On the back of that reputation, get appointed head of a bigger college. Preston was appointed head of Stoke College in 1993.

3) Bring your girlfriend with you and promote her. Preston brought to Stoke his devoted colleague from Amersham, Helen Chandler, and appointed her an assistant director.

4) Revel in the new "free" and unaccountable atmosphere for heads of colleges under privatisation. Get yourself (and your girlfriend) a lot of money, not forgetting the perks. Preston got a salary of £90,000 (Chandler got about £45,000), plus "company" car, trips abroad, etc.

5) Indulge yourself in endless bullying and hectoring of staff, students and their unions.

6) Suck up to prominent local councillors and businessmen, make them college governors, and impress them with endless flattery and "free enterprise" rhetoric. Stoke College governors were almost all pillars of the business community.

7) Get far too much taxpayers' money from the quango, the Further Education Funding Council, by ridiculously inflating the number of students you expect to enrol. The FEFC tells the *Eye* the college roll is "18 per cent under target", and the college owes a staggering £3.4m.

8) When the going gets tough, make full use of your sick pay scheme. Since September, when the news of the vast debts started to break, Preston and Chandler have both been off sick — but not too sick to renovate a pub they have bought in Wales, through their jointly-owned company The Pub Doctor Ltd. While sick, of course, they have been on full pay from the taxpayer. The FEFC, the guardian of public funds, says it knows very well that Preston and Chandler have been off sick doing up their pub for three months, but "cannot comment on the case as a disciplinary hearing is imminent".

The FEFC says it "does not agree that the troubles at the college are due to the incorporation (privatisation) of colleges". These are due, they say, to "weakness in management and control systems at this particular institution". They plan to get the money back by cutting the college grant in future (ie by making students and staff pay for the council's total failure to control their reckless and cosseted principal).

Figure 9.4 A comment on management in an FE college. Source: Foot (1996, p. 27)

of institutions and their managers who are spending large amounts of public money. Meanwhile, NATFHE and lecturers continue their case to resist the erosion of their working conditions, their living standards and to try to improve the quality of provision offered in the colleges.

Case study – the Liverpool dockers

The docks have always been an important part of Liverpool and for a time in the early part of this century, Liverpool was the leading sea port in the UK. In September 1995 the docks were the site of the start of one of the longest-running struggles in modern UK history. Dockers working for a private contractor, Torside, were ordered to work overtime at a rate they disputed. Protests followed and within 24 hours 80 dockers were sacked. The sacked workers mounted a picket line and all 329 dockers employed by the Mersey Docks and Harbour Company refused to cross it and were sacked. Since being sacked the workers have been presented with a number of final offers ranging from new jobs on individual contracts to redundancy payments, but the dockers have continued their fight to get their old jobs back. The dispute has mobilized many people and once a week the picket is composed of women and children organized by WOW (Women on the Waterfront) composed of partners, mothers and sisters of the sacked workers.

The dispute over overtime payments is part of concerns among the dockers that changes instituted in the 1980s are leading back to the casual labour system that operated in the past, and was the basis for a number of disputes.

Casualization has become a part of the 1990s struggle since the sacked dockers found their jobs had been taken by casual labourers employed by PDP Services. Their contract provides for an hourly rate of £4 with no overtime rate and provides that the contract can be terminated when the contractor determines. It also states that there is:

no obligation on the contractor to provide the worker with any guaranteed number of working hours in any day or week. There will be periods when no work is available.
(Quoted in Pilger, 1996, p.16)

This type of activity has fuelled the fears of dock workers that casualization, which they fought so hard to end, is returning to the docks with all the uncertainties and indignities that that involves.

Socialist journalist John Pilger (1996) is in no doubt that the reason for this is the changes brought about by the New Right governments of the 1980s and 1990s:

The truth is that the number of dockers' jobs has spiralled down to about 300, a tiny fraction of the figure a few years ago. As for 'wealth creation', profits have soared from less than £9 million in 1989 to more than £31 million last year – the year the company jettisoned its dockers. . . .

It was taxpayers' money that floated Mersey Docks and Harbour Group in 1970, and taxpayers' money that wrote off £112 million in loans, and funded up to £200 million worth of redundancies, and paid out £37.5 million for the regeneration of the dock area. Add to this £76 million of City Challenge funding. Since 1989, the company has received some £13.3 million in European Regional Development Funds. According to the Liverpool Echo, 'directors of Mersey docks have received phenomenal grants to create employment' – while unemployment has gone up. Inexplicably, the company's literature boasts of its success in something called the 'free market'.
(Pilger, 1996, p. 16)

He points to the large sums of money made by some individuals out of the spate of privatizations in the dockyards in the 1980s and also points to the 38 per cent pay increase the managing director of Mersey Docks' received just before the dockers were sacked.

The dispute is therefore a microcosm of the way the changes instituted by the government have led to changes in working conditions which make conditions for workers worse and allow a few to enrich themselves.

Discussion point

To what extent do you agree that this dispute illustrates the return of a form of casualization to the docks?

In their study of the dispute, Jane Kennedy and Michael Lavalette (1996), sociologists from Liverpool University, place the dispute in the context of the long-running struggles against casualization and flexible labour in the docks, and also its implications due to the widespread promotion of 'flexible working practices' (see also Section 7.4) throughout workplaces in the UK.

However, they are also concerned to highlight the great levels of solidarity that still exist and are illustrated by the action of the dockers in this dispute. The issue of the notion of class and who are the working class is also part of the analysis since, although dockers are manual workers, they are also service workers. This highlights the fact that we cannot equate service work with being middle class. Kennedy and Lavalette (1996) also consider the arguments over strategy within the union between those who tend towards the belief that in the context of changes to the law and earlier defeats for workers, solidarity is not a realistic option, and those who argue that this is the key to winning this dispute and thereby re-asserting the importance of traditional trade union principles.

Arguments over union strategy in contemporary Britain

Divergence in strategy has been the subject of a debate about trade union strategy as a whole between the broadly Weberian approach of Eric Batstone (1984, 1988) and the Marxist approach of Ralph Darlington (1994).

Batstone argues that it is important to note that the onslaught on the unions by the Conservative governments in the 1980s did not destroy them and that there are important levels of continuity between the 1970s and 1980s in terms of shop-steward and local union organization. In other words, unions were able to continue to represent their members. This point is not at issue in the debate however, which concerns the reasons why unions have continued to be effective in some instances, and by implication, the choices to be made over strategy for the future.

Batstone argues that the success of trade union shop stewards in the 1980s and in the future depends on leading stewards adopting a realistic stance towards bargaining with management. Such bargaining would allow them to improve their members' conditions. In essence, the point here is to argue that successful trade unionism depends on the development of sophisticated bargaining skills rather than industrial action.

On the basis of his study of trade unionism on Merseyside, Darlington (1994) is critical of this idea:

My aim is to put Batstone's resolute endorsement of a 'sophisticated' shop steward organization that engages in 'strong bargaining relations' with management to the test of empirical research through the prism of an alternative Marxist theoretical framework.

(Darlington, 1994, p. 5)

Darlington argues instead that the development of these sophisticated shop stewards, which did involve reforms in the 1970s – for instance increasing the level of paid time off for union officials and providing them with more facilities – could be seen as an indicator of the bureaucratization of grassroots trade union organization. At its worst, these developments also involved trade union representatives almost acting to police their members, diffusing their potential to take action by talk of the way strikes would harm negotiations.

In other words, Darlington is arguing that while some gains might have come from negotiations, in the long run the divisions between union members and union representatives that this entailed would lead to a reduction in the ability of the unions to fight if the need arose. His solution is for a return to rank and file unionism with a renewed emphasis on industrial action as the basis for negotiations so that workers are all part of the union action.

It is clear that in the 1980s and 1990s the development of 'new realism' in the Labour Party (see also Sections 2.10 and 17.2) and the trade unions led to a number of instances where ordinary union members felt that their union was acting with a concern to secure negotiations rather than to get involved in industrial action, and the resulting tension between and within local union representatives is a reflection of the arguments identified by Batstone and Darlington. These tensions were evident in the 1984–5 miners' strike and it is also clear that they play a role in the Liverpool dockers' strike as Kennedy and Lavalette (1996) make clear in their book on the dispute.

9.6 Unemployment and society

If there are questions surrounding the measurement of work in official statistics (see Section 3.11), this is also true of unemployment.

The first measure of unemployment is the monthly 'claimant count of the unemployed'. As its name suggests, this is compiled by adding together the total of people eligible for certain social security benefits, notably unemployment benefit, income support and national insurance credits. The rate of unemployment on this basis is arrived at by taking the total number of the unemployed so defined as a percentage of the workforce. There are however questions over the validity of this as a measure of unemployment.

First, this count only exists as a by-product of the administrative procedures surrounding welfare benefits. It is really entitlement to benefits that it measures and therefore someone who is working but nonetheless entitled to benefit might be included. Also if the rules concerning benefits and entitlement to benefit change, this will change these figures even though it has no direct effect on whether someone has a job or not. As an example of this, in April 1983 the government changed regulations to the effect that men over 60 who were without work were no longer required to sign on. This had the effect of reducing this count of unemployment by approximately 107 000.

The main alternative definition and measure of unemployment arises from the *Labour Force Survey*, conducted quarterly. This utilizes the definition of unemployment developed by the International Labour Office (ILO), which is people without a paid job who were available to start work and had looked for work. It is thus not based on eligibility for benefits and is therefore not affected by changes to the benefit system.

These two measures of unemployment provide very different figures of unemployment, a point which can be grasped by considering Table 9.9, based on material produced by the Department of Employment (now Department for Education and Employment, or DfEE).

Activity

a Explain in your own words the differences between the two measures of unemployment shown in Table 9.9 below

b Consider the effect of adopting one of these measures on the gender differences in unemployment as officially measured.

c Consider which of these two measures you think best measures actual unemployment.

I, A, E

If we look at figures from the national Census (see Section 3.11) then the number of people describing themselves as unemployed differs from the official count. In a critical discussion of official statistics, Miles and Irvine (1979) point out that the 1971 Census found 1 365 775 people who described themselves as unemployed while official Department of Employment figures for that year gave a total of 773 800 unemployed. Clearly people themselves think of unemployment in ways which differ from the official definition.

The validity of the official statistics surrounding both employment and unemployment is a debate that continues to this day. January 1997 saw the issue of the December 1996 unemployment statistics. The unemployment figures for that period were 1 884 700 according to the claimant count but 2 230 000 according to the *LFS* (for November 1996). The one month discrepancy would not explain much of the total discrepancy of 345 000 between the two figures and as a result, leading politicians argued over the figures. John Major claimed that the 45 100 reduction in the number out of work and claiming benefit producing the lowest figure for six years had 'broadened the smile' (quoted in *The Guardian*, 16 January 1997) on Britain's face, while Labour employment spokesman, Ian McCartney, said figures from the OECD showed that 18.9 per cent of British households had nobody working in them, the fourth highest rate in the industrialized western countries (also quoted in *The Guardian* 16 January 1997).

Guardian journalists Larry Elliot and Sarah Ryle (1997) pointed out the parameters of the debate over the latest figures:

Figures from the Office for National Statistics show that claimant-count unemployment has fallen by 350,000 in the past year, with half the fall in the latest three months. . . .

The Treasury admitted that it too, was sceptical, saying that the Chancellor Kenneth Clarke, preferred an alternative measure of unemployment – the Labour Force Survey.

According to the LFS . . . unemployment is more than 300,000 higher than on the claimant-count measure, and dropping far more slowly.

In the year to last autumn, LFS unemployment declined 166,000 while claimant count unemployment fell by 243,000.

(Elliot and Ryle, 1997, p. 2)

Table 9.9 Two contrasting measures of unemployment (GB in millions)

	Spring 1993			Spring 1992		
	All	**Men**	**Women**	**All**	**Men**	**Women**
Claimant count	2.86	2.20	0.66	2.61	2.01	0.60
Less						
Claimants not unemployed on ILO definition	1.00	0.73	0.27	0.85	0.61	0.24
Of which:						
(1) Not seeking work	0.62	0.44	0.18	0.53	0.38	0.15
(2) Employed	0.38	0.29	0.09	0.32	0.23	0.09
Plus						
People defined as unemployed on ILO count but not claiming	0.95	0.43	0.52	0.89	0.39	0.50
Total ILO unemployment	2.81	1.90	0.91	2.65	1.79	0.86

Source: Adapted from *Employment Gazette*, (October 1993, p. 459)

Discussion point

How do you think we should measure unemployment?

Types of unemployment

Social scientists distinguish between three broad types of unemployment:

- frictional
- structural
- cyclical.

Frictional unemployment refers to the fact that when workers change jobs there may be a short gap between leaving one job and starting another. Since this is short-term unemployment and only occurs because people take a break between jobs, it is not regarded as a problem.

Cyclical unemployment is so called because it is related to the ups and downs of the economic cycle. In periods of economic boom the number of jobs available rises and an economy may approach full employment, but if the economy moves into depression, firms will usually respond by cutting their costs, most notably by making people redundant. Commenting on this phenomenon in relation to the recent experience of the UK, Nick Madry and Mark Kirby (1996) point out that:

in the last 15 years the economy appears to have gone through a complete cycle, starting with a large recession between 1980 and 1983 followed by an economic boom which reached its height in 1987–8 and then another recession starting in about 1990 which appeared to be coming to a slow end by late 1994.

(Madry and Kirby, 1996, p. 119)

The third type of unemployment, structural unemployment, occurs when there are changes to the structure of industry or to the particular skills required in an industry and the skills which people possess which were once needed in industry are needed no longer. One of the key examples of this in the UK in recent years has been the declining demand for workers in industries such as mining and shipbuilding. Areas previously largely reliant on these industries for employment such as Clydeside, Yorkshire, the North-East and South Wales have as a result of their decline suffered large levels of unemployment.

The relative balance between cyclical and structural unemployment is important since if the majority of unemployment is of a cyclical nature, the level of unemployment can be expected to fall as the economy picks up. However a return to economic prosperity will not by itself cure structural unemployment, and therefore if most unemployment is of a structural nature, this might be expected to continue into the future unless other policies are adopted to try to reduce unemployment, such as retraining or support for regional redevelopment.

Explanations for unemployment

Keynesianism and the failure of the free market

John Maynard Keynes (1936) was an extremely influential economist whose work centrally influenced government economic and social policies after World War II up until the mid-1970s.

Keynes argued that the experience of mass unemployment in the 1930s showed that the market left to itself did not, and would not, provide full employment as its supporters argued. More importantly he argued that an economy might reach a point of equilibrium (a position where there is no pressure to change) with mass unemployment which would therefore become a long-lasting feature of society. (See also Section 14.3.)

He therefore argued for a rejection of free-market economics and for the state and government to take a much more active role in the running of the economy with the aim of achieving certain objectives including full employment. The experience of the Second World War was important in showing that the state could direct the economy (as happened in wartime) and this provided the basis for the radical change in government economic and social policy based on the work of Keynes and Beveridge (see also Sections 14.1 and 14.3).

One potential problem with this schema was the worry that wage rates would rise excessively in a time of full employment and it was this which led successive governments to attempt to effect policies of wage restraint. This led to the clash between the trade unions and the Labour government of 1974–9 which came to be known as the 'Winter of Discontent'. It provided the backdrop to the General Election of 1979 which brought Margaret Thatcher and the Conservative Party to power (see Section 17.2). Armed with a New Right ideology they set about reasserting the importance of the free market.

The New Right and the failure of the state

The central insight of the New Right (see Sections 2.10 and 14.3) is that the free market is inherently superior to state intervention. They were therefore strongly opposed to the kind of Keynesian interventionism that had characterized government over the last 30 years. They argued that the role of government was to create a stable low-inflation environment where business and enterprise could flourish and only in this way could jobs be created and unemployment thereby reduced.

New Right economist Milton Friedman (1980) argued that the state causes problems for economic growth owing to its tendency to spend more than it raises in taxes and this requires it to borrow to fund its activity. This borrowing is known as the public sector borrowing requirement (PSBR) and Friedman argued that this extra demand for borrowing pushes up interest rates which therefore push up the costs of private business. He therefore argued that the level of government borrowing needed to be reduced and a strict control kept on the money supply to reduce inflationary pressures. This is known as monetarism.

Friedman also argued that there is a natural level of unemployment and this is made higher by trade union demands for more wages and by welfare expenditure (see Section 14.3). Both of these place upward pressure on the wage rate and as a result workers price themselves out of jobs and are also reluctant to reduce their wage rates owing to the level of welfare benefits.

Did the New Right policies work?

Harvey and MacDonald in their summary of trends clearly believe that such policies not only did not reduce unemployment but were a contributory factor in the rise of unemployment seen in recent years:

Monetarist policy has resulted in an increase in unemployment, not a reduction. Although unemployment may have increased as a result of technological changes and the 'world recession' during the 1980s, Britain has a worse record of unemployment than the United States and Europe. Between 1980 and 1986, employment in the United States rose by 10 per cent, but fell in the European Community by 2 per cent. In Britain it fell by 3 per cent. Most of the increase in employment that occurred during the brief boom of 1983 to 1986 was due to an increase in part-time jobs (MacInnes, 1987). What is more, the real increase in unemployment has been concealed by changes in the way it is officially measured.
(Harvey and MacDonald, 1993, p.71)

Harvey and MacDonald also quote the findings of Richard Layard and Stephen Nickell (1986) who, being neo-Keynesian economists, are not surprisingly critical of New Right monetarist policies. Layard and Nickell's work considered several factors which might have contributed to the rise in unemployment in the 1980s, such as the level of unemployment benefits, trade union power and overall

lack of demand in the economy. They found that 80 per cent of the rise of unemployment was due to the last-mentioned factor, and this is seen as a direct result of the monetarist inspired attempt to reduce money in the economy, and therefore demand. In effect they are saying that the primary cause of the rise in unemployment was the monetarist policies undertaken by the Conservative governments of the 1980s.

A further attack on the general thrust of the New Right policies was launched by Will Hutton (1996). In his book *The State We're In* he delivered a critique of their whole approach, again arguing that the justification for these changes could not be found in purely economic arguments:

The New Right economists' undilutedly classical arguments about boosting 'labour market flexibility' and 'controlling the money supply' in truth spoke to longstanding Tory prejudices; here was the theoretical justification for tackling social security scroungers, bashing trade unions and cutting taxes and government spending.
(Hutton, 1996, p.91)

The effect of unemployment

Moving from being employed to being unemployed will clearly have an adverse effect on financial income. Changes to benefit rates in the 1980s made this even more true. Will Hutton (1996) points out that unemployment benefit as a percentage of average earnings for male workers fell from 16.3 per cent in 1979 to 12.4 per cent in 1992 for single men, and from 26.2 per cent to 20.1 per cent for married men. However, sociologists have also been concerned to consider the possible other social consequences of unemployment, in terms of both individuals and society as a whole.

The most notable large-scale research on these issues arises from the extensive social survey on unemployment and social change conducted by sociologists, Duncan Gallie, Catherine Marsh and Carolyn Vogler (1994). They were clearly concerned to place the individual experience of unemployment in the context of concern over unemployment as an increasing issue of social concern:

Gallup interviewers ask a monthly quota sample of adults in Britain what they think is the 'most urgent problem' facing the country today. Unemployment dominated replies throughout the 1980s, being the issue most frequently named as either the most urgent or the second most urgent problem.
(Gallie *et al.*, 1994, p. 1)

Unemployment, or fear of unemployment, appears to have an effect on peoples' lives, but in order to investigate the basis of these fears it is necessary to consider some of the concrete evidence on the ways unemployment affects people. Beyond the financial problems caused by unemployment lie other issues.

First, unemployment is bad for your health (see also Section 13.2). Two pieces of research in recent years have reinforced this view. In the USA, Harvey Brenner (1979) found that societies where unemployment increased by 1 million experienced a rise in deaths from various health disorders of up to 275 000 people. In the UK, Alistair Graham (1985a) found that families living on benefits, which obviously includes the unemployed, were twice as likely as other groups to suffer from health problems.

In their book, *Investigating Work, Unemployment and Leisure*, Nick Madry and Mark Kirby (1996) quote the following findings in relation to the UK:

According to The Observer *(27 September 1992) the British Regional Heart Survey, based on studies of 253 British towns over ten years, found that those who were unemployed at any time during the five years prior to the research were more than one and a half times as likely to die in the next five years as employed men. In relation to morbidity as opposed to mortality, the Office of Health Economics published statistics showing that the number of prescriptions issued on Merseyside was 9.7 per person in 1991 compared to 6.9 per person in the South West Thames Regional Health Authority. The respective unemployment rates in these two areas were 12.5 per cent and 4.2 per cent.*
(Madry and Kirby, 1996, p.138)

There is also evidence of the psychological effects of unemployment. While the unemployed suffer higher levels of suicide and psychological ill-health, Brendan Burchell (1994) found that this was also true of those suffering economic insecurity in the form of working on casual, short-term or other flexible working arrangements (see also Section 9.4). He found that their psychological profiles were closer to the unemployed than to those in secure employment. This finding is significant given the major increase in the demand for flexible working conditions and the greater use of part-time and casual labour. The changes introduced into the labour market and actively promoted by the New Right governments of the 1980s and 1990s are found to have damaging consequences psychologically for those involved.

The reasons for the effect of unemployment or casualization on psychological health are themselves a matter of debate. Many argue that it is a direct result of the financial stress involved. However Marie Jahoda *et al.* (1972) argue that it is more to do with the loss of the routine in people's lives which having a job creates, and also the sense of identity (see Chapter 10) associated with involvement in a certain job.

Discussion point

How important do you think jobs are as a source of personal identity for people today?

One of the most important sociological findings about the distribution of unemployment which underlines the importance of these effects is that found by Jean Martin and Ceridwen Roberts (1984), in their survey of women and employment, namely that wives of unemployed men are much more likely to be unemployed themselves than are the wives of employed men. In terms of households this finding will clearly lead to the negative effects of unemployment impacting much more on some households than others. The key reason for this relationship is the feature of the benefit system whereby a couple's benefits are reduced by the level of the woman's earnings, since this creates a negative incentive for women whose husbands are unemployed to be working (see also Section 14.4). It clearly has implications for the distribution of income in society by creating work-rich (and therefore more income-rich) households and work-poor households with very low standards of living.

Unemployment has negative consequences for the individuals directly affected, and the extent of unemployment in the 1980s and 1990s has made it one of, if not the, most important contemporary social issues. The reasons for this are not hard to understand. First there is the direct cost of unemployment to the economy, and therefore society, involving the loss of tax revenue and the cost of unemployment and other benefits. Secondly there is the indirect cost to the standard of living of the economy in the sense of the loss of the goods and services which could have been produced by the unemployed if they had been employed. And finally there is the cost in terms of the links between poverty, deprivation and crime. Writing in the *New Statesman and Society*, David Dickinson (1994) showed there was a clear link between unemployment and crime (see Chapter 11), particularly for young males.

9.7 Organizations: from rationalization to McDonaldization

Organizations are designed to achieve specific goals. For example hospitals are designed to treat the sick, the Inland Revenue is designed to assess and collect taxes, and schools are designed to educate people. This specificity of goals differentiates them for other social entities such as families or communities whose roles are more general. As can be seen from this list, organizations are an important component of modern life. The study of organizations considers some of the important implications of this, including the growth of bureaucracy in society.

Max Weber, rationalization and bureaucracy

The modern study of organizations starts with Max Weber's outline of the characteristics of bureaucracies and rationality (see also Section 2.3). Martin Albrow, in his book on bureaucracy (1970), underlines the importance of this to his overall work:

Weber considered rational bureaucracy as a major element in the rationalisation of the modern world, for him the most important of all social processes. Among other things this process involved growing precision and explicitness in the principles governing social organization.
(Albrow, 1970, p. 43)

Weber contrasted these rational bureaucracies with the basis of traditional societies where individuals' actions are based on habit and custom. The growth of rational thinking with bureaucracies was a key organizational innovation. Decisions would now be taken on the basis of clear notions about how a certain goal should be achieved utilizing scientific knowledge.

Crucially, Weber argued that bureaucracies would not take decisions on the basis of personal relations and networks but would be impersonal, purely rational decision-making machines. This involved the setting down and application of clear rules and a hierarchical structure to ensure that these rules were rigorously applied to achieve set ends. These rules would leave little room for personal discretion with the aim of creating an atmosphere where officials act impartially and impersonally and on a rational rather than an emotional basis. The officials who staff bureaucracies would therefore be appointed on the basis of their possession of expert or technical knowledge and the ability to apply this in a rational way.

Bureaucracy and democracy

It is clear that Weber thought that this type of organization potentially possessed technical superiority over traditional personalized forms of decision-taking (see Section 17.4) which were open to favouritism and patronage. However it is also clear that Weber saw the potential for rationalization to lead to society becoming enveloped in an 'iron cage' of bureaucracy. What he was trying to square in his theories was the balance between cold scientific modernist rationalism and the defence of the individual in the face of these impersonal bureaucracies.

The problem Weber considered was how the inherent tendency of bureaucracy to accumulate power could be prevented from reaching a point where it controlled the policy and action of the organization it was supposed to serve. . . . Weber's analysis of bureaucracy led to a plea for adherence to representative government . . . It was not ideally democratic. But it did the most that could be expected under the conditions of modern rationalized society.
(Albrow, 1970, pp. 47–9)

It was this which led Weber to develop his famous distinction between power and authority (see Section 17.4), recognizing that not all power might be legitimate. Weber called for strong political leadership to act as decision-makers to set the goals for bureaucracies to carry out and also to defend individual freedom from their encroachment. Jürgen Habermas (1972) has argued that in stressing that social scientists should not get involved in deciding political aims, Weber's formulations left little defence against decisions being imposed by force, as was the case with the rise of Hitler. As can be seen, discussions about the rise of organizations and bureaucracy were developed in a time when the outcomes were extremely important. It is the attempt to arrive at a balance between the perceived positive and negative aspects of bureaucracies, clearly seen in Weber, which has characterized continuing debate in the sociology of organizations.

The limits to rational bureaucratic control

Responding to Weber's ideas, Robert K. Merton (1952) (see Section 2.4) argued that certain elements of the ideal-type of bureaucratic behaviour as outlined by Weber might be dysfunctional because the impersonality might lead to friction between bureaucrats and the public, and also because bureaucrats trained to operate strictly by the rules might not know how to react if faced by a situation not explicitly covered by the rules.

The notion that pure impersonality might be dysfunctional leads on to a consideration of informality in organizations.

Discussion point

Would you prefer to be dealt with impersonally in a bureaucracy or on the basis of personal considerations?

The informal aspects of organizations

The clear implication of this is that we cannot study

organizations purely in terms of a study of their formal rules and procedures. Tony Watson (1995) points out that:

To understand formal work organizations sociologically, therefore, we need to see them as general patterns of regular behaviour which include the whole range of informal, unofficial and even illegitimate actions and arrangements which occur.
(Watson, 1995, p. 235)

He illustrates this through a diagram which shows the influence on organizations of both the formal and the informal organizational structures, and of the wider structures of society (see Figure 9.5).

This notion and approach can be seen in the work of Peter Blau (1955). In his book *The Dynamics of Bureaucracy*, Blau argues that we need to consider the ways in which formal regulations are actually applied and how they are modified in that process. He studied an employment agency, and found that informal agreements and strong common norms led to a more productive work environment. In this case encouraging competition was seen as harmful to productivity and to the fulfilment of the overall goals of the organization. Secondly this study considered two sections within an organization sharing a common goal and common rules and regulations, but none-

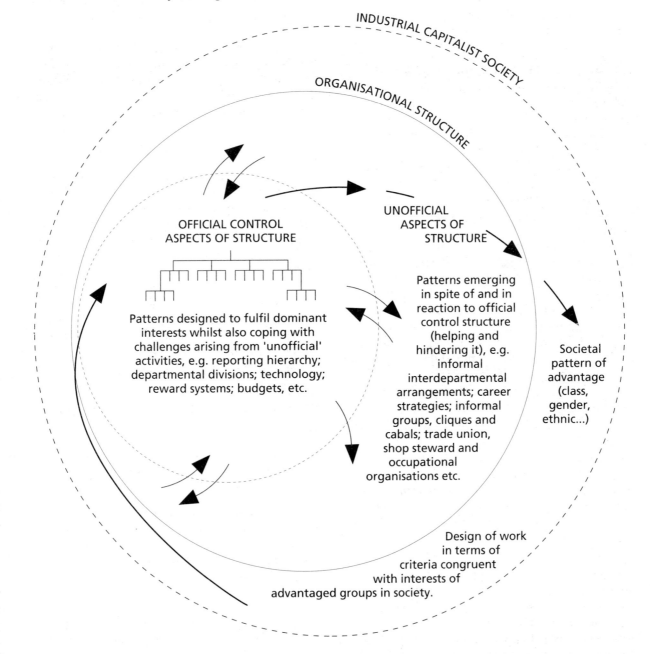

Figure 9.5 A sociological model of the modern work organization. Source: Watson (1995, p.238)

theless operating very differently. This underlines the importance of examining the actual way organizations work, rather that the way they are supposed to work.

In a second study, Blau even found that breaking the rules can produce greater efficiency, in contrast to Weber's original stress on bureaucracy and the formal rules. He studied the operation of a federal agency inspecting business compliance with employment laws. Here he found that while there were clear rules about confidentiality of cases and the reporting of offers of bribes, these were flouted and this helped produce greater efficiency overall. These informal work norms increased efficiency, but only by compromising on the bureaucratic rules which Weber had seen as the basis of efficiency.

Taylor and scientific management

As well as debates about democracy, the early twentieth century also saw the rise of the application of notions of rationality to work, notably in the form of scientific management, inspired by the American engineer Frederick W. Taylor (1911; 1964, orig. pub. 1903). At the time the work environment was changing owing to the rise of both competition and trade unionism and Taylor set out to improve the efficiency of production through the application of his science to industry.

His key argument was that failures in production were the result of bad management caused by managers leaving the organization of day-to-day labour processes to the workers, the only ones who had the skills to understand the detail of the actual process. Taylor argued that management needed to seize control of the work process and to do this they needed a scientific understanding of that process. He set about providing it. His most famous experiments to prove the usefulness of his approach involved altering the work patterns of a worker named Schmidt. Grint (1991) reports on the results of these experiments:

Through the close monitoring of Schmidt's work practices in shovelling pig iron, including rest times, operating methods etc., Taylor managed to persuade Schmidt to increase his productivity by 400 per cent, in exchange for a wage increase of 40 per cent.
(Grint, 1991, p.186)

This provides a clear insight into the central mechanism which Taylor believed to be the key: the use of productivity incentives to encourage a higher work rate. His desire to break jobs down into the simplest tasks, so reducing the level of skill required and therefore the wage rate, can also be glimpsed by his description of Schmidt as having the mentality of an ox.

Discussion point

What view of workers do you think Taylor holds? To what extent do you agree with him?

Taylor was clearly not interested in providing job satisfaction or in encouraging workers to think; in fact his scheme was designed precisely to eliminate this, since their knowledge was the basis of their control of the work process, a control Taylor consciously set out to destroy.

Taylor's approach was most famously developed in the Ford Model T plant in Detroit from 1913 onwards. This led Antonio Gramsci to term this development 'Fordism'.

Fordism was based on standardized mass production techniques, the innovation of the assembly line with the use of some mechanized techniques and the breaking down of other tasks through the application of scientific management. The result was that cars were produced more cheaply, though without any great level of choice (the famous 'any colour as long as it is black').

The key problems with this model were the spur to later developments in organizational theory. Briefly these were, first that work on the assembly line was generally miserable and alienating and often led to high labour turnover, which required Ford to raise wages but with the problem that this ate into profits. Secondly the dependence of Fordism on economic stability was exposed by the growth of competition in the 1920s and the later economic depression of the 1920s and 1930s. Finally, it was argued that mass production offered little choice to consumers who in the post-World War II era began to demand more choice. (See also Section 9.4.)

Factors influencing organizational behaviour

If we cannot view organizations simply as embodiments of rational bureaucratic control, and apply Taylorist principles to make them efficient – owing to the identification of informal factors within organizations, and the limitations of scientific management and mass production – then this leads to discussion of other possible factors which impact upon organizations and organizational behaviour.

Charles Perrow (1970) argues that there have been three broad trends in this type of analysis. First there was the rise of a concentration on interpersonal relations and group norms within organizations, exemplified by the human relations approach. Secondly some have concentrated on technology as a key factor in affecting how organizations work, leading to debates about the possibilities of automation and the use of computers to overcome problems. Finally he identifies the institutional school of theorists who concentrate on the environment within which organizations operate and the way people draw ideas from the culture around them in deciding how organizations should work.

Human relations and interpersonal approaches

Elton Mayo and human relations

The Hawthorne Works of the Western Electric Company in Cicero near Chicago were the site for a series of experiments which led to the development of the Human Relations School of Organizational Theory. Human Relations theorists argued that the concentration on pay rates and incentive schemes in Taylor's scientific management was insufficient to ensure higher productivity since it ignored the human and social aspects of work. Mayo (1933) argued that the key role of managers was to ensure that work groups' social sentiments were developed, but in a way that fostered greater productivity. This led to the question of how to do this and to the Hawthorne experiments. Researchers varied the working conditions, for example the level of lighting, of a group of workers over a five-year period. However they found that whatever they did, productivity increased, even when they reduced the lighting. This led to the famous 'Hawthorne effect' when they concluded that the reason for the increases in productivity was the attention being paid to this group of workers (see also Section 3.9), who had developed a strong social cohesion through their common experiences.

This led to the conclusion that managers should pay attention to their workers' needs at the workplace, which went beyond the purely financial. Managers must make sure that the personal and social needs of workers as humans are met in the workplace if productivity is to be maximized.

A neo-human relations school took this development further by arguing that the work itself needs to be reorganized. This meant moving away from the monotonous work on Taylorist assembly lines and instead introducing job rotation and team working, as seen in Volvo plants in Sweden.

In the 1980s this perspective came under criticism from managers who argued that it spends too much time on satisfying workers rather than customers. Human relations approaches have also been criticized from the Left by those who argue it is merely using psychology to make happy workers. However the aim is still the same, to get more productivity out of them. It might make work less oppressive, but no less exploitative.

The limits to rationality

Another approach centred on how people work inside organizations is Simon's (1957) concept of 'bounded rationality' which stressed the limits on human rationality. March and Simon (1958) argued that people are only 'intendedly rational' in that everyone has limited capabilities and does not have the ability to know the full consequences of any action. In this situation people will choose the first satisfactory option when faced with a choice, rather than try to work out the optimum solution. This is a problem inherent in all organizations. This model emphasizes the structural aspects of organizations rather than the individual decision-making process emphasized by the human relations school.

In a later development of this approach, Cohen *et al.* (1972) studied American universities and argued that their decision-taking could be likened to a 'garbage can model', by which they meant that decisions resulted from whatever happened to be thrown into the decision-making process. The result was what they describe as 'organized anarchy' far removed from the notion of decisions being reached rationally.

The key criticism of this approach is that it assumes that conflicts that emerge are broadly the result of interpersonal problems which can be solved by adaptation rather than reflections of real underlying conflicts, a problem it shares with the human relations approach.

Technology

The most obvious example of a concern with technology in organizations is the work of Robert Blauner (1964). He argued that the level of technology was the key factor affecting the level of alienation workers suffered at work. The concept of alienation was first developed by Karl Marx (see Section 2.3 and 9.2) to describe the sense of self-estrangement and loss of control suffered by workers in the workplace. Blauner set about operationalizing this concept by measuring the degree of control workers feel they have, the degree to which they feel a sense of purpose in their work, the degree to which they are socially integrated into their work and the degree to which they are involved in their work. Alienated workers suffer powerlessness, meaninglessness, isolation and self-estrangement.

He argued that it was possible to identify four different stages in the use of technology and he examined one instance of each in America in the late 1950s. In craft production (printing) the workers are not alienated since they have control over their work and experience a sense of purpose. The next stage was mechanization and here he explored the textile industry and machine-minders. Their alienation was higher since they were tied to the machines with little sense of control and with little sense of purpose or meaning in their work. The next stage was the development of mechanization into assembly line work, exemplified by car factories. Here Blauner found the highest levels of alienation. Workers have little or no control over their work, the speed of which is determined by the assembly line and with no sense of meaning since they do the same repetitive tasks all day long. Blauner's study therefore contributed to the critiques of assembly line production seen as the embodiment of Taylorism. However in the final stage of technology, that of automation, Blauner's study of a chemical plant led him to argue that alienation was lower here than on an assembly line since work involved monitoring and checking production and the maintenance of complicated equipment. The implication was that the spread of automation could reduce alienation.

His work has been subject to a number of criticisms, most notably those of Eldridge (1971). The latter argued that Blauner changed the meaning of alienation from its original Marxist notion where it was centred on objective relations in production, which are the same regardless of the technology employed, and secondly that he overstated the importance of technology in determining the level of alienation in various industries. For instance, Nichols and Beynon (1977) found that only a minority of workers at six of the seven chemical plants they studied were control-room operatives. Thus Blauner was making generalizations on the basis of the experience of a minority.

A more recent focus on technology has centred on the effect of the introduction of computers and information technology (IT). In the work of Piore and Sabel, this technological innovation is seen as central to the possibilities for the development of a renewed craft form of work based on flexible specialization, although their rather optimistic predictions are not shared by all.

Freeman and Soete (1994) argue that although computerization has led to the development of a number of high-skill jobs, the increased productivity resulting from the use of IT has also led to the devastation of employment in manufacturing industry. Shaiken (1979) also argues that computer-controlled design meant that machine tool operators were deskilled (see the section later on Braverman). Furthermore, some, for example Lyons (1993), have pointed to the way computers allow for greater control and surveillance of workers by management and therefore contribute to the creation of the surveillance society noted by Michel Foucault (see also Section 17.4).

A pure focus on technology has also been criticized by those who argue that it is necessary to examine the way technology interfaces with the social aspects of work, leading to the development of the socio-technical approach through the work of the Tavistock Institute (Trist *et al.*, 1963). Since work is a social activity, a sole reliance on technology will not create an environment that maximizes productivity. This leads back to the neo-Human Relations School, and the adoption of team working, an innovation inspired by Tavistock Institute Research.

Activity

Suggest ways in which computers could be used to provide greater control and surveillance of workers by management.

A

The organization in its environment

The third approach to studying organizations has come to be known as the institutional approach. It emphasizes the way the organization is part of a wider environment which influences both the organization and the behaviour of those within the organization. In particular it is concerned with the way that the values of organizations can be affected by links with the outside community. The best exponents of this viewpoint are Philip Selznick (1957) and Charles Perrow (1970, 1986) whose own evaluation of the institutional approach is:

The major area of contribution of the institutional school must surely be the emphasis upon the environment.
(Perrow, 1970, p. 185)

What he means by this is the way in which organizations interact closely with their environments. Central to this is the distinction which Selznick makes between organizations and institutions.

He argues that organizations are purely goal-driven entities (organizations) while others develop into bodies in which people invest their lives and which embody some more deeply embedded values (institutions). Underlying his distinction is the notion that an organization's goals can be shaped by the values of the community in which it is located, and it is this which determines the process of institutionalization. By infusing organizations with some set of values, the feeling of being part of something is enhanced as is the feeling of contributing to the wider society. Thus people feel enriched through such involvement. This fits in with the functionalist consensus framework within which it operates. (See Section 2.4.) However we need to ask whether someone working on the assembly line in a car plant gains this sense of enriching themselves in relation to the wider community through their job. The answer is probably not, and this points to the need to consider the possibility for the wider conflicts of society to be expressed inside organizations.

> ### 💬 Discussion point
>
> To what extent is your school or college influenced by its surrounding environment? To what extent does it influence the surrounding environment?

Organizational and managerial theories

Later developments of this school of thought have merged with managerial theory to consider organizational forms. Alvin Gouldner (1954, 1957) studied operations at a mine following the appointment of a new manager. He argues that the old manager allowed the workers a degree of self-control and this can be seen as more akin to traditional authority on Weber's ideal-types. Relations between bosses and workers were less impersonal and less based on rules and regulations.

However the new manager was determined to bureaucratize to cut costs and raise productivity. This meant that unofficial practices were outlawed and strict rules applied. These changes were strongly resisted by the miners, to some degree successfully. Gouldner therefore stresses that there are variations in the degree of bureaucratization and the resistance by the miners shows that the process of bureaucratization is not inevitable.

The notion was also taken up in the work of Burns and Stalker (1966) who on the basis of studies of 20 firms argued that it was possible to distinguish between mechanistic organizations and organic organizations (see also Section 2.3). They argued that mechanistic organizations are characterized by a high development of the division of labour co-ordinated by managers who adopt a top-down communication model. Individuals pursue and are responsible for only a limited number of tasks. They argued that this sort of organization is best suited to times of stability.

In contrast, in organic organizations there is much less emphasis on rigid hierarchies and instead people's skills are employed wherever they are seen as appropriate within the organization. They argue that this organic approach is much more suited to times of great change since this requires greater emphasis on innovation and creativity which gets stifled in more hierarchical systems. However they point out that the need by some individuals to retain some notion of their place in a hierarchy and a con-

centration on status differentials may impede the development of organic organizations.

The influence of the environment on organizational form and operation has been questioned recently owing to the apparent ease with which Japanese firms are able to locate abroad and fit in, despite originating from a very different cultural environment. Thus it may be that organizations can shape their environments. This is the conclusion reached by Richard Florida and Martin Kenney on the basis of their study of Japanese corporations located in North America:

Transferring organizational practices and forms from one society to another means that they must be uncoupled from the environment in which they are embedded and recreated in a new environment. The transplants provide clear evidence that organizational forms can be effectively lifted from an originally supportive context and transferred to a foreign environment. Furthermore, they show that organizations can mold the new environment to their needs and to some degree create the conditions of their own embeddedness.
(Florida and Kenney, 1996, p. 76)

Post-Fordism, post-modernism and the end of bureaucracy?

Stewart Clegg (1990, 1992) argues that bureaucracy in organizations was characteristic of 'modern' societies but that the move to post-modern times (see Section 2.10) has undermined the usefulness of this style, and organizations can no longer be seen to inevitably develop in the way Weber expected. The most important variable factor he identifies in the way organizations develop is the culture of the society around them.

In explaining the success of Japanese organizations, Clegg argues that we need to take into account the way the cultures of these societies have influenced organizational developments, but the fact that not all organizations have developed in exactly the same way is due to global forces such as cultural ideas like post-modernism (see Section 10.11). These stress that consumers desire more individualized products with a greater concern for quality than cost and as a result the division of labour evident in Taylorism and Fordism can no longer provide the goods people want. This stress on the cultural aspects distinguishes the explanation for these developments from the more technologically driven explanations such as flexible specialization and post-Fordism (see Section 9.4). However what they both share is an emphasis on Japanization as the model for future organizational developments.

The extent to which these are really very different is questioned by a number of writers. Thompson (1989) argues that while these organizations expect much greater levels of flexibility from their workers, they often retain extremely detailed rulebooks and it is clear that the key aim is still to increase productivity. As a result the performance of workers is still closely monitored.

He argues that the notion that these developments signify the end of bureaucracy is mistaken since there are still important features of bureaucratic operation present, notably hierarchies, rules and norms; and in some ways the latter has been enhanced with the growth of notions of corporate culture, where people are invited to fit in or go elsewhere. If this is true, then there is still a need to consider the possible ways in which there will be conflict within organizations, ideas about which have been developed by Marxist and interactionist sociologists.

Marxism and organizations

Michael Burawoy (1979) argues that the sociology of organizations grew out of the demise of industrial sociology. He argues that the growth of the theories of the 'end of ideology' (Bell, 1973) and convergence theory (Kerr *et al.*, 1973, orig. pub. 1960) rested on the belief that the problems of capitalism had been overcome.

The result of this, Buroway argues, is a shift to a consideration of organizations in general and a concern with studies of bureaucracy, based on the work of Max Weber. The result was that:

with the subsumption of industrial sociology under organization theory, the distinctiveness of the profit-seeking capitalist enterprise is lost . . . Descriptions of change are elevated into spurious explanations of change through the constitution of natural laws – the ineluctable processes of rationalization, bureaucratization, the pursuit of efficiency, and so on.
(Buroway, 1979, pp. 5–6)

However, he points to the contradiction in that all the variants of organization theory rest both on the notion that there is an underlying consensus in society, but also on the need for organizations for the purpose of social control. This, he says, makes the whole subject of organization theory paradoxical since:

if there is underlying harmony and consensus is not problematical, then why is social control important or necessary? And conversely, if social control is so important, then how can we take consensus as given?
(Buroway, 1979, p. 8)

He argues that the two themes derive from Durkheim (consensus) and Weber (power, authority and social control) (see also Section 2.3) and theorists have squared the circle by assuming conflict to be patho-

logical or accidental. Workers are studied in order to try to understand the way to increase productivity. The ideological foundations of the various elements which together constitute organization theory are therefore shown to be pro-capitalist and pro-managerialist, believing in principle that the source of conflict can be removed. Instead Burawoy argues that conflict and consent in the workplace:

must be grasped in terms of the organization of the labour process under capitalism. Conflict and consent are not primordial conditions but products of the particular organization of work.
(Buroway, 1979, p. 12)

This requires an analysis of the labour process under the specific historical conditions of capitalism.

Braverman: capitalism and the labour process

Harry Braverman (1974) was concerned to link the actual labour process and the way it changes to a wider political economy of society. He argued that under capitalism, the labour process is one where the capitalists are represented by managers whose job is to extract surplus value from the workers. However the key problem which they face in this respect is that they cannot buy labour, only potential labour power, and they therefore have to devise ways to extract the maximum labour power from workers. In order to push down costs and increase productivity, work is divided up so that skilled workers can be replaced by unskilled workers. Central to this is the separation of the processes of design and execution of tasks. Braverman calls this a process of deskilling and he argues that the replacement of craft workers by workers on mass assembly lines exemplifies this process. He argues that the process of deskilling will continue and his own work considered the deskilling of many white-collar jobs (see also Sections 4.6 and 4.7).

This approach has been criticized, mainly by arguing that Taylorism was not typical and therefore it is not possible to draw conclusions of a general trend to deskilling from studies of Taylorism.

Braverman has been criticized from a Marxist perspective by Burawoy (1979, 1984) who argues that both Marx and Braverman's notion of the labour process rest on the way effort is coerced out of workers through control. He argues that on the basis of his observations, workers worked hard almost voluntarily. There is therefore a need to understand why workers consent to work hard as part of an understanding of the labour process. His answer is that through ideology the seeking of profit is presented as normal and as being the basis of the worker's remuneration. An understanding of ideology is therefore necessary to see how capitalists manage to get workers to consent to work hard. This is easier under conditions of monopoly capitalism which can be contrasted to the labour process in competitive capitalism:

Anarchy in the market leads to despotism in the factory. The second type of labour process, the hegemonic organization of work, is based on consent predominating over coercion . . . Subordination of the market leads to hegemony in the factory.
(Buroway, 1979, p. 194)

Marxism, bureaucracy and the state

A second aspect of Marxist concern with organizational theory is Weber's notion that bureaucratization was an inevitable force in modern society. Weber had used this as an argument against Marx's notion that the state would disappear under communism, since he argued that the charismatic authority vested in revolutionary leaders was only temporary in nature, and if any communist regime wished to survive it would have to adopt bureaucratic procedures. Revolutions would therefore lead to a strengthening, not the disappearance of the state. (See also Section 17.3.)

These ideas were challenged by Lenin who argued that the structure of the state was determined by the fact that it arose to deal with class conflicts and that for the purposes of this, parliamentary democracy provided the best shell for capitalism since it gives the appearance that the elected representatives run society, whereas all important decisions are taken behind the scenes. The growth of the state and bureaucratization are seen as arising from the pressures of class struggle in a capitalist society. As a result, Weber's defence against bureaucracy (greater democratization) was seen as ineffective by Lenin, who argued that the only guard against such tendencies was the complete smashing of the state and its replacement by a proletarian dictatorship, meaning the greater expansion of democracy (see Section 17.1) for workers and at the same time the suppression of those who would oppress and exploit them, namely the capitalists.

Erik Olin Wright (1978) argues that there are similarities between the two in that both disapprove of parliaments which are mere talking-shops and both worry about the potential for bureaucratic domination. However, Wright argues that Lenin makes an important distinction between bureaucrats and technicians which Weber does not. Lenin argues that while the technical aspects of production had become more complex, the control functions such as accountancy had not. The reason these are in the control of bureaucrats is therefore not a technical

requirement, but a political decision to control the workers. This means workers can do these jobs with some training and therefore the division between the bureaucracy and society can be overcome. With the development of soviet organization and direct democracy, the tendencies to bureaucratization would be eroded. In the concrete context of post-revolutionary Russia, the problems of the low cultural and economic level of Russia would mean that the state could not be destroyed immediately, but the failure of revolutions elsewhere led to the isolation of Russia. These processes were further embedded by Stalin, leading to a complete reversal of Lenin's notion of the erosion of the state. Wright (1994) argues that the later development of bureaucratic rule in the Soviet Union can be seen as the result of the way a bureaucracy can consolidate its rule if the Communist Party no longer genuinely represents the workers. He therefore argues that the lessons to be learnt are that communist parties need to retain clear connections with the working class and remain organically linked to them through involvement in communities and workplaces. Again this suggests that bureaucratization should not be seen as inevitable and stresses concrete ways to avoid this problem.

Interactionism: institutions as social control devices

Goffman and total institutions

The earlier section considering the work of Philip Selznick highlighted the distinction he made between organizations and institutions, where the values of the community have been incorporated. A rather more critical view of institutions can be found in the work of Erving Goffman (see also Section 2.7). His work emphasizes the way that institutions such as prisons and psychiatric hospitals, which ostensibly reflect the concern of society for people being treated, are in fact mechanisms of social control.

He argues that we need to talk of total institutions which are characterized as places where people exist cut off from wider society and where their lives are totally regimented and controlled by bureaucratic regulations.

His most famous work in this vein was *Asylums* (1968), a study of psychiatric institutions, based on observations while working in one such hospital (see also Section 13.8). He argued that while the inmates of such places do enter with their own culture, the process of institutionalization may result in the loss of this culture and therefore the loss of ability to deal with the everyday aspects of life outside such an enclosed environment. The clear divisions between staff and patients and the strict regulations result in the loss of the feeling of self (the 'mortification of the self'). In their lives in total institutions, inmates find that things they take for granted in the outside world such as going to the toilet or sending a letter now require permission. The feeling of being an individual is stripped away.

However, while emphasizing the extent of bureaucratic control exerted on individuals in total institutions, Goffman does also argue that the responses to their situation may vary. He argues that some may choose to withdraw from all aspects of life in the institution beyond those that are compulsory, others may challenge the institution, or accept the view of the institution and try to become perfect inmates and even in some cases come to prefer life inside the institution. He emphasizes that the majority of inmates simply try to get by. Since Goffman emphasizes that by and large most inmates do retain some notion of their self, the stated aims of such institutions – which is to reform people in some way – are not achieved and he himself argues that they instead function merely as dumping grounds for people. Such a view was instrumental in the development of critiques of incarceration as the basis of treatment of the mentally ill which fed into later debates about community care.

Discussion point
Should people be treated in psychiatric institutions or in the community?

However, the interactionist focus on the construction of meaning through interaction within total institutions has been criticized for ignoring the impact of wider society. On the basis of a study of prisons in California, John Irwin (1970) argued that inmates' responses to imprisonment depended to a large extent on their experiences prior to imprisonment, which undermines Goffman's notion of understanding institutional life as separate from that of wider society, a view underlined by research by Stan Cohen and Laurie Taylor (1971) of inmates of Durham Prison. They argued that their behaviour showed a degree of resistance to institutionalization which went beyond the view elaborated by Goffman.

Contemporary theories of bureaucracy, rationality and organizations

Michel Foucault: The surveillance society

The notion of institutions as mechanisms of social control has more recently been taken up in the work of

Michel Foucault (1967, 1977). Foucault argues that the development of modern institutions concerned with social control, such as prisons, can only be traced back to the eighteenth century with the development of systematic rules of punishment and control which replaced the personal power of rulers to make arbitrary decisions. The rise of prisons is linked to the rise of new forms of knowledge and technologies including the development of the human sciences, particularly psychology and psychiatry. (See also Sections 13.9 and 17.4.)

Discussion point
Are psychology and sociology part of the solution to societal problems or part of the problem themselves?

This, along with the developments of modern medicine, allowed for the development of a new form of disciplinary power concerned with control of human bodies, and the attempt to understand the reasons why people deviate from normal behaviour and then to modify their behaviour, a process Foucault refers to as normalization. These new technologies of disciplinary power can be seen to underlie such developments as the workhouse, devised under the Poor Law (see Section 14.1), and psychiatric hospitals.

All of these new disciplinary powers depend on knowledge inside institutions, and this says, Foucault, can be seen in the Panoptican design of prisons, which allow warders to observe all inmates from a central viewing point. This notion is developed further into the idea of a surveillance society where watching people and gaining information about them becomes a central part of society. Thus, argues Foucault, all institutions come to resemble prisons with minute scrutiny over the activities of those within them.

Discussion point
In what ways and to what extent does your school or college resemble a prison?

While this form of control may not be as painful as the pre-modern forms of punishment, Foucault argues that this should not blind us to the fact that it allows a greater degree of social control, albeit more subtle, but nonetheless impinging even more on individual freedom.

Foucault's notion of a surveillance society has also been applied more recently in the work of David Lyon (1993). He argues that the construction of large computer databases creates the basis for a greater level of surveillance, although he argues that we need to consider the fact that people often actively consent to be surveyed in this way through, for example, providing their details on credit card applications.

McDonaldization

Credit cards are also the subject of a study by George Ritzer (1995) who argues that they are a particular case of the McDonaldization of society. Rather than penal institutions, Ritzer (1993) believes that fast-food restaurants are the current model for organizations:

a process by which the principles of the fast-food restaurant are coming to dominate more and more sectors of American society as well as the rest of the world.
(Ritzer, 1993, p. 1)

> ### Discussion point
> How far do you agree with the notion that more and more areas of socety are becoming dominated by the principles of McDonalization? Is this a good thing?

McDonald's, for Ritzer, is the epitome of the way that consumer culture can be seen as an extension of Weber's rationalization thesis where things are produced for consumers according to strict calculation and predictability, utilizing the material environment to control the behaviour of human beings with, for example, fixed menus, limited options, uncomfortable seats and queue control barriers. Food is therefore bureaucratically produced and dispensed in rational, modernist, Fordist ways:

the fast-food restaurant is Fordist in various ways, most notably in the degree to which it utilises assembly-line principles and technologies. ... While there may be changes in the economy which support the idea of a post industrial society, the fast-food restaurant and the many other elements of the economy that are modelled after it do not.
(Ritzer, 1996, p. 443)

Thus rationality is alive and well, though the key model now is fast-food restaurants rather than government bureaucracies.

9.8 Leisure and society

The sociology of leisure developed out of the study of work because leisure was seen as the time available after work was completed. As the amount of time taken up by work declined with the growth in productivity allowed by industrial production, it was therefore assumed that the amount of time available for leisure would increase.

It is in this context that sociologists and other commentators developed notions of the move towards the leisure society which was popular in the 1950s. The optimistic mood of the time contributed to ideas of society where work seen as coerced time would gradually reduce in terms of time usage, leaving people free to spend more time on leisure activities.

In fact there is little evidence to suggest that the rather rosy picture painted in these early theories ever approached reality. It certainly does not fit contemporary reality where under the pressure of New Right demands for greater economic efficiency, people are working longer hours, not shorter. Despite this, leisure is now firmly established as an area of sociological study even though the leisure society may not have arrived.

Patterns of participation in leisure

A sociological analysis of leisure starts with the suggestion that, like other forms of human activity, leisure is not something people do in a purely individualistic way, but that participation in leisure is structured by the same types of inequalities operative in other areas.

Social class differences in leisure participation

In her study of patterns of leisure, Sue Glyptis (1989) argues that it is clear that participation in sports and entertainment activities is clearly structured by social class (see Chapter 4). For instance she found that 34 per cent of professional workers are involved in indoor sports compared with only 15 per cent of unskilled manual workers. The reason for this is unequal access to income, since generally charges are levied even when leisure centres are run by public authorities. She also pointed to the importance of car ownership in relation to certain leisure activities, and the fact that this is clearly unequally distributed.

Marxist sociologists John Clarke and Chas Critcher (1985) note the growing importance of the provision of leisure activities as a commercial activity and point therefore to the fact that access to this is dependent on money, which leads to inequalities in access. They argue that leisure needs to be analysed within its social, economic and political context.

> ### Activity
> Suggest three ways in which commercialism has increased in the field of leisure provision in recent years.
> **A**

Since income is unequally distributed, and has become more so in the 1980s and 1990s (see Section 14.8), the kind of inequalities in access to leisure facilities noted by these studies will probably have risen in recent years. This is yet another indicator of the continuing importance of social class as a structure in society, despite the seeming sociological fashion to deny this. As Stephen Edgell (1993) comments in his book *Class*:

what needs to be explained is not the presumed demise of class, but the tenacity of class-based patterns of inequality and politics, and much else besides. In the meantime, class rules and classlessness remains a dream rather than a reality. (Edgell, 1993, p. 122)

While Edgell was not specifically talking about leisure, his point is nonetheless valid in relation to this topic.

Gender and participation in leisure

If leisure is conceptualized as activities undertaken in the time available when all necessary 'enforced' activities have been undertaken, then it is clear that in relation to males, this largely means the time available after paid work has been completed. This is of course true also for women with the important difference that generally notions of necessary activities for women would also include taking major responsibility for domestic labour. (See Section 7.5 and 9.1.)

On this basis the number of hours free time per week available to women on average is less than that available to men. In 1991–2 women in full-time paid employment had 3.3 hours free time per day compared with 4.8 hours free time for males in full-time employment. Even women in part-time employment had less free time than males in full-time employment. This differential in time available will clearly affect the level of participation in leisure activities by gender. This, for Christine Delphy (1984), is to be explained on the basis of the continuing material context of the position of women in our society, and this round-the-clock responsibility is a structural constraint in their lives which limits the possibilities for involvement in leisure. Rosemary Deem's (1990) research on leisure participation in Milton Keynes pointed to the importance of these time constraints on leisure participation for women, but she also highlighted another factor, which she calls patriarchal control (see also Section 5.3). What she means by this is the way that the extent and type of women's involvement in leisure activities is constrained by the potential reaction of males, from potential sexual harassment of females in pubs through to discouragement of women going out with men from their male partners or discouragement of them going to

places where they might meet other men, such as nightclubs. Green *et al.*'s (1990) study of Sheffield came to similar conclusions, particularly emphasizing the way that male partners acted to discourage women from engaging in certain activities, again usually those centring on pubs and clubs. A similar conclusion was reached by Wimbush (1986) on the basis of a study of young mothers in Edinburgh. This notion of the way women's leisure activities are controlled by men thus seems to be a factor commonly found in studies of women's leisure participation.

🗩 Discussion point

How far do you agree that women's leisure activities are subject to patriarchal control?

Ethnicity

Because of the greater levels of unemployment suffered by ethnic minorities, lower average levels of income will impact on leisure participation in much the same way as class inequalities, and of course in relation to actual individuals such inequalities interact together. (See also Chapter 6.)

There may also be cultural or religious norms and values which tend to segregate people in terms of leisure activities. However, whether this segregation is a matter of reaction to actual or potential racism or simply a cultural choice is a matter of debate, and it is also clear that young members of ethnic minorities are becoming more adept at creating their own styles of leisure and cultural expression by merging together cultural forms from their ethnic identity with more westernized influences, such as the rise of Bhangra music.

Sivanandan (1990) argues that there is a need to consider the way that aspects of ethnic minorities' lives have been affected by racism and the colonial legacy (see also Section 6.2), but he goes on to argue that the response to this has often been a form of resistance within which cultural and leisure pursuits feature.

🗩 Discussion point

How can you resist culturally? To what extent do you think this happens?

A similar point is made by Paul Gilroy (1987) who argues that cultural identity has been a central element in the resistance to racism, and this has often been expressed through involvement with music, dance, carnivals and sports clubs. In a later work, Gilroy (1993) emphasizes the way in which global cultural styles are mixed together and this means that contemporary black cultural forms do not draw upon or feed into notions of fixed ethnic and national roots, but instead point towards a more flexible identity which engages with themes of modernity while not feeling fully integrated within them. (See also Section 10.7.)

Sociological explanations for inequalities in leisure participation

Post-modernity and leisure

Chris Rojek (1985, 1993) argues that it is possible to outline three stages of the development of the sociology of leisure. The first stage comprised the studies which were focused on the development of leisure provision within local authorities and arose broadly in the 1970s. The main criticism of this approach was that leisure was viewed in isolation from other aspects of society.

This led to the development of critical studies of leisure based mainly on Marxist and latterly feminist perspectives concerned with analysing the reasons for the way leisure developed and the structural inequalities which lead to inequalities in access to leisure facilities.

The third phrase he identifies is defined by the rise of debates about post-modernity and the impact of this on leisure activities. This has widened the scope of leisure studies to include concern with social identity and the body, and consumer culture and consumption as forms of leisure participation. Veal (1993) argues that this means that there is a need for theorists of leisure to concern themselves with the ways in which individuals and groups express and construct lifestyles through leisure tastes and activities.

Sheila Scraton and Peter Bramham (1995) argue that it is possible to analyse swimming and consider the way the experience of swimming has been transformed in ways which indicate this shift to postmodernity:

The shift from modernity to postmodernity can be illustrated in many leisure experiences, for instance swimming. Rather than the physical education of 'serious' swimming in Victorian public baths and washhouses, policed by officious baths attendants, swimming has been transformed into water-based fun in leisure pools, with water chutes, slides, wave machines, inflatables, fountains, popular music,

Activity

a Think of another popular leisure activity and draw up your own summary of changes in recent years.

b How far does this support the idea that we are living in post-modern times?

I, A, E

aqua-rhythm classes (aerobics in the pool) with laser lights, stylish swimming costumes, casually overviewed by spectators in tropicana restaurants, grazing on fast-foods, whilst drinking diet Cokes.
(Scraton and Bramham, 1995, p.22)

Post-modernity and tourism

Post-modern themes have also been applied to the analysis of tourism. John Urry in his book *The Tourist Gaze* (1990) argues that Jean Baudrillard's idea that we now live in a world where it is not possible to distinguish between the real and the simulation is applicable to tourism, since package tourism does not provide access to the real authentic experiences of the region being visited, but instead a constructed package of contrived events in an artificial environment.

Discussion point

Is package tourism providing a contrived and artificial environment or a genuine holiday?

However, our desire for tourism also reflects a wish to seek new experiences and create new sensations and simulations. Urry goes on to argue that we may now need to talk of 'post-tourism' since many people actually now play along with the simulations offered by package tours and have given up any attempt to seek out authentic cultural experiences.

Figurational sociology and Norbert Elias

Elias developed a particular approach which has come to be known as 'figurational sociology' (see Section 2.9). However, this has been applied to the sociology of leisure and more particularly sport in a number of ways. His notion of the civilizing process and of interactions being part of a wider set of figurations has been applied to sport by the work of Eric Dunning and others at Leicester University. Dunning (1971) argues that sport has developed over time from folk games where there was a high toleration of physical violence and an emphasis on force rather than skill, to modern sport which is clearly regulated through codified rules and where there is a low toleration of physical violence. The connections between sport, masculinity and different forms of interdependence were also explored in their work on football hooliganism (Dunning *et al.*, 1988). The fact that football hooliganism can be analysed within a perspective which talks about the growth of civilization emphasizes the way that there can be setbacks in this process.

Pierre Bourdieu and cultural capital

A Marxist-influenced approach is more evident in the work of Pierre Bourdieu (see also Section 2.5) whose concepts of cultural capital and the *habitus* are applicable to the study of leisure, though can also be applied much more widely in relation to, for example, education (see Section 8.2).

In his book *Distinction* Bourdieu (1984) applies himself to a consideration of theories of leisure participation. He argues that the choices we make are never totally without constraint and in effect his argument is that structural constraints are very real.

He argues that while we can most certainly explain inequalities in participation in leisure and cultural activities on the basis of economic inequalities, these factors alone cannot explain all inequalities since when these have been taken into account, there is still a degree of choice in what we engage in. For example, going to watch a Premiership football match costs about the same as a visit to the opera and therefore the choices people make about which of these to engage in cannot be fully explained by reference to income alone.

It is here that his notion of cultural capital comes into play. Bourdieu suggests that our experiences in childhood and our particular social backgrounds create a *habitus*, a certain set of partially unconscious tastes, preferences and perceptions, which provide the basis for this cultural capital. Members of the dominant economic class can use their power to define their tastes and preferences as superior to others. This has similarities to the debates about the relative merits of high culture and mass or popular culture.

Dominant classes can also use their economic capital to purchase cultural competence in these areas, seen as high status through particular sorts of education such as public schools and Oxbridge. This allows them to develop the level of cultural competence to engage freely with high culture, whose attraction is also partly the fact that those without the cultural competence to appreciate it will in effect be excluded. Cultural capital therefore serves as an exclusion mechanism to shore up inequalities in participation in leisure and cultural activities.

9.9 The globalization of work and leisure?

The topic of globalization has recently become a very important issue in sociology and there is certainly a need to consider it in relation to work and leisure (globalization is also discussed in Sections 10.10, 12.5, 15.11, 16.8 and 17.6). Malcolm Waters argues that usage of the term started around 1960, but it was only in the late 1980s that sociologists really began to discuss the issue. Today in the 1990s, bookshelves are heaving under the weight of books discussing globalization and it is indeed clear that it is an idea sociology students will need to discuss.

Waters provides the following basic definition of the likely end-state of the process of globalization:

In a globalised world there will be a single society and culture occupying the planet. This society and culture will probably not be harmoniously integrated although it might conceivably be. ... Importantly territoriality will disappear as an organizing principle for social and cultural life. In a globalised world we will be unable to predict social practices and preferences on the basis of geographical boundaries.
(Waters, 1995, p. 3)

Discussion point
To what extent do you think we live in a globalized world?

This means that our experiences can no longer be confined to a national context and if, as Giddens (1989) puts it, globalization 'decisively conditions' our fate, nation-states are no longer the most important social organization and the borders between them are no longer seen as being as solid as they once were. However, in his discussion of the concept, sociologist Kevin Robins (1997) points out that:

The global economy exists in the context of, and must come to terms with, the realities of existing societies, with their accumulated, that is to say, 'historical' cultures and ways of life. ...

Globalisation is frequently seen in terms of the 'disembedding' of ways of life from the narrow confines of locality. But increasingly, we are coming to recognise that it is – paradoxically, it seems – also associated with new dynamics of relocalisation. Globalisation is, in fact, about the creation of a new global–local nexus, establishing new and complex relations between global spaces and local spaces.
(Robins, 1997, p. 4)

While this potentially has impacts on a whole series of social activities, we will concentrate here on the effect on work and leisure.

The global economy and work

Classical sociological discussions focused on the effects of changes such as the Industrial Revolution in a largely national context. However, it is now argued that we are entering an era characterized by the rise of a new division of labour (Fröbel *et al.*, 1980) based on the division of work between countries. This can mean that whole categories of production previously associated with the advanced industrial nations of the West are now moved to locations in other countries such as the Newly-Industrializing Countries (see Section 12.5); or alternatively that some processes involved in the overall production of a certain commodity are located in other countries, meaning that its production is multi-national. An example of this is the oil company Shell, familiar through its petrol stations. However, the actual structure of the company overall reveals the myriad multi-national links connected with that familiar petrol station (see Figure 9.6).

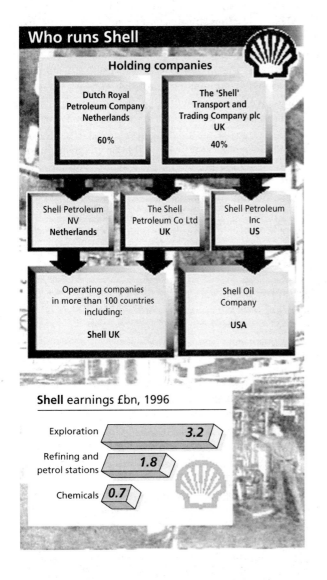

Figure 9.6 Who runs Shell. Source: *The Guardian*, 15 February 1997 p. 22

Why does this matter?

While multi-national production has been around for some time, it is argued that the scale of these operations has grown so great that we are now witnessing a qualitative change in the way production and work are organized. If true, this will have major implications for an individual's work opportunities.

Insofar as major companies are now moving to operate around the globe, it is argued that they can no longer be seen as British or American multinationals but instead need to be seen as transnational corporations, who are willing and able to operate across the whole globe and who therefore possess no national loyalty to the country they originate in. Their investment policies will therefore be determined by consideration of profit levels rather than with any concern for their own national economy overall. This, it is argued, can be seen in the increasing level of investment in other countries by major corporations. Gill and Law (1988) in their study of the global economy point to an increase of such investment from US$14.3 billion in 1914 to US$386.2 billion in 1978, and furthermore that the majority of this growth has taken place since the 1960s. In more recent times, it is estimated that the level of US companies acquired by foreign (i.e. non-American) owners rose from US$10.9 billion in 1985 to US$40.4 billion in 1987. Since the level of investment affects the level of jobs produced, it is argued that the effect of investment policies becoming more global will lead to greater competitive pressures on wage levels and ultimately on jobs with the potential for large rises in unemployment for those countries unable to attract foreign investment.

The ability to move large sums of money around the globe has been increased by the rise of the various markets in money such as the Eurodollar market and the changes to regulations about the movement of money. These were initiated by the New Rights' reforms aimed at freeing up the movement of money and goods across national frontiers. The Eurodollar market effectively grew up in the wake of the Vietnam war and consists of american dollars circulating in Europe and never returning to america. This is therefore American money outside of the control of the American government. Its growth in recent years has been phenomenal, from US$132 billion in 1973 to US$1200 billion in 1980 and US$2000 billion in 1984.

The Conservative governments in the UK made a number of changes to facilitate movement of money around the globe. In 1980 they abolished exchange controls on money and in 1987 the 'Big Bang' initiated trading in stocks and shares via computer, meaning large sums of money can be transferred around the world at the press of a button. Lash and

Urry (1994, p. 289) report that every day US$600 billion of foreign exchange is traded in London, which is equivalent to the value of trade for the whole of the world for a year.

🗨 Discussion point

To what extent does it matter that US$600 billion of foreign exchange passes through London every day?

It is argued that all of these changes have contributed to a weakening of the ability of an individual nation state to regulate its economy, and therefore to determine the kind and number of jobs that will be available. This can be seen in the UK by contrasting the period between 1945 and roughly 1980 and the period between 1980 and the present day.

After World War II, economic orthodoxy shifted towards the idea that the government should actively intervene in the economy to achieve desirable economic, social and political objectives such as full employment and high levels of economic growth. It was argued that these would feed through into increased living standards. This meant that the government made adjustments to levels of taxation and public expenditure with these objectives in mind. To some degree, governments achieved success in this respect since in the UK between 1959 and 1967 unemployment averaged only 1.8 per cent.

The contrast with today can be seen if we look at more recent levels of unemployment in the UK, where it stood for example at 9.7 per cent in April 1994 and 8.7 per cent in November 1995. This return of mass unemployment is said to be one of the potential indicators of the effects of globalization. It is important to remember that it is also the effect of the radical shift of economic policy effected by the New Right governments (see Section 2.10) of the 1980s whose return to the policies of the free market led to the return of levels of unemployment last seen in the UK when free market polices were last in vogue in the 1930s. Globalization is not therefore the only possible explanation. Nonetheless, since the key players in the world market said to be at the centre of the process of globalization are capitalist companies who are also seen as generally favouring free market polices, their growth has contributed to the rise of pressures to continue with these policies.

More directly, it is argued that since these transnational coroporations (TNCs) make investment decisions on a simple cost and profitability basis, national governments no longer have any real ability to manage economies by determining taxation

rates. While in the post-war period, companies had little alternative but to pay any level of taxation set by the government, it is now argued that the ability to move money around the globe so easily means that if they do not like the level of taxation set, they will simply disinvest and move their money elsewhere to where taxation rates are lower.

The key argument therefore is that governments risk investment capital flowing out of their country as a result of their tax policies, with the implication that mass unemployment will continue. The further implication is that high levels of unemployment and the consequent lower levels of tax revenue will threaten the ability of national governments to fund the kind of welfare benefits people have been used to (see also Sections 14.2 and 14.3). If governments respond to this by raising levels of taxation, more companies might choose to relocate their operations elsewhere resulting in further job losses.

The only alternative, it is argued – primarily by New Right thinkers and government ministers – is to attract foreign investment to this country but in order to do that it is necessary to create profitable conditions for companies in this country, which generally involves a growing flexibility of labour and therefore lower wage rates and lower numbers of people employed to undertake a particular task. It is, for this reason that John Major's government resisted all attempts by the European Union to place limits on wages and hours of work and to generally try to introduce some regulation of working conditions across Europe. This policy has led to some describing the UK as the sweatshop of the world. *Times* reporter Wolfgang Munchau (1995) summarized this as follows:

Britain is the sweatshop of Europe with the longest working hours in the European Union. . . . It is the only EU country where working time has increased by over an hour since 1983.
(Munchau, 1995, p.12)

He reports that while working hours went down in ten of the then twelve countries of the EU between 1983 and 1992, in the UK and Eire they went up.

Summarizing, if the process of globalization identified by some commentators is actually happening and if it happening at an increasing pace, then the prospect for workers in the UK is the choice between either retaining their present working conditions but thereby risking unemployment if companies disinvest, or alternatively accepting a worsening of their working conditions in order to attract this mobile capital and therefore retain their jobs. Neither seems a particularly attractive option and both rule out any kind of social-democratic or socialist government radically changing the situation.

Discussion point
Are nation-states finished?

This might therefore be called the doomsday scenario concerning the potential effects of globalization. Such a situation need not involve actual disinvestment since through the process of transfer pricing multi-national and trans-national corporations are able to minimize their liability to corporation tax. Transfer pricing involves the ability of subsidiary companies of TNCs being able to set the price at which they sell goods or services to each other. By manipulating these prices, TNCs can ensure that profits show up in those areas and countries where taxation rates are lowest. The following fictional example in Table 9.10 shows how this might work:

Table 9.10 Transfer pricing inside a trans-national corporation

Subsidiaries	Company X	Company Y
Located in	Country A	Country B
Tax rate	40%	25%
Company X	sells at low price to	Company Y
Company X	buys at high price from	Company Y
Effect	High costs	Low costs
	Low revenue	High revenue
	Low profits	High profits
	Low tax liability	High tax liability

If TNCs operate like this, and if they are an important part of an economy, then effectively it will be very difficult to raise taxes, which anyway may not be paid since the profits will be salted elsewhere through the transfer pricing mechanism.

Critical responses to the globalization argument

It is important to realize that not everyone accepts the argument that we live in a globalized world. It is therefore necessary to critically assess the validity of the ideas.

In relation to the new international division of labour thesis, which particularly focuses on the shift of many production-based jobs to areas in the developing world, one of the key criticisms of this idea is that most foreign direct investment (FDI) (the money behind globalization) actually remains very much rooted in the advanced western world. Gill and Law

(1988) point out that nearly half of all FDI went to just four countries: Canada, the USA, the UK and West Germany (now part of the unified German state). Secondly the main argument presented for the idea that investment will flow to the developing world is the lower costs involved. However, looking at the actual distribution of FDI which does go to the developing world shows it going not to the lowest cost countries, but instead to middle-income countries in Latin America and South-East Asia.

It is also important to remember that wage rates have been rising in these countries. In South Korea following the end of the military dictatorship there was large scale strike action in the 1980s. The government of President Kim Young Sam has responded by arguing that increasing wages threaten economic growth and as a result at the end of 1996 the government forced through new laws weakening job security and attempting to provide more job flexibility. In response the South Korean workers and trade unions have been engaged in a massive level of strikes against this new law. This shows that the pressures and conflicts which are said to be caused for western Europe by the rise of economies like South Korea, actually affect those economies as well. The idea that capitalism can solve its problems by shifting production to the newly industrializing countries is therefore open to question (see also Sections 12.5 and 12.6). In fact it might be argued that changes in the advanced industrial western countries are the ones creating global pressure. This bizarre reversal of the new international division of labour thesis was certainly the justification offered for the new draconian labour laws introduced in South Korea at the end of 1996. South Korean Labour minister Jin Nyum said :

The managers and owners of our companies complain that it is so difficult to do business in Korea that they have to move operations to Wales and Scotland in the United Kingdom . . . Those who are concerned about our economy pondered . . . how we could incorporate the lessons from the British experience.
(Quoted in Higgins, 1997, p. 3)

Discussion point
To what extent does this statement undermine notions that we are living in one globalized world?

The author of the *Guardian* article, Andrew Higgins (1997) makes clear the connection with arguments about globalization, providing two contrasting views of it within a short paragraph:

President Kim promoted the word segyehwa – globalisation – as a national slogan and now uses it to

explain the new labour law. Labour activists, foreign and local, are unimpressed. Globalisation means one thing: money rushing around the globe and leaving people to mop up the mess left by jet-setting capital.

(Higgins, 1997, p. 3)

It is also open to question whether the flow of FDI to the developing countries is actually slowing down. Lloyds Bank (1995) report that the share of FDI received by developing countries has fallen from a peak of around 30 per cent in 1967. One key cause of this is the higher interest rates in the advanced industrial economies of the West caused by the adoption of monetarist economic policies by the New Right governments of Reagan and Thatcher (see Section 2.10). As Lloyds Bank comment:

There were signs during 1994 that the surge in capital flows to developing countries was slowing . . . As the recovery in the industrialised world continues, the external environment may become less auspicious for capital flows towards developing countries.

(Lloyds Bank, 1995, p. 4)

If flows to developing countries fall when the economies of western Europe are recovering, it may signal that their desire to shift funds to the developing countries may in fact reflect their inability to create profitable returns in the advanced industrial economies of western Europe. Globalization might therefore be seen as a reflection of the underlying economic weakness of capitalism in the advanced nations rather than as a measure of its strength. This is broadly the position taken by Marxist social scientist David Gordon (1988) who argues that:

These changes are best understood not as a symptom of structural transformation but rather as a consequence of the erosion of the social structure of accumulation which conditioned international capitalist prosperity during the 1950s and 1960s. . . . we have all been staggering from the blows of economic crisis, including the multinationals.

(Gordon, 1988, p. 25)

This points to the degree of globalization being a cyclical matter, rising and falling partly in relation to the economic cycles in the advanced industrial economies.

A second type of criticism of the globalization argument is that it ignores the continuing importance of the nation state in creating the conditions necessary for capital accumulation. This view is exemplified by the work of Paul Hirst and Grahame Thompson (1995, 1996) who argue that:

The extreme globalisation theorists paint a picture of a world set free for business to serve customers

. . . Such a world free for trade has been the dream of classical economic liberalism since its inception. It is also an illusion. Markets and companies cannot exist without the protection of the public power. The open international economy depends ultimately on Western (particularly US) force and upon active public regulation backed by legal enforcement.

(Hirst and Thompson, 1995, p. 427)

The continued existence of military forces and their primary organization through nation states does then, to some extent, question the notion that national borders and national organizations and institutions are becoming insignificant. This reliance on military force was illustrated clearly during the Gulf War (see also Section 15.3). The interests at stake here were western access to oil, and the oil companies clearly fit into the description of multi-national and trans-national companies. However, faced with the Iraqi military, Operation Desert Shield was organized by diverse national militaries, containing a multitude of nationalities for political purposes, but undoubtedly led by the US military. The point is that, insofar as there is still the need for military protection, there is still the need for viable organizations to organize a military response, most notably the nation state.

In summary, therefore, while it undoubtedly describes a process which is very real, both the extent and the significance of globalization are open to debate.

Globalization and leisure

In some ways the response to the impact of globalization differs in relation to leisure as compared with that of the effect on work. Broadly, talk of globalization and work tends to be couched in terms of jobs lost as production is shifted to other parts of the world. However in relation to leisure, the movement of cultural products and practices around the globe and their incorporation in leisure pursuits is generally viewed in a positive light as extending the range of choice available. For example, the emergence of TV chefs such as Delia Smith and Keith Floyd, and their use of food products from around the world, has led to an enormous increase in the type of products stocked in supermarkets. We can now eat pizzas one night, Thai food the next and have a chicken dansak the next night. Since Indian food (or more particularly chicken tikka masala) is now said to be the most popular food in Britain, should we really describe it as Indian food and is this not now the epitome of British food, having eclipsed roast beef (not helped by the BSE problem) and Yorkshire pudding? Aidan Foster-Carter, talking at a conference at Leeds University, offered as an example of globalization in this context, the fact that Asda used to sell a chicken tikka pizza!

Activity

a Make a list of the way your leisure and cultural activities have been affected by the process of globalization.

b Have these changes had a positive or negative influence on your life?

A, E

The effect of global processes on cultural activities including leisure are the subject of debate (see also Section 10.10). There are fears that the domination of multi-national companies, particularly in the media field (which in terms of time spent constitutes an important area of leisure) will lead to cultural homogenization. The domination of American film and TV companies leads to fears of the eradication of more local cultural forms.

On the other hand, the growth of such multinational links does provide the possibility that we can become aware of other forms of cultural output. For example, the growth of World Music through WOMAD festivals has brought a diverse range of musical styles from around the world to the attention of people in the UK. In one weekend it is now possible to experience music ranging from Cajun and Zydeco from the USA to Qawwali from Pakistan and Gamelan from Java and Bali.

While global links around the world facilitate our awareness of this music, its appeal in reality lies in the fact that it is based on genuine local roots. Fears that globalization might undermine this by homogenizing all musical forms can therefore be contrasted with more optimistic arguments suggesting that commercial companies wish to retain its authenticity and that through the interchange of musical styles, a more hybrid form of music will emerge. (See also Section 10.10.)

The importance of the coverage of sport in Rupert Murdoch's BSkyB satellite TV system is a clear indication of the growing links between the media and sport which through this link is being affected by the global pressures evident in other aspects of leisure. This issue has already led to controversy. One of the most recent changes was in relation to rugby football, where money from BSkyB TV even led to the sport changing its playing season. Whether or not these developments will enhance the enjoyment of rugby fans remains to be seen, but it is likely to widen differentials within sport between those sports that do attract money from TV companies such as BSkyB and those that do not.

Further **reading**

There are three books written specifically for A level students which cover this topic area:

- Deem, R. (1988) *Work, Unemployment and Leisure*, London, Routledge.

- Horne, J. (1987) *Work and Unemployment*, London, Longman.

- Madry, N. and Kirby, M. (1996) *Investigating Work, Unemployment and Leisure*, London, Collins Educational.

More in-depth analyses of some of the debates covered in this chapter and in the books above can be found in the following:

- Clarke, J. and Critcher, C. (1985) *The Devil Makes Work*, London, Macmillan.

- Clegg, S. (1990) *Modern Organisations*, London, Sage.

- Grint, K. (1991) *The Sociology of Work*, Cambridge, Polity.

- Hirst, P. and Thompson, G. (1996) *Globalisation in Question*, Cambridge, Polity.

- Watson, T. (1995) *Sociology, Work and Industry*, 3rd edn, London, Routledge.

Back issues of the periodical *Sociology Review* (formerly known as *Social Studies Review*) also contain many articles on this field of sociology and many others.

Exam **questions**

1 Examine the consequences of bureaucratic forms of organization.   [25 marks] (IBS, AS, Paper 2, Summer 1995)

2 Evaluate sociological explanations of the impact of technological change on the experience of paid employment.   [25 marks] (IBS, Paper 2, Summer 1996)

3 Assess the view that the 'Scientific Management' and 'Human Relations' approaches to the study of organisations can be criticised for bias in favour of management.   [25 marks] (AEB, Paper 2, Summer 1993)

4 To what extent do you agree with the view that leisure in Britain since 1945 has become commercialised and home-centred?   [25 marks] (NEAB, 1998 Syllabus, Specimen Question, Module SL04)

Coursework **suggestions**

1 **Conduct a study of your school or college as an organization and consider whether it is characterized by the growth of a rational bureaucratic structure, or is more like the surveillance model outlined by Michel Foucault**

   Consider why it would matter and whether the answer is the same for all groups within the organization.

2 **If you have a part-time job, conduct research using this as a resource**

   For instance you could consider the extent to which the firm you work for has adopted flexible working practices and whether these have been welcomed by the staff or not. Alternatively you could examine the firm you work for in terms of the distribution of jobs by gender, age and ethnicity to consider whether there is evidence of segregation within the company.

3 **Investigate the extent to which the leisure activities of people in your area have been affected by globalization**

   This can cover a whole range of issues including food, leisure institutions, tourism, sport and you may wish just to focus on one area. If you find evidence of global influences, you need to consider which of the various theories of globalization best explains the patterns you have found.

10

Culture and identity

10.1 Socialization, culture and identity

What would human beings be like without society? We know from the rare cases in which children have been denied access to human company for long periods that interaction with other people is a vital ingredient in human development. The 'wild boy of Aveyron' was found wandering from a wood in Southern France in 1800. He had apparently spent most of his eleven or twelve years on his own in the wild. He was unable to communicate, other than through shrieking; he was fearful of other people, lacked social skills and took no interest in personal hygiene. Although after some time he learned to dress himself and became toilet-trained, he was never able to learn more than a few basic words.

In a much more recent case in California a quarter of a century ago, a baby girl was locked away in a closed room by her father who was ashamed of her hip defect. Genie spent several years away from human company, being fed by her father but denied any social interaction with others. Her father refused to talk to her and communicated merely by growling at her. After escaping with her mother, Genie received extensive help from doctors and child development experts but it was clear that permanent damage had been done. While she learnt to walk, to dress herself and became toilet-trained, she remained introverted and was never, even as an adult, able to master language beyond the level of a four-year-old.

In the case of both Genie and the 'wild boy', it appears that the absence of social interaction had severely stunted human development. Some psychologists believe that there is a crucial stage in psychological development at which point children learn language and, perhaps, other social skills extremely rapidly. The cases of Genie and 'the wild boy' suggest that if this crucial stage is missed then the acquisition of language and social skills becomes much more difficult. In other words, social interaction with other human beings is crucial to the process of becoming fully human.

Socialization and identity

Sociologists call the process through which we learn how to fit into society 'socialization':

Socialization is the process whereby the helpless infant gradually becomes a self-aware, knowledgeable person, skilled in the ways of the culture into which she or he is born.
(Giddens, 1993a, p. 60)

The family, the peer group, the community and, in modern societies, the formal education system and the mass media all contribute to the process of socialization in which we acquire the beliefs, habits and skills necessary to play an appropriate role in society. Socialization does not end with childhood but continues through life as we adjust to new situations and enter new communities (for example, changing jobs or moving to new neighbourhoods). Someone entering middle age may reflect on memories of what they were like when they were young and almost feel they are looking at a different person. This is because the human personality is dynamic rather than fixed, and develops as it is exposed to socializing experiences throughout life. This is how our sense of our own identity, or who we feel ourselves to be, is constructed.

It was often assumed in the past that the social nature of human behaviour distinguished human beings as a species from other animals. Animals, it was believed, were guided much more by patterns of instinctive, rather than socially learnt behaviour. Research now shows that much animal behaviour has a stronger social dimension than previously assumed. Studies of monkeys, for example, confirm that social dynamics are extremely important in shaping behaviour within monkey groups. Very recently, it was reported that young elephants in a South African game reserve, separated from their parents at a very early age, are now behaving in ways which we might term 'juvenile delinquency'.

Culture, norms and values

What precisely is learnt through socialization? Sociologists distinguish between values and norms. Values are the fundamental beliefs which underpin a community or society and provide general principles for human behaviour. In most societies, the influence of religion through history means that many fundamental values are derived from religious teaching. Beyond this, western societies are likely to reflect values associated with liberalism and capitalism. These would include respect for individual freedom, self-discipline, and hard work. Other societies, for example in the Far East, may attach a greater importance to collective rather than individualistic commitment. Such values stress the importance of remaining loyal to one's family, community and, perhaps now, the commercial company one works for. Some values are formalized as principles of law and are enforced through the formal agencies of social control. Others remain as general organizing principles for life and are fostered through the agencies of socialization.

If values operate as general principles, *norms* are specific rules which govern human behaviour in particular situations. Once again these may vary widely from society to society and from community to community. Examples include appropriate behaviour while eating (in some societies belching loudly is regarded as good manners, in others as rather vulgar); rules governing courtship and 'going out'; rules governing behaviour in public places, and so on (see Figure 10.1).

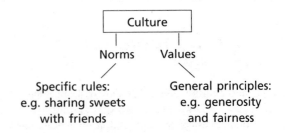

Figure 10.1 Culture, norms and values

The 'experiments' of Harold Garfinkel, an ethnomethodologist (see Section 2.7), demonstrated just how important norms are in maintaining social order and how quickly social order can disintegrate if such norms are deliberately sabotaged. We may take them for granted in our everyday lives but we quickly notice when they are broken.

Activity

Take a simple routine situation which is familiar to you, such as eating breakfast with your family or sitting in the canteen with your friends. In a five-minute period make a list of all the values and norms which you think are governing behaviour. **U, A**

Culture and biology

When sociologists refer to the *culture* of a society they include all behaviour learnt through socialization rather than that which is governed by instinct. Culture includes the norms and values of a society, together with behaviour which is governed by a sense of tradition, shared history and common identity. Culture is expressed through routine behaviour and through language, visual work (painting, design, etc.) and other forms of symbolic representation. When sociologists use the term culture they are normally referring to 'a whole way of life' within a society or smaller community. This is an important point because sometimes in other intellectual traditions it is used in a much narrower sense to refer just to 'great' works of art, music or literature (see Section 10.3).

There is a continuing debate about just how much of our behaviour as human beings is learnt or shaped by socialization and just how much is determined by instinctive patterns and governed by genetic inheritance. Clearly, both genes and socialization contribute to human behaviour but in what proportion? This, of course, is the heart of the debate over 'nature' (biology) or 'nurture' (culture). It is a crucial issue which has very important implications for our understanding of such topics as gender roles and sexuality, criminal behaviour, performance at school, differences between ethnic groups, and so on. (For more detailed discussion of this debate see Sections 5.1, 6.4, 8.9 and 11.1.)

However, it is worth noting that in recent years the weight of 'popular opinion', as measured by media discussions and newspaper articles, has been shifted significantly towards the biological view by advances in genetic science. Geneticists can now understand much of the genetic code to be found within DNA. It is now possible to identify and manipulate certain genes which regulate particular functions within the human body. These scientific breakthroughs have encouraged sociobiologists (theorists who attempt to explain social behaviour in biological terms) to make ambitious claims about the extent to which human behaviour is genetically determined (see Sections 5.2 and 6.4). There are claims that heterosexual courtship, homosexuality, differences in educational performance between social groups, and even the desire to make lots of money, are more or less determined by genes.

Most sociologists remain sceptical of the most ambitious of these claims. While they acknowledge the importance of genes, they question whether genetic theory can really explain the enormous variation in human behaviour between different cultures (see, for example, the evidence of variations in gender roles and sexuality, in Section 5.2). It is one thing to point to the influence of instinct in shaping human wants for food, shelter, sex, comfort, and so on. It is quite another to try to explain all the different ways in which such wants are expressed in purely biological ways. Our biology tells us to eat but it does not tell us to choose McDonald's rather than a French bistro. Both men and women may have sexual appetites which are genetic in origin and this may be nature's way of ensuring the evolution of the human species, but we do not spend all day trying to jump into bed with one another. There are important values and norms which operate to regulate sexual conduct and lend it a special meaning or significance for us. This is clearly the influence of culture.

Activity

Describe briefly your own sense of identity. Who do you think your are? Where do you belong and what makes you the person you are? To what extent do you think your own identity has been shaped by culture and socialization? To what extent do you think your own identity has been shaped by biology and genetics?

Now share this information in small groups. On the basis of the information provided by the members of the group, discuss the conclusions you can draw from this exercise about the respective importance of biological, genetic and cultural influences on your identity. Compare your conclusions with those of other groups in your class. **U, A, E**

10.2 **Theoretical approaches to culture and identity**

Some of the fundamental debates within sociology confront us when we explore the range of theoretical writing on culture and identity. As the main theoretical approaches are described below (see Figure 10.2), remember that each one has something to contribute to the following debates.

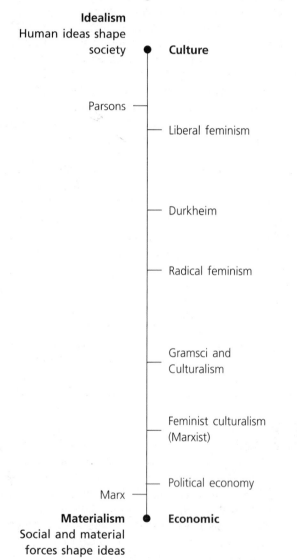

Figure 10.2 Structural theories: idealism and materialism, culture and the economy

To what extent do social actors have the capacity to change social structure or create culture, or is it the case that social structure and culture largely shape our behaviour? In other words, does society shape personal identity or do we actively construct our identities through social interaction? This, in turn, prompts questions about the relationship between culture and the social structure. Does the former shape the latter or is it the other way around? Some theories attempt to chart a 'middle course', describing a process of interaction between the two.

This relates to an important philosophical argument about material forces and ideas. Is it the case that our material environment (for example, economic conditions, class structure, etc.) has a powerful influence on the kinds of ideas that circulate in society; or is it, alternatively, the case that certain ideas become influential and decide how economics and other aspects of material reality are organized?

This section starts by reviewing the structural tradition in the sociological study of culture.

The structural functionalist tradition: Durkheim

Following Durkheim, functionalists are primarily interested in culture and identity in the context of exploring how social order is maintained. Why is it that despite the rapid rates of change experienced in modern societies, for most of the time social institutions and social relations remain orderly, stable and predictable? As discussed more fully in Section 2.4, functionalists point to the importance of a shared, common consensus around key values, which can regulate social behaviour and ensure that change occurs in orderly ways. A common consensus or shared culture, then, is placed at the heart of functionalist concerns.

Durkheim, for example, believed that a number of the social problems to be found in modern industrial societies, including rising suicide and crime rates, were precisely a product of a weakened value system and a consequent lack of social integration. However, Durkheim did not believe that such consequences were inevitable. On the contrary, he believed that the values and culture of modernizing societies evolved, as the division of labour advanced. Modernizing societies developed new 'organic' forms of social solidarity or common value systems. The values and beliefs of such societies were likely to be more general and abstract than the customs and traditions of pre-modern, rural societies. If the values and beliefs which made up the culture of traditional rural societies referred to specific activities and tasks involving everyone (for example, working in the fields), the values and beliefs of modern, industrial societies operated at a more general level which allowed both the lawyer and the factory worker to relate to them.

In fact, Durkheim argued that individualism itself, 'the cult of the individual' (1938a, p. 172; orig. pub. 1893), becomes a central value in industrial societies. Members of society become committed to the principle of individualism but recognize also the inter-dependence of one individual on another. We learn that to enjoy our own individual freedom we must acknowledge our obligations and dependence on others in society. This is the key to the 'organic solidarity' or cultural system which binds modern societies together. This is an argument which Durkheim deployed with vigour against those who put forward the kinds of arguments we now associate with Hayek and the New Right (see Section 2.10). For Durkheim, individualism was a potential threat to social stability but it could be harnessed provided that members of society acknowledged that with growing individualism there came also an increasing inter-dependence between individuals.

American structural functionalism: Talcott Parsons

Similar themes emerge in Talcott Parsons' (1951) writing about culture and social structure. However, in Parsons' work there is a stronger interest in the precise ways in which culture becomes internalized within individuals – just how particular cultural values are learnt or absorbed by individuals. Once again, Parsons' theoretical approach is discussed in more detail in Section 2.4 and his analysis of the family (see Sections 7.1 and 7.2) is also relevant to this section.

Briefly, Parsons adopts a 'systems approach'. Just as the human body can be understood as a system organized around a series of sub-systems, so also can the social world. Parsons distinguishes the cultural system from the social system and these, in turn, are distinguished from the personality system. While the social system is made up of the sets of social roles we are required to perform (all these are located within yet further sub-systems including the economic, the political, the family, etc.), the cultural system consists of the general values and beliefs which shape and regulate social behaviour. More precisely, according to Parsons, through disseminating key values, the cultural system ensures that the various parts of the social system are integrated and co-ordinated, and that specific objectives are shared by all – what he describes as 'goal attainment'. In other words, the cultural system ensures that everyone works towards more or less the same common goals.

The key link between the cultural system and the social system is the process of socialization which, Parsons believes, ensures that most people internalize values derived from the cultural system and then operate according to them when performing their roles (mother, employee, daughter, neighbour, etc.) within the social system. The expectations associated with these roles reflect the key values of the cultural system. Although in his early writing Parsons (1937) placed more emphasis on the ability of actors to

choose between options or courses of action, in much of his work the impression we are given is of a system in which the behaviour of individuals is powerfully shaped by the impact of the cultural system, particularly through socialization. The system retains stability because for a great deal of the time individuals behave as if 'programmed' to conform to the functional requirements of particular roles.

In places Parsons acknowledges the complexity of human identity. For example, he argues that because we all perform a variety of social roles in our daily lives, we are exposed to a variety of social relationships and a variety of socializing influences. However, in describing early or primary socialization, Parsons often gives the impression that he envisages the family almost as a 'personality factory', moulding and shaping human identity according to one common cultural pattern. Parsons believes that the process of socialization involves a series of adjustments in the personality system of the child as it is exposed to increasingly complex social relations: first the mother–child relation, then interaction with other family members, then interaction with others outside the family, and so on. In Parsons' terms:

[the] *personality is in this respect a kind of 'mirror image' of the succession of social systems into which it has been integrated, organised in depth over a . . . series of stages.*
(Parsons, 1956, p. 357)

Through this process, Parsons argues:

. . . the cultural patterns and value systems institutionalised in the social system, are internalised in the personality . . . these are not merely the 'same kind' of cultural values, they are literally the same values.
(Parsons, 1956, p. 358)

To put it bluntly, we exist as human personalities only to the extent to which we have taken society into ourselves. As social beings we are no more than the values, beliefs and expectations which operate in the social systems of which we are parts. This is a 'classic' structural approach which places much more emphasis on the extent to which social structures or systems shape human behaviour rather than the extent to which human behaviour can change or impact on social arrangements (social action theory). These issues are explored in more depth in Sections 2.4–2.8 which deal with sociological theory.

Parsons on culture and social change

One criticism often levelled at functionalism in general is that it has a static rather than a dynamic view of culture, and that consequently it has difficulty in explaining how culture changes. However, as Ian

Craib, a social theorist, points out, Parsons does describe the ways in which the social system interacts with the cultural system through a series of mutual adjustments. As Craib (1992) sees it, the problem is not that Parsons ignores cultural change but that he refuses to single out one factor as the most important cause of change. Whereas traditional Marxists, for example, argue that, broadly speaking, changes in social and economic structures in society shape culture (rather than the other way around), Parsons takes a multi-dimensional approach in which each social and cultural sub-system has the capacity to shape every other one.

A number of conflict theorists, including Weberians and Marxists (see Sections 2.5 and 2.6), believe that Parsons fails to deal with the ways in which conflicts over material resources – wealth, housing, territory, the means of production, etc. – can shape and change culture. From this point of view, cultural change is not merely a consequence of smooth adjustments between sub-systems but a reflection of social instability and antagonism between social groups. Parsons places, perhaps, too much emphasis on the smooth unfolding of ideas in the shaping of culture.

Another familiar criticism often levelled at functionalism and Parsons, in particular, is that it operates with an 'over-socialized' conception of the social actor. However, it is worth pointing to the relevance of this criticism in relation to identity. For Parsons, personal identity is forged through socialization. Critics suggest that this 'over-socialized' view of human identity ignores the importance of non-sociological dimensions of personality – the psychological, the physiological, etc. It exaggerates the extent to which society 'programmes' individuals to conform to socialized patterns of behaviour and underestimates the extent to which personal identity is made up of a complex set of influences in a modern society.

Discussion point

Durkheim and Parsons believe that it is important to encourage the creation of one common culture shared by all to unify society. Some critics argue that a healthy society should be multi-cultural. In other words, a variety of different cultures within one society should be welcomed because cultural diversity can strengthen a society. What do you think?

Following from this is one final but very important critical point. In Parsons' work there is an emphasis on the sharing of a common culture around one set of core values. It is this which integrates and ensures that we all work to common

objectives. And yet, as we shall see in relation to, for example, ethnicity, this is an over-simplified description of most modern societies. The work of Gillespie (1995), discussed below, shows that young members of ethnic minorities in the UK of the 1990s may construct their identities in complex ways from a variety of sources, the dominant common culture being only one. (This issue is also discussed in Sections 6.5 and 6.6.)

Marxism and neo-Marxism

Karl Marx wrote very little specifically on the themes of culture and identity, but nonetheless his ideas remain a vital influence on contemporary cultural debates. This section concentrates on three areas of Marx's work:

- his philosophical discussion regarding the origins of ideas and culture
- his writing on ideology which will be discussed only briefly as it receives more detailed attention in relation to the mass media (Section 15.1)
- his view of the relationship between culture, identity and human labour.

Where do cultural ideas come from? Marx described himself as an historical materialist and this gives us a clue as to Marx's position in relation to this question. Philosophical idealists argued that 'ideas come first' (see Figure 10.2). In other words, human beings generated ideas which were then implemented in history to construct social institutions, organize the economy, develop a polity and create culture (Parsons comes close to adopting this position). On the other hand, crude materialists argued that the material world came first; the material conditions in which we lived (the economic environment, the social structure, etc.) shaped or even determined the kinds of ideas which human beings produced. Ideas are no more than a reflection of the material environment. Marx tried to avoid the crudity of both these views. Instead, he argued:

Men make their own history but they do not make it directly as they please; they do not make it under circumstances chosen by themselves, but under circumstances directly encountered, given, and transmitted from the past.
(Marx, 1969, p. 360; orig. pub. 1852)

In other words, we do have the capacity to develop new ideas and new cultural approaches and we can use these to make new arrangements or new 'history', but we have to do this within real, material constraints. These constraints are the social arrangements which we always inherit from previous generations.

Implicit in Marx's writing is a particular view of human beings and their potential. Although under capitalism work may be an unpleasant experience for many, we are not naturally lazy or reluctant to engage in labour. Quite the contrary, human beings become social through their experience of work and the co-operative relationships involved in making and producing things (see also Section 9.2). So according to Marx the experience of labour is crucial to the development of culture. Language, customs, traditions, and even our sense of ourselves as individuals, are all intimately bound up with the shared experience of human labour. Whereas for Parsons self-identity is forged through the internalization of cultural symbols, for Marx the individual develops identity through engagement with the material world and working relationships. The problem, of course, is that under capitalism this is an alienating and frustrating experience.

Discussion point

To what extent do you agree that your individual identity is bound up with the experience of human labour? Have things in this respect changed since Marx's era, or not?

Marx on ideology and culture

Marx's writing on ideology takes this argument further. In *The German Ideology*, Marx and Engels (1977; orig. written 1845) argue that we get our ideas (and our approaches to culture) from active engagement with the world. One version of this argument can be found as the 'dominant ideology thesis' discussed in Section 15.1. Marx argued that as in capitalist societies ruling classes typically own and control the means of mental and cultural production (newspapers, publishing houses, theatres, museums, even music halls), it is likely that ideas and cultural activities reflecting their interests and tastes will circulate more speedily around society. Subordinate classes may generate their own alternative and critical ideas, but they will experience greater difficulty in circulating these. Given the limited circulation of critical or oppositional ideas, subsequent Marxists have suggested that 'the ruling ideas' do, in fact, permeate the consciousness of working-class and other subordinate groups.

One of the most important criticisms levelled at Marx's approach to the analysis of culture is that it is flawed by an 'economic reductionism'. Marx's base–superstructure model (see Section 2.3) appears to imply that cultural phenomena, however complex, can be 'explained' simply by referring to the economic processes at work. The criticism is that not all, if any, patterns of social and cultural behaviour can be reduced to matters of economics. There can be

many reasons why a film director may wish to produce a particular film, or a writer publish a novel, and there may be an even wider number of reasons why audiences enjoy a particular film or a particular book. While the base–superstructure model does seem to imply an over-simplified view of the relationship between the social, the cultural and the economic, in other places Marx does reject economic reductionism and seems to acknowledge a more complex interplay between social, cultural and economic processes. Theories of hegemony and the work of Antonio Gramsci represent an attempt to save twentieth century Marxism from the charge of oversimplistic economic reductionism. Further criticisms of Marxist approaches will be considered below.

Gramsci and culturalism (theories of hegemony)

Theories of hegemony (often referred to as culturalism) take as their starting point the emphasis Marx placed on the capacity of social groups or classes to actively create culture through engagement with the material world, including subordinate as well as ruling classes. They draw partly on the thinking of the French Marxist Althusser (discussed in more detail in Section 2.5) and more extensively from the Italian Marxist Gramsci.

Althusser, in trying to avoid the danger of economic reductionism, conceded that ideology might have a 'relative autonomy' or semi-independence from economic processes. However, he still insisted that 'in the last instance' the main ideas circulating in society contributed to the reproduction of capitalism through, for example, education. Gramsci also rejected economic reductionism but, being a political activist rather than an academic, he put rather more emphasis on the importance of individuals acting politically in the process through which ideas and culture might change.

Gramsci, writing from a Fascist prison cell in the 1930s, starts by asking why socialist revolutions failed in Germany and Italy after the end of the First World War, despite the fact that most of the 'objective conditions' specified by Marx for working-class revolution were present in both countries. The answer, Gramsci argued, had to lie at the level of ideas and culture. Although the economic and political conditions were in place, socialist parties had failed to win the battle of ideas.

Gramsci concluded that the development of class consciousness was never an automatic process simply triggered by the 'right' economic conditions. Rather, the dominant or ruling class in society would engage in a continual struggle to secure support for ideas which actually legitimated its interests. To the extent that it was successful in making its ideas appear like 'common sense', it had secured a hegemonic position. Hegemony occurs when competing ideologies:

. . . come into confrontation and conflict, until one of them . . . tends to prevail, to gain the upper hand, to propagate itself throughout society – bringing about not only a union of economic and political aims, but also intellectual and moral unity.
(Gramsci, 1971a, p. 181)

Normally, in a capitalist society the ideas and ideology of the capitalist class would secure hegemony, but it was the task of working-class intellectuals and organizations to try to counter these ideas with alternative perspectives. Whereas some Marxists seem to imply that ideological indoctrination is a finite process – individuals are indoctrinated once and for all – Gramsci suggests that there is a continual struggle through key cultural institutions in which the dominant class seeks to establish its perspectives as 'common sense' and subordinate classes may more or less resist this. Thus, a capitalist ruling class can never take its hegemony for granted; it has to engage in an active effort to secure and preserve it on a daily basis.

The idea of culture as a sphere of ideological struggle in which social classes engage in a battle of ideas has proved enormously attractive to some neo-Marxists. The Centre for Contemporary Cultural Studies (CCCS) at Birmingham University applied Gramsci's ideas in an attempt to interpret working-class youth subcultures as embryonic, or emerging, counter-hegemonic responses (see Section 10.5). Other researchers, extending the idea of social conflict to include the dimensions of ethnicity and gender as well as social class, grew interested in the ways consumers and media audiences might 'resist' the dominant or 'preferred' hegemonic message and, instead, decode or interpret media messages in subversive ways which challenged the perspectives of the powerful (Fiske, 1989; see Section 10.9).

A strength of the culturalist approach is that it reminds us that consumers and audiences are active and less vulnerable to manipulation than is sometimes supposed. However, critics argue that it can go too far in over-estimating the extent to which social groups can 'resist', and for presenting a 'cultural populism' which is little different from the free-market views of the New Right (McGuigan, 1992). The debate over cultural populism is considered further in Section 10.11.

The political economy approach

The political economy approach insists that the starting point for a neo-Marxist analysis of culture must lie with the process of cultural production and consider:

- the interests of the companies and corporations involved in the cultural industries
- the implications of producing culture through market mechanisms.

If these issues are not explored first, political economy theorists argue, then it is easy to overlook the important ways in which structures of power shape and limit the ways in which audiences or consumers get access to cultural products.

Two leading political economy theorists, Golding and Murdock (1991), suggest that unless the analysis starts with these issues, the impression is given that consumers are sovereign, freely expressing their cultural wishes in the marketplace. They argue that consumers may consume in different ways but always within limits determined by the structure and working of the capitalist cultural industries. The evidence on which the political economy approach bases its argument is discussed further in Section 10.8.

Neo-Marxists who draw on hegemony theory are sometimes critical of the political economy approach, suggesting that – like orthodox Marxism – it suffers from an 'economic reductionism' which over-simplifies and reduces complex cultural patterns to crude economics (Strinati, 1995). The ideas that influence writers, artists, producers or directors originate from a variety of sources, not simply the need to satisfy the 'bottom line'. Similarly, a political economy approach, the critics argue, tells us little about the creative and sometimes subversive 'pleasures' consumers and audiences can derive from the culture produced by capitalism. In their defence, researchers using a political economy approach acknowledge that consumers are not merely manipulated by the corporations of the cultural industries. Nevertheless, as Golding and Murdock argue:

Consumption practices are clearly not completely manipulated by the strategies of cultural industries but they are equally clearly, not completely independent of them.
(Golding and Murdock, 1991, p. 30)

Varieties of feminism

As discussed in more detail in Chapter 5, there is not one tradition of feminist theory but, in fact, several. The most important for the purposes of studying the relationship between culture, identity and society are liberal feminism, radical feminism and neo-Marxist culturalist feminism.

What all feminisms share is, first, the view that popular culture has played an important part in the subordination of women to the interests of men; and secondly that, in failing to identify this fact as a central theme for research and analysis, other theoretical approaches to the study of popular culture contribute to this subordination. For example, many feminist critics have pointed to the way in which popular culture has, at least in the past, strongly associated femininity with the sphere of consumption ('shopping'), non-work and domesticity. Beyond this, however, there are important differences between the main feminist approaches.

Liberal feminism

Liberal feminists point to the importance of popular culture in reflecting the main sexist or 'malestream' values of society, and in reproducing traditional sex role stereotypes. Such stereotypes, particularly in advertising, magazine publishing and television, encourage girls to lower their expectations and to regard male dominance of work and public life as 'normal'. Frequently, liberal feminists used quantitative content analysis (see Section 15.2) to establish the prevalence of masculine images or stereotyped female images in advertising and the mass media (for example, Gaye Tuchman, 1981).

Liberal feminists advocate campaigns to promote women into senior positions within television, advertising, journalism, and so on. They do not believe that either the dominant ideology or the structural arrangements in society make this impossible. Much can be done 'within the system'. Once this happens, the powerful messages helping to construct female identities will change and girls will begin to feel themselves more 'empowered' by popular cultural imagery.

Radical feminism

In contrast, radical feminists argue that the ideology of patriarchy is so all-pervasive that it is unlikely that simply securing more senior positions for women in cultural industries would make much difference. This is because the ideology of patriarchy is related, on the one hand, to deep-seated biological and psychological characteristics in men, and on the other hand to the commercial drives of the culture industries.

Radical feminists point, for example, to the phenomenon of the 'male gaze' (see Section 15.7) to be found in film, television, magazines and even newspapers. Men have a voyeuristic inclination to enjoy the representation of women as 'objects' and the cultural industries, whether controlled by men or women, will exploit this for profit.

Feminist culturism

More recently, feminists drawing ideas from the neo-Marxist culturalist tradition have focused attention on the female audience. Culturalist feminists follow Gramsci in searching for evidence of conflict at the level of ideas within capitalist societies. They believe that such conflicts will flow not only along the dimension of class but also gender. Researchers such as Geraghty (1991), Hobson (1989) and Ang (1985), using audience ethnography, have described ways in which female audiences can derive pleasure, sometimes subversive, from soap operas and programmes which appear at first glance to reinforce sex role stereotypes. (See also Sections 10.5 and 10.7.)

Activity

Write a short paragraph explaining the position of each theory featured in Figure 10.2, using the knowledge gained from the foregoing sections. Remember that none of these theories is 'totally' materialist or 'totally' idealist – they differ in the *extent* to which they see ideas shaping society or social and economic forces shaping culture and ideas.

U, I

Social action and culture

Structural theories differ in many respects, but they all assume that culture exists as a reality independent of the individual; that the social structure shapes and constrains patterns of cultural life and that the social structure plays an important part in shaping individual identity.

The theories described below all place more emphasis on the active involvement of social actors in the creation of culture, or they go even further to deny the validity of the concept of structure in the first place (see Figure 10.3).

• Culture created as social actors interact with social structures	• Culture constructed as social actors interact in groups	• Culture as a set of discourses • Validity of social structure as a concept rejected
• Weberianism • Structuration theory	• Symbolic inter-actionism	• Post-structuralism • Post-modernism

Figure 10.3 Action and post-structural approaches to culture

Weberian sociology and symbolic interactionism

This section will confine itself to drawing attention to the ways in which some of the 'classic' Weberian and interactionist work, discussed in more detail in other chapters, can be used to explore themes of culture and identity.

In *The Protestant Ethic and the Spirit of Capitalism* (1930, orig. pub. 1905) and his other writings on world religions (discussed in more detail in Section 18.6), Weber traces the interplay between economic forces and religion, as a set of cultural ideas. Unlike some Marxists who have argued that protestantism represented an ideology which legitimated and helped to reproduce capitalism, Weber argues that the cultural ideas associated with religion had a force and logic of their own; they significantly contributed to social change and did not merely 'reflect' underlying economic developments or the ideology of a capitalist class. The rising capitalist entrepreneurs of the seventeenth century, for example, were motivated to develop and expand capitalist trading relations, partly through a desire to organize business in a rational way, and partly because their salvationist beliefs led them to find signs of salvation in business success.

Thus, for Weber culture had as much explanatory significance as economic or political forces. Subsequently, neo-Weberian social action theorists have applied these ideas to the analysis of a variety of examples of stratification. In each case, the emphasis has been on the interplay between cultural definition and economic processes, as in the work of John Rex on race and stratification within the inner city (see Section 6.4), or Goldthorpe and Lockwood on the position of 'affluent workers' (Section 4.7).

Symbolic interactionists are less inclined than Weber to emphasize the permanence of the social structures which emerge as individuals act on the cultural definitions or meanings which guide them. Instead, they tend to describe a more fluid process in which social actors interact to construct cultural arrangements, but the emphasis is on the ways in which such cultural arrangements can change, depending on the nature of particular patterns of interaction. Culture is generated, then, through social interaction and the exchange of meanings or interpretations.

This theoretical approach stimulated a rich range of empirical, ethnographic studies of the process of cultural construction, and a number of these are described in more detail in the chapters on deviancy, community and education (see Sections 8.3, 11.5 and 16.1). Some of the earliest research on local subcultures was produced through this approach by the Chicago School in the USA, including Whyte's study of young street corner culture (1943), Cressey's study of the culture of the commercial dance hall in the late 1920s (1932), and Clifford Shaw's study of prototype muggers (1966).

Drawing on the writing of George Herbert Mead and John Dewey, symbolic interactionists have spent a considerable amount of time exploring the relationship between culture, social interaction and identity. This is discussed in more detail in Section 2.7. Mead's division of the human mind between the 'I' and the 'Me' emphasizes the importance of social interaction with others in the construction of identity (the 'I' monitoring the response of others to the impression 'Me' gives when performing a social role). For Dewey, Mead and subsequent symbolic interactionists, personal identity is essentially social in origin; but unlike Parsonian functionalism, for example, symbolic interactionism emphasizes the fluidity and flexibility of identity. Whereas within the Parsonian framework the emphasis is on the way in which our identities are moulded as we learn to perform particular roles through socialization, symbolic interactionism is committed to charting the ways in which identity can change as patterns of interaction change and individuals are exposed to new cultural environments. Social identity is not fixed or permanent but fluid, changeable and dynamic. Becker's 'classic' study of dance or jazz subcultures and marihuana use in the 1950s illustrates this very well (see Section 11.5). Individuals may come to see themselves as 'part' of the dance subculture and, perhaps, as 'marihuana users', but this depends on how much they interact with other members of the subculture and the nature of the symbolic meanings that are exchanged (Becker, 1973).

In response, structural sociologists point to the lack of attention to important macro features in interactionist writing. They argue that the account of cultural behaviour interactionists provide is incomplete unless there is also a consideration of how structure, power and history impact on and limit the development of culture and identity. In turn, interactionists point to the lack of attention in structural sociology to the importance of the processes through which identity is constructed at the micro level.

Structuration theory

Anthony Giddens offers the concept of structuration theory as one attempt to marry a sociology of structure with a sociology of action. His ideas are discussed in more detail in Section 2.9, but his approach has provided a number of important insights relevant to the study of culture and identity.

Giddens uses the term 'structuration' to describe the interplay between social structure and the action of individual social actors; each one affecting and shaping the other. We continuously create structure through our interaction with others but, equally, structure continually constrains and limits what we can do. This theme provides the key to understanding Giddens' more recent work on the relationship between culture, self-identity and globalization (1991). Giddens' important work is discussed in more detail in Section 10.10. The issue of globalization is also discussed in Sections 9.9, 12.5, 15.11, 16.8 and 17.6.

Post-structuralism and the break with 'modernism'

The problems associated with applying just a sociology of structure or just a sociology of action to the study of culture and identity have prompted a number of sociologists to turn to the writings of French 'post-structuralists', among them Jacques Derrida and Michel Foucault. Both are, perhaps, best understood as philosophers rather than sociologists, but their ideas have had considerable influence in recent years, in many ways overlapping with the themes developed by post-modernists.

The ideas of Foucault and Derrida are sometimes regarded as representing a break with 'modernist' sociology precisely because they abandon the assumption that it is possible to use sociological concepts to analyse the structure of society as a separate reality. In this way, they anticipate the development of post-modernism (see also Section 2.10).

Derrida and Foucault reject the assumption that there is a structural reality below the surface of social life which directs human behaviour, but of which we are not always aware. Rather, there is an interest in the ways in which knowledge, language and culture operate in society.

Derrida, like structuralists, starts with the idea that society can be understood as a system. He draws on the insights provided by semiologists (see Section 15.2) to suggest that social life, itself, can be understood as being made up of systems of signs or images which we recognize and respond to in our social behaviour. However, Derrida – unlike Talcott Parsons – does not believe that such systems of signs (or in Parsons' terms 'values') are fixed or permanent. The meanings of signs and images change and fluctuate in unpredictable ways and changes in one sign will trigger changes in other related symbols. In other words, the cultural system which Parsons described as essentially stable and predictable is, for Derrida, essentially unstable and unpredictable.

It is Foucault, however, who has had most influence in demonstrating how post-structuralist ideas can be applied in researching themes of culture and identity. Foucault shares with Derrida a scepticism regarding structuralist analysis and an interest in the way language or discourse works in society. In particular, Foucault seeks to develop an approach to power which departs from the conventional perspectives found in sociology, and this has considerable bearing on his analysis of culture. (Foucault's approach to power is also discussed in Section 17.4.)

First, Foucault does not believe that power is something owned or possessed by a ruling élite, class or bureaucracy (in contrast to Marxist and Weberian approaches). He rejects the idea that power is always concentrated in central institutions such as the state, financial institutions or large corporations. Neither does he think that power can be analysed through the conscious plans or intentions of powerful individuals (Smart, 1985, pp. 77–8). Rather, Foucault develops a post-structuralist approach to the relationship between power and culture. Power is 'relational'; it works through discourse or systems of language and knowledge. Every kind of knowledge brings with it particular power relationships. Thus, for example, the discourse of western medicine implies a particular power relation between doctors and patients. Students and staff working within contemporary British education institutions have had to become familiar with the discourse of modern business and the power relations associated with it. Thus, talk within education institutions is now frequently of 'business plans', 'mission statements', 'quality control' and 'marketing', and with this new discourse or 'power–knowledge relation' new patterns of control are established.

For Foucault – in contrast to structural sociology – power has to be explored at the micro level through the various ways in which 'power–knowledge' relations distribute power in varied and specific ways. Foucault does not believe that social actors are always subordinated to dominant structures in society. On the contrary, although 'power–knowledge' relations express power and may coerce, they also generate resistance. In other words, power can activate responses amongst those it is constraining: prisoners organize 'prison protests', the inmates of asylums challenge the dominant discourses of psychiatry, staff and students in the university may find ways to subvert the 'business plan' or satirize the 'mission statement'.

What does this all mean for the study of culture? Whereas both Marxists and Weberians place most emphasis on tracing inter-connections between cultural power and economic structures, for Foucault power exists within culture but in terms of a huge variety of different 'power–knowledge' relations. Culture is shaped not merely by social class or the workings of the state but by lots of different 'power–knowledge relations', or discourses. Foucault argues that we all find ourselves enmeshed in a complex web of different discourses, each offering particular ways of understanding aspects of our behaviour. Thus, there are discourses which offer ways of understanding our sexuality; there are discourses which offer ways of understanding the way we feel about ourselves as employees, people with ethnic identities, men or women, family members, as hospital users or benefit claimants, even as DIY enthusiasts. Culture is created through the complex web of discourses or 'power–knowledge' relations which are created in society *and* the distinct resistances which each discourse may activate amongst social groups and individuals. To take the first example, there is now a flourishing lesbian and gay culture which has arisen partly through resistance to dominant discourses which 'normalize' heterosexuality and marginalize other forms of sexuality (Foucault, 1979a). (See also Section 5.4.)

Foucault argues that our sense of self-identity actually comes from the way in which we are positioned in relation to particular forms of knowledge or discourses:

. . . certain gestures, certain discourses, certain desires come to be identified and constituted as individuals.
(Foucault, 1979a, p. 98)

One outcome of the spread of 'power–knowledge' relations is the constitution of 'the subject', or the individual with a sense of self and a subjective understanding of their place in relation to others. For example, discourses about sexuality offer a series of important concepts with which individuals 'position' (or think through) their own sexual identities (Foucault, 1979a). We use the words, phrases and vocabularies of sexuality to actually think about ourselves as sexual subjects.

Recent applications of Foucault's ideas

Ien Ang (1991) has used Foucault's ideas to explore the way in which television companies relate to their audiences. She shows that television programme planners think about their audiences in terms of classification systems or discourses. Audiences are grouped according to age, income, gender, and so on. Planners seek to 'control' viewing through their programming strategies but, Ang argues, such classifications or discourses are no more than crude generalizations which do not really capture the lived experience of watching television for different individuals and families, each with their own unique tastes and interests. Consequently, the attempts of television planners are always doomed to at least partial failure as audiences *resist*.

Similarly, Redhead (1990) traces the way in which

a variety of discourses about pop and rock music (for example, the terms 'house', 'garage', 'hip hop', 'metal', etc.) provide us with ways of understanding not only music but our own identities in relation to such music. These discourses are partly circulated by the music industry and the music press, but they are also circulated through the ways in which both musicians and audiences *resist* the pressures of the commercial mainstream.

Criticisms of Foucault and post-structuralism

Critics of Foucault often argue that the main assumptions of 'modernist' sociology should not be abandoned. They insist that it is still possible to use sociological concepts to move towards a more or less objective understanding of the underlying reality of society.

Poulantzas, for example, a Marxist, argues that post-structuralism ignores the importance of *sources* of power, which he insists are still to be traced to key structures in society such as the organization of capital. In particular, Poulantzas argues that Foucault under-estimates the importance of the state in modern societies: although a variety of political struggles may occur, ultimately power is still concentrated in the institutions of the state, and the state in turn still generally reflects the interests of capital. Although Poulantzas accepts that Foucault has made an important contribution to our understanding of how individuality is constructed, his concept of power is rather vague: what actually counts as 'resistance' and how should it be defined? The danger is that we become fascinated by the pluralistic variety of local struggles but lose sight of the 'bigger picture' of power.

Similarly, some feminists are worried by the implication that we should abandon the attempt to analyse the 'truth' of exploitation and patriarchy. While feminists welcome the opportunities Foucault's work suggests for analysing discourses involving gender struggles, there is a reluctance to abandon the assumption that feminist research deals with the 'real' concepts of 'justice' and 'equality' and the 'real' impact social structures have on women's and mens' lives (Hartsock, 1990). (This debate is also discussed in Section 5.5.)

Modernity, modernism and post-modernism

The rate of change in contemporary societies is so rapid that it has prompted some sociologists to argue that we should distinguish between the era of *modernity* and the *post-modern society*.

Modernity here refers to the era in which capitalism could provide most people with a degree of certainty and security in their lives. For much of the twentieth century, for example, people in the UK could expect to stay in the same kind of occupation for most of their lives; family life was the norm, and the welfare state provided a 'safety net' against poverty. National governments appeared to be able to plan ahead using 'rational' economic and social policies, often devised on the basis of 'objective' knowledge produced by social and natural scientists.

Now the world looks rather different. Many of the old certainties have disappeared: many people face job insecurity, family life is much more diverse, and governments are keen to discourage people from relying on the welfare state. In a globalized world economy, neither individuals nor governments appear to be able to claim control over their own destinies. For more discussion of these changes see Sections 7.3, 9.3, 12.5, 14.2, 15.11 and 17.6.

Some theorists argue that the impact of these changes is so significant that we should distinguish between the era of modernity and the new era of post-modernity. Such theorists also contend that the social science approaches which developed during the era of modernity are no longer able to describe the complexity of the post-modern world. In particular, they associate the era of modernity with '*modernist*' sociology. Modernist sociology assumed that it was possible to use sociological concepts in a rational way to understand the structure of society and to devise policies, on the basis of this, to help make social progress. Many (but not all) *post-modernists* follow Foucault and Derrida in denying the possibility of studying the social structure of society as an independent reality which can be approached using objective concepts. We can no longer pin our hopes on the capacity of a rational sociology contributing to social progress. Rather what we should do is concentrate on the ways in which language, knowledge and cultural ideas are used by social groups to accumulate power.

Not all sociologists accept this argument. Some question whether such high levels of uncertainty are really a new phenomenon, because life during the 1930s – in the middle of the era of modernity – was pretty insecure for many people living in an economically depressed Europe, with political instability and looming war. Post-modernist theorists also sometimes fail to do justice to the extent to which 'modernist' sociology was aware of the problems in attempting to analyse social structure as an objective reality. Sociologists, after all, had been grappling with the problem of whether or not it was possible to analyse an objective social reality for many years, and theorists following Weber and Mead had developed a critique of structural sociology before World War II. (See also Sections 3.1, 3.2 and 3.3.)

Varieties of post-modernism

We need to distinguish between *post-modernity* and *post-modernism*. While some writers point to changes in society which they believe mean that society has moved beyond the modern, to an era of post-modernity, not all these writers fully embrace all the concepts of the theoretical approach known as post-modernism. In other words, it is important to distinguish between post-modernity, as a description of social and cultural change, and post-modernism as a theoretical perspective.

Post-modern theorists, such as Baudrillard, Lyotard and Jameson agree that modern capitalist societies have entered a qualitatively new period in their development, a stage in which questions of culture and identity become much more important. All agree, for example, that in the post-modern era there is a loss of faith in grand belief systems or 'meta-narratives', including science, religion and political ideologies. 'Science' is just another way of looking at the world, along with religions, 'new age' philosophies and subcultural beliefs. There is a preoccupation with cultural style but a reluctance to regard one style or tradition as essentially superior to any other. In other words, for these theorists, the post-modern public applies a relativist approach both to knowledge and culture.

However, while the public may be relativist in its thinking about knowledge and culture, there are important differences between post-modernist theorists regarding the status of sociological knowledge and theory. Lyotard (1993) and Baudrillard (1988) embrace a fully relativist position – all grand theory or meta-narratives are regarded as the products of particular cultures, rather than capturing fundamental truths or objective knowledge. They abandon modernist ideas regarding the possibility of analysing the underlying reality of society. Baudrillard, for example, believes we live in a 'media saturated' world, in which the mass media become so pervasive and powerful that 'reality' and the media representation of 'reality' collapse together. Neither the public, nor social scientists, are able to distinguish reality from the media *representation* of reality.

However, Jameson (1991), in describing post-modern culture as the 'cultural logic of late capitalism', is reluctant to abandon entirely Marxism's insistence that it is possible to describe the 'reality' of capitalism. Jameson agrees that significant changes have occurred in culture and lifestyle but still employs an analytic framework which places the workings of capitalism at the centre of the explanation.

Similarly, post-modernist feminism is reluctant to abandon all the assumptions of modernist analysis. French post-modernist feminists, such as Jardine

(1985), argue that theorists should expose the way in which patriarchy creates myths about the essential nature of masculinity and femininity. Jardine argues that post-modernist theory can be used to expose or 'deconstruct' this meta-narrative as just a particular discourse, rather than an 'ultimate truth'. Individuals do not have basic or essential male or female natures; rather there is vast range of feminities and masculinities, each constructed through language and discourse. Jardine argues that in the post-modern world gender roles are no longer fixed or based on the 'certainties' of the modern era.

Activity

For each of the following theoretical perspectives, write one or two sentences to summarize its position in relation to the issues listed in (a) to (e). Figures 10.2 and 10.3 may help you:

functionalism; Marxism; feminism; Weberianism; symbolic interactionism; structuration; post-structuralism; post-modernism.

a Is the emphasis more on social actors creating culture or on individual identity being shaped by culture?

b Is there more emphasis on ideas and culture shaping the social structure or on social and material forces shaping culture and ideas?

c Is it assumed that despite some differences, most social groups share a common culture which has a unifying effect; or is it assumed that society consists of a plurality of different cultures?

d Are judgements made about what counts as 'good' or 'bad' culture (this is an issue which is explored further in the next section)?

e For each perspective, outlinine why it can be described as 'modernist' or 'post-modernist'.

U, I, A

However, a problem arises at this stage, for post-modernist feminism. In rejecting the validity of all meta-narratives, the post-modernist approach also appears to imply that feminism, as a meta-narrative, can no longer be regarded as offering a universal truth about power and the position of women. Many feminists, including some attracted to post-modernist approaches, are reluctant to accept this implication. As Sabina Lovibond comments:

How can anyone ask me to say good-bye to 'eman-cipatory metanarratives' when my own emancipation is still such a patchy, hit or miss affair? (Lovibond, 1990, p. 161)

Feminist theorists such as Lovibond and Hartsock (1990) accept that post-modernist concepts are useful in highlighting the fluidity and flexibility of gender positions, and the part that certain discourses play in their construction. But they are unwilling to fully embrace the relativism of post-modernist philosophy which implies that feminism is just another metanarrative. (See also Section 5.5.)

A more detailed account of post-modernist approaches may be found in Section 10.12, together with a critical assessment.

10.3 Culture, modernity and the study of popular culture

Defining culture and assessing quality

Raymond Williams (1961), in an important early study of the development of modern culture, identifies three different approaches, each of which defines culture in a distinct way.

The 'ideal'

The first definition is termed by Williams the 'ideal'. Writers employing this definition assume that culture is a 'state or process of human perfection' (1961, p. 57). Only the very best in intellectual and artistic endeavour would be included as examples: the greatest literature, most moving opera and drama, most skilfully constructed poetry, most beautiful painting and so on. In other words, what is often termed *high culture* rather than *popular culture*.

The study of culture, according to this approach, involves the application of universally agreed criteria or rules (which apply at all times across all societies) for assessing the quality of particular examples. It is assumed that it is possible to apply universal rules for separating the 'good' from 'bad' because human experience – the range of human emotions – is also universal and great art successfully describes the 'truth' of this human condition.

With its insistence on including only the very 'best' in human creative endeavour, the ideal definition can be regarded as narrow. It is assumed, for example, that only a small minority of creative artists or intellectuals actually make culture. This is an important point: Williams argues that such narrow definitions of culture were 'selective' in the sense that they served to exclude large numbers of people and secured a privileged position only for those with the 'instincts' or 'skills' to appreciate fine artistic or intellectual work.

The 'documentary'

A second way of defining culture is termed by Williams the 'documentary' approach (1961, p. 57). This is a slightly broader definition which considers not just artistic or intellectual products which satisfy the criterion of near-perfection, but all those works which represent 'the body of intellectual and imaginative work' a society has produced. In other words, writers employing the 'documentary' definition consider not only the very best in art and intellectual activity, but all examples which represent or 'document' the 'culture' of a society.

Recently the British government, in its approach to the schools curriculum, has appeared to embrace this kind of approach, with policies encouraging a concentration on 'English' literature and 'English' history. Ministers have argued that all school pupils should have an appreciation of their English heritage in terms of art and history. (This issue is discussed in more detail in Section 8.10) This definition is slightly broader but the focus remains on art and intellectual work, created again by a minority of artists and intellectuals within particular societies.

Williams argues that frequently even with this definition there remains an assumption that universal aesthetic or intellectual criteria can be applied in order to assess what counts as 'culture'. Shakespeare *is* counted as culture but the television show *Blind Date* is not.

'Social definition'

Williams identifies a third approach as the 'social definition' (1961, p. 57). Whereas the first two approaches are most closely associated with traditional teaching in Art and English as academic disciplines, this approach owes its origins to early anthropology and sociology. Although an English academic by profession, Williams himself, together with Richard Hoggart (see Section 10.4), can be credited with developing the argument for embracing this much wider definition of culture. Williams argues that the term 'culture' can also be taken to mean 'a particular way of life' and that the study of culture could also include:

. . . certain meanings and values not only in art and learning but also in institutions and ordinary behaviour. [It] will also include analysis of elements in the way of life that to followers of the other definitions are not 'culture' at all.
(Williams, 1961, p. 57)

In other words, culture could be understood as:

. . . a whole way of life, material, intellectual and spiritual.
(Williams, 1963, p. 16)

This is a much broader definition. Not only artists and intellectuals but all members of society are engaged in the process of making culture, on a daily basis, as part of their ordinary lives. Culture is no longer understood as 'separate' from ordinary people: it is something made and consumed by everyone – in local communities, on local streets, inside families and pubs, as well as in opera houses and 'serious' theatres.

This radical break with previous definitions allowed researchers and academics to begin to take popular culture seriously, and for cultural studies to evolve as a discipline in the 1960s. However, there is an important implication regarding the assessment of the quality of culture. If 'culture' is part of ordinary life and all are involved in its production, is it still possible to distinguish between the 'good' and the 'bad'? The implication appears to be that all cultural work, irrespective of its worth, has to be treated with the same degree of critical respect. The previous two definitions assume that there exist *universal* and *absolute* criteria for assessing the value of a cultural product. These criteria are timeless and unchanging. The 'social' definition, on the other hand, seems to imply a *relative*, rather than absolute, approach. Cultural standards are understood as being relative to particular societies at particular times.

Discussion point

To what extent do you think it is possible to make objective judgements about the quality of cultural products? Is it important to distinguish between 'good' and 'bad' television, books, films, etc., or should we simply allow consumers to make their own choices without imposing any concept of 'cultural standards'?

Recently, several classical musicians have been angered because their recordings of 'lighter' musical pieces (for example, songs taken from Hollywood musicals) have been banned from the United States' classical record chart. This implies the imposition of an absolute judgement. What do you think? What *is* the difference between pop/rock and classical music?

It is interesting to note, however, that neither Williams nor Hoggart were entirely comfortable with relativistic approaches. Although each writer wished to broaden and democratize the study of culture, neither wished to abandon entirely the insistence on 'standards' and 'quality'. Indeed, Richard Hoggart continues to actively campaign against the influence of relativism in contemporary cultural discussion (Hoggart, 1996).

Activity

Imagine yourself to be a television scheduler working for a national television organization such as the BBC or ITV.

a Draw up a schedule of television programmes for one day based on your knowledge of current mainstream programmes – you can pick from all current channels, including satellite and cable.

b Write a paragraph providing a rationale for your programming strategy. Include a consideration of the extent to which your approach is based upon 'the ideal', 'the documentary', or 'the social' definition of culture. Are you aiming to educate and inform, reflect contemporary culture, or just entertain?

Urbanization, modernity and 'mass society'

The modern world – the era of modernity – emerged through the rise of the Industrial Revolution, the spread of urbanization, and the growth of capitalist markets, in the second half of the eighteenth century, and throughout the nineteenth century.

With urbanization came the creation of large aggregates of people – the masses. Concerns about the instability and irrationality of the masses, their propensity for disorder and unruly behaviour, and the associated problem of how to 'civilize' or socially integrate them, is a preoccupation to be found in the sociological work of Tönnies and Durkheim (see Section 16.1) and in the writings of nineteenth century philosophers and cultural critics, such as the philosopher J. S. Mill (1806–73) and the author Matthew Arnold (1822–73).

Civilising culture and the danger of the masses

The thinking of Mill and Arnold has to be placed in the context of the debate over whether or not to extend the political franchise to working-class men in the 1870s. (See also Section 17.1.) In principle, Mill supported the concept of democracy, but he wondered whether the masses would use the right to vote in a responsible way. Mill pictured the masses as a large aggregation of isolated and anomic indi-

viduals, no longer regulated by the close-knit ties of the rural community. Without the social controls of the pre-industrial rural community, isolated urban individuals could be swayed or manipulated by skilful orators, music hall, or the other mass media of the day. Mill was cautiously optimistic that a programme of universal education could 'civilize' the masses through the elevation of their cultural standards. Only then could they be relied on to use political rights responsibly.

Matthew Arnold made the link between 'high culture' and civilization even more explicit. In *Culture and Anarchy*, he defined culture as 'the study of perfection', or:

. . . the best that has been thought and said in the world.
(Quoted in Billington *et al.*, 1991, p. 8 and Storey, 1993, p. 21)

The habits and pastimes, or culture, of the urban working-class masses, he regarded as anarchic, not only without cultural worth but actually dangerous because they often degenerated into social disorder. Arnold, like Mill, believed that the urban masses – who he described as:

'vast miserable, unmanageable ... raw and uncultivated'

posed a potential threat to the stability of society, particularly after the Second Reform Act of 1867, which extended the electoral franchise. The only hope was to use cultural education as a civilizing force

'to minister to the diseased spirit of our time'
(Quoted in Storey, 1993, p. 22; orig. pub. 1868).

Both Mill and Arnold can be said to belong to the tradition of 'mass society' theorists because they assume that society is divided between an educated and cultured élite, on the one hand, and the uncultured masses on the other. Both also picture the masses as unsophisticated, easily swayed and vulnerable to political and commercial manipulation.

Mass culture and folk culture

If anything, some cultural critics and intellectuals grew even more pessimistic about the condition of the 'masses' in the twentieth century.

Some critics believed that the success of Fascistism and Nazism in Europe during the 1920s and 1930s was attributable to the skill of their proponents in exploiting the mass media as tools of propaganda with which to exploit the ignorant and gullible nature of the masses. Significantly, writers from both the political Left and Right were sympathetic to the arguments of the mass society thesis.

T. S. Eliot, poet and literary critic, in a famous essay (1948) 'Notes towards a definition of culture' argues that culture is inevitably stratified, with each social class in society making a distinctive cultural contribution; but he implies that the more sophisticated cultures are developed by the higher social classes. Eliot appears to mourn the loss of the folk cultures, rich in tradition and custom, which were associated with the era of rural and craft production. Folk cultures served an important function in integrating communities. Now both the 'Englishness' of the higher classes, and the 'folk culture' of lower classes, were in danger of being washed away by the spread of cheap, commercial or mass culture.

The arguments of two literary critics, F. R. Leavis and Q. D. Leavis, who wrote respectively *Mass Civilisation and Minority Culture* (1930) and *Fiction and the Reading Public* (1932), develop these themes in even bolder terms. According to them, only a small educated cultural élite are capable of understanding and profiting from the descriptions of the human experience contained in great works of art and culture. Only this small cultured élite can pass on this precious inheritance to the next generation, but their position and authority is threatened by the spread of commercial 'mass culture', which panders to the lowest common denominator and undermines cultural standards. Folk songs and dances, the customs and traditions associated with the rural past, helped to cement social bonds and maintain social integration. The products of mass culture – popular fiction, detective stories, cinema, modern popular music – all debased or coarsened human experience and destabilized the social order.

In the 1940s and 1950s, the mass society debate developed further in the USA. Given the size of the United States, the power of American capitalism, and the success of Hollywood and other forms of American popular culture, this was inevitable. An important collection of articles, *Mass Culture: The Popular Arts in America* (Rosenberg and Manning White, 1957), set the terms of the debate. Supporters of the mass society thesis made the following kind of arguments:

Folk culture grew from below. It was a spontaneous . . . expression of the people, shaped by themselves . . . to suit their own needs. Mass culture is imposed from above. It is fabricated by technicians hired by businessmen; its audiences are passive consumers, their participation limited to the choice between buying or not buying . . . it is a debased, trivial culture that voids both the deep realities (sex, death, failure, tragedy) and also the simple, spontaneous pleasures.
(MacDonald, 1957, pp. 60 and 73)

Against this view, however, the book also contained a defence of American popular culture. One of the editors, for example, pointed both to the danger of romanticizing folk culture in the past and under-estimating the extent to which the American mass media also allowed 'high culture' to flourish (Manning White, 1957). A further critique of the mass society thesis is developed at the end of this section.

The Frankfurt School and mass culture

Whereas the ideas of Arnold, Eliot and the Leavis's can be located within a broadly conservative tradition, the Frankfurt School developed a Marxist analysis of mass culture. The thinking of the Frankfurt School in relation to the role of the mass media is described in more detail in Section 15.10.

The leading writers of the School, including Adorno, Horkheimer and Marcuse, were all clearly influenced not only by their experiences as left-wing intellectuals witnessing, at first hand, the triumph of Nazism in the 1930s, but also as Marxist immigrants to the USA in the 1940s and 1950s, where advertising and the commercial exploitation of popular culture were most visible and pervasive.

In books like *One Dimensional Man* (Marcuse, 1964) and *The Culture Industry* (Adorno, 1991), a rather pessimistic view emerges of capitalist societies in which the working-class has lost its capacity to think critically or to resist its exploitation. The drive of capitalism to make profit produces a form of popular culture which is shallow and meaningless because it is produced to a formula. They refer to:

The assembly line character of the culture industry, the synthetic, planned method of turning out its products (factory like not only in the studio but . . . in the compilation of cheap biographies, pseudo-documentary novels, and hit songs).
(Adorno and Horkheimer, 1977, p. 381)

Capitalist culture industries create mass culture. However, unlike earlier mass society theorists, the Frankfurt School did not believe that such a situation reflected the cultural or intellectual inadequacies of ordinary people but rather the power of advertising and the mass media to shape our consciousness (Strinati, 1995, p. 62).

Mass culture simultaneously helped to stimulate economic demand and maintain social control. The masses were encouraged to develop an appetite for commodities and entertainments – to crave 'false needs' – and the partial satisfaction of these 'false needs' through shopping and mass entertainment fostered docility and an absence of critical thought. In capitalist societies, we become 'one dimensional' people, lacking a culture through which we can express real emotion or feelings, merely the synthetic pleasures derived from the cinema screen and television set.

The function of popular culture

As a response to the pessimism of the mass culture thesis and the Frankfurt School, some writers influenced by functionalism developed a more positive appraisal of the role of popular culture in industrial societies.

Shils (1961) argues that the growing volume of popular culture (more magazines, the spread of television, the boom in popular music, etc.) does not represent simply more opportunities for commercial exploitation but, on the contrary, proves that the cultural interests of everyone could be catered for in western societies. Popular culture functions in a unifying way, helping to 'incorporate . . . the mass of the population into society' (1961, p. 1).

Conclusions and criticisms

Few sociologists accept the arguments either of the Frankfurt School or the mass culture thesis in their entirety. Not only does the mass culture thesis paint a rather romantic picture of the folk culture we have lost (it is easy to forget that pre-nineteenth century popular entertainments included brawling, cock-fighting, and public executions, as well as morris dancing and folk music); but it may overestimate the extent to which a mass culture has really enveloped us all. Some sociologists point to evidence which suggests that media audiences are frequently active and critical in the way they select and consume media products. (This is discussed in more detail in Section 15.9.)

Secondly, both the mass culture thesis and the Frankfurt School fail to pay sufficient attention to important differences between social groups within 'mass' audiences. The social class structure in late capitalist societies is highly complex and, together with gender, age and ethnicity, one's class position is likely to make an important difference to the way in which one participates culturally and consumes media.

Thirdly, one has to return to the problems of defining and assessing culture. Underpinning the arguments of both the Frankfurt School and the mass culture thesis are important assumptions about what counts as 'good' or 'bad' culture. These assumptions have to be teased out and considered carefully.

Activity

Compare the mass society, Frankfurt School and functionalist approaches to popular culture. Make notes identifying not only the main differences between each but also any similarities you can detect.

U, I, A

10.4 Culture, class and identity

Twenty years ago the American sociologist Herbert Gans argued that, while there were always exceptions, it was possible to relate culture and taste to social class (Gans, 1974). He pointed out, for example, that most people from upper socio-economic groups liked classical music and most people from lower socio-economic groups did not.

Drawing the same kind of distinction between the culture of social classes today is much more problematic. First, the mass media have now made the 'high culture' of cultural élites much more accessible to a wider audience, so it is no longer an intellectual minority who enjoy opera. Secondly, the relationship between culture and social class appears to vary widely around the world. Samba, for example, is regarded as a music of the young working-class within Brazil while heavy rock is popular amongst the young wealthy and privileged strata of Brazilian society. And yet, in Europe and north America, samba music is regarded as an exotic form of 'world music' popular with educated elites (Lull, 1995, p. 69).

Thirdly, and perhaps even more significantly for sociology, the debates over the changing nature of the class structure make the very concept of a 'class culture' problematic. (This issue is discussed in more detail in Chapter 4.)

There are several different ways of defining the differences between social classes in sociology (see Section 4.4). If sociologists cannot agree about the concept social class, what do we actually mean by 'working-class culture' or 'middle-class culture'? And yet, in our daily lives we do still recognize cultural signals – in terms of language, fashion, shopping, even television viewing – which tell us about the class background of the people we meet.

Working-class culture in the UK

In the 1950s it became fashionable to argue that rising living standards were changing the nature of working-class culture. Zweig (1961) argued that a new affluent worker was emerging who was becoming middle class in lifestyle and political attitudes. Certainly, sections of the working class enjoyed access to a range of cultural goods and commodities for the first time, including family cars, washing machines, televisions and holidays abroad. Richard Hoggart, for example, saw the arrival in the UK of American cultural products – rock and roll, juke boxes, American movies, etc. – as part of the creation of a mass society in which the rich and important traditions of working-class culture were being washed away.

Hoggart himself came from a working-class background. In *The Uses of Literacy* (1958) he devotes the first half of the book to detailing the richness and vitality of pre-war culture in the homes, churches, pubs, and other organizations of working-class communities. Working-class people faced a life of permanent insecurity, never being sure that their jobs would last or their rented housing would be permanent. Accordingly, working-class culture emphasized a certain frivolity – living for the moment rather than planning ahead, and taking fun while the chance was there. Nevertheless, Hoggart insists, traditional working-class culture also stood for certain values which he strongly approved of: a sense of responsibility for others in the community, tolerance, 'a goodwill-humanism' (1958, p. 142), a commitment to political involvement, and a sense of decency or knowing right from wrong.

In the second half of his book, Hoggart describes the ways in which he feared traditional working-class culture was being eroded by the arrival of mass entertainment designed to appeal to all classes. Radio, for example, made it no longer necessary for working-class people to meet together to sing their own songs. Hoggart felt something important was being lost:

No doubt many of the old barriers of class should be broken down. But at present the older, more narrow but also more genuine class culture is being eroded in favour of mass opinion.
(Hoggart, 1958, p. 285)

Critics of Hoggart pointed to the nostalgic flavour of his account of pre-war working-class culture and his inclination to ignore the tougher and more brutal aspects of living in such communities. Perhaps a more important criticism is that, while Hoggart stressed the inventiveness of pre-war working-class culture, he fails to recognize that exactly the same process might be at work 20 years later in the reaction of working-class people to commercial or mass culture (Storey, 1993, p. 47). In other words, rather than passively absorbing a 'poorer', 'classless' commercial culture, working-class people might still be adapting and using 'bits' of the commercial culture to create new equally rich forms of working-class culture.

Culturalism and working-class culture

The Centre for Contemporary Cultural Studies (CCCS) is strongly influenced by neo-Marxist hegemony theory or 'culturalism' (see Section 10.2). They have produced accounts of working-class culture which try to point to the ways in which it expresses 'resistance' to the dominant culture within capitalist societies. This contrasts with the rather pessimistic account provided by Richard Hoggart.

Writers at the CCCS identify local subcultures within what they term a 'parent' working-class culture. Phil Cohen (1972), for example, describes the ways in which working-class communities in the East End of London developed patterns of class cultural resistance to forces which threatened them, such as the decline of the local docks and the redevelopment of the East End. The redevelopment of docklands is also discussed in Section 16.7. Richard Johnson (1979) traces the ways in which working-class adults attempted to organize their own education in the nineteenth century, and Paul Willis (1977) conducted an ethnographic study of a group of working-class boys actively engaged in resistance within a Midlands comprehensive school (this is discussed in more detail in Section 8.2). Each study stresses the active and varied ways in which the dominant culture of capitalism can be resisted by working-class people.

There is a tension in the CCCS approach because, whilst stressing the capacity of the working-class to culturally resist, they also acknowledge the ways in which the cultural institutions of capitalism could incorporate or 'tame' working-class culture. Critcher (1979) argues that the commercialization of professional soccer, a game that grew within working-class communities in the nineteenth century, means that it is now controlled and organized as a capitalist leisure industry (see Section 10.8).

Discussion point

How far do you think it is now true that working-class people have lost control of sports such as soccer which were formerly part of 'their' culture?

A frequent criticism of the work of the Centre is that it is primarily preoccupied with masculine culture and that there is insufficient recognition of the ways in which class intersects with gender and ethnicity to shape distinct cultural patterns. Bourke (1994) uses a variety of historical sources to demonstrate the importance of *both* class and gender in the development of working-class culture. For example, a preoccupation with physique and the body became common amongst working-class men in the 1930s. Increasing numbers joined the League of Health and Strength, formed in 1906 to counter the danger of French and German men becoming fitter than their English counterparts. (See also Sections 5.6 and 13.1.) Bourke suggests that this was in part a response to rising rates of male unemployment which undermined men's 'traditional authority'. Their response was to try to reaffirm their masculinity in other ways.

Working-class women, on the other hand, had a

different cultural agenda to address. Cinema and popular fiction in the 1930s had begun to offer to women suggestions of a greater openness and freedom in terms of their sexuality. However, the boundaries of working-class female sexuality were still strongly defined by the fear of unwanted pregnancy, 'lost' reputation and the spectre of the 'amateur prostitute' raised by middle-class commentators. Working-class women in their day-to-day lives had to find a way through this difficult cultural minefield.

Middle-class cultures

The idea of 'middle-class culture' is familiar to all of us. The term is used, sometimes in a pejorative way, to denote particular tastes in food, books, cinema, leisure activities and even furniture and interior decor. And yet, it is much harder to define precisely in sociological terms what is meant by the term.

Surveys of attitudes tend to suggest that there are a number of different groups, all of which could be termed middle class (see Section 4.6). It may not be possible to speak of a single middle-class culture, but there is a relationship between cultural taste, social class and power which still appears to advantage people from middle-class backgrounds.

Drawing on both Marx and Durkheim, the French sociologist Pierre Bourdieu (1993b) has developed an account of the relationship between cultural taste and power. Like Gans at the beginning of this section, Bourdieu insists that it is possible to link particular cultural tastes to social class, although he does not believe that class background is the only determinant of these things. Bourdieu uses the term *habitus* to refer to the 'schemes of perception and appreciation' (p. 64) which those both producing and consuming culture operate with. In approaching culture, whether it be a work of high art or an edition of topless darts on cable television, individuals operate according to a *habitus* which involves particular responses and particular evaluations of what is offered. Bourdieu seems to have in mind, a sometimes only semi-conscious 'feel for the game' which steers individuals towards responding in particular ways. The *habitus* is the result of inculcation or socialization since early childhood which makes the adoption of particular 'positions' on matters of cultural taste, second nature or almost instinctive.

Bourdieu argues that a *habitus* will reflect the social conditions in which it is inculcated and, in particular, social class background will leave a strong impression. While there may be other factors which also influence the cultural tastes of individuals, nevertheless, Bourdieu argues that it is possible to distinguish between the *habitus* of different social classes.

The next step in Bourdieu's argument is to introduce the concept of the 'cultural field'. Just as there exists an 'economic field' in which there is competition between social classes and the possession of economic capital gives to one class an advantage, so Bourdieu argues there is a cultural field in which the possession of 'cultural capital' allocates an advantage. By 'cultural capital' Bourdieu means the particular cultural skills and knowledge required to 'appreciate' or 'understand' cultural products which enjoy high esteem; in other words, the 'code' which is necessary to decipher a painting or understand the particular significance of a novel.

The cultural field in a society is made up of the institutions and agencies which deal with the discussion and evaluation of culture – the review pages of newspapers, television programmes which discuss culture, museums, galleries, educational institutions and so on. Just as there is competition in the economic field for resources, so in the cultural field there is competition between social groups for cultural prestige and authority. The *habitus* of those from high socio-economic or middle-class backgrounds provides them with skills and knowledge – cultural capital – which allows them to compete successfully. They will, for example, possess the vocabulary and knowledge of art history required to engage in a discussion of the latest exhibition or a new 'art house' movie. The *habitus* of the working-class does not automatically pass on such cultural capital. Just as Bourdieu believes schools operate 'rituals of humiliation' to legitimate the under-achievement of working-class pupils (see Section 8.2), so he argues cultural institutions continue the process in which bourgeois or middle-class culture is awarded status and authority, and the *habitus* of the working-class is defined as lacking cultural worth.

Museums provide a good example. Bourdieu argues that museums may not charge an admission fee but this is a 'false generosity' (1993b, p. 237) because only those with sufficient cultural capital can enter and derive benefit from this 'free' opportunity. Free entrance to museums may appear to be a democratic policy which offers access to culture and art for all, but given the distribution of cultural capital between social classes, museums in practice operate like schools:

It is not infrequent that the working-class visitors explicitly express the feeling of exclusion which, in any case, is evident in their whole behaviour. Thus, they sometimes see in the absence of any indication which might facilitate the visit – arrows showing the direction to follow, explanatory panels, etc. – the signs of a deliberate intention to exclude the uninitiated.
(Bourdieu, 1993b, p. 298)

💬 Discussion point

Museums and 'heritage centres' have changed quite a lot over recent years. Do you agree with Bourdieu's view of museums, or do you think they are now more accessible to people from a wide range of backgrounds?

Thus, through the way exhibitions are presented – the language used, the knowledge of culture assumed, the layout and atmosphere of the museum – the experience of visiting an art gallery or museum is mystified, so that only those with cultural capital can make sense of it all. Those without are made to feel that it is their own *inadequacy* which makes them incapable of decoding what is going on.

Criticisms of Bourdieu

Bourdieu provides an illuminating analysis of the reasons why 'high art' often remains the exclusive preserve of an educated bourgeois élite, but there are some important criticisms. Does his theory take sufficient account of the way in which definitions of 'élite' culture and accessibility to cultural items can change? The mass popularization of opera in recent years suggests that the barriers to 'high art' can sometimes be rapidly broken down. Conversely, James Lull points to the development of 'black gold' or 'popular cultural capital' – the rising status of black American working-class culture as it receives growing recognition amongst a wider audience of young people, partly as a consequence of media and advertising imagery (Lull, 1995, p. 81).

This leads to another critical point. Some theorists, particularly post-modernists, question whether it is in the interests of capital to restrict access to 'high' art and culture. They point to the way in which commercial energies break down the barriers between 'high' and 'popular' culture in the pursuit of profit: everyone, these days, can buy a Picasso T-shirt.

Class culture in the post-modern world

Some theorists question whether it still makes sense to talk of a unified class culture, either working-class or middle-class, given recent changes in the nature of capitalism.

Claus Offe (1985a) argues that in the era of late, 'disorganized capitalism' fewer and fewer individuals share a common, unifying experience of full-time work – the experience which used to shape the culture of social classes. The very high rates of unemployment, casualized, part-time and temporary working, mean that wage labour grows less and less important in shaping people's lives. There will be ever-widening differences in culture and lifestyle between social groups, depending on their position in relation to work. Some skilled 'core' workers will continue to develop a culture around full-time work, but many other groups, on the periphery of the labour market, will develop much more varied lifestyles and identities. (This is discussed in more detail in Section 9.4.)

Lash and Urry (1987) argue that in the post-modern world there is a progressive weakening of the relationship between social class and culture. This is because the commercial drives of capitalism, the use of globalized media images in advertising and fashion, the emphasis on 'spectacle' in the mass media rather than serious social commentary, all encourage individuals to detach their identities and lifestyles from older social contexts. With so many images and symbols floating around in a 'media saturated' society, there is a decreasing connection between individuals' cultural tastes, fashion choices, or senses of their own identities, and their social class background.

Lash and Urry extend the ideas of Bourdieu to analyse what they regard as the post-modern world. Capitalist economies in the post-modern era generate an increasing number of jobs which deal with images, ideas, design or information, rather than the manufacture of 'things'. Workers occupied in these sectors – journalists, community arts workers and other public sector workers, copy writers in advertising, staff in video production companies, etc. – are described by Lash and Urry as the 'new petit-bourgeoisie'. While their position in terms of economic capital is often weak – they don't get paid very highly – they have a distinct *habitus* which can be described as 'alternative' or critical of traditional bourgeois, middle-class culture. It is more open than conventional bourgeois culture and draws ideas from a variety of cultural sources. It acknowledges the importance of popular culture, as well as traditional 'high' or bourgeois culture. Lash and Urry predict that this *habitus* is likely to become dominant in society, across all classes, partly because members of this social group occupy key positions in the media and cultural industries, and partly also because this approach is highly compatible with the marketing drives of capitalism. The recent fashion for surreal and stylized television advertisements might provide one illustration of what Lash and Urry have in mind. If these writers are correct, then, Bourdieu paints an over-simplified picture of the relationship between social class and culture: it is no longer possible to understand social class as 'determining' cultural patterns.

Critical responses to the post-modernist approach are discussed further in Section 10.11.

10.5 Youth subcultures

The concept of 'youth subculture' is used by sociologists to refer to the particular values, styles, cultural tastes and behaviour of young people, which separates out their culture from that of their parents. It is now recognized that youth subcultures can be traced back in history at least to the second half of the nineteenth century (Pearson, 1983).

Structural functionalism and youth subcultures

The approach of sociologists writing from a functionalist perspective in the 1950s was to start with the structural or institutional position of young people (Eisenstadt, 1956; Parsons and Bales, 1956). They argued that youth subcultures could be regarded as functional both for industrial societies and young people for a number of reasons.

Functionalists noted that the concept 'youth' and the status 'teenager' appeared only in advanced, industrialized societies. In other kinds of society, the transition from child to adult was managed much more quickly, often through a single initiation ritual which announced to the community that an individual had become a full adult. This is not possible in advanced industrialized societies because the transition between childhood and adulthood takes longer – it has been 'stretched' by the need to educate and train young people. Youth subcultures help young people to manage this 'stretched' period between childhood and adulthood. Through membership of a wider but close peer group, young people can gradually grow more independent of their parents and accomplish the transition to adulthood in a relatively smooth way.

Moreover, membership of a youth subculture can help young people to cope with the pressures and stresses they are likely to face, particularly those generated by the education system and the need to achieve qualifications. If the education system introduces young people to the pressure of competition and universalistic criteria (all being judged according to the same performance indicators), the subculture offers a more relaxed world where friendship and particularistic criteria still count – being valued for who you are rather than how you perform (Parsons and Bales, 1956).

Functionalism and social divisions

One of the most important contributions of functionalism was to highlight the point that age categories such as 'youth' are not biologically fixed but are social constructions: different societies quite clearly organize age categories in different ways.

There are, however, several criticisms of early structural functionalist approaches to youth. One important point is that youth subcultures do not always appear to function in a way which manages tension either for young people or society. Some youth subcultures are strongly associated with social disorder – British teddy boys were happily ripping up cinema seats in the 1950s, at the time Parsons and Eisenstadt published their work in the USA.

Secondly, it is clear that position in the class structure makes a difference. Working-class young people face different problems and respond in different ways from their middle-class peers. Thirdly, the 'gender blind' nature of most sociology written in the 1950s and 1960s meant that the important differences in the position of male and female teenagers were ignored. (This issue is also discussed in Sections 5.6 and 8.1.) The importance of class differences (but usually not gender differences) were recognized by some sociologists who drew on functionalism to analyse the development of delinquent subcultures in terms of the 'blocked opportunities' which working-class young people faced (see Section 11.4).

Culturalism and working-class subcultures

Functionalism made connections between the position of young people in the social structure and their cultural behaviour. However, functionalism was not very interested in the styles and fashions associated with particular youth subcultures. It was preoccupied with the functions but not the meanings of subcultures (Frith, 1984, p. 8). The early work of the Centre for Contemporary Cultural Studies shifted the theoretical focus towards making connections between social structure and what particular youth subcultural styles were communicating. What messages were being communicated when somebody cropped their hair, put on a Ben Sherman shirt and a pair of Dr Marten boots?

The early 'culturalist' approach of the CCCS team

combined the neo-Marxist interest in hegemony theory with an interest in what the selection of items of clothing, hair styles, music and symbols, actually 'signalled' to society. Their argument was that through the construction of particular styles (skinhead, teddy boy, and mod) the young working-class were developing a form of cultural resistance to the dominant ideology of capitalism (Hall and Jefferson, 1976). For example, the famous skinhead subculture took elements of traditional working-class culture – industrial boots, braces, an emphasis on masculinity and toughness – and turned these into a style that communicated a 'two finger' message to teachers, social workers, the police and the institutions which exerted control over their lives. The mod obsession with the latest fashions and chrome styled motor scooters conveyed the message that they considered themselves at the top rather than the bottom of the status hierarchy. In each case, according to the CCCS team, working-class youths were finding ways of expressing through culture, their rejection of the role assigned to them by capitalism.

At the same time, it was argued, each style also reflected the particular social circumstances in which working-class young people found themselves. Each subculture offered a 'magical' or symbolic solution to problems which capitalism generated but which, in reality, young working-class people were powerless to do anything about. Skinheads first emerged from the East End of London where traditional working-class communities were being destroyed by the decline of the London docks and housing redevelopment. The skinhead subculture was an attempt to re-create the working-class community in symbolic form, through the strong emphasis on collective loyalty and defence of territory against rival mobs. Similarly, mods could not in reality solve the problem of being locked into low-status work but the mod style of dress provided them with a symbolic or 'magical' way of claiming higher status.

Is a structural approach useful?

The early CCCS approach was extremely influential and inspired the development of what is now known as culturalism. However, subsequently a number of important criticisms of this approach emerged and these highlight, amongst other issues, the question of whether structural approaches can be applied to the study of culture.

Stan Cohen, drawing on symbolic interactionist themes, developed a sustained critique of the CCCS approach (Cohen, 1980). He first pointed out that the CCCS team were preoccupied with the most spectacular and glamorous examples of youth subculture; the most highly visible. But, Cohen argues, even at the height of the mod and skinhead eras, reality looked at from the point of view of most working-class youngsters was much more mundane.

The class structure does not simply determine the behaviour of young people in a straightforward way. Many young working-class people did not become mods, skinheads or teddy boys. Equally important, there were a number of middle-class youngsters who did, once each style had received media coverage.

Cohen goes on to insist that we should not lose sight of the subject's view of reality in developing our analysis – a key symbolic interactionist theme. Did skinheads see themselves as engaging in an ideological struggle against the hegemony of capitalism; and if not, does this invalidate the CCCS approach? The problem of the status of the subjects' own point of view is something that continues to surface again and again in approaching culture and identity.

Although studying at the CCCS, Hebdige (1979) developed a theoretical approach which moves away from the early work of the CCCS team. Hebdige insists that the influence of black culture and music on white working-class subcultures cannot be ignored. In the teddy boy, mod, skinhead and punk subcultures there is a large debt to black styles, particularly through music, and this prompts Hebdige to develop a theory which abandons the attempt to simply analyse youth subcultures in terms of the social class position of those involved.

Hebdige suggests that subcultures are actually much more complicated and involve the mixing and matching of previous subcultural styles to create new ones. Further to this, Hebdige argues, they involve the process of *bricolage*, a term he borrows from anthropology to describe the way in which cultures re-use ordinary objects or commodities to create new meanings. For example, punks assembled safety pins, dustbin liner bags, chains, and other household commodities, together with items taken from entirely different contexts, such as bondage gear, to create a new subcultural style. Hebdige's work moves towards the themes developed in post-modernism. He is interested in the way elements of culture, signs and symbols are used and reworked, rather than the links between culture and social structure.

Feminist approaches to youth subcultures

The CCCS account of youth subcultures devotes very little attention to the position of girls. The picture we are presented with is one in which boys react to social structure by developing masculine cultural styles. According to Angela McRobbie, who began her career at the CCCS, the early work of the Centre was blind to a number of key issues which a feminist re-reading of its work sharply highlights (McRobbie, 1991b).

The sexist nature of much of the culture and language of boys was ignored. There was a failure to consider the ways in which such language degraded girls and contributed to their subordination. The fascination with masculine and visible subcultures meant that the Centre ignored the important distinction between public space (the streets, the youth club, the shopping centre) and private space (the home and the bedroom). McRobbie argues that boys were able to colonize public space and marginalize girls – hence the need for 'girls nights' at many local youth clubs. A feminist approach would attach more importance to the domestic sphere and the politics of the family. It would explore the connections between female adolescent culture and the ways in which the family contributed to the subordination of women. McRobbie wanted to explore the ways in which young women might develop forms of cultural resistance, not only to the roles allocated to them by capitalism but also to the patriarchal ideology reproduced through the home, the school and the media.

McRobbie's work remains culturalist in that she draws on the theory of hegemony used by neo-Marxists, but she insists that the dimension of gender must be added to that of social class when considering patterns cultural resistance. While McRobbie's early work focused mainly on the 'culture of the bedroom' and the ways in which young women resisted subordination within the home, her more recent work reflects important changes in the position of young women and the cultural space which they have claimed. For example, she points to the way in which black 'ragga girls' can use sexually explicit dancing in a way which ridicules male sexism and re-asserts female control over sexuality (McRobbie, 1994, pp. 183–4). According to McRobbie, despite the sexism of the lyrics in some ragga music, it is now possible for young black women to use this music to open up public cultural space for themselves.

Youth culture in the 1980s and 1990s

In the1980s, following the decline of punk, there appeared to be a fragmentation of youth culture. Many new cultural patterns emerged, associated with certain styles of dress and particular kinds of music, but nothing that appeared to involve young people on such a widespread and spectacularly visible scale as in the 1960s and 1970s. New romantics, goths, casuals, two-tone and mod revivalists, did not seem to have the same kind of cultural power as the original skinheads, teddy boys and punks.

Paul Willis (1990) argues that the age of spectacular youth subcultures has gone for good. This is because there are now so many 'style and taste cultures' which offer young people different ways of defining identity – there is too much diversity for any single youth subculture to dominate society. The growth of capitalist culture and leisure industries has meant that almost all young people now have access to the cultural resources they need to engage in 'symbolic creativity' in their leisure time (Willis, 1990, p. 16).

Willis draws on unstructured interviews (see Section 3.8) with groups of young people in the Midlands to explore the variety of ways in which they use language, clothes, music, media products, even their own bodies, to create new cultural meanings. The elaborate designs and symbols created through blacks' hair styling provide one example. Consumption, for Willis, does not involve manipulation of a passive audience (as, for example, the Frankfurt School assumes) but a creative process in which young people are the active agents, often rejecting the frameworks offered by the fashion industry and using its products in highly original, even subversive ways:

If it ever existed at all, the old 'mass' has been culturally emancipated into popularly differentiated cultural citizens through exposure to a widened circle of commodity relations. These things have supplied a much widened range of usable symbolic resources for the development and emancipation of everyday culture.
(Willis, 1990, p. 18)

Willis' work underlines the point that the old accounts of youth subcultures are in need of substantial revision if they are to be applied to the world of the 1990s and beyond. However, critics point to weaknesses in Willis' approach, too. He is anxious to emphasize that everyone, not just artists, makes culture but this leads him to work with such a wide definition of 'symbolic creativity' that almost anything could be included. He even includes the account of one young Midlander who 'jumped into the canal pissed' as an example. Critics argue that the approach seriously underestimates the extent to which powerful capitalist media and leisure conglomerates can exercise control over consumption (see Section 10.8 on the political economy of culture) and over-estimates the extent to which we can seize opportunities to be creative or subversive, assuming we want to be (see also the debate about cultural populism in Section 10.11).

Post-modernism and youth subcultures

A central feature of the post-modern world, according to Baudrillard (1988), is the speed at which images, signs and symbols are incorporated by the 'agencies of signification' (media, marketing and advertising). Dick Hebdige (1988), who has moved closer to a post-modern perspective in his recent writing, applies this argument to developments in music and youth culture. He points to the way in which advertising and the media can 'absorb' even the most subversive and oppositional cultural products to sell new commodities. For example, songs once made famous by The Clash, a punk band with a sharp left-wing analysis, are now used in advertisements to sell jeans. Television makes even the most rebellious youth subcultures familiar and less threatening. In this way, the agencies of signification deny young people the power to shock.

Secondly, post-modern writing argues that another consequence of living in a 'media saturated' world is that symbols and elements of subcultures are removed from their original contexts and recirculated. Subcultural dress becomes a matter of surface style; it can no longer have a deeper meaning. For example, Dr Marten boots used to 'say something' about young working-class life, with a bit of menace thrown in. Now, removed from this context they simply represent a surface style, used for a variety of fashion statements.

Through the mass media, particularly television stations such as MTV, young people have access to the 'back catalogue' of previous forms of music and subcultural styles. They can engage in parody and pastiche, using earlier subcultural styles in a mocking or humorous way to play around with subcultural identities. A 'bit' of punk can be mixed with a 'bit' of mod or ted style. This is one illustration of what some post-modern writers, such as Jameson (1991), mean by the end of history – the historical context for particular subcultural styles is forgotten and the oppositional messages associated with them are forgotten, too. Everyone, young or old, middle-class or working-class, can 'play' with subcultural styles but they will not actually 'mean' very much.

This is a rather bleak view of the future of youth culture. All hope of meaningful cultural activity is denied; young people face a future in which any genuine radicalism is quickly incorporated into the commercial marketing system and used to sell more commodities. Some writers influenced by post-modernism present a more optimistic analysis. Dick Hebdige, for example, points to the way in which the technologies of the post-modern age permit more democratic or participatory forms of music to emerge. Samplers and computers allow many more young people to make music in cheaply built home-made studios. Nevertheless, Hebdige does not expect the return of the spectacular forms of cultural resistance associated with the 1960s and 1970s.

Activity

Explain why functionalist and culturalist approaches to youth subcultures can be described as examples of modernist sociology. What is different about post-modernist approaches?

U, I, A

There are some reasons to question the view that subcultural resistance is a thing of the past. Steve Redhead (1993) points to the rise of 'rave' as a subculture which clearly did develop an oppositional approach in the late 1980s. Through the music which represented a clear break with 'guitar music', the use of illegal drugs, the organization of large parties on unauthorized land, and the use of all sorts of costumes to heighten the fun, 'rave' looked suspiciously like a genuine youth subculture. As Redhead describes, it represented a sufficient degree of cultural resistance for the state to respond with new laws and tougher policing. A similar point can now be made about the varieties of dance music and 'jungle'. Although some forms of 'jungle' have been incorporated and are now to be heard within the commercial mainstream (jungle now provides the beat for many television advertisements, BBC Radio 1 now has a jungle evening), it is also the case that some forms of jungle form a non-incorporated 'underground' in less well known dance clubs with flourishing independent record and fanzine producers. Perhaps the future for youth subcultures is not quite so bleak.

Discussion point

How far do you agree that youth subcultures are now dead.

10.6 Culture, identity and ethnicity

Ethnicity refers to the beliefs, customs, religious practices and understanding of belonging which give individuals their senses of identity. Culture and identity are inextricably bound up with ethnicity.

Migration and first-generation experiences

For the first African–Caribbean and southern Asian families coming to settle in the UK in the 1950s and 1960s, the experience of migration had a powerful impact on their senses of identity and culture. Contrary to some of the myths about the UK which circulated in former colonies, on arrival many immigrants faced open hostility in the response of whites and experienced discrimination in labour markets, housing and education (see Chapter 6). Several researchers have discussed the impact of these experiences on first-generation immigrants.

Frequently, the response to racism was to find ways in which ethnicity could be reasserted as a form of protection against the hostility of white society. Cashmore and Troyna (1990) show that the inclination to 'turn inwards', to seek support from within the migrant community was reinforced by employment and housing market patterns which encouraged a concentration of migrants within particular parts of each town.

Amongst West Indians, Cashmore and Troyna point to the growth of Pentecostalism and other forms of Christian worship quite separate from the Church of England, as examples of a turning inwards, away from white society. Ken Pryce's famous study (1979, 1986) of the African–Caribbean community in the St Paul's area of Bristol confirms the importance of religion for first-generation migrants. (This study is considered in more detail in Section 16.3.) In a similar process of 'turning inward', Cashmore and Troyna suggest (1990, pp. 152–3), first-generation migrants of southern Asian origin set about the task of recreating in the UK the institutions and organizations (temples, mosques, business networks, cinemas, shops, etc.) necessary to reaffirm and reinforce important cultural traditions within new settings.

So for both southern Asian and African–Caribbean families in the 1950s and 1960s, the response to racism and harsh economic conditions was a strengthening and reaffirmation of traditional forms of ethnicity and identity, but often in ways which sought to accommodate rather than openly challenge white society.

Political and subcultural responses

Winston James (1993) suggests that the experience of racism actually unified the culture and identity of African–Caribbeans in the UK. In the West Indies, blacks were often divided by differences of culture and tradition between islands and by the hierarchy of colour which was imposed by colonialism (individuals were ranked according to the darkness of their skin with the lighter coloured enjoying a higher status). In the UK, James argues, a 'monolithic racism' regarded all West Indians, whatever their island of origin or shade of skin, as blacks:

Although island loyalties still remain, the people of the Caribbean have been brought together by London Transport, the National Health Service, and,
most of all, by the centripetal forces of British racism to recognise their common class position and common Caribbean identity.
(James, 1993, p. 240)

This experience had the effect of drawing African–Caribbeans together; in the eyes of whites they 'were all the same'. As a response, James argues, a shared oppositional culture began to grow amongst African–Caribbeans living in the UK which organized around the label 'black'. Some younger political activists within the southern Asian communities also argued that the common experience of racism in the UK meant that southern Asians should unite around the label 'black'. Despite obvious differences in tradition and culture, Asians and African–Caribbeans should develop a common political identity.

The 1970s and early 1980s was a period in which evidence of cultural resistance on the part of minority communities to racism and the culturally oppressive aspects of white society became much more visible. At its most dramatic, this took the form of rioting and street disorder, but cultural resistance was expressed in other ways, too (see Sections 6.5 and 16.8). Sociologists drew on structural and conflict theory to explain the development of black subcultures with distinct styles of dress, forms of music and cultural beliefs. Cashmore and Troyna (1990), for example, argue that Rastafarianism appealed to young African–Caribbeans because of their experience of racism and discrimination in capitalist labour markets (Section 18.7 contains a case study on Rastafarianism). It represented a way of asserting a black identity and a critique of an oppressive system (referred to as 'Babylon'). Similarly, Hall *et al.* (1978) linked the spread of young black street culture to the impact of structural forces. Given the way in which British capitalism directed young blacks towards low-paid work or the industrial reserve army, young blacks attempted to resist by adopting a range of street 'survival strategies' and social networks, forming a young black subculture. Although employing an ethnographic methodology, Pryce (1979) describes the same process in Bristol, through which black 'teeny bobbers' and 'hustlers' survived discrimination in labour markets and conflicts with the police by developing distinct and separate subcultures, based on the assertion of black values and identity.

Migration and the concept of diaspora

It was sometimes supposed that the children of migrant families might face a 'culture clash', being educated in British schools, mixing with white children, learning English and yet experiencing pressure to retain traditional customs within the migrant home and community. Early research exposed this view as an over-simplification. Ballard (1979), for example, using in-depth interview data, was able to show that even in the 1970s, young southern Asians did not feel they had to choose between two cultures but, rather, devised a variety of ways to negotiate between the culture of their community and the values of the wider society, producing their own synthesis of Asian and British values (see also Sections 6.5 and 8.6).

More recently, sociologists have returned to questions of ethnicity and identity as central research themes. Rather than picturing immigrant cultures as passive and subject to dilution, the new approach recognizes the dynamic processes which can develop when different cultures interact. The term 'diaspora' is used to refer to this process of cultural dispersal.

Thus, sociologists are now interested in the impact and influence of the southern Asian diaspora, the black diaspora, the Irish and Italian diaspora, and so on. One example has already been discussed. As we have seen in Section 10.4, the rising status of black working-class fashion and music within western popular culture now has an enormous influence in many parts of the world. This is partly because black populations have been dispersed to so many different societies, and partly now as a consequence of the global reach of the mass media which highlight particular aspects of black style, music and fashion. As Paul Gilroy (1993) argues, the spread of such cultural influences through the influence of global media and communication networks actually undercuts nationalist value systems (for example, 'the English way of life'); although he also notes that this can sometimes produce a violent counter-reaction in which some groups strongly reassert nationalist values. (Gilroy's work is also outlined in Section 6.5.) The influence of other diaspora is now highly significant and is reflected, for example, in the popularity of 'world music' or the spread of different styles of cooking.

The new ethnicities

Rattansi (1994) argues that the use of images of ethnicity by advertising agencies and the mass media produces a very important change in our understanding. It becomes obvious that ethnicity is not fixed or determined by biology or, for that matter, the social structure. On the contrary, we must now understand ethnicity as much more fluid, subject to change and a product of the ability of individuals to synthesize or create new cultural identities from the influences around them, including the mass media and popular culture:

... ethnicities ... are products of a process to be conceptualised as a cultural politics of representation, one in which narratives, images, musical forms and popular culture more generally have a significant role.
(Rattansi, 1994, p. 74)

Rattansi places this insight in a post-modern theoretical framework which is discussed at the end of this section. However, he acknowledges a debt to an important and influential essay by Stuart Hall called 'New ethnicities' (1992b). Hall was concerned specifically with black cinema, but his arguments are regarded as possessing a wider significance.

Hall argues that in the 1970s black film makers faced two fundamental tasks: first, to open up access to cinema and television for black artists; and secondly, to counter the negative images of blacks in mainstream film and television. In these conditions, the cultural umbrella label 'black' was used to unite artists and cultural producers from a variety of ethnic backgrounds who shared a common interest in opposing racism. However, Hall senses that in the 1980s important changes occurred. There grew an awareness of the importance of different kinds of ethnicity and the ways in which ethnicity intersect with class, gender, and age (see also Sections 6.5 and 6.6). It is now acknowledged that it not only makes a difference if you are black or white but whether you are, for example, a young male or a young female from a Punjabi family, or a middle-aged middle-class Indian in a professional occupation, or a working-class Bangladeshi from a rural village background. And all these different ethnicities intersect with the idea of Britishness: it is possible to be black and British, or young female southern Asian and British, and so on.

Recent films and television programmes have begun to explore the complexity of ethnicity and the variety of ways in which ethnic identity is constructed. Films like *My Beautiful Launderette*, *The Budda of Suburbia*, *Bhaji on the Beach*, and *Mississippi Masala*, which all achieved mainstream success, reflect these themes. These films strike a chord, particularly with young people, because they discuss the process through which identity is actively constructed, through the influence of popular mainstream culture, the continuing importance of minority cultural traditions, and the synthesis of different ethnicities. This is reflected in other popular cultural forms, too. Apache Indian, for example, has used a mixture of American rap rhythms and southern Asian Bhangra styles, to sing about themes which relate directly to the experience of young southern Asians living in the UK. He has enjoyed significant mainstream success, including a stint as a BBC Radio 1 disc jockey. Apache Indian provides an example of what Stuart Hall refers to as 'cultural hybridity' – the process through which a variety of cultural influences are synthesized to produce new cultural forms.

Case study – Television, ethnicity and identity in Southall

Marie Gillespie (1995) conducted an important piece of empirical research into the ways in which young Punjabis in Southall, West London, drew on the traditional culture of their community, their sense of Englishness and the influence of popular culture, including television soaps and McDonald's, to construct distinct identities. Gillespie worked as a teacher in a local school and used ethnographic methods, supplemented by quantitative data gathered through a social survey (see Sections 3.5 and 3.7).

Gillespie describes the ways in which parents and grandparents in Southall use communication technology to reaffirm a commitment to Punjabi culture and tradition. Such media also help to reinforce Hindi and Punjabi language skills. As Gillespie notes:

Language . . . is a potent symbol of collective identity and often the site of fierce loyalties. In the context of a British society which constructs linguistic difference as a problem rather than as a resource, the desire to defend and maintain one's linguistic heritage becomes strong.
(Gillespie, 1995, p. 87)

On the whole, Gillespie shows, young southern Asians in Southall are still strongly committed to the traditional culture of their communities. However, there is evidence of gradual change and young people are critical of some aspects of the culture and traditions which their parents uphold. *Izzat*, or family honour, is of prime importance to families in Southall, and this can place quite severe restraints on young people. The fear of provoking gossip within the community and endangering the *izzat* of one's family acts as a significant mechanism of social control, and this is sometimes resented by young people who feel that they are under continual surveillance by the community.

At the same time, young Punjabis mix with white and black students at school and college and are attracted to some aspects of young white and African–Caribbean culture. Whilst often retaining a commitment to the idea of the traditional Punjabi marriage, many young Punjabis now form romantic attachments, with boys and girls 'going out' together, sometimes without the approval of their parents. The mix of traditional Punjabi and non-traditional attitudes is reflected in the survey data which found that while 58 per cent of Southall's youth aged between 12 and 18 years thought that 'going out with a boy or girl was normal', 67 per cent thought that 'parents should be more understanding about it', and 75 per cent thought that 'people should be free to marry whom they liked', almost half the sample still indicated that they would prefer to marry within their culture (Gillespie, 1995, p. 210–19).

Secrecy can add to the sense of romance but also heightens the risk of gossip. Gillespie shows that young people in Southall use the resources provided by popular culture to open up more space for themselves. While there are no fast-food outlets in Southall, a trip to McDonald's in a neighbouring area provides an opportunity to meet members of the opposite sex, free from community surveillance, and a change from the parentally approved diet of the home.

Gillespie spent a considerable time exploring the consumption of television with the young people she knew. Television soaps were hugely popular – particularly *Neighbours*, which is a little surprising, given that it concerns mainly white Australian middle-class families living in the suburbs. Gillespie shows that young Punjabis can identify with the programme precisely because it revolves around gossip and family life. Just as *izzat* can place pressures on young people in Southall, so the gossip-mongers in *Neighbours* generate problems for young people in the soap storylines. One Punjabi girl compared an aunt, who reported to her family her flirting with boys, with the notorious Mrs Mangel in *Neighbours*:

. . . when you think of a soap you think of that woman and that's why you begin to hate that person in the soap, like when they show Mrs Mangel and Madge is having a go at her and then I think of this aunt on my road that I really hate cos she's an old gossip and it makes you feel good and you wish you could have a go at her yourself.
(Gillespie, 1995, p. 152)

Soaps also provide a way of talking about problems. By discussing the plots of soaps with their friends, young Punjabis can indirectly talk through a lot of the problems they have to deal with regarding family and personal relationships.

Black and southern Asian diaspora converge in Southall. African–Caribbean music and dress styles enjoy a very high status, particularly amongst Punjabi boys. Black slang, expressions and gestures are sometimes incorporated into young Punjabi street style, though Punjabi parents do not always approve of these developments, and young Punjabis also draw strongly from the styles, traditions and history of their parents. Some young dress codes, for example, signify support for the Khalistan movement (Sikh separatism).

Gillespie's study provides empirical evidence of the ways in which the complex range of ethnic and cultural influences is drawn on by young people on a day-to-day basis.

The 'post-modern frame' and the critics

Rattansi (1994) uses a post-modernist framework to make sense of the developments Hall and Gillespie describe. He argues that ethnicity and cultural imagery are more fluid and flexible in the post-modern world – they are no longer so rooted to particular social circumstances, such as social class, ethnic group or economic structure. We are more able now to pull particular sets of images or styles 'off the shelf' to create our own identities, although Rattansi is anxious to emphasize the continuing importance of key objective processes in society, such as the impact of racism.

Critics often draw on structural sociology to examine these arguments. Mahmood (1996), for example, makes two points. It may be a mistake to over-emphasize the novelty of the process of cultural synthesis and the emergence of hybrid cultures: the merging of cultures is as old as the process of migration and military conquest. Secondly, there are dangers in becoming so preoccupied with the process through which individuals construct cultural identities, that we forget that cultural change is frequently driven by the exercise of political power, often in ways which are oppressive to minorities. Similarly, Cathy Lloyd comments that we should not allow a fascination with the growing diversity of culture and identity to distract attention from issues of inequality and power, both within particular societies and between the different regions of the globe (Lloyd, 1993, p. 227).

Activity

Make a list of the different cultural influences which shape your own lifestyle. Think about food, clothing, music, holidays, sport, television and film, and anything else that might be relevant. To what extent does your experience confirm the emergence of 'hybrid identities'?

A, E

10.7 Culture, identity and gender

A plausible case can be made for the view that changes in gender roles are impacting on both the production and consumption of popular culture. First, as women participate more extensively in labour markets (see Section 9.3), so they also should gain more recognition as significant consumers of popular culture. There is some evidence to suggest that this is the case: more magazines, books and television programmes are targeted at key female audiences, and more services are available in the market to support female cultural participation, from women's minicab firms, to pubs with male strippers (see 'John Ball's Diary').

Secondly, on the production side, there is some evidence to suggest that women are, at last, securing positions of seniority within the cultural industries. The BBC, for example, has set itself the objective of filling 40 per cent of its senior managerial positions with either female staff or staff recruited from ethnic minority backgrounds by the year 2000. Women's magazines have long represented a sector in which female journalists have occupied a majority of the senior editorial positions.

John Ball's Diary

THREE lean, mean and clean lads have come up with a novel way of making money.

An advert appearing in this newspaper reads: "Ladies, fed up with those everyday household chores? Now you can have your home professionally cleaned by your own male housemaid. Fully/semi clothed."

For £15-an-hour Don Russo, Jay James and Nick Jones, will cook, clean, iron, polish and scrub, fully clothed in a suit or a maid's outfit or whatever tickles your fancy.

For £22.50 an hour they will do the same while sporting nothing more than a G-string and frilly apron.

When a colleague mentioned that some frustrated women may be looking for hidden extras Mr Russo gasped and said: "Oh no, we are a straight commercial cleaning service and nothing else."

He said: "We think our prices are quite reasonable to go around cleaning a strangers house with our chests and legs hanging out."

Source: *Bedfordshire on Sunday*, 29 September 1996

Thirdly, changes in values and the expectations associated with traditional gender roles have opened up more opportunities for women to participate as creative artists in such areas as drama, music, film and literature. The days when girls were allowed to 'decorate' pop bands as 'singers' but were denied opportunities to write or play music have gone.

Fourthly, changes in gender role expectations have impacted on youth subcultures. Club and dance culture appears to open up more opportunities for girls.

Feminist perspectives

The above points represent the 'good news', but critics argue that there is another side to the story.

Within families we know that women do not always share equally in the consumption of goods and services; media and cultural services targeted at men's interests, from sports videos to pornography, still far outweigh the provision for women in the marketplace. Despite recent changes in recruitment patterns, men still occupy most of the controlling positions in a majority of cultural industries – only one national newspaper, for example, is currently edited by a woman.

The BBC had originally hoped to meet its equal-opportunity targets by 1996 and has had to reschedule this to the year 2000. By 1995 only 20 per cent of its senior executives were women (BBC, 1995, p. 97). Every commercial television company is obliged to monitor equal opportunities, but very few have appointed a significant number of women into senior positions. In a recent survey, Thomas and Klett-Davies

(1995) concluded that female cultural performers worked more days than men but were paid less per day. And the greater use of part-time, casualized and fixed-term contracts in the cultural industries now is also likely to impede womens' progress. In terms of content, too, critics argue that much of the imagery used to promote pop bands, films and videos continues to use women's looks and bodies in exploitative ways.

Table 10.1 Staffing of TV Stations

Company	Female staff (%)	Ethnic staff (%)
Anglia	37	1.5
Border	41	0
Carlton	55	7.4
Central	41	4.6
Channel	47	1.0
Grampian	35	1.0
Granada	41	2.0
HTV	42	3.0
LWT	40	7.5
Meridian	45	2.8
Scottish	41	1.8
Tyne Tees	36	1.6
Ulster	37	1.3
Westcountry	48	1.9
Yorkshire	46	1.6
GMTV	56	5.9
Channel 4	57	9.7

Source: ITC Annual Report and Accounts, 1995

Activity

From Table 10.1, which TV stations employ the highest and which the lowest proportions of women? From Figure 10.4, in which electronic media areas do men earn more than women, and in which do women earn more than men?

To what extent does this evidence support the view that women are now securing equal opportunities with men in the cultural industries? How would sociologists explain the patterns revealed in these figures? (You may wish to read the rest of this section before answering this.)

I, A, E

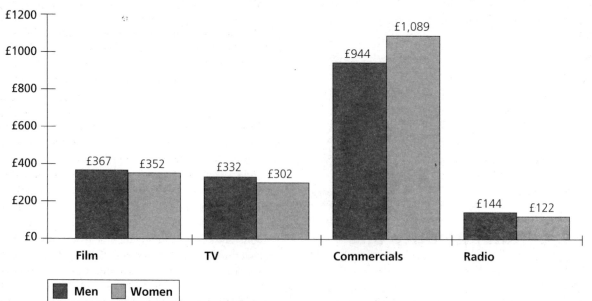

Figure 10.4 Average fee per day for men and women in film, television, commercials and radio in 1993–4 (exclusive of high maximum numbers). Source: Thomas and Klett-Davis (1995)

Feminist explanations

There are important differences between traditions of feminist thought (see Chapter 5) and these prompt different degrees of optimism regarding the possibility for women to enjoy greater freedom in the production and consumption of culture.

Radical feminists are sceptical about the possibility of change. The arrival of women in senior positions within cultural enterprises will make little difference, they argue, for two reasons:

- The imperatives of the commercial marketplace will continue to demand that magazines, films and other cultural products use sex and womens' bodies to sell commodities, whether or not women make editorial decisions.
- Patriarchal ideology is so deeply embedded in modern societies that both men and women consume culture through the 'male gaze' (see Section 15.7). In other words, both men and women simply take it for granted that women will be represented as sexual objects in film and other cultural products, and that it is 'natural' for them to be 'enjoyed' by men in this way.

Culturalist feminism: watching the detectives

Critics of radical feminism argue that it has two weaknesses. First, as a theory it encourages an ahistorical approach. In other words it suggests that patriarchy has been dominant throughout most of our recent history and so it fails to address the possible mechanisms of social change which might either modify patriarchal ideology or even replace it. Secondly, critics argue that at the empirical level there is actually evidence of change which radical feminism either underestimates or ignores.

Some feminists develop the ideas associated with Gramsci and hegemony theory to trace the ways in which feminist struggle can challenge the hegemony of patriarchal 'common-sense'. Gamman and Marshment (1988), for example, argue that while commercialism and patriarchal values continue to dominate a great deal of popular culture, there are opportunities within the mainstream to question patriarchy, if not develop feminist perspectives. They question whether radical feminism is correct in insisting that there are deep-seated psychoanalytic processes within the male mind which always and inevitably lead to culture being constructed through the male gaze. Gradual change is possible, they insist:

Change is more often the product of a slow struggle that goes on day by day, within capitalism, and within patriarchy: to shift the balance of power

... Popular culture is a site of struggle ... where meanings are contested and where dominant ideologies are disturbed.
(Gamman and Marshment, 1988, pp. 1–3)

One example of popular culture which has apparently reflected the changes in the construction of gender, discussed at the beginning of this section, is the genre of television 'cop' shows. There have been several series in which the central character has been a female detective. Recently, *Prime Suspect* has proved a particular success in the USA, as well as in the UK, winning top awards for both its acting and writing. However, the prototype for the female cop show is the long-running American series *Cagney and Lacey*. Lorraine Gammon (1988) analyses this show in detail to assess the extent to which it permits a 'feminist' reading (or interpretation) to emerge.

The show focuses on two women who are as effective as men in doing their tough work, but not like men in their attitudes or behaviour. The show explores in considerable depth some of the issues which feminists have placed at the top of their political agenda, including rape, child abuse and pornography. The interaction between characters sometimes develops a critique of sexism: male power hierarchies are gently ridiculed. But, Gammon notes, there appear to be significant constraints on the extent to which a feminist analysis can emerge. *Cagney and Lacey* are still often portrayed in 'caring' roles; neither character is permitted to stray too far from the conventional expectations associated with female roles. Indeed, one of the actresses was replaced in the second series because she did not look 'feminine enough'. The show has explicitly distanced itself from feminist politics and the leading actresses have publicly disowned feminism. Despite all this, Gamman argues that while a full-blown female gaze may not be constructed, the show does offer a variety of 'glances' with 'feminist implications'. In other words, the show touches on or hints at themes which invite a feminist interpretation.

Sexualization of the male body

One quite striking recent development in popular culture is the proliferation of imagery which places the male body in a sexual context. A television advertisement for jeans, in which a young man in a launderette removes all but his briefs, may have started the trend, but it has spread through advertisements, fashion magazines and into the world of pop music. Almost every month brings a new crop of young men, with varying degrees of musical talent, but bodies which are 'fit' enough to be represented in differing states of semi-nudity for publicity shots and music videos. As McRobbie comments:

The beauty stakes have gone up for men, and women have taken up the position of active viewers. (McRobbie, 1994, p. 186)

Men too, it seems, are being turned into sexualized commodities. This, of course, poses a set of interesting theoretical questions. Is there such a thing as a 'female gaze'? If there is, what does this mean for radical feminist theory which assumed that the male gaze was derived from psychoanalytic processes related to male child development: there was something within the male psyche which turned men into voyeurs. Is the 'female gaze' related to comparable processes within women's psychoanalytic development? But, if this is the case, why has the 'female gaze' only found public expression in recent years?

Discussion point

Is it possible for women now to behave as voyeurs by 'enjoying' looking at men's bodies? Is this evidence of equality between the sexes?

According to Suzanne Moore (1988), in order to approach the sexualization of the male body, we need to move beyond theories which deal only with psychoanalytic processes. We have to recognize that female and male sexual identities (how we see ourselves sexually and how we see others) are no more fixed by psychoanalytic processes than they are by biology. Female and male sexual identities are fluid and can change; women have *learnt* to 'enjoy' male bodies. However, Moore notes that the 'female gaze' is not identical to the 'male gaze'. She argues that it is more subtle. Women do not necessarily enjoy full-frontal shots of men, and early commercial attempts to exploit a 'female gaze' – such as *Playgirl* magazine – failed because they did n`ot recognize that women would not enjoy the crudest forms of erotic representation to be found in *Playboy* (Moore, 1988, p. 57).

Nevertheless, it is clearly the case that cultural producers are keen to satisfy the newly crystallized taste amongst women for commodities which develop more sexually explicit themes. Not all commentators regard this as a further step towards equality between the sexes. McRobbie argues that the commercial exploitation of both male and female sexuality further extends oppressive social relationships, rather than truly opening up new opportunities, either for women or men.

Case study – Men and fashion: a post-structuralist analysis

Men are now presented with a proliferation of commodities seeking to cater for them as consumers of fashion. Frank Mort (1996) draws on Foucault's post-structuralist framework in order to explain this new development.

While earlier theories have typically understood consumption as being determined by, for example, the power of capitalism to manipulate the masses (see the Frankfurt School in Section 10.3) or the power of high-status social groups to set trends for social groups beneath them (see Section 10.9), Mort rejects the models employed by structural sociology. He argues that if we employ Foucault's 'historical archaeology' (an analysis based on careful examination of specific power–knowledge relations rather than general trends, using secondary sources and historical materials) we find that consumption patterns are much more complex than general structural theories imply. The emergence of a culture which was preoccupied with male fashions and masculine identities in the 1980s was the product of the way in which a number of distinct social groups developed particular forms of knowledge. Power, according to Mort, was exercised within systems of consumption by these social groups: consumption was not determined by the 'power' or 'effect' of 'external' forces, such as the class structure.

Mort's detailed analysis helps to make this point more clearly. In comparison with the 1950s, he argues, important changes occurred in the way masculinity was represented through fashion and clothes design, advertising and retailing during the 1980s. There was a movement away from traditional masculinity: it became much more acceptable for young men to be deeply preoccupied with image, style and 'the way they looked'. A much wider range of products became available with which men could groom themselves, from deodorants to hair gel. Most importantly, Mort implies, fashion and advertising now offered a much wider range of male identities, many of which departed radically from the respectable image of the heterosexual middle-class white male.

Mort explains this in terms of a 'complex tangle of alliances' between key social groups and individuals who developed new forms of knowledge about fashion and masculinity. Mort uncovers:

. . . a coalition between independent journalists and designers, photographers, models and urban flaneurs. These experts claimed to provide answers to a set of pressing questions about the disintegration of established consumer patterns and the emergence of new ones.
(Mort, 1996, p. 8)

The thrust of Mort's analysis is to demonstrate that a cluster of separate factors and interests coincided during the 1980s to produce a new understanding of masculinity and fashion. To begin with, a number of factors had already made the issue of masculine identity less clear-cut. (See Section 5.6.) The traditional sources of masculine authority, such as lifetime careers, were no longer secure, and the feminist critique of traditional forms of masculinity had also encouraged some men to question their own behaviour. Secondly, a sustained consumer boom developed in the same period; those with sufficient income began to spend more and more on clothes and consumer goods. This helped to stimulate a resurgence in the British fashion industry. These conditions provided opportunities for 'talented individualists' to develop careers as 'cultural professionals', providing advice and guidance on new trends in consumption, style and fashion. *The Face*, which emerged as an independent magazine in 1980, and later *Arena*, offered such 'cultural professionals' opportunities to disseminate new ideas, which included new ways of representing male dress and design.

Following Foucault, Mort is interested in the way particular social groups are able to exercise power through the promotion of different forms of knowledge. The journalists, designers and photographers working for *The Face* and similar magazines were a tightly knit group of metropolitan 'entrepreneurs' who were able to make a living by trading on their knowledge or cultural expertise.

However, there is one problem posed by the theoretical approach which Mort employs. Although he attempts to avoid structural theory – and, in particular, 'top down' or 'trickle down' models of consumption which picture consumption trends percolating down from the top of the social structure (see Section 10.9) – Mort's own analysis places a great deal of emphasis on the 'taste leadership' of the 'culture professionals', based in London. Not only, perhaps, is there a danger in over-estimating the influence of a small group of metropolitan fashion enthusiasts across the rest of the country (would their influence, for example, be obvious on the terraces at Hartlepool football club?), but Mort's analysis comes close to reproducing another version of the same 'top down' or 'trickle down' theory.

10.8 Cultural industries: the political economy of cultural production

Researchers using a political economy approach, such as Golding and Murdock (1991), insist that before exploring the varied ways in which we consume commodities and construct cultural identities, we should not overlook the capacity of capitalist enterprises to shape the options and resources which are available to us.

First, culture is now more than ever a commodity to be sold in the form of media products, clothes, fashion accessories, leisure opportunities, sportswear and other consumer goods. The media and cultural sectors of most capitalist economies are dominated by a relatively small number of very large companies, often multi-nationals and with interests in a wide range of media and cultural activities (see examples in Figure 10.5).

Increasing concentration of ownership (fewer and fewer larger and larger companies) is reinforced by the trend towards mergers between already large media companies. Walt Disney, already a huge film and leisure conglomerate, has recently taken over ABC and Capital, one of the largest US television networks in a $19 billion deal. The Time corporation, the largest publisher in the USA, merged with Warner Communication (records, music publishing, film and television) in 1989 to form Time Warner, which in turn is now merging with Turner Communications, to form the biggest media and leisure conglomerate in the world. The size and dominance of these organizations often allows them considerable control over the ways in which cultural markets develop and products are marketed.

To provide just one recent example, the arrival of digital audio recording technology into western European and American markets, although available in Japan since 1986, was delayed for a number of years because the companies involved wanted to exploit the sales potential of existing technologies and were concerned about the potential for consumers to make high-quality unauthorized recordings (Blake, 1992, p. 14).

Large cultural conglomerates can also exploit their interests across a range of sectors of cultural production to reinforce and consolidate their power. Rupert Murdock and News Corporation used the newspapers owned in the UK to promote the image of BSkyB Satellite TV, also part-owned by News Corporation. BSkyB purchases a large volume of material from Fox studios, a television production company also owned by News Corporation in the USA. News Corporation's television can be promoted through the listings magazines which Rupert Murdock owns in various countries. Sony, the Japanese electronics manufacturer, now owns record companies to produce the software to be played on its Walkman and CD players. Sony also has interests in Hollywood to cash in on the use of rock music in films and 24-hour cable television. The process through which a company exploits its interests in one sector to enhance its profits in another is some-

GERMANY

Bertelsmann

Family planning business built up by unflashy, idealistic Reinhard Mohn into global communications company, rivalling Murdoch and Time-Warner. In 1986 acquired US publisher Bantam-Doubleday (via which it owns Transworld) and the Arista, Ariola and RCA record labels – 14 per cent of the world music industry. Now involved in America Online.

■ **Interests**

Publishers in Germany, Spain, UK (Transworld: imprints include Bantam, Corgi, Black Swan); book clubs with 25 million subscribers

BMG Entertainment: music publisher/distributor

Gruner & Jahr: 70 magazines in Germany (including *Spiegel*, *Stern*), France (including *Femme Actuelle*, *Voici*), Italy, Spain, Austria, Poland, Switzerland, UK (including *Best*, *Prima*). 9 newspapers in Germany.

Stakes in 4 German TV channels (including RTL) and 7 radio stations

■ **Connections**

Merged broadcasting interests with CLT in April; already linked (though relations now tense) to Havas/ Canal Plus as digital allies and partners in Vox and Premiere. Arch-rival: Kirch.

ITALY

Fininvest

Milan-based vehicle for Silvio Berlusconi (right), the "Pope of Television" and short-lived Italian PM. Centred on print, advertising and TV (with 45 per cent of the national TV audience), the empire also encompasses hypermarkets, financial services and AC Milan.

■ **Interests**

Italy: 3 ad-funded channels. Stake in Telepiu pay-TV (already digital)

Publitalia (ad sales)

Mondadori: newspapers, 30 magazines (including *TV Sorrisi*, *Panorama*, *Vera*)

Abroad: Stakes in Spanish and German TV stations

■ **Connections**

Kirch has stake in Fininvest's Mediaset (TV and advertising) division, and is fellow shareholder in Telepiu and German sports channel.

UK

News International

British arm of Australia's News Corporation, owning 40 per cent of BSkyB. Benefiting from nerve, ruthlessness and Tory government support in his empire-building, Rupert Murdoch now controls 38 per cent of the UK national press and enjoys complete hegemony in British pay-TV.

■ **Interests**

4 newspapers (*Sun*, *News of the World*, *Times*, *Sunday Times*)

4 Times supplements

HarperCollins publishing

Digi-Media Vision (digital technology)

BSkyB: 10 satellite channels (more in multichannel package)

Germany: stakes in Vox, Premiere channels

Holland: Sky radio

■ **Connections**

Linked to Bertelsmann in grand alliance, but now seemingly sulking and semi-detached. Partners Granada in BSkyB, Kirch in Premiere. Murdoch-Berlusconi talks, on acquiring an Italian TV channel, came to nothing.

Figure 10.5 Examples of large multi-nationals.
Source: *The Guardian*, 8 July 1996

times described as a process of 'synergy' (synthesizing two activities to produce more energy).

As Golding and Murdock (1991) argue, the declining vitality of cultural institutions in the public sector, such as the BBC, local public libraries, and community arts projects, together with the emphasis many governments have put on privatization policies in recent years, have further strengthened the position of the large corporations.

Another point made in the political economic analysis is that the large corporations often have cautious and conservative management strategies which stifle cultural innovation. Large corporations feel most comfortable sticking to the 'tried and tested' formula, which has proven commercial success, rather than risking investment in new cultural approaches. Thus, new authors find it increasingly difficult to interest publishers who prefer to invest in guaranteed commercial successes – a Jilly Cooper 'bonkbuster' or a Jeffrey Archer novel. Similarly, new pop and rock bands often struggle to win the backing of the big record companies who can rely on established artists and their back catalogues to keep the profits rolling in; and television production companies find that they more frequently have to work to a commercial formula (for example, costume drama with a leading part for an American actor) in order to interest the large television stations.

The large corporations also exercise significant influence through their sponsorship of sport and cultural activities, and the importance of advertising revenue which they generate. When BSkyB bought the rights to televise Premier League soccer in 1991 it had an audience of under one million, but by 1996 this had topped five million, built around its coverage of soccer. No wonder it was willing to pay £674 million to secure the rights until the year 2001. The television rights for the 2002 soccer World Cup have just been sold for $2.2 billion to a German media conglomerate. BSkyB now exercises considerable influence over the organization and delivery of sport; Premier soccer is now played on Sundays and Mondays to suit the television schedules, and Rugby League has actually switched seasons from the winter to the summer. Sport is now a major business with soccer clubs, rugby clubs, horse racing, and television now fully integrated within the commercial leisure industry. (This issue is also discussed in Section 9.8.) Similarly, in the field of music, both popular and classical, corporate sponsorship is a frequent element in subsidizing productions and 'world tours'.

Discussion point

How far has sport become a business? Is this a good thing?

Finally, the political economy approach points to the way in which the market delivers cultural goods in an uneven and unequal fashion. The consumption of cultural goods is stratified along the main dimensions of social inequality. Use of new cultural technologies, such as the Internet, depends on access to expensive technology which has to be updated frequently. While, in 1989, over 34 per cent of the highest income groups had access to a personal computer at home, only 0.8 per cent of the lowest income group enjoyed this (Golding and Murdock, 1991, p. 29). Although most households have a television, access to video recorders, camcorders, and even telephones is heavily stratified. As more sporting and cultural events are allocated to pay-TV, this 'problem' will become more acute. This prompts some political economy theorists to question whether privately controlled media and cultural industries can offer 'cultural citizenship' to all sections of society.

Critics of the political economy approach raise two issues. First, they point to the empirical evidence of diversity and creativity in the ways people – even those in subordinate positions, at the bottom of the social structure – consume and use cultural commodities. The big corporations may be able to control markets but they cannot anticipate all the ways in which people use their products. For example, Lambretta scooters were originally aimed at housewives but were taken up by mods to become symbols of young working-class freedom and rebellion. Blank audio tapes are supposed to be used for legitimate recording only but are actually used on a daily basis by people around the world to subvert the private ownership of musical rights.

Secondly, big corporations frequently misjudge

Solvency in the professional game
Lisa Buckingham

MANCHESTER United and Blackburn Rovers may be in the same league on a Saturday afternoon, but in terms of their finances they are light years apart. In what is now distinctly a game of two halves, performance off the pitch is as crucial as "doing the business" on it.

Blackburn, fourth in the Premier League in 1992–93 and runners-up last season, sustained losses of nearly £6.4 million, finishing a decidedly sick 22nd in football's financial table. United, on the other hand, complemented its Premier League win with pole position in the financial tables on a profit of £4.2 million.

The discrepancy is explained not only by the size of United's gate – which offers a weekly capacity of 45,000 – but by the club's off-pitch success with more than half of its income derived from merchandising, television, sponsorship and other sales.

According to accountants Touche Ross, the average football club now earns between 35 and 40 per cent of its revenues from such secondary activities. The figure has risen by about 20 per cent in the past four or five years and is likely to increase by the same amount again in the coming few seasons – only, of course, if clubs refrain from following

Millwall into barmy diversifications such as pubs.

Although television money and rewards from success in cups provide the icing on the cake, spin-off income is growing faster. Seven Premier League clubs, plus Burnley, are managing a 25 per cent or better operating return on turnover partially thanks to this business. Premier League clubs earned average operating profits of £1.46 million in 1992–93 while all other divisions turned in operating losses.

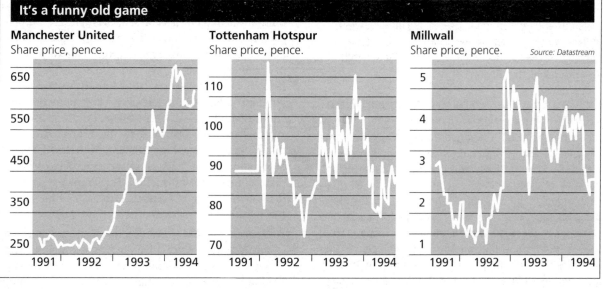

It's a funny old game

Manchester United
Share price, pence.

Tottenham Hotspur
Share price, pence.

Millwall
Share price, pence. *Source: Datastream*

---

markets and sales figures flop: consumers resist by simply not buying. Thirdly, in starting with an analysis of production rather than cultural resistance, culturalists and other theorists argue that the political economy approach falls back into the trap of economic reductionism (see Section 10.2).

Nevertheless, the political economy approach is valuable in reminding us that most of the cultural options available to us bear in some way the imprint of multi-national consumer capitalism.

> **Activity**
> a Using all the evidence presented in this section, write a paragraph which summarizes how this supports the political economy perspective.
> b What criticisms might other sociologists make of the political economy approach?
>
> **I, A, E**

10.9 Consumption

Some sociologists, such as Saunders (1987), go so far as to argue that it is now consumption rather than production which generates the most important divisions within modern societies.

Saunders argues that consumption is a crucial issue for people because, in contrast to the world of work where they are often powerless, they can exercise more control over how they consume and can invest a sense of identity in the process – a 'home of one's own' is a common desire. Critics point out, however, that it is still what occurs in the sphere of production which largely decides what and how households consume. Much depends on whether households contain full-time 'core' workers in secure jobs with higher wages, peripheral workers in low-waged, insecure occupations, or the unemployed (Burrows and Butler, 1989). This debate is also explored in Chapters 4 and 9.

Explaining patterns of consumption

Marx distinguished between the use value of commodities and their exchange value. While in terms of practical usage, most of us could manage without a Picasso print on the wall or an electric toothbrush in the bathroom, these commodities are often exchanged (sold) for quite high values in the market. This distinction has been developed by some theorists (e.g. the Frankfurt School, see Section 10.3) into an analysis of consumption which suggests that members of the public are often manipulated by advertising and encouraged to develop 'false' desires for commodities which have little use value.

However, critics of this argue that the manipulative power of big business alone cannot explain the huge growth in demand for consumer goods. They suggest that the meanings and motives which prompt consumers to buy commodities have to be taken more seriously. An early attempt to do this is found in the work of Thorstein Veblen (1857–1918), an American sociologist, who developed an analysis of the newly wealthy middle class in North America (1953; orig. pub. 1912). Veblen's theory of 'conspicuous consumption' suggests that affluent social groups will use their purchasing power to claim social status through the visible display of commodities which signal high social standing. The North American *nouveaux riches* (newly rich) attempted to copy the consumption patterns of the European aristocracy in an effort to promote their social status. Thus, particular foods and drinks, particular styles of clothing, horse riding and European holidays all became fashionable during the late nineteenth century amongst this social group.

After World War II, 'working-class affluence' brought opportunities for 'conspicuous consumption' to many more people:

> *By the 1950s, following a pattern already established in the United States, first in Britain, then in the rest of Western Europe, 'mass consumption' . . . began to develop amongst all but the very poorest groups. Groups which had to do paid work of various kinds, from mining to typing, unlike [Veblen's] leisure class . . . who had to do little if any paid work, became 'consumers', too.*
> (Bocock, 1993, p. 21)

In analysing post-war consumption, sociologists were tempted to simply elaborate Veblen's original ideas. Thus, Willmott and Young (1973), for example, developed another 'top-down' model in which they argued that lower-middle-class and working-class families aspired to model their consumption patterns on upper-middle-class lifestyles. According to their model of 'stratified diffusion', as soon as incomes permitted, first lower-middle-class and then working-class families adopted middle-class consumption and cultural habits.

More recently, sociologists have regarded 'top-down' models – which assume that lower socio-economic groups always seek to emulate or copy higher income groups – as over-simplified or even just plain wrong. Campbell (1995, p. 109) makes three criticisms:

- There is little hard sociological evidence to suggest that many lower income groups do consciously seek to emulate middle-class consumption patterns, other than in terms of the simple aspiration to be more comfortably off. Are the cultural patterns associated with middle-class consumption necessarily attractive to other groups? We have already seen (in Section 10.4) that the French sociologist Bourdieu points to important differences between the *habitus* (systems of taste) of working-class and middle-class groups.

- Campbell argues that there is some evidence to suggest that consumption patterns which first emerge amongst groups at the bottom (for example, black American working-class styles of dress) can be taken up by mainstream fashion and spread in popularity amongst higher income groups.

- The arguments presented in these theories are based mainly on conclusions drawn from external observation, rather than the subjects (consumers), themselves. Consumers' own accounts of their purchasing behaviour are not accorded a high priority.

An example provided recently by Dick Hebdige illustrates why some sociologists believe it is important to invest more time in investigating the meanings associated with consumption, particularly from the consumers' point of view:

When I first moved into my present home, I was intrigued by one car in the street – a great spotless Thunderbird, its maroon bodywork and sculptured chromium accessories glistening all year round, irrespective of the weather. This Thunderbird is the single most conspicuous anomaly in the Victorian terraced street in which I live. It is a Cathedral amongst hovels. It is out of scale, out of place (its real home is Detroit or Dallas), out of time (its real time is pre-1974, pre the Oil Crisis). I immediately assumed – drawing on my stock of Hollywood derived cultural stereotypes – that the car belonged to a pimp, a gangster, or a 'big shot' of some kind . . . These assumptions turned out to be unfounded. The car is owned by one of the gentlest, most gracious and modest men I know. Mr H is a slight, mild-mannered Turkish Cypriot who lives with his wife in a run down, sparsely furnished ground floor flat in the house opposite.
(Hebdige, 1996, p. 81)

Hebdige uses this example from his own domestic life to illustrate some of the weaknesses in the theories of consumption discussed so far. Mr H has lovingly devoted hours to the care and preservation of this car; he spends as much time washing, polishing, tuning and retuning his car as he does in his flat. The car represents a source of pleasure for the owner which goes far beyond a simple attempt to 'copy' the consumption patterns of higher income groups. Indeed, it represents a style and era far removed from the contemporary English middle class. But, at the same time, the car is not an object

which can easily be placed within the *habitus* of the London working class, as Bourdieu might expect.

What has to be recognized is that commodities can often provide a very complex source of meanings and pleasures for consumers: they may be pleasurable because they are a source of pride, because they constitute a mechanical or intellectual challenge, because they evoke nostalgic images of earlier eras or distinct cultural influences, and so on. For some cultural theorists, what this suggests is that an analysis of consumption has to *start* with the symbolic meanings associated with sets of commodities.

Activity
Explain what is meant by a 'top-down' model of consumption, and assess the criticisms which some sociologists make of this kind of sociological explanation of consumption. **U, A, E**

Semiology and the symbolic meaning of consumption

During the last two decades semiology has been commonly used as a method through which the meaning of images, symbols and commodities can be explored. Semiology, however, does not employ an interpretative approach like symbolic interactionism. Rather, it depends on the theorist's ability to decode sets of popular symbols (or 'signs' to use the term employed by semiologists). (This issue is also explored in Section 15.2.)

Ferdinand de Saussure (1857–1913) first developed semiology as a method for analysing language as a symbolic system. However, it was Barthes (1915–80) who first applied this approach not only to language but to all aspects of popular culture including photographs, advertisements and actual commodities. Barthes (1973) believed that all cultural symbols, including commodities, signified (communicated) certain meanings which might combine in a system to create a cultural 'myth'. For example, 'Coca Cola' means more than just a can of soft drink – for many people it *signifies* 'the American way of life' (see Figure 10.6).

| First level of signification | 'Coca Cola' (signifier) A fizzy soft drink (signified) |
| Second level of signification | Youth, fun, the American way of life (myths) |

Figure 10.6 Levels of signification

Barthes' semiological approach has been used by other analysts who have explored, for example, the ways in which 'myths' about masculinity, femininity and power have been used in advertisements for cars, deodorants, after-shaves, clothing and chocolates amongst other things (Williamson, 1978; Myers, 1986). It is still quite easy to find some advertisements attempting to associate particular products with images of masculinity and power, or traditional images of femininity, or suggestions of power and authority.

Many advertisements continue to rework 'myths' about gender, class and power, but advertising in the 1990s is often considerably more subtle than 20 years ago. Advertisements now sometimes portray a 'new man' who is caring, sensitive and willing to do his share of housework and childcare. Some critics suggest that this is yet another 'myth' rather than a reflection of real change.

Coca Cola provides another recent example of the growing sophistication of advertisements. A recent campaign tied its product in with the 1996 European Soccer Championship. 'Eat Football, Sleep Football, Drink Coca Cola' represented a considerable departure from the earlier Coca Cola ads which frequently depicted happy children or young people, 'from around the world', singing an uplifting song, globally united through their common love of Coca Cola. The soccer ad, in contrast, was shot in grainy black and white to emphasize 'documentary realism'; it portrayed scenes of rowdy terrace excitement, used a heavy rock beat, and the slogan of the advertisement, flashed across the screen at repeated intervals. The effect was both striking and a little disturbing. Coca Cola, here, was being associated with something disorderly and unruly – qualities not immediately associated with the bourgeois values of capitalism. But, of course, this is the whole point of the advertisement: to suggest that Coca Cola has an appeal or 'an energy' which transcends classes, cultures and stadium terraces – just like soccer.

Discussion point

Are television advertisements no longer sexist, or are they now sexist in more subtle ways?

Semiology offers one way of beginning to explore systematically the meanings associated with advertising and consumption, but Barthes devotes little attention to two important issues:

- The meanings or myths associated with consumption patterns clearly do change over time,

as we have seen in the case of the representation of gender; but we need to know more about how this occurs.
- Without conducting research, how can we be sure that audiences 'read' myths in the way Barthes suggests? How can we be sure that consumers derive pleasures from commodities because of the association between product and myth, as argued by Barthes?

In other words, in the absence of thorough audience and consumer research, there is a huge danger that semiology produces an idiosyncratic interpretation which reflects the preoccupations of the researcher rather than widely held, popular myths.

Excorporation and incorporation: the work of John Fiske

Although Barthes recognized that images and commodities could be polysemic (offer multiple meanings), he failed to explore fully the ways in which ordinary people might contest or refuse the conventional meanings associated with consumption. Critics argue that he under-estimated the importance of cultural resistance in consumption.

Neo-hegemony theorists or culturalists (see Section 10.2) have been particularly interested in the potential semiology offers for analysing social conflict as it is expressed at the level of culture and ideas. The Centre for Contemporary Cultural Studies (CCCS) has employed semiology extensively in its analysis of dominant and subordinate cultures. However, John Fiske takes the semiological analysis of consumption considerably further.

Fiske argues that while there is a tremendous energy within capitalist societies which encourages consumption through advertising, marketing and the media, consumers do not always 'consume' in the ways in which capitalism anticipates. They may use commodities in a subversive way. They may engage in semiological guerrilla warfare, creatively employing their own semiology to give images and commodities new meanings. Fiske describes this as 'excorporation' – the process through which commodities produced by capitalism are used in new or different ways (excorporated) by subordinate groups to create oppositional meanings and cultural resistance (Fiske, 1989a, pp. 15–18). Dr Marten boots were excorporated by skinheads; Vespa motor scooters were excorporated by mods.

This leads Fiske to assert that it is precisely the resistance of oppressed or subordinate groups which *makes* popular culture:

Popular culture is always a culture of conflict, it always involves the struggle to make social meanings that are in the interests of the subordinate

and that are not those preferred by the dominant ideology. The victories, however, fleeting or limited, in this struggle produce popular pleasure, for popular pleasure is always social and political.
(Fiske, 1989b, p. 2)

For Fiske, then, only that which involves consuming commodities to make oppositional or subversive meanings actually counts as popular culture. This is quite a controversial position to take and some of his own examples clearly illustrate why. Arcade video games make huge profits but, according to Fiske, allow people often with little autonomy in their real lives to enter a world which they can control using their skill and knowledge. Shopping malls may be symbols of consumer capitalism but the young unemployed can excorporate the public space within, engaging in cultural opposition both by evading security personnel and enjoying the pleasure of window shopping but not buying. Most controversially, Fiske argues that young women can excorporate Madonna as a commodity (her music, films, books, posters, etc.), in opposition to dominant sexist and patriarchal values. This is despite, as Fiske concedes, Madonna being voted number three 'Sex/Lust Object' in a 1985 American magazine. Nevertheless, according to Fiske the 'meaning' of Madonna is a site of:

. . . semiotic struggle between the forces of patriarchal control and feminine resistance, of capitalism and the subordinate, of the adult and the young.
(Fiske, 1989b, p. 97)

But do consumers and subordinated social groups really decode or excorporate commodities in the way Fiske claims? Fiske does refer to empirical, usually ethnographic, research on particular social groups to support some of his arguments, but he does not always do this consistently. The great danger is that, once again, the interpretation made by the academic rather than by 'ordinary people', is allowed to shape the semiological analysis.

Also, is Fiske correct in arguing that popular culture is 'always a culture of conflict' involving the subversive rejection of dominant values? It is possible to think of plenty of widely popular cultural activities which do not, on the face of things, appear to involve cultural resistance – going fishing or watching daytime television, for example. If we follow Fiske, either these are ruled out as examples of popular culture, or we have to make the claim that someone sitting at the canal side with a fishing rod is engaged in an act of cultural resistance.

Post-modernism and consumerism

For post-modernists the dominance of a consumer culture is one of the defining features of the post-modern society. As we have seen (in Section 10.4), Bourdieu believes certain codes or rules shape the way in which social groups consume. He argues, for example, that social class governs taste. The meaning of commodities will signify 'middle class' or 'working class'. However, according to some theorists such as Mike Featherstone (1991a, pp. 18–25), one of the distinguishing features of the post-modern world is that these codes are breaking down. We now all have greater freedom to 'play' with the meaning of commodities and to select commodities from a range of social contexts. Rather than 'inheriting' particular styles and tastes through upbringing and occupation, we can playfully construct our identities by combining permutations of commodities, all signifying in different ways. Thus, commodity stockbrokers may read *The Sun* but shop in Saville Row, while miners may choose Laura Ashley wallpaper but drink in the working-mens' club.

Mike Featherstone lists the following reasons. First, in its drive to make profit, consumer capitalism produces more and more, formerly 'exclusive' goods, thus lowering the price and thereby making them more widely available. Secondly, the mass media have eroded many of the old distinctions between 'high' and 'popular culture' (see Section 10.3). Thirdly, he points to the proliferation of style magazines and television programmes which now allow a wide range of social groups to acquire knowledge of 'fashion' and 'taste'. Finally, like Bourdieu (Section 10.4) and Mort (Section 10.7), Featherstone points to the role of a particular social group – 'the new cultural intermediaries' – who work in fashion, design, the media, marketing, information and cultural industries. Typically, such workers have been to university or college but are distinct from the traditional middle class. Free from the influence of conventional bourgeois values, they use their cultural expertise:

. . . to ransack various traditions and cultures in order to produce new symbolic goods, and in addition provide the necessary interpretations on their use.
(Featherstone, 1991a, p. 19)

Two critical points developed by Campbell (1995) in a recent review are worth highlighting here. First, there is a danger in:

treating the attitudes and practices of certain sections of the affluent middle class . . . as if they were typical of consumers as a whole.
(Campbell, 1995, p. 114).

The interest in lifestyle, consumption and identity to be found in certain parts of Hampstead and Islington may not be reproduced across all sections of society. Secondly, Campbell suggests, it may not be safe to assume that meanings suggested or signified by different commodities will actually be understood in precisely the same way by all social groups:

. . . it is rare for anyone to be completely mystified by the goods that others have purchased or by the way that they are being utilised. This is not the same, however, as claiming that all, or even most, members of that society would be in a position to agree on what 'meaning' should be attributed to the fact that a particular individual has purchased a pair of blue jeans or chooses to wear them to go shopping.

(Campbell, 1995, p. 115)

Activity

Is Fiske correct to insist that popular culture always contains expressions of resistance to dominant values? Consider this question with examples and illustrations of your own.

I, A, E

10.10 **Nationalism, globalization and self-identity**

By globalization, sociologists usually mean the process whereby societies, communities and individuals are increasingly *interconnected* around the world (McGrew, 1992). Social processes in one part of the world impact on those in other parts. The cultural implications of globalization have been of particular interest. (The sociological arguments about globalization and its implications are also explored in Sections 9.9, 12.5, 15.11, 16.8 and 17.6.)

Globalization is sometimes portrayed as a process in which the individual is helpless; a process through which the multi-national cultural conglomerates come to dominate popular culture across the world in a relentless way. Critics, including some Marxists, would argue that this is, indeed, happening. Cultural homogenization (the wiping out of regional and local cultures) will accelerate as the same fast-food outlets, the same cola advertisements, the same fashions, the same satellite television shows, and the same popular music, proliferate around the world. After all, Rupert Murdock, owner of News Corporation, with huge media interests in America, the UK, Europe and Asia, has indicated that his strategy is to find the cultural common denominator which will allow him to market the same cultural commodities through all the parts of the globe in which he has an interest. The common formula, he thinks, is sport plus rock music.

In considering the relationship between national identity and globalization, Stuart Hall (1992b, p. 300) identifies three possible scenarios:

- *Cultural homogenization.* National identities and culture are eroded by the impact of global cultural industries and multi-national media.
- *Cultural resistance.* National and local cultures may be strengthened if members of nations and local communities consciously resist the impact of cultural globalization. The French state, for example, has recently passed legislation intended to reverse the creeping Americanization of language and culture. In most parts of the globe there are cultural resistance movements of one kind or another, each struggling to preserve a sense of national, regional or local identity.
- *The emergence of 'new identities of hybridity'.* Globalization may encourage a circulation of cultural elements and images which allows local communities to create new 'hybrid' identities. Gillespie's study of Punjabi youth in Southall (see Section 10.6) clearly demonstrates the impact of global influences in the process of constructing a new youth subculture but they are fused with strong traditional influences as well.

A number of writers favour the cultural homogenization thesis and there is considerable evidence to support their views. Twenty years ago Tunstall (1977) pointed to the global dominance of American culture. More recently, the experience of Canada has prompted writers to conclude that global communication systems make it very difficult for nation states to protect national cultural identities even when they use state legislation (Perlmutter, 1993; Collins, 1985). Canada has been anxious to limit the impact of US media on Canadian cultural life but it has been unable to prevent a steady movement of audience away from the Canadian national broadcasting system towards US satellite stations which reach across the border, or the dominance of Canadian cinema by US-based multi-nationals. This is despite the efforts of the Canadian government in encouraging national cultural projects. In Europe now, similar fears are being expressed about the dominance of multi-national media conglomerates and their impact on national cultures, particularly since many European governments have deregulated to allow market forces a greater influence in media markets (Petley and Romano, 1993; Blumler, 1992a).

However, there are some important criticisms of the cultural homogenization model which encourage a more optimistic interpretation. As Robins (1991) points out, even if multi-national media conglomerates enjoy an increasing influence, this may not lead to the eradication of cultural differences. He argues that successful global conglomerates will commercially exploit local cultures and identities, rather than try to eradicate them. This is what Sony, the Japanese electronic and media corporation, calls 'global localization'. The Coca Cola Corporation describes itself as 'multi-local', rather than multi-national.

Further evidence to support this thesis is provided by a study of MTV in Europe (Sturmer, 1993). MTV, the television rock music station, was launched in 1981 when it reached 1.5 million households. By 1991 it reached 201 million households in 77 countries, across five continents. Given the global reach of MTV and the nature of popular music, this example might be regarded as a good illustration of the cultural homogenization thesis. However, as Sturmer shows, the situation is more complex. The European branch of MTV (MTVE) is based in London but broadcasts to the whole of Europe, including Scandinavia and eastern Europe. It is largely independent of its US parent company; its choice of videos and programming strategy represent a conscious attempt to avoid Americanization. There is a strong emphasis on European music, such as 'Euro pop' and 'indie', while attempts are made through audience request shows to establish a relationship with European audiences. However, Sturmer does note that the uneven distribution of wealth and living standards within Europe means that MTVE's marketing strategy is oriented more towards northern Europe, with less attention given to the local cultures and identities of young people in southern and eastern Europe. Perhaps the most important evidence concerns the response of audiences. Are they embracing a 'Euro-culture'? The varying degree of success of MTVE suggests that local cultural differences are still very important in determining audience responses. MTVE is hugely popular in Sweden but less successful in Italy. Most interestingly, MTVE's rap programme *Yo!*, which *is* imported from the USA, has enjoyed a very mixed response. While it is one of the more popular shows across Europe as a whole, it is much less successful in the UK and France where there are very strong indigenous rap and jungle music scenes. This may indicate that in certain circumstances local culture can resist global influences. For Sturmer:

The differing reactions to Yo! in Germany and the UK, or to the channel as a whole in Sweden, Poland or Italy, indicate that as MTVE strives to build its European profile it is at the same time reflecting and helping to create a range of diverse and surprising 'imaginary continents' for and with its young audience.

(Sturmer, 1993, p. 65)

Activity

Make a list of the arguments and evidence for and against the cultural homogenization thesis.   **U, I, A**

The third possible scenario identified by Hall is the emergence of 'new identities of hybridity'. Hall points out that globalization through the spread of western cultural influences around the globe is as old as colonialization and certainly not a new phenomenon. What is new is the volume of migration from one society to another in the second half of the twentieth century. By 1990, one in every four Americans came from an African–American, Asian–American or American–Indian background. In Europe, migration has brought strong cultural influences from, for example, North Africa, Turkey, Senegal, Zaire, the Caribbean, Bangladesh, Pakistan, India, Kenya, Uganda and Sri Lanka. These are the new post-colonial diaspora (dispersions of peoples and cultures). In this way, globalization has made much more complex the issue of national identity: there is now a 'pluralization of national cultures and national identities' (Hall, 1992b, p. 307). The simple existence of *different* cultures within one nation makes the concept of a 'national culture' much more problematic but it also makes the emergence of new cultural identities possible through a process of cross-fertilization. Section 10.6 contains examples which appear to illustrate Hall's theory (see Rattansi and Westwood, 1994; Gillespie, 1995; Hall and du Gay, 1996). However, Hall makes it clear that the emergence of new hybrid cultures is not inevitable. First, local communities may respond to the influence of globalization through a fierce reassertion of tradition and fixed ethnicity (he points to the rise of national and religious fundamentalists around the world). Secondly, cultural exchange is never an even or equal process. The cultures of minority communities will also reflect the experience of racism and the opportunities for creating new subcultural identities will be constrained by the continuing dominance of white mainstream culture in schooling, the mass media, and so on.

Anthony Giddens: globalization and self-identity

In *Modernity and Self-Identity*, Anthony Giddens stresses the interplay between global structures and self-identity:

The self is not a passive entity, determined by external influences; in forging their self-identities, no matter how local their specific contexts of action,

individuals contribute to and directly promote social influences that are global in their consequences and implications.
(Giddens, 1991, p. 2)

For Giddens, one of the defining features of living in the period of 'late modernity' is that the cultural choices we make always have global consequences. In buying a new pair of trainers, for example, we reinforce an economic relationship between a multinational sportswear company and low-wage workers thousands of miles away (see Section 12.5).

At the same time, the structural changes bound up in the process of globalization have important consequences for our self-identities. Giddens identifies two key mechanisms here. First, he points to the reorganization of time and space. Members of traditional societies experienced time and space in more or less fixed and stable ways; the experience of both time and space was rooted in the local setting (pre-industrial agricultural workers would rise with the sun, work in the local fields and stop at sundown). The dynamism of modern societies changes this: time is separated from space and both are separated from local settings. The speed of modern transport means that time is no longer a powerful determinant of our experience of space or distance – we climb into a jet and travel hundreds of miles in a relatively short period of time. Giddens calls this growing separation of time and space and locality, 'time–space distanciation'.

Secondly, Giddens refers to 'disembedding mechanisms'. In the past, social relationships were rooted in tangible, concrete settings. For example, in the past factory workers would receive a pay packet at the end of each week which would be physically handed to them by a clerk within the factory office. Now most wages and salaries are paid into bank accounts directly by computer transfer; the social relationship of payment has been removed from the local context or as Giddens puts it 'lifted out'. The 'symbolic tokens' (for example, money, plastic credit, etc.), which in the post-traditional world are increasingly important, all act as 'disembedding mechanisms' because they lift social relationships out of local contexts. Similarly, we increasingly depend on 'experts' (financial advisors, health experts, therapists, scientists, etc.) for guidance in social life, and these too act as 'disembedding mechanisms' because they exist independently of the local context.

What all this means is that we depend on globalized systems, far removed from our own local control. We have no choice other than to trust the 'expert systems' on which we depend.

So far we have looked at the ways in which globalized structures intrude on the experience of the

Activity

Make a list of the 'disembedding mechanisms' and experiences of 'time–space distanciation' in your own life. Think of things like using banks and building societies, going on holiday, shopping, leisure activities, travelling, going up in a lift, etc. **U, A**

individual, but Giddens is at pains to emphasize the interplay between individuals and the global structures. *This is, of course, the main theme of structuration theory* (see Section 2.9). Giddens argues that another distinctive feature of the post-traditional modern world is the reflexivity of individual self-identity. We are more aware of our own identities and more self-conscious about the ways in which identity can be socially constructed: 'The self becomes a reflexive project' (p. 32) – a project in which we self-consciously relate personal change to wider social changes. Giddens points to the ways in which individuals rebuild their lives (and their identities) after the traumatic experience of divorce, as an example. The greater reflexivity of the self in the modern world is related to the faster pace of change in personal and social life (rising divorce rates, for example) and is assisted by some of the 'expert knowledge' systems which are available. Thus, individuals may employ counselling, therapy, even sociology, to try to make sense of their lives and build their own sense of identity.

The risks posed for the individual in personal and social terms should not be under-estimated, but the arrival of late modernity also allows a new freedom to contemplate and explore new forms of self-identity. Modernity 'balances opportunity and potential catastrophe in equal measure' (Giddens, 1991, p. 34).

Critics suggest that the impact of technology on our understanding of time and space can be over-estimated. Few of us give more than a little thought to the process of 'time–space distanciation', we just get on with our working lives and holidays (Ferguson, 1990). Others argue that in considering the 'pull and push' between the efforts of individuals in constructing their lives and the constraints imposed by global structures, Giddens rather underplays the power of the latter (Tomlinson, 1994).

10.11 **The debate over post-modernism and cultural populism**

Post-modernism is a slippery term which is used by writers to refer to several distinct things.

Featherstone (1991a) points out that the term is variously used to refer to:

- new developments in intellectual and cultural theory (what we shall call the 'theory of post-modernism')
- the suggestion that our subjective experience of everyday life and our sense of identity has somehow changed significantly in recent years ('the post-modern condition')
- the view that capitalist or industrial societies have reached new and important stages in their development (the shift from modernity to post-modernity).

Leading post-modernist writers include Lyotard (1993), Jameson (1991) and Baudrillard (1993, 1998), although there are important differences between them.

The end of meta-narratives and cultural depthlessness

According to Lyotard, the post-modern world is characterized by a spreading cynicism about 'meta-narratives' or general belief systems, including world religions, political ideologies such as socialism or liberalism, and even science and reason, itself. We have become disillusioned and no longer expect the world to become a better place. Meta-narratives have partly been discredited because, in an era of global media in which we learn more and more about other peoples' beliefs and lifestyles, it becomes less and less possible to regard one lifestyle or one belief system as the 'true one'. As Lyotard puts it:

Eclecticism is the degree zero of contemporary general culture: one listens to reggae, watches a Western, eats McDonald's for lunch and local cuisine for dinner, wears Paris perfume in Tokyo and retro clothes in Hong Kong; knowledge is a matter for TV games.
(Lyotard, 1993, p.42)

Discussion point

Have we become disillusioned with *all* meta-narratives and, if so, why?

According to post-modernists, the collapse of meta-narratives is connected with the new 'depthlessness' of culture – 'a new kind of superficiality' (Jameson, 1991) . This is because without meta-narratives or fundamental truths, culture cannot claim to offer insights into the 'real' nature of things. Post-modern culture simply 'picks and mixes' in terms of fashion, music, lifestyle and even subcultural belief, whereas in the former modern era culture still 'meant something'. According to post-modern writers, youth subcultural styles no longer express anything more than fashion statements, unconnected to deeper values or experiences.

Similarly, Strinati (1995) suggests, post-modern television and film become preoccupied merely with surface style and imagery, rather than deeper underlying themes which might relate to 'the realities' of the human condition. Action blockbuster movies dwell on the spectacular special effects, rather than strong plots, and television drama departs from the 'realist' plots of the 1960s (which attempted to deal with serious issues like homelessness or poverty) and embraces a surreal world in which 'reality' is often confused; for example, *Twin Peaks*, or more recently *X-files* and *American Gothic*. Kaplan (1987) identifies pop and rock videos as perfect examples of post-modern culture because they abandon all notion of narrative structure – there is no attempt to 'tell a story', rather the power of a rock video lies purely in the collage of images mixed with music.

According to post-modernists, cultural standards become meaningless (see Section 10.3). Without meta-narratives, it makes little sense to 'judge' the quality of cultural products according to a cultural standard: one cultural standard is as good as any other, all are relative.

The cultural, the economic and the agencies of signification

According to Jameson and Baudrillard, with the decline of engineering and manufacturing in many advanced capitalist economies, the provision of cultural and media services becomes the key economic sector. In the UK, for example, the record industry is one of the leading export sectors of the economy.

Both Jameson (1991) and Baudrillard (1988) argue that Marx failed to appreciate the qualitative transformation which occurs once cultural artefacts, signs and images become the most important commodities in the market. Jameson does not abandon Marx altogether: he acknowledges that it is still the drive for profit which leads *capitalism* to invest in marketing, advertising, public relations and the other cultural or image industries.

Baudrillard, in contrast, moves much more sharply away from Marx, insisting that in order to understand the post-modern society we must develop a 'political economy of the sign' (or image). The trading of signs or images, as opposed to 'things', is now the dominant pattern of market relations and the task must be to explore the 'codes' which govern such exchanges (Baudrillard, 1988, pp. 57–97). It is semiology rather than economics which holds the key to understanding the principles or 'codes' governing such transactions, and it is the 'agencies of signification' – advertising agencies, marketing consultants, public relations firms, and the mass media – which play a crucial role in circulating these codes. For example, the 'designer labels' attached to jeans, shirts and coats all 'mean' something according to a code recognized by most young people. Levi 501s 'mean' one thing, jeans bought at Tescos something else entirely.

Activity

Consider the following commodities: jeans, cars, furnishings, food. Write a short summary describing the codes which operate in relation to each example.

A

For Baudrillard, we live in a world which is 'media saturated'; a world in which we are bombarded by media and advertising messages through multi-channel television, globalized electronic and cable networks, a profusion of radio stations, newspapers, and street billboards. Baudrillard argues that the consequences of this are profound. The 'codes' generated by the agencies of signification become our rules for organizing our lives. So powerful are these codes, according to Baudrillard, that we lose the ability to distinguish between reality (for example, the 'real' practical value of a commodity) and its image. We begin to buy images rather than actual 'things'. Thus, for Baudrillard, the post-modern world is a world dominated by 'simulacra' (literally, false or deceptive images) in which we no longer even try to distinguish reality from image, the two blur together.

Post-modern identity

While Baudrillard is pessimistic in his reading of the post-modern world, not all post-modernists share his vision. Hebdidge (1988), who has moved closer to post-modernism in his later writing, and Chen (1992), present more 'optimistic' accounts. We are no longer inhibited by social categories such as class, ethnicity, gender or even age in our choice of styles and fashions. Mixing and matching from a variety of subcultural styles and contexts can be a creative and pleasurable experience. We all now have a detailed knowledge of the history of earlier subcultural patterns, through the work of the mass media in continually providing retrospective accounts, via pop videos, old TV favourites recycled on cable channels, and Hollywood films, so we can select from a huge cultural warehouse of new and retro styles. Post-modern identities, then, are diverse and pluralistic – not shaped by the constraints of social structure.

This cultural knowledge which we all possess makes us sophisticated decoders of culture, fashion and mass media. For 'optimistic' theorists, the post-modern condition means having many more cultural options.

However, a more pessimistic picture is presented by others. The semiological power of the cultural codes generated by late capitalism leads Jameson (1991) to doubt whether sustained political opposition to their dominance is possible. Baudrillard goes further: for him, the media encourage a process of 'massification' (Kellner, 1989, p. 69), producing mass audiences and homogeneous patterns of consumption. The only way in which the masses can resist is through passive and silent alienation. They may watch the parade of images and symbols without absorbing any deeper message, merely channel hopping from one television station to another. And even if there were any evidence of resistance amongst the post-modern public, this would quickly be neutralized by the mass media, eager to search out more examples of 'spectacle' as entertainment. Thus, radical demonstrations or protests are represented as 'entertaining' news items without attention to the underlying political issues provoking action. Indeed, the mass media, by bombarding us with so many messages all the time – 'an ecstasy of communication' according to Baudrillard – actually disempower us. We are simply overwhelmed by the sheer volume of information and images. We become immobilized, incapable of discerning the relevant or critical from the mundane.

Critiques of post-modernism

Post-modernism is important because it represents one attempt to deal with significant new developments in culture and experience as we move towards the next millennium. The rapidly increasing number of media outlets and the increasing emphasis on consumption must make a difference to our subjective experience and sense of identity – the way we feel. However, not all sociologists believe that post-modernism offers the most appropriate set of theoretical concepts for dealing with these important developments. The following are five of the most important criticisms.

First, several critics have argued that post-modernism, particularly in the work of Baudrillard, merely rehearses the old Frankfurt School's 'manipulation theory'. Accordingly, it is vulnerable to the same criticisms. It is too pessimistic and underestimates the capacity of the audience to think critically. Alternative research presents a picture of a much more critical media audience (Morley, 1992; Philo, 1990).

Secondly, as Strinati comments:

. . . the idea that the mass media take over 'reality' clearly exaggerates their importance. The mass media are important but not that important.
(Strinati, 1995, p. 239)

Baudrillard suggests that the distinction between reality and media image collapses. However, 'modernist' sociologists are often highly critical of this 'extreme relativism'. John Eldridge, of the Glasgow University Media Group, for example, argues that it is one thing to acknowledge the influence which ideology and values have on our attempts to understand the real world; it is quite another to insist that all such attempts are *merely* ideological and equally flawed, or that, as Baudrillard believes, there is no real social world in the first place, merely our ideological perceptions of it. For Eldridge (1993), one of the key tasks of sociology is to continue to test media coverage against alternative, independent measures of reality. He considers that post-modernism's abandonment of this project represents 'intellectual vertigo . . . a failure of nerve'.

Thirdly, Kellner (1989) argues that post-modernism rests on a 'media essentialism'. Baudrillard's approach, he suggests, places too much emphasis on the importance of media technology in determining the way in which society develops ('technological determinism') and ignores the importance of social relationships – the ways in which social groups use the media technology. Many sociologists would insist that in order to understand how the mass media work, it is necessary to explore the *social* relationships involved in the ownership and control of the media, or the political connections between media and political élites, or the ways in which audiences can use media, sometimes in ways which resist dominant ideological messages. Without considering social relationships, it is difficult for Baudrillard to explain how signs or images *change* over time. This happens, of course, because far from passively consuming, social groups appropriate signs or symbols and use them to construct new and sometimes, oppositional meanings.

A fourth problem concerns the distinction between the modern and the post-modern (Chen, 1992; McRobbie, 1994). How do we know that we are living in the post-modern, in a qualitatively different kind of society to the modern? Post-modernists are sketchy on this issue and provide different answers depending on whether they are describing changes in social structure or particular forms of cultural production. Giddens (1991) convincingly argues that most of the forces transforming our current subjective experience are essentially the culmination of developments in modernity, not the consequence of a major new historical development.

Finally, the critics of post-modernism point to its own ideological role. The rejection of all previous meta-narratives is, itself, another meta-narrative. How can post-modernists be so confident in announcing the end of modernist belief systems unless, implicitly, they argue from the vantage point of their own meta-narrative (Strinati, 1995, p. 241)? Critics point to the social context in which post-modernism became fashionable and to the kinds of social groups amongst whom post-modernist ideas seemed to have the strongest appeal. Post-modernist concepts are most popular with cultural experts and academics – designers, creative workers in advertising and marketing, journalists and cultural theorists in university departments – all social groups who are likely to favour a theoretical approach which suggests that their expertise is becoming ever more vital in society. Critics argue that post-modernist ideas, with their emphasis on consumption and image rather than underlying social problems, reflect the priorities of the affluent and a reluctance to confront the less palatable realities of late capitalism (Norris, 1993; Callinicos, 1989).

Activity

Make notes for and then write an essay that evaluates critically the following statement: 'Our identity and cultural experience are shaped by the post-modern condition'. Use sociological arguments and evidence.

U, I, A, E

The problem of cultural populism

In recent years, theorists of popular culture have been concerned to avoid what they regard as two great pitfalls. First, writers have sought to avoid the danger of 'élitism'. That is they wished to avoid the 'mistakes' made by, for example, the advocates of the mass culture thesis and the Frankfurt School. Both the Frankfurt School and mass culture critics, like Arnold, Eliot and Leavis, in attacking commercialism in the culture industries, implied that much popular culture was 'inferior' to other cultural forms. Such judgements were criticized for betraying a form of élitism.

Secondly, it became unfashionable to present arguments which could be interpreted as examples of 'economic reductionism'. Both Marxist and non-Marxist theorists tried to avoid the 'danger' of economic reductionism by employing theoretical approaches which directed attention to cultural issues (magazine content, tastes in shopping, television audiences, and so on), rather than questions of how the institutions of cultural production were organized. First culturalism and now post-modernism have grown in popularity because they appeared to offer ways in which both élitism and economic reductionism could be avoided.

Harris (1992) argues that those theorists who began to employ Gramsci's ideas in the 1960s and 1970s (culturalists) did so in ways which tended to 'close off', rather than open up, empirical research or theoretical development. Harris argues that other kinds of sociology have been more 'open' in the sense that researchers have been prepared to be 'surprised', or to acknowledge data and historical evidence which did not fit neatly into their theoretical frameworks. It is a little too easy, Harris suggests, to read into audience or consumer behaviour 'evidence' of 'resistance', particularly if qualitative, ethnographic methods are used. The danger is that culturalists 'find' what they assume to be the case at the beginning; and then forms of popular cultural activity which are not compatible with the theoretical and political assumptions of the researchers are ignored. Little attention, Harris notes, has been given to popular but politically less palatable cultural pastimes like blood sports (for example, illegal dog-fighting) or 'consumer pathologies', such as the playground bullying of 'style fascists', who victimize those without designer clothes and trainers.

McGuigan (1992) condemns what he regards as a collapse into 'cultural populism'. McGuigan reminds us that the pioneers of cultural studies, including writers like Raymond Williams and Richard Hoggart, were motivated by a desire to see ordinary people's experiences and culture taken more seriously in the curriculum offered in schools and colleges. That is not the same thing as assuming that *any* kind of popular culture should be embraced uncritically simply because it is popular amongst ordinary people. Recent approaches, McGuigan argues, are so eager to avoid the mistakes of old mass society or manipulation approaches that they end up offering an entirely uncritical endorsement of popular culture. This point might be applied to both culturalism and post-modernism. Any kind of popular culture is welcomed because it offers opportunities for 'resistance'. But, McGuigan points out, evidence of 'resistance' is often thin and, at the same time, the mechanisms of real political power are often ignored. Recent approaches, he argues, have also been too anxious to avoid the charge of economic reductionism.

In consequence, the economic aspects of media institutions and the broader economic dynamics of consumer culture were rarely investigated, simply bracketed off, thereby severely undermining the explanatory and, in effect, critical capacities of cultural studies.
(McGuigan, 1992, p. 41)

McGuigan suggests that what is required is an approach which tries to relate a political economy of popular culture to a sociology of consumption and identity. In other words, sociologists and cultural theorists should retain an interest in the various and diverse ways in which we all consume commodities and construct identities; but they should not lose sight of the point that many of our cultural options are shaped by the interests of cultural and media conglomerates, the working of capitalist markets, the power of the state, and the routines and professional values of workers inside the cultural industries – artists, producers, film and video directors, journalists, advertising executives, and others.

Activity

Write a short, critical essay on the culturalist approach to the study of culture and identity.

U, I, E

Further **reading**

Two articles that provide helpful introductions to some of the key themes in this topic are:

- Sugrue, B. and Taylor, C. (1996) 'From Marx to Man. City', *Sociology Review*, Vol. 6, no. 1.
- Sugrue, B. and Taylor, C. (1996) 'Cultures and identities', *Sociology Review*, Vol. 5, no. 3.

The following are good introductions to the topic as a whole:

- Billington, R. *et al.* (1991) *Culture and Society*, London, Macmillan.
- Strinati, D. (1995) *An Introduction to Theories of Popular Culture*, London, Routledge.

The following provides a specialized introduction to one key theme, although the text is quite demanding in places:

- Bocock, R. (1993) *Consumption*, London, Routledge.

The following book is an excellent example of empirical research which is both accessible and interesting, providing important insights relevant for the study of ethnicity, culture, identity and the sociology of the mass media:

- Gillespie, M. (1995) *Television, Ethnicity and Cultural Change*, London, Routledge.

For those interested in the history of style, fashion and gender images, there is:

- Mort, F. (1996) *Cultures of Consumption: Masculinities and Social Space in Late Twentieth Century Britain*, London, Routledge.

Back issues of the periodical *Sociology Review* (formerly known as *Social Studies Review*) also contain many articles on this field of sociology and many others.

Exam questions

1 a Briefly explain two ways in which 'adolescence' is a social process.   [4 marks]

  b Identify and briefly describe what sociologists have seen as the key features of one post-war 'youth subculture'.   [4 marks]

  c What aspects of social change since World War Two have been seen as causing the emergence of youth subcultures?   [7 marks]

  d Critically assess the view that youth subcultures express class, ethnic, gender and other differences between young people rather than a 'generation gap'.   [10 marks]

  (IBS, Paper 1, Summer 1996)

2 How far is it possible to identify a single undifferentiated youth culture in post-war Britain?

    [25 marks]

  (IBS, Paper 1, Summer 1995)

3 'The dominant images [of youth] until very recently were of free-spending and pleasure seeking young people, enjoying the best years of their lives; now the pictures are of depressed young adults lying in bed or watching television until their Giro cheques arrive.'(Source: 'Celebration to the marginalisation of youth', in G. Cohen (ed), *Social Change and the Life Course*, London, Tavistock, 1987.) To what extent is this an accurate account of the changing character of young people in Britain?

    [25 marks]

  (NEAB, 1998 Syllabus, Specimen Questions, Module SL04)

Coursework suggestions

Identity and culture is a good area to select for project work because variety of empirical evidence is readily to hand in the form of:

- cultural products (magazines, television programmes, advertisements)
- people to interview about their ideas of identity (fellow students, parents, teachers)
- cultural institutions (museums, arts centres, restaurants, leisure and film complexes)
- official documents (publications produced by the Department of Heritage, the Arts Council, etc.).

Here are some suggestions for research hypotheses:

1 'Television soap operas provide symbolic resources which young people can use for the purpose of discussing and constructing identity'. Examine the summary of Marie Gillespie's work in this chapter to get ideas about how to test this hypothesis.

2 'The current generation of lifestyle magazines for men reproduce traditional forms of sexism and masculinity'. You will need to consider the various research techniques available for analysing mass media content in order to tackle this one.

3 'Government cultural policy is based on the assumption that one culture should unite the nation'. You will need to analyse a range of secondary material produced by government departments in order to test this hypthesis. Which departments would be most relevant?

4 'When purchasing new trainers, young people are primarily guided by their awareness of the cultural and symbolic significance of their choices, rather than the use value'. This hypothesis might lend itself to a quantitative approach. What methods might be most suitable? What theoretical approaches can be evaluated in the light of findings and data generated by this hypothesis?

Deviance

11.1 Key issues in the sociology of crime and deviance

Deviance is an often exciting and popular area of investigation for sociology and sociologists. Deviance, and more significantly that specific form of rule-breaking known as crime, is not only a *sociological problem*; it is defined by some, especially ruling groups, as a *social problem*. Whereas some see that the purpose of sociology is to explain and describe human behaviour in a detached fashion, others – often working within this topic area – wish to use sociological insights to produce social policy that limits the effects of crime and helps policy-creators and decision-makers to reduce or limit the amount of so-called 'undesirable activities'.

In 1993, prime minister John Major said of crime that 'we should condemn a little more and understand a little less'. This has important implications for the pursuit of a sociological understanding of crime and deviance. Are sociologists guilty of supporting the activities of deviants in society by not condemning their activities, or must understanding come before society can genuinely attempt to solve or reduce social problems?

Discussion point

To what extent does sociology side with the 'underdog' too often to make the insights produced by sociologists of value?

A great deal of the sociology of deviance attempts to add to, evaluate and replace what we could call 'common sense' understandings of crime and deviance. In the pursuit of a sociological understanding of crime it is not enough simply to seek answers, although this is a good starting point. Answers must be sought to specific questions, and answers must take into account both the theoretical and empirical dimensions of sociological analysis. However, before we can discuss, analyse and evaluate some of these theoretical and empirical contributions made by sociologists and sociological thought to an understanding of crime and deviance, we must be clear on our use of these terms and of others central to this topic area.

Crime

The category of crime is usually associated with behaviour which breaks the formal, written laws of a given society. The punishment of crime is likely to be more serious than the punishment of 'deviance' in general but, obviously, different crimes and different laws are treated in varying ways.

Deviance

To 'deviate' means, literally, to move away or to stray from, set standards in society. Deviance, then, is a much more general category than crime, and is used by sociologists to refer to behaviour that, while being different, is often not controlled legally.

It must be made clear, however, that to distinguish between crime and deviance like this is to do a disservice to the complexities of these concepts. It is of more value to think of deviance as a wide category, of which crime is a smaller part. Thus, all crime is deviance, but not all deviance is crime.

To deviate from social standards, however, is not to say that the deviant in question has performed a negative act (as defined by the standards of a given society). Although crime is usually associated with negative action, it is perfectly possible for one to deviate in a positive fashion: one could be held in high social regard, for example, for contributing outstanding and original knowledge in the sciences. Thus, the modern-day and much heralded physicist, Stephen Hawking, could be seen as a deviant: his book *A Brief History of Time* has become an outstanding popular bestseller even amongst the non-scientific book-buying public, and it is certainly true to say that his knowledge of modern science *deviates* from the norm in society.

Norms

As the name suggests, norms are the normal ways of behaving in society. A norm refers specifically to a given behavioural pattern. This is what we do in our everyday lives to behave *normally*. As with the relationship between deviance and crime, all laws are norms but not all norms are laws. If one breaks a norm one is considered as deviant. Sanctions – or punishments – against one who breaks norms depends on the severity of the norm and the public nature of the norm-breaking action. Such sanctions can range from a simple 'disapproving stare' to, on extreme occasions, social exclusion from a group.

The social construction of deviance

Norms are the products of social construction. Behaviour can vary in being normal or abnormal depending on the situation a social actor is in. Norms also vary across both time and space – they vary within a society historically, and between societies. (See also Section 10.1.)

Values

A value has a special relationship to a norm. Values

are the specific cultural goals towards which norms are directed. Whereas a norm prescribes actual behaviour, a value justifies that behaviour – it is the reason why some actions are approved of more than others.

Activity

Using the following examples of cultural styles, describe how these 'normal' ways of behaving vary across both time and space:

men's earrings
women's tattoos
men's ponytails/long hair
women's shaven/short hair

I, A

The problems of a 'sociology of deviance'

The term 'sociology of deviance', as an overarching theme for this chapter, has its problems. Whereas some sociologists investigate deviance in its everyday, general sense, others almost exclusively study the specific form of deviance known as criminality. In the literature, these two terms have also become associated closely with one another; so much so, that what is called the 'sociology of deviance' contains a vast and complex array of different theories, terms and interests. As Downes and Rock (1995) comment:

The very title of the discipline which we shall describe, the sociology of deviance, is a little misleading. A singular noun and a hint of science seem to promise a unified body of knowledge and an agreed set of procedures for resolving analytic difficulties. It suggests that the curious and troubled may secure sure answers to practical, political, moral, and intellectual problems. And, of all branches of applied sociology, the demands placed on the sociology of deviance are probably the most urgent. Deviance is upsetting and perplexing and it confronts people in many settings. Turning to sociology, enquirers are rarely given certain advice . . . They will not be offered one answer but a series of competing and contradictory visions of the nature of people, deviation, and the social order.
(Downes and Rock, 1995, p. 1)

The academic study of crimes and criminality, why crime occurs, who commits crime and how crime can be reduced, solved and eradicated, if at all, is known as criminology. Sociology and criminology exist in a special but problematic relationship to one another. Whereas some would claim that criminology is a smaller part of sociology, others claim that criminology is much wider, since it draws on a whole variety of disciplines – sociology being but one.

Activity

Referring to the quotation from Downes and Rock, answer the following questions:

a What is meant by 'applied sociology'? What does applied sociology do that may be different from other, more theoretical or general sociology?

b Why do Downes and Rock suggest that 'enquirers are rarely given certain advice' from the sociologists of deviance? Why might this be a problem for the public and governmental perception of sociology as a subject?

c If this particular area of study is characterized by 'a series of competing and contradictory visions', what implications does this have for the claims of sociology to be a science?

d To what extent do you think it is a serious problem if sociologists cannot agree? Why do you think this is?

U, I, A, E

Social problems and sociological problems

A distinction needs to be made between social problems and sociological problems. Social problems are those defined by society itself – problems such as crime, delinquency, civil unrest etc. (see Section 16.8) seen by either the majority by consensus or the ruling élite from above, to represent aspects of behaviour considered to be undesirable.

Social problems can also *become* sociological problems – objects of sociological measurement, definition and study. However, sociological problems are much wider including issues of theories, methodology etc. (see Chapters 2 and 3). Whereas some sociologists claim sociology should be the study of social problems and accept these problems without question, others – especially Marxists and interactionists – question social problems: in whose interests does it serve to define an aspect of society as a 'problem'? Marxists and other 'radical' sociological positions suggest that definitions of crime and deviance and laws and social rules tend to benefit those in powerful positions in society.

'Correctional criminology'

Hester and Eglin (1996) suggest that criminology is a practical or applied branch of sociology. They refer to both sociological and criminological theories, and to theorists who seek practically to solve crime and deviance as 'correctional'. Hester and Eglin, adopting what they refer to as a 'subversive' approach to the study of crime using symbolic interactionism, ethnomethodology and conflict structuralism (see Sections 2.7, 2.8 and 2.10), believe it is a mistake for sociology to set out to solve the problems of society, for three main reasons.

First, they believe that such 'correctional' research is often forced to adopt positivistic approaches (see Section 3.1) to the study of crime. It ends up as an exercise in the measurement of criminal frequencies. More seriously, for Hester and Eglin, they believe that ultimately this type of sociology does little more than serve the state. It becomes the mouthpiece of governmental political power. They note that at the extreme this positivistic approach becomes untheoretical, dealing only with measurement and its associated issues while failing to use or explain more deep-rooted issues of cause. This becomes what Jock Young refers to as 'administrative criminology'.

Secondly, Hester and Eglin are critical of the assumptions about human nature used in so-called correctional criminology. They believe that this type of explanation fails to understand that crime, like all social action, is socially meaningful to those involved – and to those who react to it. This level of meaningful analysis is absent from most correctional criminology. Thus, humans are treated as objects or passive victims of the environment rather than creative actors.

Thirdly, Hester and Eglin suggest that correctional criminology fails to recognize that crime, like all so-called social problems, is defined by society. It is not an innate, static or objective phenomenon but the product of political, cultural and historical forces.

David Matza, in *Becoming Deviant* (1969), identifies the five key components of a 'correctional criminology' of which, like Hester and Eglin above, he is highly critical:

1 Sociological problems are all those defined as social problems within society itself. They are identical.
2 Sociological concerns should come solely from wider social concerns.
3 The purpose of sociology is to solve such wider social problems.
4 The main focus of investigation is the causes (aetiology) of criminal behaviour at the expense of a study of the process of power and ideology involved in the construction of the rules, the breaking of which defines crime.
5 The methodology is derived from positivism (see Section 3.1).

From the above critique of what we will from now on refer to as correctional criminology, a number of key issues are raised seemingly from within something approaching a Marxist and/or interactionist theoretical framework.

We can suggest that within a Marxist framework any study of crime and/or deviance must take into account the process of power involved in the creation of rules in society. Attention must be given by the sociologist to the activities of the ruling class in using laws and rules to support their activities.

Equally, from an interactionist stance, we can take the position that crime and/or deviance can only successfully be understood by seeing it as a meaningful activity created by society since rules must exist for deviation away from the rules to be possible.

The work of John Lea and Jock Young (1993), *What is to be Done about Law and Order? Crisis in the Nineties*, takes an overtly correctional approach in its study of crime known as 'New Left realism', despite being influenced by left-of-centre politics and by Marxist and interactionist sociologies, and it is far from apologetic about this stance. As Jock Young states:

Let us state quite categorically that the major task of radical criminology is to seek a solution to the problem of crime and that of a socialist policy is to substantially reduce the crime rate.

(Young, quoted in Hester and Eglin, 1996, p. 4)

Discussion point

To what extent should sociology be used as a means through which to 'change the world'?

Sociological and non-sociological theories of crime and deviance

Sociologists are not the only academics to study crime and deviance. The specific study of crime – criminology – is itself made up not just of sociological ideas, but also other non-sociological ideas.

Within criminology roughly three types of explanation for crime can be identified: sociological, psychological and physiological. Many researchers and theorists have used some sort of combination of these theories. Our interest in them, though, is only fleeting – an attempt to understand the sociological approach better through a comparison with other approaches. As a rough guide, the following distinctions can be drawn:

- **Sociological theories** locate deviance and crime as a *response to the society* in which they occur.
- **Psychological theories** locate deviance and crime *within the psyche or mind of the individual*: the product of inborn 'abnormality' or of 'faulty cognition processes'.
- **Physiological theories** locate deviance and crime *within the biological make-up of the individual*.

💬

Discussion point

To what extent do you think that criminals are 'born' or 'made'? What do sociologists believe, and what implications might this have for social policy?

A key difference between sociological and non-sociological ideas concerns the relationship of the individual to his or her environment. Whereas sociological theories tend to understand crime and deviance as a response to society or to the social environment, psychological and physiological theories tend to look towards the individuality of the criminal. The criminal is seen to have 'abnormal' or special qualities or characteristics which make them deviant/criminal.

As Hester and Eglin (1996) comment, non-sociological theories have offered a whole range of interpretations in order to explain the criminality of the individual:

- biological 'inferiority'
- chromosome abnormality
- nutritional deficiency
- extreme introversion
- extreme extroversion
- body shape
- a dominant sexual drive.

Activity

The above non-sociological explanations for criminal behaviour are listed in a random order but contain examples of both psychological and physiological thinking. Sort the list into these two categories. **U, I**

It is useful to remember that ideas very rarely become extinct. They are often dormant for periods of time, sometimes decades, only to reappear at a later time, renamed and suddenly popular once more. Sociologists are equally as guilty of 'following the crowd' or 'jumping on the bandwagon', as they are of producing original and highly imaginative theories. Although some ideas, especially those dating back in time, may appear dated or even ridiculous to the contemporary reader, many still have their modern-day expressions.

Cesare Lombroso: classical physiological theory

Writing in 1876, Italian army doctor Cesare Lombroso is considered by many to be the founder of the scientific biological school of criminology.

Lombroso's now infamous work *L'Uomo Delinquente* (1876) first developed the idea of the 'atavistic criminal'.

Atavism, a term originally used by Charles Darwin, suggests that in the process of human evolution some individuals can represent a genetic 'throwback' to a previous stage in the history of human growth. Darwin commented:

With mankind some of the worst dispositions which occasionally without any assignable cause make their appearance in families, may perhaps be reversions to a savage state, from which we are not removed by many generations.
(Darwin, quoted in Taylor *et al.*, 1973, p. 41)

Taking up this idea, Lombroso contended that the criminal individual was born so. Physical indication of criminal potential could be identified through specific bodily characteristics, all of which suggested that the bearer was a throwback to a more primitive age. These physical characteristics included abnormal teeth, extra nipples, extra or missing toes and fingers, large ears and overly prominent jaw bones.

The logical, and quite frightening, conclusions of this idea, from a social policy point of view, is that criminal types can be easily identified and therefore action can be taken against them *before* they commit crime! Since criminality, for Lombroso, was inborn, action against crime would have to involve exclusion from society, or indeed capital punishment.

Criticisms of Lombroso's position

A number of criticisms of Lombroso have been made by contemporary sociologists. Two can be summarized as follows:

- Those identified in society as criminals may be so identified owing to how they look physically, rather than their physiological characteristics actually having a causal effect.
- Although those in prison may be more typical of a specific physical 'type', it may be that this is the effect of social or environmental factors – such as diet, access to fitness – and therefore associated with class and occupation (manual work) and subculture, rather than with a biological predisposition towards criminality.

Hans Eysenck: psychological theory

A well-known author who has adopted the 'psychological' approach to studying crime and deviance is Hans Eysenck (1970). In his work *Crime and Personality*, Eysenck attempts to correlate – or, to demonstrate a link between – criminal behaviour and the 'personality type' of the individual. Eysenck claims that criminality is the result of genetic and largely inherited predisposition: some individuals are more likely to become criminals given the sort of person they are. In adopting what he would see as a scientific or positivistic approach, Eysenck claims that tests conducted in prison on inmates indicate that prisons have more extroverts amongst their populations than the population does at large. Therefore, he asserts, extroversion is the inherited psychological basis of criminality.

Eysenck claims that extroverts are more likely, given their genetic make-up, to be under-socialized, and therefore to lack the internalization of norms and values which guide the rest of the population. He draws very specific differences between the two personality types of introversion and extroversion, suggesting that all human personality types exist along a continuum somewhere between these two points. At the extremes of this continuum:

The typical extrovert ... craves excitement, takes chances, acts on the spur of the moment, and is generally an impulsive individual ... He prefers to keep moving and doing things, tends to be aggressive and loses his temper quickly; his feelings are not kept under tight control and he is not always a reliable person.
(Eysenck, quoted in Taylor *et al.*, 1973, pp. 56–7)

It is interesting to note that some of the above characteristics are remarkably similar to modern-day definitions of hyperactivity and attention deficit disorder (ADD). On the other hand:

The typical introvert is a quiet, retiring sort of person, introspective, fond of books rather than people: he is reserved and reticent except with intimate friends ... He does not like excitement, takes matters of everyday life with proper seriousness, and likes a well-ordered mode of life. He keeps his feelings under close control, seldom behaves in an aggressive manner, and does not lose his temper easily.
(Eysenck, quoted in Taylor *et al.*, 1973, p. 57)

Criticisms of Eysenck's position

A number of sociologists, especially Ian Taylor, Paul Walton and Jock Young (1973) have taken issue with the ideas of Eysenck on both methodological and theoretical grounds. These criticisms can be summarized as follows:

- Research in prison on inmates is not necessarily the same thing as research on all criminals in general. Many criminals are not caught, or are not imprisoned, and some people who are innocent are wrongly imprisoned.
- Perhaps Eysenck is measuring the effects of imprisonment on the personality, and not the characteristics which led to imprisonment.

- Those who have the characteristics identified as being 'extrovert' by Eysenck, although not committing more crime than introverts, may be stopped by the police, arrested and sentenced more because their behaviour is of a more 'obvious' nature.
- Some commentators, such as Walter B. Miller (in Downes and Rock, 1995) have associated 'immediate pleasure seeking behaviour' with working-class subcultural values. It may well be the case, as argued by Box (1981, 1995) that the working classes are more likely to be arrested and imprisoned owing to stereotypes which operate amongst the courts and police concerning what a 'typical criminal' is like.

Modern physiological and psychological theories

There have been a number of recent science-based research programmes into the biological and psychological sources of criminal and other antisocial behavioural characteristics (Moir and Jessel, 1995). These research programmes, mainly funded within American and British university departments, seek to find a medical cure for crime, based on the assumption (shared with Eysenck) that criminality can be treated biologically. These medical-based modern explanations for criminality include:

- various mental health explanations, such as schizophrenia
- the existence of a medical condition described as 'episodic dyscontrol': a condition similar to an epilepsy type 'explosion' in areas of the brain
- a dramatic inactivity of brain functions in the prefrontal area of the brain, the areas usually associated with making plans and strategies
- explanations based on a version of hyperactivity – or as it is sometimes called, hyperkinesis.

Stanley Cohen: a sociological criticism of medical models

Cohen (1977) is highly critical of the types of explanation for criminality offered by non-sociological sources. In particular, he is suspicious of those theories based on a medical model of the criminal – the suggestion that criminals, or deviants in general, are 'pathological', 'ill' or 'sick', and that they therefore require 'help' or 'treatment'.

Cohen suggests that such approaches, while appearing to be based on a desire to 'care for' or 'help' and 'rehabilitate' the individual, are actually based on strong and powerful mechanisms of social control, and are often the justifications given by the state for repressive activity against so-called deviant minorities: individuals or groups which have the potential to embarrass the state unless hidden, controlled or condemned.

Cohen advocates a 'sceptical' stance, a left-of-centre, Marxist and interactionist influenced approach. Within this sceptical approach, what Cohen terms 'official criminology', or psychological and/or medical models of criminality, are to be mistrusted. They support the state and highlight the differences between the normal and the abnormal. They fail to discuss the vital question, *normal according to whose definition?*

Sociology and common sense

Cohen goes further and suggests that the medical/psychological models of criminality fit easily within society's commonsense understandings of deviance. Over time, through the mass media in particular, the ideas associated with these theories – ideas such as criminality representing sickness, mental ill-health, a response to disturbing childhood experiences etc. – have become part of the lay person's or public's frame of reference:

. . . the layman's understanding of deviance is based on the more visible types that are classified and presented to him every day. Pressed to explain the fact of deviation, he will probably redirect the question by talking about the type of person the deviant is thought to be: brutal, immature, irresponsible, vicious, inconsiderate, degenerate. These labels are the traditional ones of sin and immorality on to which newer concepts have been uneasily grafted following the increase in prestige and credibility given to psychiatrically derived vocabularies. Thus the sexual offender is not degenerate but sick: he has a 'kink', a 'warped mentality', or a 'twisted mind'. These labels are comfortable ways of looking at things, because they leave us with the satisfaction of knowing that the problem is somewhere out there. The fault lies in the individual's genetic composition, his mind, his family, his friends, or society as a whole.

(Cohen, 1977, pp. 10–11)

Discussion point

Why is sociology so critical of 'commonsense' thought? What makes sociology a better way of viewing the world?

Some commonsense, non-sociological theories on crime, however, do mirror quite closely the ideas of sociologists. Although lacking in the key characteristics of a sociological approach (namely, research and a theoretical perspective), the public sometimes – and politicians often – come close when discussing the social causes of crime. For example, as Tony Blair, when he was Shadow Home Secretary in 1993, commented:

Any sensible society acting in its own interests as well as those of its citizens will understand and recognise that poor education and housing, inadequate or cruel family backgrounds, low employment prospects and drug abuse will affect the likelihood of young people turning to crime. If they are placed outside mainstream culture, offered no hope or opportunity, shown no respect by others, and unable to develop respect for themselves, there is a greater chance of their going wrong.

(Quoted in *New Statesman and Society*, 1993, p. 5)

Activity

Use the quotations above from Tony Blair and Stanley Cohen to answer the following questions:

a What are the causes of crime identified by Blair?

b Which of the points identified by Blair are sociological and which are psychological?

c Can you think of any other sources of criminality in the modern world? Explain your examples.

d Referring to Stanley Cohen's quotation, why might it be a source of 'comfort' for the public to identify the sources of criminality to be 'somewhere out there'?

e Why might the same be said for governments?

I, A

11.2 Measurements of and research into crime and deviance

Of great concern in the literature associated with the sociology of crime and deviance is the validity of criminal statistics. Whereas some, especially those involved in aspects of social policy creation, view criminal statistics as a good indication of the nature of crime and criminal behaviour in society, others are more critical. Most sociologists, however, believe criminal statistics to be of value, but for some, the value of statistics lies in the opportunity it presents to demonstrate how unrealistic and fabricated such statistics actually are. The issue of the usefulness of official statistics more generally is discussed in Section 3.11.

The contemporary pattern of crime

According to Reiner (1996), a brief survey of current crime figures points to a number of clearly identifiable patterns:

- Between the two world wars the level of crime, according to the statistics, remained relatively constant.
- *Recorded* crime has increased sharply since then. In 1950, for example, 500,000 crimes were recorded, a figure that rose to 5.7 million in 1993.
- During the 1980s the recorded crime figure doubled.
- The 1994 and 1995 crime statistics illustrate a 6 per cent fall in recorded crime.

As Reiner asserts:

In the last 40 years, we have got used to thinking of crime, like the weather and pop music, as something that is always getting worse.
(Reiner, 1996, p. 3)

Recorded crime – key points

- 5.3 million notifiable offences were recorded by the police in 1994, a fall of 5 per cent or 268,000 over 1993.
- 4.9 million or 93 per cent of these offences were against property (including burglary, theft, criminal damage and fraud).
- Vehicle crime fell by 10 per cent to 1.4 million in 1994, the largest percentage fall for at least 40 years.
- Burglary fell by 8 per cent to 1.3 million in 1994, incorporating a 7 per cent decrease in domestic burglaries.
- Violent crime (i.e. violence against the person, sexual offences and robbery) rose by 6 per cent in 1994, the 312,000 offences accounting for 6 per cent of all offences.
- Within violent crime, robberies rose by 3 per cent, the smallest increase for six years; offences of violence against the person and sexual offences were up by 7 per cent and 2 per cent respectively.
- Recorded crime fell in all but four police force areas, with all eight of the metropolitan forces recording falls.

Source: *Criminal Statistics, England and Wales, 1994* (HMSO) (published 1995)

The common-sense and media-hyped picture of criminal statistics is often found unsatisfactory by sociologists. The key to the sociological criticism of official crime statistics is based on the inadequacies of a measurement of crime based on 'recorded' levels. Clearly not all crime is discovered, and not all

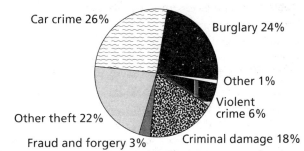

Figure 11.1 Notifiable offences recorded by the police by type of offence in 1994, in England and Wales. Source: *Criminal Statistics, England and Wales, 1994* (HMSO) (published 1995)

Activity

From the statistics provided in Figure 11.1 and Table 11.1, and the box 'Recorded crime – key points', describe the trends they show concerning the nature of crime in contemporary social life.

crime is recorded. This is a key point we will return to later.

The historical dimension of 'social problems'

Although some sections of the mass media, and some statistics on crime, would have us believe that contemporary society is characterized by a rise in the frequency and violent nature of crime, it must be remembered that deviance is a feature of every society and crimes of this nature have always existed.

Politicians, especially those of the Right who are traditionally 'strong' on law-and-order policies, have with great relish debated the so-called rising crime 'problem', trading media-friendly sound-bite politics. As Sir Keith Joseph warned in 1977:

For the first time in a century and a half, since the great Tory reformer Robert Peel set up the Metropolitan Police, areas of our cities are becoming unsafe for peaceful citizens by night, and some even by day.
(Quoted in Pearson, 1983, pp. 4–5).

In a similar vein, also in 1977, the Chief Constable of Merseyside proclaimed:

. . . the freedom and way of life we have been accustomed to enjoy for so long will vanish . . . what we are experiencing is not a passing phenomenon but a continuing process of change in our way of life . . . our customary ways of behaving and our traditional values are being radically modified.
(Quoted in Pearson, 1983, p. 5)

Table 11.1 Crimes recorded by the police[1]

Country	1990	1991	1992	1993	1994	1987 –93	1987 –94	1993 –94
						Percentage increases		
England and Wales	4 543 600	5 276 200	5 591 700	5 526 300	5 258 100	42	35	–5
Northern Ireland	57 198	63 492	67 532	66 228	67 886	4	6	3
Scotland	535 864	592 774	589 562	543 013	527 064	13	10	–3
Republic of Ireland	87 658	94 406	95 391	98 979	101 036	16	18	2
France	3 492 712	3 744 112	3 830 996	3 881 894	3 919 008	22	24	1
Belgium	353 492	382 667	386 474	388 150	577 902 [2]	32	-	-
Germany	4 455 333	5 302 796 [3]	6 291 519 [3]	6 750 613 [3]	6 537 748 [3]	-	16 [4]	–3
Austria	457 623	468 832	502 440	493 786	-	26	-	-
Netherlands	1 052 510	1 083 730	1 168 490	1 173 643	1 202 482	13	15	2
Norway	235 256	223 122	234 992	248 001	225 059	25	13	–4
Sweden	1 076 289	1 045 306	1 051 770	1 031 015	975 690	9	3	–5
Denmark	527 421	519 775	563 821	546 894	546 926	4	4	0
Finland	438 094	391 940	393 109	385 985	383 351	22	21	–1
Portugal [5]	-	-	-	307 328	330 010	-	-	7
Italy	2 501 640	2 647 735	2 390 539	2 253 503	2 173 448	21	16	–4
Greece	330 803	358 998	379 652	358 503	303 311	18	0	–15
USA [6]	14 756 000	14 873 000	14 438 200	14 141 000	-	5	-	-
Canada	2 627 193	2 899 988	2 847 981	2 736 626	2 633 830	15	11	–4
Japan	1 636 628	1 707 877	1 742 366	1 801 150	-	14	-	-
Australia [7]	1 149 478	1 274 893	1 273 948	-	-	-	-	-
New Zealand	449 479	484 507	499 033	502 460	488 533	24	20	–3

1 More serious offences; in many countries defined as against the 'penal code' or 'criminal code' and excludes less serious crimes (misdemeanours); the range of offences covered differs between each country and comparisons based upon absolute figures are therefore misleading. Source: Mainly statistical contact points in each country; such data are not all readily available in published documents
2 Belgium introduced a new method of data collection in 1994; comparisons with earlier years are therefore not possible
3 Includes former East Germany in 1992 and 1993 but part of East Germany in 1991
4 Comparison based upon West Germany only
5 Portugal introduced a new unified collection system in 1993 covering their three police forces; comparisons with earlier years are not possible
6 FBI Uniform Crime Index covering murder and non-negligent manslaughter, manslaughter by negligence, forcible rape, robbery, aggravated assault, burglary, larceny – theft of motor vehicles and theft, but excludes offences such as drugs, included in other countries' figures
7 Data for financial years 1992 = 1991/92 etc.

Source: *Criminal Statistics, England and Wales, 1994* (HMSO) (published 1995)

Violent crime: an old or new fear?

What these fears illustrate, according to Pearson (1983), is the temptation for each generation, especially those of the post-middle-age bracket, to look back through rose-tinted glasses and with nostalgia at the past: to see society before the present 'unruly age' to be a 'golden age' where all was at peace and harmony reigned.

When viewed in this fashion, current trends in criminal statistics immediately take on new possibilities and interpretations. Do they represent not so much a genuine increase in the amount of crime, but rather the increased reporting and awareness of crime – the result of fear, reflected in and reinforced by the media, of the contemporary age?

Drawing on a wide variety of sources, social historians Hay *et al.* (1988), in their work *Albion's Fatal Tree*, go to great lengths to illustrate the violent and dangerous nature of the past – in particular the eighteenth century in England. They point to a whole range of crimes and criminal activity widespread in those times, including smuggling, street robbery, highway robbery, wood theft, poaching, anonymous and threatening letter-writing, forgery, arson and, of course, murder. This explanation suggests that crime did not experience a dramatic increase since the eighteenth century, but the creation of the law, run in favour of a ruling élite for the protection of their property, criminalized the actions of the poor – actions which had always existed.

Moral panics and hooliganism

In looking at moral panics closer to our own times, Pearson comments that modern-day fears of football hooliganism are nothing new, and in fact date back to at least the mid-nineteenth century. Pitch invasions, attacks on referees and players and conflicts between rival fans were a regular feature in local newspapers of the time.

A REMEDY FOR RUFFIANS
Hooligan. 'What are you up to, Guv'nor!'
Policeman. 'I'm going to introduce you to the 'harmless, necessary Cat"!'
Source: *Punch*, 10 September 1898. (Pearson, G., 1983, p. 78)

Pearson dates the word 'hooligan' back to the summer of 1898 (as illustrated by the pen and ink drawing from *Punch* that year), when it was used in newspaper headlines to describe the activities of youths during the August Bank Holiday. Pearson suggests that the word may have been first popularized within the music halls in the 1890s. He cites the music hall song below, introduced by Irish comedians O'Conner & Brady in 1890, to demonstrate that the word 'hooligan' was popular in comedy routine songs of the period:

> *'Oh, the Hooligans! Oh, the Hooligans!*
> *Always on the riot*
> *Cannot keep them quiet*
> *Oh, the Hooligans! Oh, the Hooligans!*
> *They are the boys*
> *To make a noise*
> *In our backyard.'*

A similar line of argument to Pearson's is provided by Stanley Cohen (1980). He suggests that:

More moral panics will be generated and other, as yet nameless folk devils will be created. This is not because such developments have an inexorable logic, but because our society as present structured will continue to generate problems for some of its members – like working-class adolescents – and then condemn whatever solution these groups find.
(Cohen, 1980, p. i)

Recorded and unrecorded crime

The reason why official crime statistics are potentially so invalid is due, claim many commentators, to the problems of recording crime. Official governmental and police records – recorded by and for the Home Office – represent only those crimes known to the police. Given their nature, there is no way they could do anything else. It is, however, ridiculous to claim that all crimes committed in society are known to the police. It is worth noting that the police only have access to three, interrelated sets of figures:

* crimes detected
* crimes reported
* criminals apprehended (crimes solved).

Box (1995, 1981) from a Marxist perspective, and Heidensohn (1989) from a feminist perspective, amongst others, have commented on the reasons why many crimes go unreported. To summarize:

1 The public may fear the consequences from the criminals themselves if they turn to the police.
2 The public may fear the police themselves, or may not believe that the crime will be solved: 'there may be nothing the police can do' might be the stance taken by members of working-class communities.
3 In cases such as rape, sexual assault or domestic violence the victim may feel embarrassed, or fear that the police may not treat them with sensitivity.
4 In some close-knit communities, there may be a tendency to deal with criminality within the community, by the community and not to involve the police.
5 Some crimes may be seen as too trivial to report.
6 Some victims may not even be aware they are a victim. This is especially true in fraud cases.

The 'hidden figure' of crime

The recorded figure of crime does not by any means cover all crimes committed. This has massive impli-

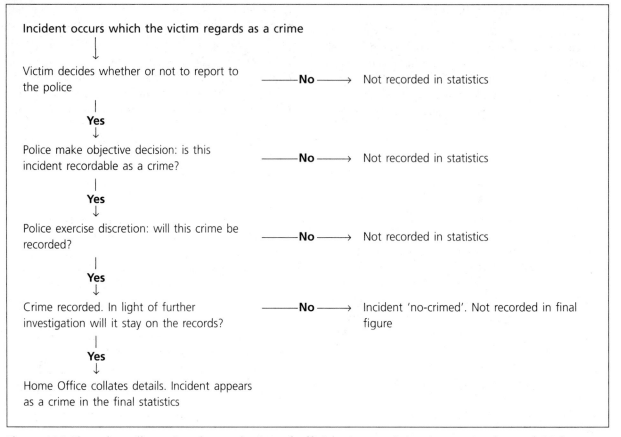

Incident occurs which the victim regards as a crime
↓

Victim decides whether or not to report to the police ————**No**———→ Not recorded in statistics
|
Yes
↓

Police make objective decision: is this incident recordable as a crime? ————**No**———→ Not recorded in statistics
|
Yes
↓

Police exercise discretion: will this crime be recorded? ————**No**———→ Not recorded in statistics
|
Yes
↓

Crime recorded. In light of further investigation will it stay on the records? ————**No**———→ Incident 'no-crimed'. Not recorded in final figure
|
Yes
↓

Home Office collates details. Incident appears as a crime in the final statistics

Figure 11.2 Flow chart illustrating the production of official crime statistics. Source: Sanderson (1994)

Activity

Using the 'flow chart' in Figure 11.2, write a description of the process through which official crime statistics are created. Then address the following question: 'How can the construction of official crime statistics be open to the interpretation of various different groups?'

I, A

cations for the usefulness of official criminal statistics: if they do not give a valid figure, then what use are they? Many would claim that they tell us more about the construction of crime statistics than about the rate of crimes.

We can best understand the problems and limitations of official crime figures with reference to Figure 11.3, which is based on an estimate (see below) that some 70 per cent of all criminal activity goes unrecorded. The 30 per cent of crime recorded is 'just the tip of the iceberg': it is visible, but more important is the undisclosed or hidden figure. This can have profound implications for the crime rates for any particular year, because an increase in recorded crime may not represent a real increase in the rate or total of all crime – it may well be that

people are reporting more. Equally, a decline in the crime rate may not indicate that less crime is occurring, but that instead much less crime is reported and recorded.

As Figure 11.4 illustrates, official crime statistics are further made problematic by the fact that crime, by its very nature, is often secretive. Thus, although offences are recorded, not all offences are solved: without knowing who committed a particular crime,

Discussion point

Are official statistics as valid as they are presented? How can sociologists use them, if they do not show the whole picture?

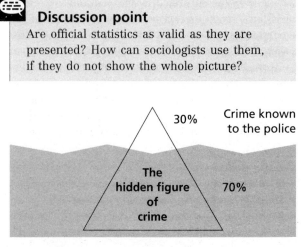

Crime known to the police — 30%

The hidden figure of crime — 70%

Figure 11.3 The 'hidden figure' of crime

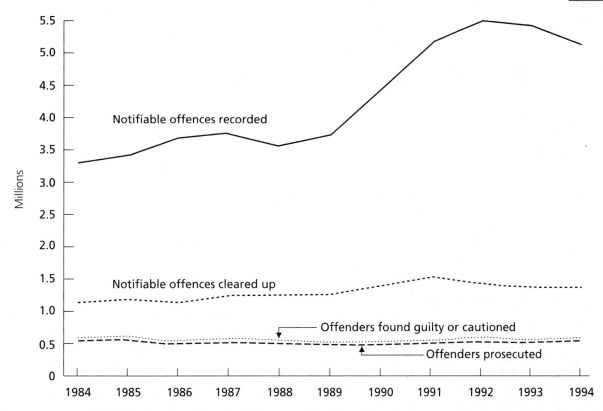

Figure 11.4 Recorded crime, prosecutions and 'known' offenders, 1984–94. Source: *Criminal Statistics, England and Wales, 1994* (HMSO) (published 1995)

it is very difficult to begin to make assumptions about 'types' of criminals and the crimes they may or may not commit.

Moral panics and official statistics

Moral panics (see also Section 15.5) and police initiatives can have a dramatic effect on the crime rate. By exaggerating a particular issue the public may be led to report it more, out of an increased but artificial or unrealistic sense of concern. Thus, the rate increases and governments and the police may well respond to such an increase in order to be 'seen to tackle the problem' in the eyes of the public. Further police attention may lead to more arrests and once more, the crime rate rises! This process is known as 'deviance amplification' (see Figure 11.5).

The British Crime Surveys

The British Crime Surveys of 1981, 1985, 1988 and 1993, produced by the Home Office, were an attempt to get at the hidden figure of crime. They found that official measurements grossly under-represented the 'real' nature of the frequency of crime. It is estimated that only about 30 per cent (just under one-third) of all crimes were reported and therefore recorded.

Of those crimes that *are* recorded, not all are solved or 'cleared up'. Equally, not all crimes are met with the same penalty, nor put on trial in the same fashion: not all crimes 'cleared up' will be seen to have been done so by the public.

As Jenkins (1991) comments, problems with the 'clear up' of crimes provide governments with huge problems – especially considering that the Conservatives originally came to power in 1979 suggesting:

. . . the number of crimes in England and Wales is nearly half as much again as it was in 1973 . . . the next Conservative government will spend more on fighting crime even while we economise elsewhere.

(Quoted in Jenkins, 1991, p. 17)

The other major finding of the British Crime Surveys was that the crimes feared the most – usually rape, assault etc. – were over-represented in the official figures. There is obviously more of a tendency to report this type of crime, given its serious nature.

The British Crime Surveys are based on a research strategy known as the 'victimization survey'. Rather than focus on crimes known to the police, instead the emphasis is given to crimes known to the victim. In a relatively simple fashion, members of the public are asked to list crimes they have been the victim of in a given time period. This technique is particularly effective in getting at the 'hidden figure' since it does not rely on the public to report crime, nor does it accept official measurements uncritically.

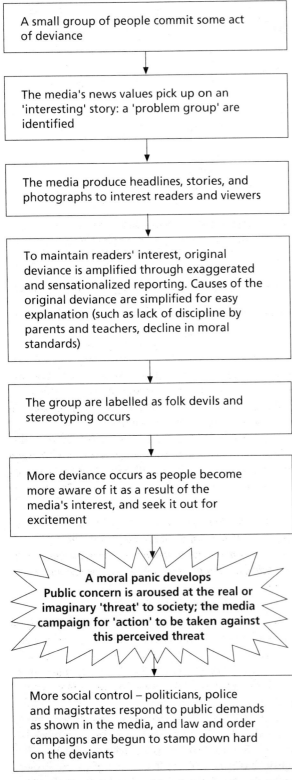

A small group of people commit some act of deviance

The media's news values pick up on an 'interesting' story: a 'problem group' are identified

The media produce headlines, stories, and photographs to interest readers and viewers

To maintain readers' interest, original deviance is amplified through exaggerated and sensationalized reporting. Causes of the original deviance are simplified for easy explanation (such as lack of discipline by parents and teachers, decline in moral standards)

The group are labelled as folk devils and stereotyping occurs

More deviance occurs as people become more aware of it as a result of the media's interest, and seek it out for excitement

A moral panic develops
Public concern is aroused at the real or imaginary 'threat' to society; the media campaign for 'action' to be taken against this perceived threat

More social control – politicians, police and magistrates respond to public demands as shown in the media, and law and order campaigns are begun to stamp down hard on the deviants

Figure 11.5 Deviancy amplification, moral panics, and the media. Source: Browne (1992)

The major drawback of victimization studies is that they miss recording those crimes regarded as 'victimless' crimes by respondents. Crimes such as drug selling/taking and vandalism against unowned/public property are known as victimless. Who, for example, is the victim and in some cases is it possible to separate the victim from the criminal? Are not the drugs pusher and taker both criminals, and equally as unlikely to report the crime to either the police or a researcher?

Activity
Create a list of other examples of 'victimless crime'.

A

Self-report studies

Another technique open to sociologists keen to uncover the hidden figure of crime is self-report studies (see the example in Figure 11.6). These work in much the same way as victimization studies but ask the respondents to admit, quite literally, to crimes they have committed within a given time period. Such studies tend to be slightly invalid: working-class youths, for example, may exaggerate in order to gain prestige within their peer group, whereas others may not trust the researcher and so lie.

The political nature of the crime debate

'Law and order' has always been a traditional vote-winner in British politics. Every year, and in particular at every election campaign, we hear from politicians that they wish to be 'tough on law and order', or that they will 'win the fight for law and order'. At these moments in the political calendar, the official crime figures are used by all sides to 'prove' that they have the most successful policies on crime, and that everyone else has failed the British public. These debates are often based on competing definitions and interpretations of the official figures, conveniently ignoring the limitations discussed above.

For example, the 1995 figures (Travis, 1996a) showed a 10 per cent fall in recorded crime since the 1993 measurement. The Home Office responded with the claim that the government was 'turning the tide in the fight against crime' – a claim difficult to disprove, but equally difficult to substantiate given the fundamental problems with the official figures as outlined above. It is interesting to note that whereas the Conservative government hailed a success in the falling rate of crime, the Labour Party pointed out that, within the overall decline in reported and recorded crime, street robberies had apparently

Acts of delinquency

1 I have ridden a bicycle without lights after dark.

2 I have driven a car or motor bike/scooter under 16.

3 I have been with a group who go round together making a row and sometimes getting into fights and causing disturbance.

4 I have played truant from school.

5 I have travelled on a train or bus without a ticket or deliberately paid the wrong fare.

6 I have let off fireworks in the street.

7 I have taken money from home without returning it.

8 I have taken someone else's car or motor bike for a joy ride then taken it back afterwards.

9 I have broken or smashed things in public places like on the streets, cinemas, dance halls, trains or buses.

10 I have insulted people on the street or got them angry and fought with them.

11 I have broken into a big store or garage or warehouse.

12 I have broken into a little shop even though I may not have taken anything.

13 I have taken something out of a car.

14 I have taken a weapon (like a knife) out with me in case I needed it in a fight.

15 I have fought with someone in a public place like in the street or a dance.

16 I have broken the window of an empty house.

17 I have used a weapon in a fight, like a knife or a razor or a broken bottle.

18 I have drunk alcoholic drinks in a pub under 18.

19 I have been in a pub when I was under 16.

20 I have taken things from big stores or supermarkets when the shop was open.

21 I have taken things from little shops when the shop was open.

22 I have dropped things in the street like litter or broken bottles.

Acts of delinquency

23 I have bought something cheap or accepted as a present something I knew was stolen.

24 I have planned well in advance to get into a house to take things.

25 I have got into a house and taken things even thought I didn't plan it in advance.

26 I have taken a bicycle belonging to someone else and kept it.

27 I have struggled or fought to get away from a policeman.

28 I have struggled or fought with a policeman who was trying to arrest someone.

29 I have stolen school property worth more than about 5p.

30 I have stolen goods from someone I worked for worth more than about 5p.

31 I have had sex with a boy when I was under 16.

32 I have trespassed somewhere I was not supposed to go, like empty houses, railway lines or private gardens.

33 I have been to an '18' film under age.

34 I have spent money on gambling under 16.

35 I have smoked cigarettes under 15.

36 I have had sex with someone for money.

37 I have taken money from slot machines or telephones.

38 I have taken money from someone's clothes hanging up somewhere.

39 I have got money from someone by pretending to be someone else or lying about why I needed it.

40 I have taken someone's clothes hanging up somewhere.

41 I have smoked dope or taken pills (LSD, mandies, sleepers).

42 I have got money/drink/cigarettes by saying I would have sex with someone even though I didn't.

43 I have run away from home.

Figure 11.6 Example of a self-report study. Source: Campbell, 1981 (in Browne, 1992)

Activity

Consider applying the survey in Figure 11.6 to yourself. What are the problems of some of the questions asked? How might these problems be overcome? Originally this questionnaire was applied to girls, so what changes might have to be made for it to be totally suitable for boys?

I, A, E

risen by 14 per cent and violent crime by 2 per cent since the previous year.

Reiner (1996) suggests that the decline in the official statistics was largely a recording phenomenon: whereas victimization studies still suggest that crime is continuing to rise, many people are reluctant to report all crimes they have experienced. Although we would expect property crime to be reported the most (because insurance companies demand that all claimants report their experience to the police), Reiner suggests that the reverse is happening:

The decline in victim reporting is linked to fears about the consequences for household and other insurance cover. In high crime areas there is a real concern about losing insurance cover or at least facing stiffer conditions and/or higher premiums for re-insurance if too many crimes are reported.
(Reiner, 1996, p. 4)

It has become increasingly difficult to attempt to analyse in any meaningful way what the official statistics show. It has been suggested by some commentators that official statistics are interesting from a sociological point of view, but only for providing us with an understanding of the social and political processes involved in their construction – not as an absolute or 'real' measurement.

Activity

Write about 500 words to explain how interactionists (see Section 11.5) would view the nature and usefulness of official crime statistics. What criticisms might be made of the interactionist view?

U, A, E

We must remember that crime does not occur in a 'social vacuum' but is an everyday reality, especially for the urban working classes. The committing, reporting, policing and recording of such crimes represent major social actions and interactions.

Crimes of the rich and powerful

Other criminal activities that are often missed by official and many sociological measurements of crime are those conducted by the powerful in society (Frank Pearce, 1976). A distinction can be drawn between:

- *crimes of the powerful* – largely those committed by ruling groups, élites and governments
- *white-collar crime* – crimes committed by professional people, such as tax evasion, business fraud, industrial espionage, insider-trading
- *corporate crime* – crimes committed not so much by individuals but rather by boards, chairpersons etc., including the breaking of the Health and Safety at Work Act.

As Steven Box (1995) comments:

. . . it might be prudent to compare persons who commit other serious but under-emphasized crimes and victimizing behaviour with those who are officially portrayed as 'our' criminal enemies. For if the former, compared to the latter, are indeed quite different types of people, then maybe we should stop looking to our political authorities and criminal justice system for protection from those beneath us in impoverished urban neighbourhoods. Instead maybe we should look up accusingly at our political and judicial 'superiors' for being or for protecting the 'real' culprits.
(Box, 1995, p. 3)

This view by Box (and shared by Pearce) that the 'real' criminals are those who make and even enforce the rules is a good example of a Marxist critique of official definitions and measurements of crime. Whereas, under capitalism, working-class criminality is emphasized and working-class activities and localities policed on a regular basis, others are ignored and allowed therefore to continue in their criminal ways. For Marxism, the real issue is not whether the crime rate is high or low, real or unreal, but why some actions and groups are over-represented by official measurements.

Box adds a fourth category to the 'crimes of the powerful', that of police crime. He suggests that 'beating-up' suspects, arresting the innocent, intimidation, blackmail, bribery, fabricating and ignoring evidence are all routine in the 'dirty business' that is the reality of law enforcement. It is, however, difficult to substantiate this claim. As Box recognizes, although it is common sense that all these activities exist in higher numbers than the odd 'bad apple' exposed by the media on an infrequent basis, proving this through evidence is a different matter.

Case studies of the powerful in society and the criminal world

1 Politicians and the Mafia

In 1994, Italian society was shaken by revelations of links between top political leaders and the Mafia. Alexander Stille's (1997) book on the subject reveals the intricacies of the links. The leader of the right-wing Christian Democrats and three times Italian Prime Minister Giulio Andreotti was alleged to have regularly used top Mafia links to remain in power. He was alleged to have attended conferences with Salvatore Riina, a top Mafia boss whose contact in Palermo was Salvatore Lima, a former mayor of the city and a finance minister in Andreotti's government despite numerous mentions in an anti-Mafia commission. In what appeared to be a warning to top political contacts to respect the Mafia code of 'omerta' or silence, Lima was murdered in March 1992. It is also suggested that certain journalists critical of the Christian Democrats were removed from the scene. In return, it is alleged, the Mafia benefited from numerous government contracts through front companies. Stille points to £50 billion in extraordinary aid between 1986 and 1990 which seemingly disappeared into projects without any apparent benefit to the local population.

2 Police accused of 'dirty tricks' war on BA passenger

In 1994, various newspapers carried articles recounting the bizarre events surrounding accusations of police 'dirty tricks'.

A file on allegations that Metropolitan Police officers at Heathrow took part in a sustained 'dirty tricks' campaign against a British Airways shareholder who made a complaint against the company is to be sent to the Crown Prosecution Service.

Scotland Yard said results of the police complaints unit investigation were being sent to the CPS and the Police Complaints Authority. BA also confirmed that it had handed Scotland Yard its internal files on allegations by John Gorman, 37, a former police officer, that he was the victim of a sustained campaign of 'dirty tricks' following his complaint. Mr Gorman told BBC's *Newsnight* programme that on a BA flight from London to New York in January last year he swallowed broken glass in an in-flight drink.

Staff on the aircraft apologized, but when, after having expensive medical treatment for the injuries caused by the glass, he sought compensation, BA accused him of being a 'Virgin stooge'. Mr Gorman took this to be a reference to the airline's battle with Richard Branson's Virgin Airlines over alleged 'dirty tricks' but he says he has never had any involvement with Virgin.

Three months after Mr Gorman lodged his claim, seven officers from Heathrow police station, accompanied by a senior BA investigator, raided his home and arrested him for 'conspiracy to defraud British Airways'.

Mr Gorman alleges that he was subsequently subjected to a vicious campaign of 'dirty tricks' involving hate mail, telephone threats and an attack by two men who burst into his home. They sprayed him with gas, banged his head against the wall and said: 'This is what you get when you mess with British Airways.' They also took documents referring to the compensation claim which were subsequently returned to Mr Gorman by a BA lawyer who said he was unaware they were stolen. Some of the telephone threats, including one in which the caller said: 'We'll get you next time', were allegedly traced by BT to British Airways' Heathrow offices. Another, in which Mr Gorman was told: 'Any morning now, nice and early, we are going to arrest you' was allegedly traced to Heathrow police station.

Mr Gorman, a former member of the Metropolitan Police anti-terrorist branch, was forced to retire after the Brighton bombing because of the effects of asbestos he inhaled while digging victims out of the rubble. He now lives on his police pension and disability allowance.

A statement from British Airways said: 'The John Gorman matter is in the hands of the police with whom British Airways has co-operated fully from the beginning. Neither the police nor British Airways has been able to determine who may have been responsible for any of the acts about which Mr Gorman complained. Those matters are the subject of continuing police investigations. British Airways has made available to the police all the information it has regarding Mr Gorman's allegations. We take them very seriously.'

Source: Michael Smith, *Daily Telegraph*, 31 August 1994

Activity

Suggest which of the categories devised by Frank Pearce and Steven Box (outlined above) the two case study examples above – relating to allegations about criminal behaviour – might fit.

I, A

The future: recent social policy

It could be argued that government policy is now concerned less with the ultimate solution to crime – if such a thing actually exists – and more with what is called 'target-hardening' (Reiner, 1996). By this is meant that anyone likely to be a potential victim of crime – individuals, families, companies, local councils – must undertake better crime-prevention measures. We are asked to move crime away, by making ourselves more of a hard target. Reiner describes this as a 'burgle my neighbour' approach – criminals are moved on to 'softer' targets.

Right realism

The policy of 'target-hardening' amongst the New Right is referred to in the sociological literature as 'Right realism'. This can be seen as an alternative claim to that of Lea and Young's 'New Left realism' already described above. 'Right realism' points the finger of responsibility at the individual: if you are the victim of crime, it says, you may well have yourself to blame.

Crime and the free-market economy

Reiner (1996) sees the increase in the recorded crime rate in contemporary times as representing a real increase in the amount of crime present in today's society. He explains this rise of crime by reference to 'socio-economic factors'. Thus:

- To explain the rise of crime after the Second World War, we need to understand that increased affluence in society from the 1950s onwards has created more opportunity for crime because we own much more property.
- Since the 1950s a cultural change has taken place with regard to the young's deference to authority. It is no longer true to say that acceptance of authority is automatic.
- The establishment of a society based on a free-market economy has created a greedy and selfish society. Poverty and the establishment of an 'underclass' has widened the gap between the rich and the poor. (See also Sections 4.8 and 14.8.)

11.3 **The functionalist analysis of crime and deviance**

Sociologists' concern with the study of deviance, like many other ideas, issues and concepts, can be traced back to the thinking of Durkheim. But perhaps now we should ask whether a functionalist analysis is still of value to sociologists. (More detail on Durkheim and functionalism in general terms can be found in Sections 2.3 and 2.4.) As Downes and Rock (1995) note:

At times, a package deal is presented in which functionalism, positivism, empiricism, evolutionalism, and determinism are collectively linked with a 'consensus' approach to social problems and a conservative approach to their solution.
(Downes and Rock, 1995, p. 90)

In other words much functionalist sociology has been found wanting in its explanations of society in recent years. It has become a 'routine conceptual folly for students to demolish before moving on to more rewarding ground', to use the words of Downes and Rock once more.

Yet despite this trend towards 'functionalist bashing', its role in the history of sociological thought is firmly secured. Equally, its linkage with modern liberal- and conservative-based approaches such as neo-functionalism and the New Right means that its history and heritage is still of relevance to the contemporary sociology syllabus.

Discussion point
How would sociology be 'worse off' without functionalism?

Unlike other major theoretical perspectives such as Marxism, interactionism and feminism, no specific 'functionalist criminology' exists to speak of, with its own individual interpretations of crime statistics, the source of criminality and potential policy solutions. Rather, functionalism takes a passing look at the issue of deviance in general, rather than crime in particular, while in the process trying to explain whole social trends and patterns. The explanation of deviance is vital to this macro analysis but it does not contain the seeds of a 'break-off' into the distinctive field of criminology in its own right. According to Downes and Rock:

Being peripheral and ad hoc, [modern-day] *functionalist criminology may be represented as a somewhat piecemeal accumulation of arguments. It is*

not integrated, organized or coherent, and it has not been the subject of lengthy debate. Others may have criticised what it has done, but those who have been attacked have not usually turned round to amend, defend or clarify their work.
(Downes and Rock, 1995, p. 97)

While functionalist criminology, especially in contemporary times, does not have a large, organized or particularly popular voice, this is not to say that within the work of Durkheim the concept of deviance has been ignored. Far from it. Equally, this is not to say that functionalist analyses have not informed and shaped the development of non-functionalist perspectives within criminology since the idea of *anomie* had a great influence on many American and British subcultural studies from the 1920s to the 1950s.

It must be recognized that Durkheim's work, as an individual, does not represent the totality of functionalist belief, and equally, the totality of functionalist belief does not recognize necessarily all that Durkheim wrote. (See also Section 2.3.)

The historical context of Durkheim's work

Durkheim's major concern was with the analysis of social order: how stability is created and how the collective will is maintained in the face of individualism. These concerns are hardly surprising if we consider the specific socio-cultural context within which Durkheim worked. Sociologists, like artists, musicians and scientists, are shaped by the world they live in, even if their object of study is this world.

Colin Sumner (1994) identifies the historical influences on Durkheim as rapid social change, unlike anything experienced in Europe before:

The crucial stages of industrialization were over by 1870 and 1882–1900 was a period of commercial and industrial depression. France was establishing itself as the second colonial power through gaining administrative control over important parts of North Africa, Indo-China and West Africa. Culturally, it was increasing in self-confidence and optimism as it gradually asserted itself against the influence of German culture . . . In penal policy, the use of the guillotine was giving way to the birth of parole . . . As in other spheres, the old ways sat uneasily next to the new. Times were changing and consequently so were ways of seeing.
(Sumner, 1994, pp. 7–8)

Durkheim's image of modern society needs to be understood within these 'changing times'. Durkheim's sociology, like Comte's before him, was an attempt to engage with the problems of the era – so solutions can come only after understanding and reflection. Durkheim's concern with order and consensus is not, then, one of presumption. He does not assume that consensus is unproblematic; on the contrary, his sociology is concerned to understand how order is possible in times which may lead to disorder, in times where rapid social, cultural and economic changes throw into darkness the previous sense of order.

Deviance, crime and disorder were thus vital for Durkheim's explanations of the future of social life at his time of writing.

The functions of deviance

For Durkheim, *deviance is functional for society*, provided its social expression is not too much or too little. At first glance this claim may appear to contradict much of functionalist thought concerning the importance of social *stability*. However, Durkheim recognized that all societies experience some level of deviation from norms and values, and in periods of social change – not unlike those he experienced in France during his own lifetime – new moral codes develop. During their creation the newer rules may be out of step with the old ones for a time. As Durkheim explains:

A society can only survive if it is periodically renewed: that is to say, if the older generations cede place to new ones. Therefore it is necessary for the first to die. Thus the normal state of societies implies the illness of individuals; a certain rate of mortality, like a certain rate of criminality, is indispensable to collective health.
(Durkheim, 1988, pp. 106–7; orig. pub. 1895)

Moreover, for Durkheim a small amount of deviance can have a reinforcing function in bonding society together against 'the common enemy'. This point has been made by functionalists concerning the amount of air time given to crime in the contemporary mass media (see also Section 15.5). We are shown how *not* to behave and thus have our collective sentiments enhanced:

Never do we feel the need of the company of our compatriots so greatly as when we are in a foreign country; never does the believer feel so strongly attracted to his fellow believers as during periods of persecution. Of course, we always love the company of those who feel and think as we do, but it is with passion, and no longer solely with pleasure, that we seek it immediately after discussions where our common beliefs have been directly attacked. Crime brings together honest men and concentrates them. We have only to notice what happens, particularly in a small town, when some moral scandal has just occurred. Men stop each other on the street, they visit each other, they seek to come together to talk of the event and to wax indignant in common.
(Durkheim, 1988, p. 127; orig. pub. 1893)

Thus, Durkheim suggests that too much crime and deviance will lead to instability, yet too little does not allow a social group to bond together. Equally, deviance is often a forerunner of a new set of collective sentiments: the criminal may be 'before his time'.

Activity

Make a list of historical and contemporary figures who might fulfil the forerunner role suggested by Durkheim, i. e. who might be said to have been *before their time* (e.g. Jesus of Nazareth). Should these people be considered as criminals?

A, E

Durkheim's definition of crime

For Durkheim, crime is a category which can be defined only by reference to the specific social norms and values of the society in which it occurs. Durkheim does not regard some actions as deviant *absolutely* – he recognizes that given the whole total of human social experience, actions accepted in some societies are condemned in others. Crime is that which contradicts the collective sentiments of the social group:

. . . an act is criminal when it offends strong and defined states of the conscience collective . . . we must not say that an action shocks the conscience collective because it is criminal, but rather that it is criminal because it shocks the conscience collective. We do not condemn it because it is a crime, but it is a crime because we condemn it. As for the intrinsic nature of these sentiments, it is impossible to specify them; they have the most diverse objects and cannot be encompassed in a single formula.
(Durkheim, 1988, pp. 123–4; orig. pub. 1893)

Too much crime and deviance – or rather, too little collective sentiment and order – becomes a problem for society: individuality rises and the status-quo breaks down. This situation is referred to as *anomie* by Durkheim: the loss of shared and dominant guiding principles or 'normlessness' (see also Section 2.3). In these situations, social actors have the potential to behave in an unrestrained way, ignoring the group and its rules:

Thus we can understand the nature and source of this malady of infiniteness which torments our age. For man to see before him boundless, free, and open space, he must have lost sight of the moral barrier which under normal conditions would cut off his view. He no longer feels those moral forces that restrain him and limit his horizon.
(Durkheim, 1988, pp. 173–4; orig. pub. 1925)

Durkheim suggests that the rise of *anomie* is the principal concern for the industrial age, given the wide-ranging and rapid social changes that have occurred. This concept is of great value, both within functionalist sociology (particularly in Durkheim's own analysis of suicide) and as taken up by other writers since Durkheim's death (see also Sections 2.3 and 11.11).

Criticisms of Durkheim's position

This section considers briefly three main criticisms of Durkheim's analysis of deviance, and of his functionalist position in general.

First, as Percy Cohen (1968) has illustrated, Durkheim's ideas on crime and deviance are *teleological*: they suggest that there is a purpose to the existence of all social phenomena, the necessary purpose of deviance being to bond the social group. This is difficult to imagine because it treats society as a living thing, an object which forces individuals to follow, like sheep or robots, the wider social pattern.

Secondly, as Downes and Rock argue, it is difficult to test the functionalist theory of crime. It seems to be a 'have your cake and eat it theory', where crime may invalidate the functionalists' claims of social stability, but is seen to 'really' function to create such stability by showing people how not to behave. Thus, functionalists are able to 'prove' stability in life, even where conflict is shown to exist instead!

Thirdly, functionalism fails to provide an adequate answer to the question 'functional for whom?' Crime may be defined as that which goes against the good of the community, but who decides what the good of the community is? It is at this point that Marxist analysis suggests that functionalism supports the ideological interests of the ruling group in society.

In view of these criticisms, will functionalist ideas on deviance continue to be influential? Despite the many critics of functionalism welcoming the claims of its death as a theory, we must not look too far into the future and assume that this is a certain trend (see also Section 2.4). Bear in mind that some critics and commentators are at pains to stress the death of a particular theory for their own personal and ideological reasons: 'functionalism is dead, long live my own theory!' The last words here can be those of Downes and Rock:

It may be that functionalists have tended to overplay their hand, but at least they appear sometimes to be playing the right sort of game. And it should be noticed, too, that functionalism still seems to be persuasive and pervasive enough to surface in a variety of disguises throughout sociology.
(Downes and Rock, 1995, p. 114)

11.4 Subcultures: deviance as a 'collective solution'

A central concept in many sociological analyses of deviance – and in particular delinquency – is that of a 'subculture'. This concept has been adopted by functionalist, Marxist and interactionist theorists and refers to the existence, within society, of smaller groups with their own identities, some of which are compatible with wider social values, others of which can be seen as being antagonistic (see also Sections 10.2 and 10.5).

The Chicago School

The Chicago School refers to what was the first large-scale and lasting Anglo-American sociology department, opened in 1892 and based at the University of Chicago. (The Chicago School is also discussed in Sections 6.4 and 16.1.) The first chairperson of the School, Albion Small, modelled the department along the lines of a typical German University: the lecturers employed were required to conduct many research programmes in the surrounding areas and to give regular seminars.

Downes and Rock (1995) suggest that the creation of the Chicago School marked the break-off point in contemporary criminology and the sociology of deviance, between the early 'shadow criminologists' and the first organized, theoretically informed sociologists of deviance:

The University of Chicago sociology department was distinctive because it accomplished a decisive break with the haphazard, solitary, and ill-maintained studies which we have identified as proto-sociology.
(Downes and Rock, 1995, p. 61)

The School was thus not just a sociology department *in* Chicago, it was a sociology department *of* Chicago. Its members were encouraged to investigate their surroundings. Given that these were the city of Chicago, and its associated subcultures of criminality and deviance, there was a rich, full and easily accessible source for these beginnings in organized criminology. The School was made up of a wide diversity of academics with varying interests, united by one common goal – the understanding of deviant subcultures in Chicago, through methodological techniques associated with interactionist sociology. (See Sections 2.7 and 3.2.)

Urban ecology

A central, early approach to the study of deviant and delinquent subcultures is known variously as the 'ecological' perspective or 'urban ecology'. This is often associated with Robert Park, a student at the

Chicago School in the late 1800s and later its head. Park borrowed the idea of ecology from biology: the idea that in the natural world plants, animals and other lifeforms exist in a pattern with each other. Some crops grow better when nearer to others, some insects develop in habitats in which others die. The land is seen as a giant set of connections and inter-relationships – an ecological system.

This idea of a 'system' was certainly in keeping with functionalist ideas of a 'social system' which were developing at about this time. Park took the idea of ecology and applied it to the 'hidden' and 'inner workings' of the city. He contended that the city could best be understood as a series of concentric circles or 'zones'. Around the outside of a city we have at the periphery the commuter belt or outer suburbs, then the middle-class residential suburbs, then the working-class housing district, and finally the inner city, part of the 'zone of transition' (see Figure 11.7). This label was chosen to reflect the rapid flux of people moving in and out of the central area. At the very centre of the city, in the middle of these concentric circles, is the 'central business district'.

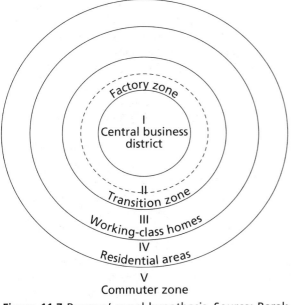

Figure 11.7 Burgess' zonal hypothesis. Source: Barak (1994)

The members of the Chicago School concentrated their research into deviance in the zone of transition, supposing it to contain the highest amounts of deviant, criminal and delinquent activity. The 'slum'-style cheap housing and rapid patterns of migration and immigration were imagined to contribute to a lack of community feeling in this zone. This lack of community was in turn thought to contribute to increased levels of crime.

In many respects, this theory represents a return to the idea of *anomie*: normlessness in the inner city is seen to be to blame for deviance. *Anomie* exists in the centre of the city because the rapid turnover of the population does not allow ties to be established.

Edwin Sutherland, another member of the Chicago School writing in the early to middle 1900s, also studied the higher levels of deviance in the central zone. He suggested that much deviance could be explained by 'differential association' – the contact with others already involved in criminal activities. In this way, young people 'learn the ways of crime' by copying and joining in with the activities of older and established criminals.

Criticisms of the Chicago School's position

A number of criticisms can be raised. Principally, the idea of the 'zone of transition' does not explain what is known as 'white collar crime', which by definition would not take place in working-class areas. Moreover, a number of the School's ideas are based on the proposition that crime is a response to social disorganization, but we could argue that some criminal activities are very organized.

Robert Merton: strain theory

Functionalist-based ideas such as *anomie* also had an effect on the work of Robert Merton. Writing in the mid-1930s, Merton understood crime and deviance to be a response to the inability to achieve social goals. This is often referred to as a 'strain theory' of crime, since Merton highlights a tension or strain between:

- the cultural goals of a society
- the legitimate or institutionalized means to achieve these goals.

Merton's work can be seen to be influenced by the 'American Dream': provided one works hard, successes such as a good job, money, a good house and a luxurious lifestyle can be yours. Merton highlights the idea of the internalization through socialization of the norms and values of society. However, he proposes that when the values or culture goals are internalized, many people fail to live up to them, or to achieve them. A dysfunction of this 'strain' or tension is deviance.

Discussion point

How is it possible that society 'causes' problems or tensions for some of its members?

Varieties of deviant responses

Merton suggested the following five main ways (the last four of which are deviant) in which individuals may respond to the strain between goals and the means of achieving them in society:

1 *Conformity* – Even though the goals may be accepted but the means to achieve them are unavailable, the rules of society are still followed. This is therefore not a deviant response.

2 *Innovation* – An individual accepts the goals but is unable to achieve the means. Instead, the goals are sought through alternative, illegitimate (deviant) methods such as robbery.

3 *Ritualism* – Some individuals, although aware that they will never achieve the goals despite having some of the means, continue to work within the system, but never aspire to reach any higher or to develop any further. These people simply 'go through the motions', in a job for example, and lose sight of the goals. Merton classifies this as a deviant response.

4 *Retreatism* – Those who lack the means and have not accepted the goals may drop out of (retreat from) society, possibly becoming recluses or turning to alcohol or other drug abuse.

5 *Rebellion* – Some individuals reject the dominant social goals and the means to achieve them, but then replace these with their own set of values. This could explain acts of politically motivated terrorism or 'freedom fighting'.

Merton is highly critical of driving social values in western societies, based as they are on what he sees as competition and greed. He suggests that this encourages individuals to break the law:

In societies such as our own, then, the pressure of prestige-bearing success tends to eliminate the effective social constraint over means employed to this end. 'The-end-justifies-the-means' doctrine becomes a guiding tenet for action when the cultural structure unduly exalts the end and the social organization unduly limits possible recourse to approved means.
(Merton, 1989, p. 139; orig. pub. 1938)

Criticisms of Merton's position

Although Merton develops many different explanations of deviant behaviour, he treats deviant responses as exclusively the actions of individuals. He therefore fails to take into consideration the highly communal aspects of some deviance. He ignores the evidence that deviant subcultures exist. These subcultures may well respond to the world along similar lines to those outlined by Merton, but they must be seen as *collective* responses.

Activity

After thinking about Merton's ideas of the 'strain' between the goals of a society and the means to achieve them, compile three lists as follows:

a the dominant goals of contemporary society in the UK

b those groups who may lack the means to achieve the goals you have identified

c contemporary groups who fit one or more of Merton's four 'deviant responses' to social situations.

Does the idea of 'strain' help to explain the criminal activities of some groups in society?

I, A, E

The influence of Merton

Other American sociologists, especially within the middle to late 1950s, have taken issue with Merton's emphasis on deviance as an individual's response. Albert Cohen (1955) and Cloward and Ohlin (1960), for example, understand deviance to be a collective solution by like-minded and like-situated individuals to structurally imposed problems. By this they mean that deviance – and especially delinquency – is the result of groups being excluded from the goals of society because of their position in the social structure – usually a class position. Therefore, these writers equate a lower class position with crime and delinquency.

Albert Cohen argues that although groups of working-class youths may originally accept the wider social goals, their growing awareness of their inability to achieve the goals leads to the development of 'status-frustration', where the goals are ultimately rejected. Instead, new and deviant goals are created and a delinquent subculture is formed.

Cloward and Ohlin take these ideas further. They contend that as well as 'legitimate opportunities' varying for the successful achievement of wider social goals, 'illegitimate opportunities' also differ. Thus, some young people are able to join a local gang, or to take up a life of crime, but others lack even these choices. These individuals become 'double-failures' and often retreat into a life of violence, drug-abuse etc.:

Much of the criminological literature assumes . . . that one may explain a criminal act simply by accounting for the individual's readiness to employ illegal alternatives of which his culture, through its norms, has already made him generally aware. Such explanations are quite unsatisfactory, how-

ever, for they ignore a host of questions regarding the relative availability of illegal alternatives to various potential criminals.
(Cloward and Ohlin, 1989, p. 143; orig. pub. 1960)

11.5 Labelling theory: the symbolic interactionist perspective

A significant development in the sociology of deviance is 'labelling theory', a term often given to the symbolic interactionist perspective. Central to this is the wish to study the meanings and motives of the actor, and the meanings his or her actions have for society. (This approach to sociology in general is discussed in Section 2.7.)

There are some problems associated with the term 'labelling theory'. In certain respects many different sociological theories are 'theories of labels' because they deal with negative or 'stigmatized' labels and how they affect the individual. However, the phrase 'labelling theory' will be used here, to refer to the particular branch of interactionist sociology concerned with how deviant labels are created, imposed and resisted through interaction. (Labelling in education is also considered in Section 8.3.)

Action and reaction

The key to understanding labelling theory is to draw a distinction between social *action* and social *reaction*. Howard Becker (1973) makes the point that deviance is not a quality inherent within an act, but is defined by a 'label' or reaction to an act by society. No actions are by nature criminal or deviant – it depends on the norms of the society, and the reaction of members of society in different situations and contexts. As Becker states:

All social groups make rules and attempt, at some times and under some circumstances, to enforce them.
(Becker, 1973, p. 1)

In his now classic text, *Outsiders: Studies in the Sociology of Deviance*, Becker asserts that:

. . . social groups create deviance by making the rules whose infraction constitutes deviance, and by applying those rules to particular people and labelling them as outsiders . . . the deviant is one to whom that label has successfully been applied.
(Becker, 1973, p. 9)

Within that short sentence we have the basic tenets of the whole labelling theory approach: deviance is

about public or social reaction, and not the initial individual action. Deviance is only 'deviance' if publicly labelled as such, through the process of interaction in which meaning is established.

Labels

Deviance, then, is considered a matter of labelling, a social judgement. Or, to use other terminology, a 'stigma' – a reaction which judges the behaviour of an individual or group, and in so doing comes to define the nature of that person's subsequent actions. If the labelling process is complete, then one may become an 'outsider' to the mainstream society:

Since deviance is, among other things, a consequence of the responses of others to a person's act, students of deviance cannot assume that they are dealing with a homogeneous category when they study people who have been labelled deviant. That is, they cannot assume that these people have actually committed a deviant act or broken some rule, because the process of labelling may not be infallible; some people may be labelled deviant who in fact have not broken a rule. Furthermore, they cannot assume that the category of those labelled deviant will contain all those who actually have broken a rule, for many offenders may escape apprehension and thus fail to be included in the population of 'deviants' they study.
(Becker, 1973, p. 9)

This approach takes us away from a sociological study of why people commit crime, or why they act originally in a deviant fashion, and turns its attention to why and how people become *seen* as a deviant by others. It is not important if the 'outsiders' concerned have actually committed a deviant act – deviance is not about what you do, but about how others perceive and react to what they think you have done.

The deviant career

Becker sees the path a person follows in becoming a fully fledged socially defined deviant as a 'deviant career': a number of stages one has to pass through before the label has any lasting effect. He makes the point that those who ultimately end up as deviants in the eyes of society are not the only ones who think about committing a deviant action. Perhaps, he notes, we should ask why people conform, rather than why people deviate, since the impulse to deviate is seen to be within us all.

The concept of a deviant career allows Becker to discuss the idea that deviant behaviour may be so labelled, but it is also learned: deviance is a product of interaction with others, through which deviance becomes 'meaningful', and understood by those involved. One of the most valuable ideas to come from the interactionist perspective is this emphasis on the 'shape' of interaction associated with each crime, and the emphasis given to the face-to-face and learnt nature of criminal activity.

External and internal control

Becker also raises the possibility that the initial labelling process which leads to a deviant career may come from *within* the individual so labelled, rather than from others. Since we are all socialized into the culture of our society, it is possible that we can 'police ourselves': we can act as our own 'public reaction', and know we are 'doing wrong' even if the wider social reaction is absent:

... even though no one else discovers the non-conformity or enforces the rules against it, the individual who has committed the impropriety may himself act as enforcer. He may brand himself as deviant because of what he has done and punish himself in one way or another for his behaviour.
(Becker, 1973, p. 31)

The self-image

Central to this labelling theory, as to all symbolic interactionist sociology, is the concept of the self. The self or self-image refers to that aspect of human consciousness through which we interact with others, define social situations and strive for meaning. Thinkers such as Charles Horton Cooley describe the self as a 'looking-glass' – it is the product of others' reactions to us, created through interaction (see also Section 2.7). As social actors, therefore, we 'reflect' back to others their thoughts about us.

If an individual is defined as a deviant by social reactions, he or she may well begin to act out this 'career' and learn how to become a 'better deviant' – to find such behaviour meaningful. This is known as a self-fulfilling prophecy and is a key concept in the labelling theory's approach to crime. Perhaps some individuals who are relatively powerless in society are put on paths towards deviant careers as a result of increased social reactions, over a period of time, defining for them their understanding of 'their self'.

Edwin Lemert: primary and secondary deviance

For Lemert (1989a, b), another leading interactionist figure writing originally in the 1950s, an essential distinction can be drawn between two types of deviance:

- *primary deviance* refers to an initial action committed by an individual
- *secondary deviance* refers to the social reaction to the initial action.

Secondary deviance is the true reality of deviance for the labelling theorists. *Deviance is not the act, but the reaction.* Owing to social reaction, the individual accepts the label and starts the deviant career. Lemert suggests that there are a number of stages or processes which lead from primary deviance to secondary deviance and the acceptance of the social judgement:

1 primary deviance
2 social penalties
3 further primary deviance
4 stronger penalties and rejections
5 further deviation – perhaps illustrating resentment against those doing the labelling
6 crisis reached by those doing the labelling – formal action taken by the community
7 strengthening of the deviant actions as the label is applied
8 finally, the ultimate acceptance by both the individual and the wider community of the deviant's status.

Lemert appears to suggest, then, that primary deviant acts are not necessarily defined as deviance by those who commit them. Equally, primary deviance can be committed, but if no social reaction follows then the individual involved will not pass on to the second deviance stage – will not accept the label.

Lemert further suggests that the definition of oneself as a deviant, once the label has been applied by a wider social source, is often a sudden and dramatic change in the self-image:

Self-definitions or self-realizations are likely to be the result of sudden perceptions and they are especially significant when they are followed immediately by overt demonstrations of the new role they symbolize.
(Lemert, 1989a, p. 196; orig. pub. 1951)

Many have been highly critical of what could be seen as the 'determinism' in this labelling approach. We can contend that the labelling process or the deviant career must not be seen as fixed or inevitable. It is possible that social actors are able to resist labels, and to fight back against them. (This issue is also considered in Sections 8.3 and 10.2.)

Activity

Using all the ideas and key concepts of labelling theory, as presented in this section, write a short piece explaining how they could usefully describe 'anti-school' behaviour in the classroom.

U, A

Case study – Deviance amplification

In his classic essay, 'The role of the police as amplifiers of deviancy, negotiators of reality and translators of fantasy', Jock Young (1977) provides an excellent example of the processes known as deviance amplification.

Young was interested in explaining the ways in which the police influence labels of criminality. Taking a group of marihuana smokers in Notting Hill, London, between 1967 and 1969, he conducted an observation study (see Section 3.9). Young suggests that owing to increasing segregation between members of the police force and members of the public, the police have come to rely much more on stereotypes of criminals and criminality as produced through the police force's cultural values. These stereotypes guide police actions on a day-to-day basis and inform the definitions of 'criminal situations' within which the police operate.

Young suggests a three-stage process through which deviant stereotypes are created within the 'police cultural world view', and the labelling effects these can have for those who come under the police's professional gaze. First, he says, police officers *translate the fantasy* (exaggerated stories) of the media:

. . . the policeman, because of his isolated position in the community, is peculiarly susceptible to the stereotypes, the fantasy notions that the mass media carry about the drug-taker.
(Young, 1977, p. 27)

Next, police officers *negotiate the reality* of what they see in everyday situations according to the stereotypes they have accepted from the media:

. . . in the process of police action – particularly in the arrest situation, but continuing in the courts – the policeman because of his position of power inevitably finds himself negotiating the evidence, the reality of drug-taking, to fit these preconceived stereotypes.
(Young, 1977, p. 27)

Finally, through the process of arrest and conviction, drug-takers become labelled and their self-image comes to accept this label, leading possibly to more deviance. Thus the police play the role of *amplifying* deviance:

. . . in the process of police action against the drug-taker changes occur within drug-taking groups involving an intensification of their deviance and in certain important aspects a self-fulfilment of these stereotypes. That is, there will be an amplification of deviance, and a translation of stereotypes into actuality, of fantasy into reality.
(Young, 1977, pp. 27–8)

At times of media moral panics (see Section 15.5) an amplification of original deviance can occur if deviant labels are accepted into the self-images of those so labelled. Young, in adopting a symbolic interactionist stance, identifies the police as a key agent in this labelling process.

In terms of the behaviour of the middle-class, so-called 'hippy' drug-takers of Notting Hill who formed Young's sample, their deviant actions intensified once the police action against them also intensified. As Young notes at the beginning of his essay:

The starting point of this article is W. I. Thomas' famous statement that a situation defined as real in a society will be real in its consequences. In terms, then, of those individuals whom society defines as deviants, one would expect that the stereotypes that society holds of them would have very real consequences on both their future behaviour and the way they perceive themselves.
(Young, 1977, p. 27)

11.6 Marxist criminology: the old and the new

The basis for a Marxist analysis of crime and deviance, as in other areas, is an analysis of the wider social conditions or social structures which lead to the creation of deviance – the 'political economy'. Marxist views on deviance adopt a 'conflict–structuralist' stance.

Marxist political economy

As identified by Marx, the economic base or the infrastructure is seen to determine the precise nature of the superstructure. In other words, the ways in which the economy is organized shape all other aspects of that society, including its culture, normative system and what does and does not become defined as deviant. (The general Marxist approach in sociology is also examined in Sections 2.4 and 10.2.) In this view, deviance in a capitalist society can only be truly understood through reference to the nature of that society.

Deviance in a capitalist society

Orthodox Marxists contend that capitalism is itself a crime, and it causes crime. It is, they say, based on oppression and economic exploitation of the majority, and creates a competitive, 'dog-eat-dog' world in which greed, violence and corruption flourish – which are the only means of survival for some.

The most basic question is 'deviant for whom?' Marxism suggests that deviance means *to stray from the norms and values of the ruling classes* – they control the means of production, and are therefore the 'intellectual rulers' in society. They have the power to define working-class activities as deviant, and in doing so, to control them. Under this world view, the legal system is seen as being ideological: it maintains the illusion of fair play, but is in fact biased towards those laws which support the narrow interests of the ruling economic élite. (See also Section 17.4.)

Marxism and the neo-Marxisms

Marxism as a theory is by no means homogeneous: within Marxism itself there is a great deal of internal conflict and debate. It is possible to identify the existence of two very general camps:

Orthodox Marxism

Orthodox Marxism assumes that the ruling classes use their power to control, fight against and punish the working classes. In the case of deviance, the legal system and the police are weapons or tools in the class struggle to be mobilized against those who 'step out of line'.

Willem Bonger (1916) provided a very early interpretation of Marxist ideas on crime and deviance. Bonger shared with Marx himself a belief that, by nature, humanity is altruistic and not competitive – a very different idea from that of modern right-wing control theories. Bonger suggested that capitalism itself, as a form of economic organization, makes humanity greedy and selfish.

Richard Quinney (1973, 1977), in common with Bonger, also argues that under capitalism the law is used to oppress the working classes. He suggests that what we now regard as 'criminal' will disappear only once capitalism itself has disappeared. He contends that there will be no greed and profit-seeking under socialism; also, the ruling class will not exist to use the law as a weapon to define as deviant those working-class activities they do not wish to allow.

Neo-Marxism

While not rejecting the ideas of the more orthodox approach, neo-Marxists take this analysis further, often by suggesting fruitful ways of evolving the development of Marxist sociology by combining it with other ideas – especially those from interactionism and, more recently, feminism.

Within this neo-Marxist camp there are further 'subdivisions', for example:

- *New criminology* – In 1973, Ian Taylor, Paul Walton and Jock Young published a book entitled *The New Criminology: For a Social Theory of Deviance*. In this they advocated the development of a 'fully social theory of deviance': in other words, to expand on and to elaborate existing ideas while borrowing heavily from interactionism.

- *New Left realism* – Aiming an attack against what they saw as the excesses of both right-wing and left-wing theories, in 1993 John Lea and Jock Young (having moved further on from *The New Criminology*) suggested that we should become 'realistic' about crime and deviance. We should understand that crime is a harsh reality for many working-class people and not something to be glorified in a 'Robin Hood' way.

> ### Discussion point
> Why are there so many different varieties of Marxist theory?

Despite offering many different ideas and exploring many different research interests, the two neo-Marxisms outlined above do agree on a vital issue: *crime is the product of inadequate social conditions*. In making this claim, they reflect the original ideas of traditional or orthodox Marxists such as Bonger and Quinney.

A new criminology?

The book *The New Criminology*, published in the early 1970s, was seen by its writers to mark both a new beginning and an end in criminology. No longer were functionalist or even the non-sociological approaches of psychology or physiology seen as acceptable theoretical paradigms within which to work. Instead, a new theory was required – Marxist in orientation, open to interactionist ideas, but firmly rooted in the orthodox Marxist concerns with political economy, with the social and economic conditions within which crime occurs. Taylor and his co-writers argued that they have:

. . . redirected criminological attention to the grand questions of social structure and the overweening social arrangements within which the criminal process is played out. We are confronted once again with the central question of man's relationship to structures of power, domination and authority – and the ability of men to confront these structures in acts of crime, deviance and dissent – we are back in the realm of social theory itself.
(Taylor *et al.*, 1973, p. 268)

To develop this 'fully social' theory of deviance – to move criminology on into the future of 'new criminology' – Taylor and colleagues drew on some very 'old criminology' and some (in their day) 'quite recent criminology'. They recommended that all explanations of crime and deviance should address seven basic issues or levels:

- the wider origins of the deviant act
- the immediate origins of the deviant act
- the actual act
- the immediate origins of the social reaction
- the wider origins of the deviant reaction
- the outcome of the social reaction on the deviant's further action; and finally
- the nature of the deviant process as a whole.

According to Taylor and his colleagues:

A criminology which is to be adequate to an understanding of these developments, and which will be able to bring politics back into the discussion of what were previously technical issues, will need to deal with the society as a totality. This 'new' criminology will in fact be an old criminology, in that it will face the same problems that were faced by the classical social theorists.
(Taylor *et al.*, 1973, p. 278)

In the establishment of this 'new criminology' they wish to advocate a change in social conditions, to achieve a revolutionary change in socialism.

Activity

Consider the seven points identified by Taylor *et al.* in *The New Criminology*, and make a note of the other ideas and theorists you have come across so far who make a similar point, or have raised a similar issue. Then answer these questions:
a How 'new' is/was the 'new criminology'?
b How is this mixing of approaches useful in contemporary sociology?

I, A, E

New Left realism

Not all fears of crime are equally realistic. Crime is not an equal opportunity predator. The chance of becoming a victim will vary according to where you live, how you live, who you are, and who you know.
(Reiner, 1996, p. 4)

At the time of the first British Crime Survey in 1983 (based on data from 1981), the government claimed that it was irrational to fear crime: the public's concern over burglary and assaults was the product of media sensationalism which in turn resulted in more reporting, and so on (Jenkins, 1991).

In response to the Home Office's claim that it was irrational to fear crime, the mid-1980s saw the rise of a new approach to law and order by left-wing thinkers. The 'New Left realist' approach developed by Lea and Young (1993), and popular amongst some London councils, suggested that some citizens, particularly the urban working class, *should* fear crime. Lea and Young claimed that the majority of crime was committed by working-class people, yet the majority of victims of such crime were also working class – often from within the same communities. Therefore, to ignore the reality of crime – not to be 'realistic' – was to ignore the very serious consequences for the day-to-day lives of working-class citizens.

As a response to what they saw as the inadequacies of official figures on crime, Lea and Young conducted the Islington Crime Survey, based in a small area of London. This revealed that the working-class residents were thoroughly rational to fear crime. For example, in one year a third of all households had experienced a serious crime such as burglary, robbery or assault.

Lea and Young are critical also of some neo-Marxist attempts to politicize black working-class crime. They suggest that such 'idealistic' approaches to crime ignore the fact that for many – including many black members of urban areas – crime is an unpleasant and harsh day-to-day reality. Lea and Young do largely accept the official crime statistics and the trends in relation to ethnicity that they show. They suggest that poor economic conditions, inadequate housing in 'ghettoized' areas, unemployment and wider social racism result in more crime committed by people living under such unacceptable conditions, not less crime.

Lea and Young are critical, too, of political, media and sociological treatments of crime – from both left-wing and right-wing ideological assumptions:

We are caught between two opposing views on crime: the mass media and a substantial section of right-wing opinion are convinced that the crime rate is rocketing, that the war against crime is of central public concern and that something dramatic must be done to halt the decline into barbarism. The left, in contrast, seeks to minimize the problem of working-class crime; . . . [it has] spent most of the last decade attempting to debunk the problem of crime. It has pointed to the far more weighty crimes of the powerful . . . It sees the war against crime as a side-track from the class struggle.
(Lea and Young, 1993, p. 11)

Lea and Young criticize what they term the 'left idealists' – those who seek to understand working-class crime as a stylized fight against the rich and powerful, a tactic in the 'class war'. Instead, they recommend that a New Left realism about crime must seek to 'navigate between these two currents'.

Victimology

Victimology is the name given to the sub-field of criminology which is concerned with the study of the victims of crime. It has been developing since the late 1940s and has been responsible for the British Crime Surveys. Victimology seeks to understand crime by trying to assess why those who are victims of crime were chosen as targets by criminals: to search for an underlying logic and order behind what are frequently seen as random or illogical events.

Walklate (1994) identifies the three main ingredients of realist 'victimology' which highlight the differences between this and the approach described above:

- the wish to understand 'real-life' problems as experienced by people
- the wish to investigate the relationships between crime and the age, gender, class and ethnicity of both the criminal and the victim
- to use local community based victimization studies (such as the Islington Crime Survey) as a means of influencing local council policy.

New Left realist ideas offer a sociological perspective on combating contemporary crime which raises some vital issues for the policing of the UK, especially the inner cities and other working-class areas. (See also Section 16.8.)

What is to be done about law and order?

The ideas of Lea and Young, outlined in their publication *What is to be Done about Law and Order? Crisis in the Nineties*, and the work of several others, has refuelled the contemporary criminological stage with argument, theorizing and debate. The New Left realists are unhappy about what they see as the crisis of explanation reached in modern British criminology, what they refer to as the 'aetiological crisis' – a lack of adequate explanations for the causes and prevention of crime. They have approached this crisis in two ways:

- At a theoretical level, they wish to address the dominance of state-sponsored right-wing control theories, which they see as wholly inadequate in their attempt to simply 'move crime on' through a policy of target-hardening.
- At a methodological or research level, they have conducted and supported numerous small-scale victimization studies in Islington, Merseyside, Fulham and other places, in order to attack what they see as the inadequacies of the British Crime Surveys.

Considering themselves to be orientated towards the left in politics, the New Left realists are critical of what they see as the dominance of 'left idealism' in contemporary British sociology.

However, Lea and Young suggest that to see all working-class crime as a fight against capitalism in the wider class struggle, as they claim the idealists do, is to fail the working classes. They argue that the working classes *do* commit the most crime, particularly street crime; but equally, they *suffer* from the largest amount of crime, living as they do in inner-city and other urban areas (see Figure 11.8).

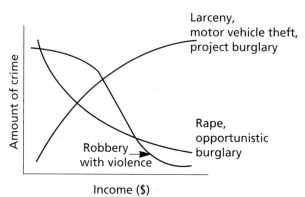

Figure 11.8 Types of criminal victimization by income. Source: Lea and Young (1993)

Realism concerning the victims of crime

Lea and Young accuse the Left idealists of suffering from a contradictory position over crime: on the one hand the latter criticize crimes of racism and crimes against women (largely carried out in urban areas by the working classes), but in the same breath support working-class crime as a form of redistribution of wealth. Lea and Young argue that the Left idealists cannot have it both ways.

Realism concerning the causes of crime

The New Left realists do not wish to reject totally the notion of crime as a politically motivated activity. They understand that the motivation for some crime is, particularly in urban areas where the difference between the wealthy and the poor is so marked, from a sense of deprivation; but they also recognize that this is a thoroughly inadequate and ineffective start for any socialist style struggle against capitalism.

For Lea and Young, on the other hand, the causes of crime are manifold:

- *Social deprivation* – Low incomes, poverty, unemployment and poor living conditions lead to crime.
- *Poor political representation of the working classes* – Frustration at the inability to solve problems through political channels leads to an increasing sense of hostility against 'the establishment'. (See also Chapter 17.)

- *The nature of working-class subculture* – Developed out of a sense of frustration, the lifestyles chosen by some working-class people to solve their problems of living in a capitalist society often emphasize antagonism – against the police and authority in general.

Realism concerning the policing of crime

Lea and Young offer a number of solutions to crime, but stress that, ultimately, a radical socialist transformation of society is needed because the problems of day-to-day life as experienced by the working classes are largely a response to a divisive class society.

Community policing

They advocate a return to community policing, in contrast to recent moves towards a 'military style' approach that they blame for the growing number of riots in inner-city areas from the 1980s onwards. (See Section 16.7.) Local community policing is needed to encourage members of working-class areas to stop seeing the police as 'the enemy', to start trusting the police once more and to report crime on a regular basis:

The causes of the shift towards military policing in the inner cities and peripheral housing estates we saw as a combination of economic decay and rising crime, police racism and the stereotyping of young people from these areas as criminals tout court *and developments in police technology which put more officers in cars and fewer on foot patrol, with a resulting decline in contact with the community.*
(Lea and Young, 1993, p. xix)

The point is made that distrust of the police and under-reporting leads to a general fear of crime because nothing appears to get done about it. This fear of crime in turn can lead to an increase in actual criminal acts (see Figure 11.9).

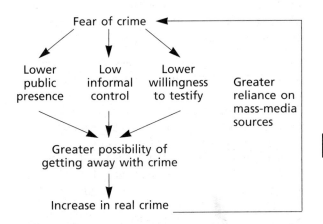

Figure 11.9 The fear of crime. Source: Lea and Young (1993)

In keeping with this idea, Lea and Young also argue that police marginalization from the community over trust will also result in more crime. Criminals are less at risk of being caught, and the police themselves, frustrated with a lack of support and information, may need to break normal legal operating procedures in order to make arrests. In doing so, they could appear to the community as even less trustworthy (see Figure 11.10).

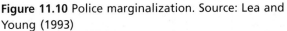

Figure 11.10 Police marginalization. Source: Lea and Young (1993)

Minimal police involvement

Lea and Young advocate a return to 'consensus policing' (see also Section 16.7), whereby the public are encouraged to go to the police for help, asking them to become involved in the community – in contrast to the trend towards armed and rapid-response patrolling.

Social change

Finally, Lea and Young make the point that however much police reform is advocated or attempted, no real progress can be made without adequate social change of a long-term variety:

As long as the basic combination of economic decay, rising crime and lack of local democratic control over policing persist in the inner cities and poorest areas, then a shift towards consensus policing is a utopian dream. Whatever the training programmes say, the pressures generated by the ghettoised police subculture to stereotype ethnic groups, working-class young people and inner-city areas will continue.
(Lea and Young, 1993, p. xx)

11.7 Studying gender and crime

A great deal of feminist sociology is concerned with reinstatement of the female voice in sociology. (This issue is discussed in more detail in Chapter 5.) Regarded as 'malestream', the discipline is seen to reflect largely the achievements and interests of male academics while concentrating on men as the object of study. This is why the non-feminist sociology of crime and deviance has contributed to the invisibility of women.

Frances Heidensohn (1989, 1996), amongst other recent feminist and feminist-influenced commentators, has made the popularization of a feminist interpretation of crime a major priority. Through the work of Heidensohn, Smart (1976), Pollack (1961) and E. Leonard (1982), a place has now been found for the female criminal and the female victim in the contemporary research literature.

Before turning to the contemporary analysis of

Discussion point

Is sociology male-dominated? Why has the work of women researchers been undervalued?

female crime, we should first attempt to investigate why the invisibility of women has been a problem. Heidensohn offers three reasons for the invisibility of women in criminology:

1 'The lack of glamour' – It may be felt by male sociologists that crime traditionally associated with women, such as shoplifting, lacks the same excitement and interest as 'male crime'.

2 'The low social threat' – Since it is often assumed that male crime is of a more violent and dangerous type, women's crime is ignored since it is of no real social threat.

3 'The lower recorded levels of female crime' – Since the official figures tend to show marked differences between male and female crime, the latter is often ignored and the compliance of women with laws and norms is often assumed.

For Heidensohn all three of these factors have contributed to the exclusion of a detailed and well thought-through feminist analysis of crime, until recently. As she comments:

Not so very long ago, students searching textbooks on crime for references to either gender or women would find few or none. That is no longer so, although there has been no comprehensive revolution; criminology has not yet been born again. (Heidensohn, 1989, p. 94)

Heidensohn suggests that although the female voice is now being recognized, this trend has yet to develop fully into a truly detailed use of feminist criminology in mainstream or orthodox thought. At present, the issue of women and crime is still not of central importance and has been tackled only superficially:

- by the lengthy analysis of official crime statistics
- as an add-on, a 'sociological added extra', but still not of central value (Heidensohn refers to this as the 'cosmetic touch' approach).

Early physiological theories (such as that offered by Lombroso – see Section 11.1) assumed a biological difference in the make-up of men and women which produced a marked difference in their potential for criminality. Lombroso believed that women were, by nature, born docile, reserved and lacking a sexual appetite. Thus men were naturally prone towards criminality, but those women who did commit crimes did so because they suffered from an abnormal sexual appetite. Heidensohn notes how these so-called 'scientific' or 'medical' biological theories have had a powerful controlling effect on women throughout history. These medical models still enjoy some popularity today. For example, shoplifting by women is often explained away using the psychiatrist's term 'kleptomania'. This is frequently used to explain the activities of premenstrual and menopausal women.

Conformity and non-conformity

Criminologists and even the more broadly interested sociologists of deviance have been uncomfortable with the study of female criminality because, logically, it leads to the superficially dull topic of conformity and not to the excitements of deviance. (Heidensohn, 1996, p. 12)

In opposition to her male 'traditional' criminological counterparts, Heidensohn suggests that the lower levels of recorded rates for female crime do not make it less interesting as an object of study but more so:

I simply want to point out that, paradoxically, an examination of female criminality and unofficial deviance suggests that we need to move away from studying infractions and look at conformity instead, because the most striking thing about female behaviour on the basis of all the evidence considered here is how notably conformist to social mores women are. (Heidensohn, 1996, p. 11)

Thus, sociologists should be asking why women conform more, rather than why they deviate less. By asking the question in the reverse sense to the traditional sociological approach to crime and gender, Heidensohn hopes to place women firmly centre-stage in the sociological debate.

In adopting the feminist strategy advocated by Heidensohn above, we should take female conformity seriously. This has implications for our interpretation of official crime statistics. Are we to believe the official figures which suggest that women commit less crime than men? Or, alternatively, are explanations which rest on a 'chivalry factor' more convincing? Do women commit crime, but of a certain sort? As in other issues in the sociology of crime and deviance, women's criminality rests on two different interpretations of the official crime statistics:

- View 1 – The official figures are *incorrect*. Women do commit a large proportion of crime, although not necessarily of the same type as men. However, they are often treated leniently.
- View 2 – The official figures are *correct*. Women conform more than men.

Discussion point

To what extent (or in what different ways) do women 'conform' more than men in society?

View 1 – Women commit crime but are treated more leniently

Pollack (1961) suggests that a 'chivalry factor' operates to protect women from becoming labelled as criminals. The argument is that the largely male-dominated police force and Crown Prosecution Service (CPS) are more likely to informally caution women than to officially prosecute. For Pollak, women's invisibility from official crime figures has contributed to a myth of female criminality. In this view, women do commit crime, but it is not reported, recorded or prosecuted as often as for their male counterparts. The official crime figures are therefore an illusion.

A similar point is made by Steffensmeier (cited in M. Leonard, 1995) who suggests that women tend to be treated more leniently by the courts and therefore do not end up in prison. The argument is that judges are reluctant to separate a mother from her children, whereas prison is more suitable for men since they are not seen to adopt the 'caring role'.

Allen (1987) illustrates how mental health explanations for female criminality often reduce the punishment given to female offenders – both in terms of the length of time of imprisonment and the format 'custodial care' takes. For example, women are often given psychiatric care as an alternative to prison since it is believed by the courts that women are more emotional than men and therefore more prone to emotional crisis.

E. Leonard (1982), however, suggests that this 'chivalry factor' is itself an illusion. If women are treated with more leniency, we must also look at how gender differences relate to, and operate with, other factors such as ethnicity, class and age. It is unrealistic to assume that these are separate, as in fact they combine to make up the 'life chances' of the individual (see also Section 5.7). Women are, in fact,

sometimes treated more harshly by the courts than men would be. As Abbott and Wallace (1990) suggest, this is particularly true of crime committed by adolescent girls, who are more likely to be put into care 'for their own protection'. There is a tendency to 'sexualize' the crimes of girls and to protect girls from their own promiscuity, whereas teenage boys are viewed by society as needing to 'be a lad'.

View 2 – Women commit less crime and conform more

Box (1981, 1995) suggests that women have less power and less opportunity to commit crime, given the manner in which they are socialized, protected by their parents during adolescence, and employed in jobs which exclude opportunities for risk-taking and deviance – given their service and/or caring nature, such as nursing, teaching, secretarial work etc.:

[Girls'] *potential autonomy is hedged in by parental close supervision; they have fewer legitimate opportunities through which they might obtain some escape from this manifestation of patriarchal control. ... the sex-differential in rates of delinquency/crime can be accounted for by the fact that in comparison with their male age peers, adolescent girls are relatively less powerful and this crucial social difference persists into adulthood.*
(Box, 1995, p. 187)

Box goes on to suggest that women find it difficult to reach the upper levels of the crime world. There are few 'employment opportunities' in organized gangs, unless through taking on a role associated with the deviant expression of sexuality such as prostitution.

A similar point is made by Smart (1976), who contends that women and girls do commit significantly fewer crimes and acts of delinquency because they lack the means and opportunities. While their brothers are allowed out in the evening, girls are forced to adopt a 'bedroom-orientated' culture by having friends to visit. They have restrictions placed on their behaviour and movements. (See also Section 10.7.)

Familist ideology

In adulthood, childbirth and marriage provide further mechanisms of control, restriction and surveillance:

Marriage and domesticity provide powerful controlling mechanisms to ensure the good behaviour of adult women. They are all the more powerful since they can largely be imposed with the willing, even eager, acquiescence of women themselves.
(Heidensohn, 1996, p. 180)

This 'familist ideology' provides a powerful source

of social control in all stages of life. (This issue is discussed in more detail in Section 7.5.)

Will female equality change the crime rate?

Critics of the 'Women's Movement' used to suggest that the more powerful women got, the more they would become deviant. Box suggests that it is time sociologists took this once right-wing argument more seriously in contemporary society.

There is an irony in a feminist perspective on crime and deviance. Taken to its logical conclusion, the implication seems to be that women will have equality only when they too can commit major crimes and be treated equally by the police and courts. In other words, will equality lead to more women being arrested and going to prison?

Claiming that the social, economic and cultural liberation of women will lead to an increase in traditional 'masculine' behaviour is to misunderstand much feminist thinking. This is, however, a very important issue, given the wide disagreement in the views of feminists concerning the validity or otherwise of criminal statistics. As Box comments:

It might have been possible to dismiss this ironic slur as yet another attempt by male criminologists to shore-up patriarchal control by warning women and politicians of the dreadful consequences which follow any concession to feminist demands for more social integration and economic equality. Yet this particular ploy is no longer so obviously available, because in recent years female criminologists too claim to have seen the 'darker side' of the Women's Movement.
(Box, 1995, p. 189)

Box sees no clear-cut answer to this debate:

This debate is bewildering because rhetoric and anecdote often substitute for rigorous analysis of relevant data.
(Box, 1995, p. 191)

The debate is riddled with political and ideological motives from both sides. The Right see it as an excuse to damage the reputation of the Women's Movement. The Left, looking towards female crime as a response to suppression and patriarchal control, claim that under a truly equal society crimes against women and crimes by women will be much reduced since the traditional difference in power between men and women will also have been challenged. As Simon comments:

[Female crimes of violence] *typically arise out of the frustrations, the subservience, and the dependency that have characterized the traditional female role.*
(Simon; quoted in Box, 1995, p. 190)

In conclusion, although Box suggests that this fear

of a surge in female crime is largely a media moral panic (see Section 15.5) designed to discredit feminist thinking, he does note that as groups become increasingly more economically marginalized in a society, through unemployment, and inadequate welfare benefits (see Sections 9.6 and 14.4), there is an increase by this group in property offences, although often minor. Therefore it may not be liberation which leads to an increase in female crime, but rather the opposite – an increased economic marginalization of women due to economic policies based on the free market in both the UK and the USA. Even if this were not the case, and liberation did lead to an increase in minor property crime, as Box puts it, 'it would be well worth it in comparison with the price paid now by powerless women' (p. 200).

Women as victims

We should not view women exclusively in terms of being victims who are helpless against the stronger male. To do so would be to reinforce much 'malestream' sociological analysis of the past where women were discussed only in the 'crime chapter' of textbooks in this context (see also Chapter 5). However, crime against women in society is a legitimate area for investigation. Again we can quote Heidensohn:

One of the most important gender issues raised in recent years has concerned the sex of the victim and of the perpetrator of violent crime. By and large . . . the feminist critics have not succeeded in directly putting gender into the main currents of criminological thought. But if the academy has been slow to respond, the polity and public opinion have reacted more rapidly and considerably. Campaigns to promote awareness of and to seek help for battered wives and rape victims, and more recently the victims of sexual abuse in the family and of sexual harassment at work, have all met with some degree of public response and even policy changes.
(Heidensohn, 1989, p. 98)

A large part of feminist sociology is to make visible otherwise invisible 'gendered crime'. Heidensohn uses the concept 'gendered crime' to refer to that in which women are victims of men – such as domestic violence, rape and harassment. Such crimes are frequently invisible in the official crime statistics because they are characterized by a reluctance or fear to report. Many of these crimes are hidden away not just from the records, but from public attention, being located within the family or home.

The increasing attention of feminist analysis paid to these areas has massive implications for other sociological topic areas, and not just crime and deviance. For example, research into abuse and rape within the home has highlighted a 'dark side' which makes traditional images of the 'caring–sharing' or symmetrical family problematic. (This issue is also discussed in Section 7.7.)

The starting point for a feminist analysis of crimes against women is to assert that violence against women, particularly of a sexual nature, cannot necessarily be understood through reference to sexuality alone. Traditional accounts of rape, for example, locate the act within a faulty sexuality or a 'damaged masculinity'. Heidensohn suggests, however, that these are not expressions of sexuality – faulty or otherwise – but of power. These acts can be seen to represent on a small scale the exercise of male power over women in society in general. As Wilson comments:

Rape is an act of violence against women. It is a hostile and sadistic act. It is a violation of a woman's autonomy and a negation of her independence.
(Wilson; quoted in Heidensohn, 1989, p. 106)

Or, from a radical feminist perspective, Brownmiller suggests that:

. . . rape and fear of rape are used as a weapon of control by men over women as a conscious process of intimidation by which all men keep all women in a state of fear.
(Brownmiller; quoted in Heidensohn, 1989, p. 108)

The female fear of crime

What the official measurements of crime, such as the British Crime Surveys, do show is the marked difference between the male and female fear of crime, especially amongst the elderly, and in inner cities.

Heidensohn suggests that a paradox exists in how traditional criminology treats the female fear of crime. In placing an emphasis on the female fear of street crime, conducted by a stranger to the victim, little attention is given to the fact that crime against women is greatest in the home, between husband and wife, or mother and son. Stanko (1988) suggests that in emphasizing the fear of impersonal crime against women – that committed by a stranger – the ideology of the family is once more reinforced. It is seen as a universally warm and safe place, ignoring the discipline and control the family traditionally exerts on its female members.

Implications for policy formation

Heidensohn comments that women's fear of crime, highlighted by sociological and criminological research, feminist or otherwise, has had an effect on recent policy formation – especially the attention given by local councils in the inner cities to adequate street lighting, women-only registered taxis, self-defence classes and closed-circuit television (CCTV) monitoring. (CCTV is also discussed in Sections 3.3

and 16.7) Although such policies are still only piecemeal, they do represent a growing concern with women's issues unlike anything seen before. Feminist sociology, suggests Heidensohn, has to be thanked for this, but the fight against 'gendered crime' is far from over.

11.8 Studying 'race', ethnicity and crime

The relationship, if any, that exists between ethnicity and crime is another popular topic for study by sociologists, especially since the so-called inner-city riots of the 1980s when issues of marginality, deprivation and criminality came to the attention not just of academics, but also of the general public via the media (see also Chapter 6 and Sections 15.8 and 16.7). This section will identify three basic positions on the relationship between ethnicity and crime.

The first position is associated especially with Paul Gilroy (1982a, b) and Stuart Hall *et al.* (1978), writing at the neo-Marxist Centre for Contemporary Cultural Studies (CCCS) based at Birmingham University (see also Section 10.6). They suggest that higher levels of criminality amongst the British black population are 'mythical', the illusion being largely the result of distorted media attention and inadequate official statistics.

The second position, also connected with Gilroy, goes further to suggest that crime by blacks, especially antagonism to police authority, is a legacy of colonial struggle, the origins of which are located in West Indian history and associated with the Rastafarian movement. (Rastafarianism is discussed in more detail in Section 18.7.) From this perspective, although blacks do not commit more crime, they do commit crime of a revolutionary and political nature. Gilroy also suggests that the over-representation of ethnic groups in the official figures is a result of selective police practices arising from 'police racism'.

The third position, from a New Left realist perspective, is adopted by Lea and Young (1993). They suggest that although anti-colonial political struggle, media exaggeration and police racism may all exist, this does not adequately explain the over-representation of some ethnic groups in the official figures – especially young, working-class African-Caribbean males. Instead, the increased levels of social deprivation and marginalization experienced by this group explain their use of crime as a response to their situation.

Mugging: hegemony and ideology

Hall and his colleagues, in their book *Policing the Crisis: Mugging, the State, and Law and Order* (1978), criticize what they see as the exaggerated and at times racist reporting of black criminality in the British popular press. In taking the example of an apparent dramatic increase in 'mugging' in the 1970s, Hall *et al.* suggest that official crime figures can be used as political weapons at times of economic crisis to justify a failing capitalist economy. In this way, a myth or illusion of black street crime has been created to act as a scapegoat, to draw the public's attention away from the real social problems of the time – unemployment, inflation etc.

The mugging moral panic

We are concerned with 'mugging' – but as a social phenomenon, rather than as a particular form of street crime. We want to know what the social causes of 'mugging' are. But we argue that this is only half – less than half – of the 'mugging' story. More important is why British society reacts to mugging, in the extreme way it does, at that precise historical conjuncture – the early 1970s. If it is true that muggers suddenly appear on British streets – a fact which, in that stark simplicity, we contest – it is also true that the society enters a moral panic about 'mugging'. And this relates to the larger 'panic' about the 'steadily rising rate of violent crime' which has been growing through the 1960s. And both these panics are about other things than crime, per se. The society comes to perceive crime in general, and 'mugging' in particular, as an index of the disintegration of the social order, as a sign that the 'British way of life' is coming apart at the seams.

(Hall *et al.*, 1978, pp. vii–viii)

As this extract illustrates, a moral panic (see Section 15.5) developed in the UK in the 1970s, sponsored or created by the media, government and police, regarding a 'new' form of crime from America, previously unheard of in Britain – 'mugging'. This developed into a moral panic concerning the safety of our streets, which ultimately led to a widespread belief that a previously golden age of law and order had come to an end.

Hall and his co-writers suggest, however, that mugging is simply a new name for a very old crime, that of street robbery with violence. As Pearson's *Hooligan: A History of Respectable Fears* (1983) illustrates, violent crime has a long history in Britain, whatever its name might be. (See Section 11.2.)

What is particularly interesting, note Hall and colleagues, is the particular time when this moral panic occurred – it coincided with a period in the UK's economic history that they describe as a *crisis*. These two factors are seen to be linked: rising economic problems and rising so-called 'new' street crimes are, in the media, blamed on the black population – so avoiding a more serious crisis in confidence in capitalism amongst the white British population.

A hegemonic or 'legitimation' crisis (see also Sections 10.2 and 17.4) is thus avoided: the government's 'right to rule', and more significantly the ruling élite's capitalist economic policies, are preserved. Hall *et al.* do not suggest that this antagonism amongst the white working classes against the black working class is deliberately created – it does, however, serve well the purposes of the ruling economic élite at this 'crisis time'.

These writers note that the moral panic has resulted in ever-increasing 'military models' of policing – where we see a shift from a community-based approach towards a reactionary police force, capable of responding with speed and force to violent situations, yet largely invisible to the general population and increasingly trusted less. This is a model of modern policing which has alienated both the white and black sections of the working classes. (See also Section 16.7.)

As illustrated by the article 'London muggings rise despite £13m campaign', street crime is still equated largely with young black men.

London muggings rise despite £13m campaign

ALAN TRAVIS

SCOTLAND Yard's £13 million Operation Eagle Eye campaign against street robbers has had only a limited impact in its first year, according to the Metropolitan police annual report published yesterday.

The official London crime figures show there were 4,000 more street robberies, a rise of 14 per cent, in the year to the end of March 1996.

The campaign, launched in August last year, drew strong criticism because it appeared to be targeted mainly at young black men.

But the commissioner, Sir Paul Condon, yesterday defended it, saying it had capped the increase in snatch thefts and robberies of personal property which had been increasing by 20 to 30 per cent a year.

He cited figures showing street muggings had fallen between November 1995 and June 1996 by some 5 per cent. Detections also doubled, to 19 per cent of street robberies being cleared up.

"Not only have we capped street robbery, but we are bringing it down dramatically," he said. Police figures show that 69 per cent of those arrested for street robberies as a result of Operation Eagle Eye have been young black men. After the launch of the operation, Sir Paul said that in some parts of London most muggers were black.

Source: *The Guardian*, 31 July 1996

The Empire strikes back

Another text from the CCCS, *The Empire Strikes Back: Race and Racism in 70s Britain* (1982), is devoted to a detailed study of the nature of this topic. (See also Chapter 6.)

Amongst the contributors to that volume is Paul Gilroy, who claims that black criminality is a political struggle against the racism and capitalist economics of British society. Gilroy's position has a point in common with that of Taylor *et al.* in *The New Criminology*. They too suggested, within a neo-Marxist framework, that working-class crime can often be seen as a response to poor social conditions and to political marginality – that some working-class crime is political in nature because it is a product of capitalist inequality, yet at the same time, it strikes out against capitalist society.

Gilroy contends that:

Police theorization of 'alien blackness' as black criminality shows where the filaments of racist ideology disappear into the material institutions of the capitalist state.

(Gilroy, in CCCS, 1982, p. 145)

Gilroy suggests that police racism is to blame for the over-reporting of black criminality within the official figures. He goes on to claim that in recognizing this as a day-to-day problem and a major feature of the black experience, especially for those living in the inner cities, we can begin to understand why some black crime is a political and revolutionary response to capitalism and racism.

> ### Activity
> Study the cartoon from the May 1981 issue of the magazine *Police*.
>   Describe what messages this sends out concerning the nature of potential police stereotypes of black criminality in the early 1980s.
>
> **A, I**

Case study – Inner-city riots

The inner-city streets of the UK witnessed serious mob violence in, *inter alia*, the St Paul's district of Bristol (in 1980), the Railton Road area of Brixton in South London (1981), Southall in West London (1981), Toxteth in Liverpool (1981), and the Lozells Road area of Handsworth, Birmingham (1985). (See also Section 16.7.)

John Benyon (1986), in summarizing the main sociological interpretations of these riots – largely, but not exclusively, linked by the media and police to the activities of young black and Asian youths – identifies three main approaches:

Source: *Police*, May 1981
'If I'd not been told this wasn't a race riot but only their way of getting rid of frustration, I would be really worried.'

1 the 'conservative' view, which suggests that collective violence is needless and without justification (this view was held by much of the media and the government of the day)
2 the 'liberal' perspective, which suggests that collective action is often a last-hope response to inadequate social conditions such as deprivation
3 the 'radical' response, which sees collective action as purposeful, meaningful and politically motivated.

Using this distinction, we can suggest that whereas Gilroy adopts a 'radical' approach, New Left realists such as Lea and Young adopt a more 'liberal' approach. What is interesting to note is that both would regard themselves as influenced by Marxism. That shows us just how wide a perspective this is.

Benyon suggests that we should, in our analysis of these events, draw a distinction between the 'sparks' and the 'tinder'. The tinder is the underlying cause of a riot, the sparks being a specific event or set of events that set off the tinder. (See also Chapter 6 and Section 16.7.) Benyon identifies eight characteristics that were common to the 1980s riots – the underlying causes or tinder. He claims that these riots can only be understood with these underlying causes in mind. They were:

- high unemployment
- widespread deprivation

Race discrimination rife within criminal justice, say probation officers

DUNCAN CAMPBELL
CRIME CORRESPONDENT

RACIAL discrimination is still rife within the criminal justice system, according to a report published today. The higher echelons of the judiciary, police, and the probation service remain white, and black people are five times more likely to be stopped and searched.

There are no black High Court judges, justices clerks, or chief probation officers, and only a limited number of prison governors, circuit judges, and ushers, according to the National Association of Probation Officers and the Association of Black Probation Officers.

Since 1989 black prisoners have risen from 14 per cent of the prison population to 17 per cent. Blacks make up 5 per cent of the outside population.

There has been a 100 per cent increase in reported racially-motivated attacks in that time. However, the report notes that the Crown Prosecution Service and the Probation Service have improved their rates of recruitment of black staff in recent years.

The report finds:

- Judges: Five out of 514 circuit court judges are black, compared with three out of 480 in 1992.
- Magistrates' courts: 17 of the 370 deputy justices' clerks and 21 of the 1,470 ushers are black. Of administrative staff, 398 out of 9,038 are black.
- Magistrates: No figures are available for the current numbers of black magistrates. In 1989, 4.7 per cent of all new appointments were black and this rose to 8.1 per cent in 1995.
- Crown Prosecution Service: There has been an increase in ethnic minority staff from 5.9 per cent in 1991 to 7.5 per cent in 1995. Recruitment is highest at the level of legal assistant, executive officer, and administrator.
- Police: In 1989 there were 1,306 ethnic minority officers in a force of 122,265, a percentage of 1.06. This had risen in 1995 to 2,223 out of 127,222, a percentage of 1.75.

Of those officers 158 were sergeants, 36 inspectors, eight chief inspectors and one a superintendent (since the survey was completed an Asian assistant chief constable has been appointed in Lancashire).

- Prison service: The service started monitoring in 1993 when five governor grades out of 1,013 were black, an unchanged figure. In 1993, 354 prison officers out of 19,325 were black. This had risen to 467 out of 19,278 in 1995, a rise from 1.8 to 2.4 per cent.
- Probation service: In 1989 the ethnic minorities provided 127 probation grade staff out of 6,651. By March 1995 the figure was 585 out of 7,905, an increase from 2.6 to 7.6 per cent. Senior probation officers rose in this period from three to 42, or 0.26 to 3.4 per cent. In March 1995 there were no chief probation officers.
- Legal profession: In 1989, 1.3 per cent of solicitors were from an ethnic minority, and 5.3 per cent of the 5,600 barristers. By June 1995, this had risen to 4 and 6 per cent respectively. The survey also found that reported racially-motivated crime had risen by at least 100 per cent, but diverged widely by area.

Ann Divine, vice chair of the Association of Black Probation Officers, said that while discernible progress was being made, there was still much to be done.

Harry Fletcher, assistant general secretary of the National Association of Probation Officers, said: "Despite greater attention to ethnic minority interests, the system has not really changed."

Source: *The Guardian*, 12 August 1996

- racial disadvantage
- racial discrimination
- political exclusion
- powerlessness
- distrust of the police
- hostility towards the police.

As Roger Matthews (1993), an advocate of the New Left realist perspective, has noted: crime, in all its varieties, is a complex social phenomenon, not easily attributable to one factor (see Figure 11.11). He comments:

... crime is, in an important sense, a socially-constructed phenomenon. Its meaning is profoundly influenced by considerations of time and space. Its construction is based on the interaction of four key elements – victims, offenders, the state and the public. These four dimensions constitute what realist criminologists have termed 'the square of crime'. (Matthews, 1993, p. 28)

In a similar vein, all crime (not solely that committed by or against members of ethnic groups) can be seen as a complex form of behaviour – a multidimensional process of meaningful intended and unintended action, interaction and labelling. In this sense, as Figure 11.11 illustrates, crime is a product of 'interaction' between the state, the offender, the victim and the informal mechanisms of social control which operate in society.

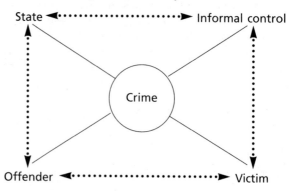

Figure 11.11 The square of crime. Source: Matthews (1993)

In more recent times, many have noted how members of ethnic minorities may be disadvantaged and discriminated against, not just by the activities of police and criminals, but within the wider criminal justice system. The article 'Race discrimination rife within criminal justice, say probation officers' (opposite) illustrates this allegation.

11.9 Control theory and policing

Control, prevention and victimology

The New Right realist camp have adopted what has become known as a 'control' approach to crime. This approach attempts to limit the frequency of crime by a policy of 'target-hardening' – moving potential law-breakers on towards easier or 'softer' targets in the hope that the effort involved in this will deter them altogether. (See Section 11.2.)

Control theory operates with a view of criminal nature as being essentially rational: crime is committed when the chances are highest of getting a maximum reward with the minimum of risk. This has implications both for crime prevention and for policing. Does it mean, to use a popular media image, that policing cannot stop the 'rising sea of crime'? Control theory also has implications for those of us in society unfortunate enough to become victims. Does it mean that those who have experienced crime have an individual responsibility to 'target-harden', or should this be a collective or community responsibility?

Increasingly, the concept of 'crime prevention' has become an important reality for many people, especially those who are defined, whether rightly or wrongly, as vulnerable and in fear of crime – such as women and the elderly, and those who have experienced the majority of total crime committed in the UK in recent times, in urban areas and inner cities. The desire to prevent crime has developed as a response to a crisis of confidence in the ability of governments, the police, the courts and social workers to reduce it. David Smith (1988a) suggests that since the mid-1970s we have lost faith in what he terms 'the rehabilitative ideal', the idea that criminals and criminality can be treated or re-educated.

This desire to prevent crime has not, however, been accepted with open arms by all. Jock Young (see Smith, 1988a; Hester and Eglin, 1996), for example, is critical of what he calls 'administrative criminology'. He sees modern, Home Office sponsored crime-prevention policies to be nothing more than piecemeal – a token gesture based on *ad hoc* initiatives, badly funded and poorly researched through what he believes are the inadequacies of positivistic methodology. The Right, on the other hand, have embraced these preventative measures.

Control theory

Control theory is based on the idea of the 'reasoning criminal'. Human actions are seen as the response by an individual through calculated reasoning to the situations around him or her. It is often referred to as 'situational control theory' because it emphasizes that crime occurs only if it is allowed to in specific situations. Crime is not a universal action; it is not always committed for the same reasons, but is specifically related to the ease, opportunity and absence of risk or detection that each situation presents.

Philosophical roots

Control theories of one type or another have an intellectual heritage which travels back in time, through Emile Durkheim to Thomas Hobbes (a seventeenth-century English philosopher) and Jeremy Bentham. These control theories are therefore influenced by functionalism (see also Section 2.4).

Hobbes believed that human nature was greedy and competitive. Humans were only communal because they could profit from not living in a constant war of all against all. This is referred to as a 'social contract' – order, harmony and social stability are only possible by the creation of rules and moral laws (the contract) which groups follow because they are in their best interests. If the rules are broken, chaos will be created.

Bentham founded what is known as 'utilitarianism' (see also Section 14.1). This philosophy suggests that human nature is concerned with the search for pleasure and the avoidance of pain. The individual constantly takes stock of, or reflects on, his or her actions, situation and choices. The individual is seen as a calculating being who assesses the sum total of pleasure and pain in every situation before acting. If a given action will lead to a surplus of profit or pleasure then this will be the path to take.

Contemporary control theory similarly has an image of the *criminal* as seeking reward, while avoiding situations where the dangers of being caught, arrested, identified or having time wasted which could be spent on another crime are obvious from the outset. Thus, so the idea goes, highly visible car locks, burglar alarms on houses and bars on windows will deter the rational criminal who will look for another target.

CCTV: Big Brother is watching you

Perhaps the biggest investment in recent years, based on control theory lines, is the development of Closed-Circuit TeleVision (CCTV) monitoring in large urban areas. Initial research appears to indicate that these schemes, while not reducing the number of crimes committed, have had an effect on arrest rates and clear-up rates (Travis, 1995; Campbell, 1995c).

A new generation of theorizing

Control theory based on right-wing tenets, and the left-wing counterpart New Left realism, developed out of what Paul Rock (1989) described as a 'theory bottleneck' – the theoretical stalemate reached within the sociology of deviance during the 1970s and 1980s. From the late 1980s the expansion of criminology, both theoretically and in terms of university posts and research places, slowed to a halt. There has been no new generation of 'upstarts' eagerly fighting with the old order for their place in the limelight in the sociology of deviance. As Rock comments:

Over time ... people get tired of rehearsing the same intellectual criticisms over and over again. ... The charms of theoretical debate decline, especially when the debate is between members of a group who have known one another for a very long time and can predict what the others will say and how they will reply in return. The outcome has been a decline in the rate of intellectual innovation. To a large extent, the sociology of deviance is preoccupied with an agenda that was established in the 1970s.
(Rock, 1989, p. 3)

Discussion point

Why does sociology have so many different types of theories? How is this of value?

However, this intellectual bottleneck, this lack of interest in debate or theorizing, has recently been overcome. Contemporary debates concerning the merits of right-wing control theory versus New Left realism place the sociology of deviance firmly back into the heated debates and intellectual innovation which characterized its growth through the 1960s and 1970s.

New Right realism

New Right realism, in adopting control theory, has attacked what it sees as the liberal and left-wing ideology of many sociological accounts of crime, law and order. Right realists accuse social theorists of providing not a reason but an *excuse* for criminal behaviour while engaging in unnecessary abstract theorizing.

New Right ideas became popular in many quarters in the UK during the Thatcher Conservative administrations, and simultaneously in the USA in the 'Reagan years' (see also Section 2.10). They are frequently linked to political and economic 'free-market' policies which seek to reduce the welfare state (see also Sections 14.2 and 14.3) and put social responsibility firmly on to the individual's own shoulders. These ideas are expressed clearly in the works of Wilson (1975) and Van den Haag (1975).

Chris Tame (1991) raises problems with the label 'New Right'. He suggests that in the last few decades this term has:

... been applied to intellectual and political movements ranging from racism, fascism, socio-biology, the 'moral majority' and Christian fundamentalists and the like to any expression of anti-socialism, and to the revivals of both classical liberalism and traditionalist thought.
(Tame, 1991, p. 27)

However, leaving this problem of definition to one side, Tame also notes that in popular usage – especially in politics and the media – the term 'New Right' has:

... of late been once more applied to a very real phenomenon, the rise of schools of thought and writers whose common characteristic is a rejection of, or critical stance towards, the dominant worldview of socialism/Marxism in myriad forms, of doctrines of social determinism and social engineering, and of state interventionism in personal, political and economic life.
(Tame, 1991, p. 27)

The central features, or emphasis, of a New Right policy on crime and law and order, according to Tame, are the concepts of freedom, justice and responsibility. Although in a very general sense we could argue that most political ideologies have something to say about these concepts, the approach offered by the New Right is distinctive because it is made up of two traditions: liberalism and conservatism.

In the case of policing (or rather, of establishing law and order), New Right theorists such as Van den Haag suggest that strong and public punishments are necessary. To echo a famous slogan of the British Conservative Party, these New Right theorists wish to be 'strong on law and order' – to show criminals and the wider population that disorder will not be tolerated and will be treated accordingly. Added to this idea is the concern that rehabilitative measures do more harm than good: they are ineffective and as a result encourage criminals to commit even more crime. Social workers in particular are seen as being 'too soft' on the perpetrators of crime.

Case study – The call for a children's curfew

Interestingly, many social ideas and policy suggestions from the Labour Party in the mid-1990s were based on a similar call for individual and family responsibility, giving them common ground

Parents face delinquent bill

JAMES MEIKLE

LABOUR yesterday backed suggestions that affluent parents should pay for the behaviour of their delinquent offspring.

It endorsed measures to tackle youth crime being considered by the Audit Commission, the public spending watchdog, even as the commission stressed it had yet to develop an official view.

Alun Michael, Labour's home affairs spokesman, said: "Given that the burden of crime has increased so massively over recent years, it is right that a share of that should come from those who contribute to it."

Speaking on GMTV's Sunday programme, he said the commission, "which has done a very serious piece of work on this", had understood and analysed the point Labour had been making – "that there is a need to nip things in the bud to reduce youth offending".

Labour is keen to capitalise on the idea that prevention is better than cure for juvenile crime. It plans to try out curfews for young children on housing estates, and will welcome any report that suggests the present system is not working.

Simon Hughes, the Liberal Democrat spokesman on urban affairs and youth issues, said early reports of the commission's study sounded encouraging. "Parents should take more responsibility for anti-social acts committed by their children," he said.

"Youth provision should be properly co-ordinated but, above all, the teaching of good parenting to all youngsters before they leave school, nursery education for all three and four-year-olds, and activities for all young people outside school hours, including a nationwide expansion of youth services, will all make a difference." Punishment regimes had been shown to have failed badly.

According to the *Sunday Times*, the commission paper finds existing arrangements "expensive, inefficient and ineffective", and criticises punishment-led regimes such as boot camps which have led to a 25 per cent rise in reoffending.

Estimates of between £5 and £10 billion have been put on the cost of damage and replacement caused by juvenile crime. A further £1 billion is spent by police, the Crown Prosecution Service, the courts and local authorities on dealing with young offenders.

The commission is said to propose the creation of a single agency for the custody of young people and a national strategy to promote good behaviour. Parents should be made to accept their responsibilities to their children.

"Social services agencies which have to help and support children because their parents refuse to house them, for example, should have powers to recover some of the costs from parents."

While the paper concedes these powers would be of limited relevance to poor parents, it adds parents should be required to pay compensation for the consequences of anti-social behaviour and vandalism by their children. There is also backing for parenting lessons, of which a number already exist with different levels of formality.

Source: *The Guardian*, 19 August 1996

---

with the New Right realists (see also Section 2.10).

Embracing what is broadly a control theory of crime, 'New Labour' advocated the adoption of a children's curfew, with children being asked to stay indoors – unless accompanied by an adult – after a certain time in the evening. This idea places the responsibility for juvenile criminal activity and delinquency firmly in the hands of the parents – it is up to the family to police itself – and is possibly a recognition that the police force can no longer be reasonably expected to afford the time to patrol the streets as a 'visible presence'.

This idea, that families must face up to their shared responsibility for curbing delinquency, adopted by those on the Left and the Right for different reasons and to different extents, is reflected in the article 'Parents face delinquent bill'.

11.10 Prisons, punishment and social control

Within the field of deviance and crime, sociologists and criminologists are interested not just in individual and collective deviant behaviour but also in how the state responds.

Durkheim: the functions of punishment

For Emile Durkheim crime represents those actions which go against the collective sentiments of a society. Durkheim recognizes the relative nature of crime and deviance: an act is not criminal because of its inherent properties, but rather because it breaks the collective rules.

Like many other social theorists, Durkheim charts a change in systems of discipline, freedom and punishment in modern social types. He notes that modern societies are supposedly based less on essentially 'revengeful' repressive punishments for criminality, and more on dispassionate necessity. Crime is punished, according to modern-day 'commonsense' wisdom, out of a need to preserve the best interests of the group – not through an emotional response:

Today, it is said, punishment has changed its character; it is no longer to avenge itself that society punishes, it is to defend itself. The suffering which it inflicts is in its hands no longer anything but a methodical means of protection. It punishes, not because chastisement offers it any intrinsic

satisfaction, but so that the fear of punishment may paralyse those who contemplate evil. It is no longer anger, but a well thought-out precaution which determines repression.
(Durkheim, 1988, p. 124; orig. pub. 1893)

Durkheim himself is sceptical of this commonsense image of the change in forms of punishment in modern times. He would rather point to the continuing similarities between the past and the modern social types with regard to the functions of discipline and punishment:

The nature of a practice does not necessarily change because the conscious intentions of those who apply it are modified. It might, in fact, still play the same role as before, but without this being perceived . . . There is no radical division between the punishment of today and yesterday, and consequently it was not necessary for the latter to change its nature in order to accommodate itself to the role that it plays in our civilised societies. The whole difference derives from the fact that it now produces its effects with a heightened awareness of what it does.
(Durkheim, 1988, p. 125; orig. pub. 1893)

Durkheim goes further to suggest that modern punishment is often based on the need or desire for vengeance. The reason for this, he says, is that crime hits at the most important aspect of social stability, which is morality; and if morality is attacked on a frequent basis then the social order will soon collapse. Durkheim appears to imply that the social group do have the capacity for revenge if what it holds most dear is threatened – the identity of the group itself. (See also Sections 2.3 and 10.2.)

A 'radical' interpretation of social control

The Durkheimian perspective on the nature of punishment is of value because it attempts to re-evaluate 'commonsense' thought. It is essentially 'debunking' – it pulls apart what we might imagine to be the case, and examines social life more deeply. Thus, Durkheim claims that there is a difference between what society may say or conventionally believe about punishment and what actually occurs. In this case, Durkheim claims that modern-day punishments are not very dissimilar from older punishments and that they both perform the same functions.

More recent commentators have also attempted to 'debunk' or critically investigate apparent distinctions between modern-day and older forms of punishment and discipline. Amongst these, of particular interest are Stanley Cohen and Michel Foucault.

Activity

On 2 March 1757, Damiens, the regicide, was condemned 'to make the amende honorable before the main door of the Church of Paris', where he was to be 'taken and conveyed in a cart, wearing nothing but a shirt, holding a torch of burning wax weighing two pounds'; then, 'in the said cart, to the Place de Grève, where, on a scaffold that will be erected there, the flesh will be torn from his breasts, arms, thighs and calves with red-hot pincers, his right hand, holding the knife with which he committed the said parricide, burnt with sulphur, and, on those places where the flesh will be torn away, poured molten lead, boiling oil, burning resin, wax and sulphur melted together and then his body drawn and quartered by four horses and his limbs and body consumed by fire, reduced to ashes and his ashes thrown to the winds'.
(Foucault, 1977, p. 3)

The extract above describes a public execution in 1757 in France. Taking a Durkheimian perspective, describe how this type of punishment might be considered functional for the social group (that is, the French people).

I, A

Although offering quite different accounts of modern systems of discipline and punishment, they can be seen as similar in one important way. Whereas Durkheim believed modern punishment, however ordered or whatever its relationship to the past, was essentially positive since it performed a number of bonding functions, Cohen and Foucault are much more sceptical: they see punishment as largely repressive and often determined in the interests of ruling élites. They therefore offer us a far more 'critical' or 'radical' interpretation of punishment. They share a concern to highlight previously hidden mechanisms of social control which, they contend, operate in contemporary society.

Visions of social control

Sociologists, philosophers and historians are becoming increasingly interested in facets of discipline and punishment in society which may not be obvious at first glance. In his book *Visions of Social Control: Crime, Punishment and Classification*, Stanley Cohen (1994) attempts to expose these facets and classify contemporary forms of control.

viduals' and groups' activities are determined and controlled.

Activity

Social control is a central concept in much sociology, especially within the sociology of crime and deviance.

a Define 'social control'. Use a dictionary of sociology if you wish.

b For each of the three perspectives Marxism, functionalism and feminism, write a paragraph describing how the perspective interprets the role of social control in society. Include a reference to the value-dimension implicit within these perspectives – that is, whether they would interpret social control as negative or positive. Give reasons for your answers.

U, I, A

When thinking about the concepts of 'discipline', 'control' and 'punishment', many of us may first imagine scenes of imprisonment or torture. Although these are very well established methods used in various societies for controlling so-called deviants, they are not by any means the only methods. The more 'radical' thinkers wish to point to other forms of control, many of which are part of our everyday life and experiences. These hidden systems of control may include the following:

- *Specialist language* – A number of commentators such as Cohen and Foucault (but from different theoretical orientations) have illustrated how language performs a controlling function. It shapes thought and therefore dictates action. The specialist knowledge of élite groups such as doctors, psychologists, scientists etc. is seen to contain its own language, unintelligible to others. In this way the medical profession, for example, is able to control patients and to justify an élitist position in society.

- *Systems of classification* – Both Cohen and Foucault also recognize that 'classification' plays a part in social control. For example, in the classroom – especially in primary years – teachers put children into ability 'sets'. (This issue is discussed in more detail in Chapter 8.) In doing this, individuals stop functioning as individuals and instead take up a place in an overall classification of ability. Such labels may subsequently dictate how others react to these social actors, and ultimately, what these social actors may think of themselves.

- *Timetabling* – Actions are very often controlled by the use of schedules and deadlines. In factories, hospitals, schools – virtually everywhere – indi-

Cohen, in discussing his attempts to expose and classify contemporary forms of social control, illustrates his aim as a theorist. It is one which many other commentators have adopted in some form:

I am critical of a society which classifies too much. This book itself, however, is primarily an exercise in classification, in ways of looking, in modes of making sense. It belongs to the type of sociology which tries to make the world look different: a strange terrain appears imperceptibly to be familiar or, just as interesting, a familiar terrain begins to look a little strange.
(Cohen, 1994, p. 1)

For Cohen, the traditional sociological use of the term 'social control' has become redundant because the perspectives of Marxism, functionalism and feminism – to name but a few – all interpret the concept in a different manner, and through a different set of values. He suggests that the term should instead refer to:

. . . those organized responses to crime, delinquency and allied forms of deviant and/or socially problematic behaviour which are actually conceived of as such, whether in the reactive sense (after the putative act has taken place or the actor been identified) or in the proactive sense (to prevent the act). These responses may be sponsored directly by the state or by more autonomous professional agents in, say, social work and psychiatry. Their goals might be as specific as individual punishment and treatment or as diffuse as 'crime prevention', 'public safety' and 'community mental health'.
(Cohen, 1994, p. 3)

In conducting his 're-mapping' of the 'terrain of social control' in contemporary life, Cohen engages in penology (the study of prisons). He, like others, is highly suspicious of the official state-sponsored forms of social control such as imprisonment, and he is especially concerned to re-evaluate or to rewrite the history of penology. Like Foucault, Cohen suggests that the official reason given for policies of incarceration and decarceration are not all they might seem to be. He wishes to revise the history of punishment:

We will have to move continually between the realm of words and the realm of deeds. The relationship between these worlds is a problem for the student of social control no more nor less than it is in any other area of social inquiry . . . This is what is meant in the debates, respectively, about 'motive' and 'ideology'. What is perennially at issue, is how surface reasons can differ from real reasons, or how

people can say one thing, yet be doing something which appears radically different. . . . Perhaps such gaps between appearance and reality or between words and action, exist because people cannot ever comprehend the real reasons for their actions. Alternatively, they understand these reasons only too well, but use words to disguise or mystify their real intentions. Or perhaps the stated verbal reasons are indeed the real ones, but because of the obdurate nature of the world, things somehow turn out differently.
(Cohen, 1994, p. 11)

The 'master patterns' of social control

Cohen argues that the 'master patterns', or the major changes, that have occurred in the history of state-sponsored social control are not necessarily those that appear to have been made. He suggests that our commonsense understanding, and the state-validated image of historical changes in punishment, imprisonment and social control, are of an illusory nature. In putting this critical notion forward, Cohen is attempting to create a 'revisionist' history of punishment. Four principal changes or developments are supposed to have taken place in the history of punishment up to the present day:

- the increased influence of the state in social control through the creation of police forces, laws, prisons etc., plus the increased use of state-sponsored 'care' or 'treatment' of deviants
- the specialization of agencies of deviance control: the separation into separate categories or classifications of the 'sick', the 'mad' and the 'dangerous' and the creation of separate bodies of knowledge to deal with them
- segregation of these various deviant types themselves into different geographical spaces such as hospitals, prisons, asylums etc.
- finally, at the end of the great 'first transformation', the decline of public physical punishment in favour of a much more so-called 'humane' treatment of the deviant individual.

These changes are well documented; but Cohen argues that other, less visible, changes are taking place that are not so well documented or publicized.

Decarceration

The great 'second transformation' in the history of punishment is the increasing process of decarceration in the western world, especially in the UK. The tendency is to close down prisons, asylums etc. as part of a great reform – an enlightened and liberated method of dealing with and controlling deviants.

Putting aside the obvious economic factors that may lead the state towards a policy of decarceration,

Cohen suggests an altogether more suspicious function. He detects within the so-called enlightened policy of decarceration, not a truly humane or liberal reasoning, but the desire to increase the marginalization of traditionally non-deviant groups: to widen and blur boundaries of legitimate state-sponsored social control. (See also Section 14.2.)

Blurring and widening the boundaries

Cohen contends that with decarceration and the development of a care-in-the-community policy, the traditional boundaries between deviant and non-deviant behaviour will become blurred. With the increasing use of the medical profession, social workers and educational professions as state agents of social control, more and more individuals can be controlled, since the traditionally deviant and traditionally non-deviant interact and live side-by-side.

Moreover, along with blurring occurs the widening of social control. More and more people become subject to these contemporary mechanisms of discipline. Social control moves out widely across more of society.

Michel Foucault

Foucault adopts a 'post-structuralist' stance. Like Cohen he is concerned with how modern systems of punishment contain previously invisible or hidden forms of control and are legitimated by the state and others as being humane or liberated.

In his key text *Discipline and Punish: The Birth of the Prison* (1977), Foucault charts a 'revisionist' history. Using a historical-based methodology which he refers to as 'archaeological' and as 'genealogical', Foucault wishes to explore and to dig behind the surface layers of the appearance of reality. This is largely what is understood by the term 'post-structuralist' – a desire to investigate social reality at a deep-structural level, to discuss those rules and regulations which exist behind the surface, usually based on language. (See also Sections 2.10 and 10.2.)

Foucault suggests that social life is controlled by what he terms 'discourses' or specialized sets of knowledge. These discourses – such as penology (the study of prisons), medicine (the study of the body and health), pedagogy (the study of forms of education), psychology (the study of the mind) etc. – operate on the human body to dictate and regulate action and shape self-identity. Our understanding of our 'self' – of who and of what we are – is seen as the sum total of all the discourses that have operated on us.

Foucault notes an interesting historical rupture or 'break' where the birth of the prison, the hospital, the asylum, the school and the factory all derive from a method of discipline originally found in the workhouse. All these institutions are seen to be based on the same form of social control which regulates minds and actions by the use of timetables, space, classifications and exercise. Foucault claims (in a similar way to Cohen) that these are the hidden mechanisms of social control – the underlying forms of discipline and punishment which are a key feature of modern social life, even if we are largely unaware of their existence. (See also Section 9.7.)

11.11 Suicide, madness and illness as deviance

This chapter has discussed many different theories of crime and deviance by reference to both classical and contemporary theories. In the sociological discussion of deviance, however, it is important for us to remember that, although many commentators equate deviance with that specific form of rule-breaking known as crime, it is actually a much broader category than that. This final section of the chapter will demonstrate that sociologists have been concerned with many other forms of deviance, including suicide, ill-health and mental illness. (See also Section 13.8.)

Durkheim and the sociology of suicide

Suicide as a topic has become popular in sociology largely through the efforts of Durkheim. In his now classic text *Le Suicide*, published originally in France in 1897, Durkheim (1979) wished to explain his sociological method. He chose what he considered, at the time, to be this most individual and personal act and attempted to illustrate how it was really the product of social collectivity (see also Section 2.3).

Prior to this the topic of suicide had already received much intellectual attention, with various theories developed to explain how suicide rates varied over time, and between societies. These pre-Durkheimian theories sought to explain patterns of suicide through reference to:

- biological factors such as heredity and racial predisposition
- psychological factors such as the suffering of an individual from an 'unstable mind'
- meteorological and 'cosmic' factors such as climate, temperature and the movement of the planets.

For Durkheim, rather unsurprisingly, these explanations were inadequate. Instead, he focuses in particular on the bonds of solidarity through which a social group is drawn together.

Durkheim chose the topic of suicide as a challenge: it represented a great test of the claims of scientific knowledge made by positivists such as himself and Comte before him. He used a comparative method, studying the rates of suicide between different societies at different times. Vital for Durkheim is the belief that social reality exists outside of the individual consciousness and will:

Sociological method as we practise it rests wholly on the basic principle that social facts must be studied as things, that is, as realities external to the individual.
(Durkheim, 1979, pp. 37–8; orig. pub. 1897)

By focusing on the official (coroners') suicide records for a number of societies, Durkheim identifies four types which he relates to the degree of solidarity experienced in society:

- *Egoistic suicide* occurs when the bonds or ties which usually unite a group together weaken and increased individuality occurs.
- *Altruistic suicide* occurs when the bonds or ties which usually unite a group together are so strong that over-integration occurs. Individuals sacrifice themselves for the good of the group.
- *Anomic suicide* occurs when the individual is not regulated by the norms and values of the group or by the social order.
- *Fatalistic suicide* occurs when the individual is regulated too much – when the norms and rules of a society are so rigid they stifle the individual and oppress too much.

Egoistic and altruistic types of suicide occur owing to too little or too much integration, whereas anomic and fatalistic suicide occurs owing to not enough or too much regulation. Egoistic and anomic suicides were seen by Durkheim to be particular problems of industrial societies.

For Durkheim, suicide rates – and the types of suicide involved – were directly related to the religious practices in the wider society. For example, he noted that Roman Catholics had a much lower rate of suicide than Protestants. He explained this by suggesting that Catholics were more strongly bonded to the social group than Protestants, given the Catholic emphasis on collectivity.

An interactionist critique

Using the methodological insights of phenomenology, a number of commentators have attempted to develop a critique of Durkheim's original research into suicide. (See also Section 3.2.) This interactionist approach suggests that social facts do not exist: reality does not exist outside of an individual, but rather, individual consciousness is reality in society. Suicide, like any other aspect of social life, deviant or not, is thus a product of social construction: it does not create or mould the individual, but rather, individual action creates the social reality.

Applied to the deviant act of suicide, this interactionist critique turns its attention to what its supporters see as the unreliability of official suicide rates. Like official crime statistics, suicide rates are seen as a social construction: they tell us more about the activities and ideas of coroners than they do about the actual nature of death or suicide itself. They tell us about the interaction between doctors, the family, coroners and the police and the attempts each of these groups make in defining the 'real meaning' of the death, through the search and classification of so-called 'indicators of suicidal intent' such as a note etc.

Viewed in this way, suicide statistics are created and shaped through strong social and cultural forces. Thus, Catholic societies may well have a lower rate of officially measured suicide than Protestant societies, but this is not the same thing as a 'real' or 'objective' rate of suicide. It might just be the case, as argued by Atkinson (1977), that Catholic coroners and coroners in Catholic societies are less inclined to record a death as a suicide for religious reasons.

Ill-health as deviance

Some sociologists have turned their attention to ill-health or sickness as a form of deviance. Given the importance of productive work for industrial societies, commentators such as Talcott Parsons have suggested that health care in western societies, being largely state-sponsored, allows the surveillance and regulation of those simply trying to get time off work (Turner, 1987, 1989). Thus a person is legitimately ill if 'signed off work' by a doctor, but if he simply declares himself to be 'ill' without evidence he is considered a deviant. (See also Section 13.9.)

Parsons termed this function of the medical profession 'the sick role', the idea being that it is a method of controlling those who potentially are deviant since they are giving up their social responsibility in an industrial society by not working. As Turner comments:

The social control and regulation of sickness is brought about by what may be termed the sick-role mechanism. The consequence is that in western societies general practitioners are concerned with clinical situations where they are professionally obliged to certify illness in order to explain the patient's failure to comply with social expectations.
(Turner, 1987, p. 40)

In order to become 'normal' and no longer deviant, the individual in question has to give up their auton-

omy over their actions and submit to the authority of the health-care regime. To ignore this would also be an act of deviance, especially if in doing so one then became ill over a long period:

To be sick required certain exemptions from social obligation and a motivation to accept a therapeutic regime. It was for this reason that Parsons classified sickness as a form of deviant behaviour which required legitimation and social control. While the sick role legitimizes social deviance, it also requires an acceptance of a medical regime. The sick role was therefore an important vehicle for social control, since the aim of the medical regime was to return the sick person to conventional social roles.
(Turner, 1987, p. 41)

Mental illness and deviance

As with suicide and ill-health discussed above, some sociologists have used the investigation of mental health (see also Section 13.8) as an opportunity to extend and elaborate on the concept of deviance to ensure that our understanding of deviance is not simply and solely limited to that of crime.

Symbolic interactionism

The symbolic interactionist perspective (see Section 2.7) – with its emphasis on participant observation (see Section 3.9) as a methodological tool, and its quest for the meanings, motives and definitions of the social situation – enables sociologists to explore the social reactions and labelling processes in the classification of an individual as being 'mentally ill'.

In his work *Asylums*, first published in the early 1960s, Goffman (1987) explores the labelling process in what he calls the 'total institution' of an asylum. He identifies a process he calls 'the mortification of the self', through which the 'outside self' of an individual entering the asylum is stripped away and replaced by an 'institutional self'. Goffman defines a total institution as:

... a place of residence and work where a large number of like-situated individuals, cut off from the wider society for an appreciable period of time, together lead an enclosed, formally administered round of life. Prisons serve as a clear example, providing we appreciate that what is prison-like about prisons is found in institutions whose members have broken no laws.
(Goffman, 1987, p. 11)

The mortification of the self is largely achieved through rituals, entered into on joining the asylum (or for that matter the prison), aimed at the establishment of a new, deviant and institutional label. For example, individuals may be required to have a medicated shower or bath, to have their hair cut and photograph and finger prints taken, and to receive 'new clothes'.

Using the terminology of Becker (see Section 11.5), Goffman suggests that the 'deviant career of an asylum inpatient' is fully established once he or she learns to, and accepts the need to, withdraw from the routines of everyday life. Instead, the patient starts to act in ways associated with being mentally ill – features of behaviour *learnt while inside the institution*:

The last step in the prepatient's career can involve his realization – justified or not – that he has been deserted by society and turned out of relationships by those closest to him.
(Goffman, 1987, p. 136)

Post-structuralism

Michel Foucault has been particularly interested in the establishment of what he calls a 'genealogical' methodology – an idea derived from the work of Nietzsche. Foucault (1989a, b) suggests that the creation of deviant labels such as 'mentally ill' or 'mad' can be understood only by reference to their opposites: insanity cannot be understood except by comparing it with sanity, for example. Foucault explains that these two 'opposite' concepts are dependent on each other for their existence – we cannot have one without the other – so it is impossible for 'madness' as a deviant label to exist without 'normality'.

Foucault observes that both opposite concepts are 'born' in history at the same time, yet behaviour which may be classified as deviant, or in this case as 'insane', exists long before the creation of these controlling categories. Before the creation or birth of the concepts 'madness' and its opposite (what Foucault terms 'civilization'), so-called insane behaviour was openly tolerated and accepted on a day-to-day basis.

Moreover, the birth of madness and its opposite, civilization, are linked historically to the creation of total institutions aimed at the exclusion of these deviants from 'normal society'. Each 'birth of opposite' is followed by the creation of an architectural space in which those so labelled can be put. Thus, reasons Foucault, the birth of the asylum (or, in his words, the 'clinic') gives rise to the birth of insanity. Before the creation of this space and the exclusion of these people so labelled, so-called insane behaviour is tolerated, widespread, yet 'unnamed' and therefore uncontrollable. Social control can operate only with a given 'audience' in mind. Deviance will 'exist' in the eyes of society only when it has been named and labelled.

Further **reading**

Accessible texts designed to introduce the key debates in this field include:

- Aggleton, P. (1991) *Deviance*, London, Routledge.
- Marsh, I. (1986) *Crime*, London, Longman.
- Moore, S. (1996) *Investigating Deviance*, 2nd edn, London, Collins Educational.

Another text, treating the subject in some depth, is:

- Heidensohn, F. (1989) *Crime and Society*, London, Macmillan.

Important studies which are accessible and of theoretical and empirical significance include:

- Lea, J. and Young, J. (1993) *What is to be Done about Law and Order? Crisis in the Nineties*, London, Pluto Press.
- Pearson, G. (1983) *Hooligan: A History of Respectable Fears*, London, Macmillan.

Back issues of the periodical *Sociology Review* (formerly known as *Social Studies Review*) also contain many articles on this field of sociology and many others.

Exam **questions**

1 'The usefulness of crime statistics in sociological research depends on the theoretical approach adopted by the sociologist.' Critically explain this view.   [25 marks]
(AEB, Paper 2, Summer 1996)

2 'Many sociological approaches to deviance have ignored the extent to which females are involved in crime.' Discuss the evidence and arguments for and against this view. [25 marks]
(AEB, Paper 2, Summer 1995)

3 'The prisons are full of the poor and the powerless, whereas the crimes of the powerful remain invisible or are not seen as crimes at all.' Explain and evaluate the validity of this statement.   [25 marks]
(NEAB, 1998 Syllabus Specimen Question, Module SL05)

4 a Briefly outline what sociologists mean by a 'moral panic'.   [4 marks]
   b Briefly identify and illustrate two aspects of the relationship between ethnicity and crime in the UK.   [4 marks]
   c Outline the weaknesses suggested by sociologists in the police statistics on the relationship between ethnic groups and crime.   [7 marks]

d Examine the claim that 'popular' views of black criminality are 'myths'.   [10 marks]
(IBS, Paper 2, Summer 1996)

5 Discuss the strengths and weaknesses of labelling theory as an explanation of deviant behaviour.   [25 marks]
(IBS, Paper 2, Summer 1996)

Coursework **suggestions**

1 **An investigation into the fear of crime**
An investigation could be conducted into whether the fear of crime is rational, given the official crime rate in a particular area. You could interview and/or questionnaire local residents in a given geographical area, paying close attention to class and gender as factors which may contribute to the fear of crime. This fear could then be measured against the official figures.

2 **Assessing ecological theories about crime in an urban area**
This could be a sociological project based primarily on library sources or on secondary sources. Official crime records in a chosen urban area could be 'mapped' on to a map of the area. The ideas of urban ecology as developed by the Chicago School could then be examined to determine whether or not they seem realistic.

3 **Looking at attitudes to crime and criminality amongst the social classes**
Taking account of age, class and gender as variables, an attitude survey could be administered in order to compare people's stereotypes of criminality.

World development

12.1 **Thinking about development**

Development sociology is about the social situation of those countries and regions often described as the 'third world'. However, it is not simply about these countries, since their existence today has been affected by social, political and economic relationships between the countries of the 'first world' and the 'third world'. Two examples can be cited to illustrate this point:

- Slavery involved the transportation of Africans to North and South America, and areas of the UK – notably Liverpool and Bristol – grew rich on the basis of the slave trade. This enforced movement of labour affected economic and social development in both Africa and the Americas.
- On a map of North Africa, the borders between countries are mostly perfectly straight lines. The reason is that these borders were not drawn up by the people who lived there, but were imposed on them by colonial powers. The nineteenth century involved conflicts between advanced industrial nations, each trying to grab the biggest share of the rest of the world. (See also Section 6.2.) More recently, part of the cause of the Gulf War was Iraqi objections to borders drawn up by colonial officials.

The world as we know it today is therefore the result of social processes that have been going on for many centuries. Sociological study can be brought to bear on this since social relationships and social change are clearly involved.

The sociology of development as a specific topic area first emerged in the 1940s and 50s. The problem was, according to the Marxist social scientist Colin Leys:

... how the economies of the colonies of Britain, France, Portugal and other European powers, colonies comprising some 28 per cent of the world's population, might be transformed and made more productive as decolonization approached.
(Leys, 1996, p. 5)

This notion is highly problematic: to define somewhere as requiring development (and therefore at the present time under-developed) requires an understanding of what constitutes development and under-development.

Some problems in measuring development

Is development to be measured in terms of economic factors such as the level of output of an economy, or the extent of industrialization? Or do we need to take social and political factors into account as well, such as the level of literacy, the level of education provided or the extent of democratic decision-making? In the early stages of the sociology of development it is clear that development was defined almost exclusively in economic terms, but nowadays alternative ways of looking at development are popular.

The most commonly used measure of the economic production of a country is known as its gross national product, or GNP. Figures on economic *development* commonly use a related statistic, GNP *per capita*. This is simply the GNP divided by the population, to allow comparisons between countries of widely differing population size. GNP *per capita* measures the annual output of tradeable goods divided by the total population, to arrive at a figure which is expressed in monetary terms – most usually American dollars. *World Development Report 1993* (World Bank, 1993) shows that the GNP *per capita* for the UK was $16 550, compared with $22 240 for the USA, and $380 for Benin. On this basis it is possible to conclude that the most developed country is the USA, followed by the UK and finally Benin.

However, if we consider some other statistics this certainty disappears. One way is to look at the provision of the basic conditions of life. Infant mortality (IM) statistics measure the number of deaths in the first year of life per 1000 live births. Figures for 1991 showed the following: USA, 9; UK, 7; Benin, 88 (Thomas *et al.*, 1994). On this basis the UK is more developed than the USA.

A third way to look at development is to consider the extent to which people in these countries have some control over their lives – a kind of democracy index. Writing in a report produced by *New Statesman and Society*, Smyth *et al.* (1994) gave each country such an index figure: the higher the figure the more democratic that country was considered to be. (The issue of differing definitions of democracy is discussed in Section 17.1.) Their rating for the UK was 75 and for Benin it was 77. According to this Benin is more developed than the UK.

Thus, depending on which figures you use, the rank order of development changes radically. To underline the point of the example, it shows us that:

- there is more than one way to measure development
- different measures may provide different hierarchies of development
- the definition adopted will affect exactly who we are talking about when we refer to the developed or undeveloped world.

We therefore need to look at the way in which sociologists and others have debated the meaning of development itself.

Economy-centred measures

Because in reality development started off quite clearly as a concern of economists, sociologists' earliest attempts to measure development were taken from economics.

Economists are concerned to measure the amount of wealth produced by an economy, on the not unreasonable grounds that the greater the economic productivity of a nation's economy, the higher the potential standard of living. The World Bank (an international organization) uses GNP *per capita* as a measure of development and divides the countries of the world into five categories. These categories and their boundaries for 1988 are reported in the *Third World Atlas* (Thomas *et al.*, 1994):

1 *Low-income countries* (GNP *per capita* below $545), including India, China and Mozambique.

2 *Lower-to-middle-income countries* (GNP *per capita* between $545 and $2200), including Mexico, Poland and Morocco.

3 *Upper-to-middle-income countries* (GNP *per capita* between $2200 and $6000), including Algeria, South Africa and South Korea.

4 *High-income economies* (GNP *per capita* more than $6000), including Germany, Saudi Arabia and Japan.

5 *Non-reporting non-members* who do not provide information to the World Bank. This group consists largely of countries that previously formed part of the 'second world' (states in Eastern Europe and the former Soviet Union). This point should highlight the fact that the World Bank was and is perceived very much as a pro-capitalist organization and was ignored by socialist countries or those declaring themselves such.

Problems with GNP *per capita*

Even though it is relatively easy to rank countries on this basis and to develop a picture of the world, this measure is not without its problems. Attempts are made to estimate the level of the production of goods and services that are not marketed – that is, goods produced and consumed in the same household – but there is a lack of valid and reliable data (see also Section 3.5) in many cases, and this often means that subsistence work is under-valued in the statistics offered. Since this is an important component of production in developing countries, there is under-counting of actual production. This is a problem we need to be aware of.

It is also questionable whether more goods being produced and sold actually means greater benefit. For example, traffic jams on crowded roads such as the M25 lead to more petrol being consumed, which increases the GNP but also increases pollution. Is

more 'better' in this case? Equally, if two countries with the same level of economic production per head of population spend that money differently, the lives of the people in those countries will be very different. For example, money spent on arms cannot pay for more education. This is an important issue because much of the debt built up by third-world countries comes from the purchase of arms (see Figures 12.1 and 12.2).

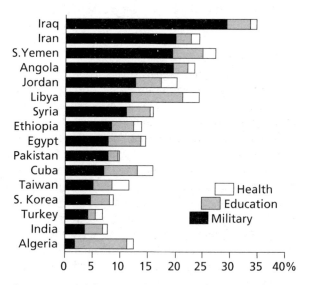

Figure 12.1 Public expenditure on military, education and health by major arms importers as a percentage of GNP, 1960–88. Source: Thomas *et al.* (1994, p. 64)

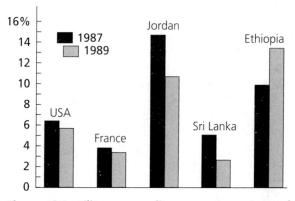

Figure 12.2 Military expenditure as a percentage of GDP for selected countries, 1987–89. Source: Thomas *et al.* (1994, p. 64)

Thomas *et al.* (1994) report that military expenditure by 'developing countries' reached a peak of $155 billion in 1984, a staggering amount of money; and although it has since reduced, the 1990 figure was still $123 billion. The four main exporters of arms to developing countries are the USA, Russia, France and the UK – showing yet again the importance of links between developing and developed countries in influencing the lives of people in both.

A third problem with GNP *per capita* is that, although it measures the average level of production per person, this represents reality only if the benefits of that production are shared equally among the whole population – which of course they are not. In 1988, for example, Morocco and Botswana had similar levels of GNP *per capita* (about $1000) and Brazil and Hungary also were comparable (at about $2000); but the percentage of GNP taken by the poorest 40 per cent of the population varied enormously between these countries. In Brazil it stood at 8 per cent, in Botswana 9 per cent, in Morocco 22 per cent and in Hungary 26 per cent.

We can see, then, that GNP *per capita* is useful in considering the level of economic development of countries, but there is not a direct relationship between increases in GNP and increases in the standard of living of the population. Although it is impossible to conceive of a country with a very low GNP sustaining a luxury level of living for all its people, countries with a high GNP do not necessarily provide this either. Economic measures can be criticized for missing out lots of factors not easily measured in terms of economic categories. As a result, some development theorists have argued that a specifically social dimension needs to be considered.

Social indicators of development

Social indicators of development go beyond simply looking at how productive an economy is, to consider how that monetary wealth is used and how it affects the social structure.

The GNP *per capita* of the United Arab Emirates (UAE) in 1991 was $20140, compared with $2520 for Malaysia. Economically it was therefore approximately eight times as developed; yet the average life-expectancy and the illiteracy levels were roughly the same (life expectancy: UAE, 72; Malaysia, 71; illiteracy rate: UAE, 45 per cent; Malaysia, 46 per cent) and the average years of schooling were higher in Malaysia (5.3) than in the UAE (5.1) (Thomas *et al.*, 1994).

The 'physical quality of life index'

Two measures of social development are widely used. The first is known as the 'physical quality of life index' (PQLI), developed by Morris (1979). This measures three things – life expectancy, infant mortality and adult literacy – and provides an index based on an average of all three indicators for each country. The idea is to reflect the distribution of social benefits. The index is based on results rather than the amount spent on achieving them. It is clear that GNP *per capita* and PQLI do not necessarily go together (Figure 12.3).

Activity

a Identify the following from Figure 12.3:
- a country in Africa with a similar GNP *per capita* to Bangladesh but a much higher PQLI
- a country in the Middle East with a similar GNP *per capita* to Spain but a much worse PQLI.

b Summarize the pattern shown by the chart.

c Make a note of five countries with low PQLIs relative to their level of GNP *per capita*, and five with a high PQLI for their level of GNP *per capita*. Try to investigate why these outcomes occur.

U, I, A

This approach does indicate that GNP *per capita* figures on their own leave something to be desired, though the PQLI is also subject to criticism. Barnett (1988) quotes the views of Hicks and Streeten (1981) who argue that, although the index claims to measure quality of life, in fact all it seems to measure is the *quantity* of life: that is, it measures how long people live or how many infants live, but says nothing about the quality of that life.

Discussion point

Which is better, a high GNP *per capita* or a high PQLI? To what extent do you think they go together?

The 'human development index'

The second social indicator of development, the *Human Development Index* (HDI), was devised by the United Nations. It considers life expectancy, educational attainment (measured by adult literacy and average years of schooling) and finally the satisfaction derived from income:

By averaging the three indicators an HDI value from 0 to 1 is calculated. The UNDP's Human Development Report 1992 *gave Canada the highest HDI at 0.982 and Guinea the lowest at 0.052.*
(Thomas *et al.*, 1994, p. 22)

The figures quoted relate to 1990, and the equivalent figure for the UK in that year was 0.964.

While the early development theories did indeed rely almost exclusively on economic data, this is now more a matter of debate. Third-world countries influenced by socialism tend to place relatively more emphasis on social welfare programmes (such as the literacy programme implemented by the Sandanista government in Nicaragua), so the implementation of

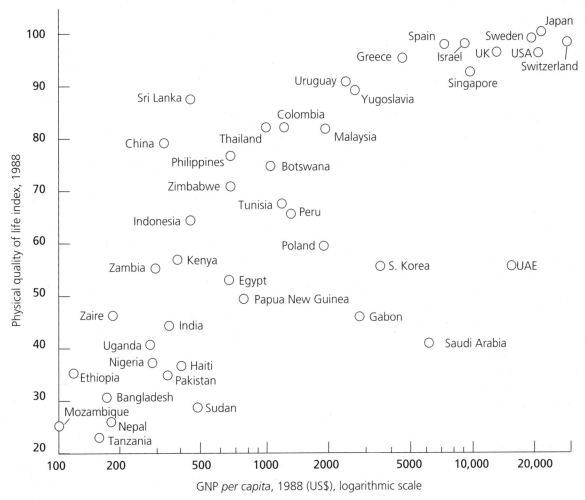

Figure 12.3 PQLI and GNP *per capita* for selected countries, 1988. Source: Thomas *et al.* (1994, p. 20)

political ideology is one of the key actors that can explain why two countries with very similar levels of GNP *per capita* end up with very different scores on the HDI index.

Concluding comments

Leslie Sklair, in his study of capitalism and development, argues:

Conventionally, a distinction has been made between economic growth ... and development, which has somewhat wider social and political implications. The crucial difference is that development includes everything that is already included in economic growth plus criteria of distribution of the social product, democratic politics and the elimination of class, gender and ethnic privileges.
(Sklair, 1994, p. 165)

The link between these and economic growth forms part of the ongoing debate between the two key classical sets of development theorists, namely the modernization theorists and the dependency theorists. It is therefore important to bear in mind

the contrasting meanings attached to the word 'development' when reading through the rest of this chapter.

12.2 **Evolution and modernization theory**

The origin of sociology lies in attempts to understand the implications for European society (see also Section 2.2) of the industrial and French revolutions. The whole notion of social change and the transition from pre-industrial to industrial society was therefore already part of sociological theory. In his survey of development sociology, Foster-Carter (1985) points out that this led to a clutch of theories which essentially saw societies going through a series of transitions from one type to another:

One very common tendency, going back to the sociological classics, is to picture development not so much as a series of stages but as a basic dichotomy, or pair of opposites. ... Tonnies' 'gemeinschaft/

gesellschaft' (community/association), or Durkheim's 'mechanical vs. organic solidarity'.
(Foster-Carter, 1985, p. 112) (See also Sections 2.3 and 16.1.)

Modernization theory clearly belongs in this category since it is based on dividing the world's societies into traditional and modern. It came largely out of the ideas of functionalism, developed in American sociology in the 1950s and '60s (see also Section 2.4) though probably its most famous exponent, W. W. Rostow was an economist, not a sociologist. This point highlights the fact that the term 'modernization theory' covers a variety of approaches with slightly differing emphases. These approaches have enough in common, however, to be categorized together.

Leys (1996) points out that capitalism, owing to the 'Cold War' climate at the time modernization theory emerged, was seen as almost natural since there was no systematic conception of its origins. Theorists, as a result:

. . . rarely acknowledged the extent to which their thinking reflected their own political commitments. (Leys, 1996, p. 6)

This cannot be said to be true of Rostow: his main book on the subject was subtitled *A Non-Communist Manifesto*.

So what developed in this atmosphere? Leys points out that the first flowering of development theory was purely economic in character and rested on the proposition that economic planning applied to developing countries would solve all their problems. This was not a success. There were criticisms of the quality of political leadership in developing countries, and there was a belief that more empha-

Table 12.1 Data for 1990 from *The Third World Atlas*

Country	GNP per capita	Human Development Index (HDI) 1990	Life expectancy	Mean years schooling	Adult illiteracy (%)
Argentina	2790	0.832	71	8.7	5
Bangladesh	220	0.189	51	2.0	65
Botswana	2530	0.552	68	2.4	26
China	370	0.566	69	4.8	27
Guinea-Bissau	180	0.090	39	0.3	64
India	330	0.309	60	2.4	52
Indonesia	610	0.515	60	3.9	23
Iran	2170	0.557	65	3.9	46
Kenya	340	0.369	59	2.3	31
Lithuania	2710	0.881	71	9.0	4
Norway	24220	0.979	77	11.6	1
Poland	1790	0.831	71	8.0	4
Saudi Arabia	7820	0.688	69	3.7	38
Senegal	720	0.182	48	0.8	62
Sri Lanka	500	0.663	71	6.9	12

sis needed to be placed on cultural rather than purely economic factors. As a result a new emphasis developed which came to be known as modernization theory. Although modernization theory continued to place great emphasis on economic growth (most clearly in the case of Rostow), it moved away from a purely economic model.

Classical modernization theory: W. W. Rostow

Rostow (1960) argued that there are a number of stages to development and the transition from traditional to modern society. His work nonetheless contained all the key elements of the classic modernization approach in that it was based on the idea of gradual evolution; it implied that there was only one path to development which all countries must go through; it presented the vision of an end result of development (generally seen as the USA) as being prosperity and political stability; and it suggested that under-developed societies need to follow the path set by developed societies. The implication of this is squarely that under-developed countries are thus because they lack something.

Rostow's model is based on an analysis of the British industrial revolution. He argues that all countries need to go through the following stages:

1 *Traditional.* Agricultural, ascriptive societies with low levels of science and technology.
2 *Preconditions for take-off.* Characterized by an increase in trade, industry and communications, plus the emergence of a modernizing élite able to use scientific and technical knowledge to promote investment and growth.
3 *Take-off.* Rostow argues that this occurs when investment grows to at least 10 per cent of national income, alongside social and political reforms to further encourage this.
4 *The drive to maturity.* This occurs when investment growth continues, as do social and political reforms conducive to continued economic growth.
5 *The age of high mass consumption.* This is basically a description of advanced industrial societies where economic production is at a consistently high level and social and political choices can be made about the society. Rostow broadly considered these to be between high individual consumption (USA), high levels of welfare provision (parts of western Europe) or social and political power (the former USSR).

The key idea is therefore that advanced industrial societies have achieved their place in the world through policies of high investment and political reform.

It follows from this that less-developed societies need to increase the level of investment in the economy until growth occurs automatically (the take-off and drive to maturity stages). Modernization theorists argued that what determined whether such a development occurred or not were social and cultural factors in the societies themselves.

Internal factors: technology, capital and culture

Modernization theorists largely concentrated on factors internal to the countries being considered. That is, they sought to locate the factors inhibiting development or the lack of factors promoting development solely within a country itself.

The key factors mentioned were either technology and investment (broadly economic factors) or enterprise and the removal of traditional cultural practices. Although it is important to state that both of these factors were mentioned by all the classical modernization theorists, there were differences of emphasis.

The first emphasis, largely associated with Rostow, talked about the importance of the level of investment and the level of scientific and technical knowledge. A country wishing to develop needed to concentrate on industrialization, and the utilization of more advanced technology. However, the more technologically minded modernization theorists realized that undeveloped countries could not simply produce this technology overnight and instead argued that it should be diffused from those who have it. This is essentially providing the theoretical reasoning behind the idea of development *aid*. It was also argued that developing countries, in building up their industries, should produce goods that in purely economic terms the advanced countries could produce more cheaply. Such an idea has similarities with the work of more radical economists like Raul Prebisch (1959), one of the precursors of dependency theory. More importantly, such an idea conflicts totally with the New Right view that the market should rule – that countries should produce only those goods at which they are most efficient (see Section 2.10). The emphasis on technology has led to this variety of modernization theory being criticized as technologically deterministic – believing that changes in technology will lead to changes in the rest of society.

A second version concentrated more on the cultural values of a society. This trend developed by applying the ideas in Weber's Protestant ethic thesis (see also Sections 2.3 and 18.6) to the less-developed countries. According to this model, the key problem is a lack of enterprise, and development therefore requires the growth of a culture which values such activity. In effect this was an application of Talcott Parsons' functionalist analysis of evolutionary development to the less-developed countries.

Parsons (1951) identified modernity with societies based on achievement and individualism, and he counterposed this to traditional societies based on ascription (where your place is determined by your status at birth) and collective traditional rituals. In applying Parsons' functionalist ideas to development, Hoselitz (1960) identified the key cultural assets of modern societies as educational equal opportunity, the impersonal rule of law and individual freedom. The point here is that simply increasing economic investment will not of itself create the conditions for modernization; instead these require cultural change as well.

In the work of Parsons, Hoselitz and more recent modernization theorists such as Apter and Rosberg (1994), the key to social evolution is the political sphere. In an attempt to identify a social group who would be able to effect such change in society, modernization theorists looked to the political élite. This led to an emphasis on education to try to create a modernizing élite in countries where none existed, although Leys (1996) argues that this has had a minimal impact on actual aid policies.

Psychological notions of personality as the key to development were developed as a variation on this theme. One example of this is the work of McClelland (1961), who argued that the key cultural factor missing in undeveloped countries was the need to achieve. He argued that it was possible to measure the extent of this, and he concluded that there was a clear correlation between this personality trait and economic performance.

There are a number of criticisms of McClelland's approach. Ian Roxborough (1979) argues that there is no clear evidence of a consistent correlation between 'the need to achieve' and economic growth, and further argues that such an approach is an example of psychological reductionism, which cannot fully explain complex sociological phenomena. He also points to the way such approaches completely ignore structural factors – a point that can be made about all modernization theory, with its clear 'cultural' emphasis.

Although it is often felt that modernization and functionalism died during the 1970s, such an approach is still favoured in some circles today. For instance Apter and Rosberg (1994), writing about sub-Saharan Africa, argue that structural-functionalism provides a powerful theoretical tool concentrating on norms, values, roles, motivation and interests as key elements, which together can provide the basis for development analysis.

The emphasis on political élites did lead to another debate by modernization theorists concerning the extent to which modernization also involves the promotion of democratic political structures. Leys (1996) argues that classical modernization theory involved the belief that democratization was an important element of modernization. Such views were influenced by the then dominant pluralist theories (see Section 17.3) which suggested that democratization was a sign of political maturity.

Huntington (1968) totally rejected this notion and instead argued that the maintenance of order, not democracy, was the key need of developing societies. Leys (1996) argues that his influence can be seen in later writers. Writing from a New Right perspective, Lal (1983) argues that ruthless and undemocratic governments were sometimes needed in the developing world to overcome special interest groups. In a critique of this approach, Kiely (1995) points out that this contradicts the New Right emphasis on minimal government and therefore shows that, when push comes to shove, it is economic freedom they are concerned with and not necessarily any other kind of freedom (see also Sections 2.10 and 17.4). The market comes before democracy.

However, it must be added that more recent work in the modernization theory vein tends to reject this negative assessment of democracy and has moved back to the more positive assessment of democracy seen in classical modernization theory.

Modernization theory in context

At the end of the Second World War it was clear that a new order was needed, to replace both the declining hegemony of Britain and to ensure that the prior period of instability – which had seen both the depression of the 1930s and the rise of fascism and the war – was not repeated. The basis for this order was laid out at a series of conferences in the late 1940s. One of the most important elements was the construction of a series of international institutions designed to regulate the world economy according to the economic doctrines of John Maynard Keynes, which advocated an active role for government in economic and social regulation, and which overthrew the orthodoxy of free-market economics which were considered to have failed (see also Section 14.1). The Bretton Woods agreement set up both the World Bank and the International Monetary Fund, two organizations that today have continuing massive influence in the developing (and the developed) world. These were funded by money from governments and states, so politics were therefore central to conceptions of development theory.

The end of the war also saw the end of large-scale colonialism and increasing numbers of ex-

Activity

Within the broad approach of modernization theory, differences of emphasis can be discerned. Some emphasize the need for the addition of economic factors such as capital and technology for the undeveloped countries to develop, while others place more emphasis on cultural factors. Equally, some tend to talk in terms of a dichotomy of traditional and modern societies, while others appear to present a more complex picture of the process of transition.

Construct a table to reflect these differences within modernization theory. Allocate modernization theories to the categories you have devised, explaining in each case why you have placed them in that category.

U, I, A

colonies achieving independence; for example India in 1947, Indonesia in 1949 and Vietnam in 1954. It should not be assumed that all of this independence was achieved painlessly. It was often the result of a long struggle against colonial powers, perhaps best exemplified by the struggle of Gandhi in India, but also including a whole host of military conflicts after the war such as Suez, Malaysia, Korea and Vietnam.

The key reason for this was fear that independent governments might opt for communism, which was seen as a particularly potent threat in Asia owing to the example of Maoist China. This in essence is what the Vietnam war was about, and Rostow was a key advisor on the issue. Some of the major themes of modernization theory are also explicable on this basis, such as the promotion of industrialization and urbanization.

The Cold War climate and the McCarthyite witch-hunt against Marxism in the USA were also important. Referring to Marx in this period 'was not merely considered unscientific, but in the USA it could easily cost you your job' (Leys, 1996, p. 6). This clearly had an effect on what was actually promoted. Yet it is important to realize that while often virulently opposed to Marxism, the brand of sociology that developed at that time in the USA did recognize the importance of state involvement in social and economic planning, and can be differentiated from the contemporary New Right which loathes such ideas.

Modernization theory is a version of liberalism which is somewhat to the left of much contemporary free-market thinking. The Cold War added a dimension which distorted thinking but promoted the importance of ensuring that development in the

Activity

This activity aims to allow you to summarize the key themes of modernization theory discussed in this section, and to provide you with some key themes of dependency theory to be discussed in the next section. This should help you to structure your notes.

The eight statements below are adapted from Foster-Carter (1985), who provides them as summaries of some of the key characteristics of the two leading classical theorists of development, Rostow (modernization) and Frank (dependency). Four statements apply to each, and the eight statements can be organized into four pairs of contrasting characteristics. On the basis of your reading of modernization theory, try to identify the four that apply to it. You can then sort the statements into opposite pairs. Check with your tutor that you have got it right. Use these headings to make short summaries as to why each is a characteristic of modernization theory.

Keep a handy note of the other four statements and repeat this exercise for dependency theory when you have read Section 12.3.

1 *Stagnationist* – For the satellite, and in some sense for the system as a whole, nothing ever changes: the structure remains the same.

2 *Externalist* – All decisive and determining change is seen as coming from, and imposed by, outside forces.

3 *Evolutionist* – It sees socio-economic change as unfolding through a fixed set of stages.

4 *Internalist* – All the crucial dimensions of change are internally generated within each society.

5 *Recapitulationist* – The presently underdeveloped countries have to follow precisely the same basic path as did the now developed countries in their day.

6 *Bilinear* – Metropolis and satellites pursue totally different paths from the beginning, determined by their different structural roles in the system.

7 *Discontinuist* – Far from following in the footsteps of metropolitan development, the satellite starts out on a different road, but will have to make a radical break with the entire system if it ever really wants to develop.

8 *Unilinear* – All countries must pass by the same route, in the same order.

I, A

newly independent countries went according to the plans hatched in the USA.

Criticisms of modernization theory

Dependency theory developed as a conscious critique of modernization theory. The former is covered in detail in Section 12.3, so in this section we will instead look at some other points that have been made.

Kiely (1995) makes a number of criticisms of modernization theory. First, it assumes that the transition from traditional to modern society is unproblematic and requires only more capital or more enterprise. Secondly, it paints a very rosy picture of the reality of modern societies. The development of position by achievement rather than ascription is quoted as one of the key characteristics, and there is no doubt that the modernizers saw the USA as a fully developed society. However, the assumption that the USA in the 1960s was a meritocracy (see Sections 4.9 and 8.1) is quite simply false. This is particularly true in relation to black Americans.

Thirdly, modernity may create as many conflicts as it destroys, so the consensus view of modernity held by most modernization theorists is also wrong. Kiely cites the 'green revolution'. This was the aid-financed agricultural revolution reliant on introducing better strains to increase productivity and end hunger. Although productivity was increased, problems emerged. Bernstein *et al.* (1992), in their study of rural livelihoods, argue that in relation to India the key problem was unequal access to items – notably water – necessary to produce a crop from the new seeds. As a result, Kiely points out, in effect the richer farmers gained much more from this and social inequalities and consequential conflicts were increased.

12.3 Capitalism, colonialism and dependency theory

The most notable classical counterpart to modernization theory was dependency theory. While modernization theorists sought to identify the internal factors blocking development, dependency theorists argued that this missed the most important factor: under-developed countries existed in a world economy whose structure was determined and dominated by the developed capitalist countries. This was a key external factor actively affecting the development prospects of the third world. This fed into an impulse to try to gain economic and social independence on the part of nations now formally politically independent. Nationalism was thus a major ingredient of this new trend. (Nationalism is discussed in more detail in Sections 6.5, 10.10, 16.8 and 17.6.)

ECLA and import-substitution industrialization

A group of economists who were working for the UN's Economic Commission on Latin America (ECLA) believed that the situation whereby third-world countries produced raw materials and first-world countries produced manufactured goods was, in the long term, detrimental to the former since the price of raw materials was falling. This meant they needed to achieve more exports to pay for the importation of manufactured goods from the first world. Their solution to this was an attempt to gain economic independence by promoting industrialization in Latin America. This is called import-substitution industrialization (ISI). (This approach is considered in detail in Section 12.6.)

ISI appealed to the rising business class in Latin America and was directed against the ruling landowners and mining interests who exported raw materials. The latter's stranglehold over wealth meant there was not a market for indigenous industry, and so wholesale structural reform was needed to produce conditions where ISI could work. Overall the analysis therefore included both internal and external obstacles to development.

ISI was not a total success. The failure of this approach led radical thinkers to look again at the arguments presented. It is out of this that dependency theory was born, as Roxborough makes clear:

Change in the Third World is primarily the consequence of the externalisation of Western European capitalism through the formation of the world market and through various forms of imperialism and colonialism. One attempt to deal with this fact is embodied in the various theories of dependency, most of which spring from attempts to rethink the ECLA analysis in the light of the failure of its programmes of ISI to overcome under-development.
(Roxborough, 1979, p. 42)

Classical dependency theory: A. G. Frank

It is with André Gunder Frank (1969, 1979) that the term 'dependency theory' is most closely associated. Frank was clearly influenced by the ECLA group but also by Marxism and the Cuban revolution. He rejected the orthodox Marxism advocated by the Stalinist communist parties of Latin America. This asserted that the key problem was that backward elements in those societies (notably the landowners) were stopping the development of capitalism, which they saw as a necessary first step towards an eventual struggle for socialism. In order to help these developments, they therefore advocated an alliance between the progressive bourgeoisie, the proletariat and the peasantry. Frank rejected this two-stage approach, arguing that the so-called progressive bourgeoisie were not progressive and were part of the problem. What was needed, he said, was an alliance of workers and peasants against both dominant groups to effect a socialist revolution.

Frank's central insight was that it was not correct to conceive of the third world as undeveloped (or traditional, as modernization theorists would have it) since it had in fact been actively affected by processes of colonialism and imperialism. (See also Section 6.2.) Development in these societies had been distorted as a result. He termed this the 'development of under-development'. Societies were not undeveloped, they had been actively underdeveloped, and under-development was a consequence of active relationships spanning the globe.

Frank argued that this could be conceived as a series of links between the metropolis (the advanced capitalist countries) and satellite areas. The relationship between rural and urban areas in satellite areas was also part of the chain. The key implication of this is that the ruling class of satellite countries are exploited by foreign capital, but also exploit their own subordinate classes. As a result, economic surplus from production flows upwards (to the local ruling class) but also outward to the metropolis. He further argued that this system had been in place since the sixteenth century, the date he gives for the beginning of capitalism. Latin America had therefore been part of the world economy for a long time and its situation could not be explained by reference to its being traditional, as modernization theorists argued.

If active under-development results from these relationships, the solution is clear: a revolutionary break with this system is needed. This mixed together elements of nationalism and Marxism (a common mix in the third world). In contrast to modernization theory, links with the metropolis will not be beneficial but harmful. Thus development is not possible without breaking the links to the world capitalist system. Foster-Carter (1985) makes the point that Frank argued that it was precisely those areas which had had the most links in the past which were most under-developed today, and he argues that the strongest case Frank provides for this is the northeast of Brazil. Originally the most advanced and successful part of Brazil, it was used up by capitalists and 'thrown on the scrap-heap'.

Frank therefore argues that it is precisely those groups seen as representing the modern in modernization theory who are in fact responsible for the creation of the traditional structures they claim to want to break down. This is precisely what he means by the development of under-development.

Criticisms of classical dependency theory

The notion that no development is possible without a break from capitalism has been questioned on an empirical basis. The 1964 military coup in Brazil and the consequent promotion of export-oriented free-market reforms was a clear target of criticism by the dependency theorists, but Brazil did experience economic growth in the late 1960s (largely by increasing the rate of exploitation of workers). While it is easy to say that this development was conditioned by Brazil's place in the world capitalist system, and that this growth quickly altered as the 'debt crisis' of the 1980s set in, the emergence of the East Asian Tiger economies in the late 1980s has again provided examples of countries experiencing development – which rather undermines the notion that this is impossible.

A second criticism of classical dependency theory is that, while it clearly points to the problems of the notion of development contained in modernization theory – principally that under-developed countries cannot simply follow the path laid down by the developed nations – it offers no real alternative notion of what development is. Leys (1996) argues that the practical points flowing out of dependency theory are either utopian (complete independence from the world economy and a self-sustaining revolution) or too vague. He argues, on the basis of his work in Kenya, that dependency theory never identifies social forces that might be able to effect transformation.

Dependent development

In response to these criticisms – notably the point that some countries have experienced development – Fernando Cardoso (1973) developed his notion of 'dependent development' to explain what had happened in Brazil. While this approach avoids the argument that no development is possible under capitalism, it stresses that the development that takes place is dependent owing to the structures of capitalism within which such development takes

Activity

Cardoso became President of Brazil. If you have access to a CD–ROM newspaper, look up recent references to Brazil and Cardoso and write a report of the policies he is following based on your findings. Can you relate these to the outline of his arguments above or identify any changes?

K, U, I, A

place. He also argues that such a form of development only benefits some, and is therefore socially exclusive. This still leaves unclear the actual mechanism of how the surplus is transferred. It is this point that has led to the growth of theories of unequal exchange (see below).

Theories of unequal exchange

The origins of this approach lie in the work of Arghiri Emmanuel (1972). He argued that the key reason why surpluses moved from the under-developed to the developed were through the unequal exchange that occurred. What he means by this is that the price of goods sold by under-developed countries is less than it should be and the price of goods sold by developed countries is greater than it should be. This means that workers performing the same task are paid less in the under-developed world than in the developed, and that somehow unequal trade relationships are maintained.

In order to explain how this comes about, Emmanuel focuses on the internal structure of a society by arguing that workers in the advanced industrial economies were able to maintain high wages through trade union pressure, while workers in the under-developed nations had weak trade unions and were therefore unable to emulate this.

This theory has been most substantially criticized by Marxist thinkers, such as Mike Kidron (1975), who argue that its focus on relations of exchange rather than production relations means it considers trade rather than capitalism. This has been a long-standing debate, since most dependency theorists do advocate a definition of capitalism based on the growth of a world market and production for that market, while Marxists insist it is the way production is organized that is crucial.

Following on this point, Marxist sociologists have argued that it is not clear that the group Frank and others identify as most exploited, namely subordinate classes in the third world, are so. Kidron (1975) argues that on a Marxist basis, looking at the proportion of surplus value taken by the capitalists, the working classes in the metropolis might be most exploited. Although they have higher wages, they are more productive and are thus more exploited.

While this might seem an arcane point, it has key implications. Dependency theorists were in effect saying that the working classes of the metropolis gained at the expense of the working classes of the satellite. A socialist strategy of international class solidarity was therefore effectively ruled out. In contrast, if the ability of the metropolis to exploit satellite countries is dependent on the surplus they extract from workers in the metropolis, then there is a clear case for working-class internationalism.

Modes of production theory

Marxist writer Ernesto Laclau (1971) asserts that Frank was wrong to say that capitalism has existed since the sixteenth century. He argues that he can only do so by defining capitalism as production for the market – in which case the ancient Greeks were also capitalists. Laclau argues that the central point about capitalism is the way in which surplus-value is extracted, and it is therefore on the basis of production and production relations, not circulation and exchange, that such definitions and theories must be built. Out of this criticism of dependency theory came the growth in the 1970s of 'modes of production' theory, heavily influenced by Althusserian structuralist Marxism. (See Section 2.5.)

This aimed to put production relations rather than exchange relations back at the centre of analysis. The idea was developed by a number of writers (Laclau, 1971; Foster-Carter, 1978; Taylor, 1979). The basic idea was developed out of the Althusserian notion of a social formation composed of a number of relatively autonomous elements. Theorists therefore argued that more than one mode of production can coexist within any social formation, though in a way which is favourable to capitalism. This allowed Marxists to reject Frank's argument that capitalism had existed on a world scale since the sixteenth century, while still being able to recognize the existence of situations where production involved unfree labour. This idea was applied, for instance, to South Africa (Wolpe, 1980) where it was argued that the apartheid restrictions allowed lower wages to be paid, as well as to the maintenance of domestic production by women, again allowing them to be paid lower wages.

While the idea appeared to offer a way to investigate the growing diversity of the world, and to incorporate local situations in an overall analysis of an unevenly developed world, the continual discovery of more and more modes of production threatened to get out of hand. This is exemplified in Schuurman quoting Foster-Carter's presumably satirical point that every village might have its own mode of production.

Kiely (1995) argues that modes of production theories can be criticized as functionalist since both the existence and the non-existence of pre-capitalist modes of production are seen as functional for capitalism. Also, as might be expected from structuralist Marxism:

It also subordinates agency to structure, and assumes that social phenomena are explained by their functionality for capitalism, rather than by the actions and struggles of human beings themselves. (Kiely, 1995, p. 69)

The talk of modes of articulation arguably had an effect on the growth of the 'regulation school' of Marxism (this approach is discussed in more detail in Sections 9.4 and 12.4), though for the most part this has led to a move to post-Marxism. (See also Section 9.4.) Marxism itself seems to have returned to more orthodox approaches in the 1980s and 90s. These are examined in Section 12.4.

World systems theory

One of the key problems of dependency theory is outlined by Frank himself. He stated that dependency theory:

... maintained the orthodoxy that (under)-development must refer to and be organised by and through (nation-state) societies, countries or regions. However this orthodox tenet turns out to be wrong. (Frank, 1991a, p. 37; quoted in Leys, 1996, p. 32)

This statement reflects Frank's later allegiance to the world systems theory developed by Wallerstein. Wallerstein (1974) was certainly influenced by dependency theory and he utilizes some of its key concepts such as core, periphery and unequal trade. However, his argument was that the definition of economies and social systems could not be done on a national basis since in reality all were now part of one international world capitalist system.

Discussion point

How do you think the communist states which used to exist in eastern Europe (the 'second world') fit into this analysis?

In order to deal with the phenomenon of the newly industrialized countries (see Section 12.6), Wallerstein introduces the notion of the 'semi-periphery'. He argues that it is possible for countries to move from periphery to semi-periphery, and even to the core, in a way that seems to contradict the arguments of the original dependency theorists. Nonetheless, since all such development is contained and constrained by the one world capitalist system, it can still be considered as dependent. This can be seen in the words of another world-systems theorist, Samir Amin:

So long as an under-developed country continues to be integrated in the world market, it remains helpless ... the possibilities of local accumulation are nil.
(Amin, 1976, p. 13)

Growth by the NICs, since it is dependent on exports and development of this sector absorbs most of the capital, so none is left for local accumulation.

Amin (1974, 1976, 1977) saw this as a key element in the distortions suffered by countries in the peripheries:

The social structure of the periphery is a truncated structure that can only be understood when it is situated as an element in a world social structure. (Amin, 1976, p. 294)

Analysis at a national level is only superficial, missing the essential point that the world is a unitary capitalist world system. The NICs therefore need to be seen as examples of non-self-sustained development. Amin also argues that the debate about unequal exchange had been hampered since the debates about relative productivity (and therefore which working class was most exploited) had been conducted at a national level. He argues that capital mobility meant that there was only one world level of value, meaning the value of one hour's labour in one part of the world was equal to that in another. In this, he rejected the points made by Laclau against Emmanuel, though he also argued contrary to Emmanuel that the working classes of the core do not automatically benefit from surplus being removed from the periphery, thereby maintaining the possibility of united international working-class action.

Activity

Make a list of the similarities and differences between classical dependency theory and world systems theory. Use examples to illustrate these.

I, A

Critique of world systems theory

Smith (1995) argues that Amin's notion of development uses core capitalism as the standard against which peripheral countries can be measured, with differences being identified as 'distortions'. She argues that this implies a 'correct' path of development, namely by the core capitalist countries. Similarly, Leys argues that the approach does not fully escape the logic of modernization theory, and its concepts of core and periphery can be seen almost as mirror-images of those of traditional and modern.

Schuurman (1993) argues that the concepts of core and periphery, even with the semi-periphery added, cannot do justice to the diversity of the third world. He also asserts that the political implications of the theory – which are autarky (meaning totally self-sufficient development) or world socialist government – are unrealistic.

Kiely (1995) suggests that the emphasis on autarky as a solution led Frank and Amin to neglect class and popular struggles in under-developed countries, and this further led them to identify with some questionable strategies:

Frank and Amin's policy of 'delinking' from the world economy and support for 'self reliant socialism' led to a rather uncritical approach to the Khmer Rouge in Cambodia.
(Kiely, 1995, p. 52)

The Khmer Rouge leader, Pol Pot is infamous for leading a regime which was very bloody and ultimately highly ineffective.

Concluding comments

The history of dependency theory shows the interweaving between third-world nationalism and various types of Marxism. Dependency theory clearly reacted against the orthodox Stalinism of Latin American communist parties, and much of its later development was inspired more by Maoism. This, however, was rather upended by China's historic about-turn in the 1970s when, following a visit by right-wing US President Richard Nixon, China moved towards a much more conciliatory and almost friendly approach to the USA – and therefore to capitalism. Partly as a result, both forms of Marxism went heavily into decline, and Frank himself now appears to talk only of radical democracy in a post-Marxist manner.

12.4 Contemporary theories of development

By the 1980s, both the two leading theories of development seemed to be in danger of collapse, leading to what some have termed an impasse in development theory. The idea that development theory had reached an impasse and needed now to go beyond it was first identified by David Booth (1985). He argued that there was a need to move forward, using empirical material to develop new theories as a way out of the impasse. This certainly inspired sociologists to rethink some central issues in development theory, with a profusion of new approaches. The sense of change is neatly summarized by Schuurman:

Back in the 1960s and 1970s, . . . the subject used to be divided into 'the good' (neo-Marxists), 'the bad' (modernization theorists) and 'the ugly' (computerised doomsday specialists). . . . [See Section 12.10.] Now, well into the 1990s, things have changed. The good feel bad, the bad feel good, and the ugly underwent plastic surgery. In the 1980s the subject of development theories moved into what became known as an 'impasse'. Teaching develop-

Activity

a Complete the activity at the end of Section 12.3.
b Decide whether the four following quotes suggest a dependency approach or a modernization approach (there are two of each). Justify your decisions in a short summary.

1 'Relations between countries, in space and time, are at least as important as what goes on within a society. In this sense, the evolving international context makes it likely – some would say certain – that stages or patterns of development are not everywhere the same.
(Foster-Carter, 1985, p. 106)
2 It was implicitly assumed . . . that the new nations would follow the same path as that taken by western European nations, and the theoretical paradigms developed to explain the transition from feudalism to capitalism in western Europe were imported wholesale, and with very few amendments into the study of Africa, Asia and Latin America.'
(Roxborough, 1979, p. 13)
3 'The attainment of a modern society was seen as a strategic goal for these new nations, and this was defined as a social system based on achievement, universalism and individualism.'
(Kiely, 1995, p. 37)
4 'The capitalist world is based on a chain of metropolis–satellite relations, divided by nations and regions within nations. The metropoles exploit the satellites through the expropriation of economic surplus, which the former use for their own economic development.'
(Kiely, 1995, p. 44)

U, I, A

ment theories was no longer a relatively clear-cut case.
(Schuurman, 1993, p. ix)

Of course, it is also the case that there have been attempts to go beyond that impasse, and Schuurman's book represents one such. Some of the themes that have been central in these debates are as follows:

• There has been an emphasis on the diversity of countries and a critique of the usefulness of the very notion of a third world.
• There has been a decline and virtual disappear-

ance of the notion of a united third world as a political entity, and a decline in the appeal of third-world nationalism.

- There has been a decline in the type of Marxism predominant in sociology in the 1970s, namely Stalinism and Maoism. Although there were other Marxist tendencies (see Section 2.5), notably Trotskyism and the Marxist-influenced New Left, all variants of Marxism have declined in recent years following the events in eastern Europe in 1989.
- Associated with the rise of the New Right, there has been a resurgence of free-market policies and their application in the developing world through the policies of the IMF and the World Bank.
- There has been a move away from an exclusive concern with macro-sociological theories based on social structures, and a growth of theories emphasizing social action and micro-sociological studies.

Theories do not normally arise in a vacuum, and so it would be foolish to suppose that the themes of dependency and modernization are simply no longer appropriate. This section will therefore summarize some of the more recent theories, and seek to show how these arise out of comment and discussion on the older theories.

The New Right: a return to market forces

The 1980s and 90s witnessed the resurgence of theories of the free market, most famously espoused by Reagan in the USA and Thatcher in the UK (see Section 2.10). It was not long before such ideas affected the developing world, since international institutions with whom they dealt – notably the IMF – had long been advocates of free-market economics and monetarism. It is also the case that after the mid-1970s funds for investment came increasingly from the private banks rather than from governmental aid agencies. Writing in the journal of the OECD, Michel (1996) points out that in the mid-1980s official development finance was still the major source of finance, but by the mid-1990s private flows of money to developing countries totalled $110 billion – far exceeding the official development flow of $70 billion.

The New Right believed that private investment is always better than public sector investment, on the grounds that the private sector is more efficient and more responsive to consumer demand. The New Right identified the internal blockages to development as state involvement in the economy, rather than the cultural factors identified by the early modernization theorists. This led them to argue that the notion of development economics was flawed because it was based on the idea of state inter-

vention. Development theory was, therefore, part of the problem rather than the solution (Lal, 1983).

According to the New Right, the key to third-world development was to reduce state involvement and open up the domestic economy to free trade with the rest of the world: the East Asian 'miracle' (see Section 12.6) could be repeated anywhere else. This, however, is open to question. There are a number of historical and unique factors in these countries which would make such replication difficult, and Kiely (1995) is critical of those who attempt to develop such an East Asian model. Despite this criticism it is clear that the World Bank and the IMF view these countries as potential models of free-market development.

While accepting that such an approach will lead to greater income inequality in developing countries, New Right theorists argue that this is a good thing and necessary for markets to work. Berger (1987) also argues that ultimately such adherence to the market will lead to greater levels of democracy and individual freedom.

The increasing importance of private finance for investment in developing countries has led to much greater weight being attached to these ideas. (Banks can always be relied on to support notions of unfettered free-market activity.). The impact of the world recession and the debt problem which led to bank loans drying up for a period in the mid-1980s, and governments in developing countries being forced to go cap-in-hand to the IMF, also reinforced the hegemony of free-market economics at the time.

Critics of the New Right suggest that there is no clear evidence that free-market solutions work; the example of the East Asian NICs cannot in reality be cited as an example of free-market capitalism. (This issue is discussed in more detail in Section 12.6.) Further, they point to the massive rise in inequality within developing (and developed) societies (see also Section 14.8) as a result of such policies, and argue that such an approach often means hugely greater hardship for some. This is intensified by the increased importance of private finance which tends to orientate itself to the more developed parts of the under-developed world, thus increasing the division between rich and poor and underlining the point that policies based on the free-market will at best provide development only for some – those potential investors view as a source of profit.

This point draws on research which shows that more development often occurs the greater the level of income equality. Journalist Ed Balls saw this as a rejection of free-market ideas:

In developing as well as developed countries, faster growth and rising income equality appear to go hand in hand.
(Balls, 1994)

The resurgence of classical Marxism

Marxists reacted against the pro-capitalist view of the world contained in modernization theory, though they shared its emphasis on economic growth as the key to development. Equally, while Marxists shared a desire for radical change with dependency theory, they rejected its nationalist orientation and insisted on the centrality of classes.

This rejection of the dependency view is perhaps best seen in the rather idiosyncratic Marxist approach of Bill Warren (1980). He rejects the idea that capitalism had a negative effect and under-developed the third world. Instead he argues that it represented social progress and a key development in the move to socialism. Capitalism destroys old traditional social structures and allows countries to develop industry.

Warren's ideas are based on those of Marx (see also Section 2.3), in the sense that the latter was quite clear about the gains in terms of productivity and technique that capitalism offered compared with pre-capitalist regimes; and this is also reflected in Marxist theorists' refusal to romanticize the past. It is the case, however, that Marx did also stress the major problems that capitalist upheaval caused in, for example, India; and in this sense Warren does not so clearly follow Marx.

Nonetheless, the 1980s did see a resurgence in approaches representing a return to a more classical interpretation of Marxism, such as the work of Hyden (1983) and Sender and Smith (1986).

In his study *The End of the Third World*, Marxist writer Nigel Harris (1987) argues that the third-worldist ideology which is the political counterpart to dependency theory was always largely a myth and has certainly been eroded today. He argues that the analysis of development needs to be centred in terms of class, not nations which were the ultimate building-blocks of dependency theory. His analysis centres on the effect of the growth of the NICs and the internationalization of capital (see also Sections 12.5 and 12.6). He argues that individual countries are now forced to respond to these pressures, but in doing so they try to industrialize primarily in terms of flexible labour with a high level of authoritarian control. This builds up resentments which lead to movements, which eventually destroy capitalism.

A further Marxist thinker, also critical of dependency theory, is Kitching (1989). He asserts that the ideas behind dependency theory are romantic sentimentalism based on peasant production, finding its expression in nationalism and populism, which he sees as looking forward and backward at the same time. He argues that this rural bias offers no real future, and instead industrialization is the only real basis for development.

While Marxism and modernization theory (see Section 12.2) share the belief in the centrality of economic growth and industrialization, the cultural and individualist emphasis – and ultimately the pro-capitalism – in modernization theory marks it out clearly as a liberal theory. This is a clear difference.

Neo-Weberian views on development

Neo-Weberian approaches start off as a critique of the way Weber's work (see Section 2.3) was interpreted by Talcott Parsons and thereafter incorporated into modernization theory. One of the key arguments is that this leads to a very static conception of culture. (See also Section 10.2.) The effect of this can be seen in the attempt to identify blockages to development central to modernization theory, which is based on the idea that there is only one path to development, and on a denial of other possible cultures of development.

However, neo-Weberianism also rejects the alternative view – seen in Marxist and dependency theory – which sees politics and culture as essentially determined by the economy. The alternative argument that societies are composed of a number of largely autonomous elements is central to contemporary neo-Weberian thought. (See also Section 2.3.) In practical terms, this often leads to a focus on the source of power and greater attention to political structures as compared with Marxism. This can be seen in the work of Theda Skocpol (1979). Her study of revolutions and developments stresses the centrality of the breakdown of the administrative apparatus of the state as a key element affecting social change.

This approach has led to concern with the policies advocated by states and a greater concern to view them as having autonomy from economic interests. As Booth states:

Variations in state structures or 'modes of domination', as distinct from societal structures and modes of production, are now established as worthwhile objects of enquiry in a way that they were not 15 years ago.
(Booth, 1993, p. 53)

Neo-Marxist views on development

The desired escape from economism has also influenced neo-Marxist views on development. In an attempt to develop a non-economic reductionist account based on some elements of Marxism, Nicos Mouzelis (1986), in considering development in the Balkans and Latin America, argues that it is possible to look at the military regimes in those regions and to view the military as having their own interests independent of capitalism. He asserts that while Marxism is a superior theory of social change when compared with modernization theory, such an approach is needed to avoid its one fatal flaw, that of economism. Mouzelis argues, therefore, that it is important to consider a mode of domination as much as it is to consider the mode of production. This emphasis on domination takes his theory very close to the classic concerns of the neo-Weberians.

A similar move away from a pure emphasis on economic production can be seen in the work of the French 'regulation school' represented by Lipietz (1987) and Aglietta (1979). They argue that post-war development in Europe was based on a Fordist regime of mass production and mass consumption. (See also Sections 4.10 and 9.4.)

They further argue that this system went into crisis in the 1970s and since then capitalists have adopted a variety of techniques, centred around the notion of flexibility, which they characterize as post-Fordist. In relation to the third world, the relevance of this analysis is that one of the forms of flexibility they suggest capitalists are undertaking is relocation into areas with cheaper wages. The effect of this is the creation of a 'peripheral Fordism' in the third world characterized by all the attributes of a 'bloody Taylorism'. (See also Section 9.7.) The argument is essentially a development of dependency theory in that it sees development in the third world as crucially structured by developments in the advanced capitalist countries, but it gives greater autonomy to non-economic elements, crucially the norms, values and laws which make up a mode of regulation.

Kiely (1995) argues that the key problem of this approach is the inapplicability of Fordism to an analysis of the third world. Fordism in the advanced economies involved giving workers high wages to ensure they could buy goods, but this is not true in the third world. He also argues that the theory is similar to functionalism in that it views a stable regime of accumulation as the norm, and it is still therefore a structurally determinist theory which does not treat social relations and conflict convincingly.

Post-Marxism

A further move away from Marxism has resulted in the growth of post-Marxism, a trend heavily influenced by post-modernism. This approach rejects Marxism as an example of a totalizing doctrine that has been rejected by post-modernists. The former Marxists who make up the post-Marxist approach have therefore instead argued for the centrality of radical democracy in development. This can be seen in the work of Laclau and Mouffe. The key problem is that no one really spells out what radical democracy means, and in effect such an approach ends up

simply as a radical gloss on pluralist and social democratic analysis.

Classical modernization theorists argued that democracy was one of the inevitable things that would appear as a result of development. Such a view was not supported by events in the real world, where military dictators and authoritarian regimes were common until recently. It is, however, the case that democracy is seen as more important today and some now see it as the basis for further development – reversing the line of causation of modernization theory.

Kiely (1995) argues that a problem with such theories is that the type of democracy they mainly refer to is liberal democracy and what is compatible with the free market. While such democratization has sometimes led to significant gains in terms of civil rights, it can do nothing about the rising inequalities caused by the free-market policies operating within it; and the effects of these might in the long term destabilize these democratic regimes, leading back to authoritarian rule.

Social action approaches

In developing what he calls an 'actor-oriented approach', Norman Long (1991) criticizes previous development theories for being far too deterministic in assuming that people's behaviour is constrained by societal and international structures. Development theories were very macro-oriented and focused almost exclusively on structures (capitalism, imperialism), while ignoring the fact that these structures had to be created and re-created by social actors. Long also argues that the traditional social actors invoked (class and gender) are not really social actors at all but abstractions, and he focuses instead on governments, state bureaucracies, companies and the church. These play an important role by mitigating or modifying the effects of global structures on a society.

In their explorations of developing societies, these social action researchers have also avoided using terms imposed from outside – such as capitalism and peasant – and instead have used people's own self-descriptions.

This does force thinkers to focus on the way that action by groups is not something that can be assumed to happen. In this respect, neo-Marxist work on how classes come to be formed, and the subjective element of class action rather than the objective notion of class structures, might come closest to integrating the concerns raised in this approach. (See also Section 4.3.)

Long's work has forced development theorists to think seriously about the fact that societies are made and changed by social actors and are not simply constructed by abstract structural forces.

Activity

On a larger copy of the accompanying chart, briefly summarize the information provided in Section 12.4.

THEORY:	New Right	Marxist	Neo-Marxist	Post-Marxist	Neo-Weberian	Social action
Explanation for global inequalities						
Likely future developments						
Effect on the third world						
Key concepts						
Authors						

I, A

12.5 Globalization and world development

At its simplest, the term 'globalization' encompasses the way in which the world is becoming more interconnected so that processes in one area have a major impact elsewhere. It is a very fashionable term, but this has unfortunately meant that it is not often given the critical scrutiny it deserves.

Convergence theory

Perhaps the best early example of a theory which today would be labelled as global is convergence theory, represented by Kerr *et al.* (1973). This was seen as a development of modernization theory.

The basic idea was that all countries were moving to a point where they would be incredibly similar: they were converging, growing more alike. The cause of this was seen as the process of industrialization. It had an initial Cold War effect in that it implied that political arguments were unimportant – whatever was said, socialism would end up like capitalism because they were both based on industrial production. The path for the developing countries could also be clearly grasped, since they too would converge on the model provided by the advanced industrial nations.

A new international division of labour

Central to the process of globalization is the idea of a new international division of labour (NIDL). (See also Section 9.9.) This idea was developed by Fröbel

et al. to explain the movement of corporations to the third world. They argued that it reflected the splitting up of the world into sectors with different characteristics, and for capitalists the third world represented a source of cheap labour.

Arguments for the NIDL thesis

The key assertion is that the 'old' division of labour, based on developing countries exporting raw materials to be processed elsewhere, has now broken down, with manufacturing industry instead being divided up around the globe:

Trousers for the Federal German market are no longer produced in München-Gladbach, but in the Tunisian subsidiary of the same Federal German company.
(Fröbel *et al.*, 1980, p. 9)

The World Bank estimates that the share of world output taken by developing countries will reach 60 per cent by the year 2020. *The Economist* (1994a) points out that the fastest growing economies at the moment are to be found in the NICs of East Asia (see also Section 12.6): economic growth there averaged 7.5 per cent between 1974 and 1993, compared with 2.95 per cent in the developed world. *The Economist* points to one of the key reasons for this, namely cheap labour: to employ a production worker in Germany costs $35 an hour, compared with $5 in South Korea and $0.5 in China, Indonesia and India.

Countries that wish to develop need to attract mobile foreign capital in the present economic climate, and one way to do this is to provide a cheap, docile labour force. This clearly has implications for the social side of development.

Arguments against the NIDL thesis

Not everyone accepts that the above process is happening, or at least at the pace and with the implications contained in the NIDL thesis.

In their study of the global political economy, Gill and Law (1988) pointed out that two-thirds of foreign direct investment (FDI) went to the advanced industrial economies, and the money that went to the developing world did not go to countries with the lowest wages but to middle-ranking countries in Latin America and East Asia. *New Internationalist* (1994) showed that 70 per cent of foreign investment in the third world went to just ten countries, and these were mainly NICs, not poor countries with the cheapest wages. Gordon (1988) has pointed out that the share of world manufacturing taken by the third world in 1984, at 13.9 per cent, was lower than their share in 1948 (14 per cent). Lloyds Bank (1995) points out that the share of FDI going to the developing world has fallen recently from a peak of 30 per cent in 1967.

Thus this alternative view suggests that the portrayal of a world ever more dominated by international capital flows may be rather a large exaggeration.

The political implications of this argument are important. (See also Section 17.6.) If globalization is happening in the way the NIDL thesis suggests, then international capital is all-powerful and nation-states can have very little individual impact. Democracy in any effective sense is at an end. If this is *not* true, there is still the scope for political action at national and international levels to have an effect.

Contemporary theories of globalization

A positive appraisal of the role of trans-national corporations (TNCs) in the third world has been given by what Schuurman calls 'post-imperialist theorists', notably the approach contained in the articles in Becker and Sklar (1987). They argue that theories of imperialism see the impact on the third world of capitalism in general, and the TNCs in particular, as always negative. They assert that, on the contrary, TNCs may bring many benefits, such as access to capital, technical expertise and markets. They also argue that TNCs might help progressive modernizing élites to overturn the political power of traditional political forces. TNCs could therefore help the process of development.

An alternative view on this is given by Sklair (1991, 1994), a development sociologist who has consistently argued for the need to devise a sociology of the global system. He says that two significant developments have contributed to the process of globalization:

- the new international division of labour and the TNCs, discussed above, and
- the global scope of the mass media.

Sklair points out that many other theories have attempted to come to terms with these developments, but he says that we need a sociology of the global system focusing on trans-national practices. He attempts to provide this in his own work, where he argues that we are now seeing the development of a trans-national capitalist class working through political practices, together with an economic wing (the TNCs) and a cultural wing (the promotion of consumerism through the mass media). (See also Section 10.9.)

This builds on the dependency approach, in that Sklair asserts that capitalism can offer only a distorted form of development to the third world. It also builds on the world systems approach, although Sklair's emphasis on political and cultural transnational practices avoids the charge of economism often laid at the door of world system theorists. He

argues that although the pro-capitalist case for TNCs rests on the claim that they will bring increased prosperity, in fact the evidence appears to suggest otherwise:

> . . . *although the TNCs have sometimes made substantial profits from their third world operations, the overall development effects have been less than outstanding, even in terms of that (distorted) form of 'development' that they sought to create.*
> (Sklair, 1994, p. 174)

At the centre of his analysis are the actions of the trans-national capitalist class comprising TNC executives, globalizing state bureaucrats, capitalist-inspired politicians and professionals and consumerist élites. He says that these operate to coordinate the system and ensure that where local practices threaten their operations these are marginalized or incorporated into the global capitalist system. In his view the ideology of consumerism and the way it is spread by the media are central to this process.

An extremely useful book, *Globalisation* (Waters, 1995), provides a summary of theories. Waters also argues that these need to be considered under three headings, the economic, the political and the cultural, and he includes a diagram illustrating how these processes have developed (see Figure 12.4).

Figure 12.4 The path of globalization through time. Source: Waters (1995, p. 159)

What this demonstrates is that it is possible to derive theories of globalization based on economic, political or cultural processes. Since most contemporary variants of sociology tend to favour one of these as the key process, this shows that globalization might become one of the most important issues

First read the article 'India's consumerism fuels sharp rise in dowry deaths' and then answer the following questions.

a Which local practice is being transformed according to this article?

b Explain in your own words how the ideology of consumerism might be seen to be contributing to this process.

c Which of the groups identified by Sklair as part of the trans-global capitalist class, if any, might be contributing to the problems identified in the article?

d To what extent does this example support Sklair's argument that local practices are marginalized or incorporated into the global capitalist system?

I, A, E

for sociological debate into the future, and one where the old arguments can still be heard.

Critiques of the notion of globalization: does it matter?

Gill and Law (1988) point out that the bulk of FDI goes not to the third world but to the developed countries. This should make us question the validity of using the term 'globalization', at least in relation to the economic sphere. It might be argued that this is simply a more pretty name for what is in fact a new form of imperialism, dominated as before by the advanced industrial nations.

Hirst and Thompson (1995, 1996), leading critics of the idea of globalization, argue that it mistakenly implies that there is a declining role for the nation-state. They consider that the whole edifice of international production and trade requires the support of various forms of state regulation, so the idea that we have gone beyond the nation-state is wrong:

The open international economy depends ultimately on western (particularly US) force and upon active public regulation backed by legal enforcement.
(Hirst and Thompson, 1995, p. 427)

So, does globalization matter? In the developed world the debate has centred around the extent to which it implies that the nation-state is finished, and whether jobs are disappearing to third-world countries. The same questions are evident in the third world. The issue of whether it is possible to achieve some kind of national economic independence in the face of a capitalist world economy was the basic question asked by dependency theorists and third-world nationalists. Globalization arguably makes these debates more important.

India's consumerism fuels sharp rise in dowry deaths
MOLLY MOORE

IN an era of unprecedented economic advances, when India boasts the world's fastest growing middle class, it is also experiencing a sharp escalation in reported dowry deaths and bride burnings.

Police say reported dowry deaths have increased by 170 per cent across the country in a decade, with 6,200 recorded last year – an average of 17 married women burned, poisoned, strangled or otherwise killed each day because of their family's failure to meet the dowry demands of their husband's family.

Indian officials say families of every religious, social and economic background are turning increasingly to dowry demands as a means to escape poverty or acquire the modern conveniences advertised daily on television.

"We are becoming a very materialistic and consumer-driven society," said Sundari Nanda, who heads the New Delhi police department's Crime Against Women cell. "For such a society, dowry becomes a way of betterment for those in the process of climbing up."

Even the poorest Indian families often spend more than £1,880 on a wedding – the equivalent of nearly 10 years' wages for the average worker.

In recent years women's organisations, such as the Women's Vigilance Society, have begun helping abused wives. In New Delhi, an estimated 150 shelters and homes for abused women have opened.

Under a 1961 Dowry Prohibition Act, giving and taking dowry is illegal, punishable by jail and fines.

Even so, few cases make it to court. The husband's family may bribe police to cover up dowry-related murders. By the time Mr Chand arrived in the village 20 miles outside the capital where his daughter, Asha, had been killed, police had declared the death accidental.

With the help of the Women's Vigilance Society he forced police to bring charges against his daughter's in-laws and arrest her husband and mother-in-law. Although Asha was said to be the fourth case of dowry death in the village in as many years, it was the first in which police filed charges.

Source: Adapted from *The Guardian*, 13 April 1995

12.6 Industrialization and NICs: the end of the third world?

For many years there has been a debate about the best policy for a country to follow to industrialize itself successfully. We have seen that modernization theorists argued essentially for developing countries to follow the lead given by the developed nations. This was considered too ethnocentric by many theorists in the developing nations, who sought to outline a course for industrialization that would lead to economic as well as political independence for these nations. Third-world nationalist approaches first alighted on the idea of import-substitution industrialization (ISI), but ultimately this was not a success.

Their approach was also frowned upon by developed nations and financial institutions such as the IMF and the World Bank. This was partly because the strategy was intended to gain independence from them, and partly because it was influenced by socialist rather than capitalist ideas. They argued that successful industrialization and development *required* countries to integrate themselves into the world economy, implying a strategy of export-oriented industrialization (EOI).

Discussion of the relative merits of ISI and EOI has taken place in relation to the experiences of what are called newly industrializing countries, or NICs. This grouping includes, *inter alia*, Brazil, Argentina and Mexico, and the East Asian economies of Taiwan, South Korea, Singapore and Hong Kong. The latter have been at the centre of recent debate because of the economic success they have experienced.

A related debate concerns the question of whether the term 'the third world' is still useful, owing to the growing diversity of countries covered by it.

Import-substitution industrialization

A radical approach to the barriers to development was taken by a group of economists working for the United Nations' Economic Commission on Latin America (ECLA), whose director was an Argentinian, Raul Prebisch (1959). Although more radical than that of the modernization theorists, this approach shares the idea that industrialization is the key to development and that government-led economic planning has a key role.

In contrast to the 'cultural' emphasis of modernization theory, the ECLA team argued that there were key structural barriers to further industrialization in Latin America. Important among these were the forms of land ownership, and the links between Latin America and the rest of the world. The development of Latin America had to be understood in relation to these linkages because it had developed by orientating itself to the outside world, as a supplier of raw materials and foodstuffs for industrialized nations.

If conventional free-market economics were to be believed, this specialization should benefit all parties, but the ECLA group pointed out that this was not the case. The amount of money that people spend on food has a limit, they argued, so income from exporting foodstuffs does not improve greatly as

the standard of living of those in industrialized economies rises. More and more goods need to be exported to pay for the increasing demand for their *imported* goods. Eventually this would place a strain on Latin American economies and a continuation along this path would lead to economic ruin.

The answer proposed by the ECLA economists was to stop relying on earnings from exporting primary products. They should industrialize, thereby becoming less dependent on imports from elsewhere. Their strategy became known as import-substitution industrialization, or ISI.

In effect, governments of the NICs needed to protect their infant industries by discouraging imports. These industries also needed a domestic market, and this led ECLA to call for land reform and other social changes to reduce inequality and allow more people to afford the products the countries would produce.

The policy achieved support from the US government (in the form of its Alliance for Progress) which wished to avoid further revolutions in the area, and believed that reductions of inequality would help achieve this aim.

However, although it did have some early successes, ISI was ultimately a failure. Roxborough (1979), a development sociologist whose work has mainly been concerned with Latin America, identifies two main reasons for this:

- To set up their domestic industries these countries needed to import capital goods (machinery and technology). As a result the import bill rose instead of falling, and so there was a need for more, not less, concentration on the exporting of primary products.
- To discourage imports of manufactured goods, taxes on imports (tariffs) were raised. But to get around these tariffs, foreign companies merely set up subsidiaries in Latin American countries.

A third problem was that these industries concentrated on providing goods for the rich in their countries, thus ignoring the needs of the mass of the population.

Export-oriented industrialization

The key alternative conception of industrialization promoted by the IMF and the World Bank involved opening economies up to the world markets and basing industrialization very much on the production of goods for export. This involved the production and exporting of manufactured goods, thus shifting the third world (or parts of it) away from reliance on the export of raw materials.

One of the reforms required by ISI was the achievement of greater equality to create a mass market for manufactured goods. This linked it up with radical political approaches. If, however, you are relying on the export market no such reforms are immediately necessary. EOI was often associated with the rise of authoritarian military governments in Latin America, such as Brazil after the 1964 coup and Chile after the 1973 coup.

The rise of the NICs

It is from this background that the newly industrializing countries emerged as a recognizable group, as Foster-Carter makes clear:

A very different approach . . . increasingly emerged in the late 1960s and 1970s, especially in parts of Latin America and East Asia. (The contrast between Brazil before and after the 1964 military coup is probably the most striking example.)
(Foster-Carter, 1985, p. 121)

This points towards identification of the NICs. The list includes Brazil and Mexico and the four 'Asian Tiger' economies of South Korea, Singapore, Hong Kong and Taiwan. Foster-Carter argues that their novelty lies not so much in the promotion of exports, but rather:

- the promotion of exporting of manufactured goods, and
- close involvement of the state in economic promotion.

The second of these propositions is controversial and has led to debate about the reasons underlying the success of the NICs. Their economic success is, however, beyond question. When measured by their GNP *per capita*, their growth rates are astounding and dwarf those of the developed countries (see Tables 12.2a and b).

It is clear that over the last 35 years the East Asian economies have overtaken the Latin American economies in terms of GNP *per capita*. (A contributing factor in this was the effect of the 'debt crisis' in Latin America in the 1980s.) Attention has

Table 12.2a Indicators of GNP *per capita* for five NICs

	GNP per capita world ranking 1962	Growth GNP per capita annual averages 1965–90	GNP per capita 1990 (US$)	GNP per capita world ranking 1990
Hong Kong	40	6.2	11 490	19
Singapore	38	6.5	11 160	20
South Korea	99	7.1	5 400	27
Brazil	67	3.3	2 680	36
Mexico	51	2.8	2 490	40

Source: Adapted from Jenkins (1994b, p. 73)

More recent figures highlight the growing divide between the Latin American countries and those in East Asia, no doubt partly reflecting the effects of the Debt Crisis on Latin America:

Table 12.2b Indicators of GNP *per capita*, 1994

	GNP per capita 1994 (US$) (current prices)	Growth GNP per capita annual averages 1980–94	GNP per capita world ranking 1994
Hong Kong	21 650	N/A	19
Singapore	23 360	N/A	18
South Korea	8 220	7.7	26
Brazil	3 370	0.3	40
Mexico	4 010	0	33

Source: World Bank (1996) Table 1 and individual country entries.

shifted very much towards East Asia in an attempt to discover the basis of their success.

Activity

List these countries in order of their positions in the world ranking (GNP *per capita*) in 1990 and 1994. Looking also at the ranking for 1962, summarize how the order changed. Which has seen the greatest improvement in its relative position and which the least?

Why have the NICs been so successful?

New Right and neo-liberal thinkers have argued that the main reason for the economic success of the newly industrializing countries lies in their adoption of free-market policies, which are thereby vindicated. Other countries are urged to follow their example.

It is possible to cite a number of examples of such New Right thinking. Berger (1987) and Fukuyama (1992) both include references to East Asia as capitalist 'miracles' for others to follow. Little (1981), a neo-classical economist, argues that their success was down to the adoption of good policies (meaning free-market ones) and favourable internal factors. Belassa (quoted by Harris, 1987), a development economist, argues that Taiwan and South Korea were successful precisely because they did not plan economically but operated within the free market. Richards (1993, 1994), in articles in the *OECD Observer*, gives a hybrid view which recognizes government involvement but still places the major emphasis on neo-liberal economic policies:

An immediately evident explanation for their success is that the three governments have systematically applied consistent trade liberalisation, conservative fiscal and monetary policies and market-oriented structural policies. There is another

reason, less instantly obvious; their governments have deliberately encouraged the adaptability of human resources.
(Richards, 1993, p. 24)

This view of their development has, however, been strongly challenged. Harris (1987), a Marxist social scientist, argues that the level of state planning in at least three of the East Asian NICs made them comparable to the centrally planned regimes of eastern Europe. He is clearly critical of the New Right's view of their development:

The process of accelerated economic growth in the newly industrialising countries appears to be everywhere associated with the expansion of the public sector and the role of the state. It has not been 'free enterprise' nor multinational capital which has led the process, but the deliberate and persistent efforts of governments.
(Harris, 1987, p. 145)

The factor of state involvement is echoed by Foster-Carter (1985), and Kiely (1993) emphasizes that the key weakness of New Right analyses of East Asian economies is that their success was due to the state getting prices 'wrong'; that is, allowing exports to be priced more cheaply than they otherwise would have been. If market prices had been applied this export growth would probably not have happened.

If the New Right view of *laissez-faire* development is wide of the mark, in what way was state involvement important? Jenkins (1994b) contends that the state was able to set performance targets, to retain a fair degree of authoritarian control (particularly over labour and trade unions), and to push through land reform. The success of land reform in East Asia, in contrast with the failure of such moves in Latin America, is one of the key factors in the turnaround in the 1980s.

Other writers have argued that the promotion of high educational standards in the East Asian NICs is also an important state-led factor.

The East Asian experience has been described both as a model of the success of free-market capitalism, and as showing the importance of certain state involvement in economic planning and development. Implicit in all this is the attempt to devise a model for others to follow.

Replicating the success of the NICs

The World Bank and other international organizations clearly believe it is possible for other countries to replicate the success of the NICs. Jenkins (1992) summarizes the message of neo-liberalism as follows:

Although entrepreneurial ability and the responsiveness of producers will vary from country to country, this will only affect the time it takes for these

policies to be successful. Thus any country which adopted sound neo-liberal policies could expect to reap the benefits which have been enjoyed by the East Asian NICs.
(Jenkins, 1992, p. 189)

Jenkins (1994b) is, however, critical of this view for a number of reasons. These fall broadly into two arguments: the success and benefits are not totally as rosy as sometimes painted; and they are not generalizable. In relation to the first point, Jenkins says that many dependency theorists have questioned the reality of development in East Asia, focusing on the following:

- There is exploitation, meaning low wages, long hours, bad working conditions and the repression of trade unions (although Jenkins points out that in East Asia wages are rising and more forceful trade unions are appearing).
- There is an urban bias, which will lead to over-urbanization and consequent problems.
- There are environmental costs associated with massively increased levels of pollution.
- Most of the NICs have fallen far short of democracy. Over the last three decades many have involved military governments, although this has lessened in recent years.
- The development is fragile because export bias leaves the countries vulnerable to changes in the rest of the world. It is perhaps most clear in this sense how such development might be described as 'dependent development'.

Activity

The significance of authoritarian control in South Korea, and the characteristics of the NICs in general, was the subject of a 'debate' between the journalist John Pilger and Aidan Foster-Carter in the *New Statesman and Society*. The relevant articles are contained in the 10 March 1995 and 17 March 1995 editions (pp. 26 and 21 respectively).

a Obtain copies of these two articles from a library. Make notes on them by listing the contrasting claims and counter-claims made by these two writers.

b On the basis of these articles and any other information you are familiar with, assess the relative strengths and weaknesses of the two contrasting positions.

K, I, A, E

What can be said about the generalizability of the model? Dependency theorists have made the point that there is a limit to the demand for exports from the third world, and if every other country were to follow the EOI route prices would inevitably fall. Also, in an economic climate dominated by recession in the developed world, the market for exports is fairly saturated at the moment. Foster-Carter (1985) sees this as dependency theory's strongest argument.

Jenkins (1994b) also emphasizes the need to see the rise of the East Asian NICs as due to specific factors and configurations which cannot automatically be generalized to the rest of the world.

The end of the third world?

Harris (1987) argues that the emergence of the NICs has led to the end of 'third worldism' as an ideology that emphasized a degree of independence from the rest of the world. The nationalist inspiration behind such a notion has been destroyed by the emergence of a global capitalist market and the integration of the NICs into it. Third-world nationalism failed and the unity implied by the concept has been undone by the fact that, while the NICs enjoyed growth, many other parts of the globe did not benefit at all. The strength of the international capitalist order means that a nationalist response to this is doomed to fail, so only class solidarity can work. Class divisions were ignored by nationalist ideologies, and Harris argues that they are now more important than ever. He says that this shows up the myth of the notion that state control had overcome the market, but it also points to a potential source of future instability in the NICs. Their development was based on authoritarian control of labour power and this has built up resentment which may be the basis of future protest about the nature of such regimes. South Korea in early 1997, with riots and labour unrest, is an example of this.

This is not simply an argument about the diversity of the world beloved of liberal thinkers, but an argument that the world is more integrated and that nationalism is no longer a suitable political response. Socialism based on classes is more relevant than third worldism based on nation-states.

To the more standard liberal argument that the third world has disappeared owing to the growing diversity of countries that the term was used to describe, some authors have said that the term still has applicability and that the third world is increasing owing to the collapse of the 'second world'.

Activity

The move from socialism to the market in Vietnam is examined in the article 'Poorest suffer in new Vietnam'. Read the article and answer the following questions.

a Which country might be talked about as 'Asia's newest economic power'?
b Summarize the differences between urban and rural life in Vietnam.
c What changes in economic policy are identified by the article?
d What are the positive effects of this?
e What are the negative effects?

U, I, A

Poorest suffer in new Vietnam
PHILIP SHENON

IN the poorest part of the country, talk about Vietnam as Asia's newest economic power is a distant whisper.

The rice farmers who tend the arid, gritty soil along Vietnam's central coast say they are thankful their crops can fetch higher prices in newly free markets. But the land here in Quang Tri province is so unproductive that even when prices go up, most farmers measure the impact in pennies.

Among the province's 400,000 people, many farming families earn less than £130 a year. In some years, when the land is washed over by salt water that floods in from the South China Sea, there is no crop at all.

"I have seen pictures of Hanoi and the other big cities, and I think they must be like paradise," said Ho Thi Dong, a labourer, aged 40. "But here in the country I think life has become more difficult. The government cannot help us like before."

As the Vietnamese government abandons socialism to make way for the free market, the services millions of Vietnamese had come to depend on under communist rule are crumbling.

In government schools, students are being asked to pay for their books, and, in some cases, for classes.

Vietnam's health care system, once free and considered a model for the developing world, is giving way to a private system.

For farmers, there is no longer the promise that in years of flooding or drought the government will provide seed and fertiliser.

The loss of government services is one thing in Hanoi, or Ho Chi Minh City, the financial centre, formerly known as Saigon. Under a free market and with billions of pounds in new foreign investment, Vietnam's cities are booming, and most city-dwellers have never lived so well.

But the new economic system means something else in Quang Tri province, where the people are as poor as any on earth, where few foreign investors visit, and where the opportunities of the free market can be swept away by flood or drought.

Source: *The Guardian*,
22 November 1994

At the heart of this is where to place the old centrally planned economies of eastern Europe since their dismemberment in 1989. The introduction there of free-market medicine has led in many cases to economic collapse and severe hardship for the people. This is seen by some as a prime example of the expansion of the third world.

12.7 Aid and development: help or hindrance?

The theoretical basis for aid lies in the diffusionist approach of modernization theory.

On this view, development consists of those who've got it giving it (or some of it) to those who haven't. (Foster-Carter, 1985, p. 112)

The 'it' can be capital, technology, institutions or cultural values. Aid is therefore meant to assist the process of modernization. It takes the form of either grants or loans.

Sources of aid

Aid takes one of two forms. The first is bilateral aid, which consists of one country giving to another directly. The second is multilateral aid, provided by many countries to many countries, and administered and applied by international organizations such as the European Union, the World Bank and various agencies of the United Nations, such as Unicef.

Vidal (1991) reports that the level of aid supplied by the British government in 1991 was £1500 million, compared with £300 million raised by the top 400 charities. Governments, not charities, are the prime movers in the aid stakes.

Jackson (1994), a member of the radical development pressure group World Development Movement, reports that the 22 advanced industrial countries which are members of the Organization for Economic Cooperation and Development (OECD) provide 89 per cent of the world's aid, and this proportion has been rising in recent years owing to the decline of aid provision from the former Eastern Bloc countries. Very few countries have actually made good on their pledge at the Rio Summit in June 1992, endorsing a UN recommendation, that countries should give 0.7 per cent of GNP in aid.

In the case of the UK, the trend has been downwards for a number of years. In February 1993, *New Internationalist* reported that the percentage of GNP given in aid had fallen from 0.56 in 1960 to 0.27 in 1990, as Figure 12.5 shows.

However, figures produced by the Overseas Development Agency (ODA, 1994) show that this percentage had risen slightly to 0.31 per cent in 1993. They also reveal that there has been a trend towards more UK aid being dispensed multilaterally.

Where does aid go to?

Aid is commonly thought of as help to the poorest people in the poorest countries, but this is a somewhat mistaken impression. Figures from the Overseas Development Administration for 1992 (ODA, 1994a) show that the total amount of UK bilateral aid, translated into pounds per head of population, was £0.52 for Bangladesh and £0.68 for Malaysia. (See also study on Pergau Dam later in this Section.)

Figure 12.5 The fall and fall of British aid. Source: World Bank/ODA/*New Internationalist*, February 1993

The statistics further show that the percentage of UK bilateral aid going to 'low-income countries' fell from 71.6 per cent in 1989/90 to 64.3 per cent in 1993/94, while bilateral aid to 'upper-to-middle-income countries' rose from 5.1 to 7.7 per cent. Most went to the poor but the proportion they receive is falling.

It is also clear that historical and political ties affect the distribution of aid. British Commonwealth countries, for example, feature heavily on the British list. On the political front, Hayter and Watson (1985) – in their study of the World Bank, the IMF and western aid agencies – make the point that western hostility to left-wing governments affects aid payments. They cite the cases of Chile, Indonesia and Brazil, to whom aid virtually stopped when socialists were in power but was restored almost immediately when right-wing military regimes took over.

Non-governmental organizations in support of aid

One set of groups who support the idea of aid are the various charities, aid agencies and pressure groups associated with the developing world. A number of these produced *The Case For Aid: A Manifesto* (Actionaid *et al.*, 1996), which argues that aid is necessary to combat poverty, and they see this as a major achievement since 1950. While supporting the idea of aid in principle, they are critical of its actual application, and in particular the way the amount committed to aid by the UK government has been cut in recent years, and the way aid has been guided by immediate political interests. They call for a long-term vision of aid to be developed based on the idea that it is in the common interest of all, is a moral good and actually works:

At the right levels, and properly targeted, aid can work. It can help people who are not reached by other capital flows. The international campaign to reduce poverty – in which aid has played a key role – remains one of the greatest achievements of this century; this effort must be renewed for the twenty-first century.
(Actionaid *et al.*, 1996)

While recognizing that aid is only one part of this, and efforts must also be made in the areas of debt, unfair trade, and the arms trade, they ask for:

- an increase in aid towards a target of 0.7 per cent of GNP
- a greater focus on poverty relief and the provision of basic services
- steps to make sure these policies are applied across all governmental organizations.

A similar campaign by Voluntary Service Overseas (VSO, 1996) highlights the role of aid in relieving poverty, supporting emerging democracies and saving lives, and also argues for an increase in the aid budget. Various literature is produced, of which one example is reproduced here as Figure 12.6.

LAST YEAR THESE PEOPLE COUNTED ON OVERSEAS AID.

200 thousand Ghanaian villagers had clean water

200 million people received an education

200 land mine victims in Cambodia were given new limbs

THIS YEAR OVERSEAS AID IS COUNTING ON YOU.

Since 1979, the British government has been cutting aid.

In last November's budget, aid was slashed by a further 5.4%.

Join VSO's campaign to send 10,000 postcards to the government to show that people like you believe AID COUNTS. Please return this card today.

IF YOU WOULD LIKE TO KNOW MORE ABOUT WHY AID COUNTS

PLEASE RING VSO's Aid Counts Hotline on 0181 246 6879.

Voluntary Service Overseas
Changing Attitudes   Changing Lives

Figure 12.6 A VSO leaflet from 1996

Trends in aid

Hayter and Watson (1985) calculate that the real value of aid provided by the Development Aid Committee of the OECD members rose from $14.7 billion in 1970 to $21.2 billion in 1981, but since

Activity

Find out the current total level of development aid provided by the UK as a percentage of its GNP. If you have trouble locating this figure, look at recent issues of *New Internationalist*, or try to find in your local reference library the latest report of the Overseas Development Administration, the section of the Foreign Office charged with administering development aid.

What is the recent trend in UK aid? Write a short summary of your findings.

I, A

that time the amount has fallen considerably. This is one of the contributory factors which has led to talk of the 1980s as the lost decade for development.

Aid as 'helpful'

The case for giving aid is usually based on the idea that it does fulfil the role set out in modernization accounts; namely it helps development. The ODA justifies aid in the following terms:

Aid from Britain helps people in the developing countries to escape the awful grind of poverty and to live longer, healthier and more fulfilled lives. Most of all, through health, population, economic and education programmes, aid helps to give people choices over their own lives and their children's future.
(ODA, 1994b)

UK aid has, for example, been used to provide electricity at a market in Bangladesh, a tree nursery in Tanzania, support for primary education in India, health clinics in Tanzania, and access to safe clean water in Somalia.

Aid as 'a hindrance'

We will look at three forms of criticism of aid. There is the argument that countries become dependent on it and it therefore saps their enterprise – this is essentially a New Right argument. (See Sections 2.10 and 14.3.) Then there is the argument that aid is spent on inappropriate goods or is inefficiently administered – this is associated with radical social democratic critics. Thirdly there is the argument that the beneficiaries of aid are not the third-world countries but the donors – this is generally associated with radical Marxist and nationalist writers.

Aid as a form of dependency culture

The Economist (1994b) has argued that the economic logic behind the idea of aid is weak:

The present approach, however well meaning, seems to have wasted a lot of money.
(*The Economist*, 1994b, p. 69)

Aid is supposed to make up for some countries' shortage of capital, but *The Economist* argues that the low rate of savings which contributes to this lack of capital is caused by rich individuals failing to save. Aid in some sense therefore subsidizes the expenditure of these rich people. It can also be seen as a way for rich countries to buy political support.

Aid is spent almost entirely on consumption rather than investment, and will not therefore aid development. Neither does it have a clear impact on improving health and infant mortality rates. It is argued that since democratic governments are more likely to help the poor this should be a criterion for aid, a suggestion that the UK government seems to have taken up.

In a study of the ethics of development, Corbridge (1993) provides a critical summary of New Right views on the issues of aid, loans and the 'debt crisis'. He says these range from the belief that aid and loans reward the inefficient and the profligate at the expense of the efficient and the frugal, to the belief (Bauer, 1991) that by talking about relief from debt some agencies avoid their moral duty to encourage individuals and countries to be responsible for their own problems. This becomes in effect a version of the dependency culture thesis whereby aid and debt relief lead people to become slovenly and reliant on handouts. (See Section 14.3.)

Corbridge criticizes this view as a stark moral prospectus and argues that it is wrong since such an approach would mean the poor suffering more. He rejects the analysis since it ignores the inequalities created by the injustice of the international finance system. This points towards the argument that these countries are not poor through their own inefficiency but through the 'rigged' nature of the world capitalist order.

Aid as inappropriate and inefficient

Many aid interventions centre on large-scale technological projects. The concern is that there is often insufficient local research or involvement, leading to aid projects either having no beneficial effect or being positively harmful. A few examples will illustrate this argument.

In 1968 the World Bank awarded a large civil engineering contract to a consortium of European firms to build the Tarbela dam on the Indus River in Pakistan. As well as mishaps such as jammed sluices and 500 000 cubic yards of earth being inadvertently swept away, the project led to 80 000 people being relocated from the area that was to become the reservoir. Seven years later not a single drop of water had reached a single farmer (George, 1976, p. 237).

An operation in Somalia imported refrigerators operating on 110 volts, whereas Somalia operates a 220-volt electrical system. Prefabricated health centres doubled in cost to $2 million because it was decided to include two flush toilets instead of one. There was no water system or plumbing to which these could be connected in the camps (Hancock, 1989, p. 12).

In 1979–80 an American private charity sent 19 tonnes of survival food and drugs to Kampuchea during a famine. The food was so old that San Francisco zoo-keepers had stopped feeding it to their animals and some of the drugs had expired 15 years previously (Hancock, 1989, p. 13).

In 1984 a French TV company organized 'Trucks for Hope' to go across the Sahara to Sahel. Almost as much money was spent on the satellite link as on the convoy, and most of the equipment was smashed because of the speed dictated by the needs of TV (Hancock, 1989, p. 16).

A UN project to develop fish-farming in Egypt spent $50 million building deepwater ponds on soil that when wet absorbs 110 per cent of its volume in water and turns into a slurry, and is therefore totally unsuitable for fishponds. Nearby, at no cost, local smallholders established their own small ponds in the Lake Manzalah area and were harvesting 27 000 tonnes of fish (Hancock, 1989, p. 123).

In 1972 in Botswana the World Bank and other agencies gave $5.4 million to develop sheep and cattle ranches in the Western Kalahari. This led to over-grazing and an economic return estimated at below zero. In 1977, $13.4 million was given to finance 'Livestock II' to establish a further 100 ranches. Over-grazing and an inconsequential economic return resulted. In the early 1990s $10.7 million was given for 'Livestock III'.

Aid as imperialism

The central thrust of the work of Teresa Hayter (1971, 1985) has been to expose the conditionality of aid, the way it comes with strings attached. Aid donors can and do use it to effect leverage on potential recipients. Hayter says we should consider aid as imperialism, a way for rich western countries to continue to dominate and affect the affairs of formally independent states. She argues:

The governments of the rich countries of the West and their ruling class claim, with considerable hypocrisy, that they are providing 'aid' to help the third world. . . . But much of this aid fails to alleviate poverty . . . and its overall purpose is the preservation of a system which damages the interests of the poor in the third world. To the extent that it is effective in this underlying purpose, aid from the major Western powers therefore probably does more harm than good to the mass of the population of the third world.
(Hayter, 1985, p. 1)

The way aid is manipulated for political ends is also a source of criticism. Perhaps the most notorious example of this comes from the USA: 'To give food aid to countries just because people are starving is a pretty weak reason' (Denny Ellerman, US National Security Council; quoted in George, 1976, p. 210). The way food aid was used to try to gain customers for US agriculture is also clearly outlined in the following account:

This increase in commercial sales is attributable in significant part to increased familiarity with our products through the concessional sales and donations programs. . . . the economic development built into food aid programs measurably improves US export sales opportunities.
(Food for Peace Law, Annual Report 1966; quoted in George, 1976, p. 198)

The suggestion that aid does not help the recipients is given further credence by figures showing that the 1980s and 90s have witnessed net capital transfers from the less-developed to the more-developed countries. Vidal (1991) shows that in 1985 African nations received $3 billion in emergency aid *but repaid more than twice that amount in debts to banks*. He also shows that the tied nature of much of this aid creates a boomerang effect. He quotes the UK government as saying that every £1.00 given to world agencies to distribute in aid earned the UK about £1.50.

Case study – Aid and the Pergau Dam affair

Part of the aid money distributed by the UK is classed as being for trade provision (ATP), which provides subsidies to UK firms to help them gain orders in the developing world. This was at the centre of the Pergau Dam affair which led to much concern with the way aid money was being allocated.

The Pergau Dam is in Malaysia and it came to the world's attention after £234 million in UK aid was provided to pay for it. The World Development Movement, a UK pressure group, launched a court case arguing that this was an example of where aid had become intertwined with deals over arms sales. It was stated that ATP money was being used to provide aid to countries that had placed orders for military equipment with UK firms. In 1994, the UK Foreign Secretary admitted that aid and trade issues had become entangled (Nelson *et al.*, 1994). They had become entangled because part of a protocol covering a £1 billion arms deal between Britain and Malaysia linked millions of pounds of new British aid to this deal via a mathematical formula. In simple terms, it implied that the more arms Malaysia bought, the more aid would be forthcoming. It was further revealed that the plan for the dam was only won by a UK company because of the aid which was seen to be supporting a 'grossly overpriced and uneconomic proposal'. A successful challenge through the courts to this use of aid money meant the budget for aid had to be restored by replacing the £234 million.

Development organizations were concerned that aid was not going to the poorest countries (Malaysia is relatively affluent), and there was also the suggestion that this money was being used to subsidize commercial ventures by companies with close links to the Conservative Party. Hugh Bayley, a Labour MP, revealed that £8 million in aid was awarded to companies that donated to the Conservative Party, and £20 million went to companies with former ministers as consultants during 1992–93 (Hencke, 1994).

The Pergau Dam affair caused a scandal and led to further revelations – notably that British aid was being given to Indonesia in the form of a £60 million payment for a power station in Samarinda and £16 million to build a road. Again it was alleged that this was something to do with arms deals with the UK. Indonesia had difficulty in buying arms because of its appalling human rights record. Since the Indonesian invasion of East Timor in 1975, approximately a third of the population had been killed and there were allegations that British-made Hawk jets had been used in this slaughter. Durham and O'Shaughnessy (1994) argued that Britain had taken a lead in meeting the arms needs of Indonesia by negotiating an estimated £2 billion deal, and it was further alleged the aid provisions were 'sweeteners' for this.

Pressure for reform following these events led in 1993 to tightening up the rules relating to aid and trade, to try to ensure there would be no repetitions.

The 'debt crisis'

Modernization theory included a key role for the state and the idea of economic planning. The world economic shock of the 1970s spurred by the OPEC-inspired oil price rises of 1973 had a number of implications. It led to economic recession in most of the advanced industrial economies, and bank coffers filled up with petrodollars from the increased profits of the oil-producing countries. Secondly it led to the collapse of stable currency exchange rates, undermined by US balance-of-payments crises partly caused by the cost of the Vietnam War. This led to the creation of the Eurodollar market, further filling the banks' coffers.

Thus the banks found themselves flush with funds at a time when state regulation of their activities was breaking down. Bankers can make profits only by lending money out; but since in recession-hit Europe and North America there were few takers the banks turned to the developing world for new customers. There, states anxious to gain funds for investment to follow the path of modernization were ready customers.

In her study *A Fate Worse Than Debt*, George (1988) points out that total US bank exposure in the third world grew from $110 billion in 1978 to $450 billion in 1982. The move to a greater emphasis on private lending rather than public lending also fitted

in with the rising economic mood. This business was very profitable for the banks. In a study of lending by the major American banks, Aronson (1977) calculates that by 1977 they were making over 50 per cent of their profits by overseas lending. Most of this lending was to governments in a small number of countries, notably Brazil, Mexico, Argentina, Peru, the Philippines and South Korea.

There is some evidence that such an approach had initial successes. In their study of the protests arising from the effects of 'structural adjustment' policies (see below), Walton and Seddon (1994) quote economic growth figures for 1973–80 as 2.8 per cent in the advanced capitalist economies and 5.4 per cent in the developing countries as a whole. The military governments that emerged in Brazil, Argentina and Chile racked up economic growth by squeezing the poor and upping the rate of exploitation, and economic recovery in the advanced economies kept export earnings high. It is true that some money borrowed was invested in foolish projects which produced nothing, and it is also clear that money went on arms expenditure and some ended up in the pockets of third-world dictators. These facts should not detract from the point that much was invested and did lead to initial growth.

However it soon became clear there were problems. Far and away the most important factor was the economic policies adopted by the UK and the US governments (see Section 17.6). Central was the doctrine of monetarism, which meant cutting back on the supply of money in order to reduce inflation. Massive rises in domestic interest rates created a recession in advanced industrial economies, leading to a fall in export markets for developing nations. The latter also had to bear huge interest payments on their borrowings. For them this represented an external shock that had nothing to do with the efficiency or otherwise of the way they had used the borrowed money.

Thus was born the 'debt crisis'. Repayments on the loans reached unsustainable proportions, and Mexico was the first to declare in 1982 that it could not afford its repayments.

Crisis for who?

In the wake of Mexico's statement, bankers worried about their money. The banks were heavily exposed in Latin America. The quest for profits had led them to lend ever-larger amounts, and by 1982 the nine biggest US banks had lent nearly three times their total capital to the third world (Jackson, 1994). In relation to Latin America, George (1988) quotes figures showing that by 1984 the British banks, Lloyds and Midland, had lent 165 and 205 per cent, respectively, of their capital in loans to four countries. Naturally they were now worried about whether they would get their money back. If Latin American countries defaulted on their debts, the scale of the problem was large enough to bring the whole financial system of the West crashing down.

In the face of this crisis the US administration, despite an allegiance to the ideas of monetarism and free markets, rushed to pump money into the system – thereby contradicting their own monetarist policies. Over one weekend about $9 billion was found or promised to Mexico, the vast majority of which was government-funded money.

Meltdown of the system was thus averted, but the debts remained and in the face of the crisis new bank lending dried up. The banks increased their accounting provisions against bad debts, which allowed them to claim tax relief. Jackson (1994) points out that by the end of 1991–92 the UK banks had received £2.25 billion in such relief, a figure larger than the UK's annual aid programme. Their profits did not suffer. George (1988) reports that the top American banks' profits went up between 1982 and 1985. With regard to the main UK banks, Jackson states that since 1982 they have:

. . . amassed a profit of £15 billion, sustained by an estimated net transfer (payments minus new lending) of some £8.5 billion from the major debtors between 1983 and 1987 alone. Clearly the 'crisis' has not been all bad for the banks.
(Jackson, 1994, p. 103)

The bill has been picked up by two groups:

- tax-payers in the advanced industrial countries whose taxes fund the institutions who bailed the banks out, and have to contribute more to make up for tax relief paid to the banks
- more tragically, the ordinary people of the debtor nations who have paid the price for the adjustments made to repay the bank debts.

The IMF and structural adjustment plans

In the wake of the 'debt crisis', private commercial lending dried up and developing countries were left with little alternative but to ask for assistance from the World Bank and the IMF. The World Bank is charged with promoting development, and the IMF is involved because in many cases it acts as factfinder for the Bank, and membership of the Bank is conditional on membership of the IMF. These institutions will provide help only if certain conditions are met, and it is the nature of the conditions applied that have caused controversy. New loans to help countries with debt problems were made conditional on undertaking certain reforms.

Both the World Bank and the IMF subscribe to free-market beliefs that:

- economic growth can come only from opening up national economies to the world market
- development requires governments to pursue policies of economic stabilization
- wealth will trickle down from the rich to the poor.

'Structural adjustment plans' (SAPs) form the centrepiece of the demands made on borrowers. Walton and Seddon (1994) describe their introduction in 1980 and state that 37 were implemented between 1980 and 1986. Typically they involved 19 policy measures with up to 100 separate conditions. Jackson provides the following brief description of a typical set of policy requirements:

The classic IMF treatment consists of short, sharp, shock-tactics of financial belt-tightening to skim off foreign exchange for debt payment. The strategy relies on cutting imports (to save foreign currency), increasing exports (to earn more of it), and cutting government spending.
(Jackson, 1994, p. 109)

While in economic terms some of these policies would lead to some degree of stability, the overall economic effect is very recessionary. With up to 40 countries trying simultaneously to increase their exports the result is a glut of products, a fall in prices and therefore export earnings. For example, despite increasing its exports of rubber by 31 per cent, Thailand saw its earnings from this fall by 8 per cent.

It is also debatable whether these policies provided any relief overall to third-world countries. Swift (1994) points out that their overall debt increased from $751 billion in 1981 to $1355 billion in 1990, and the 1980s saw a net outflow of money from the indebted countries of $200 billion (Corbridge, 1993). Average debt stood at 85 per cent of export earnings in 1970, but by 1987 this had reached 331 per cent. A UN agency concluded in 1989 that:

. . . austerity measures imposed on the poorest countries by the International Monetary Fund as a condition for new loans have produced no results.
(Quoted in Walton and Seddon, 1994, p. 101)

It should be noted that there are methodological problems involved in differentiating between the effect of an IMF structural adjustment programme and that of the underlying crisis which led to the intervention. As Brydon and Legge point out in relation to their study of women in Ghana:

We . . . can undertake research into the now, the aftermath of the imposition of policies included in stabilization-and-adjustment packages . . . but it is extremely difficult to gauge just how adjustment has changed local communities and the lives of women in them. What was it like 'before'? Is it now better? . . . or worse?

(Brydon and Legge, 1996, p. 63)

In attempting to deal with this dilemma, Brydon and Legge called on their knowledge of Ghana before a SAP was applied, and thus were able to contextualize its effects somewhat. However, for many others this is a real problem. Although most radical critiques of the IMF assert that its actions exacerbate problems by promoting free-market policies which contribute to further export dependency and social inequality, it is important to be aware that life was probably not perfect before the arrival of the IMF on the scene. This does not let the IMF off the hook: it merely points to the need for research to place its actions in the wider pre-existing social context.

There has also been great concern at the human and social cost of SAPs. George (1988) points out that, according to one study, of 196 objectives applied by the IMF only once was the aim specifically included to protect poor people from the effects of adjustment.

It is the poor who have suffered most, often seeing their standard of living drop dramatically. Cuts in government spending often include cuts in food subsidies and in educational and health provision. Walton and Seddon (1994) estimate that in some countries the loss of real income in the 1980s varied between 10 and 40 per cent, and they also quote UN figures showing that over 1000 children a day continue to die in Africa – a grim statistic the UN puts down to the effects of the 'debt crisis' and the fall in commodity prices.

Watkins (1996), a journalist, reported on the continuing effects of a structural-adjustment programme in Zimbabwe. Unemployment, he wrote, is up to 50 per cent and those with a job have seen their incomes fall by a third. Health spending has also fallen by a third and infant mortality rates have doubled since 1990. Education spending has fallen by 30 per cent.

Other examples include Morocco, where people were faced with an average price rise for food items such as oil, sugar, milk and flour of 133 per cent while wages rose by 53 per cent. In Zaire, 7000 primary school teachers were dismissed for budgetary reasons, and in 1984 some 46 000 teachers (a fifth of the total) were fired. Zambians faced food price rises of between 50 and 100 per cent. In Kenya real wages declined by 20 per cent and were lower in the 1980s than they were in the 1960s.

If we look at some of the countries in Latin America the scale of cutbacks in wages and social welfare expenditure can be glimpsed (see Table 12.3).

Table 12.3 Wages and social welfare expenditure trends in Latin America

Country	Earnings*	Government spending on (%)			
		Education		Health	
	1988	1972	1989	1972	1989
Bolivia	46	31.3	20.3	6.3	6.6
Brazil	109	8.3	4.2	6.7	6.1
Chile	105	14.3	10.1	8.2	5.9
El Salvador	63	21.4	17.6	10.9	7.4
Mexico	72	16.4	12.3	4.5	1.7
Panama	123	20.7	19.1	15.1	19.8
Peru	95	23.6	15.6	5.5	5.5

* per employee. Index figures 1980 = 100
Source: Adapted from Walton and Seddon (1994, p. 103)

The people of the developing countries are not simply victims who passively accept this erosion of their living standards. Much of the developing world has seen food riots in response to the adjustments demanded by international financial agencies. Walton and Seddon (1994) list a total of 146 such riots in 39 different countries between 1976 and 1992. Twelve countries had a single riot in this period, including Egypt, Turkey, Tunisia, Niger and Iran. In other countries the scale of protest was much bigger, as Table 12.4 shows.

Table 12.4 Some austerity protests, 1976–92

Country	Date of first protest	Total number of protests
Peru	July 1976	14
Argentina	March 1982	11
Chile	October 1982	7
Bolivia	March 1983	13
Brazil	April 1983	11
Haiti	May 1985	6
Yugoslavia	November 1986	7
Poland	March 1987	6
Venezuela	February 1989	7
India	February 1992	3

Source: Adapted from Walton and Seddon (1994, p. 39)

George has commented on this situation as follows:

Will the IMF succeed where Marx failed? Riots – which might well one day become revolutions – are more frequently set off in our time by the Fund's austerity programme, prescribed as a means to pay off debts, than by the 'communist subversion' the West claims to fear.

(George, 1988, p. 77)

Walton and Seddon (1994) argue that the two key factors which lay behind these protests were (a) urbanization and (b) the involvement of international agencies such as the IMF in domestic political and economic policy. Urbanization, they assert, results in high levels of trade union, political and community organization capable of organizing mass protests in a way which scattered peasant communities cannot. Government implementation of structural adjustment plans were behind price rises and wage cuts that were the spur to these riots.

Alternatives to structural adjustment

A criticism levelled by the Brandt Commission (1980, 1983) was that debtor nations were dealt with on a case-by-case basis and this failed to recognize that their debts arose from conditions in the world economy beyond their control. The central thesis of the report was that the crisis was an issue faced by developed and developing nations alike (north and south in the report's terminology), and that if it was not considered globally it would lead to a global crisis. Essentially this is a critique of the pure free-market economics.

The IMF and the World Bank themselves have in some senses recognized the criticisms that have been levelled against their structural adjustment plans, and this has resulted in two reforms:

- The Baker plan of 1985 aimed to achieve adjustment with growth and argued that the developed countries must take up some of the burden. In concrete terms this seems to involve more flexible repayment schedules to avoid the short sharp shock effect of the SAPs, and greater encouragement for more private bank lending.
- The Brady plan of 1989 talked of the need for revaluation and writing-off of some of the outstanding debts.

Both of these approaches recognized that turning developing countries into economic basket-cases was perhaps not a good long-term strategy.

12.8 Social divisions in developing countries

The sociology of development often takes nations as the basic starting point: either they are undeveloped or under-developed. The problem with this is that it obscures the divisions *within* countries.

The UN's Human Development Report for 1995 (UN, 1995) pointed out that between 1960 and 1991 the share of income held by the 'top' fifth of the world's population rose from 70 to 85 per cent and the share of the 'bottom' fifth fell from 2.3 to 1.4 per cent. The wealthy used to have average incomes 30 times those of the world's poor and they now have average incomes 60 times those of the world's poor.

Class differences

Oxfam (1995) reports that Mexico has the fastest growing number of billionaires, totalling 13 in 1994. Their combined wealth was more than double that of the poorest 17 million Mexicans. While it is clear that Mexico's average income is lower than that in the UK, the vast majority of people in the UK are not billionaires (see Section 14.8) and are therefore considerably poorer than the 13 Mexicans cited above. Class analysis allows us to investigate the internal economic divisions within societies. (See also Chapter 4.)

In Guatemala the average large estate is 27 000 times the size of a typical family farm (Harrison, 1993). Land holdings are still unequal in Latin America, reflecting the failure of measures of land reform. The military coup in Brazil was prompted by fears of such reform in the north-east sector of the country, and the intervention of the military in many countries in Latin America is the main reason for the failure of land reform. A second reason is that such regimes advocate free-market policies and see no need to deal with inequality.

Chile was used as a testing-ground for free-market economics after the 1973 military coup. The economist Milton Friedman (see Section 2.10) visited the country and advised the military government it must cut state expenditure by 20 per cent. The 1980 constitution adopted by Chile was modelled on Hayek's Constitution of Liberty (see Section 2.10) and bore the same name. In 1975 government expenditure fell by 27 per cent and wages fell from an index of 100 in 1970 to 47.9 in 1975. Unemployment in some shanty towns reached 80 per cent. The model was lauded by New Right thinkers across the world as Chile's economic growth accelerated. A former Conservative Cabinet Minister, Cecil Parkinson, speaking in the Chilean capital, Santiago, in 1980 said: 'There's a good deal of similarity between the economic policies of Chile and those of Great Britain' (quoted in O'Brien and Roddick, 1983).

With the rise to power in the West of staunch followers of New Right thinking, such as Margaret Thatcher and Ronald Reagan, free-market policies and an increase in inequality on a global scale were inevitable. This is precisely what the 1980s and 90s have seen (see Sections 2.10 and 14.8): the pursuit of profit has been enshrined as the key aim and the cost has been paid by the poor:

You pay £50 for a pair of trainers. The 45 people who made them share just over £1.

trodden underfoot
In 1994 Nike spent £187 million on advertising. Money saved by cutting just two TV adverts (a 1% cut in their advertising budget) could lift 18,000 Indonesian footwear workers out of extreme poverty.

Multinationals Nike, Reebok and Adidas dominate the shoe industry. They all use factories in Asia to produce their trainers cheaply.

Figure 12.7 Part of a World Development Movement leaflet

In 1990 some 2830 million people lived in the poorest countries. Their average income in dollar terms was only $330 per person and their total income was only $930 billion. Although they made up 53 per cent of the world's population, they enjoyed only 4.4 per cent of the world's income.
(Harrison, 1993, p. 452)

In some places this has led to the return of virtual slavery. Harrison (1993) reports on the way some labourers in Brazil sold themselves into debt bondage to get a job in the Amazon basin. This involves being given 'free' transport, shelter, food and clothing in exchange for two years' labour without wages. He points out that during that time the debts the men would run up for more food supplies would keep them in bondage until they retired or died.

In Pakistan, carpet-weavers buy young children through a bonded labour scheme. Iqbal Masih was sold for £160 at the age of four and was murdered in 1995 at the age of twelve. He had been organizing against the bonded labour scheme since he was ten and some have suggested that this led to his death. At a UN conference in 1994 he described the life of a bonded labourer:

'We had to get up at four and work 12 hours. We were chained to the looms, but after work we were usually released and could go to sleep.'
(Quoted in Gannon, 1995)

In a report in the *Sunday Times*, Lees and Hindle (1995) stated that the balls supplied in the UK to the Football Association and the Premier League by Mitre, which cost up to £50 to buy, are produced by six-year-old children in Pakistan being paid 10p an hour. Figure 12.7 shows a breakdown of the production costs of trainers supplied by leading companies (World Development Movement, 1996). It seems that the combination of multi-national companies aiming to make profits and an international financial climate which promotes such profit-seeking behaviour can only result in greater inequalities.

Discussion point

It might be argued that the use of child labour is morally reprehensible, but it might also be argued that the small amount of money they earn is nonetheless better than nothing. What sort of stance on this issue do you think we should take, and what action would you suggest to ensure this stance is recognized?

Ethnic differences

The mass slaughters in Rwanda and Burundi in recent years demonstrate the continuing influence of ethnic divisions (see also Chapter 6) – though the imposition of artificial national divisions by colonialists in Africa and other parts of the world undoubtedly contributed to the tragic events. (See Section 6.2.) Again however, we need to understand that such divisions also occur in advanced industrial nations.

Unicef reports that infant mortality rates of black

Activity

The crises in Rwanda, Burundi and Zaire escalated fairly dramatically in October/November 1996. Try to locate newspaper reports on this issue, or scan recent copies of *New Internationalist*.

What does this show of the importance of social divisions in developing countries and the way these have been shaped by the history of relations between the advanced industrial nations and the developing world? Write a short report as a case study and discuss your findings in a group.

K, A

children in the USA were more than twice those of white children. This means that the infant mortality rate for black children in the USA is greater than that of children in Sri Lanka, Puerto Rica, South Korea and probably other countries generally considered to be part of the third world. (See also Section 13.4.)

If we continue to use the term 'third world' it now must mean not a geographical but a social location. On that basis many black people in the USA have more right to be considered part of the third world than people in South Korea, and certainly more right to be part of it than the 13 Mexican billionaires.

Gender issues in development

In an attempt to consider the issue of gender inequality across the world, the UN's *World Development Report* (UN, 1995) introduced two quantitative measures.

- The first, the 'gender-related development index' (GDI), is based on the 'human development index' (HDI) outlined in Section 12.1. The GDI measures the same indicators, covering basic needs, but also takes note of gender inequalities in each of these areas.
- The second, the 'gender empowerment measure' (GEM), measures women's participation in economic and political life and general involvement in decision-making.

These indicators reveal that there are still substantial gender inequalities (see also Chapter 5). Even countries with high levels of HDI do not necessarily score highly on the GDI. This can be seen in Table 12.5.

While these measures reveal that there are continuing gender inequalities, they also show that some developing countries score higher on this basis than some developed ones. For example Barbados scores higher than the UK on both measures, and Cuba scores higher on the GEM index.

It is also important to consider trends over time. Here the measures reveal that there has been a clear reduction of gender inequality since 1970. The GDI figures for all countries have increased since then, and the increase has been greater in the developing countries than in the developed (Table 12.6).

The same cannot be said of the GEM. This implies that while there has been progress in the provision of basic needs to women their involvement in decision-making remains very low. The highest possible value of this index is 1.0 and the lowest zero. The actual figures show there are only nine countries over 0.6 and 35 have values lower than 0.25. Among some of the lowest are the East Asian economies of South Korea (0.255) and Singapore (0.424) which are currently in vogue as development 'miracles'. (See Section 12.6.)

Table 12.5 Comparison of HDI and GDI ranks, 1992.

Country	HDI rank	GDI rank	HDI rank minus GDI rank
Greatest improvement in rank			
Poland	43	22	+21
Hungary	42	23	+19
Slovakia	33	16	+17
Czech Republic	31	15	+16
Latvia	40	24	+16
Russian Federation	44	29	+15
Thailand	48	33	+15
Estonia	35	21	+14
Jamaica	66	52	+14
Lithuania	56	44	+12
Greatest fall in rank			
Spain	8	34	−26
United Arab Emirates	37	57	−26
Bahrain	36	56	−20
Saudi Arabia	61	81	−20
Algeria	64	83	−19
Costa Rica	24	42	−18
Yemen	98	116	−18
Libyan Arab Jamahiriya	58	75	−17
Netherlands	4	20	−16
Egypt	75	91	−16

Note. The HDI rank is by the 130 countries included in the GDI
Source: *UN Human Development Report* 1995, p. 78

Table 12.6 Change in average GDI values, 1970–92

Group	GDI 1970	GDI 1992	Percentage change
All countries	0.432	0.638	48
Industrial countries	0.689	0.869	28
Developing countries	0.345	0.560	62

Source: *UN Human Development Report* 1995, p. 5

To the extent that this is copied elsewhere, it seems that gender will be an issue with potential for marginalization in development. The UK score on the GEM is only 0.483, making it one of the lowest among the developed countries.

Regional disparity is also revealed by reference to the GEM, as shown by Figure 12.8.

One of the problems with such measures is that they simply combine statistics that are already available. They cannot, for example, focus on the distribution of income within individual families. (See also Sections 5.2 and 7.5.)

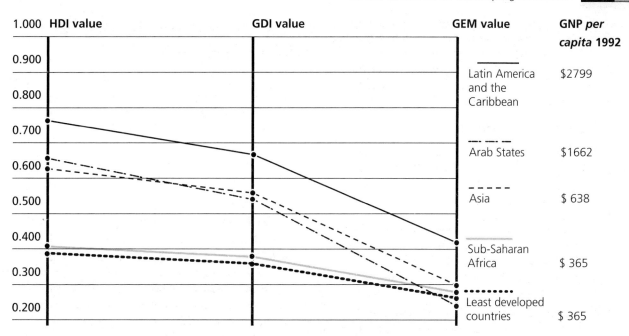

Figure 12.8 Regional comparisons of opportunities. Source: UN *Human Development Report 1995*, p. 78

💬 **Discussion point**

Which other features of life are likely to be under-stated or invisible in such figures? To what extent is this simply a technical problem?

Aspects of continuing gender inequality

Despite the general improvements noted above, in some countries there are still problems of female infanticide and gender disparities in death rates. Narasimham (1993) reports that of 8000 abortions in a Bombay clinic in the late 1980s, all but one were of female foetuses. According to the United Nations (UNDP, 1995), in China there are only 94 females for every 100 males, a divergence far beyond what would arise if nature were allowed to run its course. UNDP estimates, therefore, that about 49 million women appear to be 'missing'. In Singapore, young females aged up to four years have a death rate 125 per cent that of young males, and there are 13 countries where the death rate for young girls is higher than for young boys.

This problem is not confined to children. It is the biological norm for women to live longer than men, but in her study of women and development, Momsen (1991) reports that there are six countries – Bangladesh, Bhutan, India, Nepal, Pakistan, Papua New Guinea – where women's life-expectancy is shorter than men.

One clear impact of development on women can be seen in the massive rise in 'dowry deaths'. Dowries are the amount a woman's family must pay to her husband's family on marriage, and the threat of such a potential bill is often seen as a cause of female infanticide. Even if women survive infancy they still face possible death if their family cannot meet the dowry demands. Mies (1986) gives figures of 351 deaths of women in India thought to be associated with dowry disputes in 1975, rising to 2670 in 1976 and 2917 in 1977. A more recent figure for 1994 was 6200 such deaths (Moore, 1995).

Much of the new industrialization by transnational corporations (see Sections 9.9 and 12.5) relies heavily on female labour. Sklair (1989), in a study of the 'export-processing zones' in Mexico, reports that the majority of employees are women although the proportion has fallen from 78 per cent in 1975 to 64 per cent in 1988. He argues that the main reason for the recruitment of women is the belief by TNCs that they are docile, nimble-fingered and not interested in unions (see also Section 9.3), and their treatment reflects this belief. This creates something of a dilemma concerning:

. . . whether girls and women are actually better off inside or outside the factories that offer them employment.
(Sklair, 1989, p. 168)

The employment of women is high in the East Asian NICs of Hong Kong, Taiwan, Singapore and Hong Kong, reaching more than 40 per cent. It is also growing in areas where the textile industry has rooted itself. Oxfam (1996) cites the case of Bokul, an individual from Bangladesh:

'I sewed on collars. I was paid £4.64 a month. I often worked overtime and was not paid. I worked from 7 am till 10 pm or sometimes all night, for seven days a week. I had 30 minutes for lunch and we had to eat at our machines – we were not allowed to leave the factory.'

Theories of gender and development

Writing from a radical feminist (see Section 5.3) perspective, Mies (1986) argues that the recruitment of women occurs in ways which reinforce patriarchal structures to the benefit of capitalism, so that the process of industrialization and development reinforces gender roles rather than breaking them down. The TNCs involved in such industrialization are generally controlled by men. She provides an example of an advert produced by the Malaysian government:

'The manual dexterity of the oriental female is famous the world over. Her hands are small and she works fast with extreme care. Who, therefore, could be better qualified by nature and inheritance to contribute to the efficiency of a bench-assembly production line than the oriental girl.'
(Mies, 1986, p. 117)

Mies' view is that such governments are acting like pimps in offering young women to foreign capitalists.

With regard to education and health (see also Section 12.9), Mies argues that although provision for female education and for birth control has increased, this has occurred only so that women can be better integrated into becoming more productive workers – to the benefit of capitalism rather than for their own needs.

Mies, writing in the 1980s, was equally unimpressed with women's lot in the communist states of eastern Europe. She argues that capitalist and Marxist theories of development share a conception of 'work' that ignores the enormous amount of unpaid tasks done by females to keep the system going.

Writing from a more socialist feminist (see Section 5.3) viewpoint, Stead (1991) points to the experience of Nicaragua. Here women formed 30 per cent of the revolutionary army that overthrew the Somoza dictatorship, and by 1983 they formed 42 per cent of the economically active population. Between 1982 and 1984, some 3283 midwives were trained and health and education standards were improved dramatically. This points to political ideology as a key factor in affecting the way women are integrated into development, and also suggests a rather more positive appraisal of socialist development than Mies allows for.

12.9 Education, health and development

It is appropriate to consider some of the central debates concerning education that have taken place within the sociology of development (see also Chapter 8). Essentially these can be boiled down to two issues:

- the quantity of education provided
- the type of education provided.

The quantity of education provided

To be illiterate is to be helpless in a modern state run by way of complex laws and regulations. The man who cannot read or write is at the mercy of those who can. He is totally dependent on the sometimes questionable honesty and competence of lawyers and officials.
(Harrison, 1993, pp. 304–5)

To underline his point, Harrison recounts the problems faced by a Colombian peasant in 1975 who lost the land he had worked for 30 years, the only basis of his livelihood, owing to irregularities in legal documents he could not read.

Today, illiteracy is still a problem – albeit perhaps the problem in which the greatest progress has been made in recent decades. We are told that illiterates as a percentage of the world's population fell from 59 per cent in 1960 to 35 per cent in 1990 (Harrison, 1993). However, owing to a rise in the population the actual number increased from 701 to 916 million over that 30-year period, and Oxfam (1995) reported a figure of 960 million. ITEM (1995) says that there are still four countries in the world where more than 80 per cent of the population are illiterate – Djibouti, Solomon Islands, Somalia, Burkina Faso.

Illiteracy is not equally distributed within nations, and about two-thirds of the total of 960 million are women (see also Section 12.8). Although the gap between men and women is falling it remains highest in Africa, Arabia and South Asia, areas where women also have the lowest levels of involvement in paid employment. This points to a clear link between education and economic inequality, a fact further underlined by the universally recognized importance of the success of the education system in propelling the East Asian economies on their recent growth. (See Section 12.6.) The world is, however, far from being a meritocracy (see Section 4.9), since a World Bank study (1994) found that educational inequalities could account for only about 20 per cent of income inequalities.

Many aid agencies have over the years stressed

education as a priority area, which has had the result of lessening inequalities. The 1995 Human Development Report focused on gender inequalities and reported that:

Women's literacy rate increased from 54 per cent of the male rate in 1970 to 74 per cent in 1990. . . . Girls' combined primary and secondary enrolment in the developing world jumped dramatically, from 38 per cent in 1970 to 68 per cent in 1992. East Asia (83 per cent) and Latin America (87 per cent) are already approaching the high levels in industrial countries (97 per cent).
(UNDP, 1995, p. 3)

They also report that the biggest improvements occurred in the Arab states, thereby lessening somewhat the gender gap in that region.

Investment in education in the late 1980s and 1990s became more uncertain in the face of demands for public expenditure cuts to meet the requirements of structural adjustment plans (SAPs) (see Section 12.7). Oxfam (1995) reports that spending on education in Zimbabwe – which had stood at 112 Zimbabwean dollars before structural adjustment in 1990 – fell to 79 dollars in 1993. In Zambia, expenditure on education fell from 90 billion kwacha in 1981 to about 30 billion in 1993. The gains of the past now seem to be in danger of being lost.

It should also be noted that, despite the improvements in participation listed above, massive inequalities of educational provision still remain:

With over 60 per cent of the world's students, the South has only 11.6 per cent of the world's total educational budget.
(Graham-Brown, 1991, p. 33)

The type of education

Quantitative indicators of the amounts spent on education do not tell us what the money is being spent on. A continuing area of concern is that more is spent on education at the tertiary and university levels than at the primary level. Research by Carlos Filgueira in Latin America (quoted in Watson, 1982) showed that, between 1960 and 1970, higher education in that region expanded by 70 per cent while the decline in illiteracy was only 15 per cent. Table 12.7 provides more up-to-date figures on enrolment for all parts of the third world and a comparison with developed countries (see also Chapter 8).

Higher education is inevitably more expensive than primary education. Although important, it uses up limited funds which might be better spent on primary education. Primary education could benefit virtually all, while higher education benefits only some – most usually those who are advantaged already – and therefore contributes to an increase in inequality.

Table 12.7 Growth of enrolments, 1960–80[1]

Region	Level of education	Number enrolled (000s)			Percentage increase 1960–80
		1960	1970	1980[2]	
Developed countries	Primary	124 077	137 711	125 454	1
	Secondary	46 429	70 519	80 574	72
	Higher	9 599	21 105	29 719	214
	Total	180 105	229 335	235 747	31
Africa	Primary	19 312	33 372	61 284	218
	Secondary	1 885	5 353	13 798	636
	Higher	185	479	1 366	709
	Total	21 382	39 204	76 448	259
Latin America	Primary	27 601	47 062	64 549	134
	Secondary	3 039	7 428	17 655	493
	Higher	573	1 640	5 156	831
	Total	31 213	56 230	87 360	182
South Asia	Primary	73 595	121 296	168 854	128
	Secondary	16 196	37 439	61 561	298
	Higher	1 818	4 821	9 819	411
	Total	91 609	163 556	240 234	163

[1] Does not include the People's Republic of China, the Democratic People's Republic of Korea, and Namibia
[2] Adjusted for country differences in the length and official age span of elementary schooling
Source: Graham-Browne (1991, p. 35)

Activity

Examine Table 12.7 on page 499 and answer the following questions:

a In which region was there the greatest percentage increase in educational enrolments between 1960 and 1980?

b In which educational sector of which region was there the greatest percentage increase in educational enrolments between 1960 and 1980?

c Which regions had the highest number of enrolments in 1980 in the three sectors of education identified?

Theoretical debates about educational provision and content

Here we can identify how the two main strands of classical development thought, modernization and dependency theories (see Sections 12.2 and 12.3), are reflected in debates about education.

The theory of human capital

Functionalist and modernization theorists (see also Section 8.1) argued that education was central to modernization, industrialization and development, since it would provide the basis for enhanced skills and changed values.

The theory of human capital was developed by Theodore Schultz (1961). It became central to educational policy (see also Section 8.12) in the 1970s and 80s in the form of demands for an increasing vocationalization of education. In relation to the sociology of development, it was seen as one of the elements missing in modernization theorists' attempts to seek out the causes of under-development.

It was argued that investment in education, provided it was tied into developing the skills necessary for industry, would be an important basis for development. Also, such human capital could to some extent make up for shortages in money capital.

The theory of human capital suggests a direct link between education and industrial development, provided that education supplies what industry requires.

Education as cultural imperialism

As might be expected, these views were not accepted by those influenced by dependency theory. In her study of the effects of neo-colonialism on education in Latin America, Beatrice Avalos (1982) argues that mimicking of the structure of the developed nations (implied by modernization theory's unilinear view of development) was one of the principal causes of an over-emphasis on higher education at the expense of primary education, noted earlier. Furthermore, she argues that the emphasis on the needs of industry reinforced this, owing to the wish of many industrialists to see their workers given minimal education. Universal literacy therefore took second place to the requirements of industry.

Avalos argues that aid agencies were reluctant to expand educational provision to the majority because of concerns over the most prominent campaigns for mass literacy, led by Paulo Friere in northeast Brazil (Friere, 1982; Friere and Shor, 1987; Friere and Macedo, 1987).

In his writings on education, Friere believed it should be more than simply a tool for teaching the basic literacy skills required by industry, but should instead be a means whereby an individual learns to examine his or her situation critically. This led to conflict because the USA's 'AID' mission was concerned that the nature of discussions in the programme centred on conflicts between peasants and landowners. As a result, funding for the programme was stopped in January 1964 and aid became increasingly concentrated on secondary and higher education.

In the writing on education of Buchanan (1975), a Marxist, the effect of mimicking the developed world is again considered to have had a negative effect. He argues that this reflects the desire of some people in colonial times to enter the lower echelons of the colonial administration, which meant taking exams and courses devised by the colonial powers. This has left a legacy of an expensive and not particularly useful educational infrastructure.

A more radical position was taken by other theorists who argued that the impact of links with the developed countries through the processes of colonialism and imperialism had actually retarded or under-developed educational provision and standards. In a study of the effect of colonialism in Vietnam, Hick provides this startling example:

Unesco computations indicate that some 80–85 per cent of the population were literate at the time the French colonists arrived in the middle of the nineteenth century, and that the literacy rate had fallen to between 15 and 20 per cent when they finally left in 1954.
(Hick, 1982, p. 110)

The notion that education is not in itself always a good thing can be grasped by the fact that some see it as a form of cultural imperialism. (See also Section 10.10.) The Senegalese writer, Sheikh Hamidou, argues that the education system is the basis of the real power of the old colonial authorities:

More effectively than the gun it makes conquest permanent. The gun coerces the body but the school bewitches the mind.
(Quoted in Buchanan, 1975, p. 31)

This theme is taken up by Carnoy (1974) in *Education as Cultural Imperialism*. As the title of his book suggests, he sees education and its content as part of the legacy of imperialist domination. He asserts that there is no evidence to support the notion that mass education will benefit the majority of the population without a corresponding change in the social structure, and it may reinforce these structures and therefore inequality:

Neoclassical development theory views schooling as being a 'liberating' process, in which the child is transformed from a 'traditional' individual to a 'modern' one. This transition is supposed to enable the child to be creative as well as functional. Schooling is also supposed to enable the graduate to contribute to the economy, polity and society. But in dependency theory, the transformation that takes place in school cannot be liberating, since a person is simply changed from one role in a dependent system to a different role in that same system. While the latter may be more economically satisfying, it still leaves the individual in a conditional situation, one dominated by the metropole culture.
(Carnoy, 1974, p. 56)

Activity

a Summarize the views on the content, nature and provision of education of both the human capital approach and the dependency theory approach.

b Make a list of the arguments for and against each approach in terms of their contribution to development. (Hint: It is important to think about what you mean by development.)

I, A, E

Health and development

The social construction of starvation

The Ethiopian famine in the early 1980s led to the creation of Band Aid and Comic Relief, and much TV coverage. Yet the media tends to overlook the fact that such starvation and under-nourishment are not sporadic events but a continuing daily reality for many people.

In a study of famine and hunger, Crow (1992) quotes two estimates of the number of people who are under-nourished and therefore at risk of starvation.

- The first, produced as part of a study into world hunger (Chen, 1990), calculated that 31 per cent of the world's population – some 1570 million people – are in this situation.
- The second, produced by the World Bank (1986), provides a lower figure of 340–730 million people, or roughly 8–15 per cent of the world's population.

Whichever figure you choose to believe, these are massive numbers of people who do not have enough food, the most basic of all human needs, which those in the West take largely for granted. Why is this happening?

The media's treatment of famines tends to portray them as freak natural disasters which are simply unfortunate. This hides the whole truth:

Famine is . . . not the only form of hunger or malnutrition. In many parts of the world where famine has not occurred in recent years, sustained nutritional deprivation is . . . experienced by a significant proportion of the population. This long-term condition of chronic hunger is rarely given international focus but it may kill more people globally than the acute crisis of famine does.
(Crow, 1992, p. 15)

This points towards an explanation of hunger that does not focus on its exceptional occurrences, or indeed on the economic scarcity of food, but instead on a continuing process of social structural inequality (see also Section 13.2). This point is brought home clearly in the work of Lappé, a nutritionist (Lappé, 1975; Lappé and Collins, 1980):

To diagnose hunger as caused by scarcity of food and land is to blame nature for people-made problems. There are at least 500 million undernourished and starving people in the world. This hunger exists in the face of abundance; therein lies the outrage. . . . Measured globally, there is enough food for everyone now. The world is producing each day two pounds of grain – more than 3000 calories and ample protein – for every man, woman and child on earth. . . . Thus, on a global scale, the idea that there is not enough food to go around simply does not hold up.
(Lappé and Collins, 1980, p. 21)

A possible criticism of this view is that it focuses solely on the *distribution* of food, whereas a long-term solution would need to focus much more on a redistribution of *productive potential*. However, in either case, production or distribution, the current set-up is the result of human action. This is therefore what we might term the 'social construction of starvation', because it is a people-created not a natural problem.

The institutions set up to try to solve the problem

may often be seen as part of the problem itself. In his book *The Lords of Poverty*, Hancock (1989) examines the activities of a number of organizations involved in development. (See also Section 12.7.) He reports that, at the annual joint meeting of the World Bank and the IMF, the total cost of the 700 social events laid on for delegates during the week of the conference was estimated at $10 million – enough, for example, to supply vitamin A tablets to 47 million children at risk in the developing countries. The social events were sometimes lavish:

Ridgewells, a well-known Washington catering company, prepared twenty-nine parties in one day alone. ... A single formal dinner catered by Ridgewells cost $200 per person. Guests began with crab cakes, caviare and crème fraiche, smoked salmon and mini Beef Wellingtons. The fish course was lobster with corn rounds followed by citrus sorbet. The entrée was duck with lime sauce, served with artichoke bottoms filled with baby carrots. A hearts of palm salad was also offered accompanied by sage cheese soufflés with a port wine dressing. Dessert was a German chocolate turnip sauced with raspberry coulis, ice-cream bonbons and flaming coffee royale.

(Hancock, 1989, p. 38)

The 1985 meeting took place in Seoul in South Korea (see also Section 12.6):

In order to make space for a parking lot big enough to accommodate the fleet of limos used by delegates, the Korean government helpfully razed to the ground the poverty-ridden red-light district adjacent to the hotel – demolishing a total of 128 buildings.

(Hancock, 1989, p. 40)

Discussion point

How useful do you think these meetings are in helping to achieve the objective set out by the President of the World Bank, to 'look at our world through the eyes of the most underprivileged, ... share their hopes and fears, ... serve their needs, ... help them realise their strength, their potential, their aspirations'? What changes, if any, would you make to these operations? What problems and conflicts might be faced by anyone attempting to make changes?

Starvation is a hugely important health issue, and scandalously so. The 'green revolution' has led to higher crop yields, but because of problems associated with unequal access to water its benefits have not been equally shared. It is therefore the subject of much criticism, though it should be underlined that it did at least achieve an increase in agricultural production. One critical response to food aid (see Section 12.7) can be seen in the work of George (1976, 1988), who argues that the political aspects of food aid policy of the developed world are a key contributory factor to 'how the other half dies' – the title of her first book.

Health divisions and problems in the third world

Anyone with a cursory knowledge of the sociology of health (see Chapter 13) will know that the poor suffer the worst health. An example of this appeared in India in 1994 as bubonic plague developed into its pneumonic version. Over 1000 people were affected and at least 50 died. The outbreak was centred on Surat, a city made up of many migrant workers, with little or no infrastructure. A further example is the sale of human kidneys for £12000. These kidneys had been removed from up to 1000 poor villagers in India who were told they needed a medical examination and who then had a kidney removed under anaesthetic.

On the African continent a major problem is the spread of the AIDS virus (see also Section 13.9). Since this affects the most economically active part of the population, its spread will have knock-on effects in terms of economic production, paying for children's education and even producing subsistence foods.

Another issue causing concern has been the marketing of western baby-milk products in the third world. The concern is simple: these products rely on access to clean water to mix with them, not something that can be guaranteed for large numbers of people. Furthermore the milk is often over-diluted to make it go further. A Unicef estimate says that 4000 babies each day die from unsafe bottle-feeding, and this has led to a big campaign against the promotion of bottle-feeding by western food producers (see Figure 12.9).

Critical perspectives on health initiatives

In a study of health provision in the third world, Hardiman and Midgley (1982) found that the ratio of people to doctors was 62 times higher in rural areas of Kenya than in urban areas.

Foster-Carter (1985) also points to concerns over the operations of western TNCs (see Section 12.5) in the health field. He considers how drug prices are kept high through legal monopolies, and the way in which certain drugs that are banned as unsafe in the developed world nonetheless find their way to the third world. For example, Brown (1994) found that pregnant women in Brazil were given thalido-

A baby <u>dies</u> every 30 seconds from unsafe bottle feeding

- **Nestlé** aggressively promote their baby milks to mothers and health workers to ensure that infants are bottle fed. Such promotion is condemned by UNICEF and WHO.

- If babies are given bottles, they are less able to suckle well. This makes breast-feeding failure more likely.

- The water mixed with baby milk powder in poor conditions is often unsafe. This leads to diarrhoea and often death. *Each day, 4000 babies die because they are not breastfed, says UNICEF.*

- Baby milk is very expensive: it can cost over 50% of the family income.

- Poor people often have to over-dilute the baby milk powder to make it last longer. The baby is then likely to become malnourished.

- Breastfeeding is free, safe and protects against infection. Even undernourished mothers can breast-feed.

- **But Nestle know that if they don't get babies on the bottle they don't do business.**

Don't let them get away with it – Boycott Nescafé.

Figure 12.9 A campaign leaflet produced by the organization Baby Milk Action

mide between 1965 and 1994, even though the drug was banned worldwide in 1962. Brazil had been allowed to produce the drug to combat leprosy, but lack of control had meant the pills were given to pregnant women. It is estimated that between 1000 and 4000 thalidomide-affected babies were born. In July 1994 the Brazilian government finally outlawed the use of thalidomide by women of child-bearing age.

It is not only medical companies that affect health adversely. What happened in Bhopal in 1984 is probably the best example of another type of TNC affecting health. In December of that year a chemical plant owned by the American Union Carbide company exploded, killing thousands. The official death toll was 5325, and up to 100 000 more were still ill ten years later. A newspaper campaign advert alleged that most of these had received little or no compensation or help:

Actuaries value the life of an American at $500 000. Union Carbide got away with less than $2000 per Indian life.
(Pesticides Trust, 1994)

In a study of health from a Marxist perspective, Navarro (1982) argues that it is not possible to understand health issues in the third world without putting them in the context of imperialism. (See also Section 13.4.) The political structure affects the distribution and effects of famine and malnutrition. Navarro's approach is based on dependency theory. He argues that we need to understand the 'under-development of health'. This includes the way in which equipment and practices are imported from developed nations, even though they often do more harm than good. He cites the case of Bogotá in Colombia, a city where malnutrition is the main problem but where there are three expensive open-surgery units in operation, costing money that could provide free milk to 25 per cent of the children every day for a year.

Navarro also points to the fact that many doctors trained in the third world now work in the USA. This means that the cost of training is born by third-world countries but the benefit goes elsewhere. An example of this occurred recently in South Africa: regulations there were changed in 1996 to require doctors to practise community medicine for two years before they qualified, this being seen as an attempt to limit the export of medical expertise.

Navarro argues that the classic modernization approach said there was too little capital and expertise in the third world. He suggests that the problem is too much high-tech equipment and practices being exported to the third world, and the way this creates a two-tier health system with little money or resources given to basic health care and prevention:

Contrary to Rostow's assumption, it is the intrusion of the values of the developed countries along with their technology and 'entrepreneurial, market, international' capital into the poor societies, that creates the source of underdevelopment.
(Navarro, 1982, p. 24)

12.10 The environment and development

Development has been clearly linked with industrialization as a way to improve living standards. However, the 1970s and 80s saw the rise of environmental critiques of industrialization in both the developed and the developing worlds. (See also Section 17.5.) It is now argued that continued industrialization might lead to environmental pressures that could result in ecological disaster.

The neo-Malthusians and the population debate

Malthus (1798) thought that the growth of population always outstrips the growth of food production, and so famines would result if populations were allowed to grow. He campaigned against the Poor Law on the grounds that it would sustain population rises. (see Section 14.1.)

Neo-Malthusians have since argued that continued economic growth on a global level will lead to environmental breakdown. They have sought a 'no growth' policy and a clear approach to population control. Ehrlich (1972) campaigned for US food aid to be reduced and instead for resources to be diverted into birth-control measures. (See also Section 12.7.) In a critical review of this approach, Simons (1988) asserts that this led to support for programmes of mass (often compulsory) sterilization which were carried out in India.

Perhaps the most famous publication in this vein was *The Limits to Growth* (Meadows *et al.*, 1972). On the basis of computer models this book predicted that the world would be overcome by overpopulation and raw material shortages. As well as supporting measures for population control, it argued for a 'zero growth' economic strategy.

Critics point out that all this assumed that no technical advances would occur, and that it restricted itself solely to physical factors and did not consider social and economic changes that could have been made. The approach also received criticism in the third world where it was argued that this was simply a way for the rich industrialized West to avoid helping developing countries to achieve growth. In arguing in support of economic growth, Beckerman (1974) summarizes this criticism:

A failure to maintain economic growth means continued poverty, deprivation, disease, squalor, degradation and slavery to soul-destroying toil for countless millions of the world's populations.
(Quoted in Adams, 1993, p. 213)

Worries about population growth had a serious effect for a while, but the criticisms levelled at the neo-Malthusians have minimized this. Contemporary environmentalists have moved away from their notions of 'zero-growth'. What remains is concern over the sustainability of continued industrialization.

The notion of sustainable development

The term 'sustainable development' originates with the Bruntland Report (1987). This was an attempt to consider how it was possible to reconcile industrialization and development with environmental concerns. The report's definition of sustainable development was:

. . . development that meets the needs of the present without compromising the ability of future generations to meet their basic needs.
(Quoted in Smith, 1992b, p. 282)

This phrase avoids the problems of the zero-growth option but it remains vague. Commenting on the above definition, Adams says:

This is neat, but far from a clear base upon which to build new theoretical ideas about development.
(Adams, 1993, p. 208)

He says it is more of a slogan than a theory. This is also true of another Bruntland saying, namely 'Think globally but act locally'.

Environmental ideas which attempt to promote industrialization at the same time as caring for the environment are very popular. In a survey of the debate over industrialization and the environment, Smith (1992b) identifies three key approaches:

- the neo-liberal approach, which stresses the market
- environmentalism, which stresses small-scale development
- a structuralist approach, emphasizing the effect of the unequal relationship between north and south.

The neo-liberal approach

The problem with the market is that some goods are treated as if they are free and have no cost:

One of the central themes of environmental economics . . . is the need to place proper values on the services provided by natural environments. The central problem is that many of these services are provided 'free'. . . . Examples might be a fine view, the water purification and storm protection functions of coastal wetlands, or the biological diversity within a tropical rainforest.
(Pearce *et al.*, 1989; quoted in Jackson, 1994, p. 183)

Conventional economic calculations did not include these factors, and as a result it was felt that free markets were unable to offer environmental protection. Pearce *et al.* (1989) argue that it is possible to include environmental pollution as a cost by putting a value on the environment. Market incentives should be used, such as green taxes and making polluters pay the cost of cleaning up.

One of the problems with this is that, if we view the environment as an economic resource and simply look at it in monetary terms, there is a danger of arriving at some point where it is beneficial in cost terms to pollute! In other words, there is no guarantee that the environment will be protected.

The market notion certainly falls short of more radical environmental arguments, largely because it ignores the problems caused by the market system and assumes these can be reformed away. It is also the case that the level of regulation suggested by these ideas might lead companies to move to areas with less environmental regulation. In his study of Mexico, Sklair states:

Some of the major polluters are US businesses that have established maquiladora plants in Mexicala. [. . .] compared with Mexico, the US and particularly California, has very strict environmental protection laws. . . . a growing trend in the maquila industry is for US corporations to relocate along the border as much for the freedom to pollute as for the low labour costs.
(Sklair, 1989, p. 95)

A second problem is that Mexico is unwilling to enforce environmental laws, so as to protect jobs.

Environmentalism

Environmentalists suggest that if development and the environment are to coexist then the nature of development must in some way change. This is reflected in notions of the use of appropriate technology and more small-scale development, as in the views of Schumacher (1973). At the same time there is some consideration of the need for consumption patterns to change in the developed countries.

A more recent environmentalist approach from a sociological perspective is that of Beck (1992). He argues that the positivist belief in inevitable progress needs to be rejected, and we need to consider forms of risk that affect everyone. His thesis is that environmental problems affect us all, and he argues that the old theories of inequality cannot explain this. He neatly summarizes this as 'poverty is hierarchic, smog is democratic' (p. 36). The implication is that the environment provides the basis for action involving everyone.

Does there need to be a reduction in consumption in the advanced industrial nations? While these countries are on average well-off, and so it might appear they could reduce consumption, the averages mask great inequalities. For example, poverty statistics for the UK regularly show large numbers of people in that category. The issue of the distribution of wealth and power has to be addressed.

Jackson (1994) exemplifies a radical environmental perspective which incorporates some structuralist arguments. He argues that poverty and environmental degradation are clearly linked. Problems cannot be solved simply by more growth since often the poor do not benefit from growth. However, 'zero growth' is not an answer either. Jackson seeks an emphasis on the *quality* of economic development to replace the present emphasis on quantity. The needs of people must come first, by (a) building livelihoods to meet essential needs, (b) defending the poor's environment, and (c) letting the poor have their say. The emphasis on external constraints – such as the 'debt crisis' – which affect the choices people can make about the environment brings Jackson close to a structuralist position.

The structuralist approach

This approach builds on the insights of dependency theory. It argues that the crucial element in achieving sustainable development is the need to consider structural inequalities between the developed and the under-developed world, and to recognize that it is pressures caused by these inequalities that contribute to environmental problems.

One of the concerns is that debt-ridden developing countries are mortgaging the future of the earth to gain much-needed revenue in the present. There is a clear link between debt and the environment. George describes the practice as 'financing ecocide':

The environment is a little-noticed victim of the debt crisis in the third world, yet one day we shall pay the price for the damage this crisis does to ecosystems.
(George, 1988, p. 155)

A similar link between the structures of the world and environmental problems can be seen in the work of Redclift (1987, 1994) which explores the contradictions between development, sustainable development and the environment. He argues that the notion of sustainable development as exemplified in the Bruntland Report is far too optimistic about capitalism's ability to deal with environmental problems, and ignores the key structural inequalities which make the under-developed world dependent on the developed. This leads to cultural differences in the meaning of sustainable development. The 'north' engages in what Redclift calls 'environmental managerialism' whereby problems are treated as something to be solved through technical means. This ignores the real political and economic framework in which under-developed countries exist, and the way in which the penetration of their technologies has created problems in the under-developed countries. Thus commercial interests often predominate:

The interests in unsustainable production far outweigh those in conservation. This state of affairs is not a historical accident, but the result of powerful social classes acquiring ideological legitimacy from new forms of agricultural production, rather than from environmental sustainability.
(Redclift, 1994, p. 132)

The environment is considered only after development objectives, conceived within a capitalist framework, have been set. Answers about the environment and the transformation of nature remain partial while they remain locked into a market paradigm such as capitalism. Redclift argues that Beck's notion that the politics of risk are replacing the politics of distribution is a reflection of this partial view, since

Activity

The three broad positions outlined in this Section are taken from the work of Smith (1992, p. 286). He provides the following three summaries of the positions. The words identifying which position he is referring to have, however, been removed. Match the statements up with the three positions, namely neo-liberalism, environmentalism and structuralism. Explain your answer in a short summary.

- *Summary A* – 'provides a varied mix. The argument for "low input" technology and local initiatives is an attractive one, particularly for the less developed world, but the "no growth" solution is not, neither is it politically acceptable'.
- *Summary B* – 'the system of industrial capitalism is sufficiently flexible and adaptable to allow sustainable development to be achieved globally, based upon market principles'.
- *Summary C* – 'explaining the "real" world situation in terms of structural economic dependency within a dominant global political economic context that is capitalist. . . . transformations are required if these inequalities are to be addressed and environmentally sound solutions found'.

U, I

it abstracts environmental concerns away from issues of structural inequality that for Redclift are at the heart of the matter.

Case study – Concern over the disappearing rainforests

Deforestation is occurring at an increasing rate, often to try to develop agriculture, although the soil when exposed is not very fertile and the result is often a process of desertification.

Friends of the Earth calculate that Amazonia holds 20 per cent of all the birds on the earth; and while the UK has 1143 different plants, Costa Rica – five times smaller – has over 8000. Some 70 per cent of the plants with anti-cancer properties come from the rainforests, as do much of the world's food-stuffs such as coffee, tea, sugar, bananas, oranges, cocoa, plus a whole variety of cereals and nuts.

One of the reasons for deforestation in Brazil is the Polonoreste Project, partly financed by the World Bank. This involves the resettlement of peasants from the south who have been dispossessed of their land to grow soybeans to generate export earnings to pay off Brazilian debts (see also Section 12.7). The root cause of this is inequality and Brazil's external debt. Most commentators now agree that Brazil is the most unequal society in the world: according to Jackson (1994) some 2 per cent of landowners control 60 per cent of the nation's arable land. The Brazilian trade-union and political leader Lula Da Silva has argued that: 'If the Amazon is the lungs of the world then debt is its pneumonia'. The five countries with the biggest area of rainforest – Brazil, Indonesia, Zaire, Peru, Colombia – are all among the top debtor nations.

In her study of the effects of debt, George (1988) describes the Polonoreste project as 'the rape of Rondonia'. When it is considered that this project has led to the deforestation of an area the size of the UK, the concern is understandable. Furthermore, since the soil once exposed is totally unsuitable for agriculture, settlers are forced to expose ever more strips of rainforest to survive. A final aspect of this is the destruction and in some cases wiping out of the indigenous peoples of the area, such as the Amerindian tribespeoples. At least 87 Indian groups have been killed off. More than 200 million people live in the rainforests as a whole and a further 1 billion rely on the rivers coming out of the forest.

Concern over the project led to legislation in 1986 in the USA, requiring environmental reviews in multi-lateral development agencies (such as the World Bank operations). It would seem that the World Bank now recognizes some of the problems caused by the project and has attempted to modify programmes to incorporate environmental concerns.

A further project (Grande Carajas) partly funded by the EU will lead to deforestation of an area equal in size to the UK and France put together. Jackson alleges that this will lead to the destruction of 16 per cent of Brazil's Amazon rainforests. The forests are being cut down for timber, to be replaced by cattle ranches for the production of cheap beef and large hydroelectric dams and other industrial developments. George (1988) points out that even when it is done for timber use, this is incredibly inefficient with 90–98 per cent of the trees not used when an area is logged.

It is the phenomenon of global warming that has brought concern over the rainforests to its present high status, although the vast majority of emissions which contribute to global warming come from the developed industrial world (69 per cent of global carbon dioxide emissions come from North America and Europe and 72 per cent of CFCs are produced in the same area). Destruction of the rainforests is a minor part of the problem here, but it can seem like a solution and costs advanced industrial nations little. Scientists suggest that global warming will result in a rise in sea-levels which will lead to the disappearance of 36 countries, including Bangladesh and the Maldives.

Activity

What solutions to the problem of the rainforests might be offered from (a) a neo-liberal perspective, (b) an environmental perspective, and (c) a structuralist perspective? Which do you think would achieve most, and why?

I, A, E

Further **reading**

An indispensable book for this topic is:

- Thomas, A. *et al.* (1994) *The Third World Atlas*, 2nd edn, Buckingham, Open University Press.

A number of topic books are devoted to this subject, each of which provides a comprehensive run-through of all areas in detail:

- Barnett, T. (1988) *Sociology and Development*, London, Hutchinson Educational.
- Harris, G. (1989) *The Sociology of Development*, London, Longman.
- Webster, A. (1990) *Introduction to the Sociology of Development*, 2nd edn, Basingstoke, Macmillan.
- Foster-Carter, A. (1993) 'Development', in Haralambos, M. (ed.) *Developments in Sociology*, vol. 9, Ormskirk, Causeway Press.

More recent theoretical and empirical developments are covered in a number of books:

- Schuurman, F. J. (ed.) (1993) *Beyond the Impasse: New Directions in Development Theory*, London, Zed.
- Leys, C. (1996) *The Rise and Fall of Development Theory*, London, James Currey.
- Seabrook, J. (1993) *Victims of Development: Resistance and Alternatives*, London, Verso.
- Kiely, R. (1995) *Sociology and Development: The Impasse and Beyond*, London, UCL Press.

Back issues of the periodical *Sociology Review* (formerly known as *Social Studies Reveiw*) also contain many articles on this field of sociology and many others.

Exam **questions**

1 'Official Development Assistance (Foreign Aid) benefits the donor more than the recipient.' Explain and discuss the above statement.

[25 marks]

(NEAB, 1998 Syllabus Specimen Question, Module SL04)

2 Assess the argument that the concept of under-development is more useful than the concept of development in explaining global inequalities.

[25 marks]

(AEB, Paper 2, Summer 1994)

3 Evaluate the view that there has been a process of globalization, in which societies operate within an integrated world-wide system.

[25 marks]

(AEB, Paper 2, Summer 1995)

4 Critically discuss the view that economic growth is only one aspect of development.   [25 marks]
(AEB, Paper 2, Summer 1996)

Coursework **suggestions**

1 **Investigate the relative usefulness of the various measures of development**
It is clearly impossible to undertake primary research on this topic, but it is perfectly acceptable to submit research undertaken using secondary research methods. It is therefore possible for you to investigate the relative usefulness of the various measures of development that have been outlined in this chapter, namely GNP *per capita*, PQLI and HDI. You could consider as a hypothesis the statement: 'It is not possible to consider development adequately by using only one measure of development'.

2 **Investigate the hypothesis that aid does more harm than good to developing countries**
Again this is essentially coursework using mainly secondary sources. You will need to obtain up-to-date information about aid (perhaps focusing on that given by the UK). You could try to interview activists in relevant voluntary organizations to elicit their views.

3 **Conduct an in-depth study of the activities of trans-national corporations**
This could be either in one industry or in one region of the world. It will be necessary to consider the argument about whether or not their activities are beneficial, and to whom any benefits (or the opposite) might accrue.

Health

Chapter outline

13.1. **Defining health and illness**

People often greet each other by asking how they are. The terms well, healthy, or poorly have commonsense meanings. However, a closer look into the way members of society consider issues relating to health and illness reveals a more complex picture.

Discussion point

As a starting point to consider some of the problems in defining health, discuss the following questions. What does it mean to be unwell or well? Is pregnancy a form of sickness? If not, why do women go to a doctor when pregnant? If someone goes to a plastic surgeon to change the way they look, should they be considered unhealthy?

Definitions of health

Sociologists and others have distinguished between positive and negative definitions of health. The World Health Organization, which monitors health throughout the world for the United Nations, defined health in a positive way as:

... *not the mere absence of disease, but total physical, mental and social well-being.*
(WHO, 1955)

It could be argued that this definition means that most of us are unwell for most of the time, since it is an extremely wide definition particularly in relation to its notion of social well-being. It is also the case that this definition is difficult to operationalize and therefore apply in considering changing levels of health. In considering definitions of health in his book *Investigating Health, Welfare and Poverty*, Trowler (1996) points out that:

In practice the medical profession (and the population at large) tend to define health in a negative way: 'The condition in which there is an absence of disease or disability'.
(Trowler, 1996, p. 2)

Negative definitions of health tend to stress the objective lack of disease, but this suggests that we should not feel ill unless we have a physical ailment. Aggleton (1990), a sociologist, argues that this is problematic as we do not always feel pain when we are unwell. It is also the case that such general notions of health ignore the way in which we differ as individuals and the enormously different expectations of health among social groups.

Health and illness

We need to recognize how the interactions between objective and subjective measures affect the way that individuals and social groups react in relation to notions of health.

It is for this reason that Field (1976), discussing the social definition of illness, suggested that we need to distinguish between the objective indicators of disease and the subjective feelings of illness. Since it is perfectly possible to feel ill without actually being objectively unwell, and it is also possible to be suffering from disease or ill-health without feeling ill, the two measures could provide differing views on the extent of health or illness in the population.

Activity

Suggest examples of how it may be possible for a person to be ill but healthy, or unhealthy but not ill.

I, A

The subjective experience of illness is in fact a clear component in the construction of supposedly objective indicators of ill-health. The simple reason for this is the requirement that individuals must have sought medical help if they appear on health statistics (at least those compiled by doctors and hospitals). Statistics are compiled on the cause of death (mortality statistics) and the prevalence of ill-health (morbidity statistics), but people will not appear on the latter unless they feel subjectively ill enough to consult a doctor. This leads to the phenomenon known as the 'clinical iceberg', explained by Michael Senior (1996a):

Not all illnesses are reported to the doctor. The morbidity figures only show a small proportion of illnesses. [This] shows how the morbidity figures examine a tip of an illness iceberg. The majority of illnesses are not expressed in the figures because a large number of people do not report every illness symptom to their doctor. The idea that only a proportion of a set of illness is revealed by the morbidity figures is known as the 'clinical iceberg'. (Last, 1963) According to Last only 6 per cent of 'illness' is known about because 94 per cent of people do not report their symptoms to a doctor.
(Senior, 1996a, p. 19)

It is also the case that doctors vary (see Section 13.7) in relation to their willingness to classify people as suffering from ill-health. This insight is behind interactionist views on health that stress the ability of doctors to label people as suffering from ill-health or not and the differential treatment that patients from different social groups receive.

The idea that health is merely an objective biological category has to be challenged. Health, ill-health and illness can be seen as social constructions which involve the interaction of doctors and patients – an interaction that includes the involvement of factors other than purely objective measures of health and ill-health.

Sociological aspects of health and illness

A full understanding of the prevalence and distribution of health and illness in a population requires a fully sociological view that goes beyond the purely biological and medical knowledge about health and disease. Seedhouse (1986) identifies a number of other definitions of health, which highlight the impact of the social on this area of life.

An example of a sociological approach was functionalist (see Section 2.4) sociologist Talcott Parsons' (1972) work which saw health as the ability to perform expected roles at an optimum level. He also argued that being sick should be seen not merely as a biological phenomenon, but as a specifically defined social role, namely the sick role. (This argument is also discussed in Section 13.9.)

We can also consider the way in which the experience of being ill is differentially experienced by social groups. Approaching the issue from a social psychological viewpoint, and based on studies in France, Herzlich (1973) found three dimensions of health. Aggleton summarizes her approach as follows:

First, she identified a conception of health as a state of being – the absence of illness. Second, she identified a view of health as something to be had – a reserve of physical strength as well as the potential to resist illness. Finally, she identified an understanding of health as a state of doing – the full realisation of an individual's reserve of health. (Aggleton, 1990, pp. 13–14)

Changing conceptions of health and illness

It is usually agreed that knowledge, including our knowledge about health and illness, can be separated into three distinct cultural paradigms: magic, religion and science. Science in the form of medicine is associated with the rise of rationalism and modernity (see Sections 2.2 and 9.7). However, there are those who argue that we are now living in high-modern or even post-modern times (see Sections 1.10 and 10.11) and this has led to the development of a new approach to the sociological understanding of health and illness which will be examined in Sections 13.3 and 13.9.

... ernatural forces are sometimes asso-

ciated with the ability to cause suffering. This may be a punishment of an individual, or sometimes a whole community, for an offence against a god or a powerful individual. The 'cure' is seen as the need to call in the *shaman* to remove the curse, which obviously gave these individuals considerable power and status in their own society.

Religion (see also Section 13.8) is often seen as a powerful aspect of illness and large numbers of people pray when someone is seriously ill. Until fairly recently, mental illness (see Section 13.8) in particular was equated with possession by demons. There is still a strong belief that suffering can be a test of faith. In many societies children with mental handicaps are seen as being the favourites of their god.

Modern, western medicine can be described as using a mechanical model of illness, seeing the body as a machine which sometimes breaks down and requires repairs. This is a highly scientific view of health, where each illness has an identifiable cause and, in time, an effective cure. Jewson (1976) has shown how the power relationship between doctor and patient changed with the increasingly medical model of illness. He suggested that in the past, for those few who could afford it, consultation by a doctor was based mainly on the symptoms identified by the patient. It was only in the nineteenth century that hospitalization became commonplace (see also Section 13.5); until that time hospitals were most often avoided whenever possible as they were seen as places which people were extremely unlikely to leave cured – if at all. Since then medicine has gone from strength to strength.

Criticisms of the biomedical model

Many writers have questioned the assumptions of the medical model, that is the view that illness is always caused by an infection, that doctors will be able to cure it and that preventative measures are highly effective. Such assumptions underpin homeopathic, herbal and other 'alternative' therapies as well as medical drug-based therapies. The biomedical model assumes that disease is abnormal, that every illness has a specific cause and it is experienced in the same way in all societies. Medicine is seen as a scientifically neutral way of explaining and dealing with all forms of illness.

Trowler (1996, p. 171) suggests that people are now 'treated as objects to be manipulated by medical technology', although Walker and Waddington (1991) claim that this is no longer true for all illnesses. They show how people with HIV and AIDS, the patients and their pressure groups (see Section 17.5), often know more about the disease than the doctors, creating a more equal relationship between professional and sufferer.

The medical view of health is challenged by some illnesses for which doctors have no agreed definition, such as RSI (repetitive strain injury) and ME (myalgic encephalomyelitis). In relation to changing conceptions of health and illness, Turner (1987) points out that the change over the twentieth century from mainly acute illnesses (meaning relatively short-term ill-health, such as pneumonia) to chronic illnesses (meaning long-standing ill-health, such as heart disease and cancer) has two main implications. First, stress is now often seen as a major factor in the causation of illness, and secondly sociological skills become, to some extent, more important than medical skills for many GPs.

One effect of the growing medicalization of healthcare highlighted by Doyal (1995), in her study of gender and health, has been the gradual replacement of mainly female, informal carers, often using herbs and incantations, by mainly male professionals who are seen as experts, offering treatments that many of their patients do not understand.

In a review of sociological models of health suggesting the need to move beyond the medical model, Taylor (1994) highlights five main factors which have challenged this view:

- the replacement of infectious diseases by degenerative diseases as the main killers in society
- the challenges to doctors' claims that they single-handedly improved life expectancy, when writers such as McKeown (1979) have demonstrated the primary importance of improved sanitation
- the evidence that medicine causes much illness (e.g. Illich, 1990) (see Section 13.7)
- the evidence of widespread inequalities in health and healthcare in many societies
- the social problems encountered by many people with disabilities (see Section 13.8) based on the expectations and assumptions of other people in society.

It is as a result of these views that sociologists have argued that the social aspects of health and illness have to be an integral part of the overall study of this aspect of society. We cannot simply use the information provided by biology and medicine to analyse health, but need to incorporate our knowledge of the experience, roles and distribution of health and illness and the way these are affected by wider social structures and actions.

Individual, social and societal considerations

Turner (1987) argues thus:

Whereas disease is a concept which describes malfunction of a physiological and biological character, illness refers to the individual's subjective aware-ness of the disorder, and sickness designates appropriate social roles.
(Turner, 1987, p. 2)

He therefore believes that the study of health and illness needs to be explored at three levels: the individual, the social and the societal (see Table 13.1).

Table 13.1 Turner's three levels of health and illness

Level	Topic	Perspective
Individual	Experience of illness	Phenomenological assumptions about what it means to be healthy or ill
Social	Cultural categories of sickness	Sociology of roles, norms and deviance ('sick role')
Societal	Healthcare systems and politics of health	Political economy of illness (social inequalities in health)

Source: Adapted from Turner (1987, p. 4)

Phenomenology and subjectivity

The first of Turner's three levels in Table 13.1 is clearly related to the phenomenological approach (see Section 2.8) and is therefore based on the insight that it is important to consider the subjective experiences of individuals when considering the distribution of illness.

Since phenomenology extends to the argument that everything is socially constructed (Berger and Luckmann, 1967), the ability of scientists to arrive at any objective notion of health is denied anyway. Studies based on this approach would clearly be critical of the biomedical model which largely excludes the notion of subjective experience.

Such an approach can be criticized for denying that social reality exists and for denying the importance of social structures in society in affecting the distribution of health.

Functionalist approaches to health, illness and the sick role

Linking individual subjective experience into the notion of the social was most famously undertaken by Talcott Parsons (see Section 2.4) with his argument that ill-health is in some respects functional since it fulfils a defined role in society – the sick role. Parsons (1951) also claimed that the 'sick role' adopted by people who are unwell performs a specific social function in modern industrialized societies. He suggests that the role is based on a number of assumptions:

- the sick person is exempt from normal responsibilities such as work
- the sick person needs, and must seek, professional medical help
- sick people must demonstrate the desire to get better.

The function of the sick role is to prevent a subculture of the sick developing, whereby the release of responsibilities makes sickness seem like a desirable state.

Activity

What processes do you have to follow in order to legitimate illness at school or college and/or at work? How does this illustrate the operation of the 'sick role'?

A

Parsons' views have been subject to a number of criticisms. First, it is clear that the approach suffers from what critics of general functionalist theory have called the 'over-socialized conception of humanity' (Wrong, 1969). In defining the sick role, Parsons tends to assume that everyone will play by the rules and adopt the rights and responsibilities of the role. This, however, might not be the case. In particular, the contrast in this theory between the active role assigned to doctors and the passive role assigned to patients can be open to question. This is clearly the case recently with the rise of AIDS which has experienced highly active patient groups and knowledgeable patients themselves challenging doctors' arguments. It is also the case that the level of stigma associated with certain forms of ill-health (again AIDS is an example) might lead people to hide their condition.

The consensual nature of society assumed by functionalism tends to obscure the potential for conflict (see Section 2.6) within the experience of ill-health, and this is contained within Parsons' theory of the sick role. He assumes that sickness is a status which can be exploited, but it can also be argued that sick people are themselves exploited – by doctors, medical companies and health insurance companies. In her study of the sociology of health, Hart (1985) points out that this is a very passive view of illness which largely ignores the function of the medical profession as an agent of social control. (See also Section 11.9.)

The active–passive relationship outlined by Parsons also came into question with later interactionist studies of the doctor–patient relationship. These questioned both the notion of the doctor as a professional working only on objective knowledge, and the idea of the patient as a willingly passive body upon which doctors worked. The issue of the

doctor–patient relationship is explored more fully in Section 13.7.

It can also be argued that, while those suffering from acute diseases could be accorded the treatment described by Parsons, this might not apply equally to those suffering from chronic illnesses who are expected to 'soldier on'. This is important since, as pointed out earlier, the twentieth century has seen a gradual shift from acute to chronic ill-health. As time goes by, this might further invalidate Parsons' argument (see Section 13.9).

Marxism and the political economy approach

The basis of the political economy approach is the existence of societal structures (for example, capitalism) wider than that contained in the notion of the doctor–patient relationship, and the way these structure social relationships in the field of health and illness. This is most notably associated with Marxist approaches. Marxists (see Section 2.5) tend to argue that capitalism generally makes people ill and doctors – especially psychiatrists and psychologists – are agents of social control (see also Section 9.7). Sedgwick (1982) argues that the health of plants or animals or humans are all human inventions. Just as weeds are those plants we do not want, sickness is deviancy from the norm (see Section 10.1) of 'good health'.

However, in a capitalist society sickness is defined as the inability to work, and the doctor is the gatekeeper who permits us limited time off work. When sickness cannot be clearly defined, workers may be seen as deficient in their jobs rather than unwell.

Table 13.2 Percentage reduction of mortality from 1848/54 to 1971 in England and Wales

	Percentage of reduction
Conditions attributable to micro-organisms	
Airborne diseases	40
Water- and food-borne diseases	21
Other conditions	13
Total	74
Conditions not attributable to micro-organisms	26
All diseases	100

Source: McKeown (1979)

The evidence in Table 13.2 suggests that industrialization vastly improved the health and longevity of the population, although public health initiatives such as the provision of clean water rather than medical developments *per se* are often seen as the key basis of this. While Marx recognized that industrial society and capitalism produced advances in health compared with pre-capitalist society, he argued nonetheless that much illness is caused by the capitalist system, while its definition and treatment serves the interests of the ruling class.

It has been argued that capitalist production methods are inherently unhealthy because it is expensive to protect workers adequately. Pearce (1976), from a Marxist perspective, showed in his study of the crimes of the powerful that, despite extensive health and safety legislation, firms are rarely prosecuted. (See also Section 11.6.) In their study of health from a broadly Marxist political economy viewpoint, Doyal and Pennell (1979) also point out that housework is similarly unhealthy and alienating. (See also Section 7.5.) Even *not* working makes us ill because unemployment in a capitalist society causes stress and loss of status, with an increased risk of ill-health, depression and suicide (see Section 9.6).

The limits of social constructionist arguments

While all of the foregoing approaches have seen a purely biomedical model of health as deficient, and have therefore underlined the need for a fully sociological approach, this has sometimes led to the argument that illness is purely a social construction – most evidently in the case of phenomenological approaches. Although their critique of the purely objective positivist (see Section 3.1) approach of the biomedical model is in a sense an important corrective, there are also problems within the modified approach. Sheeran (1995) comments:

Students of the sociology of health are sometimes asked to explain how taken-for-granted concepts like health and illness are 'socially constructed' rather than biologically determined. . . . Sometimes, however, introductory presentations of the 'social constructionist' perspective encourage the uncritical acceptance of ideas which are in fact the subject of controversy.
(Sheeran, 1995, p. 8)

This particular controversy relates to the argument that illness is purely a social construction, the implication of which is that medical science has no objective basis at all and is therefore not of any great use, and even merely a form of power. While the phenomenologists and interactionists have long argued that phenomena are socially constructed, the lack of any real conception of power (see Section 17.4) and wider structures in their analysis has often led to their views being rejected. However, their 'relativist' conceptions are shared by a more recent approach which most certainly does have a conception of

power, namely the post-structuralist work based on the ideas of Michel Foucault. (See also Sections 2.10 and 17.4.)

On the basis of Foucault's work, which included detailed analysis of the rise of hospitals and clinics, it is argued that contemporary medical science is merely a particular form of power and has no claim to represent any universal truths. Relativist arguments have therefore resurfaced in post-modernist and post-structuralist inspired accounts of health and illness. (See also Section 9.7.)

Post-modern theories of health and illness

While Foucault's writings are extremely complex and far-reaching, his views on health and medicine can be summarized briefly as follows.

Medicine is a form of knowledge where different paradigms of health and illness affect the way people understand, explain and talk about health – what Foucault terms the 'discourse' of medicine. However, knowledge cannot be separated from power, so definitions of health and illness depend on who has the power to define the state our body is in.

This surveillance aspect of medicine is not a new phenomenon. Medicine (and sociology) originally developed from the need to supervise and control the large populations which began to develop in towns at the beginning of the industrial revolution. What has changed is how recent forms of supervision, control and ways of seeing the world are closely focused on the body and reproduction. (See also Sections 13.3 and 13.9.)

Discussion point

To what extent do you think it is acceptable for doctors to monitor the behaviour of their patients and adopt the surveillance role described here?

Nettleton (1996), in an article considering paradigms of health and medicine, agrees that there is a loss of faith in the biomedical model and suggests that there is a new paradigm of health and illness with an emphasis on people being increasingly expected to take responsibility for their own well-being. For example, they should avoid 'risk-taking' behaviours such as smoking cigarettes or drinking too much alcohol.

The role of health professionals is increasingly one of surveillance, as they monitor and supervise their clients' actions and advise them of the rational course to avoid ill-health. In this way, much illness can be seen as a result of wilful self-damage on the part of the patient. This clearly has the potential to

1.5m die from Aids in year as grip on poor grows

CHRIS MIHILL

THE Aids and HIV epidemic is continuing to spread across the world with a dramatic growth in many countries, including those of eastern Europe, the head of the United Nations' Aids programme warned yesterday.

Releasing new figures to mark World Aids Day on Sunday, Peter Piot, executive director of UNAIDS, told a press conference in London that 8,500 people were being infected by HIV every day across the world.

During the past year there were 3.1 million new HIV infections, and 1.5 million deaths, bringing the total number estimated to be living with HIV to around 23 million. Since the illness was recognised in the early 1980s, there has been a cumulative total of 29.4 million HIV infections, with 8.4 million Aids cases and 6.4 million deaths.

"The HIV epidemic is far from over.

It is gaining momentum in many countries and continues to strengthen its grip on the world's most vulnerable populations," Dr Piot said.

He said the majority of the 2.7 million adults infected over the past year were aged under 25, and half were women. There were 400,000 new infections among children in 1996, bringing the total number living with HIV to more than 800,000.

Dr Piot said there was rising concern over the "sky rocketing" increase in HIV in many parts of the former Eastern bloc. In some Black Sea towns in the Ukraine, the percentage of HIV infected people among injecting drug users rose from 1.7 per cent in January 1995 to 56.5 per cent 11 months later.

He said HIV was spreading rapidly in Asia, and in parts of southern Africa rates among pregnant women had reached 40 per cent.

Although a heterosexual explosion of HIV had not occurred in the UK, the

Living with HIV/AIDS

Estimated proportion of persons living with HIV/AIDS, percentage by region, 1996

Region	Percentage
East Asia & Pacific	0.2
Central & east Europe & Central Asia	0.2
Australia & New Zealand	0.1
North Africa & Middle East	0.9
Western Europe	2.2
South & south east Asia	23
North America	3.7
Latin America	6.0
Caribbean	1.2
Sub-Saharan Africa	62

number of such infections was slowly increasing and if prevention efforts ceased the situation could rapidly worsen, Dr Piot said.

Source: *The Guardian*, 29 November 1996

Activity

Read the article '1.5m die from Aids in year as grip on poor grows' and the box 'Risk factors'. To what extent could the material in the article and box support the argument about the increasing importance of surveillance in health and medicine?

I, A, E

Risk factors

- By the year 2000, 13 million women will have been infected with HIV; 4 million will have died.
- Approximately 42 per cent of adults with HIV/Aids are women, and the proportion is increasing.
- Mother-to-child transmission accounts for more than 90 per cent of all infections in infants and children. Around 30 per cent of all infants born of HIV mothers will themselves be infected before or during birth, or through breast-feeding.
- In the UK, there are 3950 women with HIV and 1206 with Aids. The largest group is in the 20–24 age range.
- The proportion of Aids cases in the UK attributable to sexual intercourse between men has consistently declined. Over the same period, the proportion of cases attributed to heterosexual exposure has risen from 4 per cent to 23 per cent.
- Only 7 per cent of trials and new treatments in this country are geared towards women.

Source: *The Guardian*, 28 November 1996

marginalize groups who cannot afford the healthy diets and exercise regimes required by the health-oriented in society.

The realist view of health: limits to social constructionism

Sheeran (1995) argues that although the social construction of health argument is often used as a demonstration of the power of sociological explanations, it overstates its case by denying any biological component of illness. Realist sociologists (see Section 3.3) reject this view, but since they also reject positivism they aim for a more sophisticated approach which does not reject the possibility of objective knowledge while still retaining the important insights about the subjective experience of illness.

Sheeran says that the problem arises partly from the comparison between illness and deviance (see Sections 11.3 and 11.5), which forms a basis for both the early functionist work of Parsons on the sick role, but more importantly for the later interpretivist and phenomenological views on the social construction of illness:

However, many physical illnesses, especially those which result in death, are not simply deviant in some settings and not in others. Neither are they voluntary. In the end they provide an awful finality to social life from which none of us can escape. According to

Twaddle (1973), at least some illnesses must therefore have a biological reality and causation which places limits on interpretation, whereas deviance is always a subjective evaluation of a behaviour or condition.
(Sheeran, 1995, p. 9)

While the subjective experience of illness may be explained by social constructionist arguments which point to its relative nature, this does not necessarily mean that objective accounts of ill-health should be abandoned. It is perfectly reasonable to assert that the subjective experience of illness and the objective reality of ill-health do not always coincide, and that therefore an approach based purely on a positivist biomedical model is deficient; but this lack of continuity does not *of itself* prove that there is no objective knowledge and that medical science is merely one form of power.

In fact, much of the evidence for the importance of the subjective experience of illness comes from comparing the subjective feelings of individuals with objective knowledge of their condition as defined by medicine. This is an extremely useful insight; but to say that only 6 per cent of patients who are in ill-health visit a doctor (see page 511) does rely on some objective knowledge of whether they are in ill-health for its usefulness.

Sociologists should therefore seek to utilize both data gleaned from medical science (*objective* information on mortality and morbidity, for example) and information on how people *feel*. They need to consider critically the overall validity (see Section 3.6) of any data presented. This does not mean sociologists have to throw the objective baby out with the positivist bathwater.

13.2. Social class and health inequalities

Sociologists and other social researchers have clearly shown that health and ill-health are affected by the social status of individuals. In particular it has been shown that a person's social class, gender and ethnic background will have an effect on the chances of suffering ill-health. However, overall, the most obvious difference is between the rich and the poor – in other words between class groups (see Tables 13.3 and 13.4).

Measuring inequalities in health

One of the key problems with identifying differences in health and illness between social classes is the way in which such groups are classified. Different systems may be used and they may produce different outcomes (see Section 4.4).

In an analysis of social class inequalities in health,

Table 13.3 Death rates by occupation

Occupation unit	Direct age-standardized death rate per 100 000	SMR[1]
Relatively low death rate		
University teachers	287	49
Physiotherapists	287	55
Local authority senior officers	342	57
Company secretaries and registrars	362	60
Ministers, senior government officials, MPs	371	61
Office managers	377	64
School teachers	396	66
Architects, town planners	443	74
Civil servants, executive officers	467	78
Medical practitioners	494	81
Relatively high death rate		
Coal miners (underground)	822	141
Leather product makers	895	147
Machine tool operators	934	156
Coal miners (above ground)	972	160
Fishermen	1028	171
Labourers and unskilled workers, all industries	1247	201
Policemen	1270	209
Deck and engine room ratings	1385	233
Bricklayers' labourers	1644	274

1 SMR is Standardized Mortality Ratio. Figures in the column below 100 indicate a below-average mortality rate and those above 100 an above-average rate.

Source: Adapted from Townsend *et al.* (1988)

sociologists from Nuffield College, Oxford University (Bartley *et al.*, 1996) suggest that different schemes of classification may indicate different patterns of health inequality. Therefore they look at two different forms of classification to compare mortality differences in social class between 1976 and 1980 and between 1986 and 1989. The Registrar General's (RG) classification scheme is seen as 'commonsensical' because it incorporates many people's assumptions about class differences. It is based on the status criterion of 'general standing in the community', although it is not always clear how status is related clearly to skill or income. They suggest that:

Because of the lack of clarity over what the classification actually does measure and how well it measures it, it is difficult to develop a more precise explanation of the size and trends of social variations in health that it produces.
(Bartley *et al.*, 1996, p. 459)

Bartley and colleagues propose the use of an alternative schema: the Erikson–Goldthorpe (E–G) system of classification (see Chapter 4). This system is deliberately designed to examine differences in the work

Table 13.4 Prevalence in 1994 of reported *limiting* chronic sickness in Great Britain, by sex, age and socio-economic group of head of household (percentages)

Socio-economic group of head of household	Males					Females				
	0–15	16–44	45–64	65 and over	Total	0–15	16–44	45–64	65 and over	Total
Professional	6	8	14	34	12	10	10	18	34	14
Employers and managers	7	10	20	34	15	6	10	24	39	16
Intermediate non-manual	9	11	27	34	17	3	12	28	36	18
Junior non-manual	8	10	25	47	16	10	14	21	43	23
Skilled manual and own account non-professional	8	15	31	46	22	5	13	27	43	18
Semi-skilled manual and personal service	8	15	32	45	21	7	15	31	50	24
Unskilled manual	6	20	40	34	23	8	19	34	45	28
All persons	8	13	27	41	18	6	13	27	43	20

Source: *Social Trends*, 1996

situation of particular occupational groups. The focus is mainly on conditions of employment, level of job security and promotion opportunities. They argue that, because it is based on objective criteria:

The E–G class schema is a validated measure of employment conditions designed without reference to health data.
(Bartley *et al.*, 1996, pp. 460–1)

They argue that the usual way of measuring differences in rates of premature death and long-term illness between class groups (the RG classification) might actually underestimate the true level of inequality, whereas the E–G classification (which is less widely used) is more accurate. They compared the efficiency of both systems of classification to explain the health experiences of two samples (see Section 3.5) of employed men over a ten-year period (1976–86). Both systems showed considerable health disadvantages for men employed in unskilled and semi-skilled manual work, although the E–G classification also demonstrated a higher risk of death for lower routine non-manual and service workers and a much lower risk of death for agricultural workers. Bartley and colleagues also confirmed that the class differences in health experiences identified by the RG classification were valid (see Section 3.6). Therefore, much of the discussion below can be accepted as being based on real inequalities, even if a different schema might make their measurement more accurate.

Explanations of social class inequalities

First it is necessary to look at some definitions. *Mortality rates* measure the deaths per thousand of

a particular social group who die of that disease at that age. *Morbidity rates* measure the number per thousand of the population suffering from a particular long-term illness such as heart disease or cancer. *Standardized mortality and morbidity rates* (or ratios) compare the number in each group to a figure of 100: therefore a standardized mortality rate (SMR) of 120 would imply a higher than average level of death or ill-health, while anything under 100 shows a lower than average rate.

The statistics in Figure 13.1 and Table 13.5 show quite clearly that mortality and morbidity rates are higher for almost all diseases for people in Classes IV and V than they are in Classes I and II. Interestingly enough, these differences have persisted, despite significant improvements in healthcare (see Section 13.5) for almost all social groups over the past century, and despite the availability of free, high-quality healthcare for all since 1948 through the NHS.

Table 13.5 Standard mortality rates (SMRs) of males aged 15–64 in England and Wales

	1971–75	1976–81	1982–85	1986–89
Social class in 1971				
I	80	69	61	67
II	80	78	78	80
IIIN	92	103	98	85
IIIM	90	95	101	102
IV	97	109	113	112
V	115	124	136	153
All social classes, including men not assigned to a social class	100	100	100	100

Source: Office of Population Censuses and Surveys/*Social Trends*

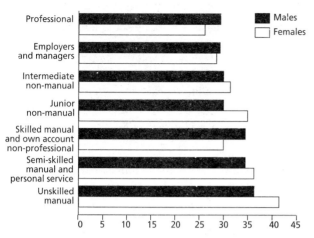

Figure 13.1 Prevalence in 1994 of reported chronic sickness in Great Britain, by sex and socio-economic group of head of household. Source: *Social Trends*, 1996

The fact that these patterns exist at all suggests that there may be social rather than just biological explanations for the differences. Although there have been follow-up studies, the most significant information presented – with proposed explanations – came from the Black Report originally published in 1980 (see Townsend *et al.*, 1988). A key finding of the report was that social class was inversely related to mortality and morbidity rates. Other findings can be summarized as follows:

- People in lower social classes were in some cases experiencing comparatively worse health than in the 1950s.
- There was under-utilization of the NHS in comparison with need among working-class people.
- British rates of infant mortality were in many cases higher than those in many other 'developed' countries. (See also Section 12.1.)
- There was a strong inverse relationship between social class and mortality rate, especially in relation to age of death, accidents to young people, infant mortality and maternal mortality.
- An inverse relationship was found in many cases between social class and morbidity.

Activity

Suggest as many reasons as you can why people in lower social classes might die earlier and suffer more from disease and ill-health than people in higher social classes.

A

Explanations from the Black Report

The Black Report examined four explanations of the patterns of inequality it identified.

The artefact explanation

Artefacts are things made by people. This explanation suggests that class inequalities in health do not really exist; they only appear to exist because of the way class is constructed. There are four important points here:

- The number of people in the lower class groups is in decline (see Section 4.7), so statistics on health inequalities among the poorer classes are based on fewer people.
- The few workers remaining in lower-class jobs are still experiencing better health than in the past.
- These figures tend to mask the higher levels of degenerative disease among (especially) middle-class women – such as Alzheimer's – as women and middle-class people live longer.
- This explanation also criticizes the classification of people by occupation.

The authors of the Black Report did not find this explanation convincing, arguing that:

Informed examination of successive census reports shows that the poorer occupational classes have contracted less sharply than often supposed, [and] *indicators of relatively poor progress in health apply to much larger sections of the manual occupational classes than just those who are 'unskilled'.* (Townsend *et al.*, 1988, p. 105)

The social selection explanation

The argument here is that people who experience poor health tend to find it difficult to get good jobs and so either move into, or remain in, lower-class occupations. This means that people are in lower social classes because of their poor health, rather than their class causing poorer health.

There is some evidence in support of this theory. Based on research on women in Aberdeen, Illsley (1986) concluded that taller women tended to move up occupational class at marriage while shorter women tended to move downwards. Since height can be taken as an indicator of health, this research tended to support the social selection model. On the basis of data from a National Survey of Health and Development, Wadsworth (1986) found that seriously ill boys were more likely to suffer a fall in social class than others.

However, the longitudinal research contained within the National Child Development Survey – following a group of children born in 1958 – also found that while some social mobility was related to health, such differences in health experiences could not explain the degree of social class gradient in health that existed. Equally the famous study of 17 000 Whitehall civil servants (Rose and Marmot, 1981; Marmot *et al.*, 1984a) found that, among those with no detectable disease at the start of their career, there were still much greater death rates among men in the lower grades of the civil service. Whitehead (1987) therefore argues that:

There is some evidence that health selection operates at younger ages, and new evidence for men over 50 that no such selection effect is evident after this age. Estimates of the size of the selection effect suggest that it accounts for only a small proportion of the overall differential between the social classes.

(Whitehead, 1988, p. 289)

The behavioural/cultural explanation

This view tends to blame ill-health on the sufferers because they do not follow a healthy lifestyle. Supporters of this view suggest that working-class people smoke and drink too much, eat the wrong kind of food and take little exercise. This view argues that the prudent would not waste money on cigarettes and alcohol, would live on healthy vegetable casseroles and would walk everywhere for exercise. The fact that some do not do this suggests a deficient culture and value system.

While the authors of the Black Report were willing to concede that this factor played a role in health differences, they viewed it as less important than structural material factors. However, its high profile in political debates in the 1980s led to the inclusion of questions about smoking-related diseases, notably coronary heart disease and lung cancer in research on Whitehall civil servants by Marmot *et al.* (1984a). The findings of this research indicated that even with non-smokers the risk of these diseases was still strongly associated with the grade of job held, thereby pointing to the inability of this model to explain most health inequalities. The research showed that cultural/behavioural differences accounted for only 25 per cent of the social-class inequalities they discovered.

The structural/material explanation

This view is favoured by many sociologists and social democratic politicians. The evidence for it was seen as the most convincing by the producers of the Black Report. The point here is that the material situation of the poor is seen as the most important factor in determining their poorer health.

Lower income earners are more likely to live in substandard housing which may be damp, overcrowded and in some cases possibly dangerous.

Many manual workers experience unhealthy and potentially dangerous working conditions and statistically they have more – and more serious – accidents at work. Manual workers often do work that is physically and mentally draining, leaving little energy for relaxation or exercise, while low income (see Section 14.8) may lead to poor diet and stress, resulting in increased smoking and drinking, for example, with potentially dangerous consequences for long-term health.

Other stress factors for manual workers are also statistically more common as they are more likely to divorce and have a far greater risk of unemployment (see Section 9.6), both of which might adversely affect income and health. Finally, working-class people tend to receive less education and information on childcare and healthy eating etc., as well as having less money to spend on these things.

Wilkinson (1986) studied the effect of changes in income on health and found that those occupations which increased their incomes relative to average earnings experienced a relative decrease in mortality rate, and those occupations which experienced a fall in their earnings relative to the average level experienced a relative rise in their mortality rate. This study provides evidence in support of the importance of material factors in social-class health inequalities.

Summarizing the evidence on the relative importance of the cultural/behavioural and the material/structuralist explanations, Whitehead (1987) argues:

The evidence that health-damaging behaviour is more common in lower social groups continues to accumulate, especially concerning smoking and diet. But can such life-style factors account for all the observed differential in health between different social groups? The short answer is: no. When studies are able to control for factors like smoking and drinking, a sizeable proportion of the health gap remains and factors related to the general living conditions and environment of the poor are indicated. In this context there is also a growing body of evidence that material and structural factors, such as housing and income, can affect health. Most importantly, several studies have shown how adverse social conditions can limit the choice of life-style and it is this set of studies which illustrates most clearly that behaviour cannot be separated from its social context.

(Whitehead, 1987, p. 304)

As discussed earlier it is also argued that working-class people tend to have limited contact and receive inferior treatment from the NHS in three key ways. What Dr Tudor-Hart (1971) called 'the inverse care law' operates as follows:

- In poorer areas doctors are less likely to set up practices, so there are fewer doctors to deal with more sick people in, for example, inner-city London than in the leafy suburbs of Surrey.
- Studies on inequalities in healthcare, such as Cartwright and O'Brien's (1978) study of GP consultations, have shown that middle-class people ask more questions of their doctors. Cartwright and O'Brien also found that the average length of consultation was 6.2 minutes for middle-class patients but only 4.7 minutes for working-class patients.
- Most doctors find it easier to interact with middle-class patients, giving them more time and being more prepared to refer them for further treatment.

Discussion point

To what extent do you think it possible or desirable to eliminate the 'inverse care law' described above? Suggest policies to reduce each of its elements.

Class and social support networks

Nettleton (1995) suggests some further explanations for class inequalities in health and illness. She argues that working-class people have fewer support networks to help them deal with stressful life events such as loss of a partner or status. Not only is this more likely to happen to working-class people, but they have fewer resources to draw on for help.

Furthermore, as both Nettleton and the Black Report point out, working-class people suffer more unemployment (see Section 9.6) which is itself seen as a significant influence on both mental and physical ill-health (and suicide), as well as leading to a number of other stress factors such as higher divorce rates. Studies of areas where factories have closed down in both the USA and the UK show higher levels of ill-health, especially in the months when the redundant workers knew they would soon be unemployed. Also, longitudinal studies show higher levels of mortality among unemployed men (little research has been carried out on unemployed women).

Private healthcare

Since the 1970s there has been a massive increase in the provision and use of private medicine, and this is probably one (but certainly not the only) reason why health inequalities continue to widen.

In a study of doctor–patient relationships in private-sector healthcare, Wiles and Higgins (1996) investigated the idea that private patients – most but not all of whom are likely to be middle class – receive better

treatment than those using the NHS. Certainly some of the evidence they examine shows better treatment for private patients in both outpatient and inpatient hospital care. Relationships tended to be less formal and patients were treated more as individuals rather than cases. (See also Section 9.7.) The main reason the people they studied gave for seeking private healthcare was time: they were treated more quickly, were given more convenient times for appointments, were allocated more time by their doctors or consultants and received information back more quickly. They felt they had more right to ask questions and some saw their doctor as a friend. They thought they were entitled to better treatment as they were paying for the time. They also felt entitled to contact the doctor directly if necessary and that there was an atmosphere of mutual respect.

Activity

The foregoing debates are illustrated by the article 'The poor odds for survival' on p. 520. Summarize the two main explanations for class inequality in survival from breast cancer presented in this article. Say which one you agree with and give reasons. Can you think of any other explanations, based on your knowledge of structural and cultural explanations?

I, A, E

This suggests that although middle-class patients generally get better treatment from their GP, they often seek to enhance their hospital treatment by paying for an experience which they hope will involve mutual respect as well as the ability to buy more professional time at a more convenient time. Interestingly, a number of black working-class women were also found to be prepared to pay for private medical treatment. Also looking at private medicine, Thorogood (1992) found that this was usually in order to pay for a second opinion from a general practitioner rather than to access hospital treatment. However she concluded that the women in her study used their money:

. . . to buy back some equality, to regain some power and control in this area of their lives.
(Thorogood, 1992, p. 37)

She suggests that their use of private medicine was designed to override their inequalities of 'race', gender and class, but it is still rare for white working-class people to use private medicine extensively. Thorogood argues that the use of private healthcare by the women she studied was designed to overcome some of the disadvantages they experienced in the NHS. Wiles and Higgins' (1996) study of middle-class

The poor odds for survival

TODAY, somewhere in the UK, two women will be told they have breast cancer. They could be the same age, their cancer might be equally advanced, they may even attend the same hospital, and yet one is more likely to die than the other. The woman from a wealthy, comfortable background has 35 per cent more chance of surviving five years than the woman from a poor home.

Cancer has never been a respecter of equality. It is well known that poorer people are more prone to contracting cancer. But new evidence shows that people from deprived backgrounds are also more likely to die from cancer than the more affluent, even when the cancer is caught at the same stage. Even though breast cancer is, unusually, more common among better-off women, they still have a better chance of survival than the more deprived.

Michael Coleman, professor of epidemiology at the London School of Hygiene, has carried out the two biggest studies which conclusively show large class inequalities in cancer survival at similar stages of disease.

He followed 155,682 people diagnosed with the 10 most common cancers between 1980 and 1989 in the South Thames region of England. The most affluent survived seven of the 10 cancers longer than the most deprived, defined by the social characteristics of patients' district of residence. The figures show 8 per cent of affluent patients survived lung cancer for five years, compared to 6.5 per cent of deprived patients. For breast cancer the figures

were 71 and 60 per cent. The same class divide was found for cancers of the colorectum, bladder, prostate, uterus and cervix, regardless of age, stage of cancer, other causes of death and which hospital provided treatment. The figures show the risk of death for the most deprived is between 11 and 59 per cent higher than for the most affluent.

A closer analysis of breast cancer patients reveals women in leafy Surrey have more chance of surviving 10 years than women from deprived east London do of surviving five years.

The studies throw up two possible explanations for the inequalities, says Prof Coleman, who is also deputy chief medical statistician at the Office for National Statistics. Deprived patients' circumstances – including diet, immunity and social support – may affect survival, or such patients may receive inferior care.

The Government's blueprint for cancer services – known as the Calman report – was published last year and has already acknowledged that hospitals have widely different success rates, due mainly to individual doctors' experience. Prof Coleman believes research should focus on whether treatment differs within the same hospitals. "We should ask the question as to whether the treatment given to people of all socio-economic classes is equally adequate."

Although the study provides no evidence that doctors discriminate against deprived patients, he says: "If because of where you live or how you speak or

how you dress, your GP refers you to a consultant who treats you less well or less efficiently because of your social group, that is obviously unfair."

Doctors vehemently deny discrimination on social class – although research for Age Concern has shown bias against older patients, while a study last month in the BMJ found that children from ethnic minority groups received inferior asthma treatment.

"We absolutely do not discriminate," says Richard Sainsbury, consultant breast surgeon at Huddersfield Royal Infirmary. He believes the variations are probably due to poorer general health or to "less good" GPs in deprived areas referring women for treatment at a late stage.

But a Glasgow GP, Dr Una MacLeod, is less convinced. For 420 women from the most and least deprived parts of Glasgow, who were diagnosed with breast cancer in 1992–93, she is comparing their treatment, home life and survival until 1998. The study follows earlier research in Glasgow, showing that differing survival rates between classes were not due, as expected, to deprived women consulting their GPs later.

In some areas, doctors are beginning to tackle geographic variations in breast cancer survival – in line with the Calman recommendations – by ensuring all patients see the most experienced surgeons at the same clinic in the quickest possible time.

Source: *The Guardian*, 21 August 1996

people found time the most important factor rather than quality.

It is important to remember that class differences do exist but are also misunderstood. Many people still believe that diseases related to stress, for example, are more commonly suffered by managers than manual workers, despite evidence to the contrary.

13.3. Gender and health inequalities

The paradox of gender, mortality and morbidity

While women seem to be disadvantaged (see also Chapter 5) in almost all aspects of social life –

income, employment status and wealth (see Section 14.8), for example – they are on average likely to live longer than men in all social classes. However, there is a paradox. Although women enjoy lower rates of *mortality* than men, they also record higher rates of *morbidity* (limiting chronic sickness) in all but a few specific occupational groups at particular ages (refer back to Table 13.4). Trowler (1996) further claims that 14 per cent of women report acute health problems compared with only 12 per cent of men.

In almost all societies, women tend to live longer than men. (See also Section 12.8.) In 1991 life expectancy in the UK was 79 years for women and 73.6 years for men. Male babies and children die in greater numbers and men are far more likely to die before the age of 75, whatever other social factors are considered.

Chronic illness statistics from *Living in Britain*, (1994) show that in that period women were more likely to find their illness debilitating (21 per cent women *vs* 18 per cent men), women were more likely to see their GP (women six times a year compared with men's four), and women were more likely to be in hospital (13 per cent/6 per cent). There are twice as many registered disabled women as men (mainly due to greater longevity, however); 57 per cent of hospital admissions for mental illness are women, especially for emotional disturbance, anxiety disorders, depression and dementia; and women are found to be twice as likely to suffer from stress, often turning to drink and cigarette addiction. In contrast, men appear more likely to become violent or suicidal as a result of stressful life events.

Explanations of gender differences

According to Trowler (1996) there are five key explanations for the differences in morbidity and mortality between men and women.

Genetic explanations

Genetic explanations suggest that women suffer from greater ill-health owing to biological differences. They often need to consult doctors about contraception, pregnancy, menstruation and menopause. Only women can contract cervical cancer, while their stronger immune response means they are more likely to suffer from arthritis. Perhaps most importantly, their lower mortality rate means that women are more likely to seek treatment for 'degenerative' diseases related to old age.

However, men suffer (and die from) more heart disease, at least until about the age of 50. They are the only ones to get prostate or testicular cancer, and more men inherit genetic weaknesses, such as haemophilia. Also, in recent years men in western societies have been more at risk from AIDS-related illnesses and deaths.

Artefact explanations

Artefact explanations look at the way the statistics are constructed. Morbidity statistics are collected from consultations with doctors. In this case the statistics may be misleading because they ignore ethnicity, geography or class, for example. The fact that women tend to have lower status jobs (see Section 9.3), are more likely to take children to the doctor and live

longer may be more significant than the fact of their sex. However, this explains nothing about why women go to the doctor more often. It certainly does not necessarily mean that men are healthier, just that they are less likely to consult a doctor when ill.

Stress explanations

Stress explanations are increasingly relevant to doctors and other medical personnel. It is now widely agreed that stress can affect health considerably. Some feminists (see Sections 2.10 and 5.3) argue that being a housewife is an extremely stressful experience, owing to the isolation, loneliness, lack of support and status and poor rewards involved (see Section 7.5). However, it also seems to be the case that many women now find the double and even triple shift of paid work, domestic work and emotional work increasingly stressful.

Cultural/behavioural explanations

Cultural/behavioural explanations suggest that men are likely to die earlier overall because they are more involved in risk-taking behaviour such as violence (see Section 11.7), and are neglectful in terms of their habits and diet. They choose not to consult doctors and so die from the results of these behaviours more than women. Men have until recently tended to smoke more and drink considerably more alcohol than women, although this is now changing. Class differences, especially in smoking and among young people, are now far more significant than gender differences, with increasing numbers of women dying from smoking-related diseases.

Structural/material explanations

Structural/material explanations emphasize the structural factors which affect the health of women (and men). Most women have to accept the major responsibility for childcare (see Section 7.5) and looking after the health of others – especially with the growth of 'care in the community' (see Section 14.2). Structural and material issues are the focus of the ideas of most feminist writers on gendered health inequalities. Women also still bear the brunt of domestic labour, the emotional burdens of most relationships, poor pay and conditions at work (see Section 9.3) and more exposure to poverty (see Section 14.6) and poor housing, especially among single women and single mothers – although some of these factors are changing for middle-class women. However, Nettleton (1995) points out that class differences between women are still less significant than for men. (See Table 13.4.)

This view also seeks to explain greater female morbidity. The socialization of women means that they accept responsibility for everyone's needs, lead-

Activity

Suggest reasons why women are more likely to visit a doctor than men, even when suffering from the same degree of ill-health.

A

ing them to suffer greater stress and stress-related illnesses. Although some women choose to do this, it is argued that they are not making a free choice owing to structural constraints and expectations in society. For example, as Hicks (1988) points out, the majority of informal carers in the UK are women, often caring for other women.

In a study of the importance of this type of care in the context of the 'care in the community' initiative, Land (1991) points to statistics from the *General Household Survey* showing that informal care is now an important aspect of healthcare overall. One in seven adults are providing informal healthcare which in total represents some 6 million people, of whom 3.5 million are women. The peak age range for such caring is 45–64, with nearly a quarter of all women of this age acting in such a role.

Women might have to leave a paid job to care for an elderly mother or mother-in-law, while single daughters or those without children are expected to take the chief responsibility for caring for parents. Single women, who are generally dependent on their own income, are often particularly vulnerable to these expectations. Many women find caring for others, and the expectation that they should do so, a further stressful burden on their lives. However, as Hicks also points out, a considerable proportion of carers are men looking after an elderly and often disabled spouse.

Activity

Evaluate the above arguments about mortality and morbidity rate differences between males and females. Which do you consider the most convincing?

I, A, E

Feminist views on health and illness

Women and medical care

As mentioned above, the vast majority of carers – formal as well as informal – are female, although this fact has tended to be ignored or treated unproblematically by many sociologists when looking at the medical profession. Marxist feminist writers such as Doyal (1995) have shown how the development of the medical profession basically involved the wresting of medical knowledge from women by men. Thereafter women remained as 'helpers' to the mainly male doctors and surgeons (see Table 13.6).

Witz (1992) argues that men have used exclusion strategies (see Sections 5.4 and 9.3) such as limiting women's access to medical schools. However, there are still some areas that are mainly closed to men, such as midwifery. Although most obstetricians are still male, the Winterton Report (1992) proposed an enhanced role for midwives.

Many feminist writers have criticized the 'medicalization' of childcare. Graham and Oakley (1981) found that women tended to see pregnancy as natural, while obstetricians tended to see it as a medical problem which needed to be organized to fit into the bureaucratic (see Section 9.7) needs of the hospital. Some births are induced, which might be seen as allowing for babies to be born at a time convenient to the hospital rather than when the babies and their mothers are ready. Using in-depth interviews (see Section 3.8), Oakley (1984) found that many women felt that the (mainly male) doctors they saw denied them much control over their pregnancy and childbirth.

Martin (1989) found that women tended to see their bodies in a medicalized way and so in need of control. It could be argued that this is the basis of many eating disorders which are generally much more likely to affect young women. It is also noticeable that the majority of contraception advice is directed far more at women than men, leaving them mainly responsible for birth control. Male-oriented forms of contraception such as condoms and vasectomies have fewer possible side-effects than those for women, such as the pill or coil, yet the latter are far more widely used.

Feminism and the body

One of the main developments in the sociology of health and illness has been the attention paid to the body by feminist writers. The ideas of early feminists have been criticized by what Annandale and Clark (1996) call 'feminist post-structuralism', (see Section 5.5) which challenges earlier feminists' views of the way that mainly male doctors have sought to exploit and control women through medical technology.

Nettleton (1995) argues that the medical regulation of bodies, especially female bodies and female sexuality, can be illustrated through the examination of reproduction and, especially, reproductive technologies. According to Stanworth (1987), these

Table 13.6 Hospital medical staff in England, 1985: females as a percentage of total in grade

Consultant and Senior House Medical Officer	23
Associate specialist	12.5
Senior Registrar	23
Registrar	21
Senior House Officer	32
House Officer	39

Source: Trowler (1996), adapted from *Health and Personal Social Services Statistics for England 1986*, London, HMSO, 1986

include fertility control technologies such as contraceptives, childbirth control technologies such as Caesarean births, screening techniques such as amniocentesis and, most interestingly, conceptive technologies such as fertility treatments, which Nettleton calls 'new reproductive technologies' (NRTs). Oakley (1984) suggests that the ability for brain-dead women to give birth by Caesarean section means that the mothers are not always seen as autonomous human beings, and this is reflected in many other aspects of NRT.

In an article about *in vitro* fertilization (IVF), Denny (1994) investigates the way debate about this surfaced in radical feminist accounts (see Section 5.4). While some radical feminist writers, particularly Firestone (1974), see such techniques as a way of freeing women from the burden of reproduction, others such as Rich (1977) view it as a way for men to gain control of reproduction and therefore undermine women's power in this area. Analyses such as the latter tend to see NRTs as controlling women in two main ways: through pro-natalist ideology and men's power and control over reproduction technology. Writers such as Rowland (1985) suggest that 'pro-natalism' (the idea that women are unfulfilled unless they have children) is promoted by the message that infertility is a medical and social disaster for women. While Denny found that some of the women she studied did feel pressurized to have children in order to be 'a complete woman', many felt this as a biological urge rather than simply a result of social pressures.

A number of feminist writers have emphasized that the ways in which males control the process of *in vitro* fertilization allows them power over the reproductive processes of women. While many feminists such as Stanworth (1987) and Rowland (1985) argue that women experience so much pressure on them to reproduce and that they are blinded by science into accepting techniques such as IVF, Denny rejects the idea that women are so easily duped. While she accepts that there are indeed subtle forms of control related both to pro-natalist culture and male control of the medical profession, she argues nonetheless that women retain an important degree of control over the process and are rarely totally powerless. She concludes:

The experiences of individual women have been lacking from most radical feminist literature, women have been portrayed as powerless victims, accepting whatever a male dominated and powerful medical profession offers them. In contrast . . . oppression is a very complex process, and one in which women are very rarely totally powerless.
(Denny, 1994, p. 75)

Black feminists (see also Sections 5.4 and 6.6) such as hooks (1984) suggest that women do not have a common cultural experience of oppression due to their sex, and Denny's study supports the view that women experience their bodies in a variety of different ways. This view is developed by Annandale and Clark (1996) who suggest that radical feminism, with its emphasis on a single female experience, has been replaced – at least in the sociology of health – with a post-structuralist stance which stresses the diversity of women's experience (see Section 5.5). They look at traditional feminist views on health and illness and suggest that these have now been challenged for a number of different reasons.

Post-structuralist feminists vary considerably in their views but, according to Annandale and Clark, they share an emphasis on the body as a constructed entity, where gender is only part of the process. This means they look less at the crucial differences between women and men as stressed by earlier feminist writers, and argue that sex and gender are part of a continuum of masculinity and femininity, whereby sexual behaviour is not bound by biological sex at all.

Similarities and differences in women's health

Doyal (1995), taking an explicitly feminist stance by focusing specifically on the health of women, points out that women are generally disadvantaged in all areas of sickness in all parts of the world. While there are clearly different experiences between women from a variety of ethnic and class backgrounds, the main difference can be seen among the health experiences of women from the developed and 'developing' countries. (See also Sections 12.8 and 12.9.)

She also argues that the way to understand the gendered experiences of women's health is to examine the inadequacies of biomedical explanations of health and illness.

The main factor to look at when assessing the health of women is the impact of poverty and relative deprivation on the health and illness of women, rather than biological or medical differences between men and women. It was really only with industrialization that women seemed to begin to live longer than men, although now the phenomenon is found in most societies apart from very poor countries such as Bangladesh. Far from being the 'weaker sex', females tend to be stronger from birth onwards. The higher mortality of males in industrialized societies seems to be linked to the dangers of many (male) manual jobs and men's more risky leisure activities and patterns of consumption. (See also Section 10.7.)

Doyal argues that to understand the factors affecting women's poorer health beyond basic biology, we need to look at what makes up their lives in terms of production and reproduction, paid work and domestic work, lifestyle and consumption patterns and experiences of support and abuse. She concludes that the greater morbidity of women shows that many experience economic, social and cultural obstacles which prevent them from fulfilling their physical and psychological needs. She asserts:

Women's right to health and the formulation of appropriate strategies for its realisation must be a central concern, not just in feminist politics, but in wider campaigns for sustainable development, political freedom and economic and social justice. (Doyal, 1995, p. 232)

A new paradigm of health and medicine?

Nettleton (1996) identifies the shortcomings of the biomedical model which has dominated medical discourse, especially those which stress intervention and cure in healthcare rather than prevention and care. She argues:

We have begun to witness a profound shift in health policy and in the ideological basis of medicine. (Nettleton, 1996, p. 33)

This change is our loss of faith in the biomedical model and a new emphasis on the prevention of disease. Nettleton suggests that such a model is now increasingly compared with a socio-environmental model which, in contrast to the biomedical model, emphasizes how people are increasingly encouraged (and expected) to take responsibility for their own health and healthcare.

The three key issues at the heart of this new paradigm can be seen as: risk, surveillance, and 'the rational self' (Nettleton, 1996, p. 34).

Risk

Risk, says Nettleton, is now the focus of much medical research. Such research may save money for the NHS as people require less treatment if they look after their own health. It also medicalizes social activities such as diet and exercise.

People are more confused than ever about what to eat, drink or avoid in their diet. According to Nettleton, the maximum 14 units of alcohol a week recommended for women – with possibly dire consequences if they risk exceeding the limit – was apparently arbitrarily raised to 21 in December 1995 in order to placate an alcohol industry that had not got the cuts in taxes they had been expecting owing to an uproar over VAT on fuel. There is also limited

sympathy for HIV sufferers who have admitted to 'unsafe' sex practices. Women tend to be bombarded with advice, often confusing and sometimes frightening, about their health, although men, too, are now sometimes identified as targets by the health industries.

Surveillance

General practitioners are now in the first line of surveillance, and women in particular are virtually forced to have their children vaccinated, themselves checked for various cancers, and their elderly mothers injected with anti-flu viruses. This is often done at considerable benefit to the doctor, although many doctors suggest that they are poorly rewarded for the jobs they do for the state. Doctors are rewarded financially for achieving vaccination and monitoring quotas for activities like smear tests – which may prove beneficial to women, although the number of scares about mistakes in such testing may reduce its credibility.

There is also surveillance on women's lifestyles as consumers (more women are obese than men); as sexual beings through family planning advice; and, of course, as chief carers for the nation's youth (see Section 7.5). The home is still considered an important arena of primary healthcare where women usually take the main responsibility for the health of all the members of the family.

The rational self

The medical discourse of risk and surveillance – that is the way people talk about health – creates a particular concept of the self. This means that women in particular are expected to act in ways that promote and enhance health because it is rational and sensible for them to do so. After all, not many people wish to follow patterns of behaviour which they firmly believe will damage them physically.

This is an interesting argument and one that is used to dispute the culpability of cigarette manufacturers. On the one hand, the manufacturers argue that cigarettes are not very addictive and so people can make a rational choice about whether to smoke. On the other hand, anti-smoking groups like ASH argue that, knowing the links between cigarette smoking and lung cancer, no rational person would continue to smoke unless it were extremely addictive.

Discussion point

To what extent might arguments about the rational self also be applied to (a) unprotected sexual activity and (b) the consumption of Ecstasy tablets or other illegal drugs?

This protocol means that all people are expected to be aware of – and do something to avoid – 'risk-taking' behaviours such as smoking, drinking, over-eating or lack of exercise. Health professionals increasingly monitor and supervise their clients' actions and advise them of the rational course to take to avoid ill-health. (See also Section 9.7.) In this way, much illness can be seen as a result of wilful self-damage on the part of the patient. This clearly has the potential to marginalize groups who cannot afford the healthy diets and exercise regimes required by the health-oriented in society. Health professionals make judgements as to our suitability for, or our entitlement to, certain types of treatment, again depending on a number of 'rational' criteria. Although everyone is encouraged to monitor their health-related behaviour, Nettleton sees in many of the Department of Health publications issued over the past twenty years:

> ... *an underlying assumption that the responsibility for changing health behaviours lay in the hands of women, or more particularly, mothers.*
> (Nettleton, 1996, p. 37)

Men's health

It is important to recognize that there now also seems to be a growing concern with the health of men (see also Section 5.6). Increases in mortality from male-only diseases, particularly testicular and prostate cancers, may be mainly to do with a lack of knowledge and the reluctance of men to talk about their bodies. Awareness of such issues seems to have been raised by the apparent success of women's health groups in improving female well-being, or it may be that there are now perceived to be a larger number of men without a wife to 'look after' them.

Activity
a Study the accompanying contents page from the December 1996 issue of the magazine *Men's Health*. Analyse the structure of the contents of this magazine and the balance of articles.
b Consider a similar health magazine aimed at women and suggest how and why it might be different.

I, A

13.4. Ethnicity and health inequalities

Defining 'race' and ethnicity

Aggleton (1990) points out that the problem of defining ethnic origin (see Section 6.1) makes it difficult

---

Men's Health
VOLUME 2 • ISSUE 10 • DECEMBER 1996

FEATURES

46 **Beat colds and flu for good**
Arnold Schwarzenegger, Steven Seagal: no one ever beat off the bad guys when suffering from a sniffle. Try our effective cold remedies and save the world.

53 **Why moving house could save your life**
Life expectancy, healthcare and crime vary greatly throughout the country. We tell you which areas to avoid. Clue: Don't even visit Glasgow.

62 **Doctor, No! James Bond's killer lifestyle**
Mad, drunk and syphilitic – a team of experts analyses the secret agent's habits.

70 **I'm afraid there's been a bit of an accident**
Getting the best out of your casualty department – If you're going to put your head between some railings, read this first.

76 **20 ways to be instantly sophisticated**
Is it correct to spear a saveloy with a chip fork? Your etiquette queries answered.

86 **Ski better now**
New skis which make you look like you grew up in the Alps, and dated Heidi.

96 **Be a sex god**
Acts of intimacy can improve with practice – try these exercises at home.

102 **Make a million. 10 famously difficult things made easy**
Save a penalty, understand modern dance, teach an old dog new tricks – simple.

108 **Shape up without trying**
Burn fat and get fit while shopping, dancing and appreciating art: here's how.

114 **Turn your home into a health spa**
Everything you need for that spa feeling ... without expensive membership fees.

124 **Heating elements**
Hats and scarves that won't make you look like Scott of the Antarctic.

126 **Nightlife special**
Become a party smoothie
Have whole semi-detached housefuls of people eating out of your hand.
Dress perfectly every time
Never be mistaken for a doorman/magician/one of the Dixieland combo again.

138 **Something to chew on**
How to cut your dental bills in half.

144 **Conquer bad breath**
Incredibly smelly food pitched against the latest mouth fresheners.

---

to measure structural differences between the health and healthcare patterns of ethnic minority groups. So there is a paucity of evidence, but the evidence that does exist is fairly convincing. For example, stillbirths are more commonly found among mothers born in Bangladesh, Pakistan and the Caribbean than among UK-born mothers (see Figure 13.2).

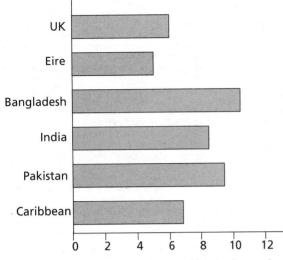

Figure 13.2 Stillbirths per 1000 total births, by mother's country of birth, England and Wales, 1984. Source: Whitehead (1987)

In a study of mortality rates among immigrants, Marmot *et al.* (1984b) found higher than average SMRs (standardized mortality rates – see Section 13.2) for a number of groups born in Africa, the Caribbean and women from the Indian subcontinent. However, country of birth tells us little about the health experiences of the children of migrants who are born in the UK.

Smaje (1996) claims that the concepts of ethnicity used in health research are often applied in discussions about whether poor health among some ethnic groups is due to cultural factors – 'ethnic' lifestyles – or structural factors such as poverty and racism. He argues that such definitions would make more sense in terms of a model based on subjective factors within particular situations. This may prove problematic for much current health research which is based on statistical data collected by epidemiologists who study rates of disease, and clinicians who focus on specific illnesses. Neither type of researcher spends much time analysing the categories they use or investigating the social meanings of their findings.

Recent arguments about the nature of ethnic identity are discussed in Chapters 6 and 10. It can be said here that most definitions of ethnic membership used by health practitioners are over-simplified and possibly invalid because they focus on either where people were born or their generalized lifestyle. So, for example, being the daughter of Sikh Indian migrants, living in Birmingham and training to be a doctor in a changing NHS, leads to a particular identity formed not only from ethnic background. Such

a view of the complexities of identities and cultures will also have implications impacting upon healthcare, such as recognizing and campaigning for the particular health needs of Asian women.

While this debate can be used extensively to criticize ethnic classifications which certainly affect the analysis of health statistics, it is still important to discover whether certain groups have certain needs and the extent to which they are being addressed or ignored. The lack of hard data gathered on the basis of these new theoretical developments requires us to make use of the data that are available, even though the categories may be challenged.

Patterns of health difference among ethnic groups

In an article considering the debates surrounding 'race', ethnicity and health inequalities, Culley and Dyson (1993) seek to explain why such differences might exist. The majority of premature deaths among, for example, Pakistanis or African–Caribbeans are from heart attacks and cancers, just as among the white population. This does *not* mean that inequalities between racial groups do not exist, although it is not always easy to gain access to such information. African–Caribbeans seem to suffer from higher rates of high blood pressure than the indigenous population, but this measurement tells us nothing about cause.

Although country of origin is recorded in medical records, the increasing number of people who would describe themselves as both British-born and black, for example, makes such a classification less useful. Despite these problems, Culley and Dyson provide us with some interesting information.

African–Caribbeans, Indians, Pakistanis and Bangladeshis are all more likely than the national average to die from liver cancer, tuberculosis or diabetes. Africans and African–Caribbeans are more likely to suffer from strokes and hypertension. Asians (i.e. Indians and Pakistanis) generally suffer more heart disease but fewer deaths from most cancers than the average, while their children are more likely to develop rickets and adults osteomalacia (brittle bones). Overall, African–Caribbeans and Asians are more likely to be diagnosed as schizophrenic and compulsorily placed in mental institutions. As Trowler (1996) points out, this is despite the evidence which suggests that immigrants generally suffer lower rates of mental illness than average. (See also Section 13.8.)

Several indicators suggest poorer maternal health of women born in Africa, the Caribbean and the Indian subcontinent than those born in the UK. Most of the research into poor maternal health has concentrated on women from the Indian subcontinent

Activity

a In Table 13.7, identify one cause of death that has a lower than average rate, and one that has a higher than average rate, for all the ethnic minority groups specified.

b In Figure 13.3, identify the ethnic groups (by mother's country of birth) with the highest and second highest rates of infant mortality and perinatal mortality. The definitions are as follows: *infant mortality*: deaths of infants under one year of age per 1000 live births; *perinatal mortality*: stillbirths and deaths in the first week of life per 1000 live and stillbirths; *neonatal mortality*: deaths in the first 28 days of life per 1000 live births; *post-neonatal mortality*: deaths at ages over 28 days and under one year per 1000 live births.

Table 13.7 Causes of death by country of birth

African	*Higher rates:*	Strokes, high blood pressure, violence/accidents, maternal deaths, tuberculosis
	Lower rates:	Bronchitis
Indian sub-continent	*Higher rates:*	Heart disease, diabetes, violence/accidents, tuberculosis
	Lower rates:	Bronchitis, certain cancers
Caribbean	*Higher rates:*	Strokes, high blood pressure, violence/accidents, diabetes, maternal deaths
	Lower rates:	Bronchitis

Source: Culley and Dyson (1993), adapted from Whitehead (1987)

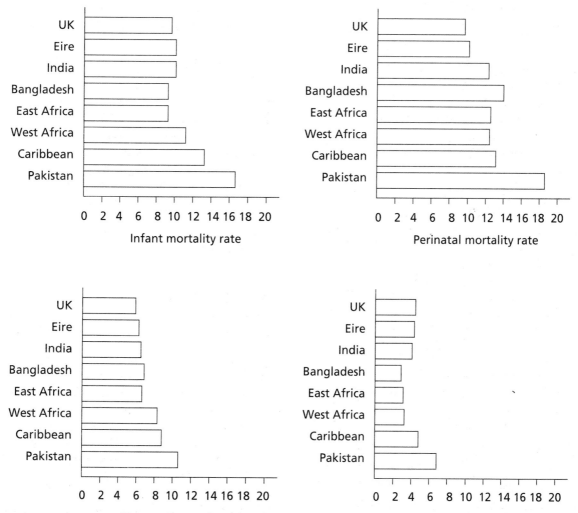

Figure 13.3 Infant, perinatal, neonatal and post-neonatal mortality by mother's country of birth, England and Wales, 1982–85. Source: Jewson (1993) p. 70

and has tended to assume poor antenatal and post-natal care rather than deprivation as the main cause of high infant mortality among women from Pakistan or Bangladesh – although Blackburn (1991) has shown significant poverty among many groups of black women in the UK.

Explaining ethnic differences in health

Although we can identify, despite the limited availability of reliable statistics, differential (and usually significantly poorer) health among ethnic minorities, the explanations have yet to be discussed. Culley and Dyson propose four possible factors: genetics, culture and behaviour, social class, and racism.

Genetic factors

Genetic arguments focus on the inherited disorders that seem to affect some groups in particular, such as sickle-cell anaemia which is largely found among Africans and African–Caribbeans. Thalassaemia is another blood disorder found in people mainly from the Middle East and the Indian subcontinent.

Hunt (1995) argues that such biological differences do need to be identified and suitable screening and counselling facilities made available. It can be seen as a form of covert racism to marginalize diseases which occur mainly among non-white groups and prioritize wider screening for relatively rarer diseases distributed throughout the population.

Cultural factors

Cultural factors include things such as diet, lifestyle and beliefs and attitudes towards healthcare. They are usually stressed by health 'experts' when attempting to explain the high level of particular health problems among certain ethnic groups. Poor attendance at postnatal and antenatal clinics among Asian mothers is seen to explain high rates of still-births and infant mortality in this group. However, reasons for low attendance, such as language, transport or educational barriers, are rarely discussed. Again, high rates of heart disease are blamed on the use of clarified butter (ghee) in much Asian cooking, but this tends to ignore structural factors such as stress, isolation, alienation and poverty which offer the most convincing explanations for class differences in health and illness (see Section 13.2).

Attempts to explain and deal with ethnic differences in, for example, rates of heart disease have often focused on cultural factors. Culley and Dyson suggest that many of these attempts seem to be misguided, being based on an ideological view of ethnic cultural inferiority (see also Sections 4.8 and 6.5) rather than facts. Blaming smoking and fat consumption for high levels of heart disease among Asians – when the rate of smoking is slightly lower than the average (especially among women) and fat consumption often far lower than that of other groups – seems to ignore much of the empirical evidence available.

Hunt (1995) also discusses cultural factors, but makes the important point that sweeping ethnic generalizations about health inequalities tend to ignore gender and class differences. The lifestyles of different cultural groups are often seen as strange or inferior. For example, high infant mortality rates among some Asian women was attributed to their ignorance about antenatal facilities rather than looking at the assumptions of western medicine which might exclude women who could not be treated by a male doctor or travel alone to clinics.

As can also be seen when looking at class-based health inequalities, cultural explanations are useful to politicians because:

- they blame the 'victim' for their misfortune (see also Section 6.5)
- they ignore structural factors such as deprivation and racism
- they advocate change among the groups concerned rather than society as a whole.

Discussion point

Areas where doctors may have limited knowledge of other cultures include diet, religious needs, language, sexual mores, hygiene and death rites. Discuss how doctors might ensure that each of these needs is considered in developing medical care for groups with religious or cultural beliefs different from their own.

Social class factors

The social class explanations outlined in Section 13.2 relating to inequalities in health suggest that poor health among many ethnic minority groups is indeed mainly due to class differences. In general, unemployed people suffer poorer mental and physical health, and the ethnic groups with the highest levels of mortality, morbidity and diagnosed mental illness – such as Pakistanis, Bangladeshis and African–Caribbeans – also suffer far higher levels of unemployment than the average. (See also Section 9.3.) As Culley and Dyson point out:

Recruitment patterns of African–Caribbean and Asian migrants mean that they are concentrated in low-paid manual occupations and particularly in industries that are most hazardous to health (e.g. laundry, textiles and clothing industries) and/or have been especially hard-hit by successive recessions (e.g. textiles and footwear industry) (Brown, 1984). Excessive shift-work, lack of job security and fringe benefits, low pay and high likelihood of unemployment are all likely to lead to poorer health amongst black and ethnic communities.

(Culley and Dyson, 1993, p. 26)

The most convincing evidence comes from differences in mortality and morbidity rates between groups. Indians, who suffer relatively low unemployment and social deprivation in the UK, have lower rates than Pakistanis and Bangladeshis, who are more disadvantaged than the average. African–Caribbeans, who are socially and economically disadvantaged on the whole, also suffer higher than average levels of heart disease and high blood pressure.

Racism

Culley and Dyson argue that racism adversely affects the health of ethnic minority groups in six main ways.

First, it leads to them being concentrated in hazardous, alienating and unrewarding jobs which have been shown to correlate closely with ill-health for all groups. The associated poverty affects diet, and leads to stress and stress-related illnesses such as high blood pressure.

Secondly, there is strong evidence to suggest that ethnic minorities are more likely to suffer high rates of unemployment. In recessions in particular, rates of unemployment of black people soar. Rising unemployment has been linked to high suicide rates and higher levels of mortality and morbidity.

Thirdly, housing may be an issue. For example, Bangladeshis in Tower Hamlets in east London tend to occupy some of the most overcrowded and low-quality housing in the country. Poor housing has been shown to lead to bronchial problems and other respiratory infections, especially among children. For them, poor health may affect education (see Section 8.6) and future opportunities as well.

Fourthly, racism means that black people and Asians are more likely to be attacked and subjected to abuse, and many individuals and families live in constant fear of such attacks. Again, it is difficult to obtain accurate figures (many members of ethnic minorities choose not to report harassment for a number of reasons), but evidence shows that rates are high and increasing in many parts of the UK. Apart from the physical effects of attacks, psychological problems from abuse and the fear of abuse are common.

Fifthly, unequal access to medical care is experienced by some ethnic minority groups. This may be less to do with direct racism than what might be termed 'institutional racism'. (See Section 6.1.) This means that language differences may present a barrier, as may lack of access to a woman doctor for some Asian women. Some doctors may only have limited knowledge of certain illnesses that affect particular ethnic groups. Mares *et al.* (1987) appeared to find that people from ethnic minority groups were more likely to complain of irrelevant and discriminatory treatment.

Culley and Dyson's sixth point is that the NHS can be seen as discriminatory is in the employment of black people. Members of ethnic minorities are widely employed by the NHS, but they are not equally distributed throughout the service (see Section 9.3). As in most other sectors of employment, black people are disproportionately employed in manual jobs, ancillary work, in the lower status jobs in nursing and, as doctors, in the less prestigious sectors such as geriatrics and psychiatric care. Some health authorities have made a determined effort to improve their treatment of black patients and employees, but this is far from widespread, especially with the increasing financial constraints on doctors and hospitals.

Concluding comments

As Hunt (1995) points out, the factors which lead to health disadvantages for ethnic minorities are complex. Culley and Dyson argue, however, that material deprivation remains paramount. The high levels of under-employment and unemployment among some ethnic minority groups (especially African–Caribbean and Bangladeshi men) and the consequences of their deprivation continue to underpin all the biological and cultural explanations. To ignore any of the factors identified may be problematic, but to ignore structural and material factors, including overt and covert racism, seems to deny the health realities for many people in our society.

Ideological debates about 'race' and health

In an introduction to the book he edits, Ahmad (1993) asserts that research into 'race' and health now forms a large industry in itself, but one that offers few benefits to ethnic minority groups. Most research is based on statistics and draws simplistic conclusions from spurious correlations. Consequently, he argues, much research in this area literally labels black people as sick. Both the terms 'race' and 'biomedicine' are socially constructed and utilized to legitimize positions of power and authority. He therefore says that the term 'race' was developed to legitimize the colonization (and enslavement, it could be added) of groups defined as inferior (see Section 6.2). Biomedicine (the 'medical model' of illness) has long been used to restrict and punish deviancy.

Ahmad sees a similarity between images of a good (subservient) patient and a good (docile) black person. Patients are not expected to challenge their doctors just as black people are not expected to query their status in society. Many migrants to the UK are treated as outsiders, much as 'alternative' medical treatments are marginalized. Therefore, he argues, both concepts are used to strengthen the control of the powerful groups in our society and rarely can or will either be challenged.

In conclusion, it can be argued that there remains within (and beyond) the NHS general assumptions of racial inferiority and 'difference'. While this explains some of the particular problems experienced by black people, their most extreme disadvantages appear to remain a structural combination of disadvantage and racism in the labour market with continuing discrimination in many other sectors of their lives. This does not mean, however, that ethnic minority groups are helpless victims in their own oppression.

As Ahmad points out, there has always been a tradition of black community action, including action on health, and this needs to be extended and expanded to ensure fair access to resources where the needs of all ethnic groups are taken into consideration. He concludes:

Although the scope for reducing racial inequalities in health lie largely outside of the NHS, equity of healthcare provision ... is also of paramount importance. These struggles for equitable health and healthcare are essentially located in the wider struggles for equity and dignity which have been a part of black people's history.
(Ahmad, 1993, p. 214)

13.5. **The establishment of a national health service**

A brief history of healthcare developments

As Doyal and Pennell (1979) and many other Marxist (see Section 2.5) writers have pointed out, we cannot understand the development of medical treatment without understanding the structural, historical, economic and political changes which have surrounded such practices. The idea that modern medical practices somehow emerged as a result of certain discoveries by great scientists such as Pasteur or Lister tends to ignore the political dimension of healthcare.

Doyal and Pennell argue that in pre-industrial societies care of the sick was for the most part undertaken by women. Healing was based mainly on folklore knowledge of herbs and remedies. While this is very different from the biomedical model which dominated medicine throughout the twentieth century, it can also be said that informal care of the sick still remains mainly in the hands of women and that there is considerable interest today in herb-based treatments for many ailments, especially those which seem to resist conventional medical treatment.

Midwinter (1994) reminds us that healthcare in medieval times was haphazard, with whole families and even villages being devastated by plagues and epidemics. A third of the population died in Britain during the Black Death – a virulent form of bubonic plague – between 1348 and 1350, and the plague recurred sporadically until late in the seventeenth century. However, the thinly spread population tended to keep most diseases within fairly local boundaries, and it was only with the growth of towns that diseases due to sewage and water pollution became an extensive problem.

Jewson (1976) suggests that 'scientific medicine' developed through three main stages. From the Middle Ages to the later eighteenth century medical care was available only to wealthy people who usually retained their own doctor. Diagnostic tools were limited, so the patient's own account of his or her symptoms was the most important guide to any problems.

From the beginning of the nineteenth century, hospital medical treatment became more widespread. From a post-structuralist viewpoint, Foucault (1976) identifies this as one of the key aspects of the growth of surveillance in modern society. (See also Sections 9.7 and 11.10.) Most of the prisons, workhouses and asylums and hospitals were built during the nineteenth century, arguably to contain and control the criminal, the poor and old, and the mentally and physically ill. Doctors became more organized – and more powerful – as a profession, and patients became cases rather than patrons. There was an increasingly biomedical view of ill-health, with the sick body seen mainly as a malfunctioning machine that needed to be fixed. Many diagnostic tools were developed at this time such as stethoscopes and thermometers, but both diagnosis and treatment remained relatively limited and based on little scientific knowledge.

Probably the most important developments at this time were in the field of social medicine. The development of the 'germ theory of disease' by Pasteur and Koch, antibiotics by Lister, vaccination by Jenner and anaesthetics by Wells and Sampson were the main advances in scientific treatment of the sick throughout the nineteenth century. Hospitals were now beginning to be seen as places to be cured in rather than to die in (when they were avoided by those who could afford to do so). Further advances in the treatment of disease can be attributed to social reformers such as Chadwick whose insistence that water must be clean to avoid the transmission of diseases has led to the virtual elimination of typhoid and cholera among the populations of wealthier countries.

Throughout the last part of the nineteenth century, medical officers were appointed to coordinate local authority healthcare, the first of these being in Liverpool in 1847 (Trowler, 1984). Their main concerns were to improve sanitation in the burgeoning towns as urbanization (see Section 16.6) became increasingly widespread. Land Enclosure Acts drove people from the land while factories promised paid jobs. However, this largely unplanned exodus led to considerable suffering. It is in this period that governments started seriously to consider the health needs and implications of the changing society, most notably through the 1848 Public Health Act. Midwinter points out that:

Although the 1848 Act was, in practice, feeble, its passage has been hailed as the most significant moment in world public health history, simply because it originated the notion of public intervention.
(Midwinter, 1994, p. 55)

Introduction of the National Health Service

Continuing developments led to the beginnings of the welfare state (see Section 14.1). The National Health Service came into being with the passing of the National Health Act 1948, with the aim of providing universal healthcare, free at the point of delivery. This occurred with considerable opposition from doctors and, in many cases, politicians who opposed the extra spending required to provide the service. Before this time the majority of the population had had to pay for their healthcare. Although the change was popular with the majority of the population, doctors were generally not happy to give up private practice to become employees of the state. Consequently, the Minister of Health at the time, Aneurin Bevan, said he had to 'stuff the consultants' mouths with gold' in order to gain their consent to working within the state medical sector.

This left the doctors as independent contractors who were paid a fee to work for the state while still maintaining the right to private practice. The retention of a private sector has been seen by some as one of the main causes of funding problems within the NHS, while others argue that private income has subsidized the NHS for many years. Although most private medical staff are trained within the NHS, private health income is sometimes used to subsidize state hospital beds. In 1995 the NHS was the largest provider of private healthcare in the UK.

Discussion point

To what extent does the provision of private healthcare within state hospitals breach the equal treatment principle underlying the NHS?

The structure of the NHS as established in 1948 is usually described as a compromise between (a) the needs of people for local provision and accountability, and (b) the desire for doctors and administrators to remain largely free from the constraints of local authority controls. This meant that GPs were largely independent of their local health authorities, who, however, provided most community and environmental services such as maternity care and health visiting. The third, regional structure was established to supervise hospitals and this resulted in areas getting care from doctors, hospitals and local health services with different areas of authority.

This tripartite system of the NHS meant that the universal and collective aims of the welfare state were to some extent undermined by the professional freedom which doctors and hospitals demanded. Doctors made many of the spending decisions about how money was to be spent on healthcare, especially as they also had considerable representation on the governing bodies of hospitals and other decision-making bodies within the NHS. It was believed that their medical expertise and professional ethos would lead to rational and disinterested policies which would rapidly reduce the demand for their services and improve the health of the nation.

Reorganization of the National Health Service

The structure of the NHS as established in 1948 survived with few changes until 1974. The tripartite system, with responsibilities shared by regional hospital boards, specialist authorities and local executive councils, was designed to be accountable and accessible, but was criticized for being expensive, inflexible and bureaucratic (see Section 9.7). Morgan *et al.* (1985) show that political compromises led to growing dissatisfaction with the NHS on three main points:

- Costs quickly became an issue owing to growing demand and a lack of centralized financial control.

- The three administrative structures led to inconsistencies and lack of continuity in treatment.
- It did little to reduce inequalities in geographical provision and between sectors. Most money went to the big teaching hospitals centred mainly in London and the South East which focused on the acute sector of treatment, leaving relatively little money for the treatment of the chronically sick such as the elderly and disabled.

This led to a comprehensive reorganization in 1974 – although that, too, was based on compromise in an attempt to serve the needs of all the interested parties. The NHS was reorganized into a number of regional health authorities, area health authorities and district health authorities. Each DHA was to have its own community health council to deal with complaints, although these too have been criticized for being ineffective and out of touch with the needs of ordinary people. One major improvement was the alignment of local boundaries, but the medical profession maintained most of their control over primary care and their influence on advisory committees at local, central and regional levels. The main improvements were a closer watch on financial allocation and an attempt to reduce some of the geographical and sectoral inequalities identified in the 1960s.

The reorganization started in 1974 had many critics, and more widespread changes were introduced in the 1980s, establishing the more market-oriented system we are becoming familiar with today.

Factors affecting the development of healthcare in the UK

According to Taylor and Field (1993), the political differences between Labour and Conservative parties are rooted in the early commercial battles between employee and employer which characterized early industrialization. The move from agricultural to industrial production, and more recently from industrial production to the provision of services, has important consequences for the current structure of employment and unemployment in the UK. Health and healthcare are, of course, intrinsically linked to economic factors. The introduction of the NHS in the immediate post-war period was:

. . . partly in response to demographic need, consumer demand and medico-technological development, but was made possible by the buoyant national and international economic climate.
(Taylor and Field, 1993, p. 22)

Population changes have also influenced the nature of the NHS. Declining infant mortality and increased life expectancy – mainly but not solely due to improved nutrition and living standards – have

placed what some would consider to be intolerable burdens on the NHS as it was conceived by Aneurin Bevan. This has been compounded by the burden of 'new' diseases such as cancers and HIV/AIDS, which are expensive to treat and, in many cases, incurable.

One response to this has been an emphasis on 'care in the community'. There is a great requirement to increase turnover in hospital bed occupancy, so that often hospitals may seek to release patients to what some people consider to be inadequate situations outside of the hospital. Although a package of care is negotiated for each patient, for the generation who tended to regard Beveridge's welfare state as being there 'from cradle to grave' this is not seen as acceptable. Furthermore, as more women enter paid employment there are often fewer of the traditional carers – married women – available to look after the disabled, elderly or chronically sick. This constitutes a crisis, and not only for the NHS and the growing numbers of sick and elderly people in need of care; Hicks (1988) points out that 1.3 million people are left to care and cope, often with little government support.

Modern pressures on the NHS

The ideal contained in the Beveridge Report that the NHS would eliminate disease – one of the Five Giants of social evil – was shattered by the ever-greater demands placed on it by an increasingly health-conscious and long-lived population. While those who proposed and introduced the NHS can be seen as collectivists in their desire (however reluctantly in some cases) to provide a health service to provide for the needs of all, the collectivist consensus has virtually disappeared with the combination of growing demands and national economic decline.

Pressures on the NHS include an ageing population, expensive technological developments, a highly skilled workforce in the health sector, and rising consumer expectations. According to Taylor and Field (1993) this has led to pressure on health costs, resulting in a perceived financial crisis in the health service and a breakdown of the post-war consensus on free, universal health provision which existed at the time of the introduction of the NHS.

Despite the belief that greater good health due to NHS provision would result in a drop in demand, it is clear that demand for healthcare has risen and continues to do so (see Table 13.8). Taylor and Field argue that, the four main factors affecting increased health spending are:

- an ageing population
- improvements in technology
- increasing labour costs

NHS patients may have to pay

DAVID BRINDLE

CHARGES may have to be introduced for treatment on the National Health Service, Sir Duncan Nichol, the service's former chief executive, is to warn in an interview to be broadcast next month.

Ministers will be angered by his remarks at a time when they are seeking to reassure people before the general election that the NHS under the Conservatives will continue to provide free health care on demand.

Sir Duncan, who was chief executive from 1989 to 1994 and oversaw the introduction of the Government's NHS market system, sparked controversy last year when he chaired an independent inquiry which concluded that the service could not continue without policy changes to meet rising demand for health care.

One option set out by the inquiry was to allow patients to buy additional services such as better hospital food or clinic appointments at times of their convenience.

In his interview for a BBC television series on the NHS, Sir Duncan appears to go still further.

His comments are screened immediately after a prediction by a doctor working for BUPA, the private health insurer, that people will in future pay to see their GP or even to have some hospital treatments.

Sir Duncan, who is now a director of BUPA and professor of health services management at Manchester university, says: "Charges of this kind would represent income to offset the costs of the NHS and so help to relieve the pressures on it."

Asked what he would say to people who accused him of undermining fundamental principles of the service, he replied: "I would say that the last thing I am attempting to do is undermine the principles of the NHS and turn it into some other sort of creature.

"What I am arguing is that we need to be honest and open about the pressures on it and we need to be allowed to think about all the possibilities that could continue to ensure that we have a health service."

Source: *The Guardian*, 29 August 1996

Table 13.8 Spending on the NHS, 1949–79

Year	NHS expenditure		Total NHS cost
	As % of GNP	£ million	(index 1949=100)
1949	3.9	437	100
1959	3.8	792	126
1969	4.4	1733	200
1979	5.3	9082	303

Source: Adapted from Taylor and Field (1993)

Activity

Some writers argue that the UK can no longer afford a free and universal national heath service. Use information in this section and in the article 'NHS patients may have to pay' to draw up a list of potential reasons why the continuation of a free and universal NHS is seen as problematic. Make a list of the suggested solutions to this problem and evaluate their respective merits.

U, I, A, E

- higher expectations of both health and healthcare.

In the 1990s, critical comments about the welfare state and collectivism generally – especially but not only from the New Right (see Sections 2.10 and 14.3) – have led to important changes in the perception and organization of the NHS. Currently the main criticisms of the NHS include the following:

- The welfare state is inefficient and private provision would be better.

- High taxes required to fund welfare are depriving other sectors and reducing money available for private investment.
- State welfare leads some people to become so dependent on welfare provision that they lose the ability to provide for themselves.

Activity

Taylor and Field's figures in Table 13.8 show NHS expenditure as a percentage of GNP, a measure of the nation's economic production. Use your library to look up GNP figures for the years 1984–93 shown in Table 13.9 on page 534 and work out NHS expenditure as a percentage of GNP for these years. Write a summary of the trend shown by these figures.

I, A

13.6. Contemporary debates on healthcare

The New Right and the NHS

The financial crisis identified within the NHS – and the welfare state generally – was accompanied by a change in views about state healthcare among members of the Conservative government of the time and many of their supporters. The New Right presented a very negative view of the role of the state. (See Sections 2.10 and 14.3.) Drawing particularly on the work of the economist Milton Friedman and

Table 13.9 Government expenditure on the National Health Service (£millions)

	1984/85	1985/86	1986/87	1987/88	1988/89	1989/90	1990/91	1991/92	1992/93
Current expenditure									
Central government									
Hospitals and community health services[1] and family health services[2]	14 976	15 932	17 086	18 870	21 110	22 197	25 276	29 075	32 049
Administration	473	475	553	627	682	855	979	1 119	1 249
less Payments by patients:									
Hospital services	−84	−92	−99	−106	−347	−407	−453	−510	−540
Pharmaceutical services	−149	−158	−204	−256	−202	−242	−230	−248	−265
Dental services	−197	−225	−261	−290	−282	−340	−418	−445	−483
Ophthalmic services	−52	−14	−1	−1	-	-	-	-	-
Total	−482	−489	−565	−653	−831	−989	−1 101	−1 203	−1 288
Departmental administration	137	142	171	193	206	192	228	283	308
Other central services	218	283	324	336	326	471	535	658	711
Total current expenditure	15 322	16 343	17 569	19 373	21 493	22 726	25 917	29 932	33 029
Capital expenditure	990	1 091	1 160	1 212	1 309	2 071	1 848	1 791	1 883
Total expenditure	16 312	17 434	18 729	20 585	22 802	24 797	27 765	31 723	34 912

1 Including the school health service
2 General Medical Services have been included in the expenditure of the Health Authorities. Therefore, hospitals and community health services and family practitioner services (now family health services) are not identifiable separately
Source: Central Statistical Office/*Annual Abstract of Statistics 1995* Key Data 1994, p. 75

the philosopher Friedrich Hayek, they argued that state provision of medicine and other forms of welfare was bad for the individual and for society. George and Wilding (1985), social policy analysts, summarize the New Right critique as follows:

- The welfare state interferes with individual freedoms.
- Governments are weakened by the incessant demands of pressure groups.
- The large-scale bureaucracy required is wasteful and inefficient.
- More efficient private forms of provision are stifled.
- People become dependent on the state and are therefore unable to take responsibility for their own healthcare.

In the UK, New Right views tend to be expressed by members of the Conservative Party, although there is some disagreement about the levels of state healthcare that should be made available. Liberal Democrats and members of the Labour Party, although disagreeing on some basic assumptions about the ways in which society should operate, are more likely to adopt a social democratic view of social welfare. This view tends to support the provision of free and universal healthcare as a right for all citizens, as the case was presented in 1948. Therefore Labour and Liberal Democratic politicians challenge most of the New Right's arguments about the role of the state (see Table 13.10).

Reforms in the NHS

In order to reduce or eliminate many of the problems identified by the New Right, the NHS was reformed by the provisions of the Health and Community Care Act 1990. The key stated aims were to:

- improve institutional efficiency and accountability
- reduce bureaucratic and economic waste
- broaden the choices of patients for their healthcare needs.

Activity

1 Using Table 13.10 and any other relevant material you have, write short speeches for Conservative and Labour politicians expressing their views about healthcare provision.
2 This table was originally written in 1984. To what extent is it still accurate today?

I, A, E

There was no stated attempt to replace public with private healthcare, although the private system of enterprise was seen as an appropriate model for the provision of health treatment.

The main changes included an increase in private and voluntary provision to improve competitiveness between private doctors and hospitals and those in the state sector, and a transfer of funds from the secondary sector (hospitals) to primary care (GPs, district nurses etc.) so that more people could be treated and cared for by community doctors and nurses as hospital outpatients or in their own homes. There are a number of aspects to these changes which remain unpopular, as more people tend to be discharged from hospital more quickly than they may have been in the past.

Table 13.10 Perspectives on the NHS

Issue	Marxist	Market liberal	Social democrat
Nature of society	Divided by classes with opposing interests	United by common interests	United by common interests and values
Social order maintenance	Coercion and ideology operate to suppress conflict	Self-interest and the common good are the same, therefore social order is maintained by pursuit of self-interest	Humanitarian social policies prevent any conflict which may be engendered by the ill-effects of capitalism
Attitude to NHS	*Anti:* It represents the interests of the ruling class and embodies the class, colour and sex inequalities in society	*Anti:* It impedes the free play of market forces when over-expanded	*Pro:* It alleviates the ill-effects of capitalism, produces political legitimacy and prevents civil unrest
Desired changes to present system of healthcare	Must be changed in the context of wider social changes including socialization of NHS and abolition of capitalist drug companies	Severe reduction of NHS or its abolition is necessary. It should be replaced by private healthcare	Extension of NHS provision is necessary, especially in such areas as psychiatric and geriatric care
Attitude to private medicine	*Anti:* It is available for the few and is parasitical on state resources. As with other profit-making enterprises, it is detrimental to the general good	*Pro:* It is a source of wealth, leads to better healthcare, improves consumer choice and is beneficial for the NHS	*Anti:* It represents the expression of private interests rather than the general public's interests

Source: Trowler (1984)

Discussion point

In what ways is discharging patients more quickly a beneficial development? Are there any groups who might lose out by this?

Economic changes in the NHS

One particularly dramatic and controversial change was the introduction of an 'internal market', whereby hospitals and other groups offer their services to doctors (many of whom are now managing their own budgets) or to district health authority managers. They then choose the best value treatment for their patients from a range of options. This means that doctors who choose to be 'fundholders' can, in theory, shop around among a number of hospital trusts – the groups that run hospitals – in order to purchase the best and most cost-effective treatment for their patients.

The general aim was to introduce the managerial practices of the private sector – where the main aim is usually profit – into state health provision in order to improve efficiency and accountability and thus make the NHS more cost-effective. It was claimed that the NHS should be able to compete effectively with private and voluntary provision and monitor its own spending.

Many opponents of the New Right argue that what they really want is wholesale privatization of all healthcare, but that this would be politically unacceptable. As it is, these reforms have attracted both support and criticism, and even some Conservative politicians now argue that there are too many managers in the 'new' NHS. Some of the problems with these changes exist because many of the aims appear to contradict each other. For example, one of the key aims of the changes is to improve patient choice, but some forms of care in the community (see Section 14.2) seem to restrict choice for some patients. Elderly people, for instance, may find it difficult to get the level of care that they feel they need within their own home. There is also a suggestion that health needs are increasingly defined in terms of financial rather than purely health criteria. However, there is now much more openness about the need to ration healthcare, although some traditional social democrats, such as Tony Benn MP, argue that rationing of healthcare is not inevitable.

The majority of politicians from all political parties – and many sociologists – now tend to reject the latter view. In their review of health policy in the UK, Blakemore and Symons (1993) suggest that although spending on healthcare has always been relatively low and well-managed, the fact that it is paid for out of taxation means that the government is constantly under pressure to reduce spending in this area if there is public pressure to reduce taxes. Consequently they suggest that by the 1980s:

Rising expectations of health services coupled with advances in medical treatment and the growing need for treatment from an ageing population have contributed to something of a crisis in healthcare.
(Blakemore and Symons, 1993, p. 195)

Ham (1992), a social policy specialist, shares this view. He regards some form of health rationing as almost inevitable in the future. While some opponents of health reforms tend to blame Conservative policies for the NHS's difficulties, Ham shares what appears to be the most widely held view that any government would face the same problems. The crisis of an ageing population and reduced capability for funding is one shared by most other advanced, western economies. With regard to current and future health provision, Ham says:

The debate about the future has arisen out of concern at the expenditure implications of demographic changes and medical advance. . . . With resources for growth likely to be limited throughout the 1990s,

whatever party holds office, the rationing of healthcare will become increasingly difficult and controversial.
(Ham, 1992, p. 236)

The purchaser–provider split

A major change to the NHS introduced by the 1990 legislation was the introduction of a split between purchasers of healthcare (the health authorities and the GPs) and the providers (hospitals and GPs). This radical change, which is depicted in Figure 13.4, was effected in order to introduce a market into the system and so make it more economically efficient:

A system of 'contracts' for providing healthcare was introduced. For example, District Health Authorities must, as purchasers, ensure that they have drawn up contracts with local hospitals to guarantee the supply of a comprehensive range of services and medical operations. Each contract stipulates cost, quantity and quality of the services to be provided over a year. Equally, fund-holding GPs must also draw up contracts with providers.
(Blakemore and Symons, 1993, pp. 196–7)

Trust hospitals and fundholding GPs

An increasing number of hospitals have become independent trusts, meaning that they are funded by central government directly rather than by local

> ### Discussion point
>
> One of the most controversial issues raised by the changes in the NHS has been to do with this apparent need to ration healthcare. It has been suggested that some treatments, such as tattoo removal, should no longer be available from the NHS. To what extent do you agree that treatment for certain things should not be available? Which services, if any, do you think this should apply to?

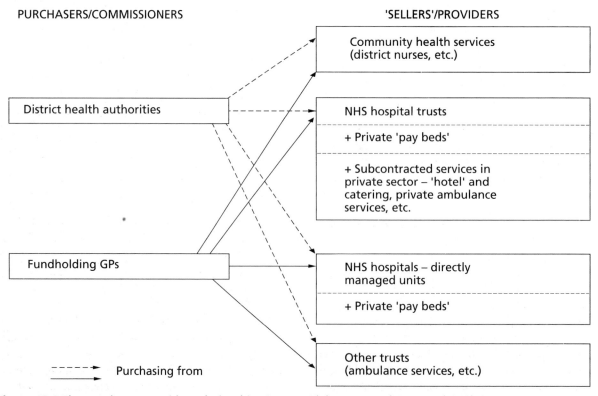

Figure 13.4 The purchaser–provider relationship. Source: Blakemore and Symons (1993)

health authorities. This makes them accountable to their own management board rather than to local authority appointed officials. A somewhat similar arrangement has been introduced for fundholding GPs who, while not being accountable to a board of managers, directly manage their own funds which they receive from their regional health authority. This, too, is an attempt to introduce competition into the NHS with the intention of improving efficiency.

Evaluation of changes in the NHS

Critics of the purchaser–provider arrangements argue that the NHS was already relatively cheap for the nation, and that the outcome will be a two-tier system with better provision for those who can afford to pay. Even without resorting to private medicine, it is clear that some patients are able to get better treatment from their GP than others. This challenges the principle of equality of access, but may improve provision for some.

While the purchaser–provider split may well improve efficiency, there is also the possibility that some trusts may eventually go bankrupt (like any other company) if they cannot attract contracts. There is, however, clearly a difference between a group of people without access to a local newsagent – or even Post Office – and leaving people without accessible healthcare.

Blakemore and Symons (1993) query the ability for the market-style NHS to improve its services to all patients. They may be more rather than less restricted in their choice of treatments as the GP will be tied to various contract arrangements. There could also be financial limits on the drugs and other treatments they may be prescribed. Many patients requiring expensive treatments fear that they will be rejected by GPs, but there is no evidence to support this claim. There may also be an emphasis on the quantity rather than the quality of care – for example the number of patients treated and discharged rather than the state of health they are in when they leave. Finally, there is little evidence that the market-style system is really more cost-effective or less bureaucratic than the system it replaced.

The three most noticeable consequences of NHS reform, according to Bilton *et al.* (1996), are:

- *marketization* – that is the introduction of an internal market into transactions between different sectors of the health service
- *privatization* – with an increasing emphasis on the private provision of much health treatment, and
- *managerialism* – whereby health professionals are increasingly managers and accountants and the majority of nursing is provided in the community by informal carers.

Hospitals 'on brink of collapse'

DAVID BRINDLE

THE hospital service will be "close to collapse" this winter with a block on non-urgent treatments in many parts of the country, a doctors' leader warned last night.

James Johnson, chairman of the consultants' committee of the British Medical Association, said evidence from many parts of England and Wales pointed to "massive" health authority deficits, rising waiting lists, and large-scale staff shortages.

Ministers and senior NHS officials have admitted that health authorities and trusts face a tough winter and that waiting times will grow because of budget constraints. But they will regard Mr Johnson's remarks as alarmist.

He was speaking after the consultants' committee had held an unscheduled debate on the developing "crisis" in the hospital sector. Members cited problems which include:

- A freeze on elective, i.e. non-urgent surgery and investigations at Queen's Medical Centre, Nottingham, for patients of non-fundholder GPs in Nottingham, and of fundholders in south Derbyshire.
- A mental health trust in Avon, said to be failing to meet its statutory duties towards mentally ill patients because of four budget clawbacks in a year.
- Deficits ranging from £900,000 to £18.8 million among London health authorities. The Merton, Sutton and Wandsworth authority in south London has said it will not pay for any elective surgery next year.

Mr Johnson said: "From reports I have heard today, I fear the hospital service will be close to collapse this winter. Elective procedures will virtually cease in many parts of the country."

Health authorities had to realise that hospital wards should not be shut and opened at will to control the cash flow. When it came to the reopening of services, skilled staff would no longer be available.

"In the meantime patients who are not emergencies but who genuinely need treatment are waiting in pain and distress," Mr Johnson said.

The BMA is compiling a full dossier of the picture across the country, to be released after a meeting of its ruling council next Thursday.

It is calling on the Prime Minister to acknowledge the scale of the problems in the NHS in his speech today to the Conservative Party conference.

A Department of Health spokesman said the NHS budget was 72 per cent higher in real terms than in 1978–79.

The Government had been awarding real-term annual increases and the health service now took just under 15 per cent of total public spending compared with 12 per cent in 1978/1979.

Source: *The Guardian*, 11 October 1996

These changes are partly a result of the demedicalization of healthcare. An ageing population in particular means that a vast number of illnesses are

Don't fall ill if you're a child in Hackney

Paul Foot

M Y LOCAL Hospitals Trust – The Royal – has come up with an exciting new plan for Hackney's Queen Elizabeth Hospital for children. The hospital meets all the conditions laid down by the Government for closure. It is in constant demand, is highly respected, even loved, throughout the area, and its dedicated staff look after some of the poorest children in Europe.

Obviously it has to go. Until now, protesters have been partly placated by the promise that the Queen Elizabeth will not be closed until all its facilities are available at a spanking new mega-hospital at Whitechapel. Now the geniuses at the Trust – its chairman is a former boss of MI6 – threaten to close the hospital before the new hospital is even started. The Trust will, I assume, be issuing notices to children in Hackney instructing them not to fall ill until the next millennium.

Can we be sure even of that deadline? The Whitechapel hospital is being built under something called the "private finance initiative". This means it will be run for profit, with the NHS relegated to the role of "customer". But will the hospital be built at all? That depends on the election and the economic crisis which will follow. A Conservative government will start by cutting hospital-building programmes. A Labour government will start by cutting hospital-building programmes.

Source: *The Guardian*, 21 November 1996

either terminal or the result of old age – or both. As medicine is increasingly successful at curing or preventing acute illnesses, such as heart attacks or infections, the caring aspect of medical care has been devolved to informal carers. This is not necessarily a bad thing, as long as carers are valued, rewarded and supported adequately.

At the moment there is perceived to be a shortage of carers because women (traditionally the carers) are increasingly entering the paid labour market. This means that for many people with needs in the community there are no informal carers, leaving many vulnerable and even dangerous people without adequate support in the community. However, an increasing number of carers are older men looking after a disabled wife, which may lead to additional problems for themselves and the community supports they require.

O'Donnell (1992) suggests that the re-election of a Conservative government in 1992 led to the consolidation of these reforms. He saw two key aspects to these changes:

- an emphasis on selective provision and the idea that free healthcare should be available only for

those who cannot afford to pay, in order to target resources to the most needy
- a change in the principles governing the NHS, so that treatment is no longer based on need but accepts at least the principle of rationing and, in some cases, ability to pay.

O'Donnell (1992) summarizes the advantages and disadvantages of the reforms. He writes:

The stated aim of the . . . reforms is to limit the cost of health services without cutting patient care or, put simply, to increase productivity in the provision of health services. The mechanism for doing this is to introduce an element of competition by creating a limited medical marketplace.
(O'Donnell, 1992, p. 25)

While many social scientists examine the NHS in terms of its ability to provide an effective and affordable service for individuals in an advanced society like the UK, Marxist perspectives (see Section 2.5) tend to regard the NHS as a tool to help manage the crises of capitalism. This means that the NHS looks after those who cannot maintain themselves adequately in order to be fit as workers. It also legitimates capitalism, by showing how well capitalist societies look after their citizens.

Marxists such as Navarro (1978) suggested that the crisis in the NHS which led to the reforms outlined above is a response to a decline in capitalist profitability in the 1970s. However, Turner (1987, 1992) suggests that this argument ignores the different types of capitalism and health systems found in different societies. For example, state health provision in the USA was never as widespread as in the UK or Scandinavia. Furthermore, many Marxists do not acknowledge the hard-won benefits that the NHS has provided for workers, despite the inequalities outlined in other sections of this chapter.

In the end it all comes down to what money is allocated to healthcare, and how it is distributed. This

Activity

a Read the two articles 'Hospitals "on brink of collapse"' and 'Don't fall ill if you're a child in Hackney'. Identify the points being made about the NHS in each.

b Using material from the articles and other information, summarize and evaluate current political debates about spending and services in the NHS. Suggest reforms in each case which might make it both more efficient and more responsive to patients' needs.

I, A, E

is and will remain a long-standing political debate – and one that may affect us all at some time in our lives. It also remains at the forefront of much political debate about the way government money should be allocated and the whole complicated issue of the role of the NHS.

13.7. **Limits to medicine and healthcare**

One of the key aims of doctors and, to a lesser extent, nurses is to be accepted as a specialist profession. Doctors in particular still enjoy considerable admiration in our society and this is used to justify their high rewards and status. Their education, skills and expertise lead to them being granted a degree of power. If this is used for the benefit of all this is fine. However, the power inequalities (see Section 17.4) their position creates does leave open the possibility that medical care is determined for the benefit of the doctor rather than the patient. This possibility is the basis for many critical views on healthcare.

Functionalists (see Section 2.4) believe that we live in a society where the most able people are allocated to the most important roles in society. They therefore argue that doctors are respected and well-paid because their job is so important that only a relatively few extremely able people can do it. Barber (1963) claimed that there are four essential attributes of a professional, which are exemplified by doctors. These are:

- a body of systematic and generalized knowledge with a long period of specialized training
- a concern for the community rather than motivation based on self-interest
- a code of ethics strictly administered by a professional body such as the British Medical Association (BMA)
- generous economic rewards to demonstrate their high standing in the community.

Illich: iatrogenesis and nemesis

There have been a number of criticisms of the foregoing views from different perspectives, especially from Illich (1990) who argued that professionals are the cause of most of the problems in society, and doctors are probably the worst of all. The titles of his books show that he has scant respect for professionals, especially the medical profession.

Illich argues that although doctors claim to have vastly improved our health and longevity, virtually eradicating such diseases such as typhoid, tuberculosis and cholera, most contagious diseases were in decline owing to improved sanitation before the development of vaccinations. He points out that well-fed people are far better able to fight disease than the nutritionally deprived. He also identifies the fact that doctors can do relatively little about the main modern epidemic killers such as heart disease and cancer.

Rather than doctors working in our interest, Illich argues, most medical treatment is useless or, worse still, downright dangerous. Non-infectious illnesses in particular are best treated by prevention and early diagnosis rather than expensive, and often disabling, medical treatment. He goes on to say that medicine is bad for us in four key ways, which he describes as either iatrogenesis or nemesis. 'Iatrogenesis' means caused by itself, so he is talking about medical treatments that make us ill. Nemesis was the Greek goddess of retribution, so here Illich is suggesting that medical treatment finally results in making us sicker as individuals, and as a society.

Clinical iatrogenesis

This covers the negative effects of medical treatments; the side-effects of drugs, the addiction promoted by tranquillizers, the patient who comes out of hospital sicker than when he or she went in. Examples of this include the thalidomide scandal in the early 1960s. (See also Section 12.9.) Expectant mothers given tablets for morning sickness subsequently gave birth to children with truncated limbs. It took years of campaigning – most notably by the *Sunday Times* – before Distillers, who produced the drug, finally offered their victims compensation. Furthermore, Illich argued, widespread use of antibiotics leads to people (and viruses) becoming resistant, and the World Health Organization is currently arguing for greater restraint in the use of antibiotics for just this reason.

Social iatrogenesis

Even worse, in some ways, is the way in which doctors use the medical model of illness to diagnose and treat reported symptoms of illness. Illich suggests that most illness is actually caused by the boredom, alienation, monotony, materialism and lack of autonomy experienced by most people in contemporary industrial societies. However, doctors blame the individual rather than society, and so not only hide the true causes of illness but, unsurprisingly, are unable to treat them.

Cultural iatrogenesis

In an over-medicalized society, people become defenceless consumers of medicine just as they mindlessly consume other products of industrial society. (see Section 10.9.) This is instilled by teachers in schools (where we passively consume educational knowledge in order to get the credentials we need) and encouraged by other professionals such as lawyers and advertisers as well as doctors. In this way people become unable to diagnose, treat or deal with not only illness but also other problems in society. They can no longer respond in a healthy way to illness, death or any other kind of suffering because they always turn to someone else.

Medical nemesis

Illich claims that our lack of autonomy means that we consume medicines and seek help from doctors which ultimately makes us less well, personally, socially and culturally. Medical developments constantly cause problems that lead to the need for 'medical' solutions. He argues that the only way – if it is possible – to restore individual and social health is for people to take control of their own healthcare and wrest it away from the doctors who only make things worse.

Activity

Explain Illich's four concepts in your own words and provide an example of each.

I, A

Other criticisms of the medical profession

Parry and Parry (1976) argue that medical professionals operate mainly in their own interests, limiting entry, criticism and competition to maintain their high rewards and status. However the autonomy of doctors is not as high in many parts of the world as it is in the USA, where most doctors practise privately. This at least reduces the level of medical lawsuits in the UK in comparison with the USA.

Johnson (1972) argues that many professionals owe their allegiance to their employers rather than their patients. In some cases doctors and nurses have lost their jobs for reporting inefficiencies in the NHS. Doctors also seem to be losing the respect of some members of the public, and a few have been attacked on night visits. However, their response – to suggest that they no longer make home visits at night – was not popular with the public. Doctors are also increasingly open to lawsuits.

Discussion point

To what extent should patients, managers, lawyers or others who are medically unqualified be free to question judgements made by qualified professional medical staff?

Doctors, managers and patients

There is considerable interest in the relationships between doctors and managers and between doctors and patients. A study by Goss (1969) suggested that, in most medical institutions, doctors' views tended to carry more weight than managers'. This debate is increasingly important with the growth of managerialism within the NHS, where these relationships remain problematic.

Doctors are sometimes criticized for their poor communication skills and their inability to interact effectively with patients, especially when there are class or cultural differences. Not only is there the previously discussed 'inverse care law' according to Tudor-Hart (1971), whereby doctors are situated in areas of lowest need, but consultation is also class-differentiated. A study by Cartwright and O'Brien (1976) showed that average consultations with middle-class patients tended to be over a minute longer than those with working-class patients, and the doctor seemed to know less about the latter group.

Although evidence suggests that many doctors still tend not to listen to their patients as much as they could, Walker and Waddington (1991) show improved interactions between doctors and homosexual men in the treatment of AIDS. They propose that this is because many gay men are actually better acquainted with the medical details about HIV and AIDS than the majority of doctors, who encounter these diseases only rarely. This suggests that interpersonal skills training for doctors and a better-informed public could reduce the professional barrier between doctor and patient, and that this needs to be provided for all members of society.

Nettleton (1995) says that our awareness of many of the above debates suggests that the medical professions and industries may be in decline. There is, undoubtedly, a growing belief in the need for personal control over health and in the use of 'alternative' medical treatments. Sharma (1992) argues that this is evidence of the growing power of consumers – in this case of medical expertise and treatments – in a post-modern society. Bakx (1991) sees it as evidence of a general decline in our faith in the biomedical model.

Furthermore, the autonomy of doctors in the UK is being undermined by the increasing managerialism of the NHS. It can also be argued that people without formal medical training are more involved in the treatment of ill-health, for example as homeopaths, aromatherapists and various types of masseurs. Although the medical knowledge of some lay people is improving, Nettleton (1996) claims that this may be due to the fact that we live in an increasingly medicalized society. Most alternative medicine and self-health groups operate in parallel with biomedical treatments and are often only sought as a last resort.

A report by the British Medical Association (1993) asserts that the medical profession welcomes alternative practitioners, but is keen to lay down their guidelines and to ensure they operate within the biomedical model. In this way challenges to the medical profession can more easily be controlled.

Medicine and capitalism: the profit motive

Some writers argue that there is a link between capitalism and the power of the medical profession. In the USA, McKinley (1977) asserted that the profit motive which drives capitalism has overwhelmed the delivery of healthcare. Even in the UK, it can be argued, healthcare is now more of a commodity than a right. The arguments about the rationing of healthcare show its increasing commodification. There are now a number of treatments, such as hip replacements and varicose vein removal, which are now rarely offered at NHS hospitals, forcing patients to resort to private treatment. It is also now true in the UK that the majority of dentists no longer offer NHS treatment to working adults who join their practice.

It seems unlikely that all medical professionals become involved purely to make a lot of money, although there are potentially considerable rewards to be had. However, it has been argued far more convincingly by Marxist writers that drug companies and medical equipment manufacturers can, and do, make excessive profits from the production and sale of related commodities.

Doyal and Pennell (1979) found that most drug companies justify their high prices and high profits by their claim to also be a high research industry. However, as they pointed out, most 'new' drugs are actually slightly modified versions of existing ones, so the main aim is to increase market share rather than produce dramatic improvements. They also note that drugs are aimed at cure rather than prevention of illness, while doctors are bombarded with advertising, so that much of the research and development expenditure goes on marketing. Research into 'real' new drugs is often guarded secretly to ensure that one company makes all the profits.

Navarro (1976) argues that not only do drug and medical equipment companies make huge profits, but medicine itself operates to maintain the ideological control of the ruling class. The NHS, for example, justifies exploitation and legitimates capitalism by providing a means to keep the workforce healthy and satisfied. Like Illich, discussed above, he claims that the medical model directs attention away from the real (capitalist) causes of much ill-health.

Medical surveillance and control

Rather than seeing medicine as losing its power, Turner (1987, 1992) argues that the medicalization of society has largely legitimated the increased surveillance of our bodies to the extent that medicine now has control over all our life processes. Drawing on the ideas of Foucault, he suggests that our bodies have been subjected to a process of rationalization (see Section 9.7) and standardization which means that medical professionals have the power to decide what are – and what are not – acceptable behaviours and forms of appearance in our society. He says:

The body has become the focus of a wide range of disciplines and forms of surveillance and control, in which the medical profession has played a critical part. The birth of the clinic and the growth of the teaching hospital have been significant institutional developments in the development of what Foucault has called the medical gaze. This framework provides an organizing principle for looking at the problem of sickness at the level of the individual body, the growth of institutional regulation and control at the level of the clinic and hospital, and finally the emergence of a bio-politics of populations whereby the state through its various local and national agencies constantly intervenes in the production and reproduction of life itself.
(Turner, 1987, 1992, p. 218)

Activity

Turner argues that the medical profession regulates us as individuals, in institutions (such as schools as well as hospital) and in terms of reproduction. To what extent do you consider your life might be regulated now or in the future by medical limitations imposed by the state in each of these cases?

A, E

13.8. Mental illness and disability

Definitions of mental illness

Deciding whether somebody is 'mentally ill' requires two judgements:

- Is the individual's behaviour odd enough to be considered outside the scope of normal human functioning?
- Is the reason behind this behaviour 'mental'?

Throughout history and up to the present day there have been problems with establishing concrete criteria for making such judgements. This is partly due to the fact that 'abnormality' is mainly socially constructed: society determines what is abnormal and there are no objective criteria. Therefore what tends to be considered abnormal is that which does not fit in with a particular society's definition of normal.

What exactly is meant by normal? Again there is no baseline; rather 'normality' is defined by a society at a particular time in history, and it is different for different social and cultural groups.

Acknowledging that abnormality is socially constructed highlights many problems. It raises questions like the following:

- If we are not sure what kind of behaviour is normal then have we any right to treat or try to change those who we consider 'abnormal'?
- What are the consequences for the individual who we consider to be 'abnormal'?

Discussion point

Discuss the questions raised above and consider to what extent you agree that they pose real problems.

A further challenge is deciding what has caused someone's abnormal behaviour. Historically many causes have been identified, including magic, spirits, the devil, demons, lack of conscience and physical malfunctioning. Although modern psychologists lean towards finding physical causes behind mental illness, the influence of psychoanalysis and behaviourism has led many to look for causes in their clients' learning environment or their interpersonal relationships rather than their physiological make-up alone.

The history of the explanations and early treatment of mental illness shows that there has long been a recognition that some behaviours are not considered normal and hence require treatment. However, the scientific ways of thinking that have dominated the twentieth century have demanded that societies provide some kind of yardstick against which normality and abnormality can be measured, allowing categorizations to be made. It is no longer acceptable to state, for example, that an individual's behaviour is so abnormal as to be considered the result of a mental illness simply because it does not accord with the norms (see Section 10.1) of a current social group or era. Homosexuality and unmarried motherhood were until quite recently both considered to be symptoms of underlying pathology.

Today a number of criteria have to be considered before making a judgement about abnormality, and problems with each criterion need also to be assessed. Over the years a number of criteria have emerged, but none is without problems. Here we consider four: deviation from the statistical norm, deviation from the social norm, maladaptiveness of behaviour, and personal distress.

Deviation from the statistical norm

This criterion suggests that behaviour should be considered abnormal if it is statistically infrequent. For example the majority of the population is heterosexual, so in this view homosexuality can be defined as abnormal. However, this criterion does not distinguish between desirable/acceptable behaviour and undesirable/unacceptable behaviour. A person who is extremely intelligent, artistic or happy would be described as abnormal, whereas feelings of depression and anxiety are so statistically common to count as 'normal' under this criterion.

Deviation from the social norm

Behaviour which differs from what is expected in society may be considered to be abnormal. This criterion also implies what people ought or ought not do, with transgressors being labelled 'bad' or 'sick'. But this criterion does not constitute a very reliable or valid definition of abnormal behaviour as abnormality is defined by the norms of that society alone, so we may end up labelling people unfairly. For example, anti-communists in the former Soviet Union were often defined as mentally ill and committed to asylums. Needless to say, such a view would not be held in the USA, where communists have been imprisoned or rendered unable to work. Hence behaviour that is considered normal in one society may be considered abnormal in another. Hearing voices and seeing visions are regarded as normal or even special in some societies, whereas such events often lead to a suspicion of schizophrenia in our society. Furthermore, concepts of normality change over time.

Maladaptiveness of behaviour

Many social scientists believe that the most important criterion is how someone's behaviour affects the well-being of the individual and/or the social group. Therefore behaviour is abnormal if it is maladaptive in this sense. Some kinds of deviant behaviour interfere with the welfare of the individual (e.g. alcoholism – though this also affects others) whilst other behaviours such as violence are more harmful to society.

Personal distress

This criterion considers the individual's subjective feelings of distress rather than their outward behaviour. People described as 'mentally ill' often

Make up your mind

DAMARIS LE GRAND

PEOPLE who use the psychiatric services and those who offer health and social care in the Bristol area have joined forces to launch a new way of responding to mental distress – a new way of assessing mental health needs.

The Avon Mental Health Measure is a radical departure from the "traditional" assessment, just what is needed. Between one in four and one in eight of the population will experience a mental health problem. A large part of our health and social care budget is spent on mental ill-health and the economy loses hundreds of millions of pounds in absenteeism and social security payments. Yet those needing help often find it difficult to have their needs properly assessed. The Avon Mental Health Measure wants to change this.

Most people who see mental health professionals for help are entering a world of coded language, where the problem is often seen as a medical label ("depressive", "schizophrenic" etc.) and treated with what the agency can provide rather than what someone needs. The measure, designed by a partnership of service users and professionals, challenges these perspectives.

Co-ordinated by Bristol social services, it represents a real breakthrough. Supported by Mind, the National Schizophrenic Fellowship and the health trusts in Avon and funded from a number of sources, including Avon Health Authority, the main input is from people with personal experience. For the first time, service users, psychiatrists, social and voluntary sector workers sat down together to try to work out how the voice of the user can be heard and understood.

Designed over a three-year period, the measure lets people examine 25 aspects of their life – their housing, mood swings and money management, sleep disturbance etc. – and to indicate how well they feel they function within each. People can express strengths, abilities and concerns as well as problems. This gives a full personal profile – essential to planning realistic and relevant care.

The measure has been extensively tested, and research into its effectiveness still continues. Service users have found that the measure helps them take control of their lives in a way not previously possible. One commented: "The measure helped me realise how ill I was and helped me and my worker work out what I really needed." Another found that: "It made me realise how chaotic my life was and has given me and my doctor a new way of looking at it."

Psychiatrists and social workers have also seen its benefits. Pamela Charlwood, Chief Executive of Avon Health Authority believes that: "The work done in Avon to develop the measure is a real step forward in enabling people to play a more active and assertive part in describing their own experience and situation."

Source: *The Guardian*,
27 June 1996

feel very unhappy (although not always while in a manic state). Sometimes personal distress is the only symptom of abnormality.

It is clear that none of the above categories provides a wholly adequate definition on which to start categorizing behaviour as normal or abnormal. Johonda (1958) suggested that most psychologists would agree with the following categories to indicate emotional *well-being*:

- efficient perception of reality
- self-knowledge
- the ability to exercise voluntary control over behaviour
- feelings of self-esteem and acceptance, the ability to form affective relationships and normal levels of productivity (a chronic lack of energy and feelings of fatigue and lethargy are often symptoms of psychological tension).

Activity

The article 'Make up your mind' demonstrates that new ways of categorizing mental illness are being developed. Explain in your own words the advantages of the method described in the article.

I

Sociological debates about mental illness

Trowler (1996) demonstrates that mental illness is socially distributed, so challenging many of the assumptions of the medical model. More women than men are likely to die while suffering from mental disorders, although this may be allied to the fact that they live longer, and the degenerative diseases associated with age. Working-class mothers seem to be more prone to depression than middle-class mothers. Black patients appear to be more likely to be admitted to mental hospitals than white patients with similar symptoms.

Activity

Suggest reasons why each of these differences may occur?

I, A

The systemic (or 'radical') approach, based mainly on the views of Laing and Esterson (1974), suggests that 'mental illness' is largely the result of faulty interactions between the individual and his or her family or significant others. Laing and his colleagues clearly demonstrated the 'dark side of the family', whereby family interactions drove a teenager to a state defined as 'schizophrenic' (see Chapter 7). Laing therefore claimed that it is the world that is mad rather than the individual.

This approach is also found in the work of Goffman (1987). Writing originally in the late 1950s, he showed that mental asylums – like other 'total institutions', including prisons, convents and military establishments – operate a system which is more likely to create than cure mental problems for the inmates. (See also Section 9.7.) He showed how the aim of institutionalization is to destroy the personal self-image of the individual and replace it with an institutional self-concept, which makes the inmate more acquiescent and obliging. Goffman called this 'the mortification of the self', a demonstration of the way that vulnerable people in particular are led to destroy and rebuild their personality by the institutions apparently designed to protect and help them. He also outlined the types of response people may offer to such attacks on the self. These include:

- withdrawing into a world of their own
- rebellion against the staff
- in complete contrast, over-identification with the staff to the point where they may attempt to take on many of their roles
- institutionalization, where inmates lose the desire to leave the institution or make any decisions for themselves.

Although Goffman's ideas were part of the liberal attack on asylums as a way to treat people with mental illnesses, the modern solution, 'care in the community', is not without its critics. (See Section 14.2.)

While many of these 'micro' sociological approaches provide insights into the working of places where people experience problems, they do not really take into account the wider social causes of mental illness. A more 'macro' sociological approach is needed to examine the impact of poverty (see Section 14.6), social isolation, alienation at work, divorce, unemployment (see Section 9.6), inequality, racism and the stresses that they cause for the individual. One of the unfortunate effects of 'care in the community' is that it often returns people to the very stresses and problems that caused their illness in the first place. However, this does not mean that supportive, therapeutic communities cannot work.

It can – and has been – argued that there is no such thing as mental illness. Foucault (1976) asserts that the definition of people as being mentally ill developed from the idea of reason and rationality which came to dominate modernist thinking (see also Section 9.7) and formed the basis for judging who

was and was not 'sane'. He pointed out that the King's Fool or the jester often had considerable power in court because he could say what others could only think. Today, people who say very extraordinary things for no apparent reason may be called insane, and even sedated or incarcerated.

Foucault's viewpoint is similar in some ways to that of Szasz (1973). Writing in the early 1960s, he suggested that mental illness was a label used to control those who challenged the existing order. It is impossible, he said, to objectively observe symptoms of mental illness (unlike symptoms of physical disease). Various labels are attached to people – such as 'schizophrenic' – if their behaviour does not conform to the dominant ideas in society.

It is important to be aware that, although mental illnesses may be 'just' labels that other people attach to those who suffer panic attacks or see hallucinations, the majority of those who live through such experiences find them very frightening. However, it may also be the case that people find the world they live in – and especially being inside a mental hospital – equally or even more terrifying.

Mental disability

Although more people than ever before are surviving for longer with both physical and mental disabilities, there is relatively little material available on this issue in the sociology of health and illness. While disabled people may reject the label of sickness, they can certainly be seen as disadvantaged within society.

Midwinter (1994) suggests that the rapid population increase in the nineteenth century made society aware for the first time of the existence of a large number of people with disabilities, especially those defined as 'mentally handicapped'. The only system designed to provide for them was the Poor Law (see Section 14.1). Mentally handicapped (and chronically sick) people were often placed first in asylums, from where their release only took them into the workhouse, though this was never the intended function of such places. In either place there was little positive treatment, whether the person concerned was classified as 'mad' or 'feeble-minded'.

Provision changed little, especially for the 'mentally handicapped', until after the Second World War. New treatments and programmes were introduced, such as 'token economies' for the mentally disadvantaged and a considerable range of somatic treatments for those defined as suffering from forms of mental illness like schizophrenia. Drugs or electro-convulsive therapy (ECT) remained the preferred treatments for those defined as mentally ill or mentally disabled.

A Royal Commission was set up in 1957 to investigate 'mental health and mental deficiency'. This led to the Mental Health Act 1959 which attempted to set up a system of definitions and treatments for the approximately 350 000 people experiencing mental suffering. The Chronically Sick and Disabled Person's Act 1970 identified certain provisions required from the local authorities, and this legislation was extended in 1981.

While these measures all sought – not always effectively – to help the mentally disadvantaged, nothing brought about change quite so dramatically as the NHS and Community Care Act 1990. While the aim was to integrate people back into the community, the lack of resources has been a constant reason for criticism, and a survey by MIND suggests that the 'mentally ill' still suffer high levels of discrimination and abuse.

Taylor and Field (1993) assert that it is wrong to act as if all people with a 'mental handicap' have a medical condition rather than a social condition. Although there is quite often an organic or genetic cause for a handicap – which is true for severe mental handicaps like that arising from Down's Syndrome – they argue that the same cannot be said for all forms of mental handicap:

Mild mental handicap is linked to poverty and deprivation, and its genetic causes are uncertain in most cases. A growing body of opinion suggests that adopting the 'medical model' has serious negative consequences, leading to the infantilization and the inappropriate application of the sick role to people who were not sick, but had learning difficulties.
(Taylor and Field, 1993, pp. 148–9)

'Normalization' and community care

Attempts to introduce a process of 'normalization' for people with a range of mental health problems have included the promotion of positive role models, and practical training for people with learning difficulties. However, the cornerstone to this process has been moves to integrate these people into the 'normal' community. It has to be said that the community may not be all that welcoming in some cases.

Community care has three features that differentiate it from institutional care:

- it takes place outside any institution
- individuals are treated as far as possible as normal members of the community
- support comes mainly from lay carers – especially family members, supported by health and welfare workers. (See Section 14.2.)

Community support, however, often becomes patchy

and there seems to be an increase in the number of people suffering from a range of mental disorders who have effectively been made homeless.

As long ago as 1979, Scull argued that some people who 'returned to the community' might not be safe, for themselves or for others. Despite this warning, the 'normalization' approach may possibly reduce the impact of the medical model in the identification and treatment of people experiencing 'mental illness' and those with learning difficulties. To an extent, 'care in the community' seems the best way of supporting people who have, for whatever reason, problems in coping with living. However, finding a caring community and providing care which is supportive, genuinely caring and also safe and secure remains a real challenge for welfare services today.

13.9. New directions in health: the sociology of the body

Lyon (1994) argues that the move towards postmodernity has changed the focus of sociology from production to consumption (see Section 10.9). Turner (1987, 1992) suggests that we are in fact moving towards a 'somatic society', where the body is the focus of political and cultural activity. Nettleton (1995) says that changes in society have profoundly changed the way we see our bodies. People tend to be far more knowledgeable about their own bodies than they were even 20 years ago:

The boundaries between the physical body and society are becoming increasingly blurred. In this respect the sociology of the body represents an important and fruitful area of study.
(Nettleton, 1995, p. 100)

She suggests that there are six key social changes which have made the sociology of the body of increasing importance and significance to an understanding of society today.

The first social change she identifies is the growing genre of feminist literature wherein women explicitly reject male domination of medicine and control of their bodies. This was discussed more fully in Section 13.3.

Secondly, dramatic technological changes, especially in the sphere of reproduction, have widened the political and ethical debate about, for example, the storage and disposal of frozen embryos that have been produced as a result of fertility treatments. These technological changes lead to a number of medical, religious and ethical debates about abortion, reproduction techniques and euthanasia.

Outraged couple try to adopt embryo

A CORNISH couple, outraged by the "recklessness" and "wastage" of in-vitro fertilisation are campaigning to adopt one of the 4,000 frozen embryos before they are destroyed by next Wednesday's deadline.

Stephen and Joanna Thomas, from Redruth, are pressing for reform to the law which insists that embryos can only be "adopted" with the consent of their genetic parents. Hospitals must destroy all embryos which have been stored for more than five years unless they have the consent of its genetic parents to extend the storage under regulations enforced by the Human Fertilisation and Embryology Authority.

Hospitals have failed to make contact with the parents of hundreds of embryos.

"I would offer my womb as a safe place, to give them a life. I'm surprised more infertile couples are not coming forward. These embryos are so valuable," said Mrs Thomas.

Mr and Mrs Thomas had a daughter before developing fertility problems: they rejected in-vitro fertilisation (IVF) on moral grounds. They then adopted a son with special needs.

"We don't see this as a golden opportunity for us to have another baby. This is the first time that this nation has en masse destroyed thousands of embryos. A moral decision is being made by this government and we are preparing to finish thousands of individual people's lives," said Mr Thomas, who describes himself and his wife as Christians of no denomination.

Life, the Catholic pressure group, is to launch an appeal this weekend for couples to "adopt" an embryo. They are asking the Government for a six-month moratorium and a change in the law so that abandoned embryos can be adopted without the explicit consent of the parents.

The Human Fertilisation and Embryology Authority (HFEA) said donating frozen embryos to volunteering couples without the consent of the genetic parents is illegal. "As in all medical treatment in Western Europe, consent over your body, your organs and your genetic material is fundamental," said a spokeswoman, Jennifer Woodside.

Most couples going for IVF only use donated embryos as a last resort. If an infertile couple, such as the Thomases, specifically asked for a donated embryo, the matter would be a clinical decision, added Ms Woodside.

Dr Peter Brinsden of the Bourn Hall clinic, Cambridge, which pioneered IVF, said it would be "totally unethical" to allow embryos to be adopted without the consent of the parents.

Source: *The Guardian*, 27 July 1996

Activity

Organize a group debate about the sociological issues (which involve the questions of morality in society) raised in the article 'Outraged couple try to adopt embryo'. Before actually engaging in the debate you should first decide the question(s) to be debated and then each use library resources to do research. Write your own evaluation following the debate. **K, U, I, A, E**

For example, BBC2 television broadcast a series of programmes about ageing in August 1996, the schedule including:

4 August	*Staying Alive*	About potential conflicts between age groups as a result of an ageing population
5 August	*Life Without End*	About anti-ageing treatments
6/8 August	*The Seven Ages of Man*	Celebrities talking about getting older
7 August	*Wrinkly Vision*	About American senior citizens in US comedies

Discussion point

To what extent do you think the issues debated in the BBC2 programmes are an accurate reflection of the experience of ageing? Suggest other issues you might include in any future set of programmes on ageing.

Thirdly, says Nettleton, demographic changes such as an ageing population and declining fertility rates in western industrialized societies have focused medical and social awareness on the problems associated with ageing and death. Debates about euthanasia are relevant here, as are those about the treatment of medical diseases and the social care of older people.

Fourthly, the experience of AIDS has led to a reappraisal of health and illness in a number of ways. Not only does it remind us of the limitations of medical technology and professional expertise, it also kills relatively young people in an era when such early death is comparatively rare. However, despite the terrible suffering of many people with AIDS, it has also led to considerable development of medical self-help groups and provided a model for other sufferers of chronic illnesses.

Fifthly, Nettleton reminds us of Featherstone's (1991a) thesis that the 'cult of the body' now forms an important aspect of the consumerism which structures much of post-modern society. (See Sections 10.9 and 10.11.) Many people are obsessed by looking fit, slim and young. It is now almost the norm in some parts of America for women to have breast enhancement surgery, while the sale of 'health and fitness' videos (often featuring svelte fashion models) is now big business, as are health clubs, slimming books and fitness studios.

Finally, Nettleton says the effect of what some people might call 'body and health fascism' on people with chronic illnesses or particular needs in our society – or even the merely overweight – is worthy of sociological debate. She argues that due to ageing and other forms of technology, we have in our society more people with chronic illnesses and disabilities than ever before.

Sociological perspectives on the body

A number of perspectives on the body have been developed over the past few years to place it at the focus of sociological debate. Nettleton (1996) outlines recent sociological views which may provide some insights into our understanding of health and illness. Naturalistic views are similar in most ways to the biomedical model of the body. Currently the most popular version is sociobiology (see Sections 5.1 and 6.4), which regards the majority of human behaviour and interaction as a result of our biological (especially genetic) make-up. For example, homosexuality is presented as the result of a 'gay' gene, as Doctor Simon Le Vay terms it, and differences in behaviour between men and women are regarded as mainly a result of genetic needs in terms of mating requirements. However, many of these ideas can be criticized as an ideological critique of feminist arguments that gender roles are culturally determined.

Some social constructionists such as Foucault (1976) argue that the body and illness are nothing more than the discourses used to describe it (see Section 13.1). Others such as Connell (1987), in her study of gender and power, accept the material basis of the body but believe that its structure is largely the result of social expectations. In this case the greater strength of men is built through the expectations (and encouragement) that young males are more physical. In some societies most of the heavy physical work is carried out by women. This weaker relativist view has been developed by a number of writers.

Douglas (1966) argued that parts of the body are classified in different societies according to different systems of purity and pollution. In her introduction concerning our notions of the body, Leder (1992) suggests that we take our bodies for granted until they refuse to work properly (an implicit biomedical model), which is why many sociologists have ignored the importance of human action in relation to the body. In his influential book on the body and social thought, Shilling (1993) describes the body as an unfinished biological and social entity which is transformed by the expectations of society. In a society where we often feel at risk, he says, social groups seek to impose more and more control over our bodies in four categories: personally, religiously, medically, and legally.

Activity
Suggest ways in which individuals and social groups seek to control the body in each of Shilling's four categories. To what extent is resistance or conflict involved?

A, E

Turner (1987, 1992) complains that discussions about the 'reality' of the body are meaningless; rather it is important to accept that it is both biologically and socially constructed. He focuses on the increasing control and surveillance of the body (and the whole population) by the medical and legal professions, often at the expense of religion. Much of this view develops from the work of Foucault, who wrote a great deal about the control of the body within institutions and by those who judge what is 'normal', such as lawyers, doctors, teachers and social workers.

In a work which has inspired the growth of the figurational approach (see Section 2.9) in sociology, Elias (1978) showed how the processes of civilization from the Middle Ages onwards led to a far more regulated view of the body and shame about many of its functions. Nettleton (1995) argues that this has had a particular effect on nurses, who tend to have to deal with such embarrassing functions. In a study of nursing, Lawler (1991) demonstrates the ways in which nurses negotiate crossing these social boundaries through a system of implicit rules which mean that the patient must comply with the nurse's instructions. There are rules about the modesty of the patient which are shared by both and protected by the nurse. This is why nurses tend to wear uniforms, decide when relatives may stay or leave, and obey certain rules about what is discussed and in what language.

The sociology of the body is at the forefront of much academic sociological work. It provides insights into a number of different arguments about health and illness, and illuminates recent sociological theory, particularly post-modernism and problems of relativism. It adds a new dimension to our understanding of debates about people with disabilities and the relationship between gender and health. It also helps our understanding of many of the key ethical and moral debates of the late twentieth century.

Chronic illness and disability

Field, writing in Taylor and Field (1993), suggests that we need to be aware of the difference between:

- *impairment* – any interruption to the normal functioning of the body
- *disability* – which refers to a loss or reduction of activity
- *handicap* – which focuses on the social problems caused by either of the above.

While finding it difficult to generalize about chronic illness and disability, he identifies a number of similarities. He notes especially that as age rises so do the numbers of chronically ill and disabled in the population; poorer people from lower social classes are disproportionately affected by such disadvantages, as are women who also make up the largest group of informal carers for people with long-term illness. However, the most disabling feature of any form of impairment seems to be the negative reactions from many institutions and individuals in society.

In relation to chronic illness, Nettleton (1995) also identifies a number of important points. Chronic illness usually affects the family and others as well as the sufferer, especially with the move towards caring in the community. (See Section 14.2.) Furthermore the chronically ill are required to adopt a particular attitude in society – as they cannot be expected to get better they should not be too demanding, as they have already challenged aspects of the 'sick role' (see below). She concludes:

Chronic illness can impact upon sufferers' daily living, their social relationships, their identity (the view that others hold of them) and their sense of self (their private view of themselves).
(Nettleton, 1995, p. 69)

Writing in the 1950s, Talcott Parsons demonstrated the functions of the 'sick role' as a form of deviance in society. Sick people are allowed a certain escape from normal obligations, but only if they seek to get better. People will tolerate certain behaviour among the sick, but this is only legitimated through seeking medical advice (although a number of studies have shown that the majority of people do not go to a doctor when they feel unwell, in which case legitimation is sought from friends or relatives). For people with chronic illness the situation is different. Although they require legitimation (and in many cases may find it very difficult to obtain), they are also usually attempting to maintain some form of social normality alongside their illness.

In a large number of cases the chronic illness is not disclosed, particularly for those problems which may lead to some sort of stigmatization, such as colostomies. People often have to develop coping strategies to enable them to maintain 'normal' lives. We also are far more intrusive about medical matters and less trusting of those with any history of medical problems. American presidential candidates are now expected to reveal all details of their medical history, although the two main Allied leaders during the Second World War, Churchill and Roosevelt, were both chronically sick – a matter that was hidden from the public by a voluntary agreement of the press.

Disability

Physical disabilities are often associated with chronic illness. Nettleton argues that disabilities are a result of the way society is organized rather than the true physical capabilities of an individual. However, we often define people as disabled and treat them differently from the rest of the population. For many this affects their self-image in a negative way, although people with such different abilities may focus around them as a form of political action or awareness. Unfortunately, people with particular needs are often stigmatized (by being presented as having 'special needs'), as well as being disadvantaged by the environment and by people's attitudes towards them.

Lonsdale (1990), in her study of women and disability, found that women thus afflicted were denied in terms of their sexuality and often encouraged not to have children.

Just as chronic illness can affect a person's self-identity, so can living with a disability. Charmaz (1983) suggests that many people with a physical disability lose their sense of self, resulting in them being more suspicious of, and dependent on, others. They often find it difficult to form and maintain relationships as they are expected to restrain 'negative' feelings about their illness. However, Charmaz also found that re-affirmation and creative living can allow many people with a disability to improve self-image and interactions with others.

Davies (1994) argues that, despite the relatively large number of people involved, disability tends to be ignored by sociologists. He suggests that this is mainly because:

- few sociologists themselves suffer from a disability
- reactions to people with disabilities tend to be emotional, including embarrassment, guilt and fear – so these groups tend to be ignored
- the medical model of disability tends to mean that sociologists have regarded it as outside their domain.

However, Davies argues that disabilities are in fact socially constructed in a number of different ways. The tendency to define a disability as an impairment or handicap suggests that such people are inferior rather than different from the apparently 'able-bodied'. Many critics such as Shearer (1981) and Barnes (1992) argue that it is the environment and attitudes of others which set people with disabilities at a disadvantage rather than their physical or mental impairment. For example, many people (not just those who find walking difficult) would benefit from more ramps or lower steps on to buses.

Davies also pointed out that whereas discrimination on grounds of gender or ethnicity are closely regulated (see Sections 5.4 and 6.2), no law existed specifically to protect those with disabilities from exploitation or discrimination. The Disability Discrimination Act 1995 has introduced a Code of Practice for employers to reduce discrimination against employed people in the workplace. The effects of this legislation on medical (and non-medical) perceptions and treatment of people with disabilities remain to be seen.

Davies argues that society tends to possess very negative attitudes about those with disabilities – stigmatizing, stereotyping and de-sexing them – and this is often reinforced in the media (see Section 15.4). All this is exacerbated by the limited interactions between most people with and without disabilities. For many, people with disabilities are seen as deviants, trapped within a medical model and unable to conform even to the expectations of the 'sick role'.

Groups such as 'The Campaign to Stop Patronage' have challenged the assumptions of the public by organizing demonstrations where people with disabilities show that they are quite able to present their own viewpoints and define their own needs. For some sociologists, Davies concludes, the fight against the stigmatization of, and discrimination against, people with disabilities can be seen as the latest – and possibly the last and most challenging – civil rights battle.

Field (1993) suggests that people with chronic illness or disability have to learn to cope with and make sense of their 'problem'. Physical and practical management of the condition is important and this will depend on a number of different factors, including the severity of the condition, when it starts to have a limiting effect, how stable it is and how visible it is. The last factor may well affect the level of stigmatization and, very significantly, it can influence confidence and self-esteem as well as occupational opportunities.

The sociology of death and dying

In our medicalized society the majority of people die in hospitals, hospices or care homes, even though most people say that they would prefer to die in their own home and much informal care is provided to aid this. Support is available for terminally ill people, but respite care for the carers – to give them a break – is often limited and some treatment is less easily managed or monitored outside an institutional setting. Palliative care – the relief and management of pain – is often a major concern for the relatives of people dying from cancer, and this may be particularly difficult to control in a non-institutional setting:

The desirability, and even the possibility, of a 'home death' depends primarily on the human resources available to help both with the control of symptoms and the constant attendance and extra domestic work which such care entails.
(Field and James, in Taylor and Field, 1993, p. 157)

For these reasons, many carers regard hospital or hospice care as preferable for the sick person and for themselves. The levels of community support and input from primary healthcare officials is also important if the aims of 'care in the community' are to be achieved in the care of the dying.

Although issues of death, dying and bereavement are profoundly important, relatively few young people experience death as a real personal trauma. This may make it difficult for people to deal with dying and death as natural events later in their life.

Death now appears mainly to be experienced by specific social groups. For example, many elderly people frequently lose family and friends, whilst most young people have limited knowledge of bereavement. Deaths from AIDS are presented as largely confined to 'gay' men and their friends. In general, people are expected to 'get on with their lives' after a close bereavement and there is little formal time available for mourning. If they find themselves unable to 'cope' with the death of someone, they are advised to try counselling – suggesting that people do need to talk about death but are rarely encouraged to do so informally.

There are few family bereavement rituals available for many people, especially if they have no religious affiliation. The treatment of the terminally ill also remains a key area of concern for health policy in our society, relating to debates about palliative care, euthanasia and the 'right to die' for people with degenerative diseases or terminal illnesses. One of the main advantages of the promotion of terminal care in the community has been the growth of the hospice movement, where care of the very highest quality is often available for those in the last stages of terminal illness. It also allows a chance for dying to be acknowledged and discussed in many cases, a practice which has generally been frowned upon in many hospitals:

It is not uncommon for hospice in-patients to be unaware that they are dying at the time of their first admission. For relatives and hospice staff admission is a clear signal that death is imminent and that now is the time to talk about their prognosis to the person who is dying.

(Field and James, in Taylor and Field, 1993, p. 160)

Kübler-Ross (1970) and Glaser and Strauss (1965) have examined how social situations affect the awareness of, and communications with, dying patients. The greater number of people being cared for in the community (see Section 14.2), and in the hospice movement, may allow people to speak more freely about dying in a demedicalized context. This could mean that death is no longer a 'taboo' subject in our society. It might also be part of the greater openness between health professionals and those with whom they deal.

Further **reading**

Both of the following provide concise and accessible introductions to the sociology of health:

- Aggleton, P. (1990) *Health*, London, Routledge.
- Trowler, P. (1996) *Investigating Health, Welfare and Poverty*, 2nd edn, London, Collins Educational.

More details and some contemporary updates can be found in:

- Doyal, L. (1995) *What Makes Women Sick: Gender and the Political Economy of Health*, Basingstoke, Macmillan.
- Gabe, J., Calnan, M. and Bury, M. (eds) (1991) *The Sociology of the Health Service*, London, Routledge.
- Senior, M. and Viveash, B. (1997) *Health and Illness*, London, Macmillan.
- Taylor, S. and Field, D. (eds) (1993) *The Sociology of Health and Health Care*, Oxford, Blackwell.

Back issues of the periodical *Sociology Review* (formerly known as *Social Studies Review*) also contain many articles on this field of sociology and many others.

Exam **questions**

1 **a** Briefly explain what sociologists mean by the sick role. [4 marks]

   b Identify the ways in which sick people are stigmatized by the rest of the population. [4 marks]

   c Explain the view that 'health' is a social construct. [7 marks]

   d Compare the impact of medical developments with that of environmental progress in improving health in an industrial society like the UK. [10 marks]

   (IBS, Paper 1, Summer 1995)

2 Critically assess the view that mental illness is a 'social construct'. [25 marks]

   (IBS, Paper 1, Summer 1996)

3 'The medical profession exercises a monopoly power over health care and does so largely in its own interest.' Assess this view. [25 marks]

   (AEB, AS Level Paper 2, Summer 1993)

4 Critically examine the relationship between social class background and the nature and distribution of different types of illness.

   (AEB, Paper 2, Summer 1994)   [25 marks]

5 'The purpose of the NHS has always been to distribute health care resources equally among all groups of the population. In this, however, it has failed.' Assess this view in the light of sociological evidence and arguments.

   [25 marks]

   (AEB, AS Level Paper 2, Summer 1995)

6 Assess the view that improvements in the health of the population are the result of better health care. [25 marks]

   (AEB, Paper 2, Summer 1996)

7 'Society gives doctors the power to label a person sick.' Examine the implications of this statement for an understanding of the nature of ill-health. [25 marks]

   (AEB, AS Level Paper 2, Summer 1996)

Coursework **suggestions**

1 **Investigate inequalities in health**

   Use secondary sources to investigate and examine the extent to which current statistics demonstrate any changes in inequalities in health over recent years. You could compare your findings with other pieces of research, such as the 1980 Black Report. Consider whether the conclusions reached in the Black Report are still supported by more recent data.

2 **Investigate the provision of healthcare**

   Carry out a survey of people in your local town centre to discover whether any of them are carers and, if so, what kind of things they do and how much support they receive. Look at the social composition of those who act as carers. For example, what percentage of them are women? Do men and women have different problems as carers? If possible, complete an in-depth case study on one or more of the informal carers that you interview.

3 Do a case study of NHS provision in your area

Undertake case-study research in your local area to identify how the NHS works and how this has changed. You could contact local hospitals, doctors and clinics to get first-hand accounts. You could also carry out interviews to get ideas about how people perceive the changes that have taken place, and whether they have seen any decline or improvement in the services they get. Older people are a particularly useful source of such information.

14

Wealth, welfare and poverty

Chapter outline

The wealthy and those in poverty live in different but linked worlds whose existence is mediated by the actions of institutions such as the welfare state. This chapter seeks to consider the empirical and the theoretical arguments surrounding the changing way in which welfare has affected lives in the UK, along with some attempt to place this in a comparative context.

14.1 The origins of the welfare state *page 555*

This section focuses on the UK. It outlines some of the historical landmarks that have left an important mark on the contemporary UK welfare state.

14.2 Recent changes in welfare provision *page 558*

This section considers the effect on the welfare state of the rise to power of the New Right, and the competing solutions offered to its perceived crises. In particular it looks at concrete changes to the welfare state in the 1980s and 90s and the arguments and debates these have generated. The contemporary welfare state has been said to be an example of welfare pluralism since there are a number of providers, in particular the community, the family, the private sector and the voluntary sector, all of which now operate alongside the state.

14.3 Theoretical approaches to welfare *page 563*

This section considers the way in which sociologists, in particular Marxists, social democrats, feminists and the New Right, have attempted to locate the role of the welfare state in considerations of social structure and social change. The argument that it is no longer possible to think of welfare in terms of a welfare state but as an integral part of the whole social structure is considered. This notion is captured by the concept 'welfare regime'. One way of considering the UK experience is to compare it with other countries.

14.4 The welfare state as a system of stratification *page 571*

Since 1945 the notion of a welfare state has implied governments actively intervening in the distribution of income via the taxes and benefits systems. This section considers how the welfare state operates to construct social stratification, by asking the questions: Who pays? Who benefits?

14.5 Defining poverty *page 577*

Despite the general increase in living standards, poverty remains remarkably persistent. But so too do sociological and governmental debates about what exactly is meant by poverty. This section considers the absolute/relative argument, plus newer debates focusing on consensual notions of poverty and poverty and citizenship.

14.6 The extent of poverty in the UK *page 582*

Building on the theoretical debates about the definition of poverty, this section considers how this leads to conflicting empirical accounts of the extent of poverty.

14.7 Poverty: conflicting explanations and solutions *page 589*

This section addresses the conflicting sociological explanations offered for the cause of poverty and the implied solutions that these point towards.

14.8 The changing distribution of income and wealth *page 594*

The poor do not exist in isolation but as part of a wider stratification structure. This section looks at the changing nature of the distribution of income and wealth in the UK.

14.9 Conflicting explanations for the distribution of income and wealth *page 597*

This section shows how competing sociological theories of the distribution of income and wealth form part of wider theories of the social stratification system.

14.1 The origins of the welfare state

For the beginning of the welfare state many analyses look to the period immediately after the Second World War and the implementation of the Beveridge Report. It is possible, however, to see concern by the state for the condition of the population going back much earlier.

Welfare and the state

Once a centralized state machinery had been created – which in the UK occurred around the time of Henry VIII – the question of the extent to which it should intervene in the running of society became necessary. At the time there was a great fear of social disorder following the Black Death, and so questions of social control and social welfare became intrinsically linked:

It was undoubtedly fear of social disorder in the two and a half centuries following the Black Death which gradually converted the maintenance of the poor from an aspect of personal Christian charity into a prime function of the state.
(Fraser, 1973, p. 28)

There were also those who wanted state welfare on the basis of social justice. Many accepted that poverty was the result of economic forces beyond the control of any one individual, and this led to the establishment by 1536 of measures allowing parishes (i.e. local areas) to collect money for the poor, although private charities remained the main source of assistance for the poor until the 1660s.

The Poor Law

The Poor Law Act of 1601 was occasioned by fear of social disorder, there having been a large rise in the number of vagrants. The Act put into place formal classification of the poor who were to be divided up into:

- the impotent poor (the aged and the sick) who were to be provided accommodation in almshouses
- the able-bodied poor (the unemployed) who were to be provided with work in workhouses
- the persistent idlers who were to be sent to houses of correction.

The basic idea was to provide three very different policies for these three groups. However, since it was implemented by local government, differences often occurred and in many ways the system was never fully operational.

The original Poor Law system remained in place for the next 200 years although various influences changed its mode of application.

- Owing to the rise in Puritanism, the application of the law was made much harsher. This led to poverty being seen as a sign of individual deficiency and a punishment for sin. Support for the poor by the Church began to decline.
- As a result of industrialization the numbers employed in agriculture decreased, and this led to a massive increase in unemployed labour which was not fully taken up by the new factories. Even those who did obtain work in factories faced appalling conditions and low wages.

The Poor Law was made much stricter and more punitive with the threat of the workhouse increasingly used to deter people from claiming relief; beggars and vagrants were given a choice between forced labour and a whipping.
(Cole, 1986, p. 11)

Discussion point
Do you agree with the idea that the poor should be punished?

The 1834 Poor Law Amendment Act

The rise of new economic doctrines which form the basis of contemporary free-market economics (see Section 2.10) criticized the all-embracing nature of the Poor Law.

The Poor Law Commission recommended changes to the system to reflect the idea that the poor needed to accept the economic disciplines of the emerging new order. Out of all this emerged the 1834 Poor Law Amendment Act.

Reflecting the changing ideology most clearly was the principle of less eligibility. This meant that conditions in the workhouses were to be made worse than the lowest-paid employment as a conscious effort to discourage people from applying for help. Relief outside the workhouse was denied to any able-bodied person, and a strict moral order was maintained in the workhouses with clear separation of the sexes, even husbands and wives. Historian E. P. Thompson quotes Poor Law assistant commissioners as saying:

Our intention is to make the workhouses as like prison as possible ... Our object is to establish therein a discipline so severe and repulsive as to make them a terror to the poor and prevent them from entering.
(Thompson, 1968, p. 295)

Despite this, he quotes figures showing the number of workhouse inmates rose from 78,536 in 1838 to 197,179 in 1843.

The Act concentrated on the idea that people became poor through their own personal deficiencies or laziness, and that this should not be rewarded. Instead people should have their behaviour patterns modified. There was little if any recognition of the effect of societal economic and social change in causing poverty and distress. Unemployment was assumed to be caused by wilful laziness rather than lack of jobs. See also Section 9.6.

The workhouses were notoriously fearful places. The treatment of the poor in these times – and revulsion at it – is one of the main sources of inspiration for the novels of Charles Dickins (1812–70). Implementation of this Act led to massive protests. Historian John Knott (1986) reports that there were riots in many areas following the setting up of the new workhouses: 1835 saw riots in Eastbourne, Chesham and Ipswich. Later there were many cases of protesters attempting to burn down the new workhouses. The level of protest indicated the horror and revulsion that ordinary people felt against the new legislation, and this anger was to feed into the growth of the Chartist movement in the 1840s.

The moral definition of the poor

Underlying intervention by the state in the name of welfare is an essentially moral distinction between the deserving poor and the undeserving poor.

- The deserving poor were those who society (or the dominant elements within it) defined as poor through no fault of their own, meaning essentially those suffering from old age, disability or chronic illness of some sort.
- The undeserving poor were seen as those who were able to work but attempted to avoid it to live off the state.

This distinction – albeit with changing names attached – is a fairly constant element of state intervention in the social policy arena. (See also the debate on the underclass in Section 4.8.)

Activity

Suggest examples of groups seen as 'the deserving poor' and those seen as 'the undeserving poor' in contemporary UK society. How valid do you think this distinction is? **A, E**

Foundations of the modern welfare state

By the third quarter of the nineteenth century, ideas about the causes of poverty had changed. There was a realization that poverty was not necessarily the individual's fault.

One reason for this was the first major economic recession faced in Britain between 1873 and 1896. Secondly, research into poverty among the elderly. Since these were people who had worked all their lives, the idea that their poverty could be explained by idleness was clearly wrong. Research in the 1890s showed that 40 per cent of the working class aged over 65 were on poor relief and therefore in poverty (Baugh, 1987).

Further important reasons for the change in attitude include:

- In 1880, education was made compulsory (see Chapter 8). As a result education authorities compiled evidence on the state of schoolchildren, and many were found to be badly clothed and fed.
- A large wave of strikes hit the nation in the 1880s, leading to awareness of the low wages received by skilled workers.

The growth of social science at the turn of the century was exemplified by two massive surveys on poverty undertaken in London by Charles Booth (1902) and in York by Seebohm Rowntree (1901). Booth reported that the main causes of poverty in London were unemployment and old age. Rowntree found that 28 per cent of the population in York were poor, mainly owing to low wages. (See also Sections 14.5 and 14.6.)

The changing political climate

One important political factor leading to greater concern with poverty and social welfare which dates from this time is the rise of trade unionism (see Section 9.5) and socialist movements. The 1867 Reform Act widened the right to vote (see Section 17.2) and meant that working people began to have a say in societal affairs.

Another shift in political philosophy was the changing definition of liberalism. In the nineteenth century (and again recently since 1979) liberalism as a political philosophy had tended to mean emphasis on the free market (*laissez-faire*) and individualism. The state was viewed negatively as an institution which acted to limit individuals' freedom. Oxford philosopher Thomas Green redefined liberalism and argued that the state could act to provide an environment which allowed people to be free. Liberalism as a political philosophy was therefore reconciled with a positive role for the state.

The Liberal reforms of 1905–15

By the time of the election of a Liberal government in 1905, it was clear that changes in relation to social welfare were going to be a major part of their legislative programme. The idea that certain services should be provided by the state – and financed out of a national insurance scheme – were behind this.

A number of pieces of legislation were passed which provided an important basis for contemporary provision, most notably the Old Age Pensions Act in 1908 and the National Insurance Act in 1911. The first of these introduced pensions paid out of taxation to all people over 70. This was because most of the surveys quoted above had shown that the elderly were one group very much at risk of poverty. The second Act introduced health insurance and unemployment insurance.

Towards the Beveridge Report

The First World War massively increased the role of the state in the economy and provided an example of some degree of centralized planning. The free-market ideas of nineteenth-century liberalism were further eroded with the onset of the Great Depression of the 1930s which led to mass unemployment and hardship. This also placed great pressures on the existing system of welfare assistance. The idea behind this system was that people would make payments out of their wages and would in turn receive payments when they were unemployed. It worked on the assumption that unemployment would be fairly rare and short-lived. These assumptions were not true in the 1930s, so that payments into the system declined while demands on it rose.

Although wages rose between 1899 and 1936, Rowntree (1937) in a follow-up survey of York found that 4 per cent of the population were still in primary poverty, and he estimated that poverty affected 53 per cent of the working classes at some point in their lives. Old age and unemployment were still the most serious causes of poverty.

The failure of the free-market economy to provide the benefits its proponents claimed it would led to wholesale revision of economic doctrine, to provide a much more active role for the state in the economy and in the provision of welfare.

The Beveridge Report

The Five Giants

The Beveridge Report (1942) pointed to the piecemeal and chaotic introduction of changes into the system and argued for a new comprehensive system. Beveridge said that such a system needed to be put into place to cure what he called the 'Five Giants' of Idleness, Squalor, Want, Disease and Ignorance. Effectively these relate to the areas of unemployment, housing (see Section 16.7), poverty, health (see Chapter 13) and education (see Chapter 8).

The report argued for state intervention to ensure that everyone could live without fear of want. The state would guarantee a minimum standard of living for all its citizens. Beyond this, incomes were to be left to the free market, allowing for individual incentive and enterprise. It argued that a comprehensive system of national insurance needed to be introduced, supported by a variety of forms of national assistance.

In order for the system to work (bearing in mind the problems of the 1930s), Beveridge considered that it should be underpinned by full employment, a National Health Service and a system of family allowances. (See also Chapters 7, 9 and 13.)

- National Insurance was to be unified through payment of contributions by both employee and employer, a system that survives to this day.
- The NHS would reduce illness, and therefore the burden of claims due to illness and disability.
- 'Family allowances' were introduced to help those in poverty from low wages, but also as a conscious attempt to boost the falling birth rate.

The ideas in the report were implemented in a series of Acts, most notably the Education Act 1944, the National Insurance Act 1944, the Family Allowances Act 1945, the National Health Service Act 1946 and the National Assistance Act 1948. It should be noted, however, that at the time there was much reluctance to enact all the proposals owing to concerns about cost and the principles underlying the notion of welfare. As a result, Beveridge's proposals were never totally implemented, but his ideas served as the clear inspiration for welfare reform up to the 1970s.

The assumptions behind the Beveridge proposals

Government economic policy immediately after the Second World War was influenced by the ideas of the economist John Maynard Keynes (1936). He contended that the government should intervene to ensure that full employment was maintained. (See also Section 9.6.) Full employment was also an important condition for the existence of a welfare state according to the Beveridge Report.

Beveridge also assumed that for most of their lives women would not be employed: his report contained the assumption that married women would be full-time housewives. As a result, married women often received benefits only as dependents of men, and if they were employed were encouraged to opt out of most national insurance payments. This raises a number of important implications.

- The system placed women in a position of dependency on men in many respects. (See Section 5.3.)
- The overall provision of welfare was based on the asssumption that there would be hours of unpaid work by women in the home. (See also Section 7.5.)

This, feminists argued, showed that the welfare state operated on a 'familial ideology' (see Section 7.1) and treated women as second-class citizens.

Discussion point

How valid or acceptable are these assumptions today? What implications does your answer have for the welfare state?

14.2 Recent changes in welfare provision

This is the end of an era for the British welfare state. The post-war settlement has not stood the test of time and both Conservatives and Labour are intent on re-emphasising the market.
(Bryson, 1992, p. 89)

The crisis of the welfare state

A universalist welfare state can operate only on the basis of nearly full employment, since this maximizes tax revenue and minimizes demand for benefits related to unemployment. This position was broadly maintained until the early 1970s in the UK. However, the long-term relative decline of the UK economy led to an economic crisis and rapidly rising unemployment. Mass unemployment returned and has been a continuing phenomenon since that time. (See Section 9.6.) This crisis was to reveal the extent to which a welfare state was dependent on a prosperous economy. This meant in effect that it was reliant on capitalism – rather than overcoming it.

O'Donnell (1987) points out that this crisis left social democratic thinkers in a dilemma. Should they help the private sector and thereby create the flourishing economy which would provide the surplus for a welfare state? Or should they concentrate on preserving public-sector welfare services by squeezing the private sector?

These events were to lead to many social democratic thinkers reappraising their ideas. Mishra produced a book entitled *The Welfare State in Crisis* (1984). He argued that there was a need for much greater integration of social and economic policy owing to their interrelated nature (as the crisis had so clearly demonstrated). This would imply more state control of the economy and the institution of corporatist arrangements, as for example in Sweden and Germany.

Writing from a Marxist perspective, O'Connor (1981) points to the main way in which the welfare state fell into crisis in the late 1970s. He argues that the welfare state performs both an accumulation function (it helps provide the basic trained and healthy labour force capitalism needs) and a legitimation function (since it is often premised on arguments about fairness and social justice people see its existence as a mark of the legitimacy of the regime). (See also section on Habermas in Section 2.9.) However, he points out that there is now a problem because the cost of this legitimation function is cutting into the accumulation function: the welfare state is becoming too expensive and is threatening capitalist profitability.

Gough (1979) argues that in order to solve this crisis capitalism might try to make the workers 'pay' through lower wages and reduced welfare. It might be said that this presents a picture of the effect on the welfare state and welfare generally of the election of a government committed to New Right ideology.

The New Right and the welfare state

The 1979 General Election brought to power a government with a radically new approach to public expenditure and the welfare state. Since then, government policy has been influenced by New Right thinking (see Section 2.10), leading to a number of changes.

Probably the most important change has been the ending of the Keynesian commitment to full employment. The New Right argued that there was a 'natural level of unemployment' caused mainly by wages being too high, largely as a result of the actions of trade unions (see Section 9.6). The market would therefore solve unemployment by creating downward pressure on wages. However, this also required that the differential between wages and benefits needed to be increased by means of downward pressure on benefit levels.

Despite this there was little change in social welfare expenditure until the late 1980s, notably through the 1986 and 1988 Social Security Acts. Arguably 1988 was an important turning point with a much more radical application of New Right thinking to the welfare state after this point. We can summarize some of the main changes to the provision of welfare that have occurred in the period since the late 1980s.

- Grants previously provided to cover costs other than normal weekly expenditure – for example to purchase a cooker – have been replaced by payments from a Social Fund which are (a) discretionary and (b) largely repayable loans.
- Eligibility for benefits to 16 to 18-year-olds were removed on the grounds that places on training schemes were available for all. A lower rate of Income Support payments was introduced for those under 25.

- The value of the state pension is to be reduced for those retiring early in the twenty-first century by ending the link between earnings and pensions.
- Eye tests attracted charges and there was a much greater use of private charges for dental treatment.
- Some benefits – for example housing benefit and child benefit – were not increased in line with inflation. This led to real, though not nominal cuts in the value of such benefits.
- All earnings-related supplements to benefits – such as unemployment benefit – have been withdrawn.
- Responsibility for the administration of sickness payments and maternity benefits was shifted on to employers.
- Prescription charges have been increased by considerably more than the rate of inflation: for example, between 1979 and the late 1980s by 540 per cent.
- 'Right to buy' legislation has been introduced, leading to the sale of council homes to their tenants.

Activity

Using the earlier description of New Right thinking on the welfare state, try to explain how each of the changes noted above might be justified with reference to New Right theories.

I, A

All the changes might be summarized in the following way. First, there has been a shift from universal provision towards selective provision. The balance between benefits available to all (universal) and those available only to some via a 'means test' (selective) has been clearly altered towards greater reliance on selective provision.

Secondly, there has been privatization and marketization. This is notable in the case of the sale of council houses, and with the introduction of market principles into education (see Section 8.11) and the NHS (see Section 13.6).

Thirdly, there has been a shift towards community care: looking after the elderly, the disabled and the mentally ill has been moved from care in institutions to care in the community. However, it is often pointed out that this effectively means care by the family. (See also Section 7.6.) It is clear that care in the community is considerably cheaper for the state than institutional care.

Fourthly, there has been a shift away from seeing the state as the sole provider of welfare. The responsibility of the state has been reduced by encouraging private provision (notably through the encouragement of private pensions) and by emphasizing the charitable and voluntary sector.

Beyond the crisis?

Lowe (1993), in his book *The Welfare State in Britain Since 1945*, characterizes the experience since 1976 in the following way:

After 1976 there was unquestionably an historic break in the development of Britain's post-war welfare state. The commitment to 'full' employment was abandoned. So too was corporatism. Expenditure on the five major social services . . . also declined in relation to GDP and each service was radically restructured.
(Lowe, 1993, p. 328)

Despite this, he still feels it is a matter of debate whether this constitutes a fundamental transformation. He argues that, although there was an end to the commitment to full employment, the amount of expenditure on the welfare state stayed broadly the same. This was caused by the lack of a coherent alternative and the relative inefficiency of market provision in areas such as health and housing. This analysis therefore questions the widespread perception that the 1980s and 90s witnessed moves which threatened to destroy the welfare state. It is clear, nonetheless, that all commentators agree it has been changed in some important respects.

Hutton (1996), a journalist and economic commentator, asserts that the usual arguments about the need to reduce welfare expenditure in a time of austerity are based on false assumptions. He alleges that cuts are spurred by political ideology rather than economic need, and that the twenty-first century will see a large rise in the amount of tax revenue available to fund welfare payments. According to Hutton: 'apart from Iceland, Britain runs the meanest, tightest, lowest-cost social security system in the world'. This can be seen by a comparison with welfare expenditure in the EU. (See Figure 14.1.)

Sally Witcher (1994), Director of the Child Poverty Action Group, states that there is a need to challenge the myths that have created a sense of crisis in welfare provision – particularly the arguments that the UK has a high rate of taxation, and that it is possible to identify a distinction between the deserving and the undeserving poor. (See also Sections 4.8 and 14.8.) She argues that these myths have contibuted to a situation where it is possible to consider cutting social security. This, she feels, is not based on sound analysis:

[The CPAG does not] *accept that underlying growth in social security will exceed future growth in the*

France	23.3
Italy	19.5
EU average	18.7
Germany	17.7
Canada	15.5
US	14.2
UK	13.9
Japan	12.8

Figure 14.1 Social security spending as a percentage of GDP, 1994. Sources: *The Guardian*, 16 October 1995/OECD

economy ... expenditure on benefits is largely a reflection of problems or policies elsewhere, like high unemployment, lack of affordable high-quality childcare and deregulation of the housing market. ... Benefits are inadequate, even for the minimalist role of alleviating poverty. An increasing emphasis on means-testing creates poverty traps and work disincentives.
(Witcher, 1994, pp. i–vii)

Discussion point

Talk of a crisis in the welfare state has recently led to discussion about whether the UK can still afford it. To what extent do you think a welfare state is (a) necessary and (b) possible for the twenty-first century?

Contemporary welfare provision

Because we so often talk about 'the welfare state', it is easy to forget that there are other agencies beside the state which provide welfare. This situation has been described as 'welfare pluralism'. There are private-sector providers in the shape of private schools and medical services (see Section 13.6), and there has also been a greater emphasis on the voluntary sector in recent years. The move away from institutional care which was often criticized for being bureaucratic and unresponsive has also been fuelled by the policy of 'care in the community', though there is a question-mark over who exactly in the community provides such care.

The private sector

Although there has always been some private-sector provision in areas where it could exist alongside public-sector provision (notably health and education),

there has been less success in promoting private-sector provision as the main provider of services.

Since 1979 there have been a number of instances where the UK government have sought to encourage private provision of welfare, most notably by encouraging people to take out private insurance plans for their welfare needs. Welfare state theorist, Julian Le Grand (1990), points out that the number of people covered by private health insurance rose from 2.2 to 5.2 million between 1976 and 1986. However, despite the rise, this is still less than 10 per cent of the population.

In the mid-1980s the government produced proposals to transfer sickness insurance and pension insurance to the private sector, but these were never followed through owing to criticisms and the reluctance of the insurance companies to take up policies for all employees.

In the face of this the Conservative government opted instead to try to encourage employees to opt-out of the state pension scheme and transfer to private provision, by providing tax relief for those who chose to do so. However, this scheme received a setback when it was revealed that many of those who transferred would receive less benefit than they would have from the state pension.

The Conservative government further introduced private-sector involvement in the welfare state via the requirement that providers of certain services should be decided by competitive tender. While this has had an important effect in terms of jobs in the sector, the services subject to this regime were mainly ancillary services such as cleaning and catering. Core provision of care remained largely in state hands. Nevertheless there are some recent examples of private-sector provision moving into such core areas, as the article 'Granada to run hospital' demonstrates.

Market approaches have also been introduced into these care sectors via the setting up of quasi-markets. The Health and Community Care Act 1990 provided for a split between purchasers and providers of services. (See Section 13.6.) Similar initiatives were also put to work in the education sector where significant sectors – such as further education and polytechnic higher education – have been removed from LEA control. Le Grand characterizes the significance of this as follows:

This shift from the state as funder and provider to the state primarily as funder with perhaps only a residual role as provider will undoubtedly create enormous changes in the way services are delivered and employees treated.
(Le Grand, 1990, p. 351)

In their survey of the restructuring of welfare in the

Granada to run hospital

The first scheme in which the private sector will design, finance, build and operate a hospital directly for the National Health Service is due to be announced by Kenneth Clarke, the Chancellor of the Exchequer, in tomorrow's Budget. The proposal would mean that Granada, more commonly associated with television and motorway service stations, would run a 150-bed section of a hospital.

Mr Clarke is expected to give the go-ahead to the £35m project to rebuild large parts of Wycombe and Amersham General Hospitals, which are part of the South Buckinghamshire NHS Trust.

The privately financed project has been put together by the Health Care Group, a consortium of the builders Taylor Woodrow, Granada, which will run the building, and the finance house, Nexus.

The scheme will be announced to off-set capital cuts in the Budget which are expected to hit not only NHS hospitals but the roads programme, housing, schools and other parts of Government spending.

The South Bucks development will be followed shortly with approval for a £26m 166-bed new paediatric wing at St James's University Hospital, in Leeds, and a flagship £100m project to rebuild the whole of the Norfolk and Norwich NHS Trust. That will provide a 700-bed privately financed and run facility leased to the NHS on a green field site in the city.

The private consortium will finance and run the buildings, but, as with the other projects, medical care will continue to be provided by directly employed NHS staff.

Thereafter, Stephen Dorrell, the Secretary of State for Health, expects about one scheme a month to go through over the next year.

Source: *The Independent*, 27 November 1995

UK in the 1980s, Clarke and Langan (1993) make the point that the level of inspection and regulation of these services may be problematic owing to cuts in the funding and staffing of public-sector inspection bodies in these areas.

Supporters of private-sector provision argue that its expanding role in the welfare state is likely to lead to more efficient use of resources and provides some degree of choice to members of the public. Critics often argue that the importance of the profit motive means that private-sector provision will be limited to certain areas, leading to an effective two-tier welfare state. Fully private provision, they say, would lead to choice for those with money but no choice for the rest.

Burchardt and Hills (1997) estimated that the cost of private welfare insurance for a married man on average pay (about £400 per week, in April 1996) would be £900 per year to cover just three things: mortgage protection, unemployment risk and health insurance. This is equivalent to 6p on the rate of income tax. Thus, even for someone on average earnings, private provision of welfare is likely to be beyond their means.

The voluntary sector

A number of voluntary organizations provide care, for instance the Salvation Army, Barnados, NSPCC and MIND. These are not statutory bodies set up by parliament but their views are often taken into account since they have a degree of expertise and experience.

Government policy in the 1980s sought explicitly to encourage more voluntary-sector provision. In 1984 the Secretary of State for Social Security said that to ignore this sector would:

. . . go against the wishes of many of those actually in need of care [and] would reduce the opportunities now open to so many tens of thousands of people to give something back to their own local community by participating in social support.
(Quoted in Knapp, 1989, p. 240)

In his study of the economics of private and voluntary welfare, Knapp estimates that the total amount of public-sector support for voluntary organizations between 1983 and 1986 was £3151 million. Much of this arose from the requirement that local authorities services should be subject to compulsory competitive tendering.

To the two advantages of voluntary provision outlined by the former Secretary of State might be added others. For example they often specialize and can therefore bring expertise to bear. This might lead to innovative provision of services. Since they often use unpaid volunteers, voluntary organizations are often very cost-effective.

There are also inherent weaknesses in voluntary provision. First, precisely because it is voluntary it cannot be guaranteed. Secondly, it may be unequally provided across the country. Thirdly, it is unlikely to have the monetary resources to contemplate large-scale provision, and thus can exist realistically only as a secondary level of service relying on either state or private-sector provision as the main provider. Finally, voluntary services are not directly accountable via democratic mechanisms in the way that state providers are.

The family

Families acted as key providers of care and welfare before the setting up of the comprehensive welfare state. Now, much functionalist-inspired discussion about the loss of functions of the family (see Section 7.2) suggests that it plays a smaller role. But does it?

Within the Beveridge Report we have seen that there were assumptions about the continuing role of the family, especially that married women would not seek paid employment because they had another job to do. That, of course, meant the unpaid job of housewife. This clearly provides a largely hidden but substantial subsidy which reduces the cost of state provision, most notably in the case of childcare. The 1980s saw attempts to buttress this housewife role. Families (in effect women within families) were seen as primary carers, with the state and other social services seen as secondary back-up services. In a speech in 1977, a future Conservative Cabinet Minister argued this quite clearly when he said:

Quite frankly, I don't think that mothers have the same right to work as fathers do. If the good lord had intended us to have equal rights to go out to work, he wouldn't have created men and women. These are biological facts ... We hear a lot today about social work – perhaps the most important social work is motherhood.

(Patrick Jenkin; quoted in Clarke and Langan, 1993, p. 66)

Clarke and Langan point out that despite this the number of women in paid employment rose over the period of Conservative administrations in the 1980s, which additional role they took on while still maintaining primary responsibility for care within the family. In other words the burden on women has increased. Sociological research by Finch and Mason (1993) on family responsibilities showed the continuing importance of family and kinship obligations, even despite the rise of the welfare state. They found that over 90 per cent of their sample had given or received financial help from relatives, and over 60 per cent had shared a household with an adult relative other than their parents at some time. (See also Sections 7.4 and 7.5.)

Clarke and Langan (1993) argue that one of the major reasons for the increase in the number of patients treated by the NHS is the reduced amount of time people spend in hospitals. Recuperative care is effectively transferred from the state to the family, usually women.

Clearly the transfer of work from the state to the family involves a reduction in state expenditure, but it also has other effects. First, many of the jobs within the welfare state, and in the NHS in particular, were occupied by women, so a reduced emphasis on this lessens employment opportunities for women. Secondly, insofar as women are now expected to

undertake increased unpaid care roles in the home this places a further restriction on the types of paid employment they may take.

Care in the community

One main criticism of the welfare state concerned its bureaucratic and unresponsive nature. This criticism was particularly aimed at institutional care within the welfare state. In his famous study, *Asylums*, interactionist Erving Goffman (1968) demonstrated that care for the mentally ill within institutions had negative effects on their health. (See also Sections 9.7 and 13.8.) Similar points can be made about the negative perceptions that surround homes for the elderly. There has therefore been a consistent criticism of institutional care from an interactionist/libertarian strand within sociology.

In response to this, an alternative framework of care has been developed which has become known as 'care in the community'. What this means is that the elderly, the mentally ill and the physically handicapped are looked after not in separate institutions but within society. It is argued that this is possible owing to the range of service providers in this age of welfare pluralism. It is also argued that such care avoids isolating people away from the rest of society, which is seen as one of the key negative effects of institutional care.

One final advantage of care in the community is that it is cheaper. According to *New Society* (1987), looking after a single elderly person then cost about £295 a week in an NHS hospital and roughly £135 a week in residential care, whereas the cost of care in the community was just under £100. This clearly has an appeal to those who wish to reduce public expenditure. Despite this, it is suggested that the vast majority of local authority spending on the elderly and those with disabilities goes on residential care: Gray *et al.* (1988) quote figures of 73 per cent for residential care and 18 per cent for community services.

A major problem is that a lack of funding and resources means there are in reality not enough community support facilities. Concerns over this have focused attention particularly on the number of suicides and homicides committed by the mentally ill. A government report (quoted in *The Guardian*, 16 January 1996) showed that in the previous year there had been 240 suicides among mentally ill people; of these 53 were in-patients, 154 out-patients and 33 discharged within the past year. (See also Section 13.8.) These figures appear to show that there are more suicides among those outside institutional care than inside, which has led to pressure to improve provision of care in the community.

It is precisely because of this lack of real service

Activity

Suggest ways in which the involvement of families in welfare provision has increased in recent years.

A

backup that Alan Scull (1984) refers to the policy as one not of care in the community but of 'decarceration' – emphasizing that essentially it involves removing people from institutional care but with no real notion of how then to look after them, leaving vulnerable people open to private landlords and others with no care background. It is suspected that a large proportion of the rise in the homeless in the UK can be accounted for by people who have been ejected as large institutions closed.

While 'care in the community' has been a slogan supported by many people since the 1940s, no one was ever really sure what exactly it meant. It gained support as a result of the problems identified with institutional care, but such radical critiques of psychiatric care now seem to serve the desire to reduce costs. It would seem that in reality, for many vulnerable people, care in the community means being left to fend for themselves. This might be characterized as counterposing care in the community to care by the community.

Towards the end of 1996 something of a sea change emerged when the government admitted that the 'care in the community' policy had failed (reported in *The Times*, 6 November 1996). The Health Secretary outlined plans for a new debate and legislation on care for the mentally ill, based around some degree of 24-hour in-hospital provision. Whether this will satisfy all the critics of care in the community remains to be seen.

Discussion point

To what degree can care in the community be seen as a realistic possibility rather than an aspiration?

Welfare pluralism

While there has been support in many quarters for the growth of welfare pluralism – on the grounds that there are several alternative ways to provide care and we should explore all of them – it has also been criticized as an ideological smokescreen for the transformation of the welfare state from a universalist to a selectivist provider, and as a justification for public expenditure cuts. In looking at the way in which the meaning of care in the community has changed, Walker (1989, p. 204) argues that the promotion of care in the community fits in with neo-liberal philosophy (see Section 2.10) in the following ways:

- antagonism towards public expenditure on the welfare state
- increasing emphasis on self-help and family support

- extension of the scope of the market in social relations
- the breaking down of the social democratic consensus.

14.3 Theoretical approaches to welfare

The New Right, the state and welfare

New Right thinking is based on the belief that a free market is much better than the state at providing economic growth and improved living standards. This belief is reflected in the New Right's absolute rejection of Keynesian economics which stressed the need for the state to actively intervene in the economy. (See also Sections 2.10, 13.6 and 17.3.) Similarly, they are very critical of the Beveridge Report for 'discouraging individualism, self-reliance, voluntary organizations and private initiatives' (Marsland, 1992, p. 146).

Willetts (1992), a New Right theoretician and Conservative MP, makes the further point that centralized planning is impossible owing to the complexity of modern life. The free market should therefore be restored to its role of importance. This in turn means that the scope of the state must be reined back.

New Right philosopher Friedrich Von Hayek argued that any state expenditure threatened individual liberty (since it is financed out of coercive taxation measures), and so in order to defend freedom the state should be kept at an absolute minimum. The idea that the state acts to secure social justice is one that Hayek rejected, seeing it instead as a back-door way to secure moves to socialism and equality.

Saunders (1995), a sociologist with New Right sympathies, argues that it is possible to see the welfare state as contributing not to a growth in human happiness but to a growth in human misery:

Universal state welfare was established in Britain from the mid-1940s, and both the crime rate and the decline in the conventional two-parent family began to rise a decade or so later. . . . This is not to suggest that state welfare directly causes crime and family breakdown, but it is possible that it has enabled these changes to occur. Single parenthood, for example, was not a viable option for most women before various welfare reforms from the 1960s onwards provided financial support for it.
(Saunders, 1995, pp. 91–2)

Furthermore, welfare expenditure, by eroding personal responsibility, creates a culture of dependency. Green (1988), a New Right social thinker, argues that this is so in the case of free healthcare provided by the NHS (see also Section 13.6), which he argues has:

. . . undermined the capacity of people for self direction and spread a child-like dependency on the state.
(Green, 1988, p. 5)

Some people become 'hooked' on welfare benefits like a drug, sappping their will and energy and therefore not helping them at all to fend for themselves. A former Conservative Cabinet Minister, Sir Keith Joseph, explains this most clearly:

The only lasting help we can give to the poor is helping them to help themselves; to do the opposite, to create more dependence, is to destroy them morally, whilst throwing an unfair burden on society.
(Quoted in Lowe, 1993, p. 303)

Murray (1984), an American New Right political scientist, has made much the same point in relation to the anti-poverty policies in the USA. He argues that instead of providing more for the poor they have simply provided more poor. (See also Section 4.8 on the underclass argument.)

In the UK, Marsland (1996) has given a systematic analysis of the welfare state from a New Right perspective in his book *Welfare or Welfare State?*. He contends that it needs to be substantially contracted, with many of the services it provides coming instead from a free market. In this extract he outlines its negative consequences:

We seem to have got ourselves stuck in a posture of neurotic obeisance to the Nanny Totem of the welfare state. . . . the welfare state inflicts damaging levels of moral and psychological harm on its supposed beneficiaries. It has seduced the British people away from their natural independence of spirit and their traditional commitment to hard work, honesty and high standards. It has transformed much of the population into deferential conformists with an irrational inclination to spasmodic rebellion and a cynical eye to the main chance. It has made of its primary clients – perfectly normal, capable men and women before the state got to work on them – a festering underclass of welfare dependants fit for nothing better than passive consumption of an ever-expanding diet of 'bread and circuses'.
(Marsland, 1996, pp. 6 and 20)

In summary, the New Right believe that state expenditure has negative economic consequences and state welfare expenditure can contribute to negative social consequences. Conversely, a reduction in the welfare state and a greater emphasis on a free market and personal responsibility will lead to a better society.

Discussion point

To what extent do you agree with Marsland that the welfare state has negative moral and psychological consequences for its clients?

Social democratic approaches to welfare

It is perhaps with the broad approach labelled 'social democratic' that the notion of a welfare state is most closely associated. Social democrats believe that the liberal democratic state is the best institutional mechanism to foster democratic control in society, and further that such a state machinery can be used to attain desirable social objectives such as greater equality or equality of opportunity.

This trend really came to the fore in the wake of the economic and social crisis of the 1930s which led to the discarding of the ideas of free-market liberalism (the forerunners of today's New Right). The experience of the Second World War convinced these people that government planning could work, and with the development of Keynes' economic theories this soon became the orthodoxy. If the government was able to influence the economy to achieve economic ends, then why should not the same methods be applied to social objectives? This is the origin of theories of the welfare state. There is a clear link between economic and social objectives here since one of the key assumptions underlying the Beveridge Report was that government would seek to achieve and maintain full employment.

Social democracy is based on the belief that free-market capitalism is wasteful, inefficient and unjust. However, the construction of a new society will come not from revolution but from gradual evolution within parliamentary democracies. (See also Sections 2.5 and 17.1.)

George and Wilding (1994), welfare theorists, provide the following list of reasons for social democratic support of the welfare state, showing its economic and social benefits over free-market capitalism.

- It can eliminate want and suffering in society.
- State expenditure on welfare, particularly on education, provides a form of investment in the future, creating greater economic prosperity.
- Education spending also allows everyone to fulfil their individual potential and thus creates a more egalitarian society. (See also Sections 4.9, 8.5–7.)

- It can help promote feelings of altruism (willingness to help and consider others), for example through the free giving of blood.
- It can create conditions of social integration since everyone is treated equally.
- Welfare can help compensate for the negative aspects of economic change (e.g. through unemployment benefits). (See also Section 9.6.)

Activity

Suggest ways in which each of the above aims could be achieved.

Assess the extent to which the contemporary welfare state does seek to achieve these aims.

A, E

The welfare state is therefore seen as a key mechanism to achieve a more ethical, civilized and just society. This notion is encapsulated in sociologist Marshall's (1963) notion of the growth of 'citizenship rights' (see also Section 17.5), which all citizens are entitled to as of right (hence the name). He argued that the meaning of citizenship had developed over time, from:

- *civil citizenship* – meaning individual freedom, essentially freedom of speech, freedom of thought and belief, the right to own property and the right to justice; through to:
- *political citizenship* – which entails the right to vote and participate in political decision-making; through to:
- *social citizenship* – which involves in addition to the others the right to economic welfare and security, including the right to education, work and healthcare.

As can be seen from this list, the notion of social citizenship essentially entails provision of the services conventionally associated with the welfare state.

The initial success and popularity of the welfare state led some social democratic thinkers in this tradition – notably Anthony Crosland, as a Labour government minister – to argue that essentially the UK was no longer a capitalist or class-divided society. Crosland emphasized the importance of the economic and social reforms introduced by the post-war Labour government as an important element in the construction of the welfare state. Political factors are therefore a central if not the only element in analyses based in this tradition.

This can be seen clearly in the work of probably the leading theorist in this approach today, namely Gøsta Esping-Andersen. In a comparative analysis of the rise of welfare states, he argues that the impor-

tant factors determining the shape of welfare regimes is the nature of class mobilization and of class coalitions in the political structure. (See also Section 4.7.)

A final factor of great importance today is the social democratic support for universal provision of welfare benefits. There are a number of problems associated with means-tested benefits which lead them to take up this position. Among these are the stigmatization associated with the means test, the greater administrative cost of means-tested benefits, the problem of creating poverty traps (see Section 14.7), the generally lower quality of services provided only for the poor, and the fact that welfare provision intended for everyone is better able to withstand onslaughts on welfare expenditure by the political right (see above).

While undoubtedly the social democratic perspective relies heavily on notions of social justice and ethical considerations of how society should be organized, it is far from clear that the actual welfare states that have grown out of this tradition in fact do very much to make society more just, equal or fair. As George and Wilding point out:

[There is] *convincing empirical evidence . . . that universal provision does not reduce income inequalities in society.*
(George and Wilding, 1994, p. 86)

This has led to criticisms of this perspective from the Left, and an ongoing debate by sociologists about who actually benefits from the welfare state (see Section 14.4). Universal provision has also been attacked by the Right, who argue that to provide benefits for those able to provide for themselves is an expensive waste.

One of the major problems with the social democratic perspective is that it clearly does imply a high level of state expenditure on welfare. This has to rely on improved economic performance by the nation. However, moving towards 'market socialism' and abandonment of the idea of the state playing the leading economic role make such changes more reliant on capitalism. What arises seems to be a much watered-down version of democratic socialism, which places a question-mark over whether democratic socialism is still a step in the transition to socialism:

It is doubtful whether the new brand of market socialism that so many democratic socialists aspire to today poses any real threat to capitalism. The socialism of the future will contain more elements of capitalism than past brands of socialism did.
(George and Wilding, 1994, p. 101)

The 'middle way'

George and Wilding (1994) develop this category to capture the point that not all non-Socialists are supporters of the New Right. There exists a body of opinion broadly in favour of some kind of welfare state, but opposed to use of it for egalitarian social engineering – as embodied in the social democratic view that the welfare state is a stepping stone to greater equality. They suggest that both Keynes and Beveridge can in reality be depicted as holding this position, which they characterize as anti-collectivist but not anti-interventionist. It encompasses the one-nation strand of Conservatism and the Liberal Democrats.

What the latter share is opposition to socialism, but a belief that the free market left to its own devices does create certain problems that need rectifying through intervention by the state. This leads to a stress on 'fairness' and 'equality of opportunity', and the way in which the welfare state can help to consolidate society by, for example, promoting policies to make the family unit strong. Underlying this is the idea of a contractual relationship between the individual and the state, leading welfare to operate to promote integration of society as a whole.

Marxist approaches to welfare

Marxists (see also Section 2.5) argue that the welfare state is a mechanism to both stabilize and reproduce capitalism, but also that certain elements of it represent concessions which the working classes have won from capitalism. Perhaps the best example to illustrate this is Marx's idea that legislation to reduce the hours of factory work resulted from centuries of class struggle between workers and capitalists. However, he also argued that it would in the end benefit the capitalists too since their workers would not be so tired and therefore be more productive.

Marxists also argue that reforms are often introduced to head off disruptive action by the working classes. The extent of the class struggle is therefore the key determinant of the nature of any welfare state that develops. However, it is also the case that calculations by the capitalist class will play a part, and this leads on to an analysis that sees the welfare state as a form of social control. With regard to social security, Ginsburg (1991) argues that it keeps wages low by setting benefit levels low, and by ensuring that able-bodied unemployed are required to work seeks to instil and maintain industrial discipline.

different emphasis is placed on this by O'Connor 1984). While accepting that the welfare state to maintain the accumulation of capital, he it also has to perform the sometimes con-ction of legitimating the system. (See

also information on Habermas in Section 2.9.) This leads to a crisis because while everyone wants more public services they do not want to pay the necessary extra taxes. He asserts that this may lead to government expenditure exceeding government revenue. Instead of providing a stable situation for renewed capital accumulation, this may lead to instability and economic and political crises. The welfare state may therefore in some cases be dysfunctional (see Section 2.4) for capitalism.

Offe (1984), who is associated with the Frankfurt School (see Sections 2.5 and 10.3), has argued that in fact the idea of a pure *laissez-faire* capitalism as outlined by the New Right would not work because the ensuing social unrest would undermine the stability required for capital accumulation. Nonetheless he does see the welfare state as constituting a cost to the capitalist system. His conclusion is that 'while capitalism cannot coexist with the welfare state, neither can it exist without the welfare state'.

This is moving away from earlier Marxist positions – which tended to see the welfare state as unproblematically creating the conditions for continued capital accumulation – towards a position that argues that there is a cost to capitalism; a necessary cost, but a cost nonetheless. The implication is that the capitalist class may choose to, and may succeed in, dismantling most or all of the welfare state. The lack of a coordinated response to 'attacks' on the welfare state from the New Right has tended to confirm this view. Offe now argues that capitalism may be able to survive with a very minimalist welfare state for the poor and with the rest of the population surviving on private welfare.

Feminist approaches to welfare

The assumption contained in the Beveridge Report that married women would not want to seek paid employment had important implications for the way the welfare state developed. (See Section 9.3.) For example, many benefit payments are dependent on a past record of National Insurance contributions that usually come through paid employment, so women who have not worked regularly are placed at a disadvantage. This type of issue has been discussed by feminist writers. Williams (1989), for instance, argues that because the development of the welfare state after 1945 was based on this questionable view of the role of women, in many ways it served to reinforce women's dependency in the home. (See also Section 7.5.)

Lewis (1991) is concerned to highlight the important campaigning role of women inside the Labour Party in actually bringing about welfare state reforms. However, she also points out that as a result of the way it was implemented the welfare state rarely prioritized women's concerns. This can be seen, for example, in the failure to provide a comprehensive, publically funded system of childcare.

Feminist writers have also been concerned with the welfare state as an employer, since the majority of its employees are women.

Overall, therefore, while the welfare state may have led to some improvements in living standards, feminist writers (see also Section 2.6 and Chapter 5) have been concerned to highlight the ways in which gender assumptions remain embedded in its structure.

Activity

Use the information given so far in this section to allocate the following thinkers to one of the theoretical approaches –

New Right, middle way, social democrat, feminist, or Marxist:

David Willetts	J. M. Keynes
Milton Friedman	Jane Lewis
David Marsland	W. Beveridge
Fiona Williams	James O'Connor
T. H. Marshall	Claus Offe
Charles Murray	D. G. Green.

I, A

Recent thinking on welfare regimes

The theoretical positions on welfare outlined above continue to be held today. However, the 1980s and 90s have seen a number of innovative approaches to thinking about the welfare state. This section looks at a few examples.

Post-Fordism and the welfare state

It has been argued (e.g. by Jessop, 1994) that the Keynesian welfare state was the ideal type of the Fordist economic regime (see Section 9.4), with full employment and income support measures to encourage and perpetuate mass consumption. If there is indeed a crisis in the welfare state, it can be seen as an element of the crisis of Fordism. While mass production ensured there were the funds to provide for the welfare state, welfare provision strengthened the working classes and organized labour. This meant that wages grew faster than productivity, which led to a crisis of accumulation. The move towards post-Fordism, with its emphasis on flexibility and divisions within the workforce (between core and periphery), is an attempt to deal with this (see Section 9.4). The effect of this transformation on the welfare state might be characterized as in Figure 14.2.

Activity

Investigate one particular area of welfare state provision and analyse recent changes using the framework suggested in Figure 14.2. Evaluate the extent to which this is a useful way to characterize recent changes in provision.

I, A, E

	Fordism	Post-Fordism
Needs	Mass universal needs	Diversity of individual needs
Provision	Monolithic Bureaucratic Professional-led	Welfare pluralism Quasi-markets Consumer sovereignty Reorganized welfare work

Figure 14.2 The welfare state: from Fordism to post-Fordism?

While the notion of greater plurality of welfare provision (see Section 14.2) and the greater emphasis on markets are clearly examples of the development of flexibility, seen as characteristic of post-Fordism, there are nonetheless criticisms of the use of the concepts Fordism/post-Fordism to describe the welfare state. These are as follows.

- Ultimately this is an economically determinist type of analysis which attempts to explain changes in the welfare state as deriving from changes in the economy.
- It under-estimates or ignores the importance of political struggle in establishing the welfare state and maintaining it.
- Since the analysis is centred on production it is not really able to take into account social relations other than class. This means that gender and ethnicity in particular are ignored. (On this debate see Section 2.6 and also Chapters 4–6.)

'Decommodification' and the welfare state

Gøsta Esping-Andersen is undoubtedly one of the most influential theorists of welfare at the present time whose concept of decommodification has led to radical new thinking. He argues that we need to consider how the welfare state does more than simply modify existing stratification systems, to understand the way in which it is a stratification system in and of itself. This places welfare right at the heart of analysis of the changing distribution of income and wealth. (See also Section 14.8.)

Esping-Andersen (1990) analyses the welfare policies in eighteen advanced industrial economies and suggests that we can establish three distinct types of what he calls 'welfare regimes'. The reason he uses this term rather than the more common 'welfare state' is precisely to argue that we cannot analyse welfare simply by looking at the actions of the state; we must root it in a number of factors, in particular the relationships between state welfare policies, the employment structure and the general social structure.

He argues that it is essential to consider the importance of class political mobilization as an explanation for the type of welfare regime. This argument is in line with the social democratic approach which stresses that politics can make a difference. The crucial question is, therefore, the way in which the working classes are mobilized to seek changes to the system. Esping-Andersen thus rejects the idea found in both functionalist and Marxist analyses that the welfare state arises because it is functional for industrial/capitalist society and that this explains its development and character:

To emphasize active class-mobilization does not necessarily deny the importance of structured or hegemonic power. But it is held that parliaments are, in principle, effective institutions for the translation of mobilized power into desired policies and reforms.
(Esping-Andersen, 1990, p. 16)

In the course of developing a comparative picture of different types of welfare regimes, Esping-Andersen introduces the concept of decommodification. What he means by this concept is the extent to which people can survive without having to work for a living:

Decommodification occurs when a service is rendered as a matter of right, and when a person can maintain a livelihood without reliance on the market.
(Esping-Andersen, 1990, p. 22)

For example, in the UK the NHS provides a health service free at the point of delivery (apart from some charges for prescriptions and appliances), and even if you do not have a job there are benefits like unemployment benefit and income support that ensure you survive.

Decommodification overcomes inequality and this creates the basis for social cohesion.

The importance of this concept is that it can be used to consider the extent to which a welfare state really offers people a choice about how they live their lives, or whether it forces them to go to work by pro-

viding only a minimal safety-net for those totally unable to do so.

Esping-Andersen's views have not been without critics. Most notably his model is criticized for being centred on class divisions while ignoring other social divisions in society, especially those arising from gender and ethnicity, making it difficult to apply to certain policy areas:

The application to family policy of cross-national models such as Esping-Andersen's, derived from examining benefits predominantly for male workers, is problematic to say the least.
(Ginsburg, 1991, p. 83)

Williams (1994), a feminist sociologist, argues that the concept of decommodification can mean different things to men and to women. Decommodification enhances males' ability to enter the labour market on their own terms, but they are also aided in this process by the domestic labour (see also Sections 7.5 and 9.1) supplied by women which is also decommodified. In this sense some women may wish for commodification – that is, payment for the work they do – rather than endorsing decommodification.

Discussion point

To what extent do you think diverse social groups would welcome decommodification?

In summary, those writers who are critical of Esping-Andersen's position focus on the centrality of class relations and the labour market in his analysis and the relative absence of other social structures (notably the family), and therefore the invisibility of other social divisions (notably those based on gender).

Activity

Critically evaluate the usefulness of the concept of 'decommodification' in the analysis of welfare provision.

I, E

Comparative welfare regimes

One of the ways in which we can assess the effect of a welfare state is to look at the social structures and social relations prior to its development. Many studies of the UK contrast the pre-welfare state situation with that prevailing after implementation of the Beveridge Report (see Section 14.1). However, a problem with this type of analysis is that it focuses on one nation-state, which tends to make it appear as if international links have no impact.

Such thinking encourages another way of considering welfare states or welfare regimes, namely that of comparative studies of the operations in various countries. It is useful to consider the extent to which particular societies' welfare regimes are similar or significantly different. Such analyses can therefore also be used to consider the relative importance of international forces and more specifically national factors.

On the basis of his concept of decommodification (discussed earlier), Esping-Andersen divides the eighteen countries he studied into three distinct welfare regimes: the conservative model, the liberal model and the social democratic model (see Table 14.1). The higher the score the greater the decommodification.

The liberal model is the one where the idea of the importance of the market is strongest, and so the welfare regime tends to involve a weak residual welfare state with mainly means-tested benefits. He argues that the clearest examples of this type of regime are the USA, Canada, Australia and Switzerland.

The conservative model arises, he says, in countries where the free market never really caught on. He argues that welfare regimes in these countries are characterized by the relative unimportance of private and occupational welfare as the state takes a stronger role, to maintain the present social structure. Status differentials in society are maintained and divisions between groups based on occupational

categories are reinforced. There is a clear earnings-related method of delivering welfare; entitlements to benefits are therefore unequal, so maintaining old inequalities in the system. Such systems also tend to have a large moralistic element owing to the influence of the Church in these societies. Therefore benefits seek to uphold the traditional family structure as an important element in providing welfare. Examples of this type of regime include Austria, Belgium, France, Germany and Italy.

Esping-Andersen's third model, the social democratic, is one in which the principle of universalism is most fully developed. Here, welfare regimes are based on the idea of citizenship and social rights, and so benefits are made available to all, including the middle class. Welfare is fused with employment via the commitment to full employment in this model. Examples of this type of regime include Denmark, Finland, Norway, Sweden and the Netherlands.

The UK is not easy to classify on this basis according to Esping-Andersen. He says there are few elements of the conservative model here, but there are clear elements of both the liberal and the social democratic model.

Bryson (1992), a welfare sociologist, also adopts a comparative approach in her study of welfare and the allocation of benefits. She argues that advanced capitalist economies were routinely referred to as welfare states but that quite recently this has changed:

We have witnessed a significant change of political direction by both conservative and non-conservative governments. The change involves a stated intention to rely more on the market and to reduce state interventions.
(Bryson, 1992, p. 1)

In this sense the changes of the 1980s and 90s can be understood as a backlash by those dominant groups in society who lost out as a result of the reforms of the 1960s and 70s. These changes occur on a global level. (See also Sections 9.9, 10.10, 12.5, 16.8 and 17.6 on debates about globalization.) She argues that such global pressures have affected countries differentially. Japan has been the least affected by the pressure to marketize, while the Scandinavian countries have been most affected.

On a comparative level, Bryson argues that a key feature in the 1980s was a movement away from institutional welfare, where the state was seen as the normal first-line provider of welfare, back towards a residual model which sees the state intervening only when other institutions such as the family, the market and private charities fail. This, she says, can be seen most in the USA, Canada and Australia.

Table 14.1 The rank-order of welfare states in terms of decommodification score

Australia	13.0
United States	13.8
New Zealand	17.1
Canada	22.0
Ireland	23.3
United Kingdom	23.4
Italy	24.1
Japan	27.1
France	27.5
Germany	27.7
Finland	29.2
Switzerland	29.8
Austria	31.1
Belgium	32.4
Netherlands	32.4
Denmark	38.1
Norway	38.3
Sweden	39.1
Mean	27.2

Source: Esping-Andersen (1990, p. 52)

Activity

Figure 14.3 contains summaries of the characteristics of Esping-Andersen's conservative, liberal and social democratic regimes. Using this and information from the section on recent changes in the UK's welfare state, consider how you would locate the UK welfare state. In what direction do you think it is moving?

I, A, E

Conservative welfare regimes
- These see the individual as subordinated to the family or the state.
- They pay large welfare benefits to certain groups such as civil servants to create a class loyal to the state.
- The main form of benefit is of the social insurance type based on contributions made through employment. This creates distinctions based on a person's place in the employment structure and therefore in society.
- Corporatism is used to bind people together but also to recognize status differences between groups.
- They believe in the importance of upholding the traditional family structure owing to the influence of the Church.

Liberal welfare regimes
- These see the individual and individual freedom as most important.
- They believe that the market is the best system for distributing resources and the state should act only in clear cases where the market fails (e.g. short-term unemployment).
- They believe state benefits must not undermine the need for incentives in a market economy, or the work ethic. Therefore benefits tend to be low and means-tested to avoid discouraging people taking paid employment.
- Means-tested benefits are the predominant form, so benefits are only paid to some, notably those with low incomes, creating a selective welfare state.
- They create divisions between those reliant on low benefits and those able to obtain higher remuneration from employment.

Social Democratic welfare regimes
- These believe that the equality of democracy needs to be matched with a wider equality in the economic and social spheres.
- Welfare benefits are based on a notion of citizenship and therefore seen as a right.
- This means that welfare benefits need to be available to all, leading to a universal welfare state.
- They believe that such a system can limit inequalities and overcome divisions between the working and the middle classes.
- The welfare state may be an important element in the transition to socialism.
- They are committed to full employment both in principle and because the high level of benefits paid are dependent on it through tax revenue.

Figure 14.3 Features of Esping-Andersen's three types of regime

Bryson also asserts that important historical and cultural differences play a part in the way international pressures for change have an effect. While all those countries with a high degree of institutional welfare have a high degree of material wealth, not all wealthy countries have high levels of institutional welfare. Here she cites the examples of Japan and the USA. Japan's system can be explained by an historical cultural tradition of great reliance on the family as the basis of welfare, whereas the USA has had a much greater cultural acceptance of the market. As a result governments in those countries spent less of their economic wealth than countries like Sweden. She argues that by looking at how much the government of each country receives in tax revenue as a percentage of its overall economic production (gross domestic product or GDP), the effects of these differences can be seen. This is illustrated in Table 14.2.

Table 14.2 Government receipts as a percentage of GDP, 1984–85

Sweden	59.8
France	48.5
Germany	45.4
UK	42.8
Australia	34.1
USA	31.1
Japan	30.3

Source: Adapted from Bryson (1992, p. 74)

According to Bryson, Australia has a welfare state based largely on securing high wage levels and providing residual and means-tested benefits only for those not in work. In the USA she sees a much greater emphasis on private charity through organizations such as the Rockefeller Foundation and the Ford Foundation, and a clear anti-welfare state feeling. This means that although benefits paid through contributions are largely exempt from change, provision for others is minimal and subject to cuts.

She notes that while the Nordic countries developed the most comprehensive universalist model of welfare states, this did mean that a higher proportion of national income went on the welfare state. International market pressures have led them to consider changes in recent years. Since 1976 there have been moves to place greater emphasis on the market, but not without ramifications: the Swedish government fell in 1990 over protests at moves to limit the growth of welfare spending.

Bryson concludes that, while there are important historical differences that are reflected in how welfare states have developed, all have tended to privilege the interests of dominant groups over the rest.

All have retained some degree of attachment to a *laissez-faire* notion of a welfare state, reinforced by moves towards free-market doctrines in the 1980s and 90s. The main cause has not been an economic over-burden caused by the welfare state, but resistance by privileged groups to any measures seeking to erode that privilege.

14.4 The welfare state as a system of stratification

One common image of the welfare state is of an institutional Robin Hood which takes from the rich and gives to the poor. It is certainly the case that many of the social democrats associated with the rise of the welfare state viewed it in such terms, and part of the hostility towards it shown by the New Right is also based on their fear that it involves such a procedure. The question, therefore, of who benefits from the welfare state has been an important and continuing one, in both political and sociological circles. While social democratic thinkers might assert that it is possible for the welfare state to promote greater equality, Marxists and latterly feminists have strongly questioned this. It is also clear that the advent of the New Right to government led to the ending of the notion of the welfare state as a redistributive institution.

Welfare regimes as creators of social stratification

Esping-Andersen (1990) suggests that, in order to consider fully the effect of the welfare state on stratification, we need to link consideration of its actions with the concept of citizenship developed by T. H. Marshall (see also Section 17.5). This would allow consideration of the way in which the welfare state actively promotes certain kinds of social stratification:

The welfare state is not just a mechanism that intervenes in, and possibly corrects, the structure of inequality; it is, in its own right, a system of stratification.
(Esping-Andersen, 1990, p. 23)

We have already seen, in Section 14.3, that Marshall identified three types of citizenship. He saw the rise of the welfare state as moving towards an era of social citizenship where everyone was entitled to social participation in society. Welfare regimes based on liberal ideology tended to develop residual modes of welfare benefit whereby the state acted merely as a safety-net. This creates a division between those living on benefits, who tend to be poor, and the rest of the population who live off their earnings from employment. The division tends to be large because benefit levels are low to discourage those seen as work-shy from applying. This is further reinforced by the stigma attached to means-tested benefits:

The poor-relief tradition, and its contemporary means-tested social-assistance offshoot, was conspicuously designed for purposes of stratification. By punishing and stigmatising recipients, it promotes social dualisms.
(Esping-Andersen, 1990, p. 24)

Clearly this model fails to ensure that all people are entitled to social participation, and therefore creates inequalities between citizens.

In contrast the conservative model, rooted as it is around social insurance based on workplace contributions, generally contains at least two distinct levels of benefits, since it is designed expressly so that welfare entitlements maintain class and status differentials.

Esping-Andersen argues that because both the liberal and conservative systems were set up explicitly to create or maintain social inequalities, this led to great hostility towards them, particularly from the labour movement. He points out, however, that often schemes promoted by the labour movement benefited only the most organized workers, and excluded others, thereby setting up divisions inside the working classes. (See also Section 4.7.)

In contrast to these approaches, the universalist model of the welfare state seeks to avoid the same problems, and seems at first sight to contain within it the notion of equality. Benefits are to be available to all at the same rate. Everyone is to be treated equally. Esping-Andersen argues, however, that this system can work only when the majority of the population are working class who will accept the modest benefits available. But with the expansion of the middle classes as a proportion of the population (see Section 4.6) this system breaks down – they supplement their state benefits with private-sector provision, thus undermining the equality of universalistic provision.

In this situation the dualistic nature of the social-insurance residual model is re-created. Esping-Andersen points out that one way in which support for the welfare state has been maintained in this situation is to promote higher levels of benefits for the middle classes via the state – by, for example, making the benefits earnings-related. This is what happened in Sweden and Norway. The point is then that the welfare state is maintained but the notion of equality that underpins it has been eroded, although it does remain universal provision.

What is novel in this analysis is the way in which

the assumption is avoided that welfare is in some way linked to greater equality. It recognizes instead how welfare regimes developed, some of which were consciously devoted to maintaining inequalities.

> ### Discussion point
>
> To what extent do you agree (if at all) that welfare regimes have been set up with the aim of maintaining existing levels of inequality?

What do we mean by 'welfare'?

A further debate about the issue of welfare states and inequality concerns the rather narrow focus of many enquiries into this topic. It is necessary to consider not only the directly observable welfare state, but also fiscal and occupational welfare.

- *Fiscal welfare* means the way in which resources and incomes are distributed through the system of tax allowances and tax rates which clearly affect the disposable income certain groups receive. (See also Section 14.8.)
- *Occupational welfare* is concerned with the existence of large amounts of what are commonly called 'fringe benefits' available to certain people by virtue of their job, such as a company car, a cheaper mortgage, or a subsidized canteen.

All this has an effect on the income and the expenditure needed to maintain a certain lifestyle, so it is important to take it into account when looking at the question of the redistributive effect of the welfare state.

> ### Activity
>
> **a** Suggest one concrete benefit which might be obtained for each of the three types of welfare outlined so far in this section.
> **b** Explain in your own words why it is important to consider all three forms of welfare in an overall consideration of the effect of welfare?
>
> **I, A**

The welfare state and social inequality in the UK

Women experience the welfare state differently from men. So too do the various classes and people of differing racial and ethnic backgrounds.
(Bryson, 1992, p. 159)

The welfare state and class inequalities

The most redistributive aspect of a welfare state is the existence of social security benefits. These do distribute income towards the poorest and they would be considerably worse off without them. However, the changes in the 1986 and 1988 Social Security Acts which replaced the system of one-off grants with repayable loans (see Section 14.2) has clearly reduced this effect somewhat. The exclusion of 16 to 18-year-olds from entitlement to income support has also had the same effect. *The Economist* in June 1994 estimated that there were 68,000 people aged 16–18 without any income at all.

A second point is that the real value of benefits has been cut since the level of supplementary benefit/income support benefits as a percentage of average earnings fell over the 1980s, as can be seen in Table 14.3. Benefit for a single person was equal to 20.8 per cent of average earnings in July 1986 but this fell to 19.1 per cent by April 1988.

Table 14.3 Supplementary benefit/income support as a percentage of average earnings

	July 1986	April 1987	April 1988
Single person	20.8	19.5	19.1
Couple	32.1	30.3	28.3
Couple + 1 child	38.5	36.4	32.9
Couple + 2 children	43.1	40.8	37.1
Couple + 3 children	47.2	44.8	41.1
Couple + 4 children	51.0	48.5	44.8

Sources: Department of Social Security/*The Guardian* 12 May 1989

Research carried out for the National Children's Home charity (reported in *The Guardian*, 1 February 1994) shows that the allowance for food contained within income support is now less (in real terms) than in the days of the workhouse (see Section 14.1). The director of the charity commented:

It is appalling as we approach the year 2000, that even an 1876 workhouse diet is too expensive for the families of one in four of our children.

The data showing this are in Figure 14.4. Changes in the 1980s therefore seem to have reduced somewhat the redistributive impact of this aspect of the welfare state.

Looking at other aspects, it seems clear that the affluent benefit much more than the poor. In a famous study on the question of who benefits from the welfare state, Le Grand (1982) investigated the beneficiaries of welfare policy in five areas, namely health (see also Sections 13.2–4), education (see also Section 8.5), council housing, public transport and social services. Of these the only one where the poor benefited substantially more than the better-off was council housing.

Table 14.4 Public expenditure (£ p.a.) per household on social services in the UK by income group, 1978

Income group (original income)	Health care	Education	School meals, milk and other welfare foods	Housing	Rail travel	All social services
Top 20%	354	444	21	57	25	902
Next 20%	323	400	24	73	11	831
Middle 20%	320	348	26	103	7	804
Next 20%	309	216	22	118	5	670
Bottom 20%	306	156	22	205	2	691
Mean	322	313	23	111	10	780

Sources: Le Grand (1982)/CSO

THE WORKHOUSE MENU

Bethnal Green 1876		**Poor Law Orders 1913**	
Breakfast	*pence*	*Breakfast*	*pence*
Bread	28	Bread	13
Gruel	2	Milk	24
Lunch		*Lunch*	
Bread	28	Beef	21
Pea soup	2	Potatoes/cabbage	5
or Meat (scrag/neck)	13	Fresh fruit pudding	20
Potatoes/cabbage	5		
or Suet pudding	12		
Supper		*Supper*	
Bread	28	Seed cake	15
Cheese	5	Cocoa	3
or Broth	5		
or Milk	6		
Total*	**£5.46** per week	**Total***	**£7.07** per week

* 1994 prices
In 1994, Income Support allows for £4.15 per week

Figure 14.4 The workhouse menu. Sources: *The Guardian*, 1 February 1994/Food Commission/NCH Action for Children

As can be seen from Table 14.4, annual expenditure on healthcare was 15 per cent greater for the top fifth of income groups than for the poorest fifth. In relation to education, expenditure on the richest 20 per cent was 284 per cent that spent on the poorest 20 per cent. One finding which surprised Le Grand was the greater benefit to the richer groups of expenditure on public transport, since it was widely assumed that they would use much greater levels of private transport. He found that the richest fifth of income groups undertook ten times as many rail journeys as the poorest fifth. This research was conducted in 1978, but later research by Le Grand and Winter (1987) shows that the trends continued.

The welfare state and gender inequality

In her comparative study of welfare and the state, Bryson (1992) includes separate chapters on men and women to emphasize the fact that their experiences in a welfare state are very different.

The Beveridge Report was clear that the presumed role for married women was in the home, and that they would be provided for via their husbands' earnings. The 'family wage' (see Sections 5.3 and 7.5) thus dictated the levels of wages and benefits which were paid mainly to men on the assumption that they were responsible for a wife and children. One vestige of this idea was the married man's tax allowance which survived until 1990.

The principal problem with this is that many of the benefits associated with the welfare state were dependent on a certain record of NI contributions made through paid employment. Women had less involvement in paid employment: in the UK in 1985 only 52 per cent of married women were in such employment. Historically the two main reasons for this were:

- a series of Factory Acts in 1833, 1844 and 1847 which reduced the hours that women and children were allowed to work
- the gendered assumptions contained in the Beveridge Report and consequently enshrined in social welfare legislation.

Some feminists have seen this as an example of a patriarchal alliance between men of all classes to exclude women from paid employment and thus increase their dependency on men. Walby (1986), for example, sees the Factory Acts as an alliance between capitalists portraying themselves as concerned with women's and children's welfare, and male workers wishing to exclude women to avoid competitive downward pressure on wages. While the reforms were seen as progressive precisely because they did appear to remove women from the dangers of factory work – and Bryson argues that in this sense they did improve women's welfare – Walby argues that they reinforced gender inequalities because of their effect on the availability of paid work for women. (See also Chapter 5 and Section 9.3.)

Bryson further argues that although the welfare state looks after men's interests better than women's, women do nonetheless gain because they are predominant as welfare recipients. This is due to three factors:

- women live longer than men
- parental support is largely given to mothers
- owing to men's superior position in the occupational structure, they are less likely to need the support of the welfare state.

Williams (1993a) echoes the argument that women's experience of the welfare state has been contradictory. She points out that much of the legislation is based on three assumptions about women:

- that their primary role is that of mother and wife
- that they live in heterosexual married relationships
- that they are financially dependent on their husbands.

This creates the following contradictory position:

On the one hand, welfare policies have provided women with material and social improvements: family allowances/child benefit, access to safer childbirth and more reliable forms of contraception as well as employment opportunities. On the other hand the assumptions behind welfare policies have often circumscribed women's lives, with the consequence that many women's needs have been overlooked or marginalised or existing inequalities have been reproduced.
(Williams, 1993a, p. 79)

The clear focus of looking at the gendered construction of the welfare state can be seen in Carol Pateman's feminist work, which argues that a divide between a public and a private domain was created and women were confined to the private sphere (the family). This left them dependent on men and in a secondary position to men who were able to operate in both the public and the private spheres. (This is explored in more detail in Section 5.4.) This has meant that many women who lived without a male breadwinner were forced into poverty.

Clearly, one important basis of the gendering of the welfare state is about the relative lack of universal provision for childcare facilities which ultimately requires that at least one partner gives up paid work for some considerable time. Since women are likely to earn less than men, it may in one sense be economically rational for the woman to give up her job in most cases, but this rests on the assumption that the male will share his earnings equally with his family. This assumption has been questioned by research into the field of family finances. Pahl's (1989) study of family finances and the organization of them has shown that women do not have equal access to, or equal control over, such finances. (See Section 7.5.)

Also, the cost of looking after children – in terms of lost income, mainly by women – is considerable. Bryson quotes the findings of one study done in the UK in 1980 which calculated that the cost in lifetime earnings of a woman bringing up two children was £122,000.

The 1980s saw a growth in 'care in the community' which seemed to reinforce the notion that a woman's primary responsibility is in the home, though at the same time there was a growth in part-time paid employment for women. Bryson argues that one effect of the continuing assumptions about women's role is that the welfare state has inserted women into a secondary proletarianized part of the workforce.

Since most gains for women have come from government intervention, any move away from government intervention threatens to make the situation worse for women.

The welfare state and ethnic inequality

A system of benefits which operates largely on the basis of contributions made through paid employment will place at a disadvantage any groups disadvantaged in the employment sphere. This is clearly the case with ethnic minorities. A further aspect of this in the case of ethnic minorities is that their employment in low-paid jobs often occurs within the welfare sector itself – particularly the health service – and therefore contributes to the maintenance of services at a lower cost. The cost to society is lowered but at the expense of poorer income for ethnic minority groups. In many ways, all of these points are to a greater or lesser extent also true of women.

One distinctive difference faced by ethnic minorities is the relationship between welfare provision and immigration control. (See also Section 6.2.) Studies have shown how many benefits are dependent on a certain period of residence, and the widespread use of passport checking through the Department of Social Security. These restrictions meant, as Williams points out, that while black workers might have been employed to build council houses, they probably were not allocated them; and while they might be employed to clean DSS offices, they probably were not entitled to the benefits they dispensed.

A key reason for this was the assumption embodied in much welfare provision that one aim was to produce a British nation that was fit to rule the Empire. (See Section 6.2.) This can be seen in the concerns over the fitness of British troops fighting in the Boer War (see Section 13.2). This led to concerns that the 'national stock' was in decline and moves to improve it were presented in terms of improving the nation. Since in many ways this talk of 'nation' was conceived in terms of 'whiteness', it created the conditions for the treatment of others differently.

In summarizing the effect of state welfare, Bryson argues thus:

The evidence shows that for societies with either universal or selective approaches, inequality is maintained. This is clearly a bottom line. Benefits from social welfare provisions do deliver assistance, and life is more secure for the needy when such benefits are available. But it is also clear that benefits do not redress inequality.
(Bryson, 1992, p. 130–1)

Fiscal welfare and inequality

Fiscal welfare relates to a nation's system of taxation. (See also Section 14.8.) It depends on the balance between taxes that hit the richest hardest (*progressive taxes*, of which income tax is an example) and taxes that hit the poorest hardest (*regressive taxes*, of which VAT is an example). It also depends on the way in which relief from taxation is given to certain activities and the question of who benefits from these reliefs. These reliefs act in effect like benefits, because money that would otherwise flow to the government in taxation payments stays with the individual.

In relation to the first of these points, the UK government after 1979 followed a policy of shifting the burden of taxation from income tax to VAT. The highest rate of income tax in 1978 was 98 per cent, and it is currently 40 per cent. Similarly the standard rate of income tax has been reduced from 33 per cent to 23 per cent. While everyone benefits from this, the richest benefit most. At the same time the rate of VAT has increased from 7 per cent to 17.5 per cent. Since this tax is levied as a percentage of the price of a good, people with different incomes buying identical goods pay the same amount of tax, which is therefore a higher proportion of the income of the poorest in society. Research by Cope (1987) shows that the level of income below which no income tax is payable stood at 80 per cent of the average industrial wage in 1983, but by the late 1980s this had fallen to 25 per cent, thus drawing larger numbers of lower-paid workers into taxation.

Overall, therefore, the tax system does not take from the rich proportionately greater than the poor; if anything it is the reverse and this trend has accelerated in the 1980s. Westergaard (1995) points out that if we look at the total net addition to disposable income caused by the tax and benefits system changes between 1979 and 1989, some 46 per cent went to the richest 10 per cent of households and only 8 per cent to the poorest 40 per cent of households.

The issue concerning tax relief presents a picture of even greater inequality. This is an important form of public expenditure since it constitutes a cost to the government in exactly the same way as other more direct forms of public expenditure. Bryson (1992) points out that the cost to the nation of these exemptions and reliefs was greater than in any other heading of public expenditure in 1990–91. Prest and Barr (1985), in a study of the operation of public finance, argue that the effect of this is that the proportion actually contributed to taxation revenues by each income group in the 1980s was roughly the same, despite the apparent progressivity of income tax rates.

An important set of tax reliefs applies to houseowners, who generally do not include the poorest people. (See Section 16.8.) Tax relief on mortgage interest payments substantially reduces the cost of the mortgage, and gains from the sale of one's home are excluded from capital-gains tax. The benefits on these will be greater the greater the value of the house, which generally is linked to income.

The government has tried to encourage greater private provision of welfare by giving tax relief on private pension contributions – which tend to be taken up more by the better-off. There are further reliefs available for charitable contributions, which includes many private schools, thus reducing the cost of educating children privately – again something indulged in much more by higher income groups.

In the UK, up to 1990 an allowance was paid to married men exempting some of their wive's earnings from tax. Since 1990 the allowance has been claimable by either men or women in certain circumstances, thus reducing a gender inequality in the system. Westergaard (1995) declares, however, that this change may create more class inequality since it will favour prosperous households at the expense of poorer ones.

It is also the case that fiscal welfare can only be received by those with an income, so women who do not have paid employment lose out.

One illuminating way to show the effect of both social welfare and fiscal welfare was devised by the Child Poverty Action Group in 1991. They showed that the benefits available from fiscal welfare meant that the total benefits paid to someone earning £40 000 a year and their family were only £1 per

Table 14.5 Benefits for wealthy equal handouts for jobless (£/week)

Married couple with a single earner (aged 44) on £40,000 pa		Unemployed married couple with two children aged four and six	
Married couple's and personal allowance at 40%	13.64	Income Support	57.60
			12.35
			12.35
			7.35
Mortgage interest tax relief	33.46	Rent rebate	23.43
Personal pension relief	61.54	Community Charge benefit	10.58
Nat. Ins. personal pension subsidy	8.11	Free school meals	2.85
2% personal pension incentive	6.08	Free welfare milk	2.10
Personal equity plan dividend	4.62		
Total	**127.45**	**Total**	**128.61**

Sources: Child Poverty Action Group/*The Observer* 17 March 1991

week less than those paid to an unemployed person and their family. This can be seen in Table 14.5.

Occupational welfare and inequality

In the British welfare state the amount of time spent in paid employment has an effect on the state benefits that are available. This has an important effect, owing to the greater likelihood that women's paid employment will be disrupted (by looking after children) and of a part-time nature (see Section 9.3) where the contributions made will be lower. One very important effect of this is that women are less likely to attain a record of sufficient contributions to qualify for a full state pension.

A number of benefits are paid to people by their employer – in common parlance these are called 'fringe benefits'. Obviously it is necessary to be in employment to get fringe benefits, so the unemployed and full-time housewives are excluded. This is another case of inequality in occupational welfare.

However, even among the employed, occupational benefits can serve to reinforce existing inequalities. Oppenheim and Harker (1996), for example, show how the distribution of occupational benefits is clearly gendered (see Table 14.6), and other research shows that occupational benefits tend to be skewed towards the higher-paid. In a study in Australia, Jamrozik *et al.* (1981) showed that those in the top earnings bracket received 3.8 times the occupational

Table 14.6 Percentage of jobs where employer provides benefits, by gender

	Male full-timers	Female full-timers	Female part-timers
Pensions[1]	73	68	31
Sick pay[1]	66	58	27
Paid time off	64	48	30
Unpaid time off	54	54	57
Company car or van	30	10	5
Free/subsidized transport	31	24	17
Goods at a discount	47	40	31
Free or subsidized meals	39	47	25
Finance/loans	21	20	12
Accommodation	14	17	5
Life assurance	39	19	5
Private health	31	22	9
Recreation facilities	40	36	24
Maternity pay	n/a	31	16
Childcare	1	13	10

[1]Above basic government scheme
Sources: *Unequal Jobs, Unequal Pay*, ESRC, The Social Change and Economic Life Initiative, Working Paper 6, 1989/Oppenheimer and Harker, 1996, p. 105

benefits of those at the bottom. A study in the UK by the Low Pay Unit in 1984 found that a company director on £25,000 a year could receive as much as £12,500 more in fringe benefits.

Concluding comments

Social welfare on its own does not seem very redistributive. If we take into account all types of welfare, including fiscal and occupational, it seems that the better-off benefit considerably more than the rest and that the welfare regime serves to reinforce exist-

Discussion point

Of all the types of welfare discussed – social, fiscal and occupational – which do you think is the most important and which the least important in contemporary society in the UK?

ing class, gender and other inequalities. Much of this extended welfare regime remains hidden and most media concentration is on the iceberg of social welfare payments. This serves to protect the main beneficiaries from scrutiny, and the benefits themselves serve to keep certain groups privileged without too many questions being asked.

14.5 Defining poverty

The distinction between absolute and relative poverty centres around whether our conception of human need is based on biological notions or social notions. Oppenheim and Harker of the Child Poverty Action Group provide the following definitions of absolute and relative poverty:

A definition of absolute poverty assumes that it is possible to define a minimum standard of living based on a person's biological needs for food, water, clothing and shelter. ... [Relative] poverty is defined in relation to a generally accepted standard of living in a specific society at a specific time and goes beyond basic biological needs.
(Oppenheim and Harker, 1996, pp. 7 and 9)

Definitions of absolute poverty

The Poor Law (see Section 14.1) required that the principle of lesser eligibility be applied to those seeking relief: the support they were given should be less than that available through work. The administrators of the Poor Law had to arrive at a level of support which would allow people's basic biological needs to be met. This led to the idea of a subsistence level of poverty. The idea was to arrive scientifically at a set of very basic needs and to translate this into financial terms to derive a subsistence level of income.

Application of the idea of a subsistence or absolute approach to poverty is seen clearly in the work of Seebohm Rowntree (1901) in York. In order to derive a measure of poverty in York, he devised a subsistence poverty line based on the monetary value of subsistence needs. In relation to food this led him to calculate the cost of a standard diet similar to that offered in the workhouse – though as John Scott (1994) points out, as he did not include provision for fresh meat his 'diet' was even harsher than that offered to paupers in the York workhouse. In his original survey in 1899 Rowntree found that a total of 28 per cent of the population of York were in poverty. Since the main cause of poverty identified by Rowntree was low wages, his work undermined the idea behind the Poor Law which was that the main cause of poverty was indolence and laziness. This fed into pressure for social reform

leading towards establishment of the welfare state.

Rowntree (1937, 1941; and Lavers 1951) conducted follow-up surveys in later years. These showed that the proportion in poverty had fallen to 18 per cent in 1936 and 1.5 per cent in 1950. This situation was also seen as a success story for the welfare state.

Rowntree's work is important for the effect it had on sociological and government thinking on the issue of poverty. The suggestion that the problem of poverty had been solved certainly fitted in with the notion of affluence which became influential in both popular and sociological thinking in the 1950s and early 60s.

Defining relative poverty

Not everyone was convinced that the problem of poverty had been solved by the 1960s. That period witnessed the rediscovery of poverty largely through the work of Abel-Smith and Townsend (1965). In a study comparing the incidence of poverty in 1960 with that in 1954, they found that there had been an increase, from 7.8 per cent of people in 1954 to 14.2 per cent in 1960. Abel-Smith and Townsend demonstrated that far from the welfare state removing poverty, the levels of benefits paid out were so low and required such strict behaviour of the recipients that poverty could still exist and grow despite the welfare state.

The trend identified is completely the reverse of that seen in the series of studies undertaken by Rowntree, and at first sight this seems a contradiction. It is not, because Abel-Smith and Townsend were using a very different definition of poverty – which came to be known as 'relative poverty'. This rests on the idea that our needs in contemporary society are more than simply biological needs, but include the need to be able to participate in the normal activities of society. Townsend outlined the condition of relative poverty as follows:

Poverty can be defined objectively and applied consistently only in terms of the concept of relative deprivation. . . . Individuals, families and groups in the population can be said to be in poverty when they lack the resources to obtain the types of diet, participate in the activities and have the living conditions and amenities which are customary . . . in the societies to which they belong.
(Townsend, 1979, p. 31)

According to this, poverty must be defined in relation to a socially recognized standard of living, as opposed to some biological notion of subsistence. An important implication of this is that what counts as poverty differs from society to society and from time to time, as social experiences and social expectations change in a way that biological needs generally do not. Deprivation consists of more than simply biological want; it means lacking the resources to meet socially expected ways of living and therefore to make choices about how to live one's life.

Townsend followed up his early work with a national survey on poverty and a later survey of poverty in London, allowing comparisons with Charles Booth's (1902) pioneering social survey of London. In order to operationalize his definition of poverty to conduct this empirical work, Townsend constructed a deprivation index. This consisted of a list of 60 items that acted as indicators of lifestyle, the absence of which would constitute evidence of deprivation. He felt these items both reflected a range of lifestyles and allowed him to test the sort of lifestyles that are common to the majority of the population. To create his deprivation index, Townsend selected 12 items the lack of which were all linked to low income. He then set out to discover the percentage of households who lacked these items (see Table 14.7).

Table 14.7 The deprivation index

Characteristic	Percentage of population
1 Has not had a week's holiday away from home in last 12 months	53.6
2 *Adults only*. Has not had a relative or friend to the home for a meal or snack in the last 4 weeks	33.4
3 *Adults only*. Has not been out in the last 4 weeks to a relative or friend for a meal or snack	45.1
4 *Children only* (under 15). Has not had a friend to play or to tea in the last 4 weeks	36.3
5 *Children only*. Did not have party on last birthday	56.6
6 Has not had an afternoon or evening out for entertainment in the last two weeks	47.0
7 Does not have fresh meat (including meals out) as many as four days a week	19.3
8 Has gone through one or more days in the past fortnight without a cooked meal	7.0
9 Has not had a cooked breakfast most days of the week	67.3
10 Household does not have a refrigerator	45.1
11 Household does not usually have a Sunday joint (3 in 4 times)	25.9
12 Household does not have sole use of four amenities indoors (flush WC; sink or washbasin and cold-water tap; fixed bath or shower; and gas or electric cooker)	21.4

Source: Townsend (1979, p. 250)

The question arises of how many items a household must lack in order to suffer from deprivation and be classed as in poverty. Townsend used statistical techniques to show that there is a point at which lack of household resources leads to a qualitative reduction in social participation. This he found occurred when there was a household income of less than 140 per cent of the 'supplementary benefit' level. This level of income constituted the threshold of deprivation. As a result he concluded that 22.9 per cent of the population were in poverty. Townsend asserted that this statistical measure of deprivation constituted an objective measure of relative poverty. This reinforced the earlier claims by Abel-Smith and Townsend that it was possible for poverty to exist even given the existence of the welfare state and its associated benefits.

Townsend's work also calculated the extent of poverty using two other indicators. Although Townsend himself did not favour these measures they have continued to play a part in the ensuing debate. They are:

- the state's effective standard of poverty, simply measured by calculating the number of people living below an income, achieved by adding together the existing levels of supplementary benefit (now income support) and an amount for housing costs – on this basis 6.1 per cent of the population were in poverty
- the relative income measure which calculates the number of people living on less than half average income – on this basis 9.2 per cent of the population were in poverty.

Activity

Outline in a table the various stages in a research project to measure the extent of poverty. It should draw out the contrast between absolute and relative definitions of poverty, and show the effect of the difference on the way the research should be conducted.

I, A

Absolute versus relative: the continuing debate

Arising from the different definitions, estimates of the extent of poverty in the UK in the period after the 1960s vary widely, from 1.5 to 22.9 per cent. This discrepancy clearly has implications because poverty is seen as a serious social problem which governments must address.

Clearly, the adoption of a relative definition of poverty is explicitly a critique of the adequacy of an absolute definition. So far, in order to provide a clear contrast we have not delved into the details. This subsection will highlight the points of argument.

Points in favour of an absolute definition

First, a clear strength of the absolute measure is that it provides an easily understandable and universal notion of a poverty line.

Secondly, in many ways the absolute definition of poverty fits in with many people's everyday conception of what poverty is. For instance a recent British Social Attitudes survey (Taylor-Gooby, 1990) found that 60 per cent of people thought of poverty basically in subsistence terms.

Thirdly, the methodology behind the absolute approach to poverty was very influential in the development of the Beveridge Report (see Section 14.1) and therefore in the construction of welfare state policies to deal with poverty. Since government policy still operates by setting levels at which benefits will be paid, the idea of research based on the validity of these effective poverty lines still remains. So long as benefits remain based on a subsistence idea, subsistence-based research will remain attractive.

Points against an absolute definition

First, in the studies based on such a notion, the construction of a subsistence existence to define a poverty line has most often been done by 'experts', and without consistency. Rowntree included the price of tea in his original survey though it is clear that the nutritional value of this is negligible. The notion of a changing absolute is contradictory.

Secondly, even if the inconsistencies were removed, there is still the real problem of attempting to arrive at one measure of subsistence which is universally applicable. For instance the cost of living may vary from one part of the UK to another and from one social group to another.

Thirdly, it is not certain that all those researchers identified with an absolute measure of poverty in fact used such an approach. This is most clear in the case of Charles Booth since, as Trowler (1989, p. 43) points out, his definition includes phrases that indicate a more relative approach. He defined the poor as those whose income is only just sufficient for a 'decent independent life' and the very poor as those unable to live according to the 'usual standard of life in this country'.

Fourthly, despite the apparent scientificity, it is clear that a set of value judgements entered into the work of the early researchers. Beveridge himself stated that the issue of what was needed for human subsistence was ultimately a matter of judgement, and in many cases judgements have more often been made on the basis of moral rather than scientific distinctions. The distinction between the deserving and the undeserving poor, made not on the basis of levels of income or resources but on the basis of individual behaviour (see also Section 4.8), was part of the Poor Law categorization of the poor, and this distinction lingers on in the work of Booth and Rowntree.

It is of course quite possible to draw up a similar list of pros and cons associated with relative measures.

Points in favour of a relative definition

First, in support it could be said that such a measure is more able to reflect accurately the way in which poverty is a social construction since such conceptions are rooted in notions of the normal standard of living, which will obviously vary from society to society and from time to time.

Secondly, insofar as relative measures of poverty are based on the extent to which people are able to match the normal standards of involvement in society, such conceptions link discussion of poverty to other areas of social life rather than treating poverty as an isolated phenomenon. Debates about poverty are therefore linked into notions of citizenship (see Section 17.5) which affect everyone, not just the poor.

Thirdly, since relative measures of poverty do not rely on building up a single subsistence line, they are better able to reflect the diversity of lifestyles found in contemporary advanced industrial societies such as the UK. In particular in relation to Townsend's concept of deprivation, since it is not entirely reliant on the notion of income or the lack of it, it is possible to identify two different societies with essentially the same sort of distribution of income and therefore patterns of inequality, but with radically different levels of poverty, since the latter would be affected by the different societal norms operative in these two societies.

Points against a relative definition

First, despite the move away from a subsistence measure, relative poverty definitions still tend to operate with a poverty-line. Townsend, for instance, created an effective poverty-line in terms of a point where normal participation gives way to deprived participation. The reason for doing this is his argument that it is possible to arrive at an objective measure of poverty. This view has been subject to much criticism, notably from Dorothy Wedderburn (1974) who argues that the list of items which made up his deprivation index were chosen arbitrarily. As such, the index represents his subjective view and this therefore undermines its claim to objectivity.

A second criticism aimed at Townsend's index by Piachard (1987) is that, while Townsend saw lack of choice as a key element in defining poverty, his index does not take choice into account. Vegetarians would choose to go without meat on a Sunday (or indeed on any other day) but this would appear as a deprivation on Townsend's index. By definition, vegetarians do not feel deprived if they do not eat meat. Townsend's list therefore makes a choice seem like a lack of choice or a deprivation. While this criticism is valid for some specific items on Townsend's list, it is questionable whether it is of general applicability. It is more difficult, for instance, to see how lack of a fridge could be put down to choice.

Thirdly, much of Townsend's empirical work has in fact investigated the extent of poverty measured by using fixed empirical measures – such as the level at which benefits are paid. His survey of London, for example, found that 7 per cent of Londoners were living on incomes below the level at which benefits were paid. The term 'living in the margins of poverty' is more often used to describe those living below Townsend's theoretically derived poverty line (i.e on income above the benefit level but less than 140 per cent of that level).

In the same vein, Sen (1983) has argued that all relative definitions have an absolute core in that they use fixed measures such as nutritional requirements to measure relative living standards. It is also often felt that using an absolute measure is easier for campaigning purposes as it is more easily understood by the general population.

Fourthly, it has been argued – most prominently by those of a New Right persuasion – that relative poverty is simply a measure not of poverty but of inequality. They argue that if we take the measure of relative poverty based on those who earn less than 50 per cent of average earnings, such people will always exist unless we achieve a society with nearly even distribution of income. Relative poverty is therefore seen as an ideologically motivated attack on inequality, disguised as a measure of poverty. As an example, Marsland argues that:

*The so-called relative concept of poverty is a pure nonsense designed to keep alive the guttering flame of Marxist and socialist critique of capitalism. Its implication, which is self-evidently ludicrous, is that there is worse poverty in Britain than in Uganda. . . . It underpins ludicrous headlines such as 'Third of Britons live in poverty' (*Times Higher Educational Supplement, 11 March 1994*) . . . As John Moore put it, in commenting on Poverty lobby manipulations of income data, 'It is utterly absurd to speak as if one in three people in Britain today is in dire need. These claims are false and they are dangerous'.*
(Marsland, 1996, p. 47)

Another criticism can be levelled against the main alternative way of operationalizing relative poverty, the measure adopted by Townsend himself of income

below 140 per cent of the benefit level. There are two points of criticism here.

- Since the levels of benefits are not objective but are set by politicians, any measure based on the benefits system is inevitably mired in the same non-objective political process.
- The logic of this measure leads to the conclusion that if benefits were abolished poverty would be as well; or conversely, an increase in benefits would lead to an increase in poverty. This is clearly contrary to the real effect of such potential measures.

Fifthly, the indicators used to measure relative poverty (namely income less than 50 per cent of average income or below 140 per cent of the benefit level) are open to the criticism that the percentages chosen are arbitrary and subjective.

Sixthly, it has been argued by Roll (1992) that a relative definition would deny the existence of poverty in a country where everyone was starving and/or where there was a drastic but evenly spread fall in everyone's living standard. (See also Section 12.8.)

Concluding comments

The debate seems intractable. It does have political and ideological elements, since any definition of poverty provides the basis for its measurement – and therefore pressure on government to do something about it. Variations of both definitions continue to exist, though contemporary versions have become more sophisticated than the original formulations, as the next subsection shows.

Activity

Outline the policy implications of the choice between defining poverty in absolute or relative terms. You could do this by listing the kind of policies each definition would lead to for a government attempting to alleviate 'poverty'.

A

Contemporary definitions of poverty

Starting with those studies which operate within the broad framework of the absolutist tradition, it is clear that the enduring appeal of this approach is its easy application to applied social research with the aim of getting the government to do something.

Precisely because decisions about benefits are not dry academic exercises but are taken in a political context, scope for research was created by the decision of the government to set the initial levels of benefits below those recommended by Beveridge. The actual levels of benefit appear to have been set some 40–45 per cent lower than those shown to be necessary in Rowntree's 1936 survey. Since governments have failed to consistently uprate benefits in line with inflation, a difference can still be shown to exist today between subsistence needs measured in ways similar to Rowntree's and the actual benefits paid out. One stark illustration of this is research which shows that the amount of money paid out to cover food for children would be insufficient to buy the minimal diet laid down in the workhouse in 1876 (at today's prices). (See page 573.)

Piachard showed in 1979 that amounts allowed for children in supplementary benefit payments covered only about 66 per cent of the actual cost of raising a child, and child benefit for working parents covered about 50 per cent of such cost. Bradshaw *et al.* (1992; quoted in Oppenheim, 1993, p. 50), using a budget standard drawn up using actual patterns of expenditure, showed that income support would provide 34–39 per cent of the cost of their modest but adequate budget. Similarly a study conducted in 1993 to estimate the cost of a modest but adequate family budget and a low-cost budget using methods similar to Rowntree's showed that benefit levels did not meet such basic subsistence needs. A two-adult, two-child family received 31 per cent less in state benefits than the survey suggested was

	Total weekly expenses (£) (excluding rent)	Total benefit (£)
Pensioner (owner occupier)	67.06	57.15
Pensioner (LA* tenant)	53.36	57.15
2 adults, 2 children** (LA* tenant)	141.40	105.00
Lone parent 2 children** (LA* tenant)	110.72	85.60

All households are assumed to receive the maximum benefits and rent is therefore excluded as it is covered by housing benefits.
*LA = Local Authority
**Children aged between 4 and 10

Figure 14.5 Keeping the family on low-cost budgets (£ per week, April 1992 prices). Source: *The Guardian* 11 November 1992

needed on their low-cost budget. This can be seen in Figure 14.5.

It seems, therefore, that contrary to popular belief the levels of benefits paid out by the welfare state are often far from generous, and in many instances fall below what is deemed necessary by studies conducted using methodology similar to the originators of the notion of absolute poverty.

Of course, it is true that until the mid-1980s most sociologists appeared to accept the thrust of the case for defining poverty in relative terms rather than absolute, and as such the notion has spurred research, most notably the two Breadline Britain studies conducted in 1983 and 1990 by Mack and Lansley (1985, 1992). They accepted that poverty should be defined in relative terms and therefore centre on the notion of deprivation. However, in order to avoid the criticism levelled at Townsend – namely that his list of items was arbitrarily selected by himself – they set out to arrive at a consensual measure of need by asking a sample of respondents whether they thought items on a list were necessities or not. This allows them to argue that their standard of necessity is not one set by themselves but by the prevailing societal norms, shown by the results of their survey.

In order to ensure that the items in their 'deprivation index' were considered necessities, Mack and Lansley included only those felt to be necessities by at least 50 per cent of their respondents. Having constructed an index, they could then set out to discover the number of households lacking such items. The findings from their first survey are set out in Table 14.8.

Clearly from this table the question then arises of how many items one needs to lack in order to be in deprivation. Mack and Lansley's answer is that lacking three or more necessities represented a point where deprivation had a pervasive impact on

Table 14.8 Multiple deprivation 1983: percentage lacking necessities

No. of necessities lacked	All adults	Bottom 10% income	Top 30% income
0	66	29	82
1 or more	34	71	18
2 or more	19	52	7
3 or more	12	39	4
4 or more	10	34	3
5 or more	8	29	2
6 or more	5	21	1
7 or more	4	19	0

Source: Mack and Lansley (1985, p. 107)

people's lives, and this therefore became their cut-off point. From Table 14.8 we can see that 12 per cent of the population were in poverty in 1983, a total of 7.5 million people, which even includes 4 per cent of those in the top 30 per cent of income earners.

In 1990 Mack and Lansley found that the number in poverty had increased to 11 million people (20 per cent of the population) including more than 3 million children. They comment:

These are much higher than the equivalent figures for 1983. They present a stark alternative to images of universal gains in prosperity.

(Mack and Lansley quoted in Frayman, 1991, p. 10)

Some of the findings from the 1990 survey are outlined below.

- Roughly 10 million people in the UK today cannot afford adequate housing; for example, their home is unheated or damp or the older children have to share bedrooms.
- About 7 million go without essential clothing, such as a warm waterproof coat.
- There are approximately 2.5 million children who are forced to go without at least one of the things they need, like three meals a day, toys, or out-of-school activities.
- Around 5 million people are not properly fed by today's standards – they don't have enough fresh fruit and vegetables, or two meals a day, for example.
- About 6.5 million people cannot afford one or more typical household good, like a fridge, a phone, or carpets for living areas.
- At least one of the necessities which 'make life worth living' – hobbies, holidays, celebrations etc.' – are too expensive for about 21 million people.
- More than 31 million people – over half the population – live without minimal financial security. They say they cannot save £10 a month, or insure the contents of their homes, or both.

The innovative use of a questionnaire (see Section 3.7) designed to elicit what people themselves (as opposed to panels of experts) considered to be necessities has led to this being called the 'consensus' notion of necessities and of the level of goods needed to avoid 'being in poverty'. This approach has been more recently applied in research by the Child Poverty Action Group (Middleton *et al.*, 1994).

Discussion point

To what extent are definitions of poverty now determined by political ideologies rather than scientific objective evidence? Will this always be the case?

14.6 The extent of poverty in the UK

Precisely because there is no fundamental agreement about definitions of poverty, there is no one universally accepted measure of the extent of poverty today. An ideological edge was given to the debate by recent Conservative governments reversing their earlier acceptance of the notion that poverty should be measured in relative terms and moving back towards an absolute approach. As a result, the extent of poverty today can vary from the negligible amount seen to exist in the statement made by John Moore in 1989 (then a Conservative Cabinet Minister) announcing the shift back to absolute measures, up to approximately 22 per cent of the population according to the findings of the Breadline Britain 1990s survey.

Although there has never been an official poverty-line in the UK, because governments have consistently failed to devise one, benefits are calculated to provide for a person's basic needs and to avoid creating a disincentive to work. The level at which benefits are paid might therefore arguably be seen as a proxy for such a poverty-line. The main alternative choice is to measure the proportion of the population living below 50 per cent of average income, after housing costs. Using this measure, Oppenheim and Harker (1996) provide a summary of recent trends in the extent of poverty (see Figure 14.6).

It is clear that, on this measure, the extent of poverty has risen quite dramatically in recent decades. In his book on poverty and wealth, Scott argues that this reflects:

... a marked reduction in inequality between 1968 and 1979, followed by a sharp rise over the following decade.

(Scott, 1994, p. 92) (See also Sections 4.10 and 14.8.)

The picture of a marked rise in the number in poverty is still true even if we use the alternative measure of the proportion of the population below the level of income support. Statistics show that this number has risen from 6 per cent of the population in 1979 to 8 per cent in 1992 – some 4.7 million people.

Since income support is paid at a level which meets basic needs it is sometimes difficult to see how people living below this level survive. The explanation for this rests on the evidence that means-tested benefits are not claimed by all of those eligible to receive them. Oppenheim and Harker (1996) reveal that about £2 billion worth of means-tested benefits to which people were entitled went unclaimed in 1992, which underlines the scale of this problem. As a result their actual income falls below that set out

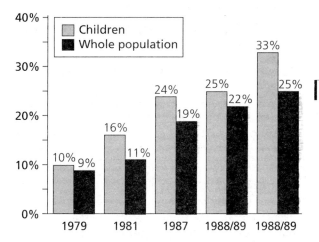

Figure 14.6 Proportion of children and population living in poverty between 1979 and 1992/3 (living below 50% average income after housing costs). Source: Oppenheim and Harker (1996, p. 37) using data from DSS, *Households below average income, 1979–1988/9* and *1979–1992/3*, HMSO, 1992 and 1995

in the benefits legislation. This can be seen in Table 14.9.

The view that poverty is rising is, however, unlikely to be shared by government ministers. One of the key criticisms of these contemporary measures of poverty arises from the New Right contention that this in reality reflects not a rise in poverty but a rise in inequality. This was perhaps made most explicit by the Secretary of State for Social Security in a statement in May 1989 against the poverty lobby:

Their purpose in calling 'poverty' what is in reality simply inequality is so they can call western material capitalism a failure.

(John Moore, quoted in *The Guardian*, 12 May 1989)

He went on to argue that poverty in the sense of 'want' had been eliminated, and that the poor today had affluence beyond the dreams of the early poverty researchers This view affected the government's policy.

Table 14.9 Take-up rates for various benefits (the percentage of those eligible actually claiming)

Name of benefit	Nature of benefit	Take-up rate (%)
Income support	Means-tested	81
Family credit	Means-tested	51
Housing benefit	Means-tested	80
Retirement pension	Not means-tested	100
Child benefit	Not means-tested	100

Source: Department of Social Security (1992), *Social Security Statistics*, London, HMSO, p. 349

In response, the poverty lobby – notably the Child Poverty Action Group – has published a number of studies using the government's own official statistics to challenge this picture.

Official statistics on poverty

Two important series of data are published by the government which provide indications of the level of poverty. Until 1988 the government provided statistics on low-income families (LIF), but since then this measure has been replaced by statistics on households below average income (HBAI). While these provide a rich source of data, they have one problem in common: both are derived from the annual *Family Expenditure Survey* (FES) which omits the homeless and people living in institutions from its sample. (See also Section 3.5.) Since these are groups likely to contain many people with little money, statistics derived from this source are bound to underestimate the extent of poverty.

Until 1988, LIF statistics used to measure the extent to which there were families surviving on incomes less than the value of basic state benefit: income support (IS), previously supplementary benefit (SB). Using both the officially published statistics and the later calculations of the extent of LIF produced by independent researchers, Oppenheim (1990, 1993) and Oppenheim and Harker (1996) conclude that the numbers in poverty increased from 6 million (12 per cent of the population) in 1979, to 10 million in 1987 (19 per cent), 11.3 million (20 per cent) in 1989, and 13 million (25 per cent) in 1993.

From 1989 the government replaced the LIF statistics with HBAI. One of the reasons for this was the conviction that the statistics in fact measure inequality rather than poverty *per se*, in line with the government view as outlined in John Moore's speech quoted above. It also reflects the government's opposition to the use of the IS/SB scales as a poverty benchmark, and the suggestion that households are more appropriate measures of income since they often share resources. It has been pointed out (Alcock, 1993) that this is a contested claim since families rather than households are more likely to share resources. (See also Section 7.5.)

Nonetheless since one of the commonly used measures of poverty is those households on less than 50 per cent of average income, this has been used to provide such a measure. The Child Poverty Action Group has published figures derived from these statistics and argue that they present similar results:

Despite their different approaches, what both methods reveal is that:

• *In 1992, 4,740,000 people (8 per cent of the*

population) were living below income support level. In 1979, 6 per cent of the population were living below the supplementary benefit level.

- *In 1992, 13,680,000 people (24 per cent of the population) were living on or below the income support level. In 1979, 14 per cent of the population were living on or below the supplementary benefit level.*

- *In 1992–3, 14.1 million people (25 per cent of the population) were living below 50 per cent of average income after housing costs. In 1979, 9 per cent of the population were living below 50 per cent of average income after housing costs.*

So, whichever way you measure it, poverty has grown significantly over recent years and by 1992–3, between 13 and 14 million people in the United Kingdom – around a quarter of our society – were living in poverty.

(Oppenheim and Harker, 1996, p. 24)

Using DSS publications, Alcock argues that these trends show that:

Despite government claims of growing affluence for all over this period, the 1988–9 figures also show a decline in real terms (against inflation) of 6 per cent in the incomes of the bottom 10 per cent of the population.

(Alcock, 1993, p. 17)

The extent of this growth in inequality can be further glimpsed through statistics from the *Family Expenditure Survey*. These show that between 1979 and 1994 the highest earners (the top 10 per cent) increased their income in real terms by 62 per cent while the income of the poorest tenth fell (again in real terms) by 17 per cent. (See also Section 14.8.)

This does demonstrate greater inequality. However, the growth in inequality on the HBAI figures has been shown to be less than would have been the case if the old LIF statistics had been continued (Johnson and Webb, 1990). There is, therefore, suspicion that this change in the presentation of official statistics (see Section 3.11) may have been motivated partly to minimize the apparent extent of growing inequality.

The New Right criticism that there has been an attack on inequality dressed up as an attack on poverty could still be validly made, and it is also clear that they would hold very different views on the positive or negative implications of the growth in inequality. (See also Section 14.9.) Saunders (1995), probably one of the best known sociologists who broadly supports the New Right position, has argued that, while it is true that capitalism creates considerable inequalities, it nonetheless raises the living standards of both the wealthy and the poor. Inequality, he says, is necessary since this is the

engine which provides the motivation for the creation of wealth which will raise the living standards of all:

The enhanced wealth created by capitalism has benefited all social classes and . . . the luxuries enjoyed by the few in one generation rapidly become the norm for the majority in the next . . . for capitalism thrives on mass markets and cannot survive on demand from the rich alone.

(Saunders, 1995, pp. 13–14)

Increased inequality will clearly increase the numbers in poverty on relative measures, but Saunders argues that this inequality will also increase the standard of living of those at the bottom by first creating greater incentives for the wealth creators at the top of society. This is known as the 'trickle-down thesis' and is the New Right's defence of greater inequality. Thus the evidence of greater inequality would not be accepted by New Right thinkers as a bad thing, but rather as a good thing (with certain concerns that it does not go too far). Saunders asserts that capitalism has raised the general standard of living so much that 'what we call poverty today would have represented "affluence" just a few generations earlier'. He argues, therefore, that the reconceptualization of poverty from absolute subsistence measures to relative poverty is the result of capitalism since it has increased the living standards and therefore the relative standards of all.

Discussion point

To what extent do you agree with Peter Saunder's statement?

What are the implications of this viewpoint?

The distribution of poverty in the 1990s

In the 1980s the number of poor households in the UK (see Section 14.8) increased dramatically. A European Commission report stated that almost 25 per cent of poor households in Europe were in the UK. It went on to show that the number of poor people, defined as those who spend less than 50 per cent of the national average, had increased in the UK from 1980 to 1985, reaching 10.3 million people, while the number in other EU countries remained broadly static.

A report by the Joseph Rowntree Foundation (1995) claims that, since the late 1970s, income inequality has been growing more rapidly in the UK than in any other country with the exception of New Zealand.

Narrowing the focus to look at the numbers in poverty (measured by those living on less than 50 per cent of average income) shows that they have increased from 9 per cent of the population in 1979 to 25 per cent in 1993. However, this does not tell us anything about who these people are, or whether those in poverty in 1993 were significantly different from those in poverty in 1979. This requires us to consider the *distribution* of poverty. There are two ways of looking at this, as Oppenheim and Harker explain:

We can look at the composition of the poor – which groups make up the bulk of those in poverty; we can also assess the risk of poverty – which groups are most likely to be poor. These two things are different – e.g. lone parents make up only a small proportion of the total number of people in poverty as they are a small group; however, they have a high risk of poverty.
(Oppenheim and Harker, 1996, p. 34)

Activity

Study Figures 14.7 and 14.8 and identify the following social groups:

a the social group by family status which comprises the smallest proportion of the poor

b the social group by economic status which comprises the largest proportion of the poor

c the social group by economic status which has the smallest risk of being in poverty

d the social group by family status which has the largest risk of being in poverty

e one social group by economic status which comprises a fairly small proportion of the poor but with a moderately high risk of being in poverty

f one social group by family status which comprises a relatively large proportion of the poor but with a fairly low risk of being in poverty

g two social groups in each of the status diagrams with the highest risk of being in poverty (excluding 'others').

In contrast with the earlier figures produced by Oppenheim (1993), a few changes can be highlighted. The elderly now cromprise a smaller proportion of the poor than in 1989, while lone parents and the unemployed comprise a larger proportion. Equally, pensioners now face a lower risk of being in poverty (40 per cent of households with

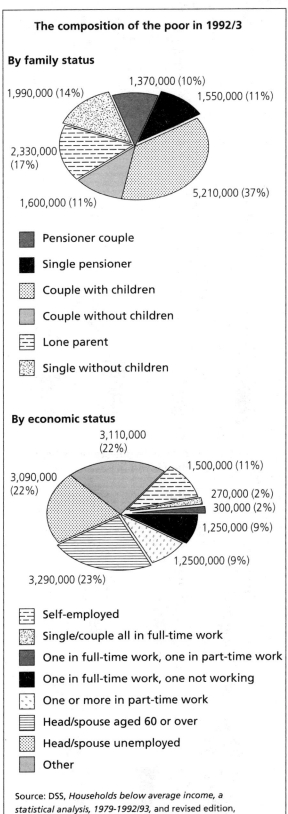

The composition of the poor in 1992/3

By family status

1,370,000 (10%)
1,550,000 (11%)
1,990,000 (14%)
2,330,000 (17%)
5,210,000 (37%)
1,600,000 (11%)

- Pensioner couple
- Single pensioner
- Couple with children
- Couple without children
- Lone parent
- Single without children

By economic status

3,110,000 (22%)
3,090,000 (22%)
1,500,000 (11%)
270,000 (2%)
300,000 (2%)
1,250,000 (9%)
1,2500,000 (9%)
3,290,000 (23%)

- Self-employed
- Single/couple all in full-time work
- One in full-time work, one in part-time work
- One in full-time work, one not working
- One or more in part-time work
- Head/spouse aged 60 or over
- Head/spouse unemployed
- Other

Source: DSS, *Households below average income, a statistical analysis, 1979-1992/93,* and revised edition, HMSO, 1995.

Figure 14.7 The composition of the poor, defined as living below 50 per cent of average income, after housing costs. Source: Oppenheim and Harker (1996, p. 35)

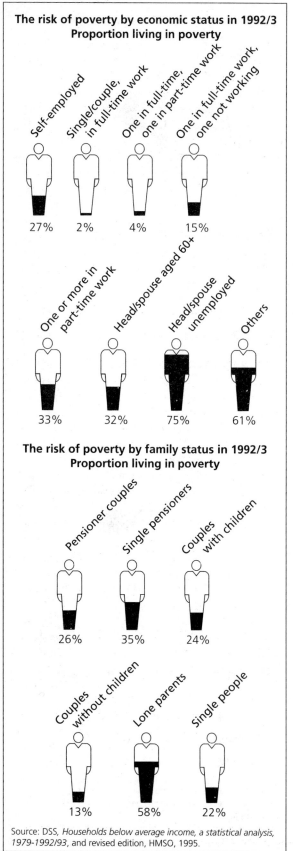

The risk of poverty by economic status in 1992/3
Proportion living in poverty

Self-employed	Single/couple, in full-time work	One in full-time, one in part-time work	One in full-time work, one not working
27%	2%	4%	15%

One or more in part-time work	Head/spouse aged 60+	Head/spouse unemployed	Others
33%	32%	75%	61%

The risk of poverty by family status in 1992/3
Proportion living in poverty

Pensioner couples	Single pensioners	Couples with children
26%	35%	24%

Couples without children	Lone parents	Single people
13%	58%	22%

Source: DSS, *Households below average income, a statistical analysis, 1979-1992/93*, and revised edition, HMSO, 1995.

*Defined as living below 50% of average income after housing costs.

Figure 14.8 The risk of poverty. Source: Oppenheim and Harker (1996, p. 40)

head/spouse aged 60+ were in poverty in 1989) and the unemployed and lone parents face a greater risk (69 per cent of households with head/spouse unemployed were in poverty in 1989, and 50 per cent of lone-parent families were in poverty in 1989).

A number of social groups have consistently appeared in studies and commentaries about poverty because they have always constituted a great proportion of the poor. These groups are pensioners, the sick and disabled, single parents and the unemployed. This shows that vulnerability to poverty is not equally spread but is affected by gender, age, disability and class. Those social divisions which lie at the heart of all social stratification therefore perhaps unsurprisingly lie at the heart of the construction and distribution of poverty. However, as Oppenheim (1990, 1993), Oppenheim and Harker (1996) and Alcock (1993) point out, the relative importance of these groups among the poor has changed dramatically over the last 25 years (see Table 14.10).

Activity

a From Table 14.10 identify the groups that have increased as a proportion of the poorest fifth and those that have decreased, between 1979 and 1992/3.

b Using material from this chapter, suggest possible reasons for these changes and consider their relative importance. **I, A, E**

Table 14.10 The changing composition of the poorest tenth between 1979 and 1992/3 (percentages, after housing costs)

	1979	1988/9	1992/3
By family status			
Pensioner couple	20	6	4
Single pensioner	11	8	4
Couple with children	41	44	47
Couple without children	9	10	15
Lone parent	9	10	11
Single without children	10	22	19

Sources: Oppenheim (1993, p. 47) and Oppenheim and Harker (1996, p. 40)

We can identify two major reasons for this: changes in the labour market (see Chapter 9) and family structure (see Chapter 7). The end of the Beveridge-inspired commitment to full employment, and the reassertion of the ideas of the free market with a greater emphasis on flexibility, has led to the return of mass unemployment. In April 1994, official unemployment figures showed there were 2,734,400 out of work, representing 9.7 per cent of the workforce. This is extremely high compared with annual averages of 1.7 per cent for 1951–64 and 2.0 per cent for 1964–70. The result is higher levels of poverty since income for the unemployed is well below average income. For instance, Micklewright (1985) estimated that for a single man with no children, unemployment benefits would equal 27 per cent of the average male manual wage. (See also Section 9.6.)

Secondly, the number of single-parent families has increased over the period. Eight per cent of families with children were lone parents in 1971, but this rose to 12 per cent in 1979, 16 per cent in 1989 and 20 per cent in 1991. The vast majority of these (over 90 per cent) are headed by women. It is also the case that the proportion of single mothers in employment has decreased from 49 per cent in 1979 to 41 per cent in 1993. (See also Section 7.4.)

As a result these two groups (the unemployed and lone parents) constitute a much greater proportion of the poor than in the past, and consequently other groups have fallen as a proportion of the total poor. One of the most important outcomes is a shift from those groups traditionally seen as part of the deserving poor (the elderly, the sick and disabled) to groups often seen as part of the undeserving poor (the unemployed, single-parent families). As a result the extent to which consideration of poverty and the poor is burdened with moralistic distinctions has grown. (See also Section 4.8.)

Gender and poverty

Women appear in a number of the groups most likely to suffer poverty. Women's life expectancy is longer so they are more likely to feature among pensioners in poverty. Also, about 90 per cent of single-parent families are headed by a woman. Changes to family structures – in particular the rise in divorce, which is the most common cause of single-parent families – have led to greater numbers of women being identified among those in poverty.

In 1992, 5.4 million women and 4.2 million men were living in poverty (on or below the income support level) according to Oppenheim and Harker (1996).

In their studies of women and poverty from a broadly feminist perspective, Glendinning and Millar (1987, 1992) refer to the growth in usage of the term the 'feminisation of poverty'. By this is sometimes meant that the extent of poverty suffered by women has increased. However, one problem with this notion is that it can serve to hide the extent to which women have always experienced poverty. Lewis and Piachard (1992) pointed out that 61 per cent of adults on poor relief at the beginning of the century were women, while Oppenheim (1993) calculates

that 62 per cent of those dependent on state benefits in 1991 were women.

Glendinning and Millar therefore argue that the only consistent usage for the term must be a growing awareness of the extent to which women suffer from poverty.

One of the main reasons for the majority of the poor being women relates to their secondary position in the labour market (see also Section 9.3). Glendinning and Millar say that, although women are participating in greater numbers in the labour market, they have not achieved equality of pay, and many have found themselves in insecure, low-paid, part-time work: something like 80 per cent of part-time workers are women. Callender (1992) says that, despite the fact that unemployment remains higher for men than women, the insecurity of such jobs has made women much more susceptible to unemployment. She points out that between 1979 and 1986 male unemployment rose by 146 per cent and female unemployment by 276 per cent. In a study looking at the interrelationship between gendered employment and pension entitlements, Bernard et al. (1995) say that the increasing phenomenon of early retirement may lead to increased risk of poverty among older women owing to their interrupted career patterns and low earnings during their employed lives, since this will largely determine their financial circumstances in retirement.

A second area of concern is the treatment of women in the social security system and the effect this has on their likelihood of being poor. Because the British welfare system is based largely on an insurance model where contributions made by those in work count towards their benefit, the historical lesser involvement of women in the labour market has had the effect of reducing their eligibility for benefits. Women are less likely than men to have made full national insurance contributions and therefore are more likely to be ineligible for a number of benefits.

Changes in the nature of the welfare state have exacerbated these divisions. The re-emergence of an emphasis on care in the community has in many cases meant care by women (see also Sections 7.6, 13.6 and 14.2): this has further reduced their ability to enter the labour market. Also, the change to greater amounts of welfare being dispensed via occupational pensions has meant that women have less access to these, again owing to their secondary position in the labour market.

Arber and Ginn (1991, 1995) have written extensively about the situation faced by women and the interrelationship between gender and age. They consider the extent to which there is pressure on women to retire if their husbands retire early.

Although they point out that such situations do exist, and such pressures may lead women to retire early with negative financial consequences, in some ways the pressure on women to fit in with the employment pattern of their male partner may be less among those in their 50s since the male is more likely to have a pension and therefore not be reliant on means-tested benefits. It is the rules concerning partner's earnings within these benefits that lead to women of unemployed men being much more likely to be unemployed themselves among younger age groups.

In another piece of work on this issue, Groves (1992) points out that while pensions often make provision for widows based on their husbands' contributions, such rights may well be lost to the wife when couples divorce, though the man would retain such rights. Given that the divorce rate is increasing and that women live longer than men, this will increase the likelihood of a woman falling into poverty in retirement.

The increasing numbers of lone-parent families also largely affects women. The need to provide childcare and the problems of doing so on the lower wages women get make this group particularly susceptible to the risk of poverty. While married mothers were participating in larger numbers in paid employment in the 1980s, the proportion of lone mothers (with children under 15) in paid employment declined from 45 per cent in 1981 to 39 per cent in 1990 (Bartholomew *et al.*, 1992). Government plans to end the lone-parent benefit on the grounds that it encourages single parents met with a barrage of criticism, because it was argued this would mean that single parents became even more dependent on the state because it would adversely affect only those in employment (see Figure 14.9).

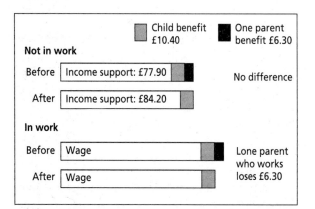

Figure 14.9 The effects of scrapping one-parent benefit on a family with one child. Source: *The Guardian*, 5 September 1995

Ethnicity and poverty

A specific question on ethnicity was included in the Census only in 1991, owing to fears about the use to which such data might by put (see Section 6.3). It is also the case that the DSS does not classify claimants by ethnic origin. There is therefore a paucity of official information on this issue.

However, Alcock (1993) says there is evidence to show that black people are likely to feature among many of the social groups who are known to suffer a greater risk of poverty. Here again it is both the employment structure and the institutions of the welfare state which seem to be the main culprits.

Amin and Oppenheim (1992), in a survey of poverty and ethnicity produced for the Child Poverty Action Group and the Runnymede Trust, point out that unemployment for black people is much higher than for whites. Table 14.11 provides recent figures on such divisions.

Table 14.11 Unemployment* rates (percentages) in the UK in 1994, by sex, age and ethnic origin

	Men		Women	
	All aged 16+	16–24	All aged 16+	16–24
Whites	11	18	7	12
Ethnic minorities	25	37	16	27
Ratio W/EM	2.27	2.05	2.28	2.25

*ILO unemployment rates
Source: Adapted from Oppenheim and Harker (1996, p. 116)

Activity
From Table 14.11, identify the social group where the ratio of the unemployment rate for ethnic minorites compared with white people is highest, and the social group where it is lowest. What does the information in this table suggest about the relative importance of ethnicity and the other social divisions shown in the table?

I, A

It is also evident that ethnic minorities have employment prospects that are skewed towards the lower-paid jobs (see also Section 9.3). In the third Policy Studies Institute research report on ethnic inequality in the UK, Brown (1984) found that while only 3 per cent of white men were in unskilled manual jobs, 9 per cent of West Indians were and 6 per cent of Asians were. A survey in the city of Leicester found that average pay for full-time workers among both ethnic minority men and women was 82 per cent of that for white men and women. The higher levels of unemployment and lower pay makes it much more likely that ethnic minority groups will need the support of the welfare state. Here, however, there are a number of problems.

The difficulties range from outright racism towards claimants from ethnic minorities, to a number of requirements in the legislation which make it less likely that ethnic minorities groups will be eligible. Alcock (1993) points out that their life-experience of immigration to this country as adults and possibly spending periods abroad means they are less likely to qualify for full benefits based on NI contributions. This makes them more dependent on means-testing, but it has been shown that they are less likely to claim such benefits. In a study of Batley in West Yorkshire, Gordon and Newnham (1985) found that 39 per cent of immigrant families were not claiming benefits to which they were entitled, compared with 23 per cent of the indigenous population. Likely reasons for such reluctance are racism, and problems of language and/or cultural differences.

One further important reason may be fears over their status in this country, fuelled by recent debates about illegal immigrants. Alcock (1993) quotes evidence to show that, although it is not meant to be a routine requirement, the practice of checking the passport of an ethnic minority claimant acts as a powerful disincentive to claim. Residence requirements also make recent immigrants ineligible for a number of benefits, notably those relating to disability.

As a result of racism, they are also likely to suffer from wider deprivation, for example in relation to housing, education and health:

Poverty as deprivation includes a broader range of disadvantages, exclusions and powerlessness resulting in a quality of life which is poorer and more restricted. For black people in Britain the existence of racism at all levels within the social structure means that most of these broader features of deprivation are also likely to affect them disproportionately.
(Alcock, 1993, p. 153)

Oppenheim (1993) points out that since the ethnic minority population has a younger age profile than the population as a whole, they will have been disproportionately affected by changes to the benefits system, such as the freezing of child benefit in the mid-1980s and the cuts in income support for young people.

14.7 Poverty: conflicting explanations and solutions

Proposed solutions depend on the various explanations of the causes of poverty. These tend to fall into two broad camps, the individualist/cultural and the structural. What differentiates them is the abiding moral element to British social policy: should those in poverty be viewed as unfortunate victims requir-

Activity

If the term 'poverty' carries with it the implication and moral imperative that something should be done about it, then the study of poverty is only justifiable if it influences individual and social attitudes and actions.
(Piachard, 1987, p. 61)

a Make a list of the arguments for and against this statement.

b Assess this issue by considering the relative strengths of the two lists you have drawn up and coming to your own conclusion about which contains the stronger case.

I, A, E

ing help, or as profligate idlers requiring motivation or punishment? (See also Section 4.8.) The notion of the deserving and the undeserving poor is still alive and well, as Lister points out:

There has always been a tendency to categorize poor people . . . according to their respectability or 'deservingness', i.e. according to moral rather than economic or demographic characteristics.
(Lister, 1991, p. 194)

This can perhaps best be seen in the growth of the notion of an 'underclass' (see also Section 4.8), certain versions of which certainly contain the implication that the reason people are poor is because of their own behaviour.

However, one of the problems the poor face is that the cost of unhealthy food is cheaper than more healthy food, and the growth of out-of-town supermarkets has confined the poor without private transport to using local shops which tend to be more expensive. This can be seen in Figure 14.10.

The political implications of this for social policy are clear. If we adopt a structural explanation of poverty, then the government should do something to alleviate the distress. On the other hand, a cultural approach implies less the need for government financial assistance than for campaigns to get the poor to change their behaviour. These campaigns need not necessarily imply spending more money. Indeed, some writers in the tradition of the New Right (see Section 2.10) argue that spending more to help those in poverty is actually part of the problem, not a solution.

Structural approaches to poverty

This term covers a variety of perspectives, ranging from Marxist and feminist approaches through to social democratic arguments. (See also Sections 2.5 and 2.6.)

£14	£9.80
Weekly cost per person of a healthy diet – 1986	**Weekly spending in a low income family – 1986**

Increase in food price (1982–6)

Healthy food		**Not so healthy food**	
Wholemeal bread	17%	White bread	15%
Green vegetables	17–51%	Biscuits	19%
Salad vegetables	29–37%	Sugar	13%
Root vegetables	22–42%	Beef, lamb, pork	9–14%
Fresh fruit	16–45%	Bacon	13%
Fruit juice	64%	Sausages	13%
Poultry	26%	Whole milk	17%
White fish	44%	Butter	9%

Figure 14.10 The rising cost of eating well. Source: *The Observer*, October 1995

Poorest claimants are refused help

NICHOLAS TIMMINS

Almost a quarter of a million applications for a loan to the Social Fund have been turned down because those seeking help were judged too poor to be able to repay, according to official figures.

The fund, set up in 1986, provides the emergency safety net for people on income support who take the interest-free loans to buy furniture, cookers or other capital items, with the repayments deducted from their benefit. However, those with existing loans or who already have direct deductions to meet fuel or other debts can be refused a loan on the grounds that they have too little benefit left to make the repayments.

Refusals on the ground of inability to pay have more than doubled since 1992–93, up from 44,890 to 116,095 last year, according to figures provided by Ian Magee, chief executive of the Benefits Agency, to Alan Milburn, Labour MP for Darlington. Precise comparisons are difficult due to a switch from counting applications for loans to counting the number of items refused. But refusals on one count or the other now total almost 250,000 over the past three years.

Mr Milburn said the figures showed that Peter Lilley, Secretary of State for Social Security, was betraying his pledge to target help on the most needy. "The very people that the Social Fund was designed to help now find they are too poor to qualify," he said. "Even before ministers take the axe to social security spending again, thousands of vulnerable people are being left without a vital lifeline."

Source: *The Independent*, 16 October 1995

Social democratic perspectives

Social democracy encompasses a wide spectrum of people who broadly share the belief that a market economy left to its own devices will create large income inequalities and therefore poverty, but that such a situation can be changed through government intervention acting through the parliamentary system. Clearly this is one motivation for setting up the welfare state based on the principle of full employment and universal provision of certain benefits.

The key cause of poverty according to writers in this tradition is the operation of the labour market, and in particular the creation of high levels of unemployment (see Section 9.6). Townsend (1979) certainly sees the operation of the labour market as a central cause of poverty. Since participation in the labour market is seen to be the main source of income for most people, exclusion from work is likely to be a weighty factor.

Changes to the labour market in the 1980s and 90s under the impact of the New Right promotion of a 'flexible' enterprise economy (see Section 9.4) led to a rise in the numbers unemployed and to the creation of a whole raft of new jobs, often part time and often poorly paid. Opportunities for the unemployed to remove themselves from poverty by finding well-paid jobs have been reduced. Changes to the taxes and benefits system have also meant the widening of inequalities (see Section 14.8) and a reduction in the real value of benefits, leaving those dependent on them for their income worse off. One example of this is the shift from grants to loans in the social fund which has led to some in need being refused assistance precisely because they are poor. This can be seen in the article 'Poorest claimants are refused help'.

💬 Discussion point

To what extent do you think the refusals outlined in the article 'Poorest claimants are refused help' are justified?

A second example of how government operation of the social security system affects the level of poverty is the 'poverty trap'. This affects those in low-paid employment: a large proportion of any increase in earnings is clawed back in reduced entitlement to social security benefits. In the past this meant that for some, for every extra £1 earned, they lost more than £1 in benefits and therefore lost out overall. Oppenheim and Harker (1996) point out that in 1985/6 there were some 290 000 familes who stood to lose between 70p and 99p out of every extra £1 earned because of this, and by 1993/4 this figure had increased to 640 000 familes. Thus the poverty trap catches more people today. Thirdly, changes to the Jobseeker's Allowance in 1996 meant that education workers on termly contracts, such as school-meals workers and crossing patrol staff could no longer claim for benefits during the school holidays. A worker earning £3000 a year will lose nearly £500 a year as a result (Harman, 1996).

Townsend argues that there is a need for government intervention through policies aimed at reducing inequalities in income and wealth, greater industrial democracy (see Section 9.5) to give workers more say in how companies operate, the abolition of unemployment through a right to work, and the institution of incomes to dependants such as children and housewives so that involvement in the labour market is not a precondition for a decent income. The idea that the social security system is based on outdated notions of how people live their lives is also made by Oppenheim and Harker:

Designed for a full-time male workforce, it discriminates against those who have been low paid or unemployed, against those who have worked part-time and people who have come to this country from abroad.
(Oppenheim and Harker, 1996, p. 4)

In an application of the idea of government action to eliminate poverty, Rentoul (1987) uses Townsend's notion of the need to redistribute income and wealth. Using Mack and Lansley's estimate of 10 million people in poverty from their 1983 study, Rentoul estimated that £12 billion would be needed to eliminate poverty. He argues that this money could be raised by placing a ceiling of £22,000 on incomes, made up of £16,400 in wages and the rest from interest on personal assets of £110,000. Rentoul calculated that 2 per cent of the adult population lived above this 'wealth line'.

In many ways, social democratic approaches have been influenced by the ideas of T. H. Marshall on citizenship. (See also Section 17.5.) Marshall argued that citizenship involved entitlement to certain rights and that historically these rights had been defined largely in relation to individuals and property: the right to free speech, to vote and to own property (see Section 14.3). However he argues that there is also an arena of 'social citizenship' and the welfare state should therefore be about providing certain things as a right to all.

Scott (1994) identifies what he calls a further radical concept of citizenship developing in the work of Townsend and he utilizes this to consider both poverty/deprivation and privilege in society using a largely radical Weberian framework. (See also Sections 2.6 and 17.3.) His point is that although Marshall argued that a social democratic concept of citizenship would begin to overcome the problems of inequality created by unfettered capitalism, the way in which the welfare state developed in the UK meant that, by and large, citizenship rights were gained not by all adults but only by those participating in the labour market. As such therefore the welfare state has to be further reformed so that citizenship rights are available to all, whether they participate in the labour market or not. This provides the theoretical basis for the radical proposals set forth by Townsend and also Rentoul.

As can be seen from this, central to social democratic approaches are the importance of the institutions of the welfare state and the belief that it is possible to extend citizenship to all by removing both deprivation and privilege through political and institutional change:

Questions of class analysis, then, are highly germane to the questions of poverty and wealth, but these are to be seen as social statuses that arise from the ways in which the status of citizen is institutionalised in a society and enters into complex interrelations with its class system.
(Scott, 1994, p. 174) (See also Chapter 4.)

Marxist perspectives

Marxists agree with social democratic thinkers that the cause of poverty is to be located in the nature of free-market capitalism. Marxists (see also Section 2.5) disagree with social democratic thinkers about the solution because they do not believe that the welfare state and notions of citizenship can overcome the inequalities created by capitalism. Since, they say, poverty is a permanent feature of capitalism, the only solution is the revolutionary overthrow of capitalism and the institution of a communist society where production is based on human needs, not profit.

Central to the writings of Marx was the idea that capitalism operated by workers producing more in value than they were paid in wages, leaving this 'surplus value' to be accumulated by the capitalists (see Section 2.3). The lower the wages, the higher the income of the capitalists. The creation of poverty is thus the obverse of the creation of great stocks of wealth. Marx's 'immiseration thesis' (see Chapter 4) predicted that over time more and more people would become poor relatives to the capitalist class with their wealth at the top of society (see Section 4.5). Competition between capitalists would largely be solved by pressures for cuts in wages or greater productivity from workers, all of which would be backed up by the threat of unemployment if workers resisted. Such a threat existed, argued Marx, because the capitalists maintained a permanent reserve army of unemployed labour. (See also Section 9.6.)

Since capitalism requires this permanent phenomenon of a reserve army of labour, there is a need to provide basic subsistence payments to enable such people to survive while they are not wanted. All capitalist states will therefore develop basic welfare systems. These will serve not to eliminate poverty, but merely to ensure that the poor can physically survive.

The Marxist approach to the welfare state does not accept the possibility outlined by social democratic thinkers that it can overcome the inequalities created by capitalism. The reasons for this are perhaps best explained by neo-Marxist writer Claus Offe. He points out that the welfare state faces a number of key structural limits to its powers. The most important of these is its reliance on tax revenue from private production and borrowing from private financial institutions to fund its activities. This means that in order to fund its activities it needs to ensure the continued profitable operation of capitalism:

The welfare state, rather than being a separate and autonomous source of well-being which provides incomes and services as a citizen's right, is itself highly dependent upon the prosperity and continued profitability of the economy.
(Offe, 1984, p. 148)

Marxist theorists are not greatly impressed by the social democratic vision of the possibility of the welfare state creating universal citizenship and being able to effect the kind of reforms as outlined by Townsend. What is needed is a social revolution to overthrow the capitalist basis of society.

Feminist perspectives

Feminists have also been critical of the welfare state for the way in which the gendered division of labour between the male breadwinner and a dependent full-time housewife is reinforced in its structures (see also Section 5.3). This means effectively that most of the benefits it dispenses require participation in the labour market and this serves to exclude large numbers of women, or at best confine them to a secondary status. The operation and construction of the welfare state therefore serves to reinforce exiting gender inequalities and as such can be described as operating in a patriarchal way. (See Section 5.4.)

For feminists the solution to poverty would be an end to such assumptions. This would involve a variety of changes, some of which might concentrate on removing barriers to the involvement of women in the labour market – such as the provision of state-financed childcare facilities – plus the institution of greater benefits for those who do not want to participate in the market. This would enable women (and indeed men) to make choices about the way they lived their lives and remove the risk that women would fall into poverty either through having to take responsibility for bringing up children or through being economically dependent on a male. (See also Section 5.7 on Demos research.)

Whether or not such reforms are possible in a capitalist society – or indeed in a socialist society – are the subject of debates within feminism.

Individualistic approaches

The key reason for poverty identified by individualistic thinkers is the behaviour and culture of the individuals in poverty. This was perhaps first expressed in the notion of the undeserving poor which formed part of the Poor Law legislation. More recently it has been expressed in 'the culture of poverty' and in the cultural version of the underclass thesis. (See also Section 4.8.)

The culture of poverty

On the basis of his studies of the urban poor in Mexico and Puerto Rico, Lewis (1961, 1968) argued that the poor have a distinctive set of attitudes, norms and values which include a sense of resignation and fate. This cultural attribute makes them different from the rest of the population. His list of attributes of this culture of poverty runs to some 62 traits, including things such as feelings of helplessness and marginality, early sexual experience and violence in the household.

Lewis argued that, although middle-class researchers might find it hard to understand, such a way of life provided something positive for poor people and therefore it would be perpetuated. The culture of poverty is passed on from generation to generation. Lewis argued that in the USA something like 20 per cent of those in poverty could be said to live in this 'culture of poverty'.

Since that time the concept has come into more general usage, and often tends to be presented as the *reason* for poverty: these people are in poverty because of their own behaviour and attitudes, or at best, that of their parents. Their fatalistic attitude to life leads them to fail to take up opportunities and so they remain poor. They tend to live life for the moment, spending rather than saving, and not getting involved in political or community groups campaigning for change. (See also Section 2.10.) Even if some of their poverty is due to the structure of society, their failure to get involved in any attempt to change it is due to their culture, not to structural factors.

Although Lewis was sympathetic to the people he studied, the idea that culture was central to the causes of poverty has been most notably taken up by the political Right, notably by Sir Keith Joseph in the UK. He argued that there was a cycle of deprivation and saw culture as the key element which kept the cycle going. Since this appears to let society off the hook for poverty, and instead labels the poor as essentially culturally deficient, this viewpoint has attracted criticism for at least two reasons.

- The notion of a culture of poverty is deficient because it is not precisely specified, and furthermore culture is a consequence not a cause of poverty (e.g. Bilton *et al.*, 1988).
- Evidence shows that the children of those in poverty are not necessarily likely to remain in poverty, as the culture of poverty thesis would suggest.

An example of the second criticism can be found in the work of Brown and Madge (1982). In a study set up to test the 'cycle of deprivation thesis', they found no evidence to support the idea that deprivation is culturally transmitted. This clearly questions the extent to which a culture is passed on through the generations.

A further criticism is based on the idea of situational constraints: that the behaviour of poor people is to be explained on the basis of social and economic constraints which keep them in their present situation. If the poor express fatalism, it is because of the way these constraints are a reality, not because they are failing to take up opportunities that really exist. The poor have the same aspirations as everyone else but these situational constraints stop them from achieving them (Liebow, 1967).

The dependency culture

A more widespread concept in the individualistic approach today is that of the 'dependency culture'. This is similar to the 'culture of poverty', but the explanation of the source of that culture is distinctive.

Here, the origin of the culture of dependency is the welfare state. New Right thinkers argue that the welfare state, by providing the poor with money for doing nothing, removes their incentive to go out and find work. (See Section 2.10.) They therefore stay unemployed and become dependent on their benefit payments. This leads to a loss of dignity and pride and to failure to take up new opportunities.

Marsland (1992) asserts that this idea provides the basis for arguing against universal welfare provision. He says that the cause of poverty is the socialist ideology underlying the setting-up of universal welfare benefits since this saps people of the need to strive to survive. Socialism, by ridiculing competition and the competitive market, undermines the pursuit of excellence and the ability of capitalism to produce the increased living standards it undoubtedly is capable of. The solution, therefore, is that benefits must be made more selective and people

should be encouraged to rely more on family and community support if they fall into difficulties. Further, the benefits system should seek to encourage people to improve themselves by, for example, providing training schemes which help to keep people in tune with the skills required to obtain a job. Reducing the cost of social welfare would also allow a reduction in taxes, which would provide a spur to further economic growth and create more job opportunities.

Critics of this approach point out that when we last had unfettered capitalism the levels of poverty were high, largely owing to low wages. Having a job in an unfettered capitalist economy is therefore not a guarantee that one will not suffer poverty. A further criticism is that all the evidence shows that in means-tested benefits the poor are least likely to apply, either because of the stigma attached or because they do not understand the system. Middle-class applicants are more likely to benefit. (See also Section 14.4.)

The underclass debate

Cultural explanations of poverty have been given a further twist by discussion of the idea that there is an 'underclass'. (See also Section 4.8.) This term has been the subject of intense debate owing to the two very different meanings attached to the word. Pilkington (1992) identifies a cultural and a structural view of the underclass.

The cultural view

The cultural view is very much, though not exclusively, associated with New Right thinkers and has been very influential in the USA, most prominently through the work of Murray (1984, 1989, 1994). This type of argument continues the line developed by the culture of poverty thesis, though in contrast to Lewis, these writers are very unsympathetic and in some cases overtly hostile to the people they are describing. Murray argues that the key cause of such an underclass is the growth of illegitimacy, which led to the growth of groups with distinct value systems. Again the emphasis is on the idea that people are poor because of their distinct values and behaviours and it is therefore their fault.

This view has been subjected to numerous critiques. Heath (1992) collected data on the attitudes of those defined as being in the underclass and found no evidence to support the idea that they held distinct cultural values. In fact, they seemed more likely to want to work than those in households where someone already had a job, and in all other respects held attitudes very similar to the rest of the population.

There seems to be an absence of hard evidence to support the notion of a distinct culture among the poor.

The structural view

The structural view is associated with Weberian sociology (see Sections 2.3 and 2.6) since it argues that we cannot understand poverty and deprivation simply on the basis of the class structure alone: we need also to consider the way status divisions interact. This view also highlights the fact that structural constraints in society may lead to the growth of the poor who are more or less permanently dependent on benefits, not because they don't wish to find a job, but because mass unemployment means there are not jobs for everyone. The distinction is to pointedly divide them off from the working class. Runciman (1990), a neo-Weberian sociologist, therefore includes the underclass as a separate class in his schema, and Labour MP Frank Field (1989) has concentrated on the way changes to welfare state provision have excluded certain groups from the standard of living and citizenship rights obtained by others.

The clear implication of this view is that the underclass are the victims of changes beyond their control, usually changes in the job market and welfare benefits.

Concluding comments

The distinction between the cultural and the structural views of the underclass has been blurred by recent interventions. Dahrendorf (1987) argues that although structural factors play the major part in the *creation* of an underclass, this then develops its own culture. This idea has been shared by Frank Field (1996). Writing for the right-wing think-tank, the Institute for Economic Affairs, he says that the welfare system created after the Second World War does contain incentives for bad bahaviour. In particular he argues that means-testing, by treating the poor badly, lays the ground for the emergence of a 'yob culture'. He is still mainly focusing on the structural deficiencies of means-tested benefits, but the notion of a yob culture brings him closer to the cultural view of the underclass.

The concept of an underclass has been strongly rejected by Marxist thinkers. They contend that the poor are a part of the working class and exhibit no cultural differences from them.

The concept of an underclass is discussed in more detail in Section 4.8.

> **Discussion point**
>
> To what extent is it possible to identify distinct structural and cultural approaches to the idea of the existence of an underclass?

14.8 The changing distribution of income and wealth

Income

The most important statistics relating to the distribution of income came from the Royal Commission on the Distribution of Income and Wealth which reported periodically until 1980 (when it was abolished by the government). Statistics from its research show some degree of redistribution of income from the top tenth to the next 60 per cent, but little change overall (despite some improvement in the 1950s and 60s) for those at the bottom of society (the bottom 30 per cent) – see Table 14.12.

Since 1979 there has been a definite move back to greater inequality. The main reason for this has been the preference for the 'free market'. Markets operate on the basis of reward and sanction and thus serve to create greater inequality. The level of inequality has risen faster in the UK than anywhere else, except New Zealand, between the late 1970s and the early 1990s, according to research by the Joseph Rowntree Foundation (Hills, 1995). This can be seen in Figure 14.11. One facet of this is that while average income rose by 36 per cent between 1979 and 1992, income for the poorest tenth (after housing costs are deducted) fell by 17 per cent (Mann, 1995). One important element of this has been changes in the labour market. Unemployment has more than doubled since 1979, but it has been unequally experienced.

> **Activity**
>
> **a** Identify countries on Figure 14.11 that are members of the European Union.
> **b** To what extent are UK trends out of step with other members of the EU? Justify your answer.
>
> **I, E**

Oppenheim and Harker (1996) report that a construction worker is ten times more likely to be made redundant than a lawyer. At the same time there have been widely documented cases of individuals massively enriching themselves, which has led to a widening of income differentials. Also, changes to the tax and benefits system – such as the cutting of income tax and the matching increase in indirect taxes – have benefited those at the top while disadvantaging those at the bottom. The Joseph Rowntree Foundation's enquiry into income and wealth published in 1995 found income and wealth distributed as shown in Figure 14.12.

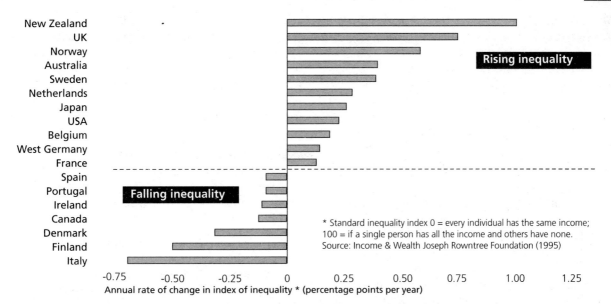

Figure 14.11 International income inequality trends. Source: Mann (1995, p. 7)

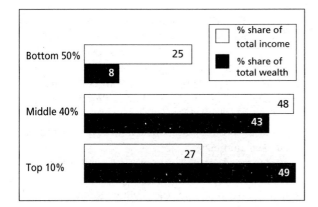

Figure 14.12 Distribution of income and wealth to the income groups. Source: *The Guardian*, 15 February 1995

Table 14.12 Historical trends in percentage shares of total income

	Before tax			After tax		
	Top 10%	Next 60%	Bottom 30%	Top 10%	Next 60%	Bottom 30%
1949	33.2	54.1	12.7	27.1	58.3	14.6
1954	29.8	59.3	10.9	24.8	63.1	12.1
1959	29.4	60.9	9.7	25.2	63.5	11.2
1964	29.0	61.4	9.6	25.1	64.1	10.8
1967	28.0	61.6	10.4	24.3	63.7	12.0
1974	26.8	62.3	10.9	23.6	63.6	12.8
1979	26.1	63.5	10.4	23.4	64.5	12.1

Source: Atkinson (1983, p. 63)

The *Family Expenditure Survey* shows that between 1979 and 1994 the top 10 per cent of earners saw their income rise by 62 per cent in real terms

Activity

Write your own summary of what the information presented in Table 14.12 shows in terms of the changing distribution of income between 1949 and 1979.

(i.e. after taking inflation into account) while the poorest tenth saw their income fall by 17 per cent. This increase in inequality was accompanied by an increase in the number of people living in poverty or on the margins of poverty.

Wealth

The twentieth century (or at least its first seventy years) saw a gradual redistribution in wealth. The richest 1 per cent of the population owned 69 per cent of wealth in 1911, but this had reduced to 42 per cent by 1960. Equivalent figures for the richest tenth are 92 per cent down to 83 per cent.

A similar trend emerges with later figures. The most wealthy 1 per cent fell from 21 per cent in 1976 to 18 per cent in 1991. What is most notable is the limit of the redistribution of this wealth. While the very wealthy appear to have lost out, they appear to have lost out to the not quite so wealthy. The rest do not seem to have increased their level of wealth at all. The least wealthy 50 per cent of the population owned 8 per cent of wealth in 1976 and this was unchanged in 1991.

A major reason for the redistribution of wealth noted above appears to have been the transfer of assets among family members to avoid death duties, so it is unclear whether these are 'real' redistributions. Inheritance still constitutes an important

Activity

Read the following extracts and then answer the questions.

1 'Signals accumulated steadily over the 1980s that, while levels of living improved "on average" and people already well off became very much better off, material circumstances for the poor at best stayed much as before and at worst actually deteriorated. Estimates for the full decade 1979–89 confirmed the trend by showing real increases in disposable income to the order of nearly 40 per cent on balance for the wealthiest one-fifth of households, but a mean fall of some 4.5 per cent for the poorest one-fifth. So much for "trickle down of new wealth to the bottom".' (Westergaard, 1995, p. 131)

2 'It is true that capitalism does create and perpetuate considerable economic inequalities between the social classes, but it also raises the living standards of rich and poor alike. For all the academic criticism of "trickle-down" theories of economic growth, it is clear that the enhanced wealth created by capitalism has benefited all classes and that the luxuries enjoyed by one generation rapidly became the norm for the majority in the next.' (Saunders, 1995, p. 13)

3 'Controversy has arisen over the question of whether the Conservative government of the 1980s favoured higher-income groups, at the expense of the low paid, in its social and economic policies. It is certainly clear that, during the 1980s, the trend towards greater equality of income distribution went into reverse.' (Scott, 1994, p. 106)

a Using information here and in Section 14.9, explain the meaning of the phrase 'trickle down'. Identify one argument for and one against this concept.

b Suggest two examples of the 'social and economic policies' of the 1980s which might have affected the distribution of income and wealth.

c Investigate sociological arguments opposing those put forward by Scott. Use these to (i) write a defence of government policy in the 1980s, and (ii) evaluate the validity of Scott's argument.

U, I, A, E

source of wealth. Harbury and Hitchens (1979) found that among the top 0.1 per cent of the population in property-holding terms, 51 per cent were inheritors in 1957 but this had fallen to 36 per cent in 1973. However, among the extremely wealthy (those left more than £1 million), the fall was less marked – from 9 per cent in 1957 to 7 per cent in 1973.

Discussion point

Emile Durkheim argued for a law to effectively abolish inheritance. Do you agree that such a change should be made?

One form of wealth that increased in the 1980s was the ownership of company shares: by 1988, 21 per cent of people owned some shares, often the result of the privatizations of the period. However, Scott (1994) points out that the richest 1 per cent of the population owned 75 per cent of all privately owned shares.

The other main area of growing wealth is in housing. (See also Section 16.8.) The growth of owner-occupation in the 1980s increased the stock of wealth. Scott sees this as one of the main reasons why there was a degree of redistribution of wealth in the early 1980s, but it is debatable whether this constitutes marketable wealth since the money can only be realized by selling one's house and thus making oneself homeless.

Westergaard (1995) is another to claim that the trend for wealth to be less unequally distributed was stopped or reversed in the 1980s. Using material from *Social Trends*, he argues that if we exclude the value of personal dwellings, the share of the richest 1 per cent of the population in marketable wealth

Activity

Since 1989 the *Sunday Times* has produced an annual survey of the UK's richest people. It is published in April or May each year. The size of the study has gradually expanded and it now covers the richest 500 people. Locate a copy of the latest edition of the survey and calculate the following as percentages:

a those who are women
b those who are titled aristocrats
c those who were educated at a public school
d those who were educated at an Oxford or Cambridge college
e those who currently live in (i) the South East of England and (ii) Wales.

K, I

rose from 26 to 28 per cent, and of the richest 5 per cent of the population from 45 to 53 per cent. Even with the value of personal dwellings included, the share of the richest remained constant throughout the 1980s.

14.9 Conflicting explanations for the distribution of income and wealth

Activity

Draw up a table in which you can summarize the theories on inequality outlined in this section. Include the names of key thinkers together with short summaries of their views, your own conclusions on whether they think inequality is a good or a bad thing, and your own criticisms of each view.

U, I, E

Functionalist theories of inequality

Functionalists argue that inequality is functional for society in that it ensures that those with the most potential talent are encouraged to develop through lengthy spells in education and training, with the promise of higher incomes when they qualify. (See also Section 2.4.) In order to ensure that society's functional prerequisites are best met we must ensure people fully utilize their talents.

For Davis and Moore (1967), inequalities arise from the different values placed on various roles by the societal consensus. Since there are so many roles in contemporary societies, inequality is inevitable (Parsons, 1951, 1977). However, since functionalists believe that selection to fill various positions is done on the basis of merit, they see this as legitimate. In other words, they argue that there is equality of opportunity to find one's place in a society offering different levels of reward. (See also Section 4.9.)

Discussion point

Do you agree that inequality is inevitable in contemporary society?

The main problem with this view is its tautological nature. When asked to provide some evidence that some occupations are more functionally important than others – and therefore deserve higher wages – the response is that they are more important because they are paid more. This becomes a completely circular argument.

In an attempt to get round this, Davis and Moore tried to argue that there were other ways of considering functional importance. However, it can be argued that if it is possible to find jobs of high functional importance to which only low rewards are attached, this rather undermines this as a theory of inequality. The rise of the New Right has seen the re-emergence of similar themes to those raised by functionalists in the 1950s.

The New Right and inequality

Saunders (1990b, 1995) suggests that all societies have been unequal in some way. He therefore supports the functionalist argument that inequality and a stratification system are inevitable. He also argues that such inequality is beneficial, both because it performs the selection mechanism identified by functionalists, and because inequality is a motivating force:

Successful entrepreneurs may well accumulate a fortune, but in so doing, they will have added to the productive power and wealth of the society as a whole. . . . a few entrepreneurs become rich, some others fail and go bust, and meanwhile the rest of society grows more affluent as it gains by their efforts.
(Saunders, 1990b, p. 53)

Discussion point

How might inequality be a motivating force? Do you think it is?

Saunders goes on to consider whether there are any other ways in which such inequality might manifest itself. He broadly accepts Davis and Moore's functionalist argument that inequality is inevitable because otherwise talented people would not be motivated to fill important positions. However, he does argue that there is an alternative to high income inequalities to ensure that this happens. For example, such a position could be arrived at through coercion, where a powerful societal authority could cajole people to take certain positions.

The central authority Saunders has in mind is basically the state, and he is therefore attacking versions of socialism based on centralized state authority. It should be noted that there is a difference here from the earlier functionalist accounts, since they did not hold such a negative view of the state as New Right thinkers do. Indeed they held that the state and government were responsive to the value consensus in society.

In summary, then, Saunders argues that the only alternative to the market is an oppressive coercive society, and since that is undesirable we must accept the inequality which is the basis of a market society, since it both preserves individual liberty and provides the beneficial effects identified by functionalist thinkers:

The value of egalitarianism is not necessarily unattainable, but it could only be realised at the price of individual liberty. Equality and liberty are incompatible objectives. If we desire one, we must sacrifice the other.
(Saunders, 1990, p. 67)

Discussion point
If Saunders is right and we have to choose, which of these two objectives do you think society should pursue?

New Right thinking on this has been criticized on a number of grounds. With regard to the 'trickle-down theory' – which put in simple terms means that in order to make the poor richer we must first make the rich richer – critics have pointed out that while the first stage of this is easy to do, the second stage often does not appear (as was seen in Section 14.8 and elsewhere). On the other hand Saunders contends that the poor today are considerably better off than the poor of yesteryear.

It is also possible to question whether societies based on a free market provide better levels of economic growth than centrally organized societies. State involvement has been an important feature in the economic growth achieved by the newly developing economies in South East Asia (see Section 12.6). It might also be argued that the liberty that Saunders sees as the reward for putting up with inequality is not obviously greater in capitalist than socialist societies. Capitalism has clearly coexisted with examples of highly repressive regimes such as the old South Africa and the military regime in Chile (see Section 12.8), and it is not clear that those in poverty enjoy much real liberty.

A final criticism is that the system of preserving liberty through the market seems to lead to consistent inequalities in the degree of liberty. Saunders argues that money does not discriminate since one person's money is as good as anyone else's. While this is true, the unequal distribution of money, necessary in his view to secure liberty, does seem to be unequally distributed remarkably consistently by class, gender and ethnicity. This rather questions whether the market system is as blind to existing social divisions and as open to all as Saunders suggests.

Marxist views on inequality

In contrast to views that inequality is necessary and broadly beneficial overall, Marxists are clear critics of inequality. For them inequality exists only because some groups exploit others. In simple terms, the rich are rich because they steal from the poor. Inequality is therefore something which is based on a fundamental conflict of interests and on an unjust system. (See Section 2.5.)

The basis for this is Marx's theory that the source of all value in society is labour and that all types of society have contained groups who do little labour themselves but live off the work of others. This occurs precisely because of the unequal ownership of property which means that profits accrue only to the owners of production. The rest of the population are forced to work to live, because all other avenues for the majority of the population to make a living have been closed off. They therefore have the 'choice' of selling their labour-power or starving. (Though see the criticism of this position by Anthony Giddens in Section 2.9.)

The argument continues that the productive potential of capitalism cannot be fully realized because the overriding concern is profit. In order to fully utilize the productive potential there is therefore a need to overthrow capitalism and institute a society based on needs. For Marx this was likely to occur not only because of the crisis-prone nature of capitalism, but also because workers would become increasingly fed up of being exploited and impoverished and would rise up against the system. Even if everyone's wages were to rise, as long as surplus value is being extracted – which will always occur under capitalism – the poor will get poorer in relation to the rich as time goes on. As the capitalists pile up surplus value, the gap between them and the poor increases.

It is important to realize that this is what Marx meant by 'immiseration', because the higher average living standard of today compared with the time he was writing is often presented as a refutation of Marx's ideas. Clearly it is not. What matters is the relative distribution of income, not the absolute. The 1980s provide evidence for Marx's immiseration thesis, since the distribution of income has become much more unequal.

Discussion point
How convincing do you find this Marxist viewpoint?

The most important critiques of Marxism are based on the experiences of those societies that have been organized on avowedly Marxist lines, which have shown no tendency for reduced inequality and have proved very unpopular – as can be seen by the uprisings in 1989 in the eastern European bloc. In reply, most contemporary Marxists (e.g. Wright, 1994b, 1997; Westergaard, 1995) argue that in fact these societies were not really Marxist anyway.

Another criticism levelled at Marxism is that its concentration on production and the inequalities that arise therefrom leads to a relative overlooking of the possibilities of other forms of inequality and other bases of stratification – notably those based on gender and ethnicity. (See Chapters 5 and 6.)

Weber and inequality

Weber thought that there is more to inequality than simply the economic arena, though he did recognize that as important. He argued that social inequalities can also arise on the basis of status differences and on the basis of differences in political power. This is encapsulated in the famous trilogy of 'class, status and power'. (See also Section 2.3.)

With regard to economic inequality based on class, Weber agreed with Marx that this existed but he argued that the two-class model developed by Marx was inadequate. He offered a very different definition of class as a group of people who share a similar market situation and who will therefore share similar life-chances in the labour market, including similar levels of income. What this means is that those with different levels of skill will be able to command higher wages and therefore will be in a different market situation from other wage-earners. Weber therefore rejects Marx's notion of a unified proletariat and suggests that wage-earners are in a number of distinct classes. As society becomes more complex the levels of differentiation will increase, and so the number of classes will increase as old classes fragment as skills become more precisely differentiated, leading to different market situations. The end result is a picture of the class structure with a potentially unlimited number of classes.

However Weber also argued, in contrast to Marxism, that economic power was not the source of all power. Instead there are distinct spheres and bases for power in society. He said that status divisions arise from notions of social honour and commonality of lifestyle, and that this may not necessarily correspond to class divisions. Weber developed this idea from caste divisions. One important element of the caste system is that your caste is determined at birth and stays with you for life. As such this analysis can be applied to the position of women and ethnic minorities in our society. Weber

argued that status is a superior way of looking at the subjective aspect of inequality since it is integral to a status group that they feel a common identity, whereas this is not automatic with people in the same class.

Parkin (1972, 1979) has argued that Weberian sociology can explain gender divisions by using the notion of social closure. This means a strategy of erecting barriers to stop other groups entering positions with high pay and status. Men it could be argued have excluded women through social closure. (See also Section 5.3.)

The final element of Weber's theory is that of political power. Unlike Marx, Weber argued that economic power does not automatically confer political power. Instead he argued they were parallel but different sources of power and neither was primary. Political change and actions of the state can affect the economic arena just as much as economic changes may have an impact on the political process. Many contemporary Weberians (Giddens, 1973, 1985c; Mann, 1986, 1993) argue that the problem with much Marxist analysis is that it ignores the important role played by political power and the state independently of capitalists. (See also Sections 2.6 and 17.3.)

The main criticism of Weberian sociology is that the theory of social class outlined in it tends simply to lead to static lists of the hierarchy of the class structure without necessarily explaining the dynamics of the relationship between them. The concept of social closure is, however, one attempt to do precisely that.

A second criticism is that much of Weber's analysis is based on the very over-arching interpretation of power produced by Nietzsche. In this view power is omnipresent and will always be so. If power is the source of inequality, then this presents a view that inequality is an ever-present phenomenon in society.

Discussion point

Will inequality be an ever-present phenomenon in society?

Feminism and inequality

Feminist sociologists have dubbed the earlier views on inequality as 'malestream' (see Abbott and Wallace, 1997). What does this mean?

If your position in the class structure is defined by your place in the sphere of production, what can be said about women who are full-time housewives? They stand outside the class system in a direct sense, yet it would be absurd to argue that such women do not experience inequality (see Section

4.11). Feminists have therefore argued that a more adequate theory of stratification needs to consider the way in which inequalities arise other than on the basis of class. (See also Chapter 5.)

In this respect, radical feminists have argued that gender divisions and sexual oppression are more important than class differences. They say that such inequalities arise not from capitalism but from a system of patriarchy, meaning rule by males. Males everywhere oppress women and one important facet of this is that women have less income and wealth than men. Radical feminists tend to stress the way in which men physically oppress women through physical violence and rape, but also through a system of laws which make it much less likely that women can own property. Developing a materialist feminism, Delphy and Leonard (1993) argue that as a result of patriarchy we should see women as a separate class from men.

A second factor in feminist theories is that an exclusive focus on the workplace ignores the way in which gender divisions in the rest of society influence and constrain the way women participate in the sphere of paid employment. This is most obvious in the case of childcare. Radical feminists argue that it is in this reproductive sphere of society that the ultimate basis for inequality lies, rather than in the productive sphere as Marxist theories of stratification suggest. The assumption that women will bear the primary responsibility for childcare clearly affects the length of time they spend in paid work, and whether it is part time or full time. The fact that the onerous tasks associated with domestic labour are unpaid (see Section 7.5) also affects the amount women can earn, and makes many economically dependent on males, further reinforcing male power over women. An adequate theory of income inequality therefore needs to take into account the gender assumptions operating in all spheres of society.

Marxist and socialist feminists have tried to construct a theory which shows how gender (and indeed ethnic) inequalities interact with class inequalities through placing effective limitations on women's involvement within the employment sphere. To what extent this is a successful blend is still very much a matter of debate (Walby, 1990; Bradley, 1996).

Critics of feminist analyses suggest that they tend to break down because of arguments over differences among women themselves; for example divisions between white and black women. These divisions have caused massive splits in the feminist movement and lead one to question whether gender is any more capable of providing a full explanation of income inequality than any other concept.

Westergaard (1995) has argued that class inequality remains fundamental because in the 1980s there was increasing inequality in income distribution but the difference in income distribution between men and women narrowed. Gender cannot therefore explain this trend in the 1980s, leading to a reassertion of the primary importance of class analysis.

Discussion point
To what extent do the divisions among feminist thinkers weaken the feminist case?

Further **reading**

Good introductory books on this topic are:

- Trowler, P. (1996) *Investigating Health, Welfare and Poverty*, London, 2nd edn, Collins Educational.
- Cole, T. (1986) *Whose Welfare?* London, Tavistock.

Further detail can be gained from the following:

- Bryson, L. (1992) *Welfare and the State*, London, Macmillan.
- Scott, J. (1994) *Poverty and Wealth*, London, Longman.
- Alcock, P. (1993) *Understanding Poverty*, London, Macmillan.
- Oppenheim, C. and Harker, L. (1996) *Poverty: The Facts*, 3rd edn, London, Child Poverty Action Group.

Back issues of the periodical *Sociology Review* (formerly known as *Social Studies Review*) also contain many articles on this field of sociology and many others.

Exam **questions**

1 Assess the argument that rather than eliminating poverty, the welfare state has created a form of 'dependency-culture'. [25 marks]
(AEB, Paper 2, Summer 1992)

2 The claim that 'the poor are themselves to blame for their poverty' is a feature of some explanations of poverty. Critically examine the sociological arguments for and against this statement. [25 marks]
(AEB, Paper 2, Summer 1991)

3 a Briefly distinguish between absolute and relative poverty. [4 marks]
  b Briefly explain what is meant by the concept of the 'cycle of poverty'. [4 marks]
  c How has recent social policy affected the number of young people and children living in poverty? [7 marks]

d Evaluate the view that the elimination of poverty is inseparable from the reduction of general inequality. [10 marks]
(IBS, Paper 1, Summer 1995)

4 Examine the causes and the consequences of the adoption of community care policies in the last ten years [25 marks]
(IBS, Paper 1, Summer 1996)

Coursework **suggestions**

1 Conduct a study of poverty in your local area
You could do this utilising the methodology adopted by the Breadline Britain studies. This involves first devising a questionnaire to arrive at a list of necessities, and then using a sample of the population to quantify the extent of poverty in your local area. You could then compare your findings with the latest nationally published figures and note any important differences. This should also include consideration of the social distribution of poverty in your locality.

2 Conduct a survey to consider the relative importance of types of welfare
You could conduct a survey to consider the relative importance of the three types of welfare identified in this chapter – namely, direct, fiscal and occupational. The purpose of this would be to see how the distribution of each of these types of welfare varies across different social groups.

3 Conduct a case study of 'care in the community'
You could conduct a case study of the operation of 'care in the community' in your locality. You could try to interview people involved in the provision of welfare, such as professionals employed by local authority social services departments, voluntary workers and welfare campaigners. Ask then about how effective care in the community has been and if they think it has provided overall benefits or not. You might wish to focus on changes to institutional care, for example for the elderly, and apply the theories of Goffman and Foucault to see which theory best fits the changes you have identified.

The mass media

15.1 **Perspectives on the role of the media in society**

The mass media has an increasingly large role in contemporary advanced industrial societies. Very few households do not own televisions or music systems of varying degrees of sophistication, and very few people do not have daily access to television, radio or print news. Among the young in particular, rapidly advancing home and personal computer technologies take up a large space in patterns of leisure consumption in day-to-day life (see also Sections 10.8 and 10.9). As the statistics in Tables 15.1 and 15.2 illustrate, consumption of the media is a major preoccupation for many members of society.

Activity

Using the statistics in Tables 15.1 and 15.2, write short summaries of the following:

a how people use their free time
b what the most popular leisure activities in the home are – for the young, the old and for males and females.

The mass media is capable of connecting individuals on opposite sides of the world through developments on the information superhighway, and the future of the mass media looks strong in terms of the rewards for those individuals and companies at the forefront of its development. It should therefore come as no surprise that the mass media and its many relationships to society and the individual are a rich source of argument and debate for sociologists.

Defining the mass media

Before starting to analyse any social phenomenon it is important to be clear on some important key terms – the media is no exception to this.

- *Medium* refers to a single source of information or technique of passing on information.
- *Media* is simply more than one medium.
- *The mass media* is a term used to refer to more than one source of information designed to reach out to many people – a mass audience.

As Figure 15.1 (see page 604) illustrates, it is possible to further subdivide the mass media into those that are 'representational' (i.e. they represent something) and those that are based on, or use, electronic technologies.

Activity

Refer to Figure 15.1 and answer the following two questions.

a What is the main difference between 'representational' and 'mechanical/electronic' media?
b where would the recent developments in the 'world wide web' be placed on the diagram?

Table 15.1 Use of free time (hours per week)

	Age 16–24	Age 25–34	Age 35–44	Age 45–59	60 and over	All aged 16 and over
Television or radio	14	15	13	17	26	19
Visiting friends (may include eating)	7	5	4	4	4	5
Reading	1	1	2	3	6	3
Talking, socializing and telephoning friends	3	3	3	4	4	3
Eating and drinking out	6	4	4	4	2	3
Hobbies, games and computing	2	2	1	3	3	2
Walks and other recreation	2	2	1	2	3	2
Doing nothing (may include illness)	1	1	1	2	2	2
Sports participation	3	1	1	1	1	1
Religious, political and other meetings	-	1	1	-	1	1
Concerts, theatre, cinema and sports spectating	1	1	-	-	-	-
Other	1	-	-	-	-	-
All free time	**41**	**36**	**31**	**39**	**52**	**41**

Source: ESRC Research Centre on Micro-social Change, from *Omnibus Survey,* May 1995

Table 15.2 Participation[1] in home-based leisure activities 1993–4 (percentages)

	16–19	20–24	25–29	30–44	45–59	60–69	70 and over	All aged 16 and over
Males								
Watching TV	99	100	99	99	99	99	97	99
Visiting/entertaining friends or relations	96	97	97	97	94	94	91	95
Listening to radio	93	95	95	94	91	86	83	91
Listening to records/tapes	96	96	93	86	76	66	50	79
Reading books	55	58	56	60	61	59	58	59
Gardening	24	22	37	52	62	65	55	51
DIY	34	44	61	68	65	58	35	57
Dressmaking/needlework/knitting	2	3	3	3	3	3	4	3
Females								
Watching TV	99	99	99	99	99	99	98	99
Visiting/entertaining friends or relations	98	98	99	98	96	95	94	96
Listening to radio	97	95	92	91	88	84	77	88
Listening to records/tapes	97	96	92	88	75	62	42	75
Reading books	75	70	70	71	71	74	67	71
Gardening	11	23	34	51	57	54	39	45
DIY	16	35	39	40	34	23	10	30
Dressmaking/needlework/knitting	19	30	30	37	44	48	38	38

[1] Percentage in each age group participating in each activity in the four weeks before interview
Source: General Household Survey, Office of Population Censuses and Surveys

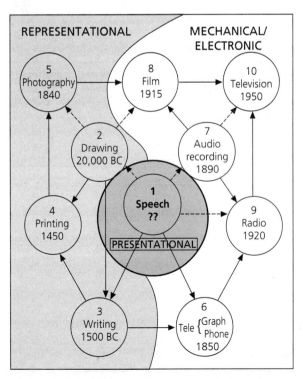

Figure 15.1 Kinds of media. Source: Hart (1991)

Studying the mass media

The mass media itself is of interest and concern to many members of, and groups in, society, some of which are involved in the media, or use the media to gain publicity for their particular opinions, causes or ideologies. Recent moral panics or moral crusades led by some sections of the media (see Section 15.5), against other sections, include concerns over computer pornography, government propaganda at times of national emergencies, and the ever-occurring theme of the representation of violence and sexually explicit material.

The mass media has become an important tool used in political campaigns, often played against the backdrop of concerns of bias and censorship from all sides of the political spectrum. News broadcasting, in particular, has come powerfully into its own, in the apparently 'instant' reporting of major world events such as national disasters, elections and warfare.

As with any topic in sociology, it is possible to apply a number of different theoretical perspectives in attempting to understand the role of the media in contemporary society. A number of these perspectives represent a rich tradition of sociological thought dating back to the early developments of the mass media itself, whereas others are more recent, attempting to build on existing sociological knowledge in order to explain newer and possible future media developments. Many new sociological perspectives, ideas and debates are intended as a 'conversation' with the ghosts of other past and popular sociological ideas. For this reason it is often easier to understand contemporary theoretical discussions by first understanding a history of sociological thinking.

What follows in this first section is a brief introduction to ideas and research which form the background to more recent discussions and debates.

'Orthodox' Marxism

Marxists treat the media as an agent of ideological control, in much the same way as they would view the operation of institutions such as the education system or a religious belief system. (See also Sections 8.2, 10.2, 18.6.)

Marxists believe that the media creates false class consciousness – to take the minds of the masses away from the harsh realities of capitalist society. Through deliberate manipulation and censorship the media contains images and messages which are seen by this perspective to amount to little more than propaganda.

The classic Marxist treatment of the issue of false class consciousness comes from Marx and Engels' *The German Ideology* originally written between 1845 and 1846. In this work, Marx and Engels state:

The ideas of the ruling class are in every epoch the ruling ideas, i.e. the class which is the ruling material force of society, is at the same time its ruling intellectual force.
(Marx and Engels, 1974, p. 64)

Here Marx and Engels illustrate their belief that ideas in society flow from the top of the wealth and power structures downwards to the masses (see also Section 2.5). The masses are seen as victims in this war of ideas. This classic statement, known as the 'dominant ideology thesis', is applied by later and modern-day Marxists to institutions such as the media. The most popular ideas, values and attitudes in society come from the ruling class. In this respect, some modern-day Marxists claim that the media has taken over from religion as a prime source of ideological control.

This orthodox Marxist account of the role of the media as an agent of oppression in the 'class struggle' has its criticisms. Some commentators suggest that the idea of a dominant ideology simply

Discussion point

Are the 'dominant ideas' always those of the 'dominant class'? Are social actors able to replace or resist media messages with those of their own?

fails to take into account the wealth and diversity of ideas which exist in society, both pro-establishment and anti-establishment (subversive). Abercrombie *et al.* (1980) believe that there is a lack of a dominant ideology in contemporary western capitalist nations.

Another criticism made against the orthodox Marxist account of the role of the media in ruling-class control is that the theory is extremely deterministic and possibly over-crude: it treats social actors as 'passive robots' who are tricked into believing opinions which operate against their class interests and which are created by a conspiracy of the ruling class.

Neo-Marxist approaches

There are many different ways to read and interpret Marxist sociology and the so-called 'orthodox' account is but one. Other commentators commonly referred to as new or neo-Marxists suggest that individuals are capable of resisting these media messages, yet these messages do nevertheless exist.

The Frankfurt School

The Frankfurt School, with its own particular brand of Marxist-based sociology termed 'critical theory', developed from the Institute of Social Research at Frankfurt University, Germany, in 1923. This represented a major attempt by western Marxists to reconstruct and evaluate Marxism as a political project and as an intellectual and academic set of beliefs in the light of the rise of Hitler in Germany and the rise of Stalin in the then Soviet Union. The central aim of the Frankfurt School was to create a truly humane and free society based on classless principles, to be achieved through the liberation of the masses.

Theodor Adorno and Max Horkheimer (1944), members of the Frankfurt School, sought to explain the rise of fascism in Nazi Germany by looking at the role the media played as a source of political propaganda. Central to their analysis are the interrelated concepts of 'the culture industry' and 'mass culture'. (See also Sections 10.3 and 10.8.)

With the rise of mass communication and so-called technological advances in media products, Adorno and Horkheimer argue that culture has been reduced to a 'mass culture' where the culture industry – the creation of literature, art, theatre etc., into business – has turned culture into an empty and meaningless product to be bought and sold and ultimately thrown away. Such mass culture lacks any genuine attempt to discuss the human situation or to improve on it.

Adorno and Horkheimer suggested that the media of their time, and especially the media of Hitler's Germany, contained no element of social commentary or criticism. It therefore represented a proruling élite view of the world as being 'normal' while at the same time, through advertising, encouraged members of society to perpetuate the economy by buying commodities. The Frankfurt School believed this process to operate not only in Hitler's Germany but also in western capitalist countries, and especially in America with the then developing Hollywood film businesses:

The whole world is made to pass through the filter of the culture industry . . . the easier it is today for the illusion to prevail that the outside world is the straightforward continuation of that presented on the screen.
(Adorno and Horkheimer, 1993, p. 33; originally written in 1944)

Neo-Marxism and hegemony

The newer Marxisms are often described as being 'hegemonic theories'. The concept of hegemony was introduced to sociology by Antonio Gramsci (1971b) and is used to represent a state of physical and mental control where one ruling class dominates another subject class. Coercion, or physical force, is effective in society, but for only a little while. However, ideological control – the domination of the minds of the masses – is more effective and longer lasting. (See also Sections 2.5, 10.2 and 17.4.)

Hegemony refers to the success of a nation-state or ruler to control or dominate another. In its contemporary sociological use, the concept is used to refer to the control of a subject class through their own participation and consent. Modern-day Marxists believe this to be one of the functions of the media.

Neo-Marxism has its origins in the observations made by Gramsci, concerning the lack of 'success' of the Marxist project – even in societies such as Italy and Germany which could be seen to contain the 'correct' and 'fully mature' economic, historical and social conditions needed for revolutionary action. That the revolution had not happened – and did not look like it would happen – lead Gramsci to investigate why this was so. What held a society back from revolution?

Gramsci's answers to this question marked the point of departure of neo-Marxism from orthodox Marxism. Gramsci contended that class conflict did not happen just in political revolts, but also at the level of consciousness. Before a revolution could occur – even if the so-called 'necessary economic conditions' are in place – class consciousness has to be ready also. This key observation placed institutions of ideology and hegemony – such as the mass media – at the forefront of a neo-Marxist analysis of society. A lack of revolutionary potential could be explained by the ideological battle waged against the masses through the media.

Activity

Study the following list of points.

- Modern society is based on class conflict.
- The mass media contributes to false consciousness in society.
- Whereas the ruling class own the media, managers control the day-to-day running.
- The ruling class rule as the controllers of ideas.
- Bias does exist, but it is not a deliberate capitalist conspiracy.
- The media is the mouthpiece of the ruling class.
- The ruling class own and control the media.
- The purpose of sociology is to expose ideological rule in society.
- The nature of media ownership has changed since the death of Marx.
- The media contributes to hegemony in society.

Some of these ideas are associated with the orthodox Marxist perspective, some with the neo-Marxist perspective, others with both. Rewrite the list, dividing it into three sections, one each for the three combinations above.

U, I

The Glasgow University Media Group

The Glasgow University Media Group (GUMG) (1976, 1980, 1982) represents an attempt at the hegemonic analysis of bias in television news coverage on a variety of news events such as elections, strikes, warfare and health issues. The GUMG points out how bias is not the result of deliberate or conscious conspiracy by members of the ruling class, but is instead part of the day-to-day process of how news is made by professionals working within a culture which presents a pro-capitalist viewpoint as normal and natural while excluding or ignoring other views. Thus the media creates a 'hegemony' or total dominance of one viewpoint.

John Eldridge (1993), a founder member of the GUMG, believes that it is impossible for television news not to be biased since it is manufactured by individuals who are effectively 'creating reality' by choosing to include some stories while excluding others:

However natural, actual and immediate it all looks, television is a massive feat of social construction. Yet it is not reality that is constructed but a semblance of it. And how could it be otherwise?
(Eldridge, 1993, p. 4)

Pluralism

The pluralist perspective in media sociology stems from an analysis of the range of sources of power in what are seen as contemporary western democracies. Pluralism is a belief in competition within compromise and consensus. (See also Sections 17.4 and 17.5.)

Applied to the media, a pluralist analysis would suggest that although bias exists, it does so in order to represent the interests of the buying public who have purchasing power and exercise a free choice over where to give their custom.

Discussion point

Does shareholding and privatization increase public power or is this situation nothing more than an ideological invention?

Pluralists believe that democracy is achieved through the very culture industry attacked by the Frankfurt School. Audiences have the power to make one media product successful, while closing down another owing to lack of demand.

Pluralists claim that a dominant ideology does not exist through enforced ideological control and the manipulation of the media by a ruling class élite since every taste and political view is represented in the media. The most popular of these is bought by the public and becomes the most successful.

Feminism

The feminist analysis of the media, sharing many similarities with the Marxist analysis, looks towards the media as an agent of ideological control. The media is a source of the socialization of traditional gender roles and constructs an ideological 'femininity' to be followed by girls and women alike. (See also Section 2.6 and Chapter 5.)

For example, feminists would claim that women's body shape is defined or policed by the media. Biased language often contains references which socialize women into a subordinate position in society, and women's occupational roles are often highly stereotypical in TV adverts.

The central concept in any feminist analysis of power in society is 'patriarchy' or 'rule of the father' (this is discussed in more detail in Chapter 5). This concept is used by feminists as a means by which aspects of everyday life can be critically labelled as contributing to the inequalities between the sexes. In their fight against male bias, or patriarchy, sociologists taking a feminist perspective have pointed to the need to actively challenge and pull apart or 'deconstruct' representations of femininity in the media.

The audience: active or passive?

A key feature of the debates between most sociological perspectives concerns the role of the audience. Do individuals – or even groups – believe media messages? Is it realistic to speak of 'the masses' and are they complete victims of ideological influence? In presenting this key issue of sociological debate, a simple answer would be to create a dichotomy of extreme positions: either audiences are active and able to interpret from the many media messages on offer, or audiences are passive and able to be 'tricked' by manipulated messages which may support a ruling élite view of the world. (See also Sections 10.3 and 10.9.)

Pluralists would argue that audiences are able to actively select from media messages. On the other hand, some Marxist and some feminist theorists would argue that audiences are often controlled by the media. As we can see, the issue of bias in the media and the issue of the effect of the media on society are closely related. Contemporary sociological approaches to these problems try to treat different audiences differently. Some may be affected by what they hear, see or read, but others will not.

Angela McRobbie, illustrates through her research that magazines aimed at a young audience contain highly ideological messages. McRobbie (1983) takes as an example *Jackie* magazine, aimed at pre-teen girls, and through content analysis demonstrates the existence of patriarchal ideology. She claims that this 'ideology of adolescent femininity' attempts to define for young girls how they should live their teenage and adult lives. Magazines like this contain articles, problem pages and photo-stories all of which are concerned with a limited number of themes: the importance of romance in a girl's life, the importance of finding a 'good boy', and the importance of 'looking good'. (See also Section 10.7.)

However, McRobbie does not assume that readers of these magazines are necessarily influenced by them in a passive fashion. She suggests that sociological research into the content of the media needs

Activity

Study the two newspaper front pages in Figure 15.2, produced on the day of the 1992 general election in the UK. How are they biased, if at all? Whose interests do they represent? Using the three theories of orthodox Marxism, neo-Marxism and pluralism try to think through the eyes of these theories. How would they interpret these front covers? Write one detailed paragraph per theory.

I, A

to take a two-sided approach: it needs to identify bias and whose interests are represented by such bias; but equally, research needs to demonstrate the extent to which audiences 'read' this bias in a critical fashion.

💬 **Discussion point**

Are audiences active or passive in their consumption of the media?

The New Right

The New Right is not so much a sociological perspective as a set of political ideas which have become influential in British society since 1979 with the arrival of the first Thatcher Conservative government. (See Section 2.10.)

Of central concern to the New Right's views on the media are the issues of ownership and censorship. Like those of pluralism, New Right ideas are influenced by a belief in the fairness of a free market economy to meet the needs of the public/consumers/audiences in a democratic fashion. The public have freedom of choice and demonstrate this through their patterns of consumption.

Among those who believe in New Right ideas, we often find 'moral panics' (see Section 15.5) created concerning the content of the media and its perceived potential to corrupt the morality of society. Recent moral panics which have led to the reopening of the censorship debate have included the death in February 1993 of two-year-old James Bulger – which raised issues of single-parent families and the dangers of violent media in contributing to increased levels of delinquency and criminality.

Figure 15.2 Front pages of the *Daily Mirror* and *The Sun*, 9 April 1992 (© Rex Features)

Many of us are familiar with the name Mary Whitehouse among other 'moral crusaders' who from time to time rekindle criticisms aimed at the media for indoctrinating its audience.

Activity

With the five theories covered in this section in mind, copy and complete the following table. This should help you to understand these theories and act as a summary for your notes.

	Orthodox Marxism	Neo-Marxism	Pluralism	Feminism	The New Right
View of society					
Key concepts					
View of the role of the media in society					
View of bias in the media					

U, I

Post-modernism

Contemporary approaches to the study of culture in all of its forms include increasingly popular ideas on 'post-modernism'. This concept, despite its wide variety of meanings and definitions, is used to refer to many aspects of social life from musical forms and styles, literature, and fine art through to philosophy, history and especially the mass media. (See also Sections 10.2 and 10.11.)

Post-modern sociologies contain the observation that in post-modernity, as opposed to modernity, we witness the decline of absolute truth and the rise of *relativism* – where no single dominant meanings can be widely agreed on in society regarding the nature of social life. When asked in an interview to define post-modernism, the French post-modernist Jean Baudrillard (1993a) commented:

There's no clear or appropriate answer to that. Basically, if post-modernism exists, it must be the characteristic of a universe where there are no more definitions possible. It is a game of definitions which matters ... they have been deconstructed, destroyed ... it has all been done. The extreme limit of these possibilities has been reached. ...all that are left are pieces.

(Baudrillard, 1993a, pp. 94–95)

In his essay 'Simulations', Baudrillard (1983a) attempts to explain the differences between 'reality' as lived by individuals in their day-to-day life, and the so-called 'reality' portrayed by the media. Baudrillard, like other post-modernists, contends that everyday reality and media reality have become blurred. Individuals obtain what they experience as real knowledge about the real world from the media, but this is actually reproduced knowledge about an entirely simulated or reproduced world. This he calls the 'hyperreal'.

Umberto Eco (1987), an Italian post-modernist philosopher and literary figure, defines the hyperreal as 'that which is more real than real'.

In using this concept of the hyperreal, some post-modernists claim that with the increased importance of the media in contemporary society, the nature of the relationships between the media and audiences is changing. Baudrillard claims that audiences, especially of television, have undergone a rapid and profound change in their experiences.

Audiences live their lives through the simulations of reality given by the media. Thus, the knowledge and experience social actors believe they have of 'real life' becomes indistinguishable from that given to us by the media. An example of this was the 'instant' 24-hour images of warfare produced by Cable News Network (CNN) from the Gulf war. Audiences felt they had experienced the war themselves, yet they only did so through manufactured television images. (See also Section 15.6 which contains a detailed case study of the media and warfare.)

15.2 Methods of media analysis

It is possible to draw a distinction between techniques that involve the analysis of media content and those that involve the analysis of audiences' responses to media content. This section discusses two main approaches to studying the content of the media.

Principles of content analysis

Content analysis is a highly successful technique used by a number of sociologists to investigate the content of the media. Since the media comes 'ready made', it is relatively easy to gain access to the required broadcast or publication and relatively cheap to build up a sample.

Discussion point

How can sociologists investigate and expose the 'hidden messages' in the media?

Content analysis allows a researcher to measure or simply add up the frequency of a given message. Provided the method is agreed by a team of researchers beforehand, and clearly discussed in research, replication of this type of 'counting' is possible. For example, feminist researchers may be interested in counting the frequency of so-called traditional gender-roles in a whole variety of media products, from children's books, shopping catalogues, television advertisements and other sources. Marxist-orientated sociologists may wish to study the frequency with which a pro-establishment viewpoint occurs in the media.

When conducting content analysis, researchers often use 'coding schemes' – lists of categories to 'look' for. Thus, when 'coding-up' a piece of media text (be it a picture, text, or a TV advert) the research uses a prearranged set of codes or categories and simply measures the frequency of occurrence of these codes.

One of the popular starting points for media research among sociologists is to analyse the language used in the media. Does the media contain words or phrases that may contain a biased, one-sided viewpoint? A clearly identifiable example of this type of bias can be seen in newspaper headlines – especially in the tabloid press, where bold statements are often necessary to capture the public's attention and persuade them to purchase today's 'big story'. (See also the chart 'Mad dogs and Englishmen'.)

News items, be they transmitted or published through radio, television or print, are based on and created by a process of selection. The construction of the news involves decisions made by media personnel as to the relative merits and importance of each story or item. At some points in the year, most notably the 'silly season' during the summer parliamentary recess, some stories are given attention they would not merit at other times, except perhaps as the short, light-hearted item at the end of a broadcast.

The decision as to what item is 'most important' is reflected in the order of the scheduling of the items. In television and radio broadcasts, priority of story is reflected by the brief headlines often used as an introduction to the longer programme. Audiences share a common-sense understanding that these items are the most important since they come first. Equally, newspaper front-page headlines serve the same function.

A simple method of conducting content analysis into the biased and selective decisions media personnel make is to measure the frequency of particular types of news stories, and where they are scheduled in an overall broadcast or publication. Over a period of time it should be possible for the researcher to see any patterns, if they exist, in the type of items given importance over others.

Mad dogs and Englishmen

We have	They have
Army, Navy and Air Force	A war machine
Reporting guidelines	Censorship
Press briefings	Propaganda

We	They
Take out	Destroy
Suppress	Destroy
Eliminate	Kill
Neutralize	Kill
Decapitate	Kill
Dig in	Cower in their foxholes

We launch	They launch
First strikes	Sneak missile attacks
Pre-emptively	Without provocation

Our men are ...	Their men are ...
Boys	Troops
Lads	Hordes

Our boys are ...	Theirs are ...
Professional	Brainwashed
Lion-hearts	Paper tigers
Cautious	Cowardly
Confident	Desperate
Heroes	Cornered
Dare-devils	Cannon fodder
Young knights of the skies	Bastards of Baghdad
Loyal	Blindly obedient
Desert rats	Mad dogs
Resolute	Ruthless
Brave	Fanatical

Our boys are motivated by	Their boys are motivated by
An old-fashioned sense of duty	Fear of Saddam

Our boys	Their boys
Fly into the jaws of hell	Cower in concrete bunkers

Our ships are ...	Iraqi ships are ...
An armada	A navy

Israeli non-retaliation is	Iraqi non-retaliation is
An act of great statesmanship	Blundering/Cowardly

The Belgians are ...	The Belgians are also ...
Yellow	Two-faced

Our missiles are ...	Their missiles are ...
Like Luke Skywalker zapping Darth Vader	Ageing duds *(rhymes with Scuds)*

Our missiles cause ...	Their missiles cause ...
Collateral damage	Civilian casualties

We ...	They ...
Precision bomb	Fire wildly at anything in the skies

Our PoWs are ...	Their PoWs are ...
Gallant boys	Overgrown schoolchildren

George Bush is ...	Saddam Hussein is ...
At peace with himself	Demented
Resolute	Defiant
Statesmanlike	An evil tyrant
Assured	A crackpot monster

Our planes ...	Their planes ...
Suffer a high rate of attrition	Are shot out of the sky
Fail to return from missions	Are zapped

Source: *The Guardian*, 23 January 1991

'The camera never lies' so the saying goes, but in terms of the selective use of camera angles, pictures do not necessarily show the whole story. For example, demonstrations can be made to look far more dramatic, violent or hostile by zooming in on a small group and avoiding coverage of other less violent moments. Equally a protest against a leading public figure may be made to appear less important by concentrating on less violent moments.

Here, sociologists are faced with the possibility of combining content analysis with another research method, such as questionnaires or interviews. (See also Chapter 3.) Members of a demonstration or other newsworthy event can be asked whether media pictures and images reflected their own, real-life experiences.

Newspaper content analysis

By far the easiest and most accessible form of content analysis is the measurement in newspapers of biases in language, pictures, and use of space and headlines. In analysing a daily newspaper, the sociologist would expect to:

- measure the sizes of headlines and surface areas of stories to see which type of stories were given most coverage
- measure the frequency and type of words used to see whether they are biased or emotive
- assess the images used in pictures
- assess the order in which stories are presented from front cover to back cover
- study the content of political comments, editorials and news stories for openly one-sided views.

As the chart 'Mad dogs and Englishmen' demonstrates, the language used in the media can often contain bias which is not always obvious until it is presented in a different form, in this case side-by-side. The 'vocabulary' relates to news coverage of the Gulf war.

Problems and limitations of content analysis

In turning the essentially qualitative (images, words, order, etc.) into the more quantitative (frequencies, figures etc.) the subtlety of biased messages may be lost. It is important to remember with content analysis that the whole of the product is greater than its parts. The overall effect of a biased piece of reporting may be lost in pulling it apart in order to represent it as a series of figures.

Another major problem with content analysis is that the 'coding scheme' used is often open to personal interpretation. These codes are sometimes guided by the ideological and personal values of the researchers themselves. It is quite possible to 'see' what you think is bias if you go looking for it in the first place. Having said this, though, content analysis does tend to be more reliable (see Section 3.6) than semiology, discussed next.

Activity

Perform content analysis on a sample of newspapers to look at the issue of gender bias in the media. You will have to organize the size and type of your sample and think about what research has already been done into this issue to use as a theoretical background to your work. Present your findings as a short report. Use the following chapter headings: *Introduction; Existing research; Methodology; Results; Evaluation.* Remember to be as theoretical and evaluative as possible.

A, E

Semiology

Semiology can be defined, by the literal meaning of the word, as the scientific study of signs. Semiology as a technique or academic discipline developed from linguistics – the concern to study the meanings, origins and uses of language, and how humans communicate in a shared way through language. (See also Section 10.9.)

Semiology takes as its starting point the view that language is a series of learnt or socialized codes, a series of messages or meanings. In semiology codes or 'signs' are studied for the meanings they communicate – but these codes are believed to exist in all human life, not just language.

Human behaviour and social action are treated as one vast 'text' which can be studied in the same way as a piece of writing. Signs help us to understand our day-to-day life since they stand for or 'signify' a particular meaning. For example, in order to establish in the first few seconds of a film that a character is a business person, we would probably be given an image or a sign of that person with a smart suit and briefcase. This sign would represent a cultural image which is socialized into the minds of members of western Europe and communicates a common-sense message.

In studying the signs in a piece of media 'text', researchers using semiological methods seek to 'read' the text in such a way as to decode or deconstruct it – to pull apart and uncover each of the codes to establish the meaning being communicated. Semiologists believe that audiences of the media, and social actors in day-to-day life, deconstruct the signs around them.

Some signs communicate codes which could be seen as being ideological. For example, a television advertisement featuring an apron-clad woman in a kitchen could be seen to contain patriarchal ideology (see Chapter 5).

Problems and limitations of semiology

Perhaps the major criticism of semiology comes from a positivistic methodological stance (see Section 3.1). Semiology is unrepresentative and often subjective. Firstly, it is not true that the audience and the researcher share a common meaning of a sign, nor is it correct to assume that fixed meanings will exist over time. Again, this takes us back to the debate concerning the participation of the audience of the media with the signs and ideology contained in the media. Do audiences accept signs and dominant meanings pre-constructed for them; or are they free to re-create meanings and to read the media in a subversive way, rejecting ideology?

Activity

1 Analyse a sample of five television adverts using the methods of semiology. In order to do this, ask yourself the following questions.
   a What 'sign' is being used?
   b How do we recognize the sign?
   c What dominant or intended meaning do the creators of the advert wish us to receive?
2 Write a paragraph describing the limitations of this method. Concentrate on the issue of the 'subjectivity of your reading'.

A, E

15.3 Current media policy and political debates

The media and its freedoms and constraints in contemporary social life are of great significance for politicians (see Chapter 17), media workers and sociologists, as well as for the public as audience members and possibly as pressure group members. Even if you are simply engaged with the media as a reader of a newspaper or a viewer of television, issues of freedom, choice, control and quality affect your life. Three issues will be discussed in this section.

* Do 'free-market' policies enable freedom of choice for the consumer?
* Does market competition lead to erosion of the quality of broadcasting?
* Will we witness a decline in the 'moral standards'

of the output of the media – and if so, what effect will this have on the audience?

Some commentators have suggested that we live in a 'media saturated society', by which they mean that the world has become so exposed to mass communications that it is difficult now to think of life without them. If this is the case, a critical understanding of recent media policy becomes all the more important: if the media is a central force in contemporary life, shaping the lives of millions, what economic, cultural and global forces shape the media itself? (See also Sections 10.8 and 10.9.)

Discussion point

To what extent do you think the mass media is the most significant technological development of the present age?

Television technology as a cultural form

From a neo-Marxist stance, cultural critic Raymond Williams (1990) has suggested that television has not so much shaped contemporary times, as been itself shaped by the times. We need to be very careful when attributing a 'cause' or 'effect' to any social phenomenon:

It is often said that television has altered our world. In the same way, people often speak of a new world, a new society, a new phase of history, being created – 'brought about' – by this or that new technology: the steam-engine, the automobile, the atomic bomb. Most of us know what is generally implied when such things are said. But this may be the central difficulty: that we have got so used to statements of this general kind, in our most ordinary discussions, that we can fail to realize their specific meanings.

(Williams, 1990, p. 9)

Rather than the shape of contemporary social life being caused by television, Williams argued that the form and content of television could be seen as a product of contemporary social life. The question of whether television technology is a cause or an effect is an important and profound starting point for the investigation of contemporary media culture. (See also Section 10.3.)

Writing in 1975, and looking forward into his future of media broadcasting (which is of course our past and present), Williams commented that:

There is still an unfinished struggle and argument over the institutions and control of sound and vision broadcasting: the conflict that has been clear for two generations between 'public service' and 'com-

mercial' institutions and policies. It would be a major error to suppose that this conflict is over; indeed the signs are that it is now entering one of its most acute and difficult phases.
(Williams, 1990, p. 135)

Williams argued, with amazing foresight, that contemporary media debates and arguments would focus on issues of public and commercial broadcasting and control. This prediction has largely been proven to be the case. Debates over media policies in the late 1990s can be seen to focus on the nature of, and differences between, public and commercial broadcasting.

Public and commercial broadcasting

The term 'broadcasting media' refers to media transmitted through the air – terrestrial TV (and satellite TV) and radio. To be technically correct, cable TV is not a form of 'broadcasting' by this definition because it is not transmitted through the air but received via cables. For the sake of convenience, however, cable TV is often included in definitions of 'broadcasting', especially since many programmes for cable TV are produced originally by traditional stations and production houses for 'broadcast'.

Broadcasting can be further subdivided into 'public' and 'commercial'.

- *Public broadcasting* in the UK refers to the BBC. The audience pays a licence fee which acts as a funding mechanism. The top positions at the BBC are government-appointed.
- *Commercial broadcasting* is sometimes referred to as 'independent' broadcasting. Traditionally, this concept was used to refer to regional companies which transmitted via the Independent Television (ITV) network. Recently the independent sector has grown owing to the introduction of Channel 4, Channel 5, satellite and other technologies.

Broadcasting: the widening of choice?

Discussion point
To what extent have 'free-market' policies led to a freedom of choice in the public's consumption of broadcast media?

There has been much contemporary debate about whether consumer choice has been increased by the widening of independent broadcasting. We can identify two basic responses to this issue.

- *Widening media products increases the freedom of consumer choice and therefore the power of the audience.* This 'free-market' position is held by some pluralists (see Section 17.4) and some

members of the New Right (see Section 2.10) but not by all. Developments in technology which bring an ever-increasing choice of products into the home are seen to represent the increased democracy of the media. This view is based on a belief in an 'ideal future' of broadcasting where the audience enjoys an almost unlimited choice.
- *Freedom of choice cannot exist when the public can consume only what they can afford to buy.* Some commentators – including many who are 'left-of-centre', but also increasingly some pluralists – have suggested that this is not a democratic situation, far from it. (See also Section 17.1.) Additionally, there will be only a very limited 'choice' as more and more stations buy products from similar sources – products that are increasingly similar in nature and content. With a rather pessimistic tone, these commentators see a future where audiences are exposed to repeats of cheap, poor quality programmes, where ultimately there is no choice. (See also Section 10.3.)

Ownership and control of the modern media

The traditional 'battleground' for debates over the level of democracy in the media, especially between pluralist and Marxist viewpoints, is often referred to as 'the ownership and control debate'.

The orthodox Marxist view on media ownership, as an example of the ownership of any of the means or forces of production (see also Section 2.5), is to argue that ownership and therefore ultimate control rests in the hands of a narrow group – the ruling class so defined by their ownership in the first place. The Marxist view on the media relates directly to their ideas on media bias: the ruling class own the media and therefore are able to directly control its output.

Pluralists take issue with this view, which they see as simplistic and naive (see also Section 17.4). Pluralists would argue that with the rise of joint-stock companies (share-holding), ownership and control have become split. Although a narrow élite may own a majority holding of a media company, the owners are forced to employ controllers to run the organization on a day-to-day basis.

Modern-day Marxists, such as those who adopt the neo-Marxist or hegemonic approach, contend that this development, although highly significant, does not mean that ruling-class interests are any less represented in the media, nor does it mean that controllers, or professional managers have ultimate freedom from their share-holding, élite owners.

Marxists are highly critical of the development of large-scale multimedia conglomerations, such as

The whole world in his hands ?

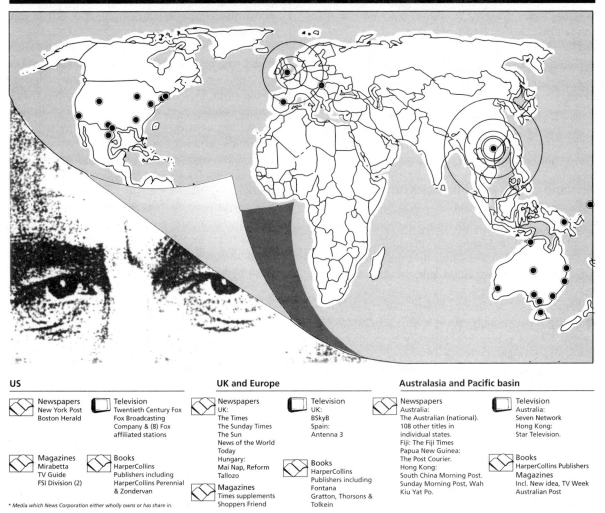

US		
Newspapers New York Post Boston Herald	**Television** Twentieth Century Fox Fox Broadcasting Company & (8) Fox affiliated stations	
Magazines Mirabetta TV Guide FSI Division (2)	**Books** HarperCollins Publishers including HarperCollins Perennial & Zondervan	

* Media which News Corporation either wholly owns or has share in.

UK and Europe		
Newspapers UK: The Times The Sunday Times The Sun News of the World Today Hungary: Mai Nap, Reform Tallozo	**Television** UK: BSkyB Spain: Antenna 3	
Magazines Times supplements Shoppers Friend	**Books** HarperCollins Publishers including Fontana Gratton, Thorsons & Tolkein	

Australasia and Pacific basin		
Newspapers Australia: The Australian (national). 108 other titles in individual states. Fiji: The Fiji Times Papua New Guinea: The Post Courier. Hong Kong: South China Morning Post. Sunday Morning Post, Wah Kiu Yat Po.	**Television** Australia: Seven Network Hong Kong: Star Television.	
	Books HarperCollins Publishers **Magazines** Incl. New idea, TV Week Australian Post	

Source: *The Guardian*, 2 August 1993

News Corporation owned by Rupert Murdoch, depicted here in the graphic (see also Section 10.8). Marxists perceive the development of media oligopolies (where control of a market is in the hands of a few large companies only) as serving ruling-class interests in the ideological war between the masses and the ruling class. The media audiences of contemporary western societies are being subjected to a limited range of opinion, given that a limited number of key individuals still have ultimate control: share-holding does not benefit working-class democratic ownership of the media, given the large sums needed to hold a majority share.

In contrast to this Marxist view, pluralists believe that owing to the rise of the joint-stock company, media ownership and control have become divided. A 'managerial revolution' has occurred (see also Section 4.5). The classic example of this argument comes from Burnham (1945). Burnham claims that the rise of the professional manager is an indication of increased democracy in the workplace.

Professional managers are left to do their job by owners and investors, who can come from all aspects of the social system. This is very much the image of the 'share-owning' democracy supported by the New Right, as illustrated by increased privatization of British industry since the 1979 general election. (See also Chapter 17.)

Public power or mass culture?

Discussion point

Do the media audience (the public) have the power to control the content of the media – or are they simply exposed to what ever media bosses wish them to consume?

The recent concern with the widening of media products in society throws up problems with a great deal of orthodox pluralist, Marxist and New Right thinking. As a result these positions are currently 'reinventing' their traditional ideas in the light of these changes.

The key issue, then, is whether the widening of media products leads to increased public power through consumer choice, or to increased levels of 'mass culture' (see also Section 10.3) – poor quality, uncritical, unintellectual programming which hinders the powers of the audience to reflect critically about society.

Within this second, more pessimistic view, that this so-called 'wider' media choice will lead to negative outcomes, we find sociologists who would usually or traditionally be opposed to each other, sharing what appear to be similar views – although they have often arrived at these views through very different theoretical assumptions and routes. For example, some Marxists and neo-Marxists may find themselves with some pluralists and members of the New Right in expressing concern over the 'quality' of the media. An equally 'odd' combination are the feminists and New Right theorists who both condemn the alleged increase in pornography from satellite and cable TV, and CD–ROM and Internet mediums.

The New Right

It is worth noting that what we have come to refer to as 'the New Right' in sociology (see Section 2.10) is a combination of two, perhaps contradictory beliefs.

- Some New Right thinking, especially since the beginning of the Thatcher Conservative administrations in 1979, has openly supported the economic mechanisms of the 'free-market' in society. This is seen as providing greater individual choice and therefore contributing to an increase in the democratization of social life.
- Another slightly 'older' ingredient in 'new' right thinking is a desire to return to 'traditional' morality or values – to re-emphasize religion (Christianity) and the family as the source for 'moral well-being' and social stability. This could be seen in John Major's 'back-to-basics' campaign. (See also Section 7.6.)

The second tradition blames rising crime and other 'indicators' of a decline in moral standards on the increase in single-parent families, the supposed lack of moral authority and discipline in schools, and the increase of undesirable products in the media which contain violence, swearing and sexually explicit materials.

Community radio: local power?

A good example of the widening of media choice can be seen by looking at radio. In response to the 1990 Broadcasting Act we have seen, in recent years, the slow growth and expansion not just of television broadcasting but also of radio – especially as a result of the government's desire to expand 'local' or 'community' radio stations.

As John Tulloch (1990) notes, the growth of community radio may have particular significance not only for so-called 'minority tastes' but also for 'minority groups' previously 'outside' the mainstream of broadcasting. In particular we may see the expansion in future years of radio broadcasting of both a truly community-based multicultural nature, plus specific stations and programmes aimed at ethnic audiences.

At present, however, the expansion of community radio is severely hampered by a lack of financial revenue arising from initial problems with finding advertising sponsorship – the major drawback of broadcasting in a free market.

Deregulation and public choice

As Paddy Scannell (1990) asserts:

Today the key topic in debates about broadcasting is deregulation. Should the state cease to control and regulate broadcasting, and let market forces shape its future development?
(Scannell, 1990, p. 20)

The Peacock Committee, charged in 1985 by the Conservative government to look into the issue of deregulation, has suggested that it should occur. Its 'Report of the Committee on Financing the BBC' (1986) recommended that an alternative to the still existing 'licence-fee' method of funding the BBC should be sought. If the BBC is to become simply one of many channels in a new free-market, openly competitive, 'deregulated' system – seen by the Conservative government to encourage freedom of public choice – then the compulsory purchase, by the audience, of a licence fee for a channel they may decide not to use no longer makes sense. As Scannell further notes:

For Peacock, broadcasting was a commodity – a marketable good like any other – provided for consumers, and the establishment of consumer sovereignty in broadcasting through a sophisticated market system was the aim of the report.
(Scannell, 1990, p. 21)

The Peacock Committee saw the future of television with a 'pay-per-programme' or 'pay-per-channel' funding mechanism.

Broadcasting in the 1990s

Following on from the recommendations made in the Peacock Report was the publication in 1988 of the White Paper *Broadcasting in the 1990s*. Included in the recommendations of this White Paper were:

- replacement of the ITV network with a new Channel 3 based on regional franchises
- creation of a Channel 5 (and a Channel 6 if possible) whose franchises would be auctioned
- introduction by the BBC of a pay-as-you-watch subscription service in the future.

The 1988 White Paper, more than any other previous media legislation, clearly illustrates New Right free-market ideas at work. However, many years on from its publication several of its ideas and recommendations are yet to be developed, or are still in a development stage. For example, ITV – now referred to as Channel 3 – has seen franchises given to four new holders:

- Carlton – which has taken over the old Thames Television network
- Meridian – which has replaced TVS
- Westcountry Television
- GMTV – which has replaced the TV-AM breakfast slot.

Channels 4 and 5

Channel 4 was launched in 1982 to provide for 'minority tastes', away from the mainstreams of BBC 1 and ITV (as, equally, was BBC2, which started broadcasting in 1964). In practice, this was to mean a move away from light entertainment, towards educational programming, programmes directed at issues concerning community or 'marginal groups', British sponsored drama and arts/cultural broadcasting. There is a common-sense belief that Channel 4 and BBC2 are supposed to be the 'arts' channels.

Channel 5, as set out in the 1988 White Paper and launched in March 1997, is to provide further diversity of tastes by offering yet another channel and thus increasing the 'freedom' of the audience. We might hold a pessimistic view of this, considering how much cable and satellite broadcasting of late has arguably not widened choice, but simply allowed increased exposure to repeats, and MTV (covered in more detail in Section 10.10), Sky sports coverage and CNN news coverage – which are accessible through a wide variety of other mechanisms.

A New Right perspective

Cento Veljanovski (1989) argues that media broadcasting must be left to a free market. Deregulation, from the point of view of the New Right, puts power into the hands of the consumer. Veljanovski rejects what is commonly referred to as the 'wall-to-wall Dallas' image, by which the quality of media products reduces to the 'lowest common denominator' – being the lightweight chat shows, soap operas and game shows unwelcomed by some.

Deregulation: should we bury pluralism?

With the move towards deregulation gaining momentum, a number of sociologists have begun to reappraise the future of media democracy. This process of reflection has also fallen on existing sociological ideas and theories. Have pluralist ideas, in particular, stood the test of time? As James Curran (1991), who adopts an 'up-dated' pluralist approach, notes:

New times call for new thinking . . . The domination of public service broadcasting in western Europe is weakening in response to a combined commercial and political onslaught. And the rapid expansion of TV channels is transforming the media landscape in a way that calls for an intellectual adjustment.
(Curran, 1991, p. 82)

As he notes, originally pluralist views emerged and developed in a very different social and cultural context. This occurred not long ago in terms of actual years – but at a time dramatically different in terms of the developments in the media during the last ten years.

When pluralism was first developed, the media was in the hands of a small élite who competed with one another for the audiences' attention over their limited media products. Curran suggests that since this situation has changed it is time to reject orthodox pluralism: to recognize this and move on from its dated values:

The result is a legacy of old saws which bear little relationship to contemporary reality . . . it is time that they were given a decent funeral.
(Curran, 1991, p. 82)

Curran is relatively optimistic about the ongoing deregulation, although he does warn against the full deregulation of all television into the commercial sector. He believes that since the majority of advertising and sponsorship monies would move to TV, other forms of the media would suffer, such as radio. He argues that realistic media 'democracy' where the audience has a real choice in purchasing and consumption will only be possible in a structure based still on a 'core public sector', but combined with an increased private sector. Curran believes that this combination will realize the old pluralist ideal of freedom of choice: The media will become:

. . . an open system of dialogue, and give added impetus to the collective, do-it-yourself tradition of civil society.
(Curran, 1991, p. 111)

The media marketplace

Jay Blumler (1991), adopting a revised pluralist perspective, is another to argue that we should feel slightly anxious over total deregulation. He describes a totally deregulated media as a 'new-style American television system', and means by this phrase that a totally free media marketplace would lead to a devaluing of the quality of some media broadcasting. For Blumler, the benefits of the free-market are:

- greater viewer choice (in terms of quantity)
- intensified commercialism
- greater entertainment programming.

However, Blumler is also wary for the future quality of news and public affairs broadcasting. He believes that while entertainment programmes will get funding and audience attention, the important 'factual' programmes – which are vital for us to think about the world around us – may lose quality.

Blumler's image of the future of TV news suggests that, although democracy within the media will increase for the audience, democracy through the media may become more problematic. In other words, our freedom of choice will expand, but our exposure to, and critical knowledge of, political ideas will contract. We will find it difficult, therefore, to participate fully in a democratic society which relies on its members having an informed political choice at the ballot box. Where will the information about political choices come from, if all we are fed is entertainment?

Blumler (1992) argues further that the 'march of the market' raises vital doubts within pluralist theory concerning the preservation of specific aspects of media 'quality' once taken for granted. These 'vulnerable values', which we currently hold dear but which may suffer in a totally free market, are:

- *programme quality* – through increased pressure to make programmes cheaply for maximum profit
- *diversity* – minority tastes may be cut if few purchase them
- *cultural identity* – the specific 'national identity' of any one country may be eroded by an increased exposure to other countries' media products (see also Section 10.10)
- *the welfare of children and juveniles* – this may suffer as children's television may be created solely to sell related toys, and not to stretch the mind.

Contradictions for the Left and Right

Samuel Brittan (1989) argues that the 'case for the consumer market' is such that freedom of choice will only be enlarged by increased freedom in broadcasting. However, he stresses that this is very different from the 'anything goes' panic among some pluralist and New Right thinkers, since, he suggests, even a deregulated media will still be 'regulated' by legal constraints such as the 1959 Obscene Publications Act.

Brittan recognizes, however, the contradictions within the thinking of the New Left and New Right camps on the issue of deregulation:

- the New Left are against censorship, yet unhappy about public choice in the media, whereas
- the New Right desire public choice – but only provided they do not choose 'undesirable' and 'immoral' material such as pornography.

Is freedom in broadcasting possible?

Brittan highlights the tension that deregulation will bring between the so-called audience 'free choice' and increased broadcasting 'controls' to ensure that the 'free choice' is the 'right one'. He concludes:

Constant vigilance will continue to be the price of liberty in broadcasting, as in all other walks of life. (Brittan, 1989, p. 50)

15.4 The social construction of news

Hegemonic sociologists (see Section 10.2) such as those working at the Glasgow University Media Group, who adopt a neo-Marxist orientation to the media, have made a major contribution to the sociological study of the media by asserting that news productions are inevitably and 'normally' the result of selection, interpretation and therefore bias. This is an important point to realize when starting to think critically about the creation of news stories and other programmes.

News is not a neutral, objective reality which exists in a vacuum ready made and separate from those in the media who report it. News simply would not exist without the media: it is an ideological term which suggests that some events in society desire our attention because they are more important than other events. As Figure 15.3 illustrates, 'news' (or

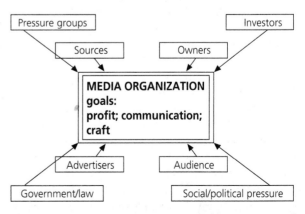

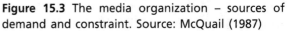

Figure 15.3 The media organization – sources of demand and constraint. Source: McQuail (1987)

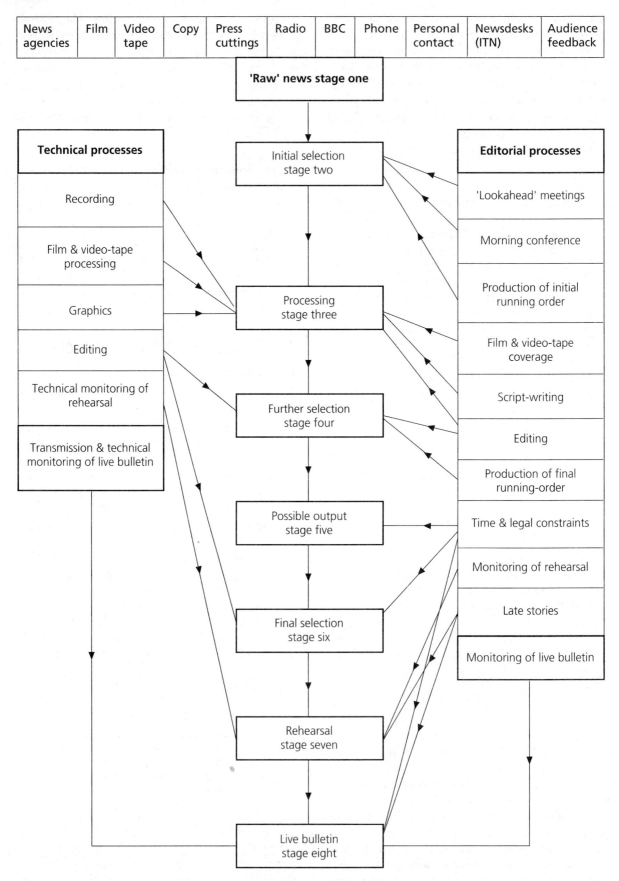

News agencies	Film	Video tape	Copy	Press cuttings	Radio	BBC	Phone	Personal contact	Newsdesks (ITN)	Audience feedback

'Raw' news stage one

Technical processes

Recording

Film & video-tape processing

Graphics

Editing

Technical monitoring of rehearsal

Transmission & technical monitoring of live bulletin

Initial selection stage two

Processing stage three

Further selection stage four

Possible output stage five

Final selection stage six

Rehearsal stage seven

Live bulletin stage eight

Editorial processes

'Lookahead' meetings

Morning conference

Production of initial running order

Film & video-tape coverage

Script-writing

Editing

Production of final running-order

Time & legal constraints

Monitoring of rehearsal

Late stories

Monitoring of live bulletin

Figure 15.4 The daily evolution of Channel 4 News. Source: Blanchard and Morley (1982)

any media product for that matter) is not made away from all other outside influences.

Neo-Marxist sociologists, however, point out that events are only considered important by the public if they are presented by the media as being important news in the first place.

We can identify a number of influences on the media in the process of the creation or social construction of news programmes or publications.

News values

'News values' are the decisions which guide the overall look or feel of a newspaper or television news programme, and the values they follow concerning what types of stories to concentrate on at the expense of others. These news values can evolve over time to give a news product its own distinctive character, or they can be highly stylized from the initial launch of a product aimed at a particular audience group through market research. But however news values evolve, their existence shows that news is not created in a totally neutral way – it involves decisions and selections.

Discussion point

Why is it important to think of the news as a product, as something which has been manufactured?

As we can see from Figure 15.4, a news programme goes through many different stages in the 'news production progress'. A number of groups and individuals come into contact with what will be the finished news item.

Many sociologists see these groups or individuals as 'gatekeepers' who 'set the news agenda'. Through manipulating values as to the worth of some stories to be included as 'news' and others to be excluded, the media personnel control, regulate and oversee what information or biases are given to the buying public and what are not.

Media organizations and institutions thus 'set the agenda' for audiences. Although pluralist sociologists would argue that audiences are given what they want because they have the power to purchase on the media marketplace, Marxist sociologists and others critical of the role of the media in society would suggest that audiences are given a very limited selection of ideas and views to choose from in the first place.

The act of agenda-setting is, however, a very complex one involving many different stages, processes and influences – from both within and without the media organization in question. As Figure 15.5

shows, the media does have the potential to affect or shape the public agenda, but the media is itself shaped by the agenda of the public and the government of the day.

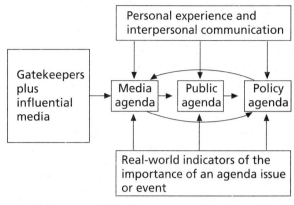

Figure 15.5 A model of agenda-setting. Source: E. M. Rogers and J. W. Dearing in J. Anderson, ed. (1987), *Communication Yearbook 11*

Professional culture

The GUMG have highlighted the existence of a professional culture among media personnel. Upon entering the profession, media workers at a number of different levels undergo a process of secondary socialization whereby they learn the culture and values (see also Section 10.1) of the particular organization they have joined. The GUMG argue that this professional culture is essentially based on white, European, male, middle-class, middle-of-the-road values. In this way the cultural messages of the media reflects the hegemony of dominant groups in society.

Activity

Copy and complete the following table. This should act as a summary of the ideas in this section so far, indicating how perspectives would interpret them.

	Definition	'Orthodox' Marxism	Neo-Marxism	Pluralism
News as a production				
News values				
Gate-keeping				
Agenda-setting				
Professional culture				

U, I

The office routine

Galtung and Ruge (1976) suggest that the day-to-day set-up and running of media organizations are constrained by office or bureaucratic routines. Media organizations are limited by the fact that their office culture is based on the rapid turnover of periods of 24 hours. The outside world is more often than not presented as a series of sudden, unrelated events, sometimes forgotten by the start of the next 24-hour period. Given this constraint it is sometimes difficult for media organizations to develop a sense of gradual build-up and background to events.

By being unable, or sometimes unwilling, to present news items as a series of unfolding events which culminate in a large, more newsworthy event, reporting may tend to over-simplify stories. Realistically, there is little choice in this. The character of newspapers and television broadcasts are such that they are designed to be short, sharp and relatively easy to digest.

The object of any media product, ultimately, is to sell to an audience, either by the public directly purchasing their chosen product or by viewing and listening figures in television and radio ratings wars. Often news will be made as dramatic as possible in order to sell. An example of this is the front pages of British tabloid newspapers.

Personalization

Chibnall (1977) notes how news stories often contain the technique of 'personalization'. By this it is meant that it is often easier for an audience to understand an item, and to remember and reflect on it, if it is presented in a way that says something about the individual viewer's life. This effect can be achieved by presenting stories from an individual's viewpoint, giving an item a 'personal touch' by focusing in on a particular family and their life.

It is useful to think of the processes of agenda-setting, gatekeeping and the influences of the office routine, professional culture and news values as all working together. This could be referred to as 'shaping the news flow'.

News flow can be complex and multidimensional. The creation of a newsworthy event, and its transmission between different news sources – international, foreign, regional, community etc. – can be best seen as a chain or flow. After the initial event the piece of 'news' in question is passed from journalist to journalist, each time in a shortened or slightly modified form depending on how these media agencies see the intended audience – the 'receiver'. Once the news has been 'received' by the audience it may be transmitted again, this time through word of mouth, and once more modified as this process occurs. Finally, the reaction of the receiver is transmitted back to the original source through critical debate, public opinion polls, audience complaints, letters to media organizations etc.

The concepts of gatekeeping, agenda-setting and news values may suggest that the media is solely responsible for the creation of the 'news'. But it must be remembered that the news is a social construction, made out of social processes – in particular the social interaction, or 'give-and-take', between governments, official sources, the public, media personnel and pressure groups. The 'news' is a product of bargaining between many different groups. It is not, however, a truly equal bargain – some groups such as the government do have more power, but not necessarily all of the time.

Activity

Using copies of *The Sun* and *The Times* newspapers *from the same day*, write a list of the news values each has. Explain how they are different, and how you can judge this from the use of space, running order and the other issues raised above.

I, A

Case study – The press coverage of Greenpeace

In a detailed case study of the relationships between environmental pressure groups and the media, Anders Hansen (1993) notes that:

... the prominence of certain social issues, at certain times, is relatively (although not exclusively) independent of the severity of such issues ... Nor does their fall from prominence in these arenas necessarily signal that the issues have been successfully resolved. It may simply be that they have been overtaken, and perhaps squeezed out altogether, by other, newer, issues.
(Hansen, 1993, p. xv)

The media attention given to environmental issues, then, like all other 'news', is frequently subject to the definitions of those who put the news together as to what is 'current' or 'topical' and what is not; or, to put it another way, what is 'important' or 'of significance' and what is not.

Taking the environmental movement Greenpeace as an example, Hansen contends that for some social movements, media publicity, and its effective use, is the key to getting its message across to the public, and hence gaining popular support. The successful use of media coverage through organized 'publicity stunts' enables these groups to reach a wide audience, and in doing so, to embarrass those they are protesting against – such as those hunting endangered species, dumping waste etc. However:

It is one thing for environmental groups to achieve massive media coverage for a short period of time and in relation to specific issues. It is quite a different task to achieve and maintain a position as an 'established', authoritative and legitimate actor in the continuous process of claims-making and policy-making on environmental matters.
(Hansen, 1993, p. 151)

In trying to identify and explain the nature of the press coverage received by Greenpeace, Hansen conducted a content analysis of five years' worth of two British newspapers – *The Guardian* and *Today*, between January 1987 to December 1991. Although Greenpeace is one of the more successful environmental groups to have developed in the 1980s (based on its membership figures, and especially considering it started as one of the very smallest) it nevertheless trailed behind Friends of the Earth in the amount of coverage received during the period of this study. For the period 1987–91 the numbers of articles were:

- Friends of the Earth – 1031
- Greenpeace – 896
- World Wide Fund for Nature (WWF) – 304
- Royal Society for the Protection of Birds – 328.

Only 120 articles mentioned both Greenpeace and Friends of the Earth together. Hansen concludes that:

. . . although there is some overlap between the two environmental pressure groups, they gain coverage independently of each other in the large majority of articles. This indicates that these two key environmental pressure groups may play rather different, and perhaps complementary, roles in terms of the issues which they help to put on the media agenda and bring to public attention.
(Hansen, 1993, pp. 153–4)

Hansen notes that these two groups have not allowed their rivalry to play a significant part in their press coverage. Rather than fighting against each other to the benefit of the press, they have concentrated on the issues they wish to put across, and on taking and directing the media agenda, rather than being directed by it.

A simple count of the frequency of being mentioned in the press does not, however, tell us much about the nature of that coverage, nor how successful each group has been in getting its ideas and causes in print. Hansen notes, in response to this, that Greenpeace is able to obtain press coverage on a wide range of issues. For example, the ten highest mentioned issues were (as percentages of all articles):

- nuclear power/arms/waste – 21.5
- exploitation of natural resources – 11
- waste disposal/management – 11
- conservation/endangered species – 10
- sea/beach pollution – 7
- air pollution/acid rain – 5
- ozone layer/global warming – 5
- discussion of governmental environmental policies – 4
- the 'Rainbow Warrior' affair – 3
- other environmental groups – 3.
  (Hansen, 1993, p. 157)

As this indicates, Greenpeace is relatively prominent in media coverage, and is relatively successful in getting its own agendas across; or, to put it another way, in shaping the 'news', in shaping the agenda-setting process. In this way, Greenpeace has been able to project an image of a 'legitimate' or 'expert' party on its chosen subject (environmentalism) and in this respect is a 'credible' source for the media to turn to. It has been successful in making itself appear an 'authoritative' voice, largely through the use of a 'scientific' legitimation claim, where it appears expert because it has a number of 'scientists' who speak on its behalf, while also using its own opinion poll research and environmental testing – which it makes accessible to the media, thus increasing the likelihood that it will be contacted by journalists seeking an 'easy source of information'. (Environmental pressure groups are also considered in Section 17.5.)

In this way, 'unofficial sources' sometimes do have the ability to shape the agenda-setting process.

15.5 Moral panics and the media

In the competition to sell to their audiences, the media not only simplifies but also exaggerates: sensational stories are popular and sell well. A 'moral panic' is a term coined by sociologists to refer to an exaggerated fear or outrage by the media and the audience, over an issue that has been blown out of proportion by the media in the first place.

Often the media is the first to act as moral crusader for the morality of society and to speak for public opinion in condemning the supposed actions of various groups in society. But far from always reporting some events neutrally, the media can amplify acts of deviance. (This is discussed in Section 11.2.) It can:

- exaggerate these acts to report an apparent rise in deviant actions
- arouse increased public concern which may have

an effect on crime figures based on public reporting

- actually increase particular deviant acts by making such appear interesting to an audience, or by labelling individuals as deviants. (See also Section 11.5.)

Folk devils

Whereas 'moral panic' refers to public and media responses to an issue or group, the group targeted by a moral panic in question, fictional or not, is referred to as a 'folk devil'.

Discussion point

How do audiences respond to moral panics? What types of group are labelled as folk devils?

Case study – The creation of mods and rockers

A classic example of a moral panic is provided by Stanley Cohen in his book *Folk Devils and Moral Panics* (1980), first published in 1972. Cohen's research of the 1964 mods and rockers disorders at British seaside towns, most notably during Easter bank holidays at Clacton, illustrates the extent to which media sensationalization can have an effect on audiences, including the public, police and the government.

Cohen demonstrates that the newspaper accounts of these riots tell stories of horrific terror, chaos and large-scale rioting. Clacton was pictured as being at the total mercy of rival gangs who, through mob behaviour, destroyed property, intimated the public and fought with one another.

Although these images may have become more and more familiar on subsequent occasions, they were by no means a true account of the first mods and rocker disturbances. Cohen argues that there were no opposed rival gangs until after the media moral panic had begun. There were minimal numbers of motorbikes and scooters used by these young people – their so-called main symbol of group membership – and the most serious offences originally committed were nothing more than threatening behaviour and minor vandalism.

However, owing to over-reporting, a self-fulfilling prophecy had been created whereby more members of the public became worried, police activity was increased as a response, and young people themselves created and joined these gangs that had been presented to them by the media as a fashionable and exciting lifestyle option. (See also Section 10.5.)

Ethnicity and moral panics

The Centre for Contemporary Cultural Studies (CCCS) at Birmingham University has produced a range of material focusing on the representation of ethnicity in the British pro-capitalist media. Taking a neo-Marxist stance, and especially influenced by the concept of hegemony as developed by Gramsci, Stuart Hall *et al.* in their book *Policing the Crisis* (1978) explain media prejudice, racism and the creation of the 'mugging' moral panic within the context of a crisis in capitalist legitimation since the 1970s. (See also Section 11.8.)

Orthodox Marxist sociology suggests that the inevitable break-up of capitalism will occur owing to periodic crisis points – where capitalism will be seen by the masses as no longer able to deliver what it promises. Rising unemployment, a declining standard of living and a rising cost of living will lead to the development of 'true consciousness'. Then the working classes will change from 'a class in themselves' and become 'a class for themselves' (see Section 4.7), this being the forerunner to any mass revolutionary action. Such economic crisis leads to a legitimation crisis, which is considered by Marxists such as Gramsci to be an even more serious threat to capitalism. (See also Chapter 17.)

A legitimation crisis, or a crisis in hegemonic control, occurs when the ruling class, through the state, is no longer able to win over the 'hearts and minds' of the general population. The very authority of the ruling class is challenged. Hall *et al.* argue that this very situation occurred in the first half of the 1970s in the UK.

Although rejecting an orthodox Marxist approach to media bias, Hall and colleagues nevertheless argue that the British mass media served the interests of the state at this time of crisis, and acted to divert public attention away from the problems of capitalism. A moral panic was created aimed at the scapegoat or folk devil of the 'black mugger'. In doing this, the media, especially the British press through sensationalism and exaggeration, turned the problems faced by a capitalist economy onto an 'outsider': Mugging was defined as a new crime imported from 'violent America', and sweeping the country like a plague.

It was noted, however, that the crime 'mugging' is merely a catch-all phrase for a number of different violent street crimes which were by no means new to the UK. In defining the mugger as a black and creating a widespread moral panic, the media helped to develop racism. However, this too served the interests of the state, since while the white and black working classes are divided the possibility of collective mass revolutionary action remains small.

Discussion point

How do the stereotypes of 'race' and ethnicity used in the media, especially in the reporting of the news, define reality for the audience?

'Primary definition' and the role of 'official sources'

Hall *et al.*'s work in *Policing the Crisis* has proven to be of great importance for subsequent media analysis, especially concerning the issue of 'primary definition' – the claim that official sources will dominate over non-official sources in most reporting of events. This tendency for official sources to create the common or 'primary definition' of a social situation through the media is seen as further evidence of hegemony in society – ruling-class definitions of events rule but without direct action taken by the ruling classes themselves.

Recent work within the Glasgow University Media Group has taken issue with this claim. It is suggested that journalists, pressure groups (and other examples of 'non-official sources') and 'official sources' are in competition and negotiation with one another, and news reporting is a product of the interaction of these agencies. This idea can be clearly seen in the work of Paula Skidmore, a member of the GUMG, who has researched the issue of whether there has or has not been a moral panic over sexual abuse of children in recent years in the media. (See also Section 7.7 on child abuse.)

Case study – The media reporting of sexual abuse of children

Paula Skidmore (1995) argues that rather than seeing a moral panic over sexual abuse of young people, we have witnessed a 'moral clampdown' – an altogether different process – aimed at the social work profession.

A content analysis of all references to this type of abuse in newspapers and on TV in 1991 in England – sponsored by the Economic and Social Research Council's (ESRC) Child Sexual Abuse and the Media Project, based at Glasgow University – shows some 1668 press items and 149 TV news items. Skidmore notes that of these items, 71 per cent of the press items and 83 per cent of the TV items were what she terms 'case-based' – were based on the reporting of an event or incident, rather than a more general piece discussing intervention, protection etc. Therefore, the media coverage of this issue can be seen to be reactive rather than proactive. It becomes a 'newsworthy' subject only once a 'scandal' breaks, and not beforehand.

Of these 'case-based' news items, positive representations of the social work profession were rare. When discussing the effects of this reporting on the audience, Skidmore contends that the audience:

... remembered, in general terms, social workers being wrong, parents fighting for their rights and police as 'goodies'. ... However, people were often less 'anti-social work' and recognized negative media coverage as not being true of the profession of the whole. Participants often believed social workers were being scapegoated.
(Skidmore, 1995, p. 22)

This observation is vital. It suggests that although social workers were portrayed in a negative light, the audience did not necessarily accept this image of them – even though they did remember it. As Skidmore further comments:

There is evidence therefore that audiences deconstruct and resist dominant media constructions around CSA [child sexual abuse]. People draw on personal and professional experience, their different structural positions within society, and diverse political frameworks in order to challenge or reinforce media accounts and develop alternative explanatory frameworks.
(Skidmore, 1995, p. 22)

Skidmore's research could be seen to throw some doubt on Hall *et al.*'s assertion that official sources are more likely to take dominance in news reporting. In the case of reporting issues of child sexual abuse, the media is presented with a problem of 'specialism' – it is unclear which journalists should cover the story 'in-house' since 'child abuse experts' do not professionally exist – they haven't been needed until recently. More often than not these stories are reported in a similar fashion to crime stories. The journalists are thus dependent on any information, official or otherwise, and the creation of a 'common-line-of-media-enquiry' is based very much on the negotiation of a number of different agendas from a number of different organizations and sources.

Interestingly, this research also notes that the media is currently faced with a situation of 'child abuse fatigue' – a growing general reluctance to spend more time on these stories; a feeling that too much reporting has already taken place.

What appears to have taken place in the reporting of cases of child sexual abuse, after the initial sensationalism, is not a moral panic but the reverse – an inability (or an unwillingness) to consider this practice as potentially as widespread as claimed by social workers and some feminist groups. Instead of a moral panic, then, we see an attempt by the media to scapegoat the social work profession: to suggest that these cases are not widespread, but are falsely started owing to the 'incompetence' of social workers to detect cases correctly:

Instead of just the abuser as a deviant 'folk devil' we often see the social work profession 'scapegoated' for their inadequate or incompetent intervention to protect children. This has often focused on an expressed belief that there cannot be the level of abuse of children that child protection professionals or feminist groups suggest. Social workers are therefore portrayed as zealots looking for abuse where none exists. In this sense, instead of a moral panic about child sex abuse in the media, we have increasingly seen a moral clampdown.
(Skidmore, 1995, p. 22)

Activity

There have been many contemporary media moral panics. Compile a list of all those you can remember and their relevant folk devil. It might be useful to ask other people of differing ages which ones they can think of. If you do this you must have a clear definition of a moral panic and a folk devil for them. Finally decide whether there are any common links between the entries on your list.

U, I, A

15.6 Political bias

Many groups and organizations in society are interested in, and concerned about, the potential the media has for spreading political bias and propaganda. These interested groups include, of course, sociologists, but also pressure groups, governments, governmental 'watchdogs' and political parties (see also Chapter 17). Sociologists have been concerned with bias in the media since the very beginning of a sociological interest in the subject of the media in general.

Discussion point

Why is it important for sociologists, and other interested parties, to be able to identify possible bias in the media?

Politics and public belief

Greg Philo (1994), a neo-Marxist member of the Glasgow University Media Group, contends that the dominance of a New Right Conservative government in the UK since 1979, and the electoral failures of the Labour party, could be explained by the success of Conservative administrations in using the media as an effective campaign tool:

To understand public beliefs about politics we must analyse how political parties have used the media. The crucial issue is how successful they have been in establishing strands of political belief which make sense and 'work' with voters.
(Philo, 1994, p. 46)

Philo suggests that although sometimes the media gives a biased account of the world to the audience – which they may or may not believe – at other times the media is a resource or 'campaigning tool' over which the political parties fight, each trying to give a good impression to an audience. He suggests that the Conservative governments' use of key phrases time and time again in the media – through speeches, interviews, party political broadcasts and other forms of political 'advertising' – placed Conservative policies firmly into the public consciousness. These popular political phrases included:

- 'there is no alternative'
- 'a share-owning/ home-owning democracy'
- 'popular capitalism'
- 'enterprise culture'
- 'the miracle economy'.

Some of these phrases not only acted as shorthand for Conservative policies, they were also used to attack and discredit in an effective manner Labour ideas and previous Labour governments:

- 'the winter of discontent'
- 'picket-line violence'.

The importance of the mass media for politicians and politics is perhaps best illustrated by the fact that the advertising company Saatchi & Saatchi were employed by the Conservatives as image gurus. Political broadcasts since 1978/9, based on Saatchi & Saatchi ideas, used music and images in dramatic ways much more than previous campaigns. According to Philo, electoral success was the result of the careful manipulation of these phrases or media messages. However, as Philo comments:

We have to consider the crucial question of how the audience responds to political and economic messages. What people understand, remember and what they believe depends in part on the nature of the message. But understanding, memory and belief also vary with factors such as practical experience and knowledge as well as the political, class, and cultural histories of the different groups receiving the message. New information from the media is

interpreted through these complex patterns of pre-existing knowledge and belief.
(Philo, 1994, p. 70)

Although the media presents a 'ready made world', the audience, suggests Philo, is sophisticated enough to reflect on this world and to compare it to experience already gained.

It is also important to recognize that not all of the mass media in the UK supports the Conservative Party all of the time. As illustrated by the front pages of the *Daily Mirror* reproduced below, sometimes the tables are turned, and the press can come out in favour of the Labour Party.

Activity

It has been argued by some that the *Daily Mirror* has in recent years moved away from its traditional support for the Labour Party. Build up a collection of contemporary *Daily Mirror* front covers and editorials. Do they support the Labour Party more than other parties, or not? How can you tell?

I, A, E

Case study – The politics of HIV/AIDS reporting

An understanding of the media sensationalization of some stories and the trivilization of others often

provides the sociologist with a keyhole view into the news values of the particular media product or organization under study.

David Miller and Kevin Williams (1993), while working for the GUMG, focused their research into HIV/AIDS reporting and the interaction between the news media and the sources of information used in reporting, in particular government 'official' sources. Miller and Williams suggest that news is not simply a manufactured product based solely and always on the dominant assumptions of media personnel which support and justifies a ruling élite. Instead news is created through a process of negotiation between reporters, other media personnel and the sources of information themselves:

The interaction between the news media and the social institutions they report is a key issue for the sociology of journalism. What appears in the news is the outcome of a process of negotiation between the reporter and the source of information. In the 'dance' between reporters and official sources some see the officials as leading, while others argue that reporters do. However this dance is subject to a number of agendas, personal, organizational and political, that are brought to bear on the reporter and the source within their own organisation.
(Miller and Williams, 1993, p. 126)

HIV/AIDS media coverage has often been factually misleading, politically motivated and sensational-

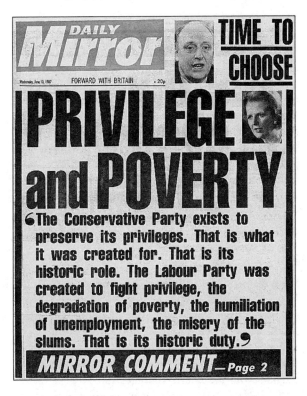

Figure 15.6 Front pages of the *Daily Mirror*, 1 June and 10 June 1987

ized. In this respect, it is similar to many other news stories. However, Miller and Williams are highly critical of what they see as the mistake made by other sociological research. It is not possible nor desirable to treat the mass media as a 'machine' or unified whole. It is equally undesirable to assume that the media always takes the side of dominant social élites.

Official sources of information do not always have a smooth access to the media, and often fail to set the news agenda as previously assumed by some. The opposite is also true: 'alternative' or limited resourced groups and opinions do sometimes gain access where and when official sources are unable to do so. In the case of HIV/AIDS reporting, Miller and Williams focus on the work since 1987 of the Health Education Authority (HEA).

The aim of the HEA was to promote messages of safe sex and safe drug-use through the media, focusing in particular on the issue that anyone can be at risk regardless of their sexuality. However, the HEA met with many problems when trying to use the media as a form of public education.

- The HEA workers were largely distrustful of journalists and so failed to develop good working relationships.
- The HEA failed to produce good quotable material that the media could use.
- Health education has a relatively low status in the eyes of journalists.

These factors combined to limit the space and air time given to the official viewpoint, and this study serves to illustrate the fact that the media does not always blindly follow the official line.

Peter Beharrell (1993), also working for the GUMG, makes the point that when discussing the British press, regardless of the issue in question, it is a mistake to assume that reporting is uniform across the whole range of papers on offer to the public. Taking the case of the reporting of HIV/AIDS issues, Beharrell suggests that there has been a whole range of responses by the press to these issues:

The press reporting of AIDS shows both similarity and diversity. The coverage has not all been negative or simply sensational.
(Beharrell, 1993, p. 241)

Responses to HIV/AIDS in the press can differ between papers and over time within the same paper. In some cases a variety of opinions can be found within a single edition, depending on the journalists and columnists in question. These points have been largely ignored, argues Beharrell, by other sociologists who assume a dominant ideological value-system which totally controls and guides the nature of press reporting:

The mainstream media reporting of AIDS is not uniform. It draws on a number of competing perspectives which are rooted in institutional arrangements, social movements and struggles. These involve not simply differences of strategy or policy but ways of understanding, with specific languages and terminology. They are in a wider sense ways of thinking about AIDS, frames of reference with their codes and conventions, priorities and assumptions.
(Beharrell, 1993, pp. 210–11)

Beharrell suggests that early representations of HIV/AIDS in the British press tended to create images based on the idea of a 'gay plague'. Little differentiation was made between HIV and AIDS, and moral panics were created around the idea of 'innocent victims' who caught the disease from carriers who needed to be identified, exposed and isolated. (HIV/AIDS is also discussed in Chapter 13.)

Beharrell argues that racist images were often constructed around Ugandan and Kenyan 'foreign carriers'. For example, Africa was described as the 'land of the living dead'. Newspapers also often portrayed women and young children as passive, innocent victims who are helpless and therefore dependent on the help of the male, western world. (See also Sections 12.7 and 12.9.)

However, these patriarchal, homophobic and racist representations were not created by the whole of the press. Beharrell argues that whereas *The Sun*, *Daily Express* and *Daily Mail* did, at times, contain the above ideology, *The Guardian*, *The Times* and *The Independent* treated this with scepticism. The *Daily Mirror*, however, focused on the safe-sex messages as provided by the HEA – not surprisingly, however, given that the then owner Robert Maxwell had become the co-founder of the National AIDS Trust. This indicates the variety of press reporting, and as Beharrell claims, evidence that assumptions regarding a dominant ideology in the media are unrealistic.

Case study – The media and warfare

The role of the media at times of national and international conflict is a much debated political, as well as sociological, issue. In recent times the television viewing public have been presented with so-called 'instant' or 'as-it-happens' media coverage of conflicts such as the Gulf war.

Periods of warfare are generally considered as times when governments both censor the media, and use it as a tool of propaganda. Under the legitimation of a 'national emergency' some information is labelled as 'state secrets' and subsequently controlled. Journalists are often dependent on government agencies for information or 'news' and both formally and informally information can be withheld, made open or 'leaked' as misinformation, all in the name of national security.

The BBC at times of war

Philip Schlesinger (1992) suggests that there is a long-established 'myth of independence' surrounding the BBC's role at times of war. For example, during the Second World War the government had the powers to legally and officially commandeer the BBC, and at times such a policy was advocated by Winston Churchill. Although it did not, this is not to say that the BBC was allowed to go totally unrestrained:

Instead, the BBC was politicized by making it into an emergency service, and incorporating its top echelons into the government information machine . . . there was nothing so crude as planting a censor in the makeshift newsroom. It simply was not necessary as Reith and his staff knew what had to be done, and moreover, fully accepted its propriety.
(Schlesinger, 1992, p. 18)

From this account, a more 'hegemonic' stance is identified rather than an orthodox Marxist view. The government of the day did not need to control the BBC overtly because the corporation, under the control of its Director-General Reith, controlled itself in line with the government as a matter of course.

The Vietnam war

The relationship between government and media at times of war was a much debated issue during the Vietnam war, fought between the USA and communist-dominated North Vietnam. Some believe that the exposure of the American people to violent scenes from the battlefield led to public pressure to end the war. Others go further and claim that this is evidence of a democratic media – free from government interference and state control, allowing the audience to make up their own minds.

Kevin Williams (1993b) of the GUMG takes a very different side to the argument. He claims that the American government of the day controlled the reporting of the conflict through the selective use of information given to journalists, and in doing so was able to effectively set the agenda. Whereas some argue that the media was actively biased against the American war effort – and in effect 'lost the war' for the American government by lowering public morale and support through graphic and violent news coverage – Williams' research attempts to prove the opposite.

Williams suggests that rather than the media shaping public consciousness, the reverse is true. It is more correct to operate with a model of the audience which sees the audience or public as able to influence media coverage. The media only began to question governmental policy after public opinion had already begun to swing this way. The swing in public consciousness is seen by Williams to be a direct result of the inability of the White House itself to avoid internal confusion and disagreement regarding the war.

The Falklands conflict

During the Falklands conflict between the UK and Argentina, many serious questions were raised concerning the problems presented for governments by the British mass media at times of national emergencies. The BBC in particular came under heavy criticism at the time from the government, and also from some of the pro-establishment press such as *The Sun*, *The Times* and the *Daily Mail*.

In *The Times*, columnist John Page criticized Peter Snow, a BBC *Newsnight* presenter, for his 'superior tone of super-neutrality which so many of us find objectionable and unacceptable'. So the problem with the BBC for some people was that it was *too neutral*: as the nation's public TV broadcasting organization it should have supported the British government in order to build up public morale at a time of crisis.

Also criticized was a particular showing of the BBC's *Panorama* programme. Some Conservative MPs at the time complained that this programme, like *Newsnight*, represented little more than treason. The Prime Minister, Margaret Thatcher, at Prime Minister's Question Time in the House of Commons, responded to such criticism of the BBC:

I know how strongly many people feel that the case for our country is not being put with sufficient vigour on certain – I do not say all – BBC programmes. The chairman of the BBC has assured us, and has said in vigorous terms, that the BBC is not neutral on this point, and I hope his words will be

Activity

Use the above extract from Margaret Thatcher's speech as a basis for the following task. Choose any one theoretical perspective and write a critical report detailing why the BBC should be neutral or pro-government, depending on the beliefs of the perspective you choose. Then team up with another student who has used a different, contradictory perspective. Make a short list combining and summarizing both sides of the argument.

I, A

heeded by the many who have responsibilities for standing up for our task force, our boys, our people and the cause of democracy.
(Quoted in Eldridge, 1993, p. 9)

The Gulf war

Two main issues of concern to come out of the media coverage of the Gulf war, for sociologists, were the new developments in so-called 'instant' news coverage, and the use of language in reporting.

🗨 Discussion point

Why are audiences fascinated by so-called 'as it happens' news events?

Philip Taylor (1992) is highly critical of the claims, by some sections of the media, to instant coverage of the events in the Gulf war. In particular, the 24-hour news station in America, Cable News Network (CNN), presented its images as first-hand, as-it-was-happening, reality of events. These images and reports were often used by other news organizations, including the BBC and ITN. Taylor shares the concern of other sociologists such as John Eldridge, in questioning the role of CNN in the war.

The war has been interpreted by some as a staged media event in order to create pro-American capitalist propaganda. Rather than the coverage being instant, true, direct and totally real, Taylor points to the existence of 'news pools' controlled and organized by the military. Journalists were put into Media Reporting Teams which combined reporters from a wide number of organizations. The reports created by these teams were then made available to all other journalists – out of the 1500 journalists in the region, only 200 places in the pools had been created.

Taylor and Eldridge comment that, since the war, reporters have complained that the activities of these pools were controlled by the military, defining for them what information to have from official sources, where they were allowed to go, and which other journalists could and could not benefit from the information created by these pools. The exclusiveness of these pools resulted in direct competition between journalists which may well have hindered the collection of information if based on more equal and co-operative grounds.

Regarding the claims by satellite and cable news organizations to instant, 'reality as it happens reporting', Taylor asks:

But what exactly had they seen? . . . audiences could indeed be forgiven for thinking that they were participating in historic events as they were unfolding. But the excitement of the occasion, when peo-

ple not directly involved in matters of life and death felt that they were actually a part of what was going on, raises a number of questions about the relationship between war and the media. Was this a new variation of 'total war' in which the gap which had previously existed between soldier and civilian had been substantially narrowed by television? Or was it something else? Were people 'seeing' a war in which nations resolved their disputes for the benefit of their publics . . . were they, in other words, being manipulated into believing that they were part of something they were not . . . ?
(Taylor, 1992, p. 33)

📝 Activity

In April 1991, *New Statesman and Society* in conjunction with Channel 4 published a list of songs that were banned from BBC radio stations during the Gulf war. The list is reproduced below:

ABBA Waterloo; Under Attack
AKA Hunting High and Low
ALARM 68 Guns
ANIMALS We Got to Get Out of This Place
ARRIVAL I Will Survive
JOAN BAEZ The Night They Drove Old Dixie Down
BANGLES Walk Like an Egyptian
BEATLES Back in the USSR
PAT BENATAR Love is a Battlefield
BIG COUNTRY Fields of Fire
BLONDIE Atomic
BOOMTOWN RATS I Don't Like Mondays
BROOK BROS Warpaint
CRAZY WORLD OF ARTHUR BROWN Fire
KATE BUSH Army Dreamers
CHER Bang Bang (My Baby Shot Me Down)
ERIC CLAPTON I Shot the Sheriff
PHIL COLLINS In the Air Tonight
ELVIS COSTELLO Oliver's Army
CUTTING CREW I Just Died in Your Arms Tonight
SKEETER DAVIS End of the World
DESMOND DEKKER Israelites
DIRE STRAITS Brothers in Arms
DURAN DURAN View to a Kill
JOSE FELICIANO Light My Fire
FIRST CHOICE Armed and Extremely Dangerous
ROBERTA FLACK Killing Me Softly
FRANKIE GOES TO HOLLYWOOD Two Tribes
EDDIE GRANT Living on the Frontline; Give Me Hope Joanna
ELTON JOHN Saturday Night's Alright For Fighting
MILLIE JACKSON Act of War
J HATES JAZZ I Don't Want to be a Hero
JOHN LENNON Give Peace a Chance; Imagine

JOHN LEWIS Stop the Cavalry
LULU Boom Bang a Bang
McGUINNESS FLINT When I'm Dead and Gone
BOB MARLEY Buffalo Soldier
MARIA MULDAUR Midnight at the Oasis
MASH Suicide is Painless
MIKE AND THE MECHANICS Silent Running
RICK NELSON Fools Rush In
NICOLE A Little Peace
BILLY OCEAN When the Going Gets Tough
DONNY OSMOND Soldier of Love
PAPER LACE Billy Don't Be a Hero
QUEEN Killer Queen; Flash
MARTHA REEVES Forget Me Not
B A ROBERTSON Bang Bang
TOM ROBINSON War Baby
KENNY ROGERS Ruby (Don't Take Your Love to Town)
SPANDAU BALLET I'll Fly For You
SPECIALS Ghost Town
BRUCE SPRINGSTEEN I'm on Fire
EDWIN STARR War
STATUS QUO In the Army Now; Burnin' Bridges
CAT STEVENS I'm Gonna Get Me a Gun
ROD STEWART Sailing
DONNA SUMMER State of Independence
TEARS FOR FEARS Everybody Wants to Rule the World
TEMPTATIONS Ball of Confusion
10CC Rubber Bullets
STEVIE WONDER Heaven Help Us All

Write four paragraphs interpreting the BBC's intentions, one each from the points of view of pluralism, the New Right, orthodox Marxism and hegemonic Marxism.

I, A

Post-modern warfare?

The popular French thinker Jean Baudrillard (1995) came to even more popular and public infamy during the Gulf war when he claimed that the conflict did not actually happen (see also Section 10.11)! In a series of three articles during 1991 in the French paper *Liberation*, Baudrillard tried to stress the 'hyper-real' qualities of war coverage in the media. The articles were entitled 'The Gulf war will not take place', 'The Gulf war: is it really taking place?', and finally 'The Gulf war did not take place'. In an interview during the time of the war Baudrillard commented:

. . . the war [is] *a kind of machinery, with its gigantic montage, special effects, etc. . . . This war is a good example of a synthetic object. This does not mean that damage and destruction didn't take place. There is violence, but it is not real, it is*

virtual. There is also violence in the virtual but it's like a simulation model, a parachuted war that does not take place . . . so it was a simulacrum of a war.
(Baudrillard, 1993b, p. 206–7)

Many of Baudrillard's critics point out that claiming the war didn't happen is to offer little comfort and great insult to the thousands of ordinary citizens and military personnel who were killed or injured, and to their families. The point Baudrillard wishes to make, however, in characteristically dramatic fashion, is that for many – including many of the journalists and military personnel who were 'actually there' – the Gulf war existed only as flickering images on a TV screen. It is an example of what Baudrillard refers to as 'simulacrum' – simulated images of reality which appear so direct, instant and clear, they define what we think of as reality. Post-modernists refer to this situation – where media-reality becomes blurred with reality as perceived through the individual senses – as 'hyper-real': more real than real. As Paul Patton comments:

At the time, the TV Gulf war must have seemed to many viewers a perfect Baudrillardian simulacrum . . . Fascination and horror at the reality which seemed to unfold before our very eyes mingled with a pervasive sense of unreality as we recognized the elements of Hollywood script which had preceded the real . . . occasionally, the absurdity of the media's self-representation as purveyor of reality and immediacy broke through, in moments such as those when the CNN cameras crossed live to a group of reporters assembled somewhere in the Gulf, only to have them confess that they were also sitting around watching CNN in order to find out what was happening. Television news coverage appeared to have finally caught up with the logic of simulation. . . .

. . . It was not the first time that images of war had appeared on TV screens, but it was the first time that they were relayed 'live' from the battle-front. It was not the first occasion on which the military censored what could be reported, but it did involve a new level of military control of reportage and images . . . what we saw was for the most part a 'clean' war, with lots of pictures of weaponry, including the amazing footage from the nose-cameras of 'smart bombs', and relatively few images of human casualties, none from the Allied forces . . . the Gulf war movie was instant history in the sense that the selected images which were broadcast worldwide provoked immediate responses and then became frozen into the accepted story of the war.
(Quoted in Baudrillard, 1995, p. 2 and p. 3)

In his book *What's Wrong With Post-modernism*, Christopher Norris (1990), a critic of post-modernist ideas, suggests that Baudrillard is 'lost in the fun house'. Norris is highly critical of the way in which Baudrillard appears to seek controversy and media attention – as he did with his views of the media reporting of the Gulf war. Norris suggests that Baudrillard is prone to either take no position in his work, criticizing everything, but offering no positive solutions to problems in return; or he is prone to take a position of opposition on everything – seeking the most controversial opinion just for the sake of being 'on the other side' to the mainstream.

In his more recent work, *Uncritical Theory* (1993), Norris continues with this theme, suggesting that Baudrillard's work itself could be seen as supportive of the western world's war effort in the Gulf, since it conveniently denies that a 'real' war took place in the first place:

One could justifiably argue that Baudrillard was waiting at the end of the road that structuralism and post-structuralism had been travelling for the past three decades and more . . . It has finished by promoting a post-modern-pragmatist worldview, which blithely deconstructs the 'notional' difference between 'war' as a simulated pseudo-event . . . and war as a real-world state of affairs in which countless thousands of Iraqi civilian men, women and children were daily killed in an aerial bombardment of unprecedented scale and ferocity. Small wonder, as I say, that Baudrillards' ideas have achieved such a cult following at a time and in a context – that of the current US drive for renewed world hegemony – when few intellectuals seem able or willing to resist these pressures of ideological recruitment.
(Norris, 1993, p. 25)

15.7 Representations of gender in the media

Discussion point
To what extent are men and women portrayed differently in the media?

Feminism is concerned with how women (and men) are portrayed by the media. Feminist research has been occupied with the goal of displaying gender ideologies in the media for the same reasons, and using the same methods, as Marxists are concerned to demonstrate a pro-capitalist bias. Both these two sociological traditions are built on a belief in political action. Deconstructing what they see as false ideas in the media, for Marxists and feminists, can form the basis for a rejection of traditional socialization patterns by both women and the working classes alike. A concern with false representations in the media is a concern, by these perspectives, to establish true consciousness in the minds of the traditional victims of the media – the subordinate in society.

Varieties of feminism

It is possible to draw a distinction between three types of feminist views (see also Chapter 5) on the role of the media in contemporary society:

- liberal feminism
- radical feminism
- Marxist/socialist feminism.

As Liesbet van Zoonen (1991) comments:

Classifying feminism in three neatly separated ideological currents, is certainly at odds with the present fragmentation of feminist thought . . . Also, feminist theory and practice is often rather eclectic, incorporating elements from different ideologies as circumstances and issues necessitate . . . However, taken as ideal types . . . they are indicative of various ways in which feminists perceive the media.
(van Zoonen, 1991, p. 35)

Within the 'liberal' strand of feminist thought, stereotypes and gender socialization are seen to be the reason for the inequality of power between men and women. In this context the mass media, like education, is responsible for the continuation of these prejudices and stereotypes through the representations of femininity it creates and reinforces. Liberal feminism suggests that by removing these images, and replacing them with positive images of women, socialization can be changed and power differences in society ultimately addressed. Full equality, however, must also exist through the law.

For radical feminists, female oppression and subordination is the direct result of a male-dominated social system. Such a patriarchal society is built on men's desire to control women – ideologically and in the last instance through violence and force. Radical feminism often leads to the political/sexual choice of lesbianism – women must be free of men, otherwise inequality will always continue. Radical feminists advocate use of the media, by feminists, as a tool against patriarchy: to set up 'alternative' media which can be used to recruit women to the feminist cause:

Technological developments in print and audio-visual media made the proliferation of feminist writing, newsletters, magazines, radio and TV programmes, video and film groups possible. A host of feminist ideas would otherwise have not received a public forum.
(van Zoonen, 1991, p. 37)

Socialist or Marxist feminism has attempted to combine accounts of gender discrimination in society with those of class. Recently, (dis)ability, ethnicity and sexuality have also been added. All such forms of ideological control are ultimately seen to benefit capitalism.

Discussion point

To what extent are capitalism and patriarchy a similar source of inequality and social control? How may the media reinforce and reproduce these?

The mass media is seen to be a key institution in the process of cultural reproduction – of continuing the capitalist and patriarchal systems through hegemony. Like the liberal and radical feminists they wish to reform the existing media, while in the meantime creating socialist media of their own. Ultimately, however, inequality can only be solved by a change in the class system in society.

Ownership and control

There are two dominant interpretations of the ownership and control of the media within the feminist perspective.

The first interpretation is that the majority of media 'moguls' are men, as are the higher postholders within these media empires (see Figure 15.7). Thus it can be argued that media institutions are male-dominated: they present a male view, a patriarchal ideology, both within the organization and within the content of their own products.

An estimate produced by the Women In Journalism (WIJ) group suggests that in 1995–6 only 20 per cent of positions of significant decision-making power in newspapers were held by women (WIJ Research Committee, 1996).

Activity

Study Figure 15.7 on page 632 and interpret this from the viewpoint of feminism. What does this *suggest* about women's role within the BBC – and possibly in the media in general?

The second interpretation of ownership and control is that even those women who are able to reach the higher levels within a media organization may have to 'play the male game' in order to get there – to continue to organize programming based largely on male understandings of 'what female audiences like'.

Laura Mulvey (1975) argues that the representation of female bodies in films has contributed to the patriarchal stereotype the media uses when displaying what is defined as femininity in contemporary society (see also Section 10.7). She believes that the cinema industry operates from an overwhelmingly male viewpoint. For example, female bodies are depicted as 'playthings' for the male audience. This argument suggests that women in general in the cinema take on passive and subservient roles, often treated as sex objects.

Wolf (1990) refers to the way in which women are portrayed in the media as 'the beauty myth'. By this she means that the media presents a particular physical image of femininity as the 'normal' body image for women to have, even though this image may well be beyond the majority of 'normal women'.

Joan Smith in her book *Misogynies* (1989) – meaning 'women-hating' – explores a similar theme to Mulvey. Smith is concerned with the use (or in her terms misuse and exploitation) of the female fear of violent assault as a basis for film plots. Female fear is used as a commodity, being marketed and sold to audiences. But these films add to the stock-of-fear which already exists in wider society. In this way, the cinema industry contributes to male dominance by reinforcing an image of femininity which defines women as victims of the superior strength of the male – weak, vulnerable and in need of protection (see also Section 11.7):

Female fear sells films. It's a box-office hit. In 1960 the shower scene in Hitchcock's Psycho . . . *shocked audiences who had never seen anything like it on their cinema screens; today such scenes are ten a penny. Terror, torture, rape, mutilation and murder are handed out to actresses by respectable directors as routinely as tickets to passengers on a bus. No longer the stock in trade only of pornographers and video-nasty producers, they can be purchased any day at a cinema near you.*
(Smith, 1989, p. 16)

Discussion point

How are 'female bodies' used by the media to sell and make popular, commercial products?

Women's magazines

Marjorie Ferguson (1983) has provided feminist sociology with an analysis of magazines aimed at older women. Her sample of magazines was drawn from issues of *Woman*, *Woman's Own* and *Woman's Weekly*. Ferguson first drew a random sample of magazines between 1949 and 1974 and then, in order to determine whether the content of these

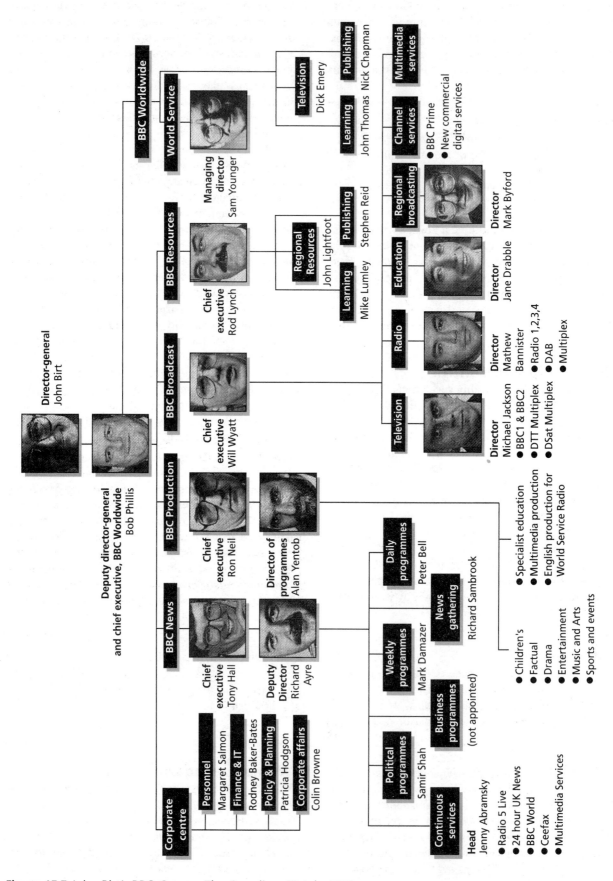

Figure 15.7 John Birt's BBC. Source: *The Guardian*, 22 July 1996

magazines changed over time, she drew a second sample between 1979 and 1980. In addition to this content analysis, Ferguson conducted interviews with media personnel in an attempt to understand the day-to-day decisions made by those who put these magazines together.

Ferguson identifies a number of dominant concerns shared by all three magazines across her first sample. These dominant themes included: overcoming misfortune, getting and keeping a partner, being a good wife, keeping a happy family. Ferguson suggests these concerns, taken together as a whole, make up a 'cult of femininity'.

Although the content of some of these themes had changed between the first and second sample dates, what remained the same was the magazines' atmosphere of instruction: these magazines teach or instruct women and girls how to behave as a 'normal' member of society. They socialize their audience into a cult of femininity. (See also Chapter 5.)

Ellen McCracken (1993) has argued that, despite the gendered nature of ownership and control changing for American womens' magazines during the 1980s, they still reflect the underlying ideological structure identified above – the use of 'utopian solutions' such as the perfect lover, dress, job etc., as the ideal goal for womens' lives. McCracken argues that women are encouraged to feel part of a 'utopian community' by these magazines – a cult of femininity.

While adopting a socialist or Marxist feminist analysis of women's role in the media, we could suggest that the media tends to present the interests of capitalism as normal and natural – as beyond question. Equally, the continuation of patriarchy – inseparable from the interests of capitalism – is also enforced by the media: women are presented with images of 'female lives' which justify and support female oppression and exploitation in society.

Case study – Women in the news: does sex change the way a newspaper thinks?

In 1995 the non-profit-making organization Women In Journalism (WIJ) was formed, its aim being to promote women's work in the media industry while monitoring the portrayal of women in magazines and newspapers. The WIJ group, whose committee members include a number of female editors and MPs, have conducted a number of content analysis studies to investigate what they see as the unfair representation of women in national newspapers and magazines in the UK. They comment:

To place the coverage of women in the news in context it is important to note two things. One is that most news decisions are taken by men. For the past two years the Women In Journalism survey of the news and comment pages has shown that 80 per cent of those at news conferences are men. This is not to say that women do not play key roles in news rooms, including that of editor on several papers. But news and comment are still male dominated and, at the moment, the ultimate decision-maker – the Editor – is a man on 18 of our 19 national daily and Sunday newspapers. The other factor is that most news is about men. Previous research has shown that, on the whole, the news pages are dominated by male figures and, in this way, it reflects the reality of our public society. Unlike men, who appear in news columns in any and all roles, women who make the news tend to fit into certain categories, namely politicians, actresses, members of royalty, crime victims, wives and women of achievement.

(WIJ Research Committee, 1996, p. 1)

The WIJ group took the 1995 'political scandal' of the 'crossing of the floor' in the House of Commons of Alan Howarth MP (from Conservative to Labour) and Emma Nicholson MP (from Conservative to Liberal-Democrat). To 'cross the floor' in the House of Commons means to switch political parties. This is very unusual and is done when the MP in question feels she or he is unable to continue to represent a party on a point of policy.

On Saturday 7 October 1995 Alan Howarth announced his decision to leave the Conservative Party, and on Friday 29 December 1995 Emma Nicholson did likewise. The WIJ group compared the newspaper coverage of these two similar events to see whether media coverage was similar – or whether it differed owing to the difference in gender of the two MPs.

The WIJ group studied five days' of newspaper coverage, looking at ten newspapers: *The Sun, Daily Mirror, Daily Mail, The Guardian, Daily Telegraph, The Times, Mail on Sunday, News of the World, The Observer* and *Sunday Times*. Both qualitative and quantitative methods were used. The result was that Howarth and Nicholson received about the same amounts of coverage:

- 60 articles for Nicholson
- 67 articles for Howarth

- 999 paragraphs for Nicholson
- 861 paragraphs for Howarth

- average length of a story for Nicholson – 17 paragraphs
- average length of a story for Howarth – 13 paragraphs.

There are some signs here, perhaps, that a bit of extra interest was given to Emma Nicholson. However, differences showed up when looking at the tone of the pieces.

In terms of the bias behind the stories the results reported were:

- *Emma Nicholson* (out of 60 stories)
  favourable – 12
  unfavourable – 19
  neutral – 29

- *Alan Howarth* (out of 67 stories)
  favourable – 13
  unfavourable – 20
  neutral – 34.

The language used, in both the text and the headlines, pointed to the frequent use of sexist and stereotypical images for Emma Nicholson. *The Observer* frequently (about 50 per cent of the time) referred to Nicholson as 'Emma' but never referred to Howarth as 'Alan'. Overall, no reference was made to the appearance of Howarth, yet Nicholson's appearance and domestic situation was frequently reported. Also, while Howarth was described as:

- 'intelligent and independent-minded'
- 'an honourable man'
- 'a principled man'
- 'intelligent and committed'

Nicholson was described as:

- 'an admirable women but not a serious politician'
- 'frightful bitch'
- 'at an emotional age'
- 'something to do with the menopause'
  (WIJ Research Committee, 1996, p. 4)

In conclusion, from looking at this brief snapshot of headlines we can see a difference in how the two MPs were represented. Alan Howarth was described as a 'man', as if tough decisions were the things that characterized being a 'man', whereas Emma Nicholson's femininity is used to create an image of an irrational women not quite in control. This work of the WIJ group is useful in highlighting the differences between the representations created in the national press of gender and sexuality.

However, proving gender bias in media representations is one thing, but suggesting that these representations might have an influence on men and women in society is altogether a different argument. For example, Brown (1990) suggests that popular culture – such as popular media forms like soap operas, situation comedies etc. – can actually exist or

be used as a weapon against patriarchal hegemony. Thus women may be able to use popular culture in a subversive fashion, questioning dominant and traditional notions of gender. (See also Section 10.7.)

15.8 Representations of ethnicity in the media

Traditionally the sociological treatment of 'race' and ethnicity in the media focused on issues of under-representation and negative images. Although many would still argue that non-white ethnicity is portrayed in a limited fashion, the argument can now be made that in cinema and television at least, conscious steps forward are being made in the creation of positive representations and role models for black and Asian groups. (See also Section 10.6.)

Hartmann and Husband: racist ideology

An important and now classic contribution to the debate about the existence of racist ideology in the mass media is provided by Hartmann and Husband (1974, 1976). This research focused on two aspects of media research:

- content analysis (see Section 15.2) of British daily newspapers between the years 1963 and 1970
- audience research directed at a sample of children in schools – both those of a multi-ethnic and relatively single-ethnic nature.

Hartmann and Husband concluded that, during the time span of their content analysis, the British press contributed to racist ideology by portraying a specific stereotypical image of black people by focusing on stories and issues that emphasized 'racial problems' and the 'strange cultural attitudes' of new immigrants. This suggests that black people are portrayed in the media as a threat to the smooth running of white British society. They are portrayed as criminals, illegal aliens etc. These images and representations manipulate racist ideas and create moral panics in wider society.

Hartmann and Husband also contended that such stories and racist images had a very limited 'reinforcing' effect on the audience – especially those who lived in areas and went to schools that were not especially multi-cultural:

Mass communications regarding 'race' will be interpreted within the framework of meanings that serve to define the situation within any social group. At the same time the way 'race'-related material is handled in the media contributes towards this definition of the situation. Attitudes and interpretations prevailing in a community are therefore seen as the result of the interplay between the on-the-ground social situation and the way 'race' is handled by the media.

(Hartmann and Husband, 1976, p. 273)

The work of Hartmann and Husband illustrates a pluralist-influenced perspective. They claim that the media is shaped by the values and attitudes of society. There is an 'interplay' between the media and the audience. Thus, media images will only change, in time, once social attitudes themselves become less racist:

The way the media define the situation is seen as resulting from the definitions prevailing in the general culture and from institutional factors that stem from the media themselves.

(Hartmann and Husband, 1976, p. 274)

Although Hartmann and Husband's study was ground-breaking at the time, work on media effects and racist ideological representations in the media has since come a long way. Now we can identify a number of problems in their study, drawing on a Marxist-based perspective.

1 They failed to link the existence of racism to the wider class-based structure of society.
2 There is no consideration of the ways in which the media represents the hegemony of ruling élites in society.
3 The audience should not be seen solely in terms of age and experience, but also in terms of how class, gender, religion, geography, (un)employment etc. affects one's understanding and interpretation of the media messages we receive.

Stuart Hall *et al.* (1978) suggest that ethnic groups are often defined in the British media as social problems, as criminals around which we often find moral panics constructed. This view of the media is shared by other commentators. For example, although the media is controlled by legal and self-policing professional codes of conduct, informal racism can be created by under-representing black and Asian people in all other aspects of the news and popular drama programmes, except as social problems.

Hall and colleagues see a link between the economic conditions in society and the significance of moral panics – in this case the creation of a 'mugging' moral panic (see Section 15.5) around young black males in the 1970s. They argue, while adopting a neo-Marxist stance, that the crisis in the economic stability of capitalism, leading to a potential legitimation crisis of capitalism, can be seen as the background for the creation of a racist stereotype of the 'black mugger'. In their view, the British press contributed to the dominant hegemony of capitalism by creating racist images which divided the white and black working classes at a time of insecurity for the capitalist rulers in society.

Racism and the press

A recent example of content analysis (see Section 15.2) on the representations of 'race' and ethnicity in newspapers is to be found in Van Dijk's *Racism and the Press* (1991). Using a mixture of content analysis and 'discourse analysis' – where the text of a news report is studied for hidden meanings, Van Dijk suggests that:

. . . during the last decades the coverage of ethnic and racial affairs in the Press, on both sides of the Atlantic, has gradually become less blatantly racist, but that stereotypes and the definition of minorities as a 'problem' or even as a 'threat' is still prevalent, in particular in the popular newspapers, while minority journalists, especially in Europe, continue to be discriminated against in hiring, promotion and news story assignments.

(Van Dijk, 1991, p. 245)

Van Dijk's research illustrates the point that news issues involving members of ethnic minorities are usually based around ideas of 'racial tension' or 'crime problems' which – as suggested by Hartmann and Husband – identifies members of racial groups as a 'problem for white society to deal with'.

Van Dijk studied the headlines on five newspapers – *The Times*, *The Guardian*, the *Daily Telegraph*, the *Daily Mail* and *The Sun* – between August 1985 and January 1986, looking at the stories related to 'race'. The two most frequently used words in such stories were 'police', which was used 388 times, and 'riot', used 320 times. This illustrates the negative context in which 'race' issues were raised in the press. For Van Dijk, this racist ideology:

. . . is not limited to news reports, but also characterizes background articles and editorials. Indeed, the editorials clearly show the dominant ideology at work in the media account of the ethnic situation. In the right-wing Press, ethnic events are primarily evaluated as a conflict between 'us' and 'them', against the background of a conservative ideology that prominently features such concepts as order, authority, loyalty, patriotism, and 'freedom'. Besides ethnic minorities, anti-racists and the 'loony left' in particular are the target of such editorial attacks. It is not surprising, therefore, that ethnic minorities are consistently less quoted than majority group members and institutions, even on subjects, such as experiences of racial attacks or prejudice, on which minorities are the experts.

(Van Dijk, 1991, p. 246)

A pluralist perspective would argue that under-representation does occur, and has occurred, but is slowly being challenged. British and American television companies are producing more self-conscious black-issues programmes, independent black television companies are beginning to have their product exposed to mainstream audiences, and black and Asian actors are being cast more in popular drama.

Ethnicity and popular drama

We can make the observation, perhaps, that some drama programmes on all channels are (albeit slowly) introducing black and Asian characters and families into broadcasting – creating more work for black and Asian actors and actresses and exposing the public to positive images. (See also Section 10.6.) But how widespread is this?

This development (if it has realistically happened) is nonetheless a recent one. For example, writing from a critical perspective which shows an awareness of black issues in the media, John Tulloch (1990) suggests that, with the exception of *EastEnders* from the BBC, many dramas still do not portray black characters and/or families in 'normal situations' – they are still used almost exclusively in storylines on issues such as racism, crime etc.:

There is little doubt that some broadcasting executives now display much greater sensitivity to the issues of black representation and this has been reflected in a number of recent one-off plays and drama serials . . . However, there is still a distinct lack of what might be described as run-of-the-mill black characters.
(Tulloch, 1990, p. 149)

Tulloch suggests that for broadcasting to become truly equal, we must move from the present situation where we are slowly seeing 'black characters' to seeing 'characters who happen to be black': where ethnicity and 'race' do not become the centrally defining characteristic of the character, but simply one of a number of characteristics – no more 'special' than any other.

Tulloch identifies the need for black audiences to lobby media corporations before dramatic progress is to be made. This is particularly significant, in these days of the 'free market' in the media, given the requirement, as laid out in the Peacock Report, for the BBC and ITV to increase to no less than 40 per cent of its programmes to be made by independent production houses:

As the largest group of outsiders in British broadcasting, blacks have little to lose and much to gain from exerting substantial pressure for a presence in the new broadcasting market that is representative of their numbers.
(Tulloch, 1990, p. 152)

Case study – Reporting of aid and famine issues

An increasingly frequent occurrence in the western media is a concern for charitable events, causes and relief. From Band Aid-style 'global' music and media events, through to telethons and celebrity popular Christmas records, public attention is often turned towards good causes which merit attention. While not wishing to devalue the worth of such causes, some sociologists are equally concerned with those charitable events, organizations and issues which do not have access to public attention through media exposure, and those which seek to create funds by using what could be described as racist images. (See also Section 12.7.)

As a critic of the way in which the media reports issues of 'natural disasters', Jonathan Benthall (1995) suggests that 'disasters' and emergencies only become defined as disasters by the world media. So powerful is the media in swaying public attention and attitudes that the media itself has the power to define what constitutes a worthy cause or dangerous situation through the act of endorsement:

Disasters do not exist – except for their unfortunate victims and those who suffer in their aftermaths – unless publicized by the media. In this sense the media actually construct disasters.
(Benthall, 1995, p. 27)

Coverage of suffering and disaster is so selective and arbitrary that media endorsement of one particular cause inevitably occurs at the expense of another. Benthall argues that this media 'hallmark' is often a prerequisite for the involvement of many world powers. On the other hand, governments may use media coverage and public attention turned towards one part of the globe as the ideal time to perform actions in another part of the world they may not wish to be scrutinized too carefully.

Some left-wing and radical political viewpoints – often hostile to western aid and charity which are seen as further opportunities for the developed world to ensnare undeveloped countries – have interpreted

Activity

Using a copy of a weekly television listings guide, answer the following questions.
a How many programmes are aimed at an 'ethnic' audience?
b How many of these programmes are comedies? Does this tell us anything?
c Among those programmes that are not comedies – what time are they scheduled and on what channels? Does this tell us anything about the scheduling decisions made?

I, A

Which picture?

You won't find Oxfam using harrowing pictures of starving children in its appeals – although some charities think such pictures are an effective way of fundraising. Why?

Behind the picture

In 1985, during the worst of the Sudanese famine, a UN representative set out on a tour of the famine zone. In tow was a film crew.

They arrived at a camp near Port Sudan where hill-dwelling Hadenowa had come to seek help. Everyone was in a desperate state. The men had all gone to find work – and money – in Port Sudan. The only people left were the old, and mothers with their children.

A guide picked up a child sitting motionless under a makeshift shelter and placed the child on the parched soil. He was being helpful, showing the visitors what was happening. "Here," he said "look at this child" and the TV crew took their pictures.

It is a familiar image of famine – one that says very little about what is really going on. But step back, as the photographer Wendy Wallace did, and the picture is very different.

Why do pictures matter to Oxfam?

Pictures have power. They can convey information and emotion. They can provoke a response and leave a lasting impression.

The right pictures can mobilize people and change the course of events. It's a power that can be used for good or bad.

Are pictures true or false?

We like to think that photographs are a piece of reality, captured on film. But they are not neutral. They have one particular view point, which can distort as well as reveal.

In Oxfam's experience the pictures we see from developing countries are an example of distortion. Harrowing pictures of starving children still feature in some charity advertising, and news from outside Europe and North America is dominated by famine, disaster and poverty.

We are being given a begging-bowl image of the Third World – which is at odds with people's actual lives.

Is Oxfam saying famine doesn't exist?

No – only that disasters and famines are the exception not the rule. And even in these situations the pictures of exhaustion and hunger we are used to seeing don't do justice to people's struggle to stay alive.

Is it always wrong to use pictures of famine?

No – but show it like it is. This means begging-bowl pictures of starving children aren't enough. Who is this picture of? What's their story? What happened to cause this suffering?

Hang on, didn't Oxfam use pictures of starving children?

In the past Oxfam – and other aid agencies – ran fundraising cam- paigns showing starving pot-bellied children. They were relatively successful in raising money, at least for a short time.

But we've learnt from our mistakes. Such poster campaigns were counter-productive. They gave the impression that people sat and waited for food – or death, and that they did nothing for themselves. It was as if Oxfam was saying the response to famine should be pity – when it should be a demand for justice and action.

How does Oxfam try to use pictures?

Pictures used well can challenge prejudice – about race or about stereotypes of men and women. They can either give people dignity, or take it away. They can help to provoke a positive and appropriate response or they can mislead.

When Oxfam uses pictures it tries to take this into account. We try to tell the story behind the picture. We try to use named people and give some idea of their lives. We try to use pictures that reflect Oxfam's practical experience, which is that people don't want hand-outs, but help so that they can help themselves.

western charity, media-led or other wise, as further evidence of western imperialism: the rich West attempting to 'save' unfortunate people who are 'unable to look after themselves'. (See Section 12.7.)

Although Benthall does not subscribe completely to this view, he does however take issue with what he sees as potentially racist photographic images presented by the western media. Images of Africans and Asians in the western media either appeal to romantic stereotypes so as to continue tourism in these areas, or we are presented with images of women and children as passive victims, dependent on others to help them. As Benthall argues:

Photography and the ensuing technologies of film and television – though in principle they can be, and sometimes are, adapted for all sorts of liberating purposes – are in practice often used to reinforce stereotypes which have a controlling function in our society.
(Benthall, 1995, pp. 186–7)

Many charities are now conscious of the way in which photographs and the media in general can be used in an ideological fashion to create an image of suffering, weakness and pity – designed to raise more money for a particular cause. As the Oxfam leaflet reproduced on the previous page demonstrates, each picture used in such campaigns must be used and chosen with extreme care. The image created must be a true reflection of the lives of those individuals, not just a snapshot which reinforces stereotypes and prejudice.

15.9 **The audience and media effects**

Discussion of the effects of the media is of great importance to the sociological study of the media as a whole. Theories of bias and one-sidedness are often based on an interest to demonstrate how ideas in the media may control the audience. Media effects can be as simple, or even as important, as socialization, whereby individuals learn the norms and values of their culture; or they may be perceived – depending on the perspective of the researcher – as negative and harmful, a source of social control used to suppress the masses by a narrow ruling élite.

Discussion point

To what extent does the media 'control' the audience, or can the audience 'fight back'?

Sociological and psychological models of media effects often spill over into the minds of public con-

sciousness. Moral panics (see Section 15.5) related to violence on television, 'video-nasties' and computerized pornography often contain simplified versions of academic ideas. However, it is important that sociologists keep an open mind when discussing these issues, because it is all too easy to be drawn into an unsociological discussion, lacking any theoretical or empirical basis.

Media effects can be intended or unintended, and short-term or long-term. This makes the study of effects a complex process. The easiest way to approach the issue is to understand the way in which sociological ideas have changed over time.

Direct effects

Models of media influence used at the beginning of the twentieth century assumed a direct effect on the audience. The media was likened to a hypodermic-syringe, capable of injecting into an audience bias, violence, ideology etc. The audience was seen as relatively passive, unable to resist media messages. An example of this type of model came from the Frankfurt School, regarding the concepts of 'mass culture' and 'mass society' (see also Sections 10.3 and 15.10). Modern societies were characterized by the decline of individual, creative and critical thought, and replaced by media mass culture. These mass societies produced indoctrinated victims of ruling-class ideology unable to resist or to reject.

This relatively simplistic model of media effects is still used today by some sociologists and behavioural psychologists. They suggest that humanity is the victim of external stimuli in the environment and that all human social action is the product of these determined responses, not of free will or consciousness.

The hypodermic-syringe model has come to inform popular and current media and public debate. The ideas of Mary Whitehouse, among others, demonstrates the concern some individuals and groups have with media violence and the influence it may have on a passive audience.

Indirect effects

The idea of direct media effects onto a passive audience has many criticisms. It treats the audience as little more than cultural robots, unable to think critically about the world around them. Media influence is assumed to be direct and unstoppable.

The work of Lazarsfeld *et al.* (1944) in America provided sociology with another model, this time emphasizing the social context of media viewing. In their study *The People's Choice*, Lazarsfeld and colleagues identified the existence of key individuals who were responsible for transmitting ideas, originating from a media source, onto a social group.

Through interaction, these 'opinion leaders' (or as they are sometimes known 'molecular leaders') take ideas from the media in an active fashion and then pass them on through discussion.

In this model, media influence is indirect or mediated. The audience are no longer passive victims of external stimulus, but are shown to be consuming the media within a social context, viewing takes place with others, and ideas can be rejected. The original study for this model investigated American voting patterns. Lazarsfeld *et al.* claimed that media influence was a 'two-step flow': first from the media to the opinion leaders, and secondly from the opinion leaders to the social group. In terms of voting behaviour, Lazarsfeld *et al.* suggested that media election campaigns made little difference to the voting behaviour of the vast majority of the audience. (See also Chapter 17.)

The two-step flow model fits within a pluralist conception of the mass media. Democracy is preserved since individuals are not passive victims. Marxist criticisms of this model point to the fact that no reference is made to the existence of a narrow ruling élite in society. The pluralist model fits the 'American dream' well – élites exist, but they do so not through ideological control, since the audience has power.

💬 Discussion point

To what extent is it useful to think of media consumption as a collective or social activity and not just an individual one?

The uses of the media

Taking the idea of a conscious, critical audience further, Blumler and Katz (1974) suggested that the important issue when discussing media effects is not to ask how the media influences its audiences, but rather to focus on how the audiences use the media to their own ends. This model, the 'uses and gratifications' approach, takes even further the pluralist notion that audiences are not 'blank sheets of paper' on which the media writes, but are capable of using the media to secure personal goals.

For example, the same television programme may be used by audience members in a variety of ways. Audience members have goals or motivations for their patterns of media consumption: some may seek information, others escapism, others yet more uses:

. . . it is clear that the need to relax or to kill time can be satisfied by the act of watching television, that the need to feel that one is spending one's time in a worthwhile way may be associated with the act

of reading, and that the need to structure one's day may be satisfied merely by having the radio 'on'.
(Blumler and Katz, 1974, p. 24)

Blumler and Katz (1974) identify five key elements in the 'uses and gratifications' model.

1 The audience is seen to be active.
2 The audience has the power to exercise choice over his/her consumption of the media.
3 The needs satisfied by the media compete directly with other sources of need-fulfilment in society.
4 The goals of media consumption can be identified by the audience themselves in a reflective process.
5 The researcher should suspend all value-judgements regarding the relative and specific 'worth' or 'merit' of these audience goals.

The uses–gratifications approach has implications for media policy-makers and programme designers:

. . . instead of depicting the media as severely circumscribed by audience expectations, the uses and gratifications approach highlights the audience as a source of challenge to producers to cater more richly to the multiplicity of requirements and roles that it has disclosed.
(Blumler and Katz, 1974, p. 31)

In other words, since the audience is shown to have multi-dimensional needs which are gratified in various ways – often differing from one individual to the next – the media must cater for these needs by producing a wide plurality of media products. Free choice, as argued by the pluralist influences on this perspective, is essential to ensure that all members of the audience can and will have their needs met.

Cultural studies

With the rise of academic interest in popular culture (see Chapter 10), the uses–gratifications approach has proved influential in making sociologists, psychologists, philosophers and other interested parties think about the audience in terms of their own motivations and 'readings' of the media. As the Italian literary figure, Umberto Eco, comments:

. . . the question that has dominated the study of mass communications since the early 1960s has been: 'What do mass communications do to audiences?' It was only in the late 1960s that people began, timidly, to ask: 'What do audiences do to (with) mass communications?'
(Eco, 1995, p. 119)

For example, recent work by the neo-Marxist-orientated Centre for Contemporary Cultural Studies uses a model of not just the audience, but of *audiences*. It is possible for the same media 'text' to be understood differently depending on the individual concerned. Therefore, even if the media contains ideology, it is still possible for audiences to resist, reject and provide alternative, 'subversive' readings.

The nationwide audience

David Morley's study *The Nationwide Audience* (1980) was an early attempt to establish how the meanings of television for the audience varies according to the characteristics of the audience. Taking the BBC news programme *Nationwide* as a subject for his study, Morley suggests – as Figure 15.8 illustrates – that the 'reading' of *Nationwide* varied considerably. There were:

- 'oppositional' readings which replaced the media-intended meaning with another
- 'negotiated' readings which altered the content of the message received and combined it with already-held ideas in the audience
- 'dominant' readings which agreed with the media-intended reading.

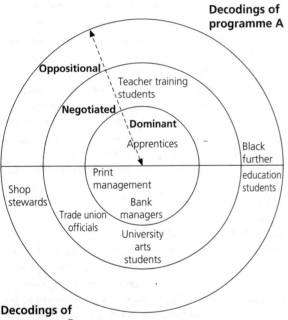

Figure 15.8 The pattern of decodings. Source: Morley (1992)

Desperately seeking the audiences

Since the arrival of the uses–gratifications approach within 'effect theory', we see the development of a concern not with effects but with 'the audience' as a key variable in our understanding of the role the media plays in contemporary society. Taking this further still, we are no longer interested in *the audience* but in *audiences*.

Ien Ang (1991) has warned against seeing the audience as a single, mass group sharing a mass identity. She suggests that sociology, cultural studies

and media studies have all been 'desperately seeking the audience' as a single entity for far too long. (See also Section 10.2.) Ang notes that in recent years the phrase 'couch potato' has become a popular addition to everyday language – used to denote someone who sits alone, watching television all day, 'channel-surfing'. Although this negative term is in popular usage, it resembles the contemporary sociological failure to recognize the power of the audience when they consume the media – especially the televisual media. Ien Ang suggests that:

[the concept] *'television audience' only exists as an imaginary entity, an abstraction constructed from the vantage point of the institutions, in the interest of the institutions.*
(Ang, 1991, p. 2)

Thus, the idea of a single, mass 'audience' is a fictitious construction, built by media companies and organizations to give them an imaginary 'market' at which to aim their products. However, Ang suggests that although audiences need to be seen as powerful interpretors of media reality, in one sense they *are* still a silent mass: they lack the real power to decide which programmes get created and transmitted in the first place:

The millions of ordinary television viewers do not generally take any active part in determing the structural frameworks of the television culture of which they are mobilized to partake. They remain the invisible audience in whose name or on whose

behalf the institutions put forward their interests, claims, defences, policies, strategies . . . Audiences can never be completely free, because they are ultimately subordinated to the image flows provided by the institutions .. .This is not to say that audiences are totally defenceless in the face of the power of the television institutions; far from it. But the 'freedom' they have (to choose between programmes, to watch a little or a lot, together or alone, with more or less attention, in short, to use and consume television in ways that suit them) can only be seized within the parameters of the system they had no choice but to accept. In this sense the television audience is not only an invisible audience; it is also, literally, a silent majority.
(Ang, 1991, pp. 5–6)

In the shadow of the silent majorities

Potentially a far more harrowing account of the audience is provided by post-modernist Jean Baudrillard (1983b). In his book *In the Shadow of the Silent Majorities; or, The End of the Social*, he paints a picture of the contemporary audience as a silent, uninterested, apolitical mass, interested only in seeking media representations of 'the social', and not able to actually act *within* 'the social'. (See also Section 10.11.)

In this post-modern world of the shadow majority, 'reality' for the audience has become hyper-real; that is, dependent on media images of reality, not actual lived experience. Baudrillard refers to the media as part of the 'simulacra' – images or pictures which simulate reality for the audience whose meaning and knowledge of the world is dependent on these 'simulations' and indistinguishable from their 'real' experiences. This situation is also referred to as the 'abyss of meaning'.

Cultural effects: stepping out of the shadows?

In his book *Seeing and Believing*, Greg Philo (1990) attempts to develop a new paradigm within which to understand the issue of media influence on different types of audiences.

Philo suggests that, although the media does contain preferred ideological messages, the audience does not necessarily simply reject or accept these. It is possible to talk of the 'cultural effects' on the audience – in some cases, some members of the audience will take on media images in an uncritical fashion, in other cases individuals will be able to understand the biased message, but to resist it. Rather than the media being an all-powerful controller of society, Philo would rather understand it as a struggle or battle-site where the audience and

media-makers fight over dominant meanings. Thus, the audience does not exist as a silent mass with a collective identity, but as active, thinking, reflective and creative *audiences* – who share cultural experiences in common:

. . . the news may offer a 'preferred' view of events, but we cannot assume that its audience will all accept this interpretation.
(Philo, 1990, p. 5)

The methodology of cultural effects

Taking the 1984 miners' strike as an example, Philo's methodology was to ask audience members, in groups, a year later, to write their own media stories based on photographs. The respondents were shown pictures of violence and asked to put together a news item. This was then followed up by interviews (see Section 3.8) where the respondents were given the opportunity to explain their thinking. Philo found that many of the audience members produced very similar stories, focusing on the violence of the picket-lines (which Philo suggests was a source of ideological bias in the news at the time) and on the phrase 'drift back to work' – as used at the time to suggest (again, wrongly according to Philo) that the strikes were failing and the miners were returning.

Taken at face value this would seem to suggest that the audience were all passive victims of the media, as the hypodermic-syringe model suggests. However, through interviews, Philo discovered that the respondents were perfectly able to create stories 'in the style of a biased media', while not actually believing these stories. The key factor in whether the audience was affected (or not) lay in the cultural and class background and experiences of the individuals themselves:

The consensus [in the media] *that violence is wrong is not likely to be matched by a common agreement on who should be blamed. For example, attitudes on whether police or pickets are more likely to start trouble may vary between different groups in the society (as between groups of working-class trade unionists and middle-class professionals). Such differences within the audience may affect the way in which information from the media is received.*
(Philo, 1990, pp. 5–6)

This new effects model aims to show that individuals have a personal life-history or biography which is the sum of all their cultural experiences so far. Individuals use this biography to interpret the media, and those who lack direct experience of the issue presented by the media may be more likely to believe it than others.

As Figure 15.9 demonstrates, the 'meaning' that a programme or item may have for any one mem-

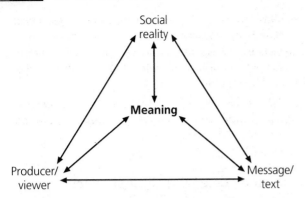

Figure 15.9 An interactive model of how meaning is constructed. Source: Hart (1991) after Fiske (1990)

ber of the audience is based on the interplay and interrelationships between the message of the text in question, the ideas of the audience member (how she or he responds to the text), and ideas which already exist in 'reality' as experienced by the individual.

15.10 **The mass culture debate**

With the development of a system of mass communications, social theorists, since the early 1900s onwards, have been concerned to chart, describe and evaluate the artistic or intellectual nature of the media. This analysis of the artistic or intellectual 'value' of modern-day cultural products is commonly referred to as 'the mass culture' debate (see also Section 10.3). We can characterize the debate by illustrating its central preoccupations and questions:

1 What effect has the creation of a 'mass communications' system had on the quality of media products?
2 What effect has the quality of media products had on the audience?

or, in a more critical (and perhaps pessimistic) fashion:

3 Have modern cultural products suffered from lack of intellectual, artistic and creative value owing to their mass production as commodities to be bought and sold?
4 Has the creation of the mass media led to a mass culture – where the media audience is an uncritical, unintellectual mass unable to value truly artistic achievement?

What characterizes this debate is a confusion of terms, all of which sound similar. Theorists in this debate discuss 'mass society', 'mass culture', 'popular culture', 'high culture', 'low culture' etc. Before we continue to discuss this debate in detail, these key terms need to be more carefully and clearly defined.

- *Culture* – This commonly used concept has two definitions, both of which are important in this debate:
  a the highest artistic and intellectual achievements of a society
  b the way of life of a group.
- *Mass communications* – This is the development of a widespread system of communications (the mass media) where a vast array of technologies and media products are on offer to the 'consumer' or audience.
- *Mass culture* – With the development of a mass communications system, some argue that the media products on offer in today's society lack the intellectual and artistic value of previous times: that the large-scale production of the media lowers its value – it is only a 'throw-away', temporary product to be consumed.
- *Popular culture* – This is a term often used as a replacement for 'mass culture'.
- *Mass society* – Those critical of 'mass culture' also contend that we have seen, or are seeing, the rise of a 'mass society' where the audience has become a faceless, uncritical, apolitical mass – open to all worthless media products, controllable by the media and the ruling class without question or criticism.
- *Low culture* – 'Mass culture' is also seen, by those critical of it, as a 'low culture'. It is made simply for money and immediate consumption, not for lasting artistic value.
- *High culture* – This is the opposite of 'low culture'. High culture is believed by some to be a thing of the past – truly critical, artistic and intellectual cultural products.

Activity

Some sociologists are highly critical of popular, or mass culture, whereas others feel it does have some value. First create a detailed list of examples of both 'high' and 'low' culture. Then write an argument for or against the value of either high or low culture in contemporary society.

A, E

Mass culture: the Frankfurt School

The Frankfurt School have claimed that contemporary societies are 'mass societies'. By this they mean that social community has been lost and, with the rise of mass communications, the media has become worthless. The media contains no genuine attempts to express critical thinking regarding the social condition, and in failing to do so stands in the way of revolutionary changes in the consciousness of the masses.

Marcuse (1966), a member of the Frankfurt School, refers to individuals in a mass society as 'one-dimensional'. By this he means that membership of contemporary society is based on socialization through the culture industry and a loss of free-thinking, intellectual curiosity and critical thought.

Marcuse suggests that these 'mass societies' are characterized by the 'paralysis of criticism' – the inability of the masses to engage with critical, enlightened and revolutionary thought. A new post-war affluence, combined with this loss of criticism, leads to the continuation of false class consciousness in society. Marcuse, in common with others in the Frankfurt School such as Adorno and Horkheimer, operates with an image of the mass media, or in their words, 'the culture industry', which sees the media feeding crass, commercial 'low culture' into the minds of the willing masses – who are tricked and duped into thinking that media 'entertainment' represents a free and active choice:

. . . the vast majority of the population accepts, and is made to accept, this society . . . The distinction between true and false consciousness, real and immediate interest still is meaningful . . . men must come to see it and to find their way from false to true consciousness, from their immediate to their real interest. They can do so only if they live in need of changing their way of life, of denying the positive, of refusing.
(Marcuse, 1964, pp. xiii–xiv)

Liberation, the end goal of the project of 'critical theory', can in this view only been achieved by waging a war on consciousness – of showing the masses that they do have the ability to achieve critical thought; but to do so they must give up the comfort and security of the mass culture delivered by the modern system of mass communications.

The Frankfurt School condemn this mass culture. Media products are seen to deliver 'low culture' as a commodity to be bought and sold for capitalist profit, rather than concentrating on genuine expressions of taste, art and intellect. This low culture, characterized by its essential sameness, is consumed by the masses who in turn lose individuality.

The Frankfurt School take this idea to its logical conclusion. They place their hope of revolutionary change for society in the hands of 'high culture'. Critics of the school point out that whereas they wish to achieve a mass Marxist revolution, they put their hopes for this in the hands of a non-working class, cultural élite. As Chris Jenks (1993) comments:

It is, in many ways, one of the grand paradoxes and ironies of contemporary social theory that a concerted, prolific and radical group of Marxist scholars should have constituted a thesis on the character, value and function of mass culture that is personified by condemnation rather than redemption.
(Jenks, 1993, pp. 107–8)

As a warning against these pessimistic and critical theories which claim that social life has been characterized by the development of a 'mass society', Raymond Williams (1963) notes that the concept 'masses' is highly problematic – it means many different things to many different theorists:

The masses are always the others, whom we don't know, and can't know. Yet now, in our kind of society, we see these others regularly, in their myriad variations; stand, physically, beside them. They are here, and we are here with them. And that we are with them is of course the whole point. To other people, we are also the masses. Masses are other people.
(Williams, 1963, p. 289)

Williams claims that whereas 'we' are always able to think for ourselves, 'the masses' are always other people who cannot. In fact, the concept 'masses' is so general it is meaningless, and certainly not capable of being measured:

There are in fact no masses; there are only ways of seeing people as masses.
(Williams, 1963, p. 289)

The 'golden age' of high culture

A number of the criticisms of low culture, from all sides of the political spectrum, are based on a 'golden age' argument. They frequently suggest that whereas the past was an age of high intellectual values, the present has become cheapened. These types of arguments, however, do not usually tend to be linked to a historical analysis. This begs the question – 'When did the golden age collapse?'

Gans (1974) suggests that with the rise of mass communications we witness not the cheapening of cultural products, but their plurality. People have much more freedom of choice and therefore more opportunities to think about the world. As Chris Jenks elaborates:

All people, within the post-industrial society, have more freedom, more choice, and clearly, more self-expression. Popular culture then is not simply an exercise in exploitation or mechanical reproduction but instead it fulfils a need and a desire of a particular, but genuine, kind of taste or tastes.
(Jenks, 1993, p. 112)

Gans argues that the Frankfurt School themselves are guilty of ideology because they have a biased dislike of popular media and assume that popularity means worthlessness where it might not. This biased or ideological dislike of 'ordinary culture' is based on a dislike of, or a lack of sympathy and understanding for, 'ordinary people'.

Williams (1990), also from a Marxist viewpoint, claims that popular culture and the modern-day media do have value. They allow for as much creativity, revolutionary thinking and self-expression as so-called 'high' or 'élite' culture. Williams suggests that to devalue 'popular' or 'mass culture' is to do a disservice to the working classes, whose culture it usually is. This so-called mass culture frequently employs the techniques of irony and satire to subvert and to make highly politicized comments.

Swingewood (1977) argues, in accordance with the title of his book, that we are witnessing the 'myth of mass culture'. Mass culture, he asserts, is neither good nor bad, revolutionary nor exploiting. Actually, it is not real – it does not exist. It is simply an ideological phrase used by some groups to win intellectual arguments while devaluing all other viewpoints.

15.11 **Globalization and the future of mass communications**

Traditionally, the largest unit for macro sociology has been individual societies themselves, or the nation-state. Recent theoretical developments in sociology, however, have attempted to study social life on a much wider, global scale. Theories of 'globalization' suggest that sociology should now concern itself with the relationships *between* societies. (Globalization is also considered in Sections 9.9, 10.10, 12.5, 16.8 and 17.6.)

The global village

In the early 1960s, cultural and media critic Marshall McLuhan (1964), famous for his early discussions of information technology, predicted that with the rise of worldwide communications systems, individuals would live in a kind of 'global village' – where communication and electronic interaction could take place between geographically separate areas.

The implications of this idea are enormous. Individuals could share cultural experiences in time and space, where before interaction was often unlikely and in some circumstances impossible. (See also Sections 10.10 and 16.8.) Taken to its extreme conclusion, this global village would represent a single common culture made up of a whole variety of cultural traditions – a pastiche of ideas, attitudes and experiences as illustrated by post-modern theories of cultural identity.

Although developments in technology and their use have been somewhat slower than predicted by McLuhan, with the rise of the Internet – the global network of satellites, cables and computers, also referred to as the 'information superhighway' – some sociologists suggest that this global village may not be far off.

Cyberspace and globalization

The areas on the Internet available for linking individuals are known collectively as 'cyberspace' (see Section 16.8). The development of this system of tele-communication came primarily from economic transactions on global stock-markets and from weapons research. Increasingly, it is possible for individual homes to use this new technology. Many homes now subscribe to cable or satellite television organizations.

Discussion point

Have contemporary media technologies significantly changed the face of global broadcasting? Have we witnessed a global media revolution?

A global culture?

Although it is unrealistic to assume that a common culture is developing across the globe, simply because people are watching the same television programmes, there is a degree of globalization occurring in the media (see Section 10.10). Countries miles apart now share common images through the buying of programmes from one television organization by another, charity 'rock events' can be shown across the world at the same time, and newsworthy events such as warfare, elections and natural disasters are transported into our homes 'as they happen'. Malcolm Waters (1995) suggests that this is evidence of globalization, though not as yet to the degree first predicted by McLuhan.

Cyberspace and post-modernism

The rapid developments taking place in cyperspace are seen by some to herald the development of a post-modern society in which virtual reality and Internet communications will exist side by side with traditional forms of communication and interaction.

Globalization as democracy

As a criticism of Marxist theories on the development of communism as a global and inevitable path, Fukuyama (1992) provides a different vision of the near future based on the notion of 'convergence'. Fukuyama suggests that the idea of a future classless society is unrealistic. We have reached the 'end of history' and our new world order is, and will be, based on liberal capitalist democracy (see also Section 17.1). The eastern and western worlds are being drawn closer and closer together, increasingly following a similar pattern of development.

Pluralists would embrace this image of globalization as the increased democratization of the globe, and see the mass media as playing a central part in this process. Through increased shared media experiences, the eastern and western worlds can develop common tastes and attitudes.

Globalization and consumption

A major theme in the analysis of the development of new technologies across the globe is the emphasis given to the development of a global 'consumer culture'. The media acts as a giant shopping catalogue where, as Featherstone (1991b) argues, individuals are able to define themselves through consuming particular lifestyles and products.

Americanization and global imperialism

Pluralists have embraced the idea of globalization as a positive development towards a democracy in which individuals are free to choose the goods they consume from the media from a vast range of different products. Other commentators are more sceptical, claiming that globalization represents a process of Americanization: the expansion of western capitalist ideas and values onto the rest of the globe.

Sklair (1991) suggests that the direction of globalization, through the mass media, flows from the western world outwards. The process is of the expansion of western trading for economic gain into new global markets. As Waters comments:

Not only the programme producers but the advertising agencies and news agencies as well as the companies that manufacture consumer products are owned in advanced capitalist societies.
(Waters, 1995, p. 148)

This process of westernization uses the media to achieve hegemony: the same consumer ideals and values are to be found across the whole of the information superhighway:

Advertising, in particular, seeks to sell products by depicting idealized western lifestyles, often under the universalizing themes of sex, status and the siblinghood of humanity – the world sings a hymn of harmony to a soft drink company of doubtful nutritional value. They mimic the opportunities for simulation already given in soap operas, sitcoms and action thrillers.
(Waters, 1995, pp. 148–9)

Further reading

Accessible A level standard texts designed to introduce the key debates in this field include:

- Barrat, D. (1990) *Media Sociology*, London, Routledge.
- Dutton, B. (1986) *The Media*, London, Longman.
- Trowler, P. (1996) *Investigating the Media*, 2nd edn, London, Collins Educational.

Further texts designed to provide more detail include:

- Abercrombie, N. (1996) *Television and Society*, Cambridge, Polity.
- Sorlin, P. (1994) *Mass Media*, London, Routledge.

A good, general 'reader' covering many classic and contemporary writings in this field is:

- Eldridge, J. (ed) (1993) *Getting the Message: News, Truth and Power*, London, Glasgow University Media Group/Routledge.

Important studies which are accessible and of theoretical and empirical significance include:

- Cohen, S. (1980) *Folk Devils and Moral Panics: The Creation of the Mods and Rockers*, Oxford, Basil Blackwell.
- Philo, G. (1990) *Seeing and Believing: The Influence of Television*, London, Routledge.

Back issues of the periodical *Sociology Review* (formerly known as *Social Studies Review*) also contain many articles on this field of sociology and many others.

Exam questions

1 Explain and evaluate the role of the mass media in the social construction of 'moral panics' in society. Illustrate your answer with reference to at least two examples of 'moral panics'.   [25 marks]
(AEB, Paper 2, Winter 1994)

2 'The "hypodermic syringe" model sees the individual as a member of a passive audience, who is easily influenced and manipulated by the mass media.' Assess this model with reference to sociological evidence and arguments.
[25 marks]
(AEB, Paper 2, Summer 1995)

3 Assess the view that it is professionals, such as broadcasters and journalists, who really control the content of the media.   [25 marks]
(IBS, Paper 1, Summer 1996)

4 a Briefly explain what sociologists mean by the concept of 'news values'. [4 marks]

b Identify and briefly explain two factors, other than 'news values', which influence what finally appears as news. [4 marks]

c What have sociologists contributed to our understanding of how media professionals work? [7 marks]

d Critically assess the view that the content of the media reflects the interests of those who own and control the media. [10 marks]

(IBS, Paper 1, Summer 1995)

Coursework **suggestions**

1 Moral panics in the British popular press

Using content analysis, and possibly a form of audience-based research such as those developed by Greg Philo in his book *Seeing and Believing*, research could be conducted on how the popular press creates and represents moral panics. The folk devil could be any current group as identified at the time of research.

Possible examples are political campaigners, strikers etc.

2 The representation of gender in television adverts

By using content analysis and drawing up a coding scheme, a sample of TV adverts could be deconstructed to see whether gender bias existed. Attention would have to be paid to the coding used, to ensure that both image and voice were taken into consideration. A replication of a previous, feminist study could be attempted.

3 Crime and ethnicity reporting in the newspaper media

Content analysis could be used in order to investigate whether the reporting of criminal activity in the media is associated with the alleged criminality of black people. Using the work of Stuart Hall as a theoretical context, images and text could be coded and analysed to see whether a bias detrimental to ethnic minorities exists. These findings could be compared with a TV report of the same crime.

Community, locality and nation

16.1 **The development of the sociology of community**

The origins of the sociology of community can be traced to European theorists Tönnies and Durkheim

(see box on page 684), who were writing towards the end of the nineteenth century. Their aim was to explain the new phenomenon of urbanization and its effect on social life (see also Section 2.2). Both saw city life having negative consequences for 'community'. People in feudal village-based society, they sug-

---

The ideas of Tönnies and Durkheim can be summarized in the following way:

Gemeinschaft or mechanical communities:
Simple, traditional society
Rural
Little division of labour
Homogeneous culture
Shared norms bring social cohesion
Intimate, enduring relationships

(Adapted from Selfe, 1987, p. 234)

Gesellschaft or organic communities:
Complex, modern industrial society
Urban
Highly differentiated division of labour
Heterogeneous culture
Contracts/legal bonds bring social cohesion
Few important close relationships, mostly
    impersonal, short-term relationships

Activity

This section traces the development of the sociology of community from early sociology to the present. As you read through it draw up a time-line from 1887 to the present, placing each theorist at the appropriate time on the line, summarizing their ideas in a few sentences or phrases. For example:

1887: Tönnies: Pre-industrial rural society
    = *Gemeinschaft* (community);
    Industrial society = _____

1893: Durkheim: _____

U, I

gested, had lived in close contact with each other, sharing beliefs and lifestyles. This was the ideal breeding ground for 'community'. Tönnies (1955, orig. pub. 1887) saw feudal/rural society based on *Gemeinschaft* (or 'community'). People were close, bonded by kinship or friendship. However, as villages grew into towns and cities these bonds faded. *Gemeinschaft* gave way to *Gesellschaft* (or 'association'), a society based on individualism and impersonal contractual relationships. Durkheim (1947, orig. pub. 1893) noted a similar trend in the movement from what he called 'mechanical' society to 'organic' society. In mechanical or rural societies people worked together on the fields, but in organic or urban societies work was highly complex and differentiated, separating people. (See Section 16.3.)

Much of the sociology of community that has followed has been a debate with the ghosts of Tönnies and Durkheim, particularly over the issue of whether a sense of community can exist in urban areas. (See the box at the top of this page.)

Simmel and the Chicago School

The next major developments can be traced to the writings of Simmel, the Chicago School and Wirth. Simmel (1903) was able to identify positive and negative features of life in the city:

Unlike Tönnies, and to an extent Durkheim, Simmel seems untouched by nostalgia for the world that preceded the advent of industrialization. He writes as an unapologetic urbanite . . .
(Kasinitz, 1995, p. 12)

There was, he said, a contradictory nature in urban living: *positively*, an opportunity for freedom and self-expression; *negatively*, the possibility of loneliness and the way that the city lies beyond individual control. Thus, in observing a highly individualized society, he offered us the idea that, at best, 'community' in modern urban areas is weak. However, he felt that the advantages of urban living far outweighed the disadvantages.

The Chicago School, a body of urban sociologists at its height between 1915 and 1950, developed two wings. (The work of the Chicago School is also considered in Sections 6.4 and 11.4.) One favoured quantitative research, most famously illustrated by Burgess' Concentric Zone Model (1925) which attempted to map the growth of cities as an ecological system. The other was built on an ethnographic tradition (see Section 3.9), based on qualitative data, giving first-hand reports of relationships in specific communities and subcultural groups. In contrast, Tönnies, Durkheim and Simmel tended to pursue 'grand theory':

The significance of the Chicago School lay in its successful pursuit of empirical research informed by theory. It turned American sociology away from armchair theorising toward firsthand and empirical enquiry.
(Bulmer, in Kuper and Kuper, 1989, p. 105)

As such it built the foundation not only for American sociology, but the discipline in general.

Wirth (1938) borrowed ideas from all the above-mentioned traditions. He suggested that a city:

. . . may be defined as a relatively large, dense, and permanent settlement of heterogeneous individuals.
(Wirth, in Kasinitz, 1995, p. 64)

As a result urban relationships were superficial and functional, based on self-interest. Out of this developed a generalized 'way of life', but very little of what we could call 'community'.

> ### 💬 Discussion point
>
> To what extent is it accurate to say that rural areas develop 'community' but urban areas do not?

Post-war theories and research

Crow and Allan (1994) suggested that the sociology of community after the Second World War developed in three distinct phases.

The first phase

The first phase, during the 1950s and 1960s, was orientated towards ethnographic style research into specific communities, including their kinship networks, local employment, and political and religious affiliations. In many ways this was similar to the ethnographic wing of the Chicago School. On the positive side they were able to provide:

. . . a wealth of information about ordinary people's lives (in particular in working-class urban districts and some of the more remote rural communities (Crow and Allan, 1994, p. 13).

However, they suggested that these studies were too descriptive and impressionistic and, as a result, it was not possible to use them for the purposes of comparison. The studies were rooted in a functionalist approach, tending 'to direct attention away from conflict and schism' (p. 14).

Young and Willmott's *Family and Kinship in East London* (1957) can perhaps be seen as an example of the general tradition of this time. (This is also considered in Section 7.5.) It considered how a friendly and supportive community, based on family ties and close neighbours, existed in the inner London borough of Bethnal Green. However, redevelopment had given some people the chance to relocate to the newly built suburb of Greenleigh, and it was noted how this created 'privatized' families and a loss of community.

Rex and Moore's *Race, Community and Conflict: A Study of Sparkbrook* (1967) was mentioned as an exception to the general trend in research into community at this time because it took a Weberian approach and therefore considered conflicts in urban areas (see also Section 6.4). They argued that it was possible to divide local inhabitants into 'housing classes'. Each housing class shared the same situation in the housing market, ranging from outright owners to tenants of rooms in lodging houses, and was the outcome of discriminatory rules and regulations. The market reinforced class and racial inequalities.

The second phase

The second phase identified by Crow and Allan emerged in the 1970s. This period was dominated by theoretical debate, at the expense of primary research. The debate was geared around critical appraisal of the concept of community and the lack of evaluative or critical assessment in the research of the first post-war phase. Attention was drawn to conflict in terms of social class and gender, both of which had previously been ignored or invisible. It was argued that, as communities did not exist in isolation, researchers needed to give an assessment of how outside forces – such as the state – affected them (see Chapter 17). Feminists such as Delamont (1980) argued that phase one studies had:

. . . a tendency to portray women's lives in a patronising manner, or to make them invisible: Women are described as 'gossiping' but men as 'discussing' in the accounts and women's roles are frequently neglected.
(Delamont, in Crow and Allan, 1994, p. 16)

Feminists have often accused male sociologists of seeing society only in terms of its public sphere, where men dominate as decision-makers of the major institutions, only acknowledging women in the private sphere, when necessary, as childrearers and homemakers (see Chapter 5). Feminists developed oral history as a research method to show how women had taken control of their own lives and made contributions to the development of their communities. Crow and Allan showed how women were involved in political action like the Glasgow rent strike of 1915, in formal employment, and in mutual support by sharing identities as housekeepers and childrearers – what Harris (1983) called an 'occupational community' in itself.

The third phase

Crow and Allan saw the third phase of post-war sociology of community occurring in the 1980s and 1990s. They said that sociologists have aimed to build on the strengths of the previous two phases: from the first phase the interest in locality studies, combined with the critical awareness of the second phase. Particularly important has been the social, economic and political context in which the studies have taken place, a time of recession and restructuring (see Section 9.4). As a result of a downward turn for world capitalism, industries have reorganized themselves, perhaps downsizing or moving particular aspects of production to areas of cheaper labour, in order to protect profits (see Section 12.5).

The aim of studies in this phase has been to examine the effect of such a context on communities and how they have responded to it. The case studies chosen for Section 16.3 are good examples of studies of this nature. They also show the awareness of this phase that within localities there may exist different (and potentially conflicting) viewpoints on group and individual levels – indeed that individuals may even offer differing accounts in private and in public.

Communitarianism

The 1990s have also been important for a reawakening of sociological, political and policy-orientated interest in the role of community, and in particular the 'loss of community' thesis. Much of the debate stems from so-called 'communitarians' (see also Section 2.10). In a similar way to Tönnies and Durkheim, communitarians feel that the individualism of the present capitalist society is isolating people and breaking up their sense of community and the stability it brings for them and society.

Etzioni's *The Spirit of Community* (1995) offers the:

... call to restore civic virtues, for people to live up to their responsibilities and not focus on their entitlements, to shore up the moral foundations of society.
(Etzioni, 1995, p. ix)

He claims that this focus has already gained the respect of key members of the UK's three main political parties. Success in the communitarian project relies on:

... building shared values, habits and practices that assure respect for one another's rights and regular fulfilment of personal, civic and collective responsibilities.
(Etzioni, 1995, p. 255)

Etzioni's focus is modern America, a nation where he says people are all too aware of their rights (and with an interest in extending them, with the help of self-interested lawyers) but who show little or no sense of their obligations to fellow citizens as a community or a nation. He feels that the same applies to the UK.

Discussion point
To what extent is it true to say that politicians agree with the communitarian agenda? Can you provide specific examples?

According to communitarians, the answer to the identified problems lies in 'moral reconstruction', for which Etzioni proposes a five-fold programme.

- Families should aim to teach their offspring full moral values. This relies on *both* parents taking responsibility for childcare, but relies on workplaces offering flexible work patterns to allow it. (See also Section 7.5.)
- Schools need to reinforce the moral values taught at home, or make up for parents who neglect their duties in this area. (See also Section 8.10.)
- National governments need to allow 'social webs' to develop and to empower them to make contributions to maintaining their own communities. This would bring people of all backgrounds together, who, by expressing a 'civil commitment', would 'build community and foster mutual respect and tolerance'.
- National society must regulate local communities and groups to ensure that conflicts do not break out and that communal obligations remain in place.
- Fifthly, Etzioni tells us 'Don't get mad; get going' (p. 249). If we have a special interest or concern we should work through democratic processes to express it; through debate will come community-wide consensus.

In conclusion he asserts that communities will work only if people have a *commitment* to good behaviour rather than being forced. As a result citizens need educating, praising when they act well and 'frowning upon' when they don't.

Discussion point
To what extent do you agree with the five-fold programme advocated by Etzioni? Can you identify any problems with it?

These themes are taken up by the many contributors to Atkinson's *Cities of Pride* (1995). Prashar (1995), for example, argues for government-supported community initiatives (a 'third sector') which would 'innovate, agitate, and interrogate so that our democracy remains vibrant and responsive'. Halliday (1995) describes how this is already being done by Community Development Trusts, voluntary groups who identify shortfalls in community provisions and work to fill them (along the lines of Etzioni's 'social webs'). Being locally based they are best able to identify local needs, but are also more visible and accountable should local people be dissatisfied with their service provision. However, she appears to differ from Etzioni by noting that communities in depressed areas, with a longer road to travel, do need financial help from government.

Criticisms of communitarian theory

Although the communitarian call to re-invoke community values has many supporters, it has also caused waves of criticism. Derber, from a Marxist standpoint, has criticized Etzioni's concentration on ordinary people while ignoring business practices which make the minority richer and create wider inequalities. He needed to make reference to 'corporate social obligations', important in a world where multi-national corporations have:

. . . produced abandoned plants and ghost communities all over America.

(Quoted by Steele, 1995; see also Section 16.8.)

Marquand (1996), who has taken a social–democratic perspective, criticizes Etzioni's lack of political awareness, suggesting that a reliance on morals and voluntary action is a 'counsel of despair'. Self-discipline and motivation have a place but we ought not to give up on local and national government leadership and co-ordinating powers. The answer is to take 'the market' out of public policy and to ensure that wealth creation schemes also include 'community values' at their heart.

Feminist theorists such as Bea Campbell, (1995b) have also found fault with Etzioni's critique of the modern family – the assertion that family breakdown is linked to community breakdown – on a number of counts. Firstly, she believed his call for both parents to take responsibility for their children was a backdoor way of restating old patriarchal ideas of the woman's place being in the home. (See Chapters 5 and 7.) When a similar argument was put to Etzioni he responded by saying:

. . . to say we should tell both parents that it is OK to neglect children because we're afraid that, initially at least, more responsibility will fall on mothers . . . disregards the needs of children and I feel very strongly that we should not do that.

(Quoted by Kelly, 1995, p. 21)

Secondly, Campbell criticized his view that lone mothers are the fault of modern society's problems. Single mothers, she said, are very active in creating self-help groups (the sort of behaviour advocated by *The Spirit of Community*) and not passive victims. Instead men are the problem:

. . . a war is being waged against the community itself by criminalized coteries of men and boys – 88 per cent of offenders appearing in court are male – and community solidarity is sustained overwhelmingly by mothers.

(Campbell, 1995a, p. 31)

Generally the lack of reference to feminism, for Campbell, is indication enough of the poverty of the communitarian perspective.

Other sociologists have been concerned about the individual in communitarian theory. For the New Right – what Etzioni calls 'liberals' or 'libertarians'

– the advocated programme infringes on personal choices. For them it is unlikely that the strong moral consensus, if established, would tolerate deviations according to the actions and beliefs of minority groups and individuals. As such it is too authoritarian: the type of power asserted in totalitarian, communist societies and not the sort expected from free democratic ones (see Section 17.1). As far as they are concerned people should be able to do what they want, as long as it doesn't harm others. Etzioni feels our actions always have knock-on effects, whether we perceive it or not.

Pahl (1995), although not of the New Right, developed this theme by suggesting that communitarianism was failing to take account of people's sense of individuality. They are not selfish and uncaring, but social beings operating in friendship networks, ready to help their friends whenever they are needed; yet their sense of individuality requires that they have their own identity. Therefore 'phoney communitarianism' had misread reality and if it had its way 'the spirit of community' would return us to the divided and oppressive communities of the past.

Activity

a Summarize the key arguments for and against communitarianism.
b Which ones stand up best to scrutiny?

I, E

In conclusion we can see that the sociology of community has developed from its earliest romanticized nostalgia to a more critical and sceptical discipline. Sociologists from a variety of perspectives have offered important extensions to the area concentrating more deeply on the effects of gender, ethnicity and general conflicts that may occur within communities. Methodologically they have also tried to be more rigorous by comparing communities within one study and aiming to develop comparability between studies. Yet, in some ways the new communitarian debate can be seen as a return full circle to the initial

Activity

a Using the time-line you have written up as your guide (see Activity on page 646), write a paragraph to explain how theories on community have changed as sociology has matured.
b Compare your time-line and summary paragraph with a partner. Discuss possible reasons for the changes in emphasis and consider how far the most recent theories have improved on the earlier ones.

I, A, E

debate about the loss of community in modern, urban capitalism. Has community ebbed away in urban areas? Did it ever exist? Or, are those claiming the end of community not able to see vibrant communities when they do exist?

16.2 **The functions of community**

This section aims to show that communities operate in functional and dysfunctional senses. Positively, they serve to bring people together, giving them a common identity and sense of purpose. This collective sense of being can lead, for example, to the development of support networks and proactive political movements of informal and formal kinds.

However, community life can have negative consequences for individuals and groups inside and outside of the perceived boundaries. Insiders may have differing levels of commitment to their group yet feel pressure to conform in their thinking, speaking and acting. This may differ according to circumstances but could cause psychological tensions and stresses. They may feel unable to conform to their community's norms and may suffer the consequent backlash. The development of cultural norms also means that there will be resulting boundaries and 'outsiders' beyond, with all the potential for conflict this may entail.

Thus it becomes clear that sociologists of community should avoid the romanticized, rose-tinted images of community life, whether in the past, present or future. 'Community' may not always be the utopia many sociologists have presumed it to be.

Structuralist orientations

The macro or structural tradition in sociology has always concerned itself with considerations of the functions that institutions or structures perform for society as a whole or its individual members. If we return to Durkheim (1893), 'community' was best seen in pre-industrial societies, characterized by mechanical solidarity, as the result of living in close proximity and engaging in face-to-face interaction. (See also Section 2.3.) The similarity of working and social lives for members of the community led to the development of social solidarity and collective consciousness – awareness and feelings of togetherness. Alternatively it could be seen as a result of social cohesion brought about by the fact that individuals are dependent on each other in a complex division of labour, as was seen in industrial society, based on organic solidarity. Thus a function of community for Durkheim was the development and retention of consensus, or social solidarity. This has been a theme recurring in many subsequent theories and studies of community.

It has often been suggested that working-class communities, in particular, have offered their members the closeness and support that a collective lifestyle brings. Writing in *Working Class Community* (1968), Brian Jackson offers a romanticized view:

Work, the old poverty cycle, the extended family, this is the settled structure of community. In turn this leads to a style of living which again adds to the structure . . . If the community is built up 'vertically' through kinship, where people of different ages – grandchild and great-aunt – are joined together; it is also built up 'horizontally' where people of the same age but different families are joined in a strong social bond. It begins in childhood . . .
(Jackson, 1968, pp. 166–7)

In particular the working-class community of Huddersfield, which he was writing about, was seen to be drawn together by economic circumstances – or, more accurately, poverty. This led community members to develop informal support networks and formalized support via friendly societies and trade unions. Young and Willmott (1957) were able to note similar facets of community in Bethnal Green, but both studies suggested that things were changing. Geographical mobility and the decline of traditional industries were having a negative effect on 'community'.

Such views of community have been much criticized for their rather romantic notions, failing to note divisions and conflicts within their subject communities. They have also been criticized for viewing them as socially isolated units without influences from beyond, such as the state or the decisions of multi-national industries.

Recent assessments of the functions of community

Recent sociologists have advocated a more complex assessment of communities. They suggest that it is too simplistic to see them as characterized by harmonious and affectionate relationships since they are bound to fluctuate between people within the community and over time. For example, although working-class communities were united in poverty, some individuals would have had more money than others. Although working in the same industry, different people would have different skills and working conditions. Such instances might just as easily have caused 'relative deprivation', where people felt aggrieved at their poverty or lack of skills compared with others they knew, and had the potential for jealousies and conflict. Thus Crow and Allan suggested that:

. . . the nature of community ties varies with different patterns of physical proximity, differences in

longevity of settlements and of people's residence there, different levels of resources (varying according to age, class and gender), and different senses of obligations between people
(Crow and Allan, 1994, p. xviii)

Bauman (1990) is keen to analyse and explain what he sees as a 'post-modern' world. He thinks that the more 'comprehensive' or all-encompassing communities become, the more 'oppressive' they will become as they begin to interfere with a variety of aspects of people's lives. The more oppressive they become, the more tensions will develop. Bauman uses the example of communes, which are most likely to develop according to this schema. Initially they seek to offer liberation from all other claims for living, but in doing so they end up doing the same, forcing members to live in a particular way. As a result he sees them as 'the most fragile and vulnerable of communities' (p. 77) likely to break apart as they become oppressive and fail to live up to the high hopes and expectations of their members. Likewise Bell and Newby (1983) said that in attempting to develop an 'ethos of loyalty' community leaders and members may initiate a framework of rules which infringe upon the freedoms of individuals. Thus we find in communities a contradictory nature:

... community without privacy feels more like oppression. And that privacy without community feels more like loneliness than 'being oneself'.
(Bauman, 1990, p. 106)

💬 Discussion point

To what extent do we need to see community in the black and white form advocated by Bauman? To what extent is there a middle ground? Give examples to justify your answers.

Many have noted how the setting of rules functions to create 'in-groups' and 'out-groups' (Bauman, 1990); 'insiders' and 'outsiders' (Cohen, 1986); 'inclusion' and 'exclusion' (Crow and Allan, 1994). Because communities seek to define who is and who is not acceptable, the result is likely to be potential or actual conflict given that the deviance of the 'unacceptable' group has been focused upon. For Bauman the 'out-group' is 'useful, even indispensable' to the 'in-group', because it 'brings into relief the identity of the in-group and fortifies its coherence and solidarity' (p. 58). However, it is not always clear who is acceptable and who is not. Boundaries are grey and can be threatened by ambivalence from members of the 'in-group' who may not really care if they are acceptable or not, or by people in the 'out-group' who are not members of the 'in-group' but wish to be. An example of the latter might be immigrant groups who, although 'different', want to be accepted as British and to 'play by the rules'. Instead they face discrimination and resulting inequalities as the 'insiders' aim to reinforce their own rules of membership.

Symbolic boundaries

A. P. Cohen, a post-modernist, has taken ideas of membership and belonging to a new level by introducing the idea of 'symbolic boundaries'. These are 'mental constructs ... boundaries which inhere in the mind' (Cohen, 1986, p. 17) which people use to decide who is and who is not a member of their community. As such they have no factual or accurate quality. They are totally subjective, changing from person to person – an individual may also be completely inconsistent in their application of their own 'symbolic boundaries'. Such boundaries have become necessary because of social changes which have blurred or erased traditional, taken-for-granted boundaries between social groups.

- Geographical boundaries – locally, nationally and globally – have been undermined by industrialization and urbanization, creating uncertainty. We can see the effect of this in the debate over national boundaries and what some see as the increasingly meddling and interventionist European Union aiming to prevent British people living their traditional lifestyle (whatever that is).
- The development of new technology has meant an immediate flow of information from anywhere in the world. Previously communities were relatively sheltered from the outside world, with local opinion leaders reaffirming locally held cultural norms. Now they may have a variety of cultural norms and values thrust upon them, attacking previous certainties.
- Developments in transport have massively increased levels of geographical mobility. Not only do communities face the threat of new cultures via the media, they may meet them face-to-face in interaction too! Geographical mobility and the mass media may, for example, threaten linguistic or dialect differences, creating a national homogeneity in the way people speak. This has been seen by some communities as a major threat to their way of life and has led to campaigns for separate language tuition in schools and for a diversity of dialects in the presenters of television and radio programmes. In Wales it even led to the development of a Welsh language channel, S4C Wales.

- Communities have differing experiences and react to similar events in different ways. This may develop the collective consciousness further but could just as easily divide members. We will consider this in Section 16.3 when looking at the effects of the 1984/5 miners' strike on three geographically separate communities.

Unable to assert physical boundaries or to isolate themselves from the threats incumbent in a 'shrinking' world, both in terms of time and space, communities may attempt to develop a distinct or separate identity through reference to symbolic or cultural differences.

Activity

Try to make a list of examples where communities have responded to perceived 'threats' to their language, morals, religion, dress or behaviour patterns. How have they responded and how successful have they been?

A, E

Cohen reminds us that communities will not respond to the same threat or stimulus in the same way. Furthermore, individual members may adopt the symbols created to make their culture distinct but may interpret them differently, but this is necessarily so. If the symbols were too precise and easily open to collective interpretation they would no longer be symbols; instead they would act as structures determining people's behaviour and producing uniformity. The job of the post-modern sociologist becomes a matter of separating the community as it appears to be – 'the community mask' (1986, p. 13) – from the diversity of interpretations held by individual members; i.e. deciding whether what they see is a 'true' representation of the group feeling or just that of a particular person (or persons). In concluding his discussion of symbolic boundaries he says:

Their symbolic character enables their [community's] *form to be held in common while also enabling individuals to attribute meanings to them. The symbolism of community thus speaks simultaneously for the collectivity to those on the other side of its boundaries and to each of its members who refract it through their individual sense of belonging.*
(Cohen, 1986, p. 17)

Playing out the role

Giddens (1984) makes use of the dramaturgical theory of 'symbolic interactionist' Erving Goffman (see Section 2.7) to suggest that members of communities play a variety of roles, varying with the

Shearer's goal is to win over Geordies

THE return to Newcastle of football's £15 million man Alan Shearer, and the fuss made about it, is a reminder that Geordies still take homecomings very seriously.

That this should survive in an era of mass communication reflects the firm attachment to the symbols of regional identity which is just part and parcel of living here.

One element is the continual debate about who does or does not belong to Geordieland. Is birth necessary and sufficient, or can belonging be acquired by sons and daughters after a suitable period of residence?

The exact geography of Geordieland is also unclear and a full research effort into the issue chaired by a trusted outsider (Melvin Bragg would do) is becoming imperative.

The local culture is weighted in favour of the oral tradition. The language is notoriously hard to replicate in print, which may go some way to explain the North East's poor performance in literature compared to its music, sport, painting and its greatest cultural forms, reunions and farewells.

Being a Geordie is a full-time job and it is exiles such as Shearer who have to work hardest to prove the right to continued affiliation.

He will certainly need to allude to legendary number nines, the fervour of local nightlife, the awfulness of beer mugs as opposed to straight glasses, the dangers of the "bad" pint and the frightening possibility that the Metro (a strangely exotic and typically over-ambitious name) may be extended to Sunderland.

Mr Stuart Boyd
Newcastle upon Tyne

Source: *Daily Express*, 31 July 1996

Activity

Consider the reader's letter 'Shearer's goal is to win over Geordies'. When is a Geordie really a Geordie? Is it possible to give an accurate answer? How would A. P. Cohen's concept of 'symbolized boundaries' answer these questions? Was it, as the letter suggests, attachment to the community that brought Alan Shearer back to the North East?

I, A

circumstances in which they find themselves. Goffman suggested that 'actors' operate in 'front' and 'back' regions. The 'front' region is their identity as they offer it to people they meet, perhaps strangers. Given that they are afraid to show their 'full hand', only aspects of this cameo are true. The back region is seen as our true selves. Giddens, however, sees a weakness in this schema:

If agents are only players on a stage, hiding their true selves behind the masks they assume for the occasion, the social world would indeed be largely empty of substance.
(Giddens, 1984, p. 125)

Such a situation is likely to cause us as much stress as revealing everything about ourselves. In order to solve this contradiction Giddens offers us the concepts of 'enclosure' and 'disclosure', suggesting that to some people, at some times, in some places, we show more of our true selves. Thus there can be a gradient between 'front' and 'back' regions. These concepts are important when we remember the assertion that living in a community can be oppressive as well as supportive. Individual members of a community may well feel pressure to mask their true feelings in order to accept 'official' versions of truth and action. Some have suggested that the need to follow the 'official' line may be more comprehensive than this, seeing community as a form of prison.

Crow and Allan (1994) quote Damer who described traditional working-class communities as 'effectively prisons for their inhabitants' (1990, p. 89). Communities act like this by making use of an effective array of social arsenal – tools such as ridicule, threats, or even (as has been the case in Northern Ireland) punishment beatings. It is likely that in a 'strong' community members will be under the surveillance of the watching eyes of their neighbours. In modern society we are just as likely to be under the roving eye of closed-circuit television (CCTV). Such surveillance will be strong enough to ensure that most members adhere to the 'collective' or common will. Those who step beyond the boundaries of acceptability face being the object of gossip, being shunned or ostracized, and possible retribution. For the consensus theorist such actions ensure the smooth running of the community for the good of all.

Activity

How would conflict theorists, such as Marxists and feminists, explain the operation of social control of community members? Do the 'norms' represent the expectations of the 'collective' group as a whole or of powerful sections within it?

A, E

Active communities

The modern sociology of community is not all doom and gloom – theorists have still seen communities inspiring positive collective action:

In practice, the idea of community as a 'spiritual unity' serves as a tool for drawing as yet non-existent boundaries between 'us' and 'them'; it is an instrument of mobilization, of convincing the group to which the appeal is made of its common fate and shared interests, in order to solicit a unified action.
(Bauman, 1990, p. 73)

Examples include the anti-poll tax campaign of the late 1980s (Bagguley, 1993), the miners' strike of 1984/5 (Waddington *et al.*, 1991), and localized anti- (or pro-) road or airport building campaigns. (See also Chapter 17.)

Activity

a Find examples of communities being 'mobilized' and helping to transform their own locality. Use back copies of local newspapers to help you develop ideas.

b Think about the functions that communities might serve, firstly for society as a whole, and secondly for its individual members. Write two lists, one for a consensus theorist and one for a conflict theorist. Remember that consensus theorists such as functionalists have tended to emphasize the positive nature of functions, and conflict theorists, such as Marxists and feminists, had tended to emphasize the negative features of structures and their functions. Which theorists appear to offer the best explanations? Why?

I, A, E

Cooke (1989), who adopts a post-modernist perspective, proposes that communities (or 'localities' as he prefers to call them) 'are actively involved in their own transformation' (p. 296), although outside forces might prevent them being able to plan the exact outcomes. Some communities are likely to be heavily involved in local policy initiatives. The level of involvement is likely to be determined by their previous histories, so success in the past is likely to encourage further action. It is also likely to ebb and flow over time and space. The effectiveness of any mobilization of the community may also be reliant on political vision, leadership and management.

Cooke's major interest was job creation and he noted how communities could have constructed locally relevant policies but have been constrained by the centralizing tendencies of national government which limits levels of spending, puts power in the hands of urban Development Corporations (which are not locally accountable) and is more concerned with looking 'outwards to a global economy' (1989, p, 305).

16.3 The loss of community thesis

Early sociological writers on 'community' tended to offer a pessimistic analysis of social development, suggesting that the close-knit communities of the past, which they saw as a good thing, were being undermined by the social changes ushered in by the process of industrialization. (See also Section 2.2.) This analysis became known as the 'loss of community' thesis and it continues today with theoretical differences between sociologists on whether community exists in modern (or post-modern) urban capitalism.

Tönnies (1887) and Durkheim (1893), writing at the end of the nineteenth century, were keen to assess the significant social changes allied to the movement from a feudalistic rural-based society to an industrial urban-based one. They assumed that in feudal society where settlements were small in size, there was a good chance of knowing everyone by name and opportunity to engage in regular face-to-face interaction with the whole population of the settlement. Similarity in location, tradition, work, religion, kinship and social activities ensured that populations were closely tied in many different ways, creating a strong communal interest. Durkheim referred to this closeness as 'mechanical solidarity' and Tönnies as *Gemeinschaft* (or 'community'). The 'new' urban society allowed no possibility that individuals could know all of the other members of their 'settlement'. Potentially, this could cause confusion, loneliness and *anomie* (a state where the individual could feel cut off from fellow citizens). Contact was based on functional, impersonal ties. This represented 'organic solidarity' and *Gesellschaft* (or 'association') for Durkheim and Tönnies respectively.

Qualitative research carried out before and after the Second World War found pockets of community in modern rural and urban settings, but it was criticized for failing to take account of any conflict that might have existed. A much-stated example was the village of Tepoztlan in Mexico. Redfield (1930) studied community in the village, adopting a functionalist perspective, and found aspects of pre-

industrial village life that Tönnies and Durkheim might have expected to find: a friendly, supportive, socially cohesive society. Tepoztlan was later studied by Lewis (1949) who, keen to improve living standards in the village, concentrated his study on the poverty and ill-health of the people. (This study is also considered in Section 4.8 and 14.7.) He found a different type of community, one split by petty conflicts, mistrust, and violence: so not all research lives up to our generalization. As Worsley (1987) pointed out, these two studies provide an excellent example of the issue of reliability in sociological research (i.e. the extent to which can we expect to repeat a study and get the same results). Had the different perspectives of Redfield and Lewis led to the alternative results or had the village actually changed?

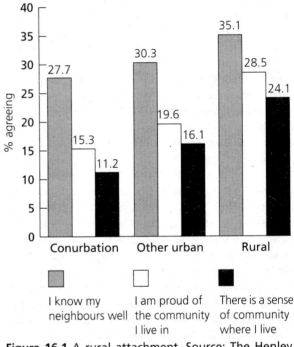

Figure 16.1 A rural attachment. Source: The Henley Centre, *Planning for Social Change*, 1992

Other pre- and post-war sociologists were keen to search for community in urban areas. Foote Whyte (1943) found it in 'Cornerville', an Italian quarter of Boston, USA; Young and Willmott (1957) in the

London borough of Bethnal Green (see also Section 7.5); Jackson (1968) in Huddersfield; to name a few. Gans (1962), after studying Italians in Boston, named such close communities in towns and cities 'urban villages'. So had they mis-read what they had seen or published accurate studies? Certainly they had provided evidence against the original assumptions of Tönnies and Durkheim.

More recently, sociology has again questioned the whole existence of 'community', particularly in the face of rapid social, cultural, political and economic change. The 'new' communitarian movement, for example, says that community is being lost rapidly and that we need to do something to stop it. 'Traditional working class communities' have been faced with the loss of their industries. Even the middle classes have faced redundancy, early retirement, unemployment, new working practices and new economic divisions (see Section 4.6). Have such economic changes led to new social networks, strengthening communities in the face of adversity; or have they further separated people through forced or chosen privatized lifestyles?

Activity

The case studies that follow will consider the above issues and others such as the role of religion, ethnicity and nationalism in creating or breaking communities. As you read through each case study, draw up a table with the following as column headings:

- name(s) of the area(s)
- name(s) of the sociologist(s)
- evidence of community (if any)
- evidence of a lack of community (if any)
- evidence of an historical loss of community (if any).

By looking at your completed table when you have reached the end of this section you will be in a much more informed position to consider whether there has been a loss of community in the contemporary era.

U, I, E

Case study – 'Split at the seams' (Waddington *et al.*, 1991)

This was a two-year study of the effects of the miners' strike (1984/5) (see also Section 9.5) on 'community' in three locations. The strike had been a bitter campaign with the employers, the National Coal Board, although many pointed to heavy government involvement in decision-making and tactics

of both the NCB and the police. 'Yorksco' had been heavily in favour of the strike, 'Nottsco' had been anti-strike and 'Derbyco' had been divided. In most other characteristics such as demography and numbers of men employed in mining they were similar, although each village in the study was seen to have had its own 'history and traditions'. Questionnaires (see Section 3.7) and interviews (see Section 3.8) were used to assess changes in community spirit during, and since, the strike.

Reactions of the three communities to the strike were seen to have depended on their past, previous job losses, inward and outward migration, transferring and bussing-in of miners from other areas. All affected the homogeneity in composition and values of the indigenous groups. The strike was seen to have led to a 'discovery' of community in much the same way as the Second World War or localized disasters had done in the past:

Like families or nations at war, striking communities mobilized a sense of solidarity on a daily basis for their own survival.
(Waddington *et al.*, 1991, p. 169)

Table **16.1** Evaluation of sense of community (percentages)

Reason for strong community	Yorksco	Derbyco	Nottsco
Everybody knows each other	31	20	25
Centrality of the pit/mining	26	24	21
Mutual support	12	9	5
History/tradition	7	10	6
Other	5	5	11
Totals	**81**	**68**	**68**
No strong sense of community	18	28	19
DK/NA	2	5	14
Number	159	133	108

Question: closed
Do you think this area has a strong sense of community?
Question: open-ended
(If yes) What gives it a strong sense of community?

Source: Waddington *et al.* (1991)

After defeat in the strike the mining communities had to cope with their loss of self-esteem, further pit closures, redundancies and new ways of working. Individual miners reacted differently, some taking early retirement or redundancy, others with indifference and others more instrumentally. This was seen to break down much of the pre-strike camaraderie.

Table 16.2 Contacts within the village (percentages)

| | Yorksco | | Derbyco | | Nottsco | |
	Mining	Non-mining	Mining	Non-mining	Mining	Non-mining
Friends	91	79	78	66	93	80
Relatives	78	72	52	57	83	65
Workmates	63	20	61	54	80	56
Number	77	82	58	75	54	54

Question: closed
Do friends/family/workmates live locally?
Workmates question asked only of those in paid work in 1988
Source: Waddington *et al.* (1991)

Table 16.3 Evaluation of neighbourliness (percentages)

	Yorksco all	Derbyco all	Nottsco all
Good/very good	72	58	66
Fair/average	21	32	29
Poor	5	9	5
DK/NA	2	1	0
Number	159	133	108

Question: closed
How good is neighbourliness in (the village)?

Source: Waddington *et al.* (1991)

Women, who played a significant part in supporting strike activities, resumed their traditional domestic roles. Families and friends aiming to return to normality had to get used to contact with others who had adopted differing standpoints during the strike.

The researchers claimed that their data showed that each locality possessed a strong sense of community (p. 14), although there were differences expressed in the different areas by different people. However, there was:

> . . . *plentiful evidence to suggest that the sense of community which sustained the strike was something which emerged and was not necessarily evident before.*
> (Waddington *et al.*, 1991, p. 29)

In fact the communities had been slowly fragmenting before the strike owing to modernization of their industry and national changes:

> *The impact of the strike varied in different parts of the communities' lives and its impact as a whole has to be understood in the context of communities already becoming less insulated from changes in the wider society.*
> (Waddington *et al.*, 1991, p. 174)

Tables 16.1 to 16.3 represent the quantitative answers gained by Waddington and colleagues in their search for 'community'.

Activity

Study Tables 16.1–16.3 and decide whether the data support the claims made by the researchers. Explain your reasoning.

I, E

Case study – 'It's not as simple as that' (McFarlane, 1986)

In this study of rural communities in Northern Ireland, McFarlane was able to show that community was a matter of 'being with your own'. This could be perceived on three levels: your own personal kin/family, people of the same religion (Protestant or Catholic), or people of your locality. The inhabitants of the four villages under study found themselves operating on any of the three levels, sometimes combinations of them, depending on the situation they found themselves in. McFarlane noted how it would be possible to make the picture more complex by taking into account individualized situations, but he opted to focus on generalized similarity and differences:

> . . . *different people emphasized different things, while people differed in the number and range of issues raised. However, there is amongst the variations in theorising a certain general structure which can be discovered (or imposed?) . . .*
> (McFarlane, 1986, pp. 99–100)

Discussion point

Debate whether generalized 'social facts' can be discovered. Is McFarlane, as postmodernists might suggest, just aiming to impose his own subjective version of truth (one truth among many); or is there an ultimate general pattern to be revealed, as positivists might argue?

He suggested that the four villages were not representative (see Section 3.5), but in choosing ones with majorities of Catholics or Protestants or a roughly equal split, he felt that the evidence allowed him to make generalizations about all rural communities in Northern Ireland.

Awareness of the sectarian divide between Protestants and Catholics was paramount to life in the villages, although some saw it as a political divide rather than a religious one. There were times when the division could be forgotten, but other times when it was to be asserted.

Allegiances were likely to come to the fore at election times or during the summer marching season. They might also be expressed more privately in terms of marriage where mixed Catholic–Protestant couplings would be frowned upon and tended, as a result, to be rare. Evidence of the divide could also be expressed in consumption where a shop- or pub-owner's religion may affect whether an individual purchased goods from that establishment.

Religion also affected people's thoughts, it led to the development of labelling where the labels 'Protestant' and 'Catholic' allowed members of the community to stereotype themselves and the 'other sort'. The stereotypes were not as simple as 'us' being positive and 'them' being negative. People might just as easily see negative traits in their 'own' and positive assets of life in the other community. (See also Sections 18.6 and 18.7.)

Interaction was also guided by religious affiliation and may have led to avoidance of others or silences. McFarlane quotes one man who said: 'The worst time's when you're in a bar and something comes on the TV about a bomb or something. You know, you just don't know what to do if there's mixed company. Everyone goes f.....g quiet and all' (p. 95). It was also made clear to the researcher that people of the 'opposite' religion were also 'your own': 'they know the same personal histories and personal foibles ... they speak the same dialect ... you feel the same in all sorts of ways' (p. 96). People therefore tried to act 'decently' (i.e. not show bitterness) – they lived in the same locality and felt the need to share it, 'everything else being equal'. In fact they thought McFarlane very cynical when he questioned jokes they made about each other and how they engaged in banter when sharing friendly interaction.

The sectarian divide was complicated by other factors. Class was seen to be important, with the middle class appearing to express far more tolerance of other people's religion, although the working class thought this was only for show. Men saw women as less tolerant of religious difference, but women suggested the alternative was true. Most thought that young men showed a 'lack of restraint', but believed this was just a phase they were going through.

Figure 16.2 shows how McFarlane expressed community relationships. He observed that the Catholic–Protestant boundary was generally seen as

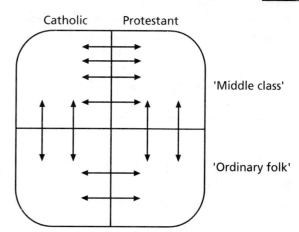

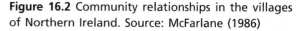

Figure 16.2 Community relationships in the villages of Northern Ireland. Source: McFarlane (1986)

more permeable among the upper 'class' ranges than in the lower ranges.

Case study – 'Glasgow's miles better' (Charsley, 1986)

This was an investigation of community in Glasgow, a place where Protestant and Catholic loyalties might also be seen as prevalent. In the chosen area of focus, marriage, the high level of mixed marriages was seen to dispel such a hypothesis. Even in instances where the couple were Protestant or Catholic many of the friends and non-family guests were likely to be of mixed background. If religious identity was not the focus of celebration, Charsley considered whether Glasgow, the city, as a single large community, or even localities within it, represented a community focus in the marriage. Evidence was lacking in both cases.

However, although evidence of celebration of local or city-wide community was lacking in Glaswegian weddings, people saw a celebration of their national community, of being Scottish. (See also Sections 10.10, 16.8 and 17.6.) Their weddings were seen to be different from (and superior to) those in England, the celebration involving a range of events, both before and on the day, which were perceived to give them an extra richness. The answer to the embracing of Scottishness and the indifference to Glaswegian identity may lie in the negative images of the city, in recent history:

[It has had] *a reputation for slums, poverty, drunkenness and violence, rooted far into the past, but repeatedly reactivated.*
(Charsley, 1986, p. 181)

The antipathy towards Glasgow is also evident in the movement to 'standard English' and a softening of accent in formal situations. At the same time a 'Glaswegian' dialect has been a requirement of membership in other situations. More recently comedians, writers and academics have given it a higher status, making this example an increasingly complex one. In conclusion Charsley tell us:

There is a broad middle ground in which the bulk of the city's population live most of the time. . . . Most who live there have no single community to preoccupy them, either in celebration or rejection.
(Charsley, 1986, p. 184)

Case study – 'Endless pressure' (Pryce, 1986)

This was a study, originally published in 1979, of a West Indian community in the St Paul's district of Bristol, a run-down inner-city area. (See also Section 10.6.) To those outside the community it is chaotic and of low status. To insiders it has its negative features (some call it 'The Shanty Town' or 'Jungle') but it is the only environment where they feel in control. This shows some linkages to the findings of Whyte's (1943) 'Cornerville'.

Full understanding of the life of West Indians in St Paul's requires reference to the movement of black people from Africa to the Caribbean as slaves, and the post-war immigration to the UK as a 'reserve army of labour' (employed when labour is scarce, redundant during economic downturns). (See also Section 9.3.) Both situations represent white colonial domination and racist imperialism (see Chapter 6). The economic situation of blacks in Britain, and St Paul's in particular, was precarious. Many would not gain employment, and those who did would find promotion limited, even in white-collar jobs. This has led them, according to Pryce, to two possible life orientations (though within each orientation he identified a number of subgroups):

- those with work will develop a 'stable law-abiding orientation'
- those without work will develop an 'expressive–disreputable orientation'.

The institutionalized racism which 'proletarianized' the West Indians of St Paul's was called 'endless pressure', the continuous repetition of harassing or stressful experiences due to poverty or other hardships. Christian churches and sects, and reggae music, had developed as an escape and/or a form of protest. (See Section 18.7.)

Pryce, who was of West Indian origin, gained access into three main but separate groups who gave him 'a kind of panoramic view of the West Indian scene' (p. 285). Becoming a recognized member of the community also helped his integration. Generally welcomed, acceptance was aided when he became viewed as an 'insider' – this even required being baptized, to get complete access to the 'saints'! Yet he said that St Paul's had a lack of community which

may not be apparent to people when they first visited the community:

Diverse groups with vastly dissimilar backgrounds do mingle freely in close physical interaction in St Paul's. But this is deceptive, for mingling of this kind does not automatically create a community spirit in the sense of conformity, consensus and vigilance about community standards. . . . Beneath the romantics' illusion of a tight-knit, friendly, organic, warm, harmonious community, the divisions are deep. There is much suspicion between groups. . . . Deeper, more intensive and meaningful interaction takes place on a single-race basis only.
(Pryce, 1986, p. 30)

Conclusion

In conclusion, can we say that there has been a loss of community? It is clear that much of our answer lies in how we define 'community' and what we expect to find as evidence of its existence. Modern society does not allow us to interact with every person we come across, as Durkheim and Tönnies thought might happen if 'community' existed. There are simply too many people and not enough time. However, as we shall see in Section 16.5 on rural sociology, it is questionable whether this ever occurred, at least in any consensual form. Some of the evidence in this section has shown that there can be high rates of interaction between members of a community, but more important may be a shared consciousness and a capacity to support each other in times of need. Importantly, we do know that contemporary communities do not exist in vacuous isolation. They are subject to internal changes, with members constantly leaving and new members arriving. The infrastructure, economic, political and religious arenas change with a resulting impact on the culture of the area. The mass media brings in ideas from elsewhere. Perhaps, it is possible to suggest that rather than having been lost, community has changed in form in order to meet new challenges and requirements of a developing society.

Activity

You were asked to build up a table as you read through the four case studies. What does it tell you about 'community' or the lack of it? Is it fair to say there has been a loss? A more accurate assessment might develop from wider reading. Figure 16.3 (see opposite) makes reference to a range of studies. You might ask your librarian to locate some of them for you.

A, E

1 M. Anwar (1985) *Pakistanis in Britain* Rochdale
2 P. Bagguley *et al.* (1990) *Restructuring* Lancaster
3 A. Bostyn and D. Wight (1987) 'Inside a community' Cauldmoss
4 D. Byrne (1989) *Beyond the Inner City* Tyneside
5 F. Coffield *et al.* (1986) *Growing up at the Margins* County Durham
6 A. Cohen (1978) *Whalsay* Shetland Islands
7 J. Cornwell (1984) *Hard-Earned Lives* East London
8 S. Damer (1989) *From Moorepark to 'Wine Alley'* Glasgow
9 R. Deem (1986) *All Work and no Play?* Milton Keynes
10 N. Dennis *et al.* (1956) *Coal is our Life* Featherstone
11 F. Devine (1992) *Affluent Workers Revisited* Luton
12 N. Elias and J. Scotson (1965) *The Established and the Outsiders* 'Winston Parva', Leicestershire
13 R. Finnegan (1989) *The Hidden Musicians* Milton Keynes
14 R. Frankenberg (1957) *Village on the Border* Glynceiriog
15 G. Giarchi (1984) *Between McAlpine and Polaris* Dunoon
16 H. Gilligan (1990) 'Padstow' Cornwall
17 M. Grieco (1987a) *Keeping it in the Family* Corby
18 J. Hanmer and S. Saunders (1984) *Well-Founded Fear* Leeds
19 C. Harris (1987) *Redundancy and Recession* Port Talbot
20 A. Holme (1985) *Housing and Young Families in East London* East London
21 L. Howe (1990) *Being Unemployed in Northern Ireland* Belfast
22 S. Hutson and R. Jenkins (1989) *Taking the Strain* South Wales
23 R. Jenkins (1983) *Lads, Citizens and Ordinary Kids* Belfast
24 B. Jordon *et al.* (1992) *Trapped in Poverty?* Exeter
25 J. Littlejohn (1963) *Westrigg* Cheviot Hills
26 T. Lummis (1985) *Occupation and Society* East Anglia
27 P. Marris (1987) *Meaning and Action* Docklands, East London
28 R. Meegan (1989) 'Paradise postponed' Merseyside
29 R. Moore (1982) *The Social Impact of Oil* Peterhead
30 B. Mullan (1980) *Stevenage Ltd* Stevenage
31 H. Newby (1977) *The Deferential Worker* East Anglia
32 R. Pahl (1984) *Divisions of Labour* Isle of Sheppey
33 M. Porter (1983) *Home, Work and Class Consciousness* Bristol
34 J. Porteus (1989) *Planned to Death* Howdendyke
35 K. Pryce (1979) *Endless Pressure: A Study of West Indian Lifestyles in Bristol* Bristol
36 J. Rex and R. Moore (1967) *Race, Community and Conflict: A Study of Sparkbrook* Birmingham
37 E. Roberts (1984) *A Woman's Place* Barrow/Lancaster/Preston
38 V. Robinson (1986) *Transients, Settlers and Refugees* Blackburn
39 C. Rosser and C. Harris (1965) *The Family and Social Change* Swansea
40 P. Sarre *et al.* (1989) *Ethnic Minority Housing* Bedford
41 J. Sarsby (1988) *Misuses and Mouldrunners* Stoke-on-Trent
42 P. Saunders (1979) *Urban Politics* Croydon, London
43 P. Saunders (1990) *A Nation of Home Owners* Burnley/Derby/Slough
44 A. Shaw (1988) *A Pakistani Community in Britain* Oxford
45 M. Stacey (1960) *Tradition and Change* Banbury
46 M. Stacey *et al.* (1975) *Power, Persistence and Change* Banbury
47 M. Strathern (1981) *Kinship at the Core* Elmdon, Essex
48 J. Tivers (1985) *Women Attached* Merton, London
49 J. Tunstall (1962) *The Fishermen* Hull
50 C. Wallace (1987) *For Richer, for Poorer* Isle of Sheppy
51 S. Wallman (1984) *Eight London Households* Battersea, London
52 D. Warwick and G. Littlejohn (1992) *Coal, Capital and Culture* Yorkshire
53 W. Williams (1956) *The Sociology of an English Village: Gosforth* Cumbria
54 B. Williamson (1982) *Class, Culture and Community* Throckley
55 M. Young and P. Willmott (1957) *Family and Kinship in East London* East London

Figure 16.3 Some recent community and locality studies in the UK. Source: Crow and Allan (1994)

16.4 Conceptual debates: 'community', 'locale' or 'locality'?

The concept of 'community' has been a matter of debate for 100 years or more. In this section we need to build towards a definite conclusion about which concept is most useful for our sociological purposes. For Durkheim and Tönnies a 'community' was a locally based settlement of people who were closely bonded, but at best it had changed, at worst been lost. Hillery (1955) showed how sociologists were unable to agree on a definition, but Lee and Newby (1983) felt able to promote three variations. Giddens (1984) emphasized the importance of 'locale' rather than 'community', but Cooke (1989) preferred the idea of 'locality' over 'locale'.

Activity

a Write down a list of at least 20 key words or ideas that you associate with 'community'.

b Use this list to help you write a definition, starting: 'A community is _____.' When you reach the end of this section you should return to your definition and compare it with those covered here, considering similarities and differences. **I, A**

Community

For Durkheim and Tönnies, 'community' existed in pre-industrial times and was seen as a location where people knew each other and interacted regularly. Forms of relationship in the following era of industrial society were seen as poorer in comparison. This has been the view of many people, and so in 1983 Lee and Newby felt the need to warn us that:

There is . . . a constant danger of nostalgia in contrasting the past with the present, a tendency to take a highly selective and somewhat rose-tinted view of the 'good old days' which can convey a misleading account of the actual changes which have occurred.
(Lee and Newby, 1983, p. 52)

However, given the view which suggests that modern societies lack 'community', they did feel the issue needed further investigation. In searching for a clear definition of what 'community' is, they told us that Hillery (1955) found 94 different definitions:

- 69 agreed that community involved interaction or social bonds within a given area
- 14 identified common links other than area
- 15 saw community as a rural area, in line with Tönnies and Durkheim.

Lee and Newby pin-pointed three major variations.

1 *Community as a geographical expression.* These definitions refer only to a specific location such as a town or ward of the town. As such they are not very useful to sociologists as there is no consideration of the people found in that geographical location.
2 *Community as a local social system.* These definitions build on the weakness of the previous type of definitions by considering that the location is the setting for social relationships. However, they do not consider the quality of those relationships.
3 *Community as a type of relationship.* These emphasize the spiritual bond or identity of a group of individuals, but the weakness is that they may lack reference to a geographical context.

Activity

Try to think of examples of communities that fit each of these types of definitions. Which of the definitions appears to be the most useful indicator of community?

A, E

After completing the above task you may feel that all three themes fall short of the mark in some way. In reality most of the sociology of community, in adopting specific definitions, falls nearest the idea of the social system.

Bauman (1990) suggests that the idea of relationships within 'given boundaries', within which consensus is sought and gained, is the most important feature of community: 'the primary natural reality' (p. 72). For him:

A community is a group in which factors which unite people are stronger and more important than anything which may divide it; the differences between members are minor or secondary by comparison with their essential . . . similarity.
(Bauman, 1990, p. 72)

So, although consensus is usually important, Bauman does not see it resulting in perfect, close relationships. In our lives relationships will go through peaks and troughs, but when the requirement is there people generally pull together; this is how Bauman saw community. In suggesting that community exists within adopted boundaries Bauman is not necessarily thinking of clearly recognizable geographical limits. They could be social, such as religious or ethnic divides, although sharing similar geography.

Locale

In many ways Bauman's ideas are similar to those expressed by Giddens (1984), although the latter is more focused on the importance of time and place. (See also Section 10.10.) His idea of what we have called 'community' is much influenced by his theory of 'structuration' and the theories of 'time-geography'. Structuration emphasizes the inseparability of structure and action – that behaviour of individuals is influenced by structures such as the family or religion, but that they can also influence the structures. (See also Section 2.9.) Time-geography considers the constraints of the clock and distance between places over what we can do. For instance we cannot pop down to the Mediterranean for lunch and be back for afternoon lessons because the distance is too great and we haven't enough time. However, 'distances' are shrinking owing to improvements in modes of transportation.

Rather than use the concept of community, Giddens offers us the concept of 'locales': 'the use of space to provide the settings of interaction' (p. 118); or in other words, the social structure or physical framework in which action will take place. He is keen to ensure that we should not make the mistake of believing that there is a one-way causation where locales create action: both are independent. He goes on to suggest that:

Locales may range from a room in a house, a street corner, the shop floor of a factory, towns and cities, to the territorially demarcated areas occupied by nation-states. But locales are typically internally regionalized and the regions within them are of critical importance in constituting contexts of interaction.
(Giddens, 1984, p. 118)

As a result of the connection between time, space

(geography) and performance (action), locales are in a continual state of ebb and flow. They cannot be seen as fixed entities. This can be seen in a house or even a city, where different areas are (geographically) segregated or 'regionalized' for different activities at different times. In the case of the house, for example, there may be a division between downstairs for day-time activity and upstairs for night-time.

Activity

Suggest ways in which social action in urban areas may vary over time and space. **A**

You might have suggested the change in use of the central business district or city centre, from day-time office/shop work to night-time leisure activities. You might also have noted how over a number of years parts of a city grow and others decline.

Although pointing out that 'regions' may be rooms or floors of houses, Giddens also considers the concept in its more usual geographical context. Using the example of the 'north–south divide', he reminds us that not only are the North and South geographically determined, they also have 'long established, distinctive social traits' (p. 122). Thus locales exist when people can come together to interact. In times past, when geographical mobility was extremely limited, this coming together had to involve people living in close proximity. More recently transportation has allowed people to travel large distances, widening and altering the contexts of communities. We now live in an age of the Internet where people can come together as one unit on a global scale, close in time although not geographically.

Giddens draws on the ideas of Goffman (see Section 2.7) to explain that what we show of ourselves changes relative to time and space. In different communal contexts we may be keen to show or mask our true feelings. Thus individuals, although they may want to do as they desire, may feel obligated to act according to the rules of their locale in order to be accepted and acceptable. Giddens asserts that:

In all societies there are social occasions which involve ritual forms of conduct and utterance, in which the normative sanctions regulating 'correct performance' are strong ... individuals are likely to feel they are 'playing roles' in which the self is only marginally involved.
(Giddens, 1984, p. 126)

Discussion point

What can locales (or communities) do to ensure that people act in ways that are seen to be acceptable?

Locality

Like Giddens, Cooke (1989) is unhappy with the concept of 'community' because he feels it is tainted by its previously romanticized uses, and often a specific geographical reference. Cooke is, however, also critical of Giddens' suggestion of the term 'locales'. He dislikes the locational component which he feels is too loose, particularly the idea that a room could be a context for what we have been calling 'community'. Cooke would like a far more geographical component, such as a town or region. He also suggests that Giddens (1984) fails to see how 'locales' can be a component part of action as well as a setting for it.

Instead, Cooke suggests that the term 'locality' is a 'strong candidate for filling the gap' (p. 10). Locality encourages us to consider how specific areas, which at first glance may even appear similar, differ in their histories, present and in all likelihood their futures too. The tradition and culture of an area, as well as leadership in the present, may draw people together in an active way or may make them passive to the influence of the outside world:

Locality is a space within which the larger part of most citizens' daily working and consuming lives is lived. It is the base for a large measure of individual and social mobilization to activate, extend or defend those rights, not simply in the political sphere, but more generally the areas of cultural, economic and social life ... the base from which subjects can exercise their capacity for proactivity.
(Cooke, 1989, p. 12)

Activity

a Write down brief definitions of your own of the terms 'community', 'locale' and 'locality'.
b Which of them is closest to the definition of 'community' you developed at the beginning of this section?
c For each definition think of examples to illustrate what you have written.
d Explain which concept you now feel is most/least useful.

U, I, A, E

Selecting the most useful concept

If the choice of options is wide, how can sociologists settle on one? In this chapter we generally take the view that a 'community' is a group of people who are socially bound and influenced, within a geographical context (from village to planetary proportions). For those that wince at using the word 'community', Crow and Allan suggest the use of quotation marks around it. It is their belief that:

There is no doubt that the communities of which we are members play a significant role in shaping our social identities and patterns of action.
(Crow and Allan, 1994, p. 1)

The task of sociologists is to determine to what extent, and in what ways, there have been changes in these identities and whether there are generalized properties, or whether each group is unique in its constitution, past and present.

16.5 The sociology of rural areas

Realities or images?

Some people have romanticized notions about rural areas. Post-modernists (see Section 10.11) argue that this imbalanced view may be enhanced if they add to the image of rurality the 'normalized' concept of 'community':

Put the two together and the effect is to multiply the mythology to something more than its constituent parts. Add 'English' and the effect is like a chemical reaction.
(Short, 1992, p. 4)

Thus we may, when asked to imagine the countryside, conjure up images of Constable paintings, or what we have seen on television – perhaps *Emmerdale*, *The Darling Buds of May* or *Last of the Summer Wine*.

Activity
a Think of these examples, and any others you may be aware of. Make a list of the images they bring to mind.
b After reading this section use the list to consider the accuracy of such portrayals of rural life.

I, A, E

Short suggests that the images presented historically of rural England were of beauty, moral character, 'strength of physique' and 'English virtue'. He quotes a First World War officer who said he was fighting for 'English fields, lanes, trees, English atmospheres and good old days in England – and all that is synonymous with liberty'. Such images have since been widely perpetuated. Laing (1992), for example, considers the role that the long-running radio programme *The Archers* has played in portraying images of 'timeless country folk'. Sociology has itself not been immune from this 'mistake': Durkheim and Tönnies promoted pre-industrial rural society as an example of (perfect) community. Even much later, according to Short:

Too many of the early post-war community studies carried out in Wales, the West of England and Scotland neglected change and thereby helped perpetuate the myth of changelessness in the countryside.
(Short, 1992, p. 11)

Thus Short argues that we must learn from the post-structuralist emphasis on symbols and images (see also Section 2.10 and 10.11), ensuring that we do not fall into the same 'rose-tinted' traps.

Rural areas used to be focused on village or hamlet settlements which were largely self-sufficient owing to the predominance of agriculture. The images arising from this might suggest a continuance of an unchanging picture, but the reality is different. Although agriculture might still account for the majority of land-use in rural areas, it does not account for the bulk of its employment or income (see Section 9.3). Instead, as with most urban areas, the major sources of employment are now manufacturing and service industries, particularly the latter (Lowe and Bodiguel, 1990).

The opposite of 'rural' might be presumed to be 'urban', but where does one finish and the other start? Sociologists in the past have assumed that there exists a 'rural–urban continuum', whereby extremes of the continuum represent 'pure rurality' or 'pure urbanism', and towns in rural areas represent a 'half-way house'. Recent writers have rather quashed this idea by asserting that few, if any, rural areas in the UK exist in the remoteness that 'pure rurality' might require. Rather they exist in an urbanized society, subject to many of the same pressures as urban areas. Recent commentators such as Lowe and Bodiguel (1990) and Hoggart *et al.* (1995) remind us that rural areas are, for example, subject to trans-national or globalizing influences (see Section 16.8). Newby (1987) and Ambrose (1992) suggest that the distinction between what is 'urban' and what is 'rural' is blurred by urban workers who use villages for dormitory purposes. Ambrose describes many rural areas as 'discontinuous suburbs'.

Rural areas, as we shall see, have not had an unchanging, timeless quality. There is, then, no easy way to define 'rural'. Here we will assume links with the green countryside and living in smallish settlements, which accounts for 80 per cent of the land area of England and Wales, but less that 20 per cent of the population.

Pre-industrial rural areas
Let us start our assessment of rural areas in pre-industrialized or feudal times. Durkheim (1893) and Tönnies (1897) saw them as consensual

communities in the purest form. However, Marx and Engels in *The Communist Manifesto* of 1848 had already suggested they were bound up in oppressive and exploitative relationships between lords and serfs (see Section 2.4).

Figures 16.4 and 16.5 show how the feudal system worked. Land was passed down to people of lower rank in the social order and those receiving it were obligated to pay for it, financially and with their actions, perhaps as soldiers or as workers on the fields. The serfs (or peasants) were unable to leave the manor; they were required to work land for their lord before they worked their own, to grow the food they needed for survival. Such oppression led to peasant revolts in England (1381) and in Germany (1524), as well as being a contributory factor to the Protestant movement of the Reformation which compared the poor life of the majority with the riches of those in the Roman Catholic Church.

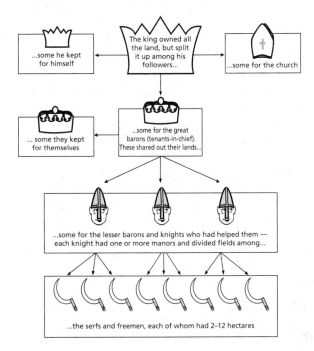

Figure 16.4 The feudal system. Source: Moss (1970)

Feminists might also point to the conflict between men and women during the feudal period. Women who failed to conform could be accused of witchcraft and executed. (See also Section 18.7 for a case study on witchcraft.) Generally women were invisible, appendages of their menfolk rather than separate beings. Such instances call into question the cosy communal images of rural life at that time.

Contemporary rural areas

In *Country Life: A Social History of Rural England*, Newby (1987) details the development of inequalities as time passed. Land-owning and farming were

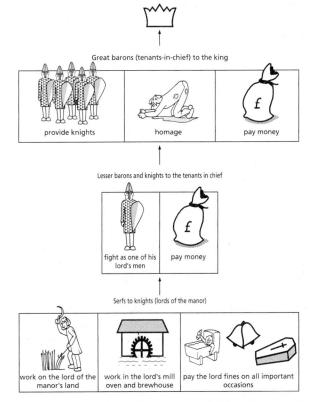

Figure 16.5 What each man did for his land in feudal times. Source: Moss (1970)

not merged until after the Second World War. This was significant because in the early industrial period the minority owned the land but were happy enough to rent it to others who worked it. Merging the ownership and production of food meant that they could maximize profits by making agriculture more 'economic' – by reducing the number of people working on the land and making those who did, and the processes they used, more 'efficient'. It is on this era that we will concentrate our thoughts.

Newby, a neo-Weberian (see Section 2.6), has contributed to a number of influential studies of rural life since the 1970s and is seen as 'an exceptional figure in British sociology for his sustained interest in rural sociology' (Crow *et al.*, 1990, p. 254), an area which many admit has not been thought of as the most exciting. In fact most studies of rural life have been done outside sociology departments, by geographers, anthropologists and agricultural economists. In particular, Newby has made use of general sociological concepts such as 'class', 'status' and 'market situations' (see Section 4.2) in order to show that rural areas are not to be seen as distinct and separate from other areas of modern life: they are subject to similar pressures and changes.

Newby has shown how the post-war reconstruction of England affected rural areas deeply. Growth in the provision of public services such as roads, electrification, health, welfare and education brought rural society 'into the mainstream of English society as a whole' (p. 211). Policy also introduced planning controls to prevent further physical urbanization of the countryside, despite warnings that it might have dire effects by exacerbating regional imbalances. Such a policy commitment was based on 'a gut feeling that the English countryside needed to be protected rather than planned in any positive sense' (p. 215). Thus rural areas saw the introduction of national parks, national nature reserves, sites of special scientific interest and greenbelts to contain the spread of major towns and cities. Rural areas were being preserved for agriculture at a time when that sector was 'down-sizing'; new industrial development was prevented when local people needed new jobs; the building of new housing was prevented, causing scarcity and rising prices.

The growth of car ownership and the motorway network ensured geographical mobility, the possibility of commuting and the process known as 'counter-urbanization' (the drift of populations from the towns and cities 'back' to rural villages):

Rural England, which had been agricultural England, swiftly became middle-class England. The new 'immigrants' brought with them an urban, middle-class lifestyle which was alien to the remaining local agricultural population . . . There therefore arose new social divisions and cleavages . . . Inevitably conflict ensued . . .
(Newby, 1987, p. 222)

The conflict became apparent over issues of housing and environmental issues. On housing the middle-class newcomers objected to the building of cheap homes, often sponsored by the local authority, for the rural poor who had been displaced by rising prices and the newcomers themselves – on the grounds that these dwellings were 'detrimental to the character of the village'!

On environmental grounds the newcomers were critical of the latest farming practices which required the destruction of hedgerows and other wildlife habitats, the use of pesticides, and interference with recreational pursuits:

Concern for the rural environment thus became a public issue partly because there was now residing in the countryside an affluent and articulate population, no longer dependent upon local farmers and landowners for housing and employment, and which was capable of mobilizing itself politically.
(Newby, 1987, p. 227)

Out of this local campaigning developed a national environmental movement: 'the "politics of the country-side" was becoming a national (which is to say,

urban) concern' (p. 229). (See also Section 17.5 for a case study on the environmental movement.)

Activity

Use resources in your library to find out where the main political parties stand on this issue. Which party seems to offer the best policies? Why?

I, A, E

Earlier sociological romantics would have been heavily critical of the 'loss of community' and the 'effects of urban immigrants', but Newby is far more open-minded. He wonders whether the newcomers have in some ways revitalized rural areas with their money, campaigning for the survival or renewal of rural services and for the protection of the environment. At the same time, he is aware that the newcomers are able to overcome the loss of locally provided services by getting in their cars, with those hardest hit being the poor, the elderly and the disabled. While accepting loss of services for lower taxes, the affluent majority of ratepayers:

. . . have demonstrated an understandable reluctance to foot the rapidly rising bill on behalf of their less fortunate neighbours.
(Newby, 1987, p. 232)

Although, in absolute terms, the weakest members of the rural community have seen a rise in living standards, there has been a relative decline in living standards compared with others. The decision as to whether the consequences have been negative or positive, says Newby, depends on the individual's point of view and the person's conception of 'community'.

Activity

a Make a list of the positive and negative consequences of the middle-class 'invasion' of rural communities noted by Newby, together with any other points you can think of.
b Decide whether it has been for better or worse.

I, E

Agribusiness: capitalism in rural areas

Newby (1987) also considers the movement from traditional agriculture to what he calls 'agribusiness' in the post-war period. 'Agribusiness' refers to industrial or factory farming methods of mass food production for (largely) urban centres which are based on 'cost efficiency' and the 'search for sustained profitability'. He calls this the 'second agricultural revolution' (p. 193).

Small family farms have been marginalized, being forced to cater for local or specialized markets (such as those existing for organic food) or to sell up to feed the increasing concentration of production in corporate hands. This, again, shows how rural areas are subject to urban practices: note how the experience of the 'small' farmer compares with that of the family shop or business enterprise. Agribusiness:

... refers not only to the increasing concentration of production on fewer, larger farms, but also to the integration of agriculture into a complex of engineering, chemical and food-processing industries.
(Newby, 1987, p. 193)

These parts of the agribusiness have developed the kind of colonialization policy faced by farmers in the developing world (see Section 12.7), 'forcing' financial and contractual agreements in their search for greater profits. According to Newby:

Farmers have simply lacked the market power to do much more than accept the bargain they have been offered.
(Newby, 1987, p. 196)

Agribusiness is likely to become a far more important sociological issue in the future. In order to maximize its profits it has sought to provide convenient food at cheapest cost, resulting in:

... a standardized product, of whatever taste, colour or nutritional value, under conditions of semi-automated technology, and then adding colouring, flavouring and nutritional elements provided by the relatively recent science of food technology.
(Newby, 1987, p. 196)

This has already led to 'food scares' regarding BSE,

listeria and food-irradiation, because such practices may have negative consequences. (See also Section 10.9.)

Criticisms of Newby's work are hard to find. We might accuse him of an English bias, but this is his clearly stated prerogative. He felt that the histories of the other UK members (and those of other nations beyond) were too difficult to assimilate into one book. This does, however, indicate areas for future research. Crow *et al.* (1990) suggest that in his earlier work Newby might have considered the wider, non-agricultural, forces shaping rural areas; although he has shown awareness of such forces in *Country Life*, the study lacks the global perspective others would like.

Feminist rural sociology

In recent times feminists (see Chapter 5) have begun to apply their theoretical concerns to rural areas. Wright (1992) put forward the work of Bouquet (1985) as a fine example of how feminists attempt to account for social change and conflict in rural areas, as opposed to the functionalist-based work of the 1950s and 1960s.

Bouquet suggests that we can identify three general periods of sex-role division within rural history. The first, in the early nineteenth century, was a period of relative equality between men and women, although Wright disagrees because men still did the heavier work. The second period, in the mid-nineteenth century, saw a separation of roles with men ploughing and women in the dairy. The third period, in the early twentieth century, saw men doing all the agricultural work, with women indoors catering for tourists, as well as doing voluntary work and fundraising in response to the under-provision of services by the state. Changes were associated with the introduction of new machinery.

Shortall (1994), adopting a less critical postmodernist stance, notes how (urban) feminists may assume a homogeneity in all women, and thus see urban and rurally based women alike having similar conflicts with men. Shortall suggests this may be a mistake. She shows how Canadian women farm-workers formed locally based networks, co-ordinated under a national structure, to campaign for female agricultural, rural and community issues. Each area had equal importance. Yet, despite their female orientation:

Hostility towards men is inconceivable in a system that depends on such a high degree of co-operation. Furthermore, farm women and their husbands are joined by marital ties and bonds of affection.
(Shortall, 1994, pp. 283–84)

This might put her at odds with Marxists and radical feminists! (See Sections 2.4 and 2.6.)

Activity

Do some research on the three 'food scares' mentioned above. What were the concerns expressed, and in particular how did they relate to agribusiness? Make a note of other 'food scares' if they arise and try to interpret them sociologically.

I, A

Discussion point

Use the evidence to develop two sides of a debate. A suggested theme is: 'This house believes that scientists have become too involved in the food production process'.

Conclusion

In conclusion, it can be said that *images* of rural areas often distort realities, so that potential conflicts can been missed. Only in more recent sociological discussion has the issue been put back on the agenda. You may feel that the subject over-emphasizes conflicts at the expense of consensus, but you will need to decide to what extent 'social solidarity' is apparent within rural areas, or subcultures within them.

Many writers claim a need for more research on this area. For example, Lowe and Bodiguel (1990) advocate the need for more work on gender, age and how the two intersect in the rural setting. A suggestion has also been made for the consideration of action and structure combined – 'an analysis of structurational processes' (Hoggart *et al.*, 1994, p. 264) (see also Section 2.9) – ranging from the actions of individual rural inhabitants to the effects of national, trans-national and global processes on rural life. Wright (1992) sees the need for more assessment of individual rural dwellers as active creators of their own meanings and 'symbolic boundaries', drawing on the work of Cohen (1986) to support her claim.

The last comment goes to Newby (1987), who identifies an important new development in 'high-tech', 'footloose' industries which are locating themselves as the new 'cottage industries' – allowing the countryside for the first time to compete with urban areas on the same footing. In all aspects of life other than land-use, he suggests that rural areas will become completely urbanized.

16.6 Theoretical perspectives on urban development

Savage and Warde (1993) suggest that there are a number of recurrent themes in urban sociology, many responding to developments in general sociological theory. They believe that:

. . . the city may be considered as a sociological laboratory for it is regularly used to address, to some degree empirically, particularly those matters concerned with the experience of modernity.
(Savage and Warde, 1993, p. 32)

They trace developments in urban sociology according to a typology which splits the discipline into theories explaining urban development by time (how cities have evolved through history) and by space (how cities expand and/or shrink with their role in the world economy). (See also Section 10.10.) This typology is illustrated in Figure 16.6.

The evolutionary or historical perspective

This might be seen as the classical modernist approach which uses grand theory to explain a universal dimension – in this case, that cities have

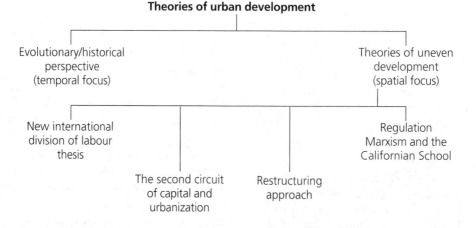

Figure 16.6 Theories of urban development. Source: Savage and Warde (1993)

evolved in a generalized pattern. The approach can be traced back to the Chicago School's ecological, quantitative wing. (See Section 16.1.) It used Darwinian concepts to explain urban change and development in terms of 'competition' and 'succession' for urban space by various social groups, which was illustrated by Burgess's 'concentric zone' model proposed in 1925 (refer to Figure 11.7 in Chapter 11). The city was seen to expand out from its central business district with land-use apparent in distinct rings. Key factors determining land-use were land prices and commuting costs. Expansion of the city was said to lead to sifting, sorting and relocation of social groups and areas.

Generally, the evolutionary approach sees the modern city as the most advanced type of settlement – traceable through historical progression – as it was best suited to meeting the needs of industrial production. However, earlier theories were unable to explain the industrial collapse and decline of many cities in the capitalist world from the 1930s. Savage and Warde (1993) argue that Hall (1980) is a good example of a recent evolutionary theorist – attempting to incorporate the development and stagnation of the industrial city, seeing early industrialization linked to population expansion by attracting migrants and de-urbanization as the population moves further away from the city, first to the suburbs and then to rural areas. Generally Savage and Warde were critical of the evolutionary approach because it failed to allow for diversity and uniqueness in urban developments. Cities exist in a world economy which could dramatically affect their development (see Sections 10.10 and 12.5) – an argument taken up by the 'theories of uneven development'. (See also Section 12.4.)

Theories of uneven development

Theories of uneven development emerged from the 1970s, many from the re-popularized Marxist tradition combining an interest in the capitalist economy with analysis of cities and urban trends.

The new international division of labour (NIDL) theory

One presentation of NIDL theory came from Fröbel *et al.* (1980). Their treatment was based on a core–periphery model. This suggested that important activities were based at the centre (or core), and as a result workers there demanded a high standard of living. (See also Sections 9.9 and 12.5.) At the periphery, those areas furthest from the core, were to be found economic activities that were less important because of their distance from key markets, and as a result people here had an uncertain and low standard of living. Fröbel and colleagues argued that

multi-national companies, aided by improvements in communications and transport, were able to re-route production to the peripheries in the search for profits. Peripheries offered low-cost labour, weaker trade unions, and less stringent planning and pollution controls, allowing corporations to maximize profits. Such arguments were used to explain de-urbanization in western cities and uneven urban development on a global basis, because some cities were better able than others to retain and attract multi-national companies and the employment they offered.

However, NIDL theory is not without its critics. Cohen (1987) suggests that the model is too economistic, and it does not account for reality as corporate units are not as geographically mobile as it would have us believe. Savage and Warde (1993) argue that the model does not take due account of state intervention or local resistance.

The second circuit of capital and urbanization

This perspective was based on the early work of Harvey (1973). It built on the weaknesses of NIDL theory by allowing incorporation of historical and geographical differences between cities.

The central idea was that cyclical increases and declines in profits in capitalist economies led to land and buildings being seen as a commodity. In times of over-production, when capital was potentially idle it was invested in land and buildings. The office block and property boom of the 1970s was seen as an example of this. However, buildings could also act as a barrier to investment when they were too old or lacked the flexibility to be used in alternative ways. Such a situation could lead to economic crises. Thus, the urban environment and the economy were seen to be closely related. Harvey's theory also noted how local resistance could prevent loss of investment and lead to the survival of the urban environment.

Savage and Warde (1993) argue that the theory lacked evidential support and had some theoretical weaknesses, particularly its inability to explain the difference between change and its causes. The theory was also accused of being too economically and class determined; other forces could play a part in urban development.

The restructuring approach

This approach was 'pioneered' by Massey in the late 1970s and early 80s (Savage and Warde, 1993). Massey concentrated on the particular strategies adopted by companies in the search of profit maximization, and how this affected spatial inequality. In order to react to changes in the economy, companies had to 'restructure' – closing some units, investing elsewhere, usually places with a more compliant, more easily exploited labour force. Such policies led in the UK to control functions of an industry being located in the South East where most professionals lived. Such a plentiful supply would help the companies to drive down labour costs. Production, on the other hand, was based in peripheral regions, where unskilled labour was plentiful. (See also Section 9.9.) This theory developed awareness of a new spatial division of labour, acknowledging that capital was more mobile than labour. It showed that social and cultural qualities of the labour force, as well as the economy, led to urban development and decline. It also allowed for reversals in fortune because the labour force could change its attitudes.

Savage and Warde, however, question whether localities have a homogeneous labour force, as well as to what extent firms consider the social system. They suggest that 'localities' are socially and culturally differentiated however they are defined. In any case, many people – especially professionals – commute from one locality to another.

Regulation Marxism and the Californian School

Regulation Marxism was concerned to explain the relationship between capital, labour and the state – particularly how the latter can regulate capital. The focus of attention for many theorists in this recent tradition has been the movement from Fordism, a society of mass production, consumption and regulation, to post-Fordism in the 1980s, where production and consumption are ever-changing – flexibility and instability have become essential. (See Sections 9.7, 10.8 and 10.9.)

Harvey's (1989) more recent work, which Savage and Warde see as typical of the Regulation School, explains that the post-Fordist era is based on newly innovated products and small batch production, which can be subcontracted in order to respond quickly to changing fashions. This has been supported by the development of new production technologies (which mean that a large skilled workforce is unnecessary) and communication technology (which improves information flow) (see Chapter 15). Post-Fordist society has also seen a significant growth of service industries to develop and satisfy people's desires for consumption.

This market re-orientation, according to Harvey, leads to urban design that is fragmenting and segregating. Information technology also ensures that:

Dispersed, decentralized and deconcentrated urban forms are now much more technologically feasible than they once were.
(Harvey, 1989, p. 76)

Savage and Warde argue that Harvey did not apply his framework in any detail to uneven development and urban change. This has been a challenge taken up by the Californian School, which has concentrated its studies on the Californian urban conglomerations of the American west coast, particularly Los Angeles. This region has seen a rise in fortunes with the development of new high-tech (post-Fordist) industries, while north-east USA (the 'Rust Belt'), based on Fordist mass production methods, has declined.

Activity

Use library resources to do some research on the histories of American 'Rust Belt' cities such as Detroit, Cleveland, Pittsburgh and Buffalo. In what ways were they linked to mass production? How have they declined since their peak, and for what reasons?

K, U, A

Savage and Warde also note how the earlier 'economies of scale', where similar industries grouped together to reduce costs, have been overtaken by 'economies of scope', where smaller firms of a variety of orientations group together to benefit from subcontracting and face-to-face interaction. They point to Scott (1988) as an example of a theorist of the Californian School. He suggested that economies of scope lead to socially homogeneous neighbourhoods of people who work in the new setting. Such a process is self-reinforcing – and, as Harvey (1989) has also argued, leads to social segregation because people who lacked the characteristics and skills of those in the neighbourhood, usually the working class and ethnic minorities, were excluded.

Discussion point

To what extent is the Californian School right to assert that we now live in a post-Fordist society? What would be the consequences of socially segregated neighbourhoods?

Savage and Warde (1993) argue that, because the Californian School is based on economic theory, it has not fully considered the consequences of this in terms of social conflict. For example, how will those excluded react to their exclusion from jobs, housing and opportunities? The perspective also fails to consider the role of the state; for example, how do its policies support or work against the new economies?

Callinicos (1989), writing from a Marxist perspective, argues that we have a long way to go before we see the end of work-based societies. Although 'dole' queues lengthened in the 1970s and 80s, Callinicos points out that the vast majority of working-aged people in western economies are still employed, mostly as wage earners. He argues that those in white-collar occupations in the service sector have had their pay and conditions reduced to such an extent that they are still wage labourers. (See also Section 4.6 and 9.7.) In California, according to Callinicos, *per capita* income fell from 123 per cent of the US average in 1960 to 113 per cent in 1984, with any benefits falling to entrepreneurs and the minority owning large property and financial assets. The state in the UK and the USA, according to Callinicos, has at best been complacent in the light of such trends.

A development of the Californian School approach can be seen in the post-modern thinking of Fishman (1995), who contrasts contemporary urbanity with the modernist metropolis. The latter was based on a single centre which was the 'hub' from which arterial 'spokes' of transport networks and infrastrutural development took place (as illustrated by the Chicago School's 'concentric zone' model). The new urbanism, based on mass car ownership and a *laissez-faire* attitude to planning, he suggested, had led to the development of 'technoburbs', urban development without dominant centres or explicit boundaries which spread along 'growth corridors':

Where the leading metropolises of the early twentieth century covered perhaps 100 square miles, the new city routinely encompasses two to three thousand square miles.
(Fishman, 1995, p. 398)

The Los Angeles region is seen as a prime example of the 'new city'. Fishman says it is 'not urban, not rural, not suburban, but possessing elements of all three' (p. 400). There is no clear distinction between areas of work, leisure or residence – all may be found in the same locality. Whereas the modernist city was defined by space, the geographical distance between separate regions with specific land-uses, he claimed that the post-modern city is defined according to time: the number of minutes (by car) from home (which is now the centre point or focus of post-modern people) to a chosen destination:

The pattern formed by these destinations represents the 'city' for that particular family or individual. The more varied one's destinations, the richer and more diverse is one's personal 'city'.
(Fishman, 1995, p. 409)

The 'de-urbanization' of the old metropolitan centres has been led by the exodus of manufacturing commerce and office work to new landscaped industrial parks (which links with the points made by Scott (1988) about 'economies of scope') – thus the concept 'technoburbs'. The middle classes and employed working classes have followed, to 'planned unit developments' located in random fashion around and within them, leaving the old (inner) city an area with cheap housing, attracting ethnic minorities, but one with no jobs to offer which results in their being 'doubly disadvantaged' (see Chapter 6). Although there are 'entry-level jobs' available in the 'new city', its new (angry) middle-class migrants have resisted attempts to build low-income housing, the net result being a lack of balanced community. This theme is discussed in Section 16.7.

The seemingly unplanned nature of land-use in the 'post-modern' city, in which a variety of activities takes place in close proximity, is often likened to a collage or 'kaleidoscope'. Jencks (1996), from a post-modernist perspective, suggests that a city can be likened to a 'slime mould' because it expands in good times and contracts (or coagulates) in bad times, which means it has a flickering quality like pulsating stars. Modernist theories, with their 'mechanistic' models, did not see this – which is why he felt they were inappropriate. The growth of 'megalopolises' (cities of over 10 million people) has been caused in part by, and led to, migration on a world level, bringing to them new peoples and new lifestyles. This may, as Fishman and others have said, lead to homogeneous enclaves, but Jencks feels that it can also cause heterogeneity in others (see Section 10.10). Thus a megalopolis can also be called a 'heteropolis'. Both Los Angeles and London are examples, although the latter is more diverse.

Focus on Los Angeles

Los Angeles has been a much-quoted and researched example of a city in post-modernity. Soja (1992a, b), identified by Savage and Warde as a member of the Californian School, notes how it has been a site of economic, social and spatial restructuring (i.e. change). Like Fishman, Soja notes how it has become a region based on high-tech manufacturing and service industries. He identifies the following causes.

- Working class resistance has been broken through selective redundancy and general unemployment.
- Capital and industries have become globally mobile, able to uproot or invest when and where it is most expedient. This uncertainty has led to a more passive workforce and allowed the introduction of new technology, thus giving corporations even more control. (See also Section 9.9, 10.10, 12.5 and 17.6.)
- Local and national subsidies attract and keep corporations and new industries.
- There has been inward migration of 'two million'

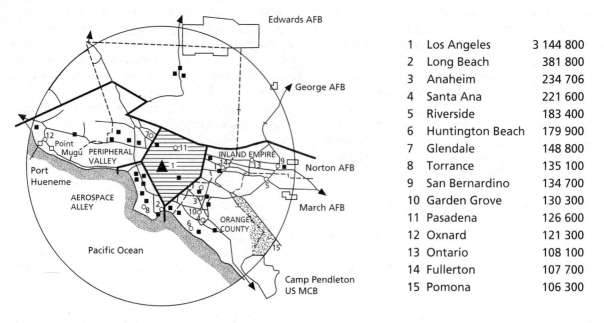

1	Los Angeles	3 144 800
2	Long Beach	381 800
3	Anaheim	234 706
4	Santa Ana	221 600
5	Riverside	183 400
6	Huntington Beach	179 900
7	Glendale	148 800
8	Torrance	135 100
9	San Bernardino	134 700
10	Garden Grove	130 300
11	Pasadena	126 600
12	Oxnard	121 300
13	Ontario	108 100
14	Fullerton	107 700
15	Pomona	106 300

Figure 16.7 A view of the outer spaces of Los Angeles. The urban core is outlined in the shape of a pentagon with the Central City denoted by the black triangle. The major military bases on the perimeter of the Sixty-Mile Circle are identified and the black squares are the sites of the largest defence contractors in the region. Also shown are county boundaries, the freeway system outside the central pentagon, and the location of all cities with more than 100 000 inhabitants (small open circles). Source: Soja (1992b)

people from 'third world' countries (see Sections 12.5 and 12.6). This, and the attracting of global capital, has made LA a 'world city'. Soja notes, as do Fishman, Harvey and Scott, that ethnic minorities have been segregated, both in terms of labour and residence.

Thus there is now a situation where:

The Sixty-Mile Circle [the Los Angeles region] *covers the thinly sprawling area of five counties, a population of more than twelve million individuals, at least 132 incorporated cities and, it is claimed, the greatest concentration of technocratic and militaristic imagination in the USA.*
(Soja, 1992b, p. 282)

The Sixty-Mile Circle is shown in Figure 16.7 above. The map shows how defence work is one of the keys to developing (and protecting) this environment, very much as a national government policy. Thus Soja adds to the post-modern account – which critics might suggest offers more description than it does cause – an analytical backbone by explaining developments in urban regions with reference to economic, political, military and social trends.

Focus on London

In identifying Los Angeles as a world city, Soja had taken up an important argument developed by, among others, King (1990). This idea suggests that urban growth needs to be seen in an international context of mobile capital and labour. (See also Section 9.9 and 10.10.) These were themes developed in some of the earlier theories of uneven urban/economic development.

King argues that a world city needs to be seen as a co-ordinating centre for global financial and trading activities. As a result we find that it is home to world banks and the headquarters to global corporations. This encourages the growth of a highly paid élite and the immigration of cheap labour from the developing world, both groups working at polar ends of the newly expanding service sector. In order for the global or world city to develop an historical tradition, international trade is required – and government policies that provide stability and encourage inward investment (although the state cannot control such investment or the policies of global corporations).

King sees London as a good example of a world city, given its role as a globally orientated financial centre. Its historical focus has generally been outward, rather than inward, orientated towards international trade from the seventeenth century. Today it is a site of massive global investment, resulting in expansion of the square mile of the City and the redevelopment of Docklands. This situation is allowed with little regard for local people who are expected to adapt in order for the changes to take place. However, the future is unclear:

London is far more dependent on the world economy than many other cities in the world ... and hence is consequently more vulnerable to changes in it. There is no guarantee that particular countries or cities will, in the long historical term, remain either at the core or the periphery. And a major collapse in the world economy will hit harder those cities whose fortunes are tightly tied to it than others which are not, as has recently been seen.
(King, 1990, p. 154)

Thus world city orientation offers the possibility of collapse and stagnation, but without it urban areas lack the financial resources to adapt and redevelop – a case of 'tails I win, heads you lose'.

Discussion point

Are Los Angeles and London unusual, or are they setting a trend which other cities will follow?

16.7 **Life in urbanity**

Recent times have seen increasing dissatisfaction with urban living, particularly in the more central areas of urban regions, and a related movement of populations to suburban and rural areas. These trends are shown in Figure 16.8.

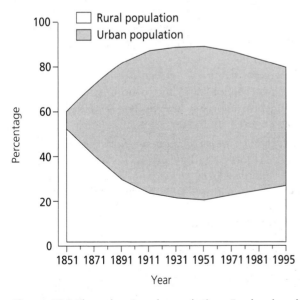

Figure 16.8 The urban/rural population, England and Wales, 1851–1995. Sources: Browne (1992)/ *Social Trends* (1997)

Activity

Write a paragraph to describe the trends shown in Figure 16.8.

Although a smaller *proportion* of people now live in urban England and Wales than in the 1950s, it is evident that the vast majority of the population still live in towns and cities. Sociologists want to know how they experience this, how urban living affects their quality of life.

Sherlock (1991) believes that cities offer major advantages: shops, friends, pubs, restaurants, theatres and cinemas are all close at hand. However, he also asserts that housing and transport policies since the Second World War have reduced the quality of 'street community', a major requirement of humankind as social animals. For Sherlock:

... all cities could be made attractive to all their citizens, and more people could be drawn to them – if strategic planning were restored, population densities maintained, public transport preferred to private cars and urban street housing re-established and improved upon.
(Sherlock, 1991, p. 20)

Discussion point

In your view, what is it about urban living that can be seen as positive and what can be seen as negative? Is it the same for all city dwellers? How do your ideas compare with those of Sherlock (1991)?

The remainder of this section deals with three subject areas that reflect sociologists' concerns about quality of life in urbanity:

* the inner city
* urban riots and urban social movements
* housing issues.

The inner city

Some common themes are evident in the various theories of the development of the 'world city', 'postmodern city' or 'post-industrial city'. In particular they have all noted how migrants from developing countries (see Section 6.2) have been attracted to the urban regions of richer countries to perform unskilled jobs in the newer service and high-tech industries (see Section 9.3). As subcontracted (or officially 'self-employed') workers on short-term and/or part-time contracts, they have been used flexibly by companies in order to maximize profits. Long periods of unemployment are likely. Many theorists see these migrants being separated, geographically and socially, from other communities; although Jencks (1996) suggests this is not exclusively so.

Contemporary sociologists have been keen to study this situation, theoretically and empirically, particularly in terms of quality of life (deprivation, policy initiatives to alleviate the problems and the consequences of both) and the potential consequences for society as a whole. (See also Sections 14.2 and 14.6.)

A classic study from the 1980s is that on Hackney by the critical journalist Harrison (1985). This provides an illustration of Jencks' point that areas flicker like 'pulsating stars'. In the past Hackney was a successful area, but in recent times its traditional manufacturing base has largely been lost, owing to cheaper and more technologically advanced bases in the UK and abroad, resulting in a life of unemployment and surviving on 'the dole' for people in the area. The people Harrison interviewed reported a lack of control over their own lives because decisions that affected the area were made beyond it – they had little chance of altering them. They also felt frustrated at being deprived of basic 'life chances' such as decent homes, environment and schools. A major consequence, as people lost hope, was a falling population as people who could move sought a better life elsewhere.

This section now looks at a number of more recent case studies which develop these themes, in an attempt to explain them in terms of the global restructuring of capital and industry that Harrison had pointed to.

Case study – Chicago

Wacquant's study of Chicago in 1989 aimed to explain what he saw as 'hyperghettoization': the 'undeveloping' of an inner area in a short space of time, owing to a complex of factors:

The plight of the ghetto is the outcome of a complex interaction of economic, social and political factors and no monocausal theory will ever satisfactorily account for it.
(Wacquant, 1995, p. 419)

The economic reasons for 'hyperghettoization' were, according to Wacquant, based around the restructuring of the capitalist economy that we considered in the previous section. Sectorally, the economy moved from the old industries, destroying the jobs previously taken up by inner-city dwellers. Occupational changes meant that what jobs they could get were poorly paid or short-term. Spatial changes in the economy meant that jobs had moved away from the city to the suburbs and regions beyond. However, these were not neutral processes, but based on:

. . . the new 'hegemonic–despotic' phase of American capitalist development – one which pacifies workforces by uprooting itself or threatening to do so, leaving workers the choice of a poor job or no job.
(Wacquant, 1995, p. 419)

Socially, Wacquant identifies institutional and individual racism as a cause of the 'hyperghettoization'. White employers (in both an organizational and an individual sense) tended to see black inner-city inhabitants as lazy, poorly qualified and unable to assume a 'work-first' mentality. This led them to overlook black applicants, or to locate away from the black inhabitants of the inner city. This further segregated the 'wealthy' whites and the 'poor' blacks (see Chapter 6).

Politically based interference was seen as the third cause of 'hyperghettoization'. Road-building policies helped the de-industrialization process and the flight to the outer regions. They also acted as buffers to prevent spatial expansion of the ghetto. The outward flight of industry, and the wealthy, was helped by government subsidies for factory and home building in the outer regions. Slum clearance programmes making way for new centrally based commerce resulted in displaced residents being forced into the remaining ghetto, making for a more concentrated, homogeneous form. Welfare policy became penal policy:

[the] *War of Poverty of the 1960s* [became] *the . . . War on the Poor of the 1980s.*
(Wacquant, 1995, p. 438)

The poor were blamed for the making of the ghetto through the 'New Right's' underclass agenda (see Sections 4.8 and 6.5) which claimed that the lifestyle of the inner-city poor, who were too lazy to work and who couldn't be bothered to help themselves, had brought the problems on their own localities. This allocation of blame allowed reductions in welfare programmes – which were accused of creating a dependent culture – and led to the development of policies criminalizing the poor, resulting in them being put in prison (see Section 11.10). Wacquant was angered by the direction in policy:

Since ghetto poverty is the product of economic and political forces and struggles, not the result of the aggregation of free individual choices or moral failures, remedies to it must likewise be economic and political.
(Wacquant, 1995, p. 435)

Case study – Atlanta

Rutheiser's (1996) study is concerned with policy initiatives in Atlanta as it prepared to host the 1996 Olympic Games. Corporate and public leaders marketed Atlanta as engendering a spirit of friendliness and co-operation between races, whereas, claimed Rutheiser:

Atlanta is, in fact, one of the poorest and most violent cities in the USA and the Olympics will do little to change that.
(Rutheiser, 1996a, p. 28)

He claims that the policy of the organizing committee – a mixture of white corporate power and black public leaders – was to create the veneer of a 'world city' and to hide the reality of its poverty. As Wacquant (1995) similarly observed in Chicago, the black poor of Atlanta had been increasingly directed and segregated into homogenized ghettos, and the downtown (i.e. centre) of the city had become increasingly a place of residence for black people as whites moved to the economically developing suburbs and regions.

The marketing strategy of the Olympic organizing committee could be seen in two allied policies.

* In an attempt to make downtown safer and more 'user-friendly' for the white middle classes, new high-cost housing development took place, excluding the black working classes.
* In preparing for the Centennial Theme Park (where the bomb exploded during the Olympics), housing and hostels for the poor and homeless were cleared and there did not appear to be plans to replace them. The city council was forced to go along with the idea because they lacked the amenities offered by the park and lacked the finance to provide an alternative. The park was proposed as a public space, but policy on access ensured that the poor or 'riff-raff' could be excluded.

Rutheiser expected that, some time after the Olympics, the park would be redeveloped for new commercial use. He saw this kind of urban revitalization as 'Jim Crow in twentieth century drag', where an appealing stage was set for international investors, and the 'ugly poor' were swept under the carpet. (So-called 'Jim Crow Laws' had been used to segregate black and white Americans – see Chapter 6.) Thus he argued that:

Bloated by a patronage-heavy bureaucracy and forced to compete with other centres for much needed investment, the City of Atlanta has been reduced to at best a junior partner in what is now more accurately described as a private–public partnership that is largely free of public oversight and accountability. . . . If private entities truly wish to act in the public interest – a development that by all means should be encouraged – there is no reason why they should not be held accountable to those they claim to serve.
(Rutheiser, 1996b, p. 288)

Case study – Los Angeles

Davis (1995) has been similarly critical of public–private policy, particularly its 'militaristic' qualities, which has been used to segregate blacks and whites into separate areas. In 1990 the city under his gaze was Los Angeles – where, he argued, public spaces used for meeting other people, interaction and developing a sense of others had been destroyed. Architectural design had developed a 'security offensive' using military fortress design to build high-class, gated, security-patrolled, camera-surveilled village enclaves in the downtown area. Commercial developments had also been designed as 'hyper-structures' with enclosed walkways and privatized 'public' space:

The new Downtown is designed to ensure a seamless continuum of middle-class work, consumption, and recreation, insulated from the city's 'unsavoury streets'. Ramparts and battlements, reflective glass and elevated pedways, are tropes in an architectural language warning off the underclass other. . . . In stark contrast, a few blocks away, the city is engaged in a relentless struggle to make the streets as unliveable as possible for the homeless and the poor . . . with its own version of low-intensity warfare.
(Davis, 1995, p. 362)

Such warfare has taken the form of a containment policy, keeping the poor black population segregated in its own area – this is effectively Wacquant's 'hyper-ghettoization'. Individual policies include the development of 'bum-proof benches' for parks, buses and other public locations to stop the homeless sleeping on them. Outdoor sprinklers with intermittent flows have been designed with a similar purpose in parks and shop doorways. Numbers of public toilets have been reduced in order to reduce the amount of time the poor spend in the wealthy downtown area – it is assumed that the middle classes will use conveniences in restaurants, museums and the like, places

Activity

Wacquant, Rutheiser and Davis individually offer extremely critical accounts of developments in inner cities in the USA.

a   Write a paragraph that summarizes their arguments, concentrating on the *similarities* between the three accounts.

b   Do the policies for revitalization of the central city need to be seen negatively? Try to think of positive reasons that public and private developers might give for their policies. Do they cancel out the criticisms?

c   To what extent do cities in the UK follow similar patterns to those in the USA? Apply examples that you know about.

U, I, A, E

'closed' to the poor. Allied to this he pointed to a war on the informal economy, essentially illegal activities, but the only way the unemployed poor can earn themselves an income:

By criminalizing every attempt by the poor – whether the Skid Row homeless or MacArthur Park vendors – to use public space for survival purposes, law-enforcement agencies have abolished the last informal safety-net separating misery and catastrophe.
(Davis, 1990, p. 366)

Inner-city policy for Davis is, therefore, not only about segregating social groups into homogeneous areas, but also persecuting the poor for being poor.

Case study – Docklands

The issues in the activity on page 675 are taken up by Deakin and Edwards (1993). Although they take a much more social democratic perspective with regard to regeneration of the inner cities, they come up with the similar conclusion that reliance on mobile capital and the private sector is unlikely to provide long-term benefits for those that most need them. Investment will be determined by economic cycles such that recession produces decline, and because investment is geared to profit those investing have little or no obligation to the local community.

Deakin and Edwards note how inner-city policy promoted by continuous Conservative administration of the 1980s and 90s was based on the concept of the 'enterprise culture' and links with the private sector (see Chapter 17). Urban local authorities were seen by ministers as slow, bureaucratic and too mixed up in left-wing ideological commitments, whereas the private sector offered drive, energy and the ability to create jobs. The private sector was the epitome of the 'enterprise culture'. 'Enterprise' incorporated self-interest, confidence, responsibility and a work ethic (compare this with the New Right account of the inner-city 'underclass' – see Section 4.8), all aspects thought to be lacking in the inner city. Allied to revitalization projects it would minimize public costs and be able to do what millions of pounds of public money had been unable to do – bring jobs, create a new culture and end the cycle of deprivation:

. . . there emerged the new orthodoxy that the root cause of the problems of the inner cities was the collapse of their economic infrastructures brought about by the emigration of firms to out-of-town sites or their death in situ, *compounded by the socially selective emigration of their populations. . . . What needed to be done was now clear: new industry, new jobs and an economically active population had to*

be attracted back to the inner areas in order to regenerate their economic infrastructures.
(Deakin and Edwards, 1993, p. 3)

Their evaluation of such a policy is based on three case studies: Trafford Park in Manchester; Heartlands in Birmingham; and Docklands in London. We will consider the last case, often seen as the 'flagship' of the Conservatives' urban regeneration policies.

Deakin and Edwards note how interpretation of the Docklands success in regenerating an area of London's dilapidated East End has caused conflict within the ranks of sociologists. 'New Right' sociologist Marsland (see Section 2.10) was quoted as saying that it was 'the most exciting, positive and potentially profitable (in every sense of that maligned word) development in Europe' (p. 96). Deakin and Edwards conclude that the answer was somewhat more complicated, with benefits and costs requiring consideration.

Positively, the Docklands project had brought physical regeneration of the infrastructure, new industry and commerce and new jobs, particularly benefiting women. However, many of the new jobs are not 'new' but due to relocation (bringing in 'old' staff), and when they are new they go to 'outsiders'. The local population do not have the skills required, are not given training and thus unemployment remains high. Formation of the nationally (rather than locally) accountable London Docklands Development Corporation (LDDC) took planning out of local government control, ensuring that local people are not 'stakeholders'. Deakin and Edwards wonder whether local authorities, with the finance that the LDDC had, might have done a better job. Their feeling is that the question could not be answered, but partnership – allied to a legal commitment from the private sector to live up to its promises – might offer the best way forward. Such an option, however, was not possible in a capitalist world and so all the public sector could do was offer financial subsidies and incentives. The benefits of recent policy, in reality, have been marginal. The assumption had been that new jobs would have a 'trickle-down effect' (see Section 2.10) on other aspects of social deprivation, but there have been few 'new' jobs:

Docklands has neither demonstrated the unquestionable superiority of market-led regeneration and led to the 'death of planning', nor demonstrated the hollowness of claims for the enterprise culture.
(Deakin and Edwards, 1993, p. 249).

Deakin and Edwards argue that:

. . . with market-led changes still in full flow and the size and composition of the population altering in response, the risk that the existing population would be squeezed out or at best marginalized was

clearly still strong.
(Deakin and Edwards, 1993, p. 112)

Yet they go on to say that:

In the Isle of Dogs, the two communities – the existing East-Enders and the incomers – will have to learn to live with one another.
(Deakin and Edwards, 1993, p. 122)

One wonders how far this is easier for Deakin and Edwards to write than it is for the communities to do – at least in any positive and meaningful sense – especially when one takes the following critical perspective into account.

Crow and Allan (1994) quote Marris who said (in 1987) that the original residents:

. . . saw themselves threatened by office developers, by an invasion of homeless families herded into huge impersonal Greater London Council estates; by the conversion of the riverside into fashionable, luxury hotels and apartments; and by main roads slashing through what was left of their disintegrating, blighted and economically marginal communities.
(Marris, 1987; quoted in Crow and Allan, 1994, p. 149)

Concluding comments

It does seem, as was once said, 'the poor are always with us', and living in an increasingly marginalized fashion in the inner cities. (See also Section 14.6.)

Activity

a Consider writing to the London Docklands Development Corporation at Thames Quay, 191 Marsh Wall, London E14 9TJ (or, if you get the chance, go to the Visitors' Centre at 3 Limeharbour, London) to find out more about the task it was set and how it was carried out. Following up some of the sociological references will allow you to develop a rounded picture of the Docklands development.

b Explain briefly how changes in capitalism and public policy have affected the inner city. To what extent can they be seen as a success or a failure?

c If the policies to change the inner city have not, in your view, been totally successful, how could they be improved?

I, A, E

This part of 'Life in urbanity' has identified some of the major structural and micro factors contributing to the phenomenon. Successive administrations in the UK, USA and elsewhere have claimed to seek solutions to the deprivation, poverty and sense of despair associated with life in the inner areas of urban regions, but sociologists (in particular) need to identify the sincerity and success of such attempts.

There appear to be numerous perspectives in answer to this. However, it is also obvious that we need to consider how the inhabitants of the inner city have responded to their isolation. Cooke (1988) claimed that:

It might be argued that such behaviour (i.e. the policies of corporations and public administration) will provoke rebellion but post-modern Britain looks no more collectively rebellious a society than the USA. The urban masses of both countries have been stupefied by the invasion of their relatively secure world of employment by Thatcherism, Reaganomics and world industrial recession, they are the subjects of more proficient surveillance than ever before and are policed in Britain, as in the USA, by increasingly abrasive methods of social control.
(Cooke, 1988, p. 489)

However, others might see inner cities as time-bombs waiting to explode. The next part of this section considers whether the inhabitants have been 'stupefied' or whether they have resisted their isolation.

Urban riots and urban social movements

We have noted that Cooke, a post-modernist, suggests that it is now likely that we will no longer see collective rebellion in urban society because the 'masses' have been 'stupefied', or ground into submission. We now consider whether such submission has been gained by the ruling élite of urban society, and if a rebellion is likely from the working classes.

M. Castells, a Marxist, began a debate in the 1970s to suggest that political resistance was likely to come from urban social movements, being groups based on consumption rather than production. This is the issue we take up here.

Urban riots became a major topic of debate in the 1980s, taking place in many of the UK's towns and cities during that decade (and since). However, these British riots were not without precedent. Field (1982) notes that instances such as collective attacks on the police, arson, widespread looting and the contagion of riots from town to town had all occurred previously during this century. We might also note that urban riots are not unique to the UK; the USA has also suffered similar disorders throughout this century, a recent prominent example being the riots in Los Angeles in 1992.

Communal and commodity riots

Janowitz (1979), looking specifically at the USA, offers a useful distinction between 'communal riots' and 'commodity riots' to account for changing patterns of collective racial violence. Communal riots were the 'typical' 'race' riots during and immediately after the First World War. They were the result of a clash between blacks and whites over rights of settlement in particular areas, with whites leading violent attacks on what they feared were expanding boundaries of black communities. British riots of 1959 which occurred in Nottingham and Notting Hill (London) could be seen as examples of communal riots. (See also Chapter 6.) According to Janowitz, commodity riots – which were large-scale outbursts within the community of black people, became more prevalent after the Second World War. He believes they represented a form of collective behaviour against the 'agents and symbols' of the wider society. They were described as commodity riots because they were associated with outbursts of looting and, he suggests, had their high point in the period between 1964 and 1967 (for example in the Watts area of Los Angeles in 1965).

Commodity riots lacked any conspiratorial quality. They were likely to be set off by an actual or perceived malpractice by the police. This led to stoning of the police, the development of a crowd and mounting tensions. The second phase of the riot would involve breaking of windows, a breakdown of local social control and perception of the temporary opportunity for looting. A final phase developed if the crowd was not dispersed and involved arson attacks and possible sniper fire and a military type response by a combined force of the police and army. Initially participants were likely to be over-represented by single, young, unemployed men who formed part of the informal street community. The looters who joined the riots after they were under way were more likely to be part of the 'respectable' adult world.

Such actions could be explained by the failure of the black civil rights movement to produce social change for the populations they represented through legal/'democratic' political channels. As such they were outbursts against the perceived 'double standards' for the black and white people, the latter being seen as politically, economically and socially advantaged.

We will see that many of the riots that have taken place in the UK and the USA since this classic 'ideal type' description have followed the anticipated pattern almost directly. Yet Janowitz lacked the ability to see this application in the future as he saw blacks 'acting' rather than 'reacting'. Since the 1960s, he believes, collective violence has been characterized by 'political racial violence', terroristic style violence by small groups of organized blacks against whites. Certainly this has not come to popular public consciousness, although ethnic minorities in the USA and UK did form vigilante defence groups to protect their communities, at various times.

Riots in the UK

British riots which took place in the late 1970s and early 80s – beginning with the St Paul's district of Bristol, studied by Pryce (1986) (see also Section 16.3) – bore a number of similarities with the US commodity riots. They virtually all started in the same way, with the spark being actual or perceived aggressive behaviour by the police. In each case the primary grievances were seen to be aggressive police practices, unemployment, poor housing conditions and the discrimination felt by the minority communities. One exception to this was in Southall in 1981, where the Asian community reacted to violence and 'violation of their community' by National Front activists – thus this was more of a 'communal riot'. The Asian community in Southall is discussed in more detail in Section 10.6.

A major government enquiry led by Lord Scarman (1982) explained that young inner-city inhabitants were being raised in insecure social and economic conditions, in an impoverished environment. They shared the same desires and expectations as the society at large, but faced discrimination which caused frustration when their expectations were not met. The report called for an effective and co-ordinated approach to tackling inner-city problems: consultation of local communities, by both private and public bodies. The needs of ethnic minorities with regard to housing, education and employment needed to be more readily recognized. However, as argued by many of the contributors to Benyon's (1984) *Scarman and After*, the two years following the report saw little evidence of a response. Disadvantage and discrimination were likely to continue, was the message, unless the problems of the inner city and ethnic minorities in particular were solved. (See also Chapter 6.)

Discussion point

Bearing in mind what the UK government has done to revitalize inner-city areas (discussed in the previous section), can we argue that it has finally responded to the Scarman Report and that urban riots are likely to be a thing of the past?

Riots in largely ethnic-minority areas such as Brixton (in 1995) and Bradford (also in 1995), as well as on council estates that have predominantly white residents like Blackbird Leys in Oxford (in 1991) and Meadow Well in Newcastle (also in 1991), suggest that violent urban protest is likely to continue, particularly if we accept the opinion of many critical commentators that their underlying structural causes have not been remedied.

The Los Angeles riot of 1992

A similar situation was evident in the USA following the trial of a group of LA policemen who were accused – and then acquitted – of unlawfully beating Rodney King, a black motorist. The beating had been captured fully on video and shown on television. The not-guilty verdict was felt to be unacceptable, not least to blacks in Los Angeles who rioted for five days before being quelled by 6000 National Guards and 1000 federal police:

Over the next few days, disturbances broke out across America as people from every background protested against the injustice of the Rodney King verdict.
(Jackson, 1992, p. 13)

Jackson reports the underlying causes as the growing polarization between wealthy whites and poor blacks, the social marginalization of the poorest blacks in inner-city ghettos, reductions in government spending on urban redevelopment, and a younger generation of black people who are not as willing to compromise as their parents had been.

Activity

Re-read the quotation from P. Cooke on page 677, beginning 'It might be argued that such behaviour . . .' Was he right then? Could he be right in the future?

I, A, E

Urban riots and urban social movements

The suggestion so far seems to be that urban riots are not infrequent forms of political protest. We now need to consider how we define those who riot and whether rioting is the only form of urban political protest. (See also Chapter 17.) In general, it would appear that urban rioters are a homogeneous, yet disorganized, group of people who feel segregated and disenfranchised. Rioting appears to be the only way they have to voice their concerns and resentment. Pure Marxists might see them as part of the working-class mass; pure Weberians might note the combination of their class and ethnic status. (See also Chapter 4.)

Such issues have come to light in the debate about 'urban social movements', a concept developed by the Marxist, M. Castells. He saw them as:

. . . organizations standing outside the formal party systems which bring people together to defend or challenge the provision of urban public services and to protect the local environment.
(Castells, 1983; quoted in Lowe, 1988, p. 456)

Although rioters are reported to be disorganized, their aim is similar so we might be able to apply some of the principles from the debate.

Castells' earlier writing was very much influenced by what he had seen in France, especially the riots and protests in Paris in 1968. Groups such as the squatter movement were geared towards stopping the massive urban renewal programmes. This led Castells to believe the protest movement was not in itself a strictly working-class movement (students had been heavily involved) based around factory production, as might have been expected by pure Marxists; but rather a movement of consumers of urban public services. Initially he saw these movements as of secondary importance to class-based ones, but after visiting the USA and noting a wide variety of social movements, he moved to the position that they arose independently of class and act as autonomous organizations 'against the logic, interest and values of the dominant class'. The importance of class-based protest had declined with the globalization of production which had reduced people's abilities to control their own lives. As Kirby (1995) notes:

. . . people try to control their lives by controlling their locality. The urban social movements are thus a defensive reaction to structural change in the world which has made the old forms of movement obsolete.
(Kirby, 1995, p. 76)

However, Castells' theory of urban social movements has been criticized on at least two counts. First, he sees their role as radical, trying to redress disadvantages in service provision, whereas many urban pressure groups now seek to protect their advantages. For example, middle-class 'nimby's' ('not-in-my-back-yard') may form groups to protect their residential areas from redevelopment for roads, new housing and the like (Urry, 1990a). Secondly, many recent urban protests have been about environmental issues rather than collective consumption of state services, which the theory of urban social movements cannnot account for (Bagguley, 1993). (See Chapter 17 for more detail on the environmental movement.)

Thus the debate about 'urban social movements' has developed into a wider contemporary debate about 'new social movements'. A particularly relevant idea for us regarding new social movements comes from Beck (1992), who suggests that class inequality has been supplemented by 'risks' to which everyone, no matter what social class, is susceptible. For example, environmental hazards and pollution are 'risks' to which all people are subject, although others might argue that inner urban residents (who tend to be poorer) are more at risk than middle-class ruralites. Certainly urban environmental protest groups have become more common. Groups such as 'Reclaim the Streets' have taken to direct action like blocking streets to make their point to car-drivers and policy-makers. Bellos (1996), a journalist, noted how single-issue direct-action protest groups were beginning a process of 'cross-fertilization' (working together), and quoted P. Deluce of Corporate Watch (an organization aiming to help others campaigning against large corporations) who said:

Pick any issue and there is a multitude of issues. Newbury . . . [scene of a protest over the building of a bypass] . . . is not just about the environment. It is also about transport, housing and biodiversity. We are interested in jobs and local communities needs. Calling them single issues is only trying to marginalize them.
(Bellos, 1996)

Bagguley (1993), in a useful attempt to clarify the debate, offers some direct contrasts between 'old' (or 'urban') and 'new' social movements, suggesting that they might be seen on a continuum between two pure types. The former are based around economic issues, with their values stemming from their relationship to the means of production. They generally have a working-class base and are represented by officials in bureacratic organizations who work towards discussion and compromise. New social movements differ in that they are concerned with issues beyond the workplace, such as the environment or human rights, based on the importance of each individual and their cultural identity. They are more likely to have a middle-class base, be organized around localized networks, and have no particular spokesperson or leader. They are likely to work towards an ultimate end with no compromise.

Concluding comments

How urban rioters are classified obviously depends on how we assess their aims and whether we think they have acted as an organized mass. It is clear that they have tended to be socially disadvantaged, working class and/or from an ethnic minority, and they have been somewhat aggrieved by a lack of service provision, which might allow us to label them 'old' or 'urban

Discussion point

a To what extent can the concept of an 'urban social movement' be applied to the recent urban rioters in the UK and the USA?

b To what extent have 'new social movements' been effective, particularly on environmental issues?

c Are there political issues in your local area that have inspired widespread opposition? Have the various viewpoints inspired urban or new social movements? How successful have they been? How can you account for that?

social movements'. However, they do not appear to have any bureaucratic organization, leadership, or in the short term be ready to compromise (they tend to be 'controlled' into submission), which might make them a 'new social movement'. They do tend to have qualities of both new and old movements, but given their spontaneous uprising and their almost as sudden disappearence it would be worth questioning whether rioters represent a 'movement' in any real sense.

What is certain is that urban living does create the conditions for a variety of communal groupings or movements. How these develop in the future will continue to be the stimulus for further sociological speculation and research.

The sociology of housing

Quality of life in urbanity is very much related to the increasingly scarce resource of housing. Sociologists interested in this area have been keen to explain how individuals and households come to live where they do, *and* why they don't live elsewhere. This part of the section on 'Life in urbanity' aims to identify the key themes and supporting evidence.

Definitions of housing type

Sociologists of housing in the UK have identified three key types of tenure:

* *owner-occupied housing* – homes for people who have bought their property or those with mortgages who are not yet outright owners
* *public rented housing* – homes rented from local authorities
* *private rented housing* – homes rented from private landlords.

There are distinct changes within and, more importantly, between types of tenure which are seen to indicate varying levels of inequality. The proportions of tenure have also been changing, as Figure 16.9 shows.

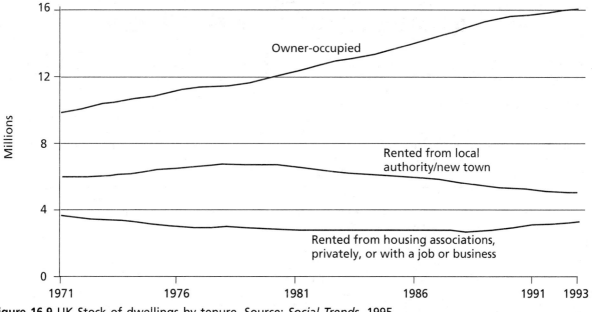

Figure 16.9 UK Stock of dwellings by tenure. Source: *Social Trends*, 1995

Activity

Figure 16.9 shows the changes in these three types of tenure from 1971 to 1993. Describe the trends in the graph and use your knowledge of recent social and political developments to account for them.

I, A

Housing and social policy

It is clear that levels of owner-occupation have increased significantly. (See also Section 10.9.) Generally such housing has higher status, so we might assume that the increase in stock represents a rise in living standards, particularly when we also note that the number of houses rented from local authorities has declined. Morris and Winn (1990) warn against making such an assumption, noting that the quality of owner-occupied housing has increasing variation. Instead, they say, government policy – particularly since 1979 – can account for a large part of the change. Policies of Conservative administrations from 1979 were aimed at reducing state involvement in people's lives by developing a wider and more significant consumer market, allowing for more choice, and making individual citizens more responsible for their own destinies. This applied to housing as much as to any other policy area. Such policies, based on political commitments rather than what Morris and Winn identified as the 'realities' of housing needs and availability, had 'led to housing inequality becoming an ever more evident part of the housing system' (p. 14).

Policy was deliberately aimed at increasing the levels of owner-occupation and private renting while reducing the amount of publicly owned housing provided by the 'nanny state'. The 'right-to-buy' policy allowed council tenants to buy their homes at a price lower than the market value. It was thought that as private owners they would take much more care of their properties and neighbourhoods, making them more responsible citizens while at the same time reducing long-term costs to the taxpayer. In reality, according to Morris and Winn, it meant that the best homes in the 'best' neighbourhoods were sold to tenants, leaving local authorities with a stock increasingly located in inner cities and the least popular areas. Councils were left principally with flats and poorly built, experimental homes from the 1960s and 70s which were costly to maintain. They concluded that:

. . . the right to buy has undoubtedly increased the incidence of housing disadvantages within the public sector and in particular has contributed to the closer correlation between council housing and low income. (Morris and Winn, 1990, p. 23)

Local authority homes were also sold 'en bloc' to private (i.e. corporate) or housing association ownership, making them 'privately rented' homes. Winn and Morris believe that this led to short-term benefits such as refurbishment (e.g. newly double-

Discussion point

If you were a council tenant in one of the areas mentioned in the article 'Inner-city estates to be privatized', would you vote to move your home into the control of new private ownership? What factors would influence your decision?

Inner-city estates to be privatized

JAMES MEIKLE
COMMUNITY AFFAIRS EDITOR

THOUSANDS of run-down homes on inner-city housing estates are to be transferred to private landlords in return for multi-million pound revamps.

The government has insisted £174 million in grants for demolition, new buildings, repairs and renovation on 29 estates will only be provided if tenants vote to move their homes out of local authority control to housing associations or new housing companies which can raise money on the financial markets.

The first stages of the regeneration strategy announced yesterday by housing minister David Curry will help break the municipal housing monopoly in some of Labour's council heartlands – including Hackney, east London, Sheffield, Durham and Sandwell, West Midlands. Other authorities – Tower Hamlets, Lambeth, Newham, and Merton (all in London) Stoke and Thameside, Greater Manchester – have also decided to give up some of their run-down estates so they can be modernised.

The schemes are expected to raise another £250 million by commercial borrowing, and those in Sandwell and Tower Hamlets will involve the first housing companies – whose boards will comprise one third tenants, one third council nominees and one third independent business people and community representatives.

The schemes were announced a year after John Major attacked the "sullen concrete wastelands" and "dreadful old eyesores" of run-down council housing, and made clear the public sector could not foot the whole bill for putting things right.

Critics argue the measures, covering 19,000 homes, hardly dent the estimated £20 billion renovation backlog. However, the Chartered Institute of Housing, representing professionals in the sector, believe such schemes could eventually double the present £2 billion annual public funding on such work by using the private sector.

Councils lost the power to build homes some years ago, but still control four-fifths of the 5 million homes in the social housing sector. Many authorities, especially ones under Labour control, have been reluctant to transfer estates to housing associations – prompting the latest scheme, for which at least another £130 million is promised over the next two years.

Mr Curry told the institute's conference in Harrogate: "The truth is the old world municipal monopoly is not going to come back. No government is going to let it rip again. But there are some places we could not give away if we tried, but I don't believe people in them should be left behind and offered no hope."

He did not believe rents would rise significantly.

John Perry, the institute's director of policy, welcomed the scheme, saying: "If it gets off the ground ... it could signal a new future for social housing."

The biggest transfers are likely to involve 7,000 homes on eight estates in Sandwell. Their transfer to three housing companies, qualifying for £40 million in grant – 10 times the council's present modernization budget – is expected to be bolstered by another £100 million in private borrowing. Ged Lucas, the borough's housing director, said: "This means we have the opportunity to make real inroads into the huge backlog of disrepair."

Source: The Guardian, 15 June 1996

---

glazed windows) but led to longer-term inequality as rents increased, displacing the poorest tenants who could not afford them. The article 'Inner-city estates to be privatised' describes a recent example of this policy.

Another related policy was deregulation of the private rented sector. Previously private landlords had been subject to a variety of controls to prevent them exploiting their tenants, who in turn had various rights which they could use to make their homes safer from interference. The 'New Right' (see Section 2.10) saw such regulation as 'anti-landlord', 'anti-market', with the result that people were put off renting their properties to those who could make use of them. The aim of deregulation was to increase the number of homes available to those who wanted the flexibility of renting their homes rather than being tied to one local authority or a mortgage. Morris and Winn suggest that this policy led to an increase in high-rent accommodation, favouring middle-class owners who let their properties to middle-class tenants who chose to rent because it suited their particular needs at the time. This failed to meet the needs of low-income households, resulting in increased homelessness.

Government policy had also been seen to make owner-occupation seem a positive option by offering subsidies to mortgage buyers, and lenders were keen to compete in this newly developing market. This increase in demand for owner-occupied housing – a finite source – led to vastly increased prices and inflationary pressures for the Treasury. The government took steps that had the effect of steadily increasing the levels of interest that mortgage buyers had to pay on their loans. As the Chancellor had hoped, the increase in interest charges reduced demand and eased inflation. However, it had the unintended and unpopular effect of decreasing house prices, many becoming worth less than their owners had paid for them ('negative equity'). Many home-owners were thus caught in a vicious circle of being unable to make their increased repayments, but unable to sell their house to escape the situation. The net result was an increasing rate of house repossessions by lenders, who sold them at the lower market rate, leaving their previous 'owners' homeless and needing rented accommodation and still having to pay off the remaining money borrowed.

Ford (1990) describes the causes and consequences of this at greater length in her essay

'Households, housing and debt'. She argues that non-payers or defaulters mostly wanted and tried to make their mortgage repayments, but effectively buried their heads in the sand when they could not to avoid negative comments from others – making the situation more difficult.

Homelessness

Homelessness became an important issue in the 1980s (see also Sections 14.2 and 14.6), but home repossessions were just one factor contributing to this. Other significant reasons were loss of a home previously offered by parents, family or friends, loss of rented accommodation, or separation from a partner. Hutson and Liddiard (1994) give deeper insights into the causes and consequences of youth homelessness. They suggest that a variety of explanations can be offered, being either structural or personal. In structural terms the following arguments are offered.

- Changes in the labour market led to low pay and unemployment, making the keeping of a home economically unsustainable. (See Section 9.6.)
- Changes to the welfare benefits system lowered the level of any alternative income – or even excluded particular individuals from this altogether. (See Section 14.2.)
- Changes in the housing market, identified above, meant that there was a lack of affordable housing.
- Demographic changes meant that this age-group represented an increasing proportion of the population. Combined with a desire to live in single-person households and reduced levels of affordable housing, the result was homelessness.

Among the many personal explanations were the desire to leave home to attain independence; the poor experience of living in care; physical or sexual abuse at home; mental illness; involvement in crime; alcohol and drug abuse. Hutson and Liddiard found that young people were most likely to see their homelessness in one of these terms. For example, a 19-year-old youth said:

I took a lot of bashing because my mother split from my father, yeah, and I stuck with my father. He used to do what he did to my mother to me . . . I thought 'I don't want to go through what she's been through! I'm off!'.

Conservative politicians tend to see youth homelessness in terms of personal choice, whereas Labour and other politicians emphazise structural conditions. John Cunningham (Labour) saw youth homelessness in the following way:

The severe shortage of adequate, affordable, fit housing is causing the crisis.
(John Cunningham, *Hansard*, 10 February 1987)

Hutson and Liddiard remind us that political statements are not only to do with ideological commitment but also whether a politician's party is in power or not. It is easier for politicians to espouse a caring attitude if they do not have the responsibility to find the financial resources to manage the problem.

Activity

If your library has a newspaper on CD–ROM, look up the issue of 'homelessness' in the index. How does the newspaper explain and evaluate the issue? Are there particular biases? Are there any contradictions? What effect will the stories have on the readers?

I, A

Housing and sociological theory

Much of this section on housing has considered political policies and economic conditions in explaining inequality of access, but sociologists have also seen causes in other arenas. Pahl's (1975) concept of 'urban managers' is a classic example. He identified them as the people with direct control of urban resources, including housing – estate agents, mortgage lenders, local government officials and councillors, and property developers. All were seen to be guided by their moral and political values.

Morris and Winn (1990) suggest that this concept fell from grace because 'urban managers' was ill-defined, and because power was wrongly ascribed to low-level officials; but they conclude that this work had been overlooked too quickly. The concept had not been fully researched, and a useful addition to it might be the concept of labelling in terms of the interactive setting between managers and clients. Ideas from the sociology of organizations might also be used to evaluate how far officials were constrained by the 'rule book'. (See Section 9.7.)

Saunders (1978, 1987), from a neo-Weberian perspective, explained the developing inequalities between owner-occupiers and non-owners in terms of the further financial gains offered by house price inflation, the ability to improve one's property, and gaining extra government subsidies. However, as Morris and Winn note, property may not always gain in value (the 1990s have shown this) and home-owners are an inhomogeneous group with widely different experiences.

Ball (1983) criticized the sociological debate over consumption of housing, arguing for a linked assessment of production processes. (See also Sections 10.8

and 10.9.) These include land purchase and development, building of the home, transfer of the completed home to the buyer, and use of the home. A whole range of groups are involved in the processes and there is potential for a variety of conflict situations, which can be assessed sociologically. Until recent times, he argued, land prices had risen so profits came relatively easily for developers. Now, however, they had to think far more widely in their assessment of costs and savings. Savings had been identified by limiting the number of housing types available, offering a blanket design while still marketing homes as 'individually' designed. Recession in the housing market led to building in small batches which had to be sold before the next batch was built. Often the first homes will be built nearest the site entrance as 'show homes' but this was an inefficient process. Small batch production had also led to subcontracting in order to avoid having a wage bill during idle periods – post-Fordism in the sociology of housing! There are many issues raised here that sociologists would do well to consider.

Concluding comments

After food, housing is arguably the most important resource available to people. Those buying their own home are usually making the biggest individual purchase of their lives, so it is strange that sociologists have not given housing more attention. From the work available to us we can see that the homes people live in, or conditions of homelessness, are determined by the complex interaction of a variety of factors. Structural conditions such as the economy, labour market and policy options by 'urban managers' affect the availability of housing and people's chances of entering the housing system. Individual choices such as how much income should be spent on housing or length of stay in one place also affect the type of tenure we find people living in. However, whether macro or micro forces have most influence on housing, it should be noted that there are variations in housing quality according to social class, gender, ethnicity and age, with those least advantaged in other areas of society also least advantaged in housing.

16.8 Nation, nationalism and globalization

This is a relatively new topic in sociological study. According to Mears (1994), the reason for this is that in the years following the Second World War it was believed that nations had stabilized and that ethnic enclaves had either been assimilated or accepted for their 'charming' difference. It is now clear that national stability has not developed into a long-term trend and that nationalist desires are being expressed, turning to bitter conflict in several areas of the world. Sociologists have been keen to find explanations. Nationalism is also considered in Sections 10.10 and 17.6.

Nations: imagined communities?

Anderson (1983), from a neo-Marxist perspective, argues that we could define a nation as 'an imagined political community – and imagined as both inherently limited and sovereign' (p. 6). 'Imagined' is used because people of a nation cannot possibly know each other and therefore cannot know if they think and behave in the same ways – they have to believe or imagine that they do. 'Limited' is used because the nation is seen to have physical boundaries; 'sovereign' because national citizens believe they are free and safe under their leaders and give them authority to lead; and 'community' because comradeship is emphasized over inequalities and divisions.

Anderson links the advent of nationalism to the development of print and literacy. Thereby the ideas of the élite were more easily geographically transferable, at a time when early science was creating new questions – and resulting insecurities – to be answered. The empires of the nineteenth century were also given credit for this phenomenon. Nationalist vocabulary made reference to kinship in order to inspire beliefs of naturalness and the safety of home. 'Collective amnesia' helped the 'nation' to forget aspects not fitting the necessary formula, and particular records were kept to remind people of the parts to be remembered, helping to create the required identity.

The functions of nationalism

Hobsbawn (1990), a Marxist historian, also sees nations and nationalism as invented, but believes it more useful to begin looking at nationalism than the physical entity of the nation:

In short, for the purposes of analysis nationalism comes before nations. Nations do not make states and nationalisms but the other way round.
(Hobsbawn, 1990, p. 10)

He sees nationalist beliefs changing in quantity and quality within any given nation, and reminds us that although people have nationalist beliefs they may also have other beliefs that override them. He also argues that, although states may hold 'official ideologies', we cannot be sure that these are held by its citizens. These are important points which many other sociologists have emphasized.

For Hobsbawn, nationalisms are not new and their effects have been overrated. He illustrates this by looking at recent developments that are claimed, incorrectly in his view, to be caused by nationalism. The break-up of the USSR, he claims, was due rather to *glasnost* and internal political changes, and the reunification of Germany was due to unforeseen external circumstances. Thus he argues:

. . . nationalism, however, inescapable, is simply no longer the historical force it was in the era between the French Revolution and the end of imperialist colonialism after World War II.
(Hobsbawn, 1990, p. 169)

Where it did arise it was due to uncertainties of modern global phenomena. As such it was a reactionary force which might complicate or act as a catalyst for other developments.

Gellner (1983) has a more Durkheimian view of nationalism, seeing it taking over the role of religion in allowing society to worship itself. (See Section 18.3 for a discussion of Durkheim's views on religion.) Like the previous two theorists, he argued that it had an imagined quality:

The cultures it claims to defend and revive are often its own inventions, or are modified out of all recognition.
(Gellner, 1983, p. 56)

It was found in the modern world because modernity required a homogeneous culture (which, like Durkheim, he thought would be taught in schools – see Sections 8.1 and 8.10). Social and geographical mobility meant that people would need to communicate in a variety of contexts, and culture would be the connecting process. Nationalism, he argues, was not the only process.

💬 Discussion point

a What is the function of nationalism?

b What are the positive and negative aspects to living in a society based on nationalist sentiments?

c When you cast a political vote, are you likely to be influenced by a party's 'patriotism'?

Globalization and national identity

Where Hobsbawn simply hinted towards the role of globalization and its resulting uncertainties creating a need for nationalism to provide a sense of safety, many other sociologists have considered this process in greater depth. Globalization is also considered in Sections 9.9, 10.10, 12.5 and 17.6.

Giddens defines globalization as:

. . . the intensification of world-wide social relations which link distant localities in such a way that
distant social happenings are shaped by events occurring many miles away and vice versa.
(Giddens, 1990, p. 64)

This process, as far as he is concerned, has been caused by the world capitalist economy, the nation-state system, the world military orders and industrial development. Robertson (1992) adds to these structural factors by promoting individual actions as a factor contributing to globalization. In adopting Giddens's 'structuration theory' – that structural conditions influence individual actors and vice versa (see Section 2.9) – he argues that global conditions can be seen to destabilize identities, with the result that individuals, perhaps through collective collaboration, re-assert themselves to enforce their 'common humanity'. Such a collective response via anti-globalist or new social movements could be in terms of a nationalist manifesto; however, it could be organized around others' 'politico-religious fundamentalist' doctrines. Whatever the doctrine, the aim was:

. . . the 'restoration' of their own social communities to pristine condition with the rest of the world being left as a series of closed communities posing no threat to the 'best community'.
(Robertson, 1992, p. 81)

A similar stand is taken by Held (1991), emphasizing the 'political' rather than the 'cultural'. He suggests that citizens of nation states are led to believe that they can participate in choosing their country's future, but globalization has affected the ability of a nation to be autonomous in its decision-making. Likewise, decisions made within a nation-state, such as whether to build a nuclear power station, affect the autonomy of other nation-states. This can result in a desire to recapture political autonomy and nationalism can become a consequence:

Globalisation is frequently portrayed as a homogenising force, eroding 'difference' and the capacity of nation-states to act independently. . . . Yet . . . the age of the nation-state is by no means exhausted. . . . The importance of the nation-state and nationalism, territorial independence and the desire to establish or regain or maintain 'sovereignty' does not seem to have diminished.
(Held, 1991, p. 210)

In particular, he notes how non-nuclear powers and peoples have tried to re-assert themselves in the light of the knowledge that nuclear powers will be unlikely to use their full arsenal to stop them. So loss of autonomy had produced an effort to regain it. The effect was a situation whereby nation-states were neither totally independent nor interdependent.

Wallerstein (1991) also notes the political dimension with regard to globalization and nationalism, arguing that the state is able to define the 'national culture'. (See also Section 10.10.) However, just as state boundaries in capitalism allow the free movement of capital commodities etc., they also allow free movement of ideas and cultural expression. Thus:

At the very moment that one has been creating national cultures each distinct from the other, these flows have been breaking down the national distinctions.
(Wallerstein, 1991, p. 97)

He goes further in suggesting that, just as there is a dialectical relationship between global and national cultural identities, there can be:

[simultaneously created] *homogeneous national cultures and distinctive ethnic groups or 'minorities' within these nation states.*
(Wallerstein, 1991, p. 98)

This relates to the movement of peoples in the world economic system and the formation of minority enclaves. Thus we have a situation whereby a multitude of identities is being created and re-created by different camps related to global contexts and consequences. (See Section 6.5 and 10.10.)

National identities in a 'post-modern' global age have been the concern of Hall (1992), a post-Marxist. For him the 'post-modern subject' is constantly open to new influences. Identity therefore has:

. . . no fixed, essential or permanent identity. Identity becomes a 'moveable feast': formed and transferred continuously in relation to the ways we are represented or addressed in the cultural systems which surround us.
(Hall, 1992, p. 277)

As a result, Hall says the 'post-modern identity' in terms of individuals or, importantly, collectivities (such as nation-states) can be 'dislocated' or lacking stability and a single point of reference. This can be negative by disorientating identity, but also positive by challenging individuals or collectivities to re-appraise their identities. The usefulness of the 'post-modern subject' in terms of globalization and nationalism is apparent when considering the disorientating effects of increasing global interconnections which challenge traditionally accepted and uniting identities by, as suggested by Held and Wallerstein, weakening the autonomy of nation-states:

The erosion of the nation-state, national economies and national cultural identities is a very complex and dangerous moment. Entities of power are dangerous when they are ascending and when they are declining . . .
(Hall, 1991, p. 25)

This is illustrated by considering the concept of 'Englishness' through the rise and fall of the British Empire. The ascendance of Englishness is seen in the rise of 'The Empire', allowing the English to place themselves in a superior position relative to all other peoples – an obviously racist and nationalized condition. This offers them stability and reassurance in their own identity. However, Hall notes the decline in more recent times of the UK as one of the world's leading economies, putting an end to the 'old logics' and discourses of identity. Thus with economic decline the air of superiority is difficult to sustain and an instability in terms of identity is created.

Activity

There is a wealth of evidence in the actions of English citizens, politicians and the media to re-assert the superiority of 'Englishness'. Make a list of these actions, and explain and evaluate the consequences of their use.

I, A, E

A future cyberstate: communities beyond nation?

The theorists associated with globalization and nationalism have tended to see the latter as a response to the former, although Robertson and Hall recognize that nationalist movements are not the only response to globalization. Both theorists would probably endorse the suggestion made by Wallerstein that such nationalist movements are only relative to their time in history. He sees them as 'transitional and transitory' – a social and psychological 'crutch'. Giddens and Held are less committal about the future. Both recognize that unchecked globalizing tendencies, and resulting responses, could have dire consequences – what Giddens terms the 'high-consequence risks of modernity'. Both theorists recognize the need for a more co-ordinated global political order if globalization is not to have lethal, perhaps fatal, consequences for the world's population. Giddens is more inclined to believe such an order will come about.

But what form will this new world order take and what will become of the nation state? Angell (1995) and Mooney (1996) both predict the death of the nation-state, with the 'new city state' and the 'cyberstate' (respectively) taking its place, emphasizing how information technology has taken power away from national governments. Angell argues that:

It will be inevitable that nation-states will fragment: rich areas will dump the poor areas. . . . One inevitable consequence of global trade will be the rise of the New City State at the hub of global

Discussion point

a Both Angell and Mooney were writing for the Libertarian Alliance, an organization campaigning for total freedom for the market and the individual, so their ideas might be considered wishful thinking rather than reality. What do you think?

b Films such as *Independence Day*, *Bladerunner*, *Mad Max*, *Escape From New York* and *Escape from LA* have offered views about the future of communities and nations. The sociologists cited in this section have also discussed their points of view. However, we don't have a crystal ball and our opinions are just as valid as those of the film-writers, if not the sociologists. Discuss the following issues.

- What is the future of the nation-state?
- Might it be torn apart by nationalist conflicts or the developing 'cyberstate'?
- Could a new global political order develop? What form might it take?
- If a new global order developed, could the nation-state find a place in it?
- Several of the films mentioned above see society breaking down and relationships being fragmented. What is the future of community and society?

electronic and transport networks.
(Angell, 1995, p. 4)

Perhaps we are already seeing evidence of this transformation in cities such as Los Angeles and London. If nation-states have a role, Angell believes it would be by acting as a 'corporation-state', providing market-based corporations with staff of the necessary expertise, and a stable economic and political environment in which to operate. If they don't they will be left behind and crumble.

Mooney (1996) sees the future in the 'cyberstate', where the world is governed by commerce (rather than politics) via information technology:

On the ground, people will organize themselves into small regional states and control their own local affairs.
(Mooney, 1996, p. 6)

Further **reading**

An excellent, up-to-date synopsis of the sociology of community is:

- Crow, G. and Allan, G. (1994) *Community Life: An Introduction to Local Social Relations*, London, Unwin Hyman.

The following text contains key readings from the historical spectrum of urban sociology, along with introductory comments:

- Kasinitz, P. (1995) *Metropolis: Centre and Symbol of Our Times*, Basingstoke, Macmillan.

The following is another fine collection of selected readings from a variety of historical and sociological perspectives, each with a short commentary to put the essays in context:

- LeGates, R. (1996) *The City Reader*, London, Routledge.

The following has short segments from primary texts, with commentary and activity type questions:

- Mellor, R. (1992) *Change in Urban Life*, London, Nelson.

The following are excellent primary studies, each with reference to methodology and the research process (see also Chapter 3):

- Pryce, K. (1986) *Endless Pressure: A Study of West Indian Lifestyles in Bristol*, Bristol, Bristol Classical Press.
- Whyte, W. F. (1981) *Street Corner Society: The Social Structure of an Italian Slum*, Chicago, University of Chicago Press.

Back issues of the periodical *Sociology Review* (formerly known as *Social Studies Review*) also contain many articles on this field of sociology and many others.

Exam **questions**

1   a   Identify two differences between the concepts of *Gemeinschaft* and *Gesellschaft*.   [4 marks]

    b   Describe two aspects of modern life which tend to break up communities.   [4 marks]

    c   What have sociological studies contributed to our understanding of conflicts within communities?   [7 marks]

    d   Evaluate the view that modern communities are the products of deprivation and discrimination.   [10 marks]

(IBS, Paper 1, Summer 1995)

2   How have sociologists attempted to explain the changes in nationalism and national identity in contemporary societies?   [25 marks]
(IBS, Paper 1, Summer 1996)

3   To what extent have sociological studies supported the popular stereotype of the countryside as an idyllic alternative to the stresses and strains of living in cities?   [25 marks]
(AEB, Paper 2, Summer 1995)

Coursework **suggestions**

1 **To assess the proposition that some people, by their roles or actions, provide the 'social glue' that keeps communities together**

People whose roles or actions might provide 'social glue' include neighbours, youth workers, Neighbourhood Watch co-ordinators, local councillors and volunteer groups. Through primary research (e.g. questionnaires or interviews) you could ask these people and/or people in the local community how important it is to have people providing such services. This could be backed up with use of secondary sources such as local newspapers. Are their actions important on their own or is it their cumulative effect that is important? Is the 'social glue' disappearing?

2 **To assess the proposition that where people live is more a matter of circumstance than individual choices**

Housing and homelessness have become important issues in the 1990s. You might research this particular hypothesis using questionnaires or interviews with local residents (always take a friend with you) or with workers at the town hall housing department, a local housing association, estate agent or those working with the homeless. Again, local and national newspapers may help support your findings. You might develop your conclusions using Giddens' concept of 'structuration'. (See Section 2.9.)

Power and politics

17.1 Democracy and political systems

In common-sense thought and language, 'politics' is usually associated with the activities of those in government (parties and individual MPs), the state in general, and sometimes with those seeking political power perhaps in a different form – such as pressure groups.

Sociologists, on the other hand, should consider 'the political' as much wider than simply the activities of elected élites: politics in its wider definition is about the exercise of power – and can be seen to occur through the whole of social life on a number of different levels, both macro and micro. For example, for feminists, 'sexual politics' is about the struggles for power between men and women in many social arenas (see Section 5.4).

Activity
Using the definition opposite – that 'politics' is about the exercise of power – make a list of 'political struggles' of a 'micro' nature which have affected your own life over the past few days.

I, A

Political sociology
Although all social life is political in a sense, 'political sociology' has traditionally focused on a number of key concerns.

- The nature of power – who has it, how did they obtain it, how is it used, and how does it change over time?

- The nature of the state – how does it exercise its power, and in whose interests?
- Who do people vote for and how does this change over time?
- The role of pressure groups and other social movements – how do they attempt to exercise power, how effective are they, and in whose interests do they operate?

A distinction must be drawn between the academic activities of political sociologists and the discipline of political science. As a rough distinction, political science focuses on the institutions of government and political parties, whereas political sociology takes a much more society-based approach and is concerned with investigating the effects of power in society – particularly that power held by the state and other ruling groups.

Discussion point

To what extent do you think it is possible to maintain the above distinction between political science and political sociology?

Varieties of political systems

Taking politics in its narrow sense to refer to the operation of government and the state, we can begin to make a distinction between the main varieties of 'political systems' in operation around the globe in contemporary social life. It is possible to identify three broad types of political system – three ways of classifying how government is organized on a social basis. It must be remembered, however, that these are 'pure' or 'ideal-typical' descriptions; in reality, some characteristics are played down in some societies or even ignored.

Totalitarianism

Carl Friedrich (1954) offers a four-fold classification of the key elements of totalitarianism:

- a single set of ideological principles which everyone must accept and follow
- a single party state led by one dictator
- the use of violence to control those who do not follow the 'correct' ways of behaving – usually through the creation of a secret police force
- total state control of all economic and social institutions.

In current usage, the word 'totalitarian' is used to describe some fascist and some self-proclaimed communist societies, especially Nazi Germany and the former USSR, although there is some debate as to whether these two types of system can be classified together under one heading, since the USSR was controlled by an élite party rather than by a single dictator.

Oligarchy

An oligarchy means to be governed by 'the few', as opposed to being ruled by a single dictator.

Democracy

The term 'democracy' has a Greek origin: *demos* = the people, and *kratos* = rule. Thus democracy means 'rule by the people'. Athens, in ancient Greece, is usually associated with the birth of democracy, using popular public assemblies and law courts to make decisions by debate and discussion. In reality, however, not all those living in Athens at that time could attend public assemblies or vote at them: only the male 'citizens' had rights of voting, whereas women and the vast slave population were excluded.

Even today the concept 'democracy' is highly problematic because many different societies of a wide variety of political systems, cultures and structures describe themselves as democratic. It must be noted that there is an important difference between *claiming* to be democratic and actually *being* democratic.

Discussion point

Why has 'democracy' become a major 'legitimation claim' in the contemporary world?

A Marxist perspective on democracy

Bottomore (1978, 1993), adopting a Marxist perspective, is highly critical of the claims to democracy made by many societies – including those of the western world. He suggests that all the time a ruling class exists, claims of democracy are nonsense. From a Marxist perspective (see Section 2.3), the concept 'ruling class' is used to refer to those who own the 'means of production' – i.e. all that is necessary to make a finished product. Even with a regular system of secret voting, those who have the real power remain unelected yet in control owing to their ownership of the means of production. Bottomore suggests that the 'popular rule' associated with democracy is impossible in capitalist societies:

One must be sceptical, therefore, of the view that the extension of voting rights to the mass of the population can establish easily and effectively – or has in fact established in the short period of time in which modern democracies have existed – popular rule, and gradually erode or eliminate the power of a ruling class. What seems to have taken place in the democratic countries up to the present time is

not so much a reduction in the power of the upper class as a decline in the radicalism of the working class.
(Bottomore, 1993. pp. 28–9)

Discussion point

To what extent can societies be 'democratic' if they have great inequalities of wealth and a dominant class which enjoys the majority of this wealth?

Bottomore is equally critical of the notion of 'equality of opportunity' (see also Section 4.9) often associated with a democratic society. He claims that the notion is frequently used as a replacement for true equality – it is used to hide the fact that in these 'democracies' the people do not rule, and neither do they have equality among one another and in relation to their 'hidden rulers', the ruling class:

... this later notion [equality of opportunity], besides having quite a different significance, is actually self-contradictory. Equality of opportunity, as the expression is habitually used, presupposes inequality, since 'opportunity' means 'the opportunity to rise to a higher level in a stratified society'. At the same time, it presupposes equality, for it implies that the inequalities embedded in this stratified society have to be counteracted in every generation so that individuals can really develop their personal abilities.
(Bottomore, 1993, p. 117)

A similar view to Bottomore's is that of Box (1983) who, also working within a Marxist perspective, suggests that claims to democracy can be used by ruling groups to hide their criminal (see also Section 11.6) and power-seeking behaviour. They can do this because under a representative form of democracy we must trust those who we vote to represent us, something they may not do properly in practice:

In a truly democratic society, the problem of power is not solved but it is contained. There is no way that people determined to behave badly, and having mastered the shameless art of deception, can be prevented from occupying positions of power. ... large sections of the public lack the inclination, ability, or power to make accountable those wielding political power, and through them, those wielding economic power. Ironically, for a nation that went to war against fascism, the democratic will to solve the problem of power has been lost; we have people in political and economic power who are not accountable to those whose lives they control.
(Box, 1983, pp. 202 and 204)

Discussion point

To what extent do you agree with this statement by Box as an assessment of government in contemporary advanced capitalist societies?

Problems with the definition of democracy

A number of commentators, including Held (1987, 1993) and Birch (1993), have raised critical issues with the definition of democracy as simply 'rule by the people'. For example, although in our contemporary times democracy may, for many, appear as the most obvious or commonsense way to organize society, this was not always the case:

Democracy seems to have scored an historic victory over alternative forms of government. Nearly everyone today professes to be a democrat. Political regimes of all kinds throughout the world claim to be democracies. Yet what these regimes say and do is often substantially different from one another. Democracy bestows an aura of legitimacy on modern political life: laws, rules and policies appear justified when they are 'democratic'. But it was not always so. The great majority of political thinkers from ancient Greece to the present day have been highly critical of the theory and practice of democracy. A uniform commitment to democracy is a very recent phenomenon. Moreover, democracy is a remarkably difficult form of government to create and sustain.
(Held, 1993, p. 14)

Once it is recognized, however, that the contemporary commitment to 'all things democratic' is a relatively recent social development, our problems with democracy do not stop there – quite the opposite. Having identified democracy as a principal form of political organization in the contemporary world, we should establish a much more detailed definition than simply 'rule by the people' which, although a simple concept to grasp, does not really tell us anything about *how* people rule. This is where, according to Birch (1993), the problems of definition start. For example:

1 Should 'the people' mean *all* the people, or only *some*? Should those in prison be allowed to vote, since if they are guilty they have not followed the rules of society?

2 Equally, should those 'proven' to be 'mentally ill' be allowed to vote. Can they make a reasoned or rational decision – and does this matter anyway?

3 The same point applies to children – they live under the control of governments, so should they

be allowed to have their say?

4 Can we call any society a democracy if it fails to allow women or some ethnic groups a vote? If not, then most of the modern-day 'democracies' have only actually been democracies for a remarkably short time.

Activity

Using information in this section, write your own evaluative answers to Birch's questions.

A, E

As can be seen from these four questions, the concept 'rule by the people' is somewhat problematic. The same can be said for the concept 'rule', since many 'democratic societies' have established quite different mechanisms to allow the people to rule:

If ruling is taken to mean the activity of reaching authoritative decisions that result in laws and regulations binding on society, then it is obvious that (apart from occasional referendums) only a small minority of individuals can be rulers in modern, populous societies. So for the dictionary definition to be operational, ruling must be taken in the much weaker sense of choosing the rulers and influencing their decisions. But how weak can this sense be and still remain meaningful? Is it essential to a democracy that governmental decisions, though only made by a small minority of politicians, should nevertheless reflect or embody the popular will? If so, how can the popular will be defined and how can it be identified in practice?

(Birch, 1993, p. 48)

Activity

Sociologists have a duty to make the concept 'democracy' as problematic as possible. This is said because they should avoid uncritical acceptance of any aspect of society. It is also vital that they draw a distinction between societies that are 'truly' democratic and those that merely claim to be so.

a Using the ideas of Bottomore, Box, Held and Birch, write a list of 'problems' with the notion of democracy.

b In small groups, suggest possible solutions to the problems you have identified.

I, A, E

Models of democratic systems

At the heart of these problems in defining the concept 'democracy' lies a conflict between two opposing definitions that lead to very different types or models of democratic systems. On the one hand democracy can mean the direct participation by all; while on the other hand, given the size of contemporary nation-states, it can also mean the election of those who are to rule. There are, then, two basic models of democracy (Held, 1993, p. 15):

- *participatory democracy*, often referred to as 'direct democracy', which Held defines as:

  a system of decision-making about public affairs in which citizens are directly involved

- *representative democracy*, which Held defines as:

  a system of rule embracing elected 'officers' who undertake to 'represent' the interests or views of citizens within the framework of the 'rule of law'.

In contemporary western societies the 'representative' model is the most common form of political system.

The limits of democracy

A number of sociologists, philosophers, economists and others have been concerned to chart what they see as the limits of the democratic system of government. They suggest that given the size of nation-states it is only realistic for representative style democracies to develop, yet within this political system it is highly unlikely that the 'people' will have all their wishes met with suitable 'collective decisions' from full-time party officials or rulers. These 'representatives' may themselves turn into an élite group, supported in their rule by the massive bureaucracies set up to administer the state. (See also Section 9.7.)

Discussion point

To what extent can 'democracy' really be achieved in a society where political participation for the majority is limited to a vote in an election every four to five years?

Max Weber, in his key work *Economy and Society* (1968; orig. pub. 1921), notes that 'party machines' – massive bureaucratic systems – are needed to control modern states to the extent that participation in the governing or ruling process by the people is often minimal (see also Section 2.3). Weber was concerned that unless parties developed in nation-states standing for different interests then democracy via the ballot box could be highly problematic – little real choice could be given to 'a people' to choose who to represent their interests – a very undemocratic situation.

The concerns of Weber about the (un)representative model of democracy are echoed in the work of Schumpeter, an economist. In his book *Capitalism, Socialism and Democracy*, Schumpeter (1992; orig.

Activity

Using a suitable local library or other centre of information, obtain copies of the most recent manifestos for the main political parties in your local area. Make lists of each of the parties' main policies on a few issues that interest you. Now answer this question. To what extent do you agree with Weber, that little real choice is given to 'the people' when deciding for whom to vote?

I, A, E

pub. 1943) argues that representative democracies inevitably end up as government by the politician, not by the people. He notes that it is very difficult to define exactly what the 'common will of the people' actually is in any given society. Usually, because this is the only way in which large-scale 'democracies' work, the 'common will' or 'common good' is defined from above and so represents only a limited proportion of the people at any one time:

It is not only conceivable but, whenever individual wills are much divided, very likely that the political decisions produced will not conform to 'what people really want'. Nor can it be replied that, if not exactly what they want, they will get a 'fair compromise'.
(Schumpeter, 1992, pp. 254–5)

17.2. Political participation: elections and voting behaviour

Societies such as that of the UK are regarded as 'liberal democracies' – sometimes referred to as 'liberal-capitalist'. Democracy is claimed to be achieved through a system of 'representative democracy' where the general population vote in free elections for those individuals or groups whom they wish to rule over them for the time being.

Representative democracy might appear normal or natural to those who have never experienced anything else, but it is important to remember that this is just one political system among many. Equally, within the category of 'liberal democracy' we can find important differences. In today's society, the concept of democracy is often associated with voting, and so a great deal of sociological literature exists on the nature of voting.

Problems for psephology

Given the contemporary unpredictable political climate we appear to live in, psephology (the study

of voting behaviour and patterns) has become even more complex and problematic. For many commentators, the post-war period in British politics has been characterized by *alignment* and *partisanship*.

Until the late 1970s it was considered the norm that working-class members of society voted for the Labour Party (with the backing of their trade union) while the middle classes voted Conservative or Liberal. This was voting in line with one's 'true class interests', or in 'alignment' with one's class position. Alternatively it could be said that voters experienced a sense of 'partisanship' with a particular political party: they were loyal to the goals, ideas and interests of one party and did not often change their mind or become what today is called a 'floating voter'.

Voting was thus seen as being relatively stable and in line with one's social position. Butler and Stokes (1969) conducted in-depth analyses of voting patterns and behaviours in the 1960s and 70s, and their results appeared to agree with this partisan and class alignment image of voting. They suggested that class loyalty was ensured through the process of political socialization within the family: the sons and daughters of manual workers voted in line with their parent's Labour loyalties, while those born to middle-class families did the same with the Conservative Party.

For example, Butler and Stokes suggest that even when the electorate as a body renew themselves with first-time voters 'coming of age', it is still possible to detect:

... the electorate's enduring party alignments. Support comes to any party for the most astonishing variety of reasons. But some of these will be general enough and enduring enough to be considered as bases of party alignment. Since the rise of the Labour Party the foremost of these in Britain has been social class.
(Butler and Stokes, 1969, p. 4)

The contemporary debate for political sociologists is therefore between two related issues.

- Is voting aligned or dealigned?
- Is voting volatile or stable?

The deviant voter

Traditionally, a great deal of psephology sought to explain the existence of 'deviant voters' – those who did not appear to vote in line with their class interests. A number of explanations for 'deviant voting' were put forward.

- Middle-class members who vote Labour may do so out of a sense of working-class loyalty if they have become upwardly mobile in their own lifetime. They might still consider themselves to be working class.

Poll piles pressure on Labour

MARTIN KETTLE

THE Labour high command's nightmare scenario, a repetition of the 1992 General Election defeat, began to take shape yesterday as the latest Guardian–ICM opinion poll confirmed a sustained Conservative comeback.

Labour's long-standing opinion poll lead over the Conservatives has been cut by three points in the last month, leaving the gap between the parties at its closest in almost two years, according to the August Guardian–ICM poll survey.

The Labour advantage has fallen in each of the past four months. It now stands at 12 points, nine points down from the 21-point lead in April.

Labour retains a large enough lead for an election victory, but the narrowing will shape the fierce pre-election contest. It will electrify the Conservatives by reinvigorating their latest anti-Labour campaign tactics, and will give Tony Blair's leadership its first serious taste of battle with a confident enemy when the political season resumes next month.

The state of the parties in the adjusted August survey shows Labour at 45 per cent (no change on July), Conservatives 33 (up 3), Liberal Democrats 19 (down 2), and others 3 (down 1).

The results in ICM's unadjusted poll underline the Conservative recovery. The unadjusted August figures show Labour at 50 per cent (no change on July), Conservatives at 30 (up 5),

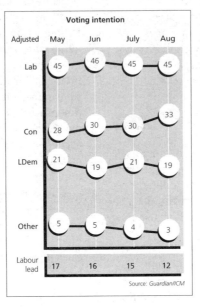

Liberal Democrats at 18 (down 2), others at 3 (down 2). The unadjusted Labour lead in August is 20 points (down 5).

With nine months to go before the expected polling day, the results show the political momentum is with the Conservatives, who last month launched a major scare campaign against Mr Blair under the slogan New Labour: New Danger.

This latest poll, which consolidates a trend among other polling organisations, will boost Tory hopes that the long-awaited feelgood factor, which

some had despaired of ever seeing, is arriving at the 11th hour via the high street and the housing market to bring them electoral relief. Mr Blair, on the other hand, will be strengthened in his view that party divisions – such as the rows about the shadow cabinet elections and the treatment of Clare Short – help the Tories.

Labour will be able to draw genuine comfort from the fact that the narrowing lead has not been caused by any fall in overall Labour support. Labour's rating of 45 per cent remains unchanged since July and has scarcely altered since May.

The ICM finding follows polls by Mori last week and by System Three in Scotland yesterday which also showed no change in the Labour rating. The reduced lead has so far been caused by Conservative gains at the expense of the Liberal Democrats and the minor parties. Labour voters are also far more solid in their voting intention than their Tory counterparts.

But a five-point swing to the Conservatives since July among C1 white-collar workers – traditionally the most volatile section of the electorate – will cause alarm among Mr Blair and his advisers, who have invested immense effort in trying to reassure this group that Labour does not threaten their achievements.

Source: *The Guardian*, 7 August 1996

- Middle-class 'caring professions' such as social workers or teachers may vote Labour out of a sense of duty to, or commitment for, the ideas of redistribution or social welfare. (See also Section 4.6.)
- Working-class voters who vote Conservative, especially if elderly, may do so owing to pre-war traditions where the Conservatives were seen still to represent the 'common man' – or, out of loyalty to a particular party during the Second World War.
- Some working-class members might 'defer' to what they see as the superiority of the middle classes to rule over them, and thus vote Conservative.

Dealignment

Since the 1970s and the work of Butler and Stokes it is possible to detect a number of changes to the

Crucial voters return to Tories

MARTIN KETTLE

THE crucial questions raised by the steady erosion of the Labour poll lead over the Conservatives – down 3 points again this month – are: who is changing their voting intentions, and why are they doing it?

The August Guardian–ICM survey reveals that the most eagerly canvassed group of voters in the country – the C1 white collar workers – have switched to the Conservatives this month in spectacular numbers, a sign, perhaps, that these 'new' Tory voters of the 1980s may be beginning to come back to the party which they associate with their prosperity and aspirations.

In July 1991, the C1 white collar section of ICM's sample opted 42–33 in favour of Labour. This month, in a dramatic reversal, they have gone 39–40 to the Conservatives. For a single month, this is a very large swing – 5 per cent. The feeling that old habits may be reasserting themselves among the electorate is underlined by an examination of the results shown in the table. ICM asked all voters whether a series of statements were more likely to be true under a Conservative or a Labour government (voters could also choose to answer: both, neither, or don't know).

Voters expect a Labour government to be more likely than the Conservatives to bring economic problems. More voters believe that interest rates will rise under Labour than the Tories (46 per cent as against 26 per cent); that inflation will go up (exactly the same figures); and that taxes will rise (43 to 27). Voters also expect more strikes if Tony Blair gets to Downing Street.

This would certainly seem to be a grim message for Labour, but it is mitigated by the apparently contradic-

VOTERS' HOPES AND FEARS

Questions: Under which government, Conservative or Labour, do you think the following is most likely to happen?

	All voters	
	Conservative	Labour
The economy will deteriorate	32	29
Interest rates will rise	26	46
Law and order will improve	24	40
Inflation will go up	26	46
Unemployment will fall	22	48
There will be more strikes	27	39
Taxes will go up	27	43
Educational standards will improve	21	51
We will have a single European currency	30	30
House prices will rise substantially	33	21
Income will be spread more evenly	11	63
Welfare payments will be concentrated on the really needy	18	57
The health service will deteriorate	60	12
There will be lasting peace in N Ireland	12	13

Source: ICM

tory finding that more people believe that the economy will deteriorate under Conservative rule (32 saying Tory, as against 29 saying Labour). Voters are also optimistic that Labour has got answers to unemployment, with 48 per cent thinking it is more likely to fall under Labour, as against 22 per cent for the Tories.

Labour's social policy strengths are underlined in the survey. Only 12 per cent think the health service will deteriorate under Labour, compared with 60 per cent for the Conservatives. Labour will be boosted by its good showing on law and order, traditionally a Tory strength.

Intriguingly, the electorate seems incapable of differentiating between the likelihood of Britain joining a European single currency under either of the two major parties; 30 per cent say it is more likely under Labour, and 30 per cent say the Conservatives.

ICM interviewed a random sample of 1,200 adults aged 18 and over by telephone between August 2–3, 1996. Interviews were conducted across the country and the results have been weighted to the profile of all adults.

Source: *The Guardian,*
7 August 1996

modern pattern of voting behaviour. It is suggested that we are experiencing a process or pattern of 'dealignment', whereby the traditional relationships between class and party loyalties are slowly being eroded.

In line with the foregoing discussion, there may be at least two processes involved here: class dealignment and partisan dealignment. Voters may no longer vote according to the 'traditional' or 'expected' fashion based on their class background, or they may have given up established loyalty to a particular party

and instead may 'float' their vote, possibly changing their mind from election to election.

The 'demise' of the deviant voter

The processes of dealignment almost certainly explains the observation that many working-class people must have voted for the Conservative Party since the 1979 election for the party to have stayed in power for an extensive period. This has implications for the idea of 'deviant voting' because it seems that the majority of society have become 'deviant voters' – and if this is true, then the term 'deviant' becomes inappropriate. Perhaps this concept is no longer useful to explain voting patterns since 1979?

Volatility

When class and partisan dealignment occur, this makes the voting system highly volatile. Today it is becoming increasingly difficult to predict the outcomes of elections, or indeed to predict an individual's voting pattern or party loyalty (if any) from their social background:

. . . while the two-class, two-party model has dominated British political science, most commentators have agreed that class, both as a social and a political force, has been steadily declining in Britain. Rising levels of affluence and the break-up of traditional communities are held to have eroded class solidarity. Labour in particular, it is said, can no longer rely on working-class support in the way that it could a generation ago, and the new breed of affluent skilled manual workers in the South of England are believed to have swung decisively to the Conservatives. The spread of home-ownership in the working class exacerbates the trend. Such changes in the character of the working class are held to explain why a left-wing ideology can no longer win the working-class vote.
(Heath *et al.*, 1985, p. 8)

The question posed by Heath and colleagues characterizes a great deal of contemporary political sociological debate regarding the nature of voting. Is it true that the Labour Party can no longer rely on the working class vote? Or, has dealignment happened? This idea is used by those who claim that we have reached 'the end of ideology' – that there has been a movement to the 'middle ground' of politics on both a national and a global scale. A 'new world order' has been established where what are seen as the ideological excesses of both the Left and Right have been replaced by 'consensus politics'.

When applied to the British electoral system, 'convergence' can be easily identified in the idea of 'embourgeoisement' as developed by Zweig (1961). The embourgeoisement thesis has been developing in many forms since the 1960s to explain what were seen as profound changes in the class structure of the UK – referred to by some as a 'post-industrial' society (see Section 4.7). When embourgeoisement occurs, we witness an expansion of the middle classes in society together with a reduction in the working classes, signalling a long-term process of upward mobility for many members of the working classes owing to changes in production technology in the workplace.

A more recent attempt to argue that this 'con-vergence' has taken place is provided by Fukuyama (1992), who suggests that the 'western liberal-capitalist ideal' is the model of democracy to which all industrial societies are slowly moving. In this sense, with the collapse of the USSR and the adoption of capitalist or market-style economics in many new eastern European nation-states, the East and the West are 'converging'.

Critics of this idea – usually from a Marxist or neo-Marxist stance – have argued that Fukuyama's model of the 'end of history' is not so much a 'con-vergence' but more a 'victory' for the West at the end of the 'cold war'. These critics claim that rather than an end of ideology, Fukuyama – and others like him – are celebrating what they see as the further advancement of capitalism on a new global stage (see Section 12.5). However, for Fukuyama, given his right-wing perspective, this 'victory of capitalism' would be welcome.

Discussion point

To what extent would you agree that ideology has ended in contemporary politics?

As Steele *et al.* (1989) contend, at the heart of Fukuyama's idea of the end of history is a capitalist-biased critique of Marxism. The claim of the 'end of history' or the 'end of ideology' is a thinly veiled attempt to provide academic and intellectual justification and legitimation for the imperialist and colonial activities across the globe of recent United States governments.

Some commentators feel that class is still an important key to understanding the nature of voting behaviour:

The withering away of class, if true, would have quite serious implications for the future of the political parties. It would suggest that a more volatile period was likely to follow in which no party could be sure of its share of the vote. However, the evidence that class has withered away is very thin . . . We are sceptical whether the social changes have been quite so far-reaching as most commentators have assumed, and we are accordingly sceptical of the more radical prognoses of the parties' futures.
(Heath *et al.*, 1985, p. 8)

Models of voting

It will be useful to begin by making a distinction between two types of voting models.

* *Expressive models* suggest that one's voting behaviour is based on social background. So class, housing, union membership, etc. affect the political choices made.

- *Instrumental models* suggest that voting is an individual action. It is not based on personal background or family socialization, but on a rational and calculated choice. Voters are seen as active consumers of party politics.

Himmelweit *et al.* (1981) develop what they term a 'consumer theory of voting', which is similar to the idea of an 'instrumental model' of voting. They point out that decision-making for voting is a well-researched area of social life for various reasons.

- The event is recurrent, so individuals' decision-making can be compared over a fairly standard period of time.
- Everyone is faced with the same limited number of options.
- Given the use of the media by political parties, most people are exposed to the same type of information on which to make their decision.

Himmelweit and colleagues note that this combination of features is rare in other areas of social life, which is why elections provide sociologists with excellent opportunities for research. They recognize that although elections potentially involve all people, they do so in a very insignificant fashion given the importance of the actual event and its consequences for the future of society:

Despite the importance of the aggregate decision, the majority of the electorate are little involved. They believe that their individual decision, being one of millions, makes little difference to the outcome, and the public as a collection of individuals does not see itself as having much influence on political events or even on the conduct of the party of their choice. This is not surprising. After all, it is only at election time that the public's views are seriously canvassed and any interest taken in their lives, their fears, their babies.
(Himmelweit *et al.*, 1985, p. 2)

and:

To be taken off the shelf, dusted down and asked to perform once every four or five years neither generates much enthusiasm for the act of voting, nor convinces the public that it is worth their while to invest in the study of political issues. It is also not easy to know where to turn for guidance. Politicians do not help. At election times each party sets out a tempting table d'hôte of policies, implying that if only their party were to come to power all their proposals would be implemented. No one mentions that the cost of implementing one policy might well jeopardize the implementation of a second equally desirable one or even threaten the continuation of long-established services that the

voters had come to take for granted. Electioneering is about persuasion, not education.
(Himmelweit *et al.*, 1985, p. 2)

This model of 'consumer voting' draws on images of the market-place. Voters are seen as consumers, purchasers of a set of ideological values. Voters are not passive but active – they participate in the political process, and an election happens *because* of them, not *to* them:

The individual, with his personal set of attitudes and beliefs, looks for the best match or the least mismatch between these and his or her perception of the platforms and the record of the parties. The voters' information gathering about the parties' stand might be searching or superficial, accurate or misleading, and his own views transient or stable. What matters is that the act of voting, like the purchase of goods, is seen as simply one instance of decision making, no different in kind from the process whereby other decisions are reached.
(Himmelweit *et al.*, 1985, pp. 11–12)

These writers suggest that the primary strength of their model is that the ideological stands of the political parties, from which consumption is made, do not need to be stable over time. Voting is like shopping: often the range of choice on offer changes or the same goods are packaged differently or located in a different area, but within a familiar framework, so consumption can still take place with relative ease.

By advocating the active nature of voting, Himmelweit and colleagues wish to 'return the voter to the centre stage' of election research. They argue that elections should be understood as a complex decision-making process more dependent on the actions of 'ordinary people' than on the specific ideological claims of élite party groups.

Criticisms of the idea of partisanship

Heath *et al.* (1985) question whether so-called 'traditional' partisanship ever really existed. Working-class members, they say, did not vote Labour out of a blind sense of *duty*, but because they felt the policies and ideology of the Labour party best served their specific interests. This, then, is a *rational* decision. Equally it may be that:

. . . on its own the new orthodoxy of instrumental voting will not do either. If people voted purely on the basis of rational calculation about the benefits the rival parties would bring them, they would never vote at all. The individual vote can make so little difference to the outcome of an election that the rational, instrumental elector would never waste his or her time and effort in going to the ballot

box. We have to introduce an expressive or moral element to explain the act of voting itself.
(Heath *et al.*, 1985, p. 9)

They conclude:

. . . we believe that it is quite unnecessary to decide for or against either theory. Any act of voting must involve both expressive and instrumental elements, and we very much doubt whether the balance between these two elements has changed much in the course of this century, let alone in the last twenty years that have marked the decline of Labour and the revival of the Liberal Democrats.
(Heath *et al.*, 1985, p. 10)

Tactical and 'pocket-book' voting

Heath *et al.* (1991) continued their analysis of recent British elections to include the 1987 General Election, which resulted in another victory for the Conservatives. They note that this election result indicates the rise of two very distinctive voting patterns: 'tactical' and 'pocket-book'.

Tactical voting

Voting tactically means choosing a party not because one feels they will make the best government – or may even receive enough votes to be in government – but because voting for this party may result in a constituency defeat for another party that one wishes to see lose. For example, in a traditional 'Tory stronghold' one could switch allegiance from Labour to the Liberal Democrats simply because the latter seemed to have more of a chance of 'getting the Conservatives out'.

Tactical voting is a particular or peculiar characteristic of 'first-past-the-post' election systems. The phenomenon can be explained through an *instrumental model* of voting behaviour: individuals make a calculated or rational assessment of the state of power and popular support in their local community, and then cast their vote accordingly.

Heath and colleagues suggest, however, that tactical voting was not widespread during the 1987 election. They calculated that only 6 per cent of their survey voted for one party while preferring the policies of another. This is a figure not far removed from the 5.9 per cent they found in 1983.

Despite attempts by the Liberal Democrats and pressure groups such as the Centre for Electoral Choice to promote the value of tactical voting among the electorate through the media, and the adoption of this tactic by some sections of the left-wing press, tactical voting is totally dependent on the ability of the electorate to assess their own particular tactical situation.

Heath and colleagues note that, of those who apparently switched allegiance in the 1987 election

from Labour to the Alliance, 84 per cent did so in constituencies where the Alliance were much more popular than Labour anyway, and stood a good chance of gaining power. This would suggest that if an 'Alliance vote' was a 'tactical vote' (a situation very hard to prove) it was at least happening in those areas where it could be a potentially successful policy. Therefore, some of the electorate (but not all) were sophisticated enough to understand the tactical situation.

Pocket-book voting

A second phenomenon associated by Heath and colleagues with the 1987 General Election was 'pocket-book' voting. This is casting one's vote for the particular party felt to be best for one's own economic circumstances, to improve one's own standard of living. This idea, originally associated with Ivor Crewe, was taken up and treated with scepticism. Heath and colleagues did, however, note that those who voted Conservative in 1983 were less likely to vote Conservative again in 1987, if they thought that as a result their own personal economic situation would decline.

They suggest, however, that 'pocket-book' voting was not as widespread as one might think. Rather they believe that, although people did take the economic 'competence' of the parties into account, it was not necessarily with regard to their own personal self-interests but for what they perceived as the interests of their class. Thus, 'pocket-book' voting can be seen as but an extension of class allegiance.

Discussion point
How far would you agree that class no longer matters in voting behaviour?

Are voters loyal?

Rose and McAllister (1990) pose the question: 'If voters are loyal, what are they loyal to?' They go on to argue that in order to understand voting behaviour, in order to understand why people vote as they do, and whether they vote out of party loyalties or not, we must adopt a 'lifetime learning model' of voting behaviour. This starts with the recognition that a number of influences come to bear on the voting process, including:

- parental socialization
- the economic conditions in which one works and lives
- the political values one has, and uses to make sense of the world
- the context of the community, region and nation in which one lives

- the performance of the parties and of governments during the run-up to an election.

This 'lifetime learning model' suggests that the activity of voting and the phenomenon of elections are dynamic or fluid processes, in a constant state of change. For example, at each election new voters are eligible to vote, and over time the ideological stances of the parties themselves may change. As Rose and McAllister comment:

The outcome of an election is not just a reflection of what voters want, nor is it decided simply by what parties do: the outcome is the product of what parties propose, and how the electorate disposes of what is offered.
(Rose and McAllister, 1990, p. 2)

They adopt what could be seen as a position which is more 'voter-led' than it is 'party-led':

When party leaders lead, voters do not have to follow. A change in what the parties propose can cause people to think afresh about whether they wish to continue giving their support to a party that is changing direction . . . Even though parties change, the concerns of ordinary people can remain stable, for they reflect a lifetime of experience. The major influences are not campaign appeals or actions taken by the government of the day. An individual's view of the world is shaped by an accumulation of experiences, beginning early in life. In the home a child learns to assimilate values and expectations of parents, friends and others in the immediate environment.
(Rose and McAllister, 1990, pp. 6–7)

Understanding how the UK votes

In their study *Understanding Political Change: The British Voter 1964–1987*, Heath *et al.* (1991) note that the General Elections of 1979, 1983 and 1987 are often presented as a 'sea-change' in popular political opinion.

Activity

Examine the statistics in Table 17.1. What trends can you see in voting behaviour since 1945?

I, A

Following Margaret Thatcher's first General Election victory in 1979, commentators such as Hall (1984) wrote of her deliberate project to challenge and change popular attitudes – to develop what she would have described as a 'self-reliant' society. To Hall, this represented a return to 'hegemonic politics' – the lure of Thatcherism was its popularist rhetoric and its power lay in its ability to obtain popular consent. Hall described the shift or popular victory of New Right policies as 'The Great Moving Right Show'.

Development of the project of Thatcherism may have enabled the Conservative Party to gain voters from those who would usually have voted Labour or Liberal Democrat, or 'traditional' working-class voters. Thus the 'success' of Thatcherism was to take advantage of the changing nature of class voting behaviour – yet in doing so, it contributed even more to the process of dealignment. With the rise of the

Activity

Suggest factors which may influence how an individual votes in an election.

A

Table 17.1 UK General Election results since 1945

	Percentage of votes				Parliamentary seats				
	Con	Lab	Lib Dem	Nat	Con	Lab	Lib Dem	Nat	Total
1992	41.9	34.4	17.8	5.8	336	271	20	24	651
1987	42.3	30.6	22.5	2.0	376	229	22	6	650
1983	42.4	27.6	25.4	1.7	397	209	23	4	650
1979	43.8	36.8	13.8	2.2	339	269	11	4	635
1974 Oct.	35.8	39.2	18.3	3.5	277	319	13	14	635
1974 Feb.	37.9	37.2	19.3	2.8	297	301	14	9	635
1970	46.4	43.1	7.5	2.4	330	288	8	5	630
1968	41.9	48.0	8.6	1.1	253	364	12	1	630
1964	43.4	44.1	11.2	0.9	304	317	9	0	630
1959	49.4	43.8	5.8	0.6	365	258	6	0	630
1955	49.7	46.4	2.7	0.9	345	277	6	2	630
1951	48.0	48.8	2.6	0.4	321	295	8	3	625
1950	43.4	46.1	9.1	0.6	298	315	9	2	625
1945	39.6	48.0	9	1.4	210	383	12	6	640

Source: *The Guardian*, 11 April 1994

New Right, many started to ask the question 'Will Labour lose again?'

Heath *et al.* (1991) note that many commentators adopted one of two main explanations to try to explain Labour's defeat in the 1983 election.

- Some claimed that some of Labour's policies were 'too left-wing' for the 'average' voter's tastes. Although policies on unemployment were favoured, policies on nuclear disarmament, for example, were felt to be simply too extreme. Those who adopted this explanation suggested that in order for Labour to gain future election success it had to move towards the 'centre ground' of politics.
- Others claimed that the Labour Party suffered a 'credibility gap'. Many of the electorate felt that Labour's very public internal divisions placed widespread doubt in the minds of voters as to their suitability for government.

Thatcherism can be seen to have acted as a bridge between the libertarian and social authoritarian elements in New Right thinking (see Section 2.10). Some, however, are sceptical as to whether Thatcherism as a distinct political ideology ever existed as such. They suggest that what we now call 'Thatcherism' was no more than an effective (in terms of gaining popular public support) set of short-term pragmatic and practical responses to changing social and economic conditions. In other words they say it was not a premeditated and formulated social philosophy.

Others, such as Hall (1984), see Thatcher's particular brand of 'popular capitalism' as a form of 'authoritarian populism' – a distinctive set of political strategies which are based on strong leadership from above and with a mass appeal. As Hall comments on the growth of New Right politics:

There can be no doubt about it: the move to the right no longer looks like a temporary swing of the pendulum. On the national political stages of Britain and the United States and at the international meetings the spotlight has veered over to the ideas and rhetoric of the New Right. Nowhere has this been more apparent than in Maggie Thatcher's austere kingdom. But it would be wrong to identify the success of the British radical right solely with the personality of Mrs Thatcher and her hard-nosed cronies. Although they have given the swing to the right a distinctive personal stamp, the deeper movement is a form of authoritarian populism which has great appeal to the average punter.
(Hall, 1984, p. 24)

Labour in the 1992 General Election

The 1992 General Election brought another victory for the Conservative Party. As with the 'landslide' of the 1983 election, when Labour suffered their greatest loses ever, the 1992 result was seen as a bitter defeat for them (although in 1992 the Conservative majority dropped to just 21 seats, a loss of 80 seats from the 1987 result). This time, still in the aftermath of the claims of the demise of Labour and the rise of the 'middle ground' in response to the 1987 and 1983 results, yet another rethink took place among British political commentators. The essential question now was not whether Labour would lose, but the even more pessimistic 'Can Labour ever win again?'

Crewe (1992) suggests that Labour could have won the 1992 election. The implementation of the massively unpopular 'poll tax' had turned many away from the Conservatives, and there was rising unemployment and concern over 'fat cat' wages to heads of privatized companies. Given this scenario, a shift back towards 'traditional' class voting patterns should have paved the way to a Labour victory. Yet, despite all this, Labour still lost. As Crewe asks: 'Why did Labour lose (yet again)?'

Crewe argues that Labour lost the 1992 election owing to the way in which the public perceived the then Labour leader, Neil Kinnock, as not competent to rule the country, and the Labour Party in general as likely to mismanage the economy. Crewe also suggests that many Liberal Democrat voters may well have returned to the Conservative Party as a method to stop Labour coming to power. Therefore, the Conservatives did not so much 'win' the election, as Labour 'lost' it. Or, to put it another way, the Conservatives won only because the electorate did not wish Labour to do so.

The political challenge

Gamble (1994), in his 'Loves Labour lost', suggested that Labour had a real political challenge on their hands after four concurrent election defeats:

Conservative dominance will not be easily overturned. The Conservatives are entrenched and their opponents are divided. The party enjoys many advantages over its competitors – in funding, membership, and press and business support. Its ideas are the ruling ideas. It has set the policy agenda for more than a decade, and it can rely on a large core vote which is concentrated in the south of England, where the bulk of the constituencies now are.
(Gamble, 1994, p. 44)

Gamble raises some very important issues here. Success at the ballot box is a much more complex process than just winning favour with the electorate. It is necessary to consider the ability a party has to attract new voters or young voters, the type and success of campaign its members can put together, and its public image in – and treatment by – the press and other media. Facing all these dimensions of a successful election campaign, Gamble did not think a Labour victory would come easily:

. . . Labour will do well to continue its advance at the next election. It would be an exceptional result for Labour to win the next election outright. But it is not impossible. Much depends on the ability of the leadership to unite the party around a set of policies and a political style that can give Labour a distinctive, radical profile and broaden its appeal. Labour will not win the kind of landslide it requires unless it breaks decisively with its past and helps to create a momentum for radical change which gives voters positive reasons for switching to Labour. Geography, social structure, and history all seem to be against it. But British politics remains unpredictable. The country is in a mess, and many of the solutions of the 1980s have been discredited. Labour has an opportunity to relaunch itself and become the focus of a new radical politics. Will it take it?

(Gamble, 1994, p. 44)

The 1997 General Election

While the 1992 General Election had been held against the backdrop of changes within the Conservative Party epitomized by the transition (in 1990) from Margaret Thatcher to John Major as party leader and Prime Minister, the 1997 General Election was held against the backdrop of the considerable transformation of the Labour Party, enshrined in the leadership of Tony Blair. The launch of 'New Labour' as an attempt to communicate a clear break with the party's past and the increasing importance of the ideas of ethical socialism and communitarianism (see Section 2.10) within the party are some examples of this.

While it was clear this transformation had led to a resurgence in support for Labour as expressed in opinion polls (see page 694) there were fears that it might lead to the danger of alienating the party's traditional base of support in the trade unions and the working class.

Despite his image as a 'grey man' leading a government staggering from one crisis to the next, John Major's Conservative administration had managed to hold on to power for the full duration of its five-year term of office (ending in 1997). The Wirral South by-election held on 27 February 1997 and won by Labour with a majority of 7888 (a swing of 17.2 per cent), did not provide much basis for optimism about the impending General Election in the Conservative camp, thus fuelling expectations that 1997 would see the Labour Party returning to power for the first time since 1979. On 1 May 1997, the General Election duly arrived and the results are summarized in Table 17.2.

Table 17.2 UK General Election 1997 – summary of results

Party	MPs elected	Share of the vote (%)
Labour	419	43
Conservative	165	31
Liberal Democrats	46	17
Others	29	9

The long-awaited victory of the Labour Party clearly undermined the idea that Labour would never govern again and that the Conservatives would hold power in perpetuity, a view often expressed in the 1980s. However, the transformation in the Labour Party since 1992 means that its significance in terms of the continuing debate about class and voting are more difficult to analyse. Does the Labour victory mean class is still important, or is it an example of its demise?

Activity

Obtain reports on the 1997 General Election from newspapers and magazines such as *New Statesman and Society* and the *Economist*. Use these, and any more substantial academic articles you are aware of, to consider how the result of the 1997 General Election will affect the models of voting behaviour outlined in this section.

I, A

In one sense, the victory of the Labour Party in 1997 means we are entering 'new times' though exactly what that will mean and whether it will be a Labour Government in free-market clothing remains to be seen. Nevertheless the transformation of the Labour Party under Tony Blair can certainly be seen as an example of trends which others have drawn more widely, including the notion that we now live in post-Marxist and even post-Socialist times.

Post-Marxism?

In contemporary political commentary the phrase 'New Times' is used by some on the Left to explain or evaluate the so-called 'death' or 'collapse' of Marxism. Since the collapse of the USSR, and the expansion of liberal-capitalism into eastern Europe, many in the West have claimed that Marxism is dead: a failed experiment. This claim can be seen as part of two wider, and related, trends:

- the crisis of confidence in left-wing politics experienced in the West over the past two decades
- the crisis of confidence within the Left itself, regarding its future, aims and goals.

In the UK in 1990 the Communist Party (CPGB) produced their 'Manifesto for New Times', outlining the future (or, at least, one of many possible futures) for left-of-centre politics in a society where New Right party politics were still dominant at the ballot box. The CPGB spelled out their reasons and interests for addressing the question: What is left for marxism in the modern world? As Nina Temple, secretary of the CPGB, notes:

The Manifesto's orientation to both the new times and a wider global perspective is essential to sustaining and renewing critical, democratic Marxism in Britain. It enables us to face honestly the corruption and authoritarianism perpetrated in eastern Europe in the name of Communism, and to recognize that with the collapse of that edifice we are left with one foot in the rubble. Only by distancing ourselves from the wreckage can we judge what remains of value from the tradition of Marxism in the twentieth century . . . The Manifesto represents a serious attempt to modernize Marxism, which demands a fundamental reassessment of the relationship between class interest and the rights of the individual and of nature. Improving that relationship means embracing pluralism and drawing contributions from other traditions.
(CPGB, 1990, 7–8)

Discussion point

What do you see as the future of Marxism in these so-called 'New Times'?

The approach to these 'New Times' adopted by the CPGB is to attempt to update Marxism, to make it more relevant to contemporary problems and more open to a plurality of Left ideas. Although the Left – 'old' and 'new' – and the Right may still be unsure what these 'New Times' are, one thing is certain: issues of power will always be central to social life, and therefore vital for sociology. These 'New Times' will provide both social actors and social scientists alike with fresh challenges and insights.

17.3 **Power and the state**

Of key importance in contemporary sociological analysis of power in society is an analysis of the role of the state. In fact the state is a relatively recent phenomenon in the overall history of humanity, but is in the contemporary world a major feature of all developed, developing and undeveloped societies. (See also Sections 2.2 and 12.4.)

The state can be seen as the organization or bureaucratic mechanism through which a government exercises power in society – whether that society in question has a democratic, oligarchical or totalitarian political system. The state includes the government, the law-making and law-keeping bodies and the civil service of a society. It operates within a given geographical space or territory, and many commentators have focused on the state's legal monopoly on legitimate force within these territories.

Defining the state

Sociologists today usually refer to a state as a 'nation-state'. The given territory in which the state operates is whole nations or countries. In ancient Greece, and taking Athens as an early example, city-states existed where the territory of state rule was confined to much smaller geographical and political spaces.

The expansion of the nation-state across the globe is a key feature of modernity and is seen to be the result of the legitimacy of nationalism as a political force. As Birch comments:

The entire surface of this planet, with the single exception of Antarctica, is now divided for purposes of government into territories known as nation-states. This is a relatively recent development in human history. Only two hundred years ago, there were fewer than twenty states with the shape and character that we should now recognize as deserving describing as nation-states . . . The transformation has come about largely because the doctrine of nationalism has both triumphed in Europe and been exported to the rest of the world.
(Birch, 1993, p. 13)

Dunleavy and O'Leary (1987) define the state according to five key ingredients.

1 *'The state is a recognizably separate institution or set of institutions, so differentiated from the rest of its society as to create identifiable public and private spheres.'*

2 *'The state is sovereign, or the supreme power, within its territory, and by definition the ultimate authority for all law, i.e. binding rules supported by coercive sanctions. Public law is made by state officials and backed by a formal monopoly of force.'*

3 *'The state's sovereignty extends to all the individuals within a given territory, and applies equally, even to those in formal positions of government or rule-making. Thus sovereignty is distinct from the personnel who at any given time occupy a particular role within the state.'*

4 *'The modern state's personnel are mostly recruited and trained for management in a bureaucratic manner.'*

5 *'The state has the capacity to extract monetary revenues (taxation) to finance its activities from its subject population.'*

(Dunleary and O'Leary, 1987, p. 2)

Citizenship

Living under the rule of a nation-state, one may become a 'citizen'. Citizenship is associated with a number of rights and duties, which differ according to the precise laws of each nation-state. For example, a citizen is required to pay taxes to support the state and to keep within the boundaries of its laws. If one breaks the law – and is caught – the state has the legitimate right to use the threat of force or actual force against that citizen.

State violence

For Weber (1968; orig. pub. 1921) the central defining characteristic of the state was its legitimate right to use coercion or violence within its defined territory (see also Sections 2.3 and 4.2). To this end, the state was an 'iron fist in a velvet glove' – underpinning its rule was a systematic use of force. Weber uses the term 'political community' to refer to the social space under the control of the state and its rules and domination through violence.

Discussion point

To what extent is the state benevolent, or is its rule based on the use of violence?

Sovereignty

Nation-states operate the right to self-rule, or to govern their affairs in an autonomous fashion within their defined territory. Nation-states are therefore *sovereign* – they have legitimate legal authority within their political space and are not answerable to outside forces.

In theory this concept of sovereignty is a clear one, but in practice the operation of nation-states in the contemporary world is not clear-cut. Some combine or give up part of their sovereignty to global political and/or economic organizations or powers, such as NATO or the European Union. Some human rights and civil rights laws and organizations cut across state sovereignties, yet are enforced differently.

Functionalism and the state

For Emile Durkheim, participatory democracy was an impossible ideal. Given the large scale of modern nations, democratic rule could only be established by using the state as a mechanism through which to define collective moral sentiments in law, and to ensure that these collective sentiments are followed.

In this view, the state is essential for the democratic process in society. It allows for increased communication between the masses and their rulers so as to ensure that the will of those who rule is also the will of the collective. Therefore the state is essential for social solidarity (see also Sections 2.3 and 2.10):

... solidarity comes from the inside and not from the outside. Men are attached to one another as naturally as the atoms of a mineral and the cells of an organism. The affinity which they hold for each other is based on sympathy ... Now, at each moment in its development, this solidarity is expressed externally by an appropriate structure. The state is one of these structures. The state is the external and visible form of sociability.

(Durkheim, 1988, p. 56; orig. pub. 1886)

Discussion point

Does the state serve the interests of the ruling group, or help to establish collective sentiment in society?

The functionalist view of power

For Parsons (1963, 1967), power is a commodity to be shared among all those in society. It is not held by an élite group who use it in their own interests. Instead, Parsons' ideas on power focus on the traditional functionalist notions of 'value consensus' and normative harmony and stability (see also Section 2.4). For Parsons and other functionalists, social goals are collective in nature: those who rule do so because they are allowed to by the majority, but only if those who rule act in the interests of the majority, following collective sentiments.

This Parsonian functionalist image of power can be compared to modern banking. Thus politicians are like brokers or bankers, being allowed to 'borrow' or 'invest' the power given to them by their subjects or citizens; but if those subjects are unhappy about the uses to which this power is being put, they can withdraw their power and put their support in the hands of others.

Functionalists see the nature of the stratification system to be such that those who obtain the highest positions, with the highest rewards, are generally those who deserve to be there. Thus, power is given from the collective to a suitable set of leaders who ensure that the collective sentiments are met in a democratic fashion. If this is not the case, then power can be withdrawn at times of elections and referendums.

Criticisms of the functionalist approach

It is worth noting that the image of power central to the work of Parsons is based on a very specific set of ideological principles – in much the same way as other perspectives are 'political' or 'ideological' in nature, such as Marxism, feminism or the New Right. Parsons sees the model of western liberal democracy as the 'best' or most suitable model of power in society. For this reason some critics – usually from a left-of-centre approach – have argued that functionalism, and Parsonian functionalism in particular, is nothing more than an academic justification or legitimation for western politics, and for capitalism in particular.

Marxists would point out, as would some feminists, that in so-called western democracies the existence of elections does nothing to change those who are truly in power, who are seen to exist behind those voted for, possibly manipulating those in government for their own ends. Furthermore, those societies characterized as liberal democracies still contain great inequalities, whether they be based on class, gender, ethnicity, age or (dis)ability. (See Chapters 4, 5, 6 and Section 14.8.) Therefore, elections do nothing to solve the problems of those truly in need – who appear to be ignored from the power of 'collective sentiments' given to political leaders to 'borrow'.

Classical pluralism

Both sociologically and ideologically, the approach adopted by pluralism owes more to functionalism than to any other perspective. As has happened with many other perspectives in recent years, some pluralists have attempted to update the theory in the light of changes in society.

The core of all pluralist thinking – as the name suggests – is that the nature and distribution of power in western liberal capitalist societies is based on a *plurality* of power centres. Politics – the distribution of power, the conflict of wills – is based on the principles of competition, conflict and compromise.

- *Competition* – Political parties, pressure groups and other individuals, communities and organizations genuinely compete with each other for the sharing out of power.
- *Conflict* – These various groups represent conflicting interests, yet in their competition some interests win at some times, others at other times. In this way, all interests are represented and catered for. (See also Section 2.6.)
- *Compromise* – Although politics is about competition or the conflict between various interests, this conflict operates within an overall framework of consensus. At the end of the day, a relatively

stable society is created since all interests are being met at some level.

It is important to note that pluralism does not assume the existence of an all-encompassing value consensus as does functionalism. Rather than a single moral unity, society is seen as split into sections, or sectional interests. It is possible for an individual to have interests represented by more than one group, and to be in harmony with other individuals over one issue, but in conflict with the same individuals over another issue. (See also Section 10.2.)

When it comes to voting behaviour, pluralists believe that an individual votes for the party which represents the majority of his or her interests at that time. Other interests, not offered by the political parties on offer, are catered for by non-political party political groups such as pressure groups which are much wider in membership, but narrower in focus.

Who controls community power?

A classic piece of pluralist research into community power structures is provided by Dahl's work *Who Governs?* (1961), in which he studies how local politics is structured in the American city of New Haven. Dahl's central question was this:

In a political system where nearly every adult may vote but where knowledge, wealth, social position, access to officials, and other resources are unequally distributed, who actually governs?
(Dahl, 1961, p. 1)

Or, to put this in more detail:

Now it has always been held that if equality of power among citizens is possible at all – a point on which many political philosophers have had grave doubts – then surely considerable equality of social conditions is a necessary prerequisite. But if, even in America, with its universal creed of democracy and equality, there are great inequalities in the conditions of different citizens, must there not also be great inequalities in the capacities of different citizens to influence the decisions of their various governments? And if, because they are unequal in other conditions, citizens of a democracy are unequal in power to control their government, then who in fact does govern? How does a 'democratic' system work amid inequality of resources?
(Dahl, 1961, p. 3)

Dahl was interested in discovering whether a single élite group were responsible for decision-making, or whether – according to traditional pluralist ideas – decision-making was the product of a plurality of local power bases whereby a variety of local interests were represented. Dahl looked specifically at the election of the mayor of New Haven, the development of local land-use and the way in which education was organized and structured.

In order to conduct his study, Dahl adopted the method of looking at the decisions made on the above issues – and at who it was making those decisions. Dahl contends that if one looks at a number of decisions made on a range of issues within a given time period, as he did, in every case where a decision has been made a number of different interests had had their say in the decision-making process. From Dahl's pluralist viewpoint, this proves the plurality of power in New Haven.

Dahl concludes that, rather than an élite group dominating these areas of local political life, power and the ability to influence the decision-making process was in the hands of the wider community – through the representation of their interests by pressure groups. He claims that those in official governmental office – such as the major and other politicians – were forced to listen to and consult the local community before making major decisions. In this way, the various interests in New Haven were engaged, from the pluralist perspective, in the democratic processes of conflict, competition and compromise.

Classical pluralism and the state

A pluralist explanation of the role of the state in contemporary society rests on the ideas of competition, compromise and negotiation.

In conjunction with other non-state agencies such as pressure groups, political parties not in government, local councils etc., a process of competition, compromise and negotiation takes place over the resources provided by the state. The power of the state is thus exercised by a variety of élites working both within the state and from without, and the various interests of the population are met.

The nature of society is such that a functionalist-style value consensus is not believed to exist. Instead there is conflict between the divided interests of the population, but a conflict which is resolved through the wider interplay of competition and conflict between élites. Unlike Marxists such as Gramsci and Poulantzas who suggest that the state's apparent role of conflict-reducer and consensus-producer is merely a 'smokescreen' or an ideological veil to hide the true inequalities of power in society, pluralists genuinely believe in this role. For them the state operates for the good of all.

Neo-pluralism: from classical to élite

Commentators have drawn a distinction between 'classical' pluralist thinking, and the more recent, revised, 'élite' pluralism.

Marsh (1983), for example, identifies a number of different ways of classfying pluralist theorizing concerning the nature of power and the role played by pressure groups in the political or decision-making processes:

The classical pluralist position ... is no longer accepted by the majority of liberal democrats as an accurate description of the distribution of power in contemporary liberal democracies.
(Marsh, 1983, p. 11)

In drawing this distinction between 'classical' and 'élite' pluralisms, Marsh provides the following definitions.

In the classical pluralist position power is seen as diffuse rather than concentrated. Society is viewed as consisting of a large number of groups, representing all the significant, different interests of the population, who compete with one another for influence over government. This competition occurs within a consensus about the 'rules of the game'.
(Marsh, 1983, p. 10)

Elite pluralism is seen by Marsh to differ from classical pluralism in two main ways:

First, there is a greater acceptance that all individuals may not be represented by groups and that some citizens are therefore under-represented by the interest group system. ... Secondly, the élite pluralist admits that groups are less open and responsive to their members than the classical pluralists assumed because all organizations tend to be hierarchically run.
(Marsh, 1983, pp. 11 and 12)

Classical pluralism, then, tends to assume that all interests are represented – that power is shared equally. However, it is possible to identify some interests which are represented more readily and more successfully than others: those which support the ideas, values and culture of élites in society – or, at least, those interests which do not expose, attack or undermine the interests of élites.

Thus, in western capitalist or industrial societies, although both capital (business) and labour (workers) are represented by pressure groups, trade unions, associations etc., many would contend that the interests of capital are taken up by those in power more than the interests of labour. Simply because a pressure group or interest exists does not automatically mean that it will be successful in influencing the decision-making or power-holding processes of society.

As Marsh illustrates, this is the point at which some have attempted to revise pluralism to develop what has been called 'élite pluralism': to suggest that whereas some groups or interests are successful, other are less so. Power is still seen as a process of competition, but now the rules of the game are recognized to be fixed in favour of some at the expense of others.

Classical élite theories

All 'élite theories' are based on the identification of a narrow ruling group who rule over the majority in society. Whereas some élite theories are left-of-centre, and therefore are highly critical of this two-tier social arrangement, others see élite rule as necessary. The approach known as 'classical élite theory' fits into the second of these types. These 'classical' ideas are usually associated with the writings at the turn of the century of Vilfredo Pareto (1963) and Gaetano Mosca (1939) in Italy.

In this approach, élites who have the power to rule the state become so as a result of superior personal qualities. Since, therefore, they are most suited to such élite positions, their rule is natural: some people are fit to be rulers and others only fit to be ruled. This unequal situation was seen by Pareto and Mosca to be characteristic of all human societies, and therefore an inevitable consequence of social life.

The ideas of Pareto are very similar to those of Niccolo Machiavelli (1469–1527), another Italian political scientist and philosopher. Machiavelli is most noted for his work *The Prince* in which he outlines his recommendations for a successful élite ruler. He draws a distinction between two types of rule which an élite or élite group can adopt: rule through legal means, and rule through force. Machiavelli believed that while the development of a legal system places humanity above the animals, sometimes the law is not enough and force must be used to secure rule. He draws an analogy between two types of animals which, he argued, élite rulers would do well to mimic. These were the fox for cunning and the lion for the use of strength and force.

Machiavelli's advice for élites is that rule over a majority will only be successful by the individual who displays courage, boldness, cunning and strength – which he refers to as *virtu*. The ideas of Machiavelli are largely associated with authoritarian, right-wing political ideas.

Pareto adopts the same distinction between the fox and the lion. However he suggests that, even with the use of cunning or strength, there will probably come a time when one set of élites will be replaced by another. The nature of élite rulers is such that they are easily corruptible, giving way to a life of power and pleasure. When this happens, élite rule 'circulates' and another set of élites come to power.

The other theorist associated with classical élite theory is Gaetano Mosca. Like Pareto and Machiavelli, he too believed that élite rule is normal, natural and inevitable – and that élites are those who possess characteristics which separate them from the 'ordinary' masses, in his case, mainly organizational skills.

Criticisms of classical élite theories

For Mosca, democracy was the government by élites who represented the interests of the people – an idea which has a contemporary expression in some pluralist thought. Mosca suggested that élites, if drawn from a variety of social backgrounds, will be able to serve the interests of the people in a democratic fashion.

From a Marxist perspective, Bottomore is critical of the association of democracy with élite rule. He claims that 'representative democracies' are:

. . . an imperfect realization of democracy, to the extent that it does permanently exclude the many from any experience of government.
(Bottomore, 1993, p. 90)

For Bottomore, all that such élite rule serves to do is further the interests and privileges of the élite few at the expense of the many.

Radical élite theory

Hunter (1953), in his work *Community Power Structure: A Study of Decision Makers*, can be seen to approach the issue of 'who governs?' from a very different ideological and methodological stance from that of Dahl's pluralism (see page 704). As an early example of 'radical élite theory', Hunter studied the number of groups involved in a local community's decision-making processes, in order to identify the existence of élites who controlled the processes and who, as a group, ruled over the population of a city.

To conduct his research Hunter used a panel of local people to identify those who they felt were in positions of significant power in the local community. He then compared these 'reputations' together in order to identify those considered most powerful. A common set of names was drawn up.

As Hunter himself notes:

It has been evident to the writer for some years that policies on vital matters affecting community life seem to appear suddenly. They are acted on, but with no precise knowledge on the part of the majority of citizens as to how these policies originated or by whom they are really sponsored. Much is done, but much is left undone. Some of the things done appear to be manipulated to the advantage of relatively few.
(Hunter, 1953, p. 1)

Hunter rejects Dahl's pluralist-based notion that the community is involved in the decision-making process through the help of pressure groups. Instead, studying what he refers to as 'Regional City', a city with a population of about a half million, Hunter identifies the existence of a narrow group of élites who exercise power over the majority – who make decisions for their own benefit and for the benefit of others like them.

C. W. Mills' *The Power Elite* (1956) was also written with the élite composition of America in mind. Although Mills felt he had been successful in identifying a number of élites in America, unlike some pluralists and Pareto and Mosca, he was highly critical of their existence – believing the existence of élites to be highly undemocratic. He identifies three élite groups which together form what he describes as the 'power élite':

The power élite is composed of men whose positions enable them to transcend the ordinary environments of ordinary men and women; they are in positions to make decisions having major consequences. ... For they are in command of the major hierarchies and organizations of modern society. They rule the big corporations. They run the machinery of the state and claim its prerogatives. They direct the military establishment. They occupy the strategic command posts of the social structure, in which are now centred the effective means of the power and the wealth and the celebrity which they enjoy.
(Mills, 1956, pp. 3–4)

These three sets of élite groups are:

- industry/business
- the military
- the American government.

Between them, capitalism in America is governed, controlled and maintained in the interests of these three groups. Clearly, not every one working in these three areas can be seen to represent an 'élite', but those in the top positions of the hierarchies of these three areas certainly do. Mills suggests that these people are known to each other, and so rule in conjunction with one another. However, he notes:

Despite their social similarity and psychological affinities, the members of the power élite do not constitute a club having a permanent membership with fixed and formal boundaries. It is of the nature of the power élite that within it there is a good deal of shifting about, and that it thus does not consist of one small set of the same men in the same positions in the same hierarchies.
(Mills, 1956, p. 287)

Thus, the power élite can be seen as a relatively stable set of élite positions along with which comes great influence and power. The owners or holders of these positions may change, but the positions themselves will continue to exist, so power will continue to be concentrated in the hands of a small power élite.

Mills suggests that those in each of the three strands of the power élite are similar people. He puts this down to the process of socialization within these organizations (training on the job) and the selection processes used to choose their personnel – and especially their 'top personnel'.

Mills thus regards the top positions of American society to be based on this three-strand power élite model. What implications does this have for those members of the general population who are subject to the power held by the power élite? Mills himself asks this question:

But how about the bottom? As all these trends have become visible at the top and on the middle, what has been happening to the great American public? If the top is unprecedentedly powerful and increasingly unified and wilful; if the middle zones are increasingly a semi-organized stale-mate – in what shape is the bottom, in what condition is the public at large? The rise of the power élite, we shall now see, rests on, and in some ways is part of, the transformation of the publics of America into a mass society.
(Mills, 1956, p. 297)

Hence Mills regards the public of America to be largely a 'mass': uncritical, unable to engage in collective action, passive to the rule and control of the power élite. (See also Sections 10.3 and 15.10.) He suggests that the rise of a 'mass society' at the very bottom of the social structure allows the activities of the power élite to go largely unquestioned, and to remain unchecked. Those at the top wield power, those at the very bottom have accepted 'their lot' and are slowly turning into a passive mass:

The top of modern American society is increasingly unified, and often seems willfully co-ordinated: at the top there has emerged an élite of power. The middle levels are a drifting set of stale-mated, balancing forces: the middle does not link the bottom with the top. The bottom of this society is politically fragmented, and even as a passive fact, increasingly powerless: at the bottom there is emerging a mass society.
(Mills, 1956, p. 324)

Categories of élite models

Marsh (1983) identifies two types or models of 'élite theories' in the contemporary sociological literature concerning the nature of rule in western capitalist societies:

- fragmented élites
- veto groups.

The 'fragmented élite model' suggests that while élites exist, they lack real direction, purpose and cohesion in their rule. These élites compete with each other for power, and therefore do not represent a stable, ruling force. Decisions are taken with the immediate concerns of the élite group in mind, with little consideration of the 'national interest'. Marsh indicates how, from the viewpoint of this model, many decisions are made by government, independently from these élites in power.

In contrast, the 'veto group model' suggests that although a number of élite groups may exist, one is dominant and therefore is in a position of power and rule. Those that do hold power, do so through their relationships with the economy: they rule by virtue of the structural positions they hold.

Marsh himself subscribes to the 'fragmented élite' model of power in society. He suggests that contemporary British society is characterized by a variety of élite groups which are not united in the holding, sharing and exercising of power: even within political parties and other élite organizations there may be division and disagreement.

In the final analysis, Marsh argues that those élite groups who do rule are usually those associated with the economy:

The crucial power of any group results not from its interest group activity but rather from its structural position in the economy . . . decisions taken by large companies or city institutions have an almost immediate direct effect on the economy, and thus on the government's prospects of re-election. Groups with such power cannot be ignored . . .
(Marsh, 1983, p. 15)

However, the nature of élite power, and its distribution, is such that it is in constant change. Power, for Marsh, is above all else a fluid and dynamic set of relationships.

Orthodox Marxism

For Marx and Engels, power is based in an individual's class location in society. From this viewpoint, power will only be 'plural' or communal in a society which is class-less: where no one ruling group owns the means or forces of production, and uses this to dominate or rule over the rest of society (see Sections 2.4 and 4.10). As Marx and Engels state in *The Communist Manifesto*:

The history of all hitherto existing society is the history of class struggles. . . . But every class struggle is a political struggle.
(Marx and Engels, 1967, pp. 79 and 90; orig. pub. 1848)

Power is seen here primarily as a result of economic ownership. This power is largely accepted by those ruled over – the working classes – owing to the use of both coercion and ideology as control mecha-

nisms. Many Marxist writers see the working classes as in a state of 'false class consciousness', unable to see for themselves the true nature of society under capitalist control: the inequalities of power are due to inequalities of wealth (see Section 14.8). In this orthodox view, the state is an instrument of ruling class power.

Élite rule or ruling classes?

A distinction is usually drawn between the concept of an élite and the idea of a ruling class – particularly the Marxist notion of a ruling class. While a ruling class is an élite in one sense, since collectively its members experience power, status and prestige over and above that held by the masses, in Marxism a class is defined in terms of its ownership of the means or forces of production. Whereas the working classes own nothing except their labour power which they sell to the ruling class, the latter, by definition, own the means or forces of production.

On the other hand, an élite or élite group can still experience the lifestyle, life-chances and power of a ruling class but not actually own the means of production. The term 'élite', then, is a much wider term than 'ruling class' and could refer to members of government, non-elected high state positions etc.

Orthodox Marxism and the state

Like the classical élite theorists earlier, Marxists too see power to lie in the hands of a privileged few, but this situation is not seen as desirable. For Marx, the 'end of history' will result in the establishment of a truly classless society where the means of production will be communal and serve to the benefit of all. (See Section 4.10.)

In the orthodox Marxist treatment of the state, it is seen as a tool in the class struggle, supporting the interests of the ruling, capitalist class. As Marx and Engels state in *The Communist Manifesto*:

The executive of the modern state is but a committee for managing the common affairs of the whole bourgeoisie.
(Marx and Engels, 1967, p. 82; orig. pub. 1848)

The origins of the state

Frederick Engels claims, in his work *The Origin of the Family, Private Property and the State*' (1972, orig. pub. 1884), that the origins of the state lie in the creation of private property. While private property did not exist, and property was collectively owned, a ruling group did not exist and therefore the state was not needed to protect and preserve their unequal rule. However, once property was established – once a surplus was produced within a society – class distinctions developed when one group claimed this property or surplus for themselves. The state is then needed to control class conflict. The newly established ruling class had 'created new organs to protect their interests', and:

As the state arose from the need to hold class antagonisms in check, but as it arose, at the same time, in the midst of the conflict of these classes, it is, as a rule, the state of the most powerful, economically dominant class, which, through the medium of the state, becomes also the politically dominant class, and thus acquires new means of holding down and exploiting the oppressed class.
(Engels, 1972, p. 160)

The state in communist society

At the 'end of history', with the establishment of a classless society, Marx believed that the state would eventually wither away because it would no longer be needed. This would happen after a temporary period immediately after the revolution in which we would see a 'dictatorship of the proletariat' of the state – using its power in the name of the establishment of a fully classless society.

Orthodox Marxist criticisms of classical pluralism

To a certain extent, Marxist and neo-Marxist criticisms of pluralism take as their starting point the observation that only some interests are successful in their representation.

Viewed from a Marxist perspective, the operation of pressure groups is not democratic, far from it. They may well create the illusion of democracy, the illusion of a representative political system; but in the final analysis, those interests which do not support the activities or interests of the ruling capitalist class will not be taken seriously, or will even be actively suppressed.

It might even be contended that some pressure groups and their leaders will not attempt to change or promote some issues for fear of damaging their reputation or potential success in other areas. By 'playing the game', by adopting the tactics whereby some issues are ignored and losses accepted and others are taken up and fought, pressure groups may be more successful – especially given that they operate on limited budgets and may not be able to afford a lengthy, time-consuming and expensive campaign on an issue they are sure to have ignored or to lose.

Problems with the orthodox Marxist theory of the state

Parkin (1979) argues that the ideas of orthodox Marxism on the role of the state in society need to be updated for contemporary times. He suggests that Marx did not have a fully developed theory of the state, just a handful of comments made about the state while in the process of discussing other issues. Secondly, the few ideas Marx did have on the state contain within them what appears to be a contradiction.

On the one hand, Marx refers to the state as an instrument of the rule of the capitalist class. As Parkin comments:

The classical statement at the conceptual level is of course the elliptical pronouncement in The Communist Manifesto *in which the capitalist state is likened to an executive committee charged with the workaday task of managing the affairs of the bourgeoisie. The state acts in a fairly uncomplicated way as the direct spokesman and protector of the exploiting class. Marx's own dismissive comment in* The German Ideology *that the state is 'nothing more than' this, seems to squash quite firmly any idea that it raised problems of any real theoretical import.*
(Parkin, 1979, pp. 121–2)

On the other hand, Parkin highlights the fact that Marx, in his work, *The Eighteenth Brumaire of Louis Bonaparte* (1984; orig. pub 1852), suggests another, much more complicated, relationship between the state and the ruling class, where the state has a *relative autonomy* from the ruling class. In this second view, Marx appears to suggest that the state does serve the interests of the capitalist class, but is not its puppet: the state serves the interests of capitalism, but without being its 'executive committee' *per se*.

In the example provided by Marx of the state of Louis Bonaparte in France *circa* 1850, we see a situation develop where a stalemate exists in the class conflict between the ruling class and the working class. Under these conditions the state itself operates as a relatively independent political force or power. The state operates of its own accord, but in doing so takes a course of action which is beneficial to the ruling class, and once more helps to preserve and protect their rule.

This idea, that the state has some degree of 'relative autonomy' from the ruling class, is a popular

Discussion point
Is the UK governed by a ruling class, by a ruling élite or by 'the people'?

Discussion point
Is the state merely a tool of the ruling class, or does it have some independence?

one in much contemporary Marxist and neo-Marxist theorizing.

The state in capitalist society

Miliband (1973) echoes the first interpretation of the ideas of Marx and Engels – as illustrated by Parkin earlier – that the state is an instrument in the hands of the ruling class. He suggests that the nature and operation of the state in society is of central importance in any understanding of the nature of political and class struggle in society:

More than ever before men now live in the shadow of the state. What they want to achieve, individually or in groups, now mainly depends on the state's sanction and support. But since that sanction and support are not bestowed indiscriminately, they must, ever more directly, seek to influence and shape the state's power and purpose, or try and appropriate it altogether. It is for the state's attention, or for its control, that men compete; and it is against the state that beat the waves of social conflict. It is to an ever greater degree the state which men encounter as they confront other men. This is why, as social beings, they are also political beings, whether they know it or not. It is possible not to be interested in what the state does; but it is not possible to be unaffected by it.
(Miliband, 1973, p. 3)

Miliband is critical of élite theories and of pluralism, both of which, be believes, operate to hide the real nature of the state in society. He believes they ignore the fact that the interests of the state are the interests of capitalism, and in particular of the ruling class themselves. Those in the state machinery operate in the interests of those who own the means of production.

Neo-Marxism

In the work of Gramsci, an Italian neo-Marxist, we see another conception of the nature of the state, different again from that of Miliband. Gramsci (1971), writing in a Fascist prison in the 1930s, stresses the role played by *hegemony* in class domination in capitalist societies. He notes that in order to secure their position of leadership, the capitalist class need to rule through a combination of both repressive and ideological means over all other classes – to dominate totally a class society. (See also Sections 10.6 and 15.6.)

Hegemony refers to rule through ideological means: to rule through the consent of the masses by manipulating and organizing this consent. The state is the tool through which this consent is manipulated and controlled – it operates to create the hegemony of the ruling group. As Gramsci suggests:

... the state is the entire complex of practical and theoretical activities with which the ruling class not only justifies and maintains its dominance, but manages to win the active consent of those over whom it rules.
(Gramsci, 1971, p. 244)

However, in order to make the rule of the ruling class seem legitimate, the state operates with a degree of 'relative autonomy' since it makes concessions with the ruled masses and is affected by popular social-democratic struggles. In this sense, the state arbitrates between the classes, yet it is not a genuine arbitration since, at the final analysis, the ruling class hegemony is protected.

Gramsci divides the operations of the state into two areas, civil society and political society:

... it should be remarked that the general notion of the state includes elements which need to be referred back to the notion of civil society (in the sense that one might say that state = political society + civil society, in other words hegemony protected by the armour of coercion).
(Gramsci, 1971, pp. 262–3)

Collectively, the two halves of the state are referred to by Gramsci as the 'integral state'. In defining the relationships between these two levels of the 'integral state', he writes:

What we can do, for the moment, is to fix two major superstructural 'levels': the one that can be called 'civil society', that is the ensemble of organisms commonly called 'private', and that of 'political society'. ... These two levels correspond on the one hand to the function of 'hegemony' which the dominant group exercises throughout society and on the other hand to that of 'direct domination' or command exercised through the state and 'juridical' government.
(Gramsci, 1971, p. 12)

Thus, Gramsci draws a distinction between the use of force or domination by the state (political society), and the use of ideological means to secure hegemony (civil society). The majority of Gramsci's work focuses on the latter at the expense of the former.

Structural Marxism

A structuralist account (see Sections 2.5 and 2.10) of the role of the state under capitalism is offered by Poulantzas (1980). Like Miliband, he stresses the importance of the state in contemporary life:

Who today can escape the question of the state and power? Who indeed does not talk about it? ... Whether overtly or not, all twentieth-century political theory has basically posed the same question: what is the relationship between the state, power and social classes?
(Poulantzas, 1980, p. 11)

However, whereas Miliband stresses the first reading of Marx, that the state is an instrument of the ruling class, Poulantzas emphasizes the second reading – that the state has a degree of relative autonomy from the ruling class.

By taking a structuralist approach, Poulantzas locates the operation of the state in the division highlighted by Marx between the economic base and the superstructure of society (see Section 2.3). Since the position of the state, in this view, is in the superstructure, it will automatically follow the needs of those who own and control the economic base – the ruling class. Unlike Miliband, he does not regard the class composition of the élites who run the state as important: regardless of who they are they are structurally predisposed to serve the interests of capitalism.

While the state is structurally determined to act out the will of the ruling class, it is not run by the ruling class on a day-to-day basis. Rather it is governed by those in government. Thus the state has a relatively autonomy, but even with this, will always work in the interests of those for whom capitalist society is structured – the owners of the means of production.

In defining the state, Poulantzas follows the work of Althusser (see Sections 2.5 and 2.10) in drawing a distinction between:

• the repressive state apparatus
• the ideological state apparatus.

As Poulantzas comments:

The State's role in the constitution of the relations of production and in the delimitation-reproduction of social classes derives from the fact that it does not confine itself to the exercise of organized physical repression. The state plays an equally specific role in organizing ideological relations and the dominant ideology.
(Poulantzas, 1980, p. 28)

This distinction is very similar to that made by Gramsci between 'political society' (domination) and 'civil society' (ideology). So the state maintains the superiority of the capitalist class not only by the use of force or repression, as through the army or police and law courts, but also through ideological means – such as through the media, education, the family and other institutions of socialization. (See Sections 7.4, 8.2, 10.1 and 15.6.)

Poulantzas suggests that too much emphasis has been given, in contemporary Marxist and neo-Marxist thought, to ideological domination. This, he argues, has been at the expense of under-stating physical domination, a feature of the state much discussed originally by Weber. While Poulantzas supports the work of Gramsci in highlighting the ideological power which keeps capitalism together in the face of economic contradictions and problems of legitimacy, we should not ignore repression altogether:

Only too often does emphasis on the state's role in ideological relations lead to underestimation of its repressive functions. By repression should be understood first and foremost organized physical violence in the most material sense of the term: violence to the body. . . . the state is always rooted in its physical constraint, manipulation and consumption of bodies.
(Poulantzas, 1980, p. 29)

Concern with the physical manipulation of bodies as a form of power also surfaced in the later work of post-structuralist Michel Foucault (see page 718).

Who rules the UK?

The debate about whether the members of an élite or ruling class rule society can be seen to be divided into several issues of concern to sociologists.

• How do we define 'élite' and 'class'?
• Is it possible for an upper class to exist, but not to be a 'ruling' class? Are these concepts interchangeable or separate? (See also Section 4.5.)
• Is it possible for a ruling class to use other 'élites' as their tools or instruments of power?
• Should we try to understand how state-élites and upper-class members rule together – how power is shared among the different types of élite groups and upper classes in society?

Suggested answers to these questions are many and varied. As Urry notes:

In Britain there are two sets of difficulties involved in the attempt to analyse whether there is a power élite (with or without group consciousness, coherence and conspiracy) or a ruling class. The first is lack of information. . . . The second is that the interpretation of this evidence very much depends on the general picture that one has of the workings of society as a whole. . . . The empirical information cannot in itself confirm or refute the hypothesis that there is a ruling class unless two other conditions exist. One is that specific criteria of this concept must be provided. The other is that a concept only makes sense and its value judged when it is placed within a whole set of other concepts which are theoretically related.
(Urry; in Urry and Wakeford, 1973, p. 8) (See also Section 3.3)

Westergaard and Resler (1976) have argued that concessions made by the state operate to increase hegemony by hiding class domination, and making the activities of the state appear legitimate. In making this claim, they are critical of pluralist ideas – where the welfare state is seen as a clear indication of the dismantling of the power of capital and the increased redistribution of wealth to the masses. For pluralists the nature of power is such that it is becoming shared by a variety of élites who represent, democratically, a variety of interests. Westergaard and Resler comment on this:

The trouble with this thesis is twofold. First, in so far as it is right, what it says is hardly worth saying. Second, its proponents studiously avert their gaze from questions that do matter. Because they then see nothing, they draw the conclusion that there is nothing to see.

(Westergaard and Resler, 1976, p. 245)

But, from their perspective, Westergaard and Resler argue that despite the development of a welfare state, power and wealth are still concentrated in the hands of a ruling class – and class conflict against this ruling group is being dampened by the arguments produced by pluralist theories. Thus social welfare is being made to seem like the establishment of equality in society, yet it is only a piecemeal, token gesture. The state still, ultimately, serves the interests of the ruling class. (See Sections 14.4 and 14.8.)

Westergaard and Resler suggest that 'power' is a difficult phenomenon to 'see' in social life, but the effects of power differences are obvious:

The continuing inequalities of wealth, income and welfare that divide the population are among the most crucial consequences – the most visible manifestations – of the division of power in a society such as Britain. Those inequalities reflect, while they also demonstrate, the continuing power of capital – the power, not just of capitalists and managers, but of the anonymous forces of property and the market. They also both reflect and demonstrate the orientation of state power.

(Westergaard and Resler, 1976. pp. 141–2)

They go further, and suggest that the problem with the pluralist notion that society is characterized by a plurality of interests and groups representing those interests is that:

. . . it tells us nothing. . . . There is no value, then, to the point that many pressures go to shape the outcome of events. It is obvious. The crucial questions concern the nature of the pressures and the direction of the outcome.

(Westergaard and Resler, 1976, pp. 245–6)

Thus, from a Marxist perspective, the pluralist notion that power resides in the competition between élites who in turn represent the interests of the local community is a dubious one. Instead, power resides in the ownership or non-ownership of the means or forces of production.

Contemporary applications of Marxism and radical élite theory

Scott's (1986) approach to the analysis of power in contemporary society appears to draw on the traditions of both Marxism and radical élite theory. Scott claims that the UK does still have an easily identifiable upper class, despite the claims made to the contrary by other traditions. However, he wishes to redefine this concept to make it more applicable to post-war capitalist societies:

Although there is widespread agreement that Britain did once have a sharply defined upper class, many researchers have argued that the twentieth century has seen its demise. This upper class was formed in the late nineteenth and early twentieth century from the landed, commercial and manufacturing classes of earlier periods, but was unable to sustain its position in the face of the economic trends of the twentieth century.

(Scott, 1986, p. 3)

Scott, however, disagrees with this interpretation. He claims that the upper class have not become an irrelevance, they do still exist and hold considerable power (see also Section 4.5). He rejects the pluralist-based 'managerialist position' which claims that, owing to changes in the production processes in industry and the development of shareholding of industry, the power and control of the upper classes has taken a back seat to the rising post-war power and influence of the manager. Instead, Scott claims that we have witnessed a 'depersonalization' of the ownership of property – where the property owned by the modern upper class is no longer the land, factories and industrial plants of yesteryear, but the assets, pension funds and insurance funds flickering on computer screens in global money markets.

Pluralists may claim that those individuals who make up the company boards which collectively own and control these monies come from wide backgrounds and are drawn from the 'new middle classes'. Scott argues, however, that close analysis of the types of people sitting on these company boards illustrates that along with these salaried middle classes there are still to be found a number of entrepreneurial capitalists who often own a majority of shares to give them control:

Top corporate decisions, therefore, are taken by a group of directors with significant shareholding interests, often with controlling blocks of shares, and with interests which are closely allied with those of the financial intermediaries. Directors and top executives are the beneficiaries of the structure of impersonal share ownership, and through their membership of the boards of banks and insurance companies are actively involved in taking decisions about the use of this impersonal 'institutional' share ownership. Top directors are tied together through the 'interlocking directorships' which are created whenever one person sits on two or more boards. Through these interlocking directorships a web of connections is created which ties together a large number of enterprises and casts the 'multiple directors' in a key role as co-ordinators of the business system as a whole.

(Scott, 1986, p. 6)

Scott himself asks, although an upper class undoubtedly exists, is it also a ruling class? He notes that those in top positions – those who have the opportunity to exercise control and power over others – do still tend to be drawn from the upper class:

Three in five top civil servants land quango jobs

ANDY MCSMITH

THREE out of five top-ranking civil servants in Britain receive jobs on quangos after retiring from service.

In his report Lord Nolan warned that the right to appoint or approve 10,000 quango appointments every year is giving Ministers 'considerable power of patronage'. He called for the creation of committees with independent members to advise on quango appointments, and a Commissioner for Public Appointments to monitor them.

The report added: 'Some argue that this is an unhealthy concentration of power . . . We share some of this concern, particularly about the absence of independent checks and balances.'

A survey by Labour MP Alan Milburn shows that 15 of the 25 civil servants who retired with the rank of permanent secretary in the past five years have quango posts.

He said: 'Whitehall is infested with a 'jobs for the boys' culture. Unlike the rest of the population, Sir Humphreys are finding nice little earners when they retire.'

Other former permanent secretaries have taken relatively modest positions on quangos, for instance as museum trustees. Sir Richard Lloyd Jones, former permanent secretary at the Welsh Office, agreed to take on an unpaid post as chairman of the Arts Council in addition to his paid job chairing the Staff Commission for Wales. But there has been no quango job for Sir Allan Green QC, who had to resign as Director of Public Prosecutions in 1991 after being caught soliciting near King's Cross in London.

Sir Duncan Nichol, former NHS chief executive, is also one of the 10 without a quango.

He received a £113,550 payoff and a £36,000-a-year pension when he left last year to become professor of health care at Manchester University and a £15,000-a-year director of Bupa, the private health organisation.

Source: *The Observer*, 14 May 1995

The various parts of the 'state élite' – cabinet, parliament, judiciary, civil service and military – are recruited disproportionately from among the economically dominant upper class. This similarity

Oxbridge retains grip on judiciary

ALAN TRAVIS

THE upper reaches of the judiciary are still dominated by those who are Oxbridge-educated, according to official figures published yesterday. This is despite the protestations of the Lord Chancellor, Lord Mackay, that the "old boy network" no longer determined the appointment of judges.

The figures, published by the Lord Chancellor's Department, show that 80 per cent of Lords of Appeal, Heads of Divisions, Lord Justices of Appeal and High Court judges were educated at Oxford or Cambridge.

More than 50 per cent of the middle-ranking circuit judges went to Oxbridge but only 12 per cent of the lower ranking district judges.

Sir Thomas Legg, the permanent secretary at the Lord Chancellor's Department, answered criticism over the Oxbridge domination of the higher courts from MPs yesterday by insisting: "It is not the function of the professional judiciary to be representative of the community."

He told the Commons Home Affairs Committee that the Lord Chancellor had to choose the senior members of the judiciary from "the most successful members of a learned profession, and from those who had been in it for at least 20 to 30 years."

But Chris Mullin, Labour MP for Sunderland South, said that the system of appointments appeared to be self-perpetuating, with all the senior judges aged between 55 and 66 and moving in limited circles.

He added that the only woman judge in the Appeal Court happened to be the sister of a previous Lord Chancellor and the daughter of a Lord of Appeal.

Mr Mullin said that a study carried out last year by Labour Research had shown that of 641 judges, 80 per cent had been to public school.

Other official figures published yesterday included a sample survey of 218 new appointments as magistrates in England and Wales. This showed that 91 were Conservative voters, 56 Labour, 41 Liberal Democrat, 24 had no political affiliation, and four voted Plaid Cymru.

Source: *The Guardian*, 18 May 1995

Activity

First read the articles 'Three in five top civil servants land quango jobs' and 'Oxbridge retains grip on judiciary', and then write answers to the following questions.

a Does the UK have a ruling élite?
b How does a ruling élite preserve its own rule?

I, A, E

of economic background is reinforced by the fact that they had studied at a small number of major public schools and at Oxford and Cambridge Universities. . . . The upper class and the political élite show a similarity of social background and are, in many cases, the same people.
(Scott, 1986, p. 7)

However, for Scott, the upper class are not a ruling class *per se*. He considers, like Gramsci (see page 710), that the state itself is a major source of power in societies and as such can, and often does, operate separately from the government and the upper class. Scott contends that the concept of 'power bloc' best describes the distribution of power in contemporary western societies:

Neither 'ruling class' nor 'élite' can be used as adequate descriptions of the British political structure. Historical patterns of class dominance must be understood in terms of the particular alliance of classes and sections of classes which constitute the 'power bloc'. A power bloc is an informal coalition of social groups, often under the leadership of one group, which actually holds the levers of political power in a society. . . . British society in the twentieth century has been ruled by just such a power bloc, headed by the upper-class members of the 'establishment'. . . . over the course of the century the cohesion of the power bloc has weakened, but it remains the basis of upper-class political dominance. . . . Britain has an upper class that dominates government, but it does not have a ruling class.
(Scott, 1986, p. 7)

The autonomy of the state

The work of Nordlinger (1981) represents what can be called a '*state-centred*' approach to understanding the role of the state in contemporary social life. Nordlinger suggests that the state as a political force in its own right has some *autonomy* over the will of the population and the will of governments. The state can be seen as an élite body which sometimes works in its own power-seeking interests, independently or autonomously from the ideas or control of political parties (see also Section 2.6).

This has important implications for the so-called democracy at work in western societies. If the state, an unelected and unaccountable body (as far as the general population are concerned), operates in its own interests, then what does this mean for 'rule by the people'?

Is there a future left for the state?

Recent debate on the nature of the state in contemporary, western 'liberal democracies' has focused on the future roles of the state. Notably, many theorists are becoming increasingly pessimistic, and believe that the future of the state will be dramatically different from its recent past.

State overload

Brittan (1975), and others more recently, have suggested that one way to interpret the future role of the state is to recognize that its rapid expansion since the Second World War will have to be reduced or stopped. In economic terms, western societies will not be able to afford 'to deliver the goods' as promised, particularly in the areas of social welfare which cost governments vast sums each year (see Section 14.2). As the state promises more and more, in order to obtain the increasingly fragile and volatile support of the population, it can in reality only afford to deliver less and less.

The New Right and the 'nanny state'

With the rise of the New Right in western politics (see Section 2.10), there can be seen a keen awareness of the notion of the state becoming overloaded. In the UK, since the establishment of the first Thatcher government in 1979, there has been – as a core ideological feature of New Right politics and policies – the rejection of what is called 'the nanny state'. It is believed by some New Right theorists that excessive reliance on the state providing social welfare – benefits, healthcare, etc. – cannot be met by the revenue generated by the state through taxation.

These theorists go further and suggest that too much public expenditure and support leads to a 'nanny state' where individuals become far too dependent on the state for support. As a result a 'dependency culture' is established where those asking for state support lack the necessary drive to look for work, or to take control over their lives and those of their families (see Section 14.3). This issue became a major arena for political conflict in the UK during the 1980s and early 1990s, between the New Right, the so-called New Labour opposition, and the middle ground occupied by the Liberal Democrats.

The New Right can best be understood as a combination of two sets of ideas:

- libertarian ideas
- social authoritarianism.

In other words, there is a combination of (a) a belief in the economic and personal freedom of the free market while wishing to erode the interventionist power of the state (libertarian), and (b) a belief in the necessity for a moral regeneration of society with strong law-and-order policies (social authoritarianism). Thus, in New Right thinking, individual responsibility needs to be encouraged – but only if individuals can be trusted to take moral responsibility. To summarize the key ideas of the New Right:

- The state should not have to take primary responsibility for the welfare of individuals and their families (see Sections 1.1, 7.4 and 14.3).
- Too much state intervention into private life leads to a 'dependency culture' where laziness and idleness cause increased poverty and unemployment. Individuals should be made to seek employment rather than rely on the state to support them (see Sections 4.8 and 14.7).
- Industry once owned by the state should be sold to private investors (privatized) so that individuals can become empowered to take charge of their own lives by owning a small part of the nation's industry (see Section 9.3).
- An 'enterprise culture' should be established where business competition is encouraged in order to free the state from the control of business.
- Strong policies on law and order are needed to control those who do not abide by the rules of society (see Section 11.10).
- Moral regeneration is needed in society. Traditional family and religious values should be restored. Also needed are strong discipline in schools and the home, and the discouragement of single-parent families (see Sections 7.4 and 8.9).

Legitimation crisis

Habermas (1988), a German social theorist with a position derived from the Frankfurt School of Critical Theory, shares the New Right's pessimism about the future of the state. In his book *Legitimation Crisis*, first published in Germany in 1973, Habermas suggests that a legitimation crisis has developed around the activities of the state and of party politics in general. While being asked and expected to deliver more and more by the population, the state finds it increasingly harder to meet these demands. Over time, the population loses faith both in the state and in the political system itself – the state is no longer seen as legitimate since in the eyes of the population it makes promises it does not keep (see also Section 2.9). As Habermas comments:

Because the economic crisis has been intercepted and transformed into a systematic overloading of the public budget, it has put off the mantle of a natural fate of society. If governmental crisis management fails, it lags behind programmatic demands that it has placed on itself. The penalty for this failure is withdrawal of legitimation.
(Habermas, 1988, p. 69)

Habermas suggests that the rise of anti-state, New Right theories in western capitalist societies is a direct response to this state crisis. Free-market policies are employed to compensate for the over-demand on the state as a response to failing legitimation. It is hoped that the logic of the market will regulate the state where the state failed to regulate governmental expense and promise. We see the adoption of a non-interventionist policy by New Right political parties where the state is not used to intervene in the economy.

Feminism: the patriarchical state

For feminists such as Pateman (1988) and Walby (1990) the state is seen as a patriarchical institution. By this they mean that it operates to legitimate male domination and power in society at the exclusion of women. (See also Section 5.3.) For example, Pateman argues that the concentration on the definition of 'politics' as something associated with democracy acts to exclude the private lives of women from the political process. Whereas politics is seen almost exclusively as something conducted by the business of governments (i.e. men) and states, the inequality experienced by many women in the private sphere – the family – goes unrecognized as a legitimate political struggle.

Walby offers a very similar analysis. She claims that patriarchy – male dominance over women – exists in six spheres of society:

- paid employment
- the household
- culture
- sexuality
- violence
- the state.

For the feminists, all these structures of 'patriarchical control' operate on women's lives in conjunction. Thus violence in the home and the exclusion of women from paid employment are related, as is the fact that overseeing all of social life is the state which, they say, turns a blind eye to the plight of women. (Walby's work and the debates surrounding it are discussed in more detail in Section 5.3.)

17.4 Contemporary conceptualizations of power in society

All sociological theories can be seen to contain a theory of power. They have all entered into a discussion or debate as to the precise nature of power and its operation in society. However, as elsewhere in sociological analysis and discussion, we find that different theories define power in various ways.

According to Westergaard and Resler (1976):

Power . . . is a rather exclusive phenomenon. Its effects are tangible. But power as such is something of an abstraction. It certainly cannot be measured in the way, for example, that the distribution of wealth can be measured. And just because it is not

hard and fast, there is no simple and agreed definition of what it is.
(Westergaard and Resler, 1976, p. 142)

In a very broad sense, politics means to seek power and power means to seek one's own will, at the expense of others (or to get one's own way). In this broad way, all aspects of social life are situations of power and the struggle for power – and therefore, all sociology is the study of power.

Authority, legitimation and coercion

A starting point for understanding what power is, and how power operates, is to see it as follows.

> 'In a situation where B acts according to the wishes of A, then A would be said to have power over B'.

Taking this definition further, many sociologists draw a distinction between power based on 'authority' and power based on 'coercion'. For Weber (1968; orig. pub. 1921), although all power is ultimately based on domination – especially by the use of violence or force by the state – it is possible to draw a distinction between legitimate and illegitimate power.

- *Authority* is seen as legitimate power. This is when a ruler is successful in securing the 'hearts and minds' of a population. In the eyes of the population, the ruler has the moral right to rule, and therefore the decisions of the ruler are accepted.
- *Coercion* is the opposite to authority. It is illegitimate power gained through the threat of force and/or the use of force.

Weber and more recent commentators have suggested that coercive power is less 'stable' than authoritative power. A ruler who wins the hearts and minds of a population can expect to enjoy a longer rule than in those societies based on force.

Frequently, coercion leads to attempts to establish authority. This may be by appealing to 'democracy', one of the greatest and most powerful legitimation claims of the contemporary world (see Section 17.1). Some governments, especially in relatively politically unstable areas such as eastern Europe and the developing world, obtain initial power through coercion, but quickly thereafter wish to establish themselves as legitimate in the eyes of their own population and the rest of the world. (See also Section 12.4.)

Weber's 'ideal-types' of authority

Weber discusses types of authority in some detail. The construction and use of 'ideal-types' is fundamental to Weber's sociology, and they enable him to discuss in 'pure' terms the essential characteristics of a given phenomenon (see Section 3.2). Ideal-types can be understood as lists of characteristics a given social phenomenon may have, against which the sociologist compares 'reality'.

Ideal types are 'pure' or 'abstract' expressions. It is not a problem if all the characteristics of the ideal-type do not 'match up' or conform with 'reality', since even in making this observation knowledge is gained of the social world. Ideal types enable sociologists to compare different societies and different time periods within the same society.

Weber identifies three 'pure types' of authority, all of which are 'legitimate' sources of power used by leaders or leading groups to secure the consent of the population:

- rational–legal authority
- traditional authority
- charismatic authority.

These 'pure types' are defined by Weber as the following sources of legitimacy.

1 *Rational grounds – resting on a belief in the legality of enacted rules and the right of those elevated to authority under such rules to issue commands.*
2 *Traditional grounds – resting on an established belief in the sanctity of immemorial traditions and the legitimacy of those exercising authority under them.*
3 *Charismatic grounds – resting on devotion to the exceptional sanctity, heroism or exemplary character of an individual person, and of the normative patterns or order revealed or ordained by him.*
(Weber, 1968, p. 215; orig. pub. 1921)

In social reality, Weber argues that these 'pure types' may well be combined together. It is perfectly possible, for example, for traditional authority to arise from charismatic authority. In this situation we may well find societies where members of a particular family are seen to have special religious or magical power (charismatic) and who therefore have always ruled and only members of this family can rule (traditional).

A 'radical' view of power

Adopting a perspective which, while not Marxist as such, owes a great deal to left-of-centre or 'radical' approaches in sociology, Lukes (1974) identifies three 'dimensions' of power. These are:

- decision-making
- nondecision-making
- shaping decisions.

Lukes is critical of pluralist notions of power – especially within the work of Dahl (see page 704). Lukes notes that pluralists only really focus on the first dimension of power – they have a 'one-dimensional' theory. He suggests that while pluralists take at face value the notion that power can always be 'seen' in decision-making, sometimes power is 'unseen', not observable. In this sense, modern western societies are far from open and democratic: they operate on a dimension of power which is hidden, closed and inaccessible to the majority. As Lukes notes:

. . . the pluralists assume that interests are to be understood as policy preferences – so that a conflict of interests is equivalent to a conflict of preferences. They are opposed to any suggestion that interests might be unarticulated or unobservable, and above all, to the idea that people might actually be mistaken about, or unaware of, their own interests.
(Lukes, 1974, p. 14)

In defining the precise nature of these three 'dimensions' identified by Lukes, we can present them as follows.

The one-dimensional view: decision-making
In this dimension, power can be seen as a battle between open interests which conflict until a decision is reached. Lukes suggests that pluralism focuses solely on this aspect of power, whereas this dimension can only truly be understood in relation to the second and third dimensions:

I conclude that this first, one-dimensional, view of power involves a focus on behaviour in the making of decisions on issues over which there is an observable conflict of (subjective) interests, seen as express policy preferences, revealed by political participation.
(Lukes, 1974, p. 15)

The two-dimensional view: non-decision-making
In the second dimension, power must be understood as operating also through a process of non-decision-making. Some issues or topics are ignored from the public agenda, and therefore they cannot be openly discussed:

. . . the two-dimensional view of power involves a qualified critique of the behavioural focus of the first view (I say qualified because it is still assumed that non-decision-making is a form of decision-making) and it allows for consideration of the ways in which decisions are prevented from being taken on potential issues over which there is an observable conflict of (subjective) interests, seen as embodied in express policy preferences and sub-political grievances.
(Lukes, 1974, p. 20)

The three-dimensional view: shaping decisions
In the third dimension, power can be identified in the process of shaping the wishes or desires of the pop-

ulation. By making some situations appear normal, natural and inevitable, the population of a society may simply go along with the rules of society and not even begin to *think* about questioning them, let alone *actually* questioning them. People's decisions can be made or shaped for them by those who rule:

. . . the three-dimensional view of power involves a thorough going critique of the behavioural focus of the first two views as too individualistic and allows for consideration of the many ways in which potential issues are kept out of politics, whether through the operation of social forces and institutional practices or through individuals' decisions. This, moreover, can occur in the absence of actual, observable conflict, which may have been successfully averted – though there remains here an implicit reference to potential conflict. This potential, however, may never in fact be articulated. What one may have here is a latent conflict, which consists in a contradiction between the interests of those exercising power and the real interests of those they exclude.
(Lukes, 1974, p. 24)

Lukes therefore wishes the concept of power to be understood as multi-dimensional. He suggests that it is important for sociologists to recognize that power is related to decisions made by a ruling group from which they benefit and which are subsequently exercised over the general population – often against their interests – even if they do not actually know what their 'true interests' are.

This view has been highly influential in much neo-Marxist sociology in recent years. Lukes' work itself appears to reflect some of the ideas of Gramsci and the idea of 'hegemony' – where rule is established in society by making such a rule appear normal, natural and beyond question. As Lukes comments concerning his third dimension of power:

Is it not the supreme and most insidious exercise of power to prevent people, to whatever degree, from having grievances by shaping their perceptions, cognitions and preferences in such a way that they accept their role in the existing order of things, either because they can see or imagine no alternative to it, or because they see it as natural and unchangeable, or because they value it as divinely ordained and beneficial?
(Lukes, 1974, p. 24)

Activity
Using the ideas of Lukes, suggest an example of each of the 'three dimensions of power' in relation to your education.

I, A

Power in everyday life

The dramaturgical analogy

Goffman, in his book *The Presentation of Self in Everyday Life* (1969; orig. pub. 1959), adopts what he describes as a 'dramaturgical' approach. By this, he compares social life to the theatre: individuals are 'social actors', they follow 'scripts', they adopt 'roles' and give 'performances'. Within this analogy is a micro-theory of power and the political nature of everyday life. (See also Section 2.7.)

Goffman suggests that in any interactional encounter we seek to define the social situation. We need to understand how others perceive us, and what meanings they give to the situation. Power is exercised in everyday life through the attempt to take control of the definition of the social situation. This is achieved by 'impression management' – by carefully manipulating the impression of our-'self' which we give to other social actors.

'Alternative spaces' of power

With the rise of post-modern theories in sociology, the conventional view of power as 'getting one's way' is becoming seen by many as problematic. The definition of power is now a controversial area. Many seek to define 'alternative spaces' or 'sites' of power; that is to say, to identify how power operates at a number of different levels in ordinary life as well as in the structures set up by government.

Recent approaches to sociological theorizing about power and politics in everyday life have tended to concentrate on the idea of a post-modern society. This contains the belief that contemporary times are different from those of the past, that significant changes have occurred in the nature or fabric of social life – including that of the political – so making our contemporary lives 'post' (or after) a previous stage. (See also Section 10.11.)

In these 'new' times social theorists are still debating quite what the nature of these times are, and the directions future social change might take. These theorists differ considerably, not only with respect to what characterizes these times, but whether their characteristics are positive or not for society.

For example, some theorists have identified what they see as the development of the 'post-political': a significant loss in the participation, interest or confidence of populations in democracy, party politics and voting in general. Whereas, for some, the development of the post-political is treated as further evidence for the decline of hope for the future of society, others see this process as simply yet another opportunity for pastiche.

Post-modern 'sites of power', rather than the traditional nation-state, are areas of social life and social living such as culture, identity, knowledge and language. The contemporary concern with these alternative conceptualizations of power is an attempt to move social theory on, to redefine traditional sociological debates.

The politics of the body

For Foucault (1991), the key to understanding the nature of society is to study the origins of 'discourses'. (See also Section 2.10.) A discourse is a set of knowledge and rules, often associated with a specialized language. For example, Foucault would consider the discourse of psychology to enable psychologists to control, label and constrain some people into 'specialized spaces' – asylums – often against their wishes. Foucault notes that discourses organize, although they are not exclusively confined to, an associated 'space' or institution in which they operate, such as the asylum or the hospital.

Power in this sense is all around us, although Foucault notes that these discourses can be resisted: we can attempt to 'reverse' the identity they give us. This 'fighting back' or resistance is referred to by Foucault as the 'politics of space'. Power is then about the discipline and control of the body. As Foucault notes:

. . . the body is also directly involved in a political field; power relationships have an immediate hold on it; they invest it, mark it, train it, torture it, force it to carry out tasks, to perform ceremonies, to emit signs.
(Foucault, 1991, p. 25)

Like many other contemporary thinkers, Foucault is also concerned with the role power plays in knowledge:

We should admit rather that power produces knowledge (and not simply by encouraging it because it serves power or by applying it because it is useful); that power and knowledge directly imply one another; that there is no power relation without the correlative constitution of a field of knowledge, nor any knowledge that does not presuppose and constitute at the same time power relations.
(Foucault, 1991, p. 27)

Knowledge *is* power because it controls, labels and constrains, it limits possibilities for the 'subject' of its gaze. Power exists everywhere like a web or maze covering all aspects of society:

Foucault argues that power is not a possession or a capacity. It is not something subordinate to or in the service of the economy. He insists that relations of power do not emanate from a sovereign or a state; nor should power be conceptualized as the

property of an individual or class. Power is not simply a commodity which may be acquired or seized. Rather it has the character of a network; its threads extend everywhere.
(Sarup, 1993, pp. 73–4)

Discipline and surveillance

Foucault emphasizes the role played by social institutions in the discipline and control of the populations of western societies. He argues that the state has an overarching control over, and use of, techniques of punishment and discipline through many and varied institutions such as prisons and asylums – and perhaps less obviously through hospitals and schools (see Sections 8.4, 11.10 and 13.9).

In his work *Discipline and Punish: The Birth of the Prison* (1991; orig. pub. 1975), Foucault notes that all these institutions use similar methods of control of the body. In making this claim he uses the concepts of 'discipline', 'punishment' and 'control' in a very broad fashion to refer to any system or set of practices which function to label, constrain, organize or regulate the human body. Of particular importance to Foucault's work is the use of timetables and taxonomies (classification systems) by institutions as instruments for the control and ordering of social actors.

The 'silent majorities' and political participation

Baudrillard (1983) is very pessimistic of contemporary social life. He writes of the development of the 'silent majorities' who, disillusioned with politics, have lost the ability even to be interested in power any more, let alone fight it. (See also Sections 2.10 and 10.11.)

Baudrillard believes that politics has 'died': the 'silent majority', the masses, are indifferent to all party politics. The masses are 'free', but only in the sense that they are unable to be represented by anyone, anything or any set of beliefs. All that are left, in this world characterized by the death of politics, are 'fatal strategies' (Baudrillard, 1990) – social theory is unable, any longer, to study the social, to investigate how and where the 'politics' is in life.

Knowledge as power

For Lyotard (1984), the 'post-modern condition' is best described as a relativity of reason. No longer, he argues, can the 'grand narrative' of the freedom of humanity through scientific reason be sustained in the light of the contemporary fragmentation of knowledge. In other words, 'scientific reason' – once a major form of legitimacy in the world – is now becoming understood as yet another 'big story', yet another

claim to truth with no objective criteria through which to measure its 'truth' (see Section 3.2).

For Lyotard there is no such thing as a universal, single truth, only *truths*. There is no such thing as reality, only *realities*. In this way, all knowledge is relative – all is as 'good' as any other. In this post-modern condition, knowledge itself has become a site for power – a battlefield. According to Sarup:

It is widely accepted that computerized knowledge has become the principal force of production over the last few decades. . . . Knowledge will be the major component in the world-wide competition for power and it is conceivable that nation-states will one day fight for control of information, just as they battled for control over territories in the past.
(Sarup, 1993, p. 133)

For Lyotard, knowledge itself is no longer a goal – it has become a commodity. It is something to be bought and sold, something to be consumed. Within the production of this knowledge, though, lies power. Who 'owns' what knowledge? How much will it cost? Will everyone have equal access as consumers? According to Lyotard:

Knowledge and power are simply two sides of the same question: who decides what knowledge is, and who knows what needs to be decided? In the computer age, the question of knowledge is now more than ever a question of government. . . . In the discourse of today's financial backers of research, the only credible goal is power. Scientists, technicians, and instruments are purchased not to find truth, but to augment power.
(Lyotard, 1984, pp. 8 and 46)

'Language-games' and power

For many contemporary thinkers, language too is a 'site for power'. Lyotard uses the concept of a 'language-game' to describe how the power that knowledge gives is expressed through the use of language. Communication between individuals is understood as a 'game' between 'players' with 'rules': each utterance is like a 'move' in the game.

In this way, language is an expression of the use of power since we are in conflict with each other. Lyotard uses the metaphor of battle to describe how power operates in these language-games:

In the ordinary use of discourse – for example, in a discussion between two friends – the interlocutors use any available ammunition, changing games from one utterance to the next: questions, requests, assertions, and narratives are launched pell-mell into battle. The war is not without rules, but the rules allow and encourage the greatest possible flexibility of utterance.
(Lyotard, 1984, p. 17)

The power that institutions have over the individual bears down on these language-games and restricts our freedom within them. That is to say, institutions shape the rules of language – they define what are 'correct' and 'incorrect' utterances, and in doing so they exercise power over us by controlling the game in their favour. In this way, institutional and bureaucratic life functions to:

. . . filter discursive potentials, interrupting possible connections in the communication networks: there are things that should not be said. . . . there are also things that should be said, and there are ways of saying them. Thus: orders in the army, prayer in church, denotation in the schools, narration in families, questions in philosophy, performativity in businesses.

(Lyotard, 1984, p. 17)

Discussion point

What is meant by 'power'? How is power a feature of all aspects of social life?

17.5 Pressure groups, citizenship and new social movements

Pressure groups

An essential distinction must be drawn between political parties and pressure groups – both of which, in the pluralist perspective, are seen to be important in the political process.

Political parties are interested in gaining power at a governmental level. In western liberal democracies, parties compete for votes by putting candidates forward for election by the population. By their very nature, political parties are national because they wish to govern the whole nation-state, and are interested in every issue of political discussion. Nationalist parties, such as those in Northern Ireland, Wales and Scotland, obviously contest what counts as a nation-state but would, if successful, still seek to govern in a redrawn map of nation-states.

Pressure groups (sometimes referred to as 'interest groups') are usually concerned with a single issue, or a set of related issues. They do not seek election, but rather operate in the political process by lobbying those in power for their help. They can be local, national or even international (global) but they do not wish to govern the nation-state.

Many contemporary pluralists have argued that the arena of political battles has slowly moved away from political parties and elections, towards the activities of pressure or interest groups. This is seen as the result of a rapid expansion in terms of both number and activities of pressure groups in the postwar period. Today, pressure groups are seen as essential to western democracy.

A further distinction can be made between pressure groups that are protective and those that are promotional. Protective pressure groups seek to look after the interests of their members. On the other hand, promotional groups try to achieve *change* by advocating or promoting a particular cause. Within these categories, many pressure groups can be seen as 'single-issue' groups, with a very narrow focus. The following are some examples from British political life:

- *protective pressure groups* include Trades Union Congress (TUC), Confederation of British Industry (CBI), The National Farmer's Union (NFU)
- *promotional pressure groups* include Greenpeace, Friends of the Earth, Amnesty International, Campaign for Nuclear Disarmament (CND).

Activity

Choose one pressure group, either from the list above or another of your own choice, and investigate its history and activities. Write up this information in the form of a short report.

K, U, A

In reality, it may be difficult to decide, in the final analysis, between classifying a pressure group as promotional or as protective. For example, on the one hand Greenpeace *promotes* environmental issues, but it could also be argued that in doing so it seeks to *protect* us from the hazards of environmental crisis. The same point could be made about CND.

Pressure groups in contemporary British politics

Marsh (1983) notes that sociologists' treatments of the role, effect and influence of pressure groups since the 1960s have changed. This is due, he argues, to changes in the relationships between pressure groups and society. Marsh identifies three main changes.

- The number of pressure groups in existence has greatly multiplied.
- Groups are becoming increasingly involved in politics.
- Groups have increased their contact with the state, yet reduced their contacts with parties and parliament.

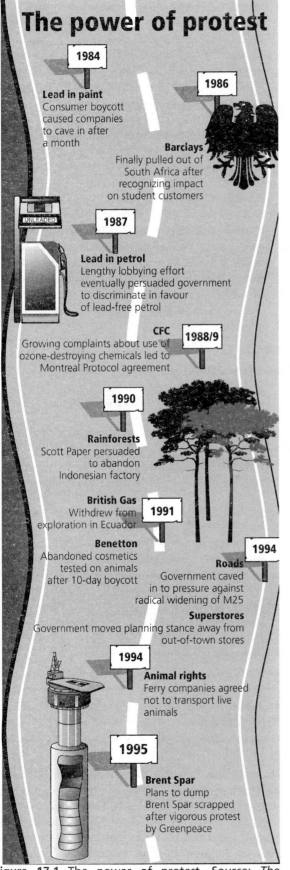

The power of protest

1984

Lead in paint
Consumer boycott caused companies to cave in after a month

1986

Barclays
Finally pulled out of South Africa after recognizing impact on student customers

1987

Lead in petrol
Lengthy lobbying effort eventually persuaded government to discriminate in favour of lead-free petrol

CFC **1988/9**
Growing complaints about use of ozone-destroying chemicals led to Montreal Protocol agreement

1990

Rainforests
Scott Paper persuaded to abandon Indonesian factory

British Gas **1991**
Withdrew from exploration in Ecuador

Benetton
Abandoned cosmetics tested on animals after 10-day boycott

1994

Roads
Government caved in to pressure against radical widening of M25

Superstores
Government moved planning stance away from out-of-town stores

1994

Animal rights
Ferry companies agreed not to transport live animals

1995

Brent Spar
Plans to dump Brent Spar scrapped after vigorous protest by Greenpeace

Figure 17.1 The power of protest. Source: *The Guardian*, 22 June 1995

Activity

Figure 17.1 depicts how pressure groups have had an influence in several major controversies. Answer the following questions.

a Over what issues (among others) have people protested in the years 1984–95?
b What changes have resulted from these campaigns?

Related to these main changes, a number of other trends can be identified. First, a number of pressure groups have resumed contact with the Labour Party, while at the same time reducing contact with the Conservative Party.

Secondly, what Marsh calls 'ideological groups' (those seeking to promote or defend legislation on ideological principles) have grown in number. Also, 'economic groups' (those seeking to promote or protect the specific financial interests of their membership) have been drawn into a more formal role in the decision-making process – and as a consequence are more able than ideological groups to effect change.

Thirdly, since the 1970s there has been an increase in 'single-issue groups' which have been largely unsuccessful in changing government policy, or even in obtaining government favour and help. Consequently these groups have instead tried to influence public opinion largely through the media, rather than governmental opinion.

Fourthly, many single-issue groups have tried to obtain the support and recognition of the Trades Union Congress (TUC) in an attempt to gain power – especially within the Labour Party.

However, despite these major trends and their consequences, Marsh is keen to emphasize that the role of pressure groups in society is in a dynamic state: it is unpredictable and open to great change.

The contributions of pressure groups to democracy

Grant (1989) suggests that pressure groups are vital for democracy in the western world:

There is a fundamental link between the existence of pressure groups and the very survival of a system of democratic government. Freedom of association is a fundamental principle of democracy. Democracy permits the existence of groups, but it could also be argued that groups contribute to the quality of the decision-making process. Those that have axes to grind may have

something to say that is relevant to the issue under consideration.
(Grant, 1989, p. 21)

Grant contends that representative democracy in fact offers a relatively infrequent choice of political view, with elections required only every five years (in the UK). It could also be said that with the increasing similarity of views between some of the contemporary, major British political parties, this choice is becoming further limited, even when an election is held.

Grant therefore sees the existence of pressure groups as essential to democracy because they often offer diverse political opinions, and a more frequent opportunity than elections for one's political voice to be heard:

Pressure groups permit citizens to express their views on complex issues which affect their lives. In systems of voting, each vote counts equally, but numerical democracy can take no account of the intensity of opinion on a particular issue. Democracy cannot be simply reduced to a head-counting exercise: it must also take account of the strength of feelings expressed, and of the quality of arguments advanced.
(Grant, 1989, p. 21)

Within Grant's discussion of pressure groups it is possible to identify nine 'justifications' for the existence of pressure groups in a western democracy – and the roles they might play. Grant uses the work of another commentator on the role of pressure groups, Des Wilson, in a critical fashion to compile these arguments – some of which Grant ultimately rejects.

- Democracy cannot exist on voting alone. Pressure groups are needed to keep the regular momentum of political debate and discussion going.
- Some groups, while living in a democracy where they enjoy the right to a free vote, are still under-represented by party politics and/or socially disadvantaged. Pressure groups can be used by these disadvantaged groups to raise their profile in the eyes of the state and the public.
- Some commentators have argued that pressure groups are able to take a long-term view of political issues, more so than political parties and governments who are immediately answerable to the population, and so may adopt increased short-term policies in order to be 'seen to do the right thing'.
- Pressure groups, it could be argued, may improve the government's knowledge of issues they might otherwise overlook – such as environmental matters.
- Pressure groups often make information open to the public by 'leaking' secret information to the media etc.

- Pressure groups may be seen to combat other pressure groups – thus increasing the variety of political and ideological choices.
- Pressure groups may fight issues, or adopt policies or strategies, that have been ignored by the media – and therefore allow an increased knowledge of the world for the population of a society.
- One argument, often used by pluralists, is that pressure groups ultimately encourage people to take responsibility for their own political actions. They can empower people to stand up for causes in which they truly believe.
- Finally, pressure groups may act as a 'safety valve' and allow potentially violent and socially disruptive people a safe outlet for their social comment and protest. For pluralists and functionalists this would be seen as a positive benefit, but Marxists would take the opposite view – perhaps seeing pressure groups as part of the ideological illusion created by capitalism to hide great inequalities of power (see Section 2.6).

Discussion point
What role do pressure groups play in democratic societies? Do they facilitate democracy?

Citizenship

Since the 1980s the concept of 'citizenship' has risen to a place of significance in British political debate. The concern with citizenship is essentially a concern with the question: what does it mean to be 'the people' in a democratic society? To have 'citizenship' – to be a citizen of a nation-state – means to live under the control of a state with 'rights' that one can exercise, and duties and obligations which the state must perform.

Marshall (1977) suggests that the concept of 'citizenship' can be divided into three different, but related, sets of 'rights':

- *civil rights* – to individual freedom, to free speech and thought
- *political rights* – to participate in the democratic political process
- *social rights* – to social welfare. (See also Section 14.3.)

Marshall says that the contemporary concern with rights is a reflection of the development of capitalism. Since capitalist economic systems are based on the principles of freedom and consumption, the development of rights and law were, he suggests, vital to the business contract. Without these rights a fair relationship between producer and consumer could not be guaranteed.

Faulks (1994) notes that on the current political stage, the concept of citizenship and the concern with rights is treated differently by the Left and the Right:

For those on the Left of the political spectrum it is seen as a useful concept around which to mobilize support for egalitarian policies; for those on the Right the notion of 'the citizen' has been utilized to encourage a greater sense of civic duty and to make public services more efficient through the operation of the government's new 'citizens' charter'.
(Faulks, 1994, p. 2)

However, it is possible to identify some problems with the concept of citizenship. Turner (1986) argues that the concern with citizenship is a reflection of the development and rise of the nation-state in 'modernity' – a term used to refer to the rise of industrial societies and in the West, the development of capitalism. However, with the onset of globalization many argue that the nation-state is no longer as important as it once was. (See also Sections 9.9, 10.10, 12.5, 15.11, 16.8 and 17.6.) The individual citizenship of a nation-state can today be overruled by the global rights given to individuals by the European Court of Human Rights and the 1948 United Nations Universal Declaration of Human Rights. For Turner, citizenship is becoming problematic – national identity and the nation-state are becoming outdated tools of sociological analysis. (See also Section 10.10.)

Lister (1990) asserts that the New Right in British parliamentary politics have narrowed our understanding of being a citizen in contemporary society. She notes that being a citizen seems almost exclusively related to 'being a consumer' and little else. Lister points out that, for members of the New Right, citizenship is seen as the product of the free-market economy: we are given the power by the market to consume, and in doing so express our freedom from the state. For the New Right, citizenship is about breaking down the state, not being supported by it (see Section 2.10).

Hirst (1990, 1993a), from a neo-pluralist stance, argues that in today's society citizens lack any real power to challenge the policies of government, except at the ballot box. One possible solution to this situation is to establish a Bill of Rights which specifically identifies the rights citizens are entitled to. In this way, a newly elected government would always have to operate within clear boundaries.

New social movements

Much of the contemporary sociological study of political struggle and protest has concentrated on the idea of 'new social movements'.

A social movement is – defined in simple terms – a non-institutional body or group which takes up a given cause or issue of a political nature. Use of the prefix 'new' to describe 'new social movements' has come about owing to the recent rise (or rather, return) of these movements in the late twentieth century.

For many decades sociology has been preoccupied with the relationships between power, the state, social class and voting – almost to the point of dismissal of 'social movements' which have been seen as adding and contributing little to the political arena. However, since the 1960s there has, arguably, been a return to these types of political expression. A number of factors can be identified for this return of (new) social movements:

- disillusionment with the ability of the state to distribute welfare (see Section 14.4)
- disillusionment with the choice of ideologies offered by institutional party politics
- the change in the class composition of society – the growth of a 'new middle class' and the development of volatility and dealignment in voting behaviour (see Sections 4.6 and 17.2).

These three related social developments are used by some as evidence of a 'post-industrial' society, one where traditional class struggle and political issues no longer exist. For Hallsworth (1994) the term 'new social movement':

... may be viewed as a concept originally developed by commentators on the political left. It was one developed specifically to refer to the wide and diverse spectrum of new, non-institutional political movements which emerged or (as in the case of feminism) re-emerged, in western liberal democratic societies during the 1960s and 1970s. More specifically, the term is most often used to refer to those movements which may be held to pose new challenges to the established cultural economic and political orders of advanced (i.e. late twentieth century) capitalist society.
(Hallsworth, 1994, p. 7)

Hallsworth also notes that in terms of the social characteristics of the members of new social movements, a fairly narrow section of the wider social community is represented. Members tend to be:

- young – usually aged 16–30
- part of what is often refered to as 'the new middle class' – those who work in the public sectors or who are born into families where the parents do
- 'peripheral to the labour market', such as students, or outside the labour market, such as the unemployed.

Inglehart (1990) notes that new social movements and the modern political arenas they have created are more concerned with non-material political issues – identity and lifestyle (See Chapter 10) and the inequalities these are subjected to, rather than economic inequality as such.

Equally, some post-modernists would claim that new social movements offer the individual the opportunity to reconstruct their identity in a post-modern society: to use identification with a wider group as a political process, to subvert how the state and other institutions attempt to control an individual's life.

Examples of so-called new social movements are:

- black power
- gay liberation
- women's liberation
- student power
- greens.

What these types of movement have in common is a move away from a traditional social-class based membership: the political movements of 'old' were largely 'workers movements' or 'labour movements', whereas those of today exist separate from production-centred politics. As Scott (1990, 1991) suggests, whereas the old workers' movements were concerned with attacking the state, economic inequality and class struggle, the 'new' social movements are more concerned with individual and group autonomy. Whereas the old workers' movements organized themselves through formal and hierarchical groups – such as unions – the new social movements are based much more on informal 'networking'.

Post-modernism and 'DIY cultures'

The term 'DIY culture' is sometimes used to refer to the lifestyles offered to the individual by new social movements. One does not so much 'join' a new social movement as 'live' one. Membership (although not in the traditional sense of this word) of new social movements is based on constructing a lifestyle from a pastiche of elements – picking and choosing from a number of choices on offer – from dress codes through food-consumption codes to sexual identity (see Section 10.9). This 'picking and mixing' has lead to some post-modernists claiming that involvement in a new social movement is an expression of a post-modern lifestyle.

New social movements and the 'failure of the welfare state'

The viewpoint held by both Offe (1985) and Habermas (1981) suggests that new social movements have arisen as a response to the realization that the welfare state can no longer meet its original promise: to distribute evenly and fairly wealth and social care (see Section 14.3). Association with new social movements is seen by Offe as an attempt to resist and reject bureaucracy in social life, to try to limit the control which the surveillance of the state has over its members.

There is an important difference between what is referred to as the 'early' and 'late' stages of capitalism. In early capitalism political protest was concerned with 'outsiders' becoming citizens – having rights which the state will recognize and protect; whereas in late capitalism, political struggle is based on the attempt to reduce state control of the individual's life.

For Habermas, the economic 'free-market' policies adopted by the state in late capitalism are seen by many to lack legitimacy – to be unable to deliver the once-promised social welfare. This realization prompts the development of new social movements. (See also Sections 2.9 and 17.1.)

Risk identities and new social movements

Beck (1992) suggests that, rather than having entered a period of 'post-modernity', instead we have reached a further stage of modernity – 'reflective modernity'. This is a claim he shares in common with Giddens (see Section 2.9) who suggests that we have reached 'high' modernity (see Section 10.10). In 'reflective modernity', Beck argues that we have created a 'risk society': the fundamental organizational principle of all lifestyles is that of the avoidance of risk or danger. Individual identity is therefore based on the adoption of a lifestyle which avoids the problems created by capitalist production and industrialization, such as pollution, exposure to dangerous levels of ozone etc. (See also Section 13.3.)

Viewed in this way, modern society (as opposed to a 'post'-modern society) poses particular problems for the individuals involved. One solution to these problems, one way to avoid the risks, is to adopt a lifestyle based on membership or association with a new social movement. Beck identifies the growth of the 'green movement' to be a specific response to living in a risk society.

Criticisms of new social movements

Callinicos (1989), writing from a Marxist perspective, rejects a post-modern analysis of the growth of new social movements. He suggests, instead, that internationally or collectively a working class can still be identified and class inequality does still exist. Further, this working class still retains powerful 'political movements' which operate alongside new social movements, rather than having been replaced by them.

Hirst (1993a), from an updated pluralist (or 'neo-pluralist') stance, is also critical of the claims made

by some that the future of political struggle is with
new social movements. He suggests that these movements are based on such loose associations and networks that they contribute virtually nothing to
political life: they are too fragmented to effectively
challenge the existing nature of the distribution of
power.

Discussion point

To what extent has contemporary political
protest moved away from a traditional
class-based notion of political struggle and
inequality? What forms do contemporary
political protests take and around what
issues?

17.6 Globalization and nationalism

In contemporary sociology few terms have been
given as much importance in recent years as
'globalization'. (Debates around this concept are also
covered in Sections 9.9, 10.10, 12.5, 15.11 and
16.8.) As Waters (1995) notes:

*Social change is now proceeding so rapidly that if
a sociologist had proposed as recently as ten years
ago to write a book about globalization they would
have had to overcome a wall of stony and bemused
incomprehension. But now, just as post-modernism
was the concept of the 1980s, globalization may be
the concept of the 1990s, a key idea by which we
understand the transition of human society into the
third millenium.*
(Waters, 1995, p. 1)

For Waters, globalization can be defined as:

*A social process in which the constraints of geog-
raphy on social and cultural arrangements recede
and in which people become increasingly aware
that they are receding.*
(Waters, 1995, p. 3)

Activity

Using the definition supplied by Waters,
create a list of aspects of your own social
life which could be seen to have been
influenced by global forces.

I, A

When applied to politics, the idea of globalization
raises a number of important questions for individuals living in the contemporary age. If globalization
is occurring:

- what beliefs, values and ideologies are foremost
  on the global political stage?
- what are its implications for nationalism and
  national identity?
- what are its implications for citizenship under the
  state?

The end of ideology?

Fukuyama (1992), from a right-wing perspective, has
proclaimed a forthcoming 'end of history' whereby
a global consensus based on liberal democracy will
become the ruling political system. Fukuyama's ideas
echo those of earlier theorists who charted the rise
of post-industrial societies in which we see the 'end
of ideology' – where the East and West converge
ideologically – and a 'new world order' is established
around democracy.

Discussion point

To what extent do we live in a 'new world
order' where East and West have converged
and 'consensus politics' rule?

Critics of this idea, particularly from a Marxist or
neo-Marxist stance, point out that rather than
an equal convergence between East and West,
what in fact lies at the heart of these ideas is the
belief in the process of westernization across
the globe. With the collapse of the USSR and related
self-proclaimed communist systems, the western
'liberal–capitalist–democratic' model of political
organization is seen to have won the Cold War.

Globalization and the 'success of capitalism'

For many of the New Right, globalization can be
equated with the collapse of so-called communism
and the establishment of free markets on a truly
international scale. Establishment of the World Bank,
the International Monetary Fund (IMF) and to a
lesser extent the European Union (EU) indicates the
growth of new markets – the expansion of a world
economy and of 'world capitalism' (see Section 12.5).

Equally, the growth of globalization can be seen
in terms other than economic ones: growth of the
United Nations (UN) as a 'peace-keeping' force, and
the European Court of Human Rights, may serve as
examples of modern international politics.

For many who take a Marxist or neo-Marxist perspective, globalization – whether economic, cultural
or military – is seen as yet further evidence of the
'Americanization' of the globe.

Although the increased expansion of global free
markets would be an opportunity embraced by many

Figure 17.2 A new world order? Source: Marxism Today, October 1990

on the New Right, globalization also holds its more sinister side for those of this political view. If applied to the international regulation of laws, globalization is seen by some on the New Right to raise problems of national sovereignty. Global courts and their laws may have the power to veto, or block, an individual nation-state's law-making process. If this were the case, national sovereignty and citizenship may be called into question.

Multi-national companies and the power of capital

Lash and Urry (1987) claim that modern societies have reached a new 'global' stage in historical development where 'disorganized capitalism' has occurred. That is to say, multi-national (or 'trans-national') companies exist separately from a particular 'home' country, and they can undermine the power of a national economy. These companies have shifted their manufacturing operations to the *underdeveloped world* where labour power is cheaper (see Section 12.5), and as a result a decline in class politics is occurring because in the West employment is changing from manufacturing to service industries – traditional working-class jobs are lost (see Section 9.9), as are the political significance of traditional working-class movements.

Sklair (1991) suggests that sociological analysis must now rethink how it conceptualizes politics in the light of these global forces.

Is the nation-state dead?

For many commentators, then, globalization and not nationalism is the prime sociological category of the present age. However, the 'death of the nation-state' is far from certain. For example, Hirst (1993b) argues that state intervention is still required to 'bail out' capitalist economies from time to time from economic crises, and therefore a truly independent, global free-market economy is impossible.

Figure 17.3 Master of the universe? Source: *The Guardian*, 7 August 1996

Fukuyama (1992) claims that the 'new world order' will be one where capitalist economics dominate the globe and 'consensus politics' emerges between the once-opposed East and West. Others such as Van der Pijl (1989) argue that globalization brings with it the development of global class struggle. Rather than class politics dying, Van der Pijl argues that the old fight between capital and labour is transferred on to a larger, global stage where trans-national companies exploit a trans-national working class who share a common alienated experience of work.

Further **reading**

Accessible texts designed to introduce the key debates in this field include:

- Kirby, M. (1995) *Investigating Political Sociology*, London, Collins Educational
- Riley, M. (1988) *Power, Politics and Voting*, London, Harvester-Wheatsheaf.

The following are designed to provide more detail than the above introductory A level texts:

- Bottomore, T. (1993) *Political Sociology*, 2nd edn, London, Pluto Press

Lovenduski, J. and Randall, V. (1993) *Contemporary Feminist Politics*, Oxford, Oxford University Press.

Important studies which are accessible and of theoretical and empirical significance are:

- Mattausch, J. (1989) *A Commitment to Campaign: A Sociological Study of CND*, Manchester, Manchester University Press
- Roseneil, S. (1995) *Disarming Patriarchy: Feminism and Political Action at Greenham*, Buckingham, Open University Press.

Back issues of the periodical *Sociology Review* (formerly known as *Social Studies Review*) also contain many articles on this field of sociology and many others.

Exam **questions**

1 Compare and contrast Marxist and New Right perspectives on the role of the state in society.

[25 marks]

(AEB, Paper 2, Summer 1996)

2 a Briefly outline what marxists mean by the relative autonomy of the state. [4 marks]

b Distinguish between the repressive state apparatus and ideological state apparatus. [4 marks]

c Outline, with examples, what marxists mean by hegemony. [7 marks]

d Assess the claim that the UK state is controlled by a ruling class. [10 marks]
(IBS, Paper 2, Summer 1996)

3 Examine the extent to which class remains the basis of voting behaviour in contemporary UK society. [25 marks]
(IBS, Paper 2, Summer 1996)

4 a Briefly define what sociologists mean by the state. [4 marks]

b Using examples of each, briefly distinguish between parties and pressure groups. [4 marks]

c Outline the elitist theory of power. [7 marks]

d Assess the strengths and weaknesses of the pluralist theory of power. [10 marks]
(IBS, Paper 2, Summer 1995)

Coursework **suggestions**

1 Conduct a study of voting intentions
Possible relationships between class, region, income, age, gender, ethnicity etc. and voting intentions could be investigated using quantitative methods. It is important to recognize in this research, however, the view by many commentators, that volatility and dealignment has made these relationships problematic. This coursework could attempt to answer the question 'Has dealignment occurred?'. You will need to pay careful attention to sample size, construction and limitations.

2 A case study of the process of political socialization and activity within the family
Choosing a small number of families – for example on the basis of different social classes, or income groups – you could investigate, using qualitative methods, the differences between the young and older members' attitudes to politics, and activities in politics. Do these differ between the ages, and/or between the classes? Gender and/or ethnicity may also be important variables.

3 A case study of the community power structure in a local town
Using the work of Dahl and Hunter as a theoretical base, you could ask the question 'Who runs this town?'. Questionnaires could be administered to local business people, government officials and people. A list of 'important people' could be drawn up and local newspapers scanned to see whether these individuals or groups get publicity or coverage for their actions and opinions. Conclude whether the chosen town is run by 'the people' or by a narrow élite.

18

Religion and belief systems

Chapter outline

18.1 Origins of the sociological study of religion

Whereas philosophers are interested in whether God exists, if God is omnipotent or omnipresent, sociology is concerned less with what God may or may not be, and more with the social effects and the social consequences of religious belief and practice. It is important to be clear on this distinction early on – there are some questions which are beyond the remit of the sociologist to answer.

The study of religious effects and consequences is not yet another add-on-extra to sociology – another branch of the discipline as a whole – but is absolutely fundamental to the birth of the sociological project in western Europe in the nineteenth century (see Section 2.2). Early sociology was the sociology of beliefs. Or, more specifically, early sociology was concerned to explain, chart and predict the replacement of a religious world view by a scientific and rational one.

For the founding fathers such as Auguste Comte and Henri Comte de Saint-Simon, sociology was to have a new area of study: humanity at the birth of a new era of history, the epoch of industrialization.

Central to this image of social change was an idea of evolution. Social history was slowly progressing towards a scientific age where sociology would be used by intellectuals to explain the social world. (See Section 3.1.) Despite this belief in science, both Comte and Saint-Simon, towards the end of their lives, advocated the setting up of secular religions, including in Comte's case the idea of a priesthood of sociologists.

Friedrich Nietzsche: nationalism and the death of God

Possibly one of the most frequently cited, often misrepresented and poetic expressions of nineteenth-century ideas on the future of religion was provided by Friedrich Nietzsche, a German philosopher whose work has experienced a revival in the more recent sociological treatment of religion, as in other areas.

In his 'parable of the madman' written in 1882, in which he claimed 'God is dead', Nietzsche was concerned to highlight what he saw as the most significant event in European history – the inability of religion (in this case Christianity) to provide purpose and meaning in social life.

Nietzsche tells the story of a madman running through a market place announcing that God has died – that society has stopped believing in God and that this has left an empty space of meaning yet to be fulfilled. The madman addresses the crowd:

'Where has God gone?' he cried. 'I shall tell you. We have killed him – you and I. We are all his murderers. But how have we done this? . . . Are we not perpetually falling . . . Are we not straying as through an infinite nothing? Do we not feel the breath of empty space? Has it not become colder? . . . God is dead. God remains dead. And we have killed him. How shall we, murderers of all murderers, console ourselves? . . . Is not the greatness of this deed too great for us?'
(Nietzsche, 1969, pp. 14–15; orig. pub. 1883–5)

Nietzsche's point is not that only madmen can come to the conclusion that 'God is dead', but rather that the realization that religion no longer provides meaning to social life will produce a society of mad people. Life will be characterized by chaos and uncertainty without the functions of religion.

Discussion point

Have Nietzsche's predictions been proved right? Has 'God died'? Are we less religious in contemporary times?

Nietzsche by no means welcomed the news that 'God is dead'. Instead, he believed this would lead to a meaningless existence. Nietzsche believed that this loss would be fulfilled by a sense of nationalism in the future. (See Sections 10.10, 16.8 and 17.6.) However, nationalism itself would not lead to a genuine search for meaning, but instead towards violent social control exercised against populations by state rulers.

Activity

Think why Nietzsche was so concerned about the loss of religion for society. What social functions does religion perform which are so vital for society? Create a list of the functions of religion for:

a the individual
b society.

I, A

The birth of sociology

Although his ideas may closely resemble a sociological treatment of the effects of religion, it is important to remember that Nietzsche was not a sociologist. The origins of sociology are generally considered to lie with two nineteenth-century intellectuals – Henri Comte de Saint-Simon, and his pupil and secretary Auguste Comte – the founding father of positivism (see Section 3.1) and the first to use the name 'sociology' in 1838 to describe his scientific analysis of industrialization. Comte, and others of the era – Condorcet, Turgot and Saint-Simon – proclaimed that sociology was the ultimate achievement of human science (Kumar, 1986).

The scientific society

Comte claimed the aims of sociology were the same as all other sciences:

The determination of the future must even be regarded as the direct aim . . . that knowledge of what social system the elite of mankind is called to by the progress of civilization – knowledge forming the true practical object of positive science – involves a general determination of the next social future as it results from the past.
(Quoted in Kumar, 1986, pp. 23–4)

Thus, sociology – the scientific study of society – was to predict the future path of history, a path considered to represent the rise of scientific thought at the expense of religious explanations of the world.

Positivism and the law of three stages

'Positivism' became the general term used by all those who believed in a general, universal scientific method shared by all sciences – social and physical or natural.

In taking an evolutionary image of social change, where each epoch or stage of history grew naturally and logically from the one preceding it, Comte suggested that positivism was the highest intellectual human achievement, the third and final stage of history – the 'positive stage':

1 *The theological stage:* society and social events are understood in terms of magic, superstition and religion.
2 *The metaphysical stage:* the development of abstract concepts to explain society and to replace superstition.
3 *The positive stage:* where science develops, based on experimentation and observation.

In taking this image of history, Comte believed science developed at the expense of religious explanations. Therefore, sociology is by nature a counter-religious or anti-religious explanation of the world. It was the highest achievement of the last stage in human and social intellectual development. The existence of sociology for Comte naturally leads to secularization – the decline of religion, the erosion of the supernatural.

Discussion point

Is sociology opposed to religion? Why might this be so? Is it possible to be both religious and sociological?

The 'religion of humanity'

Although Comte believed the future of religion was one of inevitable decline, like Nietzsche, he believed it was essential for society to have a common set of moral guidelines to encourage social stability. Whereas Nietzsche saw nationalism fulfilling the vacuums left by Christianity in western Europe, Comte (as had Saint-Simon before) once more placed his hopes in sociology. Comte believed society should be run by sociologists – similar to Plato's idea of the 'philosopher king'.

Comte tried to establish a new 'secular religion' referred to as 'the religion of humanity', around which collective rituals and ceremonies could be held in the name of positivism: a new scientific and rational set of moral beliefs for a new scientific and rational industrial era. This idea, however, lost Comte some of his support from the intellectual and scientific communities in France at the time – and most notably, eventually the loss of support from Emile Durkheim.

Modernity and religion

Comte, along with others such as Herbert Spencer and Ferdinand Tönnies, had an image of modernity

central to his sociological ideas. The modern age or 'modernity', as opposed to the pre-industrial or traditional social epoch before it, would represent the final development of a number of great social changes. Modernity, the scientific age, would be characterized by:

- the decline of community (see Section 16.3)
- urbanization (see Section 16.6)
- the rise of technological methods of production (see Sections 9.2 and 9.4)
- an increasing reliance on scientific knowledge (see Section 3.1)
- rationalization (see Section 2.6)
- the rise of bureaucracy (see Section 9.7)
- a decline in traditional forms of religion (see Section 18.4).

The founders of sociology wrote the majority of their sociology with these processes in mind, although many of them differed in their interpretations of these events.

Post-modernity and religion

More recent theoretical developments in social theory, such as post-structuralism or post-modernism (see Section 2.10), have been highly critical of this image of all social change as a process of 'modernization' – or movement towards this universal social type.

Post-modernists argue that this 'modern social type' does not represent the 'end of history' as predicted by the founders such as Comte and Marx.

Activity

Post-modernism is a popular, and frequently misused, term in modern intellectual circles. The phrase is often used because it is considered 'fashionable' to be post-modern. (See also Section 10.11.)

The term is of great importance both philosophically and sociologically. It describes a new era of history when culture is fragmented and chaotic. An individual can 'shop-for-God' by picking and choosing from a number of religious lifestyle options.

Think of the people around you, the people you know in society – your family, friends, other students etc. Try to list all the different ideas, cultures and beliefs these people have as a collective group.

Answer this question: 'To what extent do you agree that contemporary society is based on a post-modern pastiche of cultures?'

I, A, E

Society has dramatically changed in the last two decades to such an extent that this universal march towards scientific rationality and reason has all but collapsed.

The nature of a post-modern existence is such that all knowledge is relative – there are no absolute truths. (See also Section 10.11.) In this sense, post-modern images of the contemporary world believe that the dominance of scientific thought will itself decline, in the same fashion as it brought about the decline of traditional religious belief in the nineteenth century.

A new social order will develop based on intellectual fragmentation. Religion, science and other knowledge claims will all exist side-by-side, allowing individuals to 'shop' for a combination of legitimation claims through which to make sense of reality in a meaningful fashion.

18.2 **Definitions and measurements of religion**

The founding fathers believed that religion represented a pre-scientific mode of thought which would subsequently decline owing to industrialization, rationalization and positivism.

We have yet, however, to define what we mean by 'religion'. This is a fundamental question of sociological enquiry. We must be able to identify the existence and characteristics of a phenomenon before we can attempt to explain its role – past, present and even future – in social life. A starting point is often to make the observation that a wide variety of beliefs called 'religions' exists, some of which are older than others, some similar, some influenced by others. Figure 18.1 illustrates the multiplicity of major world religions, to which we can also add those described as 'new religious movements'.

The problems of definition

Defining 'religion' presents sociology with a number of problems:

1 There is no single, commonly held definition of religion. This may well increase debate within sociology as to what religion *is*, but equally it constrains debate on the issue of what religion *does*. It is difficult (though not impossible) to discuss

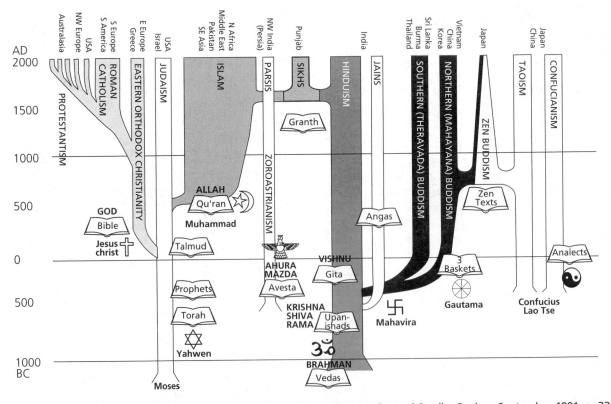

Figure 18.1 The world's religions, their symbols and sacred texts. Source: *General Studies Review*, September 1991, p. 33.

NOTES: The leading prophet or founder of the religion is in lower case and underlined. The God (or the name given to 'God') worshipped by the followers of the religion is in block letters. Judaism, Islam and Christianity are usually spoken of as monotheistic religions; and Hinduism and its derivatives – notably Buddhism – as polytheistic religions. The more learned among Hindus, however, would say that Vishnu, Krishna and others are not themselves gods, but are revelations (avatars) of the one spirit, Brahman. Certain other religions, significant in numerical terms (Shintoism, Bahai, Animism) do not feature in the diagram. The denominations and sects within (and beyond) Protestantism require a diagram on their own.

the possible functions of religion until we understand what it is we are discussing.

2 The secularization debate, the belief that religion has declined or will decline, is severely hampered by the lack of a shared definition of religion. Broad definitions tend to lead to a conclusion that religion has not declined, whereas more narrow definitions often lead to the opposite conclusion.

3 Many of these definitions of religion contain an element of 'function' about them. Given this, it is sometimes quite difficult to separate the points at which sociologists disagree. Do they disagree over the characteristics or the functions of religion?

4 This lack of a definition may well invalidate the sociological study of religion. Does the debate and argument, at the end of the day, come down to a question of definitions? Are we simply studying competing definitions and nothing more?

Despite these problems, the study of religion is a popular sociological topic area, for students and sociologists alike. While the problem of definition is sometimes left to one side, it is important to remember that it is a very real problem.

Discussion point

Why is it important for sociologists to be as clear as they can on definitions?

Early definitions: Mueller and Tylor

In 1856, Max Mueller defined religion as 'a disease of language'. By this, he illustrates an essentially social definition of religion: religion is a human enterprise, a social creation. Created by language, religion provides a ready-built world in which we can act and interact (Berger, 1990).

Mueller's definition does have its uses, because it identifies the importance of a meaningful reality in which to act; but it still fails to explain what the characteristics of a religion are exactly.

In 1871, Edward Tylor approached the definition of religion via the philosophical theory of animism: the belief that all things – human, animal, plant and other objects – have a soul. Tylor defined religion as humanity's attempts to understand the soul, both their own and others'. It was a belief in 'spiritual beings' (Berger, 1990).

From a contemporary sociological viewpoint, these definitions contain a number of elements, varying in their use for present discussion. The idea that religion constructs a meaningful reality through which the social actor understands the word and acts bears more than a passing resemblance to contemporary phenomenological ideas. (See Section 2.8.)

Emile Durkheim

Durkheim's definition of religion – the *sacred* as opposed to the *profane* – has proven highly popular and influential amongst his contemporaries, and equally amongst contemporary sociologists. (See Section 2.3.)

Turner (1991) considers that Durkheim's idea of 'the sacred' was of ground-breaking significance at the time. It marked the end of a concern with 'gods' or 'beings', and the development of an emphasis on the importance of religious *practice*. For Durkheim, religion is:

. . . a unified system of beliefs and practices relative to sacred things, that is to say, things set apart and forbidden – beliefs and practices which unite into one single moral community called a church, all those who adhere to them.
(Durkheim, 1988, p. 224; orig. pub. 1912)

Durkheim's definition has three main advantages over previous definitions:

1 It concentrates on religious practice as a central ingredient.

2 It allows comparison to take place between societies and their different sacred practices.

3 It does not consider or question the truth of religious beliefs.

As Durkheim comments:

All [religions] *are true in their own fashion; all answer though in different ways, to the given conditions of human existence.*
(Quoted in Turner, 1991, p. 243)

Phillip E. Hammond

Hammond (1985) wishes to see religion defined as 'the sacred', following the ideas of Durkheim. Hammond is highly critical of the problems previous definitions of religion have created for sociology. He claims that we have mistakenly read the founders' analysis of dominant, large-scale institutionalized Christianity in western Europe. As a result, definitions of religion have been inherited by contemporary sociology which are far too narrow. They fail to take into consideration the revival, renewal and persistence of the 'sacred' in social life.

Hammond believes we have mistakenly related religion and the sacred together, as if they are one and the same category. Instead, he wishes to understand religion as a smaller sub-category of the sacred. For example, we could point towards nationalism and science as possible examples of modern-day 'sacreds' which are nevertheless non-religious:

We cannot blame the founders. A sensitive reading of them makes clear the distinction they drew

between 'sacred' and 'religion', so that, if secularization meant the decline of religion, it did not necessarily mean as well the disappearance of the sacred.
(Hammond, 1985, p. 3)

> ### Activity
> Using the ideas of Durkheim, Hammond contends that the sacred still exists in modern society, but in a new, modern form. Create a list of all those aspects of contemporary life, such as beliefs, that may have become 'sacred'.
>
> **I, A**

The sacred: an evaluation

Although a useful and popular definition, Durkheim's use of 'the sacred' is recognized to have some problems. Turner (1991) identifies what he considers to be the two most fundamental of these.

First, hidden in Durkheim's work is the ethnocentric (see Chapter 6) evaluation of other cultures – the belief that western science, and especially positivistic sociology – ultimately is more advanced than, and therefore better than, 'primitive religions'. Talcott Parsons interprets Durkheim's sociology of religion to suggest that religions are:

. . . distorted representations of an empirical reality which is capable of correct analysis by an empirical science . . . sociology.
(Quoted in Turner, 1991, p. 243)

Thus, sociological positivism represents the 'truth' which will evaluate the less truthful views of other cultures. This is a stance Turner and many others find politically and academically objectionable.

Secondly, Turner also objects to Durkheim's lack of understanding of the subjectivity of the individuals involved in religion. He fails to look, in a detailed way, at individual consciousness.

Max Weber

Whereas Durkheim may have failed to study individuals' subjective understanding of their realities, Weber concentrates fully on this aspect of sociological study. Using the concept of *verstehen* – meaning 'to see the world through the eyes of those involved' – Weber believes the point of all sociology should be to understand the meanings and motives of social actors (see Sections 2.6 and 3.2).

Weber suggested that the definition of religion, if ever possible, should be attempted by a sociologist only at the end of a piece of research. The sociologist should allow the subjective reality of the actor to dictate the definition process. The sociologist should never impose his or her own categories on the understanding of the actor.

Bell and Berger: phenomenological approaches

Many contemporary definitions of religion are created by uniting the ideas of Durkheim and Weber. Such definitions, usually more phenomenological in nature (see Section 2.8), seek to:

- discuss the 'sacred'
- understand individual subjectivity
- not impose their own reality onto the actors in their research.

Two examples of this approach to defining religion can be identified in the work of Daniel Bell (1977) and Peter Berger (1990). For Bell:

Religion is a set of coherent answers to the core existential questions that confront every human group, the codification of these answers into a creedal form . . . the celebration of rites which provide an emotional bond . . . and the establishment of an institutional body to bring into congregation those who share the creed and celebration.
(Quoted in Turner, 1991, p. 244)

For Berger:

Religion is the human enterprise by which a sacred cosmos is established . . . By sacred is meant here a quality of mysterious and awesome power, other than man and yet related to him, which is believed to reside in certain objects of experience.
(Berger, 1990, p. 25)

Turner: a materialist approach

Bryan Turner (1991) adopts what he terms a 'materialist' approach to the study and definition of religion. Following the work of a number of different sources from Nietzsche, Marx, Weber through to Foucault, Turner suggests that the study of religion must take into account two vital issues:

- the functioning of the economy and the relationship of religion to it
- the control, discipline and punishment of the human body, and how religion contributes to this.

Turner uses Weber's ideas to view religion as a human search for meaning, but he is open to the possibility that different economic groups use and are controlled by religion in different ways.

Solutions?

Contemporary solutions to the problem of the definition of religion appear to be, either to ignore the problem as much as possible and get on with the job of doing sociology; or, as with Turner, to attempt to bring different approaches together. As Berger comments:

Definitions cannot, by their very nature, be either 'true' or 'false', only more useful or less so. For this reason it makes relatively little sense to argue over definitions.
(Berger, 1990, p. 175)

Glock and Stark

An example of an attempt to combine qualitative and quantitative approaches (see Chapter 3) to the definition and measurement of religion is illustrated in the work of Charles Glock and Rodney Stark (1965, 1968).

Glock and Stark adopt what could be described as both a positivistic and a phenomenological approach: a pluralistic method to study religion. They recommend that all sociological research on religion – its beliefs, practices and functions – should meet five criteria (or in their terms, five 'dimensions'). Thus all sociological study of religion should meet a requirement to:

1 study individuals' and groups' levels of religious belief
2 understand the amount of involvement an individual has in acts of religious worship and celebration
3 investigate feelings of supernatural, sacred and spiritual contact amongst individuals and groups
4 measure the amount of understanding and knowledge people hold of their religion
5 see how dimensions 1–4 influence the day-to-day action and interaction of these people.

Glock and Stark contend that a full sociological understanding of religion will be possible only if we adopt these areas of study.

Activity

Design a piece of sociological research which investigates religion as defined by the five dimensions suggested by Glock and Stark.

I, A

18.3 Religious practice and ritual

Early functionalist and functionalist-based theories (see Section 2.4) of the role of religion in society developed through the use of fieldwork and the study of small-scale non-western societies. The theoretical justification for the study of such small-scale pre-industrial societies is given through a use of evolutionary images of history (see Section 12.2). The so-called 'advanced' western world was seen to have progressed further along the historical path towards science, reason and rationality than these other, 'slower' developing societies. Sociologists could therefore understand more of their own culture by spending time researching societies in those 'traditional' stages of development believed to have come before modernity.

For the functionalists, it was undeniably a simpler task to study the interrelationships of harmony and consensus between social institutions on a small-scale than in an industrializing and changing western European society.

A common belief shared by these anthropological or ethnographic pieces of research was the importance of *ritual* or collective ceremony to bond society together with a set of norms and values.

William Robertson Smith: collective ceremonies

In the late 1800s, William Robertson Smith, although not himself a functionalist, proved highly influential to the sociological study of small-scale tribal communities – and especially to the work of Emile Durkheim and others.

Smith, himself a Christian minister, believed tribal religious ritual practices were a forerunner to large-scale religious practices such as Christianity. Smith concentrated on the significance of collective ceremonies for the social group. Through participation in sacrifice, the sharing of sacred meals and other important times, individuals were bonded together. The function of collective ritual was to create a consensus over group norms:

Religion did not exist for the saving of souls, but for the preservation and welfare of society . . . Ancient religion is but part of the general social order.
(Smith, quoted in Turner, 1991, p. 44)

The idea is thus that religion performs an integrative role to create social order.

Emile Durkheim: the conscience collective

Durkheim uses a wide definition of religion encompassing many different sets of beliefs and practices. In a similar fashion to W. R. Smith, he places high value on the importance of religious rituals – which function to bond society together.

Durkheim defines religion as the 'sacred' rather than the 'profane': religion is any set of practices and beliefs which are treated as sacred – set apart, special, not treated as part of the ordinary, mundane and profane world.

Given the importance of the integrative function which the sacred performs, Durkheim believed this distinction was a human universal. All societies, irrespective of their place along the path of historical development, had their sacred forms.

What is especially interesting about Durkheim's definition of religion is his insistence that religion is not solely a belief in a God or gods. Religion is characterized more by what it does, the function it performs, the collective practices it encourages:

It has often been said that religion was, at each moment of history, the totality of beliefs and sentiments of all sorts relative to the relations of man with a being or beings whose nature he regarded as superior to his own. But such a definition is manifestly inadequate . . . we know for certain, moreover, that a religion without a god exists [Buddhism]. This alone should be sufficient to show that we should not continue to define religion in terms of the idea of God . . . the only characteristic that all religious ideas and sentiments share equally seems to be that they are common to a certain number of people living together, and that they are also normally very intense . . . it is, thus, very probable . . . that religion corresponds to an equally very central area of the conscience collective.
(Durkheim, 1988, p. 222; orig. pub. 1893)

Durkheim draws an important distinction between 'religion' and 'magic':

- Religion bonds social members together – it gives a group unity through the sharing of a common faith. In this sense, religion has what Durkheim calls a 'church' – a set of shared practices which are communal and collective in nature.
- By contrast, magic has no 'church' – it has no general, collective ceremonies which bind individuals together into a conscience collective: magic may well have rituals and ceremonies, but its bonds are not lasting.

With the case of religion, however, the bonds or collective norms and values are socialized through public ritual, but are internalized and carried around in the consciousness of individuals. In this manner, even on their own, individuals are never individuals – they are always part of a shared collective. (See also Sections 2.3 and 10.2.)

Durkheim borrows from the work of Gustave Le Bon. In his discussion of collective public rituals, Le Bon conducted research into the psychology of 'crowd behaviour' in the late 1800s. Durkheim places great importance on the public or 'crowd' nature of religious ceremony. Socialization occurs through integration with others. (See Section 10.1.)

The problem of social order

Durkheim's work – especially on religion – is often presented as an attempt to answer what is known as the 'Hobbesian problem of order'. Thomas Hobbes, a seventeenth-century English philosopher posed the question 'how is order possible?' For Hobbes, the basis of human activity was competition which led to a 'nasty, brutish and short' life. Given this state of nature, how is society possible? How is the greedy individualistic will put aside for the good of the collective?

Talcott Parsons, a later American functionalist, interpreted Durkheim's work to address this problem by arguing that the external constraint of a social group and the institutions of society lead to an internal control within the individual body whereby moral codes are internalized via rituals and rites.

Totemism

In his classic text *The Elementary Forms of the Religious Life*, originally published in 1912, Durkheim (1982) uses the example of totemism as practised by Australian aborigines to illustrate how religion contributes to the conscience collective.

Totemism (the practice of worshipping a totem) simply means to take an object – usually from the natural world, a plant or animal – as a symbol of group membership. It is the method by which clans are able to identify 'insiders' and 'outsiders'.

The totem also fits into Durkheim's definition of a religion: it is a sacred object, not a profane one. The practice of totemism also involves the development of a shared moral unity designed to integrate and contribute to the conscience collective. Since these social bonds are long-lasting, totemism is considered to have a 'church'.

Durkheim contends that in religion the real object of worship is not a God or gods with special or supernatural powers, but rather the group itself. The totem is a sacred symbol of group life, of belonging to a collective. The function of religion is to give social members a concrete symbol of group life around which they can organize public group-enhancing rituals.

Bronislaw Malinowski: religion, uncertainty and meaning

Malinowski (1954), too, believes that the function of religion is to bond a moral community together. Using research from the Trobriand Islands – another small-scale non-western society – Malinowski's work both complements and criticizes Durkheim's.

In agreement with Durkheim, Malinowski believes religion contributes to social solidarity by reinforcing a value consensus (see Section 2.4). However, Malinowski believes that collective religious ceremonies operate to create solidarity only when such cohesion is threatened. Therefore, religion does not involve the worship of a symbol which stands for society; rather, it is a powerful mechanism of stability used at times of disruption, anxiety and crisis.

Uncertainty and a loss of meaning are powerful sources of social disruption for group life. The loss of a clear, stable understanding of the meaning of life, by those involved in such, would be dysfunctional for the smooth functioning of the group.

The function of religion is to create public rituals which reinforce collective norms and values at times when they are threatened. A good illustration of this argument would be death and marriage. Both these events could harm the status quo of society, albeit in different ways. By creating public rituals around these events, and thereby pulling individuals together, stability is reinforced and collective life can continue.

Malinowski applies his ideas to his fieldwork in the Trobriand Islands. At times of sea-fishing, group members are tense and anxious. Normally, for most of the year, fishing in their protected lagoon offers a safe environment. However, the sea – a potentially hostile, dangerous and hazardous environment – offers many opportunities for fear and tension amongst the group. This tension, although potentially a threat to social solidarity, can be combated via collective ritual. In this way, religion operates at times of life crises.

Discussion point

Think about the work of Durkheim and Malinowski. How might some of their ideas contribute to a form of intellectual or academic colonization or imperialism? Do they suggest that the western world is in some way better than other areas? Should sociologists think like this, if they do?

Claude Lévi-Strauss: a structuralist approach

A contrasting anthropological treatment of small-scale non-western societies is provided by structural anthropologist Claude Lévi-Strauss (1989) whose work has proved highly influential on modern-day social theories such as the development of post-structuralism (see Section 2.10).

Lévi-Strauss' work was popular in the late 1950s and 1960s and represented the beginnings of an interest in structural philosophy in French academic thought.

'Structuralism' refers to the general belief that specific aspects of social life, although appearing perhaps on a surface level to be unrelated, can in fact be interrelated at a more hidden level (or structure) beyond, above or behind the level of mere surface appearance. Social life is therefore patterned, regulated or structured in much the same way that language is thought to be.

A basic distinction can be drawn between the deep structure and the unique, individual action which occurs within a structure. Or, as is the case with language, there are the rules of language such as grammar or syntax (the structure) and speech acts which are individual (the world of surface appearance).

Taking the idea of 'structure' in a more general sense, Saussure – considered to be the founder of the 'structuralist' approach – contended that language should be studied as a system of underpinning rules and regulations, a set of codes, which pattern and regulate. We should not concern ourselves simply with the specific content of language; instead Saussure wished to identify the formal, universal laws which dictate human language in a scientific fashion.

In taking the ideas of Saussure, and applying them to anthropological study, Lévi-Strauss sought to analyse the patterns or structures inherent in human life – kinship patterns, myths, totemism, the classification of the natural world and religious customs. He believed that a common structure united all societies despite the apparent 'uniqueness' of such societies.

The not so savage mind

In his text *The Savage Mind*, first published in 1962, Lévi-Strauss (1989) argues that the 'scientific mind' of western societies and the so-called 'savage mind' of 'primitive cultures' are not simply different points along a shared historical path, one lesser developed than the other. Instead, the savage mind is as capable of 'scientific' thought as the western mind. They are both united by a deep structure.

As a point of departure, Lévi-Strauss takes the work of Malinowski, of whom he is highly critical. Malinowski, although believing totemism provides vital functions which enhance social stability, nevertheless believes (as does Durkheim) that it is a pre-scientific mode of thought. We are given the impression that totemism is a basic or 'primitive' mode of thought incapable of seeing the world 'how it really is'.

Lévi-Strauss believes that the work of Malinowski has created an illusion of understanding so far as the real meaning of totemism is concerned. At a surface level, totemism may appear distinct, but at a deep structural level it uses the same categories and methods of thought as 'modern man'. The (not so) 'savage mind' uses a vast and complex system of classification for the natural world, in a similar way to western science. Equally, the telling of myths and stories illustrates the use of the technique of analogy to explain their relationships to the world around them.

18.4 **The secularization debate**

Central to the sociological study of religion is the area of intellectual activity known as 'the secularization debate'. A very important part of the debate is the question of definition (see Section 18.2). Like the definition of religion itself, many sociologists do not agree on the term 'secularization'. Equally, there is little agreement amongst the vast secularization literature, once we decide what the concept means, as to whether or not it has happened, will happen, and whether its existence or otherwise is a cause for celebration or disillusionment.

To attempt to deal with these fundamental problems through the course of this section, a basic definition will serve: *secularization is usually referred to as the decline of religion, or the loss of the religious in society.*

Classical views

Early sociological activity was the sociology of secularization. Early sociologists, in particular Comte, Weber and Durkheim, emphasized the character of sociology as a rational intellectual activity, quite unlike the irrationality of the religious thinking preceding it (see Section 2.3). The industrial age was the dawn of a new, higher human history, one where humanity's relationship to nature changed dramatically. No longer did human societies lie in the dark shadows of nature, controlled by its forces; instead, humanity mastered the world around it. Science became the new-found guiding principle behind social change. Religion was believed to be in decline, and this was seen as a good thing.

Max Weber was one of the few founding fathers of sociology to view secularization in a slightly less than positive light. For Weber, rationality and bureaucracy would rise to prominence in modernity (modern, industrial society) but at the expense of earlier ways of thought. The modern world may control nature by science, but humanity, for Weber, would also suffer under its hands (Kasler, 1988; Kumar, 1986). (See also Section 9.7.)

Weber outlined a number of elements in the general trend towards secularization. One element was the 'desacralization' of the world view used to explain events in society. The sacred or supernatural was believed to be in decline in favour of scientific explanations.

Along with desacralization, Weber identified the process of 'disenchantment' – or rather, the 'loss of enchantment' from social thought. Traditional society was believed to be characterized by a general belief in the reality of magic. Myth and folklore played a central part in the social life of the past, but would fade out, giving way once again to scientific rationality and reason.

By this Weber means that modern social action would be based on rational motives rather than magical ones. Rational motives are those where means, ends and goals are *calculated*, rather than relying on supernatural forces. Weber was somewhat disillusioned by this process, regretting the loss of the enchanted.

For Weber, then, secularization is a process of increasing rationalization (see also Section 2.3). Weber's conception of 'rationality' was as a process whereby precise calculation is introduced into areas of social life. Rational thinking is based on the systematic breaking-down of an object for study, into smaller parts, all of which can be classified and analysed. In this way, all areas of modern life can be seen to have become rational, from health (systematic classification of the body and disease – see also Chapter 13) to music (systematic classification of notes, scales etc.).

Weber believed that along with the rise of rationality comes the rise of bureaucratic systems of management. Once again, Weber did not see this necessarily as a positive contribution to modern social life: bureaucracy is seen as an 'iron cage', limiting human individual freedom and controlling and constraining action. (See also Section 9.7.)

Discussion point

Has religion lost its 'social significance'? If so, how can we tell, how can we measure this loss?

Contemporary arguments for secularization

A number of sociologists have adopted the idea of secularization and have applied it to contemporary forms of society.

Bryan Wilson

Wilson contends that the process of secularization, as originally indicated by the founders, is a unilinear path of modern social development. Like Comte and Weber, Wilson believes that religion has made way for scientific thought, reason and rational calculation. He contends that religious practice and religious thought have both declined in western societies:

Religious 'thinking' is perhaps the area which evidences most conspicuous change. Men act less and

Activity

Study the statistics in Table 18.1, which represent modern trends in church membership.

a Write a paragraph describing what these figures appear to suggest for the idea of secularization.

b How valid do you think these figures are in indicating an 'overall trend' of secularization? What do they *not* show?

I, E

Table 18.1 UK church membership[1] (millions)

	1970	1980	1992	1994
Trinitarian churches				
Roman Catholic[2]	2.7	2.4	2.1	2.0
Anglican	2.6	2.2	1.8	1.8
Presbyterian	1.8	1.4	1.2	1.1
Methodist	0.7	0.5	0.4	0.4
Baptist	0.3	0.2	0.2	0.2
Other free churches	0.5	0.5	0.6	0.7
Orthodox	0.2	0.2	0.3	0.3
All Trinitarian churches	8.8	7.4	6.6	6.5
Non-Trinitarian churches				
Mormons	0.1	0.1	0.2	0.2
Jehovah's Witnesses	0.1	0.1	0.1	0.1
Other Non-Trinitarian	0.1	0.2	0.2	0.2
All Non-Trinitarian churches	0.3	0.4	0.5	0.5
Other religions				
Muslims	0.1	0.3	0.5	0.6
Sikhs	0.1	0.2	0.3	0.3
Hindus	0.1	0.1	0.1	0.1
Jews	0.1	0.1	0.1	0.1
Others	0.0	0.1	0.1	0.1
All other religions	0.4	0.8	1.1	1.2

[1] Adult active members
[2] Mass attendance

Source: *Social Trends 26*, (1996); original data from *Christian Research*

less in response to religious motivation: they assess the world in empirical and rational terms, and find themselves involved in rational organizations and rationally determined roles which allow small scope for such religious predilections as they might privately entertain.
(Wilson, 1966, p. x)

Wilson suggests that modern consciousness has indeed become disenchanted. The modern psyche is based on the ideologies of science, not magic:

Even if ... non-logical behaviour continues in unabated measure in human society, then at least the terms of non-rationality have changed, it is no longer the dogmas of the Christian church which dictate behaviour, but quite other irrational and arbitrary assumptions about life, society and the laws which govern the physical universe.
(Wilson, 1966, p. x)

Wilson suggests that the social significance of religion, in all its forms, has declined. Religious ideas, consciousness and explanations no longer inhabit the human mind, no longer dictate human action. Equally, religious practices no longer take up the time of the individual.

Will Herberg

In his book *Protestant, Catholic, Jew*, Will Herberg (1956) suggests that although the USA has significantly larger church attendance figures than, for example, the United Kingdom, this should not immediately lead us to assume that people are more religious in America than elsewhere, or even that those individuals and groups who attend church services – even on a regular and semi-regular basis – are more religious than those who do not. Attendance figures do not give the whole picture, and in particular they do not give an indication of the reasons or motives for attendance.

Herberg suggests that church attendance in the USA is largely an indication of a commitment to a wider community, not necessarily an indication of

Activity

The work of Wilson and of Herberg offers modern sociology very different interpretations of the process of secularization. Whereas Wilson focuses his argument on the increasing rationalization of social life, Herberg is more concerned to investigate the purposes or functions of religious services and rituals. Make a list of the key similarities and differences between these two approaches.

I, A

'religiousness'. Many people attend church services out of a sense of 'duty' to their family and neighbourhood (see also Chapter 16). These secular motivations for attending church are an illustration, argues Herberg, of an 'internal' process of secularization, of the gradual erosion of the strength of religious commitment within the church, not from the outside.

The Christian 'New Right' in America

As possible evidence against the ideas of Herberg, we can turn to the rise of evangelical Protestantism within the USA, in the late 1970s and the 1980s. Known by the label 'the New Christian Right' or 'the Christian New Right', this movement has attempted to reunite Christian religious beliefs with political life. Peter Beyer (1994) refers to the Christian New Right as a 'religio-political movement'. It is an example not only of a new religious movement, but also, in a much wider sense, of a new social movement. (See Section 17.5.) It seeks to mobilize popular public support through the use of techniques such as 'televangelism', in order to have its nominated candidates elected at the political ballot box.

Showing some resemblance to the New Right in British and American politics (see Section 2.10), the Christian New Right is a return to what is seen to be 'traditional morality'. There is, on occasions, some overlap between the 'political' New Right and the 'religious' New Right. The American Republican Party has, in recent years, been heavily influenced by Christian New Right ideas, and in particular over their choice of a vice-presidential candidate.

Family values, sexual discipline, censorship of 'corrupt views' through the medium of television, especially pornography, and a condemnation of homosexuality, are core values to the Christian New Right. As Beyer comments:

A first, quick acquaintance with the issues championed by the New Christian Right reveals a somewhat odd combination of personal moral issues, geopolitical issues and economic issues . . .While the writings of the movement trace them all to a fundamental moral and biblical message, the highly selective nature of these issues and their resemblance to the platform of the secular right in America indicate that there is more at issue than the reassertion of pure religious norms and values . . . a call to religious revival, moral regeneration, and the resurgence of the American nation.
(Beyer, 1994, p. 122)

The leaders and followers of the movement of the Christian New Right believe their ideas to be the basis for a new political and national identity in America – and a new mechanism for shaping America's role in the new global political arena of the 'new world order'.

While members of the Christian New Right would, we can assume, see their project as the start of the moral regeneration of America, the evidence suggests that the membership and influence of this movement is not yet large enough to make a significant difference on the national or global stages. It does, however, suggest that 'religious' values in the West do still exist, even if they are often combined or used in conjunction with other sources of power.

Objections to secularization

Far from following Wilson or the earlier founders, many sociologists are highly critical of the idea that religion has declined. These sociologists claim that secularization is a myth. Secularization, they say, has not happened, although some do suggest that the precise nature of religious practice and commitment may have changed.

David Martin

David Martin (1978, 1991) is highly critical and sceptical of the term 'secularization'. He suggests that it has become almost meaningless in recent sociological debate owing to the inability of sociologists to agree on a precise definition. Martin also claims that much of the literature on secularization is dependent on the ideological values of the researchers themselves. He claims that secularization is often used as a term by counter-religious sociologists. This claim, that value-freedom is absent from the sociological study of religion, could be very damaging for some people.

Martin suggests that the concept of secularization should be made redundant. It is a myth that does not take sociological debate forward, but hinders it. It should be dropped from sociological analysis.

Phenomenology and the over-secularized conception of humankind

Many modern-day phenomenologists (see Sections 2.8 and 3.2) are concerned to illustrate how religion continues to play an important function in society, especially in the consciousness of individuals. In direct contrast to Bryan Wilson, thinkers such as Robert N. Bellah and Thomas Luckmann claim that institutionalized religion may be on the decline and church attendance may have dropped, but private individual belief still continues. It is a mistake to assume that the quantitative methods used by Wilson, specifically the analysis of church attendance figures, can allow us to achieve a realistic understanding of the meaning and motives of private belief.

Many secularization theories are based on a highly unrealistic notion of a 'golden age' of religious commitment in the past. Phenomenologists are keen to reject this naive image of the history of religion. Whereas the decline in church attendance figures does not necessarily mean an end to religious belief, past high church attendance figures do not immediately indicate that all those who attended believed to the same level or extent. It may well be that the past was a time of *forced participation*, whereas the present allows more individual freedom of choice.

Bellah (1970) and Glock (1976) both suggest that it is a mistake to assume that religion has declined simply by looking at declines in its public and communal forms. Instead, Bellah claims that a process of 'individuation' has occurred. Individuals are free to search for their own religious and spiritual meanings, unconstrained by a repressive church.

While making a similar point to Bellah, Thomas Luckmann (1967, 1996) describes contemporary society as based on the processes of the transformation and privatization of religion. He suggests that although large-scale 'institutional' religious practice has declined, it would be a mistake to make the assumption that religion has declined or will decline:

... even thirty years ago it was obvious that [institutional religion's] *dominance and pervasive social reach had come to an end. The widespread view that this meant the end of religion seemed erroneous to me. Even in the heyday of secularization theories, there were signs that a new, institutionally less visible social form of religion was emerging, and that it was likely to become dominant at the expense of the older form.*
(Luckmann, 1996, p. 73)

As Luckmann comments, although religion may have declined in the public sphere of life, it has still lived on in the private sphere – at the level of private belief and individual practice. This new religious world, or newly transformed, privatized social consciousness, will still have its religious expression:

Churches and sects would henceforth have to exist in a radically transformed social structural and cultural context. The new, basically de-institutionalized, privatized social form of religion seemed to be relying primarily on an open market of diffuse, syncretistic packages of meaning, typically connected to low levels of transcendence and produced in a partly or fully commercialized cultic milieu.
(Luckmann, 1996, p. 73)

Individuals are free to 'shop around' for a set of religious meanings and values which suits them – not dictated to by a rigid, set, institutionalized form of public worship. This 'privatization' of religion is seen by Luckmann to be a liberating consequence of differentiation in wider society. (See also Section 10.9.)

Religious transformation

The arguments above suggest that the sacred has not declined, it has changed or transformed. Religion's emphasis has moved away from institutionalized public practice towards individual personal belief; away from collective rites and ceremonies towards a personal search for meaning. This leads to a situation of religious pluralism – evidence not of the break-up of religion but of its continued expression.

A return to the sacred

In discussing the idea that religion has become transformed in modern society, many commentators have returned to the ideas of Emile Durkheim. They claim, following Durkheim, that the sacred lives on, but in an altered form. Whatever the term used to describe this process of revival and renewal – transformation, privatization, individuation etc. – the central idea is that the sacred is a much wider category than just institutional religion. In his classic text, *The Elementary Forms of the Religious Life*, Durkheim (1982) suggests that:

... the former gods are growing old or are already dead, and others are not yet born ... But this state of uncertainty and confused agitation cannot last for ever. A day will come when our societies will again know those hours of creative ferment in the course of which new ideas and new formulas are found which will serve for a time as a guide to humanity; and when these hours have been once experienced, men will spontaneously feel the need of reliving them from time to time in thought, that is to say, of keeping alive their memory by means of celebrations which regularly reproduce their products.
(Durkheim, 1988: 244; orig. pub. in 1912)

and:

There are no gospels which are immortal, but neither is there any reason for believing that humanity is incapable of inventing new ones. As to the symbols with which this new faith will express itself, whether or not they will resemble those of the past, or be more adequate for the reality which they seek to represent, this is a question which goes beyond the human capacity to predict.
(Durkheim, 1988, p. 245; orig. pub. 1912)

As we can see, Durkheim believed that the role performed by religion – the sacred – was so great that when an old sacred expression 'died' another would, in time, be 'born'. Thus, the revival of privatized religion could be seen within this Durkheimian framework to represent the transformation of the sacred.

Civic religions and rituals

Many sociologists have suggested that a re-definition of the concept 'religion' is needed, in the light of the claim that there has been a transformation of the sacred in modern life: the category 'sacred' is seen to be a much wider category than 'religion', which was used quite narrowly by the majority of the founders (but not all, as the work of Durkheim illustrates) to represent almost exclusively institutional religious practice and beliefs. As one commentator, Robert Bocock (1985), comments:

Many people, including some sociologists, define modern western societies such as Britain as being 'secular'. In the sense that such modern societies are no longer dominated by religious institutions in the way the Catholic Church dominated life in the Middle Ages in Europe, then it is possible to say that they are more secular. However, such a description can overestimate both the role of the Church in the past and the decline of the influence of religious groups on many people in present day societies. So some definition of religion and the secular is needed which allows for these complications in a way which the notion of secularization fails to do.
(Bocock, 1985, p. 208)

One of these new definitions, to explain the continued existence of the sacred, focuses on what are called 'civic religions' or 'civic rituals'. Whereas a religious ritual is an organized event around a religious figure or occasion, a civic ritual is an event organized around a head of state, or a date of significance such as a day of independence or a coronation. These civic rituals celebrate citizenship in a nation-state (see Section 17.5).

Although civic rituals and religious rituals are different in focus, many have indicated how, in practice, these two types of rituals are quite similar. Bocock suggests that civic rituals could be a new expression of the 'sacred' as defined and discussed in the work of Durkheim. Such modern-day civic rituals could include:

* coronations
* royal weddings
* remembrance days
* state funerals
* independence days
* celebrations of revolutions
* ceremonies based around wars or battles.

Many commentators suggest that the civic rituals shown in Figures 18.2–18.5 have a common 'sacred'

character with more so-called 'traditional' religious practices and rituals. In this way, the annual celebration of the French revolution was considered by Durkheim as an example of a nationalist-based civic ritual which indicated the presence of the sacred in a supposedly 'secular age'.

Figure 18.2 A celebration of the French Revolution

Figure 18.3 A coronation

Figure 18.4 A remembrance parade

Figure 18.5 Celebration in Red Square, Moscow

Equally, the old Soviet Union (USSR), despite formally banning 'religion', could still be seen to have its sacred expressions – particularly in the way that the revolution was celebrated annually by parades in Red Square, and statues of Marx, Lenin and other important historical figures were erected as focal points for celebration and other national activities.

Timothy Crippen

Crippen (1988), following the ideas of Durkheim, suggests that the secularization thesis, whereby religion will slowly decline in the contemporary world, is an unrealistic way to understand the nature of modern-day religious belief and commitment. Instead, according to Crippen, we have witnessed a transformation of previous sacred symbols. He argues that 'the sacred' is a human universal, so it is present in every society, but not necessarily in an identical or common form:

Decaying commitment to 'supernatural' forms of explanation in combination with an increased reliance on 'technorational' explanations of experience represents a transformation in the way that the 'sacred' is constructed.
(Crippen, 1988, p. 320)

Crippen suggests that modern sacred symbols are based on scientific (or, as he defines them, 'technorational') images. The sacred has not declined or decayed, but the 'old gods' have been replaced by 'new gods'. For him, these are based around nationalist identities (see also Section 16.8); the most sacred symbols, along with many modern-day rituals, are those based on the 'sovereignty' of the nation-state:

... the nation-state represents the most dominant, extensive, and inclusive boundary of moral identity in modern societies. Thus, it is no surprise that so many scholars remark that nationalism is the dominant form of modern religious consciousness ... the emblems and shrines that identify and commemorate the 'nation' are among the principal sacred objects in the modern world and correspond to the dominant organizational form of sovereignty.
(Crippen, 1988, p. 325)

Discussion point

Is science the complete opposite of religion or merely its modern equivalent?

Medicalization and secularization

A contemporary topic of sociological enquiry charts the growth of common ground between the sociologies of knowledge, religion and science and medicine (see also Chapter 13). For theorists such as Shilling (1993), Bull (1990) and Featherstone (1991) the synthesis between these areas of study is an inevitable consequence of the changes taking place in late-capitalist societies in western Europe and America.

'Medicalization' is a term used by Turner (1982, 1985) and Bull to refer to the increasing dominance of the medical profession, medical personnel and medical knowledge in areas of society previously controlled by other institutions such as religion. Medicalization, then, is seen by some as a process of secularization. Religion has lost or is losing the battle for control over morality, sexuality and diet. Religion is losing or has lost control over the human body and how the body is to be disciplined. As Bull comments:

The social dominance of medicine has remained unnoticed until quite recently, yet evidence of it is ubiquitous. People have to be examined by the medical profession at every stage in the life-cycle; medical criteria define what is acceptable in town planning, automobile design, agricultural production . . . and many other areas of social life.
(Bull, 1990, p. 245)

Contemporary society is often described as having a 'consumer culture', in which individual self-identity is something to be 'bought' as a life-style package (see Section 10.9). The claim is made by Turner that religion has lost the ability to define, dictate and control this consumer culture of the 'healthy body', so it has lost a cultural battle to medicine.

According to Turner (1989, 1990) religion has been taken over by medicine. Medicine with its

Discussion point

Why are people in society more inclined to believe and obey something if it can convince them of its 'scientific nature'?

claims of being a 'science' offers a source of morality that can control the body. Sickness is no longer the result of a sinful life, instead it is the result of an unhealthy life, an equally amoral life-style.

Turner explores how medicine has taken control away from religion over diet and the morality attached to diet, this being seen as a process of secularization. He identifies two quite similar methods of control over the body through a restrictive diet, which he labels:

- religious asceticism
- medical regimen.

Turner believes that a medical regimen has taken over from religious asceticism. This process of medicalization as secularization can be illustrated by discussing the emergence of so-called 'dietary science' in the late nineteenth century. A historical 'rupture' or break is seen to have occurred between eighteenth-century and modern dietary practices. Diet in the eighteenth century was based on a highly religious form of control in which the controlling and limiting of food intake was an attempt to purify the inner body, the soul, and to control desires, especially sexual desire. Diet was therefore controlled by religious ideas in the interests of wider social stability: it enforced the norms and values of society concerning family and monogamy.

In contrast, it can be argued, in modern society diet is concerned with the outer body. Diet functions to create a healthy body. The goals are improved sexuality, longevity of life and improved physical appearance, not the avoidance of sin. This is an example of the medicalization of diet, the replacement of religious ideas with scientific ones. Turner concludes that:

Put simply, the doctor has replaced the priest as the custodian of social values.
(Turner, 1990, p. 37)

and:

The modern medical regimen implies a certain asceticism of morals as the main defence against sexually transmitted disease, heart disease, stress and cancer. In this sense, religious norms of the good life have been transferred to medicine; the result is that medicine, as an allegedly neutral science of disease, encroaches on both law and religion, in providing criteria of normality. While the sacred conscience collective withers away, medicine provides, as it were, a second-order moral framework.
(Turner, 1989, p. 214)

Resistance to civic rituals

Bocock (1974, 1985) warns that even if civic rituals are identified to exist in society, we should not immediately assume that they are valued and accepted by all, or even that those who attend such occasions accept that they are involved in a form of 'sacred' ritual.

For example, coronations and royal weddings may not be seen as being legitimate sources of norms and values (see Section 10.1) by anyone outside of the higher social classes, and may be actively resented by some working-class members and political activists.

Discussion point

Do all members of society follow the religious and secular rituals of society with an equal degree of acceptance and deference?

18.5 **New religious movements**

'Religion' and 'religious beliefs' can vary in the way they are practised according to each individual. For some, 'being religious' involves some sort of formal, public worship whereas for others the emphasis is on personal, private belief. It is thus possible to be religious in one's own mind without joining a religious organization or being part of a group.

Discussion point

How can religious classifications help with the analysis of religion in society?

On making this observation, sociologists have become increasingly concerned with the process of classifying types of religious organizations. How can we identify and explain the different ways in which groups of religious people join together in more or less public services? In answering this question sociologists have drawn a distinction between types of religious organizations.

Typologies and classifications

The act of classification, of creating a typology, is a central process in much sociology. Classifications can be extremely helpful in allowing sociologists to think about the social world and specific aspects of it. However, it is important to remember that not all typologies are exact, that they do not all perfectly mirror society. The value of typologies is that they can be compared to social life and then modified, changed and discussed.

Ernst Troeltsch

Ernst Troeltsch (1981) was one of the first thinkers in the early 1930s to attempt to classify different types of religious organizations. The distinction Troeltsch draws between 'church' and 'sect' has proved to be long-lasting and highly influential in more contemporary sociological discussions of types of religious practice.

The church

The church can be seen as the original and institutionalized form of religion in a society – dominant, and widely integrated into mainstream culture. The church is an extremely large-scale organization drawing membership from all sections of the population, although it is particularly related to the culture of the ruling or upper social groups. Although members can join, or be baptised into a church, the majority of members are born into it, following the practices of their family.

Churches are based on strong hierarchies and often have specialist priests arranged in a heavily bureaucratic system of power relations to one another and to their followers. Churches are often related to the state, so they are by nature protective of the existing role of social life and attempt to promote the ideas of a long-established ruling group in the interests of social stability. Hence they are often a conservative force.

Sects

Sects are smaller, more radical protest movements set up in opposition to a dominant mainstream church. They are less traditional than the church and less hierarchic, having an emphasis on community and fellowship. Troeltsch suggests that while churches are a source for the integration of all of society, sects appeal to very specific types of people, the marginal lower classes who may be opposed to the state.

Sects are typically highly integrative of those who do join, in some cases asking their members to withdraw from the mainstream world. Some examples include the Divine Light Mission, the Unification Church, the Church of Scientology, the Children of God, and Hare Krishna.

Activity

Using a library, research any one of the examples of sects listed above. Explain briefly their aims, and why they could be classified as sects.

K, I

Bryan Wilson

Wilson (1970) notes that since the work of Troeltsch, the task of defining sects has become more difficult:

The task of formulating general characterisations of sects has become more, rather than less, difficult since Troeltsch wrote, because of the many new combinations of elements that sects might now embrace in a world where men have far more diversified social experience . . . we are obliged to recognise the diversity among sects, as well as their

similarity, if our characteristics are to be useful.
(Wilson, 1970, p. 26)

Even when very general 'ideal types' have been drawn up to describe the nature of sects, we still must not assume that these so-called essential characteristics will not change over time. As Wilson also comments:

In actual sects we must expect that each of these general attributes will show some variation from the formulation. Sects undergo change, both in response to changes in the external environment, and by a process of what might be called mutation. Consequently, some attributes may be receding in importance, and others growing, at particular times in a sect's life history.
(Wilson, 1970, p. 28)

Wilson draws a typology or ideal-type of sects which emphasizes eight central characteristics, which may be more or less important at different times in the history of any one sect:

1 *Voluntariness:* Sects are based mainly on voluntary membership, but Wilson nevertheless identifies the growing trend for children of sectarians to join the same sect as their parents.
2 *Exclusivity:* Sects are often seen by their members to be based on a sense of 'exclusivity' where those who have joined are part of the 'few' who show their commitment by great allegiance.
3 *Merit:* Over long periods of time, Wilson suggests that some sects may offer membership on the basis of some act or proof of merit, of suitability for belonging to the group.
4 *Self-identification:* Sects, like other social groups, are a source of self-identification for those who make them up. They use a more or less flexible or rigid categorization of 'them' and 'us' depending on the sect in question.
5 *Élite status:* Some sects define themselves and their members as social elites, as a 'chosen people'.
6 *Expulsion:* As well as tests for membership, some sects often have rules, the breaking of which might lead to expulsion. Having said this, Wilson also notes that over time, with increased life, sects may take these rules less strictly than before.
7 *Conscience:* Many sects operate on a day-to-day basis by relying on the individual conscience of their members to live a 'worthy life' however this might specifically be defined.
8 *Legitimation:* No sect, or any other religious or social movement, new or otherwise, exists without a set of ideological values which give its practices and rulers legitimacy in the eyes of its followers.

Wilson warns us that these categories, created by him, are intended to:

. . . remind us that our categories are often clearer than the actual cases. The danger of sociology is that its constructs may easily be mistaken for summary statements of reality, for formulae in terms of which the world is to be grasped.
(Wilson, 1970, p. 35)

The response to the world by sects

Wilson (1985) develops a typology of seven different types of sect, in order to aid comparisons between them based on their response to the world:

1 *Conversionist sects:* These are 'evangelical' or 'fundamentalist' Christian sects, suggesting that the outside world is corrupt because humanity is corrupt. In order to change the world, humanity must be changed, or 'saved'. These sects tend to engage in mass meetings and public preaching rather than door-to-door recruiting.
2 *Revolutionary sects:* These desire to change the existing social order: a time will come when change will become necessary, whether by force and violence or through other means. The members of these sects believe they will become powerful, in this world, after this revolutionary change, through their status as representatives of God.
3 *Introversionist sects:* This type desires not to convert the population, nor to overturn the world, but rather to retire from the world: to cut themselves off in order to find a more personal spiritual experience.
4 *Manipulationist sects:* These are groups claiming that they have access to a specialized form of religious knowledge, which they must use to improve the existing goals of society, which they accept. They are after what they see as improvements in this world, and are less concerned with what might happen in the next – which will simply be an extension of the happiness found in this one, using the correct sources of knowledge.
5 *Thaumaturgical sects:* These groups seek personal messages from spiritual sources. They believe it is possible for humanity to experience the supernatural dimension. So-called 'miracles' or 'magic healing' are seen as further examples of the existence and power of the supernatural.
6 *Reformist sects:* These are based on having changed their nature from an original early revolutionary orientation to the world, slowly moving towards an introversionist type. They associate with the world, but at the same time they are concerned to maintain some distance from it.

7 *Utopian sects:* These partly withdraw from the world, yet partly wish to improve on it. They seek to remake the world along communitarian lines, often on a global scale.

Wilson stresses that sects tend to undergo changes in their history, and so these types should not be seen as fixed, but open to movement and reinvention.

Denominations

In response to Troeltsch's distinction between church and sect, others have added a third type – that of the denomination. Often associated with H. R. Niebuhr (1957), the denomination is usually thought of as an organization more like a church than a sect. Although being larger than sects and much more mainstream, denominations tend to be conservative and hierarchic. However, unlike churches, denominations are not necessarily supportive of the state and they often do not claim to hold a universal truth but are tolerant of the existence of many other religious ideas.

Rather than control the lives of members in a communal, sometimes world-rejecting, fashion as is the case with some sects, the emphasis within a denomination is on the creation of a lifestyle based on freedom of decision for the individual. They are focused on behaviour in this world, not salvation in the next.

Cults and new religious movements

Although the three-fold typology – church, sect, denomination – has its uses, especially as a starting point to encourage the sociological study of religious groups, the reality of social life is always a little more complex. A vast number of different types of religious groups exist in society, a fact which has lead some commentators to conclude that some groups defy classification as so far developed by sociological study.

More contemporary sociology has identified a fourth religious type, the cult. They are usually less rigid as an organization than the other types.

Elementary forms of the new religious life

Another way to discuss smaller, contemporary religious organizations is to use the concept 'new religious movements'. Perhaps the most detailed use of this broad concept is provided by Roy Wallis in his 1984 study *The Elementary Forms of the New Religious Life.*

Discussion point
What different relationships to wider society might small religious movements have?

Wallis draws a distinction between three types of so-called new religious movements as based on the relationship of the movement to the social world they exist in. Although the first to note that some movements do not fit readily into this typology, Wallis identified three main relationships a movement can have with the outside world:

- rejection
- accommodation
- affirmation.

In relation to the concepts already used in this section, movements that reject the world are often sects, movements that accommodate the world are denominations or offshoots from denominations, and movements that affirm the world could be seen as cults.

World-rejecting groups

These groups are largely hostile to the world around them. They ask of their members a total commitment which usually involves leaving the world behind. In practice the process of joining a group such as this would involve the giving up of past ties, material objects and often one's name – to be given a new identity by the new community once joined.

Limited contact with the outside world may be allowed for recruitment, publicity or fund-raising purposes. As a result these movements vary in size from very small one-off communities to more national and even international communities. Many media, public and government 'moral panics' (see Section 15.5) exist around these groups. They are seen as deviant and are sometimes accused of 'brainwashing' their members.

World-accommodating groups

Rather than being openly hostile to the world, these movements accommodate it; or rather, they ignore it and concentrate on more spiritual matters such as their faith and how to practise it in the most successful fashion. Although these groups will have traditional social contact and traditional social roles such as jobs and families, they are not concerned with creating or building a new or alternative community. These beliefs may help them in their day-to-day mainstream lives but are not designed solely for this purpose. Instead, these groups place great emphasis on seeking enlightenment. They are tolerant of others and of other faiths.

World-affirming groups

World-affirming groups, similar to cults, are often not actual organizations at all, but simply a loose collection of like-minded individuals. These 'groups' often lack collective public worship, a meeting place and even a fully developed set of ideas.

However, these groups do offer individuals something vital in their lives, a source of spiritual power. They seek not to ignore or reject the world but to make the world better; not by building a new society but by helping the individuals of this one become more successful, happy and able to cope with life.

They are largely tolerant of other faiths and do not demand too much commitment from their members. They recruit from as wide a group of people as possible and often sell training courses or workshops based on a particular technique aimed at unlocking the hidden spirituality in each person (such as by meditation).

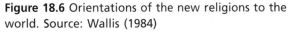

Discussion point

What image do the mass media give of new religious movements? How are they portrayed? Why do you think this is?

The difficulty of classification

As indicated in Figure 18.6, Wallis recognizes that some groups in modern social life defy classification because they occupy a 'middle' or 'intermediate' space between two or more of these types. These movements include the Jesus People, Meher Baba, the Divine Light Mission, and the Healthy Happy Holy Organization.

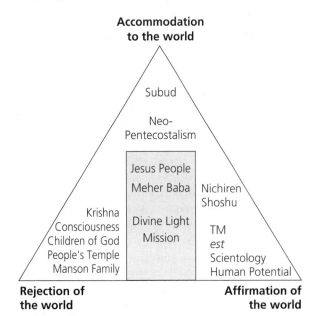

Figure 18.6 Orientations of the new religions to the world. Source: Wallis (1984)

Stark and Bainbridge

Rodney Stark and William Sims Bainbridge (1985) are highly critical of all attempts to classify religious 'types', organizations or movements. They claim that all typologies are not an actual list of identified characteristics but an assumed list of possible criteria which movements may or may not possess. As such, they are little more than speculation and do not provide sociology with the necessary degree and level of theoretical and empirical rigour needed to develop any meaningful analysis of society.

Instead, Stark and Bainbridge seek a genuinely useful method to compare and distinguish movements from one another. They suggest this could be conducted through an analysis of the levels of conflict between a movement and wider society.

Activity

As identified above, there are many problems associated with the classification of new religious groups – as there are with the definition and classification of religion in general. Answer the following question briefly:

- Are contradictory definitions of social phenomena such as religious movements useful to the discipline of sociology, or are they a hindrance to sociological analysis?

I, A, E

Some commentators suggest that an alternative method of classification could be developed based on the religious ideas and beliefs from which these new religious movements have developed. It would be possible, in this way, to classify movements as being Hindu-orientated, Christian-orientated, Buddhism-orientated etc.

However, once more, this typology would not allow us to classify all modern movements. Some are based on attempts to improve the person, to unlock human abilities through the mastery of techniques aimed at increasing one's spirituality. These groups are often not derived from a clearly identifiable past religious source but are part of what some call the 'human potential movement'.

The human potential movement

Roy Wallis and Steve Bruce (1986) note that the human potential movement, by virtue of its eclectic nature, is difficult to define in precise terms:

The Human Potential, or Growth Movement is not readily defined. The very vagueness and elasticity of its boundaries, the shifting character of its constituent elements, are among its most significant features – but they clearly hinder the task of easy definition. These labels are generally taken by those

involved to refer to a broad range of activities concerned with enabling people to realise a greater amount of the potential that they possess by way of ability, awareness, creativity, insight, empathy, emotional expressivity, capacity for experience and exploration, and the like.
(Wallis and Bruce, 1986, p. 158)

The human potential movement is concerned precisely with that – with improving the potential of its followers, with enabling them to 'grow' in various ways. The use of the word 'movement' is significant – it is not a group as such, although one could join a smaller group which was a part of the overall movement. Many are 'members' of the movement without being a member of a group or sect *per se*, just a follower or interested individual practitioner of a number of spiritual practices such as meditation, some forms of dance, some martial arts, massage, Yoga, T'ai Chi etc. As well as these more individual practices, on the fringes of the human potential movement we also find more well-defined and identifiable groups such as the Scientology movement. As Figure 18.7 indicates, the human potential movement is located at a point of wide crossover between many different types of belief.

Wallis and Bruce suggest that the human potential movement is an example of a 'general' rather than a 'specific' social movement:

It consists of a congeries of independent groups, leaders, media of communication, etc, which display no common structure of authority or membership, with divergences of purpose and practice, yet recognizing that they share in common a commitment to the attainment of personal growth by self-directed means. The ideology of such a movement is, therefore, inevitably a diffuse one.
(Wallis and Bruce, 1986, p. 165)

The human potential movement is characterized by a mixture of traditional spiritual practice plus aspects of humanistic psychology. We have witnessed a large increase in the interest of individuals with these ideas, particularly commercially, with many groups, courses and workshops set up around the country for massage, meditation, and relaxation to name but a few, plus the creation of a successful business of books and other related objects such as crystals.

A number of connections can be made between the ideas of the human potential movement and the sources from which they have come. This is depicted in Figure 18.8 on page 751.

Case study – The making of a Moonie: choice or brainwashing?

This classic study in the sociology of religion was published by Eileen Barker (1984) and has been praised for the methodological approach adopted.

The Moonies were founded by the Reverend Sun Myung Moon in 1954 under the name 'The Holy Spirit Association for the Unification of World Christianity'. Also known as the Unification Church, this religious group has been the subject of much media, public and government attention.

Barker conducted her study in the light of a media moral panic (see Section 15.5) about the so-called 'brainwashing' activities of this sect. Her research focus was the explanation of how and why people decided to join the Moonies, and to attempt to explain what sort of people they were:

This book is concerned primarily with an attempt to clarify an answer to the question with which it started: Why should – how could – anyone become a Moonie? For many people it seems so incredible that anyone should choose to become a Moonie that the simplest resolution of the question is to deny that such a choice is ever made. The assumption is that Moonies are brainwashed . . . since no one, in his or her right senses would want to become a Moonie. Becoming a Moonie must be the result of something that others do to the victim, rather than something that a convert himself decides to do.
(Barker, 1984, p. 6)

We must understand Barker's research decisions in the context of this media moral panic at the time, created by scare stories of kidnapping and brainwashing, perpetuated by the popular press in both the UK and the USA. Examples of newspaper headlines of the time are:

'Parents fight brainwashing by bizarre sect'
'Rev. Moon's plot to rule the world today'
'Moonie cult faces probe by MP into brainwashing'
'Mass suicide possible in Moon church'
'Moonies have captured my son'
'Tragedy of the broken families'
(Barker, 1984, p. 2)

Barker had two main research objectives. The first was to explain and discover the process and pattern of Moonie recruitment. The second was to classify who is recruited: are Moonies a similar or specific type of person? Heavily indebted to the work of Max Weber, Barker can be seen to attempt *verstehen* in this work:

- to understand the world through the eyes of those involved
- to investigate the motives and meanings of becoming a Moonie, rather than to rely on a media produced picture of the world.

Barker's research raises a fundamental issue of sociological methodology – the difference, in her view,

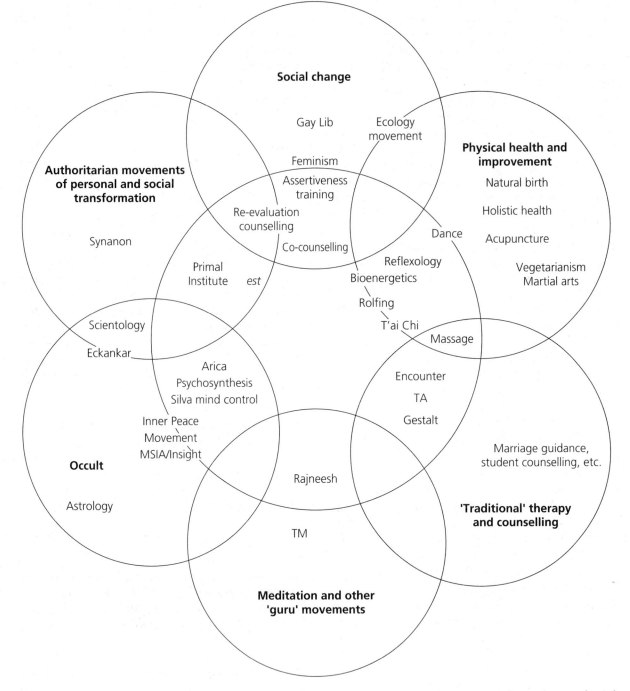

Figure 18.7 The milieu within which the human potential movement is located. Source: Wallis and Bruce (1986)

between the nature of social science and natural science (see Section 3.2).

The chemist does not try to find out what molecules 'feel' ... but some degree of subjective understanding is necessary for the sociologist ... to describe let alone understand or explain ...
(Barker, 1984, p. 20)

In order to achieve *verstehen*, she rejects the traditional divide between positivist and phenomenological methods, deciding instead to produce both

quantitative and qualitative data. This is known as 'triangulation', or 'methodological pluralism'. Barker used participant observation, in-depth interviews and questionnaires (see Sections 3.6–3.9). Although there are a number of ethical problems involved in participant observation, notably in this case the need to take on the role of a Moonie, Barker states:

I never pretended that I was, or that I was likely to become one. I admit that I was sometimes evasive,

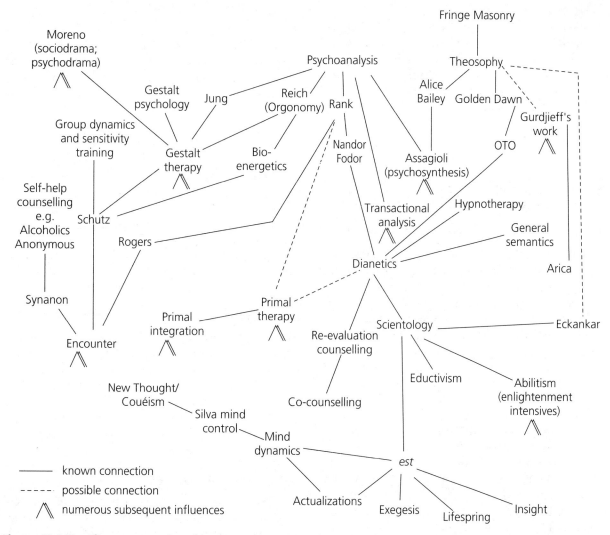

Figure 18.8 Significant connections between some major elements of the human potential movement and their sources. Source: Wallis and Bruce (1986)

and I certainly did not always say everything on my mind, but I can't remember any occasion on which I consciously lied to a Moonie.
(Barker, 1984, pp. 20–21)

Barker's research illustrated that the Moonies are highly inefficient in holding on to interested new members. The low rate of recruitment and high pattern of dropout after relatively short periods suggest that particular types of people become full Moonies – they are not brainwashed and not everyone who shows an initial interest has an equal chance of joining.

Barker suggests that Moonies come from very happy and secure family backgrounds which are usually 'respectable' middle-class homes with parents whose jobs involve some sort of commitment to public service – doctors, teachers, police etc. She concludes that individuals join the Moonies because they are offered a solution to their needs. At times of crisis in these individuals' lives, often in early adulthood,

the warm family atmosphere of the Moonies offers support and comfort. Equally, the community of the Moonies offers these individuals a chance to commit to a group of people and serve the community with them – as their parents did in wider society.

Cult controversies (1985)

In another study of the Moonies, *Cult Controversies*, Beckford (1985) interviewed 26 ex-members, 35 parents of practising members and 26 activists in campaigns against cults.

Beckford was interested in the societal reaction to the existence of cults such as the Moonies. He comments that the controversy surrounding some cults is a product of social construction: it grew, as did the increased membership of these groups, in the 1970s, in a specific cultural context. Beckford comments, that as sociologists we must:

. . . explore the social processes whereby the interactions between individual human beings and

between human groups can generate controversy. After all, controversy is not something that exists independently from human beings: they construct it. At the same time, their actions are guided by culture or shared meanings. It is essential therefore to examine not only the social construction of controversy but also its cultural setting and the meaning that it has for the people involved.
(Beckford, 1985, p. 1)

Discussion point

Why are cults such controversial aspects of society?

Some of these cults or new religious movements have attempted to fight back against the popular media and public image, to the extent that litigation has been brought against some sections of the media. In response, many western governments have picked up on the 'cult problem' as defined by the media, opening legal enquiries and in some cases passing legislation that attempts to limit the activities of some new religious movements. For example, Sun Myung Moon – the leader of the Moonies – is barred from entering the United Kingdom.

Beckford argues that the origins of these cult controversies in wider society arose from smaller-scale conflicts within the families of the young people who joined new religious movements, between them and their parents. (See also Section 7.7.) These family concerns have been taken up by outside organizations, some self-appointed and others government sponsored, who have made it their task to limit the activities of all new religious movements.

The cultural effects of new religious movements

Beckford asserts that even if some, or the majority, of new religious movements were to suddenly disappear (which does not tend to happen in social life), their place in the culture of western societies would still live on. This is because new religious movements, such as those highlighted by the media as being 'problematic', have made three distinctive contributions to western cultural life, even if not intended:

1 They have unwittingly helped to reinforce and re-establish boundaries between socially defined 'normal' and 'abnormal' religious expressions.
2 They have led to a return to a discussion over the legal rights of families and governments to forbid individuals to partake in so-called 'deviant religious activities'.
3 They have made British governments look again at the use of charitable funds to sponsor religions

and the legal definitions of 'genuine religions' used.

As Beckford notes, these changes or contributions are essentially negative in the sense that the existence of new religious movements has forced governments to respond in a negative or critical fashion to them:

. . . the cult controversy is a barometer of changes taking place in a number of different societies. New religious movements represent an 'extreme situation' which, precisely because it is extreme, throws into sharp relief many of the assumptions hidden behind legal, cultural, and social structures. The operation of many new religious movements has, as it were, forced society to show its hand and to declare itself.
(Beckford, 1985, p. 11)

The rise and functions of new religious movements

As well as measuring and labelling religious movements, sociologists are interested in the functions these movements perform, both for the individual and for wider society. In many respects, these issues of classification and function are related: the function of a movement is often used as part of a classification scheme.

The cultic milieu

Colin Campbell (1972) suggests that all cults and new religious movements represent part of a general alternative or counter-cultural set of values which attempt to undermine the dominant, mainstream cultural values and goals of a society. This set of deviant values contains all alternative systems of thought, not just religious ideas, such as unorthodox science, deviant medicine and non-conformist political ideologies.

All these counter-cultural ideas make up a 'cultic milieu', a set of values which collectively can be thought of as an alternative cultural reservoir. Members of these groups and believers of these ideas are drawn from those seeking an alternative to mainstream ideas, practices and beliefs.

We could doubt, however, whether all these deviant or alternative ideas can be classified together in this way. Although they all share in common an intolerance of the mainstream, they could also be seen as highly alternative and antagonistic to each other!

Economic and technological changes

Like Campbell, Steven Tipton (1982) uses the idea of a 'counter-culture' to explain the existence of new religious movements. Tipton claims that the development of these alternative cultural deviant values can be related to, or located in, economic and technological changes in society.

Tipton suggests that as the proportion of the economy concerned with production and not consumption declines, the fundamental nature and character of work also changes – from a 'game' between humans and nature to a 'game' between people. With such economic change (see Section 9.4), the youth in a society become disillusioned and turn against 'the system', seeking alternative and deviant values, some of which are alternative expressions of religiousness (see Section 10.5).

A second explanation offered by Tipton to explain the existence of deviant religions is concerned with technological development in society. Owing to developments in technology in the workplace, social life is less concerned with the world of work and more concerned with the world of leisure and personal consumption. In the western world, especially in the 1960s, claims Tipton, these developments freed the youth to search for their own sources of personal expression since the world of work is no longer the prime focus of life. Part of this search for expression, again, includes the development and rise to popularity of new religious movements.

Max Weber: marginalization

Weber provides an explanation for the rise of new religious movements by looking at the functions they perform for the individuals who join them. He notes that religion is not necessarily a conservative force, and so sects and cults could offer the oppressed and marginal a sense of hope, status and dignity: an alternative search for that lost in mainstream culture.

Weber argues that new religious movements are joined by the marginal – those on the outskirts of society, those not fully integrated into the dominant cultural values of society, or those not able to achieve the dominant success-indicators of society (such as wealth) owing to their structural position.

The marginalized include the poor, exploited, disadvantaged. In western societies we could identify members of some ethnic minorities, the under-educated and the working class to represent the marginalized (see Section 4.8). They often turn to small religious movements and groups offering them a chance for political and radical struggle against those seen to oppress and exploit in society. Religion can be a major political motivating force.

An example of religion acting in this fashion is the Nation of Islam, a group of political activists in the USA in the 1960s, among whom was Malcolm X. This group, referred to as the Black Muslims, preached salvation from white oppression for American black peoples through revolutionary struggle. (See Chapter 6.)

H. R. Niebuhr: deprivation

A common theme running through sociological debates on the functions of religious sects and cults is that of 'deprivation'. It is often suggested that new religious movements offer the marginal an answer to their deprivation. They are given the chance to replace that which is lacking from their lives by an alternative religious source separate from the mainstream.

Niebuhr (1957) originally applied the concept of deprivation solely to economic matters. He contended that working-class, economically unsuccessful individuals joined sects as an answer to their economic deprivation. Through their emphasis on hard work, these sects raised the economic status of their members.

Niebuhr also suggests that sects are inevitably short-lived. If their members are economically successful as a result of their work ethic, the sect changes to reintegrate members back into mainstream culture.

18.6 Classical theories on the role of religion in society

Sociologists are concerned with the role religion plays in society. A number of interpretations of this role have been presented within sociological debate. Briefly, these can be summarized as:

1 religion bonds social groups together
2 religion contributes to social control through ideology
3 religion is a form of discipline which controls the human body
4 religion stops social change
5 religion creates a meaningful reality in which social actors can act
6 religion offers the marginalized hope, status and a force through which radical social change can take place.

As can be seen from this brief list, sociologists disagree on the role religion performs. It may well be the case, though, that religion has performed, does perform and will perform all of these roles at different times and in different locations. Debate focuses on two vital issues:

• does religion contribute to the status quo?
• does religion encourage or hold back social change?

When interpreted by different theoretical perspectives, these two issues lead to the full range of possible interpretations listed above. It is important to remember that each perspective has its own associated political ideology which forms a framework or window through which these issues are discussed. While Marxists, functionalists and feminists may all agree at one level that religion does support the status quo, at another level they will disagree on whether this situation is positive or negative for the individual and for society.

Religion as social cement

Some perspectives regard religion's role, or function, as contributing to social harmony. The term 'social cement' is usually associated with theories that see harmony as a normal, natural and positive state for society.

Functionalist theorists (see Section 2.4) such as Durkheim and Malinowski believe that religion bonds social groups together into a 'moral community'. Talcott Parsons also shares this interpretation. He stresses religion's function as an agent of socialization: it contributes to the internalization of shared norms and values (Holton and Turner, 1988). (See Section 10.1.)

Religion as social control

Conflict theories such as Marxism and neo-Marxism tend to stress the control functions of religion. Religion is seen as another agent of ideology which performs a similar role to the education system and the mass media.

It is important to recognize the connections between these institutions and others in social life. Marxism, neo-Marxism and feminism, like any other theories, would not see one of these institutions as providing all of society's ideological control (see Section 17.4). They may well focus on some as more significant than others, but the nature of social life is such that all institutions operate together in a structured form. Thus, working-class subordination from a Marxist perspective is a result of both ideological and repressive controls. The working classes are controlled by all social institutions – religion being a smaller, but significant, part of a larger system of discipline. The same is true of a feminist analysis of female subordination.

Marxism

Perhaps the best-known and most widely cited Marxist views on religion come from Marx's *Toward the Critique of Hegel's Philosophy of Right* (1984b) first published in Germany in 1844. This essay is concerned with the theme of 'self-alienation', a concept Marx derived from the work of Ludwig Feuer-

bach. Although he was highly critical of Feuerbach's ideas, Marx formed from his work the idea that ideological control is sometimes a form of self-delusion: the subordinate in society can keep themselves subordinate by ideological means. The concept 'alienation' was used by Feuerbach to refer to situations where humans create intellectual forces, or ideas, in their consciousness, but then let themselves be ruled over by these ideas. Alienation means to be ruled over by the products of one's own labour. Viewed in this way, religion represents a set of ideas created by humanity but which humanity lets rule over them. Religion is a form of self-delusion which holds back revolutionary consciousness. As Marx commented:

The basis of irreligious criticism is: Man makes religion, religion does not make man. In other words, religion is the self-consciousness and self-feeling of man, who either has not yet found himself or has already lost himself again . . . This state, this society produce religion, a perverted world consciousness, because they are a perverted world.
(Marx, 1984, p. 303; orig. pub. 1844)

For Marx, then, religion is not a form of social cement but of 'social opium'. Although he agrees that religion supports the status quo and stops change, he goes further and suggests that it is ideological since it supports, hides and legitimates capitalist exploitation:

[Religion is] *the opium of the people. . . . Religious distress is at the same time the expression of real distress and the protest against real distress. Religion is the sign of the oppressed creature, the heart of a heartless world, just as it is the spirit of an unspiritual situation.*
(Marx, 1984, p. 304; orig. pub. 1844)

Marx, while recognizing that religion provides hope and dignity for those who are suffering in society, asserts that these are a false hope and a false dignity because they hide the true nature of society and the true causes of suffering: an oppressive class-based economic system. Religion creates false consciousness. It stops revolutionary feelings by promoting reward in an afterlife for compliance with the rules of this one. (See also Section 2.5.)

Friedrich Engels

In his essay *On the History of Early Christianity* (1984), first published in Germany in 1894, Engels (a close colleague of Marx) discussed similarities between early religious movements and early socialist movements. Engels notes that the history of Christianity, for example, is very similar to the sort of communist ideas both he and Marx were involved in:

Both Christianity and the workers' socialism preach forthcoming salvation from bondage and misery;

Christianity places this salvation in a life beyond, after death, in heaven; socialism places it in this world, in a transformation of society.
(Engels, 1984, p. 209; orig. pub. 1895)

However, the points of comparison, for Engels, can only be made this far. He regards religion (as does Marx) as a false search for equality and an end to suffering since it is alienated and leads to false consciousness. It gets in the way of true consciousness, which would be brought about by socialism.

Internal debates within Marxism

Since the death of Marx in 1883, great debate has taken place concerning the 'real' meaning of his ideas. Various sociologists have taken what is called a 'neo-Marxist' stance: they believe in a general Marxist sociology but with some reservations, alterations and new ideas – often brought about by combining Marxist thoughts with those of other thinkers.

Discussion point

Over 100 years on, can we still use Marx's ideas successfully to explain the contemporary world?

This issue concerning the 'real meaning' of Marxism can be divided into two branches or camps of Marxism:

- One branch emphasizes the 'materialistic' reading of Marx. Concentrating on his later mature work, they interpret Marx as a scientist studying the universal, inevitable laws governing history.
- The second interpretation is regarded as 'humanist'. Concentrating on Marx's early work these sociologists focus on Marx's concerns with consciousness, subjectivity and ideology.

These two readings have led to two interpretations of his sociology of religion. (See also Section 2.5.)

Dominant ideology

As stated in *The German Ideology*, Marx and Engels (1977, originally written in 1845) believed that the dominant ideology of every social epoch was invented, distributed and controlled by the ruling class of that epoch. From this idea, religion could be seen as yet another weapon in the class struggle, used, but not necessarily created, by the ruling class to control the masses.

However, Abercrombie and Turner (1978) are highly critical of this 'dominant ideology' interpretation of Marx. They contend that, in feudal times, although Christianity was a major part of ruling class culture, it was largely ignored by the peasantry and had little effect on their lives. The ideas of the ruling classes could not therefore control a population

if they did not share these same ideas. Abercrombie and Turner suggest that economic and repressive control were used far more effectively than religion as a means for gaining the compliance of the population. This criticism leads to the second interpretation of Marx's ideas.

Religion and class distinctions

The second interpretation is that religion has an economic character: it is related to different socio-economic classes and used by these groups in different ways.

Using the work of Engels, Turner (1991) argues that in each epoch there will develop two ideological positions, one each for the subordinate class and the ruling class. Religion does not simply bond the whole of society together into a unified whole based on a ruling class ideology of which everyone is a victim in a passive fashion. Instead, it contributes to individual class solidarity. Different classes can get different functions from the same religion:

. . . it is argued that religion satisfies the need of the dominant class to feel that its privileged social position is legitimate; however, the same religion, or some version of it, gratifies the need of subordinate groups, for comfort on this world or revenge in the next. As a narcotic, religion is the expression of human misery, but it is also a reaction against human suffering.
(Turner, 1991, pp. 79–80)

Max Weber

Max Weber was highly critical of the idea of an all-controlling dominant ideology – the idea that religion is a weapon always to be used to control subordinate classes. He believed religions provide society with a 'theodicy' – a set of abstract ideas and beliefs which explain both the existence of God or gods and evil. Weber drew a vital distinction between:

1 theodicies of privilege
2 theodicies of non-privilege.

Ruling groups have a theodicy of privilege in which they have no need for ideas of salvation from poverty: they have, after all, no poverty to be saved from! However, subordinate groups develop a very different theodicy, which is one of non-privilege as a response to their lower socio-economic position. These groups use religion to justify their pain and suffering. Sometimes a theodicy of non-privilege can have a revolutionary nature – a major criticism of Marx's idea that religion was always a 'social opium'.

Karl Mannheim

In his work *Ideology and Utopia*, Karl Mannheim (1960), like Weber, draws a distinction between the consciousness of ruling and subordinate groups. For Mannheim, ruling groups adopt an 'ideology'. Their dominant socio-economic position leads to a consciousness which is blind to aspects of their rule which could potentially undermine their rule. They feel safe in their high position.

Lower socio-economic groups, on the other hand, develop a 'utopian' mentality. They focus on chances and opportunities for change and revolution. They too are blind to social conditions which may stop their successful rise from subordination.

Mannheim thus has an image of society as a tension between different groups with different types of consciousness, battling for the 'highest positions'. He also comments that when subordinate groups rise successfully up the social strata they lose the utopian mentality and take on an ideological consciousness – they ultimately lose the ideals they started with.

Religion as a force for change

Although for very different reasons, with different interpretations, Marxism, functionalism and feminism all believe religion is a conservative force. The phrase 'conservative force' means quite simply to conserve, to protect, to keep the status quo.

Using again the work of Max Weber, however, it is possible to present an alternative understanding of this issue. Far from always stopping change and always supporting the status quo, historical analysis provides sociology with a number of instances where religion has, on the one hand, led groups to cause unintended change, and on the other to actively seek social change using religion as a political force. (See also Section 2.6.)

Discussion point

Does religion stop change or contribute to it?

Weber's ideas on historical and social change can best be described as a conversation with the ghost of Marx. Weber's influential 1920s study, *The Protestant Ethic and the Spirit of Capitalism* (1930, orig. pub. 1905), can certainly be read as a critique of Marx's ideas on historical materialism.

For Marx, history was divided into stages or epochs. Borrowing from Hegel, Marx contended that conflict produced social change. All history is based on class struggle, which moves history along the path towards communism – towards a classless society – and therefore the 'end of history' since there would be no more conflicting classes to produce revolutionary changes.

Weber, in contrast, offers a very different image of social history and the origins of capitalist devel-

opment. In doing so, he provides sociology with a criticism of the idea that religion is a conservative force. In effect, Weber argues that a very particular form of Protestant religion, Calvinism, created the social conditions which made society ready for a capitalist economic system.

Frank Parkin (1986) is critical of simplistic interpretations of Weber's work which lead to the conclusion that 'religion created capitalism'. Parkin emphasizes that Weber's intention was to study the ideas and beliefs which lead to a 'capitalist spirit' – the values of capitalism – but not actually directly to a capitalist economic structure itself. This was not a universal or inevitable development but an unintended consequence of Calvinist belief.

Calvinism: the Protestant ethic

Calvinism rejected what it saw as the decadence of Roman Catholicism. Calvinism was based on an idea or theodicy known as 'the elect': it was believed that, at birth, some individuals were pre-destined to go to heaven. These 'elect' few were chosen by God, irrespective of their conduct in this world. However, in order to cope with feelings of anxiety, the Calvinists believed that a sign of God's favour, an indication that one was a member of the elect, was success at one's 'calling' – the career an individual adopted. The Calvinists believed that 'hard work was a virtue'. If an individual worked hard and became successful, God was thereby praised; and in turn, God would give the elect few a sign (success) of their predestination. This is known as the 'Protestant (work) ethic': a lifestyle based on religious beliefs which lead to a very specific form of social action – economic activity. Other aspects of the Protestant ethic included condemnation of time-wasting, idleness, laziness and gossip.

The spirit of capitalism

Weber suggests that the meaningful social action produced by the Calvinists' 'work ethic' leads to the 'spirit' of capitalism, the essential ideology of profit-seeking and profit reinvestment at the heart of the subsequent capitalist economic system. Capitalism was thus not an inevitable outcome of scientific forces as identified by Marx, but the unintended consequence of specific religious meanings and motives.

Religion and political conflict

Weber's ideas described above serve as an example of religion not being a conservative force. Rather than holding back change, religion has created the conditions necessary for change on a major scale and of great historical significance, even if this change was largely unintended.

Other historical examples suggest that social actors can use religion and religious ideas in a self-conscious political fashion to achieve radical and often revolutionary social movement and change.

💬 Discussion point

Can religion act as a political force in creating revolutionary struggle?

Case study – The ghost dance cult

The Ghost Dance Cult of the Sioux North American Indians can be seen as an example of a religious movement which actively sought social change through religious ideas. This movement preached salvation from the bondage and exploitation of the white settlers (Brown, 1991).

The Ghost Dance is an example of a 'millenarian movement', a social movement which preaches salvation from suffering due to coming great natural changes (floods, volcanoes etc.) and a return to a glorious past, free from misery. Millenarian movements are intimately related to Christianity and normally develop among the poor and marginal either in the western world, or amongst Christian colonized areas in the non-western world.

The Ghost Dancers believed that Christ supported the plight of Indians over the settlers and that Christ had returned to encourage Indians to fight for their freedom once more. This indicates how the religion of colonial invaders often influences and becomes combined with native religions.

The Ghost Dancers represented a major political threat to the American government of the time. Conflict escalated until, in December 1890 at The Battle of Wounded Knee, the Ghost Dancers were stopped. An estimate puts those killed amongst the Sioux as nearly 300 men, women and children (Brown, 1991).

Although ultimately unsuccessful as a revolutionary movement, this example serves as another indication that religious belief can act as, to use Weber's term, a theodicy of non-privilege.

18.7 Contemporary views on the role of religion in society

Classical debates in sociology such as the issue 'is religion a conservative force?', or more widely, 'what is the function of religion?' still continue in contemporary sociological discussions, with many contemporary approaches drawing on the ideas of the classical views in their work.

The New Right

Since the 1970s, New Right thinking has had a profound effect on modern social life (see Section 2.10). The New Right see religion as a vital source of morality. New Right theories on crime and deviance (see Section 11.9) in society often blame the rise of moral degeneration of society, especially amongst the young, for rising rates of crime. The rise of single-parent families (see Section 7.3) is seen as the result of a society lacking values from a religious source.

💬 Discussion point

How might a lack of religious values lead to 'moral degeneration' and an increase in deviance? Do you think this is a fair picture of modern society?

As demonstrated by the newspaper article 'Young adrift in the moral maze', it is often a matter of media-led 'common-sense' opinion that the young in modern society are 'adrift' without a strong sense of religious commitment.

📝 Activity

Read the article 'Young adrift in the moral maze' and answer the following questions.

a Make a list of all the examples of moral confusion alleged in the article.
b Make a list of all the examples of moral standards that are still important.
c List those groups deemed to be responsible for the decline in moral standards.
d To what extent do you agree that the young are 'experiencing a moral crisis'?

I, A, E

Feminism and religion

In contrast with the New Right, feminists (see Section 2.6) are interested in the way religion is used as a source of 'social opium' – to control women. Whereas the New Right would regard social control as a positive function of religion (as too would functionalism), feminists regard religion as an instrument or source of patriarchy – male domination over women. Religion has been used, historically, to:

- control feminine bodies by labelling some women as deviant
- deny feminine sexuality, seen as a threat to social stability
- support the family – another agent of patriarchy.

Feminists are critical not only of society but also of the way in which female thinkers have been ignored and thus devalued within academic study – including some

Young adrift in the moral maze

THE RESULTS of a nationwide Mori poll for BBC Radio 1, published tomorrow, find that two-thirds of those aged between 15 and 35 believe their generation 'is experiencing a moral crisis' and that they are 'not sure any more what is right and wrong'.

Most can recall only two or three of the Ten Commandments and, when reminded of the rest, argue that only about five remain relevant.

Barely half (52 per cent) believe 'there are definite rights and wrongs in life', while 41 per cent say 'morality always depends on the circumstances'. A majority say 'people should be allowed to do whatever they like, as long as it doesn't harm anyone'.

If the self-testimony of the young appears to be that they find themselves in a moral fog, there is little doubt whom they deem responsible. It is in the nature of being young to 'diss' one's elders but in 1994 the moral stature of politicians has shrunk to microscopic proportions among the young.

More than half believe Parliament and politicians are doing a bad job at 'setting and upholding moral standards'. Only 3 per cent agree Ministers are doing a good job at upholding morality. And these young voters are the ones most eagerly wooed by Blair and Major.

If the young retain respect for the moral standards set by their own schools, doctors, parents and the police, they are disparaging of those set by the courts, business leaders and the Royal Family. (They also believe pop stars aren't very good at maintaining moral standards but most pop stars would say this proves they are being proper pop stars.)

Everyone blames everyone else. The press blames the politicians for cowardice and hypocrisy. The politicians blame the Church, the schools and publicly ailing role models such as the Royal Family – who in turn blame the press for magnifying their long-running domestic crises. The religious community, for its part, blames the Government and business.

Ann Widdecombe MP, the Employment Minister and one of the Government's most unashamed moralists, told *The Observer* that the press had to bear the blame for the low esteem in which the young hold their political leaders. But the survey reveals that the young blame the press anyway for declining moral standards.

Not surprisingly, Ms Widdecombe urged the Church to regain the moral high ground, and pointed to its decline as a key factor in the apparent moral quagmire in which the young find themselves trapped.

This is no good either: in the eyes of the young, the Church has lost its moral authority. Most believe it 'has little to offer people nowadays'. Only one in seven agrees that 'what the Church says about what is morally right and wrong has a strong influence on my life'. Most actively disagree with this.

Remarkably, half of those calling themselves Christians (a majority of the 1,200 young people surveyed) nevertheless believe the Church has little to offer.

Dr George Carey, the Archbishop of Canterbury, told *The Observer* the findings were evidence of the size of the task the Church faces. 'The poll results indicate that the churches now have to earn their influence over young people. They cannot take respect for their moral authority for granted.'

This is putting it in the very mildest of Anglican terms. The archbishop has appointed a youth officer to his Lambeth Palace staff and, too little too late or not, in a speech on Friday signalled a new resolve for the Church to be seen to be addressing moral issues.

He said people want 'clear guidance on right and wrong' and 'feel genuinely despairing when they perceive the Church to be compromising, to be translating the simple laws of morality into layer upon layer of qualification.'

Young people come up with their own moral definites now. 'The Church has no bearing at all on our lives,' said Jo Elvin, 24, editor of *Sugar*, a new monthly for 15- and 16-year-old girls.

The magazine, launched last week with a story of a 14-year-old schoolgirl mother and 'the 15 biggest sex lies

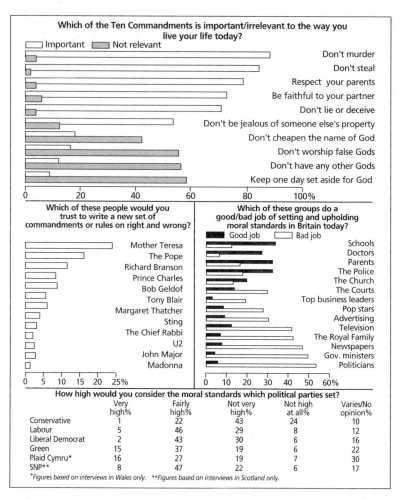

Which of the Ten Commandments is important/irrelevant to the way you live your life today?

☐ Important ▨ Not relevant

- Don't murder
- Don't steal
- Respect your parents
- Be faithful to your partner
- Don't lie or deceive
- Don't be jealous of someone else's property
- Don't cheapen the name of God
- Don't worship false Gods
- Don't have any other Gods
- Keep one day set aside for God

(0 – 20 – 40 – 60 – 80 – 100%)

Which of these people would you trust to write a new set of commandments or rules on right and wrong?

- Mother Teresa
- The Pope
- Richard Branson
- Prince Charles
- Bob Geldof
- Tony Blair
- Margaret Thatcher
- Sting
- The Chief Rabbi
- U2
- John Major
- Madonna

(0 – 5 – 10 – 15 – 20 – 25%)

Which of these groups do a good/bad job of setting and upholding moral standards in Britain today?

■ Good job ☐ Bad job

- Schools
- Doctors
- Parents
- The Police
- The Church
- The Courts
- Top business leaders
- Pop stars
- Advertising
- Television
- The Royal Family
- Newspapers
- Gov. ministers
- Politicians

(0 – 10 – 20 – 30 – 40 – 50 – 60%)

How high would you consider the moral standards which political parties set?

	Very high%	Fairly high%	Not very high%	Not high at all%	Varies/No opinion%
Conservative	1	22	43	24	10
Labour	5	46	29	8	12
Liberal Democrat	2	43	30	6	16
Green	15	37	19	6	22
Plaid Cymru*	16	27	19	7	30
SNP**	8	47	22	6	17

*Figures based on interviews in Wales only.   **Figures based on interviews in Scotland only.

ever', is not bereft of moral guidance: on the 'Nosy Page', Kelle, from the pop group Eternal, says that 'guns, violence, racism, drugs and ignorance should be obliterated from the face of the earth'. Murder is still out, said Jo Elvin – the Mori survey confirmed that the commandment 'Thou shalt not kill' still won approval of 88 per cent of the young – but old sins like theft or adultery are now grey areas, as are new dilemmas such as drug use. Racism and green issues are more likely to be seen as important moral issues to this generation.

'Young people are questioning all things, they're all finding out a morality for themselves,' Jo Elvin commented. It is unclear who are the leaders or groups that will inform the morality of this post-Church, post-absolute generation. It is certainly not Conservative politicians, who will need to examine their depleted moral credit among the young before chastising

other public figures for abandoning moral guidance.

Two in three believe Tory politicians do not have high moral standards, against less than a quarter who think they do. Labour, Liberal Democrat and Green politicians are perceived to have higher moral standards.

There is no consolation for the Tories from a question asking which of a range of public figures might best be trusted with coming up with a new set of rights and wrongs for the Nineties. Despite the overall poor showing of the Church, religious figures took the top three places – but all with small percentages. Mother Teresa is the first to carry down the new tablets of stone from the mountain – but Moses could never have worked with a mandate of 25 per cent of the vote.

However, even this is little short of popular acclaim compared to John Major: only 2 per cent chose the Prime Minister to carry out the task.

Dr John Keown, lecturer in law and medical ethics at Cambridge University, said the findings are no surprise because what moral consensus there was has now collapsed and 'we are in an age of moral relativism'.

'These are disturbing findings,' he said, 'particularly when you think of what the parents of tomorrow will teach their children about right and wrong.'

Mori conducted 1,200 face to face interviews with people aged 15 to 35 in 149 sampling points across Britain.

• An ICM poll in the *Sunday Express* found that 85 per cent of Tory voters considered the party's policies on crime to be ineffective, with 17 per cent saying they would be prepared to vote Labour because of their discontent on the issue. A Mori poll for the *Mail on Sunday* indicated Labour had a 10-point lead over the Tories on law and order policies.

Source: *Observer*, 9 October 1994

---

areas of sociology. Until recently the role of religion as a source of control of women has been largely ignored by mainstream sociology. Feminists refer to the invisibility of women in sociology as 'malestream' – illustrating the inadequacies of dominant 'male' sociology to deal with gender issues (see Chapter 5).

Case study – Witchcraft

An example of a feminist-style analysis of religion – or at least an analysis of religion which could contribute to a feminist debate – can be drawn by looking at the rise of 'witch-hunting' in western Europe in the sixteenth and seventeenth centuries. Alan Anderson and Raymond Gordon (1978, 1979) provide an historical interpretation of witch-hunting which can be seen to fit into a feminist perspective on religion and its role in society. They contend that:

Witch persecution had a misogynous ideological basis which reflected the low status of women at that time.
(Anderson and Gordon, 1979, p. 359)

They argue that, with the exception of England, in the sixteenth and seventeenth centuries women were a credible target to be singled out, labelled and controlled by this moral panic (see Section 15.5) because they were seen to be an instrument of the devil – weak and open to satanic temptation if not controlled by society. Viewed in this way, witch-hunting by the Christian church can be seen as an attempt to control female sexuality.

However, in England, although some witch scares

did occur, they were of a significantly lower rate than in other countries. This is interpreted by Anderson and Gordon to be due to the influence of a Puritan form of Protestantism which raised the status of women relative to other European societies.

A second, but complementary interpretation of European witch-hunts is provided by Turner (1989, 1990). He locates witch-hunting within the history of the exclusion of women from medical practice. Turner contends that the male-dominated Christian church scapegoated as witches 'wise women' who practised herbal medicine and midwifery at a local village level. By focusing the already existing fear of female satanic temptation on these women, the newly developing medical profession within the church was able to win an important battle over clients and credibility. (See also Section 13.3.)

Familism and sexuality

Simone de Beauvoir was another to identify the patriarchal content of religion, especially in relation to the family. As she comments:

Christian ideology has contributed not a little to the oppression of women ... [Women] could take only a secondary place as participants in worship, the 'deaconesses' were authorized to carry out only such tasks as caring for the sick and aiding the poor. And if marriage was held to be an institution demanding mutual fidelity, it seemed obvious that the wife should be totally subordinate to her husband.
(Quoted in Turner, 1989, p. 119)

Feminism identifies a strong relationship between religious ideology, familist ideology and the control of feminine sexuality. Religious ideology is seen to contain an 'ideology of the family', as the above quotation from de Beauvoir illustrates. Religious ideology presents the family structure – and women's subordinate place within it – as normal and natural (see also Section 7.5). It could be argued that the family is vital for the continuation of capitalism. For example, Weber, although not a feminist, describes how humanity needs to be organized, disciplined and controlled in society to aid capitalist production and its efficiency. The body and its sexual desires need to be ordered and regulated to avoid chaos which could disrupt capitalist organization. Religion deals with this 'problem of sexuality' for capitalism through the development and enforcement of strict moral codes. As Weber comments:

Rational ascetic alertness, self-control, and methodical planning of life are seriously threatened by the peculiar irrationality of the sexual act, which is ultimately and uniquely unsusceptible to rational organisation.
(Quoted in Turner, 1991, p. 112)

A phenomenological approach

While functionalists and the New Right see religion as a form of 'social cement', and Marxists and feminists see religion as 'social opium', there is another perspective on the role of religion in society: the belief that religion *contributes to the consciousness of the social actor*:

- it provides meaning to social life
- it legitimates norms, values and élites
- it can provide the marginalized with a set of ideas that can advocate social action to create change.

This emphasis on consciousness and meaningful social action is more of a phenomenological interpretation (see Section 2.8) of the role of religion in society. It is concerned with how religious beliefs create or contribute to a 'socially constructed reality'.

Berger and Luckmann (1967) see social actors as *symbolic actors*: they create, construct and develop reality by searching for meanings in individual events, and in doing so make sense of the world around them through 'common sense thought'. In order to act in this world, individuals need to have a sense of stability. Common sense knowledge provides stability by giving meaning and by legitimating the world. The world (or social reality) is experienced as external to the individual when it is actually created through interaction after being inherited through primary socialization.

Berger (1990) suggests that religion contributes

to this construction of a meaningful world by building what he terms *nomos*. In following Durkheim, Berger uses *nomos* to refer to a situation opposite to *anomie* (see Section 2.3). For Durkheim, *anomie* means meaning*less*ness, while for Berger *nomos* means meaning*ful*ness. Religion has the potential to help to build *nomos* by offering a particular script that actors can adopt in order to act and interact.

For Berger, religion performs a 'world-building' function:

Viewed historically, most of man's worlds have been sacred worlds . . . it can thus be said that religion has played a strategic part in the human enterprise of world-building.
(Berger, 1990, p. 27)

Threats to meaningful stability

Berger argues that, although religion provides a 'socially constructed reality' with shared meanings, there are still periodic threats to such a meaningful stability – most notably when death occurs within the social group (a similar point is made by functionalist thinker Malinowski – see Section 18.2).

Berger refers to death as a 'marginal situation'. These marginal situations push social actors to the margins or boundaries of meaningful stability. They represent moments in an otherwise stable world where commonsense understandings are called into question and doubt:

Death radically challenges all socially objectivated definitions of reality – of the world, of others and of self. Death radically puts in question the taken-for-granted, 'business-as-usual' attitude in which one exists in everyday life.
(Berger, 1990, p. 43)

Although a phenomenologist, Berger believes (as did functionalists Durkheim and Malinowski before him) that religion functions to help social actors cope with marginal situations:

Religion then, maintains the socially defined reality by legitimating marginal situations in terms of an all-encompassing sacred reality. This permits the individual who goes through these situations to continue to exist in the world of his society . . . in the 'knowledge' that even those events or experiences have a place within a universe that makes sense.
(Berger, 1990, p. 44)

Continuing the theme of the relationship between religion, stability and marginal situations, Anthony Giddens (1991, 1993b) is also concerned with death and self-identity in modern society. (See also Section 10.10.) Giddens argues, in contrast to Berger, that in contemporary late-capitalist societies (referred to

as *high-modern* societies) the social consequences of
death are highly problematic – much more so than
in early-modern or traditional eras of society.
Giddens suggests that one of the consequences of
high-modernism is to change profoundly how individuals cope with death:

*The modes of life brought into being by modernity
have swept us away from all traditional types of
social order, in quite unprecedented fashion . . . the
transformations involved in modernity are more
profound than most sorts of change characteristic
of prior periods . . . in intensional terms they have
come to alter some of the most intimate and personal features of our day-to-day existence.*
(Giddens, 1993b, p. 4)

By the process of secularization – the decline of
religion – associated with high-modernity, death is
no longer made meaningful by religion. Instead, it
has become a problem which individuals attempt to
cope with by adopting lifestyles aimed at creating a
self-identity based on health. Death is no longer
explained by religion, but avoided by lifestyle.

Case studies – Contemporary examples of religion as a source of change

One way in which religion can create meaningful
lifestyles, around which social action and interaction
can take place, is by offering people a source of revolutionary or radical potential. Returning to the ideas
of Max Weber, who believed that religion can offer
the oppressed a source of liberation, some sociologists are concerned to illustrate examples of this phenomenon in the contemporary world.

Rastafarianism

Stuart Hall (1985) argues that religion is a 'meaning
system' for both the rulers and oppressed in society.
Claims made by religions may not be empirically
correct, but they can nonetheless create a stable
sense of meaning for those who subscribe to their

ideas. In this way, Hall argues that religion can be
ideological, but he also suggests that it is not
simply nor always a matter of false consciousness.
In making this claim, Hall suggests that whereas
Marxist sociology may be correct at some times and
in some places, it is not a general nor universal law
of human behaviour.

In turning to the example of religious meanings
in Jamaica, Hall notes the existence of religious discourses or sets of meanings which are used by their
followers as an act of rebellion or resistance, both
from within Jamaica, and for young blacks in the UK
in the 1970s and 1980s. (See also Chapter 6.)

The history of Jamaican culture is dependent on
a varied mixture of a number of cultural influences:
the Spanish occupation which almost destroyed the
indigenous culture; the establishment of the slave
trade and plantation economies; and the 'merging'
of the so-called 'dominant' white culture of the colonial rulers and administrators with the colonized
blacks originally from West Africa, into a single
'coloured' population. (See also Section 10.6.) Hall
notes how, over time, non-slave or 'free coloureds'
became the Jamaican middle class while the descendants of the slave populations became the lower-
class members, all of which shared, to greater and
lesser extents, the 'creole' Jamaican culture.

Hall suggests that in this context of oppression
and colonial rule (see Sections 6.2 and 12.3), religious meanings were used as an act of resistance by

Figure 18.9 A member of the Rastafarian movement

some, against the white colonial invaders. Since the movement towards independent nationalism for Jamaica, the Rastafarian movement in particular, has shown great resistance against outside ideas, beliefs and practices.

Within the Rastafarian movement, identified by Hall as a mixture of religious, political and nationalist ideas, the emergence of the Ras Tafari brethren, based on the ideas of evangelical preacher Marcus Garvey in the mid 1920s, can be seen as a militant opposition to 'White Babylon', promising to deliver its black members to a world free from slavery, oppression and exploitation in all forms. (See also Chapter 6.)

Taking Emperor Haile Selassie I of Ethiopia as the reincarnation of Jesus, and believing that the Rastas were originally a lost tribe of Israel who would be 'delivered' back to a 'promised land', many members of the Rastafarian movement have been harassed by the police in Jamaica for their non-conformist ideas, and in particular the taking of ganja (marijuana) which is believed to increase spirituality.

In terms of cultural style and identity (see Section 10.6), Rastas wear their hair in 'dreadlocks' – an interpretation of the Bible's instruction not to cut their hair. Equally, through identification with Haile Selassie, they wear the colours of Ethiopia – green, yellow, red and black.

With its emphasis on the liberating force of religious belief, Rastafarianism has proved popular not just in Jamaica, but also in the UK, with some young blacks adopting these ideas (suggests Hall) as a means by which to resist a racist society.

Liberation theology

'Liberation theology' is a present-day general term given to a version of South American Roman Catholicism that uses Christian religious ideas as a political motivating force to create social change. As the name suggests, liberation theology believes that Christ was a revolutionary figure who practised the liberation of people from slavery, poverty and oppression. Liberation theology explains third-world poverty and deprivation to be the result of governmental corruption and exploitation which must be challenged directly, through political and violent means if necessary. (See also Section 12.8.)

In Weber's terms, liberation theology would represent a 'theodicy of non-privilege' which is used by the marginal to change society, to challenge the status quo.

The Islamic revolution

Since the sixteenth century the Shi'ism form of Islam, as practised by Shi'ite Muslims, has been the official form of religion in Iran. The 'Iranian revolution' of 1978–9 is often interpreted as an example of a traditional religion – Islam – being used to combat western economic and cultural expansion in the Middle East (Waters, 1995).

Although originally adopted by the Shah Mohammed Reza, western capitalist ideas were seen by others as a threat to traditional Islamic ideas and therefore something which should be stopped from spreading in Iran. Opponents of the westernization of Iran, such as Ayatollah Khomeini, reinterpreted Islamic ideas as a fundamental rejection of western values – especially western attitudes to sexuality.

This spread of Islamic fundamentalism, a return to radical and revolutionary interpretations of traditional ideas from the Qur'an, has led to a political rejection of western expansion in these societies.

The examples of Rastafarianism, liberation theology and the Iranian revolution serve to suggest that far from being 'the opium of the people', religion can often be used as a force for radical and political social action and social change.

Is social change always radical?

In one sense the Iranian revolution is an example of religion not being conservative because it contributed to social change, and stopped the process of the westernization of Iran. However, in another sense the Iranian Revolution *was* conservative because it sought to protect or *conserve* a traditional set of values – hence the term 'fundamentalism'.

Therefore, social change can be both radical and conservative. Revolutionary struggle, brought about by religious ideas, can lead to the overthrow of a ruling tradition and the establishment of new ideas; but equally, revolution can lead to the re-establishment of old ideas.

Religion as discipline and control

In *History of Sexuality* (1990a, 1990b, 1992) and *The Birth of the Prison* (1979), Michel Foucault – a highly influential French post-structuralist historian and philosopher (see Section 2.10) – discusses the ways in which religion controls the body, and in particular the female body. As an example of what he calls a 'discourse', a specialized set of languages which control self-identity and shape or mould human behaviour, Foucault believes that religion contributes to the levels and mechanisms of surveillance in society.

Foucault identifies a number of mechanisms of control which operate on the human body and which benefit the way in which the capitalist economy of the West operates. Looking at a critical history of education, the prison, the hospital, the mental asylum and religion, he argues that the body is subjected to diet, timetable, surveillance, and physical punishment distributed by these different institutions at different times in the history of the social body and the individual body. In particular these mechanisms of discipline and punishment operate to create, mould and constrain the self-identity and the sexuality of the individual, creating a 'self' ready to be controlled by capitalist production methods.

Rethinking the sociology of religion

In evaluating the work of Engels, Weber and Foucault discussed above, Turner suggests that it is time for sociology, and especially the sociology of religion, to start to conceptualize its object of study not as class, society or the nation-state, but rather as the human and social bodies. Religion, he argues, operates to control the human body – its actions, thoughts and desires. (See also Sections 13.3 and 13.9.)

Globalization and religion

Some religions, especially the Abrahamic-based ones of Islam and Christianity, are seen as major contributors to the process of globalization (see also Sections 9.9, 10.10, 12.5, 16.8 and 17.6). With their emphasis on the conversion of non-believers they have both become 'world-religions' stretching across traditional geographical and cultural areas.

Fundamentalist forms of religion are seen by Lechner (1990) as providing an answer to the chaos of the post-modernization of the globe, and in doing so they flourish well under such global conditions.

As Waters (1995) comments, contemporary global life is not so much a 'new world order' as a 'new world disorder'. Increasing levels of globalization produce chaos, a lack of meaning; in fact, too much diversity of meaning. This is because globalization involves the unification of many diverse ideas, ideologies, beliefs, faiths and other cultural practices into a chaotic shared culture to which everyone is exposed. (See Section 10.10.)

Lechner sees fundamentalism as a *response* to this global chaos. Religions such as Islam seek to unite together, back into a common and shared set of meanings, all those peoples alienated by and anxious about the diverse array of cultural ideas they have suddenly become exposed to. As Lechner comments, fundamentalist religions are:

. . . a value-orientated, antimodern, dedifferentiating form of collective action – a socio-cultural movement aimed at reorganizing all spheres of life in terms of a particular set of absolute values.
(Quoted in Waters, 1995, p. 130)

Further reading

Accessible A level texts designed to introduce the key debates in this field include:

- Bruce, S. (1995) *Religion in Modern Britain*, Oxford, Oxford University Press.
- Thompson, I. (1986) *Religion*, London, Longman.
- Thompson, K. (1986) *Beliefs and Ideology*, London, Tavistock.

Further texts, designed to provide more detail, include:

- Hamilton, M. B. (1995) *The Sociology of Religion: Theoretical and Comparative Perspectives*, London, Routledge.
- Turner, B. S. (1991) *Religion and Social Theory*, 2nd edn, London, Sage.

A good, general 'reader' covering many classic and contemporary writings in this field is:

- Bocock, R. and Thompson, K. (eds) (1985) *Religion and Ideology*, Manchester, Manchester University Press.

Additionally, back issues of the periodical *Sociology Review* (formerly known as *Social Studies Review*) contain many articles on this field of sociology and many others.

Exam **questions**

1 'The main function of religion in society is the control of weaker social groups by the more powerful.' Evaluate sociological arguments and evidence both for and against this statement.
[25 marks]
(AEB, Paper 2, Summer 1996)

2 Critically examine sociological explanations of the emergence and growth of religious sects in apparently secular societies. [25 marks]
(AEB, Paper 2, Summer 1992)

3 Assess the evidence for and against the claim that religion still fulfils a number of important functions in modern societies. [25 marks]
(AEB, Paper 2, Summer 1995)

4 a Identify two features of secularization.
[4 marks]
   b Identify and illustrate two criticisms of the secularization thesis. [4 marks]
   c Outline the evidence for the secularization of the UK. [7 marks]
   d Examine the reasons for the changes in institutional religion in the UK. [10 marks]
(IBS, Paper 2, Summer 1996)

5 Assess the reasons put forward by sociologists for the emergence of new religious movements.
[25 marks]
(IBS, Paper 2, Summer 1996)

Coursework **suggestions**

1 **A comparison between the religious views of the young and the old**

   This could be a mainly quantitative piece of research based on questionnaire and/or interview methods. Key issues to discuss would be how to define/measure religion and the sample type and size. Although the process of research is important, it is vital to remember that to demonstrate 'evaluation' skills you will need to discuss the problems of researching religion in great detail.

2 **Has secularization occurred?**

   This could be based on a combination of both qualitative and quantitative research techniques. A careful sample will need to be constructed, taking into consideration factors such as class, gender, age, ethnicity etc., and care needs to be taken over how religion is defined and measured. This research could, for example, take an established definition of religion such as that by Glock and Stark and use it in an evaluative fashion. The research will also need to consider both practice and belief.

3 **Science and religion**

   Using debates on secularization and the transformation of the sacred – particularly the ideas of Durkheim, Crippen, Turner and Bull – this research could investigate the question 'Is science a religion?', or 'Has science become sacred?' This coursework could be based on a combination of primary and secondary sources – particularly media sources. Examples could be sought which appear to suggest the 'sacred' or 'religious' character of science, and in-depth interviews could be carried out on people's faith in science to 'solve all'.

Copyright acknowledgements

Addison Wesley Longman for figure 4.5 from *Conflicts about Class* by Lee and Turner on p. 119 and for the diagrams from *Communication Models for the Study of Mass Communications* on pp. 617 and 619. Reprinted by permission of Addison Wesley Longman Ltd; The Associated Examining Board for the questions on pp. 59, 107, 158, 195, 232, 279, 303, 371, 463, 509, 552, 600, 645, 688, 727, 763 and 764; The American Educational Research Association for 'Myths, Counter Myth and Truths about Intelligence' by Sternburg, Robert J., *Educational Researcher*, 25 (2) 12 on p. 316. Copyright 1996 by the American Research Association. Reprinted by permission of the publisher; Ashgate Publishing Limited for the diagram from *The Experience of Work*, ed. Littler, C. R., on p. 327; Baby Milk Action for the material on p. 505; *Beds on Sunday* for the extract on p. 401; Blackwell Publishers for the extract from *Stratification and Power* by Scott, J. on p. 110, the extract from *Who rules Britain?* by Scott, J. on pp. 126–7, the extracts from *Contemporary British Society* by Abercrombie, Warde *et al.* on pp. 195–6 and 232, the table from *The Sociology of Housework* by Anne Oakley on p. 261, the extract from *Sociology, 1989* by Giddens on p. 279, the extract from *Against Postmodernism* by Callinicos on p. 340, the figure and extract from *An Introduction to Sociology* by Browne, K. on pp. 432 and 673, the table from *Girl Delinquents* by Dr Campbell, A. on p. 433, the 3 tables from *Free Markets and Food Riots: The Politics of Global Adjustment* by Walton, J. and Seddon, D. on p. 495, the table from *The Role of Medicine* by McKeown, T. on p. 514 and the table from *The Three Worlds of Welfare Capitalism* by Prof Gøsta Esping-Anderson on p. 569; Blackwell Science Ltd for the tables from *The Sociology of Health and Health Care* by Taylor and Field on pp. 535 and 538; The British Sociological Association for the extract on p. 100; Cambridge University Press for the figures from *Class Counts* by Wright, 1997 on p. 116; Cassell PLC for the figure from *Cities of Pride* by Atkinson on p. 656; Causeway Press for the extract on p. 158; Citizens Advice Bureau for the table from *A Right to Family Life* on p. 208; CPAG for material on pp. 572, 583–4, 585, 586 and 588; Dartmouth Publishing Company for the extract on p. 270; Edward Elgar Publishing for the extracts on p. 51; Reprinted from *Child Abuse and Neglect* by Baker, A. and Duncan, S., copyright 1985, pp. 457–67, with kind permission from Elsevier Science Ltd, The Boulevard, Langford Lane, Kidlington OX5 1GB, UK on p. 276; ESRC Research Centre on Micro-Social Change for the tables on pp. 169, 252, 576, 603 and 739; Express Newspapers PLC for the articles on pp. 272 and 654; Federation des Cercles le Marxisme Aujourd'hui for the diagram from *Marxism Today* on p. 726; The Food Commission and NCH Action for Children for the material on p. 571; Framework Press for the figure from *Family Household and Life Course Studies in British Society* by Alan Warde and Nicholas Abercrombie on p. 262; Goldsmiths College for the figure from *Unequal pay for equal parts: A survey of performers in the theatre and electronic media* by Thomas, H. and Klett-Davies, M., 1995 on p. 403; Greenwood Publishing Group Inc. for the figure from *Varieties of Criminology* by Barak on p. 439 © 1993 by Praeger. Reproduced with permission of Greenwood Publishing Group Inc., Westport, CT; *The Guardian* for the articles on pp. 146, 163, 258, 259, 318, 345, 367, 406, 407, 452, 454, 457, 484, 488, 516, 522, 535, 539, 540, 548, 581, 588, 595, 610, 614, 632, 682, 694, 696, 713, 721 and 727; HarperCollins Publishers Ltd. for the extracts from *How to do Social Research* by Dunsmuir and Williams on pp. 79–80, the figure from *General Studies A Level* by Swatridge, C. on p. 123, the table from *Social Class Differences in Britain* by Reid on p. 124, the table from *Topics in Sociology* by Trowler with Riley on p. 337 and the table and figure from *Investigating Health, Welfare and Poverty* by Trowler on pp. 524 and 529; HLT Publications for the figure on p. 430; HMSO for the table from *Family Expenditure Survey* on p. 138, for the figure from *Employment Gazette* on p. 144, for the figure from *Households Below Average Income* on p. 151, for the tables from *Social Trends* on pp. 169, 252, 254, 249, 604 and 681, for the extracts from *Recent Research on the Achievements of Ethnic Minority Pupils* on p. 295, for the Cabinet Office Statistics on p. 337 and for the statistics from *Criminal Statistics England and Wales* on pp. 427, 428 and 431. Crown copyright is reproduced with the permission of the Controller of Her Majesty's Stationery Office; The *Independent* for the articles on pp. 196, 218, 222, 240, 301, 305, 320, 561 and 590; The Independent Television Commission for the data on p. 402; Intercontinental Features for the cartoon on p. 344; Jedd for the cartoon on p. 453; Klein, R. for the article on p. 229; Macmillan Press Ltd. for the extract and figure from *Introductory Sociology* by Bilton *et al.* on pp. 65 and 84, for the extract from *Social Research* by Sarantakos on p. 84, for the table from *Doing Sociology* by Harvey and MacDonald on p. 85 and for the table adapted from *Welfare and the State* by Bryson on p. 570; Manchester University Press for the diagram from *Symbolizing Boundaries* by Cohen, 1986 on p. 659; Mirror Syndication International for the front covers of the *Daily Mirror* on pp. 225, 608 and 625; The National Council on Family Relations for the table from *Journal of Marriage and the Family*, 'Societal Change and Change in Family Violence from 1975 to 1985 as revealed by two National Surveys' by Murray A. Straus and Richard J. Gelles on p. 275. Copyrighted 1985 by the National Council on Family Relations, 3989 Central Ave. NE, Suite 550, Minneapolis, MN 55421. Reprinted by permission; Thomas Nelson and Sons Ltd. for the extracts from *A New Introduction to Sociology* by Mike O'Donnell on pp. 158 and 159; *New Internationalist* for the article on p. 200; *New Left Review* for the figure from *Advanced Capitalist Societies* by Wright on p. 116; *New Statesman* for the articles on pp. 151 and 595; Newell, M. for the poem on p. 226. Martin Newell is The *Independent*'s regular poet, and this poem first appeared on the paper's front page on June 26 1996; News International for the front page from The *Sun* on p. 608; Northern Examinations and Assessment Board for the questions on pp. 195, 278–9, 371, 419, 463 and 509; The *Observer* for the articles on pp. 162, 205, 259, 576, 590, 713 and 758–9; The Office for National Statistics for the data from *1991 Census, Economic Activity Volume* on pp. 121, 159 and 196. Crown copyright 1991, for the material from *General Household Survey Preliminary Findings*, 1995 on pp. 245, 247, 248, 249, 251, 253, 255, 256, 739. Crown copyright 1995, for the material from *Labour Force Survey*, 1995 and 1996 on pp. 249, 331, 332, 333, 336, 337 and 339. Crown copyright 1995 and 1996, for the material from *Social Trends 26*, 1996 on pp. 257 and 518. Crown copyright 1996, for the material from *Annual Abstract of Statistics*, 1995 on pp. 335 and 536. Crown copyright 1995, for the table from *Employment Gazette*, 1993 on p. 350. Crown copyright 1993, for the material from *Living in Britain*, 1994 on pp. 518 and 519. Crown copyright 1994, for data supplied by CSO (now ONS) 1982 on p. 572. Crown copyright 1982. Reproduced by permission of the Controller of HMSO and of the Office for National Statistics; Olympus Books UK for the extract from *Sociology Update 1991* by Denscombe, M. on p. 158; Open University Press for the extract from *The Company She Keeps* by Hey, V., 1997 on p. 103, for the extract from *Disarming Patriarchy* by Roseneil, S., 1996 on pp. 101–2 and 186, for the extract adapted from *Women in Britain Today* by Beechey, V. and Whitelegg, E. on p. 232, for the tables from *Third World Atlas* 2nd edition by Thomas, A. *et al.* on pp. 450, 467 and 469; Material from *Which Picture?* information leaflet on p. 637 reproduced with permission of Oxfam Publishing, 274 Banbury Road, Oxford, OX2 7DZ; OUP for the figure from *Social Mobility and the Class Structure in Modern Britain* by Goldthorpe *et al.*, 1987 on p. 118, for the extract from 'Post 16 Qualification Reform: Compare France', by Green, A., *Forum*, 1993, vol. 35, no. 1 on p. 323, for the material from *World Development Report 1995* on pp. 498 and 499. Copyright © by The World Bank., and for the table from *The Economics of Inequality* by Atkinson, 1983 on p. 595. Used by permission of Oxford University Press, Inc; Permission granted by Mark Paterson on behalf of Peter Moss for the material from *History Alive: Introductory Book* by Moss, P. on p. 665; Philip Allan Publishers for the extract and figure from *Let's Get Real: the Realist Approach in Sociology* by Clarke and Layder, *Sociology Review* vol. 4:2 (November 1994) on p. 73, for the table from *The Middle Classes in Modern Britain* by Savage, M. *Sociology Review*, vol. 5:2 (November 1995) on p. 134, for the table 'Some Important Dates' from *History of Black People in Britain* by Small, S., *Sociology Review*, vol. 3:4 (April 1994) on p. 203, for the line drawings from *Urban Kinship Past and Present* by Willmot, P., *Social Studies Review*, vol. 3:2 (November 1988) on p. 243, for the extract from *Women Outside Marriage* by Chandler, J., *Sociology Review*, vol. 2:4 (April 1993) on p. 251, for table 1 from *Money, Marriage and Ideology: Holding the Purse Strings* by Pahl, J., *Sociology Review*, vol. 3:1 (September 1993) on p. 262, for the extract from *Family Values and Relationships* by Jewson, N., *Sociology Review*, vol. 3:3 (February 1994) on p. 269, for the extract from *Who are you and so what?* by Clark, J. and Saunders, C., *Sociology Review*, vol. 1:1 (September 1993) on p. 304, for the extract from *Gender and Education Revisited* by Clark, J., *Sociology Review*, vol. 5:4 (April 1996) on p. 304, for the table 'The Square of Crime' from *Squaring up to Crime* by Matthews, R., *Sociology Review*, vol. 2:3 (February 1993) on p. 454 and for the table from *Links: the World Religions*, *General Studies Review*, vol. 1:1 (September 1991) on p. 732; Pluto Press for the extract from *The Unhappy Marriage of Marxism and Feminism* by Hartmann on p. 171 and for the extracts from *What is to be done about Law and Order?* by Lea and Young on pp. 446 and 447; Popular Publications for the material on p. 227; Reproduced by kind permission of *Private Eye* the article on p. 347; Punch Library and Archive for the cartoon on p. 429; Rodale Press for the material on p. 527; Routledge for the extract from *An Introduction to Sociology: Feminist Perspectives* by Abbott and Wallace on p. 36, for the figure from *Research Methods* by McNeill on p. 64, for the extract from *Social Class in Modern Britain* by Marshall *et al.* on pp. 97–8 and 147, for the figure from *Class* by Edgell on p. 119, for the table from *Social Class and Social Justice* by Marshall and Swift, *British Journal of Sociology* on p. 148, for the extracts from *Five Feminist Myths about Women's Employment* by Hakim, *British Journal of Sociology* on pp. 174–5, for the extract from *Whose myths are they anyway?: a comment* by Breugel, *British Journal of Sociology* on p. 175, for the extract from *Feminist Fallacies: A Reply to Hakim on Women's Employment* by Ginn, *British Journal of Sociology* on p. 176, for the table from *Society and Social Science: A Reader* by Anderson and Riccu on p. 266, for the material from *Reforming Education and Changing Schools: Case Studies in Policy Sociology* by Bowe, Ball with Gold on p. 311 for the figure from *Sociology, Work and Industry* by Watson on p. 355, for the figure from *Globalization* by Waters on p. 483, for the table from *Capitalism and Development* by Sklair on p. 486, for the table from *Poor Britain* by Mack and Lansley on p. 581, for the diagram from *Understanding the Media* by Hart on p. 604, for the figure from *What's this Channel Fo(u)r?* by Blanchard and Morley on p. 618, for the material from *Television, Audiences and Cultural Studies* by Morley on p. 640, for the figure from *Introduction to Communication Studies* by Fiske on p. 642 and for the material from *The Elementary Forms of the New Religious Life* by Wallis on p. 748; Reprinted with permission of Sage Publications Ltd from Pierre Bourdieu, *Sociology in Question* translated by Richard Nice on p. 89. English translation © Sage Publications, and from Bryan S. Turner, *Medical Power and Social Knowledge* on p. 513 © Bryan S. Turner, 1987; Simon and Schuster International for the map from *Community Life* by Craw and Allan on p. 661; The *Socialist Worker* for the article on p. 132; Soja, E. W. for material on pp. 671 and 672; Soundings for the extract on p. 194; Telegraph Group Ltd for the article on p. 435; © Times Newspapers Limited, 1996 for the articles on pp. 219 and 301; © Times Newspapers Limited, 1994 for the article on p. 301; © Times Supplements Limited, 1996 for The *Times Educational Supplement* articles of 17-5-96 on p. 211, of 24-4-96 on p. 300, of 24-4-96 and 15-3-96 on p. 301 and of 19-4-96 on p. 322; UNESCO Publishing for the table on p. 501; UODLE material on pp. 107, 159, 195–7, 232–3, 278, 304, 323, 324, 371, 419, 463, 464, 552, 601–2, 645, 646, 688, 727–8 and 764 is reproduced by permission of the University of Cambridge Local Examinations Syndicate; University of Chicago Press for the extracts from *Family Fortunes* by Davidoff and Hall on p. 168; Virago Press for the extract from Blood Bread and Poetry by Rich on p. 187; VSO for the material on p. 490; Waddington, D. Wykes, M. and Critcher, C. for the tables from *Split at the Seams*, OUP, on pp. 657 and 658; Wallis, V. for the diagrams from *Sociological Theory, Religion and Collective Action* by Roy Wallis and Steve Bruce on pp. 750 and 751; Michelin Wandor for 'The four demands' from *Once a Feminist: stories of a generation* on p. 184; Women's Community Press for the cartoon on p. 189; World Development Movement for the material on p. 497 from *Corporate Giants: their grip on the world's economy* briefing. Published by World Development Movement 1996.

Bibliography

Abbott, D. (1994) 'Family, conjugal roles and the labour market', *Sociology Review*, vol. 4, no. 1.

Abbott, P. and Wallace, C. (1990) *An Introduction to Sociology: Feminist Perspectives*, London, Routledge.

Abbott, P. and Wallace, C. (1992) *The Family and the New Right*, London, Pluto Press.

Abbott, P. and Wallace, C. (1997) *An Introduction to Sociology: Feminist Perspectives*, 2nd edn, London, Routledge.

Abel-Smith, B. and Townsend, P. (1965) *The Poor and the Poorest*, London, Bell & Sons.

Abercrombie, N., Hill, S. and Turner, B.S. (1980) *The Dominant Ideology Thesis*, London, Allen & Unwin.

Abercrombie, N. and Turner, B.S. (1978) 'The dominant ideology thesis', *British Journal of Sociology*, vol. 29, no. 2.

Abercrombie, N. and Warde, A. (eds) (1994a) *Family, Household and the Life-Course*, Lancaster, Framework.

Abercrombie, N. and Warde, A., with Soothill, K., Urry, J. and Walby, S. (1994b) *Contemporary British Society*, 2nd edn, Cambridge, Polity Press.

Acker, J. (1973) 'Women and social stratification: a case of intellectual sexism', *American Journal of Sociology*, vol. 78.

Acker, J. (1989) 'The problem with patriarchy', *Sociology*, vol. 23, no. 2.

Actionaid, Bond, Cafod, Christian Aid, Intermediate Technology, Oxfam, Save the Children, Voluntary Service Overseas, Unicef, World Development Movement, World Wildlife Fund (1996) *The Case For Aid: A Manifesto*, London, Actionaid.

Adams, B. (1993) 'Sustainable development and the greening of development theory', in Schuurman, F.J. (ed.) *Beyond the Impasse: New Directions in Development Theory*, London, Zed.

Adorno, T.W. (1991) *The Culture Industry*, London, Routledge.

Adorno, T.W., Albert, H., Dahrendorf, R., Habermas, J., Pilot, H. and Popper, K. (1976) *The Positivist Dispute in German Sociology*, London, Heinemann.

Adorno, T.W. and Horkheimer, M. (1979) *The Dialectic of Enlightenment*, London, Verso (orig. pub. 1944).

Adorno, T.W. and Horkheimer, M. (1993) 'The culture industry: enlightenment as mass deception', in During, S. (ed.), *The Cultural Studies Reader*, London, Routledge (orig. pub. 1944).

Aggleton, P. (1987) *Rebels without Cause: Middle Class Youth and the Transition from School to Work*, London, Falmer Press.

Aggleton, P. (1990) *Health*, London, Routledge.

Aglietta, M. (1979) *A Theory of Capitalist Regulation*, London, Verso.

Ahmad, W.I.U. (ed.) (1993) *'Race' and Health in Contemporary Britain*, Buckingham: Open University Press.

Albrow, M. (1970) *Bureaucracy*, London, Pall Mall.

Alcock, P.(1993) *Understanding Poverty*, Basingstoke, Macmillan.

Aldrich, R. (1988) 'The National Curriculum: an historical perspective', in Lawton, D. and Chitty, C. (eds), *The National Curriculum* (Bedford Way Papers 33), London, Institute of Education, University of London.

Alexander, J. (ed.) (1985) *Neofunctionalism*, London, Sage.

Alexander, J. (1987) *Sociological Theory Since 1930*, New York, Columbia University Press.

Alexander, J. (1995) *Fin de Siècle Social Theory*, London, Verso.

Allan, G. (1985) *Family Life*, Oxford, Basil Blackwell.

Allan, P., Benyon, J. and McCormick, B. (eds) (1994) *Focus on Britain*, Deddington, Philip Allan.

Allen, H. (1987) *Justice Unbalanced*, Buckingham, Open University Press.

Allen, J. (1994) 'Foucault and special educational needs: developing a framework for analysing children's experiences of mainstreaming'. Unpublished paper given at the BERA Symposium on aspects of integration policy and provision for children with special educational needs.

Allen, S. (1982) 'Gender inequalities and class formation', in Giddens, A. and Mackenzie, G. (eds) *Social Class and the Division of Labour*, Cambridge, Cambridge University Press.

Allen, T. and Thomas, A. (eds) (1992) *Poverty and Development in the 1990s*, Oxford, Oxford University Press.

Althusser, L. (1968) *Reading Capital*, London, New Left Books.

Althusser, L. (1971a) *Lenin and Philosophy and Other Essays*, London, New Left Books.

Althusser, L. (1971b) 'Ideology and ideological state apparatuses', in *Lenin and Philosophy and Other Essays*, London, New Left Books.

Althusser, L. with Balibar, E. (1966) *For Marx*, London, Allen Lane

Ambrose, P. (1992) 'The rural/urban fringe as a battleground', in Short, B. (ed.) *The English Rural Community*, Cambridge, Cambridge University Press.

Amin, K. and Oppenheim, C. (1992) *Poverty in Black and White*, London, CPAG/Runnymede Trust.

Amin, S. (1974) *Accumulation on a World Scale*, London, Monthly Review Press.

Amin, S. (1976) *Unequal Development*, Brighton, Harvester.

Amin, S. (1977) *Imperialism and Unequal Development*, Brighton, Harvester.

Amos, V. and Parmar, P. (1984) 'Challenging imperial feminism', *Feminist Review*, no. 17.

Anderson, A. and Gordon, R. (1978) 'Witchcraft and the status of women: the case of England', *British Journal of Sociology*, vol. 29, no. 2.

Anderson, A. and Gordon, R. (1979) 'The uniqueness of English witchcraft: a matter of numbers?', *British Journal of Sociology*, vol. 30, no. 3.

Anderson, B. (1983) *Imagined Communities*, London, Verso.

Anderson, J. and Ricci, M. (eds) (1994) *Society and Social Science: A Reader*, Buckingham, Open University Press.

Anderson, M. (ed.) (1971) *Sociology of the Family*, Harmondsworth, Penguin.

Andrews, A. and Jewson, N. (1993) 'Ethnicity and infant death: the implications of recent statistical evidence for material explanations', *Sociology of Health and Illness*, vol. 15, no. 2.

Ang, I. (1985) *Watching 'Dallas': Soap Opera and the Melodramatic Imagination*, London, Methuen.

Ang, I. (1991) *Desperately Seeking the Audience*, London, Routledge.

Angell, I. (1995) *The Information Revolution and the Death of the Nation State*, London, Libertarian Alliance.

Annandale, E. and Clark, J. (1996) 'What is gender? Feminist theory and the sociology of human reproduction', *Sociology of Health and Illness*, vol. 18, no. 1.

Anthias, F. (1990) 'Race and class revisited: conceptualising race and racisms', *Sociological Review*, vol. 38, no. 1.

Anthias, F. and Yuval-Davies, N. (1983) 'Contextualising feminism: gender, ethnic and class divisions', *Feminist Review*, no. 15.

Anthias, F. and Yuval-Davis, N. (1993) *Racialized Boundaries*, London, Routledge.

Anyon, J. (1983). 'Intersections of gender and class: accomodation and resistance by working class and affluent females to contradictory sex-role ideologies', in Walker, S. and Barton, L. (eds), *Gender, Class and Education*, Lewes, Falmer Press.

Apple, M. (1986) *Teachers and Texts: A Political Economy of Class and Gender Relations in Education*, London, Routledge.

Apter, D. and Rosberg, C. (1994) 'Changing African perspectives', in Apter, D. and Rosberg, C. (eds) *Political Development and the New Reality of Sub-Saharan Africa*, Charlottesville, University Press of Virginia.

Arber, S. and Ginn, J. (1991) *Gender and Later Life: A Sociological Analysis of Resources and Constraints*, London, Sage.

Arber, S. and Ginn, J. (eds) (1995) *Connecting Gender and Ageing*, Buckingham, Open University Press.

Arblaster, A. (1984) *The Rise and Decline of Western Liberalism*, Oxford, Blackwell.

Archer, M.S. (1982) 'Morphogenesis versus structuration: on combining structure and action', *British Journal of Sociology*, vol. 33.

Archer, M.S.(1988) *Culture and Agency*, Cambridge, Cambridge University Press.

Archer, M.S.(1995) *Realist Social Theory: The Morphogenetic Approach*, Cambridge, Cambridge University Press.

Arensberg, C.M. and Kimball, S.T. (1968) *Family and Community in Ireland*, 2nd edn, Cambridge, MA, Harvard University Press.

Armstrong, D. (1995a) 'The rise of surveillance medicine', *Sociology of Health and Illness*, vol. 17, no. 3.

Armstrong, D. (1995b) *Power and Partnership in Education: Parents, Children and Special Educational Needs*, London, Routledge.

Arnold, M. (1960) *Culture and Anarchy*, Cambridge, Cambridge University Press.

Aronson, J. (1977) *Money and Power*, London, Sage.

Aronson, N. (1984) 'Comment on Bryan Turner's "The government of the body: medical regimes and the rationalization of diet', *British Journal of Sociology*, vol. 35, no. 1.

Ashcroft, B. *et al.* (eds) (1995) *The Post-Colonial Studies Reader*, London, Routledge.

Assiter, A. (1996) *Enlightened Women: Modernist Feminism in a Postmodern Age*, London, Routledge.

Atkinson, A.B. (1983) *The Economics of Inequality*, Oxford, Oxford University Press.

Atkinson, D. (1995) *Cities of Pride: Rebuilding Community, Refocusing Government*, London, Cassell.

Atkinson, J.M. (1977) 'Societal reactions to suicide: the role of coroners' definitions', in Cohen, S. (ed.), *Images of Deviance*, Harmondsworth, Penguin.

Atkinson, J.M. (1978) *Discovering Suicide*, Basingstoke, Macmillan.

Atkinson, J.M. and Heritage, J. (eds) (1984) *Structures of Social Action: Studies in Conversation Analysis*, Cambridge, Cambridge University Press.

Atkinson, P. (1985) *Language, Structure and Reproduction: An Introduction to the Sociology of Basil Bernstein*, London, Methuen.

Avalos, B. (1982) 'Neocolonialism and education in Latin America', in Watson, K. (ed.), *Education in the Third World*, Beckenham, Croom Helm.

Ayres, R. (ed.) (1995) *Development Studies*, London, Greenwich University Press.

Bagguley, P. (1993) 'Urban sociology', in Haralambos, M. (ed.) *Developments in Sociology 9*, Ormskirk, Causeway Press.

Bagguley, P. and Mann, K. (1992) 'Idle thieving bastards: scholarly representations of the underclass', *Work Employment and Society*, .vol. 6, no. 1.

Bagguley, P. and Walby, S. (1988) *Women and Local Labour Markets: A Comparative Analysis of Five Localities*, Lancaster, Lancaster Regionalism Group, University of Lancaster.

Bakx, K. (1991) 'The "eclipse" of folk medicine in western society', *Sociology of Health and Illness*, vol. 13, no. 1.

Ball, M. (1983) *Housing Policy and Economic Power*, London, Methuen.

Ball, S. (1981) *Beachside Comprehensive: A Case Study of Secondary Schooling*, Cambridge, Cambridge University Press.

Ball, S. (1994) *Education Reform: A Critical and Post-structuralist Approach*, Buckingham, Open University Press.

Ball, J.S. and Gerwirtz, S. (1997) 'Girls in the education market: choice, competition and complexity', *Gender and Education*, vol. 9, no. 2, pp. 207–222.

Ballard, C. (1979) 'Conflict, continuity and change: second generation south Asians', in Khan, V.S. (ed.), *Minority Families in Britain*, Basingstoke, Macmillan.

Ballard, R. (1982) 'South Asian families', in Rapoport, R.N., Fogarty, M.P. and Rapoport, R. (eds), *Families in Britain*, London, Routledge & Kegan Paul.

Balls, E. (1994) 'East Asian experience shows link between growth and equality', *The Guardian*, 4 July.

Banton, M. (1955) *The Coloured Quarter: Negro Immigrants in an English City*, London, Routledge.

Banton, M. (1987) *Racial Theories*, Cambridge, Cambridge University Press.

Banton, M. (1994) *Discrimination*, Milton Keynes, Open University Press.

Barak, G. (ed.) (1994) *Varieties of Criminology*, Westport, Praeger.

Barber, B. (1963) 'Some problems in the sociology of professions', *Daedalus*, vol. 92, no. 4.

Barbour, R.S. (1990) 'Health and illness', in Haralambos, M. (ed.), *Developments in Sociology*, vol. 6, Ormskirk, Causeway Press.

Barker, E. (1984) *The Making of a Moonie: Choice or Brainwashing*, Oxford, Blackwell.

Barker, M. (1981) *The New Racism*, London, Junction Books.

Barnes, C. (1982) *Disabled People in Britain and Discrimination: A Case for Anti-Discrimination Legislation*, London, Hurst & Co. in Association with the British Council of Organizations of Disabled People.

Barnett, T. (1988) *Sociology and Development*, London, Hutchinson Educational.

Barrat, D. and Cole, T. (1991) *Sociology Projects: A Student's Guide*, London, Routledge.

Barrett, M. (1980) *Women's Oppression Today: Problems in Marxist Feminist Analysis*, London, Verso.

Barrett, M. (1989) *Women's Oppression Today*, 2nd edn, London, Verso.

Barrett, M. and McIntosh, M. (1982) *The Anti-Social Family*, London, Verso.

Barrett, M. and McIntosh, M. (1991) *The Anti-Social Family*, 2nd edn, London, Verso.

Barrow, J. (1982) 'West Indian families: an insider's perspective', in Rapoport, R.N., Fogarty, M.P. and Rapoport, R. (eds), *Families in Britain*, London, Routledge & Kegan Paul.

Barthes, R. (1973) *Mythologies*, London, Paladin.

Bartholomew, R., Hibbert, A. and Sidaway, J. (1992) 'Lone parents and the labour market', *Employment Gazette*, November.

Bartley, M., Carpenter, L., Dunnell, K. and Fitzpatrick, R. (1996) 'Measuring inequalities in health: an analysis of mortality patterns using two social classifications', *Sociology of Health and Illness*, vol. 18, no. 4.

Barton, L. (1988) *The Politics of Special Educational Needs*, Lewes, Falmer Press.

Bassett, P. (1996) 'Will Britain's workforce ever stand up and be counted?', *The Times*, 17 January.

Batstone, E. (1984) *Working Order: Workplace Industrial Relations Over Two Decades*, Oxford, Blackwell.

Batstone, E. (1988) *The Reform of Workplace Industrial Relations*, Oxford, Clarendon Press.

Baudrillard, J. (1981) *For a Critique of the Political Economy of the Sign*, St. Louis, Telos.

Baudrillard, J. (1983a) *Simulations*, New York, Semiotext(e).

Baudrillard, J. (1983b) *In the Shadow of the Silent Majorities – or, The End of the Social and Other Essays*, New York, Semiotext(e).

Baudrillard, J. (1988) *Selected Writings*, Poster, M. (ed.), Cambridge, Polity Press.

Baudrillard, J. (1990) *Fatal Strategies*, New York, Semiotext(e).

Baudrillard, J. (1993a) 'Game with vestiges', in Gane, M. (ed.), *Baudrillard Live: Selected Interviews*, London, Routledge.

Baudrillard, J. (1993b) 'Baudrillard: the interview', in Gane, M. (ed.), *Baudrillard Live: Selected Interviews*, London, Routledge.

Baudrillard, J. (1993c) 'The evil demon of images and the precession of the simulacra', in Dòherty, T. (ed.), *Postmodernism: A Reader*, Hemel Hempstead, Harvester Wheatsheaf.

Baudrillard, J. (1995) *The Gulf War Did Not Take Place*, Sydney, Power Publications.

Bauer, P. (1991) *The Development Frontier*, Hemel Hempstead, Harvester Wheatsheaf.

Baugh, W.E. (1987) *Introduction to the Social Services*, 5th edn, Basingstoke, Macmillan.

Bauman, Z. (1990) *Thinking Sociologically*, Oxford, Blackwell.

Bauman, Z. (1991) *Modernity and Ambivalence*, Cambridge, Polity Press.

Bauman, Z. (1992) *Intimations of Postmodernity*, London, Routledge.

BBC (1995) *Report and Accounts 1994/95*, London, BBC Publications.

Beardsworth, A. and Keil, T. (1993) 'Hungry for knowledge: the sociology of food and eating', *Sociology Review*, vol. 3, no. 2.

Beauvoir, S. de (1972) *The Second Sex*, Harmondsworth, Penguin (orig. pub. 1953).

Beck, U. (1992) *Risk Society*, London, Sage.

Becker, D. and Sklar, R. (eds) (1987) *Postimperialism: International Capitalism and Development in the Late Twentieth Century*, London, Lynne Rienner.

Becker, H.S. (1951) 'Role and career problems of the Chicago public school teacher, ' Doctoral thesis, University of Chicago.

Becker, H.S. (1971) 'Social-class variations in the teacher–pupil relationship', in Cosin, B.R., Dale, I.R., Esland, G.M. and Swift, D.F.(eds), *School and Society*, London, Routledge & Kegan Paul (orig. pub. 1952).

Becker, H.S. (1973) *Outsiders: Studies in the Sociology of Deviance*, New York, Free Press.

Beckerman, W. (1974) *In Defence of Economic Growth*, London, Jonathan Cape.

Beckford, J.A. (1985) *Cult Controversies: The Societal Response to the New Religious Movements*, London, Tavistock.

Beechey, V. (1977) 'Some notes on female wage labour in capitalist production', *Capital and Class*, no. 3.

Beharrell, P. (1993) 'AIDS and the British Press', in Eldridge, J. (ed.), *Getting the Message: News, Truth and Power*, London, Glasgow University Media Group/Routledge.

Bell, D. (1973) *The Coming of Post-Industrial Society*, New York, Basic Books.

Bell, D. (1977) 'The return of the sacred? The argument on the future of religion', *British Journal of Sociology*, vol. 28, no. 4.

Bell, N.W. and Vogel, E.F. (eds) (1968), *A Modern Introduction to the Family* (revised edition), New York, Free Press.

Bellah, R.N. (1970) *Beyond Belief*, New York, Harper & Row.

Bellos, A. (1996) 'Action marks move beyond "single issue" campaigning', *The Guardian*, 8 August.

Ben-Tovim, G. and Gabriel, J. (1982) 'The politics of race in Britain, 1962–1979: a review of the major trends and recent debates', in Husband, C. (ed.), *'Race' in Britain: Continuity and Change*, London, Hutchinson.

Bendix, R. (1963) *Max Weber: An Intellectual Portrait*, London, Methuen.

Benedict, R. (1943) *Race and Racism*, London, Routledge.

Benthall, J. (1995) *Disasters, Relief and the Media*, London, I. B Tauris and Co.

Benyon, J. (ed.) (1984) *Scarman and After: Essays Reflecting on Lord Scarmans's Report, the Riots and their Aftermath*, Oxford, Pergamon Press.

Benyon, J. (1986) 'Turmoil in the cities', *Social Studies Review*, vol. 1, no. 3.

Benyon, J. and Denver, D. (1990) 'Mrs Thatcher's electoral successes', *Social Studies Review*, vol. 5, no. 3.

Berger, P.L. (1987) *The Capitalist Revolution*, Aldershot, Gower.

Berger, P.L. (1990) *The Sacred Canopy: Elements of a Sociological Theory of Religion*, New York, Anchor Books.

Berger, P.L. and Kellner, H. (1981) *Sociology Reinterpreted*, Harmondsworth, Penguin.

Berger, P.L. and Luckmann, T. (1967) *The Social Construction of Reality: A Treatise in the Sociology of Knowledge*, Harmondsworth, Penguin.

Berle, A.A. and Means, G.C. (1968) *The Modern Corporation and Private Property*, New York, Harcourt, Brace and World Inc. (orig. pub.1932).

Bernard, M., Itzin, C., Phillipson, C. and Skucha, J. (1995) 'Gendered work, gendered retirement', in Arber, S. and Ginn, J. (1995) (eds), *Connecting Gender and Ageing*, Buckingham, Open University Press.

Bernstein, B. (1977) *Class Codes and Control*, vol. 3, London, Routledge & Kegan Paul.

Bernstein, E. (1961) *Evolutionary Socialism*, New York, Schoken Books (orig. pub. 1899).

Bernstein, H., Crow, B. and Johnson, H. (eds) (1992) *Rural Livelihoods: Crises and Responses*, Oxford, Oxford University Press.

Beveridge, W. (1942) *Social Insurance and Allied Services*, London, HMSO.

Beyer, P. (1994) *Religion and Globalization*, London, Sage.

Beynon, H. (1973) *Working For Ford*, Harmondsworth, Penguin.

Bhaskar, R. (1978) *A Realist Theory of Science*, 2nd edn, Brighton: Harvester.

Bhaskar, R. (1979) *The Possibility of Naturalism*, Brighton, Harvester.

Bhaskar, R. (1986) *Scientific Realism and Human Emancipation*, London, Verso.

Billington, R. *et al.* (1991) *Culture and Society*, Basingstoke, Macmillan.

Bilton, T., Bonnett, K., Jones, P., Stanworth, M., Sheard, K. and Webster, A. (1987) *Introductory Sociology*, 2nd edn, Basingstoke, Macmillan.

Bilton, T., Bonnett, K., Jones, P., Skinner, D., Stanworth, M. and Webster, A. (1996) *Introductory Sociology*, 3rd edn, Basingstoke, Macmillan.

Birch, A.H. (1993) *The Concepts and Theories of Modern Democracy*, London, Routledge.

Blackburn, C. (1991) *Poverty and Health*, Buckingham, Open University Press.

Blair, T. (1996) 'My radical task', *The Observer*, 15 September.

Blake, A. (1992) *The Music Business*, London, Batsford.

Blakemore, K. and Boneham, M. (1994) *Age, Race and Ethnicity*, Buckingham, Open University Press.

Blanch, M. (1979) 'Imperialism, nationalism and organised youth', in Clarke, J. *et al.* (eds), *Working Class Culture*, London, Hutchinson.

Blanchard, S. and Morley, D. (1982) *What's This Channel Fo(u)r*, London, Comedia.

Blau, P. (1955) *The Dynamics of Bureaucracy*, Chicago, University of Chicago Press.

Blauner, R. (1964) *Alienation and Freedom*, Chicago, University of Chicago Press.

Blumer, H. (1969) *Symbolic Interactionism: Perspective and Method*, Englewood Cliffs, NJ, Prentice-Hall.

Blumler, J.G. (1991) 'The new television marketplace: imperatives, implications, issues', in Curran, J. and Gurevitch, M. (eds), *Mass Media and Society*, New York, Edward Arnold.

Blumler, J.G. (ed.) (1992a) *Television and the Public Interest: Vulnerable Values in Western European Broadcasting*, London, Sage.

Blumler, J.G. (1992b) 'Vulnerable values at stake', in Blumler, J.G. (ed.), *Television and the Public Interest: Vulnerable Values in West European Broadcasting*, London, Sage.

Blumler, J.G., Brown, J.R., Ewbank, A.J. and Nossiter, T.J. (1971) 'Attitudes to the monarchy: their structure and development during a ceremonial occasion', *Political Studies*, vol. 19.

Blumler, J.G. and Katz, E. (eds) (1974) *The Uses of Mass Communication: Current Perspectives on Gratifications Research*, Beverly Hills, Sage.

Blumler, J.G., Katz, E. and Gurevitch, M. (1974) 'Utilization of mass communication by the individual', in Blumler, J.G. and Katz, E. (eds), *The Uses of Mass Communication: Current Perspectives on Gratifications Research*, Beverly Hills, Sage.

Bly, R. (1991) *Iron John*, Shaftesbury, Element Books.

Bocock, R. (1974) *Ritual in Industrial Society. A Sociological Analysis of Ritualism in Modern England*, London, George Allen & Unwin.

Bocock, R. (1985) 'Religion in modern Britain', in Bocock, R. and Thompson, K. (eds), *Religion and Ideology*, Manchester, Manchester University Press.

Bocock, R. (1993) *Consumption*, London, Routledge.

Bogenhold, D. and Staber, U. (1991) 'The decline and rise of self-employment', *Work, Employment and Society*, vol. 5, 223–39.

Bone, A. (1983) *Girls and Girls-Only Schools: A Review of the Evidence*, Report of the Equal Opportunities Commission, UK.

Bonger, W. (1916) *Criminality and Economic Conditions*, Boston, Little Brown.

Booth, C. (1902) *The Life and Labour of the People*, London, Williams & Northgate.

Booth, D. (1985) 'Marxism and development sociology: interpreting the impasse', *World Development*, vol. 13.

Booth, D. (1993) 'Development research: from impasse to a new agenda', in Schuurman, F.J. (ed.), *Beyond the Impasse: New Directions in Development Theory*, London, Zed.

Bott, E. (1971) *Family and Social Networks*, 2nd edn, London, Tavistock.

Bottomore, T. (1973) Ruling élite or ruling class?, in Urry, J. and Wakeford, J. (eds), *Power in Britain: Sociological Readings*. London, Heinemann.

Bottomore, T. (1978) *Classes in Modern Society*, London, George Allen & Unwin (orig. pub. 1965).

Bottomore, T. (1993) *Elites and Society*, 2nd edn, London, Routledge (orig. pub. 1964).

Bottomore, T. and Nisbet, R. (1979) 'Structuralism', in Bottomore, T. and Nisbet, R. (eds), *A History of Sociological Analysis*, London, Heinemann.

Bourdieu, P. (1977) *Outline of a Theory of Practice*, Cambridge, Cambridge University Press.

Bourdieu, P. (1984) *Distinction: A Social Critique of the Judgement of Taste*, London, Routledge.

Bourdieu, P. (1990) *In Other Words: Essays Towards a Reflexive Sociology*, Cambridge, Polity Press.

Bourdieu, P. (1993a) *Sociology in Question*, London, Sage.

Bourdieu, P. (1993b) *The Field of Cultural Production*, Cambridge, Polity Press.

Bourdieu, P. and Haacke, H. (1995) *Free Exchange*, Cambridge, Polity Press.

Bourdieu, P. and Passeron, J.C. (1977) *Reproduction in Education, Society and Culture*, London, Sage.

Bourke, J. (1994) *Working Class Cultures in Britain 1890–1960*, London, Routledge.

Bowlby, J. (1965) *Child Care and the Growth of Love*, Harmondsworth, Penguin.

Bowles, S. and Gintis, H. (1976) *Schooling in Capitalist America*, London, Routledge & Kegan Paul.

Box, S. (1981) *Deviance, Reality and Society*, 2nd edn, London, Holt, Rinehart & Winston.

Box, S. (1983) *Power, Crime and Mystification*, London, Routledge.

Box, S. (1995) *Power, Crime, and Mystification*, 2nd edn, London, Routledge.

Bradley, H. (1989) *Men's Work, Women's Work*, Cambridge, Polity Press.

Bradley, H. (1996) *Fractured Identities: Changing Patterns of Inequality*, Cambridge, Polity Press.

Bradshaw, J. and Holmes, H. (1989) *Living on the Edge*, Newcastle, Tyneside Child Poverty Action Group.

Bradshaw, J., Hicks, L. and Parker, H. (1992) *Summary Budget Standards for Six Households*, York, Family Budget Unit, working paper 12.

Brah, A. (1992) 'Difference, diversity and differentiation', in Donald, J. and Rattansi, A. (eds), *'Race', Culture and Difference*, London, Sage.

Braidotti, R. (1991) *Patterns Of Dissonance*, Cambridge, Polity Press.

Brandt Commission (1980) *North–South : A Programme for Survival*, London, Pan.

Brandt Commission (1983) *Common Crisis*, London, Pan.

Braverman, H. (1974), *Labor and Monopoly Capital*, New York, Monthly Review Press.

Brenner, H. (1979) 'Mortality and the national economy', *The Lancet*, 15 September.

Brenner, R. (1986) 'The social basis of economic development', in Roemer, J. (ed.), *Analytical Marxism*, Cambridge, Cambridge University Press.

Breugel, I. (1996) 'Whose myths are they anyway: a comment', *British Journal of Sociology*, vol. 47, no. 1.

British Medical Association (1993) *Complementary Medicine: New Approaches to Good Practice*, London, BMA.

British Sociological Association (1991) *Statement of Ethical Practice*, London, BSA.

Brittan, S. (1975) 'The economic contradictions of democracy', *British Journal of Political Science*, vol. 15.

Brittan, S. (1989) 'The case for the consumer market', in Veljanovski, C. (ed.), *Freedom in Broadcasting*, London, Institute of Economic Affairs.

Brody, M. (ed.) (1975) *Mary Wollstonecraft: 'Vindication Of The Rights Of Woman'* (orig. pub 1792), Harmondsworth, Penguin.

Brown, A. (1994) 'Thalidomide's horrors plague poor of Brazil', *The Observer*, 23 October.

Brown, C. (1984) *Black and White in Britain: The Third PSI Survey*, Oxford, Heinemann Educational.

Brown, D. (1991) *Bury My Heart at Wounded Knee: An Indian History of the American West*, London, Vintage.

Brown, M. (1990) *TV and Women's Culture*, London, Sage.

Brown, M. and Madge, N. (1982) *Despite the Welfare State*, London, Heinemann.

Brown, P. and Scase, R. (eds) (1991), *Poor Work, Disadvantage and the Division of Labour*, Buckingham, Open University Press.

Browne, K. (1992) *An Introduction to Sociology*, Cambridge, Polity Press.

Bruce, S. and Wallis, R. (1989) 'Religion: the British contribution', *British Journal of Sociology*, vol. 40, no. 3.

Bruntland, G. *et al.* for World Commission on Environment and Development (1987) *Our Common Future*, Oxford, Oxford University Press.

Bryan, B., Dadzie, S. and Scafe, S. (1985) *The Heart of the Race: Black Women's Lives in Britain*, London, Virago.

Bryant, C. (1985) *Positivism in Social Theory and Research*, Basingstoke, Macmillan.

Bryant, C. and Becker, H. (eds) (1990) *What has Sociology Achieved?*, Basingstoke, Macmillan.

Brydon, L. and Legge, K. (1996) 'Gender and adjustment: pictures from Ghana', in Thomas-Emeagwali, G. (ed.) *Women Pay the Price: Structural Adjustment in Africa and the Caribbean*, New Jersey, Africa World Press.

Bryson, L. (1992) *Welfare and the State: Who Benefits?* Basingstoke, Macmillan.

Buchanan, K. (1975) *Reflections on Education in the Third World*, Nottingham, Spokesman.

Budge, I. and McKay, D. (eds) (1993) *The Developing British Political System: The 1990s*, 3rd edn, London, Longman.

Bull, M. (1990) 'Secularization and medicalization', *British Journal of Sociology*, vol. 41, no. 2.

Bulmer, M. (ed.) (1982) *Social Research Ethics: An examination of the Merits of Covert Participation Research*, Basingstoke, Macmillan.

Burawoy, M. (1979) *Manufacturing Consent*, Chicago, University of Chicago Press.

Burawoy, M. (1985) *The Politics of Production*, London, Verso.

Burchardt, T. and Hills, J. (1997) *Private Welfare Insurance and Social Security: Pushing the Boundaries*, York, Joseph Rowntree Foundation.

Burchell, B. (1994) 'The effects of labour market position, job insecurity, and unemployment on psychological health', in Gallie, D., Marsh, C. and Vogler, C. (eds), *Social Change and the Experience of Unemployment*, Oxford, Oxford University Press.

Burgess, R. (1984) *In the Field: An Introduction to Field Research*, London, Unwin Hyman.

Burghes, R. and Roberts, C. (1995) 'Lone parents', in *Community Care*, 6–12 July.

Burnham, J. (1945) *The Managerial Revolution*, London, Pelican.

Burns, T. and Stalker, G.M. (1966) *The Management of Innovation*, 2nd edn, London, Tavistock.

Burrows, R. and Butler, T.(1989) 'Middle mass and the pit: a critical review of Peter Saunders' sociology of consumption', *Sociological Review*, vol. 37, no. 2.

Burrows, R. and Loader, B. (eds) (1994) *Towards a Post-Fordist Welfare State?*, London, Routledge.

Busfield, J. (1996) *Men, Women and Madness: Understanding Gender and Mental Disorder*, Basingstoke, Macmillan.

Butler, T. and Savage, M. (eds) (1995) *Social Change and the Middle Classes*, London, UCL Press.

Butler, D. and Stokes, D. (1969) *Political Change in Britain: Forces Shaping Electoral Choice*, Basingstoke, Macmillan.

Butler, J. (1990) *Gender Trouble: Feminism and the Subversion of Identity*, London, Routledge.

Butterworth, E. and Weir, D. (eds) (1975) *The Sociology of Modern Britain* (revised edition), Glasgow, Fontana.

Byrne, E. (1978) *Women and Education*, London, Tavistock.

Byrne, T. and Padfield, C. (1985) *Social Services Made Simple*, 3rd edn, London, Heinemann.

Callender, C. (1992) 'Redundancy, unemployment and poverty', in Glendinning, C. and Millar, J. (eds), *Women and Poverty in Britain: The 1990s*, Hemel Hempstead, Harvester Wheatsheaf.

Callinicos, A. (1982) *Is There a Future for Marxism?*, Basingstoke, Macmillan.

Callinicos, A. (1987) *Making History*, Cambridge, Polity Press.

Callinicos, A. (1989) *Against Postmodernism: A Marxist Critique*, Cambridge, Polity Press.

Callinicos, A. (1995) *Theories and Narratives*, Cambridge, Polity Press.

Campbell, A. (1981) *Girl Delinquents*, Oxford, Basil Blackwell.

Campbell, B. (1995a) 'Granddaddy of the backlash', *The Guardian*, 1 April.

Campbell, B. (1995b) 'Old fogeys and angry young men', *Soundings*, issue 1, autumn.

Campbell, C. (1972) 'The cult, the cultic milieu and secularization', in Hill, M. (ed.), *A Sociological Yearbook of Religion in Britain*, London, SCM Press.

Campbell, C. (1977) 'Clarifying the cult', *British Journal of Sociology*, vol. 28.

Campbell, C. (1995) 'The sociology of consumption', in Miller, D. (ed.), *Acknowledging Consumption*, London, Routledge.

Campbell, D. (1995c) 'Cameras key weapon in fight against crime', *The Guardian*, 30 December.

Carby, H. (1982) 'White women listen: black feminism and the boundaries of sisterhood', in *The Empire Strikes Back*, London, CCCS/Hutchinson.

Cardoso, F.H. (1973) 'Associated dependent development', in Stepan, A. (ed.) *Authoritarian Brazil*, New Haven, Yale University Press.

Carnoy, M. (1974) *Education as Imperialism*, New York, David McKay.

Carver, T. (1991) *Engels*, Oxford, Oxford University Press.

Casey, J. (1982) 'One nation: the politics of race', in *The Salisbury Review*.

Cashmore, E. (1983) *Introduction to Race Relations*, London, Routledge & Kegan Paul.

Cashmore, E. and Troyna, B. (1990) *Introduction to Race Relations*, London, Sage.

Cassell, P. (ed.) (1993) *The Giddens Reader*, Basingstoke, Macmillan.

Castles, S. and Kosack, G. (1973) *Immigrant Workers and Class Structure in Western Europe*, Oxford, Oxford University Press.

Centre for Contemporary Cultural Studies (1982) *The Empire Strikes Back: Race and Racism in 70s Britain*, London, CCCS/Hutchinson.

Centre for Research in Education Marketing (1996) *Student Decision-making and the Post-16 Market Place*, CREM, University of Southampton.

Chandler, J. (1991) *Women Without Husbands*, Basingstoke, Macmillan.

Chandler, J. (1993) 'Women outside marriage', *Sociology Review*, vol. 2, no. 4.

Charles, N. and Kerr, M. (1988) *Women, Food and Families*, Manchester, Manchester University Press.

Charles, N. and Kerr, M. (1994) 'Gender and age differences in family food consumption', in Anderson, J. and Ricci, M. (eds), *Society and Social Science: A Reader*, 2nd edn, Buckingham, Open University Press.

Charmaz, K. (1983) 'Loss of self: a fundamental form of suffering in the chronically ill', *Sociology of Health and Illness*, vol. 5, 168–95.

Charsley, S.R. (1986) ' "Glasgow's miles better": the symbolism of community and identity in the city', in Cohen, A.P. (ed.) *Symbolising Boundaries: Identity and Diversity in British Cultures*, Manchester, Manchester University Press.

Charter, D. (1996) 'The college in crisis', *The Times*, 13 December.

Cheal, D. (1991) *Family and the State of Theory*, Hemel Hempstead, Harvester Wheatsheaf.

Chen, K.H. (1992) 'Post-Marxism: critical postmodernism and cultural studies', in Scannel, P. *et al.* (eds), *Culture and Power*, London, Sage.

Chen, R.S. (ed.) (1990) *The Hunger Report*, Providence (RI), Alan Shawn Feinstein World Hunger Program.

Chester, R. (1985) 'The rise of the neo-conventional family', *New Society*, 9 May.

Chibnall, S. (1977) *Law-and-Order News: An Analysis of Crime Reporting in the British Press*, London, Tavistock.

Chodorow, N. (1978) *The Reproduction of Mothering: Psychoanalysis and the Sociology of Gender*, Berkeley, CA: University of California Press.

Church, J. and Summerfield, C. (1996) *Social Focus on Ethnic Minorities*, London, HMSO.

Citizens Advice Bureau (1996) *A Right to Family Life: CAB Client's Experience of Immigration and Asylum*, London, Association of Citizens Advice Bureaux.

Clark, J. (1996) 'Insights: gender and education revisited', *Sociology Review*, vol. 5, no. 4.

Clark, T.N. and Lipset, S.M. (1991) 'Are social classes dying?', *International Sociology*, vol. 6, no. 4.

Clarke, J. and Critcher, C. (1985) *The Devil Makes Work*, Basingstoke, Macmillan.

Clarke, J. and Langan, M. (1993) 'Restructuring welfare: the British welfare regime in the 1980s', in Cochrane, A. and Clarke, J. (eds), *Comparing Welfare States*, London, Sage.

Clarke, J. and Layder, D. (1994) 'Let's get real: the realist approach', *Sociology Review*, vol. 4, no. 2.

Clarke, R. (1980) 'Situational crime prevention: theory and practice', *British Journal of Criminology*, vol. 20.

Clarricoates, K. (1978) 'Dinosaurs in the classroom: a re-examination of some aspects of the "hidden" curriculum in primary schools, *Women's Studies International Quarterly*, vol. 1.

Clegg, S.R. (1990) *Modern Organizations*, London, Sage.

Clegg, S.R. (1992) 'Modern and postmodern organizations', *Sociology Review*, vol. 1, no. 4.

Cloward, R.A. and Ohlin, L.E. (1960) *Delinquency and Opportunity: A Theory of Delinquent Gangs*, Glencoe, Free Press.

Cloward, R.A. and Ohlin, L.E. (1989) 'Differential opportunity and deliquent subcultures', in Kelly, D.H. (ed.), *Deviant Behaviour: A Text-Reader in the Sociology of Deviance*, 3rd edn, New York, St Martin's Press.

Coates, D. (1984) *The Context of British Politics*, London, Hutchinson.

Cochrane, A. and Clarke, J. (eds) (1993) *Comparing Welfare States*, London, Sage.

Cockburn, C. (1983) *Brothers: Male Dominance and Technological Change*, London, Pluto Press.

Cohen, A. (1955) *Deliquent Boys: The Culture of the Gang*, Glencoe, CA, Free Press.

Cohen, A.P. (1986a) 'Of symbols and boundaries; or, Does Ertie's greatcoat hold the key?', in Cohen, A.P. (ed.) *Symbolising Boudaries: Identity and Diversity in British Cultures*, Manchester, Manchester University Press.

Cohen, A.P. (1986b) *Symbolising Boundaries: Identity and Diversity in British Cultures*, Manchester University Press, Manchester.

Cohen, M.D., March, J.G. and Olsen, J.P. (1972) 'A garbage can model of organisational choice', *Administrative Science Quarterly*, vol. 17, no. 1.

Cohen, P. (1972) 'Subcultural conflict and the working class community', in *Working Papers in Cultural Studies*, no. 2, Birmingham, Centre for Contemporary Cultural Studies.

Cohen, P. (1988) 'The perversions of inheritance: studies in the making of multi-racist Britain', in Cohen, P. and Bains, H. (eds), *Multi-Racist Britain*, Basingstoke, Macmillan.

Cohen, P. (1992) 'It's racism what dunnit: hidden narratives in theories of racism', in Donald, J. and Rattansi, A. (eds), *'Race', Culture and Difference*, London, Sage.

Cohen, P.S. (1968) *Modern Social Theory*, London, Heinemann.

Cohen, S. (ed.) (1977) *Images of Deviance*, Harmondsworth, Penguin.

Cohen, S. (1980) *Folk Devils and Moral Panics: The Creation of the Mods and Rockers*, Oxford, Basil Blackwell.

Cohen, S. (1994) *Visions of Social Control: Crime, Punishment and Classification*, Cambridge, Polity Press.

Cohen, S. and Taylor, L. (1971) *Psychological Survival: The Experience of Long-Term Imprisonment*, Harmondsworth, Penguin.

Cole, T. (1986) *Whose Welfare?*, London, Tavistock.

Coleman, J. (1958) 'Relational analysis: the study of social organisations with survey methods', *Human Organisation*, vol. 16, no. 4.

Collins, R. (1985) 'Broadcasting policy in Canada', in Ferguson, M. (ed.), *New Communication Technologies and the Public Interest*, London, Sage.

Communist Party of Great Britain (1990) *Manifesto for New Times: A Strategy for the 1990s*, London, Lawrence & Wishart.

Comte, A. (1830/77) *Cours de Philosophie Positive*, Paris, Bachelier/Ballière & Sons.

Comte, A. (1844) *A Discourse on the Positive Spirit*, London, William Reeves (trans. 1903).

Comte, A. (1851) *System of Positive Polity*, London, Longmans Green.

Comte, A. (1853) *The Positive Philosophy of Auguste Comte* (edited by Harriet Martineau), 2 vols, London, Chapman.

Connell, R.W. (1987) *Gender and Power*, Cambridge, Polity Press.

Connell, R.W., Ashenden, D.J., Kessler, S. and Dowsett, G.W. (1982) *Making the Difference*, Sydney, George Allen & Unwin.

Connor, S. (1989) *Postmodernist Culture*, Oxford, Basil Blackwell.

Connors, J. (1992) *Manual on Violence Against Women in the Family in Commonwealth Countries*, London, Commonwealth Secretariat.

Cook, L. (1983) 'Popular culture and rock music', *Screen*, vol. 24, no. 3.

Cooke, P. (1988) 'Modernity, postmodernity and the City', *Theory, Culture and Society*, vol. 5, nos 2/3.

Cooke, P. (ed.) (1989) *Localities: The Changing Face of Urban Britain*, London, Unwin Hyman.

Coontz, S, and Henderson, P. (eds) (1986) *Women's Work, Men's Property*, London, Verso.

Cope, J. (1987) *Business Taxation*, Wokingham, Van Nostrand Reinhold.

Corbett, J. (1994) 'Challenges in a competitive culture: a policy for inclusive education in Newham', in Riddell, S. and Brown, S. (eds), *Special Educational Needs Policy in the 1990s: Warnock and the Market Place*, London, Routledge.

Corbett, J. (1995) *Bad Mouthing: The Language of Special Needs*, Lewes, Falmer Press.

Corbridge, S. (1993) 'Ethics in development studies: the example of debt', in Schuurman, F.J. (ed.) *Beyond the Impasse: New Directions in Development Theory*, London, Zed.

Cornell, D.L. (1992) 'Gender, sex and equivalent rights', in Butler, J. and Scott, J.W. (eds), *Feminists Theorise the Political*, London, Routledge.

Coser, L. (1956) *The Functions of Social Conflict*, London, Routledge & Kegan Paul.

Coser, L. (1977) *Masters of Sociological Thought*, 2nd edn, New York, Harcourt Brace Jovanovich.

Coverley, B. (1996) *Successful Step-parenting*, London, Bloomsbury.

Cox, O. (1970) *Caste, Class and Race*, New York, Monthly Preview Books.

Craib, I. (1992) *Modern Social Theory*, 2nd edn, Hemel Hempstead, Harvester Wheatsheaf.

Cressey, P.G. (1932) *The Taxi Dance Hall: A Sociological Study in Commercialised Recreation and City Life*, Chicago, University of Chicago Press.

Crewe, I. (1985) 'Can Labour rise again?', *Social Studies Review*, vol. 1, no. 1.

Crewe, I. (1987) 'Why Mrs Thatcher was returned with a landslide', *Social Studies Review*, vol. 3, no. 1.

Crewe, I. (1992) 'Why did Labour lose (yet again)?', *Politics Review*, September.

Crippen, T. (1988) 'Old and new gods in the modern world: toward a theory of religious transformation', *Social Forces*, vol. 67, December.

Critcher, C. (1979) 'Football since the war', in Clarke, J. *et al.* (eds), *Working Class Culture*, London, Hutchinson.

Croland, M. (1985) *One in Five: The Assessment and Incidence of Special Educational Needs*, London, Routledge & Kegan Paul.

Crompton, R. (1993) *Class and Stratification: An Introduction to Current Debate*, Cambridge, Polity Press.

Crompton, R. (1996a) 'Gender and class analysis', in Lee, D. and Turner, B. (eds), *Conflicts About Class*, Harlow, Longman.

Crompton, R. (1996b) 'Is class dead?', *Sociology Review*, vol. 5, no. 2.

Crompton, R. (1997) 'Gender and employment: current debates', *Social Science Teacher*, vol. 26, no. 2.*

Crompton, R. and Jones, G. (1984) *White Collar Proletariat*, Basingstoke, Macmillan.

Crompton, R. and Le Feuvre, N. (1996) 'Paid employment and the changing system of gender relations: a cross-national comparison', *Sociology*, vol. 30, no. 3.

Cross, M. (1992) 'Introduction', *New Community*, vol. 19, no. 1.

Cross, M. and Keith, M. (1993) *Racism, the City and State*, London, Routledge.

Crow, G. *et al.* (1990) 'Recent British rural sociology', in Lowe, P. and Bodiguel, M. (eds) *Rural Studies in Britain and France*, London, Bellhaven Press.

Crow, B. (1992) 'Understanding famine and hunger', in Allen, T. and Thomas, A. (eds) *Poverty and Development in the 1990s*, Oxford, Oxford University Press.

Crow, G. and Allan, G. (1994) *Community Life: An Introduction to Local Social Relations*, Hemel Hempstead, Harvester Wheatsheaf.

Culley, L. and Dyson, S. (1993) '"Race", inequality and health', *Sociology Review*, vol. 3, no. 1.

Curran, J. (1991) 'Mass media and democracy: a reappraisal', in Curran, J. and Gurevitch, M. (eds), *Mass Media and Society*, New York, Edward Arnold.

Curtis, L.R. (1968) *Anglo-Saxons and Celts.*, Connecticut, University of Bridgeport.

Dahl, R.A. (1961) *Who Governs?*, New Haven, Yale University Press.

Dahrendorf, R. (1959) *Class and Class Conflict in an Industrial Society*, London, Routledge & Kegan Paul.

Dahrendorf, R. (1987) 'The erosion of citizenship and its consequences for us all', *New Statesman*, 12 June

Dale, R. (1969, 1971, 1974) *Mixed or Single Sex School?*, vols 1–3, London, Routledge & Kegan Paul.

Dalla Costa, M. and James, S. (1972) *The Power of Women and the Subversion of the Community*, Bristol, Falling Wall Press.

Dallos, R. and Sapsford, R. (1995) in Muncie, J., Wetherell, M., Dallos, R. and Cochrane, A. (eds), *Understanding the Family*, London, Sage.

Darlington, R. (1994) *The Dynamics of Workplace Unionism*, London, Mansell.

David, M (1993) *Parents, Gender and Education Reform*, Cambridge, Polity Press.

David, M. (1986) 'Moral and maternal: the family in the Right', in Levitas, R. (ed.), *The Ideology of the New Right*, Cambridge, Polity Press.

Davidoff, L. (1979) 'The separation of home and work? Landladies and lodgers in nineteenth century England', in Burman, S. (ed.), *Fit Work For Women*, London Croom Helm.

Davidoff, L. and Hall, C. (1987) *Family Fortunes: Men and Women of the English Middle Class 1780–1850*, Chicago, University of Chigaco Press.

Davies, B. (1989) *Frogs and Snails and Feminist Tales: Pre-school Children and Gender*, Sydney, Allen & Unwin.

Davies, T. (1994) 'Disabled by society', *Sociology Review*, vol. 3, no. 4.

Davis, K. and Moore, W.E. (1945) 'Some principles of stratification', *American Sociological Review*, vol. 10.

Davis, K. and Moore, W.E. (1967) 'Some principles of stratification', in Bendix, R. and Lipset, S.M. (eds), *Class Status and Power*, 2nd edn, London, Routledge.

Davis, M. (1995) 'Fortress Los Angeles: the Militarization of Urban Space', in Kasinitz, P. (ed.) *Metropolis: Centre and Symbol of Our Times*, Basingstoke, Macmillan.

Dawkins, R. (1976) *The Selfish Gene.*, Oxford, Oxford University Press.

Daye, S. (1994) *Middle Class Blacks in Britain*, Basingstoke, Macmillan.

Deakin, N. and Edwards, J. (1993) *The Enterprise Culture and the Inner City*, London, Routledge.

Dearing, R. (1993) *The National Curriculum and its Assessment – Final Report*, London, Schools Curriculum and Assessment Authority.

Deedes, W. (1968) *Race Without Rancour*, London, Conservative Party Political Centre.

Deem, R. (1988) *Work, Unemployment and Leisure*, London, Routledge.

Deem, R. (1990) 'Women and leisure', *Social Studies Review*, vol. 5, no. 4.

Delamothe, T. (1989) 'Class dismissed', *British Medical Journal*, vol. 299, 1356.

Delphy, C. (1979) 'Sharing the same table', in Harris, C. (ed.), *The Sociology of the Family*, Keele, University of Keele.

Delphy, C. (1977a) *The Main Enemy*, London, Women's Research and Resource Centre.

Delphy, C. (1977b) 'Women in stratification studies', in Roberts, H. (ed.), *Doing Feminist Research*, London, Routledge.

Delphy, C. (1984) *Close to Home: A Materialist Analysis of Women's Oppression*, London, Hutchinson.

Delphy, C. and Leonard, D. (1993) *Familiar Exploitation*, Cambridge, Polity Press.

Dennis, M. (1975) 'Relationships', in Butterworth, E. and Weir, D. (eds), *The Sociology of Modern Britain* (revised edition), Glasgow, Fontana.

Dennis, N., Henriques, F. and Slaughter, C. (1956) *Coal is our Life*, London, Eyre & Spottiswoode.

Dennis, N. and Erdos, E. (1992) *Families Without Fatherhood*, London, IEA Health and Welfare Unit.

Denny, E. (1994) 'Liberation or oppression? Radical feminism and *in vitro* fertilisation', *Sociology of Health and Illness*, vol. 16, no. 1.

Denscombe, N (1993) *Sociology Update 1993*, Leicester, Olympus Books.

Denscombe, N. (1995) *Sociology Update 1995*, Leicester, Olympus Books.

Department of Employment (1995) *Labour Force Survey*, London, HMSO.

Department of Employment (1996) *Labour Market and Skill Trends 1995/6*, London, HMSO.

Derrida, J. (1978) *Writing and Difference*, London, Routledge & Kegan Paul.

Derry, J. (1996) 'Teaching the sociology and philosophy of science', *Social Science Teacher*, vol. 25, no. 2.*

Devine, F. (1992) *Affluent Workers Revisited: Privatism and the Working Class*, Edinburgh, Edinburgh University Press.

Dewey, J. (1972) 'Communication, individual, and society', in Manis, J. and Meltzer, B. (eds), *Symbolic Interaction: A Reader in Social Psychology*, Boston, Allyn & Bacon.

Dex, S. (1987) *Women's Occupational Mobility*, Basingstoke, Macmillan.

Dickinson, D. (1994) 'Criminal benefits', *New Statesman and Society*, 14 January.

Dobash, R.E. and Dobash, R.P. (1980) *Violence Against Wives: A Case Against Patriarchy*, Shepton Mallett, Open Books.

Donald, J. and Rattansi, A. (eds) (1992) *'Race', Culture and Difference*, London, Sage.

Dopson, S. and Waddington, I. (1996) 'Managing social change: à process-sociological approach to understanding organisational change within the National Health Service', *Sociology of Health and Illness*, vol. 18, no. 4.

Dore, R. (1987) *Flexible Rigidities: Industrial Policy and Structural Adjustment in the Japanese Economy, 1970–80*, London, Athlone.

Douglas, J. (1967) *The Social Meanings of Suicide*, Princeton, Princeton University Press.

Douglas, J.W.B. (1964) *The Home and the School*, London, Macgibbon & Kee.

Douglas, M. (1966) *Purity and Danger*, London, Routledge.

Downes, D. and Rock, P. (1995) *Understanding Deviance: A Guide to the Sociology of Crime and Rule Breaking*, 2nd edn, Oxford, Oxford University Press.

Doyal, L. (1995) *What Makes Women Sick? Gender and the Political Economy of Health*, Basingstoke, Macmillan.

Doyal, L. and Pennell, I. (1979) *The Political Economy of Health*, London, Pluto Press.

Drew, D. and Gray, J. (1990) 'The 5th year examination achievements of black young people in England and Wales', *Educational Research*, vol. 32, no. 3.

Drew, D. Fosam, B. and Gillborn, D. (1995) 'Statistics and the pseudo-science of 'race' and IQ: interrogating the Bell Curve'. Unpublished paper presented at the annual conference of the Royal Statistical Society, July 1995.

Dummett, M. and Dummett, A. (1982) 'The role of government in Britain's racial crisis', in Husband, C. (ed.), *'Race' in Britain: Continuity and Change*, London, Hutchinson.

Dumont, T. (ed.) (1993) *Channels of Resistance*, London, BFI Publishing.

Duncombe, J. and Marsden, D. (1995) *Sociology Review*, vol. 4, no. 4.

Dunleavy, P. and Husbands, C. (1985) *Democracy at the Crossroads*, London, George Allen & Unwin.

Dunleavy, P. and O'Leary, B. (1987) *Theories of the State: The Politics of Liberal Democracy*, Basingstoke, Macmillan.

Dunning, E., Murphy, P. and Williams, J. (1988) *The Roots of Football Hooliganism*, London, Routledge.

Dunsmuir, A. and Williams, L. (1991) *How to do Social Research*, London, Collins Educational.

Durham, M. and O'Shaughnessy, H. (1994) 'UK in secret £2bn arms bid', *The Observer*, 13 November.

Durkheim, E. (1938a) *The Division of Labour in Society*, Glencoe, Free Press (orig. pub. 1893).

Durkheim, E. (1938b) *The Rules of the Sociological Method*, Glencoe, Free Press (orig. pub. 1895).

Durkheim, E. (1979) *Suicide: A Study in Sociology*, London, Routledge & Kegan Paul (orig. pub. 1897).

Durkheim, E. (1982) *The Elementary Forms of the Religious Life*, London, George Allen & Unwin (orig. pub. 1912).

Durkheim, E. (1988) *Selected Writings* (edited by A. Giddens), Cambridge, Cambridge University Press.

Ealing Women's Liberation Workshop Collective (eds) (1971) 'Sisterhood is ...', *Shrew*, vol. 3, no. 6.

Eco, U. (1987) *Travels in Hyper-reality*, London, Picador.

Eco, U. (1995) *Apocalypse Postponed*, London, Flamingo.

Edgell, S. (1980) *Middle Class Couples*, London, George Allen & Unwin.

Edgell, S. (1993) *Class*, London, Routledge.

Edholm, F. (1991) in Loney, M., Bocock, R., Clarke, J., Cochrane, A., Graham, P. and Wilson, M. (eds), *The State or the Market*, London, Sage.

Education and Training for the 21st Century (1991), London, DfEE.

Edwards, T., Fitz, J. and Whitty, G. (1989) *The State and Private Education: An evaluation of the Assisted Places Scheme*, Lewes, Falmer Press.

Egerton, M. and Halsey, A.H. (1993) 'Trends by social class and gender in access to higher education in Britain, *Oxford Review of Education*, vol. 19, no. 2.

Eggleston, S.J., Dunn, D.K. and Anjoli, M. (1986) *Education for Some: The Educational and Vocational Experiences of 15–18 Year Old Members of Minority Ethnic Groups*, Stoke-on-Trent, Trentham Books.

Ehrlich, P.R. (1972) *The Population Bomb*, London, Ballantine.

Eisenstadt, S.N. (1956) *From Generation to Generation*, Chicago, Free Press.

Eldridge, J. (1991) 'Whose illusion, whose reality? Some problems of theory and method in mass media research', in Eldridge, J. (ed.), *Getting the Message: News, Truth and Power*, London, Routledge.

Eldridge, J. (1993) 'News, truth and power', in Eldridge, J. (ed.), *Getting the Message: News, Truth and Power*, London, Routledge.

Elias, N. (1978) *The Civilising Process*, Oxford, Blackwell (orig. pub. 1939).

Eliot, T.S. (1948) *Notes Towards a Definition of Culture*, London, Faber & Faber.

Elliot, F.R. (1996) *Gender, Family and Society*, Basingstoke, Macmillan.

Elliott, L. and Ryle, S. (1997) 'Fall in dole queue "fiddled"', *The Guardian*, 16 January.

Ellsworth, E. (1989) 'Why doesn't this feel empowering? Working through the repressive myths of critical pedagogy', *Harvard Educational Review*, vol. 59, no. 3.

Elsted, J.I. (1996) 'How large are the differences – really? Self-reported long-standing illness among working class and middle class men', *Sociology of Health and Illness*, vol. 18, no. 4.

Elster, J. (1983) *Explaining Technical Change*, Cambridge, Polity Press.

Elwood, J. (1995a) 'Gender, equity and the gold standard: examination and coursework performance in the UK at 18'. Unpublished paper presented at the AERA conference, San Francisco, USA.

Elwood, J. (1995b) 'Undermining gender stereotypes: examination and coursework performance in the UK at 16', *Assessment in Education*, vol. 2, no. 3.

Emmanuel, A. (1972) *Unequal Exchange: A Study of the Imperialism of Free Trade*, New York, Monthly Review Press.

Engels, F. (1972) *The Origins of the Family, Private Property and the State*, London, Lawrence & Wishart (orig. pub. 1884).

Engels, F. (1984) 'On the history of early Christianity', in Feuer, L.S. (ed.), *Marx and Engels: Basic Writings on Politics and Philosophy*, Aylesbury, Fontana (orig. pub. 1895).

Engels, F. (1986) 'Anti-Dühring', in Marx, K. and Engels, F., *Collected Works*, vol. 25, Moscow, Progress Publishers (orig. pub. 1878).

Epstein, D. (1993) *Changing Classroom Cultures: Anti-racism, Politics and Schools*, Stoke-on-Trent, Trentham Books.

Epstein, D. (1995) '"Girls don't do bricks": gender and sexuality in the primary classroom', in Siraj-Blatchford, J. and I. (eds), *Educating the Whole Child: Cross-Curricular Skills, Themes and Dimensions*, Buckingham, Open University Press.

Eribon, D. (1992) *Michel Foucault*, London, Faber & Faber.

Esping-Andersen, G. (1990) *The Three Worlds of Welfare Capitalism*, Cambridge, Polity Press.

Esping-Andersen, G. (ed.) (1993) *Changing Classes*, London, Sage.

ESRC (1989) *Unequal Jobs, Unequal Pay: The Social Change and Economic Life Initiative*, ESRC working paper 6.

Etzioni, A. (1995) *The Spirit of Community*, London, Fontana.

Evans, J. and Lunt, I. (1994) 'Dilemmas in special educational needs: some effects of local management of schools', in Riddell, S. and Brown, S. (eds), *Special Educational Needs Policy in the 1990s – Warnock and the Market Place*, London, Routledge.

Evans, J. and Vincent, C. (1996) 'Parental choice and special education', in Glatter, R., Woods, P. and Bayley , C. (eds), *Choice and Diversity in Schooling: Perspectives and Prospects*, London, Routledge.

Eversley, D. and Bannerjea, L. (1982) 'Social change and indications of diversity', in Rapoport, R.N., Fogarty, M.P. and Rapoport, R. (eds), *Families in Britain*, London, Routledge & Kegan Paul.

Eysenck, H.J. (1970) *Crime and Personality*, London, Paladin.

Faludi, S. (1992) *Backlash: The Undeclared War Against Women*, London, Chatto & Windus.

Family Spending 1995-96, (1996), London, Office for National Statistics.

Faulks, K. (1994) 'What has happened to citizenship?', *Sociology Review*, vol. 4, no. 2.

Featherstone, M. (1991a) *Consumer Culture and Postmodernism*, London, Sage.

Featherstone, M. (1991b) 'The body in consumer culture', in Featherstone, M., Hepworth, M. and Turner, B.S. (eds), *The Body: Social Process and Cultural Theory*, London, Sage.

Featherstone, M., Hepworth, M. and Turner, B.S. (eds) (1991) *The Body: Social Process and Cultural Theory*, London, Sage.

Ferguson, M. (1983) *Forever Feminine: Women's Magazines and the Cult of Femininity*, London, Heinemann.

Ferguson, M. (1990) 'Electronic media and the redefining of time and space', in Ferguson, M. (ed.), *Public Communication: The New Imperatives*, London, Sage.

Field, D. (1992) 'Elderly people in British society', *Sociology Review*, vol. 1, no. 4.

Field, F. (1989) *Losing Out: The Emergence of Britain's Underclass*, Oxford, Blackwell.

Field, F. (1996) *Stakeholder Welfare*, London, IEA.

Field, S. (1982) 'Urban disorders in Britain and America', in Field, S. and Southgate, P. (eds) *Public Disorder: A Review of Research and a Study in One Inner City Area*, London, HMSO.

Fielding, A.J. (1995) 'Migration and middle class formation in England and Wales 1981–91', in Butler, T. and Savage, M. (eds), *Social Change and the Middle Classes*, London, UCL Press.

Finch, J. and Mason, J. (1991) 'Obligations in kinship in contemporary Britain: is there normative agreement?, *British Journal of Sociology*, vol. 42, no. 3.

Finch, J. and Mason, J. (1993) *Negotiating Family Responsibilities*, London, Routledge.

Fine, B. (1995) 'From political economy to consumption', in Miller, D. (ed.), *Acknowledging Consumption*, London, Routledge.

Finegold, D. *et al.* (1990) *A British 'Baccalaureat': Ending the Division Between Education and Training*, London, Institute For Public Policy Research.

Firestone, S. (1970) *The Dialectic of Sex*, London, Women's Press.

Firestone, S. (1979) *The Dialectic of Sex*, 2nd edn, London, Women's Press.

Fishman, R. (1995) 'Megalopolis unbound', in Kasinitz, P. (ed.) *Metropolis: Centre and Symbol of Our Times*, Basingstoke, Macmillan.

Fiske, J. (1989a) *Understanding Popular Culture*, London, Unwin Hyman.

Fiske, J. (1989b) *Reading the Popular*, London, Unwin Hyman.

Fiske, J. (1990) *Introduction to Communication Studies*, 2nd edn, London, Routledge.

Fiske, J. (1991) 'Postmodernism and television', in Curran, J. and Gurevitch, M. (eds), *Mass Media and Society*, London, Edward Arnold.

Fletcher, R. (1966) *The Family and Marriage in Britain*, Harmondsworth, Penguin.

Florida, R. and Kenney, M. (1996) 'Japanese automotive transplants and the transfer of the Japanese production system', in Deyo, F.C. (ed.), *Social Reconstructions of the World Automobile Industry*, Basingstoke, Macmillan.

Foot, P. (1996) 'A lack of principal', *Private Eye*, 27 December.

Foote Whyte, W. (1943) *Street Corner Society: The Social Structure of an Italian Slum*, Chicago, University of Chicago Press.

Ford, J. (1990) 'Households, housing and debt', *Social Studies Review*, vol. 5, no. 5.

Foster-Carter, A. (1978) 'The modes of production controversy', *New Left Review*, vol. 107.

Foster-Carter, A. (1985) 'The sociology of development', in Haralambos, M. (ed.), *Sociology: New Directions*, Ormskirk, Causeway Press.

Foster-Carter, A. (1995) 'A tiger's eye', *New Statesman and Society*, 17 March.

Foucault, M. (1967) *Madness and Civilization*, London, Tavistock.

Foucault, M. (1970) *The Order of Things*, London, Tavistock.

Foucault, M. (1972) *The Archaeology of Knowledge*, London, Tavistock.

Foucault, M. (1974) *The Birth of the Clinic: An Archaeology of Medical Perception*, London, Tavistock.

Foucault, M. (1977) *Discipline and Punish: The Birth of the Prison*, Harmondsworth, Penguin.

Foucault, M. (1979a) *The History of Sexuality*, vol. 1, London, Allen Lane.

Foucault, M. (1979b) 'Governmentality', *Ideology and Conciousness*, vol. 6, Autumn.

Foucault, M. (1980) *Power/Knowledge: Selected Interviews and Other Writings 1972–1977*, Brighton, Harvester.

Foucault, M. (1989a) *The Birth of the Clinic: An Archaeology of Medical Perception*, new edn, London, Routledge.

Foucault, M. (1989b) *Madness and Civilization: A History of Insanity in the Age of Reason*, new edn, London, Routledge.

Foucault, M. (1990a) *The History of Sexuality. 1: An Introduction*, new edn, Harmondsworth, Penguin.

Foucault, M. (1990b) *The History of Sexuality. 3: The Care of the Self*, new edn, Harmondsworth, Penguin.

Foucault, M. (1991) *Discipline and Punish: The Birth of the Prison*, new edn, Harmondsworth, Penguin.

Foucault, M. (1992) *The History of Sexuality. 2: The Use of Pleasure*, new edn, Harmondsworth, Penguin.

Frank, A.G. (1969) *Capitalism and Underdevelopment in Latin America*, New York, Monthly Review Press.

Frank, A.G. (1979) *Dependent Accumulation and Underdevelopment*, New York, Monthly Review Press.

Frank, A.G. (1991a) 'Latin American development theories revisited', *Scandanavian Journal of Development Alternatives*, vol. 10, no. 3.

Frank, A.W. (1991b) 'For a sociology of the body: an analytical review', in Featherstone, M., Hepworth, M. and Turner, B.S. (eds), *The Body: Social Process and Cultural Theory*, London, Sage.

Fraser, D. (1973) *The Evolution of the British Welfare State*, Basingstoke, Macmillan.

Fraser, S. (ed.) (1995) *The Bell Curve Wars*, London, Basic Books.

Frayman, H. (1991) *Breadline Britain 1990s*, London, LWT.

Friedman, M. (1980) *Free To Choose*, Harmondsworth, Penguin.

Friedrich, C. (1954) *Totalitarianism*, Cambridge, MA, Harvard University Press.

Friedson, E. (1974) *The Profession of Medicine: A Study of the Sociology of Applied Knowledge*, New York, Dodd Mead.

Friere, P. (1972) *Pedagogy of the Oppressed*, Harmondsworth, Penguin.

Friere, P. and Macedo, D. (1987) *Literacy: Reading, the Word and the World*, London, Routledge & Kegan Paul.

Friere, P. and Shor, I. (1987) *A Pedagogy for Liberation: Dialogues on Transforming Education*, Basingstoke, Macmillan.

Frisby, D. (1984) *Georg Simmel*, London, Tavistock.

Frith, S. (1984) *The Sociology of Youth*, Ormskirk, Causeway.

Frith, S. (1988) *Music For Pleasure*, Cambridge, Polity Press.

Fröbel, F., Heinrichs, J. and Kreye, O. (1980) *The New International Division of Labour*, Cambridge, Cambridge University Press.

Fryer, P. (1984) *Staying Power: The History of Black People in Britain*, London, Pluto Press.

Fukuyama, F. (1992) *The End of History and the Last Man*, Harmondsworth, Penguin.

Fuller, M. (1980) 'Black girls in a London Comprehensive school', in Deem, R. (ed.), *Schooling for Women's Work*, London, Routledge and Kegan Paul.

Gallie, D. (1994) 'Are the unemployed an underclass? Some evidence from the Social Change and Economic Life Initiative', *Sociology*, vol. 28, no. 3.

Gallie, D., Marsh, C. and Vogler, C. (eds) (1994) *Social Change and the Experience of Unemployment*, Oxford, Oxford University Press.

Galloway, P., Armstrong, D. and Tomlinson, S. (1994) *The assessment of Special Educational Needs: Whose Problem?*, London, Longman.

Galtung, J. and Ruge, M. (1981) 'Structuring and selecting news', in Cohen, S. and Young, J. (eds), *The Manufacture of News: Deviance, Social Problems and the Mass Media*, London, Constable.

Gamble, A. (1994) 'Loves labour lost', in Perryman, M. (ed.), *Altered States: Postmodernism, Politics, Culture*, London, Lawrence & Wishart.

Gamman, L. (1988) 'Watching the detectives: the enigma of the female gaze', in Gamman, L. and Marshment, M. (eds), *The Female Gaze: Women as Viewers of Popular Culture*, London, Women's Press.

Gamman, L. and Marshment, M. (eds) (1988) 'Introduction', in *The Female Gaze: Women as Viewers of Popular Culture*, London, Women's Press.

Gane, M. (ed.) (1992) *The Radical Sociology of Durkheim and Mauss*, London, Routledge.

Gannon, K. (1995) 'Killing of Pakistan's boy activist draws demands for banning of child labour', *The Guardian*, 21 April.

Gans, H. (1962) *The Urban Village*, New York, Free Press.

Gans, H. (1974) *Popular Culture and High Culture*, New York, Basic Books.

Gardner, H. (1995) 'Cracking open the IQ box', in Fraser, S. (ed.), *The Bell Curve Wars*, London, Basic Books.

Garfield, S. (1986) *Expensive Habits: The Darker Side of the Music Industry*, London, Faber & Faber.

Garfinkel, H. (1967) *Studies in Ethnomethodology*, Englewood Cliffs, NJ, Prentice-Hall.

Garfinkel, H. (1984) *Studies in Ethnomethodology*, new edn, Cambridge, Polity Press.

Garrett, A. (1996) 'Census sensibility on trial', *The Observer* (Business Section), 24 November.

Garrett, S. (1987) *Gender*, London, Tavistock.

Gellner, E. (1983) *Nations and Nationalism*, Oxford, Blackwell.

George, S. (1976) *How the Other Half Dies*, Harmondsworth, Penguin.

George, S. (1988) *A Fate Worse than Debt*, Harmondsworth, Penguin.

George, V. and Wilding, P. (1994) *Welfare and Ideology*, London, Harvester Wheatsheaf.

Gerachty, C. (1991) *Women and Soap Opera*, Cambridge, Polity Press.

Gerry, C. (1985) 'Small enterprises, the recession and the "disappearing" working class', in Rees *et al.* (eds), *Political Action and Social Identity*, Basingstoke, Macmillan.

Gershuny, J. and Pahl, R. (1985) 'Britain in the decade of the three economies', in Littler, C.R. (ed.), *The Experience of Work*, Aldershot, Gower.

Giddens, A. (1969) 'Georg Simmel', in Raison, T.(ed.) *The Founding Fathers of Social Science*, revised edn, London, Scolar Press.

Giddens, A. (1971) *Capitalism and Modern Social Theory*, Cambridge, Cambridge University Press.

Giddens, A. (1973) *The Class Structures of the Advanced Societies*, London, Hutchinson.

Giddens, A. (ed.) (1974) *Positivism and Sociology*, London, Heinemann.

Giddens, A. (1976) *The New Rules of the Sociological Method*, London, Hutchinson.

Giddens, A. (1977) *Studies in Social and Political Theory*, London, Hutchinson.

Giddens, A. (1979) *Central Problems in Social Theory*, Basingstoke, Macmillan.

Giddens, A. (1980) *The Class Structure of the Advanced Societies*, 2nd edn, London, Hutchinson.

Giddens, A. (1984) *The Constitution of Society: An Outline of the Theory of Structuration*, Cambridge, Polity Press.

Giddens, A. (1985a) 'Jürgen Habermas', in Skinner, Q. (ed.) *The Return of Grand Theory in the Human Sciences*, Cambridge, Canto.

Giddens, A. (1985b) *Capitalism and Modern Social Theory: An Analysis of the Writings of Marx, Durkheim and Max Weber*, Cambridge, Cambridge University Press.

Giddens, A. (1985c) *The Nation State and Violence*, Cambridge, Polity Press.

Giddens, A. (1986) *Sociology: A Brief But Critical Introduction*, 2nd edn, Basingstoke, Macmillan.

Giddens, A. (1987) *Social Theory and Modern Sociology*, Cambridge, Polity Press.

Giddens, A. (1988) *New Rules of Sociological Method*, London, Hutchinson.

Giddens, A. (1989) *Sociology*, Cambridge, Polity Press.

Giddens, A. (1990) *The Consequences of Modernity*, Cambridge, Polity Press.

Giddens, A. (1991) *Modernity and Self-Identity: Self and Society in the Late Modern Age*, Cambridge, Polity Press.

Giddens, A. (1993a) *Sociology*, 2nd edn, Cambridge, Polity Press

Giddens, A. (1993b) *The Consequences of Modernity*, Cambridge, Polity Press.

Giddens, A. (1997) 'Goodnight, Mr Average', *The Observer*, 26 January.

Giddens, A. and Turner, J. (eds) (1987) *Social Theory Today*, Cambridge, Polity Press.

Gilbert, N. (1995) 'Official social classifications in the UK', *Social Research Update*, July.

Gill, S. and Law, D. (1988) *The Global Political Economy*, Hemel Hempstead, Harvester Wheatsheaf.

Gillborn, D. (1990) *'Race', Ethnicity and Education: Teaching and Learning in Multi-ethnic Schools*, London, Unwin Hyman.

Gillborn, D. and Gipps, C. (1996) *Recent Research on the Achievements of Ethnic Minority Pupils*, London, Ofsted.

Gillespie, M. (1995) *Television, Ethnicity and Cultural Change*, London, Routledge.

Gilligan, C. (1982) *In a Different Voice: Essays on Psychological Theory and Women's Development*, Cambridge, MA: Harvard University Press.

Gillis, J.R. (1985) *For Better, For Worse: British Marriage 1600 to the Present*, Oxford, Oxford University Press.

Gilroy, P. (1982a) 'Police and thieves', in *The Empire Strikes Back: Race and Racism in 70s Britain*, London, CCCS/Hutchinson.

Gilroy, P. (1982b) 'Steppin' out of Babylon: race, class and autonomy', in *The Empire Strikes Back: Race and Racism in 70s Britain*, London, CCCS/Hutchinson.

Gilroy, P. (1987) *There Ain't No Black in the Union Jack*, London, Unwin Hyman.

Gilroy, P. (1990) 'The end of anti-racism', *New Community*, vol. 17, no. 1.

Gilroy, P. (1992) 'The end of antiracism', in Donald, J. and Rattansi, A. (eds), *'Race', Culture and Difference*, London, Sage.

Gilroy, P. (1993) *The Black Atlantic: Modernity and Double Conciousness*, London, Verso.

Ginn, J., Arber, S., Brannen, J., Dale, A., Dex, S., Elias, P., Moss, P. Pahl, J., Roberts, C. and Rubery, J (1996) 'Feminist fallacies: a reply to Hakim on women's employment', *British Journal of Sociology*, vol. 47, no. 1.

Ginsburg, N. (1991) 'The wonderful world(s) of welfare capitalism', *Critical Social Policy*, Summer.

Ginsberg, N. (1992) 'Racism and housing: concepts and reality', in Braham, P., Rattansi, A. and Skellington, R. (eds), *Racism and Antiracism: Inequalities, Opportunities and Policies*, London, Sage/Open University Press.

Giroux, H. (1989) *Schooling for Democracy: Critical Pedagogy in the Modern Age*, London, Routledge.

Gittins, D. (1985) *The Family in Question*, Basingstoke, Macmillan.

Gittins, D. (1993) *The Family in Question*, 2nd edn, Basingstoke, Macmillan.

Glaser, B.G. and Strauss, A.L. (1965) *Awareness of Dying*, Chicago, Aldine.

Glasgow University Media Group (1976) *Bad News*, London, Routledge & Kegan Paul.

Glasgow University Media Group (1980) *More Bad News*, London, Routledge & Kegan Paul.

Glasgow University Media Group (1982) *Really Bad News*, London, Writers and Readers Cooperative.

Glass, D.V. (ed.) (1954) *Social Mobility in Modern Britain*, London, Routledge.

Glass, R. (1960) *New Comers: West Indians in London*, London, Allen & Unwin.

Gleick, J. (1987) *Chaos*, London, Cardinal.

Glendinning, C. and Millar, J. (eds) (1987) *Women and Poverty in Britain*, Hemel Hempstead, Harvester Wheatsheaf.

Glendinning, C. and Millar, J. (eds) (1992) *Women and Poverty in Britain: The 1990s*, Hemel Hempstead, Harvester Wheatsheaf.

Glock, C.Y. (1958) *Religion and the Face of America*, Berkeley, University of California Press.

Glock, C.Y. and Bellah, R.N. (eds) (1976) *The New Religious Consciousness*, Berkeley, University of California Press.

Glock, C.Y. and Stark, R. (1965) *Religion and Society in Tension*, Chicago, Rand McNally.

Glock, C.Y. and Stark, R. (1968) *American Piety: The Nature of Religious Commitment*, Berkeley, University of California Press.

Glyptis, S. (1989) *Leisure and Unemployment*, Buckingham, Open University Press.

Goffman, E. (1971) *The Presentation of Self in Everyday Life*, Harmondsworth, Penguin (orig. pub. 1959).

Goffman, E. (1991) *Asylums: Essays on the Social Situation of Mental Patients and Other Inmates*, Harmondsworth, Penguin (orig. pub. 1968).

Golding, P. and Murdock, G.(1991). 'Cultural communication and political economy', in Curran, J. and Gurevitch, M. (eds), *The Mass Media and Society*, London, Edward Arnold.

Goldthorpe, J. (1987) *Social Mobility and Class Structure in Modern Britain*, Oxford, Clarendon/Oxford University Press.

Goldthorpe, J. (1982) 'On the service class: its formation and future', in Giddens, A. and MacKenzie, G. (eds), *Social Class and the Division of Labour: Essays in Honour of Ilya Neustadt*, Cambridge, Cambridge University Press.

Goldthorpe, J., Lockwood, D., Platt, J. and Bechhofer, F. (1968) *The Affluent Worker*, Cambridge, Cambridge University Press.

Gomm, R. and McNeill, P. (1982) *A Handbook for Sociology Teachers*, Oxford, Heinemann Educational.

Goode, W.J. (1963) *World Revolution and Family Patterns*, New York, Free Press.

Gordon, D.M. (1988) 'The global economy: new edifice or crumbling foundations', *New Left Review*, no. 168.

Gordon, P. (1996) 'The racialization of statistics', in Skellington, R. (ed.), *'Race' in Britain Today*, London, Sage.

Gordon, P. and Newnham, A. (1985) *Passports to Benefits: Racism in Social Security*, London, CPAG/Runnymede Trust.

Gorz, A. (1982) *Farewell to the Working Class*, London, Pluto Press.

Goss, M.E.W. (1969) 'Influence and authority in an outpatients clinic', in Etzioni, A. (ed.), *A Sociological Reader on Complex Organizations*, 2nd edn, New York, Holt, Rinehart & Winston.

Gough, I. (1979) *The Political Economy of the Welfare State*, Basingstoke, Macmillan.

Gough, K. (1972) 'An anthropologist looks at Engels', in Glazer-Malbin, N. and Waeher, H.Y. (eds), *Woman in a Man Made World*, Chicago, Rand-McNally.

Gould, S. (1981) *The Mismeasure of Man*, Harmondsworth, Penguin.

Gould, S. (1995) 'Curveball', in Fraser, S. (ed.), *The Bell Curve Wars*, London, Basic Books.

Gouldner, A. (1954) *Patterns of Industrial Bureaucracy*, Glencoe, Free Press.

Gouldner, A. (1957) *Wildcat Strike*, London, Routledge & Kegan Paul.

Gouldner, A. (1975) *For Sociology*, Harmondsworth, Penguin.

Gouldner, A. (1979) *The Future of Intellectuals and the Rise of the New Class*, Basingstoke, Macmillan.

Graham, A. (1985a) 'Bearing the weight of unemployment', *Community Care*, 7 March.

Graham, H. (1985b) *Health and Welfare*, Walton-on-Thames, Nelson.

Graham, H. and Oakley, A. (1981) 'Competing ideologies of reproduction: medical and maternal perspectives on pregnancy', in Roberts, H. (ed.), *Women, Health and Reproduction*, London, Routledge.

Graham-Brown, S. (1991) *Education in the Developing World*, London, Longman.

Gramsci, A. (1971) *Selections from the Prison Notebooks* (edited by Q. Hoare), London, Lawrence & Wishart (orig. written 1929–35).

Gramsci, A. (1977) *Selections From Political Writings, 1910–1920* (edited by Q. Hoare), London, Lawrence & Wishart.

Gramsci, A. (1978) *Selections From Political Writings,*

1921–1926 (edited by Q. Hoare), London, Lawrence & Wishart.

Grant, W. (1989) *Pressure Groups, Politics and Democracy in Britain*, Hemel Hempstead, Philip Allan.

Gray, A.M., Whelan, A. and Norman, C. (1988) *Care in the Community: A Study of Services and Costs in Six Districts*, York, University of York Centre for Health Economics.

Green, A. (1990) *Education and State Formation: The Rise of Education Systems in England, France and the USA*, Basingstoke, Macmillan.

Green, A. (1993) 'Post-16 qualification reform', *Forum*, vol. 35, no. 1.

Green, D.G. (1988) *Everyone a Private Patient*, London, Institute for Economic Affairs.

Green, E., Hebron, S. and Woodward, D. (1990) *Women's Leisure, What Leisure?*, Basingstoke, Macmillan.

Gregory, M. (1994) 'Flight into a minefield', *The Guardian*, 30 August.

Griffin, G. (1995) 'Introduction', in Griffin, G. (ed.), *Feminist Activism in the 1990s*, London, Taylor & Francis.

Grint, K. (1991) *The Sociology of Work*, Cambridge, Polity Press.

Groves, D. (1992) 'Occupational pension provision and women's poverty in old age', in Glendinning, C. and Millar, J. (eds) *Women and Poverty in Britain: The 1990s*, Hemel Hempstead, Harvester Wheatsheaf.

Habermas, J. (1972) *Knowledge and Human Interests*, London, Heinemann.

Habermas, J. (1976) *Legitimation Crisis*, London, Heinemann.

Habermas, J. (1981a) 'New social movements', *Telos*, no. 49.

Habermas, J. (1981b) *The Theory of Communicative Action*, London, Heinemann.

Habermas, J. (1988) *Legitimation Crisis*, new edn, Cambridge, Polity Press.

Habermas, J. (1989) *The New Conservatism*, Cambridge, Polity Press.

Hakim, C. (1987) *Research Design*, London, George Allen & Unwin.

Hakim, C. (1991) 'Grateful slaves and self-made women: fact and fantasy in women's work orientations', *European Sociological Review*, vol. 7.

Hakim, C. (1995) 'Five feminist myths about women's employment', *British Journal of Sociology*, vol. 46, no. 3.

Hakim, C. (1996a) 'The sexual division of labour and women's heterogeneity', *British Journal of Sociology*, vol. 47, no. 1.

Hakim, C. (1996b) *Key Issues in Women's Work*, London, Athlone Press.

Hall, C. (1982) 'The butcher, the baker, the candlestick maker: the shop and the family in the industrial revolution' and 'The town turned upside down? The working class family in textiles 1790–1850', in Whitelegg, E. *et al.* (eds), *The Changing Experience of Women*, Buckingham, Martin Robertson/Open University Press.

Hall, S. (1980) 'Race, articulation and societies structured in dominance', in *Sociological Theories: Race and Colonialism*, Paris, UNESCO.

Hall, S. (1984) 'The Great Moving Right Show', *New Internationalist*, March.

Hall, S. (1985) 'Religious ideologies and social movements in Jamaica', in Bocock, R. and Thompson, K. (eds), *Religion and Ideology*, Manchester, Manchester University Press.

Hall, S. (1991a) 'And not a shot fired', *Marxism Today*, December.

Hall, S. (1991b) 'The local and the global: globalisation and ethnicity', in King, A D. (ed.) *Culture, Globalisation and the World System: Contemporary Conditions for the Representation of Identity*, Basingstoke, Macmillan.

Hall, S. (1992a) 'New ethnicities', in Donald, J. and Rattansi, A. (eds), *Race Culture and Difference*, London, Sage.

Hall, S. (1992b) 'The question of cultural identity', in Hall, S. *et al.* (ed.), *Modernity and its Future*, Cambridge, Polity Press.

Hall, S. (1995) *Fantasy, Identity and Politics*, in Carter, E., Donald, J. and Squires, J. (eds), *Cultural Remix: Theories of Politics and the Popular*, London, Lawrence & Wishart.

Hall, S., Critcher, C., Jefferson, T., Clarke, J. and Roberts, B. (1978) *Policing the Crisis: Mugging, the State and Law and Order*, Basingstoke, Macmillan.

Hall, S. and du Gay, P. (eds) (1996) *Questions of Cultural Identity*, London, Sage.

Hall, S. and Jacques, M. (eds) (1983) *The Politics of Thatcherism*, London, Lawrence & Wishart.

Hall, S. and Jacques, M. (eds) (1989) *New Times*, London, Lawrence & Wishart.

Hall, S. and Jefferson, T. (eds) (1976) *Resistance Through Rituals*, London, Hutchinson.

Halliday, A. (1995) 'Development trusts', in Atkinson, D. (eds) *Cities of Pride*, London, Cassell.

Hallsworth, S. (1994) 'Understanding new social movements', *Sociology Review*. vol. 4, no. 1.

Halsey, A.H., Heath, A. and Ridge, J.M. (1980) *Origins and Destinations*, Oxford, Clarendon Press.

Ham, C. (1992) *Health Policy in Britain*, 3rd edn, Basingstoke, Macmillan.

Hamilton, M. (1990) 'Inequality and stratification', *Social Studies Review*, vol. 5, no. 5.

Hamilton, M. and Hirszowicz, M. (1993) *Class and Inequality*, Hemel Hempstead, Harvester Wheatsheaf.

Hamilton, P (1992) 'The Enlightenment and the birth of social science', in Hall, S. and Gieben, B. (eds), *Formations of Modernity*, Cambridge, Polity Press/Open University.

Hammond, P.E. (ed.) (1985) *The Sacred in a Secular Age: Toward Revision in the Scientific Study of Religion*, London, University of California Press.

Hancock, G. (1991) *Lords of Poverty*, London, Mandarin.

Hansen, A. (1993) (ed.) *The Mass Media and Environmental Issues*, Leicester, Leicester University Press.

Haralambos, M. (1974) *Right On: From Blues to Soul in Black America*, Ormskirk, Causeway Press.

Haralambos, M. and Holborn, M. (1995) *Sociology: Themes and Perspectives*, 4th edn, London, Collins Educational.

Harbury, C. and Hitchens, D. (1979) *Inheritance and Wealth Inequality in Britain*, London, George Allen & Unwin.

Hargreaves, A. (1989) 'Decomprehensivisation', in Hargreaves, A. and Reynolds, D. (eds), *Education Policies: Controversies and Critiques*, Lewes, Falmer Press.

Hargreaves, D.H. (1967) *Social Relations in a Secondary School*, London, Routledge & Kegan Paul.

Harman, C. (1996) 'Tories steal benefits from low paid', *Socialist Worker*, 23 November.

Harris, D. (1992) *From Class Struggle to the Politics of Pleasure: The Effects of Gramscianism on Cultural Studies*, London, Routledge.

Harris, G. (1989) *The Sociology of Development*, London, Longman.

Harris, L. (1993) 'Postmodernism and Utopia', in Cross, M. and Keith, M. (eds), *Racism, the City and State.*, London, Routledge.

Harris, N. (1983) *Of Bread and Guns*, Harmondsworth, Penguin.

Harris, N. (1986) 'Theories of unequal exchange', *International Socialism*, Autumn.

Harris, N. (1987) *The End of the Third World*, Harmondsworth, Penguin.

Harris, S. *et al.* (1993) 'School work, home-work and gender', *Gender and Education*, vol. 5, no. 1.

Harris, S. (1994) *Sociology Revise Guide*, London, Longman.

Harrison, P. (1985) *Inside the Inner City: Life Under the Cutting Edge*, Harmondsworth, Penguin.

Harrison, P. (1993) *Inside the Third World*, 3rd edn, Harmondsworth, Penguin.

Harriss, K. (1989) 'New alliances: socialist-feminism in the eighties', *Feminist Review*, no. 31.

Hart, A. (1991) *Understanding the Media: A Practical Guide*, London, Routledge.

Hart, N. (1976) *When Marriage Ends: A Study in Status Passage*, London, Tavistock.

Hart, N. (1985) *The Sociology of Health and Medicine*, Ormskirk, Causeway Press.

Hartley, R.E. (1966) 'A developmental view of female sex-role identification', in Biddle, B.J. and. Thomas, E.J. (eds), *Role Theory*, London, John Wiley.

Hartmann, H. (1981) 'The unhappy marriage of Marxism and feminism: towards a more progressive union', in Sargent, L. (ed.), *The Unhappy Marriage of Marxism and Feminism: A Debate on Class and Patriarchy*, London, Pluto Press.

Hartmann, H. (1982) 'Capitalism, patriarchy and job segregation by sex', in Giddens, A. and Held, D. (eds), *Classes, Power and Conflict*, Basingstoke, Macmillan.

Hartmann, P. and Husband, C. (1974) *Racism and the Mass Media*, London, Davis-Poynter.

Hartmann, P. and Husband, C. (1976) 'The mass media and racial conflict', in Cohen, S. and Young, J. (eds), *The Manufacture of News: Deviance, Social Problems and the Mass Media*, London, Constable.

Hartsock, N. (1990) 'Foucault on power: a theory for women?', in Nicholson, L.J. (ed.), *Feminism/Postmodernism*, London, Routledge.

Harvey, D. (1989) *The Condition of Postmodernity*, Oxford, Blackwell.

Harvey, L. (1990) *Critical Social Research*, London, Unwin Hyman.

Harvey, L. and MacDonald, M. (1993) *Doing Sociology: A Practical Introduction*, Basingstoke, Macmillan.

Hay, D., Linebaugh, P., Rule, J.G., Thompson, E.P. and Winslow, C. (1988) *Albion's Fatal Tree: Crime and Society in Eighteenth Century England*, Harmondsworth, Penguin.

Hayek, F. (1944) *The Road to Serfdom*, London, Routledge.

Hayek, F. (1960) *The Constitution of Liberty*, London, Routledge.

Hayter, T. (1971) *Aid As Imperialism*, Harmondsworth, Penguin.

Hayter, T. (1985) 'Introduction', in Hayter, T and Watson, C. (1985) *Aid: Rhetoric and Reality*, London, Verso.

Hayter, T and Watson, C. (1985) *Aid: Rhetoric and Reality*, London, Verso.

Hazareesingh, S. (1986) 'Racism and cultural identity: an Indian perspective', *Dragons' Teeth*, no. 24.

Hearn, G. (1987) *The Gender of Oppression: Men, Masculinity and the Critique of Marxism*, London, Pluto Press.

Heath, A. (1981) *Social Mobility*, Glasgow, Fontana.

Heath, A. (1992) 'The attitudes of the underclass', in Smith, D.J. (ed.), *Understanding the Underclass*, London, Policy Studies Institute.

Heath, A., Curtice, J., Jowell, R., Evans, G., Field, J. and

Witherspoon, S. (1991) *Understanding Political Change: The British Voter 1964–1987*, Oxford, Pergamon.

Heath, A., Jowell, R. and Curtice, J. (1985) *How Britain Votes*, Oxford, Pergamon.

Heath, A., Jowell, R. and Curtice, J. (with B. Taylor) (eds) (1994) *Labour's Last Chance?*, Aldershot, Dartmouth Publishing.

Hebdidge, D. (1979) *Subculture: The Meaning of Style*, London, Metheun.

Hebdidge, D. (1988) *Hiding in the Light: On Images and Things*, London, Comedia.

Hebdidge, D. (1996) 'The impossible object: towards a sociology of the sublime', in Curran, J. *et al.* (eds), *Cultural Studies and Communications*, London, Arnold.

Heidensohn, F. (1989) *Crime and Society*, Basingstoke, Macmillan.

Heidensohn, F. (1996) *Women and Crime*, 2nd edn, Basingstoke, Macmillan.

Heisler, B. (1991) 'A comparative perspective on the underclass', *Theory and Society*, vol. 20, 455–83.

Held, D. (1987) *Models of Democracy*, Cambridge, Polity Press.

Held, D. (1991) 'Democracy, the nation state and the global system', in Held, D. (ed.) *Political Theory Today*, Cambridge, Polity Press.

Held, D. (1993) 'Democracy: from city-states to a cosmopolitan order?', in Held, D. (ed.), *Prospects for Democracy: North, South, East, West*, Cambridge, Polity Press.

Hencke, D. (1994) 'MP reveals £20m of overseas aid funds went to firms with links to ex-Ministers', *The Guardian*, 12 December.

Hencke, D. and Norton-Taylor, R. (1992) 'Taxpayers meet bill for Baghdad forces', *The Guardian*, 17 November.

Herberg, W. (1956) *Protestant, Catholic, Jew*, New York, Doubleday.

Heritage, J. (1987) 'Ethnomethodology', in Giddens, A. and Turner, J. (eds), *Social Theory Today*, Cambridge, Polity Press.

Herrnstein, R. and Murray, C. (1994) *The Bell Curve: Intelligence and Class Structure in American Life*, New York, Free Press.

Herskovits, M.J. (1958) *The Myth of the Negro Past*, Boston, Beacon Press.

Hester, S. and Eglin, P. (1996) *A Sociology of Crime*, London, Routledge.

Hewitt, T., Johnson, H. and Wield, D. (eds) (1992) *Industrialization and Development*, Oxford, Oxford University Press.

Hey, V. (1994) *Elderly People and Community Care*, London, SSRU, Institute of Education, University of London.

Hey, V. (1997) *The Company She Keeps: An Ethnography of Girls' Friendships*, Buckingham, Open University Press.

Hick, D. (1982) 'Colonialism and education: Vietnam' in Watson, K. (ed.), *Education in the Third World*, Beckenham, Croom Helm.

Hicks, C. (1988) *Who Cares: Looking After People At Home*, London, Virago.

Hicks, N. and Streeten, P. (1981) 'Indicators of development: the search for a basic needs yardstick', in Streeten, P. and Jolly, R. (eds) *Recent Issues in World Development*, Oxford, Pergamon.

Higgins, A. (1997) 'The boom that backfired', *The Guardian*, 16 January.

Higginson Committee (1988) *Advancing A levels*, London, HMSO.

Hill, S. (1976) *The Dockers*, London, Heinemann.

Hills, J. (ed.) (1990) *The State of Welfare*, Oxford, Oxford University Press.

Hills, J. (1995) *Inquiry into Income and Wealth*, York, Joseph Rowntree Foundation.

Himmelweit, H.T., Humphreys, P., and Jaeger, M. (1985) *How Voters Decide*, Buckingham, Open University Press.

Himmelweit, S. and Costello, N. (1995) 'Work and the economy', in *Society and Social Science: Foundation Course D103*, Buckingham, Open University Press.

Hirschfield, M. (1938) *Racism*, London, Gollancz.

Hirst, P. (1990) *Representative Democracy and its Limits*, Cambridge, Polity Press.

Hirst, P. (1993a) *The Pluralist Theory of the State*, London, Routledge.

Hirst, P. (1993b) 'Globalization is fashionable but is it a myth?', *The Guardian*, 22 March.

Hirst, P. and Thompson, G. (1995) 'Globalisation and the future of the nation state', *Economy and Society*, vol. 24, no. 3.

Hirst, P. and Thompson, G. (1996) *Globalisation in Question*, Cambridge, Polity Press.

Hobsbawn, E.J. (1990) *Nations and Nationalism Since 1870: Programme, Myth and Reality*, Cambridge, Cambridge University Press.

Hobson, D. (1989) 'Soap operas at work', in Seiter, E. *et al.* (eds), *Remote Control: Television, Audiences and Cultural Power*, London, Routledge.

Hoggart, R. (1958) *The Uses of Literacy*, Harmondsworth, Penguin.

Hoggart, R. (1996) *The Way We Live Now*, London, Pimlico.

Hoggart, R. *et al.* (1995) *Rural Europe: Identity and Change*, London, Arnold.

Holmwood, J. (1996) *Founding Sociology? Talcott Parsons and the Idea of General Theory*, London, Longman.

Holton, R.J. and Turner, B.S. (1988) *Talcott Parsons on Economy and Society*, London, Routledge.

hooks, b. (1982) *Ain't I A Woman?: Black Women and Feminism*, Boston, South End Press.

Horne, J. (1987) *Work and Unemployment*, London, Longman.

Horowitz, I. (1968) *Professing Sociology*, Chicago, Aldine.

Horrocks, R. (1992) *Masculinity in Crisis*, Basingstoke, Macmillan.

Hoselitz, B. (ed.) (1960) *The Sociological Aspects of Economic Growth*, New York, Free Press.

Hout, M., Brooks, C. and Manza, J. (1993) 'The persistence of classes in post-industrial societies', *International Sociology*, vol. 8, no. 3.

Howe, D. (1996) 'Black, White and Yellow Journalism', *The New Statesman*, 6 September 1996.

Howe, N. (1994) *Advanced Practical Sociology*, Walton-on-Thames, Nelson.

Hughes, J.A., Martin, P.J. and Sharrock, W.W. (1995) *Understanding Classical Sociology: Marx, Weber, Durkheim*, London, Sage.

Humm, M. (ed.) (1992) *Feminisms: A Reader*, Hemel Hempstead, Harvester Wheatsheaf.

Humm, M. (1995) *The Dictionary of Feminist Theory*, Hemel Hempstead, Prentice-Hall/Harvester Wheatsheaf.

Humpheries, J. (1977) 'Class struggle and the persistence of the working class family', *Cambridge Journal of Economics*, vol. 3.

Humphreys, L. (1970) *Tearoom Trade*, London, Duckworth.

Hunt, L. (1986) *The GLC Women's Committee: A Record of Change and Achievement for Women in London*, London, Greater London Council Women's Committee.

Hunt, S. (1995) 'The "race" and health inequalities debate', *Sociology Review*, vol. 5, no. 1.

Hunter, F. (1953) *Community Power Structure: A Study of Decision Makers*, Chapel Hill, University of North Carolina Press.

Huntington, S. (1968) *Political Order in Changing Societies*, New Haven, Yale University Press.

Hustwitt, M. (1984) 'Rocker boy blues', *Screen*, vol. 25, no. 3.

Hutson, S. and Liddiard, M. (1994) *Youth Homelessness: The Construction of a Social Issue*, Basingstoke, Macmillan.

Hutton, W. (1987) 'Thinking aloud', Channel 4, 12 November.

Hutton, W. (1995) 'Is there a new underclass in British society?', Benjamin Meaker Lecture, University of Bristol, February.

Hutton, W. (1996) *The State We're In*, London, Vintage.

Hyden, G. (1983) *No Shortcut to Progress*, London, Heinemann.

Ignatieff, M. (1995) 'The ideological origins of the penitentiary', in Fitzgerald, M., McLennan, G. and Pawson, J. (eds), *Crime and Society: Readings in History and Theory*, London, Routledge.

Illich, I. (1990) *Limits to Medicine – Medical Nemesis: The Expropriation of Health*, Harmondsworth, Penguin.

Inglehart, R. (1990) 'Values, ideology and cognitive mobilization in new social movements', in Dalton, R.J. and Kuechler, M. (eds), *Challenging the Political Order*, Cambridge, Polity Press.

Ingleheart, I. (1971) 'The silent revolution in Europe: intergenerational change in post-industrial societies', *American Political Science Review*, pp. 991–1017.

Irwin, J. (1970) *The Felon*, Englewood Cliffs, NJ, Prentice-Hall.

ITEM (1995) *The Third World Guide 1994/95*, Montivideo: Instituto del Tercer Mundo (ITEM).

Itzin, C. and Phillipson, C. (1993) *Age Barriers at Work: Maximising the Potential of Mature and Older People*, Solihull, METRA.

Jackson, B. (1968) *Working Class Community: Some General Notions Raised by a Series of Studies in Northern England*, Harmondsworth, Penguin.

Jackson, B. (1994) *Poverty and the Planet: A Question of Survival*, Harmondsworth, Penguin.

Jackson, P. (1992) 'The dark side of LA', *Politics Review*, vol. 2, no. 1.

Jacobs, B. (1988) *Racism in Britain.*, Cambridge, Cambridge University Press.

Jahoda, M., Lazersfeld, P. and Zeisel, H. (1972) *Marienthal: The Sociography of an Unemployed Community*, London, Tavistock.

James, C.L.R. (1963) *The Black Jacobins: Toussaint L'Overture and the San Domingo Revolution*, New York, Vintage.

James, S. and Busia, A. (eds) (1993) *Theorising Black Feminisms: The Visionary Pragmatism of Black Women*, London, Routledge.

James, W. (1993) 'Migration, racism and identity', in James, W. and Harris, C. (eds), *Inside Babylon: The Caribbean and the Black Diaspora*, London, Verso.

Jameson, F. (1991) *Postmodernism*, London, Verso.

Jamrozik, A., Hoey, M. and Leeds, M. (1981) *Employment Benefits: Private or Public?*, Sydney, Social Welfare Research Centre.

Janowitz, M. (1979) 'Collective racial violence: a contemporary history', in Graham, H.D. and Gurr, T.R. (eds) *Violence in America: Historical and Comparative Perspectives*, New York, Bantam.

Jardine, A. (1985) *Gynesis: Configurations of Women and Modernity*, London, Cornell University Press.

Jary, D. and Jary, J. (1991) *Collins Dictionary of Sociology*, London, HarperCollins.

Jencks, C. (1996) 'The city that never sleeps', *New Statesman and Society*, 28 June.

Jenkins, J. (1991) 'Passions of crime', *New Statesman and Society*, 17 May.

Jenkins, R. (1992) 'Theoretical perspectives', in Hewitt, T., Johnson, H. and Wield, D. (eds) *Industrilization and Development*, Oxford, Oxford University Press.

Jenkins, R. (1994a) 'Capitalist Development in the NICs', in Sklair, L. (ed.) *Capitalism and Development*, London, Routledge.

Jenkins, R. (1994b) 'Rethinking ethnicity: identity, categorization and power', *Ethnic and Racial Studies*, vol. 17, no. 2.

Jenks, C. (1993) *Culture*, London, Routledge.

Jesson, D., Gray, J. and Tranmer, M. (1992) *GCSE Performance in Nottinghamshire 1991: Pupil and School Factors*, Nottinghamshire County Council Education, Advisory and Inspection Service.

Jessop, B. (1994) 'The transition to post-Fordism and the Schumpeterian workfare state', in Burrows, R. and Loader, B. (eds), *Towards a Post-Fordist Welfare State*, London, Routledge.

Jewson, N. (1976) 'The disappearance of the sick man from medical cosmology 1770–1870', *Sociology*, vol. 10, no. 2.

Jewson, N. (1990) 'Inner city riots', *Social Studies Review*, vol. 5, no. 5.

Jewson, N. (1994) 'Family values and relationships', *Sociology Review*, vol. 3, no. 3.

Johnson, T.J. (1972) *Professions and Power*, Basingstoke, Macmillan.

Johnson, P. and Webb, S. (1990) *Counting People with Low Incomes*, London, Institute for Fiscal Studies.

Johnson, R. (1979) 'Really useful knowledge', in Clarke, J. et al. *Working Class Culture*, London, Hutchinson.

Jones, A. (1993a) 'Becoming a "girl": post-structuralist suggestions for educational research', *Gender and Education*, vol. 5, no. 2.

Jones, P. (1993b) *Studying Society: Sociological Theories and Research Practices*, London, Collins Educational.

Jones, S. (1991) 'We are all cousins under the skin', *The Independent*, 12 December.

Jordan, W.D. (1974) *The White Man's Burden*, Oxford, Oxford University Press.

Jorgensen, N. (1996) 'Coming to terms with the family?', *Sociology Review*, vol. 5, no. 3.

Jowell, R., Curtice, J., Brook, L. and Ahrendt, D. (1995) *British Social Attitudes (11th Report) 1994–95*, Aldershot, SCPR.

Joyce, P. (ed.) (1995) *Class*, Oxford, Oxford University Press.

Kamata, S. (1984) *Japan in the Passing Lane*, London, Unwin.

Kamin, L. (1974) *The Science and Politics of IQ*, New York, John Wiley.

Kaplan, E.A. (1987) *Rocking Around the Clock: Music Television, Postmodernism and Consumer Culture*, London, Methuen.

Karabel, J. and Halsey, A.H. (1977) *Power and Ideology in Education*, Oxford, Oxford University Press.

Kasinitz, P. (1995) *Metropolis: Centre and Symbol of Our Times*, Basingstoke, Macmillan.

Kasler, D. (1988) *Max Weber: An Introduction to His Life and Work*, Oxford, Polity Press.

Kearney, R. (1993) *Modern Movements in European Philosophy*, Manchester, Manchester University Press.

Keat, R. and Urry, J. (1975) *Social Theory as Science*, London, Routledge & Kegan Paul.

Keddie, N. (ed.) (1973) *Tinker, Tailor: The Myth of Cultural Deprivation*, Harmondsworth, Penguin.

Kellner, D. (1989) *Jean Buadrillard: From Marxism to Post-Modernism and Beyond*, Cambridge, Polity Press.

Kelly, E. (1988) *Surviving Sexual Violence*, Cambridge, Polity Press.

Kelly, G. (1995) 'Off-the-self sociology', *Times Higher Educational Supplement*, 24 March.

Kennedy, J. and Lavalette, M. (1996) *Solidarity on the Waterfront: The Liverpool Docks' Lock-out*, Liverpool, Liver Press.

Kerr, C., Dunlop, J., Harbison, F. and Myers, C. (1973) *Industrialism and Industrial Man*, Harmondsworth, Penguin (orig. pub. 1960).

Key Data 95 (1995) London HMSO.

Keynes, J.M. (1936) *The General Theory of Employment, Interest and Money*, Basingstoke, Macmillan.

Kidron, M. (1975) *Capitalism and Theory*, London, Pluto Press.

Kiely, R. (1995) *Sociology and Development: The Impasse and Beyond*, London, UCL Press.

Kilminster, R. (1992) 'Theory', in Haralambos, M. (ed.), *Developments in Sociology*, vol. 8, Ormskirk, Causeway Press.

Kimmel, A. (1988) *Ethics and Values in Applied Social Research*, London, Sage.

King, A.D. (1990) *Global Cities: Post-Imperialism and the Internationalization of London*, London, Routledge.

Kingdom, J. (1992) *No Such Thing as Society?* Buckingham, Open University Press.

Kirby, M. (1995) *Investigating Political Sociology*, London, Collins Educational.

Kirby, M., Madry, N. and Koubel, F. (1993) *Sociology: Developing Skills Through Structured Questions*, London, Collins Educational.

Kitching, G. (1989) *Development and Underdevelopment in Historical Perspective*, London, Routledge.

Knapp, M. (1989) 'Private and voluntary welfare', in McCarthy, M. (ed.), *The New Politics of Welfare*, Basingstoke, Macmillan.

Knott, J. (1986) *Popular Opposition to the 1834 Poor Law*, London, Croom Helm.

Knowles, C. and Mercer, S. (1992) 'Feminism and antiracism: an exploration of the political possibilities', in Donald, J. and Rattansi, A. (eds), *'Race', Culture and Difference*, London, Sage.

Kohn, M. (1995) *The Race Gallery*, Jonathan Cape.

Kruse, A.M. (1992) ' "We have learnt not just to sit back, twiddle our thumbs, and let them take over": single-sex settings and the development of a pedagogy for girls and a pedagogy for boys in Danish schools', *Gender and Education*, vol. 4, no. 1.

Kubler-Ross, E. (1970) *On Death and Dying*, London, Tavistock.

Kuhn, T. (1970) *The Structure of Scientific Revolutions*, 2nd edn, Chicago, University of Chicago Press.

Kuhn, T. (1974) 'Logic of discovery or psychology of truth?', in Schilpp, P.A.(ed.) *The Philosophy of Karl Popper*, La Salle, ILL, Open Court.

Kumar, K. (1978) *Prophecy and Progress*, Harmondsworth, Penguin.

Kumar, K. (1986) *Prophecy and Progress: The Sociology of Industrial and Post-Industrial Society*, Harmondsworth, Penguin.

Kumar, K. (1995) *From Post-Industrial to Post-Modern Society*, Oxford, Blackwell.

Kuper, A. and Kuper, J. (1989) *The Social Science Encyclopedia*, London, Routledge.

Kuzmics, H. (1988) 'The civilising process', in Keane, J. (ed.), *Civil Society and the State*, London, Verso.

Labov, W. (1973) 'The logic of nonstandard English', in Keddie, N. (ed.), *Tinker, Tailor: The Myth of Cultural Deprivation*, Harmondsworth, Penguin.

Lacan, J. (1977) *Ecrits: A Selection*, London, Tavistock.

Lacey, C. (1970) *Hightown Grammar: The School as a Social System*, Manchester, Manchester University Press.

Laclau, E. (1971) 'Feudalism and capitalism in Latin America', *New Left Review*, vol. 67.

Laing, R.D. and Esterson, A. (1964) *Sanity, Madness and the Family*, Harmondsworth, Penguin.

Laing, S. (1992) 'Images of the rural in popular culture, 1750–1990', in Short, B. (ed.) *The English Rural Community*, Cambridge, Cambridge University Press.

Lakatos, I. (1975) *Philosophical Papers*, 2 vols, Cambridge, Cambridge University Press.

Lal, B. (1988) 'The 'Chicago School' of American sociology, symbolic interactionism, and race relations theory', in Rex, J. and Mason, D. (eds), *Theories of Race and Ethnic Relations*, Cambridge, Cambridge University Press.

Lal, D. (1983) *The Poverty of 'Development Economics'*, London, IEA.

Land, H. (1991) 'The confused boundaries of social care', in Gabe, J., Calnan, M. and Bury, M. (eds), *The Sociology of the Health Service*, London, Routledge.

Land, H. (1995) 'Families and the law', in Muncie, J., Wetherell, M., Dallos, R. and Cochrane, A. (eds) (1995) *Understanding the Family*, London, Sage.

Lane, P. (1979) *British Social and Economic History*, Oxford, Oxford University Press.

Langley, P. and Corrigan, P. (1993) *Managing Sociology Coursework*, Lewes, Connect.

Lappé, F.M. (1975) *Diet for a Small Planet*, New York, Ballantine Books.

Lappé, F.M. and Collins, J. (1980) *Food First: The Myth of Scarcity*, London, Souvenir Press.

Lash, S. (1990) *The Sociology of Postmodernism*, London, Routledge.

Lash, S. and Urry, J. (1987) *The End of Organised Capitalism*, Cambridge, Polity Press.

Lash, S. and Urry, J. (1994) *Economies of Signs and Space*, London, Sage.

Laslett, P. and Wall, R. (eds) (1972) *Household and Family in Past Time*, Cambridge, Cambridge University Press.

Lather, P. (1991) *Getting Smart: Feminist Research and Pedagogy with/in the Postmodern*, London, Routledge.

Lawler, J. (1991) *Behind the Screens: Nursing, Somology and the Problem of the Body*, London, Churchill Livingstone.

Lawson. T. (1986) 'In the shadow of science', *Social Studies Review*, vol. 2, no. 2.

Lawson, T. (1993) *Sociology for A Level: A Skills-Based Approach*, London, Collins Educational.

Lawson, T. and Garrod, J. (1996) *The Complete A–Z Sociology Handbook*, London, Hodder & Stoughton.

Layard, R. and Nickell, S. (1986) *How to Beat Unemployment*, Oxford, Oxford University Press.

Layder, D. (1994) *Understanding Social Theory*, London, Sage.

Lazersfeld, P., Berelson, B. and Gaudet, H. (1944) *The People's Choice*, New York, Columbia University Press.

Lea, J. and Young, J. (1993) *What is to be Done about Law and Order? Crisis in the Nineties*, London, Pluto Press.

Lechner, F. (1990) 'Fundamentalism revisited', in Robbins, T. and Anthony, D. (eds), *In Gods We Trust*, New Brunswick, Transaction.

Leder, D. (ed.) (1992) *The Body in Medical Thought and Practice*, London, Kluwer Academic.

Lee, D. (1990) *Scheming for Youth*, Buckingham, Open University Press.

Lee, D. and Newby, H. (1983) *The Problem of Sociology*, London, Hutchinson.

Lee, D. and Turner, B. (eds) (1996) *Conflicts About Class*, Harlow, Longman.

Lees, C. and Hindle, S. (1995) 'Scandal of football's child slavery', *Sunday Times*, 14 May.

Lees, S. (1986) *Losing Out: Sexuality and Adolescent Girls*, London, Hutchinson.

Le Grand, J. (1982) *The Strategy of Equality*, London, Allen & Unwin.

Le Grand, J. (1990) 'The state of welfare', in Hills, J. (ed.), *The State of Welfare: The Welfare State in Britian Since 1974*, Oxford, Oxford University Press.

Le Grand, J. and Winter, D (1987) *The Middle Classes and the Welfare State*, London, LSE.

Le Grand, J., Winter, D. and Woolley, F. (1990) 'The National Health Service: safe in whose hands?', in Hills, J. (ed.), *The State of Welfare: The Welfare State in Britain Since 1974*, Oxford, Oxford University Press.

Lemert, E.M. (1989a) 'Primary and Secondary Deviation' in Kelly, D.H. (ed.) (1989) *Deviant Behaviour: A Text-Reader in the Sociology of Deviance*, 3rd edn, New York, St Martin's.

Lemert, E.M. (1989b) 'Paranoia and the dynamics of exclusion', in Kelley, D.H. (ed.), *Deviant Behaviour: A Text-Reader in the Sociology of Deviance*, 3rd edn, New York, St Martin's.

Leonard, D. and Hood-Williams, J. (eds) (1988) *Families*, Walton-on-Thames, Nelson.

Leonard, E. (1982) *Women, Crime and Society*, New York, Longman.

Leonard, M. (1995) 'Masculinity, femininity and crime', *Sociology Review*, vol. 5, no. 1.

Lévi-Strauss, C. (1963) *Structural Anthropology*, New York, Basic Books.

Lévi-Strauss, C. (1989) *The Savage Mind*, London, Weidenfeld & Nicholson (orig. pub. 1962).

Levitas, R. (1996) 'The concept of social exclusion and the new Durkheimian hegemony', *Critical Social Policy*, vol. 46, February.

Lewis, J. (1991) *Women, Family, Work and the State Since 1945*, Oxford, Blackwell.

Lewis, J. and Piachard, D. (1992) 'Women and poverty in the twentieth century', in Glendinning, C. and Millar, J. (eds), *Women and Poverty in Britain: The 1990s*, Hemel Hempstead, Harvester Wheatsheaf.

Lewis, O. (1950) *Five Families*, New York, Basic Books.

Lewis, O. (1951) *Life in a Mexican Village*, Illinois, Illinois University Press.

Lewis, O. (1961) *The Children of Sanchez*, New York, Random House.

Lewis, O. (1968) *La Vida*, Harmondsworth, Penguin.

Lewis, R. (1988) *Anti-Racism: A Mania Exposed*, London, Quartet Books.

Leys, C. (1996) *The Rise and Fall of Development Theory*, London, James Currey.

Liddington, J. and Norris, J. (1978) *One Hand Tied Behind Us*, London, Virago.

Liebow, E. (1967) *Tally's Corner*, Boston, Little Brown.

Lipietz, A. (1987) *Mirages and Miracles: The Crisis of Global Fordism*, London, Verso.

Lister, R. (1990) *The Exclusive Society: Citizenship and the Poor*, London, Child Poverty Action Group.

Lister, R. (1991) 'Concepts of poverty', *Social Studies Review*, vol. 6, no. 5.

Little, I. (1981) 'The experience and causes of rapid labour-intensive development in Korea, Taiwan province, Hong Kong and Singapore, and the possibilities of emulation', in Lee, E. (ed.) *Export-Led Industrialisation and Development*, Bangkok, ILO.

Lloyd, C. (1993) 'Universalism and difference: the crisis of anti-racism in Britain and France', in Rattansi, A. and Westwood, S. (eds), *Racism, Modernity, Identity*, Cambridge, Polity Press.

Lloyds Bank (1995) *Economic Bulletin*, February, London.

Lockwood, D. (1964) 'Social integration and system integration', in Zollschan, G.K. and Hirsch, W. (eds), *Explorations in Social Change*, London, Routledge & Kegan Paul.

Lockwood, D. (1981) 'The weakest link in the chain?', in Simpson, S. and Simpson, I. (eds), *Research in the Sociology of Work*, Greenwich, CT, JAI Press. Reprinted in Rose, D. (ed.) (1988) *Social Stratification and Economic Change*, London, Hutchinson.

Lockwood, D. (1989) *The Black Coated Worker*, 2nd edn, Oxford, Oxford University Press (orig. pub. 1958).

Lockwood, D. (1992) *Solidarity and Schism*, Oxford, Clarendon Press.

Lombroso, C. (1876) *L'Uomo Delinquente*, Milano, Hoepli.

London Docklands Development Corporation (1994) *Attitudes to London Docklands: A Survey of Local Residents*, London, LDDC.

Loney, M., Bocock, R., Clarke, J., Cochrane, A., Graham, P. and Wilson, M. (eds) (1991) *The State or the Market*, London, Sage.

Long, N. and Van den Ploeg, J. (1991) 'Heterogeneity, actor and structure: towards a reconstitution of the concept of structure', unpublished paper quoted in Booth (1993).

Lonsdale, S. (1990) *Women and Disability: the Experiences of Physical Disability among Women*, Basingstoke, Macmillan.

Lovell, T. (ed.) (1990) *British Feminist Thought: A Reader*, Oxford, Blackwell.

Lovenduski, J. and Randall, V. (1993) *Contemporary Feminist Politics: Women and Power in Britain*, Oxford, Oxford University Press.

Lovibond, S. (1990) 'Feminism and postmodernism', in Boyne, R. and Rattansi, A. (eds), *Postmodernism and Society*, Basingstoke, Macmillan.

Lowe, P. and Bodiguel, M. (eds) (1990) *Rural Studies in Britain and France*, London, Belhaven Press.

Lowe, R. (1993) *The Welfare State in Britain Since 1945*, Basingstoke, Macmillan.

Lowe, S. (1986) 'Urban social movements: the city after Castells', in O'Donnell, M. (ed.) *New Introductory Reader in Sociology*, Walton-on-Thames, Nelson.

Luckmann, T. (1967) *The Invisible Religion: The Transformation of Symbols in Industrial Society*, Basingstoke, Macmillan.

Luckmann, T. (1996) 'The privatization of religion and morality', in Heelas, P., Lash, S. and Morris, P. (eds), *Detraditionalization: Critical Reflections on Authority and Identity*, Oxford, Blackwell.

Luhmann, N. (1982) *The Differentiation of Society*, New York, Columbia University Press.

Lukács, G. (1971) *History and Class Consciousness*, London, Merlin (orig. pub. 1923).

Lukes, S. (1973) *Emile Durkheim: His Life and Work*, Harmondsworth, Penguin.

Lukes, S. (1974) *Power: A Radical View*, Basingstoke, Macmillan.

Lukes, S. (1984) 'The future of British socialism?', in Pimlott, B. (ed.), *Fabian Essays in Socialist Thought*, London, Heinemann.

Lull, J. (ed.) (1987) *Popular Music and Communication*, London, Sage.

Lull, J. (1995) *Media Communication Culture*, Cambridge, Polity Press.

Lunt, I. and Evans, J. (1994) 'Dilemmas in special educational needs: some effects of local management of schools', in Riddell, S. and Brown, S. (1994) *Special Educational Needs Policy in the 1990's: Warnock and the Market Place*, London, Routledge.

Lyon, D. (1993) 'An electronic panoptican? A sociological critique of surveillance theory', *Sociological Review*, vol. 41, no. 4.

Lyon, D. (1994) *Postmodernity*, Buckingham, Open University Press.

Lyon, M. and West, B. (1995) 'London Patels', *New Community*, vol. 21, no. 3.

Lyotard, F. (1993) 'Answering the question: what is postmodernism?', in Doherty, T. (ed.), *Postmodernism: A Reader*, Hemel Hempstead, Harvester Wheatsheaf.

Lyotard, J. (1984) *The Postmodern Condition: A Report on Knowledge*, 2nd edn, Manchester, Manchester University Press (orig. French edn 1979).

Mac an Ghaill, M. (1988) *Young, Gifted and Black: Student–Teacher Relations in the Schooling of Black Youth*, Buckingham, Open University Press.

Mac an Ghaill, M. (1991) 'Black voluntary schools: the "invisible private sector"', in Walford, G. (ed.), *Private Schooling: Tradition, Change and Diversity*, London, Paul Chapman Publishing Ltd.

MacDonald, D. (1957) 'A theory of mass culture', in Rosenberg, B. and Manning White, D. (eds) *Mass Culture: The Popular Arts in America*, Basingstoke, Macmillan.

Macdonald, I., Bhavani, R., Khan, L. and John, G. (1989) *Murder in the Playground: The Burnage Report*, London, Longsight Press.

MacKinnon, M.H. (1994) 'The longevity of the thesis: a critique of the critics', in Lehman, H. and Roth, G. (eds), *Weber's Protestant Ethic: Origins, Evidence, Contexts*, Cambridge, Cambridge University Press.

McCarthy, M. (ed) (1989) *The New Politics of Welfare*, Basingstoke, Macmillan.

McClelland, D. (1961) *The Achieving Society*, New York, Van Nostrand.

McCracken, E. (1993) *Decoding Womens' Magazines: From Mademoiselle to Ms*, Basingstoke, Macmillan.

McDonnell (1990) 'The beginning and end of social class', *Social Science Teacher*, vol. 20, no. 1.*

McFarlane, G. (1986) ' "It's not as simple as that": the expression of the Catholic and Protestant boundary in Northern Irish rural communities', in Cohen, A.P. (ed) *Symbolising Boundaries: Identity and Diversity in British Cultures*, Manchester, Manchester University Press.

McGrew, A. (1992) 'A global society?', in Hall, S. *et al.* (eds), *Modernity and Its Futures*, Cambridge, Polity Press.

McGuigan, J. (1992) *Cultural Populism*, London, Routledge.

McInnes, J. (1972) *The Western Marxists*, London, Alcove Press.

McInnes, J. (1987) *Thatcherism at Work*, Buckingham, Open University Press.

McKeown, T. (1979) *The Role of Medicine: Dream, Mirage or Nemesis*, Oxford, Blackwell.

McKinley, J. (1977) 'The business of good doctoring or doctoring as good business: reflections on Friedson's view of the medical game', *International Journal of Health Services*, vol. 17, no. 3.

McLuhan, M. (1964) *Understanding Media*, London, Routledge.

McNeill, P. (1985) *Research Methods*, London, Tavistock.

McNeill, P. (1990) *Research Methods*, 2nd edn, London, Routledge.

McQuail, D. (1983) *Mass Communication Theory: An Introduction*, London, Sage.

McQuail, D. and Windahl, S. (1993) *Communication Models*, 2nd edn, New York, Longman.

McRae, S. (1993) *Cohabiting Mothers*, London, Policy Studies Institute.

McRobbie, A. (1978) 'Working class girls and the culture of femininity', in *Women Take Issue: Aspects of Women's Subordination*, Birmingham, Womens Study Group/Centre for Contemporary Cultural Studies.

McRobbie, A. (1983) 'Teenage girls, *Jackie* and the ideology of adolescent femininity', in Waites, B., Bennett, T and Martin, G. (eds), *Popular Culture: Past and Present*, London, Croom Helm.

McRobbie, A. (1991a) 'Settling accounts with youth subcultures', in McRobbie, A. *Feminism and Youth Cultures*, Basingstoke, Macmillan.

McRobbie, A. (1991b) *Feminism and Youth Culture*, Basingstoke, Macmillan.

McRobbie, A. (1994) *Postmodernism and Popular Culture*, London, Routledge.

Mack, S. and Lansley, J. (1985) *Poor Britain*, London, George Allen & Unwin.

Mack, S. and Lansley, J. (1992) *Breadline Britain*, London, LWT.

Madry, N. and Kirby, M. (1996) *Investigating Work, Unemployment and Leisure*, London, Collins Educational.

Mahmood, S. (1996) 'Cultural studies and ethnic absolutism: comments on Stuart Hall's "Culture, Community, Nation"', *Cultural Studies*, vol. 10, no. 1.

Mair, A. (1994) *Honda's Local Global Corporation*, Basingstoke, Macmillan.

Malinowski, B. (1954) *Magic, Science and Religion and Other Essays*, New York, Anchor Books.

Malthus, T.H. (1798) *Essay on the Principle of Population*, Harmondsworth, Penguin (1986 edn).

Mama, A. (1989) 'Violence against black women: gender, race and state responses', *Feminist Review*, no. 32.

Mama, A. (1992) 'Black women and the British state: race, class and gender analysis for the 1990s', in Braham, P., Rattansi, A. and Skellington, R. (eds), *Racism and Antiracism: Inequalities, Opportunities and Policies*, London, Sage/Open University Press.

Mann, K. (1995) 'Work, dependency and the underclass', in Haralambos, M. (ed.) *Developments in Sociology*, vol. 11, Ormskirk, Causeway.

Mann, M. (1973) *Consciousness and Action Among the Western Working Class*, Basingstoke, Macmillan.

Mann, M. (1986) *The Sources of Social Power*, vol. 1, Cambridge, Cambridge University Press.

Mann, M. (1988) *States, Wars and Capitalism*, Oxford, Blackwell.

Mann, M. (1993) *The Sources of Social Power*, vol. 2, Cambridge, Cambridge University Press.

Mann, N. (1995) 'Britain "second among equals"', *New Statesman and Society*, 10 February.

Mannheim, K. (1960) *Ideology and Utopia: An Introduction to the Sociology of Knowledge*, London, Routledge.

Manning, P. (1993) 'Consumption, production and popular culture', *Sociology Review*, vol. 2, no. 3.

Manning White, D. (1957) 'Mass culture in America: another point of view', in Rosenberg, B. and Manning White, D. (eds), *Mass Culture: The Popular Arts in America*, Basingstoke, Macmillan.

Mansfield, P. and Collard, J. (1988) *The Beginning of the Rest of Your Life*, Basingstoke, Macmillan.

March, J.G. and Simon, H.A. (1958) *Organizations*, New York, Wiley.

Marcuse, H. (1955) *Reason and Revolution*, new edn, London, Routledge & Kegan Paul (orig. pub. 1941).

Marcuse, H. (1964) *One-Dimensional Man*, London, Routledge & Kegan Paul.

Mares, P., Larbie, J. and Baxter, C. (1987) *Training in Multi-Racial Health Care*, Cambridge, National Extension College.

Marks, J. (1991) *An Appraisal of the Assisted Places Scheme*, London, Independent Schools Information Service.

Markham, F. (ed.) (1952) *Henri Comte de Saint-Simon: Selected Writings*, Oxford, Blackwell.

Marquand, D. (1996) 'Community and the Left', in Radice, G. (ed) *What Needs to Change: New Visions for Britain*, London, HarperCollins.

Marsh, D. (1983) 'Introduction – Interest groups in Britain: their access and power', in Marsh, D. (ed), *Pressure Politics: Interest Groups in Britain*, London, Junction Books.

Marsh, I., Keating, M., Eyre, A., Campbell, R. and McKenzie, J. (1996) *Making Sense of Society: An Introduction to Sociology*, Harlow, Longman.

Marshall, G. (1987) 'What is happening to the working class?' *Social Studies Review*, vol. 2, no. 3.

Marshall, G. (ed.) (1994) *Concise Oxford Dictionary of Sociology*, Oxford, Oxford University Press.

Marshall, G., Newby, H., Rose, D. and Vogler, C. (1988) *Social Class in Modern Britain*, London, Hutchinson.

Marshall, G. and Swift, A. (1993) 'Social class and social justice', *British Journal of Sociology*, June.

Marshall, T.H. (1963) 'Citizenship and social class', in Marshall, T.H. (ed), *Sociology at the Crossroads*, London, Heinemann.

Marshall, T.H. (1977) *Class, Citizenship and Social Development*, Chicago, University of Chicago Press.

Marsland, D. (1992) 'The roots and consequences of collectivist paternalism', *Social Policy and Administration*, vol. 26, no. 2.

Marsland, D. (1996) *Welfare or Welfare State?*, Basingstoke, Macmillan.

Martin, D. (1978) *A General Theory of Secularization*, Oxford, Blackwell.

Martin, D. (1991) 'The secularization issue: prospect and retrospect', *British Journal of Sociology*, vol. 42, no. 3.

Martin, E. (1989) *The Woman in the Body: A Cultural Analysis of Reproduction*, Buckingham, Open University Press.

Martin, J. and Roberts, C. (1984) *Women and Employment: A Lifetime Perspective*, London, HMSO.

Marx, K. (1954) *Capital*, vol. 1, London, Lawrence & Wishart (orig. pub. 1867).

Marx, K. (1956) *Capital*, vol. 2, London, Lawrence & Wishart (orig. pub. 1885).

Marx, K. (1959) *Capital*, vol. 3, London, Lawrence & Wishart (orig. pub. 1894).

Marx, K. (1968) 'The Eighteenth Brumaire of Louis Bonaparte', in Marx, K. and Engels, F., *Selected Works*, Moscow, Progress Publishers (orig. pub. 1852).

Marx, K. (1969) 'The Eighteenth Brumaire of Louis Bonaparte', in Feuer, L. (ed.), *Marx and Engels: Selected Writings*, London, Collins Fontana (orig. pub. 1852).

Marx, K. (1973) *Grundrisse*, Harmondsworth, Penguin (orig. pub. 1939).

Marx, K. (1984a) 'Excerpts from "The Eighteenth Brumaire of Louis Bonaparte"', in Feuer, L.S. (ed.), *Marx and Engels: Basic Writings on Politics and Philosophy*, Aylesbury, Fontana (orig. pub. 1852).

Marx, K. (1984b) 'Excerpt from "Toward the critique of Hegel's philosophy of right"', in Feuer, L.S. (ed) *Marx and Engels: Basic Writings on Politics and Philosophy*, Aylesbury, Fontana (orig. pub. 1844).

Marx, K. and Engels, F. (1977) *The German Ideology*, (edited by C.J. Arthur), London, Lawrence & Wishart (orig. written 1845).

Marx, K. and Engels, F. (1967) *The Communist Manifesto*, Harmondsworth, Penguin (orig. pub. 1848).

Marx, K. and Engels, F. (1968) 'Manifesto of the Communist Party', in Marx, K. and Engels, F., *Selected Works*, Moscow, Progress Publishers (orig. pub. 1848).

Mason, D. (1995) *Race and Ethnicity in Modern Britain*, Oxford, Oxford University Press.

Matthews, R. (1993) 'Squaring up to crime', *Sociology Review*, vol. 2, no. 3.

Matza, D. (1969) *Becoming Deviant*, New Jersey, Prentice Hall.

Matza, D. (1990) *Delinquency and Drift*, New Brunswick, Transaction.

May, T. (1993) *Social Research: Issues, Methods and Processes*, Buckingham, Open University Press.

May, T. (1996) *Situating Social Theory*, Buckingham: Open University Press

Mayes, P. (1986) *Gender*, London, Longman.

Maynard, M. (1990) 'The reshaping of sociology? Trends in the study of gender', *Sociology*, vol. 24, no. 2.

Mayo, E. (1933) *The Human Problems of an Industrial Civilisation*, New York, Macmillan.

Mead, G.H. (1934) *Mind, Self and Society*, Chicago, University of Chicago Press.

Meadows, D., Randers, J. and Behrens, W.W. (1972) *The Limits to Growth*, New York, Universe.

Mears, R. (1994) 'Why have sociologists neglected nationalism?', *Social Science Teacher*, vol. 23, no. 2.*

Mennell, S. (1989) *Norbert Elias: Civilisation and the Human Self-Image*, Oxford, Blackwell.

Meredith, P. (1993) 'Patient participation in decision-making and consent to treatment: the case of general surgery', *Sociology of Health and Illness*, vol. 15, no. 3.

Merton, R.K. (1952) 'Bureaucratic structure and personality', in Merton, R.K., *Reader In Bureaucracy*, New York, Free Press.

Merton, R.K. (1968) *Social Theory and Social Structure*, New York, Free Press.

Merton, R.K. (1989) 'Social structure and anomie', in Kelley, D.H. (ed), *Deviant Behaviour: A Text-Reader in the Sociology of Deviance*, 3rd edn, New York, St Martin's (orig. pub. 1938).

Michel, J.H. (1996) 'Partnerships in development', *OECD Observer*, February/March.

Micklewright, J. (1985) 'Fiction versus fact: unemployment benefits in Britain', *National Westminster Bank Quarterly Review*, May.

Middleton, S., Ashworth, K. and Walker, R. (1994) *Family Fortunes: Pressures on Parents and Children in the 1990s*, London, Child Poverty Action Group.

Midwinter, E. (1994) *The Development of Social Welfare in Britain*, Buckingham, Open University Press.

Mies, M. (1986) *Patriarchy and Accumulation on a World Scale*, London, Zed.

Miles, I. and Irvine, J. (1979) 'The critique of official statistics', in Irvine, J., Miles, I. and Evans, P. (eds), *Demystifying Social Statistics*, London, Pluto Press.

Miles, R. (1982) *Racism and Migrant Labour*, London, Routledge.

Miles, R. (1984) 'Marxism versus the "sociology of race relations?"', *Ethnic and Racial Studies*, vol. 7, no. 2.

Miles, R. (1988) 'Racism, Marxism and British politics', *Economy and Society*, vol. 17, no. 3.

Miles, R. (1990) 'Racism, ideology and disadvantage', *Social Studies Review*, vol. 5, no. 4.

Miles, R. (1993) *Racism After 'Race Relations'*, London, Routledge.

Miliband, R. (1973) *The State in Capitalist Society: Analysis of the Western System of Power*, London, Quartet Books.

Miller, D. and Williams, K. (1993) 'Negotiating HIV/AIDS information: agendas, media strategies and the news', in Eldridge, J. (ed), *Getting the Message: News, Truth and Power*, London, Glasgow University Media Group/Routledge.

Miller, E. (1992) *Men at Risk*, Jamaica, University of the West Indies Press.

Millett, K. (1970) *Sexual Politics*, New York, Doubleday.

Mills, C.W. (1956) *The Power Elite*, Oxford, Oxford University Press.

Mills, C.W. (1958) *The Sociological Imagination*, New York, Oxford University Press.

Milne, S. (1997) 'Ford in last minute talks to settle race row', *The Guardian*, 27 January.

Mirza, H.S. (1992) *Young, Female and Black*, London, Routledge.

Mirza, H.S. (ed.) (1997) *Black British Feminism*, London, Routledge.

Mishra, R. (1984) *The Welfare State in Crisis*, Brighton, Wheatsheaf.

Modood, T. (1988) '"Black" racial equality and Asian identity', *New Community*, vol. 14, no. 3.

Modood, T. (1989) 'Religious anger and minority rights', *Political Quarterly*, July.

Modood, T. (1992) *Not Easy Being British*, Stoke on Trent, Trentham Books.

Moir, A. and Jessel, D. (1995) 'A cure for murder?', *The Guardian*, 30 September.

Mommsen, W.J. and Osterhammel, J. (eds) (1987) *Max Weber and his Contemporaries*, London, Unwin Hyman.

Momsen, J.H. (1991) *Women and Development in the Third World*, London, Routledge.

Mooney, S. (1996) *From Nation-State to Cyberstate: Information Technology and the Triumph of the Commercial Ethic*, London, Libertarian Alliance.

Moore, H. (1994) 'Divided we stand: sex, gender and sexual difference', *Feminist Review*, no. 47.

Moore, M. (1995) 'India's consumerism fuels sharp rise in dowry deaths', *The Guardian*, 13 April.

Moore, S. (1988) 'Here's looking at you kid', in Gamman, L. and Marshment, M. (eds), *The Female Gaze: Women as Viewers of Popular Culture*, London, Women's Press.

Morgan, D.H.J. (1975) *Social Theory and the Family*, London, Routledge & Kegan Paul.

Morgan, D.H.J. (1996) *Family Connections: An Introduction to Family Studies*, Cambridge, Polity Press.

Morgan, M., Calnan, M. and Manning, N. (1985) *Sociological Approaches to Health and Medicine*, London, Routledge.

Morley, D. (1980) *The Nationwide Audience: Structure and Decoding*, London, British Film Institute.

Morley, D. (1992) *Television, Audiences and Cultural Studies*, London, Routledge.

Morris, D. (1968) *The Naked Ape*, London, Corgi.

Morris, L. and Irwin, S. (1992) 'Employment histories and the concept of the underclass', *Sociology*, vol. 26, no. 3.

Morris, J. and Winn, M. (1990) *Housing and Social Inequality*, London, Hilary Shipman Ltd.

Morris, L. (1987) 'Constraints on gender: the family wage, social security and the labour market', *Work, Unemployment and Society*, vol. 1, no. 1.

Morris, L. (1993) 'Household finance management and the labour market: a case study in Hartlepool', *Sociology Review*, vol. 4. no. 3.

Morris, L. (1994) *Dangerous Classes: The Underclass and Social Citizenship*, London, Routledge.

Morris, M.D. (1979) *Measuring the Conditions of the World's Poor: The Physical Quality of Life Index*, New York, Pergamon.

Mort, F. (1996) *Cultures of Consumption: Masculinities and Social Space in Late Twentieth Century Britain*, London, Routledge.

Mortimore, P. (1981) 'Achievement in schools', *Contact*, November (published by Inner London Education Authority).

Mount, F. (1982) *The Subversive Family*, London, Jonathan Cape.

Mouzelis, N. (1986) *Politics on the Semi-Periphery: Early Parliamentarianism and Late Industrialization in the Balkans and Latin America*, Basingstoke, Macmillan.

Mouzelis, N. (1993) 'The poverty of sociological theory', *Sociology*, vol. 27, no. 4.

Mouzelis, N. (1995) *Sociological Theory: Whatever Went Wrong?* London, Routledge.

Mullard, C. (1982) 'Multiracial education in Britain: from assimilation to cultural pluralism', in Tierney, J. (ed.), *Race, Migration and Schooling*, London, Holt, Rinehart & Winston.

Mulvey, L. (1975) 'Visual pleasure and narrative cinema', *Screen*, vol. 16, no. 3.

Münch, R. (1987) 'Parsonian theory today: in search of a new synthesis', in Giddens, A. and Turner, J. (eds), *Modern Social Theory*, Cambridge, Polity Press.

Munchau, W. (1995) '"Sweatshop" Britain works the longest', *The Times*, 24 January.

Muncie, J. and Sapsford, R. (1995) 'Issues in the study of the family', in Muncie, J., Wetherell, M., Dallos, R. and Cochrane, A. (eds) (1995) *Understanding the Family*, London, Sage.

Muncie, J., Wetherell, M., Dallos, R. and Cochrane, A. (eds) (1995) *Understanding the Family*, London, Sage.

Murdock, G.P. (1949) *Social Structure*, New York, Macmillan.

Murdock, G.P. (1965) *Social Structure*, New York, Free Press (orig. pub. 1949).

Murray, C. (1984) *Losing Ground*, New York, Basic Books.

Murray, C. (1989) 'Underclass', *Sunday Times Magazine*, 26 November.

Murray, C. (1990) *The Emerging British Underclass*, London, Institute for Economic Affairs.

Murray, C. (1994) *Underclass: The Crisis Deepens*, London, Institute for Economic Affairs.

Myers, K. (1986) *Understains: The Sense and Seduction of Advertising*, London, Comedia.

Myrdal, G. (1969) *An American Dilemma: The Negro Problem and Modern Democracy*, New York, Harper & Row.

Narasimham, S. (1993) 'The unwanted sex', *New Internationalist*, February.

National Union of Teachers (1988) *Women: What Does the NUT Offer You?*, London, NUT.

Navarro, V. (1976) *Medicine Under Capitalism*, London, Croom Helm.

Navarro, V. (ed) (1982) *Imperialism, Health and Medicine*, London, Pluto Press.

Negrine, R. (1994) *Politics and the Mass Media in Britain*, 2nd edn, London, Routledge.

Nelson, D., Pillai, M.G.G. and Durham, M. (1994) 'How Thatcher aid deal's golden fruit turned sour', *The Observer*, 27 February.

Nettleton, S. (1995) *The Sociology of Health and Illness*, Cambridge, Polity Press.

Nettleton, S. (1996) 'Women and the new paradigm of health and medicine', *Critical Social Policy*, vol. 24, London, Sage.

New Earnings Survey 1995, London, HMSO.

New Internationalist (1994) 'The New Globalism', August.

New Society (1987) 'The crisis in community care', 18 September.

New Statesman and Society (editorial) (1993) 'A free market for crime', 26 Feb.

New, C. (1993) 'Structuration theory revisited: some reflections on agency', *Social Science Teacher*, vol. 22, no. 3.*

Newby, H. (1977) 'In the field: reflections on the study of Suffolk farm workers', in Bell, C. and Newby, H. (eds), *Doing Sociological Research*, London, Allen & Unwin.

Newby, H. (1987) *Country Life: A Social History of Rural England*, London, Cardinal.

Nichols, T. and Beynon, H. (1977) *Living With Capitalism*, London, Routledge & Kegan Paul.

Niebuhr, H.R. (1957) *The Social Sources of Denominationalism*, New York, World Publishing Company.

Nietzsche, F. (1969) *Thus Spoke Zarathustra: A Book for Everyone and No One*, Harmondsworth, Penguin.

Nisbet, R. (1976) *Sociology as an Art Form*, London, Heinemann.

Nordlinger, E.A. (1981) *On the Autonomy of the Democratic State*, Massachusetts, Harvard University Press.

Norris C. (1990) *What's Wrong With Post-modernism: Critical Theory and the Ends of Philosophy*, Hemel Hempstead, Harvester Wheatsheaf.

Norris, C. (1992) *Uncritical Theory: Postmodernism, Intellectuals and the Gulf War*, London, Lawrence & Wishart.

Norris, C. (1993) *The Truth about Postmodernism*, Oxford, Blackwell.

Oakley, A. (1972) *Sex, Gender and Society*, London, Temple Smith.

Oakley, A. (1974a) *The Sociology of Housework*, Oxford, Martin Robertson.

Oakley, A. (1974b) *Housewife*, London, Allen Lane.

Oakley, A. (1979) *From Here to Maternity*, Harmondsworth, Penguin.

Oakley, A. (1984) *The Captured Womb: A History of the Medical Care of Pregnant Women*, Oxford, Blackwell.

Oakley, A. (1990) 'Interviewing women: a contradiction in terms', in Roberts, H. (ed.), *Doing Feminist Research*, London, Routledge.

Oakley, R. (1982) 'Cypriot families', in Rapoport, R.N., Fogarty, M.P. and Rapoport, R. (eds), *Families in Britain*, London, Routledge & Kegan Paul.

O'Brien, M. and Jones, D. (1996) 'Revisiting family and kinship', *Sociology Review*, vol. 5, no. 3.

O'Brien, P. and Roddick, J. (1983) *Chile: The Pinochet Decade*, London, Latin America Bureau.

O'Connell, H. (1994) *Women and the Family*, London, Zed Books.

O'Connor, J. (1973) *The Fiscal Crisis of the State*, London, St Martin's Press.

O'Connor, J. (1984) *Accumulation Crisis*, Oxford, Blackwell.

ODA (1994a) *British Aid Statistics 1989/90–1993/94*, London, HMSO.

ODA (1994b) *Aid That's Really Going Places*, London, ODA.

O'Day, R. (1983) 'Women in the household: an historical analysis (Unit 7: U221)', Buckingham, Open University Press.

O'Donnell, M. (1987) 'Ideology, social policy and the welfare State', *Social Studies Review*, vol. 2. no 4.

O'Donnell, M. (1991) *Race and Ethnicity*, London, Longman.

O'Donnell, M. (1992) 'Your good health?', *Sociology Review*, vol. 2, no. 1.

O'Donnell, M. (1993) *A New Introduction to Sociology*, Walton on Thames, 3rd edn, Nelson.

Offe, C. (1984) *The Contradictions of the Welfare State*, London, Hutchinson.

Offe, C. (1985a) 'New social movements: challenging the boundaries of institutional politics', *Social Research*, vol. 52, no. 4.

Offe, C. (1985b) *Disorganised Capitalism*, Cambridge, Polity Press.

Omi, M. and Winant, H. (1994) *Racial Formation in the United States*, London, Routledge.

OPCS (1995) *Marriage and Divorce Statistics in England and Wales*, London, HMSO.

Oppenheim, C. (1990) *Poverty: The Facts*, London, Child Poverty Action Group.

Oppenheim, C. (1993) *Poverty: The Facts*, 2nd edn, London, Child Poverty Action Group.

Oppenheim, C. and Harker, L. (1996) *Poverty: The Facts*, 3rd edn, London, Child Poverty Action Group.

Ortner, S. (1974) 'Is female to male as nature is to culture?', in Rosaldo, M. and Lamphere, L. (eds), *Woman, Culture and Society*, Stanford, Stanford University Press.

Osbourne, K. and Nichol, C. (1996) 'Patterns of pay: results of the 1996 New Earnings Survey', *Labour Market Trends*, November.

Outhwaite, W. (1987) *New Philosophies of Social Science*, Basingstoke, Macmillan.

Outhwaite, W. (1989) 'Theory', in Haralambos, M. (ed.), *Developments in Sociology*, vol. 5, Ormskirk, Causeway.

Outram, S. (1989) *Social Policy*, London, Longman.

Oxfam (1995) *The Oxfam Poverty Report*, Oxford, Oxfam.

Oxfam (1996) *Sweat Shirt, Sweat Shop*, Oxford, Oxfam.

Pahl, R.E. (1984) *Divisions of Labour*, Oxford, Blackwell.

Pahl, J. (1989) *Money and Marriage*, Basingstoke, Macmillan.

Pahl, J. (1993) 'Money, marriage and ideology', *Sociology Review*, vol. 3, no. 1.

Pahl, R. (1995) 'Friendly society', *New Statesman and Society*, 10 March.

Pareto, V. (1963) *A Treatise on General Sociology* (edited by A. Livingstone), New York, Dover Publications.

Park, R. (1950) *Race and Culture*, New York, Free Press.

Parker, H. (1974) *View From The Boys*, Newton Abbott, David & Charles.

Parkin, F. (1972) *Class Inequality and Political Order*, St Albans, Paladin.

Parkin, F. (1979) *Marxism and Class Theory: A Bourgeois Critique*, London, Tavistock.

Parkin, F. (1986) *Max Weber*, London, Routledge.

Parmar, P. (1982) 'Gender, race and class: Asian women in resistance', in *The Empire Strikes Back*, London, CCCS/Hutchinson.

Parry, N. and Parry, J. (1976) *The Rise of the Medical Profession*, London, Croom Helm.

Parry, O. (1996) 'Equality, gender and the Caribbean classroom', in *21st Century Policy Review Special Issue: Institutional Development in the Caribbean*, Baltimore.

Parsons, T. (1937) *The Structure of Social Action*, Glencoe, Free Press.

Parsons, T. (1951) *The Social System*, London, Routledge & Kegan Paul.

Parsons, T. (1955) 'The Amercian family: its relation to personality and the social structure', in Parsons, T. and Bales, R.F. (eds), *Family Socialisation and the Interaction Process*, New York, Free Press.

Parsons, T. (1959) 'The social structure of the family', in Anshen, R. (ed.), *The Family: Its Function and Destiny*, London, Harper & Row.

Parsons, T. (1963) 'On the concept of political power', *Proceedings of the American Philosophical Society*, vol. 107.

Parsons, T. (1967) *Politics and Social Structure*, New York, Free Press.

Parsons, T. (1977) *The Evolution of Societies*, Englewood Cliffs, NJ, Prentice-Hall.

Parsons, T. and Bales, R.F. (1956) *Family, Socialization and the Interaction Process*, London, Routledge & Kegan Paul.

Pateman, C. (1988) *The Sexual Contract*, Cambridge, Polity Press.

Pateman, C. (1992) 'Equality, difference, subordination: the politics of motherhood and women's citizenship', in Bock, G. and James, S. (eds), *Beyond Equality and*

Difference: Citizenship, Feminist Politics, Female Subjectivity, London, Routledge.

Patrick, J. (1973) *A Glasgow Gang Observed*, London, Eyre Methuen.

Patterson, S. (1963) *Dark Strangers*, Harmondsworth, Penguin.

Pawson, R. (1989) 'Methodology', in Haralambos, M. (ed.), *Developments in Sociology*, vol. 5, Ormskirk, Causeway.

Pawson, R. (1992) 'Feminist methodology', in Haralambos, M. (ed.), *Developments in Sociology*, vol. 8, Ormskirk, Causeway.

Pawson, R. and Tilly, N. (1996) 'How (and how not) to design research to inform policy-making', in Samson, C. and South, N. (eds), *The Social Construction of Social Policy*, Basingstoke, Macmillan.

Payne, G. (1987) *Economy and Opportunity*, Basingstoke, Macmillan.

Peacock Committee (1986) *Report of the Committee on Financing the BBC* (Peacock Report), London, HMSO.

Pearce, D., Markanda, A. and Barbier, E. (1989) *Blueprint for a Green Economy*, London, Earthscan.

Pearce, F. (1976) *Crimes of the Powerful*, London, Pluto Press.

Pearce, F. (1989) *The Radical Durkheim*, London, Unwin Hyman.

Pearson, G. (1983) *Hooligan: A History of Respectable Fears*, Basingstoke, Macmillan.

Pearson, R. (1992) 'Gender matters in development', in Allen, T. and Thomas, A. (eds) *Poverty and Development in the 1990s*, Oxford, Oxford University Press.

Peckham Rye Women's Liberation Workshop Collective (eds) (1971) 'Women's Liberation Workshop', *Shrew*, vol. 3 no. 5.

Perlmutter, T. (1993) 'Distress signals', in Domunt, T. (ed), *Channels of Resistance*, London, BFI Publishing.

Perrow, C. (1970) *Complex Organizations*, 2nd edn, Glenview, Scott, Foresman and Co.

Perrow, C. (1986) *Complex Organizations*, 3rd edn, New York, Random House.

Perry, K. (1996) 'Measuring employment: comparison of official sources' *Labour Market Trends*, January.

Pesticides Trust (1994) 'The international medical appeal for Bhopal', *The Guardian*, 3 December.

Petley, J. and Romano, G. (1993) 'Public service television in Europe', in Dumont, T. (ed), *Channels of Resistance*, London, BFI Publishing.

Phillips, A. (1987) *Feminism and Equality*, Oxford, Blackwell.

Phillips, A. (1991) *Engendering Democracy*, Cambridge, Polity Press.

Phillips, A. (1992) 'Universal pretensions in political thought', in Barrett, M. and Phillips, A. (eds), *Destabilising Theory: Contemporary Feminist Debates*, Cambridge, Polity Press.

Phillips, A. (1996) 'What has socialism to do with sexual equality?', *Soundings*, no. 4.

Phillips, M. (1995) 'We've fiddled the figures, thank you', *The Guardian*, 29 January.

Philo, G. (1990) *Seeing and Believing: The Influence Of Television*, London, Routledge.

Philo, G. (1994) 'Politics, media and public belief', in Perryman, M. (ed), *Altered States: Post-modernism, Politics, Culture*, London, Lawrence & Wishart.

Phizacklea, A. and Miles, R. (1980) *Labour and Racism*, London, Routledge & Kegan Paul.

Piachard, D. (1987) 'Problems in the definition and measurement of poverty', *Journal of Social Policy*, vol. 16, no. 2.

Pilger, J. (1995) 'Natural born partners', *New Statesman and Society*, 10 March.

Pilger, J. (1996) 'They never walk alone', *The Guardian*, 23 November.

Pilkington, A. (1984) *Race Relations in Britain*, Slough, University Tutorial Press.

Pilkington, A. (1992) 'Is there a British underclass?', *Sociology Review*, vol. 1, no. 3.

Piore, M. and Sabel, C. (1984) *The Second Industrial Divide*, New York, Basic Books.

Plowden Report (1967) *Children and Their Primary Schools*, London, HMSO.

Plummer, K. (1976) 'Men in love: observations on male homosexual couples', in Corbin, M. (ed.), *The Couple*, Harmondsworth, Penguin.

Plummer, K. (1983) *Life Documents*, London, Unwin Hyman.

Pollack, F. (1955) 'Empirical research into public opinion', in Connerton, P. (ed.), *Critical Sociology*, Harmondsworth, Penguin.

Pollack, O. (1961) *The Criminality of Women*, New York, A.S. Barnes.

Pollert, A. (1988) 'Dismantling flexibility', *Capital and Class*, vol. 34.

Pollert, A. (ed) (1991) *Farewell to Flexibility*, Oxford, Blackwell.

Polsky, N. (1971) *Hustlers, Beats and Others*, Harmondsworth, Penguin.

Popper, K. (1959) *The Logic of Scientific Discovery*, London, Hutchinson.

Popper, K. (1976) *Unended Quest*, Glasgow, Fontana.

Porter, S. (1992) 'Women in a woman's job: the gendered experience of nurses', *Sociology of Health and Illness*, vol. 14, no. 4.

Poulantzas, N. (1978) *State, Power, Socialism*, London, New Left Books.

Poulantzas, N. (1980) *State Power Socialism*, new edn, London, Verso.

Prasha, U. (1995) 'A new role for the third sector', in Atkinson, D. (ed) *Cities of Pride: Rebuilding Community, Refocusing Government*, London, Cassell.

Prebisch, R. (1959) 'Commercial policy in the under-developed countries', *American Economic Review*, vol. 44.

Prest, A.R. and Barr, N.A. (1985) *Public Finance in Theory and Practice*, 7th edn, London, Weidenfeld & Nicholson.

Pryce, K. (1979) *Endless Pressure*, Harmondsworth, Penguin.

Pryce, K. (1986) *'Endless Pressure': A Study of West Indian Lifestyle in Bristol*, Bristol, Bristol Classical Press.

Pusey, M. (1987) *Jürgen Habermas*, London, Tavistock.

Quinney, R. (1973) *Critique of Legal Order*, Boston, Little Brown.

Quinney, R. (1977) *Class, State and Crime*, New York, McKay.

Rabinow, P. (ed.) (1991) *The Foucault Reader: An Introduction to Foucault's Thought*, Harmondsworth, Penguin.

Randall, V. (1987) *Women and Politics: An International Perspective*, 2nd edn, Basingstoke, Macmillan.

Rapoport, R.N., Fogarty, M.P. and Rapoport, R. (eds) (1982) *Families in Britain*, London, Routledge & Kegan Paul.

Rattansi, A. (1994) '"Western racisms", ethnicities and identities in a postmodern frame', in Rattansi, A. and Westwood, S. (eds), *Racism, Modernity and Identity*, Cambridge, Polity Press.

Redclift, M. (1987) *Sustainable Development: Exploring the Contradictions*, London, Methuen.

Redclift, M. (1994) 'Development and the environment: managing the contradictions', in Sklair, L. (ed) *Capitalism and Development*, London, Routledge.

Redfield, R (1930) *Tepotzlan: A Mexican Village*, Chicago, University of Chicago Press.

Redhead, S. (1990) *The End of the Century Party*, Manchester, Manchester University Press.

Redhead, S. (1993) *Rave Off: Politics and Deviance in Contemporary Youth Culture*, Aldershot, Avebury.

Reiner, R. (1996) 'Crime and control: an honest citizen's guide', *Sociology Review*, vol. 5, no. 4.

Rentoul, J. (1987) *The Rich Get Richer*, London, Unwin Hyman.

Rex, J. (1961) *Key Problems of Sociological Theory*, London, Routledge & Kegan Paul.

Rex, J. (1973) *Race, Colonialism and the City*, London, Routledge & Kegan Paul.

Rex, J. (1983) *Race Relations in Social theory*, London, Routledge & Kegan Paul.

Rex, J. (1986) *Race and Ethnicity*, Buckingham, Open University Press.

Rex, J. (1988) 'The role of class analysis in the study of race relations: a Weberian perspective', in Rex, J. and Mason, D. (eds), *Theories of Race and Ethnic Relations*, Cambridge, Cambridge University Press.

Rex, J. and Moore, R. (1967) *Race, Community and Conflict: A Study of Sparkbrook*, London, Institute of Race Relations/Oxford University Press.

Rex, J. and Tomlinson, S. (1979) *Colonial Immigrants in a British City: A Class Analysis*, London, Routledge & Kegan Paul.

Rich, A. (1980) *Blood, Bread and Poetry*, New York, W.W. Norton.

Richards, A. (1993) 'Korea, Taiwan and Thailand: trade liberalisation and economic growth', *OECD Observer*, October.

Richards, A. (1994) 'Hong Kong, Singapore and Malaysia and the fruits of free trade', *OECD Observer*, January.

Richardson, J. (1996) 'Race and ethnicity', in Haralambos, M. (ed), *Developments in Sociology*, vol. 12, Ormskirk, Causeway Press.

Riddell, S. and Brown, S. (1994) *Special Educational Needs Policy in the 1990's: Warnock and the Market Place*, London, Routledge.

Rist, R.C. (1977) 'On understanding the processes of schooling: the contributions of labeling theory', in Karabel, J. and Halsey, A H. (eds), *Power and Ideology in Education*, Oxford, Oxford University Press.

Ritzer, G. (1993) *The McDonaldization of Society*, Thousand Oaks, CA, Pine Forge Press.

Ritzer, G. (1995) *Expressing America: A Critique of the Global Credit Card Society*, Thousand Oaks, CA, Pine Forge Press.

Ritzer, G. (1996) *Modern Sociological Theory*, 4th edn, New York, McGraw-Hill.

Roberts, H. (ed.) (1990) *Doing Feminist Research*, London, Routledge & Kegan Paul.

Roberts, K. *et al.* (1977) *The Fragmentary Class Structure*, London, Heinemann.

Roberts, M., McGee, N. and Payne, M. (1996) 'Results of the 1995 Annual Employment Survey', *Labour Market Trends*, November.

Robertson, R. (1992) *Globalisation: Social Theory and Global Culture*, London, Sage.

Robins, K. (1991) 'Tradition and translation: national culture in its global context', in Corner, J. and Harvey, S. (eds), *Enterprise and Heritage: Crosscurrents of National Culture*, London, Routledge.

Robins, K. (1997) 'What is globalisation?', *Sociology Review*, vol. 6, no. 3.

Rock, P. (1989) 'New directions in criminology', *Social Studies Review*, vol. 5, no. 1.

Roethlisburger, F. and Dickson, W. (1939) *Management and the Worker*, Cambridge, MA, Harvard University Press.

Rogers, E.M. and Dearing, D.W. (1987) 'Agenda-setting research', in Anderson, J. (ed.), *Communication Yearbook 11*, London, Sage.

Rojek, C. (1985) *Capitalism and Leisure Theory*, London, Tavistock.

Rojek, C. (1993) *Ways of Escape*, Basingstoke, Macmillan.

Roll, J. (1992) *Understanding Poverty: A Guide to the Concepts and Measures*, London, Family Policy Studies Centre.

Rosaldo, M. (1974) 'Woman, culture and society: a theoretical overview', in Rosaldo, M. and Lamphere, L. (eds), *Woman, Culture and Society*, Stanford, Stanford University Press.

Rose, D. (1995) *A Report on Phase 1 of the ESRC Review of Social Classifications*, Swindon, ESRC.

Rose, R. (1989) *Politics in England: Change and Perspective*, 5th edn, Basingstoke, Macmillan.

Rose, R. and McAllister, I. (1990) *The Loyalties of Voters: A Lifetime Learning Model*, London, Sage.

Rose, S., Kamin, L.J. and Lewontin, R.C. (1984) *Not in Our Genes: Biology, Ideology and Human Nature*, Harmondsworth, Penguin.

Rosenberg, B. and Manning White, D. (eds) (1957) *Mass Culture: The Popular Arts in America*, New York, Macmillan.

Roseneil, S. (1994) 'Gender', in Haralambos, M. (ed.), *Developments in Sociology*, vol. 10, Ormskirk, Causeway Press.

Roseneil, S. (1995) *Disarming Patriarchy: Feminism and Political Action at Greenham*, Buckingham, Open University Press.

Rosenthal, R. and Jacobson, L. (1968) *Pygmalion in the Classroom*, London, Holt, Rinehart & Winston.

Rosser, R. and Harris, C. (1965) *The Family and Social Change*, London, Routledge & Kegan Paul.

Rostow, W.W. (1960) *The Stages of Economic Growth: A Non-Communist Manifesto*, Cambridge, Cambridge University Press.

Rowbotham, S. (1973) *Woman's Consciousness: Man's World*, Harmondsworth, Penguin.

Rowbotham, S. (1989) *The Past is Before Us: Feminism in Action since the 1960s*, Harmondsworth, Penguin.

Rowland, R. (1985) 'A child at any price?', *Women's Studies International Forum*, vol. 8, no. 6.

Rowntree, B.S. (1901) *Poverty: A Study in Town Life*, London, Macmillan.

Rowntree, B.S. (1937) *The Human Needs of Labour*, London, Longmans Green.

Rowntree, B.S. (1941) *Poverty and Progress*, London, Longman.

Rowntree, B.S. and Lavers, G.R. (1951) *Poverty and the Welfare State*, London, Longmans Green.

Rowntree Foundation (1995) *Inquiry into Income and Wealth*, Joseph Rowntree Foundation.

Roxborough, I. (1979) *Theories of Development*, Basingstoke, Macmillan.

Rubin, G. (1975) 'The traffic in women: notes on the "political economy" of sex', in Reiter, R.R. (ed.), *Toward an Anthropology of Women*, New York, Monthly Review Press.

Runciman, W.G. (1990) 'How many classes are there in contemporary British society', *Sociology*, vol. 24, no. 3.

Runnymede Trust (1994) *Multi-Ethnic Britain: Facts and Trends*, London, Runnymede Trust.

Rutheiser, C. (1996a) 'How Atlanta lost the Olympics', *New Statesman and Society*, 19 July.

Rutheiser, .C. (1996b) *Imagineering Atlanta: The Politics of Place in the City of Dreams*, London, Verso.

Rutherford, J. (1988) 'Who's that man?', in Chapman, R. and Rutherford, J. (eds), *Male Order: Unwrapping Masculinity*, London, Lawrence & Wishart.

Sabel, C. (1989) 'Flexible specialisation and the re-emergence of regional ecomomics', in Hirst, P. and Zeitlin, J. (eds), *Reversing Economic Decline?*, London, St Martins.

Sacks, H. (1984) 'Methodological remarks', in Atkinson, J.M. and Heritage, J. (eds), *Structures of Social Action: Studies in Conversation Analysis*, Cambridge, Cambridge University Press.

Sacks, H. (1992) *Lectures on Conversation, 1965–1972*, Oxford, Blackwell.

Said, E. (1978) *Orientalism*, New York, Random House.

Saint-Simon, Henri de (1819) 'The organiser', in Markham, F. (ed.), *Henri Comte de Saint-Simon: Selected Writings*, Oxford, Blackwell (pub. 1952).

Saint-Simon, Henri de (1825) 'The new Christianty', in Markham, F. (ed.), *Henri Comte de Saint-Simon: Selected Writings*, Oxford, Blackwell (pub. 1952).

Sanderson, J. (1994) *LLB Criminology Textbook 1994–1995*, 5th edn, London, HLT.

Sarantakos, S. (1993) *Social Research*, Basingstoke, Macmillan.

Sarlvick, B. and Crewe, I. (1983) *Decade of Dealignment*, Cambridge, Cambridge University Press.

Sartre, J-P. (1960) *Critique of Dialectical Reason*, London, New Left Books.

Sartre, J-P. (1974) *Existentialism and Humanism*, London, Eyre Methuen.

Sarup, M. (1993) *An Introductory Guide to Post-Structuralism and Postmodernism*, 2nd edn, Hemel Hempstead, Harvester Wheatsheaf.

Saunders, P. (1978) 'Domestic property and social class', *International Journal of Urban and Regional Research*, vol. 2, no. 2.

Saunders, P. (1987) *Social Theory and the Urban Question*, London, Unwin Hyman.

Saunders, P. (1990a) *A Nation of Homeowners*, London, Unwin Hyman.

Saunders, P. (1990b) *Social Class and Stratification*, London, Routledge.

Saunders, P. (1995) *Capitalism: A Social Audit*, Buckingham: Open University Press.

Saunders, P. (1996) 'A British Bell curve? Class, intelligence and meritocracy in modern Britain', *Sociology Review*, vol. 6, no. 2.

Saussure, F. de (1974) *Course in General Linguistics*, London, Fontana (orig. pub. 1915).

Savage, M. (1995) 'The middle classes in modern Britain', *Sociology Review*, vol. 5, no. 2.

Savage, M., Barlow, J., Dickens, P. and Fielding, T. (1992) *Property, Bureaucracy and Culture*, London, Routledge.

Savage, M. and Warde, A. (1993) *Urban Sociology, Capitalism and Modernity*, Basingstoke, Macmillan.

Sayer, A. (1979) 'Science as critique: Marx vs Althusser', in Mepham, J. and Ruben, D.-H. (eds), *Issues in Marxist Philosophy –3: Epistemology, Science, Ideology,* Brighton, Harvester.

Sayer, A. (1984) *Method in Social Science*, London, Hutchinson.

Sayer, A. (1989) 'Postfordism in question', *International Journal of Urban and Regional Research*, vol. 13, no. 4.

Scannel, P. (1989) 'Public service broadcasting and modern public life', *Media, Culture and Society*, vol. 11, no. 2 (April).

Scannel, P. (1990) 'Public service broadcasting: the history of a concept', in Goodwin, A. and Whannel, G. (eds), *Understanding Television*, London, Routledge.

Scarman, Lord (1982) *The Scarman Report*, Harmondsworth, Penguin.

Schacht, R. (ed) (1993) *The Great Philosophers: Nietzsche Selections*, New York, Macmillian.

Schlesinger, P. (1992) *Putting 'Reality' Together*, London, Routledge.

Schultz, T. (1961) 'Investment in human capital', *American Economic Review*, vol. 51, March.

Schumacher, E. (1973) *Small is Beautiful*, London, Abacus.

Schumpeter, J.A. (1992) *Capitalism, Socialism and Democracy*, London, Routledge (orig. pub. 1943).

Schutz, A. (1972) *The Phenomenology of the Social World*, London, Heinemann.

Schuurman, F.J. (ed) (1993) *Beyond the Impasse: New Directions in Development Theory*, London, Zed.

Scott, A. (1990) *Ideology and the New Social Movements*, London, Unwin Hyman.

Scott, Allen J. (1988) *Metropolis: From the Division of Labour to Urban Form*, Berkeley, University of California Press.

Scott, J. (1985) *Corporations, Classes and Capitalism*, 2nd edn, London, Hutchinson.

Scott, J. (1986) 'Does Britain still have a ruling class?' *Social Studies Review*, September.

Scott, J. (1991) *Who Rules Britain?*, Cambridge, Polity Press.

Scott, J. (1994) *Poverty and Wealth*, London, Longman.

Scott, J. (1995) *Sociological Theory: Contemporary Debates*, Aldershot, Edward Elgar.

Scott, J. (1996) *Stratification and Power*, Cambridge, Polity Press.

Scraton, S. and Bramham, P. (1995) 'Leisure and post-modernity', in Haralambos, M. (ed.), *Developments in Sociology*, vol. 11, Ormskirk, Causeway.

Scruton, R. (1986) 'Authority and allegiance', cited in 'New ethnicities', in Donald, J. and Rattansi, A. (eds) (1992), *Race, Culture and Difference*, London, Sage.

Scruton, R. (1991) Speaking on the Radio 4 programme, 'Punters', 8 August.

Scull, A. (1979) *Museums of Madness*, Harmondsworth, Penguin.

Scull, A. (1984) *Decarceration: Community Treatment and the Deviant, a Radical View*, Cambridge, Polity Press.

Seabrook, J. (1993) *Victims of Development: Resistance and Alternatives*, London, Verso.

Sedgwick, P. (1982) *Psycho Politics*, London, Pluto Press.

Segal, L. (1987) *Is the Future Female? Troubled Thoughts On Contemporary Feminism*, London, Virago.

Segal, L. (1989) 'Slow change or no change: feminism, socialism and the problem of men', *Feminist Review*, no. 31.

Seidel, G. (1986) 'Culture, nation and 'race' in the British and French New Right', in Levitas, R. (ed), *The Ideology of the New Right*, Cambridge, Polity Press.

Seidler, V. (1989) *Rediscovering Masculinity*, London, Routledge.

Selfe, P. (1987) *Advanced Sociology*, London, Pan.

Selfe, P. (1995) *Work Out Sociology*, Basingstoke, Macmillan.

Selznick, P. (1957) *Leadership in Administration: A Sociological Interpretation*, New York, Harper & Row.

Sen, A. (1983) 'Poor, relatively speaking', *Oxford Economic Papers*, no. 25.

Sender, J. and Short, S. (1986) *The Development of Capitalism in Africa*, London, Methuen.

Senior, M. (1996) 'Health, illness and postmodernism', *Sociology Review*, vol. 6, no. 1.

Sennett, R. and Cobb, J. (1977) *The Hidden Injuries of Class*, Cambridge, Cambridge University Press.

Shaiken, H. (1979) 'Numerical control of work: workers and automation in the computer age', *Radical America*, vol. 1, no. 6.

Sharma, U. (1992) *Complementary Medicine Today: Practitioners and Patients*, London, Routledge.

Sharpe, S. (1976) *Just Like a Girl: How Girls Learn to be Women*, Harmondsworth, Penguin.

Shaskolsky, L. (1970) 'The development of sociological theory: a sociology of knowledge interpretation', in Reynolds, L.T. and Reynolds, J.M. (eds), *The Sociology of Sociology*, New York, McKay.

Shaver, S. and Bradshaw, J. (1995) 'The recognition of wifely labour by welfare states', *Social Policy and Administration*, vol. 29, no. 1.

Shaw, C. (1931) *The Natural History of a Delinquent Career*, Chicago, University of Chicago Press.

Shaw, C. (1966) *The Jackroller*, Chicago, University of Chicago Press.

Shearer, A. (1981) *Disability: Whose Handicap?*, Oxford, Blackwell.

Sheeran, Y. (1995) 'Sociology, biology and health: is illness only a social construction?', *Sociology Review*, vol. 4, no. 4.

Sherlock, H. (1991) *Cities Are Good For Us*, London, Paladin.

Shilling, C. (1993) *The Body and Social Theory*, London, Sage.

Shils, E. (1961) 'Mass society and its culture', in Jacobs, N. (ed.), *Culture for the Millions*, New Jersey, Van Nostrand.

Shils, E. and Young, M. (1953) 'The meaning of the coronation', *Sociological Review*, vol. 1.

Short, B. (ed) (1992a) *The English Rural Community: Image and Analysis*, Cambridge, Cambridge University Press.

Short, B. (1992b) 'Images and realities in the English rural community: an introduction', in Short, B. (ed) *The English Rural Community: Image and Analysis*, Cambridge, Cambridge University Press.

Shortall, S. (1994) 'Farm women's groups: feminist, farming or community groups, or new social movements?', *Sociology*, vol. 28, no. 1

Shorter, E. (1977) *The Making of the Modern Family*, London, Fontana.

Shutz, A. (1967) *The Phenomenology of the Social World*, Evanston, Northwestern University Press.

Simmel, G. (1890) *On Social Differentiation*, Berlin, Dünker & Humblot.

Simmel, G. (1968) *Sociology*, Berlin, Düncker & Humblot (orig. pub. 1908).

Simmel, G. (1978) *The Philosophy of Money*, London, Routledge & Kegan Paul (orig. pub. 1900).

Simon, H.A. (1957) *Models of Man*, New York, Wiley.

Simon, R. (1982) *Gramsci's Political Thought: An Introduction*, London, Lawrence & Wishart.

Simons, M. (1988) 'The red and the green: socialists and the ecology movement', *International Socialism*, Winter.

Sivanandan, A. (1976) 'Race, class and the state: the Black experience in Britain', *Race and Class*, vol. 17, no. 4.

Sivanandan, A. (1982) *A Different Hunger*, London, Pluto Press.

Sivanandan, A. (1990) *Communities of Resistance*, London, Verso.

Sivanandan, A. (1995) 'La tratison des clercs', *New Statesman and Society*. 14 July.

Skeggs, B. (1991) Postmodernism: what is all the fuss about? *British Journal of Sociology of Education*, vol. 12, no. 2.

Skellington, R. (1996) *'Race' in Britain Today*, London, Sage/Open University Press.

Skidmore, P. (1995) 'Just another moral panic? Media reporting of child sexual abuse', *Sociology Review*, vol. 5, no. 4.

Skinner, Q. (ed.) (1990) *The Return of Grand Theory in the Human Sciences*, Cambridge, Canto.

Sklair, L (1989) *Assembling for Development*, London, Unwin Hyman.

Sklair, L. (1991) *Sociology of the Global System*, Hemel Hempstead, Harvester Wheatsheaf.

Sklair, L. (ed) (1994) *Capitalism and Development*, London, Routledge.

Skocpol, T. (1979) *States and Social Revolutions*, Cambridge, Cambridge University Press.

Slattery, M. (1985) 'Urban sociology', in Haralambos, M. (ed) *Sociology: New Directions*, Ormskirk, Causeway Press.

Slattery, M. (1986) *Official Statistics*, London, Tavistock.

Slattery, M. (1991) *Key Ideas in Sociology*, Basingstoke, Macmillan.

Sly, F. (1996) 'Women in the labour market: results from the Spring 1995 Labour Force Survey', *Labour Market Trends*, March.

Smaje, C. (1996) 'The ethnic patterning of health: new directions for theory and practice', *Sociology of Health and Illness*, vol. 18, no. 2.

Small, S. (1994) *Racialised Barriers*, London, Routledge.

Smart, B. (1985) *Michel Foucault*, London, Routledge.

Smart, B. (1994) *Postmodernity*, London, Routledge.

Smart, C. (1976) *Women, Crime and Criminology*, London, Routledge & Kegan Paul.

Smart, C. (1991) 'Securing the family? Rhetoric and policy in the field of social security', in Loney, M. *et al.* (eds), *The State or the Market*, London, Sage.

Smith, D. (1988a) 'Crime prevention and the causes of crime', *Social Studies Review*, vol. 3, no. 5.

Smith, D.J. (ed) (1992a) *Understanding the Underclass*, London, Policy Studies Institute.

Smith, G. (1986) 'Pluralism, race and ethnicity in selected African countries', in Rex, J. and Mason, D. (eds), *Theories of Race and Ethnic Relations*, Cambridge, Cambridge University Press.

Smith, J. (1989) *Misogynies*, London, Faber & Faber.

Smith, M. (1994a) 'Police accused of "dirty tricks" war on BA passenger', *The Telegraph*, 31 August.

Smith, M. (1994b) 'BA is sued over "intimidation"', *The Telegraph*, 24 September.

Smith, M.G. (1962) *West Indian Family Structure*, Seattle, University of Washington Press.

Smith, P. (1992b) 'Industrialization and environment', in Hewitt, T., Johnson, H. and Wild, D. (eds) *Industrialization and Development*, Oxford, Oxford University Press.

Smith, R.T. (1988b) *Kinship and Class in the West Indies*, Cambridge, Cambridge University Press.

Smith, S. (1995) 'The ideas of Samir Amin: theory or tautology?', in Ayers, R. (ed) *Development Studies*, London, Greenwich University Press.

Smithers, A. and Robinson, P.(1995) *Post-18 Education: Growth, Change and Prospect*, London, Council for Industry and Higher Education (Executive Briefing).

Smithers, R. (1994) 'Near miss denied as inquiry starts into airliner's aborted landing', *The Guardian*, 31 August.

Smyth, G., Jones, D. and Platt, S. (eds) (1994) *Bite the Ballot: 2500 Years of Democracy*, London, Channel 4/New Statesman and Society.

Snell, M. (1986) 'Equal pay and sex discrimination', *Feminist Review* (ed.), *Waged Work: A Reader*, London, Virago.

Social Trends vol. 26 (1996), London, HMSO.

Soja, E.W. (1992a) 'Economic restructuring and the internationalization of the Los Angeles region', in Giddens, A. (ed) *Human Societies: An Introductory Reader in Sociology*, Cambridge, Polity Press.

Soja, E.W. (1992b) 'Taking Los Angeles apart: towards a

postmodern geography', in Jencks, C. (ed) *The Postmodern Reader*, London, Academy Editions.

Solomos, J. (1988) 'Varieties of Marxist conceptions of 'race', class and the state: a critical analysis', in Rex, J. and Mason, D. (eds), *Theories of Race and Ethnic relations*, Cambridge, Cambridge University Press.

Solomos, J. (1993) *Race and Racism in Britain*, Basingstoke, Macmillan.

Solomos, J. and Back, L. (1995) *Race, Politics and Social Change*, London, Routledge.

Solomos, J. *et al.* (1982) *The Organic Crisis of British Capitalism and Race: The Experience of the Centre for Contemporary Cultural Studies*, Birmingham, Race and Politics Group.

Spelman, E. (1990) *Inessential Woman: Problems of Exclusion in Feminist Thought*, London, Women's Press.

Spencer, H. (1874) *The Study of Society*, London, Appleton.

Spencer, H. (1896) *The Principles of Sociology*, London, Appleton.

Spencer, H. (1971) *Structure, Function and Evolution*, London, Nelson.

Spender, D. and Sarah, E. (eds) (1980) *Learning to Lose: Sexism and Education*, London, Women's Press.

Spiro, M.E. (1968) 'Is the family universal?', in Bell, N.W. and Vogel, E.F. (eds), *A Modern Introduction to the Family* (revised edition), New York, Free Press.

Spurgeon, P. (ed.) (1993) *The New Face of the NHS*, Edinburgh, Churchill Livingstone.

Stacey, M. (1988) *The Sociology of Health and Healing*, London, Unwin Hyman.

Stanko, E. (1988) 'Fear of crime and the myth of the safe home', in Borad, M. and Yuo, K. (eds), *Feminist Perspectives of Wife Abuse*, London, Sage.

Stanley, L. (ed.) (1990) *Feminist Praxis: Research, Theory and Epistemology in Feminist Sociology*, London, Routledge.

Stanley, L. and Wise, S. (1983) *Breaking Out*, London, Routledge & Kegan Paul.

Stanley, L. and Wise, S. (1990) 'Method, methodology and epistemology in feminist research processes', in Stanley, L. (ed.), *Feminist Praxis: Research, Theory and Epistemology in Feminist Sociology*, London, Routledge.

Stanley, L. and Wise, S. (1993) *Breaking Out Again*, London, Routledge.

Stanworth, M. (1983) *Gender and Schooling: a Study of Sexual Divisions in the Classroom*, London, Hutchinson.

Stanworth, M. (ed.) (1987) *Reproductive Technologies: Gender, Motherhood and Medicine*, Cambridge, Polity Press.

Stanworth, P. and Giddens, A. (eds) (1974) *Elites and Power in British Society*, Cambridge, Cambridge University Press.

Starbuck, M. (1995) 'Figuring out the sociology of Norbert Elias', *Social Science Teacher*, vol. 24, no. 2.*

Stark, R. and Bainbridge, W.S. (1985) *The Future of Religion: Secularization, Revival and Cult Formation*, Berkeley, University of California Press.

STATLAS UK (1995) Ordnance Survey (HMSO).

Stead, M. (1991) 'Women, war and underdevelopment in Nicaragua', in Ashar, H. (ed) *Women, Development and Survival in the Third World*, London, Longman.

Steele, J. (1995) 'Clinton policies are caught in the communitaran crossfire: commentary, *The Guardian*, 12 April.

Steele, J., Mortimer, E. and Jones, G.S. (1989) 'The end of history?', *Marxism Today*, November.

Sternberg, R.J. (1995) 'Interview with *Skeptic* magazine, *Skeptic*, vol. 3, no. 3.

Sternberg, R.J. (1996) 'Myths, mythical countermyths, and truths about intelligence', *Educational Researcher*, vol. 25, no. 2.

Stewart, A., Prandy, K. and Blackburn, R.M. (1980) *Social Stratification and Occupations*, Basingstoke, Macmillan.

Stille, A. (1997) *Excellent Cadavers*, London, Vintage.

Stoller, R. (1968) *Sex and Gender: On the Development of Masculinity and Femininity*, New York, Science House.

Stone, M. (1981) *The Education of the Black Child in Britain: The Myth of Multiracial Education*, London, Fontana.

Storey, J. (1993) *An Introductory Guide to Cultural Theory and Popular Culture*, Hemel Hempstead, Harvester Wheatsheaf.

Sturmer, C. (1993) 'MTV's Europe: an imaginary continent', in Dowmunt, T. (ed.), *Channels of Resistance*, London, BFI/Channel 4.

Strinati, D. (1995) *An Introduction to Theories of Popular Culture*, London, Routledge.

Stryker, S. (1981) *Symbolic Interactionism: A Social Structural Version*, Englewood Cliffs, NJ, Prentice-Hall.

Sumner, C. (1994) *The Sociology of Deviance: An Obituary*, Buckingham, Open University Press.

Swatridge, C. (1995) *General Studies A Level*, London, HarperCollins.

Swift, R. (1994) 'Squeezing the south', *New Internationalist*, July.

Swingewood, A. (1977) *The Myth of Mass Culture*, Basingstoke, Macmillan.

Sykes, G.M. and Matza, D. (1989) 'Techniques of neutralization: a theory of delinquency', in Kelly, D.H. (ed), *Deviant Behaviour: A Text-Reader in the Sociology of Deviance*, 3rd edn, New York, St Martin's.

Szasz, T. (1970) *The Manufacture of Madness*, New York, Harper & Row.

Szasz, T. (1973) *The Myth of Mental Illness*, New York, Paladin (orig. pub. 1961).

Tame, C.R. (1991) 'Freedom, responsibility and justice: the criminology of the New Right', in Stenson, K. and Cowell, D. (eds), *The Politics of Crime Control*, London, Sage.

Tang Nain, G. (1991) 'Black women, sexism and racism: black or antiracist feminism', *Feminist Review*, no. 37.

Taylor, F.W. (1911) *The Principles of Scientific Management*, New York, Harper & Row.

Taylor, F.W. (1964) 'Shop management', in Taylor, F.W. (ed.), *Scientific Management*, New York, Harper & Row (orig pub. 1903).

Taylor, I., Walton, P. and Young, J. (1973) *The New Criminology: For a Social Theory of Deviance*, London, Routledge & Kegan Paul.

Taylor, J.G. (1979) *From Modernisation to Modes of Production*, Basingstoke, Macmillan.

Taylor, P.M. (1992) *War and the Media: Propaganda and Persuasion in the Gulf War*, Manchester, Manchester University Press.

Taylor, P., Richardson, J., Yeo, A., Marsh, I., Trobe, K., Pilkington, A., Hughes, G. and Sharp, K. (1995) *Sociology in Focus*, Ormskirk, Causeway Press.

Taylor, S. (1982) *Durkheim and the Study of Suicide*, Basingstoke, Macmillan.

Taylor, S. (1990) 'Beyond Durkheim: sociology and suicide', *Social Studies Review*, vol. 6, no. 2.

Taylor, S. (1994) 'Beyond the medical model: the sociology of health and illness', *Sociology Review*, vol. 4, no. 1.

Taylor, S. and Field, D. (eds) (1993) *The Sociology of Health and Health Care*, Oxford, Blackwell Science.

Taylor-Gooby, P. (1990) 'Social welfare:the unkindest cuts', in Jowell, R. *et al.* (eds), *British Social Attitudes: The Seventh Report*, Aldershot, Gower.

The Economist (1994a) 'Down the rathole', 10 December.

The Economist (1994b) 'The global economy: a survey', 1 October.

Thomas, A., Crow, B., Frenz, P., Hewitt, T., Kassam, S. and Treagust, S. (1994) *Third World Atlas*, 2nd edn, Buckingham, Open University Press.

Thomas, H. and Klett-Davies, M. (1995) 'Unequal pay for equal parts: a survey of performers in the theatre and the electronic media', London, Equity/Goldsmith's College, University of London.

Thomas, W.I. (1909) *The Child in America*, New York, Alfred Knopt.

Thomas, W.I. and Znaniecki, F. (1919) *The Polish Peasant in Europe and America*, Chicago, University of Chicago Press.

Thompson, E.G. (1995) Letter on *Social Trends*, *The Guardian*, 13 February.

Thompson, E.P. (1968) *The Making of the English Working Class*, Harmondsworth, Penguin.

Thompson, E.P. (1978) *The Poverty of Theory and Other Essays*, London, Merlin Press.

Thompson, P. (1988) *The Voice of the Past: Oral History*, Oxford, Oxford University Press.

Thompson, P. (1993) 'The labour process: changing theory, changing practice', *Sociology Review*, vol. 3, no. 2.

Thorogood, N. (1992) 'Private medicine: "You pay your money and you get your treatment"', *Sociology of Health and Illness*, vol. 14, no. 1.

Tiger, L. and Fox, R. (1972) *The Imperial Animal*, London, Secker & Warburg.

Tipton, S. (1982) *Getting Saved From the Sixties*, Berkeley, University of California Press.

Tizard, B. (1994) *Black, White or Mixed race? Race and Racism in the Lives of Young People of Mixed Parentage*, London, Routledge.

Tomlinson, J. (1994) 'A phenomenology of globalization? Giddens on global modernity', *European Journal of Communications*, vol. 9, 149–72.

Tomlinson, S. (1982) *A Sociology of Special Education*, London, Routledge & Kegan Paul.

Tong, R. (1989) *Feminist Thought*, London, Unwin Hyman.

Tönnies, F. (1955) *Community and Association*, London, Routledge & Kegan Paul.

Tooley, J. (1995) 'Can IQ tests liberate education?' *Economic Affairs*, vol. 15, no. 3.

Townsend, P. (1979) *Poverty in the United Kingdom*, Harmondsworth, Penguin.

Townsend, P., Davidson, N. and Whitehead, M. (1987) *Inequalities in Health and the Health Divide*, Harmondsworth, Penguin.

Travis, A. (1995) '10,000 spy cameras for high streets', *The Guardian*, 23 November.

Travis, A. (1996a) 'Straw seizes on fall in convictions', *The Guardian*, 6 February.

Travis, A. (1996b) 'Muggings mar third year's fall in crime', *The Guardian*, 27 March.

Travis, A. (1996c) 'Deportation list hits record total of 17, 800', *The Guardian*, 25 October.

Trist, E.L., Higgin, G.W., Murray, H. and Pollack, A.B. (1963) *Organisational Choice*, London, Tavistock.

Troeltsch, E. (1981) *The Social Teachings of the Christian Churches*, volumes 1 and 2, Chicago, University of Chicago Press.

Trowler, P. (1985) 'Social policy and administration', in Trowler, P., *Further Topics in Sociology*, Slough, University Tutorial Press.

Trowler, P. (1989) *Investigating Health, Welfare and Poverty*, London, Unwin Hyman.

Trowler, P. (1996) *Investigating Health, Welfare and Poverty*, 2nd edn, London, Collins Educational.

Trowler, P. with Riley, M. (1987) *Topics in Sociology*, London, Bell & Hyman.

Tuchman, G. (1981) 'The symbolic annihilation of women', in Cohen, S. and Young, J. (eds), *The Manufacture of News*, London, Constable.

Tudor-Hart, J. (1971) 'The inverse care law', *The Lancet*, 27 February.

Tulloch, J. (1990) 'Television and Black Britons', in Goodwin, A. and Whannel, G. (eds), *Understanding Television*, London, Routledge.

Tunstall, J. (1977) *The Media are American*, London, Constable.

Turner, B.S. (1984) *The Body and Society*, Oxford, Basil Blackwell.

Turner, B.S. (1982) 'The government of the body: medical regimes and the rationalization of diet', *British Journal of Sociology*, vol. 33, no. 2.

Turner, B.S. (1985) 'More on the government of the body: a reply to Naomi Aronson', *British Journal of Sociology*, vol. 36, no. 2.

Turner, B.S. (1986) *Citizenship and Capitalism*, London, Allen & Unwin.

Turner, B.S. (1987) *Medical Power and Social Knowledge*, London, Sage.

Turner, B.S. (1989) *The Body and Society: Explorations in Social Theory*, new edn, Oxford, Basil Blackwell.

Turner, B.S. (1990) *Medical Power and Social Knowledge*, 2nd edn, London, Sage.

Turner, B.S. (1991) *Religion and Social Theory*, 2nd edn, London, Sage.

Ungerson, C. (1991) *Gender and Caring*, Hemel Hempstead, Harvester Wheatsheaf.

Ungerson, C. (1995) 'Gender, cash and informal care', *Journal of Social Policy*, vol. 24, no. 1.

United Nations (UNDP) (1995) *World Development Report 1995*, Oxford, Oxford University Press.

Urry, J. (1990a) 'Urban sociology', in Haralambos, M. (ed) *Developments in Sociology*, vol. 6 Ormskirk, Causeway Press.

Urry, J. (1990b) *The Tourist Gaze*, London, Sage.

Urry, J. and Wakeford, J. (eds) (1973) *Power in Britain: Sociological Readings*. London, Heinemann.

Useem, M. (1984) *The Inner Circle*, New York, Oxford University Press.

Van den Berghe, P. (1978) *Race and Racism: A Comparative Perspective*, New York, Wiley.

Van den Berghe, P. (1988) 'Ethnicity and the sociobiology debate', in Rex, J. and Mason, D. (eds), *Theories of Race and Ethnic Relations*, Cambridge, Cambridge University Press.

Van den Haag, E. (1975) *Punishing Criminals*, New York, Simon and Schuster.

Van der Pijl, K. (1989) 'The international level', in Bottomore, T. and Brym, R. (eds), *The Capitalist Class*, Hemel Hempstead, Harvester Wheatsheaf.

Van Dijk, T.A. (1991) *Racism and the Press: Critical Studies in Racism and Migration*, London, Routledge.

Van Every, J. (1995) *Heterosexual Women Changing the Family: Refusing to Be a 'Wife'!*, London, Taylor & Francis.

Van Zoonen, L. (1991) 'Feminist perspectives on the media', in Curran, J. and Gurevitch, M. (eds), *Mass Media and Society*, New York, Edward Arnold.

Veal, A.J. (1993) 'The concept of lifestyle', *Leisure Studies*, vol. 12.

Veblen, T. (1953) *The Theory of the Leisure Class: An Economic Study of Institutions*, New York, Mentor Books (orig. pub. 1912).

Veljanovski, C. (1989) 'Competition in broadcasting', in Veljanovski, C. (ed), *Freedom in Broadcasting*, London, Institute of Economic Affairs.

Vidal, J. (1991) 'Aid', *Education Guardian*, 12 March.

Vienna Circle (1929) 'The scientific conception of the

world', in Neurath, O. (ed.), *Empiricism and Sociology*, Boston, Reidel (orig. pub. 1929).

VSO (1996) *Aid Counts: Don't Cut It*, London, VSO.

Wacquant, L.J.D. (1995) 'The ghetto, the state and the new capitalist economy', in Kasinitz, P. (ed) *Metropolis: Centre and Symbol of Our Times*, Basingstoke, Macmillan.

Waddington, D. *et al.* (1991) *Split at the Seams: Community, Continuity and Change after the 1984–5 Coal Dispute*, Buckingham, Open University Press.

Walby, S. (1986) *Patriarchy at Work*, Cambridge, Polity Press.

Walby, S. (1989) 'Theorising patriarchy', *Sociology*, vol. 23, no. 2.

Walby, S. (1990) *Theorizing Patriarchy*, Oxford, Blackwell.

Walker, A. (1989) 'Community care', in McCarthy, M. (ed), *The New Politics of Welfare*, Basingstoke, Macmillan.

Walker, B. and Waddington, I. (1991) 'Aids and the doctor–patient relationship', *Social Studies Review*, vol. 6, no. 4.

Walkerdine, V. (1981) 'Sex, power and pedagogy', *Screen Education*, vol. 38.

Walkerdine, V. and Waldon, R. (1982) *The Practice of Reason*, London, Institute of Education (Bedford Way Series).

Walklate, S. (1994) 'Crime victims: another 'ology'? *Sociology Review*, vol. 3, no. 3.

Wallerstein, I. (1974) *The Modern World-System*, London, Academic Press.

Wallerstein, I. (1991) in King, A.D. (ed) *Culture, Globalisation and the World System: Comtemporary Conditions for the Representation of Identity*, Basingstoke, Macmillan.

Wallis, R. (1984) *The Elementary Forms of the New Religious Life*, London, Routledge & Kegan Paul.

Wallis, R. and Bruce, S. (1986) *Sociological Theory, Religion and Collective Action*, Belfast, Queen's University.

Walsh, D. (1972) 'Functionalism and systems theory', in Filmer, P., Phillipson, M., Silverman, D. and Walsh, D. (eds), *New Directions in Sociological Theory*, Basingstoke, Macmillan.

Walton, J and Seddon, D. (1994) *Free Markets and Food Riots: The Politics of Global Adjustment*, Oxford, Blackwell.

Wandor, M. (ed.) (1990) *Once a Feminist: Stories of a Generation*, London, Virago.

Ward, R. and Jenkins, R. (eds) (1985) *Ethnic Communities in Business*, Cambridge, Cambridge University Press.

Warde, A. and Abercrombie, N. (eds) (1994) *Stratification and Social Inequality: Studies in British Society*, Lancaster, Framework Press.

Warnock Report (1978) *Report of the Committee of Enquiry into the Education of Handicapped Children and Young People*, London, DES/HMSO.

Warren, B. (1980) *Imperialism: Pioneer of Capitalism*, London, New Left Books.

Warwick, D. (1982) 'Tearoom trade: means and ends in social research', in Bulmer, M. (ed.), *Social Research Ethics: An Examination of the Merits of Covert Participation Research*, Basingstoke, Macmillan.

Waters, M. (1995) *Globalisation*, London, Routledge.

Watkins, K. (1996) 'Zimbabwe 'miracle cure' fails to save the poor', *The Guardian*, 27 July.

Watson, K. (ed) (1982) *Education in the Third World*, Beckenham, Croom Helm.

Watson, T. (1995) *Sociology, Work and Industry*, 3rd edn, London, Routledge.

Webb, M. (1982) 'The labour market', in Reid, I. and Wormald, E. (eds), *Sex Differences in Britain*, London, Grant McIntyre.

Weber, M. (1930) *The Protestant Ethic and the Spirit of Capitalism*, London, Allen & Unwin (orig. pub. 1905).

Weber, M. (1949a) '"Objectivity" in social science and social policy', in *The Methodology of the Social Sciences*, Glencoe, Free Press (orig. pub. 1904).

Weber, M. (1949b) 'The meaning of "ethical neutrality" in sociology and economics', in *The Methodology of the Social Sciences*, Glencoe, Free Press (orig. pub. 1904).

Weber, M. (1951) *The Religion of China*, New York, Macmillan (orig. pub. 1915)

Weber, M. (1952) *Ancient Judaism*, New York, Macmillan (orig. pub. 1917).

Weber, M. (1958) *The Religion of India*, New York, Macmillan (orig. pub. 1916).

Weber, M. (1961) *From Max Weber: Essays in Sociology*, London, Routledge & Kegan Paul.

Weber, M. (1968) *Economy and Society: An Outline of Interpretive Sociology* (edited by G. Roth and C. Wittich), New York, Bedminister Press (orig. pub. 1921).

Weber, M. (1985) *The Protestant Ethic and the Spirit of Capitalism*, new edn, London, Unwin Paperbacks (orig. pub. 1905).

Webster, A. (1990) *Introduction to the Sociology of Development*, 2nd edn, Basingstoke, Macmillan.

Webster, F. (1995) *Theories of the Information Society*, London, Routledge.

Wedderburn, D. (1974) *Poverty, Inequality and Class Structure*, Cambridge, Cambridge University Press.

Weeks, J. (1977) *Coming Out: Homosexual Politics in Britain From the Nineteenth Century to the Present*, London, Quarto.

Weeks, J. (1986) *Sexuality*, London, Tavistock.

Weiner, G. (1994) *Feminisms in Education: An Introduction*, Buckingham, Open University Press.

West, R. (1982) *The Young Rebecca* (edited by J. Marcus), Basingstoke, Macmillan.

Westergaard, J. (1995) *Who Gets What? The Hardening of Class Inequality in the Late Twentieth Century*, Cambridge, Polity Press.

Westergaard, J. and Resler, H. (1976) *Class in a Capitalist Society: A Study of Contemporary Britain*, Harmondsworth, Penguin.

Wheelock, J. (1990) *Husbands at Home*, London, Routledge.

Whitehead, M. (1987) 'The health divide', in Townsend, P., Davidson, N. and Whitehead, M. (eds), *The Health Divide*, Harmondsworth, Penguin.

Whitty, G. (1992) 'Integrated humanities and world studies: lessons from some radical curriculum initiatives of the 1980s', in Rattansi, A. and Reeder, D. (eds), *Radicalism and Education: Essays for Brian Simon*, London, Lawrence & Wishart.

Whitty, G., Rowe, G. and Aggleton, P. (1994) 'Subjects and themes in the secondary school curriculum, *Research Papers in Education*, vol. 9, no. 2.

Whyte, W.F. (1943) *Street Corner Society*, Chicago, University of Chicago Press.

Wiles, R. and Higgins, J. (1996) 'Doctor–patient relationships in the private sector: patients' perceptions', *Sociology of Health and Illness*, vol. 18, no. 3.

Wilkinson, H. and Mulgan, G. (1995) *Freedom's Children: Work, Relationships and Politics for 18–34 Year Olds in Britain Today* (pamphlet), London, Demos.

Willetts, D. (1992) *Modern Conservatism*, Harmondsworth, Penguin.

Williams, F. (1989) *Social Policy: A Critical Introduction*, Cambridge, Polity Press.

Williams, F. (1993a) 'Gender, "race" and class in British welfare policy', in Cochrane, A. and Clarke, J. (eds), *Comparing Welfare States*, London, Sage.

Williams, F. (1994) 'Social relations, welfare and the post-Fordism debate', in Burrows, R. and Loader, B. (eds), *Towards a Post-Fordist Welfare State*, London, Routledge.

Williams, J. (1986) 'Football hooliganism', *Social Science Teacher*, vol. 15, no. 3.*

Williams, J. (1997) 'In focus: work and the trade unions', *Sociology Review*, vol. 6, no. 3.

Williams, K. (1993b) 'The light at the end of the tunnel: the mass media, public opinion and the Vietnam War', in Eldridge, J. (ed), *Getting the Message: News, Truth and Power*, London, Glasgow University Media Group/Routledge.

Williams, L. and Dunsmuir, A. (1991) *How To Do Social Research*, London, Collins Educational.

Williams, R. (1961) *The Long Revolution*, Harmondsworth, Penguin.

Williams, R. (1963) *Culture and Society 1780–1950*, Harmondsworth, Penguin.

Williams, R. (1990) *Television, Technology and Cultural Form*, 2nd edn, London, Routledge.

Williams, S.J. (1995) 'Theorising class, health and lifestyles: can Bourdieu help us?', *Sociology of Health and Illness*, vol. 17, no. 5.

Williamson, J. (1978) *Decoding Advertisements*, London, Marion Boyers.

Willis, P. (1977) *Learning to Labour*, Farnborough, Saxon House.

Willis, P. (1990) *Common Culture*, Buckingham, Open University Press.

Willmott, P. (1987) *Friendship Networks and Social Support*, London, PSI.

Willmott, P. (1988) 'Urban kinship past and present', *Social Studies Review*, vol. 4, no. 2.

Willmott, P. and Young, M. (1971) *Family and Class in a London Suburb*, London, New English Library.

Wilson, B.R. (1966) *Religion in a Secular Society: A Sociological Comment*, London, C.A Watts and Co.

Wilson, B.R. (1970) *Religious Sects: A Sociological Study*, London, Weidenfeld and Nicholson.

Wilson, B.R. (1985) 'A typology of sects', in Bocock, R. and Thompson, K. (eds), *Religion and Ideology*, Manchester, Manchester University Press.

Wilson, J. (1975) *Thinking About Crime*, New York, Basic Books.

Wilson, W.J. (1987) *The Truly Disadvantaged*, Chicago, University of Chicago Press.

Wimbush, E. (1986) *Women, Leisure and Wellbeing*, Edinburgh, Centre for Leisure Research.

Winterton Report (1992) *Report of the Social Services Select Committee on Maternity Services*, London, HMSO.

Witcher, S. (1994) 'Introduction' to Oppenheim, C., *The Welfare State: Putting the Record Straight*, London, CPAG.

Witz, A. (1992) *Professions and Patriarchy*, London, Routledge.

Wolf, N. (1990) *The Beauty Myth*, London, Vintage.

Wolpe, H. (ed) (1980) *The Articulation of Modes of Production*, London, Routledge.

Women in Journalism Research Committee (1996) *Women in the News: Does Sex Change the Way a Newspaper Thinks?* London, Women in Journalism.

World Bank (1986) *Poverty and Hunger*, Washington (DC), World Bank.

World Bank (1993) *World Development Report 1993*, Oxford, Oxford University Press.

World Bank (1996) *Social Indicators of Development 1996*, Baltimore, Johns Hopkins University Press.

World Development Movement (1996) *Corporate Giants*, London, WDM.

Woronoff, J. (1992) *The Japanese Economic Crisis*, Basingstoke, Macmillan.

Worsley, P. (1984) *The Three Worlds*, London, Weidenfeld and Nicolson.

Wright, E.O. (1976) 'Class boundaries in advanced capitalist societies', *New Left Review*, no. 98.

Wright, E.O. (1978) *Class, Crisis and the State*, London, Verso.

Wright, E.O. (1985) *Classes*, London, Verso.

Wright, E.O. (1994a) 'What is analytical Marxism?', in Wright, E.O., *Interrogating Inequality*, London, Verso.

Wright, E.O. (1994b) *Interrogating Inequality*, London, Verso.

Wright, E.O. (1997) *Class Counts*, Cambridge, Cambridge University Press.

Wright, S. (1992) 'Image and analysis: new directions in community studies', in Short, B. (ed) *The English Rural Community: Image and Analysis*, Cambridge, Cambridge University Press.

Wrong, D. (1969) 'The oversocialised concept of man in modern sociology', in Coser, L. and Rosenberg, B. (eds), *Sociological Theory: A Book of Readings*, London, Collier Macmillan.

Young, J. (1977) 'The role of the police as amplifiers of deviancy, negotiators of reality and translators of fantasy', in Cohen, S. (ed), *Images of Deviance*, Harmondsworth, Penguin.

Young, M. (1961) *The Rise of the Meritocracy*, Harmondsworth, Penguin.

Young, M. and Willmott, P. (1957) *Family and Kinship in East London*, London, Routledge & Kegan Paul.

Young, M. and Willmott, P. (1975) *The Symmetrical Family*, Harmondsworth, Penguin.

Zaretsky, E. (1976) *Capitalism: The Family and Personal Life*, London, Pluto.

Zweig, F. (1961) *The Worker in an Affluent Society: Family Life and Industry*, London, Heinemann.

* *Social Science Teacher* is the journal of the Association for the Teaching of the Social Sciences. For further information write to: ATSS, P.O. Box 61, Watford WD2 2NH.

Author Index

Subject Index